THE NEW
DECORATOR'S
DIRECTORY

THE NEW DECORATOR'S DIRECTORY

LORRAINE JOHNSON

MICHAEL JOSEPH · LONDON

First published in Great Britain
by Michael Joseph Ltd
44 Bedford Square
London WC1
1985

Johnson Editions Ltd
15 Grafton Square
London SW4 0DQ

Managing editor: Georgina Harding
Designer: Clare Finlaison
Assistant editor: Louisa McDonnell
Indexer: Valerie Lewis Chandler

Johnson Editions would like to thank the
following people who have contributed to this
book: Carolyn Eardley, Elizabeth Eyres, Mandy
Gwynne-Jones, Janet Hammond, Rupert
Harding, Carole Hughes, Hilary Hockman,
Chris Ingram, Louisa McDonnell, Susanna
Powers, Gabrielle Townsend and Zuza Vrbova.
Thanks also to Danny Robins for his work on the
finished artwork, Allen Ives for typesetting,
Anne Morgan for research, and Stanli
Opperman for taking the colour photographs of
tile and carpet samples.
Alan Dodds photograph on p95 by Richard
Bryant; John Coleman photographs on p324 by
Fiona Pragott (dresser) and Karen Norquay
(table); Habitat photographs from Habitat, as in
1985 catalogue.

Johnson, Lorraine
The new decorators directory — Rev. ed.
1. Do-it-yourself products industry — Great
Britain — Directories   2. Paint industry and
trade — Great Britain — Directories
3. Wallpaper industry — Great Britain —
Directories   4. Furniture industry and trade
— Great Britain — Directories
I. Title   II. Johnson, Lorraine. Decorator's
directory
338.7'698'02541   HD9999.D623G7

ISBN 0-7181-2292-5

Production by Landmark Production Consultants, London
Printed and bound by Bath Press, Avon

Dedicated to my mother, Ginny, Martie, Linda,
and home-lovers everywhere

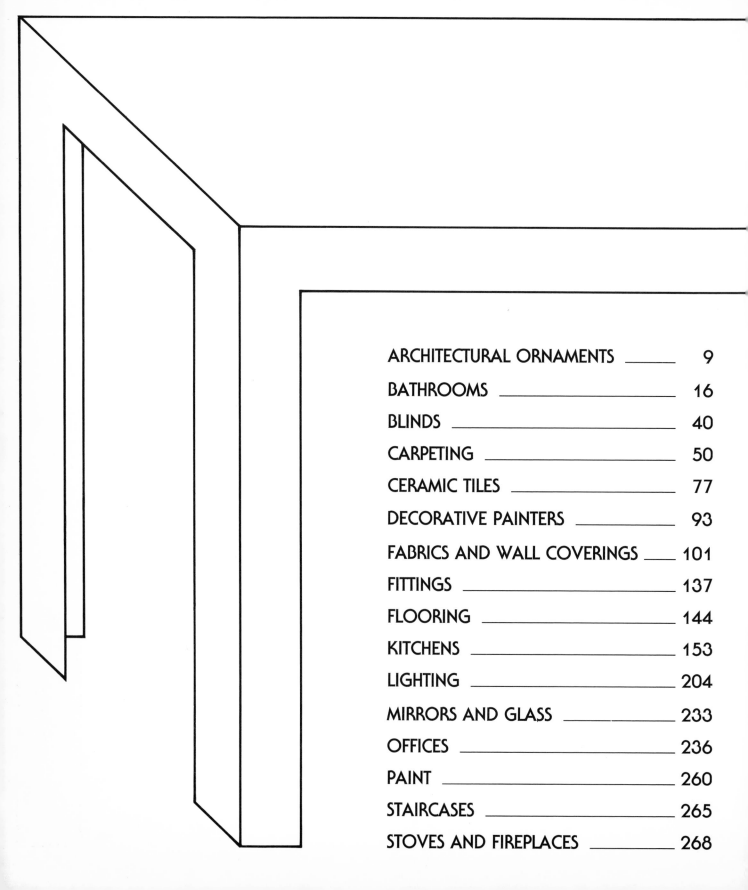

TABLE OF CONTENTS

INTRODUCTION

Half the art of decorating is knowing what's available. Furnishing a new house can mean days spent trudging around the shops in the hunt for something that little bit different. Too often the major high street retailers seem to stock only a limited and rather conservative selection, while specialist outlets are far-flung and hard to find. This book gives a bird's eye view of what is on the market, where to find it and what it costs. I hope it will not only save you time but also give you new ideas, telling you about things you never knew existed.

My own researches in the course of doing up a small house in north London a few years ago led to the first *Decorator's Directory*, published in 1981. I had spent what seemed to be an inordinate amount of time looking for what I wanted, and had discovered in the process that in fact a multitude of well-designed products were made in Britain or imported, but, for a variety of reasons, were not widely distributed. The *Directory* attempted to put consumers in touch with the manufacturers, importers and suppliers of these items.

Much has changed since 1981. New products have been developed, new trends have emerged in decorating and new companies have sprung up. Equally, some old lines have been discontinued, others have been updated, and a number of companies have gone out of business. The *New Decorator's Directory* is a completely revised and updated edition. It covers many of the same manufacturers and distributors, describing new ranges in addition to some of the older lines, plus many new companies, and attempts to fill in any gaps left by the first book.

Arranged by supplier, within sections, it describes the merchandise produced by various firms, with illustrations and basic information such as prices and measurements. Each entry is as comprehensive as space allows — it is obviously impossible to describe every range or product each company supplies so we have selected what we consider to be the most interesting or useful items.

Market coverage is very wide, from simple necessities to luxuries — prices for a coffee table, for example, range from around £35 to £16000. It is worth looking at everything, even if you're not a millionaire. Decide what you like, then see if you can afford it. And consider before you opt for something cheaper; an item that's well made from high-quality materials may seem an extravagance at first but should pay for itself in time. If something is prohibitively expensive, you may be able to find a suitable compromise — marbled wallpaper or a painted marble finish on walls and floors can be a stunning alternative to the real thing.

The Design Council have kindly assisted in the production of the book, and undertook the initial mailing to around 5000 companies. Unfortunately, many of the companies contacted did not answer or provide the necessary information. We can only assume that those firms who are included, ranging from the smallest cottage industries to large conglomerates, are rather more willing than the others to help the consumer.

ORGANIZATION OF THE BOOK

Sections are devoted to types of product (*Paint, Lighting*), to entire rooms (*Kitchens*) or to services (*Decorative painters*). Some are further sub-divided according to type or function. The large section on *Furniture*, sub-divided into 12 categories, takes up the last quarter of the book. All other sections are listed alphabetically, the entries within them also listed alphabetically by company name. Included at the end of the book is a variety of useful information, from architectural salvage dealers (invaluable for anyone restoring an old house) to some lesser-known decorating products.

HOW TO USE THE BOOK

If you are looking for a bath, for example, read through *Sanitary-*

ware in *Bathrooms* to see which firms offer the colour and style you want at a price you're prepared to pay. When you've made your choice, contact the sales department of the relevant companies — suppliers' addresses are listed at the end of the book. They will be able to put you in touch with your nearest stockist or to supply the item direct. It is sometimes possible to get a discount on a product that comes direct from the manufacturer, but always wait for the firm to offer this reduction. Don't ask for a trade discount unless you are buying in quantity.

If the examples described are nearly but not exactly what you want, it's always worth contacting the firm concerned and asking for a catalogue or for the address of the nearest stockist so that you can see their entire range.

Availability: Every effort has been made to ensure that the merchandise described will be available to readers. Inevitably you will sometimes find that a product has been discontinued, or that the designs or colours available within a range have altered slightly. If this happens, persevere: the company concerned may just have a few items still in stock or know of an outlet that has them.

Prices: Approximate retail prices for products detailed or illustrated are given wherever possible. These are bound to fluctuate to a certain extent, so if two firms have similar products in the same price bracket contact them both for specific quotations or estimates. Sometimes it has been necessary to put '*P:* on application', generally for one of four reasons: the manufacturer, wholesaler or distributor did not want to commit himself or his outlets to a predetermined mark-up (another reason for shopping around); the item is made to order and costs vary according to specification and/or market prices for materials; the merchandise is imported and its price is subject to fluctuations in the rate of exchange; the item is intended for the contract market and is normally sold only in a trade price structure (as for example in the *Offices* section).

Prices were correct at the time of going to press but inflation and changes in the cost of raw materials make rises inevitable.

Measurements: British manufacturers and distributors have not yet gone entirely over to metric measurements, and many still use the imperial system. Each entry gives first the type generally quoted by the supplier, followed by its metric or imperial conversion. Inches are rounded to the nearest 0.5cm, centimetres to the nearest ¼in; fluid ounces to the nearest 1ml, millilitres to the nearest ¼ fl oz. As with prices, measurements are given after the item described or, if they apply to all the merchandise from a particular manufacturer, on a separate line at the end of the entry.

Ranges and styles: Ranges or collections that incorporate a number of designs or pieces of furniture are in capital letters; individual models, designs, patterns etc are in quotation marks.

Design Centre Selection: Products selected for the Design Centre — the Design Council's record of British-made products of outstanding design — are identified wherever illustrated by △ in the caption. It has been impossible to identify each Design Centre selected product mentioned in the text; however, the Design Council logo ⚓ placed beside the company name at the top of an entry indicates that one or more of the products described have been selected.

Finally, if you know of, or find, a supplier that you think should have been included, please write to: The Decorator's Directory,
Michael Joseph Ltd,
44 Bedford Square,
London WC1 3DU.

We will contact the firm concerned in order to make the next edition even better than this one.

Lorraine Johnson

EKORNES Ulferts

Ekornes Ulferts offer everything from comfortable suites and easy chairs upholstered in soft fabrics or leather, to beautiful dining room furniture, flexible wall unit systems and matching occasional furniture all available in both wooden veneers and lacquer finishes. This exclusive Ekornes Ulferts range of high quality Norwegian and Swedish furniture is offered in over 70 stores throughout Britain and Ireland. Catalogue, stockist list and price details are available from:

EKORNES Ulferts

12 B St. George Street, London, W1R 9DE.

The Silent Gliss Collection for the best-dressed windows

Each domestic or office environment demands its own specific visual approach. From functional window treatments which harmonize totally with the background to treatments designed to stun the senses with their individuality.

Only Silent Gliss, the truly international specialists in creative window dressing, can offer the ideas, the technical superiority, the flair your environment demands.

Conventional Curtain Tracks
Hand-operated tracks. Cord-operated tracks. Stage tracks. Motorised tracks. The world's widest range of curtain tracks for domestic, commercial and traditional settings.

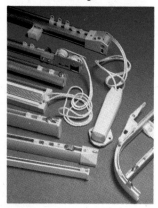

There are subtle satin silver or white finishes, and anodised black, gold or bronze finishes to match most architectural ironmongery through to the exciting Rainbow Range in 12 striking, fashionable colours.

All are made from the highest grade aluminium with premium quality nylon components. The unique 3-year guarantee demonstrates our belief in the quality and excellence of the products.

Roller Blinds
The 2200 roller blind system has a unique decelerator which ensures that it goes up very slowly, obviating the mechanical problems roller blinds normally bring. There is also a cord-operated blind for very heavy duty blinds. Wide fabric range including 51 colours in plain Trevira in 3 thicknesses, sunscreen and blackout fabrics. A logo-printing service is also available.

Panel Glide System
Attractive fabric gliding panels can be used as either a window dressing or room divider.
Electrically operated systems
Curtain tracks. Vertical blinds. Roman and Austrian blinds. The Panel Glide System. All can be motorised with neat purpose-built, reliable Swiss motors. Either push button or remote control.

Vertical Louvre Blinds
Silent Gliss gives both the office and home an extra dimension.

There are flameproofed, non-toxic, translucent louvres in 51 beautiful colours. Pure cotton louvres in 44 colours. And

Roman Blinds
The clean, modern look – perfect for co-ordinates.
Austrian Blinds
The softer "period" look.

Both feature new easy-to-assemble components for faster, more economical make-up.

Roman Blind

Silent Gliss services
Silent Gliss offers a UK-wide technical advisory and fitting service in addition to the Export Department with access to a worldwide distribution network.

eye-catching picture sets, too. In addition Silent Gliss presents the most advanced and robust blind system in the world – the new single control chain 2800 system.

Together with efficient Silent Gliss hanging drawing mechanisms

Austrian Blind

For further information, please contact your nearest Silent Gliss depot showroom.

THREE YEAR GUARANTEE 3

Export and Kent, Surrey, Sussex, Berks, Hants and South West — Star Lane, Margate, Kent CT9 4EF, England. Tel: 0843 63571 Telex: 96266.
Wales, Midlands, Notts, Derby, North of England, Scotland — Ahed House, Sandbeds, Unit 7, Dewsbury Road, Ossett, W. Yorkshire WF5 9ND. Tel: 0924 278181.
London, Bucks, Oxon, East Anglia, Middx — 5 Brewery Road, London N7 9QJ. Tel: 01-609 2646.

SilentGliss®

INTRODUCTION

Architectural ornaments are an easy way of adding interest to a boring, box-like room, or of restoring the character of a period house that has suffered through unsympathetic conversion and modernization. These non-structural components, applied after building and surface work but before decorating, can also be used cosmetically to hide a multitude of sins.

Types of traditional ornaments available range from original or reproduction mouldings and plasterwork — typically cornices, architraves, dadoes, porticos and niches—to panelling and rustic beams. These come in various materials: wood (solid or veneer), mock wood (made from polyurethane), solid or fibrous plaster, foam, fibreglass and other new synthetics. The real thing, usually more expensive, is often for perfectionists only. Many imitations are hardly noticeable, especially at ceiling height. (A word of warning, however: the range is so temptingly large it's only too easy to get carried away, adding Georgian niches alongside Jacobean panelling. In this, as in all decorating schemes, simplicity and compatibility are paramount.)

More modern ornaments, also included here, are ceiling panels used to house lighting, heating and other electrical apparatus or camouflage unsightly cracks and pipes; and ceiling tiles, either supported on a grid or applied directly, used to absorb sound and reflect light, and often incorporating lighting systems. Sometimes purely functional in appearance, sometimes these are also decorative features in themselves.

This section is divided, according to function or material, into *Plaster and plaster effects*, *Suspended ceilings* and *Wood and wood effects*.

Several firms will help with installation, but many ornaments can be fitted by anyone with some do-it-yourself skills. Be sure to consult the supplier or manufacturer first — special tools or products may be recommended to make the job easier.

● A growing number of firms specialize in salvage of items from period houses, stocking a wide range of useful and decorative pieces such as balustrades, columns, doors, beams, panelling (even entire rooms), and many smaller ornaments. These are of undoubted value, particularly for restoration. For dealers in these, see the section on *Architectural Salvage* at the end of the book.

PLASTER AND PLASTER EFFECTS

ARISTOCAST LTD

Useful range of mouldings, including reasonably priced curved cornices for bay windows and alcoves. There are 16 cornices in all, manufactured in handy lengths from either flexible

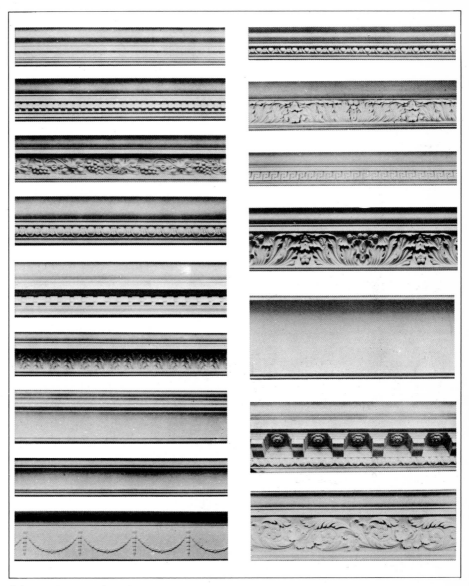

Aristocast's range of cornices

or rigid moulds. Range also includes eight niches, six ceiling roses, eight panel mouldings, and archways built to customers' specifications. *P:* cornices (flexible mould) £8.95–£10.50 per 2m (78¾in) run, (glass fibre mould) £11.65–£47.50 per 3m (118in) run; niches £31–£89.50; ceiling roses £9–£80; panel mouldings £5.20 per 1.5m (59in) run (ex VAT).

H & F BADCOCK LTD

High quality fibrous plasterwork on any scale, traditional or modern, from a company with more than a century's experience. Comprehensive service offered to architects and designers. Standard pieces include cornices in an immense variety of sections, round and oval ceiling roses, enrichments such as urns and festoons, corbels, columns and half-columns, pilasters, niches, panel moulds and patras. Badcock's will also quote for any original plasterwork to customer's design or reproduce damaged plasterwork. Fixing service provided if required. *P:* cornices £0.55–£2.69 per 12in (30.5cm) run; ceiling roses £7.65–£86.40; corbels £6.86–£22.50; columns £119–£132; half-columns £57.25–£61.60; pilasters £69.25; niches £30.75–£92.75 (ex VAT).
See following page for illustration.

PRICES AND INFORMATION WERE CORRECT AT THE TIME OF GOING TO PRESS

ARCHITECTURAL ORNAMENTS

From H & F Badcock. Top: corbels; below: half-column and pilasters

Three of Copley Mouldings' ceiling roses

G J GREEN AND VERONESE

Exhaustive range of decorative mouldings. Green and Veronese supply stock cornices, models and moulds as well as producing all kinds of plasterwork — whether ceiling, cornice, column or fire surround — to clients' individual designs. Stock range comprises more than 60 cornices, including some very deep and intricate designs, plus 3 niches, 16 ceiling roses, and 5 columns and capitals. The firm also undertakes restoration work, from small details to the most elaborate plastered ceilings. *P:* on application.

GEORGE JACKSON & SONS LTD

Wonderfully comprehensive range from the firm that made the castings for Robert Adam in the late eighteenth century. Immense collection covers every major English and French style of the seventeenth, eighteenth and nineteenth centuries, including no less than 71 fibrous plaster cornices, 12 relief cornices and bands, 69 architraves and dado rails, 92 panel

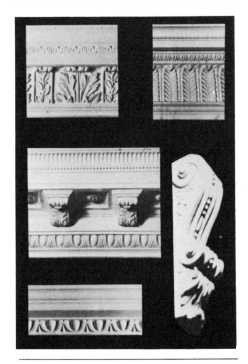

Below: centrepieces and capitals from Green & Veronese; right: cornices and corbel from George Jackson

COPLEY MOULDINGS

Rigid polyurethane decorative mouldings. Almost indistinguishable in use from traditional mouldings, they are lighter, cheaper and virtually unbreakable. Range consists of nine ceiling roses, two corbels, six cornices, two dado rails, and one panel moulding design sold in straight lengths, corners or complete door panel. *P:* ceiling roses £8.99–£25.17; corbels £9.78 each; dado rails £6.52–£8.13 per 2m (78¾in) run; panel mouldings £7.35 per 4 × 1m (157½ × 39in) straight length, £5.39 per set of four corners, £4.96 per door panel (ex VAT).

10

mouldings, 26 ceiling roses, 24 niche heads, 16 trusses, 22 capitals, plus 55 composition ornaments, 7 relief ornaments, and 14 carton pierre trophies and fibrous plaster plaques. Jackson's will gild, grain and emblazon their plasterwork, repair and restore existing plasterwork and even provide a complete decorating service. *P:* on application.

JONATHAN JAMES

High quality and complete plastering service for designers and architects, including solid and fibrous plastering and also dry lining, granolithic paving, suspended ceilings and decorative finishes. Jobs undertaken range from restoration of important period buildings to decoration of modern shopping centres and banks. Jonathan James will produce almost any design to order. *P:* on application.

J G MCDONOUGH LTD

Solid and fibrous plaster. Extremely good range of cornices, in particular, encompasses plain sections, many of the commonest Victorian designs, and rarer ones with elaborate acanthus leaf, griffin and tasselled motifs. Corbels, ceiling roses, niches and overdoors also available. *P:* cornices £1.90–£5.75 per 12in (30.5cm) run; corbels £15–£22; ceiling roses £17–£35; niches £30–£57; overdoors £70 (ex VAT)

W H NEWSON & SONS LTD

ARTCOVE ceiling centrepieces and covings. Centrepieces are made from high impact styrene in 18 different patterns and sizes. They look like real plaster, but are lightweight and easily installed. Covings, in light but strong extruded high density polystyrene, come in 15 different profiles, available in 2m (79in) lengths and with pre-cut mitres. Range also includes more than a dozen different patterns of framing, easily applied to add interest to walls or ceilings. *M:* centrepieces dia 6.5–68cm (2½–27in). *P:* on application.

RAINFORD HOUSE OF ELEGANCE

Very comprehensive range of handmade period mouldings. Made from high quality fibrous plaster, the range offers a choice of 5 niches, 15 cornices and ceiling and wall friezes, 4 corbels, 20 ceiling roses, 9 panel mouldings (with optional ready-mitred corners), archways that can be tailor-made to customer's specified dimensions, 2 interior door surrounds, pilasters and overdoors. Plaques, a Georgian canopy and a pedestal are also available, and there is even an ornamental ceiling dome for use where the dome top can be let into the roof space. *M:* ceiling roses dia 11½–38½in (29–98cm); pedestal h 35in (89cm). *P:* niches £28.50–£49.50; cornices £8.90–£14 per

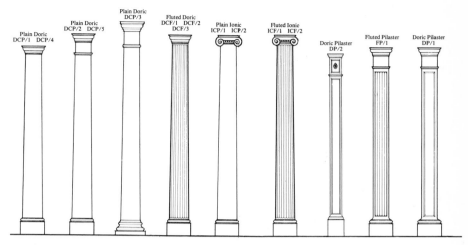

Above, from left to right: plain and fluted Doric and Ionic columns and pilasters. All from Verine

120in (305cm) run; corbels approx £14.50–£20.50; ceiling roses £8–£37; panel mouldings approx £3.50 per 72in (183cm) run; archways £194–£274; domes £139–£169 (ex VAT).

VERINE PRODUCTS & CO

Mainly large-scale mouldings, including overdoors, porches, canopies, porticos, pilasters and columns. Small selection of cornice mouldings and corbels is also offered. *P:* on application.

SUSPENDED CEILINGS

ARMSTRONG WORLD INDUSTRIES LTD

Enormous range of ceiling tiles made from fire-resistant mineral fibre that reflects light and absorbs sound, designed mainly for contract use. Designs include linear PERSPECTIVES; the large MICROLOOK and SECOND LOOK ranges encompassing a wide variety of textures and finishes; SOFT LOOK and self-explanatory SOUNDSOAK, both available in seven colourways. More unusual are GOLD LEAF in mottled old gold; shimmering silver ANTIQUE GLASS, specially sound-proofed by the addition of polyester film to the standard mineral fibre; and three-dimensional MINA-FORM, with geometric honeycomb-like coffers of varying depths, some with lights inset. Armstrong also make recessed luminaires for their ceiling systems. Most tiles can be mounted on to a stable ceiling with the correct adhesive or fixed to TRULOK grid system. *P:* on application.

PRICES AND INFORMATION WERE CORRECT AT THE TIME OF GOING TO PRESS

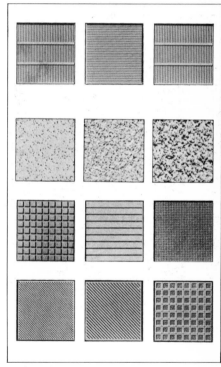

Ceiling tile ranges from Armstrong. Top row: PERSPECTIVES; below: MICROLOOK

COURTNEY, POPE LIGHTING LTD

VERSI-TILE all-purpose steel ceiling system. Contoured panels (60cm/23½in sq) are made from high grade steel and weigh only 3lb (1.36kg), reducing load-bearing on the ceiling. Four standard epoxy resin colours are available — off-white, colonial ivory, bitter chocolate and poppy red — but any special shade can be supplied to order. System can incorpo-

ARCHITECTURAL ORNAMENTS

VERSI-TILE steel ceiling system, with translucent panels for illumination, from Courtney, Pope Lighting

rate a full range of Courtney, Pope's lighting, including track, recessed luminaires and emergency units (see *Lighting*). Panels can also be used as screens or space dividers. *P:* on application.

DAVID GILLESPIE ASSOCIATES LTD

Unusual ideas for ceilings from a company that's primarily geared for architects and deliberately steers clear of mass-produced items. ZEROSPAN, made from Zerodec, consists of ceiling coffers and tiles supplied to fit 60 × 60cm (23½ × 23½in) standard grids. Coffers come in 17 designs with standard white textured finish on visible side, but paints, sprays, sound-absorbent textured coatings, gilding and other finishes can be applied. 1200 BUDGET SERIES is designed for the modern office, being non-combustible and capable of supporting all necessary supply services. The 120 × 120cm (47¼ × 47¼in) coffers can accommodate central light fittings and air conditioning grilles. Wide range of patterns and moulds already exists, but Gillespies are willing to create new designs and moulds for large installations. HEXADEC hexagonal, triangular and rhombus shapes made from moulded Zerodec can be used in an endless variety of patterns, and Gillespies can also use this material to make futuristic domes, vaults and geometric and geodesic forms. Also available are mirrored ceilings consisting of inverted pyramids of polished aluminium, and carved redwood panels that make unusual ceilings (see *Partitions*). *P:* on application.

Selection of ceiling coffers in the ZEROSPAN range by David Gillespie

From Howard Ceilings's SAFETEX 2000 range. Top: six textured panels; bottom: three fissured acoustic panels

HANDY DIRECT SUPPLIES

Suppliers of HI-LIGHT suspended ceilings, suitable for do-it-yourself installation. There are two frame systems (aluminium or steel) and a choice of decorative panels in polystyrene, textured PVC, fibreglass or mineral fibre. Available in individual parts or in frame kits. *M:* 180 × 180cm (71 × 71in) to 360 × 540cm (132 × 204in). *P:* on application.

HOWARD CEILINGS LTD

Illuminated and acoustic ceiling panels with optional inset downlighters. SAFETEX 2000 ceiling system is based on silver or gold anodized aluminium grid or frame into which textured, coloured and translucent panels are fitted. All lighting and other electrical services are hidden, giving a uniform, tidy and unobtrusive finish to any ceiling. Translucent panels with fluorescent strips placed at least 4in (10cm) above them have a high light transmission level to give even distribution of dif-

fused light. Downlighters — in brushed aluminium, gold or silver finish and with red, green, gold or blue reflector lamps — or swivel spotlights can be dropped into the textured panels to highlight particular working or display areas. *M:* each panel 24 × 24in (61 × 61cm). *P:* translucent panel £3.92; fissured panel £4.42; textured panel £3.92.

WOOD AND WOOD EFFECTS

ARISTOCAST LTD

Useful range of polyurethane cottage-style oak beams and panelling. Various sizes of main beams, planks, joists, upright posts and diagonal bracers are available. *P:* largest main beam (22ft × 12in × 8½in/671 × 30 × 21cm) £161; plank £15; joist £20; upright post £72; diagonal bracer £10.

RICHARD EPSOM

Large-scale wood carving. Exotic animal and human figures as well as traditional motifs can be featured on wall panels, pediments etc. Designs can suit both period and contemporary interiors. *P:* on application.

Carved pediment by Richard Epsom

PRICES AND INFORMATION WERE CORRECT AT THE TIME OF GOING TO PRESS

HART OF KNIGHTSBRIDGE
Pine room panelling made to order from a company best known for its pine mantels (see *Fireplaces*). Also available is the 'Harley' recess and corner cupboard in carved waxed pine, with three-shelf niche above, corner cupboard below. *M:* w31½ × h79½in (80 × 202cm). *P:* on application.

'Harley' from Hart of Knightsbridge

HOMEWORKS LTD
PANELWORKS panelling, reminiscent of the eighteenth century. Made from selected pine veneers and solid woods finished with a combination of natural and coloured cellulose, it can be ordered to fit any shape or size of room. All necessary mouldings, such as cornice, dado and skirting, are supplied. Range in-

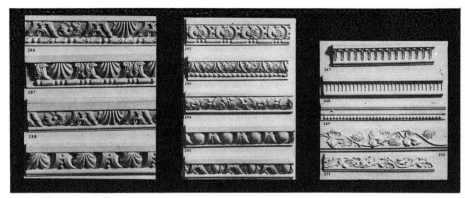

Some of George Jackson's composition mouldings

cludes book-shelves, cupboards, wardrobes and radiator casings. *P:* w100 × h260cm (39¼ × 102¼in) panelled section, with moulding, £550.

GEORGE JACKSON & SONS LTD
From pillared halls to radiator covers, all types of decorative joinery from skilled craftsmen. Joinery can be manufactured for others to fix or finished on site. Jackson's are now Britain's only manufacturers of composition mouldings, made from a resin-based product that can be moulded like clay but sets hard as wood. The mouldings are usually applied to timber and can be stained, polished, painted and treated like wood. Incredible range of 25,000 moulds makes possible some unusual detailing. *P:* on application.

MAGNET SOUTHERNS
Numerous panelling products from a huge builder's merchant chain. Timber claddings are available in redwood, whitewood and cedar, with grooved or plain surfaces and a choice of ten redwood beads and moulds. MAGNAPLANK panelling packs contain 10-11 kiln-dried boards in hemlock cedar, knotty pine, Douglas fir, hardwood or whitewood. Boards are grooved to clip into position. MAGNALUX smooth wood veneers on 4mm-ply panels come in eight types: cherry, sapele, rosewood, teak, elm, knotty cedar, oak and ash. MAGNADEC 3.2mm-ply simulated wood panels come in seven printed grains: Idaho pine, Ceylon teak, golden oak, sapele, cherry, Pacific elm and Kashmir teak. Panels can be fitted directly on to sound walls with special adhesive or attached to a batten system. Flame-retardant finish can be applied to order. *P:* MAGNAPLANK (pack to cover 240 × 82cm/ 94½ × 32¼in) £9.80-£28.06; MAGNALUX panel (96 × 48in/244 ×122cm) £31.29-£50.29; MAGNADEC panel (same size) £7.95.

W H NEWSON & SONS LTD
Enormous range of both hardwood and softwood mouldings, including architraves, cornices, picture rails, beadings, skirtings, dadoes, panel mouldings, astragals, rounds, quadrants, and dowels; some in Victorian and Edwardian styles. Newson will also make any moulding to order. COUNTRY STYLE panelling is also available. Panels can be run horizontally, vertically or diagonally, and can be slotted together and fixed by secret nailing. Available loose or packed in sixes. *M:* d1.3 × w10cm (½ × 4in), standard l2.4 or 3m (94 or 118in). *P:* on application.

OAKLEAF REPRODUCTIONS LTD
Immense selection of simulated wood ornaments in rigid polyurethane, faithfully reproduced down to blemishes and tool marks. Range includes everything from 'oak' beams and planking, 'carved' feature panels, linenfold panelling, Tudor door arches and posts, ceiling bosses, friezes, cornices, strip mouldings, corbels and pilasters to cartwheels and panels of fake books — and in designs ranging from the classical to the Jacobean. All pieces are hand-finished to ensure individual character, then stained medium oak, or lighter or darker shades to order. Other special finishes include simulated gold and silver leaf (antiqued or bright), metallic colours and even shaded paintwork. COTTAGE COLLECTION includes beams, joists, planking, plate racks and false nuts and bolts, simply fitted using nails and glue to transform a room from modern to Tudor. Oakleaf also reproduce pieces from existing originals. Standard material has British Standard Class 4 fire rating but all products are available in OAKSCREEN material, tested to Class 1 fire rating, suitable for hotels and restaurants. *P:* main beams approx £40; feature panels £13-£40; linenfold panelling approx £71 sq m (£59 sq yd); arches £28-£38; cornices £11–£43 per 2–3m (78–118in) run; friezes £14–£28 per approx 1.5m (59in) run; 17-book panel £28.34.
See following page for illustration.

ARCHITECTURAL ORNAMENTS

Simulated wood ornaments in polyurethane by Oakleaf Reproductions. Above: Jacobean-style carving; below: 'oak' beams and planking

STUART INTERIORS
Authentic-looking Elizabethan and Jacobean panelling recreated by craftsmen who special-

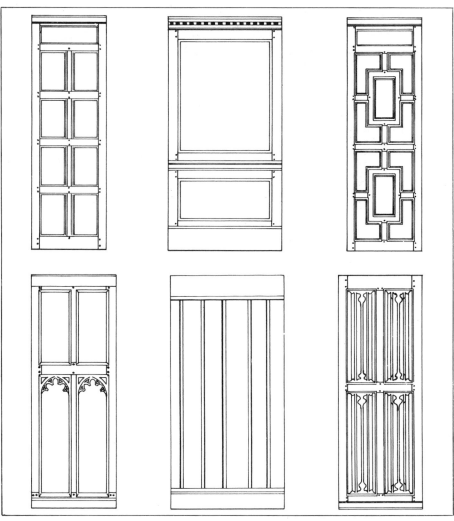

Left to right, from top: chamfered panels; large panels with arras rail; inner-frame, Gothic, plank and linenfold panelling. All from Stuart Interiors

ize in the woodwork of these periods, making everything from four-posters to staircases. Using traditional woods such as English oak, holly, yew and walnut, they will make panelling and mouldings to specification, incorporating carving if required. *P:* (per sq ft) plain panelling £14; heavy gothic panelling £20.50; linenfold panelling £31 (ex VAT).

WINTHER BROWNE & CO LTD
BRIO door, wall and ceiling mouldings, all made from kiln-dried samba, a straw-coloured hardwood. For door panels there are four profiles with matching sweeps and corner rounds, all pre-cut; available loose or in kits with option of additional ply inset panels to give greater relief. There are also four profiles for walls, suitable for skirting, architrave, dado and picture rail. These can be used for panelling too. Three cornice profiles are available, with pre-assembled corners to avoid awkward mitring. *M:* door panels standard l200cm (78¼in); wall mouldings standard l220cm (86½in). *P:* door panelling, kits from £2.95, curves from £2.10; quarter circles from 70p; wall mouldings from £2.85 per m; cornices from £3 per m.

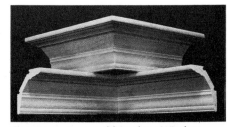

Cornice corner mouldings from Winther Browne

BATHROOMS

INTRODUCTION

The bathroom is often one of the smallest rooms in the house but there's no reason why it should also be the dullest. On the contrary, it could be the place for your most daring experiments — no one will stay there long enough to suffer. Foil paper, mirrors, even gloss paint on the walls, will brighten it up. Or go for white walls, tiles and sanitaryware — the cheapest way to create a dramatic effect, with towels and accessories providing colour and decorative highlights. If you're furnishing from scratch, there's an almost endless choice of styles: how about functional high tech, Victorian revival, glamorous 1930s, or even a decadent look in reconstituted marble?

Bathrooms tend to be short on space, so work with a graph-paper floor plan to find the most suitable lay-out. And, if you're planning basic alterations, remember that WCs are best kept on, or adjacent to, an outside wall, or near the existing outlet. Baths and sinks are more moveable but it makes sense to keep them as close as possible to existing outlets too. Baths come in varying widths and lengths — some are only 48 × 24in (122 × 61cm) — so even the smallest space can accommodate one in style. This section is divided into three. *Fittings and furniture* covers cabinets and units, panels for both walls and baths, accessories from shaving mirrors to soap dishes and toilet-roll holders, and all types of tap fittings. Taps come in three basic designs: traditional paired pillar taps, three-piece sets consisting of two separate handwheels or tap heads and a separate spout, and monobloc mixers, needing only one hole because they combine taps and spout. Taps can usually be fitted to baths and basins from any manufacturer providing the size and number of holes are compatible. Styles and materials vary from the standard chrome-plated brass fittings to exotic (and expensive) ones in gold plate, often combined with porcelain, crystal, even semi-precious stones. Accessories cover an equally broad scope and can add quite a tidy sum to the basic cost. If you're counting pennies, go for inexpensive co-ordinated plastic accessories in a colour that contrasts or blends with sanitaryware and bathroom walls.

Sanitaryware includes baths, basins — small cloakroom or hand basins as well as larger wash basins (usually on pedestals) and vanity basins (fitted into a counter top) — WCs and bidets; and also exotic items such as Jacuzzis and hot tubs, which are fast catching on for homes as well as health clubs. Here, too, there are standard shapes, sizes and colours, but also some lovely decorated ranges, and some exclusive (and expensive) designs that can turn a bathroom into a fantasy land. A chart gives a breakdown, by manufacturer, of standard colours available for vitreous china suits (basin, bidet and WC); baths, most often in acrylic or enamelled steel, are generally available in all these colours and more. White is almost always the cheapest colour, hand-painted wares the most expensive.

Showers includes shower trays, enclosures (partial and complete), curtains and rails and shower kits; also a Roman steam bath — not a shower but fitted in a shower cubicle. See *Fittings and furniture* for bath/shower mixers and handsets, and shower heads that are co-ordinated with other plumbing fittings.

● Representative products from each company are usually illustrated and prices given accordingly.

● For antique sanitaryware and fittings see *Architectural salvage* at the end of the book.

FITTINGS AND FURNITURE

W ADAMS & SONS LTD

REGAL ANTIQUE fittings, designed to complement Victorian-style sanitaryware. There are traditionally styled pillar taps for bath, basin and kitchen sink, monobloc mixers and shower mixers, pop-up wastes and plug and chain sets, all in polished brass or gold- or chrome-plated. Shelves, shaving mirrors, shower curtain rails and other accessories are also available. *P:* basin pillar taps £69 pair; bath/shower mixer with handset £265 (ex VAT).

ALBION HARDWARE LTD

Nostalgic bathroom accessories. VICTORIAN BRASS offers three choices of metal finish — polished and lacquered brass, chrome and everbright (which looks like brass but won't tarnish) — in a comprehensive range. Included is brass-mounted wall light with engraved glass globe, rimless oval mirror, glass soap tray and toothbrush/tumbler holder, double and single tumbler holders, single towel rail, hook and ring, toilet-paper holder plus spare roll holder, characterful single and double robe hooks, extendible wall-mounted shaving mirror, toilet-brush holder, shelf with a brass rail, cistern lever, cistern pull and chain, even a brass cord pull. *P:* soap dish £12–£15.50; shelf £30–£43; double hook £15–£22.50; mirror £48–£62; wall light £28–£38.

Albion's cool and pretty CHINA range covers almost the same items except that there is a double towel rail, two mirrors (rectangular or square with a frame), a free-standing soap dish and toothbrush/tumbler holder, and no shelf.

VICTORIAN toilet-roll holder from Albion

'Meadow Flower' accessories from Albion

There are two charming flower-sprigged designs — 'Meadow Flower' with cheerful rose, blue and gold sprays and 'Summer Mist' in gentle pastels — as well as plain white porcelain, and a gold line decoration on white. *P:* soap dish £8–£11.50; double towel rail £22–£28; brush holder £28.50–£32.50; mirrors £15–£55; wall light £29–£36. See *Ceramic tiles* for matching wall tiles and *Fittings* for matching door fittings.

ALLIA (UK) LTD

Wide range from the company that used to be called Royal Doulton. Stylish, geometrical AMBASSADOR mixer sets in chrome or gold-effect 'Lustrebond' for baths, basins and bidets are fitted with interchangeable ceramic tap-head inserts in colours that match Allia's sanitaryware (see sanitaryware chart). Mixers can be monobloc or three-hole, with parabolic jet or rising spray on the bidet; bath fittings include handshower with wall bracket and bath side valves with separate spout. *P:* monobloc basin mixer with pop-up waste £82–£115.25.

Allia's range of angled vitreous china accessories in standard colours plus white, ivory and vanilla silk includes wall-mounted soap dish, toothbrush/tumbler holder, towel rail and ring, shelf, double robe-hook and toilet-roll holder. The acrylic 'Carisma' vanity bar with shelves and mirror could be a useful addition, mounted alongside the bath. *P:* soap dish £9.50–£12.50; vanity bar £28.50–£33.50.

Also on offer is ARABELLA, Allia's integrated bathroom furniture system made of strips of pine or stained oak; elements include single and double base units with optional plinths, the first with double doors and the second with three doors and a set of fingerpull drawers; tall cupboards with drawers and doors

C.P. HART

Cast iron Roll Top Bath with brass ball & claw feet and Leonardo taps.

NOT JUST ON VIEW,
BUT AVAILABLE IMMEDIATELY.

Photograph by Bob Carlos Clarke.

One habit you won't want to get out of. The genuine Jacuzzi whirlpool bath.

Imagine. Your own Jacuzzi whirlpool bath. A daily experience of swirling, massaging, invigorating bubbles. Washing away your aches and pains. Relaxing your entire body. And leaving you refreshed and tingling all over.

Available in a wide range of colours and sizes, you can purchase the Jacuzzi whirlpool bath of your choice from any of Rainbow Products' authorised Jacuzzi dealers throughout the country. But do be warned: getting into the genuine Jacuzzi habit is a great deal easier than getting out.

For further information, contact Rainbow Products Ltd, Albion Wharf, Hester Road, London SW11 4AN. Tel: 01-228 9321.

Rainbow Leisure Group Limited.

and optional plinth; and mirror with strip light to go above a base unit with vanity basin(s). *M:* units w60 or 120 × h73 × d55cm (23½ or 47¼ × 28¾ × 21¾); cupboard w35 × h194 × d20cm (13¾ × 76½ × 7¾in); mirror w60 or 120cm (23½ or 47¼in). *P:* units £120.75, £226; cupboard £217; mirror £130–£202.

ARCHITECTURAL COMPONENTS LTD
Bathroom accessories in various metal finishes (brass, chrome, gold, nickel or antique bronze). Imposing 501 and 502 range has decorated round or plain square classical mounts. There are two sizes of glass shelf, various towel rails, towel ring, towel hook and robe hook, round metal-framed mirror, tall padded metal stool, two toilet-roll holders and reserve roll holder, tumbler and soap holders with tinted grey glass receptacles and a classic wall light with tinted globe. Solid brass SUSSEX range, also available in chrome or gold-plate, has only 10 items and a milder design: included is an oval framed mirror, magnetic soap-holder and wall-mounted toothbrush holder, as well as the usual holders, rails, hooks and rings. *P:* 501/502 soap dish £26–£64; SUSSEX magnetic soap holder £9–£20; soap dish £16.50–£51.

Architectural Components' SUSSEX accessories

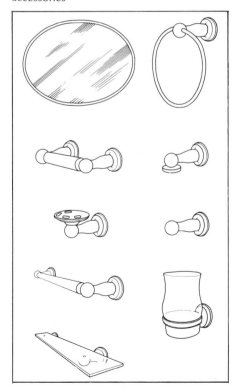

ARCHITECTURAL HERITAGE OF CHELTENHAM
Beautiful brass taps and mixers in 'Adam', Victorian and Edwardian styles, produced by Architectural Heritage in response to the demand for their antique bathroom fittings. There are bath and basin pillar taps, monobloc basin set with pop-up waste, three-piece tap set, set of waste, plug and chain, and bath/shower mixers (one with porcelain handle to the handset and adjustable mountings). Many other brass fittings are available to order. *P:* basin pillar taps £48–£100 pair; bath pillar taps £120 pair; monobloc set £120; three-piece set £135; plug and chain set £18–£35; bath/shower mixers £255.

ARMITAGE SHANKS LTD
Clean-lined STARLITE taps in Lustron 23ct gold plate or with handwheels made of acrylic simulating tortoiseshell, onyx and veined oyster in gold, brown, green, red or white. Range includes shower fittings (hand-operated or wall-mounted and thermostatically controlled) as well as bath, basin and bidet pillars, three-hole sets and monobloc mixers.
Designed to complement STARLITE tortoiseshell fittings is a set of six accessories — soap dish, tumbler holder and shelf in smoked glass, and towel rail, sliding rail for shower handspray, and towel or toilet-roll holder in Lustron 23ct gold finish only — all with acrylic 'tortoiseshell' and gold detailing.
Two ranges of ceramic accessories, one with round shapes and one with square shapes, are available in the same colours as Armitage Shanks' sanitaryware (see chart): some, like the recessed soap and sponge trays and toilet-roll holders, should be considered at the same time as tiling. Otherwise there is a wall-mounted soap tray, tumbler/toothbrush holder, double robe-hook, towel ring, toilet-roll holder with shelf above, towel rail, shelf, and toilet-brush holder in the round-ended de-

STARLITE bidet mixer set by Armitage Shanks

From Armitage Shank's STARLITE range. Top: bath mixer; below: basin mixer

sign; and an additional magnetic soap holder, kitchen-roll holder, double toilet-roll holder and pack holder in the square.
P: on application.

BERNARD J ARNULL LTD
Sleek and chunky mixers, monoblocs and shower fittings from the French firm Porcher. ORIENT, AGATE and AMBER sets come in a variety of finishes — matt as well as lustre gold, matt silver, bronze and chrome. ORIENT has three-hole fittings for baths, basins and bidets accompanied by oval heads with coloured enamel flashes to match the sanitaryware (see chart) and the option of flashes on the spouts. AGATE concentrates on monobloc fittings with flashes on the spouts. AMBER heads are made of the same ceramic as the sanitaryware and are triangular in shape, although other variations are possible. A further JADE series is economically-priced and more spindly in appearance. Typical of Porcher ingenuity is a tuckaway handshower which fits neatly into the side of a washbasin. *P:* basin mixers, ORIENT £111–£560; AGATE £135–£303; AMBER

£78–£151; JADE £64; tuckaway handshower £21.

Porcher also manufacture FEMINA ceramic accessories to match the sanitaryware using fluid elliptical shapes. Included are towel rail, toilet-roll holder, toilet-brush holder, toothbrush/tumbler holder, soap dish and shelf, in a choice of 13 colours, including shaded ones (see sanitaryware chart). *P:* soap dish £16.75–£33.55; towel rail £56–£78.

Amongst other ranges imported by Arnull is Aleria's TAHITI range with a French Empire look in chrome or gold plate and enamel in 25 shaded colours. Included are the same basic accessories as above, plus robe hooks, toilet-pack holder, mirrors, pedal-bin, tissue-box holder and several lamps with frilled glass shades. *P:* soap dish £35–£55.

Another exciting range comes from OVADIA and is made of sprayed and hand-painted wood in the client's choice of colours. All the designs have an art deco feeling, seen at its most impressive in the mirrors, criss-crossed with cut-out wooden shapes on the themes of 'Belle Epoque', 'Cygne', 'New York', 'Place Vendôme', 'Polygale', 'Retro' and 'Marquise'. There are 14 items including double and single towel rails, robe hooks, toilet-roll holder, toothbrush/tumbler holder, lights with tulip shades, and soap holders. *P:* mirror £275; soap dish and holder £63.80.

Tuckaway handshower and basin from Arnull

ARTISAN DESIGN
Custom-built and perfectly fitted vanity units, bath panels, mirrored cabinets, shelves, airing cupboards and wall panels. Each bathroom is innovatively designed in any style, in hardwood, pine or melamine, and beautifully made by a skilled craftsman. Prices are remarkably reasonable for such personalized service. *P:* on application.

B & E MARKETING LTD
Continental vitreous china accessories available in almost any colour. Rectangular ELLE range includes four different wall-fixed soap dishes with a hold for a square tumbler to the left or the right, in addition to a neat toilet-brush holder, toilet-roll holder and double robe-hook. Fluid-looking C COLLECTION offers semi-recessed soap trays (two with loops to hold a flannel), toilet-roll holder and tumbler holder. R COLLECTION has a stylish, contemporary Italian look with a toothbrush/tumbler holder, soap dishes — one for basin, one for bath and one for bidet or shower — toilet-roll holders, towel rail in three sizes, towel holder with chrome detail, plus hook and useful angled corner shelf. Further selections, which co-ordinate with the others, include two mirrors with ceramic frames and incorporated lighting (one oval with fluorescent light, one rectangular with spotlights), a liquid soap dispenser, hooks and rails, shelves (including another corner shelf) and a toilet-brush holder that completely conceals the brush. Many of the wall-mounted items can simply be fixed to the wall with adhesive. *P:* on application.

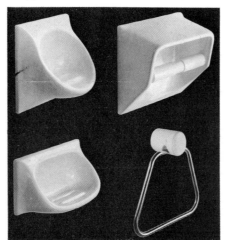

Accessories from B & E Marketing's R COLLECTION

BALTERLEY BATHROOMS LTD
Vitreous china accessories in 12 plain colours including white to complement Balterley's bathroom suites (see *Bathrooms, sanitaryware*). Basic range has wall-mounted soap dish, toilet-roll holder, towel ring, toothbrush/tumbler holder, framed mirror and wall light. To match the ROMANA suites the accessories come with gold or silver rims. In addition traditional pitchers and bowls, and an urn, decorated with flowers, are available in FLORIANA and ROSE designs and in white or champagne (which can be gilded to match the EDWARDIAN suite) while a Victorian-style chamber

pot, shelf and robe-hook go with the ROSE and EDWARDIAN ranges and there is even a ROSE patterned door knob and fingerplate.

Balterley also offer plain or decorated ceramic tap heads to match their suites and these are supplied with DELTAFLOW taps and mixers, including monoblocs, in chrome, gold or Midas gold finish for baths, basins and bidets. *P:* on application.

See following page for illustration.

BARKING-GROHE LTD
Competitively priced, space-age taps and mixers that stand out from the general run. Perhaps the most aerodynamic in design is the chrome COLANI range of bath and basin mixers, bidet and bath shower fittings; it cuts down on noise by reducing resistance to water flow. Heads have to be ordered separately since there is a wide choice of colour and finish (chrome, olive, tobacco, sand, magnolia, crocus and jasmine, as well as red/blue). Always pursuing technical excellence, Barking-Grohe are strong on monobloc one-hole fittings which take up the minimum of space and can be operated by Euromix single levers as well as by two taps. Both the LUXURY and HARMONY IN WHITE ranges offer levers, and the CLASSIC range has horizontally-positioned taps on its bath mixer for easy turning. Tap heads in these ranges are usually triangular in shape, either in smooth chrome or simulated smoked glass or brown and green onyx; 'Astral' and 'Crystal' are more traditionally round-shaped. *P:* on application.

Barking-Grohe's COLANI mixer

THE BATH STUDIO
Wide range of tapware from Dorf, Australia's leading manufacturer, including shower sets. EL TORO bath and basin sets have traditional cross heads raised on a chrome or gold spindle, with a modern, rock-hard gloss finish in white, ivory, beige, clay, grey, royal blue or warm brown. CHANTILLY is a similar design in ceramic, available in white or ivory with 23ct gold spindles and trimmings, also in 'Hampton Blue' flower-sprigged version. Also ceramic are the heads of BOOSTER CERAMIC range which come in most of the same colours as EL

Balterley's ROSE accessories with matching sanitaryware

TORO, plus an avocado and a flowery 'Springtime' version, all combined with chrome. *P:* three-hole basin mixer with pop-up waste, EL TORO £97; CHANTILLY £176; BOOSTER £87. All these can be co-ordinated with Dorf's designer accessories which include adjustable mirror, toilet-roll holder, wall-mounted soap dish, guest-towel holder, towel rail and ring, toothbrush/tumbler holder, and vanity shelf. They are available in gold or chrome finish as well as in the colours used for tapware. *P:* soap dish £13.50–£30; towel rail £27–£71.

In contrast are MANOR HOUSE traditional taps in polished brass or chrome for baths, basins and all-directional shower sets, and accessories which include a wall-mounted soap dish, towel rail and ring, robe-hook,

toilet-roll and toothbrush/tumbler holders. *P:* three-hole basin mixer £140; soap dish £40.

For simulated smoked-crystal tap heads there are reasonably-priced GLOBE and DIAMOND ranges which offer clear heads as well as shades of blue, brown, charcoal and pale green. For the real thing go to Dorf's EXOTIQUE range which has quartz-crystal heads cut by Swarovski in Austria and mounted on 23ct gold or silver chrome. *P:* bath fillers, EXOTIOUE £270; GLOBE, DIAMOND £127.

The Bath Studio also stocks VOLA bath, bidet, basin and shower combinations designed by the Danish architect Arne Jacobsen. They have clean, functional lines in eight strong colours of stoved electrostatic epoxy finish plus chrome and polished brass. Accessories include a magnetic soap holder and dispenser, towel hooks, rings and rails, toothpaste,

toothbrush and glass holders, toilet-roll holder, mirror holder, shelf, ashtray, doorknob, grab rails, flush knob and shower holder. *P:* basin mixer £80–£190; soap holder £9–£14.

BERGLEN PRODUCTS LTD

Self-assembly German OPTIFIT bathroom units which can be used in bedrooms too. There are 14 different wall, base, mirror, and tall units — even a unit for dirty linen — in louvred pine (with natural, chestnut or white lacquer finish) or plain doors in Bahama beige or white finish with knobs or loop handles and the option of a coloured vertical strip trim on the white. Basins can be set into jutting vanity tops for extra space. *P:* on application.

BISQUE

Towel radiators that warm the room, dry and store innumerable towels, and look good in their own right. Made by the Swiss company Zehnder, they come in a variety of sizes and can be bought in white stove enamel finish or ordered in more than 150 colours. *M:* h75.9 × w50cm (30 × 19¾in) to h180.3 × 75cm (70¾ × 29½in). *P:* £75–£127 (ex VAT).

Zehnder towel radiator from Bisque

CANDLELIGHT PRODUCTS LTD

Pretty rattan towel nest with towel rails and shelves for bathroom bottles and boxes. Comes in natural varnish, or sprayed white, smoke, pink, peach, peppermint or beige. *M:* d41 × w91 × h81cm (16¼ × 35¾ × 32in). *P:* from £80.

BATHROOMS

CARRON CABINET & JOINERY MANUFACTURING CO LTD

Self-assembly vanity units in three widths and three qualities plus matching wall cupboards. 'Royale', 'Vanity Fair' and 'Vanity Supreme' are made of formica laminate and finished in oyster, white, white leather and white tuscany with simulated onyx top. Wall cupboards can have mirror doors or decoration to match units. *M:* w70, 80, 120cm (27½, 31½, 47¼). *P:* on application.

CARTERS (J & A) LTD

Specialist items for the disabled and elderly to make bathrooms more safe and accessible. They range from chrome-plated steel grab bars and safety rails to wooden bath seats, mobile shower chairs and raised polypropylene toilet

'Vancouver' bath rail and wheelchair toilet rail for the disabled. Both from Carters

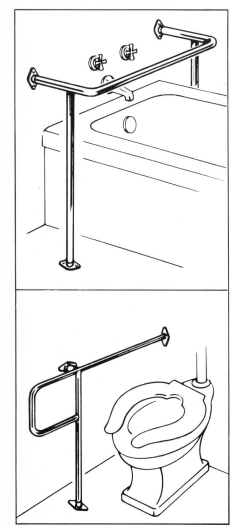

seats. There are also non-slip rubber mats for baths and showers in pastel colours. *P:* toilet seats from £12; shower chair £70.

CATHEDRAL WORKS ORGANIZATION

Marble, onyx and granite slab vanity tops, splashbacks, bath and wall surrounds from the French company Rocamat; all cut to order. More than 60 types provide a vast choice of colour and pattern but popular ones are 'Campan' marble with rust and green veining, and 'Chassagne' which can be grey, rose, beige, putty-coloured or banded. 'Saint Corneille' is speckled, sparkling, crackled or even 'floral'. Cathedral Works can also provide a complete marble bathroom, from floor to ceiling. *P:* on application.

CELMAC DISTRIBUTORS LTD

Large range of toilet seats designed with comfort, hygiene and practicality in mind. There are standard and heavy duty qualities, the latter recommended for contract installations. Different designs are available with double flap (seat and cover) or single flap (seat only) in black, white and 30 common sanitaryware colours. *P:* £10.70–£44.

CERAMIC TILE DESIGN

Ceramic soap dishes, towel rails, toothbrush holders and toilet-roll holders in 27 stock colours to match most colours of sanitaryware. *P:* soap dish £7.
Ceramic Tile Design can also supply marble basins, bath and basin cut-outs, over- and under-fittings, and soap dishes. They will have the marble cut in Italy and delivered in two to three weeks. Range of colours includes red, black, and green veining and the commoner grey and white. *P:* on application.

CHLORIDE SHIRES LTD

DA VINCI taps, mixers and shower fittings, finished in chrome, Venetian gold and gold plate, and SERENADE accessories in vitreous china, all commendably simple in design. Tap heads are either five-sided metal or transparent acrylic. The square, contemporary-looking accessories are available in the 10 colours of Shires' sanitaryware (see sanitaryware chart) and include wall-mounted towel rails and ring, toilet-roll and toothbrush holders, robe-hook and three shelves for soap, sponges and cosmetics. Matching screw covers are supplied with each accessory. *P:* on application. See also *Bathrooms, sanitaryware.*

CRAYONNE LTD

Well-designed, functional accessories in thermoplastic. CRAYONNE 1 collection of round-edged shelf, soap tray, towel rail and ring, toothbrush/tumbler holder, toilet-brush hol-

SERENADE accessories from Chloride Shires

Accessories from CRAYONNE 1 and CO-ORDINATES COLLECTION △, by Crayonne

der and a round and square mirror is already well-established (in bright red, navy, white, yellow, green and grey) as is CRAYONNE II, with a more angular look and the same items except the round mirror (in red, navy, white, beige and light green). These can be mixed or matched with a wider CO-ORDINATES COLLECTION of larger items such as a bath rack, bins, linen and shower tidies, tissue cube, a toilet seat (in white, red and navy only), and freestanding mug and soap holders. *P:* soap dish £6.90, £4.80; square mirror £25, £19.50; oval bin £11; toilet seat £18.

Using the same cheerful colours are four patterned nylon shower curtains ('Morse', 'Tramway', 'Tulips' and 'Candy Stripe') and even a 'Candy Stripe' window blind. Also available are plain bath-mat sets (standard and large rugs, pedestal mat and toilet-seat cover) in 100% looped and latex-backed cotton. *P:* curtains £21; blind £25–£36; standard mat £10.25. To complete the picture, there are two bathroom cabinets: 'Coronado' in coloured thermoplastic (white, red, navy, beige, light green and grey) with sliding mirror doors, or 'Capri' in white with hinged mirror doors and coloured trim (in white, red, navy, chrome, beige, light green, yellow and green) plus a tinted door-pocket and 'no key' medicine section inside. *M:* 'Coronado' h47 × w51 × d15cm (18½ × 20 × 6in); 'Capri' h52 × w57 × d17cm (20½ × 22 × 7in). *P:* 'Coronado' £40; 'Capri' £45.

CZECH & SPEAKE LTD
Beautifully-finished EDWARDIAN range with riser pipes and traditional brass pillar taps or levers with white porcelain fittings on its shower, basin, bidet and bath mixer sets. Nickel and chrome finishes are available in addition to polished and lacquered brass; and gold, copper, bronze and exciting black chrome finishes can be ordered specially. In addition there is a traditional pull-out handshower mixer, a thermostatically-controlled handshower and four overhead shower roses, one an enormous 12in (30cm) in diameter. *P:* basin mixer with adjustable pop-up waste £200–£300; shower roses £12–£200; bath/shower mixer

Basin mixers from Czech & Speake. Below: black chrome; bottom: CURZON

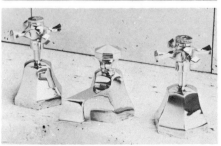

with handset £442.75–£799.25.
Included in the EDWARDIAN range are about 14 basic accessories from double towel rails to cistern lever. The brass robe-hooks with porcelain heads, double tumbler holder and tumblers, freestanding toothbrush holder, and elaborate metal bath rack are all outstanding period pieces. *P:* soap dish and holder £28–£56; bath rack £70–£130.
An interesting development is the introduction of two faceted 1920s- and 1930s-style CURZON mixers and a showerhead. They are finished to the same high standards in chrome, nickel or polished brass and the faceted taps can be rim or wall-mounted. A 1930s-style stool in cork and chrome is also available. *P:* any set £240; stool £70.

DAMIXA
For the bathroom or kitchen of the 1980s and beyond, taps in chrome and bright primaries, from Denmark. Thick, tubular hot and cold controls connect with a straight or spout mixer in a bold T-shape. Touch control through 90° turns tap on full with a flick of the wrist. There are bath/shower, bidet and basin mixers in white, red, blue, yellow, mocca or chrome with optional pop-up waste. Single lever taps are also available, and soap or hand-cream dispensers that can be fitted into the basin in the hole normally occupied by the second tap. *P:* basin mixer £55.77, with pop-up waste £62.27; soap dispenser £7.80.

FRANKE
Range of units including a diagonal vanity unit that fits into corners, saving space but providing plenty of storage. In white or Bahama beige, it has a roomy mirrored cabinet to match. *P:* on application.

GARDEX LTD
Co-ordinated plastic accessories in 30 sanitaryware-matched colours. There is a good selection of vanity units from one-piece units incorporating splashback, fixed or lifting mirror, shelf, towel rail, soap dish, toothbrush holder etc, to useful small corner cabinets and a corner-fitting shelf unit. Bath panels are also available. *P:* on application.

HABITAT DESIGNS LTD
Striking bathroom accessories. The most handsome are in dark mahogany with gleaming white porcelain mounts: a round-edged shelf, toothbrush holder with porcelain mug, soap holder, toilet-roll holder, single and double towel hooks, towel rail, mahogany cabinet with sliding mirror doors, square mahogany-framed mirror, porcelain toilet-brush holder, mahogany toilet seat and bathroom scales. Pure high tech, and also with white fittings, is a

COUNTRY accessories from Habitat

chrome-tube range including a mirror, shelf, soap dish, toothbrush/tumbler holder, toilet-roll holder, hooks and two lengths of towel rail. *P:* mahogany mirror £19.95, chrome mirror £18.50; soap dish with mahogany trim £10.95, chrome trim £7.95.
Refreshingly down-to-earth are Habitat's COUNTRY accessories made of varnished natural pine, except for a freestanding soap dish in white china. There is a round and a square pine-framed mirror, a towel ring entirely in pine, a single and double towel rail, toothbrush/tumbler holder, shelf, toilet-roll holder, plastic toilet brush holder with pine base and handle, a cabinet with sliding mirror doors, a hook rack with six hooks, pine toilet seat with chrome fittings, and surprisingly, but perfectly in keeping, vaudeville lights on a pine strip to go beside a mirror to give excellent illumination for make-up or shaving. *P:* lavatory seat £48.95; toothbrush/tumbler holder £9.95; vaudeville lights £12.95.
Also available is the cheap yet durable CRAYONNE 1 range in grey, red and white only (see separate entry) and AERO in white or red plastic-coated wire. This includes a shelf, shower caddy and soap dish with wire mesh trays, a ring tumbler-holder, a bar toothbrush holder, a toilet-roll holder and towel rail, all of which could be joined by one of three small round and rectangular mirrors framed in white, red, blue or green plastic. *P:* shower caddy £3.75; soap tray £2.75; mirrors £4.85–£7.95.
In addition there are seven kinds of shower curtain to choose from, together with red, blue or aluminium shower-rail kits and shower-rail rings: transparent plastic with a blue or red border; plain beige or white woven nylon; red and white stripe specially treated against mould; 'Raindrops' with multicoloured diagonal dashes and 'Liana' with vertical wavy lines in red, blue, yellow and green on

BATHROOMS

treated cotton. Bathmats in a practical beige, or red, green or blue stripes on beige, and bathroom scales in white with blue, green, yellow or red edging continue Habitat's primaries theme. *P:* curtains £5.75–£16.95; bathmats £5–£6; scales £14.25.

M & I J HARRISON

Classically styled mahogany, pine and oak vanity units in 12 different finishes — natural, medium or antiqued pine, red, brown or golden mahogany, medium, dark or magnolia oak, magnolia or white American oak. They are available with brass knobs and handles in single, double, multiple or corner versions, and can accommodate most types of cultured marble, tile or laminate tops and almost any inset basin. Waste bins and laundry bins can be fitted behind the unit doors. In addition there is a full range of matching bath and shower panels, dado and wall panels, airing cupboards and robe cupboards, toilet seats, plus some brass accessories mounted on matching wood — towel rails, towel ring, toilet-roll holder and robe hooks. Fully-fitted bathrooms can be made to client's specifications. *M:* single unit h30 × w21 × d33in (76 × 54 × 84cm). *P:* £279–£348.

Red mahogany vanity unit by Harrison

C P HART & SONS LTD.

Vast retail range drawn from major manufacturers. Exclusive LEONARDO range of taps and accessories from France follows the trend for Victoriana. It includes monobloc mixers and pillar taps, pop-up waste, bidet set, toilet-roll holder, fitted glass shelf, soap dish, towel ring, toothbrush holder and oval mirror; all in brass or with brass detailing, with polished, chrome-plated, red, white, blue or sugar pink or

C P Hart's LEONARDO mixer and handset

enamelled finish. *P:* bath/shower mixer with handset £182.16; shelf £52.48; soap dish £29.90; toilet-roll holder £15.56.

HEATHERLEY FINE CHINA LTD

Wide selection of accessories. Heatherley's HERITAGE range in bone china, either plain white or with simple floral patterns, includes everything from trinket boxes, soap dishes, hooks and tumblers to toilet-roll holders, toilet-brush holders and toilet brushes. It also includes a clear perspex towel rail and chrome- or gold-plated towel rings. Similar items are available in plain ceramic in a large range of British sanitaryware colours. *P:* HERITAGE trinket box £5.05; soap dish £4.50. Heatherley also make wooden accessories. There's a variety of toilet seats with chrome, brass or gold fittings, a chain pull with brass chain, large towel ring, toilet-roll brush holders, soap dish, tumbler holder and wall lights. All come in mahogany or pine with natural, walnut or mahogany finish. *P:* toilet seats from £60; chain pull £6.70; pine towel ring £12; pine soap dish £10.
There are also EMBASSY cabinets in wood, painted in sanitaryware-matched colours. These range from single drawer unit to double door cabinet, and there are five different oval, round and rectangular mirrors; all these elements can be assembled in various configurations. *P:* single drawer unit £22.60; double door cabinet £46–£60; mirrors £20–£42.50.

IDEAL STANDARD LTD

Good selection of accessories and fittings, designed with the same flair as Ideal Standard's

sanitaryware. EMPRESS, PRINCESS and DUCHESS accessory ranges include soap dishes, toilet-roll holders, glass and toothbrush holders, shelves and towel rails, all in sanitaryware-matched colours. MONOLUX, DUALUX and JETLINE monobloc and pillar taps, mixers and shower fittings are available in chrome- or gold-plated finish, or in a white acrylic finish. JETLINE also has the option of green or brown onyx and white marble tap heads. *P:* on application.

IDEAL TIMBER PRODUCTS LTD

Practical self-assembly vanity units, suitable for bathrooms, bedrooms or cloakrooms. ENGLISH ROSE range comes with a 3cm (1¼in) thick, round-edged, laminated countertop in a choice of two colours, vellum or Adriatic marble, and in three door designs: 'Lady Ann' in white textured laminate with solid oak trims and door knobs; 'Lady Jane' in sand-coloured textured laminate with solid oak trims and beige and brown enamelled door knobs; 'Lady Margaret' in laminate painted and lacquered in a profile design in blue and white. COUNTESS range comes in white or beige melamine with stylish 'gold-ring' handles and with the option of decorative gold/white or gold/brown door trims. *M:* ENGLISH ROSE w80 × d50 × 77½cm (31½ × 19¾ × 30½in); COUNTESS w76 × d47 × h75cm (30 × 18½ × 29½in). *P:* ENGLISH ROSE, 'Lady Ann' and 'Lady Jane' £79.95, 'Lady Margaret' £109.95; COUNTESS price on application.

MAMOLI

Superbly styled Italian chrome or imitor (gold finish) taps, either in geometric shapes or with more traditionally arched spouts. There is a choice of pillar, monobloc and three-piece taps and mixers for basins, bidets and baths. Certain models have swivel spouts, and pop-up wastes are an optional extra. *P:* basin pillar taps, chrome £22, imitor £40; bath/shower mixer with handset, chrome £60, imitor £112.

MARBLE STYLE LTD

Cultured onyx accessories, including wall panels. Combined or separate shampoo and soap holders, tissue dispensers and toilet-roll holders can be recessed into the wall (with or without trim moulds) in a marble effect bathroom, but there is also a plain wall-mounted toilet-roll holder, towel rail and ring with chrome or gold-plated attachments, and a wall-mounted or freestanding soap tray, in colours akin to natural marble and onyx. Vanity units to match are built by M & I J Harrison (see separate entry). Panels to go round baths or vanity units as well as from floor to ceiling are available moulded with swan, fern and sunburst designs or with incised panelling. There are even Mediterranean design floor-tiles and non-structural Ionic columns in Ortega Onyx to create a 'Last Days of Pompeii' effect. *P·* soap dish £13.70; fern wall panel (66 × 152.4 cm/26 × 60 in) £172.

Cultured onyx vanity top by Marble Style

METLEX INDUSTRIES LTD

Comprehensive collection of bathroom accessories, including 40 types of bathroom cabinet with mirror doors (some with diffused lighting, drawers, shaver socket and digital clock), over 30 types of mirror, 14 types of towel rail or ring, 14 toilet-roll holders as well as many kinds of holder, hook, shelf, bracket, rail and rack. Cork-topped stools and boxes are also available. NATURAL CHOICE range is made of pine with brass fittings and includes two cabinets, a 'three-way' combined toilet-roll holder, towel bar and shelf unit, single toilet-roll holder, soap tray and tumbler/toothbrush holder (with tinted plastic), towel ring, smoked-glass shelf, tissue-box holder, toilet-roll storage box, double hook and pine-framed mirrors. Plastic CONTOUR is contemporary-looking and comes in white, glade green, light beige, deep blue and crystal (lightly smoked bronze). It includes a wall-mounted soap dish, magnetic soap holder, double and single tumbler holder, toilet-roll holder, toiletry shelf, bath rack, hooks, towel rail, nailbrush and holder, wall tidy, and wall mirror as well as a freestanding waste bin, linen-tidy stool, vanity stool, toilet-brush holder and mirror. MEDALLION is a timeless brass-plated range with grab bar, towel rails and ring, shelves, hook, draining soap dish and toothbrush/tumbler holder, toilet-roll holder, plus two mirrors — a freestanding shaving or make-up mirror and a wall-mounted extending one. *P:* soap dishes £4.35–£7.50; mirrors £10–£47.

Metlex also make a large range of basic hotel and contract fittings, such as metal soap dishes, multiple clean towel racks and a standard basin stand with chromed rod legs; plus TIP-RO contract washroom equipment, soap dispensers etc. *P:* on application.

PRICES AND INFORMATION WERE CORRECT AT THE TIME OF GOING TO PRESS

'Blue Diamond 11' bathroom cabinet from Metlex

PATRICKS OF FARNHAM

Real marble vanity tops cut to fit client's own basin, with tap holes, draining soap recesses and polished edges as required. Patricks will also produce bath panels, wall claddings and entire bathrooms in marble. There are 10 possible choices of grade and colour: three

Marble cladding by Patricks of Farnham

dark greens, black and gold mix, various brown, beige and pink tones, white and grey, each with a different grain. *P:* 24 × 66in (61 × 167.6cm) vanity top with two overbasin cutouts, three tap lever holes per basin, two hand-polished soap dishes with drain channels, ¾in (2cm) thick marble, £580.

PETIT ROQUE LTD

Marble vanity tops, splashbacks, bath panels and matching wall tiles in a choice of beige, cream, white, black, green and pinky browns. *P:* on application.

See following page for illustration.

PIPE DREAMS

MIX & MATCH taps, three-hole and monobloc mixers in chrome with interchangeable rings — so you can ring the changes to match the decor! Rings come in a range of colours including primaries, pastels, black and white. Matching accessories are available. *P:* (with single gold ring) monobloc £198.35; three-hole £295.

This specialist bathroom shop stocks a good collection of both traditional and modern bathroom accessories and sanitaryware picked from major British and European manufacturers. See also *Lighting.*

MIX & MATCH taps from Pipe Dreams

PLASTIC FINISHES LTD

LUSTRAPLAS polystyrene and glass-fibre laminate bath panels to match and fit most

LUSTRAPLAS panels by Plastic Finishes

Marble vanity top from Petit Roque

manufacturers' standard baths. Vacuum-formed models have interlocking ends and matching flat and angle strips are available to hide the corner joins in simpler models. The seven designs are commendably plain. *P:* on application.

PLUSH FLUSH

Beautiful accessories for luxurious bathrooms, based on a range designed by Jean-Claude Delepine in Paris. BROADWAY taps have a turn-of-the-century look, with shower fittings, monobloc and pillar bath and basin sets and pop-up wastes in shining brass. MANHATTAN provides showers and three-hole fittings with smooth, twentieth-century good looks, the tap spouts shaped in a fluid arc. But these are just two standard ranges from an almost infinite variety: Plush Flush can provide almost anything to specification, in burnished brass, antique silver or gold, inlaid with malachite, coral, lapis lazuli, tortoiseshell, mother-of-pearl or whatever strikes the customer's fancy. And their designer in London, Peter Gurner, will construct marvellous bathrooms around them using such materials as Portuguese marble, Italian mosaics and African hardwoods. *P:* on application. See illustration in *Bathrooms, sanitaryware.*

S POLLIACK LTD

POLLY LIVING LUXURY bath, basin, bidet and shower mixer sets, including monoblocs, in opulent styles and materials. Tap heads come not only in hand-decorated ceramic, cut crys-

tal and gold (or combinations of the same) but also in gem stones and malachite, usually in fluted and knobbed designs but also with interesting 'Melon' and 'Cane' shapes. Gold-plated spouts are plain 'Colonial', classic 'Reeded', bamboo 'Cane', or 'Dolphin' and 'Winged Swan'. There are also shower arms in the same styles and pull-out handshowers for baths. *P:* three-hole basin mixer with gold heads £245; with swan spout and malachite heads £955.

Co-ordinating accessories with the swan and dolphin devices and in gold/crystal include tumbler holder, soap holder, towel ring, towel rail, robe hook, toilet-paper holder and bath pulls. An additional shelf, toilet-brush set, mirror, wall light and jar are available in the hand-painted ceramic ranges — MARBLE, FIORITA, DE LISLE, CHATEAU DUN, BLACK PRINCE and CORNICHE — to tie in closely with the sanitaryware and give a total designer look. There are even towels, a robe and a mat scalloped and embroidered in cream or colour with the same devices — a swan, a dolphin, an urn, palm fronds or harebells — to complete the picture. *P:* ceramic soap dish £40–£55; mirror £95–£120. See also *Ceramic tiles.*

REGENCY BATHROOM ACCESSORIES LTD

Wide-ranging collection of luxury fittings. Twenty-two ranges include designs with sculptured spouts such as SWAN, GOTHIC SWAN, DOLPHIN and, most unusual of all, GRECIAN LADY. There are also ornate designs such as VICTORIANA, GREEK KEY and FLORAL; classic shapes such as REGENCY and the fluid, curv-

ing REGENCY NOVA and ARABESQUE; and more angular, contemporary designs such as MODERN. All come in chrome or gold plate, MODERN in a mixture of the two, ARABESQUE with white enamelling and coloured enamelled motif. All ranges include combination sets and monoblocs for bath, bidet, basin and shower, plus co-ordinated accessories including towel rails and rings, soap dishes, toilet-roll holders, tumblers and toothbrush holders, hooks and wall lights. There is also a selection of mirrors, stools, shelves and waste bins. *P:* on application.

ST MARCO'S LTD

Amazing range of Italian units, accessories and fittings to match equally striking sanitaryware. Accessories come in diverse styles. The designer of the SEGNO range has constructed a towel rail, shelf, hook, soap holder, toilet-roll holder, toilet-brush holder and spotlight track for wall and mirror all from bent brass tubing (polished or chrome plated or brightly coloured); and out of bent pieces of perspex, ash or walnut, bath tray, shelf, single and double tumbler holder, sponge or soap holder and a stool. Another world away is MARLY range with reeded neo-classical mounts plated in silver, bronze, chrome or gold. Apart from rimmed and rimless oval and round mirrors and double and single wall lights with engraved glass shades, there are various towel rails, hooks and ring, grab rail, toilet-roll holder with patterned metal flap, toilet-brush holder, glass shelf, and soap and double or single tumbler holders with fluted white porcelain receptacles. Similar items brought thoroughly up-to-date in two-tone finish appear in the striking COLORADO series which has white/chrome, white/red, gold/nickel, chrome/beige, gold/white, chrome/green, chrome/nickel, chrome/brass, chrome/red, and gold disc mounts supporting bulb wall lights and plain bars and rings to make towel rails and tumbler or soap dish holders. Using the same two-tone finishes (except green) is the timeless CHARLY range, which also includes globe lights and a round-topped mirror. The MESSINA range of make-up and shaving mirrors and shaving stands in chrome or gold plate could, however, be used with all these metal accessories. Different models incorporate fixed and swivel stands, extendible arms, magnification and concealed illumination, and even holders for gold- or chrome-plated shaving brush, razor and tumbler. *P:* SEGNO towel rail £14.22, stool £37–£69; MARLY soap dish £16; COLORADO and CHARLY soap dish £17–£19.50; MESSINA extendible wall-mounted mirror with concealed light £74–£115.

An updated Edwardian look is achieved in Piemme's PRATESI bathroom furniture in lacquered dark green, dark blue, maroon or ivory decorated with gold lines. There is a washstand with four drawers and a marble top, vast bevel-edged mirror in an elegant frame, a chest of drawers and stool, plus accessories mounted on matching wood panels and using blown coloured and gilded glass for the soap dish, beaker and freestanding cotton-wool holder and brass for the towel rail and toilet-roll holder. A freestanding toilet-brush holder is also available. *P:* soap dish and holder £73; wash-stand and mirror £1,818.

Rigid polyurethane is used for units and accessories in a number of ranges, each with distinctive modern styling. Futuristic MOONLIGHT wall-mounted units have inset basin, rounded cupboard doors and pivoting corner drawers as well as special places for towels, laundry and tooth mugs. Similar systems are DOMINO (with drop-flap cupboards) and RAINBOW (with more conventional square doors). Some of the units are arranged with their elegant round or square washbasins jutting out over the wall-mounted cupboards. All come in black and white and a range of pastel and primary colours. Match them with SUNRISE polyurethane accessories in pastel colours and white — including such unusual items as a double tumbler holder with triangular tumblers, corner shelf with pivoting drawers, a long shelf with flaps, large illuminated rectangular mirror, medicine cabinet, freestanding round containers as well as wall-mounted soap trays and a space-age toilet brush and holder. Or there are HONEYMOON accessories which include several mirrors, stools with storage space, towel rails and toilet-roll holder, toilet-brush holder and robe-hooks. *P:* MOONLIGHT dressing table unit £297; RAINBOW washbasin unit with melamine basin and two-door cabinet £484; SUNRISE double mug holder £37; HONEYMOON robe-hook £52.

St Marco's BIJOUX three-hole tap set

Beautiful BIJOUX tap heads with spiral or fluted metal or coloured ceramic rope adornment are available in chrome, 24ct gold plate and Chinese lacquer (this has to be specially ordered from a choice of white, ivory, red, tortoiseshell and black). Bath taps can be mounted on wall, deck or bathside and come

with diverter, separate spout and flexible handshower; bath and bidet sets are three-hole or monobloc. The same is true of more traditional chrome-plated IMPERIAL sets which have cross-head taps, a swan neck spout on the basin and an all-in-one bath/shower mixer, with flexible shower. *P:* basin sets, BIJOUX £115–£443; IMPERIAL £86–£102.

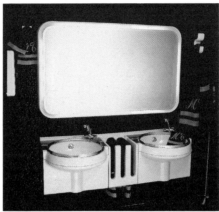

St Marco's MOONLIGHT basin units

SHAVRIN LEVATAP CO LTD

Lever taps, mixers and showers that look good in the modern bathroom as well as being easy to operate by the handicapped. There are several designs of chrome-plated basin, bidet and bath sets, and the bath mixers can have one of three shower sets attached — two handshowers with swivel head on bracket or slide rail, and a shower rose. The plastic lever handles come in white, blue, black, red, soft green or 'Duo-tone' (white/red, white/blue). *P:* three-hole basin mixer with pop-up waste £113; shower kit £25.

SHEARDOWN ENGINEERING LTD ♿

'Admix' range of concealed bidet, basin, bath and shower mixer fittings. Their standard finish is satin chrome but fittings are also available in bright chrome or gold plate. *P:* basin fitting £60; bath/shower fitting with handshower £120.

SITTING PRETTY LTD

Excellent range of reproduction Victorian taps and accessories, also some antique pieces, to complement Sitting Pretty's sanitaryware. Sitting Pretty's speciality is wooden toilet seats in mahogany or plain or coloured obeche with brass or chrome- or gold-plated fittings; also available in DIY kits. Monograms or other designs can be hand-painted on lids if requested. Beautiful mahogany cistern covers and porcelain and brass pull handles can be added. *P:* seats, mahogany £65, obeche £49.50; DIY seats

From Sitting Pretty. Top: WC with mahogany seat and cistern; below: toilet-roll holder

mahogany £45, obeche £35; cistern cover £195. Taps and accessories are available in polished brass or chrome-plated. STANDARD range includes basin and bath pillar taps, bath and shower mixers, long nose bidet pillar taps and unusual bath globecocks. *P:* basin pillars £40–£45; bath mixers £220–£235; bath globecocks £52–£58.

BATHROOMS

To continue the Victorian theme, there are brass and glass shower screens and also bath racks, soap dishes, concertina wall-mounted mirrors, towel rails and towel rings, all in polished brass. A nice finishing touch is a mahogany and brass toilet-roll holder bearing Sitting Pretty's distinctive dolphin motif. *P: shower screen £195; bath rack £48; soap dish £13; mirror £49.50; toilet-roll holder £18.50.*

SOMMER ALLIBERT (UK) LTD

Every bathroom accessory imaginable plus more than 30 bathroom cabinets. Specialist 'Doctora' first aid cabinet has generous storage space plus a safety lock. More versatile 'Starlight 600', with a light concealed within the moulded plastic frame, is one of many electrically fitted cabinets. There are also practical toilet storage units to hold paper, brush, disinfectant etc. Most cabinets come in white, beige, brown or green. *P: £25–£500.*

Bathroom furniture includes modular fitted furniture such as the self-assembly OBALIA range, in white with blue or pink trim, and the ADONIA range, in white or beige. A feature of both is the neat, integral laundry basket. *P: OBALIA prices on application; ADONIA single floor-standing unit (four drawers) £48.25, double floor-standing vanity unit with ceramic basin £132.25.*

Ranges of accessories include towel rails and rings, shelves, hooks, mirrors, wall lights, toilet-roll holders, waste bins, toilet brushes and holders, soap dishes, nailbrushes and holders, toothbrush holders and mugs, toilet seats, shower tidies, bath caddies, and even

Allibert's OBALIA units

SEVINIA PINE accessories from Allibert

stools. SEVINIA PINE range provides cheap but well designed accessories for the natural wood lover. ALCADE offers equal style with chrome trim on high quality plastic, coloured bright carmine or soft Bermuda blue. FLORINA range offers acrylic toilet seats in 21 different colours. *P: SEVINIA PINE soap dish £6.08, toilet seat £34.75; ALCADE soap dish £2.95, double-bar towel rail £9.20; FLORINA toilet seat £8.20.*

SPECTRUM LTD

High-tech Italian taps and accessories. Taps come in two ranges, I BALOCCHI and CALIBRO. Both are aggressively styled in cast brass, highly polished or with high gloss epoxy finish in bright red, green, blue, yellow and orange, and in khaki brown, dark brown, chrome grey, black and white. I BALOCCHI features taps with chunky, coloured cross-heads and spouts on chrome-plated bases; it includes bath and basin pillars (manufactured specifically for the British market), monobloc mixers with pop-up waste, concealed and wall-mounted bath/shower mixers with handsets, three-piece basin mixer with pop-up waste, bidet mixer with pop-up waste and jet, and a broad shower head. CALIBRO range centres on an unusual single pillar mixer tap, and all the fittings have matt black tips and handles to contrast the bright epoxy gloss. As well as single pillar mixers for basin and bath, with optional pop-up waste, there are two bath/shower mixers with handsets, one wall-mounted, the other concealed. To match both ranges there are accessories such as towel rail and mirror unit with integral light, soap dish and toothbrush and tumbler holders, all made of glass framed with

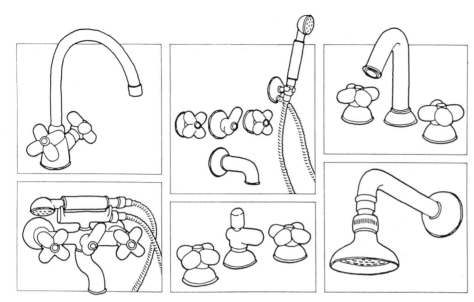

I BALOCCHI mixers for bath, basin and bidet with handset and shower head. From Spectrum

coloured or polished brass tubing. *P:* I BALOCCHI basin pillars £56 pair, bath pillars £48.50 pair, concealed bath/shower mixer with handset £200; CALIBRO single mixer tap £125–£205; toothbrush holder £17; mirror unit £200.

STEVEN TUBB
Oak toilet seats and other bathroom accessories made to order. The seat has wooden hinges and all joints are dovetailed. Steven Tubb also makes wall cupboards, a hanging four-bar towel rail as well as a freestanding one, and a toilet-roll holder. *P:* seat £70; towel rail £35; toilet-roll holder £10 (ex VAT).

TWYFORDS LTD
Two ranges of taps, INCA and AZTEC, both in chrome- or gold-plated brass. INCA range includes two bath mixers, two basin mixers and one bidet mixer. AZTEC includes pillar taps, mixers (monobloc, three-piece and with pop-up waste) for basins, baths and bidets, and a bath/shower mixer. *P:* INCA mixers £70–£400; AZTEC chrome basin taps £40 pair, gold-plated bath mixer and handset £400.
Twyfords also supply a standard range of easy-to-turn lever taps, handshowers and mixers, as well as grab rails and special seats, designed for the elderly and disabled.
RADIANTE ceramic accessories include circular mirror, shelf, soap dish, toilet-brush holder, towel rail, towel ring and toothbrush holder as well as novelty soap and toothbrush holders in the shape of a duck. All are available in most standard sanitaryware colours. *P:* mirror £64.17–£72.45; soap dish £8.15–£11.07; duck soap and toothbrush holders £11.39–£14.49.

UBM BUILDING SUPPLIES LTD
Self-assembly vanity and wall units in melamine-faced chipboard and even a dressing-table design with drawers. Units are finished in white or sand and come in two widths; the narrower offers plain doors with brass or silver knobs or real pine louvre doors; the wider is varied by the addition of special handles, decorative beading, real oak handles and trim on white doors, and wood-effect contoured edges on fawn, together with mirrored doors on the wall units. Matching melamine countertops can be cut to fit one of UBM's ceramic vanity basins (see sanitaryware chart for colours). *M:* w56, 76cm (22, 30in). *P:* base unit £49–£75; wall unit £42–£51.

WINCHMORE FURNITURE LTD
DALHAM storage units in maple with single or double vanity units and mirrors. Basin and countertop are made as one-piece moulding in pale cultured marble. Drawers and cupboard doors have rectangular carved panelling design and are finished in a paler natural shade or darker mahogany colour. Range also includes open shelving and tall units combining cupboards and drawers. *M:* single base unit w80cm (31½in) double w133cm (52¼in) × h76cm × d52½cm (30 × 20½in). *P:* single vanity unit with mirror £365; double £608 (ex VAT).

B & P WYNN & CO
Elegant French accessories and taps. From Maurice Herbeau of Lille there are beautiful hand-decorated accessories to match the typically French Herbeau basins (see *Bathrooms, sanitaryware*). There are earthenware bowls and pitchers, shelves, soap dishes, towel rings, wall lights, tumblers, and trinket boxes and earthenware-framed mirrors in each of the colours and patterns of the basins. Herbeau's taps are the classic RETRO and ornate POMPADOUR ranges, the latter with swan's neck spout. POMPADOUR also has towel rails, towel rings, shelves and soap dishes repeating the swan's head motif.
From Horus come two unashamedly old-fashioned ranges, ELOISE and JULIA. A number of bath/shower mixers, basin pillar taps, monoblocs and three-hole sets, all with wide spouts and cross-head taps, come in chrome, polished brass, matt nickel, matt bronze, old copper, white with chrome, white with gold, all gold or bright red with chrome. Particularly unusual is the JULIA wall shower with a series of two to six rotating, adjustable nozzles set into the wall at different heights giving a powerful, horizontal spray, available with wall-mounted, thermostat-controlled mixer and hot and cold taps.
P: all on application.

B & P Wynn's ELOISE monobloc, by Horus

SANITARYWARE

ALLIA (UK) LTD
From the company formerly known as Royal Doulton, three complete bathroom suites, eight other baths, five WCs, three bidets, three hand basins, five vanity basins and six pedestal basins in a possible choice of 30 colours, depending on the item. COURREGES suite has a smooth, confident appearance given to it by the famous French designer, and comes in exclusive shades of pink and blue as well as ivory silk and more standard colours (all of which can be echoed by coloured tap-head inserts); the acrylic bath is a generous ellipse and can take two bathers, and there is also a double ceramic pedestal basin available. SOVEREIGN uses elegant slab shapes which are particularly successful in the WC design (with vertical rather than horizontal cistern); it has a bow-fronted rectangular bath with cen-

BATHROOMS

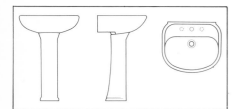

COUNTESS washbasin from Allia

tral taps and comes in a range of standard colours (see chart). COUNTESS has more modest rounded shapes with a slightly raised splashback lip on all the items, including the contoured bath with non-slip showering area. This comes in subtle ivory and vanilla silk finish as well as in selected colours such as white, wild sage, burgundy and bamboo. *P:* COURREGES single basin £200–£250, double £463–£550; SOVEREIGN basin £214–£272, WC £381–£457; COUNTESS basin £140–£168.

Other baths show the versatility of acrylic: 'Aurelia', also in Courrèges colours, is a contoured oval bath and 'Corinium' a corner bath, while 'Cressida' has a wider showering area at one end; all of these can be fitted with whirlpools, and all, in common with the cheaper baths, are fitted with cradle supports to give a high degree of stability. All but one, 'Veda', come with chrome or gold-effect hand-grips and most can be given extra glamour in one of Allia's marble-effect colours — beige marble, burgundy marble, mink marble, whisky marble and sage marble — combined with plain side panels. The matching basins, bidets and WCs are of course in plain colours of vitreous china in slightly varying shapes (one hand basin, 'Sophie', has a shell base). Two acrylic wash basins can be given the marble treatment as can the seat cover of the SOVEREIGN WC and the acrylic shower trays (see separate entry). *P:* 'Corinium' £460–£650; 'Aurelia' £432–£520; 'Cressida' £185–£259; 'Veda' £110; 'Sophie' £49; marble-effect toilet seat £73.

ARCHITECTURAL COMPONENTS LTD
Space at a premium? With a small-bore pumping system a WC can be installed below the

SANIFLO pumping system from Architectural Components

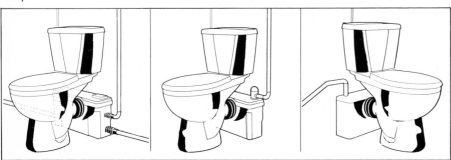

level of the sewer, septic tank or soil stack in a basement or cellar — the waste is pumped vertically and/or horizontally away. SANIFLO and SANITOP can be used with a conventional suite, while SANIPLUS takes care of the waste from a complete bathroom. *P:* £197–£300.

ARCHITECTURAL HERITAGE OF CHELTENHAM
Distinctive Victorian- and Edwardian-style sanitaryware from a company primarily involved in architectural salvage. HERITAGE suite has generously sized wash basin and WC in vitreous china with ropetwist decoration, available in plain white or ivory, or with 'Delft Blue', 'Country Garden' or 'Wild Pink Columbine' floral patterns on white. The basin is set in a decorative cast iron stand, and the WC, with mahogany seat and low- or high-level cistern, brass fittings and ceramic or mahogany flush handle, is available with matching cast iron floor brackets. Wall tiles can be made to order to match the porcelain. *P:* wash basin, plain £288, decorated £460, stand £195; WC, plain £288, decorated £460, seat £75, seat and floor brackets £165.

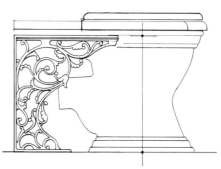

WC bracket from Architectural Heritage

ARMITAGE SHANKS LTD
Wide selection of bathroom furniture in 10 colours (see chart). There are four classic suites of basin, bidet and WC — boldly designed CLARENDON AND CARLTON and more delicate WENTWORTH and KENSINGTON — as well as a choice of other individual designs.

CLARENDON can be made more luxurious or just more lively by the addition of floral borders ('Caprice' and 'Sweetbriar') or 23ct gold patterns ('Shangri-La' and 'Versailles') which are fired into the finish of the sanitaryware. Accompanying the suites are seven contoured bath shapes in acrylic sheet, all with gold-plated or chrome hand-grips (mainly rectangular but including 'Vermont', an oval shape, 'Hawaii', a hexagonal corner bath, and 'Moritz', which is only 54in (139cm) long and ideal for limited space). Most can be fitted with whirlpools. Also available are three shower tray designs in various sizes, two wall-mounted hand basins, and a rich selection of seven wash-basin shapes. These can be fitted into the company's excellent vanity-unit range in louvred wood and/or melamine and formica laminate in a variety of finishes such as suede white, vellum, Portuguese marble, bleached wicker or fern croftweave. There is a matching two-door wall cupboard. See following page for illustration.

The charmingly nostalgic DOLPHIN suite won a prize at the 1876 Great Philadelphia Exhibition and Armitage Shanks (then called Edward Johns) have reintroduced it in all its old-world glory. Vitreous china bidet and toilet are shell-shaped, each supported by a gambolling dolphin outlined in blue on white. The blue and white wavy-topped basin can be wall-mounted on decorative cast iron brackets like the WC cistern, or inset in a period vanity unit with real mahogany doors. Other delights are a mahogany seat and polished brass chain on the WC, as well as brass and white porcelain taps for the basin and bidet, lever and handshower for the bath. *P:* on application.

Armitage Shanks's DOLPHIN suite

PRICES AND INFORMATION WERE CORRECT AT THE TIME OF GOING TO PRESS

CLARENDON suite from Armitage Shanks

Top: roll-out bidet; below: 'Pygmée' bath. Both from Arnull

BERNARD J ARNULL LTD

Luxurious ensembles of ceramic basins, bidets and WCs in unusual shapes and colours from Porcher in France. CALICEA is a typical design with narrow pedestal swelling elegantly out to support a wide basin — even a twin basin — with a generous rim; the cistern swells out to look like a chair-back on the close-coupled WC. The range is available in 13 colours (see chart), including seven of the famous Porcher shaded colours (three pastels and four deeper hues of dark rose, rich blue and browns). *P:* single basin £145–£252; WC £288–£522.

Other suites are AGORA, which is squarer-looking, ANTICA which is stylishly-rounded, FEMINA which has the softest lines, and ASTRIA which is perhaps the most economical in design. There is also POLYGALE decorated sanitaryware. Sprays of flowers are hand-painted on plain white suites and on ceramic wall tiles. Designs are 'Gentiane' (pink and yellow), 'Violette' (pink and green), 'Centaurée' (forget-me-nots in blue or coral), 'Polygale' (violet or orange), 'Campanule' (blue or red) and 'Ellebore' (pink, saffron or blue). *P:* POLY-GALE basin £331.

Baths, available in classic shapes or unusual asymmetrical designs, come in three types of material. Outstanding among the ceramic tubs (which retain heat, are quiet and stain-resistant) is 'Lutece', shaped to the body for a relaxing soak. 'Astrée', in acrylic, is a corner bath. 'Madeleine', with armrests and hand-grips, is in enamelled cast iron. Most baths can be fitted with Jacuzzi and hydrotherapy mechanisms if desired. *P:* 'Lutece' £1276–£1470; 'Astrée' £1175; 'Madeleine' £503.

For those with limited space in their bathroom there is ceramic 'Flora' which has one very narrow end to allow for awkward door openings, and cast iron 'Pygmée' and 'Revin' which are very short. There is also a roll-out bidet on castors which can be concealed beneath a vanity unit when not in use. *P:* 'Flora' £890–£1180; 'Pygmée' £319–£415; 'Revin' £279; roll-out bidet £85.

See also *Ceramic tiles.*

B C SANITAN LTD

Bathroom suites based on Victorian designs. SANITAN range consists of fluted pedestal and cloakroom basins, bidets and WCs with high- or low-level cisterns. All sanitaryware is made of vitreous china and comes in plain, gleaming white or with pretty blue, brown or multicoloured floral patterns. Co-ordinating patterned 6in (15cm) square ceramic tiles are available. *P:* basin, WC, bidet £212.75–£281.75 each; fluted basin pedestal £109.25–£161; high-level cistern £109.25; low-level cistern £103.50–£149.50; small cloakroom basin £149.50–£189.75.

SANITAN also supply a selection of Victorian-style baths. 'Victoria' fibreglass bath can be supplied with whirlpool installation and can be built in with mahogany or rattan panels. 'Karlstadt' cast iron roll top bath comes with a choice of brass or cast iron peg or claw feet. *P:* 'Victoria', bath only £437, with mahogany end and one side panel £598; 'Karlstadt' bath £483 (claw feet extra).

See following page for illustrations.

PRICES AND INFORMATION WERE CORRECT AT THE TIME OF GOING TO PRESS

BATHROOMS

Luxurious ROMANA sanitaryware has strong lines emphasized by a Greek key pattern in either 22ct gold or platinum. The same basin, bidet and WC shapes reappear in Balterley's EDWARDIAN range in white or champagne only, with traditional brass and white enamel taps and a roll top bath. This can be boxed in with solid mahogany (like the WC seat) or mahogany with rattan panels. Every suite has a full range of co-ordinated accessories also made of vitreous china. *P:* all on application.

Balterley's roll-top EDWARDIAN bath with mahogany panels

THE BATH STUDIO
Pressed-steel vanity basins by Kronit in 18 unusual vitreous enamel colours from palest jasmine to bright yellow, purple, emerald and black. Shapes are elliptical, square-edged or perfect rounds which look bang up-to-date inset in a counter with single-control lever tap. *P:* on application.

BERGLEN PRODUCTS LTD
Seamless enamelled steel vanity basins from the German company Alepe. There are 13 basin designs including an oval, semi-oval, circle, teardrop, rectangle, trapezium and even an ogee; colours are 40 rich, shiny enamels. They can be fitted into unusual wall-hung white laminate vanity tops with drawers or cupboards underneath. Alternatively, three designs of basin — round, trapezoid or semi-oval — are available moulded all in one with the vanity top itself; they can be superimposed on wall-mounted louvred mahogany or plain white, mahogany or pine vanity units. Units are available single or double with towel rail, paper dispenser or even a bottle opener built into the top. Even more remarkable is Alepe's 'round series' of handbasins which fit into a matt black tub held clear of the wall by a bracket; a modernistic tap can either be fitted in the wall above or in the basin itself, and a towel rail and tumbler-holder can be incorporated with the tub. Tubs come in different heights and can be used separately as waste bins; they are also available in shiny red and yellow enamel. *P:* on application.

Top: 'Victoria' bath with period-style suite; below: china handbasin. All from B C Sanitan

BALTERLEY BATHROOMS LTD
CARINA basin, bidet and WC suites in a choice of 12 colours including white (see chart), and five decorated styles. There are wall-mounted vanity and inset basins as well as a pedestal basin, a bidet and a quiet-action syphonic WC, all in glazed vitreous china. 'Carina Shell' has scalloped underside to the basin and scalloped cistern edge which can be rimmed in gold or platinum.
FLORIANA comes in pearl blue, milkwood and white with either full or partial flower decoration in monochromatic relief. There are six versions available in the ROSE collection;

white, pearl blue and candy pink with pink/blue summer roses; white, almond and pampas with gold/brown autumn roses; and there are co-ordinating tiles and a decorated toilet seat. 'Champagne and Roses' features a slightly different design: yellow bouquets on a creamy background.

Balterley's ROMANA suite

PRICES AND INFORMATION WERE CORRECT AT THE TIME OF GOING TO PRESS

SANITARYWARE SUITE COLOURS	WHITE	IVORY	CHAMPAGNE	BAMBOO/SANDALWOOD	ALMOND	SABLE/KASHMIR (mid brown)	WHISPER PINK	POMPADOUR/CAMEO (deep coral pink)	DAMASK	BURGUNDY	WHISPER GREEN	PAMPAS (grey-green)	AVOCADO	LINDEN GREEN (mid-green)	SAGE	WHISPER BLUE	BERMUDA BLUE (turquoise)	PACIFIC BLUE (bright)	ALPINE BLUE (mid)	SUN KING (orange yellow)	OTHER COLOURS AND FINISHES
ALLIA	•	•	•	•		•	•	•		•	•		•	•		•	•	•		•	Courrèges pink and blue; vanilla, ivory silk; marble finishes
ARMITAGE SHANKS	•		•			•		•		•		•	•			•		•			
ARNULL	•		•	•	•		•	•	•	•		•				•		•	•		two-tone colours
BALTERLEY	•		•	•	•		•			•		•		•	•	•	•				
CHLORIDE SHIRES	•	•		•		•	•			•		•	•			•		•		•	
IDEAL STANDARD	•	•						•	•	•	•		•			•		•			honeysuckle
ST MARCO'S	•	•	•				•											•			grey
TWYFORDS	•			•	•	•			•	•		•	•	•					•		two-tone colours; white satin
UBM	•	•	•	•	•	•	•	•	•	•	•	•	•	•	•	•	•	•		•	

Since manufacturers' names of colours vary, those given above only attempt to describe the shades available. Stock colours only are covered.

BONSACK BATHS LTD

Fibreglass baths in every imaginable shape, some very exotic. Their visual appeal is backed by practical design and innovative engineering. Baths are available in around 1000 colours — or any shade specified — and 12 'standard' metallic colours: bright silver, pale gold, gold orange, brilliant red, purple, royal blue, medium blue, aqua, lavender, salmon, antique brown and soft black. Iridescent mother-of-pearl finish comes in eight shades from pearly white through lustrous neutrals to red, And all can be decorated with motifs, patterns and borders such as fleur-de-lis, scrolls, Greek key, ropetwist, lovers' knots, passion fruit, laurel wreaths, daisies, 'Chinese Ming' design and 'Palace Script' initials. All the baths can be equipped with the Bonsack massage system. Bonsack offer a complete bathroom design service including preparation of drawings, colour schemes and estimates. A wide range of showers, suites and accessories are available to match the baths. *P:* all on application.

CARRON PLASTICS LTD

Ten contoured acrylic baths in more than 30 colours. Included are two sizes of corner bath — luxurious 'Alhambra' and 'Osprey' with more modest proportions and a corner seat — 'Wren', a deep standard model with integrally moulded hand-grips, 'Tern' which combines shorter length with generous width, and 'Swallow' and 'Falcon' which can be ordered with lower sides for the elderly. Most are fitted with chrome hand-grips and can be finished with matching polystyrene side panels in two neat designs. Also available are shower trays (see *Bathrooms, showers*), and a pretty oval vanity basin, 'Coral', with a raised splashback rim which can be fitted into any vanity unit. *P:* on application.

CARRON STEELYNE LTD

Sleek steel baths enamelled in 30 colours including two-tone and 'whisper' shades with several kinds of hand-grip and slip-resistant bases. Heavy gauge versions can be hushed with special sound absorbers and fitted with rigid 'Steelyne' panels; other panels are equally easy to fit with special panel clips and stainless steel fitting strips. Cheaper than cast iron, these baths are all standard rectangular shapes in two lengths, but there is a 'Lowline' version only 12in (30.5cm) high and ideal for bathing babies and invalids. There is also an enamelled 'Steelyne' vanity basin with smart stainless-steel trim. *P:* on application.

CHLORIDE SHIRES LTD

Elegantly designed bathroom suites and a series of contoured baths. Classic PRELUDE

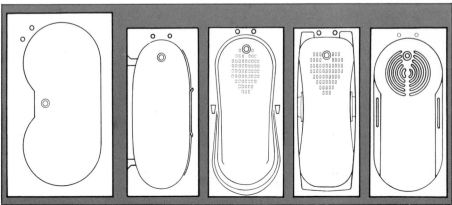

Chloride Shires' baths. From left: 'Largo', 'Sonata', 'Concerto', 'Naiad', 'Prelude'

BATHROOMS

range has basin, bidet and WC in vitreous china and co-ordinating acrylic bath with a circular area at the tap end for showering. OPUS range is much chunkier and squarer and its bath has a back-rest for comfort. NAIAD range offers compactness as well as luxury. Other ranges — which do not include co-ordinating bath designs — are the generously proportioned CAROUSEL and the more economical DENBIGH.

Of the individual baths, the most unusual is probably the circular 'Rondo' in high-gloss acrylic, with a large central bathing area and internal seating complete with arm-rests; though 'Eros', a corner bath, and 'Largo', with a double bathing area, must come close behind. 'Chelsea' has a low front to give easier access to the elderly and disabled and helpful transverse handrail (all the baths have grab rails). Almost any bath can be fitted with a gentle, massaging whirlpool.

Altogether Shires offer 11 bath designs, two freestanding square shower trays (see separate entry), four bidets, six WCs and 12 basins —including four wall-mounted hand-basins and three vanity basins (two in acrylic) which can be fitted into easy-assembly white melamine units with onyx-effect tops and plain or decorated doors. Most come in a basic choice of 10 colours, plus white (see chart); additional colours are available for baths.

CZECH & SPEAKE LTD

Hand-finished reproduction Edwardian sanitaryware. The white roll top bath is not cast iron but has an acrylic skin on a metal frame; it comes with brass claw-and-ball feet or mahogany surround. The white porcelain WC with low-level or close-coupled cistern, basin and bidet, all available to special order only, are in traditional shapes resting on squared-off pedestals. They can be supplied with polished brass and white porcelain tap fittings and accessories. *P:* bath £1130; washbasin and pedestal £160–£198; bidet £188; WC pan £176; cistern and fittings £227; mahogany toilet seat £70.

ELON TILE (UK) LTD

Ceramic wash basins and bathroom accessories, handmade and hand-painted in Mexico. Basins can be small or large, round or oval and have attractively rustic designs incorporating birds and flowers. Colours are mainly vibrant primary shades on natural cream background. Accessories include towel rail holders, recessed soap holder, toothbrush and tumbler holder, hook and toilet roll holder. Designs and colours can be varied to order. *P:* small basins from £120, large from £140; accessories from £17 each. See also *Ceramic tiles.*

PRICES AND INFORMATION WERE CORRECT AT THE TIME OF GOING TO PRESS

Decorated ceramic basin and tiles from Elon

C P HART & SONS LTD

Vast retail range drawn from leading manufacturers. Exclusives include DUKER cast iron roll top bath in true Victorian style with claw-and-ball feet in cast iron or brass; the interior is porcelain-enamelled (in white); the exterior ready to be painted to match the decor. In 1930s style is the NEO-CLASSIC suite with white vitreous china hand basin on shaped pedestal, WC with low-level cistern and mahogany seat, and bidet. *P:* roll top bath with cast iron feet £505, with brass feet £635; NEO-CLASSIC, pedestal basin £154, WC £304.75; bidet £161.57.

Hart's also stock sanitaryware by Cerabati. One exclusive is the COLOMBA range in vit-

NEO-CLASSIC suite with 'Super Repos' bath from C P Hart

reous china with clean, soft lines. WC, basins with pedestals, and bidet are available in white and six unusual pale shades — amber, buttermilk, jasmine, opaline rose, opaline blue and opaline beige. P: 60cm (23½in) basin with pedestal £51.31–£151.92; bidet £40.64–£75.83; WC with seat and cistern £143.01–£238.55.

Cerabati's COLOMBA range of sanitaryware, from C P Hart

IDEAL STANDARD

Stylish sanitaryware with an emphasis on clean lines, in 11 colours (see chart). Sinks, bidets and WCs are all ceramic while baths are acrylic. Most luxurious is the MICHELANGELO range with its distinctive squared-off shapes: the small handbasin, three sizes of pedestal basin, and floor-standing, wall-mounted and back-to-wall WCs and bidets were designed in Italy, while the complementary bath was de-

Bathroom suite from BC Sanitan

THE EDWARDIAN SUITE

A limited edition is always worth having and the Edwardian Suite from Balterley is no exception. Evoking a mood of nostalgia, the Edwardian Suite by Balterley recreates everything that is elegant and stylish about the Edwardian era. Allow your hands to caress the rich, smooth solid mahogany bath panel and surround which has been specially treated to withstand the environmental changes of your bathroom . . . Languish in a bath individually designed to give generous depth and proportions, a bath specially made to provide inherent warmth and a mirror smooth finish . . .

Feel the opulence of this very special bathroom in the co-ordinated styling of Balterley's Romana Range featuring an elegant pedestal washbasin complemented by Bidet WC and a full range of accessories. Because this bathroom is so beautifully original and created with great care, only a limited number of studios selected by Balterley can provide it. Their specially trained staff are available to advise you on design and layout, it's a small extravagance for anyone who decides they want the beautifully rare to become the unique.

Balterley

Balterley Bathrooms Ltd, P.O. Box 154 Stoke-on-Trent ST1 2PT
Tel: 0782 633118. Telex: 367391 B BATHS

Arnull of London has the ultimate bathroom and tile collections.

Porcher Sanitaryware,
Unmistakably French, Undeniably beautiful.

Cedit Designer Tiles,
Original, exciting ceramic innovation.

Visit our stunning Mayfair showroom and see the unrivalled selection of these superb products in appealing settings.

Bernard J Arnull & Co Ltd.,
13/14 Queen Street, Mayfair, London W.1.
Telephone: 01-499 3231

signed in England for the bath-loving English, and there's a shower tray to match (see *Bathrooms, showers*). Also notable is the LINDA range: the bath has taps positioned on the side to make it comfortable for two. Ideal Standard make eight individual basins for countertops or wall-mounting in cloakroom or bedroom. There are some unusual — and useful — designs such as the asymmetrical 'Mitre' and 'Cleopatra' and corner-fitting 'Angle A', plus a pretty shell-shaped basin 'Marmara'. All Ideal Standard's baths, from the compact, waisted 'Tulip' to the king-size 'Nagoya' are available with their WHIRLPOOL 2000 whirlpool system. *P:* on application.

MARBLE STYLE LTD

Four cultured onyx baths in glamorous shapes, a compact WC and bidet, a pedestal and wall-mounted basin as well as four vanity basin designs. The beauty of cultured onyx is that it has the depth and translucency of the real thing and yet is warm to the touch, stain and impact resistant, and above all immensely flexible. While the round, oval and rectangular contoured baths are moulded for comfort, with arm- and back-rests, and the vanity bowls for charm (one is shell-shaped), made-to-measure cultured onyx worktops are hygienic and hardwearing. A total marble-look bathroom can be achieved by using incised panels to go round the bath and vanity units and incised or moulded panels for the walls. Cultured onyx is just as happy with a curved shape as a straight one, and comes in a range of marble-effect colours. *P:* baths £1471–£2187; WC £781 (ex VAT).

'Hollywood' bath by Marble Style

PLUSH FLUSH

Luxurious, individual and exotic baths. Plush Flush produce baths in 20 different shapes, all made to order in innumerable possible colours and finishes including some glittering metallic ones. There's conventional 'Caribbean', circular 'Roma', pear-shaped 'Burlington', corner-fitting 'Sackville', and Japanese-

Plush Flush's 'Melridge' with 'Niagara' spout

style 'Kyoto', square with stepped sides. There's even a heart-shaped bath for the romantic. Most luxurious is 'Melridge', in fibreglass or ceralite fitted with a six-jet whirlpool system. The baths can be built in with steps leading up to them or sunk into the floor, and they come with luxurious extras such as a cushioned headrest or the 'Niagara' spout, more of a waterfall than a tap. *P:* 'Melridge' in nutmeg glitter, fibreglass £1087, ceralite £1428; whirlpool system £1718; 'Niagara' £426.80; gold-covered headrest £93 (ex VAT).
Plush Flush can supply suites, showers, accessories to match, even complete custom-designed bathrooms.

S POLLIACK LTD

The past glories of France and Italy conjured up in luxury suites of hand-painted, gold-decorated or two-toned ceramic sanitaryware. There are four designs of pedestal basin, bidet and WC suites which can be decorated in eight possible ways (or to the client's specification), three vanity basins, as well as a shower tray and 10 amazing contoured baths in glass-reinforced plastic. A pretty scrolled and fluted suite can be ordered as FIORITA or ORCHID (with blue and red flowers on white), DE LISLE (with gold palm fronds on black, white, red, blue or beige), CHATEAUDUN (with gold scrolls on white) and simulated MARBLE (in green, blue, brown or pink with cream or white). BLACK PRINCE and CORNICHE are

both simpler and squarer and look good in the deep-dyed colours with superimposed bands of gold classical decoration and devices such as an urn, swan or dolphin. There is also a plain DECO suite with strong outlines which can be decorated as wished or given a two-tone finish. *P:* basin and pedestal MARBLE £385; FIORITA £470; DE LISLE £540; CORNICHE £605.
Two of the baths, which can be decorated like the sanitaryware, are corner baths and can have a matching canopy overhead with rail and fittings: 'Le Mans' is scalloped underneath and 'Samur' has an internal seat. Rectangular 'Brissac' is suitable as a sunken bath, as is circular 'Chambord' with two diagonally-facing seats, while 'Marwa' is the last word in togetherness, called 'the sculptured bath for two'. 'Windsor', a freestanding copy of a high-backed Victorian tub with lion's claw feet, looks positively austere in comparison. Any of these can be ordered with 'Polly Jetair', a built-in massage system, which also comes with four simpler baths — rectangular 'Boston' and 'Leamington', circular 'Granada' and 'Cheltenham' for corners. They can also be ordered in almost any colour. *P:* £1120–£1325. See also *Bathrooms, accessories, Ceramic Tiles.*
See following page for illustration.

RAINBOW PRODUCTS LTD

Sizable range of hydrotherapy baths and the original whirlpools from Jacuzzi. Rainbow will

BATHROOMS

Polliack's MARBLE suite

also advise customers in fitting their 'hydro-massage' system to any acrylic or fibreglass bath. For the bathroom there are whirlpool baths, which can be used both for massage and for washing as they are filled from the taps and emptied after each use. Seven models include 'Cara', a compact oblong with three hydro air jets, and circular 'Gemini' with five jets, both available in champagne, ivory and white, or other colours to order. Whirlpool spas, larger units for installation elsewhere in the house, incorporate filter, heating and purification systems; they are kept full of water and are not used for washing. Ten models include 'Cambio', a tidy four-seater with four jets, for private use; and commercial models 'Monta-

na', a six-seater with 8-12 jets, and 'Savanna' an eight-seater with 13 jets. 'Cambio' comes in champagne, sky blue, oasis green and chocolate brown, 'Montana' in these colours plus ivory, and other colours to order, 'Savanna' in ivory only. Jacuzzi's hot tubs, spas made by traditional coopering methods in western red cedar, come in circular and oval designs in a wide range of sizes. *M:* hot tubs dia 48-84in (122-214cm), d48in (122cm). *P:* baths, 'Cara' £1695, 'Gemini' £2200, special colours £250 extra; spas, 'Cambio' £2750–£3995, 'Montana' £4950, 'Savanna' £12950; hot tubs £3225–£4995. From the German company Hoesch come 20 acrylic baths, ranging from the basic but ample 'Capri' to the giant 'Tahiti', and including no

less than five wedge-shaped corner baths. All can be supplied with whirlpool fittings. All come in 23 colours including bright red and dark green as well as more standard shades, and some models are available in two-tone finish. *P:* 'Capri', bath £275–£625, with four-jet Jacuzzi £1245–£1595; 'Tahiti', bath £937–£1480, with four-jet Jacuzzi £1907–£2450. (All prices ex VAT).

ST MARCO'S LTD
Stylish Italian baths and suites and an impressive range of accessories (see separate entry). Good quality cast iron baths come in white or champagne with clean, spare style: 'Classica' and 'Relax' (with handrails) are contoured rectangular tubs, while 'Sitty' is a short deep bath anatomically shaped. In addition there is an acrylic corner bath. NEOCLASSICA suite, in white only, has good old-fashioned 1920s shapes with strong outlines on the pedestals and round the square basin. SQUARE, despite its name, offers modern rounded-off corners and slabby shapes on basin, bidet and WC in six colours (see chart); while MODULO uses chunky cylindrical pedestals supporting large oval bowls in champagne and white. *P:* 'Classica' and 'Sitty' £230–£283; 'Relax' £306–£360; NEOCLASSICA basin £120–£145; SQUARE basin £91–£124; MODULO basin £80–£112, WC £170–£210.

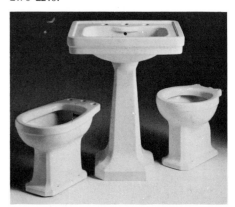

St Marco's NEOCLASSICA suite

SITTING PRETTY LTD
Splendid genuine and reproduction Victorian sanitaryware. Exclusive IMPERIAL range, made by Adamsez for Sitting Pretty, has a relief design and decorative features such as scalloped overflow and shell soap rest on the basin. Cloakroom basin, pedestal basin, bidet and WC are available in plain white, with coloured decoration on white and also in plain colours such as pale pink, pale blue, champagne, bamboo and navy. *P:* basins £195–£290; bidet £195; WC £295.
Sitting Pretty also stock ranges from BC Sanitan and from the Italian company Sbordoni,

'Montana' Jacuzzi from Rainbow

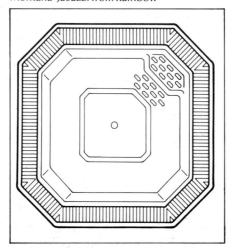

'Cambio' Jacuzzi from Rainbow

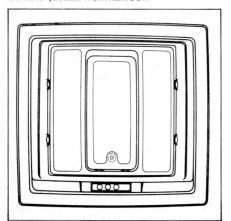

Sitting Pretty's IMPERIAL basin

and their collection of antique pieces includes cast iron roll top baths in a good range of sizes. *P:* antique baths £100–£2000.

TWYFORDS LTD

Good quality suites at competitive prices from these long-established British manufacturers. Twyfords aim to supply everything for the co-ordinated bathroom or cloakroom with ranges that match ceramic tiles by H & R Johnson and Sphinx (see *Ceramic tiles*). Collection of ceramic sanitaryware includes 16 basins (corner, wall-mounted, pedestal and inset models), eight WCs (freestanding and wall-mounted, with close-coupled or low-level cistern), and five bidets (four freestanding and one wall-mounted). There are two space-saving cloakroom basins: 'Parma', a simple recessed basin with pillar taps, and boldly styled 'Barbican', incorporating mixer taps, soap tray and integral toilet-roll holder. All come in 10 standard colours (see chart); in 'Harlequin' two-tone shades of sandalwood, pampas and avocado; some also in unique 'White Satin' finish, a smooth matt glaze that is as hard-wearing as the usual glossy glazes. *P:* basins £32–£260; WCs £160–£420; bidets £170–£270.

Five acrylic baths, in the same colours as the other sanitaryware, come in the common waisted and rectangular shapes, but there is also a giant oval model, 'Debut', and a roomy but compact corner model, 'Montrose'. Most incorporate anti-slip bases and sculpted backrests. 'Debut' also has an indented headrest. 'Astral' is a popular, compact, waisted model, sculpted for comfort; the matching suite includes a basin with an extra-deep, rectangular

bowl. There are also three steel baths: waisted, ultra-heavy gauge 'Olympian', and smaller 'Constellation' and 'Luna', all vitreous enamelled. 'Debut', 'Astral', 'Olympian' and 'Montrose' designs are all available with whirlpool installation. *P:* 'Debut' £1038.67; 'Montrose' £786.73 'Astral' £239.58; whirlpool attachments £958.33–£1150.

Twyfords have an excellent range of sanitaryware adapted for the disabled or elderly. There's 'Lowline' bath, shallower than most so that it's easy to get in and out; a WC specially built up to wheelchair height; cushioned seat and back-rest and low-level chain for the WC, plus well positioned support and grab rails. *P:* 'Lowline' £100.05; WC with seat and back-rest from £215.05; grab rails from £28.75.

ASTRAL suite from Twyfords

UBM BUILDING SUPPLIES LTD

Seven complete suites, priced economically and including twin-grip bath and shaped panel, ceramic basin and WC in 24 possible colours (see chart) depending on type and locality, plus acrylic/chrome taps, plugs and waste. CORFU is a streamlined basic suite, while MAJORCA adds the aesthetic advantage of a close-coupled WC and MADEIRA a built-in bath headrest and shaped toilet seat. A bidet

is available as an extra with the GRENADA suite which has a monobloc basin mixer and bath-shower mixer with chrome heads. Glittering Midas-gold fittings go with the JAMAICA suite while BARBADOS has extra heavy quality chrome-plated handles, cast iron 'Caribbean' bath and bath/shower mixer with adjustable head and pop-up waste. Finally TOBAGO has an 'Estoril' corner bath with all the accumulated advantages of the other suites. *P:* (entire suite) CORFU £216; MAJORCA £225; MADEIRA £286; GRENADA £373; JAMAICA £419; BARBADOS £586; TOBAGO £632–£725.

VOGUE BATHROOMS

Excellent range of 10 porcelain-enamelled cast-iron baths. Designs are modern and practical and 20 glossy colours range from white and pastel shades to rich Sorrento blue and cameo. Top of the range is generously proportioned 'Elysian' bath with side taps for extra convenience. It is also available with whirlpool installation and with chrome- or gold-plated fittings. 'Bermuda' is another bath of classic design which emphasizes Vogue's concern with quality and simplicity. 'Warwick Royale' has co-ordinating square shower tray and vanity basin, both of which can be ordered separately in the same colours as their baths. Vogue's Bathroom Ideas Bureau in London can give advice on all aspects of bathroom design. *P:* on application.

B & P WYNN & CO

French hand-decorated, hand-moulded earthenware basins, evocative of the 'belle epoque'. Made by Maurice Herbeau of Lille and exclusive to Wynn, the emphasis is on highly decorative designs of flowers and birds de-

Vogue's 'Warwick Royale'

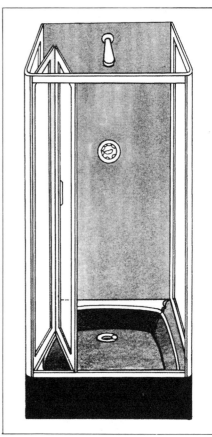

Shower surround from Allia

Wynn's 'Coquille San Jacques' basin with accessories

licately painted on white. Most unusual are the 'Coquille St Jacques' scalloped basin, 'Palourde' clam-shell basin, 'Neptune' corner basin, three fountain-style basins, and 'Toscade' basin with false reservoir urn above it. There are also designs in rich plain colours, cognac and midnight blue, and a simple, hammered copper bowl set in a wall-mounted hardwood unit, 'Carmel'. Matching hand-decorated WCs come with a standard French ceramic pan with close-coupled cistern. To complete the Francophile's ideal bathroom there are innumerable accessories (see separate entry). *P:* basins £300–£450.

SHOWERS

ALLIA (UK) LTD
Shower surrounds with centre folding door made of satin or gold aluminium and tempered glass panels, with bronze or driftwood (silvery white) finish. They can be supplied in one-, two- or three-sided versions (the panels are adjustable for out-of-true walls) and then mounted on freestanding shower trays. Two of these are in vitrified fireclay ('Stirling' comes in three sizes) and three in acrylic with side panels; all have slip-resistant bases and come in Allia's standard colours (see sanitaryware chart). Acrylic models offer a wider choice both of shape — 'Seville', for example, has a circular base — and of colour: all three come in exclusive Courrèges pink and blue and in beige, burgundy, whisky, sage and mink marble effects; and larger 'Stirling' sizes can be ordered in four misty pastels. *P:* two-sided shower enclosure £282–£393; fireclay shower tray £72–£301; acrylic shower tray £54–£106.

BERNARD J ARNULL LTD
Quarter-circle, rectangular and square ceramic shower trays from the French firm Porcher, available in white, pastels and deeper shaded colours (see sanitaryware chart). 'Emeraude' is a freestanding corner tray with a quarter-circle cabinet with sliding doors — or just a facade — made of anodized aluminium and bronzed, frosted or clear glass. 'Ocean', 'Etoile', 'Egee' and 'Major-Minor' are square or

rectangular free-standing trays and 'Soleil' and 'Auteuil' can be set into the floor. All these can have shower enclosures with sliding doors intended for corner or front entry, with side panels and back panels as required. Similar sliding glass panels can be fitted round baths, with clear, frosted or bronzed glass. *P:* 'Emeraude'shower tray £167–£290; cabinet £797–£1770; 'Auteuil' shower tray £78–£135; panel with doors £517.

BARKING-GROHE LTD
Wide range of shower kits which can be surface-mounted or concealed and include blenders and thermostats, shower heads, bath/shower mixers, handle variants and single-lever showers. They are finished in chrome, gold, bronze, pewter or white. RELEXA range of shower accessories incorporates a unique snap-coupling system for handshowers which makes possible a change from one shower style to another, for example from an effervescent 'champagne' shower to a pulsator spray, an adjustable shower or even one with a body brush. Children can have their own 'Nessie' hand-spray, with the mythical monster's head in red, blue or yellow. *P:* on application.

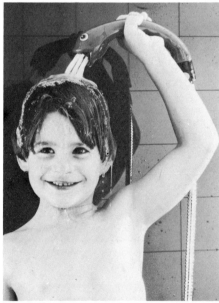
'Nessie' handspray from Barking-Grohe

CARRON PLASTICS LTD
Three sizes of shower tray in cast acrylic sheet. The largest, 'Swan', has corner seating area. The trays can be inset in a tiled recess or free-standing, and polystyrene side panels to support any standard shower enclosure can be supplied with the two smaller models. All have anti-slip pattern and are available in more than 30 colours. *P:* on application.

CARRON STEELYNE LTD
Unusual shower cabinets combining tinted acrylic panels with beechwood step, steel trim and nylon shower curtain. Shower mixers can be manually or thermostatically controlled. The heavy-gauge enamelled shower tray is freestanding with side panels and beechwood step, or designed for setting into a tiled recess. It is available in 30 standard or subtle colours and can be decorated with a design of birds on a flowering branch. *P:* on application.

CHLORIDE SHIRES LTD
Generous 'Delilah' and more economical 'Samson' shower trays in styrene, in the same shades as Shires' sanitaryware (see chart). Flat polystyrene side panels can also be supplied. For overbath showers they have 'Cadenza' and 'Cantata' — either a single hinged screen or double hinged aluminium frames with silver or gold finish and quality styrene 'crushed ice' panels. These can be screw-fixed to the side or back wall and then folded flat when not in use. *P:* on application.

DAMIXA LTD
Shower sets, chrome and gold-plated, manually or thermostatically controlled, fixed or sliding, and many other shower accessories, such as shower curtain rails, push-on sets, and a soap dispenser. Damixa's 'High Grip' shower trays, made by a specially strong construction method, are available in more than 40 colours and have a non-slip standing surface. *P:* £115.80.

GARDEX LTD
Easily assembled shower units with aluminium framework designed for durability and good value. Six models are available in 30 sanitaryware-matched colours and three sizes. All models have anti-slip shower base, which can also be ordered separately. The showers have adjustable shower heads with a choice of mixer taps and come with curtains, folding, sliding and pivot doors. *P:* on application.

IDEAL STANDARD
Three acrylic shower trays and one luxurious ceramic corner shower tray. The acrylic ones, available in the full Ideal Standard colour range (see sanitaryware chart), have circular, squared and unusual petal shapes; all are supplied with front panel but side panels are also available. The ceramic tray has curved front and slip-resistant base.
Ideal Standard also produce IDEALBLEND single lever showers, offered with a five-year guarantee against lime scale, and IDEALMIX thermostatic showers. Both come with fixed spray heads or flexible hose and handspray,

Gardex shower unit

and both are available with chrome or gold coloured finish.
P: all on application.

LANGLEY LONDON LTD
SATURDAY KNIGHT patterned vinyl shower curtains from the USA in more than 20 designs

'Bear With It' shower curtain from Langley

BATHROOMS

'Regatta' shower curtain from Langley

featuring bears, cats, birds, frogs, yachts, balloons, flowers and even a jogger. There are also plain curtains in five primary colours or clear vinyl, and two designs of fabric curtains — 'Raindrops' in white, peach or blue and 'Madame Butterfly' (with butterflies) in white, peach and black, together with liners in pastel shades. Unbreakable curtain rings come in 10 colours and have co-ordinating rod covers; the rods themselves are expandable. *M:* curtains w72 × d72in (183 × 183cm). *P:* patterns £26–£27; plain £14–£15.

LEISURE ⚠

Two steel shower cubicles — 'Fiji' and 'Tahiti'. Both units are supplied in simple self-assembly kits (including shower tray, shower sides, back panel, roof and pumping kit). They are made of colour-coated stainless steel and are completely watertight. 'Fiji' comes in natural stainless steel or white, with a choice of curtain or folding door; 'Tahiti' comes in sky blue, pampas, turquoise, sun king, pink or white with a choice of curtain or right-hand hinged door. Features of both models are the fine temperature control, automatic temperature stabilizer and variable power settings, all built into a white case with vanity mirror, and the shower head which can be fixed on to the side at any height to suit anyone. *P:* 'Fiji' £380; 'Tahiti', with curtain £435.16, with door £524.28.

MARBLE STYLE LTD

Cultured onyx shower tray and corner seat which can be combined with beautiful moulded wall panels and fronted with a glass and metal shower enclosure. Trays are in standard or exceptionally deep sizes and can have a moulded floral or sunburst non-slip pattern on the base if desired. *P:* tray £390; seat £84; panel £290–£382.

Leisure's 'Fiji'

MATKI LTD

Shower bases, surrounds and doors, and shower screens for the bath that combine good design with practicality. Bases come in most standard sanitaryware colours and are made of fibreglass-reinforced polyester with non-slip texture. Most are square but one model, 'Aristocrat', has one curved side and two straight ones, fitting neatly into a corner. 'Aristocrat' is available in two sizes. *P:* square £69–£89; 'Aristocrat' £119–£184.

Quite out of the ordinary is Matki's 'Mirage' shower surround. On the outside, it's reflective glass framed in gold or silver anodized aluminium; on the inside, it's transparent tinted safety glass. The pivot door can be arranged to open to left or right for recess or corner installation. Other screens and surrounds, with folding, sliding or pivot doors, have aluminium rails and frame with gold or silver finish, and panels in safety glass or soft or rigid impact-proof, synthetic Polython. 'Aristocrat' surround to match the shower base has curved folding door in milky white, green or smoked-look Polython. 'Pivot' square-sided surround and door is in tinted safety glass with horizontal stripes, and bath screens come in a similar pattern and in frosted textured glass. 'Showerfold' has folding door and surround

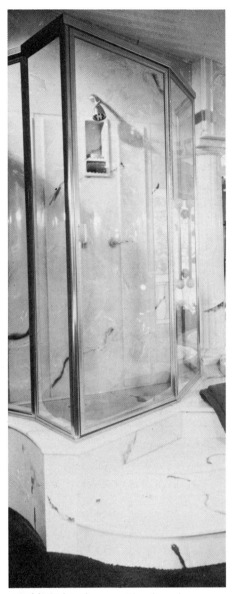

Marble Style's shower with cultured onyx panels

for shower or bath in milky white or smoked-look Polython. *P:* 'Mirage' door £198–£213, side panel £151–£162; 'Aristocrat' door £233–£360.70, complete surround and tray £352–£544; 'Pivot' door £133–£185, side panel £104–£165; 'Showerfold' door £99–£164.70, side panel £93–£133.25, bath surround door £124–£200.45, bath surround side panel £89–£124.35. See following page for illustrations.

⚠ *INDICATES ONE OR MORE OF THE PRODUCTS MENTIONED ARE SELECTED BY THE DESIGN CENTRE*

RAINBOW PRODUCTS LTD

From Hoesch in Germany, shower enclosures, bath screens, shower trays and steam baths. Nine shower trays come in a variety of geometric shapes, including a wedge-shaped corner unit. They are acrylic and come in a vast range of colours. FRESHLINE shower enclosures include three-piece sliding door, corner unit and a variety of side panels in either frosted or smoked glass with a choice of stainless steel, anodized gold or bronze framing. Range also includes unusual frameless smoked glass enclosures, shower doors and bath screen. *P:* trays £190–£575; FRESHLINE, three-sided corner unit £340, three-piece sliding door £168–£257, frameless bath screen £520, frameless corner unit £685–£715.

For therapeutic luxury, Hoesch Roman steam baths are available in a variety of sizes. Rainbow also supply self-assembly kits to transform an existing shower into a sensuous steam bath. *P:* £1150–£8000.

SILENT GLISS

LUXURY shower rails from the well known blind and curtain-rail manufacturer. Rails come in silver or gold anodized aluminium finish complete with all relevant accessories — wall supports, glider hooks, hanger rods (where necessary), dust cover, end stops and screws. Alternatively rail can be bent to suit customers' particular requirements. SLIMLINE SHOWER RAIL, in satin finish only, is a slimmer and cheaper version. *P:* LUXURY, right-angled with hanger rod for 36 × 36in (91 × 91cm) shower tray, £23.96–£43.47, without hanger rod for 72in (183cm) bath, £16.47–£33.69; SLIMLINE, for shower tray, £13.30, for bath £8.91.

PLASTIC FINISHES LTD ⚠

LUSTRAPLAS acrylic-sided shower trays with useful features. One is the patented cone system which allows the tray to fit over completed plumbing; another is the standing overflow which makes it suitable as a foot bath. Other features are a removable waste for easy cleaning and a wide rim to take any shower enclosure. Available in standard sanitaryware colours. *P:* £69.

TWYFORDS LTD

Useful selection of shower enclosures, bath screens and shower trays. ATHENA shower enclosures are designed to fit any shower tray from 24in (61cm) to 36in (91cm) square. Both pivot and double doors are available and can be arranged in recess fittings (door only), corner fittings (side and door), peninsula fittings (two sides and door) or complete enclosures (three sides and door). Made of either Cotswold clear or plain bronze safety glass, with aluminium frame finished in gold or silver, the range also includes a bath screen and shower seat. *P:* pivot door only £161–£178.25; double door only £178.25–£196.10; peninsula fitting (pivot door) £289.80–£320.85; complete enclosure (pivot door) £418.60–£463.65; bath screen £62–£68.20; shower seat £48.45–£96.90.

There are also two square shower trays, acrylic 'Halo' (with circular bowl) and lightweight ceramic 'Calypso'. Both have slip-resistant bases and come in Twyford's plain sanitaryware colours (see chart). *P:* 'Halo' £86.05; 'Calypso' £165.34.

Top: 'Aristocrat'; below: 'Pivot'. From Matki

LUSTRAPLAS shower tray from Plastic Finishes

BLINDS

INTRODUCTION

Forget nets. Forget curtains. Forget unlovely views. Consider blinds. They're not clanky, metal dust traps any more. Blinds have blossomed into one of the cheapest, most functional, yet most varied window treatments going. They can be slats or panels, silkscreened or airbrushed, wooden or paper, patterned or plain, ruched or cane, sheer or opaque, vertical or horizontal, aluminium or plastic, ready made, made to order or made at home. They also work as room dividers, draught excluders and light controllers.

Rustic, functional or luxurious, blinds are becoming increasingly popular so prices are keenly competitive, especially for plain colours. And once you have them, if you get bored, or richer — or simply change your style — you can add curtains later.

Basically, most blinds function in one of two ways: with a spring-tensioned roller mechanism, or linked by cords that are operated with pulleys. If you're good with your hands, you can make your own roller blind from a kit — most fabrics can be used, prepared with special spray-on stiffeners. Otherwise, a company can do this custom job for you, or you can buy some standard sizes ready made.

The corded variety include vertical blinds, also called vertical drapes; Austrian and festoon blinds with their extravagant swags of fabric; the more economical Roman blinds which draw up in a series of pleats; and the Venetians — not to be forgotten since they come in gleaming mirrored metal and natural wood as well as the regular, utilitarian plastic.

This section is divided into *Paper, cane and wood blinds* of all types, including internal wooden shutters that serve much the same purpose; *Roller blinds; Roman, Austrian and festoon blinds; Special blinds* designed for black-out, insulation etc; *Venetian blinds;* and *Vertical louvre blinds.* For Japanese-style sliding panels, suitable also for screening windows, see *Furniture, partitions.*

- Prices are based on the following measurements: vertical louvre blinds 36 × 84in (91.5 × 213.5cm), all others 36 × 48in (91.5 × 122cm).
- Drop measurement is shown as 'd'.

PAPER AND WOOD BLINDS

EATON BAG CO LTD

Attractive roller blinds made to measure in natural split cane, simply operated on a nylon cord pulley system and easy to clean. All blinds come with a three-year guarantee against wear and tear. *M:* max 108in (274.3cm); d limitless. *P:* £9.63.

△ *INDICATES AN ILLUSTRATED PRODUCT SELECTED BY THE DESIGN CENTRE*

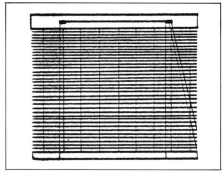

Split cane roller blind from Eaton Bag

HABITAT DESIGNS LTD

Classic roll-up cane and wood-slat blinds, in natural shade only. *M:* cane, five sizes, w91 × d182cm (35¾ × 71¾in) to w182 × d198cm (71¾ × 78in); wood, five sizes, w90 — 140 × d200cm (35½ — 55 × 78¾in). *P:* cane £5.45 – £12.45; wood £18.45 – £25.95.

PLANTATION SHUTTERS

From the United States, attractive internal wooden shutters with movable slats to adjust for light or privacy. Made from top-grade, warp-resistant Oregon pine, shutters can be stained, varnished, painted white, poppy red, electric blue, apple green, dove grey, cream or yellow, or left their natural colour. Custom-made sets are available as well as 80 standard

Plantation's pine shutters

sizes. Sets normally consist of four shutter panels hinged in pairs, but for wider windows, six panels are hinged in threes. Options are 'Full Window', half-window 'Cafe-style' and 'Tier-upon-tier', the last a useful answer for large windows with its half-open, half-closed effect. For exact fit, panels can be trimmed top and bottom and along mounting battens on sides. Delivery takes 4 – 6 weeks for standard sets, 6 – 8 weeks for custom or painted sets. *M:* custom max w18 × h80in (45.5 × 203cm); standard w28 – 76in (71 – 193cm), h16 – 48in (40.5 – 122cm). *P:* custom, on application; standard set £67.66 (h36 × w48in/91.5 × 122cm); painted 25 per cent extra.

JAMES ROBERTSHAW & SONS LTD

Pinoleum (split cane) blinds in natural colours or brightly printed. Roller blinds have taped edges and can be either spring-mounted or drawn by hand (with left or right cord control). Reefed blinds fold up in layers as Venetian blinds do, with the layers concealed at the top under a pelmet; they are fitted with self-locking mechanism and right-hand control only. Both come in five colours in addition to natural — green, yellow, brown, blue and red — and in floral prints such as 'Blue Belle', 'Climbing Orange' and 'Red Poppy' with wide bands of pattern down the sides of the natural-coloured blind. *M:* max w78in (198cm). *P:* natural £18.74; coloured £22.48; printed £24.91.

Over larger spaces, Roman blinds in slatted dark wood woven with coloured wools create a rich, dark effect. Alternatively, there are translucent pinoleum vertical louvre blinds with slatted wooden louvres in light or dark wood, loosely woven with string. *M:* max w108in (274.5cm). *P:* £54.37.

T F SAMPSON LTD △

Highly durable PLEATEX roll-up paper blinds with permanent accordion pleats. The specially developed sun- and water-resistant cellulose material gives excellent insulation for warmth in winter, coolness in summer. Blinds, all made to measure, are also available for roof lights, conservatories, pivot and roof windows and to go inside double glazing. There are nine colours: white, light green, yellow, parchment, lavender, pink, grey, burgundy and indigo. The pale shades diffuse the light; burgundy and indigo exclude it, making them a good choice for bedrooms or video rooms. Sampson offer a five-year guarantee and say blinds should give a minimum of ten years' maintenance-free service. *P:* £11.10.

PRICES AND INFORMATION WERE CORRECT AT THE TIME OF GOING TO PRESS

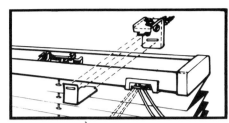

T F Sampson's PLEATEX paper blind △

TIDMARSH & SONS LTD

Beautiful TIMBERSHADE Venetian blinds made from best quality western red cedar, selected for its grain, stability and lightness. They come in natural, redwood, dark grain or white grain finish, with strong Terylene tapes and cords in complementary shades. Usually operated with a single cord, rod and handle, but electric motor is available. Wood-slat blinds have a deeper stack than standard Venetians when raised — about 3in (7.5cm) per 12in (30.5cm) of drop. Delivery free. *M:* slats 1¹¹⁄₁₆in (4.3cm). *P:* £90.80.

VIXEN-SMITH LTD

Matchstick roller blinds with individual airbrush designs. Vixen-Smith's 'Fuji' design gives a Western interpretation of a classical Japanese landscape. *P:* from £33.

ROLLER BLINDS

LAURA ASHLEY LTD

Roller blind kit comprising aluminium roller, lath to tuck the end of the fabric into, fabric stiffener, fixing brackets and wooden pull. Just add your own fabric. *M:* three sizes for max w91, 122, 183cm (35¾, 48, 72in). *P:* £6.95, £8.45, £11.45.

BLIND ALLEY LTD

Custom blinds to suit all requirements, in every shade in the spectrum. Blind Alley's own screenprint designs range from traditional 'William Morris' to art deco motifs, from conventional 'Greek Key' and 'Paisley' borders to original pictorials such as cottagey 'Cat and Curtains' or dramatic 'Manhattan'. Their imaginative airbrush designs, the *trompe l'oeil* 'Window Landscape' for example, can be modified according to size and customer's preference. Customers can also order their own designs, perhaps to show a logo or match tiles or wallpaper, and Blind Alley can supply original artwork. These can be printed, hand-painted or airbrushed on to a wide choice of background fabrics (including white, cream, beige, pastel and deeper shades) or on to customer's own fabric. Colours are individually mixed. Design, measuring and fitting service

available in London area. *P:* plain £36.36; pictorial borders £47.84; screenprints £39.95 – £49.95 extra; 'Window Landscape' £175.

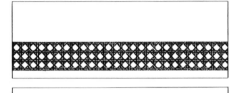

Screenprints by Blind Alley. From top: 'Cat and Curtains', 'Lattice', 'Moroccan', 'Greek Key', 'Deco Corners', 'Manhattan'

FABER (VENETIAN BLIND SERVICES LTD)

SUPER ROLLER collection with a useful range of plains, weaves and prints. Twenty-six plain colours (see chart) include bold primaries plus more subtle shades like écru, oatmeal, and dusky and petal pink. Weaves include basket-work 'Papyrus' and 'Thatch', both in a choice of colourways. Among the wide collection of patterned fabrics, border prints and special designs are 'Fiesta', a delicate cottage-style print in pink or bronze, 'Needlepoint' with a lightly drawn elderberry design, 'Alpine' with flowery sprigs in white or burgundy and brown on beige, and 'Firefly', a striking black or brown and white border print of dazzling sparklers. Blinds are available in 100 per cent cotton, cotton and polyester, or 100 per cent polyester — useful for damp atmospheres such as steamy bathrooms. There are 12 possible shapes for bottom hems with a variety of accessories, and an option of left- or right-

Below, left to right from top: Faber's 'Fiesta', 'Firefly', 'Alpine', 'Needlepoint' and their new ROLLACORD blind control with left- or right-handed clutch mechanism

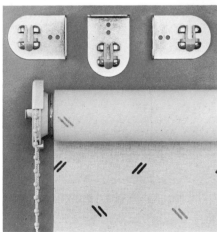

BLINDS

ROLLER BLINDS IN PLAIN COLOURS	WHITE	YELLOW	LT GREEN	BT GREEN	DK GREEN	AVOCADO	AQUA	LT BLUE	MID BLUE	NAVY	LT GREY	CREAM	CHAMPAGNE	SAND	COFFEE	DK BROWN	ORANGE	RUSSET	GOLD	RED	PURPLE	ROSE	PINK	BLACK
FABER	•	•	•		•	•		•	•			•	•	•	•	•	•	•	•	•		•	•	
FILTRASOL		•	•		•	•		•	•		•	•	•	•	•	•	•	•	•	•		•	•	
HABITAT	•	•	•	•			•	•		•	•	•	•	•	•					•		•	•	
Made-to-measure kits		•								•		•								•				
LUXAFLEX Ready Rolla	•	•	•	•		•		•	•		•	•		•	•		•			•			•	
PANORAMA	•	•		•				•	•			•						•					•	
SUNSTOR	•	•			•	•			•		•	•			•					•				
SUNVENE	•	•	•	•	•	•	•			•					•		•			•			•	
SUNWAY	•	•	•	•	•	•	•	•	•	•	•	•	•	•	•	•	•	•	•	•	•	•	•	•

See also Blind Alley, Vixen-Smith

handed control by means of Faber's unique ROLLACORD clutch mechanism. *P:* plain £22.90; weaves and patterns £32.67; special designs and border prints £39.37; right-handed control £2.09 extra.

FILTRASOL LTD
Made-to-measure blinds in more than 100 plain colours (see chart). Their quick service, they say, means you can choose a blind and have it up within days. Patterned blinds include florals, border prints and abstract or linear contemporary designs, such as cherry pattern 'Griotte', hanging trellis 'Ladybird' and gay 'Lollipop' with coloured bands. Many come in a choice of colourways. For the nursery, there are 12 colourful drawings of cartoon characters which can be printed on to all but the red, orange, dark brown and ginger blinds. Up to four can be printed along the foot of the blind according to its width. Bottom edges of all blinds can be scalloped in two styles with trims and fringes in white, natural, beige, gold and green. *P:* £21.16.

Filtrasol's transfer cartoon characters

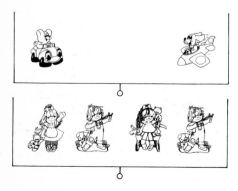

SUSANNE GARRY LTD
Blinds made to order in Susanne Garry's own fabrics (see *Fabrics & wallcoverings*). Sheers are a speciality, plain for a Japanese effect or lacy for an old-fashioned look. Accessories include matching braids and ribbons, edgings and, unique to Susanne Garry, perspex base rods with a chunky cube at each end. The clear rods can be filled with anything — cord to match surrounding furnishings or even coffee beans. *P:* blinds on application; perspex tube £8.70 per 2m (2¼yd) length; cubes £7.50 each.

HABITAT DESIGNS LTD
Roller blinds made to measure, ready made or in kits, all typically fresh and bright, from this famous firm. Made-to-measure range includes 19 well chosen plain colours (see chart); multi-coloured 'Bamboo Stripe' (with matching bedlinen); squiggly, primary-coloured 'Liana' (with matching bedlinen and shower curtain); 'Intermezzo' with diagonal broken stripes in yellow/red/blue/green or red/black/grey; 'Horizontal Stripe' with a single, broad red stripe near the base; 'Robots' featuring multi-coloured acrobatic robots; 'Jardin' with a scattering of tiny flowers; and 'Tiger Rag' with brightly coloured animals stalking through long grass. All on white cotton, except 'Tiger Rag' on white cotton/polyester. *P:* plain colours, 'Liana', 'Jardin', 'Bamboo' £24.57; 'Horizontal Stripe', 'Robots', 'Intermezzo' £22.68; 'Tiger Rag' £30.85. See also *Fabrics & wall coverings*.
Ready-made blinds include 'Rainbow' with rainbow and sky drawn in bright, crayon-like strokes; 'Suomi', a smart double pin-stripe in red, blue, green or yellow; and a cotton and bamboo blind, of fine white cotton and thin strips of split cane, translucent as paper. *M:* 'Rainbow' w120 × d165cm (47¼ × 65in); 'Suomi' w90 or 120 × d180cm (35½ or 47¼ ×

70¾in); cotton and bamboo w91, 122 or 182 × d180cm (35¼, 48 or 71¾ × 70¾in). *P:* 'Rainbow, £32.90; 'Suomi' £14.75, £16.25; cotton and bamboo £12.50, £16.50, £21.50.
Kits contain wooden roller and mechanism, brackets, cord, acorn cord pull, tacks and adhesive, with full instructions. Use them with your own fabric and Habitat's fabric stiffener or with Habitat's specially stiffened blind fabrics in cotton/viscose, available in four plain colours (see chart) and three sizes. *M:* rollers l91, 122 or 183cm (35¾, 48, 72in); special fabrics w91, 122 or 150 × d185cm (35¾, 48 or 59 × 72¾in). *P:* kits £4.45, £5.95, £9.95; stiffener (enough for 4 sq m (4¼sq yd) fabric £1.90; special fabrics £11.25, £14.25, £17.45.
Bright and different yet inexpensive is Habitat's PINIBLIND roll-up plastic slatted blind in red or royal blue with matching fittings. Comes ready-made in two sizes. *M:* w91 or 122 × d182cm (35¾ or 48 × 71¾in). *P:* £9.95, £10.95.

W A HUDSON LTD
FABRIFIX ROLLER BLIND SYSTEM for making your own blinds. Kits come with all necessary fittings apart from fabric; and twist, trellis and bobble fringes, all in white, are also available. Fabric sprayed with ROLLS FABRIFIX stiffening solution doesn't wrinkle when mounted on rollers and is sufficiently fray-resistant to dispense with side hemmings. One can of stiffening spray will treat 2 – 2.5 sq m (2¼ – 3sq yd) fabric depending on weight and absorbency. *M:* rollers l60, 90, 120, 150, 180, 245cm (23½, 35½, 47¼, 59, 70¾, 96½in). *P:* rollers £3.45, £3.71, £4.23, £6.56, £7.68, £13.46; stiffener £3.02 per can.

LUXAFLEX LTD
Made-to-measure ROLLABLIND collection with colours, patterns, textures and trimmings to satisfy most tastes. Thirty-eight plain colours range from strong primaries such as pillarbox red and deep blue fiord, to delicate pastels such as apricot and spearmint. 'Laceweave', 'Lawnweave', 'Polyweave', 'Linenweave' and 'Shantung' make up the collection of textured fabrics, in 27 mainly neutral colourways. And the collection of patterns and borders has 48 designs in 74 colourways; examples are the pretty and traditional 'Prudence', striking 'Willow' and abstract 'Stix' with random coloured rods. For those in a hurry, READY ROLLA provides 23 plain colours (see chart) and many of the same textures and patterns in stock sizes (which can be trimmed to fit). *M:* READY ROLLA w36, 48, 60 or 72 × d69in (91.5, 122, 152.5 or 183 × 175cm). *P:* ROLLABLIND plains £27.25, textures £29.31, patterns and borders £31.77–£36.50; READY ROLLA 25 per cent reduction.

PRICES AND INFORMATION WERE CORRECT AT THE TIME OF GOING TO PRESS

PANORAMA (PEEL & CAMPDEN LTD)

Reasonably priced PANAROLA blinds in cotton or cotton and polyester. As well as 11 plain shades (see chart) there are 16 floral prints ranging from 'Forget-me-nots', a trail of tiny flowers in blue or lime, to bolder 'Autumn Leaves' in rich tan and brown against white. Blinds can be left plain or finished in a choice of two scalloped bottoms with braid or fringe trims. Delivery within seven days of receipt of order. *P:* on application.

SUNSTOR LTD

Made-to-measure blinds in wide range of colours, weaves and prints. Fifty plain colours (see chart) include some unusually subtle shades: greens, for instance, include leaf, apple and pastel green, wild sage and granary sage; and there are 14 variations on the white theme. Patterns include abstracts such as 'Diagonal' and 'Horizon'; floral and other detailed prints including 'Feathers', an unusual design combining black and red feathers with a red-and-white diagonal stripe; plus pictorial and border prints such as 'Summer Sky' of clouds and swallows, or 'Sunny Days', with clouds floating across curtained windows. Six shaped finishes and a wide selection of trimmings are available. *P:* plain £25.17; textured plains and patterns £29.94; border and pictorial prints £36.28. Sunstor also make up roller blinds in customer's own fabric. Cotton, cotton mix or lace are recommended, which will be treated with dirt-resistant finish. *P:* on application.

SUNVENE LTD

Made-to-measure blinds in a selection of fabrics and plain colours (see chart), plus some predominantly floral patterns and borders. GAMBRETT, in sponge-clean, fireproofed fibreglass, comes in five plain shades — blue, white, cream, brown and champagne — and in an orange-and-brown floral print. AVON, a

Above: two of Sunvene's cotton-and-polyester blinds from the AVON range

cotton-and-polyester mix that can also be sponge-cleaned, includes all-over and border prints; 'Cherry Jam' border of bottled red cherries on a blue-and-white checked tablecloth, is the most eye-catching. LARKHALL has 17 plain shades in 100 per cent cotton and CLYDE has five muted 'linen' tones in a linen and cotton mix. *P:* AVON prints, LARKHALL, CLYDE £17.28; AVON borders, GAMBRETT £18.14.

SUNWAY BLINDS LTD

Really extensive range of plains, patterns, border prints and specials from this well known manufacturer. Among the 77 plain shades are ten variations on a 'natural' colourway in

Sunway blinds. Top: 'Cornfield'; below: PARASOL

Sunstor's range of shaped finishes and tassels

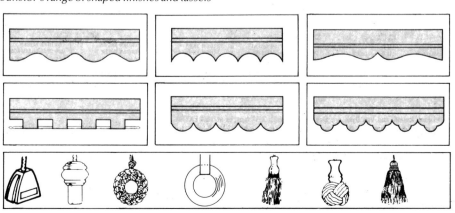

BLINDS

attractive textiles and textures, including 'Lattice', in an alternating close and loose weave, 'Diamond' with an occasional over-weave of diamond shapes and 'Barley' and 'Suki' in hessian-type weaves. There are four pastel shades in specially treated light-resistant fabrics. Forty-three fabric designs include floral patterns such as 'Whisper', with leaves and flowers in pink or blue, border prints such as 'Shogun', with oriental plants and 'Deck Chairs', with green-and-red striped chairs and parasols on the beach. More abstract designs include 'New Wave', with multicoloured wavy lines, and 'Tracery White', a white-on-white design, pretty for bedrooms and bathrooms. Six shaped finishes and a wide range of trims and fringes are available. *P:* £25.25 – £35.35.

SUNWAY MATCHMATES can be co-ordinated with Sandersons' OPTIONS range with 12 plain shades and 19 patterns to choose from. 'Cornfield' is a riot of poppies, sunflowers and cornflowers in a field of wheat and 'Rose Trellis' shows climbing flowers and rambling foliage. All blinds are made to measure. *P:* plain £25.25; patterned £41.99.

SUNWAY PARASOL ready-to-hang roller blinds come in 35 poly-cotton, cotton and cotton/linen mix fabrics, plain and patterned. *M:* w36, 48, 60 or 72in × d66in (91.5, 122, 152.5 or 183 × 152.5cm). *P:* £18.65 – £35.19.

VIXEN-SMITH LTD

Plain blinds and highly original hand-printed designs made to measure. Collection includes pretty pastel prints such as 'Sunrise' — pale blue, pink and yellow rainbows emerging from pale blue and pink clouds — and 'Seagulls' — pastel birds against white clouds and blue

Vixen-Smith's hand-printed 'Balloons' design

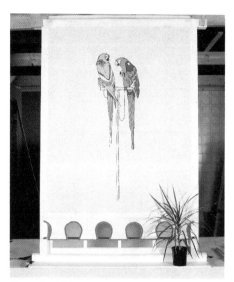

Vixen-Smith's parrots on a perch, one of several original designs

skies. Brighter colours appear in 'Balloons' and in striking single-image designs showing two gaudy parrots on a perch or a clown seated on a crescent moon. Bottom edges can be plain or shaped in eight different ways, and there is a wide range of trimmings. *P:* plain £27.56; prints from £49.32.

Vixen-Smith will also reproduce any design on to roller or louvre blinds and specialize in reproducing tile designs for co-ordinated kitchens and bathrooms. *P:* on application.

ROMAN, AUSTRIAN AND FESTOON BLINDS

LAURA ASHLEY LTD

Festoon blinds made to measure in Laura Ashley's appropriately styled COUNTRY FUR-NISHING COTTON, CHINTZ and DRAWING ROOM FABRIC (see *Fabrics & wallcoverings*). Blinds are well made, with 7cm (2¾in) deep pencil-pleat heading and 9cm (3½in) deep piped frill, weighted and lined with white or cream satinized lining fabric, and supplied with head rail, fixing brackets, hooks and gliders. They are raised and lowered by a simple silk pull cord with brass acorn, and a ratchet system allows them to be secured at any height. *P:* COUNTRY FURNISHING COTTON £49; CHINTZ and DRAWING ROOM FABRIC £54. Laura Ashley will make up matching curtains, too.

BLIND ALLEY LTD

Roman, festoon and Austrian blinds from custom blind specialists. Blind Alley will also print fabric with their own or customer's designs. Measuring, fitting and design service available in the London area. *P:* £60 + lining £9.

SUSANNE GARRY LTD

Unique three-way blind that lets down into a Roman blind, looks like a festoon blind when drawn half-way, and pulls up into formal swags. Available in three shades of cream cottom or striped. Standard blinds also made to order in Susanne Garry fabrics (see *Fabrics & wallcoverings*). *P:* on application.

HABITAT DESIGNS LTD

Ready-made Roman blinds: 'LASITHI' in pure white cotton and 'Roman' in off-white with red border. *M:* 'Lasithi' w120 or 160 × d165cm (47¼ or 63 × 65in); 'Roman' w90 or 120 × d180cm (35½ or 47¼ × 70¾in). *P:* 'Lasithi' £24.95; £31; 'Roman' £17.45; £19.45.

PENBRICE INTERIORS

For those in the London area, luxurious custom-made Austrian, festoon and Roman blinds from soft furnishing specialists. Nearly all blinds are made only after a home visit to advise and measure, with subsequent visit for fitting. Almost any fabric from an established manufacturer can be used, or one from the company's own selection. *P:* £63.25 + fabric and fixing.

Voile festoon blinds from Penbrice

SILENT GLISS LTD

Kits for Roman and Austrian blinds. Most straightforward is the 2100 SYSTEM, but three further systems offer refinements such as ratchet mechanisms and electrical operation. Kits provide everything needed apart from fabric and thread, while extension brackets, acorns and tassels are optional extras. Components also supplied separately. *M:* four sizes, w100 – 200 × max d250cm (39¼ – 78¾ × 98½in). *P:* Roman £28.94; Austrian £26.58.

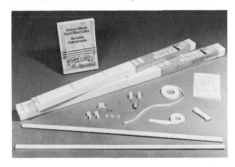

Top: Silent Gliss's Roman blind kit; below: blind made using the kit

SUNWAY BLINDS LTD

Made-to-measure festoon blinds in 44 fabrics including many from Sanderson (see *Fabrics & wallcoverings*). Sanderson fabrics include three designs in cotton/polyester (two of which, 'Country Trail' and 'Small Wonder', come from their popular OPTIONS range), each in three colourways, and four delicate designs on cream-coloured printed voile, 'In Clover', 'Country Trail', 'Rose Stencil' and 'Polka Dot'. Sunway's other festoon fabrics include six pastel-coloured French voiles, printed or plain; six heavy moirés; eight soft satins; six heavier satinized cottons and five floral cottons. *P:* on application.

VIXEN-SMITH LTD

Blinds made up either in own range of plain glazed cottons or in customer's own fabric. Three styles are available: ruched Viennese festoons, Roman (complete with lining) and Austrian. *P:* on application.

PRICES AND INFORMATION WERE CORRECT AT THE TIME OF GOING TO PRESS

Sunway's festoon blind in Sanderson 'Polka Dot' voile

SPECIAL BLINDS

FABER (VENETIAN BLIND SERVICES LTD)

For contract use, SOLITE BLACK-OUT BLIND for lecture theatres, projection rooms or any regular site for audio-visual presentations. Framed in a black anodized blind box, the blind opens and closes by a single pulley which in turn operates side pulleys for smooth efficient action. Side and bottom channels are designed for maximum light exclusion. *P:* on application.

For domestic use, DIM OUT roller blinds for children's bedrooms or any room where daylight or outside street lighting is a nuisance. Available in limited range of this company's roller blind colours (see *Roller blinds*). *P:* £33.47.

LUXAFLEX LTD

SUPER STOPLIGHT roller blind for children's bedrooms or those sleeping in the day. Specially coated to prevent light entry, blinds are

Three versions of Luxaflex's PALISADE security blind

available in five colours — coffee, green, brown, blue and pink — and one pattern. *P:* £34.66.

TWINIGHTER Venetian blind is constructed so that the slats close more tightly to exclude 90 per cent of the light, with tapes over cord holes. *M:* slats 2in (5cm). *P:* £43.32.

Luxaflex also makes an energy-saving Venetian blind, in which the concave side of the slats has special 'Thermostop' finish. Facing inwards in winter, outwards in summer, the 'Thermostop' slats reduce heat loss and heat gain respectively. Available in three slat widths in polar (white), magnolia and fawn. *M & P:* see *Venetian blinds*.

Other special products are the PALISADE security blind, firmly fixed and daunting to intruders; side-guided blinds for swivel windows; and an option of two blinds on a single head rail.

PERMA BLINDS LTD

Selection of blinds with unusual refinements. AUDIO VISUAL Venetian blind, in matt black, dark green or black and white, gives 70 – 80 per cent black-out, suitable for lecture rooms and studios. Slim matt black plastic channels on the sides and optionally on the bottom of the blind trap light, and wide tapes prevent light coming through cord holes. Also available is a 100 per cent black-out blind with metal or timber channels. *P:* on application.

RIDALUX black-out roller blind can be combined with a Venetian blind for partial or total black-out, while simpler RIDANETTE roller blind with aluminium coating on the outside gives adequate black-out for bedrooms and studios. Both suitable only for use inside double glazing. *P:* on application.

Popular CONTINENT Venetian blind with minor modifications is ideal for double glazing and meets full requirements of British noise abatement regulations (see *Venetian blinds*).

SUNWAY BLINDS LTD

Made-to-measure, light-resistant roller blinds in black, brown, white, beige, pink, green and blue. *P:* £35.35.

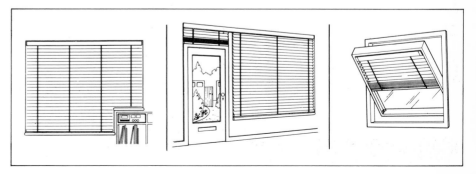

BLINDS

VENETIAN BLINDS IN PLAIN COLOURS	WHITE	MAGNOLIA	IVORY	FAWN	MUSHROOM	OYSTER	EGGSHELL	YELLOW	BEIGE	GOLDEN BROWN	CHESTNUT	DK BROWN	TERRACOTTA	RUST	ORANGE	RED	PINK	PURPLE	LT BLUE	MID BLUE	NAVY	AQUA	MINT	LT GREEN	BT GREEN	DK GREEN	AVOCADO	LIME GREEN	LT GREY	BLACK	SILVER	GOLD	COPPER
ERICSON 35	●	●	●	●	●		●	●	●	●	●	●			●	●	●		●	●				●		●			●	●	●	●	
SLIMLINE	●		●	●	●				●	●	●			●															●	●		●	
FABER	●		●	●		●	●	●	●	●	●	●			●	●	●		●	●		●	●	●				●	●	●	●		
FILTRASOL VISION	●	●	●	●		●	●	●	●		●		●		●				●	●			●	●				●	●				
HABITAT		●	●	●	●	●		●	●	●		●		●				●	●	●				●			●		●				
PANORAMA	●	●		●	●	●	●		●		●	●	●	●		●	●		●	●		●	●			●			●	●	●	●	●
PERMA	●	●	●	●	●	●	●	●	●		●	●			●	●	●		●	●		●	●	●			●	●	●	●	●	●	●
T F SAMPSON	●			●							●	●	●		●	●	●		●	●	●			●				●	●	●	●		
SUNSTOR	●		●	●	●	●		●			●	●			●				●					●				●	●				
SUNVENE				●	●	●			●		●			●	●	●	●	●	●			●	●				●	●	●	●	●	●	

See also Luxaflex, Sunway, Vixen-Smith

VENETIAN BLINDS

BLIND ALLEY LTD
Venetian blinds made to measure and printed with Blind Alley's highly original screenprint designs (see *Roller blinds*). 'New York' Venetian has a startling *trompe l'oeil* design. *P:* from £26.50.

ERICSON BLINDS LTD
Reasonably priced ERICSON 35 blinds in 25 colours (see chart) including a range of wood-effect finishes — walnut, sandalwood, teak, birch, rosewood and whiteoak. SLIMLINE blinds come in 11 colours (see chart) with matching head and bottom rails. *M:* slats, ERICSON 35 3.5cm (1⅜in); SLIMLINE 2.5cm (1in). *P:* ERICSON 35 £16.59; SLIMLINE £33.19.

FABER (VENETIAN BLIND SERVICES LTD)
Aluminium alloy blinds in good choice of strong and pastel shades. Slim FINESSE, say the manufacturers, is almost invisible when open; and SUPER comes in two broader slat widths. Thirty plain colours are available (see chart) and in the 'New Edition' option these can be mixed for stripes in standard or individual combinations. SLENDERMATIC, an acrylic rod control for both tilting and opening blinds, is available for FINESSE and the narrower SUPER slats. For sloping windows, fanlights and other awkward spaces, SV35 blinds can be made up to specification. *M:* slats, FINESSE 2.5cm (1in); SUPER 3.5cm (1⅜in), 5cm (2in). *P:* FINESSE £38.65; SUPER £33.04; 'New Edition' 10 per cent extra.

PRICES AND INFORMATION WERE CORRECT AT THE TIME OF GOING TO PRESS

From Faber. Top: SUPER; below: FINESSE

FILTRASOL LTD
Elegant SPECTRUM collection now in choice of three slat widths. VISION is a fine, slim blind, barely visible when open. It comes in the widest range of colours — 22 in all (see chart). VOGUE has a slightly wider slat giving a trace of colour to the window and comes in ten colours, while TRADITION, with the widest slat, is available in four shades. All have matching head and bottom rails. RAINBOW designs have slats in different colours; choose a set scheme or create your own. Standard designs are 'Duet' with two alternating colours, 'Quartet' with four colours creating a multi-striped effect, and 'Graduation', with four shades graded for increasing intensity. *M:* slats, VISION and RAINBOW 2.5cm (1in); VOGUE 3.5cm (1⅜in); TRADITION 5cm (2in). *P:* VISION £37.29, VOGUE and TRADITION £33.91; RAINBOW designs 10 per cent extra for more than two colours.

HABITAT DESIGNS LTD
Fine-slat Venetian blinds available by mail order in 24 colours or at the store in 34 colours, with an exceptionally good range of soft and neutral shades. All made to measure. *M:* min w61 × d61cm (24 × 24in); max w105 × d325cm (41¼ × 128in). *P:* £42.43.

LUXAFLEX LTD ⚠
Stunning array of colours in matt and gloss, and some unusual effects and finishes. Slim FINEBLIND comes in 38 plain colours, two wood-grain finishes, three border prints — 'Landscape', 'Bamboo' and 'Floral' — and in glittering 'Mirror' and lacy 'Gossamer' slats. 'Mirror' slats are shining chrome, Midas (gold) or copper on one side, matt ebony on the

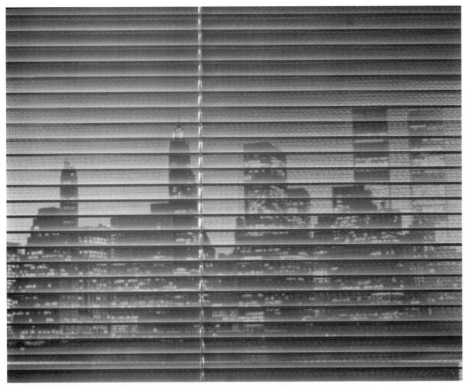

FINEBLIND, with perforated 'Gossamer' △ slats, from Luxaflex

other, creating a dramatic transformation at the flick of a wrist. 'Gossamer' slats, in five colours only, have tiny perforations; even when closed, they give a softened view of the world outside. 'Gossamer Cascade' mixes perforated with standard slats; 'Hi-tech' uses mirrored slats as highlights; and 'Decormatch' provides five striped designs in pre-set or customer's choice of colours. *M:* slats 1in (2.5cm). *P:* standard colours £44.09; border prints £49.09; 'Mirror' and 'Gossamer' £52.89; 'Cascade' £48.49; 'Hi-tech' £46.29. Broader SILHOUETTE and CLASSIC blinds each come in 20 colours. *M:* slats, SILHOUETTE 1in (3.5cm); CLASSIC 2in (5cm). *P:* £39.38. All three ranges include Luxaflex's unique 'Thermostop' energy-saving blind (see *Special blinds*).

DRAW DRAPE is a vertical Venetian blind with aluminium vanes, available in 20 colours. Slats can be removed individually for cleaning, an advantage in rooms with high condensation. Unlike most vertical louvres, however, it can only be stacked at each side. *M:* slats 2in (5cm). *P:* £58.08.

PANORAMA (PEEL & CAMPDEN LTD)

Competitively priced, stove-enamelled blinds in three slat widths and 27 colours (see chart). Up to three colours in any configuration can be incorporated into a blind at no extra cost.

Tilt wand operation, matching head and bottom rails and side guide-wires are optional extras. *M:* slats 2.5cm (1in), 3.5cm (1⅜in), 5cm (2in). *P:* 5 and 3.5cm £20.96; 2.5cm 15 per cent extra.

PERMA BLINDS LTD △

Wide selection of blinds. CONTINENT, said to be Europe's most popular blind, comes in three slat widths and 27 colours. It can be freehanging or installed between double glazing (see *Special blinds*). For small windows, ROULETT is recommended; 33 colours are available in wide slats, with a restricted choice in narrower ones. CAPRICE slimline blind gives the option of mixing slats of two colours to create an individual effect. *M:* slats, CONTINENT 2.5cm (1in), 3.5cm (1⅜in), 5cm (2in); ROULETT 2.5cm (1in), 3.5cm (1⅜in); CAPRICE 2.5cm (1in). *P:* on application.

T F SAMPSON LTD

From the PLEATEX people, reasonably priced, rust-proofed metallic blinds in 22 colours including black, gold and silver. All colours are available in the two larger slat widths, white and silver only in the narrow slats. All blinds made to measure. *M:* slats 2.5cm (1in), 3.5cm (1⅜in), 5cm (2in). *P:* £14.89 ex VAT; 2.5cm slats 50 per cent extra.

SUNSTOR LTD

Twenty-four plain shades in SLENDER, SLIM and STANDARD ranges. Two patterns, flowery 'Rose Beige' and 'Rose Brown', are also available. Fawn, gold, grey, silver, white and red STANDARD slats have glossy finishes, all others have regular silk finish. Head and bottom rails and tapes are in matching colours. ECONOMY range with white rails, is available in two larger slat widths in all colours except ivory and 'Rose' patterns. Mixed slats in co-ordinating or contrasting colours can be ordered. *M:* SLENDER 1in (2.5cm); SLIM 1⅜in (3.5cm); STANDARD 2in (5cm). *P:* SLENDER £39.14; SLIM and STANDARD £34.57; ECONOMY £24.81; mixed slats 10 per cent extra.

SUNVENE LTD

Reasonably priced rust-proofed aluminium blinds in two slat widths. Can be cadmium-plated, stove-enamelled or plastic-coated in 20 colours (see chart) from pastels to deeper shades like cherry red, with terylene webbing to match. Up to six colours can be mixed in each blind at no extra cost. Guaranteed for five years. Sunvene also offer a cleaning and repair service. *M:* slats 1⅜in (3.5cm), 2in (5cm). *P:* £17.81, £15.68.

SUNWAY BLINDS LTD

Reasonably priced range of 30 plain shades in primary, metallic and pastel tones, and in a choice of three slat widths. *M:* slats 1in (2.5cm), 1⅜in (3.5cm), 2in (5cm). *P:* 1in £42.64, 1⅜in and 2in £37.

Sunway's Venetian blinds

VIXEN-SMITH LTD

Plain and multicoloured blinds in three slat widths. Blinds with contrasting slats in two or three colours come in five designs: 'Bitter Lemon Strata', 'Russet Strata', 'Black Horizons' (stark black and white), 'Nutmeg Strata', and 'Grey Strata'. *M:* slats 1in (2.5cm), 1⅜in (3.5cm), 2in (5cm). *P:* 2in and 1⅜in £36.37; 1in £41.86.

BLINDS

VERTICAL LOUVRE BLINDS IN PLAIN COLOURS		WHITE	CREAM	OATMEAL	SAND	BEIGE	COFFEE	YELLOW	GOLD	LT BROWN	DK BROWN	RUST	ORANGE	RED	PINK	WINE	NAVY	MID BLUE	LT BLUE	AQUA	LT GREEN	BT GREEN	AVOCADO	DK GREEN	LT GREY	DK GREY	BLACK
BAUMANN		●	●	●	●	●	●	●	●	●	●	●	●	●	●	●	●	●	●	●	●	●	●	●	●	●	●
FABER		●	●	●	●	●	●	●	●	●	●	●	●	●				●			●				●	●	
FILTRASOL	'Hondo'		●		●		●	●		●		●												●			
	'Ryme'	●	●	●	●					●	●		●											●			
	'Shantung'	●		●	●		●																				
PERMA	'Designer'		●		●			●	●	●	●		●								●						
	'Glass'	●			●	●					●																
	'Shantung'	●	●	●	●	●	●					●									●						
	'Spice'	●			●	●						●															
	'Thai'				●					●				●													
	'Weave'	●	●	●	●	●		●																			
SILENT GLISS		●	●	●	●	●	●										●	●	●	●	●	●	●	●	●	●	●
SUNSTOR		●	●	●	●			●	●															●	●	●	●
SUNVENE	Glassfibre	●	●				●																●				
	Nebula		●			●	●			●							●										
	Shantung	●			●	●	●						●						●					●			
	Spice	●	●	●				●	●															●			
SUNWAY		●	●	●	●	●	●	●	●	●				●	●	●			●	●						●	

See also Luxaflex, Vertika, Vixen-Smith

VERTICAL LOUVRE BLINDS

BAUMANN FABRICS LTD
Tasteful and unusual selection of louvres in wide choice of fabrics and huge choice of colourways. SIERRA II is a finely woven, silky finish fabric, available in 43 colours including some of the boldest primaries around. SAHARA, in 29 colours, is loosely woven with random horizontal stripes against lighter backgrounds. TIRA, in 13 colourways, has bolder, more contemporary diagonal stripes, in pretty pastels against backgrounds of lilac, pink, peach or blue. COLIBRI, in linen, cotton and polyester, comes in 32 colours; a 'crocheted' weave makes the fabric semi-transparent pro-

ECETERA from Baumann Fabrics

viding light at the same time as privacy. Sophisticated ECETERA in 29 subtle colours and structures and FLAMINIA, making bolder use of colour and highlighted with a fine needle stripe, complete the Baumann range. SIERRA II, SAHARA, TIRA and ECETERA are flame-retardant. *M:* louvres, all 12.5cm (5in); ECETERA selected colours also 9cm (3½in). *P:* on application.

BLIND ALLEY LTD
Designs individually created for vertical louvre blinds, from roller-blind specialists. Design, measuring and fitting service available in London area only. *P:* artwork £15 per louvre.

FABER (VENETIAN BLIND SERVICES LTD) 🔥
Wide selection giving a choice of colour, texture and weight. Eighty-three fabrics in the FABER SUPER range include strong colours — scarlet, denim and dusky pink — in 'Hookweave', more muted tones in 'Donegal' and 'Tibet'. 'Taiweave', 'Hookweave', 'Papyrus', 'Tawny' and 'Thatch' can be co-ordinated with Faber's roller blinds. Delicate floral prints are available in 'Daphne' and 'Samos'. As well as left, right and split draw, blinds can be drawn into centre, stacked in threes, or drawn half to centre, half to both sides. FABER ESCALADE,

available in the full fabric range, is tailor-made for angled spaces. *M:* louvres 5in (12.5cm) all fabrics; 3½in (9cm) selected range. *P:* £54.59 to £108.50 according to fabric; 3½in louvres extra.

Fabric vertical from FABER SUPER range △

FILTRASOL LTD
Fifteen different fabrics in a total of 58 colourways, including five whites and off-whites. 'Shantung' in 100 per cent cotton, has a crisp, clean finish in contrast to the irregular loose weave of 'Fashion' in 77 per cent cotton, 23 per cent linen. In flame-resistant fibreglass are light 'Voile' and slightly heavier 'Charm', both with delicate grey patterns; 'Ryme', a hessian weave in eight subtle colours; and 'Hondo', a smoother weave in the brightest choice of colours — including buttercup yellow, fern green and pumpkin (a muted orange). *M:* louvres 5in (12.5cm); 'Shantung', 'Fashion', 'Hondo' also 3½in (9cm). *P:* £53.18; 3½in louvres 15 per cent extra.

LUXAFLEX LTD 🔥
Wide selection of textures and colours with an option of custom-printed designs along the top or bottom of louvres. FINESSA blinds are tailor-made to fit any space, even sloping attic windows. Each louvre swivels through 180° for precise light control and head rail is precision-engineered for smooth operation with a failsafe mechanism to avoid accidental damage. Available in 14 materials, including PVC, and 68 colourways, including metallics. With DECORMATCH these colours can be mixed and matched in standard or individual striped designs. Or fabric louvres can be transfer-printed

Luxaflex's FINEBLIND with 'Mirror' slats

Airbrushed roller blind from Blind Alley

with DECORVANE designs; 'Foliage', 'Tendril', 'Shapes', 'Rambler' and 'Angles' span the range from traditional to high tech. Matching pelmets are available. *M:* louvres 3½in (9cm), 5in (12.5cm). *P:* 5in £68.53; 3½in £78.80.
READY VERTICAL blinds, for immediate hanging, come in four widths and can be cut to fit. Available in white, beige or camel acrylic fabric. Luxaflex will also replace damaged louvres at a saving of up to 60 per cent on the cost of a new blind. *M:* w48in (122cm), 60in (152.5cm), 72in (183cm), 84in (213.5cm) *P:* from £57.

PERMA BLINDS LTD
CONSUL range in a variety of fabrics. 'Designer' and 'Shantung' in cottons and polyester offer a wide choice of colours, including olive, terracotta and pinkish coral as well as neutrals; while the more muted tones of 'Weave', 'Spice' and 'Thai' give a useful choice of whites and off-whites in tweed- and slub-effect. 'Glass' flame-resistant fibreglass fabric comes in four neutral colours, and solid and pinhole PVC blinds are also available. *M:* louvres 8.9cm (3½in); 12.7cm (5in); blinds max w6m (6½yd). *P:* on application.

SILENT GLISS LTD
Wide range of blinds in even wider range of colours from this top-quality manufacturer. SYSTEM 2700 is claimed to be the only vertical blind that can be curved to fit contours such as

SYSTEM 2800 with single control chain from Silent Gliss

bay windows. It can tilt through 180° and both tilting and traverse action are controlled with just one handle. Robust SYSTEM 2800 can also be drawn and tilted with just one control. For added sophistication, there are electronically operated blind systems. All available in cotton in 44 plain colours, in flameproof Trevira in 66 plain colours, and in Trevira printed with unusual designs from the 'Italian Picture Set' by Enzo Bertazzo. Eighteen designs, each in several colourways, include subtle 'Nodi' of hanging knotted ropes and rich 'Poggiofiorito', a vine-trellis reminiscent of Italian courtyards. The translucent Trevira lets light through while eliminating glare. *M:* louvres, standard 12.7cm (5in); selected systems 6cm (2¼in), 8.9cm (3½in), 10cm (4in). *P:* on application.

SUNSTOR LTD
Chunky and standard weaves in a range particularly favouring browns and fawns. Nine fabric collections are available, from 'Loom', loosely woven in ten muted colours, to 'Norfolk', a finer weave in natural and spice. Among the others, 'Van Dyke' is a chunky, downy fabric in shades ranging from parchment to peat; 'Amalfi' has a design of curves and droplets in brown and white; and 'Alassio' has an unusual thick-and-thin weave in grey and white. Some of the fabrics co-ordinate with Sunstor's roller blinds (see separate entry). Angled blinds for sloping windows and awkward spaces can be made to measure. All blinds come with matching control cords. *M:*

From Sunway. Below: SCENARIO; bottom: STROBE

louvres 5in (12.5cm); 'Loom', 'Norfolk', 'Van Dyke' also 3½in (9cm). *P:* £42.31-£60.32; 3½in louvres 15 per cent extra.

SUNVENE LTD
Choice of four fabrics each in an attractive selection of colourways (see chart). Silky SHANTUNG comes in white, beige, yellow, green, orange, sand, blue and tan; coarser GLASSFIBRE in champagne, brown, tango, yellow, green and white; loosely woven SPICE in white, oatmeal, barley, natural, brown, calico, tiger lily and green; and soft, fleecy NEBULA in dark beige, beige, vanilla, cork, écru and aubergine. *M:* all louvres 5in (12.7cm). *P:* SHANTUNG, GLASSFIBRE £36.21; SPICE, NEBULA £43.45.

SUNWAY BLINDS LTD
Eighty-eight colours in 26 different fabrics, including PVC. Collection covers every possible shade of fawn, beige and oatmeal through to a rich, dark russet. Fabrics range from the rough slubbed wool of SOJURN to the silky, translucent SCENARIO with a herringbone pattern. SAVANNA, the most colourful, comes in pastels plus bolder yellow, blue, red, brown and burgundy. STRAND incorporates colour in a series of woven stripes in red, yellow, brown or blue on a cream background. In white and cream PVC are SOLARIUM and STROBE; the latter has tiny perforations that can be seen through only from the inside, making it ideal for bathrooms. Louvres with pocketed and linked weights are available at no extra charge. *M:* louvres 3½in (9cm), 5in (12.7cm). *P:* on application.

VERTIKA INTERNATIONAL LTD
Simple-to-fit louvres in both bright and subtle shades. Sponge-clean louvres come in a range of fabrics from soft-latex-coated textiles to thick, roughly woven ones. Blinds are guaranteed against twisting, curling, shrinking and stretching, and all are made to individual requirements including bays and other curved spaces. Electric, mono and clutch control are optional extras. *M:* louvres 8.9cm (3½in), 12.7cm (5in). *P:* on application.

VIXEN-SMITH LTD
Plain blinds, and plain blinds hand-printed with striking designs. Fabrics include 'Shantung', 'Linen', 'Tweed' and slub-effect weaves in a choice of more than 40 colours. And the AURORA range of designs includes 'Iris' with tall blue Japanese irises, and 'Houseplants' with rubber plants, ferns, palms and ivy leaves in green and yellow—for conservatory-lovers. Fabrics can also be made up in roller blinds. *M:* louvres 5in (12.5cm). *P:* plain £47.82-£94.11; AURORA £17.78 extra.

CARPETING

INTRODUCTION

An inspired choice of carpeting can do more to create a harmonious interior than almost any other furnishing. The same colour and texture throughout a small house give a feeling of spaciousness and unity, while contrasts define space, setting apart rooms or areas.

Rugs can be used, over bare floors or wall-to-wall carpeting, to provide colour or give focus to a room. Made by machine or by hand, they come in an immense variety of patterns and textures, from intricate Isfahans through swirling Celtic designs and traditional dhurries to bold modern geometrics. And one advantage with rugs is that when you move, rugs move with you, while carpets stay put.

The quality of carpet ultimately depends on the fibre used. After silk, the stuff of the most luxurious oriental rugs, the supreme yarn for both rugs and carpets is wool — in spite of its price, still unchallenged in many areas. It can be dyed to the widest range of colours (more than 1,500), holds them better than other fibres, and won't easily catch fire. It cleans well and is certainly the hardest-wearing yarn. Wool carpets are usually mothproofed. Quality manufacturers favour 100% wool, or a mix of 20% nylon (for strength) and 80% wool — afford it if you can.

Hardwearing acrylics (Acrilan, Courtelle, Dralon, Orlon) are most like wool but soil more easily and are also fairly expensive.

Flame-resistant modacrylics (Teklan) are comparatively new, and used primarily for contract carpeting. Domestic use will no doubt increase.

Nylon (Bri-Nylon, Enkalon, Celon, Dupont, Antron, Timbrelle) is tough and fire-resistant. It can be used on its own or to add strength to blends of other fibres.

Polyesters (Dacron, Terylene, Trevira) come in good, pleasant colours but are only moderately hardwearing.

Polypropylene (Ulstron, Meraklon, Olefin, Propathene) is mainly used for hardwearing, low-priced carpets like plush piles. Stain-resistant and relatively static-free, it often has a slight sheen.

As for construction, there are basically two types of pile: long or short cut pile, and loop pile used in Wilton, tufted or Brussels weave carpets. Loop pile, made from a continuous series of loops, comes in a range of textures from thick and nubbly to closely curled. Both loop and cut piles are capable of endless variation, especially when they are combined in sculptured or textured carpets.

Of the other types, velours, or velvet pile, is very closely cut and used mainly for plain or mottled effects. Twist or hard-twist pile, with a definite twist or kink built into the yarn, has a knobbly look. Most common in plain carpets, it's sometimes combined with other piles to create unusual textures.

The complexity of design possible in a carpet is determined by the method of manufacture.

Axminsters are normally highly patterned; up to 35 colours can be used together, giving endless variety of designs.

Wilton patterns are simpler as the looms take a maximum of only five colours. But Wiltons are also the most durable, strongest and often the most expensive carpets on the market because of the high amount of pile woven into the backing.

Tufted carpets, a relatively modern invention, can be plain or patterned. Individual lengths of yarn are inserted into a pre-woven backing, creating a looped or cut-pile texture. The backing is coated twice to hold the tufts. The first tufted carpets were made from cheap synthetics. Happily they now come in better fibres, including wool.

Cord carpets can be woven or tufted, with a low-loop uncut pile. Bonded cords have a mass of fibres fixed to a hessian back and, generally very hardwearing — and about half the price of Wiltons. Look for natural and synthetic fibre mixes.

Fibre bonded carpeting, cometimes called 'needleloom' or 'needlepunch', is used mainly for tiles. Dense, felt-like layers of fibres are pushed into a backing impregnated with a bonding agent to hold them together.

A practical and often economical alternative to all these fibres is matting made from coir, rush or maize. Attractively natural, it is also hardwearing and conceals dirt well.

The carpet industry is gradually changing to metric widths of 1, 2, 3 and 4m, but the change will be slow. Some carpets are still made on looms with traditional broadloom widths. The most common are 9ft (274.5cm), 12ft (366cm), 15ft (457.5cm) and 18ft (549cm). Body carpet, the trade's name for the narrow strips used as runners on stairs and in halls, is 27in (68.5cm) and 3ft (91.5cm) wide. Try to avoid using it in rooms; the joins are never really invisible (unless it's tufted).

A simple grading scheme makes it easy to select suitable carpets for different areas. Many manufacturers make the same colours in different weights: light domestic (bedrooms only), medium domestic (light traffic areas), general domestic (sitting rooms), heavy domestic (hallways and landings), and luxury domestic. Contract quality is specifically for public places, but also useful at home in hallways and other high-traffic areas. Unfortunately, it's not always available in relatively small quantities.

This section has been simply divided as follows: *Coir, rush and maize matting, Flecked carpets, Made-to-order carpets, Patterned carpets, Plain carpets, Rugs* and *Tiles (carpeting).*

● For price comparison, there's about one fifth more carpet in a sq m than in a sq yd.

PRICES AND INFORMATION WERE CORRECT AT THE TIME OF GOING TO PRESS

COIR, RUSH AND MAIZE MATTING

AFIA CARPETS

Coir matting in two designs for economy and durability. 'Bouclé' is a ribbed cord weave and 'Panama' a basket-weave, each either bleached or unbleached. *M:* w400cm (157½in). *P:* sq yd £9.25–£12.45.

BRISTOL INTERNATIONAL

A beautiful range of eight different Swiss-made coir, sisal or sisal/coir mixture mattings, some dyed to fashionable colours. They are not cheap but they are tough enough for contract use — and they look wonderful. Least expensive is JAIPUR, 100% sisal in an open-weave waffle pattern that comes to two weights and five colours — natural, copper, celadon (pale green), slate and turquoise. The lighter weight has no backing, the heavier one a PVC waffle backing. *M:* w200cm (78¾in). *P:* sq m from £11.

The next range is MANILA, 100% sisal with cord effect, in natural only. Six different widths are available unbacked; one width comes with PVC waffle back. *M:* without backing, w90, 120, 150, 200, 230, 250cm (35½, 47¼, 59, 78¾, 90½, 98½in); with backing 200cm (78¾in). *P:* sq m from £14.25.

CONGA is 100% coir in a rough, random-effect weave. It comes in brown or natural and is available with or without PVC waffle backing. *M:* w200cm (78¾in). *P:* sq m from £13.75.

BALI is a tightly woven 100% coir herringbone pattern, available natural or bleached, with PVC waffle backing. *M:* bleached w120, 150, 170, 200cm (47¼, 59, 67, 78¾in); natural 200cm (78¾in). *P:* sq m from £15.75.

CALICUT is 100% coir with a heavy cord effect weave that comes in bleached, natural, antique pink, granite and indigo. Several different widths are available, some with PVC waffle backing. CALICUT is also available in PVC-backed tiles and, in bleached only, in a lighter weight for use as a wall covering. *M:* 104–200cm (41–78¾in); tiles 50 × 50cm (19¾ × 19¾in). *P:* sq m from £12.50.

CHEVRON is an unusual two-tone herringbone weave in 43% coir/57% sisal. It comes in blue/brown, grey/natural, green/natural and turquoise/natural, and is available with or without PVC waffle backing. *M:* w200cm (78¾in). *P:* sq m from £20.25.

COLOMBO is a beautiful hand-woven 100% coir that is made to order. The unbacked basket-weave pattern comes in single colours (natural, bleached, Havana brown, ash-pink or bronze-green) or two-tone (Havana brown/grey-blue, grey-blue/ash-pink, bronze-green/cinnamon brown, bronze-green/ash-pink). *M:* w100–400cm (39¼–157½in). *P:* sq m from £31.25.

In the real luxury bracket comes TAHITI, a bouclé-effect 100% coir that is available in

Left to right, from top: JAIPUR, MANILA, CONGA, BALI, CALICUT, CHEVRON, COLOMBO and TAHITI. All by Bristol International

bleached or natural, in a stripe combining the two colours, or in a sculptured diagonal pattern, in natural only. It comes with or without PVC waffle backing. TAHITI is also available in PVC-backed tiles. *M:* w200cm (78¾in); tiles 50 × 50cm (19¾ × 19¾in). *P:* sq m from £23.50. (All prices ex VAT.)

HABITAT DESIGNS LTD
Four coir carpetings for an inexpensive, neutral flooring finish. DIAMOND coir broadloom is an unusual diamond pattern woven from bleached and natural coir with latex backing. HERRINGBONE BLEACHED broadloom coir and HERRINGBONE NATURAL handwoven broadloom coir also have latex backing. ANJENGO coir matting, also in the traditional herringbone pattern, is sold by the metre, to be sewn together at home. Habitat also sells coir matting edge-binding tape. *M:* all w400cm (157¼in), except ANJENGO w91cm (35¾in). *P:* DIAMOND sq m £9.45; HERRINGBONE BLEACHED sq m £7.95; HERRINGBONE NATURAL sq m £6.50; ANJENGO linear m £3.20.

JAYMART RUBBER & PLASTICS LTD
Terrific selection of latex-backed natural fibre carpeting. PANAMA in 70% coir/30% sisal comes in bleached or natural; the same material is also available in red, blue, dark charcoal, green and brown under the name PANACOLOUR. BO-CON in 70% coir/30% sisal with a corded look comes in bleached or natural, and similar tiles, BO-TILE, come in natural,

From left: SISAL BOUCLE beige, PANAMA KALIF, PANAMA, SISAL BOUCLE cognac, BO-TILE bleached and natural; below: SISAL CANVAS. From Jaymart

bleached and brown. *M:* w200, 400cm (78¾, 157½in); BO-TILE 50 × 50cm (19¾ × 19¾in). *P:* PANAMA, PANACOLOUR sq m £6.90–£8. SISAL BOUCLE is 100% sisal with a smoother finish in beige and cognac (with touches of black and orange). SISAL CANVAS in 100% sisal is a basket-weave pattern in cognac only. PANAMA KALIF and DIANE 2500 are both 100% coir in natural only. *M:* w400cm (157½in). *P:* SISAL BOUCLE sq m £9.75; SISAL CANVAS sq m £15.95; PANAMA KALIF and DIANE sq m £4.95.
BRUSH-OFF is a very tough PVC-backed 100% coir with a velours finish, ideal just for doormats or for larger entrance areas that are exposed to a lot of dirt and moisture. It is available in a wide variety of widths and thicknesses and in two qualities. Colours are natural, anthracite, dark brown, dark green, red, whisky, charcoal, moss green, gold, red, red/black,

Jaymart's BRUSH-OFF

blue/light blue, brown ripple, brown/orange ripple. BRUSH-TILE offers a slightly more limited range of colours in tiles of the same material. *M:* w100, 200cm (39¼, 78¾in); tiles 50 × 50cm (19¾ × 19¾in). *P:* sq m £8.80–£13.75.

ROOKSMOOR MILLS
Traditionally woven rush and maize matting in standard sizes or made to measure to the nearest 12in (30.5cm) square. Matting is inexpensive, can be cleaned with soap and water and is not adversely affected by damp. If any damage should occur, Rooksmoor can supply needle and twine (cost £1) as well as replacement squares.
RUSH MATTING, in its natural sea-grass colour with a diamond pattern, comes in three standard sizes or made-to-measure, *M:* 9 × 6ft (257 × 183cm); 9 × 12ft (257 × 366cm); 9 × 18ft (257 × 457cm). *P:* £18.90, £37.90, £56.70; made-to-measure 45p sq ft.
RUSH BULLSEYE matting in a design of circles within squares is available in three standard sizes only. *M:* 4 × 2ft (122 × 61cm); 6 × 3ft (183 × 91.5cm); 7 × 4ft (213.5 × 122cm). *P:* £4.95, £11.95, £17.95.
MAIZE MATTING is even harder wearing and comes in two tones, either in 4in (10cm) squares of green and beige, or in 6in (15cm) squares of bark and beige. *M:* 9 × 6ft (257 × 183cm); 9 × 12ft (257 × 366cm); 9 × 18ft (257 × 457cm). *P:* £35, £70, £105; made-to-measure 75p sq ft.

E RUSSUM & SONS LTD
Two ranges of very hardwearing carpeting to use in the toughest situations. BTB COIR MATTING's vinyl chloride backing is impermeable to water, dust and loose dirt and its cut edges won't fray. It comes in four thicknesses (depending on colour) and in natural plus five colours — green (dark olive), gold, red, anthracite (dark slate grey) and brown (dark). *M:* w100, 200cm (39¼, 78¾in); thickness, 17, 20, 23, 30mm) (⅔, ¾, ⁹⁄₁₀, 1in). *P:* sq m £14.70–£18.

CARPETING

PETER SMITH ASSOCIATES (WILTSHIRE) LTD
PSA CUTFAST PVC-backed coir pile matting, suitable for any location where really tough wear is required, particularly entrance halls. Matting can be cut to any shape without fraying and laid without underlay. Large areas can be vacuumed; smaller mats may be reversed to beat out dust and grit. Available in 10 colours: bleached natural, red, whisky, gold, green, brown, charcoal, russet and two new shades — brick and blue. *M:* w100, 200cm (39¼, 78¾in). *P:* on application.

BRUCE STARKE & CO LTD
Hardwearing 100% coir carpeting. It's antistatic, flameproof, easy to lay and won't fray. TROPICOIR range is tough, latex-backed and comes in natural colour in five different weaves. HAMELIN matting is available in natural, red, olive green, cognac, russet, and a wonderful wavy-line pattern in black on red, light blue on blue, and dark brown on natural. *M:* TROPICOIR w200cm (78¾in), limited quantity also w400cm (157¼in); HAMELIN w100, 200cm (39¼, 78¾). *P:* on application.

FLECKED CARPETS

ADAM CARPETS LTD
Two 100% wool Wiltons with a slight fleck. BERBER DE LUXE is the heavier carpet with a smoother texture and a more pronounced fleck. It comes in six colours — sea spray (pale sea-green), koala (warm mid-brown), champagne (cream), honey (beige), oyster (greyish brown) and sandalwood (mid-brown). Recommended for extra heavy wear.
BERBER SUPERB has twist pile and comes in seven subtle colours — Casablanca (cream with a touch of cherry red), oasis (pale sage green), arabesque (a slightly browner pale green), Tangier (pinky beige), Maroc (sandy brown), Sahara (greyish brown), Marrakesh (medium brown).
M: both w366cm (144in). *P:* on application.

BERBER DE LUXE from Adam Carpets

AFIA CARPETS
Three ranges of flecked carpeting from this exciting carpet shop. JUDY AFIA'S CARPET in 100% wool with a woven backing is for heavy domestic use. Described as 'not quite patterned, not quite plain', there are 17 nubbly-effect colourways, which use either cream, white or fawn as the foil to hold the colours together: sand, peach, coral, peppermint, midsummer green, quail, buttercup, periwinkle, china blue, eggshell, navy, silver, jet, toffee, strawberry, powder pink and aqua. *M:* w13ft (396cm). *P:* sq yd £15.45.
BEVERLEY and FIVES are larger loop pile carpets with a flecked effect in washed pastel shades. Made from 100% wool, they are also suitable for heavy domestic use. BEVERLEY comes in peach, apricot, jade, aqua, biscuit, sapphire and lilac, while FIVES comes in peach, mid-grey, pale blue, lovat (tweedy green), off-white and apricot. *M:* w13ft (396cm). *P:* sq yd £18.

AXMINSTER CARPETS LTD
Gently flecked 'Heather Plains' design from the MOORLAND COLLECTION. A pure wool Axminster for heavy wear and medium contract use, it is available in two shades of beige, two soft greens, pink and light chestnut. *M:* w91, 366cm (3, 12ft). *P:* on application.

BMK LTD ⚠
'Pinpoint' with small dots on a contrasting background, from the ROYAL TROON range. See *Carpets, patterned.*

BRINTONS LTD
Two subtly flecked Wiltons. BROADLOOP is woven in Antron XL, suitable for extra heavy wear, with an unusual nubbly loop appearance and choice of 12 soft colours (mostly beiges, browns, greys and greens with names such as nutmeg, mace, paprika, thyme, silver sage and bouquet garni). *M:* w200cm (78¾in); other widths available to order.
BELL TRINITY in 80% wool/20% nylon with hard twist pile is also suitable for extra heavy wear. It comes in 10 muted two-tone shades and a strong red. 'Heather' is an unusual combination of brown with pale blue, while 'Seville' has the same colours in reverse, with pale blue predominating. 'Graphite' is pale blue with grey and 'Charcoal' grey with pale blue. *M:* w400cm (157½in).
P: on application.

BRISTOL INTERNATIONAL
From the Swiss company RAG, FIESTA bouclé-look flecked carpet combining two, three or four colours from an enormous range of 240 possible colours. In 100% wool with latex backing, it is available in seven different pile heights. It is also available in a single colour (see *Carpeting, plain*). *M:* w100–400cm (39¼–181in). *P:* sq m from £35.50 (ex VAT).
ROLLERWOOL is a bouclé construction 100% wool carpet with a very subtle fleck and a choice of secondary or foam backing. The version with secondary backing is guaranteed against wear from castors — hence the name — which makes it ideal for office use. Colours are lovely — ivory, sand, bamboo, chestnut, steel blue, platinum, graphite and marengo. *M:* w400cm (157½in). *P:* sq m from £20.25 (ex VAT).

CHECKMATE INDUSTRIES LTD
Two heavy contract quality carpets in synthetic fibres. ZEROSTAT BROADLOOM is loop pile in 100% Enkastat with C-foam backing. It is static controlled and exceptional wear performance is guaranteed. Available in adobe (light beige), buckskin (medium beige), bronze, bracken (dark brown), granite (grey-brown), antler (blue) and moorland (heathery green). *P:* laid price sq m approx £11.
IBOLON SUPER BROADLOOM is made from fibre-bonded 70% polypropylene and 30% nylon, also for heavy contract use. It has a dense, curly pile and is available in green, grey, blue, berber, red, mocha (grey-brown), cognac (amber), moss, cork and brown. *M:* both w200cm (78¾in). *P:* laid price sq m approx £7.25.

JOHN CROSSLEY & SONS LTD
CONCERTO velvet twist pile in 80% wool/20% nylon with the slightest of flecks. CONCERTO has received a National Association of Retail Furnishers Award. The colours are lovely soft pastels — champagne, peppercorn (light caramel), absinthe (light sage green), sandalwood (pinky-beige), cameo (apricot), tundra (grey), havana (mid-brown), autumn rose (dark peach), celadon (pale sea-green), arabesque (lilac), ascot (pale blue), mistral (pale sage green), talisman (red) and medina (mid-blue). *M:* 100, 400cm (39¼, 157½in). *P:* on application.

DLW (BRITAIN) LTD
Synthetic carpets for very heavy contract use. There are two needlepunch carpets. POLO in 65% polypropylene/35% polyamide comes in six colours — three beiges, brown, red and green. STRONG is in 100% polyamide in 18 colours — mostly subdued shades of brown, green, grey and blue. Both have the familiar 'hairy' texture of this type of carpet and both are also available in tiles (see *Carpeting, tiles*). *M:* w200 cm (78¾in). *P:* on application.
There are also two nubbly tufted loop-pile ranges in 100% polyamide, both backed in high-density foam and treated to repel dirt and static. PREMIER SCHLINGE has smaller loops and darker colours — mostly heathery mixtures of browns, plus russet, blue-grey and beige. MARSCHALL comes in 14 colours — lighter browns, four beiges and two greys. *M:* w400cm (157½in). *P:* on application.

EGETAEPPER (UK) LTD
One tufted loop-pile carpet and one design in tufted velours, all with a fleck. LOW LEVEL LOOP is a heavy duty carpet made from 100% Enkastat Plus with synthetic latex backing. Four different qualities are available — 'Apollo', 'Comet', 'Mercur' and 'Robust' — each in 14 colourways. 'Apollo' also comes in a striped version in 15 colourways.
HIGHLINE 1100 range includes the 'Texture' design with a slightly mottled appearance, also in 100% Enkastat Plus with a synthetic latex backing.
All EGETAEPPER carpets are treated with Baco FRF to retard fire and suppress smoke. *M:* w400cm (157½in). *P:* on application.

FORBO TAPIJT BV
Four stunning ranges of nubbly berber carpeting and one brilliantly different cut and loop pile with a flecked effect. PARLANDO is tufted 100% wool with a large loop pile in natural, berber colours — sahara (light brown), natural, coral (light brown with reddish flecks), havana (mid-brown), medium oatmeal, dark oatmeal, grey and grey-blue. *M:* w400, 500cm (157½, 196¼in). *P:* sq m approx £20.
PALISADE is another tufted 100% wool with a slightly more uneven loop pile. Also in natural colours — berber, beige and camel. *M:* w400cm (157½in). *P:* sq m approx £21.
ABADAN has rather bolder flecks giving it a slightly rougher, more rustic look. It is another tufted 100% wool carpet with a large loop pile, and comes in berber, natural, grey-blue, light

Below: ABADAN; bottom: MAXIM. Both from Forbo

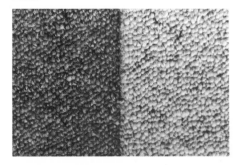

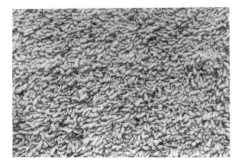

brown and sand. *M:* w400cm (157½in). *P:* sq m approx £22.50.
MAXIM, perhaps the ultimate shag carpet, has brown-flecked ivory yarns three-quarters of an inch deep — it looks almost alive! The Wilton-woven yarn comes just in beige or berber. *M:* w380cm (149½in). *P:* sq m approx £39.
Last, but definitely not least, there is the ethereal-looking IMPALA. This carpet cleverly combines cut and loop pile in the same shade to give the impression of tiny foam-flecked waves rippling across the sea. In 100% wool with Wilton construction, IMPALA comes in fashionable pastels — blue-grey, flax (beige), pearl-grey, rosewood (old rose), alabaster (pinky beige), and natural (beige). *M:* w400cm (157½in). *P:* sq m approx £36.
All these carpets are suitable for heavy domestic use, with the exception of MAXIM which is for luxury use.

GASKELL BROADLOOM CARPETS LTD
Three styles of flecked carpet that co-ordinate with one another and with the plain and patterned carpets, carpet tiles, rugs and wall coverings in the PERFECT HARMONY range (see separate entries). Top of the range is RE-PRISE, a tufted loop pile carpet in 100% wool for extra heavy wear. It comes in four colourways — flax, (two tones of beige), ice (two tones of pale blue), coral (beige with coral) and jade (beige with pale jade green).
VIRTUOSO in 100% wool, also suitable for extra heavy wear, has a less pronounced fleck. It comes in flax, light ice (very pale blue), mid ice (pale blue), dark coral, light coral, light amethyst (almost beige), light jade and mid jade.
CADENZA in 100% wool for very heavy wear has a smaller tufted loop pile and comes in dark flax (mid-brown), dark coral, mid coral and mid jade.
M: all w12ft (366cm). *P:* on application.

GILT EDGE CARPETS
FOLK LORE hard twist carpet for heavy domestic wear. The subtle textures are achieved through the use of berber-type yarn to which touches of pastel colours are added. The 80% wool/20% nylon pile comes in 12 colourways including rose, green, soft blue and grey as well as the more familiar fawns and beiges. Guaranteed for nine years. *M:* w400cm (157½in). *P:* sq yd £12.99.

GREENWOOD & COOPE LTD
Two outstanding ranges, both award-winners. NOVA COLLECTION in seven berber shades comprises 'Nova' for general domestic use and 'Super Nova' for extra heavy domestic use. Both are made from 50% wool and 50% polypropylene with a choice of jute or foam backing. Luxurious heavy deep pile has a twist in it which makes it even more durable and resi-

lient. The seven tone-on-tone shades are mainly beiges and browns with a pale blue, pale green and pale pink. Prices are reasonable, too. *M:* 12ft (366cm). *P:* 'Nova' sq yd approx £7–£8; 'Super Nova' sq yd approx £12–£13.
SAMARRA/BALAIA range, also in 50% wool/50% polypropylene with jute or foam backing, is for general domestic wear. It comes in 14 colours in a loop pile — again mainly beiges, browns and fawns, with some pinks, pale green and pale blue — all with a slight berber fleck. *M:* w12ft (366cm). *P:* sq yd approx £6–£7.

HABITAT DESIGNS LTD
Tasteful modern carpets in Habitat's characteristic style. DASH made from 50% wool and 50% polypropylene with cut pile finish and jute backing comes in just one colourway — a quiet grey with small flashes of blue, yellow, brown and rust. *M:* w400cm (157½in). *P:* sq m £10.95.
PINSTRIPE is 100% wool in narrow stripes in two flecked colourways — shades of grey and slate. Has foam backing so there's no need for an underlay. *M:* w400cm (157½in). *P:* sq yd £8.05.

HATEMA (UK) LTD
Five superb flecked all-wool berber carpets in the WOOL SPECTRUM range. Top of the range is 'Bergerac' with enormous 1cm (½in) loops and a jute backing. It comes in six colours ranging from luxurious off-white to mid-brown, and is suitable for heavy contract use.
Next comes 'Omaran', also with a jute backing, for heavy domestic and general contract use. Its loops are not as spectacular as 'Bergerac', but it still has a very chunky look. It comes in five colours — all beiges, but with flecks of different colours.
'Savanna' is another loop-pile carpet with jute backing for heavy domestic and general contract use. Comes in three beiges, one with blue flecks one with reddish flecks and one with brown flecks.
'Picardy' has a finer loop and jute backing for heavy domestic and general contract use. It comes in stone, beige, light brown, pastel blue and pastel green.
Finally, 'Macon' has a fine loop pile and foam backing, suitable for heavy domestic and general contract use. It is available in three beige tones.
M: All 400cm (157½in). *P:* on application.

HOMETEX TRADING LTD
A tufted, tight twist 'Berber look' carpet with a slight fleck from the Swiss firm Tisca. BELLA-VISTA in 80% wool/20% nylon comes in 15 colours from white through earth colours to sophisticated cognac, aubergine and blue jeans. It is suitable for heavy domestic use as well as medium contract work and gives excel-

CARPETING

lent thermal results with under-floor heating. High-density foam backing is available. Special colours can be dyed, but only for quantities in excess of 1,400 sq yd (1,170 sq m). *M:* w165in (419cm). *P:* on application.

INTERFACE FLOORING SYSTEMS LTD
Fibre-bonded needlefelt and curly looped pile carpets — finishes more often associated with carpet tiles. NYFLOOR contract range consists of four styles, all made from synthetic fibres. The effect is slightly mottled — not quite plain. For a more pronounced fleck there is a cut pile Timbrelle carpet from the DEBRON range, also available in tile form. This comes in 10 colours, each with a lighter fleck on a dark background. *M:* NYFLOOR w200cm (78¾in); DEBRON w137cm (54in). *P:* on application.

THE OLLERTON HALL DECORATING SERVICE
Two very different ranges of flecked carpeting. Competitively priced MOUNTAIN BERBER carpeting in foam or hessian-backed 50% wool/50% acrylic comes in two loop sizes. Medium-sized loops come in traditional beige to mid-brown shades plus two light greens, and small loops in eight pastels including pink and blue. *M:* w157in (399cm). *P:* sq yd £8.62.
WATERPROOF carpeting is just what it says — a tufted flecked carpet in 100% polypropylene with an impervious backing. It should be bonded to the floor. In eight colourways —grey/blue, two blues, red/brown, maroon/grey/tan, orange/dark brown/grey, two browns, two greens/grey and dark green/grey. *M:* 6ft (183cm). *P:* sq yd £10.32.

STODDARD CARPETS LTD
Two attractive ranges of flecked carpet that won't show the dirt. INTERTUFT II is made from a tufted, tightly looped 100% Enkastat fibre with either unitary backing or, for greater resilience, vulcanized cellular rubber backing. Suitable for extra heavy wear and contract situations, it is available in lovely shades of beiges, browns and greys, plus rust red, mid-blue and mid-green. *M:* w12ft (366cm). *P:* on application.
INTERBOND, in fusion-bonded 100% Antron III with either synthetic or hessian backing, is also suitable for extra heavy wear. It has a dense velours pile and comes in four browns, one greyish-brown, silver grey, dark brownish-green and brownish-orange. It is also available in the form of carpet tiles. *M:* w12ft (366cm). *P:* on application.

WILTON ROYAL CARPET FACTORY LTD
Three ranges of flecked carpets in different qualities. CRANBORNE CHASE for very heavy wear is in tufted 50% wool/50% acrylic in a

PROFESSIONAL from Wilton

medium loop pile finish. The five soft colours are teasel (mainly beige), foxglove (mainly pink), gorse (mainly pale green), thistledown (mainly cream) and briar (mainly mid-brown). *M:* w366cm (12ft). *P:* sq m £11.94.
MERIT has a cut-pile finish and is made from tufted 100% Timbrelle S, suitable for exceptionally heavy wear. Its subtle flecks almost form a zig-zag pattern in some colourways. The pattern and its antistatic treatment mean that it neither holds nor shows the dirt. The seven attractive colourways are sandstone (brown/beige), slate (pale blue/grey), jasper (rust/beige), granite (moss green/mid-brown), brownstone (two tones of brown), onyx (bright green/beige) and lichen (two tones of grey). *M:* w366 (12ft). *P:* sq m £15.75.
PROFESSIONAL with its tight loop pile in tufted 100% Enkastat is suitable for exceptionally heavy wear. It comes in eight neutral stone colours. *M:* w366cm (12ft). *P:* sq m £10.75.

MADE-TO-ORDER CARPETS

ADAM CARPETS LTD
Plain and patterned tufted carpets made to order from standard ranges or to customer's own design and colour choice. Special colours in either plain twist or velours can be supplied (minimum order 239 sq yd/200 sq m) and hydrashift machine designs are offered using up to four colours in each yarn or in combinations. Special colours or designs can often be sampled within 72 hours. Generally the carpets are produced in 80% wool/20% nylon, but new generation nylons such as Antron XL and Timbrelle S can be specified. All can be supplied with a choice of backing — secondary woven jute, unitary latex or high density foam. *P:* on application.

AFIA CARPETS
Limitless possibilities in plains or patterns for carpets, borders and rugs. A designer interprets the look the customer would like to achieve and sees the whole process through, from a first visit to the customer's home to the final installation. The result can range from a machine-made carpet adapted from stock patterns to a handmade rug or carpet of the finest wool, specially dyed. Bordered carpets and rugs are a speciality. *P:* on application.

AVENA CARPETS LTD
Literally hundreds of designs woven in any colourway for any quantity. Authentic reproductions of seventeenth and eighteenth century carpets are available as well as the most modern designs, including many by David Hicks. While specializing in worsted Brussels carpets, Avena make a range of woollen loop-pile and cut-pile qualities. They weave both body-carpet and complementary borders in 80% wool/20% nylon or 100% wool if required. Private design work can be undertaken and all designs are available in both domestic and contract grades. Looming charges on orders under 42m (46 yd). *M:* w27in (69cm). *P:* on application.

BMK LTD
Three classic velours finish tufted carpets. VELVETONE, SUPER VELVETONE and BYRON are all available in standard colours (see *Carpeting, plain*) or, for minimum quantities of 600 sq yd or sq m in customer's specified colour. *M:* w12, 15ft (366, 457cm). *P:* on application.

BRISTOL INTERNATIONAL
An amazing 240 colours in CUSTOM DESIGN WILTON. Choose from 100% wool or 80% wool/20% nylon for harder wear, and have it made up in your own design and a choice of three pile heights. *M:* w100cm (39¼in). *P:* sq m from £38.75 (ex VAT).

CARPETS INTERNATIONAL CONTRACTS
Enormous range of contract carpeting from Britain's largest supplier in this field. There are Axminsters, Wiltons, tufteds and the Queen's Award-winning range of ENDURA non-woven carpeting which has just been relaunched in two qualities with a new backing, enabling the manufacturer to hold the price steady and making installation more economical. Standard ranges are normally available from stock, but these are supplemented by a complete made-to-order service which enables any design to be produced in any construction and colour. A design studio will produce handmade samples of the design prior to the carpet being made up. For carpet that is 27in (68.5cm) wide, the minimum order is 100 linear m (109yd) for this service, for broadloom, 150 linear m (164yd); but smaller quantities can be made up at a surcharge. *P:* on application.

C P CARPETS (KIDDERMINSTER)
Traditional Wilton carpets in made-to-order designs and colourways. A choice of finish is available — velours, twist or loop pile — in any length. C P Carpets will also arrange fitting. *M:* w27, 36in (68.5, 91.5cm). *P:* on application.

PRICES AND INFORMATION WERE CORRECT AT THE TIME OF GOING TO PRESS

DESIGNERS CHOICE

Sculptured carpets, borders and rugs in pure wool made to individual pattern and colour requirements. Designers Choice list 100 different colours but will make up a new colour 'pom' to customer's specification. Similarly, they offer six different standard pile heights and plush or loop pile designs, but will make any carpet construction to order in plush, saxony, loop pile or plush and loop combinations. Variations of texture can be made within a design, and further carved and embossed — but of course the complexity and colour content will dramatically affect the cost of the carpet. *P:* from £30 sq yd. See *Carpeting, rugs* for illustration.

EGETAEPPER (UK) LTD

Special designs undertaken in synthetic fibres for as little as 200sq m (239 sq yd) in heavy duty HIGHLINE 1100 or HIGHLINE 1300. HIGHLINE 1100 is a tufted velours made from 100% Enkastat Plus with synthetic latex backing. HIGHLINE 1300 is in the same fibre with a slight twist which prevents shading and gives less of a sheen. *P:* on application.

GASKELL BROADLOOM CARPETS LTD

PERFECT HARMONY CONTRACT AXMINSTER — an exciting selection in 80% wool/20% nylon. The four colour bands in this range are coral, jade, flax and ice, to co-ordinate perfectly with the stock ranges of patterned, plain and flecked carpets, carpet tiles, rugs and wall coverings (see separate entries). The wide range of designs are mainly polka dots, grid patterns, stylized flowers, diamond lattice and fine diagonal stripes — all cool and elegant. Each design is available in three qualities. *M:* w27in (68.5cm). *P:* on application.

HOMETEX TRADING LTD

Two ranges of contract carpets from the Swiss firm Tisca, illustrating this company's flexibility. WILTON PROGRAMME offers Wilton carpets with latex backing in wide choice of yarns — 80% wool/20% nylon, ICI's nylon, Nylsuisse and Grilon fibres — and in any colour or design. Different pile weights are available in any width from 70 to 460cm (27½ to 181in).

Architects and designers will be particularly interested in Tisca's WOOL COLLECTION — 11 different carpets in many colours and textures, including two hard twists, two velours, berbertypes, Wiltons and Brussels weaves. These are available in a choice of 24 standard colours. *P:* on application.

HUGH MACKAY PLC

Made-to-order carpets from a firm that supplies cruise liners, top hotels, palaces and restaurants. Hugh Mackay will make the carpet of

Three designs from Hugh Mackay

your choice in 80% wool/20% nylon Wilton in any one of 30 standard qualities. Each quality can combine up to five colours from the 252 standard shades available. Delivery is 4–6 weeks and although there is a surcharge on small orders, this is surprisingly low considering the end product. All the Wiltons are cut pile, but Brussels weave carpet can be supplied in 100% wool only, and therefore at a somewhat higher price. *P:* on application.

ARTHUR SANDERSON & SONS LTD (THOMSON SHEPHERD)

PROGRAM and PROGRAM EXTRA tufted carpets specifically designed for the contract market. Using the revolutionary 'Graphics' machine, the PROGRAM range is tufted in an 80% wool/20% nylon yarn, and is available to order in two grades for general or heavy contract use. Designs such as 'Link' and 'Zig-Zag' are small-scale with a definite geometric look, but any graphic design can be made in any colour. Minimum order 600 sq m. *M:* w12ft (366cm). *P:* on application. Thomson Shepherd are specialists in bespoke design and offer a comprehensive range of carpets for contract situations.

Top: 'Link'; below: 'Zig-zag'. Tufted carpets from Sanderson

STEELES CARPETS LTD

Manufacturers of contract carpets and established as the leading manufacturers of high quality jacquard Wilton and 256 set Brussels body carpet. Wilton carpets can be made in an extensive range of designs and colours, from plain through tonals to four-colour designs, and there is a wide range of qualities from cut pile in 80% wool/20% nylon to cut and loops, berbers and Brussels weaves in 100% wool. *P:* on application.

They also manufacture four standard contract quality carpet ranges: STEELETWIST — a tufted twist in 80% wool/20% nylon in traditional solid colours; POINT TO POINT — another tufted twist in 80% wool/20% nylon but in a two-colour tonal design; MONACO — a tufted velvet finish carpet made from 100% Antron XL in naturals, blues and greens with a three-colour fleck; LE MANS — 100% Antron XL again, this time with a heather twist finish in naturals, blues and greens. Steeles also offer a full design and colour service. *M:* STEELETWIST and POINT TO POINT w12ft (366cm); MONACO and LE MANS 200, 400cm (78¾, 157½in). *P:* STEELETWIST sq m approx £16.50; POINT TO POINT sq m approx £17.50; MONACO sq m approx £17.50; LE MANS sq m approx £16.75.

STODDARD CARPETS LTD

Six standard quality Axminsters made to order in two widths to customer's own design. There

CARPETING

is a choice of 144 colours, usually with a limit of eight colours per design. *M:* w3, 12ft (91, 366cm). *P:* on application.

TOMKINSONS CARPETS LTD
Manufacturers of carpets since 1869. Tomkinsons' archive of patterns includes nineteenth-century French designs and designs by Voysey, Marian Pepler and also avant-garde work from members of the Memphis Group in Milan. *P:* on application.

TURBERVILLE SMITH
Patterned Wiltons in various grades and in up to five colours. Turberville Smith will weave any design, in small quantities if required. A complete after-care service is available. *M:* w27, 36in (68.5, 91.5cm). *P:* on application.

V'SOSKE JOYCE (UK) LTD
Wonderfully imaginative collaborations between designers and craftsmen. Almost any size, colour and design, traditional or modern, is possible in these hand-tufted carpets and rugs made in the West of Ireland. A trial sample is invariably produced and, if necessary, V'Soske Joyce's own consultant can oversee the whole project. A special feature of these all-wool carpets is the hand finishing; the pile can be tufted or looped to varying heights, or

Left to right, from top: V'Soske Joyce's 'Sardi', 'Jedda', 'Trellis', 'Ropes', 'Bricks' and 'Rope Border'

sheared, carved and incised to create unique effects. V'Soske Joyce also create wonderful wall hangings. (See also *Rugs*.)
YEATS LINE offers an alternative made-to-order system. Six designs are offered in 100% wool dyed in any colour to order. There is a choice of three qualities: velvet pile finish, textured surface in velvet and twist, and combination of velvet and twist forming a stripe. Geometric designs can be incised in the heaviest quality by the famous V'Soske Joyce hand-carving technique. And the special production system used for these semi-machine made carpets enables shapes up to 10m (11yd) to be produced without seams, thus reducing wastage. Standard patterns are 'Sardi', diagonal stripes; 'Jedda', a geometric design with a Middle Eastern flavour; 'Trellis', a stylized flower within a flower-shaped cartouche; 'Ropes' a diamond-shaped lattice made of twisted ropes; 'Bricks', a brick design and 'Rope Border', a border of stripes and twisted rope around a plain centre. *P:* on application.

WILTON ROYAL CARPET FACTORY LTD
Plain or patterned Wilton in any colour. There is no minimum yardage but the looming charge, which decreases as the quantity increases, isn't totally absorbed until about 40 linear yd (36.4m). *P:* on application.

PATTERNED CARPETS

AFIA CARPETS
Terrific collection of patterned carpets from all over the world. From Italy, the MILAN COLLECTION has 34 designs. Choose from star, striped or grid patterns — just a selection of those available — in exciting colours like white on midnight blue or scarlet. Made from extremely hardwearing Antron III, this range of carpets incorporates its own underlay and is laid with adhesive direct to the floor. *M:* w400cm (157½in). *P:* sq yd £24.
Other popular Afia ranges are the LINDA BARRON designs, the ROBERT WALLACE collection, PRIVATE DESIGNS by world-famous de-

Design from Afia's MILAN COLLECTION

Design from Afia's MILAN COLLECTION

signers Manuel Canovas, Halston and Jack Lenor Larsen, the EVERGREEN range of 10 designs in pure wool and finally the sumptuous LARSEN collection of three-dimensional jacquard Wiltons. More museum pieces than carpets to walk on! Prices are not cheap, but you are getting wonderful designs. *P:* LINDA BARRON and ROBERT WALLACE collections, linear yd £32; PRIVATE DESIGNS sq yd from £45; EVERGREEN sq yd £32; LARSEN collection sq yd £60 – £70.

AXMINSTER CARPETS LTD
Vast collection of patterned carpets from the firm that brought the making of Axminsters back to Axminster in Devon. All the carpets are true Axminsters in luxurious 100% wool, much of which comes from nearby Dartmoor. Axminster carpets have several well-established ranges such as BRIXHAM for very heavy wear (mainly traditional style Axminster designs, plus some floral arabesques and one design that takes its inspiration from ancient Egyptian wall-paintings); TORBAY for general wear, with a number of Persian panel designs and two tonal abstract designs, 'Variations' and 'Cumuli'; EXETER for very heavy wear, again with a number of traditional Persian-inspired designs, plus 'Sea Shells', a tonal design of shells and seaweed that comes in eight soft, modern shades and the SHALDON range which offers a very fine 'Adam Panel' design in red or green — perfect for a formal, eighteenth-century style room setting.
Two new ranges are ROYAL SEATON and ROYAL DARTMOUTH which together form the ROYAL COLLECTION. ROYAL DARTMOUTH draws exclusively on Persian motifs in soft colours like rose, cream, fern, silver green, beige and ruby red, and is suitable for extra heavy wear. ROYAL SEATON, for very heavy wear in similar shades, includes Jacobean and Adam designs (fittingly, since the first maker of Axminster carpet worked with the Adam brothers) as well as some Middle Eastern ones.
Finally, following the modern trend for pastel shades of beige, pink, green and blue, Axminster carpets have launched the MOOR-

LAND COLLECTION consisting of two qualities of Axminster — DARTMOOR for heavy wear and medium contract use and EXMOOR for heavy domestic wear. DARTMOOR offers a large number of subtly patterned, abstract tonal designs such as 'Mirage', 'Raffia' and 'Lakeland'. EXMOOR includes 'Purbeck', another gently shaded abstract design, and 'Match Points', a small, all-over design of dots and stylized flower heads in lovely shades of pink, peach, grey, green and beige.
M: all w91, 366cm (3, 12ft); some TORBAY designs also w274cm (9ft) *P:* on application.

BMK LTD &

Seven Axminsters and one tufted in 80% wool 20% nylon, all suitable for very heavy wear, plus one synthetic tufted for heavy wear. Traditional Axminster ranges of SORRENTO, MATRIX and HEBRIDEAN are augmented by four contemporary ranges, BALMORAL, ROYAL TROON, ROYAL HIGHLAND and STRATHDON.

BALMORAL is a collection of elegant, co-ordinated patterns and colours. The four patterns are 'Wide Diagonal', 'Thin Diagonal', 'Houndstooth' and 'Grid', each with a plain co-ordinate. The six sophisticated colourways are sandstone, mushroom, blue, dark rust, green and grey. Beautiful combinations can be devised, for example using 'Wide Diagonal' with a narrow border of plain carpet, next a wide border of 'Thin Diagonal' and finally a wider border of plain. *M:* w12ft (366cm). *P:* sq yd approx £25.

ROYAL TROON is another range of darker co-ordinated patterns and colours, in greens, rust, beiges and blues. 'Pinpoint', small dots on a contrast background, comes in 10 colourways; 'Pinpoint Motif', like 'Pinpoint' but with a small two-colour diamond incorporated in the design, comes in five colourways; 'Chevron', a diamond-shaped lattice, and 'Arrowhead' also come in five colourways. ROYAL TROON co-ordinates with the plain velvet tufted VELVETONE (see *Carpets, plain*) and with KINROSS (below) — the three ranges forming the CONCORDIA COLLECTION. *M:* w12ft (366cm). *P:* sq yd approx £24.50.

ROYAL HIGHLAND is a range of three designs each in dark berber, light berber and nutmeg. 'Ripple' is a tone-on-tone design with a ripple effect; 'Ogee' is a small-scale tone-on-tone ogee design; 'Square Dot' is random small-scale square dots. *M:* w400cm (157½in). *P:* sq yd approx £22.50.

STRATHDON with its contrasting trellis and flower design completes the Axminster ranges and comes in 12 soft colours — peaches, beiges, pinks, greys, greens and blues. *M:* w400cm (157½in). *P:* sq yd approx £21.50.

KINROSS is a patterned hydrashift tufted carpet in 'Crosshatch' design. It comes in 14 colourways ranging from soft pastels to bold bottle green, cherry red and navy blue. *M:*

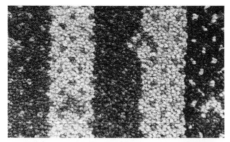

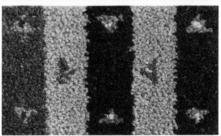

From top to bottom: BMK's 'Pinpoint Motif'△, 'Chevron'△, 'Arrowhead'△ and 'Crosshatch'

w400cm (157½in). *P:* sq yd approx £17.25.
Finally, where cost is an important factor, choose the TURNBERRY range, a patterned tufted carpet in 70% polyproplylene/30% wool, suitable for heavy wear. The small all-over diamond pattern comes in 10 attractive shades — mainly combinations of beiges, greens, blue, brown and coral. *M:* w400cm (157in). *P:* sq yd approx £10.

BRISTOL INTERNATIONAL

Stunning collection of 100% wool carpets made in Switzerland by RAG. RAG WILTON range has been designed by Jack Lenor Larsen and consists of five designs, most with a large repeat. Uses range from domestic to heavy duty according to weight. 'Bandolier' is a hex-

agonal lattice, distributing five related colour shades over a contrasting carved velvet ground. This comes in reds/oranges/browns on chocolate brown or in blue/lilacs/browns on caramel. 'Jamboree' is spectacular both in colour and texture with a thick velvet surface punctuated with inlaid angular shapes in low loop pile. One colourway is fiery in reds, browns and purples, the other cool in beiges, greys and blues. 'Millenium' is an all-over abstract relief pattern of loop and cut pile that comes in fawn/dark brown, caramel/grey, mid-brown/grey toffee/mid-brown and red/grey. 'Arabesque' is an exuberant design of stylized flowers, leaves and tendrils, with a carved velvet surface. It comes in sea-green and blue shades, yellows and browns and autumnal russets and greens. Design is also ideal for bordered rugs. 'Equinox' is a subtle combination of a large diamond-shaped grid superimposed on smaller squares in varying sizes. It comes in the same colourways as 'Arabesque'. *M:* w100cm (39¼in). *P:* sq m from £53.50 (ex VAT).

BRINTONS LTD &

Really comprehensive carpet collection. PALACE DESIGN in 80% wool/20% nylon offers 10 disciplined sprig, spot, grid, trellis and galaxy designs each in 10 subtle colourways — greys, beiges, blues, rusts, peaches, greens and tans. The carpets are of Axminster construction and suitable for very heavy wear. *M:* w400cm (157½in). *P:* on application.

Accompanying these are nine border designs and 31 shades of plain body carpet in two widths (see *Carpeting, plain*), so memorable effects can be achieved with centralized insets as well as borders, or by combining dark-on-light with light-on-dark patterns. Border designs repeat devices such as sprigs, trellises and spots from the patterned carpets as well as introducing new motifs such as classical palmettes or a Greek key design. *M:* borders w13½in (34cm). *P:* body carpet sq yd approx £23; borders linear yd approx £10.

Also in 80% wool/20% nylon is ZENITH collection in three qualities offering either traditionally intricate Axminster designs in strong reds, browns and golds, or more contemporary-looking grid and trellis designs in soft pink as well as dark blues and green or bright red and ochre combinations. *M:* w69cm (27in). *P:* on application.

Other ranges of Axminster are woven in 40% wool combined with 40% viscose rayon and 20% nylon. REGINA 442 for very heavy wear and EDWARDIAN for heavy wear offer traditional designs in popular colours, while MAJESTIC for very heavy wear has just one arabesque design in no less than 15 soft-to-medium tonal colourways — blues, greens, golds, browns, pinks, beiges and a red. *M:* w36, 144in (91.5, 366cm). *P:* REGINA sq yd approx £13; EDWARDIAN sq yd approx £12; MAJESTIC sq yd approx £13.

CARPETING

Top: PALACE DESIGN△; below: ZENITH.
Both by Brintons

For less heavy wear, SIERRA is an Axminster with one swirling design in 10 tonal colourways — beiges, pinks, green, red and blue. M: w100, 400cm (39¼, 157in). P: on application.

BROCKWAY CARPETS LTD

Two attractive modern ranges of patterned Axminsters. ITALIAN COLLECTION and NEW ENGLAND range are both made from 80% wool/ 20% nylon and suitable for heavy domestic or contract use. NEW ENGLAND's four designs are mainly dark shades of reds, browns, greens and blues in small all-over patterns. 'Dixfield' has two-tone diamond shapes on a contrast ground, while 'Milville' has a subtle design of interlinked rounded squares, giving a Spanish tile effect.
ITALIAN COLLECTION in beautiful beiges, greys and pinks would look good in any pastel-toned interior. 'Siena' is a wonderful basket-weave design, with each strand made up of four toning stripes, 'Rimini' has a crazy paving effect of linked squares, while 'Amalfi' is a clever combination of chequers, dots and dashes. The colours in this range are so subtle

that each different colourway almost looks like a totally new design. M: w400cm (157½). P: on application.

CARPETS OF WORTH LTD

Enormous selection of Axminsters in wool or acrylic to suit every taste. SABRINA, in 80% wool/20% nylon for general domestic use and BERKELEY, in the same mixture but for very heavy wear, are largely traditional Axminster designs with brown, cream, fawn, rust and red predominating in Persian-style patterns. M: SABRINA w3, 12ft (91.5, 366 cm); BERKELEY w12, 15ft (366, 457cm).
By contrast, BERKELEY VARIATIONS in the same mixture for very heavy wear has soft, almost monochromatic designs of underwater grasses, ferns and even frothing champagne. Colours are mainly beiges, pale greens, blues and peaches. M: w3, 12ft (91.5, 366cm).
AFGHAN range in 80% wool/20% nylon for very heavy wear is another range of traditionally styled Axminsters, but with rather more subtle colourings. One rather unusual colourway features beiges and browns on a dark blue background. M: w3, 12ft (91.5, 366cm).
Ten more contemporary cross-hatched and dotted designs with mainly small repeats make up the INSCAPE contract range. These are in 80% wool/20% nylon for very heavy wear. Colours are red, blue, turquoise and honey combinations. M: 12ft (366cm).
CORINTH and ACROPOLIS ranges feature mostly bold, traditional Axminster designs in the usual reds, browns and beiges. Both ranges are made from 80% acrylic/20% nylon, with ACROPOLIS for heavy wear and CORINTH for very heavy wear. One surprise in the ACROPOLIS range is a neatly stylized plant design — 'Springboard' — on a choice of red or beige background. M: ACROPOLIS w3, 9, 12ft (91.5, 274.5, 366cm); CORINTH w3, 12, 15ft (91.5, 366, 457.5cm).
P: all on application.

JOHN CROSSLEY & SONS LTD

Three elegant ranges from a company that was established in 1803. PASTORALE is a new range of Axminster carpets in 80% wool/20% nylon, suitable for very heavy domestic use. Its sophisticated textured panel design is rather like a subtly shaded patchwork quilt, juxtaposing a number of finely detailed designs. The nine soft colourways are sage, sand, clover, smoke, aquamarine, apricot, terracotta, sapphire and mink. M: w3, 12ft (91.5, 366cm).
FLORENCE, recommended for extra heavy domestic use, is also 80% wool/20% nylon. There are seven designs: 'Kirman Garden' is a Persian-style pattern in fawn, green, beige and red; 'Quadrille' is a multi-colour floral on a sage back-ground; 'Samarkand' is a Persian-style pattern in the less traditional colours of blue or damson; 'Chartreuse' and 'Tiffany'

both use the same art nouveau-type design but in different colourways — 'Tiffany' is in browns and 'Chartreuse' in greens; 'Persian' is a wonderfully intricate all-over Persian design in a choice of sage, fawn, blue or red; and finally 'Rossini' and 'Da Vinci' are two more Persian-style designs in browns, beiges and reds. M: w3, 9, 12ft (91.5, 274.5, 366cm).
SULTANA is the very top of the market — an Axminster made from 100% wool. This range has been marketed since 1884 and some of the current designs are classics styled in the Crossley studio at the turn of the century, based on fine oriental and great reproduction designs from the Victorian era. A classic range for the connoisseur, it is offered with the facility to be invisibly seamed at the factory. M: w 2ft 3in (68.5cm).
P: all on application.

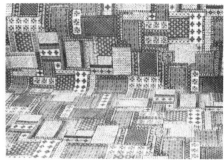

PASTORALE from John Crossley

DESIGNERS GUILD ⚘

Two ways to add pattern to your floors in Designers Guild colours. PLAIN LINE carpet is an Axminster in 80% wool/20% nylon, for general domestic use. The two-tone pattern of very fine diagonal lines on a darker background comes in 10 colours — peaches, greys, beiges, pale greens and lilac. M: w12ft (366cm). P: sq m £28.70.
If you prefer, add a border to a plain carpet or to one with a discreet pattern. BORDER is in 80% wool/20% nylon with Axminster construction. The design, based on the wallpaper border design 'Shady Border', comes in nine colours — two greys, lilac, light and dark rose, beige, eau de nil, brown or bright blue. M: w1ft (30.5cm). P: linear m £8.85.

DLW (BRITAIN) LTD

Two attractive designs in jacquard woven Wilton, made from 100% polyamide. Both are suitable for heavy wear and both have a PVA-coated backing for extra strength. CLASSIC 2000 is a small three-tone check pattern in four colourways: beige/cream/mid-brown, pink/plum/burgundy, pink/grey/navy and beige/moss green/brown. Eight other colourways are available to special order, minimum quantity 100 sq m (119½ sq yd).

CLASSIC 3000 is a large tartan pattern in three colourways: sage green/black/rust/petrol blue, mid-brown/black/rust/dark brown and light grey/black/rust/dark grey. Three other softer colourways are available to special order, minimum quantity 100 sq m (119½ sq yd). *M:* all w200cm (78¾in). *P:* on application.

EGETAEPPER (UK) LTD

Two ranges of heavy duty contract quality synthetic carpets. HIGHLINE 1100 and HIGHLINE 1300 are two grades of tufted velours made from 100% Enkastat Plus with synthetic latex backing that can be stuck direct to suitable floor surfaces. Both ranges are permanently antistatic and are treated with Scotchguard to resist soiling. HIGHLINE 1100 comes in seven designs: 'Broadway', a narrow, quite widely spaced stripe; 'Avenue', a slightly wider stripe incorporating small blocks of contrast colour; 'Bond Street', a fine, lattice-work design; 'Lido', a basket-weave design; 'Manhattan', a three-colour design of small squares on a plain background, each square with a shaded corner; 'Ambassador', narrow, self-coloured stripes; 'Monaco', small octagons with a contrast colour in the centre of each, the octagons arranged in a cross formation on a plain background.
HIGHLINE 1300 has a slight twist to the pile which prevents shading and gives less of a sheen. Designs are 'Savoy', rectangular small spots, each spot divided into two colours; 'Plaza', a pinstripe, rather like 'Broadway'; 'Carlton', a large diamond lattice-work pattern; 'Ritz', small diagonal rows of flowers with a border between each row; and 'Maxim', a diamond lattice made of lines of tiny diamonds. Both ranges come in a wide choice of colours, but the HIGHLINE 1300 range offers some particularly unusual combinations: 'Plaza' is available in black with a light grey stripe; 'Ritz' comes in black and grey and 'Carlton' has a version with an orange lattice on a black background. Some wine colours are also available.
MERAKLON RANGE for heavy domestic and medium contract applications in 100% Meraklon with synthetic latex backing is almost completely stain-resistant. The two patterns with a velours finish tufted by hydrashift machine are 'Diamond', a chequerboard effect in 11 colourways, and 'Tiara', a squiggly design in 10 colours.

'Diamond' in the MERAKLON RANGE by Egetaepper

All Egetaepper carpets are treated with Baco FRF which retards fire and suppresses smoke. *M:* all w400cm (157½). *P:* on application.

MARY FOX LINTON

Two delicious ranges for sophisticated room design. Both use simple geometric patterns in 100% wool. COOMBES patterns, in Brussels weave loop pile or smoother Wilton texture, combine two or three colours. Patterns available are 'St James', 'Hyde', 'Kew', 'Holland', 'Regent' and 'Vauxhall'. LINTON range is cut and loop pile available in any colour or two colours you want. Patterns are 'Cheverney', 'Versailles', 'Leningrad', 'Marmottan', 'Trellis' and 'Chequerboard' (made up from squares of contrasting textures). *M:* w69cm (27¼in). *P:* COOMBES linear m £25–£38.50; LINTON linear m £28–£33.

Top: 'Chequerboard'; below: 'Trellis'. Both from Mary Fox Linton

GASKELL BROADLOOM CARPETS LTD

Complete colour co-ordination of carpeting, rugs and wall coverings. PERFECT HARMONY range is divided into four tonal bands from warm to cool — coral, flax, jade and ice. Within each tone are patterned, plain and flecked carpets, carpet tiles, rugs and wall coverings (see separate entries).
FINALE range offers patterned Axminsters in

PRICES AND INFORMATION WERE CORRECT AT THE TIME OF GOING TO PRESS

80% wool/20% nylon for very heavy wear. 'Diamonte' is a trellis design with the trellis made up of small dots in two tones on a contrast background of either coral, flax, jade or ice; 'Starlight' is a two-tone dot design on a contrast background; 'Gossamer' is a more complex trellis design using more colours and 'Marguerite' combines a stylized flower in one colour with dots in a second colour on a contrast background. *M:* w12ft (366cm).
Co-ordinated borders are available in seven designs. Motifs include flowers, stripes, polka dots, Greek key, trellis and ribbon designs. Extra material has to be allowed for mitering corners, especially with the more complex designs. *M:* w9–13½in (23–34.5cm).
P: all on application.

GILT EDGE CARPETS

Dozens of designs in traditional and modern carpets. For mainly traditional Axminster designs and Axminster construction, choose from the ASTOR range (80% acrylic/20% nylon) for general domestic use, the SHIREHALL range in the same yarn for heavy domestic use, or the ROYALTY range for the luxury of 80% wool/20% nylon, also for heavy domestic use. *M:* w36, 144in (91.5, 366cm). *P:* ASTOR sq yd £10; SHIREHALL sq yd £11; ROYALTY sq yd £16.
For something more modern, choose AUDITION with its swirly arabesque design in Timbrelle pile with a new deep textured cut and loop finish. Available in nine colours: three browns and beiges, three pinks (ranging from light to dark), one grey and two greens. *M:* w36, 144in (91.5, 366cm). *P:* sq m approx £14.75.
All Gilt Edge carpets are guaranteed for either seven or nine years, depending on the type.

AUDITION from Gilt Edge Carpets

CARPETING

GOODACRE CARPETS LTD

Patterned carpets embracing modern and traditional designs. ROYAL KENDAL is a luxurious collection of 100% wool Axminster carpets in traditional patterns. 'Kirman Panel' is a Persian panel design; 'Wreath Scroll' has sinuous, swirling leaves; 'Petit Point' is a large, Jacobean-inspired stylized flower design; 'Fleur' has large bouquets of roses on a soft background; 'Byzantium' has large, star-like motifs with a Middle-Eastern influence and 'Eastern Garden' has diamond-shaped panels filled with stylized flowers. All the designs come in a huge range of colours, some with as many as 50 colours in one colourway. All are suitable for heavy contract use and the heaviest traffic areas in domestic locations. *M:* 91, 366cm (35¾in, 12ft) *P:* sq yd approx £28.

LAKELAND TWIST range in 80% wool/20% nylon for heavy domestic or light contract use comes in either an attractive floral trellis or a Spanish tile design. Predominant colours are greys, beiges, browns and green. *M:* w3, 12ft (91.5, 366cm). *P:* sq yd approx £18.

PASTEL POINTS is a modern design of dots on pale ivory, grey, blue or lilac backgrounds, or on dark green, navy, rust or wine backgrounds. Made from 80% wool/20% nylon, it is suitable for very heavy wear. *M:* 12ft (366cm). *P:* sq yd approx £23.

GREENWOOD & COOPE LTD

BEST SELLER cut and loop pile for general domestic use. This range has just one design — a large, modern, random floral pattern that comes in 10 tone-on-tone colourways. Made from 100% Timbrelle, there is a choice of jute or foam backing. Colours are mainly beiges and browns, with a red, some greens and some blues. *M:* w12ft (366cm). *P:* sq yd £5 – £6.

HOMEWORKS LTD

Wonderful collection of designs by Jack Lenor Larsen. As usual with his designs, the carpets are fantastically beautiful and the prices reflect this. For heavy domestic use in pure new wool, designs include swirls, checks and jacquard patterns. Variety of texture is a feature of the collection — velvet cut pile, different heights of loop pile, or the two combined to sumptuous effect. *M:* w69 – 104cm (27¼ – 41in). *P:* sq m from £100.

JAYMART RUBBER & PLASTICS LTD

Four very heavy duty sculptured pile carpets in polypropylene with latex backing for use in foyers, entrances and anywhere that is subject to a lot of dirt and wear. ZIGAZAGA has a chevron rib in dark brown, terracotta, biscuit, beige, blue/grey, charcoal, dark green, royal blue, dark blue and red. POLYRIB has longitudinal medium ribbing in brown/white, brown/yellow, dark brown, red, cognac, dark cognac,

A Jack Lenor Larsen design at Homeworks

green, blue, anthracite and beige. SUPER-RIB has a bolder, wider rib and comes in beige, cognac, dark cognac, brown/white. MULTI-RIB with its cord effect is available in beige, cognac, dark cognac, green, dark brown, dark brown/white, royal blue, charcoal and oatmeal. *M:* w100, 200cm (39¼, 78⅜in). *P:* sq m approx £14–£22.

Left to right: POLYRIB, ZIGAZAGA, MULTIRIB. All from Jaymart

HUGH MACKAY PLC △

Stunning choice of patterned carpets from a well established manufacturer of Wilton carpeting. All are 80% wool/20% nylon. AXMINSTER SUPER PLUSMIN is a sculptured pile Axminster — a finish that until now was unobtainable in an Axminster construction carpet. The elegant scroll design would suit modern or traditional rooms and comes in a choice of eight soft colours, each with the design in a lighter contrast colour — topaz, aspen (light green), coffee cream, parchment, copper, rose, nutmeg, pearl and champagne. SUPER PLUSMIN is recommended for very heavy wear. *M:* w91, 366cm (35¾, 144in).

Above: AXMINSTER SUPER PLUSMIN from Hugh Mackay

CATHEDRAL AXMINSTER embraces five very different designs, from the swirly abstract design of 'Jasmine' in red, to the baroque flowers and scrolls of 'Chateau' in rosé or green. This range is also suitable for very heavy wear. *M:* w91, 366cm (35¾, 144in).

COUNTERPOINT 7 provides a completely different style with its 12 neat, small-scale designs in bold reds, rusts, greens and blues. The designs include pin dot, grids, trellises, houndstooth checks and stylized flowers. Suitable for very heavy wear. *M:* w69 (27¼in).

Hugh Mackay is particularly famous for contract carpets such as CATHEDRAL CONTRACT COLLECTION and CONTRACT COUNTERPOINT. The first has some boldly coloured Persian-inspired designs, some that are reminiscent of gothic and art nouveau patterns, and plenty of strong abstract geometric designs mostly in dark blue, reds, greens and browns. CONTRACT COUNTERPOINT includes some good geometric designs using trellises, zig-zags, fine diagonal stripes and bold zebra-type stripes. The contract carpets are, of course, all suitable for very heavy wear.

And if none of the patterns in this immense range suits a particular contract installation, Hugh Mackay will make up any design in Wilton (see *Carpeting, made-to-order*). *M:* w69cm (27¼in).
P: all on application.

MERCIA WEAVERS LTD

Beautiful patterned carpets to co-ordinate with plains and rugs. 'Juliet' from ROMEO AND JULIET range has single rows of textured low loops crossing over a fine vertical tonal stripe, giving a subtle, fine grid effect overall. The 24 colours are apricot, two blues, six browns, cream, two greens, three greys, four pinks, two reds, purple, navy and black. These co-ordinate with the plain Wilton 'Romeo' (see *Carpeting, plain*). *M:* w450cm (177in). *P:* sq m approx £43.
Dramatic co-ordination can be achieved with the MARY ROSE COLLECTION of patterned carpets, plain Wiltons, borders and rugs made by Signature (see *Carpeting, plain* and *rugs*).

Below: 'Juliet'; bottom: 'Stokesay'. From Mercia Weavers

Inspired by medieval manuscript illuminations, the 100% wool patterned carpets and borders come in designs that are sinuously fantastic or pleasingly subtle. The 12 patterned carpets, all named after British castles, have either a broad integral border woven to follow round the corner so the design is not spoilt by mitering, or a narrower separate border. 'Sherborne' with a plain centre, has a wide border of fantastic twists and tendrils; 'Grosmont' also has a plain centre with a wide border of more controlled twining ivy tendrils. 'Stokesay' with its small, geometric tile design, is an example of a patterned carpet with separate border — in this case a narrow diamond pattern. Colours are heraldic (green, burgundy, dark blue), pastel (soft greens, blue and grey) or neutral (flax and fleece), to co-ordinate with the plain Wiltons in the range. The body carpet can be woven and sewn to plan at the factory to minimize waste. *M:* body carpet w69cm (27in); borders 13½, 9in (34.5, 23cm). *P:* linear m approx £23.

THE OLLERTON HALL DECORATING SERVICE

Two stain-resistant, 100% polypropylene carpets. One design is a small all-over chequerboard pattern. Foam-backed and guaranteed for seven years, it comes in triple combinations of pale greens, pale blues, browns, beiges as well as more peppery red/black/tan and blue/green/black mixtures;also a new dark blue and grey combination. The second design is a small all-over herringbone pattern in red with black, camel with grey, two tones of blue, blue with grey, dark brown with beige, light brown with peachy beige, two tones of pale green, salmon pink with grey, warm white with blue and rose pink with grey. *M:* w157in (399cm). *P:* sq yd £7.30; cut lengths available at slightly higher price.

E RUSSUM & SONS LTD

SUPER SEASONS rot-resistant indoor/outdoor flooring, especially recommended for use in cars, caravans and boats. Made from 75% polypropylene and 25% polyamide nylon with non-slip latex backing and contrasting coloured grooves for collecting the dust, can be brushed, vacuumed, shampooed — even hosed down! Comes in dark brown, cognac (orangey-brown), gold — these three on a brown background; and in red, charcoal, green, blue (navy) and beige — these on a black background. Available in rolls, cut lengths and standard size mats (see *Carpeting, rugs*). *M:* w100, 200cm (39¼, 78¾in). *P:* sq m £12.93 – £14.23.

ARTHUR SANDERSON & SONS LTD ⌂

Two attractive new tufteds and two luxurious Wiltons from a firm that is usually associated

SUPER SEASONS from E Russum

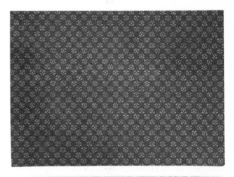

Top: LADY ANNE; below: LADY JANE. Tufted carpets from Sanderson

with wallpapers. LADY ANNE and LADY JANE are made on the new computer-controlled 'Graphics' tufting machine in 80% wool/20% nylon for very heavy wear. LADY JANE is a delicate, small-scale trellis on a choice of 12 background colours: amethyst blue, alabaster, lilac haze, autumn rust, coral, pampas green, willow green, meadow green, hazelnut, corn, honey beige and burnt almond. LADY ANNE is a snowflake design on a background of bracken, honey, cameo, Corinth (brownish-red), mulberry, nectarine, buff, jade, Atlantis (dark

CARPETING

Top: 'Trellis' from MORESQUE 111 range△, below: 'Diamond' from MORESQUE 1 range△. From Sanderson

blue), moonstone (white), vanilla or meadow (leaf green). *M:* w91, 366cm (35¾, 144in). *P:* sq m approx £21.50.

MORESQUE I and MORESQUE III are Wiltons in 100% berber wool with a cut and loop pile giving a subtle textured effect. MORESQUE I has three elegant geometric designs: 'Lattice', 'Chevron' and 'Diamond', each in three natural colours — white, flaxen beige and sandalwood. MORESQUE III comes in four two-tone designs and so is slightly more expensive. 'Strata' is in tones of stone white, beige or sandalwood, while 'Trellis', 'Mosaic' and 'Checkpoint' come in tones of white or sandalwood. *M:* w366cm (144in). *P:* MORESQUE I, sq m £35; MORESQUE III sq m £40.

SOMMER ALLIBERT (UK) LTD
TAPISOM VIKING S600 densely needled fibre-bonded carpet. This unusual 'felty' carpet is made from 100% polyamide and is suitable for heavy contract use. It is permanently anti-static and carries a five-year guarantee. There are four designs: two-tone 'Houndstooth' check on a contrast background, in orangey-brown or moss green; maze-like 'Geometric' in gold or chestnut; 'Tartan' in rust or purple; and 'Diamond' lattice in brown, dark blue or burgundy, all on light brown. *M:* w200cm (78¾in). *P:* on application.

△ *INDICATES AN ILLUSTRATED PRODUCT SELECTED BY THE DESIGN CENTRE*

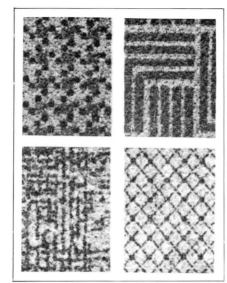

Left to right, from top: 'Houndstooth', 'Geometric', 'Tartan' and 'Diamond'. Fibre-bonded carpets from Sommer Allibert

---

STODDARD CARPETS LTD △
Five Axminsters offering a wide choice of styles. Tasteful, pastel COTTAGE COLLECTION is 80% wool/20% nylon suitable for very heavy wear. The most traditional design is 'Gold Bouquet' which comes in one beige/pink colourway only. 'Sprig' is a small, stylized flower design available in beige, apple green, olive green, mid-brown and a lovely petrol blue called blueberry. 'Tweed' is an unusual mottled design, vaguely patchwork in feel, in three beautiful pink/grey/sea green combinations. This design should not show the dirt. 'Columbine' is a small flower design with swirling stems and leaves in green, pink and blue. The range is available both contract and retail. Plain velvet pile carpets are available in all the

'Sprig' from Stoddard's COTTAGE COLLECTION△

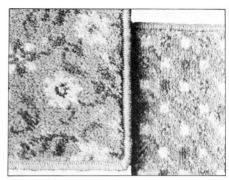

Left to right: Stoddard's 'Columbine' and 'Tweed'

background colours of the COTTAGE COLLECTION making it ideal for room-to-room co-ordination (see *Carpeting, plain*). *M:* w366cm (12ft).

MEDICI COLLECTION in 80% wool/20% nylon consists of two designs. One is based on a Renaissance Italian brocade and comes in nine colourways, each a tonal variation on a single colour. The other, with a soft pattern of small flowers and ferns, is available in three tonal colourways. *M:* w3, 12ft (91, 366cm).

GLENMORE and CAITHNESS in 80% wool/20% nylon and GLENAPPIN in 80% Acrilan/20% nylon are more traditional Axminsters, showing Persian influence both in characteristic richly coloured patterns and in stylized modern interpretations. Scale of design varies from impressive large repeats to more delicate and busy patterns. Colours are also varied with strong, practical colours giving way to softer pastel shades. *M:* GLENMORE w3, 12ft (91, 366cm); CAITHNESS and GLENAPPIN w12ft (366cm).
P: all on application.

TAMESA FABRICS LTD
Understated good looks in sculptured pile and smooth pile carpets. Sculptured pile carpets, achieved by using a mixture of Brussels and Wilton twist weaves, are made from 80% wool and 20% nylon. Neutrals are Tamesa's favoured colours.

'Kew' is a luxurious smooth pile Wilton. The background colour is crossed diagonally every foot or so by a stripe in a contrast twist weave. Colour combinations are grey/beige, grey/charcoal, apricot/pink, bronze/beige and red/white. *M:* w70cm (27½in). *P:* sq m £28.43.

TINTAWN LTD
Scrumptious Aran patterns in all-wool IRISH COLLECTION. Having been the first to introduce us to natural berbers, Tintawn have now moved into neutral carpeting with a relief pattern made by weaving short or long tufts or loops. Nine designs are available in neutral ivory and sand and in pastels such as pistachio

green and misty blue. The densely woven patterns are Aran diamonds, lattice, rosettes, spots and checks. *M:* 108, 144in (274.5, 366cm). *P:* sq yd approx £30. See also *Carpeting, rugs.* For real luxury, combine the carpet with one of six ready-made borders. Useful for either wall-to-wall installation or to surround large rugs, the co-ordinating borders come in sand or ivory only. 'Bellek' is a Tudor rose design, 'Galway' a plait design and 'Renvyle' a corded border. Three other designs are available. *M:* w23, 30cm (9, 11¾in). *P:* linear yd approx £10.

TOMKINSONS CARPETS LTD

Four Axminster construction carpets in a wide variety of designs and qualities. Top of the range is the ROYAL DEVON for heavy domestic use in 80% wool/ 20% nylon, available in pastels and traditional colourways in floral and panel designs. *M:* w36in, 9, 12, 15, 18ft (91.5, 274.5, 366, 457, 548.5cm). *P:* sq yd approx £29.99.

NEW ROYAL GOBELIN comes next for general domestic use in 80% wool/ 20% nylon in similar colours and designs. *P:* sq yd approx £25.99. BORDER COUNTRY, also 80% wool/ 20% nylon, comes in 16 designs, each with matching border, based on the sketches of the French designer Glorget. The colours are lovely soft pastels and warm peachy pinks. *M:* w200, 400cm (78¾, 157½in); border w18in (45.5cm). *P:* sq yd approx £18.99.

For an Axminster in man-made fibres, choose AXMINSTER MATCHMAKER in 100% Meraklon. Designs are wild rose and daisy patterns with matching borders, in pastel colours, warm pinks and browns. *M:* w36in, 9, 12, 15, 18ft (91.5, 274.5, 366, 457, 548.5cm); border w1ft (30.5cm). *P:* sq yd approx £13.99

'Fleur de Lys' from Tomkinson's BORDER COUNTRY range

ULSTER CARPET MILLS LTD

Florals, arabesques, cartouches and paisley designs in four qualities of Axminster 80% wool/ 20% nylon carpeting. Mainly in brown and gold combinations, with red, green and blue predominating occasionally, GLENDUN is the heavyweight, followed by GLENMOY, GLENAVY and GLENANN. (GLENMOY is complemented by two tonal ranges, GLENTONE and GLENMOY FERNGLOW.) *M:* GLENANN w36, 108, 144in (91.5, 274.5 366cm); GLENDUN, GLENMOY, GLENAVY w36, 108, 144, 180in (91.5, 274.5, 366, 457cm). *P:* GLENDUN sq m £27.50; GLENMOY sq m £23.25; GLENAVY sq m £18.75; GLENANN sq m £16.25. Aimed at the contract market are CRAIGAVON and NEW DIMENSION. CRAIGAVON Axminster has some very vivid art nouveau and art deco designs as well as some more traditional Persian and Turkish patterns on bold red backgrounds. NEW DIMENSION concentrates on smaller designs in softer colours. 'Spring Patio' and 'Summer Patio' is a three-dimensional trellis design, each on a different colour background, 'Florina' is a pretty brick red and beige stylized flower within a fine beige trellis on a slate grey background, while 'Vector' is a bold zig-zag design in browns and blues. *M:* w91cm (36in). *P:* on application.

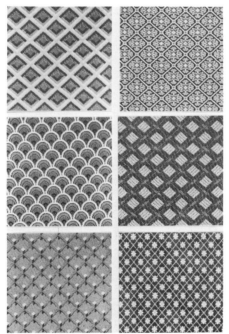

From Ulster's NEW DIMENSION range. Left to right, from top: 'Prism', 'Medici', 'Deco', 'Harlequin', 'Patio', 'Trellis'

WEAVERCRAFT CARPETS LTD

Really extensive range of broadloom carpets, all of Axminster construction. In 85% acrylic/ 15% polyamide mixtures are SECLUSIONS and FOUR SEASONS, both for general domestic use. SECLUSIONS with a four-year guarantee consists of two designs, each in six colourways; one is a hazy leaf pattern, the other gives the effect of patches of bright light breaking through clouds. Colours are tonal variations of red, moss green, mid-brown, pinky-brown, rusty brown and dark brown. *M:* 366cm (12ft). *P:* sq m approx £11.40.

FOUR SEASONS consists of five large-scale, traditional Axminster patterns. 'Carleton' combines a floral with a geometric design and comes in browns with orange, browns with red and.indigo with caramel. 'Caliph' is a bold Persian-inspired design available in brown and orangey colourways. 'Sovereign' is another Persian-inspired stylized flower design in brown with red, brown with blue or brown with russet. 'Medina', which comes in a brown colourway only, is a more geometric Persian design and 'Floral Chintz' has soft bouquets of pink and yellow roses scattered on a beige background. This range carries a three-year guarantee. *M:* w366m (12ft). *P:* sq m approx £11.40.

HYLTON PARK is a similarly-priced range in 85% acrylic/ 15% nylon, also with three-year guarantee and for general domestic use. The six designs are again largely Persian-inspired, traditional Axminster patterns, in browns, reds, russets, sage and beige. *M:* w366m (12ft). *P:* sq m approx £11.40.

STRATHMORE in 85% acrylic/ 15% nylon offers two small-scale designs with a rather more modern look. One is a two-tone stylized flower on contrasting background in light pink/ dark pink on mid-pink, rust/tan on caramel, rust/tan on dark pink, beige/brown on mid-brown, tan/caramel on rust, light brown/dark brown on mid-brown, light green/olive green on sage green and dark grey/light grey on mid-grey. The second design is a two-tone spot on a contrasting background, available in predominantly mid-brown, dark brown, caramel, navy, dark grey, red or rust colourways. This range carries a five-year guarantee and is suitable for heavy domestic use. *M:* w366m (12ft). *P:* sq m approx £13.90.

Top of the range of acrylics comes REGENTS PARK, in 85% acrylic/ 15% nylon, suitable for heavy domestic use and with a five-year guarantee. The eight designs are again traditional Persian-style patterns, but with more subtle and muted colours that lend themselves well to the pastel shades of modern design trends. One of the patterns breaks away from the traditional designs, offering a bolder, modern look in tones of brown and orange. *M:* w366cm (12ft). *P:* sq m approx £14.74.

For the luxury of wool with the resilience of man-made fibre, choose WEAVERTONE in 40% wool/ 40% acrylic/ 20% nylon. This range is recommended for heavy domestic use and carries a five-year guarantee. 'Fantasia' is a sinuous feathery pattern in almond beige, red, burgundy, terracotta, sand, brown and sage

CARPETING

green. 'Burley' is a bold abstract design in tonal shades of red, terracotta, sand, beige, brown and green. Finally 'Nimbus' is a swirly, cloud-like pattern in tonal shades of red, terracotta, sand, brown, almond beige and green. *M:* w366cm (12ft). *P:* sq m approx £14.32.
COUNTRY SHADES, with the same specification as WEAVERTONE, has a seven-year guarantee. Just one design with a faintly dappled pattern, it comes in lovely pastel shades of beiges, browns, pinks, blues and greens. Despite its pale colours, the soft pattern should help conceal dirt. *M:* w366m (12ft). *P:* sq m approx £18.70.

WILTON ROYAL CARPET FACTORY LTD ▲

A small chequered pattern in a carpet that combines velvet and twist pile. CREST and its partner CREST 42, which has denser tufting, are made from 80% wool and 20% nylon and are suitable for exceptionally heavy wear. Eight colourways are available in each quality: cinnamon (light brown/mid-brown/dark brown), cygnet (cream/light brown/mid-brown), gold (dark brown/gold/beige), paprika (dark rust/rust/coral), terracotta (salmon pink/peach/dark peach), chestnut (pink/old rose/bitter chocolate), sage (three tones of green) and cardinal (three tones of red). *M:* 91, 183, 274, 366cm (35¾, 72, 107¾, 144in). *P:* sq m £18.82.

CREST by Wilton

PLAIN CARPETS

ADAM CARPETS LTD
ROYAL SELECTION tufted twist carpet in 80% wool/20% nylon. It comes in nine lovely colours and is suitable for extra heavy wear. *M:* w400cm (157½in). *P:* on application.

AFIA CARPETS
Really wide choice of plain carpets. DERWENT in 100% Timbrelle is perfect for dens, nurseries and bathrooms as it will withstand dirt and stains wonderfully. It comes in 12 colours (including black) in any width up to 13ft (396cm) — so there's no waste, even in small rooms. Its plain velvet pile has a built-in underlay. *M:* max w13ft (396cm). *P:* sq yd £14.25.
BREMWORTH range from New Zealand uses the finest pure New Zealand wool. The four tufted carpets are all suitable for heavy domestic or medium contract use, each in 12 colours. The two plush pile carpets, 'Cellini' and 'Couture', come in mainly pale shades of blue grey, beige and peach. In twist pile is 'Pastel Lights', unusual for its type in that it too comes in soft colours. Finally, there is 'Pastel Weave' in thick loop pile, available mostly in greys, beiges and peaches. *M:* w12ft (366cm). *P:* 'Cellini' and 'Couture' sq yd £37; 'Pastel Lights' sq yd £29; 'Pastel Weave' sq yd £35.

BMK LTD
Tremendous range of velours finish and twist pile carpets from a well known company. VELVETONE is a velours finish tufted carpet made from 80% wool/20% nylon with jute backing, suitable for very heavy wear. SUPER VELVETONE is somewhat heavier, suitable for extra heavy wear. Both come in 16 colours. Slightly heavier than VELVETONE is BYRON, another velours finish tufted carpet in the same mixture with jute backing, for extra heavy wear. It is available in 11 colours. *M:* w144, 180in, (366, 457cm). *P:* VELVETONE sq yd approx £18.50; BYRON sq yd approx £22. These carpets can be made in special colours to order (see *Carpeting, made-to-order*).
BERBER COLLECTION repeats five basic shades — dark berber, light berber, sand dune (ivory), sylvan green (pale browny-green) and nutmeg — in three different carpet qualities, all 80% wool/20% nylon. These are KURLTWIST, a twist pile for very heavy wear, FORTH, a deep pile velour finish carpet suitable for heavy wear but not for stairs, and SOLWAY, a lower velours pile recommended for very heavy wear. KURLTWIST comes in 10 additional colours. *M:* w12, 15ft (366, 457cm). *P:* KURLTWIST sq yd approx £15.75; FORTH sq yd approx £17; SOLWAY sq yd approx £16.25.

BRINTONS LTD ▲
Wide selection of Wilton and Axminster plain carpeting. HEATHER BERBER is an award-winning woven Wilton in 80% wool/20% nylon. Its hard-wearing twist pile suitable for extra heavy wear, comes in 20 lovely shades, ranging from pale pastels to darker browns and greens. *M:* w366cm (144in). *P:* sq yd approx £14.
PALACE VELVET Axminster in 80% wool/20% nylon for very heavy wear comes in 31 amazing

shades that co-ordinate with the patterned PALACE DESIGN range (see *Carpeting, patterned*). There's a velours here for every colour scheme. *M:* w100, 400cm (39¼, 157in). *P:* sq yd approx £19.

BRISTOL INTERNATIONAL
The height of luxury, two beautiful ranges of pure wool carpets from the Swiss company RAG. FIESTA comes in an amazing choice of seven pile heights, each with latex backing. It has a bouclé-look and, as well as being available in any one of 240 colours, it can be obtained in mixtures of up to four colours (see *Carpeting, flecked*). *M:* w100–460cm (39¼–181in). *P:* sq m from £35.50 (ex VAT).
RODEO with its cut pile finish is available in six different pile heights and in 240 colours. *M:* w100–1000cm (39¼–392½in). *P:* sq m from £41.75 (ex VAT).

BROCKWAY CARPETS LTD
Three ranges of tufted twist pile carpets in a good choice of colours. CRAFTSMAN TWIST and MASTER CRAFTSMAN (a slightly heavier version) are both made from 80% wool/20% nylon and are suitable for heavy domestic wear. Both come in 20 colours with a wide range of beiges and pale greens.
BERBER TWIST is also in an 80% wool/20% nylon mixture for heavy domestic use. The 15 shades are gently muted, again with some good beiges and greens.
M: all w400cm (157½in). *P:* on application.

DESIGNERS GUILD ▲
ULTRA PLAIN carpet in 100% Antron Plus with luxurious-looking plush pile. This tufted carpet comes in 16 colours and is suitable for all domestic locations except stairs. *M:* w400cm (157.5in). *P:* sq m £22.20.

DLW (BRITAIN) LTD
Sixteen autumnal colours in durable cord carpeting made from needle-punched 100% polypropylene with high density foam backing. 'RO828' is recommended for general domestic or light contract use. *M:* w200cm (78¾in). *P:* on application.

EGETAEPPER (UK) LTD
Two ranges of velours finish synthetic carpets. HIGHLINE 1100 is made from 100% Enkastat Plus with a synthetic latex backing and is suitable for heavy duty contract use. It comes in 11 colours.
MERAKLON VELOUR has a firm, dense, plush pile that is softer to the touch and to the tread. Suitable for heavy domestic and medium contract applications, it has been treated with a fire-retardant, making it fire-resistant up to

Indian dhurries from Mary Fox Linton

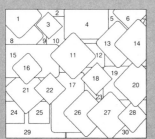

Selection of carpets: Adam Carpets' ROYAL SELECTION (1), Gaskell Broadloom's INTERMEZZO (2), Wilton's PROFESSIONAL (3), Jaymart's ZIGAZAGA (4), Gaskell Broadloom's CADENZA (5), Adam Carpets' ROYAL SELECTION (6), Gaskell Broadloom's INTERMEZZO (7), Adam Carpets' 'Berber Superb' (8), Gaskell Broadloom's ENSEMBLE (9), Stoddard Carpets' 'Tweed' in opal (10) and jade (11), Jaymart's BRUSH OFF 'Blue Ripple' (12), Stoddard Carpets' 'Sprig' in blueberry (13) and almond (14), Gaskell Broadloom's FINALE (15), Georgian Carpets' CLIFTON HEATHER (16), Gaskell Broadloom's 'Marguerite' (17), Georgian Carpets' GEORGIAN SUEDE (18), Gaskell Broadloom's ENSEMBLE (19), Stoddard Carpets' 'Sprig' in hazel (20) and 'Tweed' in coral (21), Georgian Carpets' CLIFTON BERBER (22), Gaskell Broadloom's VIRTUOSO (23), Georgian Carpets' GINA (24 and 25), Stoddard Carpets' 'Columbine' in pink (26) and blue (27), Georgian Carpets' CLIFTON MARBLE (28), Gaskell Broadloom's REPRISE (29) and VIRTUOSO (30)

British Standard 4790. It is thus the only carpet approved by the Department of Trade for use aboard UK-registered vessels. Available in a choice of 18 colours. *M:* all 400cm (157½in). *P:* on application.

FORBO TAPIJT BV

From a Dutch company, four new luxury-feel plain carpets for heavy domestic use. MIMOSA is a soft velours in 100% polyamide with foam backing and comes in 14 colours. VERONA with its slight sheen is tufted 100% polyamide with antistatic finish. The surface is somewhere between twist pile and velours and it comes in eight soft colours. PALESSE has a very dense fine gauge 100% polyester velours finish and is in 13 colours. PROMENADE is a rougher-looking hard twist tufted carpet in 80% wool/20% nylon, in six subtle shades. *M:* all w400cm (157½in). *P:* MIMOSA sq m approx £11; VERONA sq m approx £15; PALESSE sq m approx £21; PROMENADE sq m approx £22.

GASKELL BROADLOOM CARPETS LTD

Two ranges of plain carpet in 80% wool/20% nylon for very heavy wear. ENSEMBLE tufted hard twist and INTERMEZZO tufted velours are the plain carpets that co-ordinate with the flecked and patterned carpets, carpet tiles, rugs and wall coverings in the PERFECT HARMONY collection (see separate entries). Both come in the same eight colours, variations within the four tonal bands in the PERFECT HARMONY collection — flax, coral, ice and jade. *M:* w12ft (366cm). *P:* on application.

GEORGIAN CARPETS LTD

Probably the largest range of plain tufted carpets from a single manufacturer. Top of the range is the luxurious shag pile G MAJOR in 80% wool/20% nylon for very heavy wear. Next comes MANOR with an all wool pile for extra heavy wear, GEORGIAN SUEDE In 80% wool/ 20% nylon for extra heavy wear, GEORGIAN VELVET in 80% wool/20% nylon for very heavy wear, FARMER GEORGE in 80% wool/20% nylon for very heavy wear, TWEEDLOOK in 100% wool for very heavy wear, GINA in 80% wool/20% nylon for heavy wear, CLIFTON BERBER and CLIFTON HEATHER, both in 80% wool/20% nylon for heavy wear, CLIFTON VELVET in 50% wool/50% polypropylene for heavy wear, CLIFTON TWIST in 80% wool/20% nylon for heavy wear, SWEET CARESS in 100% acrylic for heavy wear and, finally, CLIFTON MARBLE in 50% wool/50% polypropylene for medium domestic use. The colour choice is enormous, embracing about 200 different shades, and if you can't find something to suit you there, consider a rug instead (see *Rugs*). *M:* CLIFTON w12ft (366cm); all others w3, 9, 12ft (91.5, 274.5, 366cm). *P:* (approx) G MAJOR sq yd £36; MANOR sq yd £31; GEORGIAN SUEDE sq yd

£26; GEORGIAN VELVET sq yd £24; FARMER GEORGE sq yd £23; TWEEDLOOK sq yd £20; GINA sq yd £19; CLIFTON BERBER, CLIFTON HEATHER sq yd £12; CLIFTON VELVET sq yd £11; CLIFTON TWIST sq yd £10.50; SWEET CARESS sq yd £10; CLIFTON MARBLE sq yd £9.

GILT EDGE CARPETS

WESSEX and WESSEX JUNIOR, plain Wiltons in 80% wool/20% nylon for heavy domestic and general domestic use respectively. Both well established ranges come in 16 colours. *M:* w3, 12, 15ft (91.5, 366, 457.5cm). *P:* on application.

GREENWOOD & COOPE LTD

Two competitively priced ranges. The very popular STARDUST range is plush pile 100% polypropylene with foam backing, suitable for light domestic use. Its 12 pastel shades are good 'bedroom' colours. *M:* w9–12ft (274.5–366cm).*P:* sq yd approx £4–£5.
CHALLENGER 4 in 100% Meraklon is suitable for general domestic use and comes with jute or foam backing. Its 14 colours tend towards the pastel shades. *M:* w12ft (366cm). *P:* sq yd approx £5–£6.

HABITAT DESIGNS LTD

COTSWOLD tufted broadloom carpet with loop pile in 75% acrylic/25% viscose, in two lovely Cotswold stone shades. Suitable for general domestic use. *P:* sq yd £6.22.

HATEMA UK LTD

Three exciting 100% cotton carpets and two wool carpets. In cotton, ARIZONA, for general domestic use, has a fine twist loop with foam backing and comes in six colours. TOPEKA, also for general domestic use, has a similar fine twist loop pile and jute backing; available in 11 colours including black. PLANTAGE has a slightly larger loop pile and jute backing; also in 11 colours. FRISON is a lovely twist pile in 80% wool/20% nylon for heavy domestic and general contract use, available in 12 smart colours including navy blue. PALETTE is a very unusual 100% wool loop pile for heavy domestic or general contract use. It comes in eight attractive soft shades. *M:* all w400cm (157½in). *P:* on application.

INTERFACE FLOORING SYSTEMS LTD

Two plain carpets in the DEBRON range, also available as carpet tiles (see separate entry). 'Supertwist' is fusion bonded 80% wool/20% nylon, in 10 colours. 'Velvet Series' is 100% Timbrelle S with a velvet finish, also in 10 colours. Both are suitable for extra heavy wear. *M:* w137cm (54in). *P:* on application.

SEE CHART FOR PLAIN CARPET COLOURS

MERCIA WEAVERS LTD

Two plain Wiltons to co-ordinate with two patterned ranges. 'Romeo' in 100% wool from the ROMEO AND JULIET range has 30 velvet plains to co-ordinate with the patterned 'Juliet'. *M:* w450cm (177in). *P:* sq m approx £36.
Plain 100% wool carpets in the MARY ROSE COLLECTION come in the same colour categories as the collection's patterned carpets — heraldic (green, burgundy, dark blue), pastel (soft greens, blue and grey) and neutral (flax and fleece). *M:* w69cm (27in). *P:* linear m approx £23. See also *Carpeting, patterned.*

THE OLLERTON HALL DECORATING SERVICE

Hundred-per-cent polypropylene pile carpet with velvet finish 'that looks just like Wilton'. The carpet comes in either standard or solid quality with double the pile height and is suitable for extra heavy wear. The Ollerton Hall Decorating Service claim it is almost impossible to stain, which makes it particularly useful in schools, hospitals, nursing homes or just in houses full of children! *M:* w157in (399cm). *P:* standard sq yd £5.71; solid sq yd £7.93; cut lengths available at slightly higher price.

Ollerton Hall's 'almost impossible to stain' carpet

ARTHUR SANDERSON & SONS LTD

Three qualities in a huge range of colours to co-ordinate with Sanderson's paint and wallpaper. HOSTESS and SUPER HOSTESS are tufted twist carpets in 80% wool/20% Timbrelle B. HOSTESS is recommended for heavy wear, while SUPER HOSTESS with a heavier pile

CARPETING

DEEP VELVET from Sanderson s

weight is suitable for very heavy wear. Both come in 21 colours. SUPER HOSTESS is also available in eight berber colours — beige, Tibetan tan (peachy tan), Arabian sand, Tunisian brown (mid-brown), desert brown (grey-brown) and desert rose (browny-pink). *M:* w91, 366, 457cm (35¾, 144, 179½in). *P:* HOSTESS sq yd £17.50; SUPER HOSTESS sq yd approx £21.

If you prefer a velvet pile, DEEP VELVET is 100% tufted wool for very heavy wear; available in 18 colours. *M:* w91, 366, 457cm (35¾, 144, 179½in). *P:* sq yd approx £25.

SEKERS FABRICS LTD

Two ranges of contract carpeting, each in 14 fashionable plain colours designed to co-ordinate with Sekers' fabrics (see separate entry). PALETTE with twist pile and CONTEXT with velvet pile are both in 80% wool/20% nylon and suitable for extra heavy wear. *M:* w100cm (39¼in), other widths to order. *P:* PALETTE sq m £23; CONTEXT sq m £44.

SOMMER ALLIBERT (UK) LTD

Two ranges of synthetic carpeting. STAR SCALA is budget-priced cord carpet in 100% polypropylene with foam backing, available in six colours. *M:* all w200, 400cm (78¾, 157½in). TITAN SUPER 510 is fibre-bonded 70% polypropylene/30% polyamide, recommended for heavy contract use and bearing an eight-year guarantee. It has a felty appearance and is available in nine colours. *M:* both w200cm (78½in). *P:* on application.

PRICES AND INFORMATION WERE CORRECT AT THE TIME OF GOING TO PRESS

PLAIN CARPET COLOURS	HEATHER	WHITE	WINE	DARK PINK	PEACH	LILAC	GREY	BLACK	DARK BROWN	BROWN	TAN	BEIGE	IVORY	PALE ORANGE	RUST	RED	LIGHT PINK	PURPLE	PALE BLUE	BRIGHT BLUE	DARK BLUE	TURQUOISE	DARK GREEN	BRIGHT GREEN	PALE GREEN	OLIVE	GOLD	YELLOW
ADAM CARPETS																												
Royal Selection			•				•			•							2		2						•	•		
AFIA CARPETS																												
Derwent	•		2							•				•			•				•	3			•		•	
BMK																												
Byron			2	•						•							3	•							2	•		
Kurltwist		•	2	•											•		4	•	3		•				•			
Velvetone/Super Velvetone		•	•	•		•	•	•			•	•					2		•		•				2	•	•	
BRINTONS																												
Heather Berber			•		2					•	2				2		2	•	4				3	•		•		
Palace Velvet		2	3	•		•	•	2		•					4		3	•	•	•		2			5	2	•	
BROCKWAY CARPETS																												
Berber Twist			2		1					•	•				2		4		2						•	•		
Craftsmen Twist / Master Craftsmen	•		3		2					•			2		•		5		2						•	•		
DESIGNERS GUILD																												
Ultra Plain	•		2	•			•	2		•					•		3			•			•		•			
DLW																												
R0828			•	•									•	•	•		3	2	4		•		•					
EGETAEPPER																												
Highline 1100					•		•						•				3		3			2						
Meraklon Velour			•	3		•	•			•							3	•	2	•	•	•			•			
FORBO TAPIJT																												
Mimosa	•			•			•		•	•					•		2	•	•	•	•	•						
Palesse			•	•			•	•		•					•		2	•	•			2	•					
Promenade					•					•					•		•	•	•			•						
Verona				•			•			•					•		2					•						
GASKELL BROADLOOM																												
Ensemble			•	•				•		•					•										•	•		
Intermezzo			•	•				•		•					•										•	•		
GEORGIAN CARPETS																												
Clifton Berber			•							•					•		2		2									
Clifton Heather			•							•							3			•								
Clifton Marble			2							•			•		•	•	•	•							•	•		
Clifton Twist			•	•													2		3	•							•	
Clifton Velvet			•	2													2	•	•					•		•		
G Major			•						2			2					3						2					
Georgian Suede			•	2			•										4	2	4				•	•	•	2	•	
Georgian Velvet			2	•			•										4	3	2				•		•	2	•	
Gina/Farmer George			•	2	•		•	•									2	2	•		•							
Manor									•								•	•	4			•	•		2			
Sweet Caress			•							•							•	•	•				•	•				
Tweedlook			•	2						•				•		•	3			•		2			•		2	
GILT EDGE CARPETS																												
Wessex/Wessex Junior	•		5				2											6					•	•				
GREENWOOD & COOPE																												
Challenger			2	•	•	•	•							•	5					•			•					
Stardust 4			2				•	2						•	4					•		•						
HABITAT																												
Cotswold															2													

PLAIN CARPET COLOURS

	HEATHER	WHITE	WINE	DARK PINK	PEACH	LILAC	GREY	BLACK	DARK BROWN	BROWN	TAN	BEIGE	IVORY	PALE ORANGE	RUST	RED	LIGHT PINK	PURPLE	PALE BLUE	BRIGHT BLUE	DARK BLUE	TURQUOISE	DARK GREEN	BRIGHT GREEN	PALE GREEN	OLIVE	GOLD	YELLOW
HATEMA																												
Anzona	●				●		●									●	●	●										
Frison		●		●	●		●	●	●						2	●	●	●	●									
Palette			●				●	●								●	●		2				●					
Plantage				2			●	●	●					●		●	●		2				●					
Topeka				●	●		●									●	3		2			●						
INTERFACE																												
Supertwist			●											●			4		●		2							
Velvet Series							●						●				3		●				●	●	●			●
MERCIA WEAVERS																												
Romeo	●	●		4			●	●	●	●	2	2				●		6			●		3	●	2	2		
OLLERTON HALL			3		●			●		2			●			2	3				2	2			●	●		
SANDERSON'S																												
Deep Velvet			●	2	●		●	●					●			2	●	●	2						3	●		
Hostess/Super Hostess		●		3	●		●	●					●	●		2	4	2	2							●	●	
SOMMER ALLIBERT																												
Titan Super 510				●	●								●	●				●			2	●						
STODDARD CARPETS																												
Elgin Velvet			●	●			●	●					●	●		●	●	2	●						●	2		
Glendonald Wilton	●	●	●	2	●		2									●	2	●	●					●				
Oban Velvet			●	●			●	●			2	●	●				2						●	●	●			
President Velvet	●	●	2		●			●					●			●	3	●	●						●			
Super Sax Wilton			●	●			●	●						●		●	2		●				●	2				
TINTAWN																												
All Wool Velvet			2				●	●		●			●	●		●	5		●				●		●	2		
New Shearling			2							●							2					●						
New Woolcomber twist																	2		2			●						
velvet			●							●		2				2	3	●	●									
Polywool cut pile			●														2		●									
loop pile																	2		●									
Sheer Velour			●										●			●	2		●				●					
Town House			●	●	●		●						●			2	2	3					●		●			
TOMKINSONS																												
Mardi Gras			●	●	●		●	●	●				●	●			3				3	3	2		●	2		
Royal Court	●			●	●		●	●					●	2		●	2	●	2				3		●	●		
Royal Household			3						2		2					2	●						3			●		
Royal Residence		●●	2		●					3		●	●			2	4	●	●				●	3	●	2		
WILTON ROYAL																												
Melody		●		●	●					●								●							●			
Charter/Super Charter		●	●	5			●					2	●	●		●	●	3	●						●	●	●	
Super Charter Berber																						●						

STODDARD CARPETS LTD

Three tufteds and two Wiltons, offering a huge choice of classic plain carpeting. ELGIN VELVET is 80% wool/20% nylon with a velours finish, for extra heavy wear; available in 14 colours. OBAN VELVET for very heavy wear 80% wool/20% nylon has a slightly thinner pile; available in 14 colours. PRESIDENT VELVET for very heavy wear is 100% wool; it too comes in 14 colours.

SUPER SAX WILTON is 80% wool/20% nylon for extra heavy wear; available in 14 colours. GLENDONALD WILTON has the most luxurious feel with a slightly deeper pile. It comes in 100% wool in 15 colours and is suitable for very heavy wear.
M: all w12, 15ft (366, 457cm). P: on application.

TINTAWN LTD

Six beautiful plain carpets with the emphasis on modern, soft pastel shades. POLYWOOL is an inexpensive but attractive range available in either cut or loop pile in 80% acrylic/20% polyester. Suitable for heavy domestic use, each type comes in four colours. M: 3, 9, 12ft (91.5, 274.5, 366cm). P: sq yd approx £8.75.

SHEER VELOUR offers a less expensive alternative to the ALL WOOL VELVET range (below), with velours pile in 50% wool/50% polypropylene suitable for all domestic locations excluding kitchens. Nine pastel colours are available. M: w100, 400cm (39¼, 157½in). P: sq yd approx £12.95.

NEW WOOLCOMBER for heavy domestic use comes in both twist and velvet pile in colours that match those of the luxury NEW SHEARLING (below) enabling you to continue a colour throughout the house, using different quality carpets for different locations. 'Twist' comes in seven colours, 'Velvet' in eight. M: w3, 9, 12ft (91.5, 274.5 366cm). P: sq yd approx £13.50.

TOWN HOUSE in 13 colours is an 80% wool/20% nylon twist pile suitable for heavy domestic and general contract use. M: w3, 9, 12ft (91.5, 274.5 366cm). P: sq yd approx £14.50.

ALL WOOL VELVET offers a comprehensive range of 16 colours in luxury 100% wool. Its cut velvet pile is recommended for heavy domestic and general contract use. M: w3, 9, 12ft (91.5, 274.5, 366cm). P: sq yd approx £18.

Top of the range is NEW SHEARLING luxury shag carpet in 80% wool/20% nylon. Available in eight soft muted shades, it is suitable for all domestic locations except stairs. M: w3, 9, 12ft (91.5, 274.5,366cm). P: sq yd approx £19.

TOMKINSON CARPETS LTD

Four plain ranges — just a selection from an old-established company. ROYAL RESIDENCE is a tufted plush pile carpet in 100% Antron Plus with jute backing. The huge range of colours consists mainly of pastel blues and greens, warm pinks and browns, but there is also a black. ROYAL COURT is a velvet finish tufted carpet also made from 100% Antron Plus. Colours include some unusual primaries. ROYAL HOUSEHOLD is a tufted plain velvet in 80% wool/20% nylon, available in soft pastels. M: 200, 400cm (78¾, 157½in). P: ROYAL RESIDENCE sq yd £16.50; ROYAL COURT sq yd £13.99; ROYAL HOUSEHOLD sq yd £16.99. MARDI GRAS in 100% Meraklon with foam backing is a budget-priced velvet finish carpet in a wide selection of pastels, naturals and traditional colours. M: w6, 12ft (183, 366cm), 400cm (157½in). P: sq yd approx £5.50.

WILTON ROYAL CARPET FACTORY LTD

Varied range from this famous factory, offering a choice of synthetic yarn or wool/nylon mixtures. MELODY is 100% polypropylene

CARPETING

plush pile suitable for heavy wear, available in 12 pastel shades. *M:* 91, 274, 366cm (3, 9, 12ft). *P:* sq m £9.45.

CHARTER COLLECTION offers three qualities of 80% wool/20% nylon tufted twist carpets: 'Charter' for heavy wear and 'Super Charter' for exceptionally heavy wear, each in 24 colours ranging from modern pastel to traditional strong shades; and 'Super Charter Berber' for very heavy wear, in eight neutral shades only. *M:* w91, 183, 274, 366, 457cm (3, 6, 9, 12, 15ft). *P:* 'Charter' sq m £15.19; 'Super Charter', 'Super Charter Berber' sq m £18.27.

RUGS

AXMINSTER CARPETS LTD

Densely patterned rugs and squares in 100% wool Axminsters. 'Soraya' and 'Chirvan' are traditional Persian-style, bordered designs on a beige background available only as squares. They are made in BRIXHAM quality for very heavy wear. Also in the BRIXHAM range, but available in smaller rug sizes as well, are 'Persian Fountains' in mink or green, 'Egyptian' with ancient Egyptian motifs on a fawn background and 'Turkey' with a Turkey red background. TORBAY range for general wear comes as large squares or smaller rugs and consists of two designs: 'Kirman', an all-over Persian design with a border, and 'Panel Persian 0397' in red, pastel pink, beech brown or sage brush green. *M:* squares 183 × 274–366 × 274cm (72 × 107¾–144 × 107¾in); rugs 137 × 69cm (54 × 27¼in), 183 × 91cm (72 × 35¾in). *P:* (for 183 × 274cm squares) BRIXHAM £125; TORBAY £110.

Below: 'Soraya'; bottom: 'Chirvan'. By Axminster

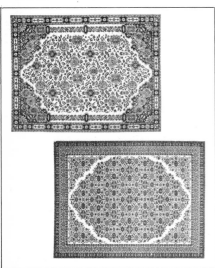

Axminster's 'Kirman'

CASA FINA

The well-known CASA FINA rug — still as colourful, decorative and generously fringed as the day it was introduced! Rugs are stocked in many sizes and in innumerable variations of 45 colours; but for a 10% surcharge Casa Fina will make up rugs to match customer's individual colour swatches. Delivery of custom rugs takes around 10 weeks. *M:* 48 × 37–161 × 110in (122 × 94–409 ×279cm). *P:* £48–£454.

DESIGNERS CHOICE

Beautiful 100% wool rugs made in individual patterns and colour requirements. See *Carpeting, made-to-order.*

Wool rug from Designers Choice

CASA FINA'S rug

DESIGNERS GUILD

Good selection of rag rugs and woven wool or linen rugs. WOVEN RAG RUGS are made from the ends of the rolls of Designers Guild fabrics and so tone beautifully with the fabrics and wallpapers. Made from 100% cotton in the UK, they may be washed by machine. Colours are peaches, pinks, greens, blues, beiges and greys. The rugs can be made to order in specific fabrics of your choice. *M:* 36 × 60in (90 × 150cm), 45 × 72in (112 × 180cm), 24 × 36in (61 × 90cm), 24 × 72in (61 × 180cm). *P:* £87, £126, £37, £76; made-to-order £71–£239.

Similar, but with a denser weave, are SOLID RAG RUGS, made in India. Each comes in one colour only — pink, beige, grey, white, green, light blue or apricot. *M:* 72 × 108in (180 × 270cm), 68 × 72in (120 × 180cm), 36 × 60in (90 × 150cm). *P:* £98, £44, £28.

LINEN FLOOR RUGS are available in 'Rib Weave' or 'Cross Weave' designs. Colours are

PRICES AND INFORMATION WERE CORRECT AT THE TIME OF GOING TO PRESS

pink with apricot, blue, beige or multi. *M:* 72 × 48in (180 × 120cm), 36 × 60in (90 × 150cm), *P:* £253, £184.

HANDWOVEN WOOLLEN RUGS come in geometric designs in dark colours like dark navy or grey with blue, or in pastel shades of grey, pink or lemon, and in a striped design. *M:* 36 × 60in (90 × 150cm). *P:* £69–£175.

EQUINOX INTERIORS LTD

Rugs like abstract paintings, by Helen Yardley. She will make, by hand, any size, any design in 80% wool/20% nylon, and has a flair for bold, roughly geometric shapes on contrasting grounds. *P:* sq m approx £200.

Two of Helen Yardley's rugs from Equinox

MARY FOX LINTON LTD

Silk dhurries fit for a modern maharaja, by Shyam Ahuja. 'Mosaic', 'Casablanca' and 'Log Cabin' are just some of the designs in wondrous pastel shades. These are also available in fine-weave cotton. *M:* silk, six sizes, 48 × 72–108 × 144in (122 × 183–274 × 366cm); cotton, six sizes up to 78 × 117in (198 × 297cm). *P:* silk. £307–£1,380; cotton £175–£432.

Other dhurries, in wool and in kelim style, are available, and any dhurry over 80 sq ft (7.4 sq m) can be woven in India to special order (for a 15% surcharge). *M:* wool, eight sizes 36 × 60–120 × 168in (81 × 152–304 × 427cm); kelim, six sizes 47 × 72–108 × 144in (122 × 183–274 × 366cm). *P:* wool £109.25–£895.16; kelim £120–£538.

Mary Fox Linton also carries a diverse range of unusual Indian rugs ranging from reasonably priced 100% cotton rag-rugs in plain colours or

Mary Fox Linton's dhurries

variegated tones to 100% wool chain-stitch and needlepoint rugs, luxury items in lovely muted colours. There are also glorious 100% wool hand-tufted and hand-knotted carpets (these in two qualities). *M:* rag-rugs and chain-stitch rugs, six sizes 36 × 60–108 × 144in (81 × 152 – 274 × 366cm); needlepoint rugs, four sizes 48 × 60 – 108 × 144in (122 × 152.5 – 274 × 366cm); hand-tufted and hand-knotted carpets, four sizes 48 × 72 – 108 × 144in (122 × 183 – 274 × 366cm). *P:* rag-rugs £46–£299; chain-stitch £149.50–£978; needlepoint £290–£1,294; hand-tufted £215–£960; hand-knotted £259–£1,800.

GASKELL BROADLOOM CARPETS LTD

Easy-to-live-with rugs. Elegant NEW CORIN-THIAN collection in 80% wool pile has five basic designs in three or four gentle colourways each: beige, grey, pale blue, pale apricot or clover. 'New Kazak' brings a traditional Middle Eastern design into the 1980s; 'Graph' is starkly simple; 'Tulip' studs tiny flowers onto a trellis; 'Stria' frames diagonal pencil lines with undulating streamers; and 'Magnolia' sculptures out a giant bloom. Special sizes can be made to order. *M:* 60 × 36in (152 × 91cm), 78 × 54in (198 × 137cm), 95 × 66in (241 × 167cm). *P:* on application.

Even more restrained in colour are NEW ROS-SENDALE rugs, a trio of bordered coffee-and-cream rugs in wool/polypropylene pile, one swirly, one linear and one in bargello zigzags. *M:* 60 × 36in (152 × 91cm), 78 × 54in (198 × 137cm). *P:* on application.

By contrast, the robust FINLANDIA collection in pure new wool semi-shag pile includes 'Bagatelle' in ivory, turquoise, red, orange, rust and brown versions, 'Chequers' in green,

Above: 'Graph'; below: 'Tulip'. Both from Gaskell

old rose and brown colourways, and 'Ripple' in brown, tan and cream mixtures. 'Bagatelle' also has a circular and an oval version in all colours except brown. *M:* three sizes 48/54 × 27 – 78 × 54in (122/137 × 69 – 198 × 137cm); 'Bagatelle' circular dia 54in (137cm), oval w78in (198cm). *P:* £25–£119; circular £55; oval £79.

PERFECT HARMONY rugs match plain and patterned carpets, carpet tiles and wall coverings in the same range (see separate entries). The rugs come in the same four colourways as the other furnishings — flax, ice, coral and jade. There is a choice of three designs: 'Octave', a shaded stripe; 'Andante', a choice of small, all-over designs; and 'Coda', a shag pile rug. *M:* 48 × 27in (122 × 68.5cm), 60 × 36in (152.5 × 91.5cm), 78 × 150in (198 × 381cm); 'Coda' also 95 × 66in (241.5 × 167.5cm) and dia 54 in (137cm); 'Octave' also 118 × 78in (299.5 ×

CARPETING

Left to right: Gaskell's 'Chintz' and 'Cameo'

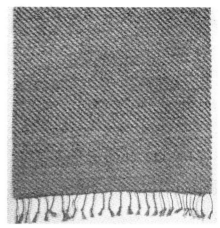

Rug by Susie Honnor at the Guild of Lakeland Craftsmen

198cm). *P:* on application.
Gaskell make two Axminster rugs for the HOUSE OF LOUIS NICHOLE collection which offers co-ordinating bed linen, wallpaper and fabric from other manufacturers. 'Cameo' has a dotted pattern in a border of stylized bows and flowers; 'Chintz' has a leaf and tendril design in a continuous tendril border. Both are 80% wool and 20% nylon and come in dusty rose and Regency blue colourways. *M:* 60 × 36in (152.5 × 91.5cm), 24 × 36in (61 × 91.5cm). *P:* on application.

GEORGIAN CARPETS LTD
Huge choice of colours and three qualities in plain rugs. G MAJOR shag pile rugs are available in 10 colours, MANOR and FARMER GEORGE qualities each come in 22 colours. (For details of construction and composition, see *Carpeting, plain.*) All the rugs have fringed edges. *M:* 27 × 54in (68.5 × 137cm), 36 × 68in (91.5 × 172.5cm), 54 × 78 (137 × 198cm), circular dia 54in (137cm). *P:* on application.

GRAHAM & GREENE LTD
Beautiful rugs, old and new, from this wonderful shop off the Portobello Road. INDIAN DHURRIES come in plain colours or stripes at very reasonable prices. Colours are apricot, cream, red, yellow, blue, green, black or white. *M:* 48 × 84in (122 × 213.5cm). *P:* £19.85. The ever-changing stock of RAG RUGS comes from Portugal and India, and Turkey provides the KELIMS, old and new. *M:* various. *P:* RAG RUGS £8.50–£35; NEW KELIMS from £110; OLD KELIMS from £135.

PRICES AND INFORMATION WERE CORRECT AT THE TIME OF GOING TO PRESS

GUILD OF LAKELAND CRAFTSMEN
Handmade rugs from members of this northern craftsmen's guild. Makers include weavers Susan Foster and Susie Honnor, and Penny Glanville, who spins and dyes (using natural moss and lichen dye) her own wool and tufts it into rugs. Susie Honnor works on a large, four-shaft loom and will accept commissions if they fit into her current work scheme. *P:* on application.

HABITAT DESIGNS LTD
Extensive collection of rugs and mats from this famous company, many available by mail order. Budget-priced JAMALI hand-woven jute and cotton dhurries come in lovely, sombre shades of browns and ochres and a choice of six simple geometric designs. *M:* 91 × 183cm (35¾ × 72in). *P:* £13.95.
For brighter colours in stripes there are PAPILLON rugs in washable cotton — fresh colours on a cream background. There is a choice of blue/beige stripes, aqua/pink/blue, blue/pink/yellow, red/yellow/blue or blue/beige/pink. *M:* 105 × 195cm (41¼ × 76¾in). *P:* £13.95.
Plain rugs come in a choice of bright colours — JAMBAI, in yellow, blue, rust or grey — or neutrals — CHENILLE in cream or soft grey. *M:* JAMBAI 90 × 150cm (35½ × 59in); CHENILLE 100 × 160cm (39¼ × 63in). *P:* JAMBAI £12.95; CHENILLE £19.95.
One of Habitat's most popular dhurry designs is ARROWHEAD — gentle background colours with a white arrowhead pattern on blue, green or pink. *M:* 140 × 200cm (55 × 78¾in). *P:* £51. SARANGA, ATOLI, CHANDINI and PURANI are all dhurries in intricate, traditional patterns in soft pastel shades. MANSA, TRIPLE DIAMOND ZARAND and SAMAN are all made from wool and cotton in traditional patterns and colours — fawns, beiges, browns and reds. *M:* 105 × 180cm–122 × 213cm (41¼ × 70¾–48 × 83¾in). *P:* £31.95–£159.

Habitat also do a good range of door mats ranging from the COCO KNOT MAT in natural coco fibre in a plaited design to coloured coir in SUNBURST, LINES or SHAPES design. *M:* COCO KNOT MAT 45 × 75cm (17¾ × 29½in); others 40 × 67cm (15¾ × 26½in). *P:* COCO KNOT MAT £4.75; others £6.95.

JAYMART RUBBER & PLASTICS LTD
Great choice of household mats at reasonable prices. Coir door mats come plain or with unusual stencilled designs — one that says 'Wipe Your Feet Stupid!' (for a family with a sense of humour), 'Wet Weather' with a design of raindrops, a wellington boot and an umbrella and the more usual 'Welcome' mat.
BRUSH-OFF PVC-backed coir (see *Carpeting, coir*) comes in standard sized doormats or choose from about 15 POLYPROPYLENE doormats with different rib or zig-zag effects. KUM KLEEN nylon-on-vinyl carpet mats will absorb 1½ gallons of moisture per sq yd which makes them ideal for bathrooms and kitchens. Jaymart also do a good range of CHINESE MATS — honeycomb seagrass doormats, rice straw mats, two-tone rush and maize mats and bullseye rush mats. *M:* various. *P:* coir mats, plain from approx £1.50, stencilled from approx £4; BRUSH-OFF from approx £5; POLYPROPYLENE from approx £2.50; KUM-KLEEN from approx £5; CHINESE from approx £1.50.

MORGAN & OATES
Beautiful range of rugs — many handwoven and all in 100% wool — available from designers and selected shops. REGATTA is a broad striped handwoven rug in colours to blend with modern, pastel-shaded interiors — soft pink, aqua blue, terracotta, pistache and buttermilk. MARL provides a classic look for home

REGATTA from Morgan and Oates

or office with its blended ground of neutral colours with fine accent stripes — handwoven in silver, parchment, slate or granite. Also handwoven is DIAGONAL TWILL, a twill rug with fine stripes and accents of colour in the borders. DIAGONAL TWILL comes in about 20 different colour combinations. *M:* runners 77 × 150cm (30¼ × 59in), 77 × 244cm (30¼ × 96in), 90 × 200cm (35½ × 78¾in); area carpets 150 × 210cm (59 × 82¾in), 180 × 275cm (70¾ × 108¼in). *P:* runners approx £120, £200, £180; area carpets approx £370, £570.
RIB RUGS are another handwoven range of a different construction, available in black with white or taupe (brownish grey) with string. *M:* 115 × 244cm (45¼ × 96in). *P:* approx £290.
JASPER, DASH LINE and ABSTRACTS are stunningly beautiful tufted rugs in wonderful colours. JASPER has a broken stripe design, DASH LINE consists of six linear designs such as grids and dashes, ABSTRACTS of larger, geometric shapes. These can be custom-coloured from a choice of about 50 shades. *M:* 140 × 250cm (55 × 98½in). *P:* approx £900 or sq m approx £245.

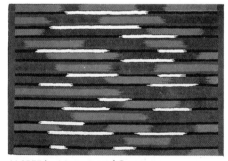

JASPER by Morgan and Oates

NICE IRMA'S LTD (FABRICATION)
Wide and ever-changing choice of ethnic rugs at reasonable prices. Working with their weavers and dyers in India, this company is continually developing new ideas and designs for rugs both plain and patterned to fit in with contemporary trends in interior design. Regular stock includes extensive range of cotton and wool rugs, dhurries and runners, and some large area rugs in wool or cotton. Patterns are usually striking Islamic geometrics, stylized flowers or stunning stripes. *M:* 24 × 36 – 96 × 120in (61 × 91.5 – 244 × 305cm). *P:* £6.50– £165.
PASTEL PLAID cotton rag rugs come in lovely soft pastel shades of pinks, blues and greens in an interesting plaid-like weave — ideal for colour without a strong pattern. *M:* 24 × 36in (61 × 91.5cm), 60 × 84in (152.5 × 213.5cm). *P:* £9.85, £46.25.

P & O CARPETS LTD
Top quality semi-antique and contemporary rugs from Persia, Turkey, Russia, Afghanistan

and China at reasonable prices. The Chinese rugs in particular are the best contract quality made. Stock is constantly changing, so sizes and prices vary. *P:* £15–£24,000.

E RUSSUM & SONS LTD
SUPER SEASONS rot-resistant indoor/outdoor flooring in standard size mats (see *Carpeting, patterned*). *M:* 33 × 60cm, 40 × 70cm, 50 × 80cm (13 × 23½in, 15¾ × 27½in, 19¾ × 31½in). *P:* £3.20, £4.53, £6.47.

ARTHUR SANDERSON & SONS LTD
Exciting dhurries and made-to-order rag rugs from this well-known firm. DHURRIES come in various different constructions such as wool, cotton and silk in weaves, chain-stitch and needle-point. Designs range from traditional Persian-style motifs to more modern patterns of trellises with Greek key borders. Colours vary from gentle pastel beiges, pinks, greens and blues, to bold reds, blues and greens. *M:* 36 × 60 – 120 × 168in (91.5 × 152.5 – 305 × 426.5cm). *P:* from £109. See illustration on following page.
RAG RUGS can be made to order in any colour in 100% cotton. *M:* 36 × 60in (91.5 × 152.5cm), 108 × 144in (274.5 × 366cm). *P:* £46, £299.

A selection of Sanderson's dhurries

SHELLEY TEXTILES LTD ⚠
Famous TUMBLE TWIST shaggy cotton rugs. In 22 lovely plain colours, they can be machine-washed so they're perfect for bathrooms, children's rooms or anywhere where spills occur. A choice of six rectangular sizes and one circular; bathroom sets and wall-to-wall fitted carpet also available. Colours are bleached gold, bayleaf green, mushroom, olive green, Kalahari (pale gold), baham beige, old gold, fern, antelope, guardsman red, bleached white, tabac, bronze, havana, horizon blue, Oxford blue, rose pink, Adriatic blue, old rose, black, mulberry and ivory. *M:* 22 × 30–36 × 72in (56 × 76–91.5 × 183cm); circular dia 42in (106.5cm). *P:* on application.
See following page for illustration.

CARPETING

Dhurry by Sanderson

Shelley's TUMBLE TWIST cotton rugs△

SIGNATURE RUGS △

Four ranges of imaginative hand-tufted rugs by Brian Boocock, marketed by Mercia Weavers Ltd. PRIMARY COLLECTION repeat geometric shapes in primary colours on white backgrounds. DYNASTY COLLECTION draws its inspiration from Chinese paintings in soft jade, grey, pink and cream, with strongly linear patterned borders. In the KAZAK COLLECTION he enlarges elements from Middle Eastern carpets and makes them strikingly modern and original by combining soft pastels with black and brown. *M:* PRIMARY, KAZAK 75 × 225cm

(69 × 89in), 183 × 122cm (72 × 48in); DYNASTY 183 × 274cm (72 × 108in). *P:* sq ft approx £10.22.

Also marketed by Mercia Weavers is Boocock's MARY ROSE COLLECTION, a refreshingly different decorative concept which draws on medieval manuscript designs. Six designs of rugs can be combined with plain or patterned carpets that have complementary border designs. *M:* 183 × 274cm (72 × 108in). *P:* sq m £23. (See *Carpeting, made-to-order*.)

'Squared' from PRIMARY COLLECTION△ by Signature Rugs

PETER SMITH ASSOCIATES (WILTSHIRE) LTD

Entrance matting specially designed to clean most dirt and dampness from shoes before

Top: 'Aquitaine'; below: 'Ming'. From Signature Rugs

normal carpeting is reached. THRESHOLD matting is made from 60% viscose and 40% nylon with unique nylon abrasion tufts, tufted into the matting at regular intervals. MATADOR CARPETREAD provides an even more determined answer to the problem of entrance dirt, with its ridged aluminium sections alternating with strips of THRESHOLD matting. Available in brown, blue, green, red and gold, THRESHOLD comes in six standard size mats, as desk mats, as tiles and with optional PVC backing. Broadloom also available, with or without PVC backing. MATADOR CARPET-READ comes in standard size mats or made to individual specifications. Both ranges are ideal for foyer and entrance areas in schools, hospit-

△ *INDICATES AN ILLUSTRATED PRODUCT SELECTED BY THE DESIGN CENTRE*

als, hotels, conference halls and other public places. *M:* THRESHOLD: mats 91 × 137cm–183 × 366cm (35¾ × 54in–72 × 125¾in); desk mats 64 × 114cm (25¼ × 45in), 104 × 127cm (41 × 50in); tiles 50 × 50cm (19¾ × 19¾in); broadloom w36, 54, 72, 144in (91.5, 137, 183, 366cm); MATADOR CARPETREAD mats 60 × 80cm (23½ × 31½in). *P:* on application.

For domestic use, choose TROJAN MATS, with an attractive shaded chequerboard effect. Available in brown, beige, bronze, green and grey, they are ideal to soften the effect of tiles in areas of heavy wear such as hallways, kitchens and dining rooms. Made from 100% polypropylene, so very easy to keep clean. *M:* 40 × 70cm (15¾ × 27½in), 67 × 130cm (26½ × 51¼), 100 × 180cm (39¼ × 70¾in). *P:* on application.

TINTAWN LTD

Four area rug designs in the IRISH COLLECTION to match Tintawn's broadloom range (see *Carpeting, patterned*). The relief patterns are created by weaving in short or long tufts and loops. Some have plain centres and elaborate Celtic borders, while others have overall patterning which draws on traditional Aran motifs. Colours are ivory or sand; three sizes available. *M:* 48 × 72in (122 × 183cm), 72 × 108in (183 × 274cm), 108 × 144in (274 × 366cm). *P:* sq yd approx £30.

'Cashel' from Tintawn's IRISH COLLECTION

TOMKINSONS CARPETS LTD

Traditional Axminster and Wilton rugs at all prices. ROYAL COLLECTION, GALLERY COLLECTION and KLEITOS are all Axminster ranges in traditional colours and designs. ROYAL is in 100% wool, GALLERY in 100% Meraklon (this range incorporates some fashion colours — pastels, browns, beiges, pinks, blues and greens) and KLEITOS rugs are 80% wool/20% nylon. *M:* 60 × 36in (152.5 × 91.5cm); circular dia 48in (122cm). *P:* ROYAL, KLEITOS approx £30; GALLERY approx £25. ROYAL TABAL Wilton rugs are made from 100% wool. 'Akira' has oriental designs in traditional colours, while 'Mandarina' and 'Bagdad' are rectangular or circular Chinese figure rugs, also in traditional colours. *M:* various. *P:* £16.99–£300.

PRICES AND INFORMATION WERE CORRECT AT THE TIME OF GOING TO PRESS

TOULEMONDE-BOCHART AT DIVERTIMENTI

Around a hundred different varieties of rugs and dhurries under one roof. They range from PRESTIGE DHURRIES in blends of the finest New Zealand wool, to modestly priced MULTI-COLOURED RAG RUGS. Nearly all the designs are created in Paris to follow current interior design trends and all the dhurries are woven in India in small villages, following age-old traditions. PRESTIGE DHURRIES range includes all-over geometric designs in bold greens, reds

Selection of designs from PRESTIGE DHURRIES range by Toulemonde-Bochart

and blues as well as softer, floral designs scattered over beige backgrounds. *M:* 125 × 179cm (49¼ × 70½in), 183 × 275cm (72 × 108¼in), 252 × 306cm (99¼ × 120¼in). *P:* £148, £350, £513.

LINEN RUGS have a slightly patchwork look, with their two-colour warp and four-colour weft. They come in three colourways — apricot with grey, black with bright pastels or multi-pastels. *M:* 123 × 186cm (48½ × 73¼in). *P:* £169.

For a bolder, geometric look, go for the TAPIS PEINT range made from jute with latex backing. Designs are hand-screened and include

CARPETING

one with a black centre and four-colour corners, and another with a bold diamond-shape in red, bounded on two sides with broad blue stripes. *M:* 160 × 230cm (63 × 90½in). *P:* £89.50.

Finally, MULTI-COLOURED RAG RUGS in cotton are attractive enough to suit most room schemes, and reasonably priced too. *M:* 60 × 120–140 × 200cm (23½ × 47¼–55 × 78¾in). *P:* £6.25–£24.95.

Dhurries by Toulemonde-Bochart

V'SOSKE JOYCE (UK) LTD
Exquisite handmade rugs to your own design with a possible four thousand colour shades to choose from. 'Craftsmanship at the service of the designer' is the way this company describes its products — rugs and carpets that blend perfectly with either modern or traditional decors. Designs can reflect the pattern of a fabric or wallpaper or, if you are lucky enough to have one, an Adam-style plasterwork ceiling as in the octagonal rug 'Osterley'. Designs can be incised using the famous V'Soske Joyce hand-carving technique. *P:* on application. See also *Carpeting, made-to-order*.

WOODWARD GROSVENOR & CO LTD
Seven finely detailed designs in the Persian style. All are 100% wool Wiltons and can be supplied with or without fringing. The designs are 'Afghan', with border and three central panels on a Turkey red background; 'Kirman', a choice of beige or gold background for a design with a deep border and large central motif; 'Tabriz', with a narrow border for the smaller sizes and a deep border for the larger ones featuring a complicated pattern of flow-

'Kashan' by Woodward Grosvenor

ers, stems and scrolls round a central panel in beiges and golds or beiges and reds; 'Shirvan', an updated all-over Persian panel design in browns, reds and beiges for more modern interiors; 'Kashan' with a central motif surrounded by delicate garlands of flowers, red or beige predominating; 'Tree of Life', a wonderfully intricate design with a deep border and central motif completely surrounded by finely drawn leaves, stems and flowers, with light or dark gold predominating; and 'Ardebil', a vivid design with border and central motif surrounded by smaller lozenge motifs on a brilliant red background. *M:* four sizes, 183 × 91–366 × 274cm (72 × 36–144 × 108in); except 'Shirvan', 183 × 91cm (72 × 36in), 229 × 137cm (90 × 54in) only. *P:* on application.

TILES (CARPETING)

CARPETS OF WORTH LTD
Patterned carpet tiles that make the joins disappear. Ideal for foyers and public areas, BONDAX tiles come in three stock designs — a restrained herringbone, a subtle chequerboard and a muted cross-hatched pattern — each in two colourways with cream, brown or steel grey predominating. Made from bonded nylon with cut pile finish. *M:* 18 × 18in (46 × 46cm).

Custom-made tiles can also be produced for special effects in almost limitless designs (minimum quantity 600 sq yd/501 sq m) and in wool/nylon or wool/acrylic combinations. *P:* all on application.

CHECKMATE INDUSTRIES LTD
Carpet tiles to suit every taste and pocket and with a huge choice of colours. Top of the range is BERLIN in 80% wool/20% Timbrelle with hard twist cut pile and PVC backing. Suitable for heavy contract use and available in laurel (grey-green), tumbleweed (light green), sea mist (grey/beige), nutmeg, cameo (rose pink), nutkin (honey beige), pumice (stone), burnt almond (rust), birch (light brown) and briarwood (dark brown). *M:* 50 × 50cm (19¾ × 19¾in). *P:* laid price sq m approx £21.

Next comes MASTERPIECE, also for heavy contract use. This is an 80% acrylic/20% nylon mixture in a twin-tone hard twist yarn with PVC backing. Available in Renaissance brown (dark brown), Etruscan tan (medium brown), Goya orange (autumnal orange), pharoah beige (beige), Florentine blue (mid-blue), Babylon green (sage green) and Corinthian gold (gold). *M:* 50 × 50cm (19¾ × 19¾in). *P:* laid price sq m approx £15.75.

HEATHLAND is a rugged loop pile tile in Antron III HF with PVC backing for heavy contract use. The colours, which have a slight sheen, are mandrake (mid-brown), foxglove (raspberry pink), fern (light green), thistle (pinky blue), gorse (mid-green), bullrush (dark brown), sorrel (beige), borage (light brown). *M:* 50 × 50cm (19¾ × 19¾in). *P:* laid price sq m approx £13.50.

ROSTAT is a fine gauge loop pile tile in 70% Acrilan/30% modacrylic with PVC backing, for heavy contract use. This range comes in taffy (mid-beige), peat (dark brown), sun (rust), harvest (light gold) and dark moss. *M:* 50 × 50cm (19¾ × 19¾in). *P:* laid price sq m approx £13.50.

IBOFLOR for heavy contract use has a hairy pile made from 55% Dorix and 45% polypropylene with an APP backing. Available in blue, berber, red, apricot, light green, camel, flame, brown, moose (mid-brown), sand, negre (very dark brown) and autumn. *P:* laid price sq m approx £12.25.

CHECKPOINT is a dense curly fibre tile made from 100% polypropylene with PVC backing for heavy contract use. It comes in beige, brass (yellowy-bronze), meadow (light greenish-yellow), brick (reddish-brown), caramel, red, blue and saddle (dark brown). *M:* 15 × 15cm (19¾ × 19¾in). *P:* laid price sq m approx £10.25.

KOMFORT is another hairy tile in 100% polypropylene with APP backing for general contract use. Available in cork (beige), tobacco (dark orangey-brown), grey, mid-brown, moss green, apricot, autumn and blue. *M:* 50 × 50cm (19¾ × 19¾in). *P:* laid price sq m approx £10.25.

For budget-priced installations choose PVC-backed MASTERFLOR tiles in 100% polypropylene with a ribbed surface. These are suitable for general contract use and come in gingernut (mustardy-brown), bamboo (light beige), sundown (rust), sherwood (bright green), slate, firedance (red), beaver (dark brown) and heather (light brown). With such a wide range of qualities and such a mouth-watering choice of colours, it would be difficult not to find something to suit! *M:* 50 × 50 (19¾ × 19¾in). *P:* laid price sq m approx £9.50.

DLW (BRITAIN) LTD

Two needlepunch ranges with the familiar 'hairy' texture, both for heavy contract use. POLO SL is made from 65% polypropylene and 35% polyamide and comes in green, red and four browns. STRONG SL in 100% polyamide offers a larger choice of colours — 18 in all. Both qualities are also available in sheet form (see *Carpeting, plain*). *M:* 50 × 50cm (19¾ × 19¾in). *P:* on application.

DUNLOP LTD

Three ranges of carpet tiles with some lovely new pastel shades. SIMPLICITY tiles in 100% polypropylene have a flat, felty appearance and are available in brown (dark brown), ochre (dull orange), caramel (fawn), green (dark grass-green), blue (navy) and coral (old rose). *M:* 40 × 40cm (15¾ × 15¾in). *P:* sq yd approx £3.99.

VELTONE, in a blend of polypropylene and nylon, have a cut pile finish that looks soft and warm. They come in brown, coffee, beige, cornflower (grey-blue), avocado and salmon. It is possible to achieve a chequerboard effect with these tiles using only one colour but alter-

nating the direction of the pile. *M:* 40 × 40cm (15¾ × 15¾in). *P:* sq yd £5.

SPRINGTEX are slightly smaller and are hard-wearing enough to use anywhere in the home. They are made of 100% polypropylene and come in Cairngorm brown (earthy brown), ebony (very dark brown), caramel, fawn, woodland green (moss green), coral (deep rose), powder blue, pastel green, ash grey and cardinal red. *P:* sq yd £5.99–£6.49.

Below: VELTONE; bottom: SPRINGTEX. By Dunlop

GASKELL BROADLOOM CARPETS LTD

ARPEGGIO fibre-bonded tiles in 100% polypropylene to co-ordinate with the plain, patterned and flecked carpets, rugs and wall-coverings in the PERFECT HARMONY collection (see separate entries). The tiles come in a wider range of colours than the carpets and include some strong dark shades. Colours are light flax, mid flax, dark flax, burnt almond, bitter chocolate (all co-ordinating with the flax carpets); jade and cypress green (co-ordinating with the jade carpets) and ice to go with the carpets in the ice colour band. *M:* w50 × 50cm (19¾ × 19¾in). *P:* on application.

JAMES HALSTEAD LTD

Three competitively-priced basics for the home. CUISINE in plain-coloured loop pile polypropylene is stain-resistant and ideal for kitchen use; it comes in three brown to beige shades, light green and blue, and bright red. Also plain, VELVET LUXURY has a cut pile finish and comes in eight colours — chocolate, cinnamon, oatmeal, Dresden blue (pale blue), crystal green (pale green), heather (pale, heathery pink), rosebud (pale, clear pink) and

CUISINE carpet tiles from James Halstead

brandysnap (mid-brown). It is intended for use in bedrooms and bathrooms. HOMEMAKER, in the same soft polypropylene pile, has a shallow herringbone pattern in chocolate/copper, copper/oatmeal, cinnamon/oatmeal and chocolate/cinnamon. These may be used on their own or combined with VELVET LUXURY for a chequerboard effect. *M:* 40 × 40cm (15¾ × 15¾in). *P:* VELVET LUXURY, HOMEMAKER, pack of 5 (1 sq yd/836 sq cm) approx £6.50; CUISINE, pack of 5 approx £3.99.

HEUGA UK LTD

The original inventor of carpet tiles, still vigorously developing attractive and resilient lines for both the contract and domestic markets. Nine contract ranges offer something for every type of installation. OLYMPIC is a low level loop pile range in 20 colours — lots of good pale greens, greys and beiges, as well as the more usual browns, blues, reds and rusts.

PASTELLE, especially aimed at contract designers, has a dense cut-pile velours finish made from new Timbrelle Grain 'S' fibre (which has anti-inflammable and anti-static properties as well as being tough enough for heavy contract use). The 20 colours with a slight mottled effect come in a good choice of pale to mid-browns, pale to mid-greens, blues, peaches and rusts.

SPECIAL RESERVE is a very dense Wilton-look tile made from Antron XL, with a luxurious wool-like feel underfoot. The 10 subtle colours are superb, with names like cassis (pale grape), calvados (pale moss green), Alsace (light grey), armagnac (light peachy brown) and bordeaux (pale wine colour).

The traditional carpet tile look may be achieved with FLOR S, LUX S, and FELT S — all

From Heuga, BISTRO carpet tile made especially for kitchens

CARPETING

three 'hairy' tiles, combining animal hair with viscose, in shades of browns, greens, blues and reds; with STRATA PLUS — a smooth, felt-textured tile made from a mixture of polypropylene, nylon and viscose; or with VORTEX — a modestly priced tile in polypropylene/nylon with a curly texture.

Most luxurious of their contract — and other — ranges is SHETLAND, pure wool loop-pile tufted tiles in six pleasantly flecked, natural berber shades.

Crowning the domestic tile ranges are FIESTA and PASTICHE. FIESTA is made from 100% polypropylene with a soft, slightly hairy feel. The eight colours are ideal for halls, playrooms, living rooms and extensions — beiges, grey, dark brown, two greens (one rather bright), bright red and light blue.

PASTICHE has been designed by two of Europe's leading textile designers to co-ordinate with the kitchen interiors of the 1980s and 1990s. The low-level loop pile is made from 100% polypropylene and has a slight sheen. The staggered bands of toning colours come in shades of brown/beige, shades of green, brown with grey and an attractive mid-blue/moss green combination.

Heuga's other two domestic ranges are HEARTH, another 'hairy' tile made from an animal hair/viscose mixture, in 10 dark-to-light shades for living rooms; and BISTRO, made especially for kitchens with a nubbly texture in six tactful shades (soya bean, french mustard, clove garlic, lobster bisque, blueberry pie and green pepper). *M:* 50 × 50cm (19¾ × 19¾in). *P:* all on application.

INTERFACE FLOORING SYSTEMS LTD

Really comprehensive range of well-proven carpet tiles for both contract and domestic use. PRELUDE PORTFOLIO is a new, fashion-conscious range of tiles for contract use featuring six designs printed on a velvet finish tile made from 100% Timbrelle S. Plain tiles come in 12 harmonizing pastel shades; the six designs use the darker shades from the range printed on to the lighter colours. 'Manhattan' features small, filled-in squares and looks very chic over a large area; 'Intersect' is a grid design and 'Arabesque' is a trellis made up of two-tone·dots.

VILLATEX range of contract tiles consists of an amazing 14 different types. 'Novella', 'Supernova', 'Terra', 'Ultra' and 'Tron' are all 'hairy' tiles of different thicknesses, made either from nylon and polypropylene or from a mixture of animal hair, nylon, polypropylene and viscose. Colours tend to be browns and beiges with the odd bright red, bright green and bright blue. The loop pile carpet tiles in the range offer a more sophisticated choice of colours. 'Seascape' in 100% Timbrelle S comes in sea greens, lilacs, greys and sandy browns, and beiges. 'Landscape' in Antron XL has a

good choice of beiges and browns, 'Piazza' in 100% Meraklon comes mainly in beiges and browns and 'Trojan' in 100% Enkastat has some muted blues, greens and beiges. The twist pile tiles in the VILLATEX range are 'Aramis' in 80% acrylic/20% nylon and 'Executive' with 80% wool/20% nylon pile in four berber colourways. 'Statesman' and 'Viceroy' are two kinds of curly type pile; 'Statesman' is particularly thick. For a velvet pile tile, there is 'Prelude' in 12 colours as in PRELUDE PORTFOLIO.

For contract situations where static is a problem, for example in modern offices where a static discharge could cause a computer malfunction, Interface have cleverly produced their COMPUTER COLLECTION. This consists of eight designs from the VILLATEX range, all of which are antistatic and have been independently tested by the British Carpet Technical Centre to ensure that they meet the stringent standards laid down by IBM and ICL.

Yet another range of Interface carpet tiles is the DEBRON range which includes 'Debron Supertwist' in 80% wool/20% nylon. This is also available as broadloom (see *Carpeting, plain*). But Interface have not neglected the domestic market and have produced 'Fair 'n Square' for kitchens and hallways and 'Nice 'n Easy' for bathrooms and bedrooms. 'Fair 'n Square' is a 'hairy' tile made from polypropylene and nylon in five dark colours and a beige. 'Nice 'n Easy' are 100% nylon with a velvet pile and come in pastel shades — dusky rose, apricot glow, cornflower, iced coffee, wild fern and cream lily. Both domestic ranges carry a five-year guarantee.

M: all 50 × 50cm (19¾ × 19¾in). *P:* all on application.

'Quartz' from PRELUDE PORTFOLIO by Interface

NAIRNFLAIR LTD

Compact but comprehensive contract range offering a good selection of textures and colours. All tiles have antistatic and fire-resistant properties. POLONAISE heavy-duty twist pile tiles are almost indistinguishable from broadloom when laid: their hard twist pile 'knits' together across the joins. In durable 70% acrylic/30% nylon, the tiles come in six earth tones — lichen, aspen, birch, hazel, bark and heather — and other colours to order. ENCORE low loop tiles for general duty are stain-resistant 100% Meraklon in seven faintly flecked shades — sapphire (grey-blue), coffee, mink, emerald (not too bright), Sienna, cinders and stone. Also low loop but for heavy duty is FORTE, in soil- and burn-resistant 100% Enkastat polyamide, guaranteed by Nairnflair and by fibre-makers Enka against wear of more than 10% in five years. Available in eight colours with pronounced fleck — five browns, green, grey and soft blue — and other colours to order. SOLO is fibre-bonded 90% blended polypropylene/10% viscose, suitable for medium duty. It comes in eight dirt-concealing colours: chocolate, natural, copper, sand, old rose (grey-pink), avocado, Atlantic, ruby. For heavy duty there's Nairnflair H, a dense directional pile, fibre-bonded tile. Made from an exceptionally hard-wearing mix of 50% nylon, 40% polypropylene and 10% other fibres, the tiles also have excellent fire resistance and give insulation against both impact and airborne sound. There are 12 colours, six earth tones and six brighter colours, including deep red and peacock blue. *M:* all 50 × 50cm (19¾ × 19¾in). *P:* (contract) POLONAISE sq m £12.96; ENCORE sq m £8.08; FORTE sq m £10.92; SOLO sq m £7.20; H sq m £10.72.

For general domestic use, Nairnflair produce three ranges: ENCORE — similar to the contract range but smaller and available in all contract shades except cinders; PRONTO — 90% polypropylene/10% viscose in seven colours (peat, natural, camel, embers (red), moss, gold, azure); and velours-look FANFARE in six colours (lake (blue), walnut, desert, forest, agate, pebble). *M:* all 40 × 40cm (15¾ × 15¾in). *P:* ENCORE sq m £16; PRONTO sq m £12; FANFARE sq m £14.

STEELES CARPETS LTD

Three contract quality ranges. STEELETILE has the same specification as STEELETWIST (see *Carpeting, made-to-order*); BERTILE is a heather berber twist in 80% wool/20% nylon that comes in naturals and pastels; LE MANS TILE has the same specification as LE MANS carpet (see *Carpeting, made-to-order*). *M:* 50 × 50cm (19¾ × 19¾in). *P:* on application.

PRICES AND INFORMATION WERE CORRECT AT THE TIME OF GOING TO PRESS

INTRODUCTION

Think tiles. They can replace carpets, with or without underfloor heating; line walls and even ceilings; cover tables and working surfaces; and be used for hearths, decorative cornices, patios.

Introduced to Europe from Moorish Spain and North Africa, glazed ceramic tiles were traditionally relegated to the floors and walls of chilly bathrooms and institutional halls. Modern tiles are still made from the same material — the most practical, long-lasting and easily cleaned available — but their appearance has changed drastically.

True, there are still the traditional designs: hand-painted blue and white tiles for kitchens, transfer-printed Victorian flowers for fireplaces; and Spanish and French Provençal-shaped floor tiles in warm, classic terracotta. But there are also deep fashion colours, mosaics in multi-faceted patterns, tiles that combine to make delightful pictures of orange trees in tubs, abstracts, geometrics in sharp black and white, and soft, smudgy tones in rectangular blocks.

The basic practical consideration is whether a surface requires heavy duty or light duty tiles, and this section is divided accordingly between wall and floor tiles. Generally, wall tiles are 6 – 11mm (¼ – ⅜in) thick, floor tiles 15 – 20mm (⅝ – ¾in). But many wall tiles are tough enough for use on worktops and on low-wear floors — in bathrooms, for example, where most of the walking is done by slippered feet. Likewise, many floor tiles could be used for wall cladding. When thinking about floors, bear in mind that printed patterns tend to disappear with wear, that neutral colours conceal the dirt, and that non-slip surfaces can be valuable wherever spills or bustling traffic are likely, not just around swimming pools. And whatever use is intended, always check the suitability of a range with the manufacturer or supplier, to save endless trouble later.

A vital word: tiles must be accurately and carefully laid — a job the supplier will usually do, although it may double the cost. Handmade versions backed, often unevenly, with clay can be particularly difficult to handle. Most mass-produced tiles are quick and easy to lay; a good handyman can do a perfectly adequate job.

Tiling is permanent. So, if a bathroom is tiled to match bedroom wallpaper, or a vanity top complements a fabric, buy extra paper or fabric to replace or repair the originals.

● Measurements in this section follow the manufacturers' practice, giving approximate conversions of standard imperial and metric sizes.

● Original Victorian and Edwardian tiles can often be obtained from dealers who specialize in reclamation. See Architectural salvage at the end of the book.

FLOOR TILES

A G TILES LTD

High standard floor tiles for contract and domestic use, from Britain's largest producer. All come with impressive collection of round edges, covings, step treads and drainage tiles. Hardwearing vitrified tiles, suitable even for airports or supermarkets, come in ten shades of brown and terracotta, plus black, in plain, speckled or 'flash' effects. Four different slip-resistant finishes are available, ideal for slippery areas such as swimming pool surrounds or workshop floors. Designs can be printed on request. M: imperial 6 × 6in (15 × 15cm) modular metric 25 × 12.5cm (9¾ × 5in). P: £7.94–£11.90 sq yd.

ROCKWARE vitrified tiles have special stain-resistant surface finish and come in three random-shaded colours: sandy Morocco, brown Barbados and off-white Gibraltar. Patterned finishes also available. M: 6 × 6in (15 × 15cm). P: £11.90 sq yd.

Glazed GEMSTONE tiles are suitable for interior and exterior floors and walls. Four neutral brown shades are available in the standard range, and GEMSTONE SPECTRUM range includes pastels citrine (yellow), rose quartz, aquamarine and tourmaline (green) as well as white and brown. M: 20 × 20cm (8 × 8in). P: £13.53 sq m. GEMSTONE PLUS tiles are guaranteed frostproof, recommended for porches and conservatories. Colours are Brazil (dark brown), Casablanca (grey) and chestnut. M: 20 × 20cm (8 × 8in). P: £13.53 sq m.

ANTIQUE quarry tiles from Germany, frostproof and impervious to stains, come in two rustic coloured finishes: elm and rosewood. M: 24 × 11.5cm (9½ × 4½in). P: £10.79 for 24. In association with H & R Johnson and Maw Tiles, AG Tiles can provide a comprehensive contract service.

SALLY ANDERSON TILES

Slip-resistant floor tiles in 40 plain colours to co-ordinate with their vast range of modular designs and system murals (see Wall tiles), some available with relating patterns. Other colours can be commissioned at extra cost. M: 6 × 6in (15 × 15cm). P: one colour, £38.16 sq yd; patterned £41.04 sq yd. SUNBURST is a circular floor motif designed to co-ordinate with CLASSIC frieze designs. M: dia 36 or 60in (90 or 150cm). P: £160.60 or £392.50 (ex VAT).

B J ARNULL & CO LTD

Beautiful Italian floor tiles. Traditional terracotta ones from Il Ferrone come in an amazing 70 shapes and sizes — including squares, rectangles, slim brick shapes, octagons and curved designs — and can be arranged in 120 different patterns. M: 25 × 25cm (9¾ × 9¾in). P: £26.95 sq m (ex VAT).

From Tecnoceramica come PAVONE floor tiles in surprising colours: bright orange, yellow and red, leafy green, sage green and two shades of grey as well as the more usual black, white and nine browns ranging from beige to rust to chocolate. Shapes include squares, rectangles, octagons, hexagons and triangles with chopped corners; there are also moulded skirting tiles. M: 20 × 20cm (7¾ × 7¾in). P: £25 sq m (ex VAT).

BARBEE CERAMICS LTD

Traditional Bavarian tiles by Korzilius. To complement their wall tiles with relief decoration, there are plain tiles for both walls and floors. Colours are Chamonix (white), Tunis (mottled beige), Provence (mottled gold) and Esterel (mixed mottled blue, yellow and brown). There are also decorated tiles with Chamonix ground and simple blue and brown floral motifs. M: 9.4 × 9.4cm (3¾ × 3¾in), 19.4 × 19.4cm (7½ × 7½in). P: plain £30 sq yd; decorated £5 each.

BOYDEN & CO LTD

Major collection including some French and Italian ranges. Colourful mosaics by the French company, Briare, are suitable for internal and external floors as well as walls (see Wall tiles). Italian company Marazzi also make a number of floor tile ranges: hexagonal CONTEE tiles come in warm earthy colours. M: 30 × 30cm (12 × 12in). P: £205.50 per 100. Rectangular SERIE 2000 tiles come in a variety of smudgy shades, from muddy brown and forest green to rich red and burnt orange. M: 20 × 10cm (8 × 4in). P: £23–£30 per 100.

CAPITAL CERAMICS

Large range of imported tiles. Classic floor tiles from Ceramano Baukeramik of Germany include elegant LINDOS: octagons with square insets, and smaller squares for walls and worktops. Octagons come in white, grey or beige; insets in white, brown, red or blue. M: 15 × 15cm (6 × 6in), 20 × 20cm (8 × 8in); insets 5 × 5cm (2 × 2in). P: £15.94–£22.74 sq yd. Or there's rustic KRETA: tough, unglazed tiles in rich terracotta or brown in squares and octagons, and with patterned or plain square insets. M: field tiles 20 × 20cm (8 × 8in), 30 × 30cm (12 × 12in). P: £19.94–£24.50 sq yd. More sophisticated is PATRAS, a classically-inspired tendril design used as a border or contrasting band beside matching plain tiles. Colours are blue and brown on sand, and corner designs are available. M: 20 × 20cm (8 × 8in). P: plain £22.50 sq yd; decorated £2.74 each. Many of Ceramano's floor tiles are also suitable for walls.

The Dutch company Capricorn offers a wide range of plain textured floor tiles in neutral shades: matt glazes include Sahara (beige),

CERAMIC TILES

Boyden's PASTILLES in 'Verdure' standard pattern, with SIALEX surround; both by Briare

orient (grey), ivory, blue (blue-grey), berber beige, Alp beige and beige-brown. Shapes include octagons, squares, small squares, skirting tiles and stair treads. FOURPLUS range of extremely tough, high-wear and frost-resistant floor tiles, though unglazed, is designed to be as easy to clean as glazed tiles. Colours available include blues and reds as well as off-white and four shades of brown. *M:* 21.6 × 21.6cm (8½ × 8½in) or 30.8 × 30.8cm (12 × 12in). *P:* £19.47–£25.79 sq yd.

CERAMIC TILE DESIGN
All kinds of floor tiles, terracotta, quarry and vitrified, plain and patterned.
Terracottas include the usual squares, rectang-

PRICES AND INFORMATION WERE CORRECT AT THE TIME OF GOING TO PRESS

les and hexagons, and a reasonably priced version of the Provençal shape. *M:* square, four sizes, 10 × 10cm (4 × 4in) to 50 × 50cm (20 × 20in); rectangles 20 × 20cm (8 × 8in); hexagons 15 × 15cm (6 × 6in), 20 × 20cm (8 × 8in); Provençals approx 15 × 15cm (8 × 8in). *P:* Provençals and small hexagons £15.95 sq yd; 50cm tiles £37.37 sq yd; 40cm tiles £31.65 sq yd; others £26 sq yd.
Of the quarries, most notable is the Wooliscroft VERSATILE range, so named because the tiles are non-slip on one side, smooth on the other, and have rounded edges. This versatility makes them popular with architects as well as domestic users. Eight colours offered are black, white, two buffs, autumn blend, red, brown and beech. *M:* 6 × 6in (15 × 15cm). *P:*

approx £11.75 sq yd.
Vitrified tiles from Czechoslovakia come with matt glaze in 29 colours — almost every colour under the sun except yellow. Particularly unusual are the two-tone blue tiles with graduated colour. *M:* 8 × 4in (20 × 10cm). *P:* from £15.30 sq yd.
Glazed floor tiles are offered in a good selection of bright as well as neutral colours (including the yellow missing on the Czechoslovakian tiles). The Spanish and Italian tiles are square or rectangular; the rectangles can be used to make contrasting borders around square tiles, giving a different, contemporary look to a floor. Patterned tiles are also available. *M:* 20 × 20cm (8 × 8in), 20 × 10cm (8 × 4cm). *P:* from £15 sq yd.
Many of Ceramic Tile Design's patterned wall tiles can also be used on floors, and the company will also make one-offs (see *Wall tiles*). What's more, their service is very comprehensive, offering ideas on what to choose and how ranges can be combined as well as selling adhesives for all purposes.

MARGERY CLINTON CERAMICS
'Oasis' floor tiles co-ordinate with Islamic lustre wall tiles, produced using the same technique (see *Wall tiles*). *M:* 15 × 15cm (6 × 6in). *P:* £52 sq yd (ex VAT).

ELIZABETH EATON
The real thing, terracotta tiles from Provence. There are eight shapes: squares, rectangles (broad and narrow), hexagons, elongated hexagons or 'batonnets' combined with squares, octagons similarly combined with small squares, and three variations on the typical Provençal curved outline, 'Mauresque', 'Vague' and 'Curviligne'. The tiles are soft fired in wood-burning ovens, which produces subtle shading variation, so should be laid random. Elizabeth Eaton advise that they are laid by a qualified tiler; and because they are porous tiles should then be wax polished or sealed (wax and sealant available from Elizabeth Eaton). *M:* squares, seven sizes, 12.5 × 12.5cm (4¾ × 4¾in) to 50 × 50cm (20 × 20in); rectangles (broad) 16 × 33cm (6¼ × 13in) or 33 × 50cm (13 × 19¾in), (narrow) four sizes, 10 × 20cm (4 × 7¾in) to 19 × 28cm (7½ × 11in); hexagons, four sizes, dia 11–34cm (4½–13½in); 'batonnets' 8 × 25cm (3¼ × 9¾in) with square insets 15 × 15cm (6 × 6in); octagons dia 21.5 or 24.33cm (8½ × 9½in) with square insets 7 × 7cm (2¾ × 2¾in) or 10 × 10cm (4 × 4in); 'Mauresque' 14 × 19cm (5½ × 7½in); 'Vague' 16 × 16cm (6¼ × 6¼in); 'Curviligne' 16 × 23cm (6¼ × 9in). *P:* £18.57–£42.60 sq m.
There is also a Spanish range IRICERAM, including a square tile, a rectangle and two hexagons. *M:* square 14 × 14cm (5½ × 5½in); rectangle 20 × 10cm (8 × 4in); hexagons 11 ×

Elon's plain octagonal tiles with square hand-painted tiles from CARRILLO range

11cm (4½ × 4½in), 20 × 20cm (8 × 8in). *P: £22 sq m.*
(All prices ex VAT.)

ELON TILES LTD

Hand-made unglazed floor tiles in warm shades from a pale terracotta to chocolate. There is a variety of traditional shapes: octagons with square insets; hexagons; squares, rectangles; rectangles with square insets; elongated hexagons; elongated hexagons with square insets; and Provençal-style (here called 'España'). For a traditionally Spanish touch, Elon's hand-painted glazed decorative tiles from Mexico — though really for walls — can be used as contrasting insets. *M:* squares 4

× 4in (10 × 10cm) to 12 × 12in (30 × 30cm); octagons and hexagons dia 8–12in (20 × 30cm); rectangles 4 × 8in (10 × 20cm), 6 × 12in (15 × 20cm); elongated hexagons 4 × 8in (10 × 20cm), 4 × 12in (10 × 30cm); 'España' dia 6–12in (15–30cm). *P:* from £24.15 sq yd. Elon's FRENCH range is suitable for domestic light wear floors as well as for walls and worktops. (See *Wall tiles.*)

HABITAT DESIGNS LTD

Glazed white or black tiles suitable for internal or external use. *M:* 20 × 20cm (8 × 8in). *P:* £6.95 for 10.

H & R JOHNSON LTD

Cristal brand satin finish floor tiles in 17 colours to match Cristal satin finish wall tiles: primrose, topaz (light brown), avocado, wild sage, sage green, spring green, turquoise, powder blue, jubilee blue, smoke grey, pearl grey, champagne, cream, light stone, pale pink and white. Suitable for medium duty floors, especially kitchens and bathrooms. *M:* 6 × 6in (15 × 15cm), 4¼ × 4¼in (10 × 10cm). *P:* large £14.40 sq yd; small £11.80 sq yd.
H & R Johnson's Encaustic Tile Department will undertake commissions for replacement of encaustic and geometric ceramic floor tiles in renovation contracts. Tiles can be produced exclusively to customers' requirements on large orders, each commission being treated individually. *P:* on application.

LANGLEY LONDON LTD

Exclusive range of tiles from Villeroy & Boch. Many of their — and Langley's own — vitrified tiles and mosaics are suitable for floors as well as walls and kitchen worktops (see separate entry) but two designs are specifically for floors: 'Palissy' and 'Primo'. The first is available in Sienna (surprisingly, an off-white) or sand, mottled and textured. *M:* 19.7 × 19.7cm (8 × 8in). *P:* £23.32 sq yd. The latter is available in Virginia (rusty red) or rusty white. *M:* 19.7 × 9.7cm (8 × 4in). *P:* £17.83 sq yd.
DIPLOMATIC by Roca, also exclusive to Langley, is a range of six glazed floor tiles in Australian beige, English blue, Grecian white, Irish green, Mexican brown and Spanish brown. They are easy to clean, scratch resistant and suitable for all interior domestic floors and for some commercial floors. *M:* 23 × 15.5cm (9 × 6in). *P:* £13.99 sq yd.
See *Wall tiles* for illustration.

MARLBOROUGH CERAMIC TILES

Twelve delicately coloured floor tiles to co-ordinate with their decorative wall ranges. There are five earthy colours — russet, nutmeg, moorland, bracken and deep coral — and seven softer shades — willow green, azure, oyster, ivory, oatmeal, matt white and coral. *M:* 15 × 15cm (6 × 6in). *P:* £12–£15 sq yd. Marlborough also manufacture a range of traditional Provençal tiles. *M:* 15 × 15cm (6 × 6in). *P:* £20–£25 sq yd. (All prices ex VAT.)

NICOBOND LTD

Four shapes of floor tile: square, rectangular, elongated hexagon and Provençal-style. Most are tough enough even for heavy traffic commercial areas and frost resistant. In addition to the traditional mottled sands, terracottas and browns there are plain white tiles, and MODUR ELLE range includes unusual greens and electric blue, all in a variety of textures; one

79

tile, 'NC4502' has a simple floral motif. *M:* 20 × 20cm (8 ×8in); 10 × 20cm (4 × 8in); hexagons 10 × 30cm (4 × 11¾in); Provençal 15 × 20cm (6 × 8in). *P:* from £8 sq yd.

Nicobond's MANDARIN MOSAICS, either Provençal-shape or square with straight, rounded or crinkled edges, can be used on floors as well as walls. Colours include various clear or mottled whites, creams and beiges, plus chocolate and rich blue (but the highly glazed finishes are not recommended for floors). *M:* 5.9 × 5.9cm (2¼ × 2¼in), 9 × 9cm (3½ × 3½in); sold in approx 30 × 30cm (12 × 12in) sheets. *P:* £1.44–£1.68 per sheet.

PILKINGTON'S TILES LTD ⚓

Two ranges of ceramic floor tiles. DORSET comprises 24 unglazed designs in squares, rectangles and Provençal shapes. There are four decorative tiles: 'Piazza', 'Copperbeech', 'Aztec' and 'Woodland'. 'Cloud' is an unusual smudgy design, available in four colours: blue, grey, green and chocolate. The rest of the range consists of plain tiles in off-white, brick red and black, or speckled neutral shades of buff and grey; and a variety of textured surfaces such as 'Pinhead' and 'Stud'. *M:* 25 × 12.5cm (10 × 5in); 20 × 15cm (8 × 6in); 20 × 20cm (8 × 8in); 15 × 15cm (6 × 6in); 10 × 10cm (4 × 4in). *P:* £10–£20 sq yd. Pilkington's simplified 'Universal Metricove' cove skirting system matches DORSET floor tiles.

The second range, VITROGLAZE, offers five glazed colours: ivory-fawn, pampas, sable, ivory russet and mid brown. Suitable for walls as well as floors, the range includes decorative tree insets. *M:* 20 × 10cm (8 × 4in); 20 × 30cm (8 × 12in). *P:* approx £9 sq yd.

DANIEL PLATT & SONS LTD ⚓

Manufacturers of contract quality CROWN quarry tiles for floors. Range comprises: floor tiles with round or double-round edges; coved skirting with a combined square/round top edge and with independent angles; sills with rounded edges, manufactured in five lengths. All are available in characteristic burnt red colour or in a shaded autumn blend. Optional anti-slip studded surface 'Superstud' is available in both colours and two sizes. *M:* 15 × 15 × 2cm (6 × 6 ×¾in), 15 × 15 × 1.2cm (6 × 6 × ⅝in). *P:* (red) £378, £298 for minimum order 1,000 tiles.

In addition, there are special surfaces: 'Morocco', which has an irregularly-grained texture, and 'Cobbles', which has irregular edges. *M:* both 15 × 15 × 1.2cm (6 × 6 × ⅝in). *P:* (autumn blend) £325 for 1,000 tiles. There's also a heavy-duty group, 'Triton', which comes in a rectangular shape with round or double-round edges, and as a square top cove. *M:* flat tile 22.5 × 11 × 3cm (8¾ × 4¼ × 1¼in). *P:* on application.

FERROLITE comes in plain or anti-slip surfaces, the latter with shot-faced or studded finish. A plain tile incorporating carborundum aggregate, 'Ferrundum', is also available. Colour options are dark red, black, chocolate, spring blend (shaded buff), plain buff, or two textured buff colours. Range comprises six sizes of flat tiles, three round-edged skirtings, four cove skirtings, plus angle beading, independent coving, a hexagon, channels and two types of grooved step treads, plus a really heavy duty tile 18mm (¾in) thick. *M:* hexagons 15 × 15 × 1.2cm (6 × 6 × ⅝in). *P:* £16.19 for 43 tiles.

RAMUS TILE COMPANY LTD

Own range under the Sumara brand name. VIVA comes in 56 colours and in triangular half-tiles as well as square — mix them to make dynamic patterns. *M:* 7.5 × 30cm (3 × 12in); 15 × 30cm (6 × 12in); 30 × 30cm (12 × 12in). *P:* £37.15 sq m ex VAT.

DENNIS RUABON LTD ⚓

Britain's largest, and Wales's only, manufacturer of quarry tiles. HEATHERBROWN, the largest range, has square and rectangular tiles in ten sizes, a hexagon, four anti-slip textures (ribbed, serrated, studded and shot-faced) plus coving with round or square edges. *M:* plain squares 9.4 × 9.4cm (4 × 4in) to 22.9 × 22.9cm (9 × 9in); plain rectangles 15 × 4.6 cm (6 × 2in) to 22.9 × 11.4cm (9 × 4½in); hexagons 15 × 15cm (6 × 6in); anti-slip 15 × 15cm (6 × 6in), shot-faced also 22.9 × 22.9cm (9 × 9in). *P:* £10–£12 sq m.

RUABON RED are medium red with a slight variation in shade from tile to tile, and come in two square sizes, one rectangular, one hexagonal, plus anti-slip and coving tiles as above. *M:* plain squares 15 × 15cm (6 × 6in), 22.9 × 22.9 (9 × 9in); rectangles 19.4 × 9.4cm (8 × 4in); hexagons 15 × 15cm (6 × 6in). *P:* £8–£9 sq m. RUABON FLAME are similarly coloured but with natural burnt look or 'flashing'. Square tile available, plus a round top coving with optional internal and external angles. *M:* 15 × 15cm (6 × 6in). *P:* £8–£9 sq m.

RYE TILES

Huge range of attractive handmade tiles in old and new designs. Rye's hand-painted and hand-sprayed designs are suitable for floors as well as walls and fireplaces, and so are their plain glazed tiles in 20 standard colours (and others to order). Their huge range of hand-printed patterns for squares or hexagons can be produced for floors in a selection of 19 colours on a Rye- or Bristol-white glazed background. The border designs in particular — traditional ones such as 'Victorian' and 'Chess Border', or the bold stripe 'Borderline' — make striking floor designs when combined

with plain glazed tiles. Prices vary according to the number of colours specified. *M:* 6 × 6in (15 × 15cm); 4 × 4in (10 × 10cm); hexagons dia 6in (15cm). *P:* £35–£37 sq yd. (See *Wall tiles* for patterns.)

BIANCO is a range of light duty floor tiles in a variety of shapes: rectangular, square, hexagonal and octagonal. All come in a white cristalline glaze. *M:* 6 × 6in (15 × 15cm); 6 × 3in (15 × 7.5cm); octagons and hexagons dia 6in (15cm). *P:* £23–£40 sq yd.

SPHINX TILES LTD

Six ranges of floor tiles. LIVINGSTONE comes in eight colours, from white with faint diagonal stripe to mottled brown; TWEEDSTONE in lizard (off-white) and oatmeal; ARTSTONE and LATTICE in brown only. Textured ANTI-SLIP comes in white and three different off-whites, and also in pale azure blue and cork brown. Largest range is PAVISOLO: square, rectangular and Provencal-style tiles in 18 shades including neutral sands and terracottas, fiery garnet and zircon, pale blue azulmar, bottle-green musgo and deep-blue kyanite and azul. All except ANTI-SLIP, Provençal PAVISOLO and four PAVISOLO colours are tough enough for heavy duty floors, even public buildings. *M:* LIVINGSTONE, ARTSTONE, TWEEDSTONE and LATTICE 20 × 20cm (8 × 8in); ANTI-SLIP 20 × 20cm (8 × 8in), 20 × 15cm (8 × 6in); PAVISOLO 20 × 10cm (8 × 4in), 20 × 20cm (8 × 8in), 20 × 30cm (8 × 12in). *P:* approx £13–£17 sq yd ex VAT.

WORLD'S END TILES

Classic floor tiles: BIANCO black diamond insets on white, and white squares, rectangles, hexagons and Provençal shapes; and ALMOND, the same shapes in beige. All suitable for medium duty. *M:* squares 6 × 6in (15 × 15cm), 4 × 4in (10 × 10cm); rectangles 8 × 4in (20 × 10cm), 6 × 3in (15 × 7.5cm); hexagons dia 4 or 6 in (10 or 15cm); Provençal dia 5in (12.5cm). *P:* £13.85–£23 sq yd.

Though ceramic, GRANITO might be mistaken for real granite. This frostproof, hardwearing tile, suitable for any use, comes unglazed in beige, green, mulberry, grey or off-white. It is also available with polished finish to order. There is a full range of treads, risers and non-slip tiles. *M:* 20 × 20cm (8 × 8in), 20 × 30cm (8 × 10in). *P:* from £12 sq m.

World's End also have a wide range of terracottas, and square and rectangular Italian floor tiles in black, white, light blue, lilac and pink. *M:* 8 × 8in (20 × 20cm), 8 × 4in (20 × 10cm). *P:* £8.50–£12 sq yd.

(All prices ex VAT.)

⚓ *INDICATES ONE OR MORE OF THE PRODUCTS MENTIONED ARE SELECTED BY THE DESIGN CENTRE*

WALL TILES

ALBION HARDWARE LTD

Enchanting Victorian-style sprigged tiles in the PORCELAIN range in three designs: 'Summer Mist', 'Meadow Flower' and 'Springtime', with soft pastels, rose or golden yellow predominating. Straight design tiles and curving corner designs can be used together to create a loop of flowers above a bath or basin. *M:* 6 × 6in (15 × 15 cm). *P:* plain white £4.90 for six; sprigged £10.70 for six.

SALLY ANDERSON TILES △

Vast range of modular designs and system murals, to order only. Choice ranges from Grecian figures and Chinese pagodas to giant butterflies and water-meadows, or by contrast, bold linear designs such as 'Multistripe' and 'Multicurve'. The MIDSUMMER range creates a stunning effect by repeating a single bold motif in various combinations across a wall; one such motif is a giant peacock feather, another a falling leaf. Most patterned tiles are used in conjunction with plain ones, and customers can plan their own schemes. Colours can be selected from about 26 translucent, high-gloss glazes, from soft, subtle aspen or orchid to strong colours such as sepia and elderberry. Up to five colours can be used in any one scheme, but obviously the number of colours chosen will influence the price. *M:* 6 × 6in (15 × 15cm); 4¼ × 4¼in (10.5 × 10.5cm); 6

Tiled mural in 'Chinese Pagodas' design, by Sally Anderson

× 3in (15 × 7.5cm); 8½ × 4¼in (21.5 × 10.5cm). *P:* from about £33 sq yd (ex VAT). Deliveries take up to six weeks.
Slip-resistant floor tiles are available in matching colours and even designs — for example, one could have a tree mural with its 'shadow' on the ground beneath! The company also produces dado friezes for restoration work, and will make special designs to commission.

B J ARNULL & CO LTD

Chic Italian tiles. Collection of modern designs by Cedit should suit all tastes. In the soft and feminine mood there's LOTO, green and pink water lilies set in an overall scheme of speckled green and blue with a touch of yellow; or LINEA ARMONIE, swaying poppies or shaded plain tiles in softest pastel pink, lilac and blue. More striking is ARIANNA, bright dots in rainbow colours forming straight lines or rounded corner squares, and MONTECARLO, tiles like white dominoes with primary-coloured dots; both are to be set against plain white background. MANHATTAN shows a city skyline silhouetted in white against blue; and PROIEZIONI is an all-line design reminiscent of computer graphics, with stripes developing into tree forms. PROIEZIONI comes in two colourways — blue, yellow, grey and green, or beige, yellow and rusty red — and both make striking borders, edging and stripes against white. To be used in the same way, there's TRATTEGGI, strong red border and inner broken red line on grey-striped background (with corner tiles); ROMBI, red and blue diamond outlines on grey and white; SEGMENTI, lines of varying widths in red and grey or pastel blue and pink; FOGLIE, stylized leaves in red with pale green outline, in white with red outline and blue stripe, or in grey with red outline; and GRAPPOLI, a naturalistic vine pattern in orange with red, or green with purple and blue stripe. *M:* 21.6 × 21.6cm (8¾ × 8¾in). *P:* £2.28 – £2.52 each. Plain tiles are also available from Cedit in 27 subtle shades: five greens, five blues, five browns, two greys, three sandy yellows, four off-whites, plus violet, lilac and deep rose.
ARMONIA range from Tecnoceramica offers a lovely palette of plain colours: black, white, mimosa (yellow) and both light and dark tones of glicine (mulberry), oasi (green), Capri (Mediterranean blue), Togo (chocolate brown), cammello (caramel brown) and vinaccia (wine-stain red). *M:* 20 × 20cm (7¾ × 7¾in). *P:* £25 sq m ex VAT.

LAURA ASHLEY LTD

Wall and floor tiles made in Italy, designed to co-ordinate with Laura Ashley fabrics and wallpapers. There are six rich plain colours, (white, rose, burgundy, cream, terracotta and china blue); six small floral designs ('Nutmeg', 'Cottage Sprig', 'Petite Fleur', 'Wood Violet', 'Scot-

From B J Arnull, some of the tiles in a range by Cedit. Left to right, from top: 'Tratteggi', 'Rombi', 'Foglie Beta', 'Grappoli Viola', 'Proiezione' and 'Segmenti Rossi'

tish Thistle' and 'Bembridge'); two geometrics ('Wickerwork' and 'Trellis'); and 'Ming', a design inspired by blue-and-white china. For lovers of the Victorian look, there is 'Quatrefoil', a large-scale Victorian print; and 'Conservatory', a Gothic plant motif adapted from a nineteenth-century textile print. All tiles come in two sizes. The larger ones are suitable for floors, but may require professional advice for fixing and are not recommended for heavy wear; the small ones are easier to apply and are ideal for walls. *M:* 20 × 20cm (8 × 8in); 15 × 15cm (6 × 6in). *P:* plain tiles from £6.50 sq m; patterned tiles from £10.50 sq m.

Laura Ashley's 'Trellis' and 'Quatrefoil'

PRICES AND INFORMATION WERE CORRECT AT THE TIME OF GOING TO PRESS

CERAMIC TILES

BARBEE CERAMICS LTD

Ultra-modern tiles from Italy and traditional ones from Germany. The Italian ones, by Bardelli, include I FILI range in dazzling shades of red, yellow, green and blue. Four variations are: plain tiles, white with narrow one-colour stripe, white with densely-packed one-colour stripes, and the same reversed. In the matching slim border tiles, all four colours have a grid on white. Subtler, square ZODIACO tiles have thin black or blue stripes arranged in a square or triangle on a pink, white, or beige ground; they can be mixed with plain ones or arranged in at least eight geometrical compositions. I GESSATI also combines striped and plain tiles, with white stripes on beige, salmon pink, black, dark grey or light grey ground; it looks good with contrasting art deco border, 'Listello Oro Deco'. *M:* I FILI and I GESSATI 13 × 26cm (5 × 10¼in); ZODIACO 13 × 13cm (5 × 5in); borders 6.5 × 26cm (2½ × 10¼in). *P:* £16.50 – £32 sq yd.

The German ones, by Korzilius, are hand-painted Bavarian tiles with rustic patterns in relief. Designed for kitchens, the decorative themes range from pretzels and strings of sausages to large realistic composites of farm animals, meadows or domestic scenes — there's even a dog seated on a sofa! All are best used as insets with Korzilius's plain tiles in Chamonix (white), Tunis (mottled beige), Provence (mottled gold) and Esterel (mixed mottled blue, yellow and brown). And, for a perfect finish, plain moulded trim pieces are available for corners and edges. Relief tiles are either coloured in blue, yellow and brown on white or left plain in Tunis or Provence shades. Pretty borders and edgings include leaf, vine and chequerboard designs and a striped moulded dado. For simpler tastes, there are also smooth white tiles with attractive floral motifs in blue and brown. *M:* 9.4 × 9.4cm (3¾ × 3¾in). *P:* decorated £5 – £10 each, plain £30 sq yd. See also *Floor tiles.*

BOYDEN & CO LTD

Exclusive French, Italian and British ranges. Fantastic mosaics from French company Briare are suitable for interior and exterior walls and floors. Range includes square, hexagonal, round and curved shapes. Round 'Pastilles' and square 'Emaux' come in 12 rich colours which look dazzling combined. For a pattern of overlapping circles, 'Ecaille' tiles come in seven soft shades, glazed or semi-matt. Round, square or hexagonal 'Mosaïque d'Or' offers a rare luxury, golden tiles. *M:* square 2.4 × 2.4cm (1 × 1in); round dia 1.8cm (¾in); 'Ecaille' dia 5.8cm (2in). *P:* £46–£60 sq m; 'Mosaïque d'Or' from £10 each.

Briare's larger square tiles come in about 50 subtly different plain shades, including a good range of pastels. *M:* 7.5 × 7.5cm (3 × 3in); 5 × 5cm (2 × 2in). *P:* £40–£60 sq m. They can be combined with decorative insets and borders

Boyden's 'Ecaille' tiles on floor and bath surround, edged with square matching border tiles; both by Briare

both geometric and floral. 'Arlequin' is a blue-and-yellow chequerboard design, 'Alpha' a bold border with white diamond outlines on pink, green, blue or red. For florals, there is the hazy 'Impression' in reddish tones on white, and simple 'Florale' with stylized silhouettes in pink, sand, light or dark blue and white. *M:* 'Florale' 5 × 5cm (2 × 2in); 'Arlequin', 'Alpha' and 'Impression' 10 × 10cm (4 × 4in). *P:* approx £40 sq m.

Plain tiles and decorative insets and panels are also imported from Marazzi in Italy. EMILIA, with six inset designs in earthy browns, terracottas and greens, has a typically Tuscan look. *M:* 15 × 15cm (6 × 6in). *P:* £20.40 for 100. 'Viserba' in the ROMAGNA range comes plain, as floral inset or unusual classically inspired border in a rich oatmeal shade. *M:* 15 × 22.5cm (6 × 9in) *P:* £38.25 for 100.

CAPITAL CERAMICS

Large collection of imported tiles. Modern Italian designs include FILERBE, in which landscapes of hills, trees and clouds are built up entirely from straight lines. Predominant colours are green and pink. And SERIE CHIC has high tech graphic background in blue, brown or green, decorated with falling leaf or bird. *M:* 20 × 20cm (8 × 8in). *P:* FILERBE £13.90–£16.20 sq yd; SERIE CHIC £13.40–£14.30 sq yd. From the German firm Ceramano Baukeramik come plain and decorated wall tiles, as well as a number of tiles for both walls and floors. Quaint 'Flower Market', 'Fish Market', 'Fruit Market' and 'Poultry Market' have a variety of insets of market stalls or items of merchandise

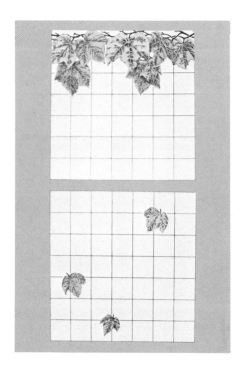

Capital Ceramics' falling leaf design in the SERIE CHIC range

to be used with plain tiles. Comes in red or blue on white or multicoloured on beige. *M:* 15 × 15cm (6 × 6in). *P:* from £4.50 each.

From Capricorn in Holland come textured tiles in natural colours for both floors and walls, and decorated tiles in the Dutch tradition. There are blue-and-white florals, other simple florals on a natural beige background, and a figure of a girl carrying bread: *M:* 10 × 10cm (4 × 4in). *P:* approx: £2.50–£5 each.

CERAMIC TILE DESIGN

One-offs in almost any colour, unusual imported and hand-decorated tiles, plus a large collection from major British and European manufacturers. Ceramic Tile Design can provide patterns ranging from antique Delft, eighteenth-century Spanish and Victorian styles to oriental and modern designs and hand-painted *trompe l'oeil* murals. Originals such as their balloon design can be supplied in panels to fit individual locations. They will make up patterns from their selection or work to the customer's own design, offering a tremendous range of colours and even attempting to match glazes to fabric samples. Service includes imaginative advice plus, where required, on-site visits for measurement and fitting. *M:* 15 × 15cm (6 × 6in). *P:*

balloon design tiles £8.05 each; hand-decorated tiles £4.50–£6.50 each; plain white tiles £5 sq yd; one-off prices on application. Imported from Turkey is IZNIK, a range of Islamic tiles in blues and terracottas copied from the tiles in the Blue Mosque in Istanbul. Can be used for walls or for fireplaces and swimming pools. *M:* 15 × 15cm (6 × 6in), borders 15 × 5cm (6 × 2in). *P:* £25.50 sq yd.

One design from Ceramic Tile Design's IZNIK range

KENNETH CLARK CERAMICS △

Five ranges of decorative tiles from these specialists in architectural ceramics, who will also undertake commissioned designs. CUSTOM CHOICE comprises 14 linear patterns that can be used to make a multitude of curves and angles. Colourways include vivid oranges, greens and blues with black lines; pastel pink and blue with white; brown and grey with darker tones; and white with blue lines — all can be combined in multicoloured schemes. SUSSEX is a range of interchangeable designs and plain tiles; chequerboards, shells, diamonds, fish, doves and florals can be grouped or mixed in a patchwork. Predominant colours are hot oranges and rich blues and greens, but there are also soft mauves and fresh blue-and-whites for doves and diamond designs. Simple blue-and-white AQUA includes two designs: 'Oriel', a geometric, and 'Daisy', with tiny flowers geometrically arranged. *M:* all 10 × 10cm (4 × 4in). *P:* plain 46p each, decorated 69p–£3.60 each. MEDITERRANEAN includes chequerboard patterns, dainty 'Hedgerow' floral, rich 'Coriander' and Celtic-inspired 'Cloister' — the last two designs in blue and terracotta. *M:* 10 × 10cm (4 ×4in). *P:* 69p–£2.60 each. Intricate TAPESTRY consists of several formal pictorials: 'Summer Garden', 'Squirrel', 'Hampstead', and 'Fishpond'. 'Fishpond' comes with corner tiles to make an attractive border around plain white tiles. All available in mustard, grey, dark blue or pale green on white, or in special colours to order. *M:* 15 × 15cm (6 × 6in). *P:* from £1.10 each.

△ *INDICATES ONE OR MORE OF THE PRODUCTS MENTIONED ARE SELECTED BY THE DESIGN CENTRE*

Kenneth Clark's CUSTOM CHOICE△

MARGERY CLINTON CERAMICS △

Beautiful tiles produced using modern silk-screen and ancient Islamic lustre techniques. There are four richly ornamented Persian Reproduction patterns copied from twelfth and thirteenth century designs: 'Kashan Cross', 'Kashan Flower', 'Kashan Goose' and 'Kashan Elephant'. *M:* 15 × 15cm (6 × 6in). *P:* 'Cross' and 'Flower' £60 sq yd; 'Goose' and 'Elephant' £64 sq yd (ex VAT). Iridescent lustre wall tiles come in eight colours: Victoria plum, red bronze, blue fire, oasis, moonlight, golden crocodile, green silver and pink ruby. *M:* 15 × 15cm (6 × 6in). *P:* from £47 sq yd. In the striking HOMAGE TO CHARLES RENNIE MACKINTOSH series, Margery Clinton re-

peats the square module which Mackintosh himself frequently used. Printed variously in matt blue, matt black or in lustre glazes Victoria plum or green silver, all on white, this range is intended chiefly for the contract market. *M:* 15 × 15cm (6 × 6in).

Margery Clinton's 'Kashan Cross' △ and 'Goose'△

CERAMIC TILES

*From Margery Clinton's 'MACKINTOSH'
series*

CUBIC METRE FURNITURE ⚠

Screen-printed ceramic tiles designed by
Minale, Tattersfield and partners and exclusive
to Cubic Metre. There are six designs: 'Rain/
Splash' with mid-blue diagonal strokes in single and crossed variations; 'Snooker Balls' with
three patterned tiles — a red ball, a green ball,
and blue and yellow balls together — for use at
random with plain white tiles; 'Jigsaw', tiles
like puzzle pieces with black outlines; 'Farfalla' with red and green stripes on two corners;
'Pasta', a collection of golden pasta shapes;
and 'Music' with two different tiles — one with
bass and treble clefs, one with continuation
lines only, all in black — forming a score. All
designs are on a white ground. *M:* 6 × 6in (15
× 15cm). *P:* 'Rain/Splash', 'Jigsaw' and 'Music'
£24.99 for 25; 'Snooker Balls' £12 for six; 'Farfalla' and 'Pasta' £27.99 for 25.

DOMUS LTD

From graphic chic to delicate Delft-like designs. SERIE ELEMENTARE lets you be the designer, in that there are 27 tiles in the range,
divided into three groups: dots, lines and
grids. Each of these motifs is printed positive
or negative on a white gound, in blue or
brown, and scaled up or down to produce designs of varying density. *M:* 20 × 20cm (8 ×
8in). *P:* £35 sq yd.
TELAIO is also based on a strong graphic element — the diagonal — and again the spaces
between the lines increase and decrease until
the tile looks almost plain. What is interesting
about the series is that the colours are mid-
tones: dusky pink, lime green, lilac and
orange, mixed and toned on a white ground,
so that the effect is pretty but clean. *M:* 20 ×
20cm (8 × 8in). *P:* £34 sq yd.
For subtle texture without pattern, consider
TRACCIA which has a light relief of lines across
its surface giving a slightly ribbed effect. Available in four styles: square, and three differently ribbed rectangles, TRACCIA 2 has heavy relief, while 1 has light relief. Colours are: white,
buff, grey, sea blue, black, bright blue, silver
and gold. *M:* 20 × 20cm (8 × 8in); 13 × 26cm (5
× 10¾in). *P:* black and white £32 sq yd; other
colours £37 sq yd.
In sparing INTUIZIONE, each tile bears just

two crossed coloured lines, but the tiles combine to form a large multicoloured grid lying
diagonally across a white wall. Also on a white
ground, original LAPIS design has naïve scrib-
bled yellow sun, blue clouds, turquoise rain,
green grass and red hearts. *M:* 20 × 20cm (8 ×
8in); 10 × 10cm (4 × 4in). *P:* £32–£35 sq yd.
Domus's collection of more traditional designs includes GRAFFITI, with naïve outlines of
fruit, fish, leaves and corn, all in mottled oatmeal, to be mixed with matching plain tiles.
BOTANICAL has delicate floral studies like
those in botanical prints, in realistic colours on
white. *M:* 10 × 10cm (4 × 4in). *P:* £5 each.
Plain colours are available in glossy white,
bright yellow, reds, oranges, blues, scarlet and
vivid green, and in softer rosy red, beige, light
blue, browns, pink and lilac. Not quite plain is
HARLEQUIN, a white tile with small coloured
triangles at the corners. There are pale terracottas and traditional black and white squares
and elongated hexagons, also available in
beige. *M:* 20 × 20cm (8 × 8in), 10 × 10cm (4 ×
4in); large terracottas 30 × 30cm (12 × 12in), 50
× 50cm (20 × 20in). *P:* £18–£35 sq yd.
Hand-painted majolica panels are available to
commission. TELAIO, INTUIZIONE, BOTA-
NICAL and some of the plain tiles and terracottas can be used for medium-wear floors as well
as walls; all the rest, except TRACCIA, can be
used for low-wear floors.

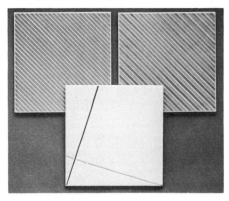

Domus' TELAIO and INTUIZIONE

ELON TILES LTD

Handmade and hand-painted tiles from Mexico. Glazed tiles come in 21 vibrant plain colours: white, Mexican white (off white), light
yellow, intense yellow, mustard, terracotta,
terracotta on white, orange, red, mauve, pink,
plum, chocolate, plain green, bottle green,
dark green, special green (a mottled blend),
Lascano (pale blue), plain blue, dark blue and
cobalt blue. *M:* approx 4 × 4in (10 × 10cm). *P:*
intense yellow, orange, red, plum and pure
white £49.68 sq yd; other colours £33.12 sq yd.
Hand-painted decorative tiles come in more
than 100 combinations of pattern and colour;
lively folk motifs such as flowers, birds and

*Worktop of Elon's hand-painted tiles in
'Seville' pattern*

leaves are common, though there are also
some ornate Spanish designs such as 'Madrid'
and 'Toledo'. Colours are traditionally Spanish
shades like terracotta, mustard, blue, green
and chocolate on an off-white background. *M:*
approx 4 × 4in (10 × 10cm) *P:* £49.68 for 72.
In addition there are 22 designs of hand-
painted fruits and vegetables, white tiles
painted with carrots, radishes, mangoes,
watermelons and a very realistic lettuce. Range
also includes number tiles. *M:* approx 4 × 4in
(10 ×10cm), *P:* £1.15 each.
Elon's FRENCH range has 12 plain colours in an
unusual mottled glaze: turquoise, miele roux
(shades of mustard and brown), mother of
pearl, antique green, shaded blue, rose, green
2 (olive), muscade (grey and brown), blanc cas-
se (white), myositis (pale blue), bleu ancien
(royal blue), and crème. They can be used on
walls, worktops and light wear floors. *M:* 4¼ ×
4¼in (10.6 × 10.6cm); 5¾ × 5¾in (16.8 ×
16.8cm). *P:* 4¼in tiles £51.75 for 72; 5¾in tiles
£32.29 for 39.

ELEANOR GREEVES ⚠

Hand-screened tiles in attractive symmetrical
floral designs especially sympathetic to period
houses. More than 20 patterns range from very
ornate 'Tudor Rose' and 'Turk's-cap Lily' to elegant 'Summer Leas', a vertical panel depicting
a climbing plant in a pot, and simple 'Rowan'
border; the last two are for use with H & R
Johnson's plain white tiles. All patterns are
printed on white, most in one colour, a few in
two. Ten stock colours are mid blue, buff, turquoise, olive, rust, lead blue, Grecian brown,
sage, lemon and amber; other colours and
combinations to order. Most tiles are suitable
for fireplace surrounds and worktops as well
as walls. *M:* 4¼ × 4¼in (10.75 × 10.75cm); 6 ×
6in (15 × 15cm). *P:* 4in tiles from £41.76 sq yd;
6in tiles from £28.08 sq yd.
See following page for illustrations.

*PRICES AND INFORMATION WERE CORRECT
AT THE TIME OF GOING TO PRESS*

Top: 'Sallie', 'Fleurs des Champs'; below: 'Thick and Thin', all from Habitat

C P HART & SONS LTD

Importers and distributors of CERABATI tiles from Paris. 'Cannage Raffia' with low relief designs of a canework pattern comes in solid white, dark blue or light brown. *M:* 15 × 15cm (6 × 6in). *P:* £16.90 sq m. Pretty 'Roseraie' comes with very flowery border design or one with posies and dots equally spaced, plus a plain white tile which also works with 'Cannage Raffia'. *M:* 20 × 20cm (8 × 8in). *P:* border tile £16.75 sq m; dotted £20.90; plain £17.75. All are suitable for walls or floors.

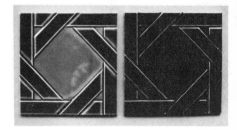

C P Hart's 'Cannage Raffia' by Cerabati

Top, left to right, from top: 'Buddleia'△, 'Fig-tree'△, 'Turk's-cap Lily', Tudor Rose'△; below: 'Summer Leas', 'Columbine'△. All from Eleanor Greeves

HABITAT DESIGNS LTD

Plain and patterned ceramic wall tiles from the famed purveyors of good taste. Plains come in white, bright red, cobalt blue, bright yellow and cream. Patterns include bright 'Redcurrant' featuring bunches of redcurrants; 'Fleur des Champs' with yellow, blue and red flowers and lime green stems, 'Thick and Thin' with bright blue borders; 'Sallie' with pale blue soft-printed pattern and matching border band; and 'Savoy Stripe' with thin red and grey diagonal stripe; all on white ground. 'Fleur des Champs' has matching wallpaper and fabric; 'Redcurrant' matching wallpaper, fabric and tinware. Tiles are sold in packs of 25; each pack includes set of useful spacer cards. *M:* all 15.2 × 15.2cm (6 × 6in). *P:* (per pack) plain white and cream £7.15; plain red £12.45; plain blue £9.85; plain yellow £10.65; 'Redcurrant', 'Thick and Thin' and 'Sallie' £14.20; 'Fleur des Champs' £19.70; 'Savoy Stripe' £17. Adhesive and grout also available from Habitat.

△ *INDICATES AN ILLUSTRATED PRODUCT SELECTED BY THE DESIGN CENTRE*

H & R JOHNSON LTD △

Cristal tiles, a comprehensive collection at budget prices from Britain's largest manufacturer, all colour co-ordinated with major British brands of sanitaryware. Plain wall tiles come in 37 gloss colours and 18 satin finish colours, the latter matching Cristal's satin finish floor tiles. In addition, NATURAL WHITES range includes plain tiles in lily, white, rose, apple and bluebell matching the Dulux paint range of the same name. Decorative CHERRY TREE has the same off-white backgrounds; the two designs — a tree in a pot and three falling cherries — can be mixed with plain tiles and used as decorative insets, borders or panels.

CERAMIC TILES

Tiles from C P Hart's 'Roseraie' range by Cerabati, with complementary border

Selection from H & R Johnson's IMAGES range

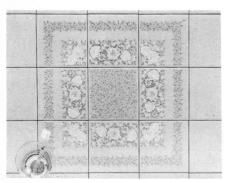

H & R Johnson's Cristal tiles in SHERIDAN range

M: plain 6 × 6in (15 × 15cm), 4¼ × 4¼in (10.75 × 10.75cm). *P:* plain £6 for 50; CHERRY TREE £1.50 for 10.
BLOOMSBURY and SHERIDAN ranges include wall tiles, floor tiles, shower curtains, roller blinds and bathroom fittings. BLOOMSBURY tiles have Edwardian-style floral panel and border designs available in the four NATURAL WHITES colourways, while SHERIDAN tiles have similarly delicate floral panels and borders in cream, pale blue, pale pink, avocado, and wild sage colourways. *M:* BLOOMSBURY 6 × 6in (15 × 15cm); SHERIDAN 4¼ × 4¼in

(10.75 × 10.75cm). *P:* BLOOMSBURY £12.80 for 25; SHERIDAN £13 for 70.
KITCHEN HARMONY range includes oatmeal plain tiles and various representational insets in brown on the same base, depicting kitchen utensils, dressers, windmills, oasthouses and willow trees. BRITTANY panels depicting pots, jars and grapes come on the same colour base. *M:* 6 × 6in (15 × 15cm); 4¼ × 4¼in (10.75 × 10.75cm). *P:* 'Willow' insets £1.50 for 10; 'Kitchen Things' insets £2.20 for 6.
'Spring Fayre' shows baskets overflowing with fruit in three of the RADIANCE range colourways: bark, honey (both light and brown shades) and topaz (light green). In the same range, 'Chrysalis' shows butterflies in six colourways: blue, honey, sepia, topaz, bark and champagne. *M:* 'Spring Fayre' £2.20 for 6; 'Chrysalis' £8.25 for 10.
IMAGES has three designs of impressionistic country scenes and plain tiles in faded pastel shades: beige, pale blue, pale pink and wild sage. *M:* 6 × 6in (15 × 15cm). *P:* plain £7.50 for 25; insets £2.20 for 6.
Cristal's popular MARBLE range of faintly marbled tiles includes off-white 'Marmora' plain tile and matching insets 'Antiquity' with classical bouquet motifs, and 'Avignon' with sprays of white blossom. *M:* 20 × 15cm (8 × 6in). *P:* 'Marmora' and 'Antiquity' £5 for 10; 'Avignon' £24.10 for 10.
H & R Johnson also offer a ceramic tile service for architects and designers, providing tiles to

order in an enlarged range of almost 70 plain colours with bright or satin finish, in ten different sizes. They can also produce a very full range of wall tile fittings, covings and mouldings in any plain colour from their range.

LANGLEY LONDON LTD

Seventy or so ranges including an exclusive collection from Villeroy & Boch of France, reputedly the world's largest ceramic tile manufacturer. Many of the vitrified glazed tiles are suitable for worktops and floors as well as walls, and the mosaics, some in unusual mottled colours, are equally versatile.
Villeroy & Boch's stunning COLLECTION BLEUE relies on charmingly naïve hand-painted bird designs and borders in blue on white. Enormous range comprises 82 designs for walls, two floor tiles, two flush strip tiles for square edgings, two convex border strip tiles with corner fittings, corner and edging tiles, and two soap tray designs. What's more, there are nine mural designs, the largest being 'The Bush' with 28 pieces, others being smaller sets depicting peacocks and cockerels, all edged with a choice of four crisp geometric borders or two with leaf designs. It is the largest single collection of co-ordinated designs Langley has ever introduced. *M:* 6 × 6in (15 × 15cm) except for border tiles. *P:* plain white wall tiles £14.91 sq yd; plain blue wall tiles £19.06 sq yd; border tiles £9.31 each; 'The Bush' £299.85.
Many floral insets and panels include a sweet trellis-and-flower border design, 'P17' and 'P37' in the ROSARIO range; available in pink or blue colourways. *M:* 19.8 × 19.8 (8 × 8in). *P:* £3.65 each. Simple SOLO series consists of a plain tile, two single design tiles with orange flowers on one and blue on the other, and a set of four tiles showing both blue and orange flowers. *M:* 15 × 15cm (6 × 6in). *P:* plain £15.69 sq yd; single £1.21 each; set of four £6.99.
MORNING series, an example of another of Villeroy & Boch's styles, consists of a plain tile, a single design tile, and a matching set of six showing a dawn scene with a bird flying from a flowering branch; available in pink and beige colourways. *M:* 20 × 15cm (8 × 6in). *P:* plain £18 sq yd; single £3.06 each; set of six £29.59.
Refreshingly different is GOLDEN NILE with Egyptian-style motifs in pale blue and gold on a sandy background and plain tiles. Co-ordinating floor tiles are also available. *M:* 19.8 × 29.8cm (12 × 8in). *P:* plain £3.29 each; patterned from £6.49 each; floor tiles £3.47 each. With a typically watery bathroom theme,

classically cool look, and more rustic cream and terracotta hexagons and brown and green Provençals. *M:* octagons 6.5 × 6.5cm (2½ × 2½in); black diamond insets 2.5 × 2.5cm (1 × 1in); hexagons 3.2 × 3.7cm (1¼ × 1½in); Provencals 9 × 5.5cm (3½ × 2in). *P:* £20.90–£29.27 sq yd.

CHELSEA rectangular mosaics come in pearly, mottled green, brown beige and blue. *M:* 10 × 7.5cm (4 × 3in). *P:* £26.51 sq yd. And RICHMOND is a mosaic in four pastel colours — matt white, powder blue, peppermint and shell beige — each with two matching flower pattern insets. *M:* 10 × 7.5cm (4 × 3in). *P:* plain £25.59 sq yd; patterned insets £1.17 each. Though not ceramic, luxurious SOLITAIRE mosaic should not be overlooked. Made from thick vitrified glass, it comes in five rich, 'marbled' colours: jade, onyx, amethyst, sapphire and topaz. *M:* 2 × 4cm (¾ × 1½in), supplied on 20 × 20cm (12 × 12in) sheets. *P:* £19.86–£21.23 sq yd.

JOHN LEWIS PARTNERSHIP ⚠

Four designs made exclusively for this well-known department store chain. 'Pastorale' has stylized flowers on a white background; 'Flik' has blue or red flecks on white; 'Graphic' is a red or blue graph design; and 'Pretty Pastels Series' has pink-and-green or blue-and-green stripes on white. *M:* 6 × 6in (15 × 15cm). *P:* 'Pastorale' 79p each; 'Flik' and 'Graphic' 62p each; 'Pretty Pastels' 49p each.

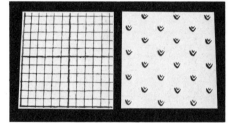

John Lewis's 'Graphic' and 'Flik'△

MARLBOROUGH CERAMIC TILES ⚠

Wide variety of patterned wall tiles. Among the most fashionable are four simple designs in fresh colours on a white background: 'Quilt', an attractive trellis pattern; 'Frames' which is bordered by two coloured lines; and the self-explanatory 'Polka Dot' and 'Asterisk'. Each is available in 12 colours — burgundy, tomato, cinnamon, ice pink, ice blue, powder blue, ice green, wild sage, champagne, pampas, avocado and apple green — and other colours to special order. 'Ice' colours are designed to match Ideal Standard's WHISPER sanitaryware. *M:* 15 × 15cm (6 × 6in). *P:* £18.95 sq yd. These can be teamed up with five border and corner designs: 'Tulip', 'Link', 'Daisy', 'Rosette' and 'Greek Key'. All are available in the above colours, and in some of the following

Above: Langley's SOLO series on bathroom floor, walls and surrounds, by Villeroy & Boch; left: examples of 'Yacht' and 'Seagull' tiles from Langley's MARINA range, also by Villeroy & Boch

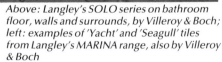

MARINA series depicts yachts, seagulls and waves; suitable for walls, floors and worktops. *M:* 9.8 × 9.8cm (4 × 4in), supplied in 29.8 × 49.8cm (12 × 20in) sheets. *P:* £18–£34 sq yd; single design £1.81 each. Of Villeroy & Boch's mosaics, the varied FLORENCE range comes in ten colours: golden brown, variegated cream, sea shell (dark grey), variegated bronze, green, russet brown, sand beige, brown beige, desert gold and orange. *M:* 5 × 5cm (2 × 2in). *P:* £29.53–£33.66 sq yd. Langley also make their own mosaics ranges for all-over use. GREENWICH series includes white octagons inset with black diamonds for a

CERAMIC TILES

additional shades: chocolate, mustard, dark blue, pink, marron, saffron, moss, yellow, champagne, oatmeal, Dutch blue, deep coral, and earthy shades Avon blue, Avon green and Avon brown. *M:* 'Tulip', 'Link' and 'Daisy' borders 15 × 7.5cm (6 × 3in), corners 7.5 × 7.5cm (3 × 3in); 'Rosette' and 'Greek Key' borders 15 × 7.5cm (6 × 3in) or 20 × 7.5cm (8 × 3in), corners 7.5 × 7.5cm (3 × 3in). *P:* 'Tulip', 'Link', 'Daisy' £1 each; 'Rosette', 'Greek Key' (small) £1 each, (large) £1.54 each.

Marlborough also manufacture plain ART GLAZES tiles in 14 colours: matt white, willow green, oyster, coral, azure, ivory, magnolia, Dutch blue, ice white, brown, Jade, honey, turquoise and oatmeal. *M:* 15 × 15cm (6 × 6in). *P:* from £12.40 sq yd. To co-ordinate with these is a wide range of decorative insets; some of the most attractive are DELFT designs. *M:* 15 × 15cm (6 × 6in). *P:* 60p each. (All prices ex VAT.)

Left: Marlborough's 'Tulip', 'Greek Key' and 'Link' border designs △; above: DELFT patterned insets, also from Marlborough, include 'Delft Scenes', 'Fruit Bowls' and 'Medallions'

MAW & CO △

Three ranges of ceramic wall tiles. CONTRASTS has delicate sprig insets and simply patterned field tiles in five colourways: white on blue, avocado, burgundy, sage green and sepia. Field tiles are also available with the colourway reversed, providing the 'contrast'. TRANQUILLITY, coloured to co-ordinate with Cristal NATURAL WHITES from H & R Johnson (see separate entry), is a range of soft floral

Maw & Co's CONTRASTS

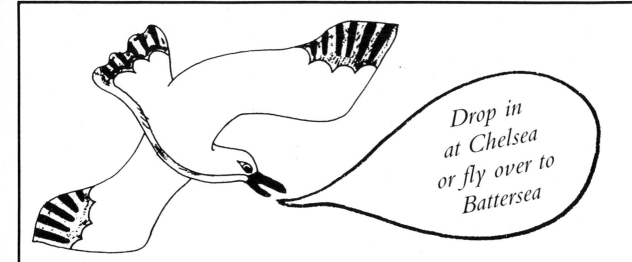

See opposite page for key

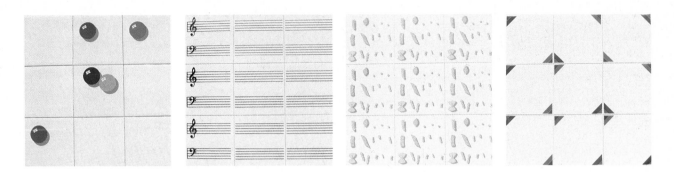

Cubic Metre tiles. From left: 'Snooker Balls', 'Music', 'Pasta' and 'Farfalla'

Selection of ceramic tiles opposite: World's End's DELFT 'Diamond' (1), DELFT inset tile from Marlborough (2), Habitat's 'Thick and Thin' (3), hand-painted bird tile from Rye (4), Jayne Simcock's 'Minstrel' (5), Margery Clinton's 'Homage to Charles Rennie Mackintosh' (6 and 27), Habitat's 'Sallie' (7), 'Delft' border from World's End (8), Skye's 'Palm' (9), Rustichiana's 'Trellis' (10), MARINA tiles from Langley (11 and 17), striped tile from Habitat (12), Capital Ceramics' LINDOS (13) and inset (14), World's End's 'Antwerp Plain' (15), BODIAM tile from Rye (16), John Lewis's 'Graphic' (18), Marlborough's 'Tulip' border (19), Rye's 'Handkerchief' (20), SOLITAIRE mosaic pieces from Langley (21 and below), Rustichiana's 'Hearts and Dots' (22), Rye's 'May' border (23), World's End's 'Antwerp Pattern' (24), MAIOLICHE D'ARTE tile from Nicobond (25), Marlborough Ceramics' 'Quilt' (26), Rye's 'Blazer' (28), H & E Smith's dado moulding (29), Rye's 'Borderline' (30), 'Delft Scenes' tile from Marlborough (31), Jayne Simcock's 'Pernod' (32), World's End's 'Flanders' (33), H & E Smith's 'Grape' (34), Rye's 'Ticking' (35), C P Hart's 'Cannage Raffia' (36), Capital Ceramics' PATRAS (37)

Selection of tiles overleaf: Nicobond's PRECIOUS plain tile (1), ALMOND tile from World's End (3), Domus's TRACCIA 2 (4, 5, 6 and 7), unglazed floor tile from Elon (8), SERIE CHIC tile from Capital Ceramics (9), Elon's intense yellow glazed tile (10), Domus's TELAIO (12, 13 and 14), hexagonal unglazed floor tile from Elon (15), A G Tiles' GEMSTONE (17) and ROCKWARE (18), glazed square tile (19) and LINDOS tile (20) from Capital Ceramics, A G Tiles' ANTIQUE (21), Elon's pink glazed floor tile (22) and 'Provence' unglazed floor tile (23), Laura Ashley's burgundy tile (24) and 'Quatrefoil' (25), SERIE ELEMENTARE designs from Domus (26, 27, 28, 29 and 30), Capital Ceramics' FOURPLUS (32 and 33), Langley's 'Palissy' (34 and 35), rectangular unglazed floor tile from Elon; also four marble tiles from Ceramic Tile Design (2, 11, 16 and 31), see Flooring

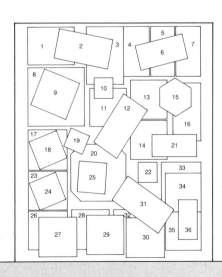

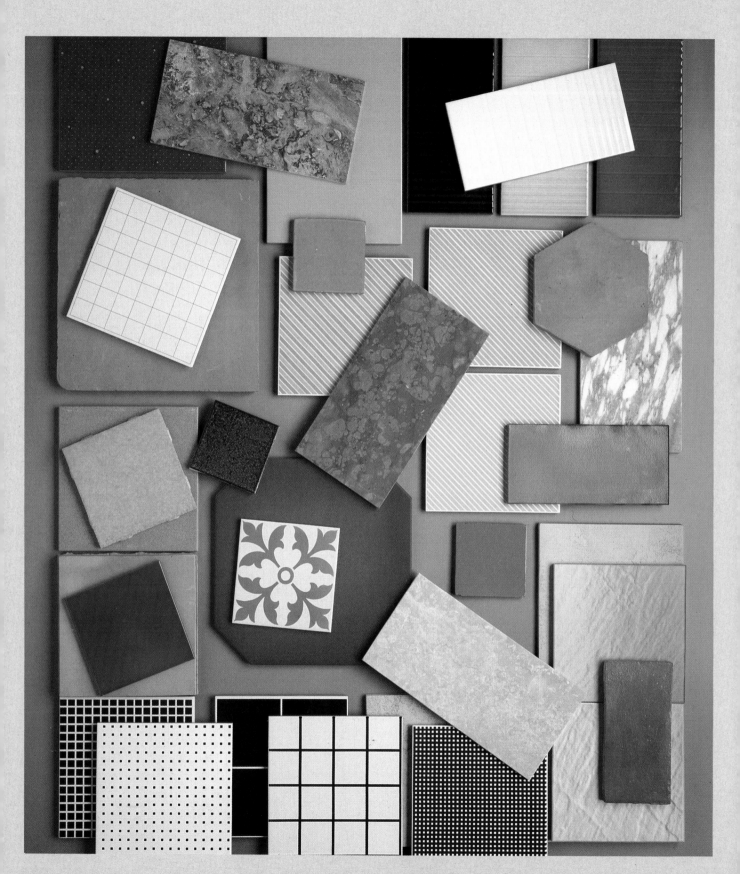

See previous page for key

patterns in bluebell, lily, apple and rose shades. Tiles can be used singly or made up into panels. BRIGHT WHITES collection is a range of six hand-screened designs: 'Daisy Chain' and 'Apple Tree' have simple modern motifs; 'Pretty Profiles' insets depict women in wide-brimmed hats; 'Cross Hatch' and 'Crayon Creations' are wild scribbly designs; and 'Delicate Dots' comprises three pointillist patterns. *M:* 6 × 6in (15 × 15cm). *P:* CONTRASTS £16 sq yd; TRANQUILLITY £9 for six; BRIGHT WHITES £18 sq yd.

Top: Maw & Co's 'Daisy Chain' from BRIGHT WHITES; bottom: 'Delicate Dots'△ from the same range

Under the name Minton Hollins, Maw offer a comprehensive range of Victorian-style tiles, many reproduced from nineteenth-century originals. Maw also produce hand-painted panels to commission using traditional majolica techniques; and for the contract market, will silkscreen individual designs on H & R Johnson's standard plain tiles. *P:* on application.

△ *INDICATES ONE OR MORE OF THE PRODUCTS MENTIONED ARE SELECTED BY THE DESIGN CENTRE*

NICOBOND LTD

Large collection of British and foreign tiles. MAIOLICHE D'ARTE is a range of five attractive Italian tiles, one plain and four with simple geometric or formal flower motifs, in shades of blue and touches of yellow on blue-white. *M:* 15 × 15cm (6 × 6in). *P:* £9.78 sq yd.

Nicobond's 21 ranges of dainty floral designs include matching plain tiles in a wide range of pale shades, some with mottled glaze. CONTRADE SENESI includes five subtle plain shades, from cream and watery blue to mossy green, and decorated tiles with wild flower motifs. *M:* 13.3 × 20cm (5 × 7¾in). *P:* £10.32 sq yd. SAMBA has plain tiles in palest beige or grey-blue with darker border; the decorated ones show flowers, grass or corn. *M:* 15 × 15cm (6 × 6in). *P:* £7.73 sq yd. PRECIOUS has floral motif on a dotted background; plain tiles have the background alone. Available in pale blue, cream and unusual dark shades of grey-brown and russet. *M:* 20 × 25cm (7¾ × 9¾in). *P:* £21.76 sq yd. Nicobond also sell their own ranges of tiling cements and grouts.

Top: Nicobond's 'NC1642' and 'NC1644' from MAIOLICHE D'ARTE series; bottom: 'NC2041' and 'NC2040' from their PRECIOUS range

PILKINGTON'S TILES LTD △

Wide selection from one of Britain's largest manufacturers, who specialize in bathroom tiles. The 67 shades in their PLAIN COLOURS AND EFFECTS range are enough to co-ordinate with any shade of sanitaryware. In addition to dozens of wistful floral designs, there are some more up-to-the-minute ranges such as MARBLE and GRID. TONES has a chic diagonal stripe in five shades: whisper pink, whisper blue, whisper green, ivory and fawn (to match Ideal Standard's WHISPER sanitaryware). *M:* 6 × 6in (15 × 15cm). *P:* £16.50 sq yd. ECHOES has

Dolphin pattern from Pilkington's SATIN range

a soft blurry pattern in the same muted colours. *M:* 8 × 6in (20 × 15cm). *P:* £17.50 sq yd. CLASSIC is a range of five attractive Victorian-inspired tiles in period colours — Afghan red, sage, plum, olive, blue or fawn on white. *M:* 6 × 6in (15 × 15cm). *P:* £17.60 sq yd. The many pictorial tiles and decorative insets include SATIN, satin-finished tiles with insets depicting water-lilies, waves, dolphins or swans. *M:* 8 × 8in (20 × 20cm). *P:* from £18.50 sq yd.

S POLLIACK LTD

Opulent bathroom sanitaryware and co-ordinating accessories, including tiles. Although the hand-painted tiles are designed to match the bath suites, there's no reason why they could not be used to add individuality to an all-white scheme. Tiles come plain, marbled or decorated, each with border tiles also available. Designs include 'Primavera' with green leaves on a brown stem, optionally also with butterflies, 'Flori Blu' with full flowerheads and 'Belle Epoch' with real gold swirls. All designs can also be supplied in mural form.

CERAMIC TILES

M: decorated wall tiles 13 × 26cm (5 × 10¼in); 26 × 26cm (10¼ × 10¼in). *P:* £7.50–£9 each. See also *Bathrooms.*

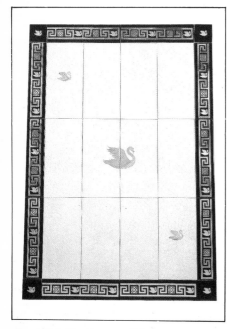

One of S Polliack's one-off designs

RAMUS TILE COMPANY

Contrasting ranges of tiles under the trade name Sumara. BELLE ARTE range includes richly coloured lily-pond design and swirling art nouveau motifs that would be ideal for a Victorian or Edwardian house. There are also delicate transfer insets: botanical 'Lily' and 'Cherry Blossom' and sepia-toned pastoral 'Angler', 'Shepherd', and 'Flautist'. *M:* 15 × 15cm (6 × 6in). *P:* £1.89–£2.84 each. TRAVERTINO is inspired by ancient Rome: crumbling columns, urns and orange trees can be combined in panels, insets and borders. *M:* 15 × 20cm (6 × 8in). *P:* plain £14.54 sq m; patterned insets from £3.75 each.

More contemporary is JEUNESSE, plain grey tiles with narrow strips in bright red, blue, yellow, green or black, providing bold borders. *M:* plain grey 15 × 15cm (6 × 6in); strips 15 × 2.5cm (6 × 1in). *P:* plain grey £10.35 sq yd; strips 50p each. And GEOMETRICA is a simple modern design in one of four base colours — grey, beige, white or ivory — over-printed with red, yellow, blue and grey grid lines. *M:* 20 × 25cm (8 × 10in). *P:* £16.13 sq m.

SYLVIA ROBINSON

Beautiful tiled panels hand-painted to commission. Sylvia Robinson has undertaken a variety of projects from a reproduction of Botticelli's Venus to *trompe l'oeil* views and vases

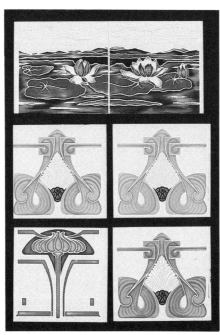

Art nouveau designs from Ramus's BELLE ARTE range

From Sylvia Robinson: a vase of flowers with decorative border tiles

of flowers. Each panel is a one-off, designed and coloured to suit the location, with a happy feel for the period of the house. *M:* 6 × 6in (15 × 15cm). *P:* from approx £8 per tile for the design shown here. (Send s.a.e. for details).

PRICES AND INFORMATION WERE CORRECT AT THE TIME OF GOING TO PRESS

RUSTICHIANA LTD

Tiles to go with SARTOR and UPSTAIRS ranges of co-ordinating fabrics, wallpapers and bed-linen (see *Fabrics, co-ordinates*). The same six fresh and pretty designs are printed on white in one, two or three of the following colours: blue, yellow, green, pink, red, beige. In one colour are 'Hearts and Dots', a sweet all-over pattern; 'La Tigre', a wavy stripe; and 'Trellis', with all-over lattice weave. In two colours are 'Ivy League' with pattern of small sprigs; and 'Hyacinth', with bunches at regular intervals. 'Carnation', with central spray and border, comes in three colours. *M:* 15 × 15cm (6 × 6in). *P:* one-colour £32 sq yd; two-colour £37 sq yd; three-colour £42.25 sq yd. Available through decorators and selected stores.

Left to right, from top: Rustichiana's 'Hyacinth', 'La Tigre', 'Ivy League', 'Hearts and Dots', 'Carnation' and 'Trellis'

RYE TILES 🔥

Huge range of handmade tiles in old and new designs. Enamel-printed wall tiles include stripes and geometrics such as 'Chevron', 'Blazer' and 'Ticking', 'Handkerchief' and 'Shirtsleeves', all imitating fabrics. There are pretties such as 'Forget Me Not' and 'Sloe'; and period-style designs such as art deco 'Big Deco' and Edwardian-inspired 'Apollo'. Enamels come in 92 colours. *M:* 4 × 4in (10cm × 10cm); 6 × 6in (15 × 15cm). *P:* 6in tiles from £22 for 36; 4in tiles from £23 for 72. Rye will also produce enamel printed hexagons with bird, insect and flower motifs. *M:* 4in or 6in (10 or 15cm). *P:* £35–£37.

There is also a range of hand-painted tiles based on delicate eighteenth-century designs showing boats or more birds and bugs. Available in innumerable permutations of colour and motif — but the number of colours, and the shades chosen, influence the price. Similar subjects are hand-painted within a soft, lightly hand-sprayed border in the BODIAM range, with matching hand-sprayed plain tiles. *M:* 6 × 6in (15 × 15cm); 4¼ × 4¼in (10.75 × 10.75cm); 4 × 4in (10 × 10cm). *P:* 6in tiles from £2 each. Most are suitable for floors and fireplaces as well as walls.

Also hand-sprayed, the SHADOW BODIAM range comprises three designs: 'Shadow Star',

'Shadow Curviligne' and 'Shadow Chevron'. As the names suggest, the technique produces a soft, blurry effect over the stencil shapes. Available in two-tone mixes of pink, blue, coral, brown, jade, green, avocado or grey, or in two-colour mixes. *M:* 6 × 6in (15 × 15cm); 4¼ × 4¼in (10.75 × 10.75cm). *P:* from £44 sq yd. These, too, can be used for walls, floors and fireplaces.

Eight eye-catching border designs, with corner tiles, are printed in Rye's bright enamel colours on a clean white background. These again range from modern to traditional: from 'Cherry', with its bright bunches of cherries, to bold 'Borderline' stripe, severe 'Chess Border' and elaborate 'Deco' and 'Victorian'. *M:* 6 × 6in (15 × 15cm); 4¼ × 4¼in (10.75 × 10.75cm); 4 × 4in (10 × 10cm). *P:* 6in tiles from £24 for 36; 4in tiles from £25 for 72. Similar floor tiles are available in 20 shades.

Rye make square and hexagonal plain glazed wall and floor tiles in 20 standard colours and other colours to order. *M:* 6 × 6in (15 × 15cm); whites only 4¼ × 4¼in (10.75 × 10.75cm); hexagons dia 6in (15cm); 4 × 4in (10 × 10cm) and 6 × 3in (15 × 7.5cm) tiles sometimes available. *P:* £29–£38 sq yd.

Hand-painted murals, panels and customers' own printed designs can be commissioned.

Hand-painted bird design and BODIAM tile with flower motif△, from Rye

JAYNE SIMCOCK ⚠

Striking original designs hand-printed in almost any colourway. Jayne Simcock's range of square wall tiles includes ten vibrant

Selection of Jayne Simcock's designs. Left to right, from top: 'Cocktail Glasses', 'Star Wars'△, 'Pernod'△, 'Pennant'△, 'Rambling Rose' and 'Minstrel'

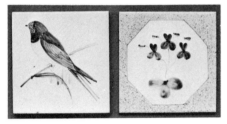

Jayne Simcock's 'Pennant' geometric△

geometrics; witty 'Cocktail Glasses' showing three long-stemmed glasses with bubbles rising from them; 'Vineyard' with a strong design of grapes, curling tendrils and foliage; and symmetrical floral 'Rambling Rose'. Her five borders comprise two with Amerindian-inspired motifs, 'Andes' and 'Totonac'; and three with classical and Egyptian motifs, swirling 'Oinochoe' and more detailed 'Amphora' and 'Dandarah'. There is a standard range of approximately 40 printed colours; special colours can be mixed if required. Border designs are available on white tiles only; square designs are usually on white or bone but coloured base tiles can be selected at 18 per cent surcharge. *M:* 6 × 6in (15 × 15cm); borders 6 × 3in (15 × 7.5cm). *P:* square tiles £24.19–£29.56; border tiles 90p–£1.15 each. Light duty floor tiles can be supplied on special request, with white base only.

SKYE CERAMICS ⚠

More than 60 silkscreen designs, some with co-ordinating fabric. Patterns include grids and polka dots, line borders and lattices, Delft and Victorian, and conventional detailed florals. 'Intermezzo' is an unusual composite linear pattern, 'Palm' a broad, simplified leaf design. Some of the tiles, such as classic 'Cane' lattice, have matching decorative border. Designs with co-ordinating fabric include dainty 'Wild Rose Trellis', 'Tumbleweed' and 'Daisy Field'; 'Maize' with diamond motif; bold 'Hills' with two broad diagonal stripes used to make up diamonds and zigzags; and 'Fitzwarren' a leafy lattice. (Fabrics are 100 per cent cotton, and Skye Ceramics can provide them plasti-

Designs by Skye Ceramics. Top: 'Palm' in two mirror-image tiles△; bottom: 'Cane'△, 'Cane Border'△ and 'Hills'

cized for shower curtains or made up into roller blinds.) Tiles are available in approximately 30 standard colours, and special colours at nominal extra charge, on white or coloured base tiles. Up to four colours can be used, depending on the design, and the number of colours determines the price. Unusual spatter-effect tiles (available in any colour or combination of colours) can also be used as a base for printing. *M:* 6 × 6in (15 × 15cm); border tiles 6 × 3in (15 × 7.5cm); 4¼ × 4¼in (11 × 11cm). *P:* 6in tiles £21.25–£29.96 for 36; border tiles £22.74–£27.46 for 72; 4¼in tiles £21.80–£27.34 for 72; one-colour spatter tiles £27 sq yd.

Skye will also make silkscreened or hand-painted underglaze or on-glaze tiles and picture panels entirely to customer specification — anything from 'Satoshi' Japanese landscape to a picture of the Roman baths at Bath, or just a pattern taken from fabric or wallpaper. (The underglaze method produces a softer effect with more muted colours than the on-glaze painting.) *M:* 6 × 6in (15 × 15cm); 8 × 8in (20.5 × 20.5cm). *P:* on application.

H & E SMITH LTD

VICTORIAN tiles with embossed peony or fruit designs, narrow embossed fruit borders, two styles of decorative moulding, plus plain and cove tiles, for lovely old-fashioned dadoes. All have highly polished glaze in colours typical of the period: bianco (white), Victorian brown and tea pot brown (plain and milk chocolate

H & E Smith's 'Grape' design with dado moulding

CERAMIC TILES

shades that look good combined), dark green and blue. 'Grape' and 'Fig' relief designs can also be hand-decorated, the shapes picked out in touches of other colour. *M:* 6 × 6in (15 × 15cm); borders 6 × 3in (15 × 7.5cm); coves 6 × 4in (15 × 10cm); mouldings 6 × 3in (15 × 7.5cm). *P:* embossed £4.50 each; plain £25 sq yd; dado mouldings £2.50 each.
H & E Smith also make plain tiles some of which are suitable both for walls and light duty floors. Squares with rounded corners come in tango red, French white and French blue. Squares, hexagons, octagons with contrasting diamonds, Provençal shapes and Dijon (elongated hexagons) come in nine colours: autumn (brown), harvest (speckled sand), almond, lime, kelp (dark green), bilberry, Aegean, bianco and basalt (dark grey). Some are available with dapple-textured surface as well as smooth. *M:* squares and octagons 6 × 6in (15 × 15cm); hexagons 6 × 7in (15 × 18cm) or 4 × 4½in (10 × 11.5cm); Provençal 5¼ × 4¾in (14 × 12cm); Dijon 8½ × 2½in (21.5 × 6.5cm). *P:* £15–£20 sq yd.

SPHINX TILES LTD
Large collection of wall tiles with a floral emphasis and pictorial insets. PORTRAIT insets show rustic scenes, BLEND insets a collection of still lifes. *M:* 15 × 15cm (6 × 6in). *P:* on application. IBIZA includes a variety of floral designs, all in Sphinx's characteristic soft shades of off-white, beige, pale blue and pink but also a contrasting border, 'Greco', and matching 'Greco Centre', both using a diamond motif in pink, green or blue colourways. *M:* 15 × 15cm (6 × 6in). *P:* £14.48 sq yd. CHATTERLEY includes 'Blue Birds', on a white ground, and vertical panels in which the birds appear framed within window panes; also a restrained linear border in blue on white or tan on beige. *M:* border 15 × 15cm (6 × 6in), 'Blue Birds' 20 × 15cm (8 × 6in). *P:* £14.48 sq yd. SIGNATURE includes two more simple borders, in reddish-brown on buff, stylized grass and humming-bird designs, and plain tiles. *M:* 20 × 15cm (8 × 6in); 15 × 15cm (6 × 6in). *P:* plain £18.62 sq yd; decorated £22 sq yd. ARCHITECTURAL range

Examples from two of Sphinx's inset ranges. Top: PORTRAIT; bottom: BLEND

comprises 12 plain colours: mushroom, African grey, alpine white, matt black, stone grey, damask, parchment, olive, dove grey, pearl, sand and ivory. *M:* 15 × 15cm (6 × 6in); 20 × 10cm (8 × 4in), 20 × 15cm (8 × 6in). *P:* from £14.48 sq yd.

WORLD'S END TILES ▲
Terrific collection of classic and modern tiles silkscreened by hand in clear, bright colours, and special designs to commission. Budget RED STOCK range offers a variety of bold grids, stripes, dots and geometric outlines in red on white. *M:* 6 × 6 (15 × 15cm); 8 × 8in (20 ×20cm). *P:* £15 sq yd.
MULTI-RANGE has fresh multicoloured patterns — 'Multi-diamond', 'Multi-dot', 'Multi-tulip' and 'Multi-stripe' — in both primary and pastel versions of red, yellow, green and blue on white. *M:* 6 × 6in (15 × 15cm); 8 × 6in (20 × 15cm). *P:* £25.50 sq yd.
BRITISH WALL TILES range includes about 50 designs, each available in 35 colourways. 'Hatched Trellis', 'Grid', 'Chequer', 'Waffle' and 'Rattan' are linear designs on white. In contrast are more ornate 'Petal 2' and 'Renaissance 2', luxurious 'Fleur de Lys' and traditional Victorian fields and borders such as 'Albion', 'Open Field' and 'Linear Flower Border'. *M:* 6 × 6in (15 × 15cm); border tiles 6 × 3in (15 ×

World's End Tiles. Left to right, from top: 'Multi-dot', 'Multi-diamond', 'Multi-stripe' and 'Multi-tulip', all from MULTI-RANGE △; bottom: two designs from 'EBB TIDE'

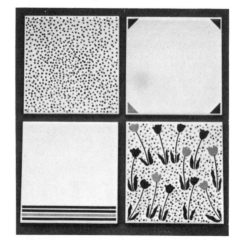

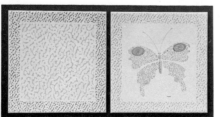

7.5cm). *P:* £21–30 sq yd.
Unusual EBB TIDE, three co-ordinating designs in pastel colours, was inspired by the look of sand corrugated by the ebbing tide. *M:* 6 × 6in (15 × 15cm). *P:* £29.90 sq yd.
DESIGNER'S RANGE includes an oriental-style border, a four-tone stripe, deco 'Palm' design, and period-style floral with contrasting border. The 35 colourways include some sophisticated combinations, varying tones of grey, pale pink and blue. The number of colours required for each design determines the price. *M:* 8 × 8in (20 × 20cm). *P:* £25–30 sq yd.
DELFT, though British made, is a range of classic Dutch designs in blue on blue-white glaze. *M:* 6 × 6in (15 × 15cm). *P:* £13.50 sq yd.
World's End also import traditional tiles from Spain and Portugal, and some beautiful Italian tiles such as Enrico Coveri's exotic jungle prints and his 'Blue Sea', cool as a Hockney swimming pool, or elegant ARIANA tiles with marbled glazes, complemented by ceramic and wood friezes and dadoes. *M:* 6 × 6in (15 × 15cm). *P:* from £23 sq yd.
(All prices ex VAT.)

World's End Tiles. Left to right, from top: 'Diamond' △, 'Delft Border' △, 'Flanders' △, 'Antwerp Pattern' △, plain white △, 'Antwerp Plain' △; bottom: a selection from the ITALIAN range

PRICES AND INFORMATION WERE CORRECT AT THE TIME OF GOING TO PRESS

INTRODUCTION

The possibilities are endless. Between them, the painters on the following pages can create almost any effect.

They'll paint original patterns and designs, imitate a motif from a fabric, wallpaper or object in the room, dress an entire wall in a *trompe l'oeil* vista. They'll gild, lacquer, apply false finishes such as marbling and tortoiseshelling, and execute a whole gamut of fashionable painted finishes. Most common of these are dragging (sometimes called graining), a striated, liney effect simulating wood; ragging (or rag-rolling), done with coiled, bunched and/or rolled rags to give an irregularly mottled surface; and stippling, a pointillistic effect applied with a special brush, which can be overlaid with other special finishes. Also popular is stencilling, which is in many ways the most adaptable finish: once cut, the stencil can be used again and again, to unite disparate objects and features in a room. Prices, of course, vary considerably from process to process, job to job — lacquering, for example, is extremely time-consuming and thus costly.

Hand-painted effects can be used individually or in combinations, and applied to practically anything, from small objects to large pieces of furniture, from door or shutter panels to an entire room.

● Most of the artists included here specialize in painted finishes alone, but a few design furniture as well. For other designers and makers of pieces to which finishes may be applied, see *Furniture, special*.

ARTISAN DESIGN

Specialists in decorative ceilings. An example of their work is a timber relief ceiling with coloured panels and gilded mouldings, inspired by Middle-Eastern designs, but they will produce all kinds of decorative effects to order. *P:* on application. See also *Kitchens* and *Bathrooms, accessories*.

JACQUELINE BATEMAN

Experienced mural painter and artist. Her work is described as 'witty and amusing, with touches of *trompe l'oeil*; her colours fresh and vibrant', and she has executed many projects for both private and commercial clients. *P:* on application.

ROBERT & COLLEEN BERY

Decorative painters who also design and make furniture. They will stencil their own delicate, flowery or Japanese-inspired designs on to panels, window shutters, blinds, glass, etc, and execute stencilled friezes and borders on walls. Friezes can be applied direct to wall or to wallcovering — even on to stretched silk. The

Timber relief ceiling by Artisan Design

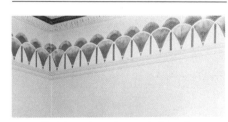

Stencilled frieze by Robert & Colleen Bery

Berys will also adapt designs from fabrics or elsewhere. *P:* frieze, basic design fee plus £5 per 12in (30.5cm). See also *Furniture, special*.

CHRISTOPHER BOULTER

Highly experienced muralist, frieze painter and designer with an unusual flair for decoration over a wide field of styles, including *trompe l'oeil*, Egyptian and baroque. He specializes in murals, but marbling or 'stone' finish can be carried out as an addition or background to the work. *P:* on application. See following page for illustration.

ANDREW BRADLEY

A fine artist who will apply all kinds of murals and decorative finishes, including marbling, stippling, stencilling and rag-rolling. His work ranges from a large mural in the children's ward of a London hospital to Austrian-style painted furniture. *P:* on application.

One of Andrew Bradley's decorative paintings

ROSEMARY CAMDEN

A marbler who specializes in fireplaces and furniture. She will work on plaster, wood or fibreglass, and can also put an attractive new finish of a preferred colour on to an ugly marble. *P:* on application.

Re-marbled fireplace by Rosemary Camden

NAOMI COLVIN

A decorator who applies special finishes to furniture. Her work is particularly suited to larger pieces such as chests, mirror frames, screens, tables and lamps, which show her bold designs and the application of the techniques to best advantage. She does traditional shellac and modern heat-resistant lacquering, all forms of gilding — even on glass — stippling and marbling. She also undertakes restoration work. *P:* on application. See following page for illustration.

PRICES AND INFORMATION WERE CORRECT AT THE TIME OF GOING TO PRESS

DECORATIVE PAINTERS

Mural by Christopher Boulter

Lacquered screen by Naomi Colvin

DAVIES KEELING TROWBRIDGE
Original decorative effects for interiors. Traditional specialist painting techniques such as stippling, marbling, stencilling, *trompe l'oeil*, etc., are used, but new styles and solutions are developed if required. A complete scheme of colour, line and texture can be carried out, from main architectural elements to the smallest detail.

Also, individual commissions are taken for the design, production and decoration of screens, window shutters, fabric, etc. The group has wide experience in both private and commercial contracts, and has worked in Europe, the Middle East, the Far East and America.
P: on application.

DECARTE
A pair of trained artists and restorers who offer an imaginative and personal service in interior decorative finishes. Frances Denny and Fiona Olivier carry out marbling, wood-graining, stippling, rag-rolling, spongeing and dragging to high standards on virtually any surface, and will paint murals or *trompe l'oeil*. They will also restore paint, gilding, lacquer and inlay.
P: on application.

ALAN DODD
Virtuoso mural painter of landscape and architectural fantasy; *trompe l'oeil* in the

Gilded mouldings and dome at the Royal Waiting Room, Windsor Station, restored for Madame Tussaud's by Decarte

Neo-classical entrance hall by Alan Dodd

Flowered stencil design by Susie Gradwell

gamut of eighteenth-century tastes. He designs and paints furniture too, and on a larger scale designs small architectural features and garden buildings. *P:* on application.

EXCLUSIVE ART
A muralist and decorator, Andrea Hayward, who will paint original compositions or children's favourite storybook characters (washable!) to order. *P:* original composition, such as a sunset or country scene, from £100; children's murals from £30 for background, £20–£50 for large figures, animals etc.; £5 for small additional details..

JOHN FISHER
An unusual mode of portrait painting. John Fisher will paint 'period' or contemporary murals incorporating family portraits, or individual freestanding 'silent companion' portrait boards. *P:* on application.

DAVID GILLESPIE ASSOCIATES LTD
Specialists in one-off effects for architects and contract designers such as decorative ceilings, domes, screens, even emblems and logos. They also do decorative wall claddings including relief murals using such materials as metal, GRP, Zerodec, wood or glass, working with a variety of techniques to produce entirely unique results. Clients supplied with preliminary colour sketches and costings. *P:* on application. See also *Architectural ornaments, Furniture, Screens.*

One of John Fisher's 'period' portraits

SUSIE GRADWELL STENCILS
Hand-painted original stencils, created either to co-ordinate with clients' own furnishing fabrics or decorative objects, such as a favourite china vase, or in themes, such as herbs, wild flowers, animals, buildings, and so on. Ingenious variations in colour and tone make a delightfully fresh and vital effect for friezes, borders or spot motifs. Susie Gradwell

also does ragging, spongeing or marbling on any interior surface. *P:* £60 per day plus fees for preparation of new designs, and expenses.

HAMPSTEAD DECORATIVE ARTS
An association of artists and craftsmen covering the entire range of decorative paint finishes on furniture and interiors: rag-rolling, stippling, dragging, spongeing, marbling, graining, exotic finishes, stencilling, gilding, *trompe l'oeil* and murals. The members of the group work individually or as a team, depending on the work required. *P:* on application. Commissions are also taken for handmade furniture; restoration and polishing are also undertaken.

Marbled frame by Hampstead Decorative Arts

DECORATIVE PAINTERS

HAND PAINTED STENCILS

Original stencil design, cutting and execution by Felicity Binyon and Elizabeth Macfarlane. Their work has been commissioned for a range of houses from country cottages to stately homes, and they will produce designs for floors, friezes, dadoes, furniture or whole rooms. Clients' fabrics can be matched if desired. *P:* on application.

Circus cat design by Hand Painted Stencils

MARK, JEAN & ROSAMUNDE HORNAK

A family of highly experienced specialist painters who, with colleagues taught by them, will undertake a wide range of jobs of any scale, great or small. Their specialities include murals and *trompe l'oeil*, false stonework, wood-

Marbled pillar by Mark Hornak

graining and marbling.
Painted silk (by Jean Hornak), painted furniture, gilding and restoration work are carried out in their studios. The hallmarks of this company's work are colour control, verve and period feeling.
P: on application.

INSIDE STORY LTD

A complete painting and decorating service. Every type of specialist paintwork, including dragging, stippling, ragging and distressed finishes, is available to be carried out by teams of master decorators, and all types of wall-coverings supplied and hung. A full advisory service suggests or plans schemes and improvements, from the simplest decorating job to a complete interior refurbishment, and repairs are undertaken. The company's own workrooms supply and make up soft furnishings of all kinds. *P:* on application.

SARAH JANSON

Specialist in architectural *trompe l'oeil* from Egyptian to neo-classical in the tradition of early nineteenth-century French 'Panoramiques', painting on walls and screens. *P:* on application. Free estimate and design.

LAURA JEFFREYS

A skilled decorator who can offer any kind of decorative finish: stippling, dragging, marbling, graining, tortoiseshelling, *trompe l'oeil*, painted borders, colour washing and lacquering. *P:* on application.

PRICES AND INFORMATION WERE CORRECT AT THE TIME OF GOING TO PRESS

Marbled dado, stencilled borders and trompe l'oeil *hanging plates by Laura Jeffreys to complement Chinese wallpaper*

LYN LE GRICE STENCIL DESIGN

Charming stencilled murals and floors by a designer and innovator who has been instrumental in reviving the technique in this country. The gradation of colour within each shape is the result of Lyn Le Grice's unique method of spray painting. She will work on rooms of almost any size, and on fabrics and furniture, in close consultation with the client. *P:* on application.
Lyn Le Grice also markets her own stencil kits. COUNTRY COLLECTION contains a festoon of fruit, leaves and ribbons; a circle of leaves and

Typical stencil design by Lyn Le Grice

Architectural trompe l'oeil *by Sarah Janson*

Details of trompe l'oeil *stonework by Mark Hornak*

Lyn Le Grice's stencilled rose border

berries; and a basket of fruit. CRAFT KIT has designs suitable for smaller areas — pheasants and bay trees, birds and posies, and a dolphin. A catalogue is available. *P:* kits £5–£7.50, individual stencils £2.25; catalogue £1 with 10 × 12in s.a.e.
Stencilling courses are held each summer in Cheltenham. A prospectus is available on sending an A4 s.a.e.

NICHOLAS LLEWELLYN DECORATIONS
Specialist decorator with many years of experience, from a family in the trade. He will paint murals and interpret clients' own ideas, mixing colours on site to match fabrics etc. Marbling, dragging, wood-graining and lacquerwork finishes are specialities. He has done many window displays using these techniques, for London interior decorators Charles Hammond. *P:* on application.

CATHERINE LOVEGROVE
A muralist who specializes in plagiarism! She will transform a wall with a copy of anything from a prehistoric cave painting to a twentieth-century poster. Have a Giotto in the garage, a Lautrec in the loo, take a bath in the tropics, wake up in Brighton Pavilion, and cook amidst Elysian fields. *P:* from £5–£20 per square foot according to amount of detail.
Catherine Lovegrove will also make an unin-

teresting window into a decorative feature by hand-painting a blind, with acrylic (washable) paint on poplin, with clients' suggested subject matter. *P:* on application.

SALLY MILES
Talented and original mural painter specializing in beautifully painted *trompe l'oeil* and landscapes. *P:* on application.

Landscape with a vista by Sally Miles

GEORGE MORRIS
Interior decorator specializing in all kinds of unusual paint finishes: dragging, rag-rolling, stippling, marbling, tortoiseshelling and graining. He will also paint *trompe l'oeil* panels, carry out gilding and gesso work, and produce painted furniture. *P:* on application.

GILBERT O'BRIEN
Specialist in ragging, stippling and marbling, and graining as applied to furniture, walls and fireplace surrounds. Also does semi-precious finishes such as tortoiseshelling on objects such as small boxes. Plus advisory decorating and design service. *P:* on application.

OLIVER & PINK
Specialists who offer to execute any imaginable paint finish, including all the decorative techniques, hand-painted wallpaper and mu-

Marbled wall decoration by George Morris

rals, at competitive rates. They will also design and make, to order, handmade tapestries and rugs. *P:* on application.

PAINTED PATTERNS
Stencilling, rag-rolling and spongeing by Rae Damerell and Belinda Cooper. They design and cut their own stencils, matching colour and tone, to soften or highlight architectural points and add interest to borders, friezes, walls or floors. Stencils are produced and colours chosen to meet each clients' own require-

Stencilled design by Painted Patterns, applied over an entire wall

DECORATIVE PAINTERS

Mural by Timothy Plant

Mexican plant mural by Jayne Simcock

Convincing trompe l'oeil *panel by Tromploy Design*

ments, and the charm of the designs lies in their individuality and hand-painted quality. *P:* on application.

TIMOTHY PLANT
A painter of delightful murals which are full of life and interest, indoors or out. He can transform a dull blank wall into an intriguing interior scene or a peaceful vista over hills and dales — or even a combination of the two. *P:* on application.

ROBERT SHIMIELD
Every sort of decorative painting technique and murals. Robert Shimield, a decorator with 10 years' experience, and his colleague Tony Merry undertake both interior and exterior jobs for private and commercial clients. Their work has ranged from a chic marbled bathroom, through a delicately sponged wall in

strawberry pink on pale green in a private house, to a landscape mural with *trompe l'oeil* effects in a café. *P:* on application.

JAYNE SIMCOCK
Designer, illustrator and muralist whose lively, modern style ranges from fairly realistic animal, plant and jungle scenes to abstract or geometric patterns. Commissions undertaken for murals and hand-painting and stencilling on walls, ceilings, floors, furniture and fabrics (blinds in particular). She also designs ceramic wall tiles (see separate entry) and can adapt these patterns to other uses. *P:* on application.

TROMPLOY DESIGN
A company which specializes in the design and execution of murals, friezes and all decorative hand-painted finishes, including marbling, dragging, stippling, etc. The versatility and adaptability of both artists and painters has

given first-class results in all the decorative techniques in which they work. The company is based in Surrey, and will undertake work in London and throughout south-east England. *P:* on application.
A range of unique highly detailed hand-painted furniture is also produced for retail in Britain and abroad.

R WOODLAND & SON
An old-established family firm of specialists in all branches of decorative paintwork. They will imitate any type of marble, will copy the grain of any species of wood, and will achieve other effects such as clouding, shading, leather and tortoiseshell imitation, as well as ragging, stippling, dragging, scumble work, antiquing and stencilling. *P:* on application.

INTRODUCTION

From revivals of classics to modern designs in shimmering silver yarn or foil, there's a fantastic variety of furnishing fabrics and wall coverings. Colour and pattern are the most obvious considerations when making a choice but other aspects are just as important. Take scale of design. Too large a pattern will overwhelm a small room, so the size of the design repeat is critical and should be checked with the manufacturer. And does the design of a curtain fabric, for example, match the pattern and scale of upholstery and wallpaper? Combining patterns can be as risky as combining colours so it's worth taking swatches of existing fabrics, wall coverings and carpets around the shops with you and checking they match before you buy. Then there's texture. The different materials should both work together and be appropriate for the job they're doing.

Fabrics come in an ever-increasing variety of natural and man-made fibres and mixes of the two. The man-made fibres are generally less expensive than natural yarns but tend to attract dust. So for easy maintenance choose a fabric that combines both types of fibre. Cotton is normally the least expensive natural material, followed by linen and wool. Silk and silk-based velvet and brocade cost the most. Printed fabrics are more expensive than plains, for obvious reasons, while special designer ranges, produced in relatively small quantities, are usually the dearest.

Curtains can be made of virtually any fabric from light-weight cheesecloth to the heaviest velvet. Sheers are probably the cheapest solution when money's tight. However, chair and sofa covers should be made from a durable fabric in the best quality you can afford. Dark or patterned covers are most practical, especially if they will get a lot of wear. Buy enough for easy-to-clean, protective arm pads — important if you decide on an extravagantly pale shade — for decorative piping and for small repairs.

Wall coverings come in an even wider choice. There's the traditional printed wallpaper or, more practical for some areas, the washable wallpaper with a protective coating. Machine- and hand-printed papers are both silk-screen printed but the latter (some printed from wood blocks) are slower to produce, often involve several complex colour registers, and are therefore more expensive. More hard-wearing than the wallpapers are vinyl wall coverings.

Other wall-covering materials are paper-backed fabrics, from luxurious fine silk to coarser linen and synthetic yarns, woven or warp-laid (with fibres in one direction only pressed on to the backing). There are mock suedes, brick wall tiles, textured panels for heat insulation and cork (sold in rolls) for sound-proofing. Many of these wall coverings are intended specifically for contract use,

flame-resistant to the standards required for hotels and offices, but could equally well be used in the home.

Co-ordinates are ranges of both fabrics and wall coverings that are designed to go together. Some ranges consist of groups of papers that mix with each other and match plain or patterned fabrics. In others, large and small versions of a basic motif are available on both fabric and paper, fabric only or paper only. Co-ordination may also be achieved by isolating an element from a complicated pattern or repeating the basic design unchanged or in reverse colourways on fabric and paper. Or paper borders, strips of the same or a complementary design, can be used to accent a paper or fabric. They can go beneath the ceiling as a frieze, around a door, or in place of picture or dado rails.

Clever co-ordination is particularly important in the bedroom, where you may want to combine different fabrics for the innumerable soft furnishings — curtains, blinds, valances, bed covers, sheets, duvets and pillows, cushions and accessories. This is another massive field, beyond the scope of this directory. A small final section, *Bed linen*, describes just a few selected ranges from major names or from specialists to give an idea of what's available.

● Obviously it is important to consider fabric width when calculating quantity and price. Unfortunately widths today vary enormously with both metric and imperial measurements currently in use. Always allow 1 – 2.5cm (½ – 1in) for the selvedge on each side of the design.

● Most papers are 51 – 68.5cm (20 – 27in) wide, sold in rolls 10m (11yd) long. Textile and contract wall coverings tend to be wider and are often sold by the metre.

FABRICS

LAURA ASHLEY LTD

A multitude of delightful, document-inspired prints. Laura Ashley have an amazing array of furnishing fabrics of all types from light-weight cottons to heaviest sateens, from chintzes to quilted and even plastic-coated fabrics. They call their cotton sateens DRAWING ROOM fabric. It's suitable for curtains and light upholstery and comprises largish-scale prints, many in complicated colourations such as 'Favorita' with exotic blooms in navy/rust/khaki or rust/green/sand on beige, 'Garlands' with green ribbons holding pink bouquets or 'Michaelmas' with bunches of the daisies in rose/green or lavender/green on a beige lattice ground. Geometric designs include 'Florentina', a flame stitch in reds, 'Louis' with royal blue stripes/cream/stone, 'Mr Jones' with a trefoil in navy/burgundy/sand, plus a few single colour designs, notably 'Clifton Castle' with twisting vines and wild tendrils in navy, sand, smoke

Laura Ashley's 'Favorita' UPHOLSTERY FABRIC

blue or plum on cream, or crimson on saffron. *M:* w120cm (47¼in). *P:* £6.95 m.

In CHINTZES they offer eight designs, two of which are also in the above sateen range. Florals predominate, with both irregular repeats — 'Bouquet' on apricot or aquamarine ground — or with regular intervals — 'Convolvulus' with single flowers in pink on a lighter pink ground. All suitable for curtains and chair covers. *M:* w122cm (48in). *P:* £6.95 m.

Sturdy, hard-wearing UPHOLSTERY FABRIC also repeats a few of the same designs such as 'Michaelmas' and 'Favorita' in heavy cotton. Six others include 'Wickerwork' with a white neo-gothic lattice on sand, 'Cricket Stripe' in sand/navy/cream, and 'Nutmeg' with precise little diamond spots in white on burgundy or moss, or sand on navy. *M:* w150cm (59in). *P:* £7.95 m.

For heavy wear consider DOUBLE-SIDED QUILTING FABRIC, ideal for bedcovers and light upholstery; it is padded with fully washable polyester wadding. Fourteen designs in seven possible combinations (they all reverse) include the afore-mentioned 'Cricket Stripe' backed with 'Nutmeg' or 'Wild Cherry' (in rose); a soft pink 'Candy Stripe' backed with 'Bindweed' plus others giving a moss, burgundy, yellow or pale cornflower colourway. *M:* w120cm (48in). *P:* £7.45 m.

The largest collection by far (with 59 designs in all) is COUNTRY FURNISHING cottons, many with co-ordinating or matching papers and fabric borders (see *Co-ordinates*). PLASTIC-COATED FABRIC is cotton treated with PVC so that it can be wiped clean. It comes in eight alternatives including a classic red 'Gingham' check, but there are also five flower-sprigged designs in cheery colours. *M:* w115cm (45½in). *P:* £6.25 m.

G P & J BAKER LTD

Huge collection of traditional and oriental-inspired cottons and chintzes with many designs derived from document prints, plus some more innovative designs.

For their hundredth anniversary, Baker launched 'Centenary Rose', an old-fashioned delight available in 100% cotton and cotton chintz, both in coral or aqua, pale yellow and white grounds. From another period is 1930s

FABRICS AND WALL COVERINGS

'Springtime', a soft floral in 100% cotton in six unusual colourways on grey and green grounds. On the oriental side there's 'Lung P'ao', also 100% cotton, with striking dragons, waves and geometric motifs in five colourways. *M:* all w140cm (55in). *P:* all £15.10 m. A more classic design from the East is the woven paisley, 'Nantes', in 54% cotton/25% viscose/21% polyester in six colourways: écru, beige, peach/rust, coral/blue, blue/peach and green/beige. *M:* w130cm (51¼in). *P:* £28.10 m. And the ENGLISH TOILE collection features familiar Baker motifs of birds and luxuriant foliage on cotton fabrics and hand-printed wallpapers (see *Co-ordinates*).

Also with a traditional appeal, JANE AUSTEN collection has six designs picked from the authoress's own patchwork quilt — florals and stripes on chintz and cotton, including 'Miss Bennett' and 'Elizabeth', one with a simple background dot, the other with the same dot overlaid with floral clusters, both in cream, lemon, beige, white, aqua and Indian red colourways. *M:* w140cm (55in). *P:* £14.10 m.

From the much more modern and delightfully fresh RIVIERA collection come six fabrics, four on heavily glazed cotton. Among them are 'Vallauris' with Matisse-like flowers and vase in five colourways on orange, lemon, aqua, mint or blue grounds; lattice 'Vallensole' and co-ordinating 'Villefranche' in seven colourways on white, lemon or pale mint grounds; and 'Mandelieu' with bright or pastel tulips, anemones and foxgloves in four colourways. *M:* w140cm (55in). *P:* £15.10 m.

Baker's 'Vallauris' and 'Mandelieu'

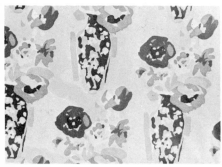

Other modernistic designs include a beautiful woven flame stitch, 'Fiametta', in six colourways — unusual ones such as blue/salmon pink and burgundy/lime green/dark green as well as the quieter light blue/mid blue and beige/silvery white. *M:* w140cm (55in). *P:* £28.10 m. There are two co-ordinating printed flame stitches on cotton chintz, suitable for curtains, cushions and light upholstery: 'Fiamma' and zig-zag 'Veneto', each in seven colourways. *M:* w140cm (55in). *P:* £15.10 m.

Another contemporary range, CALYPSO, has four stunning stripe and ikat motifs in pastel shades: 'St Martin' with lozenges, 'St Lucia' with vertical stripes, 'St Croix' with horizontal lozenges and 'St Kitts' with wavy stripes. *M:* w140cm (55in). *P:* £13.10 m.

To co-ordinate with Baker's prints there's a large collection of plain reps, MIJAS, in 42 shades, 53% cotton/47% viscose. *M:* w140cm (55in). *P:* £15.10 m. Other plains include MULLION TWILL in 45 shades ranging from rich deeps to pales. *M:* w140cm (55in). *P:* £14.10 m. And GRENOBLE is a slubbed, upholstery-weight fabric in 62% viscose/12% flax/26% cotton in 42 colours. *M:* w140cm (55in).

Baker will onion-quilt any of their printed or plain fabrics on request.

BEAUDESERT

Interior decorators with a charming shop featuring their own furniture (see separate entries), a few lovely antiques and a small collection of very special chintzes. Fabrics are faithful copies of early nineteenth-century designs printed in anything from two to ten colours on heavily glazed 100% cotton. Of the five designs the simplest is 'Cherry Trellis' with a ribbon trellis on a field with a small-scale floral pattern; it comes in three colourways: mint/forest, pink/orange, sky/cornflower. 'Tzarina' has a cluster of old roses on a dotted ground of beige, blue, peach or mint. 'Anastasia' shows small bouquets separated by a wavy leaf motif in rose/green on cream or peach. 'Fragrance' has a bigger bouquet on a subtle cross-hatch ground of peach, palest olive, yellow and lilac. And 'Beaudesert' shows bountiful bouquets tied together by swags of cords on a palest yellow or palest green ground. *M:* all 137cm (54in). *P:* £12.80–19.50 m.

Wm H BENNETT & SONS LTD

Luxurious pure silk fabrics for curtains, festoons, cushions and upholstery, at exceptionally low prices. Choose from a clutch of creamy textures such as '1200 Tussah Herringbone', '1202 Shantung Pongee', or '1204 Silk Goffer', a basket-weave design. *M:* all w45in (114cm). *P:* £7.50–£8.50 m. Or their '5001' dupion is hand-loomed in India in a dozen shimmering colours including midnight blue, mink, rose and wine plus bright green, yellow and black. *M:* w45in (114cm). *P:* £8.50 m. '2020

From left: Beaudesert's 'Beaudesert', 'Cherry Trellis', 'Anastasia'

Macclesfield', a plain, heavy upholstery silk in 10 shades is a winner for quality, appearance and value. *M:* w35½in (90cm). *P:* £6.50 m. Other popular silks to be found here are crèpe-backed satins, spun silks, shantungs and habotais. '1681 Habotai' comes in 52 shades while '1681P' is the same fabric with a choice of two prints — a floral patern or a semi-circular design. *M:* w35½in (90cm). *P:* plain £3.25 m; printed £3.95 m. Send a note of your requirements to Bennetts, and they will forward samples and a detailed price list. Prices quoted are for lengths of 3m (3¼yd) or more, but a discount is offered for orders in excess of 22m (24yd).

BENTLEY & SPENS

Batik and hand-painted designs on furnishing fabrics to order. Kim Bentley and Sally Spens specialize in creating unique designs on silk, cotton, linen and any other fabric provided it is not too heavy. They carry a good range of suitable fabrics themselves and can advise you about other sources. Each batik is drawn and dyed individually using the wax-resist method, allowing an almost limitless choice of colour and design. You can order a very small amount — just enough for a few unusual cushions — or enough to make curtains or cover a sofa. *P:* from £15 m, plus fabric.

Two designs by Bentley & Spens

BUSBY & BUSBY

Pleasant abstract designs hand-printed in durable vat colours on excellent, fully-glazed, Lancashire cotton. Lighter-weight cottons are available in five designs: abstract 'Shimmer' with soft brush-strokes and flower-inspired 'Provence', in stippled colours on a white background; 'Cascade' and 'Bandbox', swirling patterns reminiscent of marbled papers; and 'Midsummer'. Each is available in 29 colourways, but colours can also be produced to order for a minimum order of 40 metres. Busby and Busby have plans for matching wallpapers too. *M:* w120cm (47in). *P:* £14.85 m.

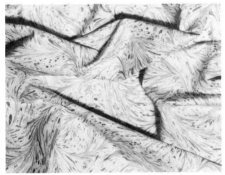

Busby & Busby's 'Cascade'

FADED GLORY range in 100% twill upholstery cloth includes the 'Bandbox' design, plus 'Pavilion' with broad and narrow diagonal stripes in two complementary colours on white and 'Pageant' with an all-over shell motif on white or reversed out. All are treated to be stain resistant and oil and water repellent. *M:* w137 (54in). *P:* £13.75 m.

Top, from left: 'Bandbox', 'Pavilion'; below: 'Pageant'. From Busby & Busby

CAMBORNE FABRICS LTD △

Top quality upholstery wools and blends manufactured in Huddersfield for contract use. Camborne Fabrics promotes the tradi-

tional virtues and proven qualities of wool — and its inherent fire-resistant nature — as a decorating fabric for use in hotels, offices, aeroplanes and ships around the world. They make 11 different qualities which are available in more than 270 colours.

A popular range is CAMBORNE, a 40% wool/60% viscose blend in 49 clear and heathery colours that co-ordinate with the CAMBORNE SCREEN range made specifically for acoustical screens and space dividers. *M:* CAMBORNE w128cm (50½in); SCREEN w162.5cm (64in). *P:* on application.

MOORLAND in 100% wool provides 10 more plains and woven check and twill designs, the twill in 12 colourways, the check in six — all in shades of oatmeal, grey, sage, rust and blue and with a lighter, off-white or oatmeal contrasting weave. *M:* w137cm (54in). *P:* on application.

A finer textured weave, COMPLEMENTS in 60% viscose/40% wool, offers three co-ordinating woven patterns: herringbone 'Coronet', zigzag 'Cascade' and diagonal 'Concorde'. It comes in nine colourways: grey/cream, rose/cream, burgundy/rose, mushroom/cream, brown/rose, rose/terracotta, sage/cream, blue grey/cream and blue/navy. *M:* w137cm (54in). *P:* on application.

In pure wool, CRAGGAN is a heavy tweed available in a good spectrum of colours from warm earth tones to blues and greys, all of them with a heathery effect. *M:* w128cm (50½in). *P:* on application.

Camborne's COMPLEMENTS △

THE CONRAN SHOP

From the purveyors of chic on London's Fulham Road, a good range of practical fabrics from India, most of them in natural fibres. Plains include 'Bamboo' with an irregular, finely ribbed surface in 25 colours from pastels to brights, from black to white, in 100% cotton. *M:* w48in (122cm) *P:* £11.50 m.

Fancy white or off-white for the whole room? A dozen or so possibilities include 'Khadi' in

Left to right, from top: Conran's '1489', 'Mahu-a-Mahu', 'Taj A', 'Bamboo', 'Moll', 'Ikat DE83/12, '1492'

beige, washable 'Khadi I' in white with an uneven slub and 'Khadi II' in white with a wavy slub. *M:* w48in (122cm). *P:* £3–£3.50 m. For a thicker fabric, again with a woven rib, there's 'Mahu-a-Mahu' in off-white cotton. *M:* w56in (144cm). *P:* £8.50 m. Or a self-patterned crisscross, 'Alicante', also in off-white cotton. *M:* w52in (130cm). *P:* £8.60 m. 'Piste' comes in white with a tiny square grid, each one punctuated with a small black dot, and in the reverse pattern. *M:* w51in (130cm). *P:* £10.70 m. Or maybe you fancy pure silk — choose from five weights from the lightest, 'Taj A' in cream, to '1489' or '1492' with darker beige subtly interwoven. *M:* 'Taj A' w48in (122cm); others w51in (130cm). *P:* 'Taj A' £9.30 m; other £14 m. Or how about a tiny white square on a ground of beige, grey or dull blue? Then there's 'Moll' from Sweden in 100% cotton. *M:* w59in (150cm). *P:* £7.75 m.

For bolder patterning, there are lots and lots of ikats in 100% cotton. *M:* w45in (114cm). *P:* £8.95 m. There's also one in 70% silk/30% cotton, '1034', with beige ground and lavender or hot pink stripe. *M:* 48in (122cm). *P:* £11.50 m.

DARTINGTON HALL TWEEDS LTD △

Hard-wearing, contract-quality upholstery and curtaining fabrics in 100% pure new wool. Dartington manufacture 12 fireproofed upholstery-weight ranges and six curtain ranges which can be fireproofed to order, all in some beautiful colour combinations.

MOSAICS offers three tonal variations: 'Fresco' in seven subtle pale shades; 'Murals' in six mid tones; and 'Icons' in 11 deep shades. All are woven in a tiny chequerboard design in three or four tones, the colourways ranging from pale grey 'Nicosia' to rusty 'Ravenna'. *M:* w127cm (50in) *P:* on application.

KALEIDOSCOPE comprises four designs: 'Renoir' relies on a dove grey and olive base with mushroom, cornflower blue, taupe or jade green accents; 'Cezanne' has a woven vertical zigzag on a pale coffee base with accents in aqua, buff, palest lilac, pale olive or grey; 'Degas' has a raised diamond texture with the

FABRICS AND WALL COVERINGS

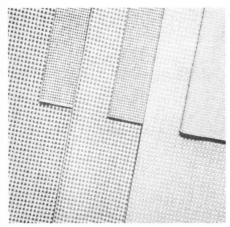

Dartington Hall Tweeds' MOSAICS △

palest lilac base and contrasting tones in grey, pale coffee, pale jade, peach or apricot; and 'Gauguin' has a richer palette with a warm grey base and a strong diamond lattice in cranberry, dark brown, dark blue, black or dark green. *M:* w127cm (50in). *P:* on application.

SUBTLE SHUTTLE is indeed subtle with three colourings: 'Monet' with an icy grey ground and six pastel variations; 'Whistler' with a warmer grey base and mid-tone second colours such as mid blue, taupe and pale olive; 'Seurat' with a rusty brown base and sharper accents in rush, rose and mid blue. *M:* w127cm (50in). *P:* on application.

All the above are suitable for upholstery, curtains and bedspreads. They can be made up in widths up to 164cm (64½in) for orders over 180m (200yd).

EDITH DE LISLE (QUENBY PRINTS LTD)

Smart, pure cotton fabrics from a Peruvian-born designer, ranging from the GOLDEN CAGE budget range to the sumptuous, metallized GOLD OF PERU. GOLDEN CAGE has eight designs, all on a diagonal or vertical grid and incorporating lattices, flowers, birds, butterflies and bees in navy/yellow, peach/yellow/mint, rust/beige/apricot, orange/lime and lime/

Selection from de Lisle's GOLDEN CAGE

pink on white. *M:* w114cm (45in). *P:* £7.50 m.

EDITH DE LISLE DESIGNS collection uses an exaggerated flame pattern, layered (fan-shaped) plume, and a crewel-inspired floral panel (with smaller-scale border and co-ordinate) to great effect, in mid blue/rust on beige, mid blue/red on off-white, mid blue/yellow/beige on white, pink/green/beige on white, apricot/mid-brown/beige on white, mid blue/mid brown/beige on white and rusty orange/green/mid blue on off-white. *M:* w122cm (48in). *P:* £13.50 m.

IKEBANA relies on similar colourways but is on heavier, 'luxury-weight' cotton and comprises six patterns, all designed to work together: 'Pomegranate' on a beige and white swirled ground, 'Prunus' with an all-over pattern of branches and clusters of blossom, 'Nara' with vertical, striped feather configurations, 'Incense' with floral stripes on the same swirled ground as 'Pomegranate', and 'Imari' and 'Lychee' with panels from all the other designs. *M:* w134cm (52¾in). *P:* £15.90 m.

'Imari' from de Lisle's IKEBANA

For those fond of metallic finishes there are two collections: STUART and the aforementioned GOLD OF PERU. STUART has five designs in five colourways: mid-blue/aquamarine, gold/yellow, rose/warm grey, peach/apricot and beige/mustard. There are period-inspired florals such as 'Morningside', 'Aviemore' and 'Queen of Scots' as well as a flame stitch, 'Highland', and a grid, 'Tartan', each with an element picked out in pearly-grey metallic. *M:* w134cm (52¾in). *P:* £19.90 m.

GOLD OF PERU uses gold more emphatically; often the design is over-printed in gold on to the horizontally-slubbed base fabric. Base colours range from a rich turquoise to rust or cooler beige. The collection features three Inca-inspired designs, 'Chancay', 'Paracas' and 'Chimu', the latter two with big birds in profile. Other patterns include 'Isabel' with thin, broken vertical stripes in gold, and 'El Dorado' with lush foliage and birds of paradise. *M:* w122cm (48in). *P:* £25.50 m.

PRICES AND INFORMATION WERE CORRECT AT THE TIME OF GOING TO PRESS

Selection from Designers Guild's ANEMONE △

DESIGNERS GUILD ⚑

Well-known collection of high quality fabrics, often pastel and floral in theme but thoroughly modern in mood. ANEMONE offers a cotton, a cotton satin and a chintz in five anemone-inspired designs that range from the graphic to the impressionistic: 'Anemone' with large blooms, 'Cluster Chintz' with bouquets on a dragged-effect ground, 'Patch' and 'Dapple' with splodges of colour suggesting petals, and 'Shadow Satin' with bolder, blurred brush-strokes. There are three colourways: cornflower blue/peach, oyster/grey and amethyst/aquamarine. *M:* w137cm (54in). *P:* £12.80-£19.50 m.

DONALD BROTHERS LTD ⚑

Established firm noted for its high quality contract furnishing fabrics and winners of several Design Council awards. Specialists in fabrics from natural fibres, they have seven superb designs in 100% wool, many with very pleasing and subtle woven self-patterns. Examples are 'Tiree' with crossing diagonals; 'Mallaig' with raised diagonal; 'Aberlore' and 'Islay' with pleasing contrasts of thick and thin skeins; 'Lewis' a diagonal, stripey weave; 'Moray' with a small chequered effect; and 'Appin' in solid tones. Most come in 12 colourways and all are flame retardant. *M:* w50in (127cm). *P:* (contract) £11.50 – £14.65 m.

In addition they do three designs using a linen/cotton mixture: 'Blanefield' in eight colours with a self-check; 'Nagshead Stripe' with a most discreet, gentleman's-tailor stripe; and similar 'Nagshead Check' with a contrasting

'Nagshead Check' △ and 'Nagshead Stripe' △ from Donald Bros

highlight, both the latter in four colour variations. *M:* 'Blanefield' w50in (127cm); 'Nagshead' w54in (138cm). *P:* (contract) £6.50–£6.95.

CHRISTIAN FISCHBACHER (LONDON) LTD⚠

Fabrics designed by the famous Collier Campbell duo. SIX VIEWS collection of furnishing fabrics has six designs in 100% cotton: 'Romany' evocative of the 1930s with bouquets of peonies and roses on grey, mint or rust ground; 'Côte d'Azur' with a medley of palm trees against blocks of colourful stripes and zigzags; 'Havana' very contemporary with

Three fabrics from Christian Fischbacher's SIX VIEWS △

bold zigzagging ribbons in bright colours; 'Water Meadow' with horizontal bands of ripples and flowers; 'Casbah' with bold ziggurat motifs giving an oriental flavour; and 'Spice Route' reminiscent of ikat-weaving. All six prints are beautifully coloured. *M:* w137cm (54in). *P:* £8.50 m.

FOURSQUARE DESIGNS⚠

A collection of refreshingly contemporary cottons from France and further afield, and screen-printed fabrics made in Britain. Of the latter, Corney & Co consistently produce pleasing designs printed on cotton, raw silk and slub silk. Three simple and satisfying designs are 'Landscape' with gently flowing lines in four bright colourways, similar 'Hollow Landscape' in gold, silver, lilac or terracotta on white, and 'Outlines' with wiggly lines in ice-cream shades. *M:* cotton w120cm (47in); silk w90cm (35½in). *P:* cotton £9–£11.50 m; silk £13.50–£15 m.

Foursquare's own collection of screen-printed cottons has similar abstracts including 'Composition 10' with primary colours and black diagonals in the style of the Dutch painter Mondrian and 'Venezia II' imitating rippling water with stripes made up of smudgy brush-strokes in two toning colours on white. In contrast, the COUNTRY collection has four pictorial designs: 'Birds of Spring' with rainbows and

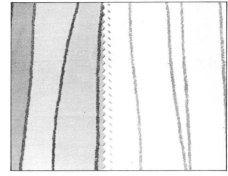

Foursquare's 'Landscape' and 'Hollow Landscape'

birds in flight; 'Rose Petals' with little petals; 'Galadriel' with leaves on cotton satin or voile; and 'Tindale Fell', a landscape, also on cotton satin or voile. *M:* cotton w120, 130cm (47¼, 51¼in); voile w150cm (59in), satin w125cm (49in). *P:* cotton £10–£15 m; voile £9.50 m; satin £8 m.

Another noteworthy English range is the POULK PRINT collection, hand-blocked in Wiltshire from designs done by Nancy Nicholson in 1929. There's 'Little Duck', Indian runner ducks in profile on a squiggly patterned cotton (also available without the ducks); 'Fig Leaf' on damask, and 'Geranium' and 'Lilies of the Valley' on cotton satin. *M:* w120–140cm (47–55in). *P:* £34–£42 m.

From France come the adventurous designs of Les Tissages Contemporaires with terrific abstracts such as the striated 'Lisalmi', the slashed 'Hamina' and dotted 'Pori' from the AURORE collection. All are printed on 100% cotton in clear bright shades, with matching sheers. *M:* w145cm (57in). *P:* £11 m.

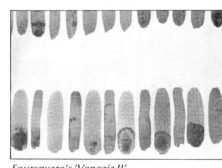

Foursquare's 'Venezia II'

MARY FOX LINTON LTD

Beautiful imported fabrics from this well-known, stylish decorator.

INTAIR collection of plain and glazed cottons from Germany has vibrant colour combinations with stripes, squares, houndstooths and plains incorporating metallized printed accents. There's also a range with unusual patterns resembling sand, shells, rippling water

From Mary Fox Linton. Above: Selection of JIM THOMPSON THAI SILK. Below: houndstooth 'Classic' and striped 'Line' from INTAIR

and clouds in both upholstery and curtain weights. There are co-ordinating fine cotton sheers in 35 colours and cotton satins with a shirred matt or sheer stripe in 18 colourways, mostly two-tones but some more unusual combinations such as red/pewter, violet/ black, grey/taupe. There's also a shirred sea-island cotton to mix with the patterns. *M:* all w150cm (59in). *P:* £15–£35 m.

Mary Fox Linton is also UK agent for JIM THOMPSON THAI SILK, both prints and weaves in fine, light and upholstery-weight silk. Lovely colours include unusual shades such as stone, old rose, peach, taupe, silvery green and lilac blue. Patterns include ikats, plaids and stripes; specifically a three-colour, ribbed, ikat horizontal stripe, 'RI4006', a narrower, four-colour variation, 'K4003', and a three-colour, ribbed silk with thin contrasting stripe and raised over-stripe, 'RI4006'. *M:* w122cm (48in). *P:* £31.50–£57.75 m.

HABITAT DESIGNS LTD

From the well-loved high street chain, dozens of refreshingly up-to-the-minute prints, all on pure cotton. Some of the best are 'Droppe' with swirls of splashed colour in primary shades on white or brown/white/yellow on grey; 'Pythagoras' a bold geometric featuring squares, triangles and stripes of green/grey/ black or red/blue/black; 'Regatta', a nautical-inspired print with light blue, navy, yellow and red flag shapes on white; 'Laululintu' with large birds, fruit and vases of flowers on bright yellow or cornflower blue; 'Modium' a bold broken stripe with pastels on yellow or brights on blue; 'Big Stripe' with just that in red/white or blue/white; and 'Chess' with a chequerboard in the same colours. *M:* all w150cm (59in). *P:* £2.60–£4.95 m.

For kids, 'Tiger Rag' has brightly coloured jungle animals creeping through the green grass and 'Balloons' has balloons in brights on white. *M:* 'Tiger Rag' w91cm (35¾in); 'Balloons' w150cm (59in). *P:* 'Tiger Rag' £5.75 m; 'Balloons' £3.25 m.

Habitat also have a very good range of PVC-coated cotton, great for play rooms and kitchens: 'Grid Check' with a grid in red, blue or green on white; 'Red Victoria' with flowers linked by a diagonal grid in white on red. *M:* 'Grid Check' w138cm (54¼in); 'Red Victoria' w145cm (57in). *P:* £6.95 m.

Habitat's 'Tiger Rag'

HAMMOND WHOLESALE LTD

Wide selection of rather grand fabrics from all over the world including chintzes, linen unions, silks, silk and linen velvets and hand-woven designs. Hammond's own document-inspired collection has new additions every season and is generously displayed in their Sloane Street showroom.

'Gaddesden' is a traditional flower pattern available as cotton chintz or as linen/cotton union in six tasteful colourways including pink on grey and blue-green on salmon in the chintz while the union is printed on cream grounds. *M:* w120cm (47in). *P:* chintz £12.95 m; union £16.95 m.

Similar to their own designs is the LEE JOFA range from America: 'Hollyhock Minor' in four colourways in 100% cotton features hydrangeas and old roses — but no hollyhocks! — in vertical bands while 'Trentham Hall' has a more overall design of intertwining vines and flowers. *M:* w127–135cm (50–53¼in). *P:* £14.25–£19.55 m.

In more modern mode is a dramatic range of contemporary designs from CHURBA of

Top: 'Gaddesden'; below: 'Hollyhock Minor'. Both from Hammond Wholesale

Rome, all manufactured in best quality Swiss glazed cotton. 'Vertical Super Position' has 5cm (2in) stripes with diagonal texturing in soft shell, honeydew, mauve, stone and smokey blue; 'Diagonal Super Position' has slightly darker diagonals running across with a vertical stripe at one outer edge; 'Super Position' has vibrantly contrasting thin stripes also in five colourways including some very unusual combinations such as brick/tangerine/pink/grey/loganberry and pale pink/grey/gold/stone; 'Waterflowers' has a subtle cross-hatched design, again in striking combinations; and 'Super Position I' and 'II' feature wavy lines in nine shades graduating from softest pinks and greys through a brilliant cherry to grape with mango. *M:* w140cm (55in). *P:* £25 m.

PRICES AND INFORMATION WERE CORRECT AT THE TIME OF GOING TO PRESS

CHRISTOPHER LAWRENCE

Luxurious and essentially contemporary designs in cotton and silk. FLORALS in 100% cotton has delicate, widely-spaced flowers with a raised outline giving the appearance of appliqué. Three floral designs include 'Delia' with tulips and other spring flowers and 'Laura' with waterlilies on a ground of ripples in pastel colourways, plus 'George' with ripples and 'Alex' with chevrons, both the latter in gold and white raised patterns. All are in 100% cotton with a rich cream ground. *M:* w130cm (51¼in). *P:* £19.57 m.

SASSO combines screen-printed designs with woven patterns in metallic ochre, white or silver. There are six designs in 100% cotton: 'Quadrato' plaid-effect checks on blue, pink, beige or sand; 'Piazza' with tiny mosaic squares in blue, yellow, beige or apricot; 'Infinito' with soft stripes of blue/apricot, beige/grey, yellow/multi, blue/green with white outline; 'Sasso' with all-over marble-effect in pinks, lavenders, blues or beiges; 'Terreno' with soft hills in sand/beige, blue/terracotta, pink/olive or green/blue; and 'Bellina' with swirling fronds in pastel shades. *M:* w131cm (51½in). *P:* £16.95 m.

OXUS offers an oriental feel, printed on either 100% cotton or silk in any of eight designs — four small scale and four large — mostly in pleasing, restrained colourways. *M:* w122cm (48in). *P:* cotton £10–£13 m; silk from £18.50 m (minimum order for silk 18m).

For more luxury, there's a beautiful, heavy-weave textured silk for upholstery and curtains. LUISA in 80% silk/20% cotton comes in plain soft or strong colours plus striped colourways which may be ordered in a virtually

From Christopher Lawrence's LUISA

infinite variety of combinations and stripe width — so that you're almost designing your own fabric! Matching borders and braids complete the sumptuous effect. *M:* w90cm (35½in). *P:* £32 m. There's also a light-weight silk with a raised slub stripe which runs horizontally across the fabric, in five colourways: green/gold, red/green/cream, grey/beige, green/maroon/beige and blue/gold/maroon. *M:* w122cm (48in). *P:* £45 m.

MARVIC TEXTILES LTD

High quality upholstery and curtain fabrics from France, Italy and America. At the base of the collection — and the bottom of the price range — are two ranges of plain glazed cotton chintzes suitable for curtains, cushions and bedcovers: CHATEL in 100% cotton in 34 colours and VALE in 50% cotton/50% Dacron in 54 colours (including rich dark burgundy, navy and black). VALE matches a seersucker, RUFFLES, in the same colours. *M:* CHATEL w150cm (59in); VALE, RUFFLES w122cm (48in). *P:* CHATEL, VALE £9.90 m; RUFFLES £11.90 m. There's also an extensive collection of printed chintzes with oriental and classic floral motifs prevailing.

Marvic's RUFFLES

From America, the RIVERSIDE collection offers glazed cotton prints in fresh, spring-like designs. The designs fall into three groups of co-ordinates, all fabrics treated with Teflon soil- and stain-repellent finish. One group consists of 'Beekman' a small multicoloured geometric, 'Hudson', a small two-tone geometric and 'Avenue', a distinctive, bold stripe which picks up all the colours in 'Beekman'; all in six co-ordinating colourways in both strong and soft shades including terracotta/peach, dark blue/green, sage/pink, apricot/pale blue, grey/pink and brown/green. The second group is 'Four Seasons', a flower and butterfly design on a variegated striped background, and 'Seasons Stripe' with just the stripe; the four colourways are ivory/pink, soft peach/pale blue, ivory/plum and yellow/green. The third group consists of batik-like 'Romantique', a subtly coloured all-over floral on a striped ground, and 'Romantique Stripe' with just the stripe;

FABRICS AND WALL COVERINGS

striped effects in three fabrics: 'Mehri' in 71% viscose/29% nylon is a reversible pocket cloth with a quilted look, iridescent in three colourways both pastel and clear; 'Sharif' in 100% viscose is a tightly woven jacquard brocade with a pattern of stripes and squares in two muted colourways; and 'Sarem' is a geometric quilted fabric with an elegant silky look, available in three soft colourways — ivory/white, opal blue/ivory and shell pink/ivory. *M:* w140cm (55in). *P:* 'Mehri' £27.90 m; 'Sharif' £23.90 m; 'Sarem' £31.90 m.

The imaginative range from Deschemaker of Paris includes some contrastingly showy tapestries: OLYMPE lamé fabrics in 13 glitter-flecked floral and geometric designs. *M:* w130cm (51¼in). *P:* £31.35–£97.80 m. And PLEIADES jacquard tapestry range offers five designs and many striking colourways, including 'Souimanga', a flame stitch. *M:* w137cm (54in). *P:* £27.92–£48.65. CANADAIR jacquards in 100% polyester for upholstery and curtains are exceptional in that they are made from inherently flameproof 100% Trevira (polyester); the eight designs offer co-ordinated geometric jacquards and seersuckers, all in lovely colours including apricot, terracotta, greens and blues. *M:* w130–140cm (51¼–55in). *P:* £21.24–£43 m. Another curtain fabric is 'Agora', a crinkled cotton chintz (a variation on seersucker) in 31 colours; it's also suitable for blinds and walls. *M:* w140cm (55in). *P:* £28.22 m.

Marvic also offer a good choice of moirés, in a variety of compositions and price brackets but all with that characteristic watermark effect.

the three colourways are ivory/blue/terracotta, pale blue/green/apricot and pink/green/mink. *M:* w137cm (54in). *P:* £19.90 m. Another American collection, WESTPOINT, provides co-ordinating upholstery fabrics in 50% cotton/50% polyester, with a number of related designs using harlequin squares or geometric stripes, plus a plain satin-finish box weave, 'Shadow Box'. Prints come in four pastel colourways, 'Shadow Box' in 14 colours to suit every permutation. *M:* w122cm (48in). *P:* £12.50–£13.70 m.

Marvic specialize in tapestries, unrivalled for their hard-wearing qualities, and have a large range of imaginative modern designs. The SAHARA pattern book shows a lovely selection of tapestries from France and Italy for upholstery, curtains and bedcovers. The FRENCH COLLECTION has an overall geometric look in subtle colours. 'Khayam' in 41% cotton/33% viscose/21% polyester/5% polypropylene is a hard-wearing jacquard with a marble effect in three colourways; 'Zarifeh' in 67% viscose/33% cotton, also a jacquard, has a pyramid design in blended colours on a solid ground in four unusual colourways; 'Harlequin' in 52% cotton/33% viscose/15%acrylic is a tightly woven geometric tapestry in three colourways; 'Teymour' in 64% viscose/32% cotton/4% polypropylene has an ikat-style pattern in three colourways; and 'Albiera' in 68% cotton/32% viscose is a geometrically quilted piqué for upholstery and bedcovers, available in 13 plain colours. *M:* w130–140cm (51¼–55in). *P:* £25.90–£29.90 m.

The ITALIAN COLLECTION offers clever

Marvic's FRENCH and ITALIAN COLLECTIONS. Above, left to right from top: 'Khayam', 'Harlequin', 'Zarifeh', 'Teymour' and (in basket) 'Albiera'. Below, left to right: 'Mehri', 'Sarem', 'Sharif'

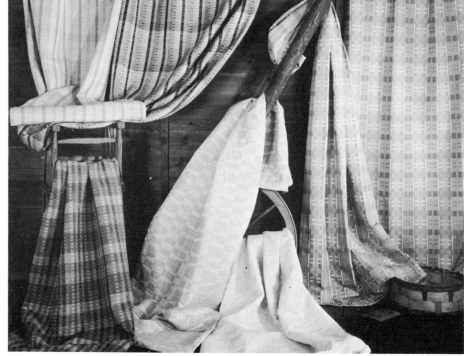

RENISHAW is an upholstery fabric in 34 colours with a slightly nubbly texture, made from 20% linen/80% viscose. *M:* w137 cm (57in). *P:* £17.50 m. 'Princess Silk' is 68% silk/32% Dacron but is a good imitation of a pure silk, in 24 shades. *M:* 130cm (51¼in). *P:* £29.50 m. And 'Countess Shantung' imitates shantung silk in 60% viscose/40% acetate in 23 shades. *M:* w122cm (48in). *P:* £13.90 m. There's also a pure silk in 24 shades. *M:* w130cm (51in). *P:* £50 m.

MONKWELL FABRICS
Manufacturers of high quality fabrics since 1889, with an emphasis on plains and jacquard weaves. An amazing selection of nine collections of Dralon velvets includes SUPREME with the largest colour range of 52 shades, and MONTROSE with both 'antique' and plain velvets in 34 colours. *M:* SUPREME w50in (127cm); MONTROSE w54in (137cm). *P:* SUPREME £22 m; MONTROSE £15.10 m.
For curtain-weight velours, there's COUNTY in 100% cotton and in 71 plain shades. *M:* w48in (122cm). *P:* £12.70 m. Or CHRISTCHURCH with crease-resistant finish in 47 mainly pastel tones, made from 81% cotton/19% viscose. *M:* w48in (122cm). *P:* £12.70 m. In deeper tones, HARMONY also comes with crease-resistant finish, but in 100% cotton and in 35 colourways. *M:* w48in (122cm). *P:* £11.70 m. In contract quality, flame-retardant velours there's VANGUARD in 15 deep-dyed shades and CARNIVAL in 70, both 100% cotton. *M:* w48in (122cm). *P:* VANGUARD £13 m; CARNIVAL £14.80 m.
VARIATIONS provides dupions in pastel tones, and in eight different textured weaves including slubs, stripes and checks. The fabrics are primarily man-made fibres, though each texture is a different mixture. *M:* w48in (122cm). *P:* £7.20–£9.50 m. SHERBORNE dupion has a satin and bouclé stripe (with vertically striped ground) in 31 colours in mixtures of acrylic and polyester. *M:* w47in (120cm). *P:* £12.20 m.
In chintz there's VERMONT in 33 plain shades (strong on blues) with seven co-ordinating small-scale designs. The co-ordinates are all pleasingly tasteful with a regular stripe available plain or as a seersucker, a thicker textured stripe, a tiny floral, a flame stitch and a self-patterned weave, all designed to make perfect co-ordination easy. In 50% cotton/50% polyester. *M:* w48in (122cm). *P:* £12.10 m.
Monkwell are famous for jacquards and make a number of ranges all in varying combinations of viscose, cotton and polyester. Consider KENSINGTON with six small-scale designs in seven colourways, delicious shades like peach and dull blue all on an off-white ground plus two larger tapestry weaves to co-ordinate: 'CR 4157', small tree pattern with birds set in a trefoil, and 'CR4067' with birds in branches. The collection also includes plain fabrics suitable for piping and other detailing. *M:* w54in (137

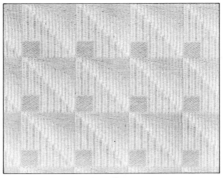

'CR4339' from Monkwell's KALEIDOSCOPE

cm). *P:* £14 m. KINNERTON has similarly tasteful jacquards. There are small geometrics, florals and the perennial pineapple motif, seven motifs in all on a coloured ground in 10 shades; plus co-ordinating plains. *M:* w54in (137cm). *P:* £14.50 m.
KNIGHTSBRIDGE has more complicated jacquards in eight designs: stripey lattice, zigzag, quatrefoil, flame, fan-shape, floral and two beautiful period tapestries — 'CR4201' with butterflies and 'CR4208' with blowsy tulips. Predominating colours are alum (pale aqua), sky, juniper (pale green) and beige. *M:* w54in (137cm). *P:* £19.50 m.
KALEIDOSCOPE is a huge range of fine or chunky jacquards — an impressive 20 designs, plus a range of four plain fabrics. More unusual ones include: 'CR4337' with diamond zigzag; 'CR4339' with a striated square within a square; 'CR4340' with a partridge in a pear trèe; 'CR4338' with an optical-effect lattice; all of these with pink, grey, green, rust, aqua, gold, rose, celadon or palest apricot predominant and in 68% cotton/32% viscose. Or there's 'CR4320' with a regular flower motif; 'CR4300' with a tiny diagonally striped trapezoid at regular intervals in mid blue, rose, peach, white or beige; 'CR4266' with a stripe and 'CR4265' with a coarse-woven lattice in beautiful combinations like peach/cornflower/cream, blue/lime/

Left to right, from top: 'CR4340', 'CR4337', 'CR4338' from Monkwell's KALEIDOSCOPE

pink, white/blue/sienna, green/blue/white and grey/peach/cornflower. *M:* w54in (137cm). *P:* £19.50 m.
TOWN AND COUNTRY has lots of traditional and modern floral tapestry designs — a total of 46 designs in 80 colourways. *M:* w50–54in (127–137cm). *P:* £13.70–£24 m. AVONDALE has six damask designs: modern raised lattice, fan-shape and small rose plus traditional double lattice, bouquet and tassels and random floral. They're 100% cotton, available in eight shades: peach, apricot, rose, blue, aqua, celadon, beige and gold. *M:* w50–54in (127–137cm). *P:* £15.70–£16.70 m.
For a huge collection of large-scale, classic printed chintz designs, 16 in all and all Scotchgarded, look at ALL SEASON II in 50% cotton/50% viscose. *M:* w54in (137cm). *P:* £11.90 m. Monkwell will Scotchgard fabrics on request.

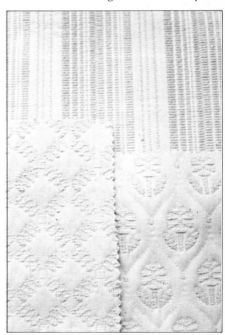

Left to right, from top: 'CR4266', 'CR4265', 'CR4230' from Monkwell's KALEIDOSCOPE

MOORHOUSE ASSOCIATES
Textile designers who hand-print their own fabrics on the premises. Thirteen striking contemporary designs range from 'Razzle Dazzle', with a grid on top of a diagonal stripe, in one of six colours on white, to 'Well Spotted' with irregular splodges of grey or stone interspersed with brighter colours. All are printed in high quality, pure cotton in machine-washable colours, available on curtain or upholstery weight Lancashire fabric. Special colourways

PRICES AND INFORMATION WERE CORRECT AT THE TIME OF GOING TO PRESS

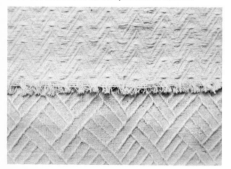

Top: 'Razzle Dazzle'; below: 'Well Spotted'. Both from Moorhouse

can be printed at no extra cost for quantities over eight yards, and you can even see your fabric printed! *M:* w48in (122cm). *P:* £4.83–£13.46 yd; upholstery weight £2 extra per yd.

NICE IRMA'S (FABRICATION) LTD

Unusual and inexpensive imported fabrics, many from India. There is a particularly good range of upholstery-weight fabrics in 100% cotton. JACQUARD WEAVES, all in creams and whites except for one apricot/white combination, feature chevrons and diamonds. *M:* w54in (137cm). *P:* £6 m. 'Complex', a ribbed weave, has small squares and rectangles in four pastel colourways on off-white: peach/ pale blue/ mid blue, lavender/mint/two blues, beige/mushroom/brown and mint/mid green/ beige. *M:* w54in (137cm). *P:* £6.60 m. 'Chalkis' has fine ribbed stripes in six colourways: beige/black, beige/pink, beige/blue grey, beige/mint, mid blue/white — these five on off-white — and red/yellow/blue on white. *M:* w54in (137cm). *P:* £5.50 m. 'Toning Fabrics' is the plainest, just a slightly ribbed effect in six

Two of Nice Irma's JACQUARD WEAVES

shades: baby blue, beige, pale grey, off-white, pale pink and mint. *M:* w48in (122cm). £6.50 m. Nice Irma's also have a large but continuously changing range of cotton ikats. *M:* w48in (122cm). £6 m. They sell cushions to co-ordinate with many designs and offer a complete making-up service for blinds, curtains, loose covers and re-upholstery.

Ikats from Nice Irma's

OSBORNE & LITTLE ⚠

Four collections of fabulous fabrics, all in 100% cotton, from this innovative firm. BOTANICA, inspired by eighteenth- and nineteenth-century document prints, features five designs with opulent blooms and foliage on a grand scale. 'Victoria' has poppies while 'Albert' has columns of roses and convolvulus on a Regency stripe. All the fabrics have a stain-resistant finish. *M:* w140cm (55in). *P:* £11.85 m.
CASAQUE from France has three rich, exotic designs in dark colourways: 'Sarong' with ikat

Osborne & Little's CASAQUE

bands in a stripe effect; 'Siam' with small leopard spots; and 'Asia' with an elaborate mix of pagodas, fruit and foliage. All have a lightly glazed finish. *M:* w150cm (59in). *P:* £15.95 m.
STRIPE, also French, has six designs, all lush, some with gold accents. 'Kim' with broad and narrow bands in a watered-silk effect comes in seven colours; 'Merina' and 'Yoruba' have floral and geometric patterns on striped grounds; 'Katarina' is a brocade with wide bands embossed with a rose motif; 'Kado' has a Regency stripe in three quiet hues; and 'Messara' is a contemporary marbled stripe. *M:* w50cm (59in). *P:* £13-£22 m.
LES TISSUS is the most unusual, with glazed and unglazed prints from the 1930s and 1940s, including 'Victoria Stripe' with verticals of moiré and checked panels in six unusual colours and 'Mayfair', featuring art-deco florals and geometric motifs in three wonderfully rich colourways including one on a black ground. *M:* w150cm (59in). *P:* £14-£24 m.
(All prices ex VAT.)

Osborne & Little's STRIPE

PALLU & LAKE LTD

Exclusive furnishing textiles.
Some of the loveliest modern weaves come from Gretchen Bellinger, who use only natural fibres. There are five silk designs: 'Isadora', finely woven pleats in 13 colours; 'Mazurka', the same cloth with a horizontal top stitch giving a grid effect; 'Malmaison', a silk shantung; 'Josephine', a shot silk; and 'Coppelia', a dupion weave. All are in earthy and metallic tones. *M:* 'Isadora', 'Mazurka' w99cm (39in); 'Malmaison', 'Josephine' w130cm (51¼in); 'Coppelia' w150cm (59in). *P:* £60–£95 m.
Also by Gretchen Bellinger are other luxury natural fabrics such as 'La Scala', a mohair plush in red, green or blue. *M:* w135cm (53¼in). *P:* £200 m. 'Pasha' is a linen velvet in seven shades. *M:* w130 (51¼in). *P:* £80 m. 'Skimmer' is in 100% linen in 16 neutral shades and pastels. *M:* w132cm (52in). *P:* £48 m. 'Applause' offers a choice of 20 shades in pure cot-

ton velvet. *M:* w137cm (54in). *P:* £80 m. And 'Croquet' is a plain hobnail reversible weave, also in six shades of pure cotton. *M:* w130cm (51¼in). *P:* £85 m. There are also pure wool fabrics in some unusually intense colours.

For traditionalists, there is an extensive range of fine woven silks and cotton damasks, velvets, tissues and plains suitable for period restorations. These are all hand-woven by the Humphries Weaving Co, the last mill of its kind in the country. *M&P:* on application.

If you are after stripes, look at the MARCATO range. 'Regatta Tela' has a thin stripe with or without a moiré finish, in nine colours. 'Bucintoro Tela' has equidistant stripes in a single combination of mint green/sky blue/yellow. Somewhat similar, 'Puparino' has a stripe in lime, yellow, aqua or hot pink on a grey ground with plain or moiré finish. 'Carolina Tela' has a vertical stripe giving an optical illusion of folding, in two colourways: aqua/ yellow or grey blue/peach. Finally, 'Silvas' is a rep in a narrow stripe, also available plain. All these are in mixes of spun rayon and cotton. *M:* w140cm (55in). *P:* £35 m; moiré designs £36 m. In 100% spun rayon in the same range there's 'Canton', a soft wide stripe in four pastel shades. *M:* w140cm (55in). *P:* £45 m.

Most of the fabrics in the stunning range from Zumsteg of Switzerland are colour-coordinated — a result of Zumsteg's special printing technique. There are gorgeous paisleys such as the large-scale 'Kasmir' and smaller-scale 'Persor', each in three colourways, and matching semi-plains like the faintly chequered 'Klio' in six colourways. All are 100% cotton. *M:* w130cm (51¼in). *P:* 'Kasmir', 'Persor' £40 m; 'Klio' £25 m. And there are lush wild silks, 'Renaissance', 'Cosimo' and 'Sandro' all with Persian-type designs in rich shades, plus 'Tuscan' and 'Chevron' in pastel colours. *M:* w140cm (55in). *P:* £60 m. With an exotic, tribal feel there's 'Veneto', a batik-inspired print, and a co-ordinating stripe, 'Rial-

Zumsteg fabrics from Pallu & Lake. Left to right, from top: 'Cosimo', 'Tuscan', 'Chevron', 'Renaissance'

Left to right, from top: Pallu & Lake's 'Persor', 'Klio' 'Kasmir'

to'. Both are designed to go with a plain basket weave, 'Jaspé Basket'. The first two are in 100% cotton, 'Jaspé Basket' in cotton/polyester, and all three come in predominantly deep shades. *M:* w130, 135cm (51¼, 53¼in). *P:* 'Veneto', 'Rialto' £40 m; 'Jaspé Basket' £45 m.

PARALLEL LINES
Delightful range of colourful fabrics manufactured in a small studio. Three designs, 'Origami', 'Rockies' and 'Roxy', feature simple geometric motifs hand-printed on 100% cotton in cheery colours such as bright blue, grass green, orange, red and yellow on a white ground. *M:* w132cm (52in). *P:* £9.50 m.

From left: Parallel Lines' 'Origami', 'Rockies' and 'Roxy'

PARKERTEX LTD
Almost all the weaves you could want, from a sister company of G P & J Baker (who are known for their document prints). The range covers a tremendous variety of weaves and

textures. 'Avignon' is a woven, textured vertical stripe in 51% cotton/49% viscose in five colours. *M:* w130cm (51¼in). *P:* £19.68 m. 'Pinner' has a diamond weave in 82% polypropylene/17% acrylic/1% nylon in five pastel shades. *M:* w125cm (49¼in). *P:* £10.98 m. 'Brindisi', a herringbone weave, and two striped co-ordinates come in a total of 45 colours made from 62% cotton/38%viscose. *M:* w140cm (55in). *P:* £14 m. 'Auvergne', a fine 100% wool with a slight zigzag weave comes in 30 lovely shades. *M:* w130cm (51¼in). *P:* £23 m. And 'New Montrose' is a quilted-effect, upholstery-weight fabric in 70% viscose/30% cotton in 11 colourways. *M:* w130cm (51¼in). *P:* £21.50 m.

The collection of tapestries includes some traditional designs with crests, floral patterns and grids, plus an art nouveau design, 'Godolphin', with leaves and flowerheads typical of the period, made from 46% viscose/30% polyester/24% acrylic. *M:* 'Godolphin' w104cm (55in); others w125-140cm (49¼-55in). *P:* 'Godolphin' £21.18 m; others £11-£30 m.

Among the brocades is 'Jaipur' in pure Indian silk in an amazing array of 45 colours including about a dozen shades of off-white. *M:* w120cm (47¼in). *P:* £20.50 m. To co-ordinate there are 'Bengal' and 'Belur', two woven vertical stripes in gorgeous hues. *M:* w120cm (47¼in). *P:* £23.10 m.

From top: 'Belur', 'Jaipur', 'Bengal' from Parkertex

For a ruched effect there are two pure cotton fabrics with puckered stripes: 'Sikkim' with a wide stripe, in eight pastel colours; and 'Sakar' with a narrower stripe in 13 colourways. *M:* w130cm (51¼in). *P:* £12.02 m.

Also in 100% cotton are three multi-purpose jacquards: 'Sherborne' in 14 colourways,

FABRICS AND WALL COVERINGS

Parkertex's 'Sakar' and 'Sikkim'

'Syracuse' and 'Versailles', more expensive and each in 15 shades. *M:* w125-140cm (49½–55in). *P:* 'Sherborne' £19.28 m; others £33.02m. Parkertex also do some nice patterned jacquards such as the MEXICO range with four designs featuring Aztec-inspired ziggurats, stripes and key effects, all in 70% cotton/30% polyester in a total of 18 colourways including lemon/mint, aqua/grey, peach/pale olive and pink/grey. *M:* w135cm (53¼in). *P:* £22.34 m.

Selection from Parkertex's MEXICO

Damasks include the traditional 'Padua', 100% cotton in 12 colourways. *M:* w130cm (51¼in). *P:* £19.26 m. There are also slubbed damasks, 'Keswick' and 'Ashover', in more than 30 colours. *M:* w125cm (49½in). *P:* £13.46 m. Flame-resistant traditional and modern damasks include 'Pentland' with diamond motif in 60% polyester (Trevira CS)/40% modacrylic. *M:* w125cm (49½in). *P:* £11.74 m.

In terms of moirés, there's 'Kintail', 100% viscose in 32 shades. *M:* w115cm (45¼in). *P:* £10.44 m. And 'Charlieu', 56% viscose/22% linen/22% cotton in 50 colours, is suitable for both curtains and upholstery. *M:* w130cm (51¼in). *P:* £15.70 m.

Parkertex's 'Kintail'

RUSSELL & CHAPPLE LTD

Long the haunt of artists buying lengths of canvas, and also of decorators in pursuit of basic bargain fabrics! The stock changes from time to time, but you can always get fine artist's linen in four widths and a superfine linen in one. *M:* fine w183, 213, 274, 305cm (72, 84, 108 120in); superfine w220 (87in). *P:* fine £5.33–£8.70m; superfine £8.31 m.

In addition there is white cotton duck in seven widths and in five weights ranging from 8oz (226g) to 12oz (340g). *M:* w91, 148, 183, 213, 244, 274, 346cm (36, 58, 72, 83, 96, 108, 136in). *P:* £1.10–£11.50 m. Coloured cotton duck is also available, in khaki and red.

For lighter-weight fabric, consider ever-popular unbleached calico sheeting, in two widths. *M:* w91, 183cm (36, 72in). *P:* 62p–£1.36 m.

Russell & Chapple also have fawn curtain lining, dyed flameproof cotton velours, white, black or grey flameproof scenic gauze, fine linen scrim, butter muslin, even green baize! Various discounts are available for orders over 20 and over 50 m (22 and 55 yd).

SAHCO-HESSLEIN UK LTD

Enormous number of high-quality upholstery and curtain fabrics from all over Europe, including some beautifully coloured warp prints. There are 30 classic brocades and tapestries. REMINISCENCE tapestry collection includes five pretty designs, three small-scale motifs, one diagonal stripe and one flame stitch, all in 40% cotton/40% viscose in a total of 25 colourways. *M:* w130cm (51¼in). *P:* £36-£40 m. 'Mestre' and 'Murano' make a lovely

Sahco-Hesslein's REMINISCENCE

tapestry duo, the first a slubby stripe in seven shades, the second a chequerboard weave in 10 shades, both in cotton/viscose in soft and varied tones. *M:* 130cm (51¼in). *P:* £36-£46 m. 'Nabucco' has a diamond pattern in 45% cotton/38% viscose/17% polyester in five natural colourings. *M:* w140cm (55in). *P:* £36 m. 'Aida' has a very thin vertical stripe and a horizontally-woven keyboard stripe, 55% viscose/45% cotton in nine colourways; 'Rigoletto' has a diamond trellis woven over a background stripe, 60% viscose/40% cotton in four colourways; and 'Tosca' has a damask-inspired classic motif, 60% cotton/40% viscose in six colourways. *M:* w130, 140cm (51¼, 55in). *P:* £35–£52 m.

Left to right, from top: 'Nabucco', 'Rigoletto', 'Murano', 'Mestre' and 'Aida'. All from Sahco-Hesslein

There are some unusual printed cottons with a partially pearlized finish, for example the impressionistic floral, 'Bogota', beautiful in pink and white with grey pearlized leaves, which co-ordinates with the striped, full glazed 'Gaeta'. *M:* w130cm (51¼in). *P:* £25 m. 'Delila' has a complex striped lattice with striped diamond infill, some of the stripes pearlized. The six colourways include a coolly elegant smoke blue/beige/coffee/grey/pearly white and a sumptuous magenta/purple/black/pearly grey. *M:* w150cm (59in). *P:* £33-£40 m.

Osborne & Little's SIENA co-ordinating wallpapers, fabric and borders

Crown's 'Edwardian' LINCRUSTA DADO

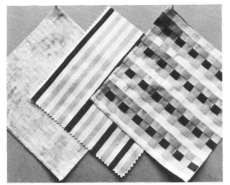

From left: 'Ducale', 'Beach' and 'Holiday' from Sahco-Hesslein

In the 100% Dralon FLAIR series are self-patterned weaves including a vertically striped herringbone, one with three differently textured small diamonds, a linen slub and a small diamond lattice. *M:* w145cm (57in). *P:* £22.50-£24.50 m.

MARBRE and FAVORITE warp-print fabrics from Switzerland, the former for curtains etc, the latter for upholstery, include some of the loveliest contemporary designs: checks, florals, geometrics and abstracts woven in one colour on a background of several subtly merging shades. The mottled background alone is also available as a fabric. 'Holiday' is a tight check in 19 colourways including a very soft salmon pink/beige/coffee/white and an elegant yellow/black/grey/white. 'Bergerac' has a bold design of large and small equilateral triangles, in seven colourways but particularly striking in black on a background of watery beige and turquoise. *M:* w150cm (59in). *P:* £33-£40 m.

Gorgeous VENEZIA series includes four co-ordinating collections with 20 different fabrics in all. SALUTE has warp prints similar to those above; one such is 'Ducale', a chequered weave of diamonds within diamonds inspired by the stonework of the Doge's Palace in Venice, in cotton/polyester. LIDO includes pearly cotton prints and 100% silks such as 'Samarkand', an abstracted paisley pattern in six colourways (including an autumnal rust/turquoise) and the marvellous striped silk taffetas, 'Beach' in nine bright colourways — each with white and three other colours — and its twin 'Florida' in the same colours but with a transparent stripe instead of white. The two remaining collections, FENICE and RIALTO, provide co-ordinating upholstery fabrics in modern and traditional styles. *M:* 'Samarkand' w140cm (55in); others w150cm (59in). *P:* 'Ducale' £40 m; 'Samarkand' £48 m; 'Beach' £42 m; 'Florida' £46 m. To co-ordinate, there are 18 plain shades in the TORCELLO COLLECTION. *M:* w150cm (59in). *P:* £42 m.

SAINT LEGER FABRICS

Fifty delightful modern prints hand-screened in Italy on pure cotton for curtains, wall coverings and upholstery, all created by the same designer, many of the designs having a hand-painted look. OCEAN makes brilliant use of grass green, blue, yellow, grey and/or clear pink with 'Riga', a wavy stripe, 'Seychelles', a shell motif, 'Naxos', an abstracted and enlarged flame stitch, and 'Bristol' a mock-chintz. All have a white background. *M:* w130cm (51¼in). *P:* £12.30-£13.80 m. PACIFIC has six stunning motifs in emerald green/pink, red/beige, bright blue/grey, yellow/orange, yellow/lime and apricot/grey. Among them, 'Acapulco' has a bold herringbone print; 'Bora Bora' has diamond shapes; 'Papua' and 'Papete' have small splodges of colour; and 'Waikiki' has alternating wave-like bands.

For co-ordinates try 'Tirreno' with pale yellow drop shapes on a striated beige ground and 'Arno' with larger mustard drops on the same ground. Or 'Shanghai', with a trio of bendy strokes in shades of beige, green, yellow, blue or apricot, co-ordinates with 'Singapore', the same fabric with the addition of a blossom motif. *M:* w140cm (55in). *P:* £14.20 m.

Saint Leger also import beautiful tapestry weaves from Italy, the DECO collection, a heavy cotton for upholstery with three small geometric weaves, in predominately pastel and neutral tones. *M:* w130cm (51¼in). *P:* £13-£15 m.

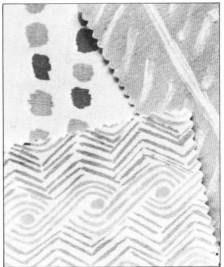

Left to right, from top: Saint Leger's 'Papua', 'Acapulco' and 'Waikiki'

ARTHUR SANDERSON & SONS LTD

Massive range displayed in Sanderson's marvellous London showroom which even has a snack bar for contemplation. Long-famed for their prints, Sandersons also do 15 ranges of plain fabric. CARTETOUCHE is glazed chintz in 50% polyester/50% cotton and in 76 colours. *M:* w48in (122cm). *P:* £9.95 m. CARTEBLANCHE, a 100% cotton chintz seersucker, comes in 21 plain shades and also in a wide self-stripe and a thin ripple effect for impeccable co-ordination. *M:* w48in (122cm). *P:* £9.25-£9.75 m. There are also three self-textured cotton satins, in 50% polyester/50% cotton in 48 colours: 'Satin Star', 'Straight' and 'Stitch'. *M:* w48in (122cm). *P:* £11.50 m.

For heavier use there's a 100% cotton tough twill with a crease-resistant finish in 31 flecked shades. *M:* w48in (122cm). *P:* £8.90 m. Or there's equally hard-wearing CATALAN cotton velours in 16 colourways. *M:* w54in (137cm). *P:* £10.50 m. AURORA offers an amazing array of 60 hues of cotton velvet with a stain-resistant silicon finish. *M:* w48in (122cm). *P:* £11.50 m. For lovers of luxury and available only through the trade, there are two ranges imported from Italy: from Ratti discharge-printed silk, wools and cottons with 33 designs of exotic paisleys and co-ordinating stripes, plus graded stripes, shadow effects, chequerboard weaves with over-printed plaids, and some with lurex accent threads; and from Luigi Bevilacqua, more traditional designs in silk, linen, cotton and/or viscose featuring damasks, brocatelles, taffetas and lampas in classic colourings such as yellow, ivory, and soft pastels. *M:* w54in (137cm). *P:* £60-£300 m.

SEKERS FABRICS LTD

Large range of patterned fabrics with matching plains that can be paper-backed for wall coverings, plus, unusually, co-ordinating plain carpeting (see separate entry).

Most impressive is the ENGLISH COUNTRY HOUSE collection, 100% cotton or glazed cotton chintz, with 12 period designs representing the major English styles. They are available both in period and modern colourings. 'Castle Ashby' features a Jacobean tree-of-life motif and has a co-ordinating striped panel fabric; early Georgian 'Standem' has beautifully faded floral configurations; 'Orchards' has small Victorian posies with a flowery border; and 'Earlywood', has bouquets in typically 1930s style. *M:* w137cm (54in). *P:* £14.90-£16.20 m.

Four other chintz ranges, all 50% cotton/50% polyester, present a wide choice of patterns. HANBURY features four designs: a flame stitch, a little cross-stitched flower, a Regency stripe with flower panels, and a plainer stripe, each in eight muted colourways. BOKHARA offers plain and puckered fabrics with stripes and zigzags, each in up to 10 medium pastel colours. AKITA and SAMARKAND offer more small designs with geometric or floral motifs such as stripes, diamonds, diamonds with inset flowers, in pale to medium shades. SAMARKAND also offers two plain-coloured glazed cottons, one smooth, one puckered, to go with the patterns. *M:* all w122cm (48in). *P:*

FABRICS AND WALL COVERINGS

Selection from Sekers' BOKHARA

smooth £13.20 m; puckered £14.40 m.

A jacquard collection, ZODIAC, with an up-to-date glossy designer look, offers six deceptively simple designs woven in two-tone satin/matt effects: swirls, stripes, herringbone, diagonals, butterfly-wing and a three-dimensional design of stacked cubes. All come in 10 colours, pale to medium tones of crab-pink, inky-blue, silver grey and orchid. The fabric is 56% viscose/44% cotton, suitable both for upholstery and curtains. Also a jacquard, BECK-FORD, in 71% cotton/29% polyester with Scotchgard finish, reverses to a satin effect. The five designs — a small basket-weave, big swirl, large trellis, irregular diagonal stripe and an art deco motif — are each woven in two-tone effects in 16 colours and can be woven with gold lurex highlights if desired. *M:* both w137cm (54in). *P:* £17.40 m.

Selection from Sekers' ZODIAC

HIRST collection in pure wool, also suitable both for upholstery and curtains, offers smooth and textured fabrics in soft and subtle colours both light and dark. There are also some tiny all-over designs in toning colours. The fabrics have been treated to give them extra fire-resistance and are suitable for all contract uses as well as retail. *M:* w137cm (54in). *P:* £23.60–£27.40 m.

DOBBIES in 52% viscose/48% cotton, is an upholstery-weight fabric in four small woven designs giving a textured look, available in 40 plain colours. All are treated with Scotchgard. *M:* w137cm (54in). *P:* £15 m.

Other plain colour fabrics are VALENCIA, a 100% cotton velours, and SAFIR, a 63% viscose/37% acetate dupion, each in 50 colours. *M:* VALENCIA w120cm (47¼in); SAFIR w122cm (48in). *P:* VALENCIA £11.20 m; SAFIR £14.90 m.

SKOPOS FABRICS

Yorkshire firm best known for their large, flame-retardant contract range but with some retail fabrics too. MARCO POLO retail range, for example, comprises six designs in 100% cotton sateen and co-ordinating 100% polyester sheers. There's self-descriptive 'Marble', 'Reed' (with ikat-style colouring) and 'Batik Flower', diagonal 'Bali Stripe', and swirling 'Cascade' and 'Cobra', each in four to eight colourways. Sheers come in standard ivory on white or in special ivory, pink or blue on champagne. Fabrics can be given flame-retardant finish for small surcharge. *M:* cotton sateen w122cm (48in); sheer w150cm (59in). *P:* cotton sateen £5.25 m; sheer £3.50–£4.50 m; flame-

From left: 'Batik Flower', 'Bali Stripe', 'Marble' sheer, 'Reed', 'Cascade', plus 'Cascade' sheer (on chair) and 'Marble' (on floor). From MARCO POLO by Skopos

retardant finish £1 m.

The Skopos contract range is distinguished by its clean, modern style. FLAME-RETARDANT PRINTED FABRICS, either cotton or cotton sateen, come in 70 or more different designs — large and small-scale block prints, floral and foliage patterns, and a particularly striking collection of geometrics, chevrons, diagonal stripes and hexagons. Each comes in three to five standard colourways, some in unusual metallized finishes. Co-ordinating bedspreads are available with most designs. There are also border-print fabrics using 10 or so of the same designs, and a few of the designs are used on panel prints. *M:* w122cm (48in). *P:* on application.

PRINTED SHEERS, all inherently flame-retardant 100% polyester, come in 30 designs including dots, dashes, zigzags and some unusual multicoloured designs co-ordinating with the cotton prints. *M:* w150cm (59in). *P:* on application.

WEAVES come in eight plain colours of flame-proofed 100% cotton or cotton sateen — white, beige, bamboo, orange, yellow, light grey, bronze and antique silver — and there are striped and chequered weaves in four colourways — blue, brown, natural and green. *M:* w122cm (48in). *P:* on application. POCKET WEAVES in modacrylic come in two designs: 'Metro' with small multicoloured rectangles and 'Honfleur' with a small diamond and floral design, each in six colourways. *M:* w178cm

FABRICS

(70in). *P:* on application. There are also two jacquard weave designs in 15 colourways. *M:* w133cm (52¼in). *P:* on application.

Skopos also do bedspreads, valances, lining fabrics and blackout-coated fabrics and a flameproof voile. A selection of designs are available on printed cotton velours. Non-standard colours can be printed on orders of over 60m (65yd) for designs of one or two colours and on orders of over 500m (547 yd) for designs of more than two colours.

SUNDOUR FABRICS

Modern abstract or geometric prints in 100% cotton with a protective Scotchgard finish. AD-LIB range has more than 10 different designs: 'Sail-Through' could be construed as a sea-scape or skyscape in three soft colourways, predominantly beige, blue or rose; 'Flash-Back' is a similar design but printed diagonally across the fabric in pinkish brown/pale blue, sage green/pale pink, rose pink/pale blue or grey/pale lilac; 'Jet-Set' and 'High-Flier' (one a reversed-out version of the other) have a bold wing-shaped print in either red or grey on cream; 'Front-Line' is a busy criss-cross pattern in either green/turquoise or sand/grey on cream; the impressionistic 'Zig-Zag' comes in soft colour combinations, sandy brown/grey, grey/rusty pink, rust/grey; 'Spark-Out' has mushroom geometric blocks on a pale mushroom background with occasional blue, black and brown over-printed triangles. *M:* w140cm (55¼in). *P:* £5.95 m (ex VAT).

Sundour's 'Sail-Through'

TAMESA FABRICS LTD

Stunning collection of plain, printed and woven fabrics. Tamesa are known for the boldness of print patterns such as 'Wheatsheaf', with large sheaves flanked by a related wheatear border, in ochre, straw and beige. *M:* w127cm (50in). *P:* £20.70 m. Another print,

'Cat's Cradle', has a continuous knot motif in one colour — black, white, grey, blue, beige or burgundy — on a natural ground. *M:* w127cm (50in). *P:* 12.18 m. 'Green Mansions' has a scattering of leaves in four colourways: two tones of grey, two of beige, maroon/navy and pink/terracotta. *M:* w127cm (50in). *P:* £13.10 m. All these are on heavy, scoured cotton.

Top: 'Cat's Cradle'; below: 'Green Mansions'. From Tamesa

Semi-sheers in linen and cotton include 'Iona' in cream with an open-weave vertical stripe; 'Lyric', woven with cream and mauve flecks; and 'Confetti' with woven pastel or ivory stripes on cream. *M:* w130cm (51¼in). *P:* £14.54–£15.58 m.

Tamesa has a terrific range of pale, pearly-coloured jacquards with striking motifs: 'Conquest' with an Inca-inspired stacked square in apricot, green, yellow or aquamarine; 'Coronet' with stylized tulips in yellow, green, pink, peach, ivory and grey, and co-ordinating 'Tiara' with more complex motifs in all these colours except grey; 'Circus' with raised stripes in orange/sea blue, mustard/olive, burgundy/navy or peach/grass green on cream. All are on 100% cotton. *M:* w140cm (55in). *P:* £22.76 m.

There's a marvellous moquette in 100% cotton, 'Griffin', with a slightly raised, irregular nap in five shades: grey, buff, beige, cinnamon, peach. *M:* w145cm (57in). *P:* £28.06 m.

Tamesa also have some ravishing, simply patterned silks: 'Royalty', a subtle, plaid-like check in apricot/yellow/aqua, rust/olive, pink/green or sea green/apricot; 'Bath' with thick and thin Regency stripes in pale grey, beige, blue, café au lait, green, red or multicolours on white; 'Myriad' with very thin lines and a broad horizontal band of subtly blended, very pale colours — green/pink, blue/aqua, apricot/peach, yellow/gold, yellow/beige, and peach/

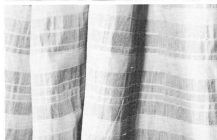
Top: 'Tiara'; below: 'Circus'. From Tamesa

yellow; 'Sylphide' with satin/matt horizontal stripes in shimmering white, oyster and pale blue; and 'Gloriana' with wide stripes in seven colourways. *M:* w127cm (50in), *P:* £53.40 m. Also silk, 'Regatta' has pin stripes in 10 pastel shades and the co-ordinating plain, 'Taffeta', has a slight slub in 13 colours. *M:* w127cm (50in). *P:* £45.96 m. And for a heavier weight, look at 'Tosca', a bold, vertical stripe-effect in exquisitely mixed muddy shades of old rose, apricot, peach and pale turquoise with accents of beige and off-white. *M:* w127cm (50in). *P:* £55 m.

Tamesa's 'Sylphide'

TARIAN DESIGN LTD ▲

Distinctive range of furnishing fabrics with bold, fresh designs by Evelyn Redgrave. All fabrics are 100% cotton with an easy-care finish or flame-resistant Trevira twills and sheers. Among the most recent designs are 'Quattro', a grey grid pattern with patches of contrasting pink/blue or yellow/grey in flame retardant twill. Its mate, 'Quintessence', has varying widths of vertical stripes in four colourways: peach/blue, yellow/grey, pink/coral and green/blue. Also available are matching plain twills in nine colours. *M:* all w112cm (44in). *P:* £10 m. Evoking images of the countryside are bold

FABRICS AND WALL COVERINGS

Selection of Timney Fowler prints

Top: 'Rio Bamba' △; below 'Quattro'. From Tarian

panoramas such as 'Alpine', 'Pastoral' and 'Rio Bamba'. The latter comes in almond/green/ coral, coral/brown, pink/grape, blue/pink, turquoise/grey, printed on cotton flame-retardant sheer and twill. A modernistic patchwork, 'Checkmate', in the same three fabrics features strokes of colour within a grid in green, lilac, pink or apricot colourways. *M:* cotton w112cm (44in); sheer, twill w130cm (54½in). *P:* £8.60 m; sheer £9.50 m; twill £9.80 m.

Tarian's 'Checkmate'

TIMNEY FOWLER PRINTS

Chic painterly designs from the studios of Graham Fowler and Sue Timney on a variety of different weights but always natural fabrics, from cottons to heavy silk. There are about 50 prints in production at any one time ranging from the neoclassical to large modern abstracts and bold stripes. Particularly impressive are the designs in black on white or black on cream, including a newsprint collage and one of beautifully sketched nudes. The prints are mainly monocolour on grounds of soft browns, creams, greens through to brighter primary colours but the company will under-

take special commissions on orders of over 50m (54½yd). *M:* w90, 120cm (35½, 47¼in). *P:* £8–£15 m; special orders price on application.

TISSUNIQUE LTD

Beautiful fabric ranges of exceptional quality and, as you would expect, not cheap. In addition to producing its own collections, Tissunique imports some of the most famous and exclusive names from the other side of the Channel, amongst them the leading Paris-based designer Manuel Canovas, noted above all as a superb colourist. His exuberant huge cotton print 'Quel Beau Printemps!' with its bright vases, pots and jugs of daffodils, tulips, hyacinths and daisies on a flecked beige background would defy any gloomy winter thoughts. *M:* w130cm (51¼in). *P:* £75 m. His other 100% cotton chintzes include gigantic bows of ribbon or lilies of the valley in extraordinary but effective colour combinations. *M:* w130cm (51¼in). *P:* £50 m. Also in cotton chintz, 'Plaid' and 'Clothilde' have similar designs, the first a large plaid-like check in contrasting colours on a plain ground, the second with a similar check over-printed over a twig-like pattern. Colourways include vibrant red or orange on deep emerald or elephant grey.

Tissunique's 'Plaid' and 'Clothilde'

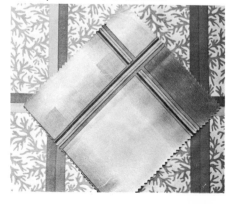

Matching twig pattern-only fabrics are also available. *M:* w130cm (51¼in). *P:* £28 m. There are also some richly coloured designs influenced by the carpets of the Middle East and an impressive modern tapestry, 'Jacobine', in cotton/viscose available in gorgeous blue, green, red or brown on a natural background. *M:* w130cm (51¼in). *P:* £60–£70 m. There are also some quieter tapestry weaves, neat designs in colourways with lots of toning naturals and greys and soft combinations such as mid blue/russet. 'Adelaide' has stripes and grouped squares, 'Amalia' has small squares and 'Anna' four grouped diamonds; all these on a ground with a faint lattice outline and in 74% viscose/26% cotton in five colourways. 'Bagatelle' in 93% viscose/7% cotton has a dotted design, sweet in white on grey; 'Bourbon' in 100% viscose has a wonderfully subtle flame pattern; and 'Constance' in 93% viscose/7% cotton has paisley comma shapes on a dotted ground. *M:* w130cm (51¼in). *P:* 'Bourbon' £40 m; others £36 m.

Left to right, from top: 'Amalia', 'Anna', 'Constance', 'Bagatelle', 'Bourbon'. All from Tissunique

Among the plain ranges is a luxurious corduroy-velvet herringbone in 100% cotton, 'Roma' in 24 shades, a range of fine pure wool, 'Harlequin', in 60 different colours, some excellent wool flannel, 'Limousine' in 20 deep colours, and an unusual cotton moiré, 'Bourbon', in 23 colours. *M:* w130cm (51¼in). *P:* 'Roma' £62 m; 'Harlequin' £50 m; 'Limousine' £75 m; 'Bourbon' £43 m.
Collections from Pierre Frey/Patifet include a wonderful pure cotton print of giraffes on a chinoiserie background in two colourways, blue/salmon pink and green/flame orange. *M:* w130cm (51¼in). *P:* £30 m. And there's a fun, nostalgic woven design, 'La Passée', of flying and floating ducks in various colourways — green on cream, black on grey, green on blue,

cream on beige, two-tone yellow or two-tone red. *M:* w130cm (51¼in). *P:* £50 m. Plain ranges include a polyester/acetate taffeta in 29 colours. *M:* w130cm (51¼in). *P:* £30 m. And the NATECRU collection offers a vast range of differently textured cottons and woven fabrics all in plain white or natural shades. *M:* w130, 140 or 150cm (51¼, 55 or 59in). *P:* £14–£36 m. Prelle et Cie collections provide the highest quality traditional design, as might be expected from this old firm founded in Lyons in 1774 which has decorated so many French chateaux and embassies. The ranges include everything you might need for classic furniture upholstery, elaborate tapestries and brocades, damasks and an impressive modern acrylic that looks like wild silk. The amazing HAMELIN range of hand-embroideries are for curtains, seat covers, quilts, tablecloths etc, made to order with often the richest and most complicated designs beautifully worked in silver or gold thread. For the wealthy only! *M & P:* on application.

The same company produces a hand-printed range of traditional cotton chintzes, THE NATIONAL TRUST COLLECTION, specially for Tissunique. Six designs have been recreated by the English designer and decorator David Mlinaric from original late eighteenth- and early nineteenth-century documents still surviving in British houses. 'Castle Coole', 'Thorpe Hall', 'Erddig', 'Stamford' and 'Stamford Borders', and 'Dunham Massey' have all been produced in the original colourway plus several new colour schemes. An additional fabric 'Royal Oak' using the familiar National Trust emblem has been designed to co-ordinate with the other chintzes in four colours: green, blue, red or yellow ochre on beige. *M:* w130cm (51¼in). *P:* £15–£25 m.

Also available from Tissunique are beautiful upholstery trimmings from the famous French firm La Passementerie Nouvelle. The range includes handmade cords, ropes and tassels, intricately woven braids, borders, tie-backs, woollen and silk fringes and some more modern-looking trims. *P:* on application.

TURNELL & GIGON LTD

Top quality Continental fabrics, plus a collection of very exclusive English chintzes. The latter, based on nineteenth-century originals, have complex floral designs in pure glazed cotton. One such is 'Arundel' with peonies in purple/yellow/pink on white, blue/pink/green on cream or peony pinks and carmines on cream. *M:* w140cm (55¼in). *P:* £22 m.

From Rome CESARI range includes both traditional and modern designs. 'C45034' is a tapestry weave in 100% viscose with a trio of soft pink or golden carnations surrounded by a pale green wreath. In contrast, 'C34663' is a subtly striped moiré in 66% cotton/34% silk, available in three colours: bright blue, golden yellow and olive green. *M:* both w130cm

Turnell & Gigon's 'Arundel'

(51¼in). *P:* £54.77 m.

An impressive range of cut velvets includes 'C6501' in 20% cotton/80% viscose with alternating stripes in rose/old blue or green/gold, gold/cream, gold/blue. *M:* w130cm (51¼in). *P:* £86.82 m. And 'C8081' in 50% polyester/50% cotton has a rope-twist stripe alternating with wider bands of swirling leaves in grey blue, green, pink or beige on cream. *M:* w140cm (55in). *P:* £108.85 m.

There are some attractive co-ordinating cottons printed with silvery and golden accents on stippled pastel grounds of pink, lime green, bright yellow and blue grey. 'C3738' is a swirling paisley; 'C3736' is a lattice of lozenges containing paisley motifs, 'C3735' has stripes and ziggurat panels; and 'C3734' has the stippled ground alone. *M:* w130cm (51¼in). *P:* 'C2724' £31.15 m; others £34.82 m.

And in a tough, upholstery-weight weave there's 'C56733', 'C56732' and 'C56743', all

Turnell & Gigon's 'C45034'

⚠ *INDICATES ONE OR MORE OF THE PRODUCTS MENTIONED ARE SELECTED BY THE DESIGN CENTRE*

matching, sporty stripes and checks in 100% viscose. *M:* w140cm (55in). *P:* £18.55 m. There's also a more subtly coloured range of heavy striped fabrics in 55% cotton/45% viscose. *M:* w140cm (55in). *P:* £20.82–£23.62 m. (All prices ex VAT.)

WARNER & SONS LTD

Fabrics known for their excellence since Warners was founded more than 100 years ago. In conjunction with Greeff Fabrics in America they have a combined collection comprising several thousand fabrics and wall coverings. Many have an Eastern flavour with designs inspired by the silk paintings of China, the weaving of India, the carpets of Persia. For example, in the BORDER PRINT collection is 'Brampore', a design taken from an early nineteenth-century bed cover from the Coromandel coast of India, with a serpentine tree abounding with huge flowers, on 100% cotton in four colourways: gold/cinnamon on slate, rose/blue on ivory, rose/topaz on walnut, turquoise/brick on sand. Other designs in the range offer peacocks, peonies and birds of paradise enough to satisfy anyone's taste for the oriental. *M:* w54in (137cm). *P:* £12.35 m.

Warners are also known for their huge chintz collection which includes such delights as 'Dupont Rose' from their nineteenth-century archive, old roses in pink/white. *M:* w48in (122cm). *P:* £12.35 m. Or from a French interior there's 'Ribbon Trellis' with swags of pink ribbon tied in a trellis design to hold small aqua-coloured nosegays on a greyish ground. *M:* w48in (122cm). *P:* £12.35 m. Both are 100% cotton glazed chintz.

Warner's 'Ribbon Trellis'

OXFORD WEAVE AND LINEN UNION collection has some detailed designs such as 'Oriental Needlework', inspired by a hand-embroidered border of deer, birds and exotic plants, in tile (terracotta)/green on sand, and 'Marabella', a pattern of daintily embroidered panels employing a variety of stitches in cinnamon/sage on mocha or ivory. Both are 100% cotton. *M:* w54in (137cm). *P:* £14.70 m. The range also includes two designs inspired by carpets, 'Shiraz' and 'Aubusson'.

FABRICS AND WALL COVERINGS

To co-ordinate with the printed fabrics there are three qualities of plains: a 60% linen/40% cotton union and a cotton rep, both in 42 colours, and a tiny herringbone weave in 100% cotton in 58 colours. *M:* union, rep w142cm (56in), weave w137cm (54in). *P:* union £12.10 m; rep £11.95 m; weave £9.95 m.

From Greeff Fabrics, consider the richly marbled 'Marble Hall' from the STATELY HOMES collection, a cotton chintz with green, pink, natural, blue or slate predominating. *M:* w54in (137cm). *P:* £12.60 m. The collection features 10 other designs in 100% plain or glazed cotton such as 'Ribbon Cascade', 'Summer Swag' and 'Garden Party', each one a real beauty, in diverse styles from the sixteenth to the nineteenth century. And their tapestry prints, all 100% cotton, include a lovely zigzag, 'Chauveron' in lacquer/indigo, brick/charcoal or rose/indigo, and 'Jocelyn', a flame stitch in bronze/blue, camel/navy, plum/beige. *M:* w54in (137cm). *P:* £12.60 m.

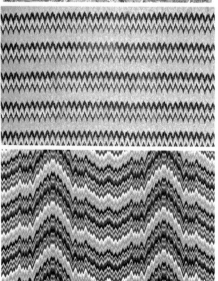

Greef Fabrics at Warner. From top: 'Marble Hall' △, 'Chauveron', 'Jocelyn'

BRIAN YATES (INTERIORS) LTD
Wonderful range of printed Italian cottons, unrivalled for colour. The company is the exclusive agent for the highly original designs of

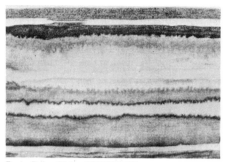

From Brian Yates' PAESAGGI

De Angelis of Milan. PRISMA SOLARE comprises four different stippled-effect geometrics in violent purples and turquoise, punk pinks and denim blue plus some quiet greens and yellows. *M:* w135cm (53in). *P:* £25 m.

The cotton satin PAESAGGI designs include interesting smudged stripes in soft, natural browns, beiges, blues and greens; also a busier broken, jagged stripe in pink/red/pale green/turquoise. *M:* w140cm (55in). *P:* £29. m. Delicate ORCHIDEE has irises, orchids and cyclamen in ultra pale blue, pink and lilac watercolour shades printed on finest cotton in semi-chintz finish. *M:* w140cm (55in). *P:* £25–£28 m.

WALL COVERINGS

ARCHITECTURAL TEXTILES LTD
Linen, wool, silk and suede wall coverings for contract use, treated with Scotchgard to resist stains, dust or dirt. All paper-backed, the TAPETEX range in linen, wool or silk comes in over 200 finishes and mainly natural or beige shades, sometimes with a hint of blue, green, pink, yellow or grey. The linen is pre-trimmed, with peelable paper backing in 60 options in narrower width and 15 in broad width. *M:* all w70cm (27½in), many also w140cm (54¼in). *P:* (contract) £4.60–£13.60 m. TAPETEX 'Suede' is a flocked viscose with a non-woven synthetic backing in 17 colours. *M:* w140cm (55¼in). *P:* on application.

There is also the TAURIDE range of high quality vinyl wall covering in six designs and 63 colourways on a cotton backing. *M:* w130cm (51¼in). *P:* on application.

MARTHE ARMITAGE
Beautiful hand-blocked, hand-printed wallpapers. There are 18 designs mostly based on plants on a white background; clients choose their own colouring since all the papers are printed to order. The papers are extremely durable and the inks are waterproof which makes hanging easier. Some of the designs can be printed on fabric and commissions for special designs are accepted. *M:* w22, 30in (56, 76cm), roll 11yd (10m). *P:* £16.50–£23 roll.

'Bamboo' by Marthe Armitage

J W BOLLOM & CO LTD
Large range of fabrics designed for exhibition or shop window display. Flame-proofed wall felts come in 84 colours. *M:* w72in (183cm), rolls 60 or 65m (66 or 70yd). *P:* £2.23–£2.53 yd. Hessian comes in a more limited range of 36 colours, but including reds and hot pink as well as the commoner natural tones. *M:* w72in (183cm), 17 selected colours also w52in (132cm), roll 60m (66yd). *P:* £1.51–£1.99 m.

Thin, flame-proofed, shiny PVC sheeting is available in 45 bright colours plus fluorescent orange and yellow and metallic gold and silver. *M:* w50in (127cm), roll 30m (33yd). *P:* roll £26–£34; cut lengths £1.02–£1.87 m.

There's also a range of simulated suede in 32 shades and leather in 30 shades including gold and silver. *M:* 'Suede' w57in (145cm), roll 35m (38yd); 'Leathercloth' w54in (137cm), roll 30m (33yd). *P:* 'Suede' £3.95–£4.40 m; 'Leathercloth' £1.75–£3.15 m, silver and gold £6.40–£6.95 m.

J W Bollom produce emulsion and eggshell paint to match all these fabrics (see *Paint*).

CAVALCADE WALLCOVERINGS LTD
Exceptionally wide range of natural and man-made fabric wall coverings, mostly paper-backed. CAVALWOOL (34% wool/15% polyester/51% modacrylic) comes either as 'Twist' — thick vertical stripes of natural coloured rope on a background of fine threads in either sand/orange or sand/light brown — or as 'Weave', a tweedy look in four neutral shades with flecks of brown or grey. *M:* 'Twist' w65cm (25in), roll 42m (46yd); 'Weave' w100cm (39in), roll 52m (56yd). *P:* 'Twist' £6.60 m; 'Weave' £13.20 m.

There are 29 plain colours of WALLFELT (35% wool/65% viscose) plus a marble effect in both white and beige, and also two mottled felts: 'Peacock' in deep turquoise and 'Fireglow' in crimson. *M:* w79cm (31in), roll 40m (44 yd). *P:* 4.95 m.

WALL HESSIAN comes in 26 shades of closely woven, latex-backed jute, though most of the neutral and earthy shades are also available paper-backed. *M:* w130cm (51in), roll 40m

(44yd). *P:* £5.15 m.

FOREST SUEDE made of flocked rayon on a cotton backing comes in 15 mainly rich warm shades. *M:* w140cm (55in), roll 50m (55yd). *P:* £9.30 m.

There are also three vinyl ranges. Fabric-backed ALPINE includes several textured finishes in neutral tones plus a heavy duty smooth finish that's highly resistant to abrasion and most stains, 'Tedlar', in white and buff. *M:* w130cm (51in), 'Tedlar' w120cm (47in); roll 50m (55yd). *P:* £2.70–£3.10 m; 'Tedlar' £6.85 m. CONFETTI, with embossed vinyl circlets on paper backing, comes in eight neutral colours plus tangerine orange and bitter chocolate. *M:* w127cm (50in), roll 30m (33yd). *P:* £1.90 m. Simulated hessian FLAX vinyl comes in 12 colours. *M:* w127cm (50in), roll 30m (33yd). *P:* £1.23 m.

Glass-fibre wall coverings suitable for painting come in five different weaves and can be used to disguise flawed walls. *M:* w100cm (39in), roll 50m (55yd). *P:* £1.20–£2.10 m.

All coverings are fire-retardant and Cavalcade will also supply appropriate adhesives. For rayon-fibre wall coverings with toning wallpaper and for linen wall coverings and furnishing fabrics see *Co-ordinates.*
(All prices ex VAT.)

COLE & SON (WALLPAPERS) LTD

Large range of excellent quality traditional-style wallpapers. OFFORD papers are all taken from period originals and include small formal patterns such as 'Windsor', a mid-Victorian geometric based on gothic designs, elaborate floral designs adapted on to wallpapers from eighteenth- and nineteenth-century French damasks, Regency stripes and a small star motif popular in the 1890s. *M:* w53cm (21in), roll 10m (11yd). *P:* £11.50–£32.50 roll.

DESIGNS IN WHITE is a collection of papers and borders with various patterns all picked out in white on an off-white or cream background, including narrow and wide stripes, large florals, oak leaves, wreaths, lacy trellis, small geometrics and a textured moiré. *M:* w53cm (21in), roll 10m (11yd). *P:* £13.80, £16.80 roll; borders 60p–£7.50 m.

A striking range of papers and co-ordinated

'02/102' with border from Cole's GILT EDGE

borders is the GILT EDGE collection where designs feature either gold or a gold sheen. There is a bold gold stripe '02/102' teamed either with red, blue, brown, mauve or green, and many colour co-ordinated plain papers shot with gold such as '02/129' with a fine spatter of gilt. A classic floral border is printed in various colours to go with the whole range. *M:* w53cm (21in), roll 10m (11yd). *P:* rolls £13.50–£19 roll; borders (10m coil) £21.50.

Cole's will also specially print their own designs in customer's colours for a minimum quantity of 10 rolls. *P:* on application.
(All prices ex VAT.)

CONTINENTAL TILES (SPECIALISTS) LTD

Real brick wall tiles in a choice of 'smooth', 'rough-hewn brushed' or 'figured' surface finish in natural brick colours: harvest gold, antique brown, rustic red and rustic brown. The brick tiles are designed to complement unglazed clay floor tiles in the same colours. All are made by Wevver of Denmark. *M:* wall tiles w23 × l5.5 × d1.8cm (9 × 2½ × ½in). *P:* £23–£27.60 sq m.

Continental's brick wall tiles

CROWN DECORATIVE PRODUCTS LTD

Well-known range of paint, co-ordinates and wall coverings. There's a very extensive collection of relief wallpapers such as ANAGLYPTA LUXURY VINYL, with a selection of mainly modern embossed designs, all in white. *M:* w52cm (20½in), roll 10.05m (11yd). *P:* £5.50 roll.

But most exciting and of real use to those restoring period houses there's LINCRUSTA DADO range, with two turn-of-the-century embossed paper designs, 'Edwardian' and 'Art Nouveau'. Both come ready trimmed in flat packs containing five panels and sufficient

LINCRUSTA 'Art Nouveau' dado from Crown

border to finish the edge. *M:* 'Edwardian' w61 × h101.6cm (24 × 40in); 'Art Nouveau' w54 × h91cm (21¼ × 36in). *P:* £38 per pack. See colour illustration.

For kids, there's the MAGIC OF DISNEY collection featuring all the best-loved characters — including Mickey Mouse and Donald Duck, Goofy, Robin Hood, 101 Dalmatians, the Lady and the Tramp — printed on white or coloured grounds. *M:* w52cm (20½in), roll 10.05m (11yd). *P:* £4.75 roll.

GASKELL BROADLOOM CARPETS LTD

A range of wall coverings from a quality carpet manufacturer to give a fully co-ordinated look to their PERFECT HARMONY range (see *Carpeting, patterned, plain, tiles* and *rugs*). The wall coverings (or 'wallcarpets' as Gaskell Broadloom call them) come in four designs, one in 100% polypropylene and the others in 100% wool. The look is soft and luxurious. 'Vignette' in 100% polypropylene looks like felt and comes in five beige to brown shades (the flax colour band of the PERFECT HARMONY collection), three pinks (the coral colour band), three greens (the jade colour band) and three blues (the ice colour band). 'Figurine' looks like strands of coarse wool, 'Pastiche' like fine wool and 'Collage', a random mixture of the two. These three wallcarpets in 100% wool each come in one shade in each of the four colour bands. *M:* w100cm (39¼in). *P:* on application.

GORDON, WATTS & CO LTD

HALLTEX decorative lining panels for walls and ceilings, manufactured in Finland. They provide good sound absorption plus thermal insulation and are ideal for all types of pinboard.

FABRICS AND WALL COVERINGS

HALLTEX from Gordon Watts

The panels are made from porous pine fibreboard. Wall panels are finished with 'Estoril' cork, yellow, green or natural hessian, beige linen, woven glass fibre in sunflower or rustica (brown), a silver-grey weave or 'Japanese grass' finish; ceiling panels are covered with embossed white paper in two textures, a weave or a striated line. All panels have both long edges grooved for neat fixing. *M:* wall panels w60 × l244cm (23½ × 96in), other lengths up to 545cm (214½in) to order; ceiling panels w30 × l305 or 366cm (11¾ × 120 or 144in); all d12mm (½in). *P:* £4–£9 sq m.

HABITAT DESIGNS LTD
A good range of wall coverings from this contemporary-minded chain store. In vinyl there are some simple one-colour prints on white grounds: 'Allegro' with strong stripes in red, green or yellow; 'Katia' with a red or blue repeating square; 'Swedish Squares' with a grid in green, blue or red; and 'Tennis' with a grey or blue chevron. *M:* w53cm (20½in), roll 10.05m (11yd). *P:* £4.45–£4.95 roll.
There are also three embossed papers, a good alternative to the ubiquitous wood chip: 'Hopsack' with a basket-weave surface; 'Herringbone' with a diagonal line in blue; and 'Hopscotch' with a square grid. *M:* w53cm (20½in), roll 10.05m (11yd). *P:* £2.55.
Habitat also make hessian, cork and woodplank wall coverings.

HAMILTON WESTON WALLPAPERS ▲
A continually growing collection of very special hand-printed historical wallpapers, reconstructed from fragments rescued from period London houses. There are six OLD PARADISE designs dating from 1690 to 1840, reproduced in the original colourways plus several new colours. The series includes the ornate chinoiserie-style 'Lambeth Saracen' (1690) in mid blue/cream, black/metallic gold, beige/burnt sienna and gold/black (original colour);

'Strand Teardrop' (1790) with vertical rows of clustered teardrops on pale blue (original), cream, beige and pink; 'Kingston Market' (1820), flowers and leaves on speckled background of light green (original), emerald green, pale blue, yellow and beige; 'Covent Garden Floral' (1830), elaborate floral ribboned design in burnt sienna on buff (original), light crimson red on rose, pale green on cream, palest blue on darker blue, white on cream and sienna on pale green; 'Fuchsia St James' (1835), twisting fuchsias in red/green on pale blue (original) or light brown background, dark green on pale green, cream/grey on white and lilac/green on heather; 'Richmond Trellis' (1840 though adapted) a deceptively modern-looking large trellis pattern in bright green on cream (original), grey/navy blue on white, burnt orange on blue, dark green/beige on apple green and mustard/pale

Top: 'Fuchsia St James' △; below: 'Richmond Trellis' △. From Hamilton Weston

blue on yellow. *M:* 'Lambeth Saracen' w20¼in (15.5cm); 'Strand Teardrop' w20½in (52cm); others w 21in (53.5cm); roll 11yd (10m). *P:* £18–£28 roll.

HATEMA UK LTD
High quality contract wall coverings for the interior designer, architect and specifier. SARI offers 300 textile alternatives. 'Classique' has thick and fine silky stripes with rose, grey-blue, sage or beige on an off-white and beige ground, while 'Structures' has a heavily textured weave in a subtle range of natural shades from white to mushroom. *M:* w100cm (39¼in). *P:* on application.
For a much tougher surface, ideal where a hallway, door or even tabletop will take lots of wear, there's SUWIDE-DURAL, a specially composed vinyl. Available in eight functional colours: off-white, beige, slate, black, light olive, khaki, light sage and dark green. *M:* w100cm (39¼in). *P:* on application.

From left: Hatema's 'Classique', 'Structures'

LEYLAND PAINT AND WALLPAPER PLC
Comprehensive and economical range of washable papers and vinyl wall coverings. SILHOUETTE is a range of blown-vinyl wall coverings that look remarkably like tiles but are much easier to apply. The 11 designs come in a total of 30 colourways. Ideal for kitchens and bathrooms, the realistic tile effects are in quiet, understated colours and, most important in these rooms, are easy to clean. *M:* w20½in (52cm), roll 11yd (10m). *P:* £7.99 roll.
COLOUR-WAVE washable papers have floral designs, textured patterns and tile and wood effects, in a total of 23 colourways. *M:* w20½in (52cm), roll 11yd (10m). *P:* £1.99 roll.
For children who can't bear to be separated from their TV favourites even in bed, there's FRAGGLE ROCK paper, featuring the Muppet-like TV characters. *M:* w20½in (52cm), roll 11yd (10m). *P:* £3.99 roll.

LUXURIOUS TEXTILES LTD
Highly original collection of wall coverings. Perhaps the most remarkable of the ranges is BEACHCOMBER including 'Autumn Leaves'

which has real leaves hand-pasted on to a paper back in four different hues, metallic orange, green, brown or metallic yellow. 'Trees' has a large, predominantly brown, tree-in-blossom design on cream hessian-look background and matching plain cream paper. 'Seagrass' has deep reddish brown grass pasted on to metallic gold paper. Plain paper is also available. *M:* w91cm (35¾in), roll 5.5, 6.1m (6, 6½yd). *P:* 'Autumn Leaves' £49 roll, 'Trees' £70 roll; 'Seagrass' £52 roll; plain £32 roll.

NEW SUEDERAMA is a collection of simulated suede in three nap finishes; it looks and feels like the real thing, and is available in a total of 60 colours. SUEDELUX in mainly browns, greys or reds has a more crinkled velvet appearance. *M:* w137cm (54in). *P:* cut lengths £5.60 m.

PROMENADE COLLECTION includes 'Sonata' which has vertical wild silk threads with characteristic slub in exotic pale colours; 'Caprice', a silky, predominantly white background with random coloured threads in either sand, blue, yellow ochre or green; 'Rondo', beige wool yarns and silky grey or bronze threads giving a striped effect; 'Symphony' contrasting velvety threads with thinner yarns for a bolder stripe; and 'Concerto', closely woven cream hessian with a very faintly coloured check design in sand, grey, pink or blue. *M:* 'Concerto' w88cm (34¾in); others w100cm (39¼in); roll 50m (55yd). *P:* £3.80–£6 roll.

PRECIOUS METALS COLLECTION is fabric-backed vinyl with a metallic finish: 'Halcyon' looks like beaten silver, gold, bronze, copper and platinum; 'Lapis' has a frosted effect in copper, silver blue and silver/white; 'Panoply' is a chequerboard pattern in either gold or red shiny foils; 'Chinese Pavilion' in chinoiserie style is on matt gold or pale blue background; 'Arboretum' has silver trees on white or mushroom and similar 'Seedling' design has little mushroom or white trees on silver. *M:* w66cm (26in), roll 9.75m (10½yd). *P:* £50 roll. (All prices ex VAT.)

Luxurious Textiles' 'Autumn Leaves'

NAIRN COATED PRODUCTS LTD

Elegant and original good quality vinyl papers from this company's subsidiary Kingfisher Wallcoverings. KINGFISHER MURALUX is a luxury screen-printed vinyl for bedrooms and

Nairn's 'Savannah'

living rooms. There are 10 mostly floral designs plus co-ordinating background papers that successfully imitate the textured look of silk and hessian coverings. One example is 'Savannah', a grass pattern on a hessian-effect background. Colours are mainly pastel. *M:* w52cm (20½in), roll 10m (11yd). *P:* £4–£8.99 roll. Kingfisher are also the manufacturers of CONTOUR — vinyl that looks deceptively like ceramic tiles. CONTOUR FRESH LOOKS collection includes several delicate designs such as 'La Mer' with its marbled 'tiles' and seashell motifs in soft green, pastel blue, stone and brown and 'Sweet Lorraine', a small tile pattern incorporating herbs and flowers in multicolours on a cream, white or off-white background. Bath and hand towels by Chortex bear the same motifs. 'September Song' has stylized flowers on a white louvred tile background in cornflower blue/green, beige/brown or green/apricot. CONTOUR TILING-ON-A-ROLL has 15 designs in 47 colourways, three of which — 'Lollipop', 'Candifloss' and 'Brighton Rock' — have ultra high-gloss finish. 'Lollipop' comes

Nairn's 'September Song'

in grey, pink, beige or green with two thin vertical stripes running off centre; 'Candifloss' is a large tile pattern in light or darker blue featuring subtle cloud effects in toning pink and white; and 'Brighton Rock' has seagulls and rainbows on random tiles in blue, turquoise and pink. *M:* all w52cm (20½in), roll 10m (11yd). *P:* £7.99–£9.99 m.

JOHN S OLIVER LTD

Exclusive hand-printed papers with some of the most dazzling designs around and a distinct emphasis on gold and silver. This highly imaginative firm has four of its own collections and in addition will print specifically to a client's colour requirement or own design. Many of the earlier designs are so up-to-date that they still remain popular: notably, the huge palm leaves 'Salmiyah Palm' from HANDPRINT collection (in glistening silver-beige on cream or electric green or white on silver foil), the enormous number of marbled and speckled papers from PLAINS OF ENGLAND, the zany zigzag 'Razmataz' from METALLIC collection (in six stunning colourways including black/white/silver, black/red/silver and black/green/silver) and, from the same range, the marvellous marbled 'Glimmer' designs in unusual colours and flashes of shiny gold. MIDAS collection consists of spongeable, mainly metallic papers with themes from the 1920s and 1940s as well as the 1980s: 'Odeon' has a huge cinema-inspired motif from the jazz age in matt gold on apricot, blue, green, cream, dove or red. (This motif is also available at half the size, as 'Nickelodeon'.) 'Ripple' is a wavy watermark pattern which comes in 12 colours and also as 'Roxy' with a 1940s-style abstract overprint. 'Razzle Dazzle' has lightning flashes in electric colours: red, green or white on silver foil, gold on cream, or gold on red. 'Marble' is a rich marbled paper in gold/bronze with brilliant veins of red, avocado or white. 'Silicon Valley' imitates the circuits of a microchip, in black on silver foil, silver on dove, gold on red or gold on cream. 'Bangkok' has a shimmering bamboo design on backgrounds of gold, red, pink, apricot, cream or turquoise,

From left: 'Razmataz', 'Silicon Valley' from John S Oliver

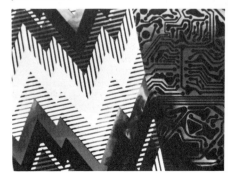

and 'Choo-sim' has the same design with an oriental floral overprint. *M:* all w53cm (20¾in), roll 10m (11yd). *P:* all £16.50–£48 roll (ex VAT). Pure cotton fabrics can be printed to match many of the paper designs and unusual paint colours can also be mixed to match.

ROUNTON DESIGN LTD △

Flexible cork wall coverings screen-printed with a non-toxic paint, in 13 colours: deep purple, crimson, indigo, terracotta, white, bright blue, green, yellow, cream, pink, turquoise, pale olive and natural. It's easy to hang using a water-based adhesive and is suitable for all walls including kitchens and bathrooms. *M:* coloured w100cm (39¼in), natural w110cm (43¼in), both d2mm. *P:* (cut lengths) coloured £7.18 m; natural £5.18 m.

STOREYS DECORATIVE PRODUCTS LTD

Huge range of inexpensive vinyl wall coverings from this popular firm under the HOMELOVER' brand name. HOMELOVER 10 has some interesting co-ordinating papers including a plain wild-silk effect, 'Dalkeith', and two floral designs, 'Poppy' and 'Poppy Field', printed over the plain paper in three pastel colours: grey, green or brown. Also co-ordinating are a tiny floral print, 'Jo Ann', and its sister paper, 'Jo' — identical except with colours reversed — in four colourways: green/white, brown/white, burgundy/white and blue/white. There are also tartan coverings in a red, blue or brown plaid pattern, shiny mock-tile papers in pastel brown, blue or green, simulated pine panelling and, for something quite different, a large panorama of scenes from the American Civil War. *M:* w50.8cm (20in), roll 10m (11yd). *P:* from £6 roll.
HOMELOVER CLASSIC has a variety of mainly floral designs with co-ordinating or contrasting plain papers, plus some textured-look ranges mostly in pastel colourways. *M:* w50.8cm (20in), roll 10m (11yd). *P:* £5–£6.50 roll.
HOMELOVER MODERN are pre-pasted vinyls and include some simple floral patterns, each with a choice of white, pastel or dark backgrounds. A smart design of matchstick-striped squares, 'Metro', is available in several candy colourways on white and in a co-ordinating plain paper — green, brown, blue or grey — with white matchstick-striped squares. *M:* w50.8cm (20in), roll 10m (11yd). *P:* £6 roll.
Storeys have also brought out a clever range of thick paper-backed vinyl to look like ceramic tiles. Aiming its designs at the kitchen or bathroom, ROLATILE has several designs that imitate the country-look kitchen with plain honey-coloured 'tiles' interspersed with patterned 'tiles' depicting fruit, oil and vinegar, pots of jam etc; a nice bathroom one, 'Coral' in green or pale cinnamon, uses four different-shaped 'tiles' with graduated shading and a fish-in-the-sea coral pattern running across

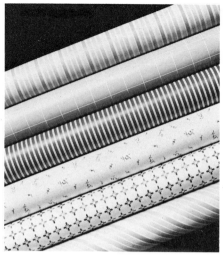

Storey's CON-TACT

several 'tiles'. *M:* w50.8cm (20in), roll 10m (11yd). *P:* £9–£11 roll.
CON-TACT self-adhesive vinyl is recommended for wall covering among other uses. Designs include stripes in soft candy colours as well as bold red/white and red/grey/white; 'Marco Check', like small pale blue tiles with white grouting; geometrics, florals, nursery prints, wood effects and the little apple and cocktail-stick prints from the HOMELOVER COCKTAILS range (see *Co-ordinates*). It is sold either in cut lengths or in rolls. *M:* w18, 27, 35in (45, 68, 90cm), roll 1.5m (1½yd). *P:* £1.10, £1.65, £2.20 m; £1.69–£2.49 roll.

TASSO DECOR INTERNATIONAL LTD

From Sweden, one of the largest ranges of contract wall coverings, in unusual but subtle colours and textures.
SONATA has a choice of two textures — one fine and warp-laid, one with a coarse diagonal weave — in 15 exceptionally good, soft colours ranging through tones of pink and red to mulberry, ivory, apricot, honey and pale blues, greens and greys. *M:* w92cm (36¼in), roll 50m (54⅔yd). *P:* on application.
ASTRA is made from 100% glass-fibre yarns coated with an acrylic compound, in 12 natural and pastel shades. *M:* w90cm (35½in), roll 8, 25m (8¾, 27⅓yd). *P:* on application.
TEMA is a textile wall covering in seven designs. 'Miami' has viscose and linen yarns woven to produce a rough linen effect and 'Atlanta' is loosely woven to produce an irregular vertical stripe, both in four colours — rose, sage, light gold and natural. 'Palma' is made from warp-laid rayon and linen yarns in palest of pale lime, grey, pink, peach, cream and white. 'Rustic' in 100% jute yarn has a bleached weft to give two tones, white and natural. 'Naturell' has an all-white woven

effect in 20% acrylic/13% cotton/33.5% rayon/33.5% linen. 'Dover' is a coarse weave in six mid tones, all with a warp of natural yarn. And 'LNK 20' and 'LNK 210' have a linen look in natural and off white. *M:* w92cm (36¼in), roll 8, 25m (8¾, 27⅓yd). *P:* on application.
TIVOLI comes in four different warp effects: silky 'Shantung' in 93% acrylic/7% rayon in four off-whites with a faintly coloured slub; chenille-effect 'Como' in linen/acrylic in six pastels and a deep rust; 'Mira' with a silk-slub effect in seven tones; and 'Messina' with a fluffy slub-effect in a fine polyester/linen/silk yarn in five neutrals. *M:* w92cm (36¼in), roll 8, 25m (8¾, 27⅓yd). *P:* on application.
All wall coverings are supplied fully trimmed and Tasso have their own adhesive.

TEROYDECOR LTD △

Beautiful warp-laid wall coverings on paper backing in 100% pure new wool or a mixture of wool and natural oriental silk. There are six ranges from designer Jean-Pierre Teroy, all with vertical yarns varying in thickness: WOOL DESIGN comes in mainly natural or cream colours with some darker variations of sand, brown or grey and a few have coloured yarns introduced giving a random striped effect in cream/green, cream/brown, cream/sand and chocolate/donkey brown. SILKWARP is available in predominantly sand, beige or grey with many subtle variations and also in several predominantly pink or green colourways. Teroydecor supplies its own adhesive. *M:* w100cm (39¼in), roll 50m (55yd). *P:* WOOL DESIGN £4.88–£6.74 sq m; SILK WARP £5.34–£5.84 sq m; adhesive (5l/8¾ pt tub to cover 25 sq m) £3.93 (ex VAT.)

From Teroydecor. Left and right: WOOL DESIGN △; centre: SILKWARP

TODAY INTERIORS LTD

Huge range of contract wall coverings for architects and specifiers. DAYMUR in polyurethane/viscose/rayon has 33 shades of suede effects, all with the appearance of crushed velvet, ranging from the palest grey and blue to the deepest navy and black. Supplied cotton- or paper-backed for easy hanging. *M:* cotton-backed w145cm (57in); paper-backed w66cm, (26in). *P:* on application.

DAYMUR from Today Interiors

DELFO has a silk-effect with a natural slub in 32% cotton/17% rayon/51% acrylic, in 24 pleasing colours including five greens, five off-whites and eight neutral as well as a red and dark blue. *M:* w99cm (39in). *P:* on application. For a similar silky-slub effect in 100% rayon there's CHROMATEX in 25 pleasing shades including three off-whites, five pinkish tones, four blues, yellows, green and browns. It matches the 10 designs in the STRIPE range which have subtly-contrasting diagonal stripes. *M:* w80cm (31½in). *P:* on application. CHENILLE in 100% acrylic has that characteristic texture of thick and thin twists in 12 colours. CHENILLE ROYALE has an even chunkier chenille texture, paper-backed in 25 shades including six browns. *M:* w80, 100cm (31½, 39¼in). *P:* on application.
All lengths supplied paper-backed, fully trimmed and cut to length unless specified otherwise. Today Interiors will also supply the correct adhesive for successful hanging.

CHENILLE ROYALE from Today Interiors

WALLPAPER ORIGINALS
Imported textured wall coverings. CRYSTAL range from Japan comes in three different textures, shimmering with mica chips, in 22 different colours. *M:* w91cm (35¾in). *P:* £6–£8.30

m. SILK LOOK from Italy, made from vertical slubbed yarns, also has three textures in a total of 32 colourways. *M:* w100cm (39¼in). *P:* £4.75–£6.50 m.

WICANDERS LTD
WALCORK real cork panels for use on walls, ceilings, chimney-breasts and doors from a company well-known for its cork floor tiles

Wicanders' WALCORK 'Barque'

(see *Flooring*). The wall tiles come pre-waxed in ten differently textured patterns from the coarse 'Harmony' to the striated 'Zebra', or 'Barque', a relief pattern on a natural or coloured background, either red, green, yellow or black. The company also supplies its own adhesive, Walbond. *M:* 'Barque' 60 × 30cm (23½ × 11¾in) in packs of four; others 30 × 30cm (11¾ × 11¾in) in packs of nine. *P:* 'Barque' £3.84 pack; others £2.81–£4.30 pack.

CO-ORDINATES

LAURA ASHLEY LTD
Ever-expanding range of document-inspired prints applied to a varied selection of fabrics (see *Fabrics*), some co-ordinated with fully washable wallpapers. COUNTRY FURNISHING cottons and papers should solve most decorating problems of those who favour period interiors. There are 59 designs for fabrics, 50 for wallpapers, including geometrics, small-scale florals, blowsy bou-

Selection of co-ordinates from Laura Ashley

FABRICS AND WALL COVERINGS

quets, stripes, flames, even a few contemporary-style prints, in just about every colour you could want: navy, burgundy, saddle (dark beige), dark green, sage, plum, smoke (dull blue), moss (green), terracotta, sand, apricot, aquamarine, rose, sky blue, china blue (bright blue), sapphire (soft cornflower), mustard (bright yellow) and poppy (red). M: fabric 122cm (48in); papers w53cm (20¾in), roll 10m (11yd). P: fabric £3.95 – £5.75; paper £3.45 – £5.25.

In addition, there are 37 wallpaper and 33 fabric borders. Paper borders have the same washable surface as the wallpapers and are co-ordinated with the 50 wallpaper designs to be used for accenting dadoes, architraves, windows, cornices etc. M: w5.5, 11cm (2, 4¼in) roll 10m (11yd); narrow borders sold in packs of two, wider borders sold singly in packs. P: £2.75 pack.

The fabric borders have a selvedge of 4cm (1½in) to allow for hemming. Use them to add a finishing touch to curtains, pelmets, tie-backs, blinds, cushions, quilts and bedlinen. M: w5.5, 11cm (2, 4¼in). P: £1.75, £1.95 m. To complete the effect, Laura Ashley has braid, bias binding, roller blind kits, table and bed linen, quilts, cushions, lampshades and bases, floor and wall tiles, lace panels and even paint (see separate entries).

Fabrics and paper from Laura Ashley's
COUNTRY FURNISHING

G P & J BAKER LTD
Famous collection of designs which are for the most part taken from document prints. ENGLISH TOILE collection has 100% cotton fabrics and hand-printed papers featuring familiar Baker motifs; for example, 'Birdsong' with trails of foliage and exotic plumed birds, 'Passion Flower' with those unusual blooms and more exotic fowl, 'Turf Inn' with carriages and landscapes, 'Cow Parsley' with trails of vines and seedheads. All are in a single colour — cornflower blue, sepia, rosy red, green, or darkest navy — on a cream ground. There's also a

small-scale co-ordinate, 'Pinleaf Stripe'. M: cotton w140cm (55in); paper w67, 76cm (26½, 30in), roll 10m (11yd). P: cotton £15.10m; paper £27 roll.

BLOSSOM (FABRICS) LTD
Softly romantic blossoms in delicate pastels silk-screened by hand on to fabrics and papers. There are 11 different fabric designs including co-ordinating smaller-scale prints. The principal design themes of harebells, primroses, tea roses, apple blossoms or honeysuckle, with appropriate foliage, are each reproduced in one or two of four colours — pink, apricot, sky blue and yellow — on a white ground. Seven of the fabrics have matching or co-ordinating washable wallpaper. Fabric is heavily glazed cotton or 100% polyester voile. M: fabrics w122cm (48in); paper w68cm (27in), roll 10m (11yd). P: cotton £11.90 – £19.35 m; paper £16.80 – £19.60 roll (ex VAT).

Fabrics from Blossom

CAVALCADE WALLCOVERINGS LTD
Two co-ordinated ranges from a comprehensive collection of wall coverings.
CANDY cleverly co-ordinates a rayon-fibre covering in 14 plain pastel shades with six multi-stripe papers. M: plain w100cm (39in), roll 60m (66yd); stripes w70cm (27in), roll 60m (66yd). P: plain £5.75 m; stripes £3.55 m.
CAVALTEX Irish linen wall coverings have co-ordinating fabrics. Mostly in neutral shades, the linen comes in a closely woven smooth finish, a more open weave and also a thick herringbone in light brown, dark brown or red. M: w100cm (39in), roll 30m (33yd). P: £5.30 – £1.40 m; co-ordinating fabric £3.95 – £12.20 m.

CROWN DECORATIVE PRODUCTS LTD⚠
Several ranges of co-ordinates from well-known manufacturers of paint and wall coverings (see separate entries). DASH range includes 40 papers that are washable, peelable and moisture resistant, plus fabrics in 100% cotton, made in England. There are 12 paper designs — six featuring florals, two stripes and two all-over patterns, 'Gem' with a white starburst on lightest beige, yellow, grey, pink or aqua, and 'Spot' with two-tone dots of colour. Only three of the 12 come with matching fab-

Stripe' △ and 'Negative Stripe' △ from Crown

ric. M: fabric w122cm (48in); paper w52cm (20½in), roll 10.05m (11yd). P: fabric £5.25 m; paper £3.25 – £4.95 roll.

In much brighter colourways comes CHERRY, mainly in four primary groups — bright red, apple green, sunshine yellow and brilliant blue — and black. The 37 papers are unpasted vinyl, designed with kitchens and bathrooms in mind. The 15 designs, all with a simple, fresh feel, range from geometric to floral, from 'Summer Flowers' with bold individual flowers on white or coloured ground, and 'Poppy' with a wild flower and grass design, to 'Stripe'. Many designs are available in a co-ordinating reverse colourway. Co-ordinating 100% cotton fabric is available in three designs: 'Stripe' in the four primary colourways on white plus cream/brown; 'Summer Flowers' in white on blue; and 'Alexa' with butterflies and grasses in yellow/green or brown/orange. M: fabric w122cm (48in); paper w52cm (20½in), roll 10.05m (11yd). P: fabric £5.25 m; paper £4.25 – £6.25 roll.

DESIGNERS GUILD⚠
High quality materials and contemporary designs in fashionable shades, from a company headed by the well-known designer, Tricia Guild. For example, in the PLAIN AND SIMPLE range (two plain fabrics and one wallpaper) there's 'Rough Diamond', a tough-textured weave available in 33 colours, and 'Moonshine', a heavy-weight cotton chintz in 40 shades. Both range from deep shades such as dark blue and pewter grey to lighter pastels. 'Network', a textured, stripe-effect washable paper in 31 two-tone combinations completes this useful range. M: fabric w137cm (54in); paper 252cm (20½in), roll 10m (11yd). P: fabric, 'Rough Diamond £12 m, 'Moonshine' £9.50 m; paper £11 roll. These also co-ordinate with

Designers Guild's PLAIN AND SIMPLE △ fabrics and paper; cushion in ANGLES △ fabric

Designers Guild prints such as ANEMONE (see *Fabrics*) and the abstract ANGLES.
Tricia Guild chose leading American manufacturers to produce the SOFT FURNISHING range, which is divided into five colour groups — blue, green, peach, rouge and natural. It en-

Designers Guild's 'Network' △ paper with ANEMONE △ fabrics

compasses more than 70 fabrics and 120 papers with 40 large prints, 24 small and 8 subtly-textured plains, plus 24 wallpaper borders. The theme is decidedly floral and pretty with designs like 'Berries', 'Misty', 'Daisies' and 'Sweet William'. Two types of fabric are available, one in 100% glazed cotton suitable for upholstery, and one in 50% cotton/50% polyester for table linens and kitchen accessories. *M*: cotton w137m (54in); mix w122cm (48in); paper 52cm (20½in), roll 10m (11yd). *P*: fabrics, cotton £14.50 – £19.50 m, mix £10 – £10.50 m; papers £17.50 – £24 roll; paper borders £3.50 – £3.90 m.

SUSANNE GARRY LTD

Huge range of co-ordinating sheers and fabrics, now expanded to include even more luxurious items. Several imported collections offer every type of design, for example, six of the latest sheers: 'Firn' with diamond-shapes, 'Journey' with leaves, 'Evian' with swags of leaves and flowers, 'Drops' with dots making up close-packed diamonds, 'Stein' with a quatrefoil and 'Solo' with slashed stripes. All are large width, white on white, in 54% polyester/36% cotton/10% silk except for 'Solo' which comes in 100% polyester. *M*: w270cm (106½in). *P*: 'Solo' £25.28 m; others £34.20 m. Susanne Garry is sole distributor for Interieur fabrics, which include some of the most unusual prints and sheers on the market. Designs include 'Antica', a lovely pearlized cotton with broad brush-strokes and gilded detail, in three colourways — pink/grey/gold, white/grey/gold and mustard/grey/gold — and similar 'Linear' with larger, sketchy stripes. *M*: w120cm (47¼in). *P*: £27.86 m. 'Retro', the co-ordinating sheer in 65% polyester/35% viscose, comes in large width and hemmed with weights, ready for hanging. *M*: w260cm (102½in). *P*: £46.73 m. Pretty 'Rose' with rosebud motif embroidered on very fine cotton, has three variations: full-width fabric, a narrow scalloped border and an even narrower scalloped, satin-backed edging. All three come in white on white, blue/rose pink, apple green/rose pink, apple green/pale blue. *M*: fabric w150cm (59in); border w40cm (15¾in); edging w6cm (2¼in). *P*: fabric £25.60 m; border £18.80 m; edging £4.82 m. A complementary sheer also with an optional scalloped edging is 'Waltz' in 100% polyester in white on white only. *M*: w260cm (102½in). *P*: £53.39 m.
A more geometric sheer is 'Nobile' with a square grid on a cheesecloth-effect ground in 100% polyester. *M*: w270cm (106½in). *P*: £31.93 m. More embroidered is 'Birch', a weeping tree pattern, and a matching embroidered voile in 100% polyester, both in pastels on cream or white. *M*: w120cm (47in). *P*: £41.75 m. For the feel of an Edwardian conservatory, consider an amazing rendition of a period Madras lace, 'Winter Garden', a 100% cotton sheer with an anemone and lattice grid in three colourways: white/écru, red/green/white and apple green/lime green/white. *M*: w175cm (69in). *P*: £38.35 m.

'Winter Garden' from Susanne Garry

A bold and exciting print, 'Jungle', offers striking abstract shapes in most unusual colourways: grey/tan/rust/burnt red/black, yellow/olive/red/mauve/black and ochre/mauve/purple/steel/turquoise. *M*: w138cm (54¼in). *P*: £48.44 m. Available with co-ordinating plain fabric in

FABRICS AND WALL COVERINGS

100% cotton, 'Batavia'. *M*: w150cm (59in). *P*:
£12.09 m.
The Swiss SAMBA collection has old favourites
such as polka dots, candy stripes, bird's feet
and diamond grids on voile and high quality
glazed cotton. Colours are pastels and a nice
grey, all on white. *M*: w150cm (59in). *P*: voile
£21 m; cotton £19.60 m. 'Hit' and 'Geo' pair a
big diagonal stripe with a matching white-on-
white voile respectively. *M*: 'Hit' w162cm
(63¾in); 'Geo' w265cm (104¼in). *P*: 'Hit'
£19.60 m; 'Geo' £26 m.

Selection from Susanne Garry's SAMBA

MATISSE has imaginative splodges of pastels
on heavy glazed cottons in six colourways. Designs range from the abstracted flower 'Impression' to the painterly stripes of 'Jealousy';
there's also a voile, 'Lucky'. *M*: all w150cm
(59in). *P*: £29.90 m. On an even larger, bolder
and brighter scale, 'Lagune' has big squares
with broad brush-strokes dividing them, in
five colourways on 100% cotton. *M*: w150cm
(59in). *P*: £29.20 m.
For a heavy, upholstery-weight fabric to co-
ordinate with most of the above, there's 'Montana' in 68% cotton/32% viscose in four brightly coloured woven patterns which reverse to
rich pastels. *M*: w130cm (51¼in). *P*: £41.89 m.
And 'Carioca' in 100% cotton offers an even
stripe in 10 unusual colour combinations. *M*:
w150cm (59in). *P*: £23.87 m.
To go with it all, Susanne Garry has chosen a
paper-backed silk wall covering with a multicoloured weave in pastel pink, turquoise and
other pastel shades. *M*: w70cm (27½in). *P*: £9
m. There's also a lovely, very fine silk wall
covering from Florence, in silver grey, orchid
and lilac. *M*: w100cm (39¼in). *P*: £18 m. Also
from Florence comes a special wall covering
design, 'Gocce di Luna', with a gondola motif
woven brocade-fashion into the cream-
coloured silk. *M*: w90cm (35½in). *P*: £5.92 m.
(The Italian silks are available only on orders
over a certain size and prices may vary.)

△ *INDICATES AN ILLUSTRATED PRODUCT
SELECTED BY THE DESIGN CENTRE*

HABITAT DESIGNS LTD
From the well-loved high street chain, a very
good range of contemporary co-ordinates.
Among the latest are 'Sakkara Dot' fabric and
paper with scattered dragon's teeth in squares
on pink, camel or pale green ground (fabric
only on camel ground), designed to work with
'Stripe', a camel rust/gold multi-stripe or 'Trellis' with coloured grid of dragon's teeth, also
on camel ground. The latter two come as fabrics only. *M*: fabric w140cm (55in); paper
w52cm (20½in), roll 10.05m (11yd). *P*: fabric
£5.60 – £6.20 m; paper £3.95 roll.
'Midi' has painterly flowers in bright squiggles
of red, blue, yellow and pink on cream or pale
yellow; 'Camille' has amorphous shapes in
apricot on grey; 'Confetti' creates a dotty
effect with squarish shapes in red or blue scattered irregularly on white for the papers, the
reverse for the fabrics; 'Petite Fleur' has red
dot flower buds on thin green stems; and
'Linea' paper with yellow, orange, green
stripes on a mint ground is designed to work
with 'Bijou' fabric in the same colours but with
dots instead. For kids there's 'Robots' and
'Algebra' with scattered numerals, both
brightly-hued on white grounds. *M*: fabric
w122cm (48in); paper 10.05m (11yd). *P*: fabric
£2.95 – £3.25 m; paper £2.75 – £3.75 roll.

From left: Habitat's 'Stripe', 'Trellis'

HILL & KNOWLES LTD
Supremely elegant English wallpapers, co-
ordinating borders and pure cotton fabrics at
realistic prices. Hill & Knowles were chiefly responsible for the border revival with their impressive range of hand-printed borders, and
many of these are still on offer.
Of the co-ordinated collections, STENCIL is
produced in eight soft colourways, each with
three papers, two differently sized borders
and one fabric. The designs, as the name suggests, are based on stencilling, the papers consisting of a small floral motif, stencilled trellis
and a plain-coloured ragged effect; the fabric
having a large stylized basket of fruit and flowers. KENT also derives motifs from stencilling
and includes a fabric with a tree bearing fruit,

*Fabrics from Hill & Knowles. Top: STENCIL;
below: KENT*

co-ordinating small floral papers and borders
plus a plain ragged-effect paper; colourways
include soft blue/yellow/brown, green/
terracotta/sand and green/blue/sand. *M*: (all)
fabric w122cm (48in); paper w52cm (20½in),
roll 10.05m (11yd). *P*: fabric £9.95 m; paper
£8.25 roll; borders 85p – £1.20 m.
Hill & Knowles also produce the fabulous RAG-
GING collection — ragged-effect paper in 21
colours, a beautiful chintz-inspired fabric,
'Birds and Leaves', plus two different borders
in each colour. *M*: fabric w122cm (48in); paper
w52cm (20½in), roll 10.05m (11yd). *P*: fabric £9
m; paper £8.25 roll; borders 65p m.

Hill & Knowles's 'Birds and Leaves' fabric

SOUTIL collection features two modern abstract designs in 14 colourways on cotton chintz including a luscious peach/turquoise/pink/cream. There are two cleverly co-ordinating wallpapers — one with a wavy stripe, the other with a minute version of the fabric — and two borders. *M*: fabric w122cm (48in); paper w52cm (20½in), roll 10.05m (11yd). *P*: fabric £19.95 m; paper £8.75 roll. (All prices ex VAT).

INTERIOR SELECTION ⚜

Specialists in co-ordinating ranges. DÉJA VU comprises papers, fabrics and borders based on Victorian themes which have been redesigned and recoloured. All fabrics are Scotchgarded, all wallpapers are washable. 'Ikat' wallpaper, inspired by Indonesian batik, has two borders — 'Ikat', a twisted rope effect, and 'Sumatra', with an ogee shape — and is designed to go with 'Java' fabric which uses a similar batik motif. 'Interlace' wallpaper and fabric with a trellis-effect and 'Borderline' border, with a smaller-scale trellis, also work well with 'Cathay Garden' paper and fabric featuring a large-scale floral design. For a more oriental effect, there's 'Cheng Tu', a Chinese lattice design dating from 1750; wallpaper and fabric are identical except for a shadow effect on the fabric in an additional colour. 'Glory' fabric and border use the same lattice design entwined with morning glories. The entire range comes in greens, reds, peaches, yellows and blues. *M*: fabric w37cm (54in); paper w52cm (20½in), roll 10m (11yd). *P*: fabric £10.60 m; paper £9.80 roll; borders £5 – £14 roll.

Interior Selection's 'Ikat' paper with 'Ikat' and 'Sumatra' borders, plus 'Java' △ fabric

KATHARINE JAMES LTD

Marvellous co-ordination in the MACHINKA FAVOURITES and TRELLIS collections. FAVOURITES 100% cotton fabrics have fresh, stylized designs of birds, butterflies and flowers, all either on a plain background or against one of two diamond trellis designs; TRELLIS 100% cotton fabrics and washable vinyl wall coverings offer the two trellis designs by themselves, either 'Small Trellis' made up from thin, wavy lines with a curlicue at each crossing or 'Large Trellis' with straighter, bolder lines and

Design from Katharine James's MACHINKA FAVOURITES

a dot in the centre of each diamond. TRELLIS also offers bed linen in 50% polyester/50% cotton — pillows, sheets, duvet covers, valances and comforters, or just the fabric by the metre — and Katharine James will make up screens and pillowed bedheads to specification. The designs, 15 in all, come in a varied selection of pastel shades and stronger colours, up to four colours hand-printed on écru, beige or white backgrounds. Examples of the attractive colourways are coral/lilac/blue/grey on white or mid blue/mustard/rust/pale green on écru. *M*: fabric w48in (122cm); paper w27in (68.5cm), roll 11yd (10m); bed linen fabric w90in (230.5cm). *P*: fabric £12.50 m; paper £15.50 roll; bed linen fabric £12 m.

MACHINKA FAVOURITES fabrics with 'Large Trellis' fabric and bed linen. From Katharine James

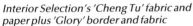

Interior Selection's 'Cheng Tu' fabric and paper plus 'Glory' border and fabric

FABRICS AND WALL COVERINGS

LEYLAND PAINT & WALLPAPER PLC

Comprehensive, and economical, range of co-ordinates from a company that specializes in vinyl wall coverings.

Part of the highly successful LOVE MATCH series, LADY LOVE MATCH features nature-inspired patterns and colourways in wallpaper, fabrics and bed linen. Pastel flowers and bold daisies in wallpaper designs come in a total of 39 colourways, with fabrics in 20 colourways and bed linen in six. *M*: fabric w48in (122cm); paper w20½in (52cm), roll 11yd (10m). *P*: fabric £4.95 m; paper £3.50 roll.

INSIGHT ready-pasted vinyls encompass designs varying from the dramatic to the delicate, from grids to florals, and somewhere in between, a simple pattern of fine vertical lines interspersed with bright cherries. There are 16 paper designs in a total of 53 colourways, plus six co-ordinating fabrics and nine paper borders. Mainly a collection for kitchens and bathrooms, some of the designs are also suitable for bedrooms and living rooms. *M*: fabric w48in (122cm); paper w20½in (52cm), roll 11yd (10m); border w4½in (11.5cm), roll 11yd (10m). *P*: fabric £5.70 m; paper £5.99 roll; border £2.49 roll.

Designs from Leyland's LADY LOVE MATCH

NAIRN COATED PRODUCTS LTD

Intelligent combinations of good quality vinyl papers and matching or complementary cotton fabrics at reasonable prices from this company's subsidiary Kingfisher Wallcoverings. GENTLE TOUCH collection consists of 12 pastel-coloured designs in a flocked finish giving a velvety feel. Patterns include small florals, random stripes and other designs. 'Flutter' has little floating butterflies in five colourways: peppermint/white, white/grey, pink/white, sky blue/white and peach/cream. 'Caress' paper has a diamond saddle-stitch pattern with bordered vertical line of flowers from another design, 'Hazy', which can be used as a co-ordinate. The papers can be dry-

Top: 'Flutter' paper with moiré fabric; below: 'Caress' paper. All from Nairn

stripped when redecorating, leaving the backing as the new lining paper. For each colourway there is a toning plain moiré fabric. *M*: fabric w122cm (48in); paper w52cm (20½in), roll 10m (11yd). *P*: fabric approx £8.50 m; paper max £8.99 roll.

PARTNERS 2 is the successor to the original PARTNERS ready-pasted coverings and fabrics. The total range of papers now consists of 75 colourways and 27 designs, including large elaborate floral prints, smaller delicate patterns and geometrics. Complementary 100% cotton fabrics come in nine designs and 29 colourways as well as five plain-coloured silk moiré effects. Some of the nicest prints are 'Gypsy' with tendrils of dull blue/rose/mustard flowers on off white, also available in wallpapers with a lovely border as 'Bolero'. A small-scale overall roundel, 'Accord', in dull blue/mustard would make a nice co-ordinate or the dull blue pinpoints of 'Minstrel' on a dusty rose ground. *M*: fabric w122cm (48in); paper w52cm (20½in), roll 10m (11yd). *P*: fabric £5.75 – £8.49 m; paper £7.99 – £9.99 roll.

JOHN S OLIVER LTD

Fabrics hand-printed and paint supplied to match this company's dazzling shiny papers. See *Wall coverings*.

OSBORNE & LITTLE LTD ▲

Fabulous wallpapers and 100% cotton fabrics from an innovative company known for their lovely co-ordinates.

SIENA has 24 marbled wallpapers and 12 matching or complementary semi-glazed fabrics plus co-ordinating border designs, each in five colourways. Two narrow borders, 'Rope' and 'Leaf', are perfect for framing walls, windows and doors, while a deeper one, 'Little Cornice', would be best as a frieze. Other borders include a deeper 'Cornice' in six colours and a gothic motif, 'Cloister'. *M*: fabric w140cm (55in); paper w52cm (20½in), roll 10m (11yd); borders w6.5–16.5cm (2½–6½in). *P*: fabric £10.95 m; paper £9.25 roll; borders £7.50–£10.75 roll.

Osborne & Little's SIENA △ with borders

With a less definite texture there's 'Nuage' from the PLAINS range with a mottled, ragged finish in a contemporary palette from deep burgundies and sea greens to lighter apricots and beiges. Choose from 38 wipe-clean wallpapers and matching fabrics in 100% cotton. *M*: fabric w150cm (59in); paper w52cm (20½in), roll 10m (11yd). *P*: fabric £13.95 m; paper £8.95 roll. From the same collection, 'Grained' offers another painted-finish look. Available as wallpaper only in 24 shades, it's designed to work with 'Granite', a lightly speckled paper and fabric available in 23 colours both pastel and deep. *M*: fabric w150cm (59in); paper w52cm (20½in), roll 10m (11yd). *P*: fabric £13.95 m; paper £8.95 roll. More modernistic painted effects are seen in

PATINA, a range of five designs, two multicoloured, three with intermeshed irregular lines giving a soft, woven look. M: fabric w140cm (55in); paper w52cm (20½in), roll 10m (11yd). P: fabric £14.75 m; paper £9.25 roll.

For up-to-the-minute style in unusually beautiful colours there's REGATTA featuring vertical stripes in a choice of three widths on wallpapers, designed to work with two fabrics: 'Waterline' with a wide, marbled stripe bordered by a rope effect and glazed 'Streamline' with a narrow stripe overlaid with a small ikat pattern. Both fabrics come in 10 colourways to go with wallpapers in 50, with lovely shades moving from mellow apricots, greys and beiges to richer greens, russets and blues. M: fabric w140cm (55in); paper w52cm (20½in), roll 10m (11yd). P: fabric £11.25 m; paper £9.25 roll.

Selection of fabrics and papers from Osborne & Little's REGATTA △

PERGOLA contrasts richly patterned fabrics with simpler wallpapers. Choose from 'Rustic' fabric with floral and lattice stripes and paper with quatrefoil and lattice; 'Parrot Tulip' fabric with tulips amidst grasses and paper with grasses alone; 'Gladiolus' with lush all-over floral fabric and fainter floral paper; and 'Flame Stitch' fabric combining four or more horizontal and vertical flame-stitch patterns and paper with a simple wavy flame stitch and optional border. M: fabric w122cm (48in); paper w52cm (20½in), roll 10m (11yd). P: fabric £11.25 m; paper £9.25 roll.

WEAVES offers a tough, 100% cotton upholstery fabric in a reversible jacquard weave plus matching wallpapers. There are two designs: 'Sunstitch', in 24 colours with brocade finish, has a sunburst motif within a grid of contrasting stitching; 'Aspen' in 10 colours, puts stylized leaves against a background of small white and coloured checks. M: fabric w145cm

'Gladiolus' paper and fabric from Osborne & Little's PERGOLA △

(57in); paper w52cm (20½in), roll 10m (11yd). P: fabric £13.50 m; paper £9.25 roll.

Other contemporary co-ordinates can be had from the Scandinavian DURO range which comprises 150 ready pasted, washable wallpapers and some matching fabrics. The clean, simple designs in pastels and bright hues feature geometrics, small florals, dots, stripes and even balloons. M: fabric w60–80cm (23½–31½in); paper w52cm (20½in), roll 9m (9¾yd). P: fabric £10.35 m; paper £8.95 roll.

Osborne & Little will undertake contract and specialist printing projects for any type of wallpaper or fabric.

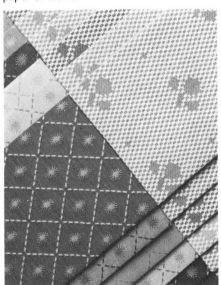

Selection from Osborne & Little's WEAVES

PALLU & LAKE LTD

Exclusive furnishing textiles and wallpapers ranging from adventurous modern prints to traditional ones in new colours. In the first category are their stock prints from America, which include JOURNEY TO CATHAY, 100% cotton chintz fabrics in nine oriental-inspired designs, each in five colourways. Co-ordinating wallpapers and vinyl wall coverings

are held in the CLARENCE HOUSE 2 pattern book. M: fabric w137cm (54in); paper w68cm (26¾in), roll 9.76m (10yd), sold in double rolls only. P: fabric £20 m; paper £16.50 single roll.

From Brunschwig & Fils comes a prestigious collection of document prints, including the MUSÉE DES ARTS DECORATIFS range taken from the archives of that Paris museum. The original designs are adapted and sometimes recoloured to suit today's tastes. Most prints come in at least five colourways and all in 100% cotton. Examples of floral prints are 'Westbury Bouquet' fabric and the co-ordinating 'Westbury Ribbons' fabric and paper border, depicting flowers and trailing ribbons. M: fabric w130cm (51¼in); paper w50, 60cm (19¾, 23½in), roll 4–6m (4¼–6½yd). P: 'Westbury Bouquet' £95 m; 'Westbury Ribbons' £60 m, border £15 m.

One of their most unusual document prints is the *trompe l'oeil* 'Mignonne', a wallpaper which gives a convincing imitation of a shimmering, heavily draped silk taffeta printed with delicate flowers. To complete the effect, 'Mignonne Border' imitates a swagged pelmet. Colourways are grey, sand, vanilla, blue, gold, celadon and dusty rose. M: w50cm (19¾in); roll 4–6m (4¼–6½yd). P: £130 roll.

Pallu & Lake's 'Mignonne' paper

A number of stencil-effect designs include the fresh, light 'Hannah' with naïve birds, flowers and fruit on a background scattered with clover and bird's-foot motifs, and 'Sidewall' with the bird's-foot motifs only. 'Hannah' comes as a 100% cotton chintz, a paper and a wide paper border; 'Sidewall' as a wallpaper only. M: fabric w137cm (54in); paper w68.5cm (27in), roll 4.6m (5yd). P: 'Hannah' fabric £60 m, border £12 m; paper £35 roll. See following page for illustration.

FABRICS AND WALL COVERINGS

Pallu & Lake's 'Hannah' wide border

PAPER MOON

Marvellous choice of unusual wallpapers with co-ordinating borders and fabrics, many of them from America. Bob Van Allen's STYLE collection has modern geometric or stylized floral designs including 'Style' — irises and tulips in yellow, blue, red or green on white or black background with tiny clusters of blue dots. 'Flair' has thin, white vertical stripes interspersed with thicker bands of blue, yellow, orange, coral and mauve while the border runs the same stripes horizontally to clever effect. 'Graphics' is a tiny white grid pattern, on a blue, beige, pale orange, brown, cinnamon, brick or green background. And 'Diamond' is a small geometric with a half-white, half-beige diamond on turquoise. Fabrics are 100% cotton or 50% cotton/50% polyester. There's also an impressive couple of papers, 'Chevron' and 'Update', which have either a diagonal silver stripe on white or a vertical silver stripe on white, blue or black. *M*: fabric, cotton/polyester w45in (114.5cm), cotton w54in (137cm)! paper w53cm (20½in), roll 10.05m (11yd). *P*: fabric, cotton/polyester £11.95 yd, cotton £17.85 yd; paper £19.50 roll; borders (5yd/4.6m roll) £9.50.

Bob Van Allen has also designed one of the most exciting collections for children — or simply for those with a sense of fun. AMERICAN COUNTRY KIDS are pre-pasted papers with borders which are often the focal point of

these designs and with co-ordinated, sensibly priced, pure cotton fabrics. 'Dancing Ducks' has delightful 'quackers' tripping randomly across the main paper and a wide border of larger, more purposeful ducks striding one behind the other. White ducks with yellow bills and feet on Wedgwood blue or dark blue/yellow ducks on white are two of the most effective colourways. 'Puppytroopers' is another winner with little animals nonchalantly parachuting in a sky of clouds and stars in blue and yellow or red on white. For the older child, 'Jungle Gym' has gigantic white checks over bright red, blue or yellow or reversed red or blue checks on white, and 'Cosmos' is a galaxy of white stars and shaded blue, yellow and red planets against a dark blue stratosphere. Most of the designs have several colour co-ordinated papers so that you could feature the main design perhaps on one wall, and use a background paper of tiny flowers or dots for the other three. *M*: fabric w45in (114.5cm); paper w53cm (20½in), roll 10.05m (11yd). *P*: fabric £9.60 yd; paper £17 roll; border (5yd/4.6m roll) £8.50 or 13.50.

MORE DECORATING WITH BORDERS caters for what it recognizes as the increasing demand for a totally co-ordinated look and often it is the border which carries the more striking or intricate part of the design while the wallpaper acts as a background: a small floral sprig paper has a border of house, school and church buildings; a deep coloured paper with flowers spaced at wide intervals provides an excellent contrast to the large, rich flower border in either dark blue/salmon/green or yellow ochre/rust brown/green; a tiny floral paper for the nursery features a border with brown bears round a honey pot and an alphabet strip beneath. The co-ordinating fabrics are 100% cotton. *M*: fabric w54in (137cm); paper w27in (44.5cm), roll 10yd (9.1m). *P*: fabric £17.40 yd; paper £23.50–£28.50 roll; borders £2 yd.

POPPY LTD

Bright, inexpensive and practical co-ordinated fabrics and wallpapers. Fabrics are 100% cotton, preshrunk and colourfast; wallpapers are washable or spongeable making them immensely suitable for children's rooms, bathrooms or halls and stairwells.

Left 'Bears'; right: 'Clowns'. From Poppy

Five design combinations include delightful 'Bears' in pink, blue or yellow tumbling across a white paper. Matching curtain fabric is available in reverse — white bears on a pastel background. 'Clowns' features pastel or primary clowns asleep with the man in the moon; both fabric and paper have white backgrounds. White 'Trees' are outlined in white on red, green, blue or yellow cotton and the pattern's reversed on the paper. The tiny white flowers of 'Yvon' are on blue, green or dusky pink fabric, reversing for the paper. 'Hedgerow' features twisting vines in green, mulberry or rust on a creamy background for both fabric and paper. *M*: fabric, 'Clowns' w60in (152cm), others w45in (114cm); paper w53cm (20½cm), roll 10m (11yd). *P*: fabric £2.99–£5.99 m; paper £2.99–£6.99 roll.

There is a made-to-order service for bed linen and curtains.

RICH & SMITH ▲

Wonderfully fresh range of fabrics plus a wallpaper and a border — all British too! Print designs have a contemporary feel although a few borrow traditional motifs such as oak leaves and florals, and they're classic enough to work with all periods and styles of furniture. All are printed on high-quality white cotton sateen, suitable for all soft furnishings and upholstery, in 13 clean, soft-toned colours: regatta (dark blue), Odessa (sea blue), haze (light blue), bottle green, sage, apple (bright green), raspberry, hibiscus (pink), peach, chestnut, mocha, wheat and buttercup. There's 'Brookfield' with a patterned stripe bordered by a dash-dot line; 'New England', a formal design of oak leaves with a bordered acorn-patterned stripe; 'Tangle' with a profusion of wiggly lines; 'Rope Grid' with squares of just that;

Left to right, from top: 'Brookfield' △, 'New England' △, 'Tangle' △. From Rich & Smith

'Fan Spatter' with tiny points of colour; 'Zag', a swirling zigzag; 'China Screen' with an all-over rose, quince and leaf pattern; and 'Sketch' with overlapping sketchy lines. *M*: w122cm (48in). *P*: £9.99 m. To co-ordinate there are plain-coloured sturdy upholstery wools in 90% wool/10% nylon in all the above shades. *M*: w130cm (48in). *P*: £20.50 m.

A heavier cotton with a grey ground can be printed with five of the designs — 'China Screen', 'Rope Grid', 'Sketch', 'Zag' and 'Fan Spatter' — in burgundy, russet, suede or grey flannel. *M*: w130cm (48in). *P*: £10.80 m. Or fans of linen can have natural linen printed in all these designs except 'China Screen'. *M*: w130cm (48in). *P*: £13.59 m.

There are five borders to complement the prints — 'Brookfield', 'China Screen', 'New England', 'Rope Grid' and 'Tangle' — all available in any of the fabric colours. *M*: roll 10.05m (11yd). *P*: £3.15–£6.30 roll.

For the walls, there's just one paper, 'Crackle' with a network of tiny white cracks (with no visible repeat), but it comes in 25 colours — all those of the prints plus wild rose, coral, alabaster, mimosa, dove grey, sky blue, pistachio and aqua. *M*: w52cm (20½in), roll 10.05m (11yd). *P*: £8.55 roll.

RUSTICHIANA LTD

SARTOR and UPSTAIRS ranges of co-ordinating fabrics, wallpapers, bed linen and ceramic tiles (see also *Ceramic tiles*). The pretty, small-scale designs feature one, two or more of the following colours: pink, red, apricot, beige, green, blue and yellow, all on a white ground. They include self-descriptive 'Hearts and Dots', 'Trellis', 'Reverse Trellis' and 'Baby Carnation', and 'Wild Leaves' with lines like blades of grass. All fabrics are 100% cotton. *M*: fabric w122cm (48in); paper w53cm (20½in), roll 10.05m (11yd). *P*: fabric £7.95 m; paper £8 roll.

Left to right, from top: 'Hearts and Dots', 'Trellis', 'Wild Leaves', 'Baby Carnation', 'Reverse Trellis'. All from Rustichiana

ARTHUR SANDERSON & SONS LTD

Massive range from these well-known manufacturers, displayed in their stunningly decorated London showroom, designed to make

'Bird and Anemone' fabric and paper from MORRIS & CO by Sanderson

co-ordination easy and decorating enjoyable. Long-famed for their prints, Sandersons celebrate William Morris's 150th birthday with a 'new' range of wallpapers and heavy-weight cotton fabrics actually designed a century ago. MORRIS & CO includes four single-colour designs for both paper and fabric, each with the swirling foliage so characteristic of Morris, including 'Bird and Anemone' on a creamy background in softly muted tones. There are 24 other exquisite hand-printed papers, first produced between 1864 and 1913, including 'Trellis', believed to be the first wallpaper designed by Morris as well as the later 'Blackberry' with a delicate, formal pattern of briars and flowers. The papers vary from single-colour designs to exclusive — and expensive — multicoloured patterns. *M*: fabric w54in (137cm); paper w53cm (20¾in), roll 10.05m (11yd). *P*: fabric £12.25 m; paper £9.95–£120 roll.

From the OPTIONS I and II ranges come 25 designs, most in three colourways, and each teamed with suggested plain fabrics, paints and papers to view, for foolproof co-ordination. Most designs date from the nineteenth and early twentieth centuries, such as 'Cornfield' by Walter Crane, a contemporary of Morris. First printed in 1903, it shows a delightful profusion of field flowers and is available as washable wallpaper and 100% cotton furnishing fabrics and also in the Sunway

'Blackberry' paper from Sanderson's MORRIS & CO

MATCHMATES range of blinds (see separate entry). From the same period come 'Edwardian Summer' with pretty sprays of country flowers and grasses, and a simpler, smaller-scale co-ordinating paper, 'Edwina'. *M*: fabrics w122–127cm (48–50in); paper w53cm (20¾in), roll

FABRICS AND WALL COVERINGS

Sanderson's 'Cornfield' paper and fabric

10.05m (11yd). *P*: fabric £7.95 m; paper £6.95–£9.95 roll.
SESAME is also inspired by a document print but has been recoloured to make a fresh, pretty collection of seven fabric and wallpaper designs, two wallpaper borders, two voiles and nine shades of plain cotton jacquard weave. All prints come in three striking colour schemes: cherry red/Oxford blue/pink, Sahara yellow/Lincoln green/salmon pink, tangerine/French grey/kingfisher blue. Designs include 'Fleur et Foulard' with its trail of peonies and

'Damascene' paper with 'Fleur et Foulard' fabric from Sanderson's SESAME

oriental flowers on a watered silk ground and 'Damascene' on the same background but with a smaller-scale, simpler floral trail. Tying the florals together is a quartet of sprig and trellis designs and a vertical stripe, 'Wavelength'. All papers are surface-printed and washable, all fabrics 'calendared' (lightly glazed). *M*: fabric w137cm (54in); papers w53cm (20¾in), roll 10.05m (11yd). *P*: fabric, calendared £11.95 m, voile £7.25 m; paper £7.95–£9.95 roll; borders £3.95–£7.95 roll.
To complete the co-ordination, there's 'Jasper', a dragged-effect design, and 'Constantine', a stylized marbled design, both in 20 shades. The fabric is suitable for both upholstery and curtains; the wallpaper is washable and matt-coated. *M*: fabric w137cm (54in); paper w53cm (20¾in). *P*: fabrics £9.75 m; paper £7.95 roll.
For an entirely different look, Sanderson's import the Fisher collections CHINA EXPORT and SIGNATURE from the USA. Modern, flamboyant and often with an oriental flavour, all fabrics are hand-printed, many with gold and silver accents. 'Tapestry de Chine' is a pearlized design in pale green, siena, black and dark green with a border and co-ordinating but slightly simpler paper; and 'Papillon' has a butterfly design. *M*: fabric w137cm (54in); paper w27in (68.5cm), roll 5⅓yd (4.9m), sold in triple rolls. *P*: fabric from £40; paper £30–£165 triple roll.
If you think of Sandersons as only selling prints, think again. They have developed an absolutely huge range of plains — over 800 fabrics and 232 wall coverings, including tweeds, hessians, silks, grass-cloths, suede effects and dupions.

SOULEIADO

Stunning Provencal prints manufactured in small factories in Tarascon and Avignon working in the local tradition. There are 57 characteristic Provençal designs on 100% cotton, lovely small-scale patterns, florals and paisleys

Selection from Souleiado's fabrics and papers

and also some larger-scale paisleys, each in up to nine colourways on a white or coloured ground, plus plain cotton in 40 colours and also a check pattern, 'Les Pionniers', in plain or glazed finish, inspired by the fabrics of the American settlers. Colours include the bright shades always associated with Provence, rich terracotta red, royal blue and sunflower yellow, plus some cooler tones. Some of the designs are available in plasticized cotton, a few come industrially quilted, and 27 come in borders of four different widths also available plain, plasticized or quilted. *M*: prints and plain cotton w130cm (51¼in); plasticized cotton w130, 150cm (51¼, 59in); borders d4, 6, 12, 18cm (1½, 2¼, 4¾, 7in); quilted cotton w130cm (51¼in). *P*: cotton prints £11.70–£17.50 m; plain cotton £8 m; plasticized cotton £18–£26 m; quilted cotton £17.60 m; borders £1.80–£3 m.
Six of the fabric designs reappear on washable wallpaper in a dozen or so colourways. *M*: w53cm (20¾in), roll 10m (11yd). *P*: £17–£19 m. If you're really keen, you can also have the designs on ceramic tiles, table and bed linen, and cushions; and Souleiado will quilt and make up quilted bedspreads or even printed panels to order.

STOREYS DECORATIVE PRODUCTS LTD▲

Good range of inexpensive tough, scrubbable, pre-pasted vinyl papers and co-ordinating cotton or cotton mixture papers. This well-established firm keeps a steady eye on fashion trends and by choosing carefully, you can do very well on a low budget. HOMELOVER ALLSORTS includes small prints, geometrics, stripes and florals and is divided into the soft pastel look and the bold neat look; each pastel colour — blue, pink, green, cinnamon and brown — has five co-ordinating papers and one fabric, each bright colour — red, green, yellow, blue, grey and brown — has three teaming papers and one fabric. Ready-made curtains are available in most colourways and there is also some very smart matching polyester/cotton bed linen. *M*: fabric w122cm (48in); curtains (three sizes) w117 × 137cm (46

Fabrics and paper from Storey's HOMELOVER ALLSORTS △

Papers from Storey's WHISPERS

× 90in). *P*: fabric £4.50–£5 m, curtains £17–£24; paper £5.50–£6 roll.

HOMELOVER COCKTAILS has three or four co-ordinating papers to each fabric. Designs include simple modern florals, criss-cross cocktail sticks and wavy stripes in lots of pastel combinations, clouds or clouds plus rainbow in pinks or blues, a little apples print in either brown, yellow, red or blue with green leaves on a white background. The little apples print is also available in CON-TACT self-adhesive vinyl (see *Wall coverings*). *M*: fabric w122cm (48in); paper w50.8cm (20in), roll 10m (11yd). *P*: fabric £5.50 m; paper £6 roll.

WHISPERS is a mix-and-match range of florals, stripes, geometrics and plain-coloured, textured-look vinyls. A misty floral print, 'Pastel', comes in three pale colourways, yellow/pink/green, rose/blue/green and blue/turquoise/green, with matching fabric. An interesting criss-cross striped pattern, 'Matchmaker', on a fine herringbone background can be teamed with a vertical-striped or herringbone-only paper. There is a plain colour, linen-look polyester/viscose/cotton to go with every design. *M*: fabric w122cm (48in); paper vinyl w50.8cm (20in), roll 10m (11yd). *P*: fabric £5.50 m; paper £6.50 roll.

TISSUNIQUE LTD
Some of the most exclusive co-ordinating papers and fabrics on the market. COTTON HOUSE from the famous Paris-based designer Manuel Canovas consists of hand-printed vinyl papers and matching pure cotton fabrics. The designs range from the ornate Chinese 'Souchong' and paisley pattern 'Golconde' to the simpler large palm-fruit print 'Penang' in raspberry, deep orange, green or blue on beige. Wallpapers are supplied untrimmed. *M*: fabric w130cm (51¼in); paper (after trim-

ming) w25½–27¾in (63–70cm), roll 11yd (10m). *P*: fabric £22–£32 m; paper £70–£240 roll.

Tissunique also supplies the CLARENCE HOUSE collections including the incredibly luxurious hand-printed reproductions of eighteenth and nineteenth century designs 'EPOCH' AND 'EPOCH 2'. One of the most expensive papers in this series is the award-winning 'Les Caprices Orientaux' reproduced (using 36 silk screens) from an eighteenth-century Chinese silk: stylized birds, bees and dragonflies are depicted on branches, fruit and flowers in exquisite colours such as blue, peach and green on an oyster background. The pure cotton fabrics match exactly. *M*: fabric w130cm (51¼in); paper w68cm (27in), roll 13.65m (15yd). *P*: fabric £44–£104 m; paper £360 roll.

Less expensive but still pricey is the stunning 'Mazar I Sharif' taken from a nineteenth-century Afghan print though deceptively modern-looking with its splash of colours like a firework display; eight colourways for both paper and fabric include orange/brown/blue, crimson/green/blue, grey/blue/pink and yellow/green/pink. *M*: fabric w160cm (55in), paper w68cm (27in), roll 13.65m (15yd). *P*: fabric £34–£56 m; paper £140 roll.

TODAY INTERIORS LTD
Co-ordinates in both bold and soft designs. ZIGZAG, designed and manufactured in the UK, offers two simple complementary designs — 'Zig', a series of wavy lines and 'Zag', a chevron pattern — on both fabric and washable wallpaper. Papers come in 26 colours, 15 solid colorations and 11 in a pastel tone on white; 'Zig' fabric in cotton/viscose/flax and 'Zag' in cotton/viscose each come in 17 colourways. Can be supplied with fire-resistant coating. *M*: fabric w140cm (55in); paper w53cm (20¾in), roll 10m (11yd). *P*: fabric £19.12 m; paper £17.52 roll.

ALESSANDRO from Manuscreens of New York offers silk-screened vinyl wall coverings and 100% cotton fabrics in good contemporary designs and fine colourways. '687-7164' features tick marks in dusty rose, grey blue and dull green on cream; '687-7150' has grey zigzags weaving across regular stripes in cranberry/darker grey on a grey ground; and in contrast '687-7101' is a pointillistic floral in softest peach/pink/sage on cream. *M*: fabric w52–54in (132–137cm); paper w27in (68.5cm), roll 7½yd (6.8m). *P*: fabric £17.50 m; paper £19–£29 roll.

ALL THAT JAZZ is a bold and exciting collection from David and Dash of Miami. Both muted and brighter shades colour high-quality cotton fabrics and vinyl wall coverings such as '537-188' with criss-cross strokes in wine/peach/grey on light beige and '536-204' with a grid made up of small white dots cut by bold diagonal white slashes on pale coffee. *M*: fabric w54in (137cm); paper w27in (68.5cm), roll 10yd (9.1m). *P*: fabric £10.95 m; paper £28 roll.

'Zag' fabric and paper from Today Interiors

TURNELL & GIGON LTD
Beautifully produced OULIVADO wallpapers and pure cotton fabrics in rich natural colours from Provence, continuing a tradition of fabrics inspired by India in the seventeenth century. The designs are usually small and intricate and many of the fabrics incorporate large complementary borders. Colours include stonewashed blue, faded red, mauvish blue, grey, black and yellow. Complementary wallpaper comes in seven colourways. *M*: fabric w150cm (59in); paper w53cm (20¾in), roll 10m (11yd). *P*: fabric £12.60 m; paper £13.50 roll (ex VAT). See following page for illustration.

Selection from Turnell & Gigon's OULIVADO papers and fabrics

WARNER & SONS LTD
Famous range from a company with more than a century's tradition. COTTON PRINTS collection of 100% cotton fabrics often with related wallpapers offers some timeless designs, most taken from period originals. 'Strawberry Hill'

FABRICS AND WALL COVERINGS

has small, topsy-turvy tulips in a border of stylized strawberries in four earthy colourways: pink/green on indigo, cherry/indigo on sand, ivory/olive on old red and brick/sage on parchment. *M*: fabrics w36in (91.5cm); paper w68.5cm (27in), roll 13.7m (15yd). *P*: fabric £9.65 m; paper £44.65 roll. Others include 'Epping Forest' with vertical panels of a stag under a tree alternating with a stripe of blossoms and medallions, an engraving-like design in old-fashioned rose, coral and blue colourways on sand or parchment, and 'Hickory Hill', a very detailed design with alternate stripes of an undulating vine and straight trellis, each entwined with flowers of several species, in three colourways on cream, natural or barn (rusty) red. *M*: fabric w54in (137cm); paper w68.5cm (27in), roll 13.7m (15yd). *P*: fabric £12.35 m; paper £41.50 roll.

Warner's 'Strawberry Hill' paper

The huge chintz collection includes a delicate design with related wallpaper, 'Silene', with twisting tendrils and small flowers and the flowers repeated in a narrow border in coral/mint on celery, white/olive on putty, cranberry/emerald on ivory and violet/olive on eggshell. In 100% glazed cotton. *M*: w54in (137cm); paper w67m (26½in), roll 13.7m (15yd). *P*: fabric £12.35 m; paper £38.80 roll.

For simple, small-scale designs, look at THE LINDEN WOOD collection, based on eighteenth- and nineteenth-century hand-blocks found in Salzburg, Austria. Eleven designs in all include 'Loden Stripe' with alternating vertical panels of paisley and flower patterns; 'Jeremy' with a cross-hatch dotted with a central flower; 'Lorraine' with a small cluster of flowers also repeated in the generous border. Each comes in delightful colours such as periwinkle (blue), persimmon (deep orange), raspberry and delphinium (blue). *M*: fabric w56in (142.5cm); paper w68.5cm (27in), roll 13.7m (15yd). *P*: fabric £10.75 m; paper £29 55–£71 roll.

BRIAN YATES (INTERIORS) LTD
Stylish fabric and wallpaper co-ordinates from the Continent with unexpected, witty designs. Fitness freaks will enjoy the SPORT collection depicting cyclists, motor cyclists, riders, windsurfers, skiers, soccer, ice-hockey or tennis

players in action against an appropriate background, for example a blue/red skier on white, yellow/white windsurfer on blue. Striking and unusually wide borders can be teamed with either the main paper or a simpler co-ordinate. 'Room-high' cotton fabrics — matching fabric with an exceptionally large width for use as wall covering — duvet covers and pillowcases complete the look. *M*: fabric w150cm (59in), 'Room-high' w280cm (110¼in); paper w53cm (20¾in), roll 10m (11yd); borders w26.5m (10½in), roll (11yd). *P*: fabric £7.25 m, 'Room-high' £12.95 m; paper £7.95–£9.95 roll; borders £9.95.

Remarkable NOVOCENTO range from De Angelis of Milan features matt papers and matching semi-chintz cotton fabrics with small, simple patterns. Unusual warm and earthy colour combinations include brick red/green/mauve, sand/green/red and yellow ochre/denim blue/red. *M*: fabric w140cm (55¼in); paper w53cm (20¾in), roll 10m (11yd). *P*: fabric £14.16 m; paper £12 roll.

NUMBER ONE papers and cotton fabrics provide a fun combination of small geometrics, flowers or trees and lively borders. The bright and fresh-looking red/blue/green/white colourways (though pastel ones are also avail-

Selection from Brian Yates's NOVOCENTO

Two of Brian Yates's NUMBER ONE borders

able) would be ideal for children, for example a top border of red watering cans on dark blue background pouring water on to a bottom border of red/green tulips on dark blue. *M*: fabric w140cm (55¼in); paper w53cm (20¾in), roll 10m (11yd); borders, roll 10m (11yd). *P*: fabric £6.95 m; paper £6.95 roll; borders £5.95 roll.

EPOK papers from Sweden are based on authentic period wall coverings and have many different borders. 'Renaissance' (dated 1570) comes in rich bronze/gold and moss green/coral pink; 'Art Nouveau' comes in soft pink/white/gold and olive/white/gold/yellow ochre; 'Art Deco' is in almond green or pink. *M*: w53cm (20¾in), roll 10m (11yd). *P*: £8.50 roll. (All prices ex VAT.)

'Art Nouveau' border from Brian Yates

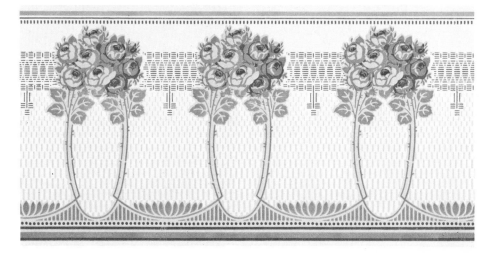

BED LINEN

● Most bed linen comes in standard sizes to fit single, double or large double (king-size) beds. Measurements are not given for standard items. Prices are generally given for double flat sheet and/or double duvet cover.

LAURA ASHLEY LTD

Selected Laura Ashley fabric designs in 100% cotton, made up into bed linen sets comprising duvet covers, flat sheets, fitted sheets and valances, each in three sizes for single, double and king-size beds, and plain or frilled pillowcases. Eight sets are available, each combining two complementary prints — either stripes or large-scale florals on one side, smaller scale florals on the other — so that duvet covers are reversible and pillowcases can be chosen in either design. There's a wide choice of colours for each. P: double sheet £14.95, double duvet cover £24.95.

To complement a bedroom scheme, patchwork quilts are available ready-made in five colours: rose, plum, sapphire, smoke and poppy; and for anyone patient enough to make their own packs of pieces, either squares or hexagons, are sold in a wide choice of colours. Each pack contains enough to make about 1 sq m (1 sq yd) of patchwork. P: single quilt £65, double £95; pack of pieces £3.95.

Laura Ashley also make cushions and table linen.

DESCAMPS

Beautiful PRIMROSE BORDER collection of bed linen, towels and table linen featuring elegant and unusual designs in subtle colours. Printed bed linen sets, most comprising flat sheet, duvet cover and pillow case come in 100% cotton or 50% cotton/50% polyester. A dozen designs include 'Papyrus' in polyester/cotton, with broad diagonal bands of wavy lines creating a moiré effect, in pink or apricot colourways; 'Parallèles' in cotton/polyester with irregular horizontal stripes in blue and red on cream or pink and orange on yellow; and pure cotton 'Mikado', a restrained design of abstract geometric squiggles on a finely striped background in tones of blue or slate. Matching towels, bedspreads and even bath robes are available in some designs. If plain is more to your taste, bed linen sets are available in 15 unusual plain colours in polyester/cotton and plain white in 100% cotton. P: 'Papyrus', 'Parallèles', 'Mikado' double sheet £25–£30.75; double duvet cover £42.60–£47.75; plain coloured double sheet £26.50–£34.50; plain white double sheet £22.55.

Deschamps also make four pretty designs for cots: 'Ricrac' with pattern of Scottie dogs, 'Calin' with coloured hearts, 'Chatons' with sleeping cats tucked up in bed and 'Nounours' with little bears on a striped background. M:

flat sheet w118 × l120cm (46½ × 47¼in) or w180 × l300cm (70¾ × 118in); duvet cover w100 × l120cm (39¼ × 47¼in) or 140 × 200cm (55 × 78¾in). P: flat sheet £20.25–£32.80; duvet cover £18.50–£42.

DORMA ▲

Massive range including collections by well-known international design companies. Three very striking designs from Marimekko include 'Sarastus' with fine, criss-crossing stripes in red, yellow or blue on white. From Mary Quant comes 'Noel Coward', a navy blue

Dorma's 'Sarastus' by Marimekko

fabric with a band of dashing stripes in red and white reversing to a tiny blue and red design on white. From the HOUSE OF LOUIS NICHOLE collection, a collaboration between major manufacturers that offers co-ordinating carpeting (see entry for Gaskell Broadloom), wall coverings, fabrics, bedspreads and cushions (see Ludvig Svensson below), and accessories, come three delicate, Victorian-inspired designs: 'Lace' in beige on cream, 'Chintz' with trailing pink and blue flowers on white, and 'Cameo' with oval cameos on a background of tiny flowers and a co-ordinating trellis pattern in dusty rose or Regency blue. Dorma also make two of their own collections, STUDIO and COUNTRY DIARY, with designs ranging from the dramatically modern to the softly romantic; plus plain sheets, valances and pillowcases in 19 pastel and deep colours and white. P: printed double flat sheet £16.95, double duvet cover £31.95; plain double flat sheet £12.50–£15.95. The soft furnishings range also includes towels and bathroom accessories, quilts, cushions, tablecloths and napkins.

HABITAT DESIGNS LTD

Bed linen and other soft furnishings in colourful designs to complement Habitat's furnishing and decorating ranges. Printed bed linen sets comprise duvet covers in three sizes — single, double and large double — and pillowcases, to be matched with plain coloured sheets. The 11 designs, all fresh and

modern, include 'Bamboo' with broad multicoloured stripes on white in pure cotton, 'Fiesta', a bold, multicoloured floral in polyester/cotton, 'Cherokee', an ikat-style print with muted bands of peach, blue, grey, red and yellow in polyester/cotton, 'Fleurs des Champs' with a small all-over floral motif in primary colours on white in polyester/cotton, and bold 'Alcatraz' with a broad black grid on white on one side reversing to narrow stripes on the other, in pure cotton. There are also two children's designs, 'Robots' and 'Balloons'. Matching towels, fabrics and accessories, even ceramic tiles, are available in many designs. In plain colours, Habitat stock duvet covers, flat and fitted sheets, valances, pillowcases and towels in a total of 11 colours ranging from white to pastels to primaries and to deep-dyed shades. P: printed double duvet cover £22.95–£23.95; 'Robots', 'Balloons' single duvet cover and pillowcase set £18.95; plain double duvet cover £21.95; plain flat sheet £14.45. The bedding range is completed by pure cotton Indian bedspreads and duvets and pillowcases in various grades. Habitat also make cushions and table linen.

HIPPO HALL

Children's bed linen in jolly designs, and also fabrics and wallpapers. Duvet covers and pillowcases feature various brightly coloured designs, a bold print on one side, a simpler print on the reverse; sheets and valances repeat the reverse print. Some characteristic combinations are 'Hippo Love' with grinning hippo families teamed with simple 'Hearts' (the wallpaper co-ordinate combines both designs); 'Aeroplanes' with fighting planes and swirling vapour trails, teamed with simpler 'Targets', coloured -circles on a stripe background, or with irregularly spotted 'Bobbles', all in blue, red and yellow; and

Hippo Hall's 'Alphabet' bed linen, fabric and wallpaper

'Alphabet' with jumbled pictorial letters, also teamed with 'Hearts'. Duvet covers are also available with one design only. *M:* duvet cover w54 × l78in (140 × 198cm). *P:* (reversible) £21.75.

ANGELA HUNT TEXTILES △

Dramatic and innovative bedwear sets of duvet covers, sheets and pillowcases, some with matching Axminster rugs. 'Splash' in 100% cotton has bold brush strokes on a white ground, edged with a scribble border, and comes in 'dark' colourway — red, black, ochre and grey — or 'light' — yellow, blue, peach and pink. Another of the designs, 'Rio', has a cheerful pattern of aeroplanes, clouds and skyscrapers that children, and many adults too, will love. For single beds only. *P:* 'Splash' double duvet cover £25.95, double sheet £12.95; 'Rio' single duvet cover and pillowcase set £22.95, single sheet £9.95.

Angela Hunt's 'Splash'

For the ultimate in luxury, Angela Hunt have a range of pure silk bedroom accessories, SATORI, with birds and flowers in pinks and beiges on a black ground. *M:* quilted cushion 14 × 14in (35.3 × 35.5cm); quilted comforter l95 × w74in (241.5 × 188cm). *P:* cushion £12.95; comforter £350.

PEMBROKE SQUARES △

Beautiful handmade crocheted bedspreads in a choice of 12 traditional designs, copied or adapted from Victorian patterns. All come in white or oatmeal cotton, and are machine washable. One design ('Traditional 1') is usually available from stock; others are made to order, taking from six to eight weeks. They can also be made in tapestry wool in a wide range of attractive colours. *M:* stock sizes 72 × 96in (180 × 240cm); 96 × 96in (240 × 240cm); 96 × 114in (240 × 285cm); 114 × 114in (285 × 285cm); other sizes available to order. *P:* £155–£319 (ex VAT).

PRICES AND INFORMATION WERE CORRECT AT THE TIME OF GOING TO PRESS

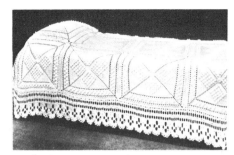

Pembroke Squares' 'Traditional 1' △

PETER REED

Fine bed linen to recall the Edwardian era, in 100% Egyptian cotton. White sheets and 'Oxford-style' pillowcases in the CLASSIC CORD range are stitched with two rows of contrasting cording in grey/burgundy, navy/ tan or harebell blue/olive green. The sheets are sold in five different sizes. *P:* on application.

RUSTICHIANA LTD

Bed linen to match SARTOR and UPSTAIRS ranges of co-ordinating fabrics, wallpapers and ceramic tiles (see separate entries). Three fresh and pretty all-over designs and a border stripe, all featuring hearts and dots, come in six colourways — green, peach, red, pink, yellow and blue — in 50% cotton/50% polyester. Range includes four sizes of pillowcase, three flat sheets, four fitted sheets, four valances, five duvet covers and four quilted comforters. *M:* double flat sheet £33.

ARTHUR SANDERSON & SONS LTD

Bed linen, bedspreads, cushions and made-to-measure soft furnishings to complement Sanderson's huge and famous decorating collection. Bed linen collection comprises duvet covers, flat and fitted sheets (single, double and king-size), plain or frilled pillowcases, box-pleated valances in six floral designs and co-ordinating lightly striped pastel shades. Matching ready-made curtains are available and all the designs have co-ordinating fabrics and wallpapers. Two of the designs are 'Juliet', a subtly coloured panelled rose and ribbon pattern with toning stripes and polka dots, and 'Dimity', a dense all-over floral in four colourways. *P:* on application.
Sanderson's soft furnishing department can make up curtains, pelmets, valances, swags, cushions and bedspreads to order in the customer's choice of fabric. Certain items are available from stock, including the luxurious, handmade king-size 'Rainbow' quilt; each comes in 12 shades of plain glazed chintz in a choice of three colourways: pinks/grey, corals/peach and blues/green. *P:* 'Rainbow' bedspread £295.

Sanderson's 'Juliet'

LUDVIG SVENSSON (UK) LTD

Beautiful lace bedspreads, curtains and cushions designed to complement the HOUSE OF LOUIS NICHOLE collection in which several manufacturers are participating to produce a unified theme in interior design (see Gaskell Broadloom entry in *Carpeting, rugs*, and Dorma entry above). Cluny lace in ecru shade is used for fitted or throwover bedspreads, bolsters, round and square cushions, curtains and tablecloths, and is also available by the yard. Ready-made net curtains echo Dorma's LOUIS NICHOLE prints. *M:* Cluny lace bedspread w36, 54, 60in (91.5, 137, 152.5cm). *P:* £153.95, £183.95, £195.95.

From Ludvig Svensson, Cluny lace bed curtains and canopy

So much hangs on a name.

Kirsch

For curtains boldly displayed on traditional poles, just one name spells quality. Smooth internal cording, effortless telescopic adjustment, fabulous styling . . . the choice of professionals . . . it has to be Kirsch.

Decorpoles

Decorpoles are everyone's top choice in genuine wood poles. Three sizes and four finishes — walnut, teak, natural and brilliant white — also available in an internally corded version. For superb fine crafted workmanship in every component . . . the traditional warmth of solid wood Decorpoles.

Kirsch

This is the track style in white metal that stays discreetly hidden behind your curtain headings. Telescopically adjustable sizes or made to measure, for straight or bay windows. All come in a superb white enamelled finish with concealed cord control. Slim, with rigid steel strength . . . that's Kirsch.

Monorail

Monorail is today's easiest way to buy quality inexpensive curtain rail. A leading name in plastic rail with track, hooks, brackets, etc. all together in one pack. For convenience and sheer curtain-hanging beauty, more and more home-lovers opt for Monorail.

Send for colour brochure to:
Antiference Ltd,
Window Furnishings Division,
Aylesbury, Bucks HP19 3BJ

Quality leaders from
Antiference
the curtain rail people

INTRODUCTION

As any successful interior decorator knows, the secret is attention to detail. Whether a scheme is modern or period, city-chic or country charming, it's imperative to get the fittings right.

This section is divided, according to function, into *Curtain fittings, Door and cabinet fittings* (which also includes items such as decorative grilles and ventilators) and *Window fittings*.

● Specific measurements are not given for door, cabinet and window fittings — most come in standard sizes.

CURTAIN FITTINGS

ANTIFERENCE LTD

Fully comprehensive range of poles and tracks in metal, wood and plastic. KIRSCH range has 12 classically-inspired designs in a variety of finishes including brilliant brass, antique brass, antique gold, antique white, pewter and walnut. *M*: dia 1–1⅜in (2.5–3.5cm), l30 – 240in (76 – 610cm). *P*: £6 – £89.

DECORPOLES are made from finest quality hardwood in four finishes — walnut, natural, white and new teak. They come with or without internal cording and in three diameters, each with matching fittings to enable different diameter poles to be used together in one room. *M*: dia 2.2, 3, 3.5cm (¾, 1¼, 1½in), l48 – 142in (120 – 360cm). *P*: £10 – £44.

Antiference also produce a range of contemporary white metal rails for all weights of curtains, suitable for fixing around bay windows, on pelmets and for valances, and a range of adjustable rods for nets and sheers. There's also a selection of decorative and functional plastic tracks and a range of curtain accessories including brackets and tape.

FABER BLINDS LTD

Light or dark wood FOLK POLE DE LUXE from a company best known for its blinds. Poles are made from seasoned Scandinavian pine with brackets and finials in seasoned hardwood. These, together with rings and other fittings, come in natural or dark oak finish. Adjustable fixing is concealed to avoid unsightly views of screws and brackets. There is a choice of six lengths and each pack contains one pole, two finials and the appropriate number of brackets and rings. *M*: 130–390cm (51–153in). *P*: 130cm pole £14.50.

HARRISON DRAPE

Comprehensive range of curtain poles, tracks and accessories. ROYALE SUITE of poles includes 'Kensington', for the heaviest drapes and available corded or uncorded; 'Chatsworth', for lighter weight fabrics where no pull cords are required; and 'Cheltenham' for the lightest materials, also with no cords. All are in steel with a choice of three finishes: polished brass, bronze-anodized or white polyester. They are easily cut to length and the reeded sections give good stiffness. A selection of finials is available with each, and 'Cheltenham' is also available with cranked or straight sockets for mounting inside the window opening. Also in the ROYAL SUITE is 'Knightsbridge', an extendible steel pole with a choice of antique brass, light wood or dark wood finishes; it is ready-corded with an overlap arrangement, and has a choice of finials. *M*: 'Kensington' dia 3.5 × l150–300cm (1½ × 59–118in); 'Chatsworth' dia 2.5 × l150–300cm (1 × 59–118in); 'Cheltenham' dia 1.9 × l120–180cm (¾ × 47–71in); 'Knightsbridge' dia 3.5 × l76–381cm (1½ × 30–150in). *P*: (rod only) 'Kensington' from £20; 'Chatsworth' from £17; 'Cheltenham' from £3.50; 'Knightsbridge' from £20.

TUDOR range offers a choice of stained or unstained wood poles. *M*: dia 2.5, 3.5cm (1, 1½in), l120–240cm, 150–300cm (47–95, 59–118in). *P*: on application.

Harrison Drape also make seven different simple uncorded curtain tracks in plastic or extruded aluminium with white, silver-anodized or gilt finishes, 'Monarch' ready-corded extendible metal track in two sizes, and 'Adaptatrack', which can be bent to fit a bay window. *M*: 'Monarch' l223–214cm (48–84in), 214–305cm (84–120in). 'Adaptatrack' l120–500cm (48–157in). *P*: on application.

W A HUDSON LTD

ROLLS metal and nylon curtain rails from a firm established in 1890. 'Regency' curtain pole has reeded rod with pineapple terminals and is available in white or gilt finish. Both 'Superglide' and 'Miniglide' are aluminium with gold, silver or white finishes, and can be bent to fit bay windows. 'Miniglide' has cord control and can be used with most weights of materials. The metal-cored plastic rail 'Nylastic' for use behind pelmets is also flexible enough for bay windows and corners. *P*: 'Regency' £47 for

3m (39in) with fittings; 'Superglide' £15 for 3m (39in); 'Miniglide' £6.50 for 3m (39in); 'Nylastic' £10 for 5m (16ft).

LUXAFLEX

Wide range of poles and tracks in metal and wood. Tracks include versatile 'Champion' with glider hooks and 'Pacemaker' for heavier curtains which has an optional extra of pleater hooks for pencil pleating if required. Both come in plain white or in gold stripe. 'Sprint' is an elegantly thin rail ideal for nets or lightweight curtains.

Poles come in metal, plastic and wood, most of them internally corded for smooth opening and closing and most available in two diameters. All the metal rods adjust telescopically. Among them, 'Essex' has a ribbed rod and simple but elegant brackets; available in antique gold or bright brass finish. 'Wellington' is a finely fluted pole with three finishes — metallized antique brass, bright brass and antique white. 'Café Rod', the non-corded version, comes with 'café rings' as an optional extra. 'Fernwood' is an adjustable metal rod with a rich walnut finish, while 'Lexington' is another elegant pole in bright brass or antique gold. Less traditional is 'Salem' with a smooth pole in brass. Wooden poles, in walnut, white and natural, are available in similar widths to the metal poles with optional internal cording in the widest size. Recess wall brackets are available to save space. *M*: 'Essex' dia 1⅛ × l30–150in (2.5 × 76–381cm), dia 1⅜ × l30–272in (3.5 × 76–690cm); wooden poles l4–12ft (1.2–3.6m).

P: all on application.

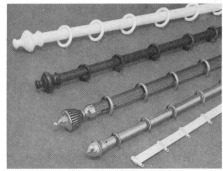

Luxaflex's wooden poles, 'Wellington' rod, 'Salem' café rod and 'Champion' track

SILENT GLISS

Reputed to have the widest range of curtain tracks in the world to suit everything from the lightest net to the heaviest velvet. Rails are precision made from high-grade aluminium and top quality nylon; they can be hand, cord or electrically operated. Bends and difficult angles can be accommodated and internal channels in the corded tracks prevent cord

Top, left to right: 'Regency' curtain pole, aluminium 'Superglide'; below: aluminium 'Miniglide', reinforced PVC 'Nylastic'. All from Hudson

FITTINGS

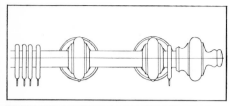

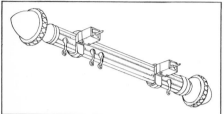

Top: wooden pole; below: pole-effect 'Nova' track (rear view). Both from Swish

from sagging and catching up. All tracks come in a satin silver anodized finish with certain products available in white and gold as well. For coloured tracks, the RAINBOW range is a recent and very appealing idea for those looking for co-ordinates or contrasts with curtains and decor. These tracks can also be used as shower curtain rails and, more innovatively, laid flat to the wall as picture rails. Colours include dark red, bright red, bright pink, bright green, bright blue, black and white to pastel green, pastel pink, peach, beige, grey, cream and yellow. *P:* on application.

SWISH

Comprehensive range of curtain tracks and poles. Versatile light and heavy duty metal curtain tracks can be supplied with or without cord controls. 'Sologlyde' will fit round a bay window and can take a deep or narrow heading. It comes in plain white, gold-decorated pattern or as 'Sologlyde aluminium' in tough gold or silver finish. 'Nylonglyde', also flexible enough to curve round a bay window, has an optional valance rail for hanging a pelmet. For putting up net curtains, dividing a room or fixing a frill around a cot, 'Furniglyde' is the best choice. *M:* l125–250cm (49–98in).

Attractive wooden poles come in four diameters and are supplied as natural pine, stained 'walnut' or painted white. Convincing 'Nova Poles' have tracks inside them for smooth operation. *M:* wooden poles dia 17–35mm (⅝–1½in), l120–240cm (47¼–94¼in). *P:* on application.

TEMPUS STET LTD

Ornamental gilded pelmets, curtain finials, tiebacks and even coronae for bed canopies — for a touch of old world splendour. All are taken from period designs. Pelmet patterns include 'Acorn and Oak Leaf' (also available in plain wood), and 'Rose Chain', composed of

rose centrepiece and four rose chains. Finial designs use traditional pineapple, acanthus and pineapple, flambeau and pomegranate motifs, and one is simple reeded. Tiebacks use ostrich feather, acanthus and Tudor rose motifs; one, 'Tiffany Fuschia', reproduces what is believed to be an original Tiffany design. Coronae come in ostrich feather, crown-like 'Madonna', delicate 'Rose Chain and Cherub' and 'Tiffany Fuschia' designs. *P:* 'Acorn and Oak Leaf' pelmet gilded, £40, ungilded, £35 per 7 × 45in (18 × 114.5cm) section; 'Rose Chain' pelmet £80 per 6 × 48in (15 × 122cm) section; finials £4.50–£10 per pair; tiebacks £18–£50 per pair; coronae £49–£110.

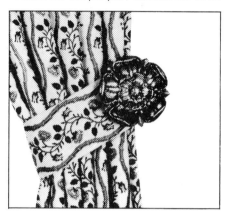

Top: Tudor-rose tieback; below: two curtain finials. All from Tempus Stet

DOOR AND CABINET FITTINGS

ALBION HARDWARE LTD

Two ranges of fittings to match Albion's nostalgic bathroom accessories (see separate entry). Both include mortice door knobs, various sizes of cupboard knobs, finger plate, lever latches, casement stays, bathroom door lock with mortice knob and bathroom lever lock. VICTORIAN BRASS fittings come in polished brass, everbright (which looks like brass but doesn't tarnish), chrome and antique bronze

finishes. Cool and pretty Limoges CHINA range comes in plain white, gold line decoration on white or two flower patterns on white. *P:* VICTORIAN BRASS mortice door knobs £9.50–£18.50, cupboard knobs £6.50–£13 pair, lever lock £21–£34; CHINA mortice knobs £8.50–£31, cupboard knobs £5.50–£16.50, lever lock £24–£28.

LEONARD BALL

Extensive range of scarce brass fittings and wooden mouldings for furniture and clocks. Wide selection of brass key escutcheons, handles, knobs, castors, furniture mounts in the form of swags, claws, rosettes, heads, capitals etc, plus brass finials in the form of eagles, balls, obelisks, pine-cones, urns, flames etc, to suit all styles of furniture. The firm also sells clock and barometer parts and undertakes repairs. For the craftsman, Ball's stock wood veneers, veneered friezes and wooden mouldings; while turned wooden components or wooden mouldings can be supplied to customer's pattern. Antique restoration service available. *P:* on application.

Cabinet handles from Leonard Ball

J D BEARDMORE & CO LTD

Wide range of traditional architectural fittings good for matching genuine antique hardware. Large range of brass grilles are suitable for enclosing radiators or covering ventilators in a period room. Elegant designs include gothic quatrefoils, diamonds and rosettes, traditional geometric motifs and rectilinearly woven wire or straps. Many of the designs are also available in aluminium or steel. *P:* approx £12 sq ft. See following page for illustration.

ELON TILE (UK) LTD

Pretty hand-painted ceramic door pulls and lightswitch plates, from Mexico. Designs are mainly rustic floral patterns in fresh colours on cream. *P:* on application.

PRICES AND INFORMATION WERE CORRECT AT THE TIME OF GOING TO PRESS

Decorative grille designs from Beardmore

M & I J HARRISON LTD

Traditional brass coat hooks. Single or double coat hooks or combined coat and hat hooks can be supplied mounted on a pine, oak or mahogany panel. *P: £10–£20.* See also *Bathrooms, accessories* and *Furniture, shelving.*

Harrison's traditional brass hooks

HARRISON BEACON

Small range of traditional polished brass door furniture. GEORGIAN SUITE offers lever handles for latches or mortice locks, key escutcheon, a mortice knob set, two letterboxes and an urn-shaped door knocker; while the equivalent items in the VICTORIAN SUITE come in a plainer style. *P: latch sets and locks £10–£22.*

Cabinet fittings come in plastic, wood, porcelain and plated steel or aluminium. Solid plastic handles come in ivory, brown, white and wood colours, all with gold trim. More ornate are 'White Porcelain' and 'Regency' knobs with curling bronzed backplates, and two rosette-patterned knobs in bronze-plated

steel. There's also a ring pull, brassed or bronzed, and a timber pull handle with bronzed ends. Much simpler are the turned oak, pine and beech knobs with traditional and practical profiles. *P: plastic 44p–£1.40 each; knobs with backplates £1.80–£3.20 each; ring pull £1.60; timber pull handle £1.80; wooden knobs 90p–£1.20 each.*

This massive range of hardware also includes brass hinges, coat hooks, chains, curtain rings, window fittings, furniture feet, and seven kinds of castors.

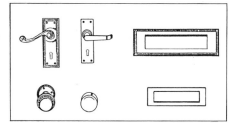

Ropetwist GEORGIAN and plain VICTORIAN fittings from Harrison Beacon

HEATHERLEY FINE CHINA LTD

Porcelain finger plates with matching door knobs, cabinet knobs and escutcheons. Each of the nine sets includes two finger plates, door knobs, smaller wardrobe knob, still smaller cupboard knob and escutcheon. Six of the sets are decorated with roses, apple blossom or songbirds, while the other three are plain white, white with gold edging and, most striking of all, black with gold edging. Also available are self-adhesive name plates ranging from 'Private' to 'Tis Here'. *P: door furniture £16 per set; name plates £1.*

Plain and decorated porcelain door knobs and finger plates with escutcheons from Heatherley

HOPE WORKS LTD

Selection of gothic wrought iron door and window fittings. LIONHEART matt black ironmongery is notable for its use of a fleur-de-lis motif. There is a wide selection of lever and pull handles, mortice knobs, door and gate latches, bolts, letterboxes, house numbers, cylinder lock covers, knockers and some long strap door hinges, or just the 'hinge fronts' to give the decorative effect without troubling with the moving part. *P: on application.*

KNOBS & KNOCKERS

Large retail range of traditional and modern door furniture, cabinet fittings, grilles, nameplates and all kinds of fittings. Clean, modern lines are shown in the STEDEN SUITE, which includes mortice knobs (one with indicator), centre door knob, pull handles, escutcheon, lever locks and latches, bathroom lever lock and snib, bell push, escutcheon, and cupboard knob and handle. Available in polished brass, satin brass, imitation metal bronze antique, chrome plated and satin chrome plated finishes. *P: mortice furniture £39.70–£45.95 set; centre door knob £68.65; cupboard knob £7.60.*

Classically English HATHAWAY and GAINSBOROUGH porcelain mortice knobs, fingerplates and escutcheons come in plain white, white with gold band and floral in blue or polychrome on white. Cupboard knobs and wardrobe knobs are available in HATHAWAY range only. *P: mortice knobs £7.30–£13.90 set; fingerplates £4–£19.35; cupboard and wardrobe knobs £1.55–£3.80.*

Other door furniture includes gothic-style ANTIQUE IRONWORK, with mortice knobs, bell push, escutcheon, letterplate, bolts and latches, and also a long hinge front with fleur-de-lis terminal. All have a matt black finish. *P:*

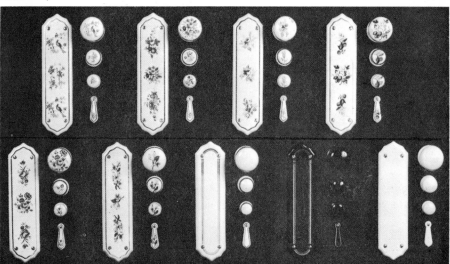

FITTINGS

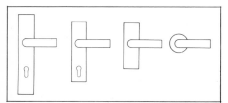

STEDEN lever handles by Knobs & Knockers

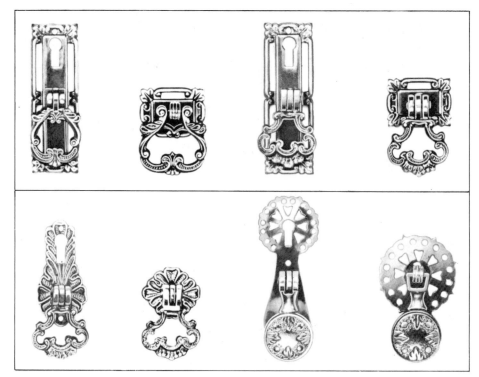

mortice door furniture £9.50 set; lever latch furniture £15.50 set; hinge fronts £10.50 pair. See also *Window fittings*.

Knobs & Knockers' cabinet fittings include some lovely polished brass drop handles, mostly Victorian in style, and brass knobs that are either plain round, plain octagonal or Georgian in pattern. Also available are two dull black iron furniture knobs. *P:* brass drop handles and knobs 85p–£3.60; iron knobs £9.50–£10.80 set.

There are also brass grilles. Choice includes diamond patterns with floral rosettes, with or without fine or large mesh backing; plain mesh; and perforated designs without additional mesh. There are five ventilator patterns available in polished brass, chrome plated or satin chrome plated finishes. *M:* ventilators h7.6 × w15.2 or 22.9 cm (3 × 6 or 9in), h15.2 × w22.9 or 30.5cm (6 × 9 or 12in). *P:* grilles, diamond £9.10–£44.65 sq ft, mesh £4.25 sq ft, perforated from £11.15 sq ft; ventilators £2.65–£19.60 each.

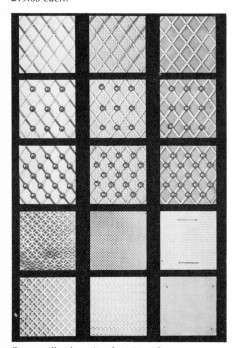

Brass grilles from Knobs & Knockers

B LILLY & SONS LTD △

More than 100 items in the SADLER SUITE, functionally styled in aluminium. Some of these door and cabinet fittings are also available in brass. Two basic designs of lever handle are available in all permutations for mortice, Yale, Union and bathroom snib locks, or without locks. There are complimentary door knobs and pulls as well as a full range of accessories including letterboxes, escutcheons, drawer and cupboard fittings, bell pushes, house numbers and other signs such as 'Push', 'Pull', telephone and male and female symbols, hooks, door stops, kicking plates, window fittings (see separate entry) and bathroom fittings (see *Bathrooms, accessories*). More select SADLER 'M' series consists of mortice levers with Yale or cylinder locks, escutcheons, bathroom snib locks and indicators, cupboard knobs and spindle fittings; it holds the British Standards Institution's Kitemark award for quality. *P:* SADLER aluminium, levers £11–£16 set, door knobs £12–£13.22 set, pull handles £4.78–£11.66 each, signs £4.26–£10.78 each, hooks £2.26 each, cupboard knobs 78p–£2.50 each; SADLER brass, door levers £18.46–£22.20 set, pulls £7.60–£51.14 each; 'M' series, door levers £11.42–£18.60.

Range of general hardware includes some very functional hat and coat hooks, fingerplates, door pulls, card frames, escutcheons and cupboard latches and fittings; all are brass in a choice of finishes including bronzed or chromium plated. *P:* hat and coat hooks 48p–£3.15. Lilly's marvellous collection of cabinet fittings

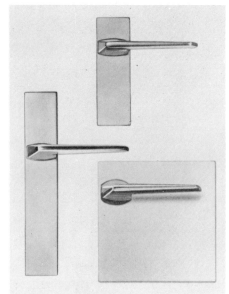

Top: drop handles for drawers; below: SADLER SUITE door levers △. All from Lilly

ranges from the basic to the antique. MODERN range of cabinet knobs, spindles, ring pulls, finger pulls and handles comes in traditional and streamlined designs with polished brass, bronze, chrome and silver-anodized finishes; there are escutcheons to match. Beautiful selection in the ANTIQUE range includes knobs and drop handles in a variety of elaborate rococo, plainer Georgian, Victorian and art nouveau styles in polished brass or brown relief finish. And the CRAFTSMEN IN BRASS range of solid brass fittings reproduces patterns introduced by Lilly in 1861, ideal for restoration of antique furniture. *P:* (knobs and handles) MODERN 45p–£2.50; ANTIQUE 55p–£2.50; CRAFTSMEN IN BRASS 70p–£3.20.

LOCKS & HANDLES
Large retail range including both traditional and modern door furniture. Georgian-style PRINCESS SUITE by Brassart is solid brass and includes door levers with plates fitted for mortice, Yale or Union locks, door pull, electric bell pushes, simple knocker, letterbox and escutcheons, as well as window casement fittings, coat hooks, chandelier hook, lightswitch and 13A socket.
In the modern idiom is SIMPLAN range by Dryad. Door handles and levers, mortice knobs, hinges, escutcheons, door stops, kicking plates and bolts are available. All have sleek modern styling and come either in cast aluminium with bright red, dark green, black, blue, brown or beige finish, or in polished and lacquered brass.
P: on application.

MAGNET SOUTHERNS
Solid brass, brass-plated and porcelain door furniture. In solid brass are plain VICTORIAN and more fanciful REGENCY and GEORGIAN ranges, the latter two with rope moldings. All

include letterplate, knockers, lock lever sets, centre knobs, escutcheon (GEORGIAN with covered escutcheon) and fingerplate (REGENCY with ornate cut-out design); VICTORIAN has cupboard knob too. Also in the GEORGIAN pattern are light switches and sockets. Modern-styled knobs (some with bathroom lock), mortice locks, letterbox flap and various latches and hinges are available in brass plate. Porcelain door sets include knobs and fingerplates and come in five styles: flower and fruit designs or gold borders on white. *P:* solid brass, lock lever set £9.96–£15.06, fingerplate £5.03–£7.48; brass plate, lock lever set £11; porcelain, mortice knob set £11, fingerplate £6.19.

NEWMAN-TONKS HARDWARE LTD
NORMBAU range of colourful nylon door furniture. Functional but stylish lever handles, mortice knobs, pull handles, escutcheons and bathroom snibs come in bright blue, red, green and yellow, plus olive, brown, black, white, and light and dark grey. The nylon material is said to have high impact and scratch

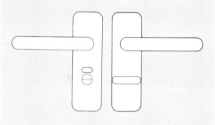

NORMBAU lever locks from Newman Tonks

resistance, to be stable to weathering, fading or ageing, and to be resistant to conventional domestic cleaners and even sea water. *P:* on application.

PERKINS & POWELL LTD
Good selection of solid brass door furniture in traditional patterns. COBDEN range includes matching mortice knobs, lever handles, letterbox, knockers, fingerplate, escutcheon, cylinder latch pull and several handsome centre door pulls, all in polished brass. For the cottage door there is a polished brass Suffolk latch set. PITTS mortice knob sets and centre door knobs come in a choice of polished brass, chromium plated, or satin chromium plated finishes.
Perkins & Powell make a useful and comprehensive range of other brass fittings, including hat and coat hooks (even a sliding wardrobe hook on a ring), card frames, hinges and brackets, ventilator grilles, curtain rings (in six different diameters) and marine fittings — including cabin hooks, flush rings and handles that serve a purpose on land as well as at sea. *P:* all on application.

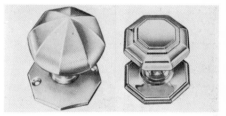

Centre door knobs from Perkins & Powell

ROTHLEY BRASS LTD
Traditional and modern brass door furniture. GEORGIAN, WINDSOR and VICTORIAN are large, traditional collections of entrance and door furniture, cabinet and window fittings, including lever handles, mortice knobs, letterboxes, pull handles, cupboard knobs and an extremely good range of electrical sockets, light and dimmer switches, and bell pushes. CURZON collection offers a limited selection of items in modern designs. Rather more bedroomy, CHINA collection of lever handles, mortice knobs, escutcheons, finger plates, wardrobe and cupboard knobs includes floral designs and a selection of smart black fittings with simple gold banding. Range of 17 brass door knockers includes a reproduction of the Romanesque door knocker from Winchester Cathedral and a head of Aphrodite. *P:* GEORGIAN, WINDSOR, VICTORIAN, mortice knobs £10.50–£36 etc, cupboard knobs £4–£9 pair; CURZON mortice knobs £26–£38 set, cupboard knobs £9–£12 pair; CHINA mortice knobs £8.30–£10.80 set, wardrobe knobs £5.80–£7.80 pair; door knockers £7–£48. See also *Window fittings.*

SIMPLAN range of door fittings from Locks & Handles △

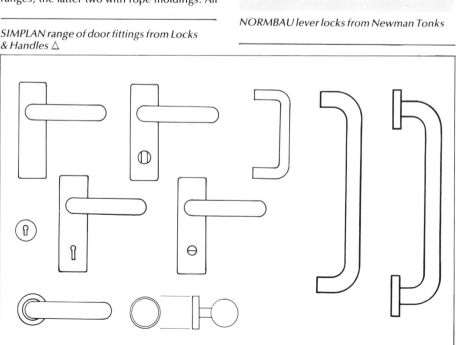

FITTINGS

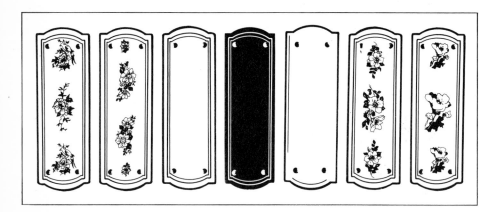

Top: CHINA finger plates; below: CURZON fittings. From Rothley Brass

VALLI & COLOMBO LTD
Stunning collection of modern cast brass lever handles, knobs, pull handles and cabinet fittings, plus keys, key escutcheons and matching coat hooks made by Fusital in Italy. Cast brass door fittings come in five ranges: OTTO A, OTTO B, OTTO G, DUE G and DUE Z. OTTO ranges are available in three finishes: gold, chrome and nerox (matt black). DUE ranges are made of a metal core coated in silicone

From left: Valli & Colombo's OTTO A, DUE Z

elastomer; DUE Z comes in brick red, cement grey and ebony and DUE G in gold, nerox, red, grey and blue. *P:* on application.

WINDOW FITTINGS
KNOBS & KNOCKERS
Large retail range including ANTIQUE IRONWORK fittings in gothic style with matt black finish. There are casement fasteners with hook or mortice plates, and also a casement stay. *P:* fasteners £3.95–£14.15 each; stays £4.70 each.

ANTIQUE IRONWORK from Knobs & Knockers

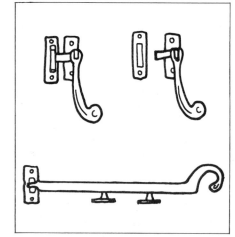

B LILLY & SONS LTD
Brass and aluminium casement fittings with uncluttered style. Lilly supply solid brass casement fittings in modern designs: two types of pin stay, a shadbolt stay and wedge, mortice plate and hook plate fasteners. The firm also makes a brass sash handle and miscellaneous brass fittings such as numerals, card frames, hooks and padlock hasps. *P:* on application.

PERKINS & POWELL
Complete range of solid brass window fittings from a firm established in 1875. For sash windows there are four types of fastener (quadrant arm, straight arm, 'Brighton' and 'Fitch' patterns), a sash hook, sash eyes, lifts, rollers, knot holders, security screws and an acorn stop with or without chain. For casement windows seven kinds of stay can be supplied, plus wedge, hook plate and mortice plate fasteners. Fittings for opening fanlights include a roller stay, a pair of quadrant arms and two fanlight catches. Usually supplied with polished brass finish but can also be chromium or satin chromium plated. *P:* on application.

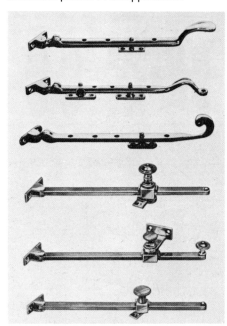

Perkins & Powell's casement stays

ROTHLEY BRASS LTD
Traditional casement and sash fittings. GEORGIAN and WINDSOR collection have casement fittings ornamented with a rope motif and include wedge, hook plate and mortice plate fasteners, as well as three patterns of stay each. VICTORIAN collection has similar casement fittings as well as sash fasteners and a screw stop set. *P:* £7.50–£16.

142

'San Giorgio' linoleum floor tiles by Sheppard Day

FLOORING

INTRODUCTION

Decorating begins at ground level. Whatever your lifestyle—or budget—it's imperative to get the floor right.

Before laying any kind of flooring, make sure the sub-floor is sound. Remove protruding nails from timber, fasten loose boards, and level the surface if necessary. Concrete, brick or tile floors must also be smooth, and free from damp.

This section is divided according to material. *Cork tiles* range from unsealed products (the cheapest) which must be coated before use, through waxed tiles that need occasional recoating, to hard-wearing, trouble-free versions finished with polyurethane or vinyl (the most expensive). All vary in thickness.

Linoleum, or lino, has been around for years, and is made of fibres such as hessian or jute which have been coated under pressure and heat with a mixture of powdered cork, linseed oil, resin and the desired pigment to produce sheets of hard-wearing flooring. It is enjoying a comeback—today's linos are far more varied and colourful than their much-maligned predecessors.

Rubber flooring is sound absorbent, and relatively inexpensive.

Stone flooring can be slate, marble, limestone or lava-derived materials. Although it can feel cold, it's undeniably handsome—and requires virtually no maintenance. Sizes and thicknesses vary enormously. Brick flooring is also included here.

Vinyl sheeting ranges from flexible, unbacked sheeting to more costly, harder wearing cushioned versions. *Vinyl tiles* are normally uncushioned, coloured right through and generally inexpensive. Relatively easy to lay, both forms need regular repolishing.

Hardwearing *Wood* flooring consists of parquet tiles, and more expensive timber planking. Both types can add to the value of your home.

● See also *Ceramic tiles, floors*.
● Architectural salvage dealers listed at the end of the book often stock stone and wood flooring.

CORK TILES

ALLIANCE FLOORING CO LTD
Competitively priced unsealed cork tiles in one light shade only but a choice of three thicknesses. *M:* 12 × 12in (30.5 × 30.5cm). *P:* £2.30–£3.65 sq yd.

MUNDET CORK & PLASTICS LTD
JOINTITE cork tiles in several natural shades from light tan to dark walnut, four different thicknesses, three different finishes and standard, medium or heavy density according to intended application. Available pre-sanded — in which case Mundet recommend sanding

again after laying and before applying waxed, sealed and waxed, or synthetic resin finish — or with these finishes already applied. Resin finish is tough and easily maintained but will not give the natural richness and gradual maturing of a wax finish. The tiles can be laid on to any even sub-floor that has been thoroughly cleaned and dried. Standard tiles have square edges but for increased stability tiles more than ¼in (5mm) thick can be tongue and grooved on request. *M:* 12 × 12in (30.5 × 30.5cm). *P:* (pre-sanded, ⅛in tiles in 50-249 sq yd quantity) standard £1.53 sq yd; medium £1.74 sq yd; heavy £1.90 sq yd.

Mundet also offer pre-cut cork skirtings, pre-cut treads with square or bull-nosed edges, cork expansion strips, cork underlay for sound insulation under various types of flooring, and CORKBOARD for thermal insulation, plus a full range of adhesives, polishes and finishes.

SHEPPARD DAY DESIGNS LTD
Hand-printed or plain cork tiles, heavy density with lacquered finish. Of the three printed designs, 'Parallel' simply has a single line running across one side of each tile; the tiles can be laid to create stripes, a chevron effect, or a pattern of squares. 'Blenheim', also available as a linoleum tile (see separate entry), has a black triangle printed across the corner of each natural-toned tile; when laid together, the triangles appear to form small diamond keystones linking larger tiles. 'Inlay' is a *trompe l'oeil* design simulating wooden boards; the 'wood' lines are printed on to each tile in varying tones of brown. *M:* all 12 × 12in (30.5 × 30.5cm) in pack of nine to cover 1 sq yd. *P:* printed £9.06 pack; plain £6.96 pack.

WICANDERS (GREAT BRITAIN) LTD
Four ranges of cork tiles and panels. Popular CORK-O-PLAST tile is made up of four layers: a PVC underside to keep out moisture and ensure stability, a layer of cork, a decorative layer of cork veneer, and finally an easy-to-clean, clear PVC layer forming a resilient surface for heavy wear. There are 13 different veneer patterns: 'Natural'; 'Natural Expand' with dark exposed flecks; 'Smoke'; 'Smoke Expand'; 'Character', small irregular rectangles of light cork in parquet-style; 'Harmony', with a light, larger patchwork effect; 'Rhapsody', a mixture of natural cork colours; 'Colorite Green' and 'Colorite Red', both expanded cork with colour showing through the natural holes in the cork; 'Accent', with a slightly textured effect; 'Allegro Tile' and 'Concert Plank', both with textured veneered patterns; 'Natural Brown', a plain dark brown tile (also available as plank, half and quarter tiles) intended for use with other designs to create individual patterns. *M:* all 30 × 30cm (11¾ × 11¾in) 'Accent', 'Natural', 'Natural Expand', 'Allegro', 'Concert', 'Natural Brown' also 90 × 15cm (35½ × 6in),

Wicanders' CORK-O-PLAST

plus quarter and half tile sizes. *P:* all patterns £12–£16 sq m.

Less expensive but less durable are CORKTEX and CORKTILE, both plain natural cork. CORKTILES are pre-sanded and ready to seal, in a choice of two thicknesses. CORKTEX are available in two thicknesses and three finishes and qualities: 'pre-polished', with factory-applied hard wax (requiring an occasional wax polishing); 'Acrylic', a tougher finish; 'Supercoat', a heavy density tile with very durable acrylic coating. Both the acrylic-coated tiles can be re-sealed with polyurethane seal. *M:* all 30 × 30cm (11¾ × 11¾in). *P:* CORKTILE £3–£4 sq yd; CORKTEX, 'Pre-polished' £5.34 sq yd, 'Acrylic' £5.43 sq yd; 'Supercoat' £8.17 sq yd. CORK-O-FLOOR panels can be used to form a floating floor to cover most existing floor coverings and overcome sub-floor problems. Selected CORK-O-PLAST patterns are bonded to pre-formed tongued and grooved chipboard panels. Panels are glued together but used loose-lay. *M:* panel 90 × 30cm (35½ × 11¾in). *P:* from £31 sq m.

LINOLEUM

FORBO KROMMENIE (UK) LTD
Toughened but stylish linoleum in a huge choice of colours. Two distinctive ranges of marbled lino are specifically designed for hard wear, hygiene-controlled areas: MARMOLEUM sheet lino in four different gauges and 34 marbled colours including bright yellow, red and blue as well as natural marble shades, and LINOFLEX tiles in 10 shades including pastels, naturals, and black and white. Tiles are backed with a fine layer of glass fibre and polyester that is highly flexible and helps prevent cracking, but at the same time gives stability and grip. After extensive testing both products were found to be bactericidal, resistant to cigarette burns and indentation, and resilient to most chemicals. To combat noise, MARMOLEUM lino is available with sound-absorbent cork backing under the name ACOUSTOLEUM. *M:* MARMOLEUM w200cm (79in); LINOFLEX 30 × 30cm (11¾ × 11¾in); ACOUSTOLEUM w200cm (79in). *P:* (contract)

MARMOLEUM from £4.81 sq m; LINOFLEX £6.49 sq m; ACOUSTOLEUM £8.07 sq m. Forbo also produce plain linoleum sheeting in eight neutral tones — rust, two beiges, olive, mid-brown, grey, grey-blue and black. Sound-deadening cork-backed linoleum comes in all these colours except the last two; it is really a specialist flooring for sports halls etc. *M:* w200cm (78¾in); plain d2, 3.2mm; cork-backed d3.2, 4.5, 6mm. *P:* (contract) plain from £4.37 sq m; cork-backed from £7.17 sq m. LINOFORM angles and covings are available for neat installation, and LINOWELD hot welding rod can be used to give a watertight, colour-matched seal.

Forbo Krommenie's LINOFLEX

HABITAT DESIGNS LTD

Three attractive designs of lino floor tiles, all coated with hard-wearing, scuff-resistant lacquer: 'Savoy', a diagonal stripe of red and white on grey; 'Pavan', with solid, pale brick body edged with a pale grey band; and 'Locarno' with pink or grey broken lines criss-crossing on a beige ground. Sold in packs of nine to cover 81 sq cm (32 sq in), complete with laying instructions. *M:* 30 × 30cm (11¾ × 11¾in). *P:* £10.75 per pack.

NAIRN FLOORS LTD ⚠

Linoleum flooring for a wide range of contract (or domestic) installations with high-point loading and natural bactericidal properties, good sound absorbency and fire resistance. Two ranges of marbled, toughened linoleum sheeting each come in 18 colours. ARMOUR-FLOR has toughened linoleum layer with jute canvas backing and extra built-in resistance to point loading making it suitable for extra heavy areas. ARMOURFLEX has similar construction but greater flexibility. It comes in three qualities: '32', suitable for heavy contract, '25' for medium and '20' for light contract areas. *M:* all w183cm (72in). *P:* ARMOURFLOOR £24 sq m; ARMOURFLEX £20–£22 sq m. Equally tough but simpler to lay in awkward areas are Nairn's tiles. ARMOURTILE '90' and '200' have unique bonded polyester web backing impregnated with a resin seal for extra stability. '200' has toughened linoleum finish, giv-

ing resistance to staining, burning and point-loading, making it suitable for extra-heavy areas. Tiles come in 10 marbled colours: six shades of beige and brown, plus blue, green, grey and red. *M:* 30 × 30cm (11¾ × 11¾in). *P:* from £17 sq m. Nairn also offer a range of standard linoleum sheeting in three gauges and four plain colours — brown, dark green, grey and black. *M:* w183cm (72in). *P:* on application.

SHEPPARD DAY DESIGNS LTD ⚠

Trompe l'oeil floor tiles, a stunning new look for lino. Designs are shaded or stippled to trick the eye into believing that the floor has a third dimension. 'Piazza' imitates stone tiles cut with mitred edges. There are 14 translucent colours: Indian red, violet carmine, Venetian rose (coral), stone pink, sand, Sienna (yellowish stone), terra verte (sage green), grey green, Antwerp (grey blue), cerulean, ultramarine, Prussian, grey flannel and gunmetal. 'San Marco', 'San Pantaleone' and 'San Giorgio' are inspired by the marble floors of great Venetian churches. 'San Marco', in grey flannel, blue grey or Venetian rose, is laid in 'brickwork' formations. 'San Pantaleone', in blue, green, or pinkish terracotta, each colour contrasted with grey and stone, and 'San Giorgio', in richer tones of Prussian blue, grey green, crimson and gunmetal, both have strong geometric

'San Marco' △ from Sheppard Day

Sheppard Day's 'Piazza' △

patterns. Both can be laid either square to the wall or diagonally. Less dramatic, 'Blenheim' has the classic black and white format: black triangles on the corner of each marbled white tile appear to form diamond keystones when the tiles are laid. The design is also available in cork (see separate entry). Complementary border tiles in the same shades can be cut to give a tailor-made finish to the floor. *M:* all 12 × 12in (30.5 × 30.5cm); sold in packs of nine to cover 1 sq yd. *P:* patterned £20 sq yd; plain £16 sq yd.

RUBBER

GERLAND LTD

3S METRO synthetic rubber studded tiles, strong, resistant to cigarette burns, acoustic and anti-slip, designed for contract use. Choose from round stud in brick, black, green, brown, blue and beige; square stud in black, brown, orange, beige and blue; low profile stud in brown, beige, orange and sage; pastille stud (circles and lozenges combined) in black only. *M:* 75 × 75cm (29½ × 29½in). *P:* (contract) £10.85–£15.66 sq m. Skating rink and sports qualities also available. See following page for illustration.

JAYMART RUBBER & PLASTICS LTD

Possibly the world's largest collection of rubber flooring. Studded synthetic rubber floor tiles for non-slip, heavy traffic surfaces come in various patterns and textures: round-studded SAFE-T-STEP, square-studded SAFE-T-TREAD, low profile PROLO, textured SAFE-T-TEX and pimple-studded FLORAFLOR. All come in five qualities — indoor, outdoor, oil-resistant, ice rink and special electrical quality for computer rooms — and in 20 colours including vivid red, green, yellow and blue as well as the commoner neutral tones. Also

Stud patterns from Gerland's 3S METRO range. Top left: pastille; right: round; below left: square

available are studded stair treads and nosings (with round or square studs), smooth risers and ribbed nosing, in black, chocolate brown, anthracite, green and olive. *M:* tiles 50 × 50 (19¾ × 19¾in); stair treads etc 100 or 120 × 48cm (39¼ or 47¼ × 19in). *P:* SAFE-T-STEP, PROLO, SAFE-T-TEX, FLORAFLOR from £10.20 sq m; SAFE-T-TREAD from £11.27 sq m; set of tread, riser and nosing £8.40.
Incredible choice of contract ribbed matting

Jaymart's SAFE-T-MAT

includes fine-ribbed PACEMAKER in three thicknesses, in black only; broad-ribbed MAT-KANDU, in black, grey, blue, red, brown, green and white, also in oil-resistant quality and selected colours in extra-thick qualities; and SAFE-T-MAT with chequerboard of ribbing available in two thicknesses in black, grey, brown and white, and in oil-resistant quality. *M:* PACEMAKER w91.5, 122cm (36, 48in); MAT-KANDU w100, 120cm (39¼, 47¼in); SAFE-T-MAT w120, 140cm (47¼, 55in). *P:* on application.

From top: Jaymart's PACEMAKER, MATKANDU

STONE

CAPITAL CERAMICS
ANTIQUITIES tiles cut from fossil-bearing limestone quarried in Bavaria. Some tiles show a distict fern-leaf motif, others have a pink vein running all through, and are cream, yellow or white in tone — though there is, of course, tremendous variation of colour and pattern. Tiles can be cut to virtually any shape or size, and are sealed against water and staining. *P:* £30–£40 sq m.

CATHEDRAL WORKS ORGANISATION
Limestone, marble and granite for internal (or external) floors, paving, stairs and wall cladding, from Rocamat, a consortium of stone quarries and workshops based in France. Eight different limestones (with honed or sawn finish) and 19 marbles (polished, honed or flame-textured) are available in sawn slabs, square tiles or larger sizes on request. *M:* tiles 30, 40,

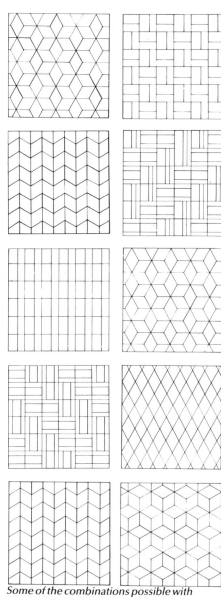

Some of the combinations possible with Cathedral Works' CAMIEU tiles

50, 60cm (11¾, 15¾, 19¾, 23½in). *P:* from £25 sq m.
CAMIEU floor tiles are hard-wearing Burgundian marble. Squares, diamonds, strips and rectangles are available in two contrasting coloured stones, 'Comblanchien' and 'Larrys'. They can be fitted together in more than 100 different designs. Tiles can be polished and are available with or without rounded edges, packed in boxes of mixed shapes to cover ½ or 1 sq m. *M:* squares 30 × 30cm (11¾ × 11¾in), rectangles 30 × 15cm (11¾ × 6in), diamonds 17.5 × 20cm (6¾ × 7¾in), strips 30 × 7.5cm (11¾ × 3in). *P:* from £20 sq m.
Granites such as 'Rose de la Clarte' (dense

pink, large grain and black mica), and 'Tarn Saint Salvy' (dark blue grey) are available in prepared slabs with polished, honed or flame-textured finish. *P:* on application.

CERAMIC TILE DESIGN

Pre-cut marble in an amazing range of colours, including red, black, green and rose-pink veining as well as the commoner beige, grey and white. Of course, the price varies considerably depending on the rarity of the stone and the thickness of the tile. Tiles are available in squares, rectangular strips and squares with cut corners matched with small black keystones for a classic pattern. Ceramic Tile Design cannot guarantee that every tile will be exactly the same colour but do endeavour to get the same veining. Marble slabs can also be cut to size. *M:* squares 30 × 30cm (11¾ × 11¾in); strips 15 × 30cm (6 × 11¾in); slabs d7–10mm. *P:* £34.50–£136.35 sq m. See colour illustration in *Ceramic tiles*.

DELABOLE SLATE LTD

Slate slabs and tiles from one of England's oldest and largest slate quarries. They are impermeable to water, resistant to chemicals and sunlight. Slabs can be cut to required shape and thickness with natural riven finish, rough ground for a relatively smooth finish or finely rubbed with carborundum powder to produce a smooth eggshell finish. Colours vary from blue-grey to grey-green with natural markings, bands or stripes (markings are more obvious in the smooth finishes). *M:* max 45.7 × 152.2cm (18 × 60in). *P:* natural £40.90 sq m; ground £48.98 sq m; finely rubbed £51.66 sq m. Quarries or tiles are small, naturally riven, rectangular or square pieces of slate with diamond-sawn edges for a clean finish. Tiles are subject to the same colour variations and natural markings as slabs, and the natural riven surface may be uneven and theretore cause some variation in thickness also. *M:* 15.2 × 15.2cm (6 × 6in), 15.2 × 30.5cm (6 × 12in), 30.5 × 30.5cm (12 × 12in). *P:* £18 sq m.

MAYBRIK (UK) LTD

Kiln-fired clay bricks just ¼in (55mm) thick, in 11 different colours, for floor covering or wall cladding. When laid, MAYBRIKS are indistinguishable from traditional 2in (5cm) thick bricks, but their slimness and self-spacing flanges make them as simple to install as ceramic or quarry tiles; there's no need to recess sub-floors, trim doors or lower the threshold as may be required for a traditional brick floor. There are two different series: 'Thinbrick' available in New England red, old Boston, black walnut, ironspot and weathered white; and 'Architectural' in black walnut, chestnut, grey flannel, mesa, Tudor red and rosewood with either glazed or abrasive finish. Both

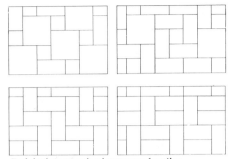

Delabole's standard patterns for tiles

series meet all British Standard requirements on water absorption, breaking strength, abrasive hardness and freeze/thaw reaction. *M:* 20 × 6cm (8 × 2½in). *P:* 'Thinbrick' £26–£28.75 sq m, corner pieces sold as singles £1.65 each; 'Architectural' £26.75 sq m.

Oak strips are available for contrasting edging. Other accessories include INNERSEAL, a deep sealer to retain colour and texture, protect against damp, grease and dirt, and HILITE, a satin gloss, water resistant, non-slip finish. Dual-purpose grout and thinset cement are also available. *M:* oak strips w2.5, 5cm (1, 2in). *P:* oak strips 98p, £1.80 linear m; INNERSEAL £13.75 per 1l can; HILITE £9.25 per 1l can,

Top: Maybrik's 'Thinbrick' laid in herringbone pattern; below: 'Architectural' with oak strip edging

SHEPPARD DAY DESIGNS LTD

Marble without the chill. See *Flooring, wood* for hand-marbled tiles made from medium-density fibreboard.

VINYL SHEETING

ARMSTRONG WORLD INDUSTRIES LTD

RHINOFLOOR domestic sheet vinyl, tough, strong and durable as its name. Available in four standards, all with 'TufTop' finish which both reduces maintenance and increases resistance to chair castors, foot traffic and impact from heavy weights. 'Super Plus' (the toughest, for heavy domestic or selected light commercial use) and 'Soft' (thickly cushioned, for medium to heavy domestic use) come in 12 patterns and colourways including cork, quarry, Provencal tile and chequered effects. 'Comfort' and 'Standard', less cushioned than 'Soft' but for similar application, come in 13 typical vinyl designs and colourways. *M:* 'Super Plus', 'Soft', 'Comfort' w300cm (118in); 'Standard' w200, 300, 400cm (78¾, 118, 157½in). *P:* (cut lengths) 'Super Plus' £14.38 sq m; 'Soft' £13.32 sq m; 'Comfort' £11.20 sq m; 'Standard £10.92 sq m.

DLW (BRITAIN) LTD

Two particularly strong and hard-wearing ranges, TRIDUR and TRILASTIC. Available in 47 designs including simulated quarry tile, Provençal tile, marble and traditional ceramic tile designs, and also modern 'Minimetric' grids and linear patterns; in a total of 164 different colourways. TRILASTIC is lighter and less expensive, constructed from three strong layers of PVC. It comes in three qualities, 'Super', 'Perfect' and 'Standard', all recommended for domestic use. TRIDUR is constructed of five layers, making it unusually durable, and is said to be resistant to indentation (even suitable for chair castors) in addition to being anti-static. Available in two qualities, 'Deluxe' and 'Exquisite', both suitable for heavy traffic contract areas, and for underfloor heating. *M:* TRILASTIC w200, 275, 400cm (78¾, 108¼, 157½in); TRIDUR w200, 400cm (87¾, 157½in). *P:* TRILASTIC 'Super' £6 sq yd, 'Perfect' £5.45 sq yd, 'Standard' £5 sq yd; TRIDUR 'Deluxe' £9 sq yd; 'Exquisite' £7.80 sq yd.

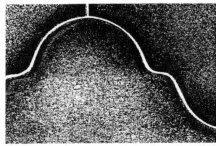

DLW's TRIDUR

FLOORING

DUNLOP LTD
Comprehensive and reasonably priced choice of self-adhesive vinyl flooring. VYNALAY non-cushioned range includes a number of patterns based on traditional ceramic tile designs. 'Spartan Brown' features the Provencal tile shape in rich brown lightened with beige. 'Venetian Sand' shows small patterned 'keystones' linking larger plain 'tiles', 'Italian Beige' interlocks small and large Provençal shapes. All these designs have hard-wearing surface, built-in shine and textured finish. *M:* w200cm (78¾in). *P:* £2.39–£2.99 sq m.

Top: VYNALAY; below: SUPERLAY sheet flooring. Both by Dunlop

SUPERLAY cushioned vinyl sheeting is available in 12 different natural effects including 'quarry tile', 'stone', 'wood block' and 'cork', each in a variety of shades. Of the stone-effect designs, 'Rossendale' shows small squares in varying tones of soft blue-grey, brown or natu-ral stone; 'Calderdale' shows ivory 'tiles' with contrasting diamond 'keystones' in any one of twelve strong colours; and 'Rydale' shows octagons and inset diamonds in chestnut brown or honey colourways. *M:* w200cm (78¾in). *P:* approx £4 sq m.

FORBO KROMMENIE (UK) LTD
Tough vinyl sheet flooring with the glass fleece construction pioneered by Forbo, a leading European company in this field. NOVILON cushioned sheet vinyls include NOVILON DE-LTA, four sophisticated modern designs in 10 colourways, the colours deeply embossed to give lasting brightness. The vinyl has thick foam and heavy-duty wear layers, making it suitable for all domestic locations. NOVA SU-PER and VIVA SUPER have improved quality with additional PVC foam and glass fibre wear layer giving warmth, comfort and sound in-sulation as well as strength and flexibility. Both are suitable for underfloor heating and have fire-resistant properties; NOVA SUPER can also withstand chair castors so is suitable for light commercial use. Both come with five-year warranty. Patterns are traditional and modern, colours including bold reds and blues as well as muted combinations. NOVA SUPER has seven designs in 17 colourways in-cluding tile-pattern 'Strada' in beige, gold and red, and mottled 'Terra' in beige, green/beige, light blue and light brown. VIVA SUPER has seven designs in 15 colourways, including che-quered 'Talina' in grey, rose/grey and light brown, 'Sonora' with an occasional diagonal motif in beige and dark beige, and 'Moderna' with two-tone diagonal stripe in light beige, blue and brown. *M:* NOVILON DELTA w200cm (78¾in); NOVA SUPER w400cm (157½in); VIVA SUPER w275, 400cm (108¼, 157½in). *P:* NOVILON DELTA £9.99 sq m; NOVA SUPER £10 sq m; VIVA SUPER £7 sq m.

Left: 'Strada'; top: 'Talina'; below: 'Moderna'. All by Forbo

Originally made for contract use in such places as hospitals and schools, tough, modern SMARAGD vinyl is also available for domestic use. Two qualities, SMARAGD and SMARAGD FOAM (the latter not suitable for wet floors) come in 20 attractive, lightly speckled colours: black, five shades from beige to brown, four shades from off-white to blue-grey, plus green, turquoise, four rich blues, yellow, two reds and two pink-speckled shades. *M:* w200cm (78¾in). *P:* approx £11 sq m.

GERLAND LTD
All types of vinyl flooring from a prolific manu-facturer. For the home, GERFLOR FLEXILAY cushioned sheet vinyl in 'all purpose', 'super' and 'luxury' qualities comes in more than 80 designs and colourways. Designs include fashionable geometric patterns and imitations

Top: 'Bali'; below: 'Quadri'. Both in GERFLOR FLEXILAY range by Gerland

of marble (including the ever-popular white with black keystones), rustic quarry and terracotta tiles, wood, cork and ceramic tile floors. Examples of ceramic patterns are 'Bali', a filigree pattern in bronze or copper, 'Ankara', an ornate design in olive or rich turquoise colourways, and 'Gand', a simpler design with small-scale mesh infill between the 'tiles', in white on white or white on blue — all in super quality. More modern is all-purpose quality 'Quadri', a grid in white and marine (blue), brick, brown, volcano red or ocean blue. *M:* w200, 300, 400cm (78¾, 118, 157½in). *P:* £6.40–£10.70 sq m.

For heavy duty there's CLASSIC solid, flexible vinyl sheeting in 16 marbled colours and two gauges, also available in tiles. (See *Flooring, vinyl tiles* for details.) *M:* w185cm (72¾in). *P:* £6.18 sq m.

For contract use there's TARAFLEX foam-backed sheeting, for heavy traffic and for sports halls. It's sound-deadening and super tough, with excellent recovery to heel and furniture indentation. 'Taralay Confort' comes

in two gauges and in strong solid colours (including vivid emerald green) and in marbled designs. 'Taralay Standard', also in two gauges, is lightly marbled. Matching stair-treads and nosings are available, plain, marbled or two-colour. Range also includes six specialist 'Taraflex Sport' vinyls, used at the Olympics at Montreal, Moscow and Los Angeles. *M:* 'Confort' w150cm (59in); 'Standard' w150cm (59in); stair treads w51cm (20in); 'Sport' w150cm (59in). *P:* (contract) 'Confort' £5.30–£6 sq m; 'Standard' £4.50–£5.90 sq m; stair treads £3.30 linear m; 'Sport' £1.40–£12.60 sq m.

Also available are ribbed vinyl sheets in black or grey for entrances, gangways and ramps where extra grip is needed, MARS felt-backed vinyl and ROBUST ANTISTATIC flooring for computer rooms. *M:* ribbed 75 × 75cm (29½ × 29½in); MARS w200cm (78¾in); ROBUST ANTISTATIC w150cm (59in). *P:* ribbed £19.60 sq m; MARS £4.35 sq m; ROBUST ANTISTATIC (contract) £6.12 sq m.

Gerland produce adhesives, welding rods and cold-joint products for use with all their sheet vinyls.

HABITAT DESIGNS LTD

Cushioned vinyl sheeting with heavy domestic rating making it especially suitable for kitchens, bathrooms and nurseries. Made of PVC with glass fibre core, it is not, however, immune to burns so is not recommended for use adjacent to solid fuel fires. There are three designs: 'Piccadilly' with red and blue stripes on white; 'Graph' with red, blue or green grid on white; 'Check' with a larger white grid on grey or red. *M:* w200cm (78¾in). *P:* linear m (2 sq m) £11.60.

JAYMART RUBBER & PLASTICS LTD

Competitively priced, low profile, studded vinyl sheet flooring. DISCO, for general domestic and light contract use, comes in eight fashionable colours: olive green, chocolate brown, dark blue, cherry red, beige, white, black and light grey. DISCO DOMO, in the same colours, is for domestic use only. *M:* w200cm (78¾in). *P:* DISCO £4.45 sq m; DISCO DOMO £2.50 sq m.

DISCO by Jaymart

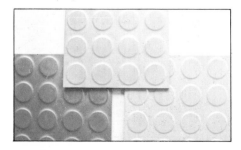

NAIRN FLOORS LTD ▲

Cushioned vinyl flooring to suit a full range of domestic applications and styles, and a variety of price brackets.

Extra tough DUROFLOR has stain-resistant demi-matt finish. Seven patterns and 16 colourways include 'Plaza', with paving effect of small interlocking shapes, in sand and terracotta; 'Napoli', with traditional Italian tile design in beige or off-white colourways; and parquet-style 'Boulogne' in two wood shades. *M:* w200, 400cm (78¾, 157½in). *P:* £10 sq m.

Softly cushioned COSYSOFT comes in seven patterns and 16 subtle colourways, all in imitation of tiles. 'Rustique' depicts small sand or terracotta tiles with an occasional floral motif; 'Arbon' is more contemporary with a chequer-board of horizontal and vertical stripes in beige/pale blue and off whites. Available with matt or gloss finish. *M:* w300cm (118in). *P:* £9 sq m.

ARENA's eight patterns and 22 colourways include some bolder tile patterns — though all in natural colours — marble effects in beige and pale brown, and a variety of parquet and wood-strip patterns, as well as 'Arbon' in an extended range of colourways. *M:* w200, 300, 400cm (78¾, 118, 157½in). *P:* £8 sq m.

AUTOGRAPH has a contemporary, designer touch. Its five patterns and 16 colourways reflect the simple lines of modern tile and fabric design. 'Minimal' has a faint floral motif on white squares, 'Lineal', a sparse grid of red, green or blue lines on white, and 'Graphical', a denser grid of brown, bright yellow, red, green or blue on white. *M:* w200, 400cm (78¾, 157½in). *P:* £7.80 sq m.

CUSHIONFLOR, first launched in 1967, still sells, with eight patterns and 22 colourways, in popular ceramic tile, quarry and parquet effects. 'Verdi' depicts tiles and irregularly shaped keystones in shades of brown, cream/beige, red/white, or blue/white. 'Flora' has a dense, stylized floral motif in green and brown on white or beige. *M:* w200, 300, 400cm (78¾, 118, 157½in). *P:* £7 sq m.

Best value for money is CLASSIC, with seven classic patterns in 16 colourways with matt or gloss finish. This range includes a mosaic pattern, 'Cramond', in red, beige, green/sand, and beige/blue colourways. *M:* w200, 300, 400cm (78¾, 118, 157½in). *P:* £5.60 sq m.

SOMMER ALLIBERT (UK) LTD

Two comprehensive domestic collections, designed to be loose-laid though adhesive can also be used.

BALANOR collection is divided into four ranges. DESIGN is the most contemporary with two outline designs: 'Diamont' with squares drawn in red, blue or beige on white, and 'Honeycomb' with honeycomb pattern in red or blue on white, or these two colourways reversed. SOFT has six simple monotone designs in pastel and neutral shades, including

FLOORING

Top: 'Diamont' from DESIGN range; below: SOFT. Both from the BALANOR collection by Sommer Allibert

cork and mosaic effects. CLASSIC offers six designs: 'Marble', 'Cottage Brick', 'Traditional Brick', 'Quarry' and Provençal 'Tomette' in a choice of pale or rich natural colours. Budget DECOR covers a wider range of styles including 'Woodblock', 'Square Mosaic', 'Floral Quarry', 'Spanish Tile', 'Cork', and 'Concorde' with octagons outlined in beige, blue or red on white. M: w200cm (78¾in). P: DESIGN, CLASSIC £9.61 sq m; SOFT £12.16 sq m; DECOR £5.72 sq m.

BALAFLEX collection is available in two widths so most rooms can be fitted without a join. A fibreglass layer and dense foam backing provide stability and resilience, and prevent shrinkage and curling. REGAL and SUPER ranges include parquet, Spanish and Provençal tile, quarry and decorated ceramic tile patterns, all in neutral or pastel shades; while DELUXE, the biggest range, includes good examples of all these styles plus 'Square Mosaic', 'Algarve' cork tile pattern, 'Travertine' marble flooring pattern (in a convincing beige) and 'Victoria Floral Tile' with delicate floral motif in cinnamon, lavender or avocado on off white. M: w300, 400cm (118, 157½in). P: £10.78 sq m.

VINYL TILES

AMTICO △
Classic natural-effect (wood, marble, brick and ceramic) and coloured vinyl tiles. Amtico place an emphasis on design and quality, but this is reflected in the price — these are by no means the cheapest on the market. Natural-

effect tiles are hand-finished so no two are identical, even varying slightly in colour, making the result even more convincing.

'Anglesey' slate-effect tiles are much larger than standard size, enhancing the impression that they really are slabs. Available in four grey to green slate shades which can be combined or used individually. M: 30.5 × 91.5cm (12 × 36in). P: £39.41 sq m.

There are four brick-effect designs with herringbone pattern or squares made up from three rectangular 'brick' shapes, in shades of white, off-white, and light and dark brick; also four QUARRY designs in beige and orangey or reddish terracotta. M: 30.5 × 30.5cm (12 × 12in), 22.9 × 22.9cm (9 × 9in). P: brick patterns £28.19–£31.05 sq m; QUARRY collection £32.91 sq m.

'Marbles' include slab-size 'Corinthian' in veined black, beige, and three grey-white colourways; 'Lorenzo Travertine' in grey-white, beige and pinkish beige; and 'Renaissance' squares in white, black, beige and yellowish green. M: 'Corinthian', 'Lorenzo Travertine' 30.5 × 91.5cm (12 × 36in); 'Renaissance' 30.5 × 30.5cm (12 × 12in), 91.5 × 91.5cm (36 × 36in). P: £32.92–£39.35 sq m.

Patterns comprise two mosaics, 'Textura' and 'Barcelona', in three white, beige and pale brown shades; a Provençal tile pattern, 'New Chateau', in three off-whites and terracotta; and four designs inspired by traditional ceramic tiles, 'Cordoba', 'Phoenicia', 'Amsterdam' and 'Lorenzo', all with darker outlines on mottled off-white or stone shades. M: mosaics 30.5 × 91.5cm (12 × 36in); others 30.5 × 30.5 (12 × 12in). P: £28.19–£37.73 sq m.

Simulating wood there are square or plank-shaped 'Wood Effect' tiles in medium and dark shades; 'Random Plank' in medium shade only; 'Stripwood' thin strips in three light to dark shades (similar to light oak, antique

Top, from left: 'Atherstone' from QUARRY range, 'New Chateau'; bottom: two brick patterns, 'Bucks County' and 'Tudor Brick'. All from Amtico

 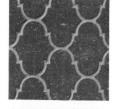

greyed pine and fresh pine); and 'Blockwood' in the same three pale shades. M: 'Wood Effect' 30.5 × 30.5cm (12 × 12in); 'Random Plank' 7.6, 15.2, 22.9 × 91.5cm (3, 6, 9 × 36in); 'Stripwood' 7.6 × 91.5cm (3 × 36in); 'Blockwood' 7.6 × 22.9cm (3 × 9in). P: £33.62–£49.90 sq m.

More basic and blatantly vinyl are the plain coloured tiles: 'Simetrica', made up from studded circles, squares or rectangles in neutral shades of grey, blue, green and mid-brown; 'Super Plains' in pure black or white; and 'Harmalux' plains in black, white, grey, blue, and five beige to green tones. M: 'Simetrica' 91.5 × 91.5cm (36 × 36in); others 30.5 × 30.5cm (12 × 12in). P: 'Simetrica' £24.09 sq m; 'Super Plains' £16.64 sq m; 'Harmalux' £6.99 sq m.

Customers can create their own effects by using standard tiles with contrasting strips or keystones. In addition to 'Stripwood' and 'Blockwood', strips are available in the same six colours as 'Harmalux', and keystones can be cut from any other tiling. M: strips 2.5, 1.3 or 0.6 × 91.5cm (1, ½ or ¼ × 36in). P: 11–86p per strip.

ARMSTRONG WORLD INDUSTRIES LTD
Patterned and plain vinyl tiles for all kinds of applications. Two ranges are suitable for commercial, light commercial and residential floors. ARLON is made of flexible vinyl and comes in 18 faintly marbled colours: grey-whites, beiges and greys, plus olive, black, orange, red and two shades of blue. Eight of the colours are available in self-adhesive tiles. ACCOFLEX UNIVERSAL, of more durable construction, comes in 17 similarly mottled colours: grey-white, two soft greys, black, seven different shades of beige, chestnut brown, olive, steel blue, terracotta, Mexican gold and cedar (dark brown with red marbling). M: 30 × 30cm (11¾ × 11¾in). P: ARLON £6.38 sq m; ACCOFLEX UNIVERSAL £5.28–£8.40 sq m.

Primarily for domestic use are CRAFTLON patterned tiles, though they may also be used for light commercial floors. Patterns are embossed on to the tiles, giving them an unusual texture. Tiles without adhesive backing are available in two gauges and eight designs: wood effect, brick patterns in terracotta, beige and white, 'Travertine' marbled effect, 'Country Style' squares with random flower motif in off whites and beige, 'Tivoli' Italian tile pattern in white, beige and brown, and Provençal tile effect in terracotta, beige, grey and mid brown. Self-adhesive CRAFTLON tiles come in six designs: 'Country Style', Provençal tile and brick effects, 'Diamond' with diagonal grid on grey, beige or red, dotted 'Solitaire' in green, brown or red on white, and modern 'Chevron' with white grid dividing up chequerboard of diagonal stripes in blue/pale blue, beige/green or rusty orange on white. M: 30 × 30cm (11¾ × 11¾in). P: standard £6.98 sq m; self-adhesive £7.90 sq m.

DUNLOP LTD

FLOORMAKER vinyl tiles, all self-adhesive. Simple 'Selflay' comes in six marbled colours: silver birch, blue, chocolate, honey, moss green and tobacco. 'Aristocrat' has glass fibre interlayer for dimensional stability and powerful adhesive for firm positioning. Twelve designs include wood, cork and marble effects plus five ornate ceramic tile patterns, all in colours from beige to brown. 'Debonair' cushioned tiles come in five designs: grey and red brick, brown marble, and three ceramic tile patterns which can be used together to produce a wider range of options. M: 'Selflay' 25 × 25cm (9¾ × 9¾in) in packs of 12 to cover 240 sq cm (8 sq ft); 'Aristocrat', 'Debonair' 12 × 12in (30.5 × 30.5cm), in pack of 9 to cover 1 sq yd. P: 'Selflay' £2.49 per pack; 'Aristocrat', 'Debonair' £5.49–£6.49 per pack.

From Dunlop. Top: 'Aristocrat'; below: 'Debonair'

FORBO KROMMENIE (UK) LTD

NOVILON self-adhesive cushioned vinyl tiles in 15 cool modern designs, made in Sweden. They can be used anywhere around the house, simply installed directly on to smooth, dry sub-floor or linoleum, vinyl, concrete or wood. Choose from tile-style patterns in soft blues, white, beige and terracotta; brick-pattern in grey and terracotta; imitation cork or cross-grain parquet; marbled beige; speckled white; or two more unusual designs — red or grey squares with triangles outlined in white on two opposing corners, laid to form composite crosses, and a chequerboard effect composed of alternate squares of vertical and horizontal stripes in grey/black and off-whites. M: 33.3 × 33.3cm (13 × 13in); in packs of six. P: £5.25 per pack.

For contract use, tough COLOVINYL semi-flexible PVC tiles come in four different gauges and 20 marbled colours — a fairly standard range including three marbled off-whites, grey, three beiges, mid-brown, three light-to-dark blues, sand, orange, rusty red, tan, three greens and black. M: 30 × 30cm (11¾ × 11¾in). P: (contract) £2.86–£5.11 sq m.

GERLAND LTD

Tiles designed primarily for contract use, some also suitable for domestic application. ARCHITECTON are solid flexible vinyl, available in 15 clear marbled colours — redcurrant, chestnut, imperial blue, old gold, black, white, ash grey, light grey, juniper (dark grey), sage green, stone grey, sand, chocolate, copra and Cotswold beige. They are free of asbestos, can be installed over underfloor heating, resist indentation and are more malleable, so less likely to chip, than most similar ranges. M: 30 × 30cm (11¾ × 11¾in). P: £4.18–£5 sq m.

CLASSIC tiles for heavy duty come in 16 lightly marbled colours: white, black, peat (dark grey), chamois and Cotswold beige, mid grey, ash grey, pearl grey, bracken (also grey), lime green, Liffey green, Riviera and marine blue, cognac, grapefruit and redcurrant. PARAGON HIGH, in heavy and extra heavy gauges, comes in a range of softly streaked, opalescent colours. P: both 30 × 30cm (11¾ × 11¾in). P: CLASSIC £6.18 sq m; PARAGON HIGH £8.35, £10 sq m.

For specialist use Gerland make ROBUST ANTISTATIC vinyl tiles for computer rooms and other places where static is a problem M: 80 × 80cm (31½ × 31½in). P: (contract) £7.40 sq m.

HABITAT DESIGNS LTD

TRAVERTINE self-adhesive vinyl floor tiles with classic natural stone appearance. M: 30 × 30cm (11¾ × 11¾in); in packs of nine to cover 0.81 sq m (32 sq in). P: £7.20 per pack.

KIBBLEWHITE & BLACKMUR LTD

Stylish choice of self-adhesive vinyl tiles, by Vigers. ITALIAN COLLECTION offers designs selected from traditional brick and ceramic flooring patterns: 'Olde Brick' squared brick pattern in grey or red; plain terracotta 'Quarry' and 'New Quarry' in grey with natural 'grouting'; 'Mountain Quarry' in red or beige with a pattern of smaller, mottled squares; 'Paver Flower' with simple ceramic-style flower motif amidst plain burnt-ochre paving; stone-coloured 'Mexican Brick' with four rectangular 'bricks' surrounding a small decorated square 'tile'; and 'Navarette' with an ornate Italian floor tile pattern. M: 12 × 12in; in packs of nine to cover 1 sq yd. P: £4.99 per pack.

DESIGN COLLECTION of cushioned, self-adhesive tiles allows room for creative flair. Although there are just four geometric patterns, tiles of each type can be laid in a variety of configurations to create totally different overall designs. 'Stripe', 'Point', 'Line' and 'Square' are each available in three pastel colourways: tones of beige and brown, pink tones and blue tones. M: 12 × 12in (30.5 × 30.5cm). P: £5.99 sq yd.

WOOD

ALLIANCE FLOORING CO LTD

Pre-sanded, sealed, felt-backed hardwood mosaic panels for do-it-yourself parquet flooring, in a variety of woods — kempas, afzelia, red meranti, walnut, agba, iroko, mahogany, Burma teak and oak. M: panels 18 × 18in (45.5 × 45.5cm). P: £5.25–£7.75 sq yd.

Kiln-dried, tongued and grooved hardwood strips also available in Tasmanian oak, Canadian oak, mahogany, Canadian maple and iroko. M: w2in (5cm), l random. P: £10.25–£11.25 sq yd.

KIBBLEWHITE & BLACKMUR LTD

Full range of real hardwood floors made by Vigers, including strips, blocks and tile or mosaic designs.

There are four different parquet systems, each with different backing and surface finish relevant to application. PARKIFLEX 'fingers' of iroko, merbau (Malaysian afzelia), teak or light oak are bonded to bitumen felt base with polymer adhesive and then die-squared in the factory. Each panel is made up of four, five or six 'fingers'. TIMBER TILE has the same composition but is available only in Tasmanian oak, a light coloured wood. SUPERPARKET is similar but panels are tongued and grooved for easy positioning and fixing, and pre-sealed with hard-wearing wax finish. Available in light, red or dark oak. Quite different, VISTAWOOD has open-mesh nylon backing that gives each panel a degree of movement. This not only means that the system can be laid on to almost any sub-floor but also gives it greater tolerance to extremes of humidity and dryness. M: PARKIFLEX, TIMBER TILE, VISTAWOOD 48 × 48cm (19 × 19in); SUPERPARKET 30.5 × 30.5cm (12 × 12in). P: PARKIFLEX £18 sq m; TIMBER TILE

FLOORING

Top: SUPERPARKET; below: block flooring. Both by Kibblewhite and Blackmur

£12.50 sq m; SUPERPARKET £15 sq m; VISTA-WOOD £16 sq m.
Also from Vigers are strips and blocks in a wide range of exotic hardwoods including maple, merbau, Tasmanian oak, iroko, teak, and oak. Both strips and blocks have tongued and grooved edges and are pre-sanded ready for

sealing and finishing on site. Vigers recommend that these are laid with VIGERFLEX C undercarriage system, joists with carefully positioned rubber mounts which can vary in depth and add to the tolerance of the finished floor. *M:* strips l100–250 × w7.5cm (40–90 × 3in); blocks l23 × w7cm (9 × 3in). *P:* strips £17–£19.85 sq m; blocks £12.50–£22 sq m; undercarriage, on application.
Vigers also produce a comprehensive range of wood adhesives, resilient edging strips, skirting scotias and doorway pieces to complete parquet installation.

MALLINSON DENNY (BUSHBOARD) LTD
PAR-K-PLY laminated wood-strip flooring, pre-treated with resin for non-slip satin gloss finish. Each strip is made up of either oak or redwood, bonded with phenolic adhesive that makes it impervious to temperature changes to prevent buckling or cracking in unheated intermittently heated, centrally heated, and even underfloor heated rooms. Special scalloped backing makes it easy to slot strips together firmly; these are then secured to sub-floor using panel pins on to wood or recommended adhesive on to concrete or vinyl. Resin finish requires no polishing and seals wood against dirt. Because the system is a natural product there might be some colour variation between strips. *M:* l35¾ or 13¾ × w2¼in (90 or 35.5 × 7cm). *P:* redwood 35¾in strips £10.04 sq yd (13 strips per sq yd), 13¾in strips £10.04 sq yd (35 strips per sq yd); oak 13¾ in strips (only) £12.04 sq yd (35 strips per sq yd).

SHEPPARD DAY DESIGNS LTD
SETTECENTO hand marbled tiles, made from medium density fibreboard. They look like marble but are easy to lay, simple to clean, and not cold to the touch. The one design is the classic 'Palladio': squares with cut corners in white with grey veining and small inset keystones coloured in imitation of blue lapis, yellow Sienna, black Portoro, green marble or pink fossilstone. Each tile is hand-painted and therefore slightly different, highly lacquered to give depth to the colour, tongued and grooved to make laying easier and give stability. *M:* 15¾ × 15¾in (40 × 40cm); in packs of five keystones in any one colour to cover 1 sq yd (91.5 sq cm). *P:* £32 per pack.

WICANDERS (GREAT BRITAIN) LTD
Three beautiful real wood flooring systems which can be laid on to existing sub-floors. WOOD-O-CORK is as easy to install and maintain as a tiled floor but with the luxury finish of wood. It is modelled on the highly successful CORK-O-PLAST composite cork tile, also by Wicanders, made up as a four-layer sandwich. A thick cork layer is backed with PVC foil for stability and grip, then covered with decora-

tive real wood veneer in pine, teak, cherry, mahogany or birch, and given PVC surface coating for durability. The result is flexible, comfortable to walk on and has good sound absorbency. *M:* planks 90 × 15cm (35½ × 6in). *P:* £22.50 sq m.
WOOD-O-FLOOR is another composite range made up from selected WOOD-O-CORK planks, bonded on to pre-formed tongued and grooved chipboard panels. Only the joints need glueing and the panels can be laid on to most sub-floors and any existing floorcoverings, providing a simple solution to a number of sub-floor problems. *M:* panels 90 × 30cm (35½ × 11½in). *P:* £38 sq m.
WOODLINE flooring consists of planks of pre-finished oak impregnated with oil and wax and subjected to infra-red heat for a long-lasting sheen that also enhances the natural grain. Five patterns are available. In random sizes are cottage-style 'Village Plank', mellow brown 'Old English' and eighteenth-century style 'Cathedral Plank' (in gunstock brown), all supplied with authentic-looking pegging though each piece is actually invisibly nailed or glued. 'Strip Oak' has a bolder grain and is available in natural or gunstock finish and in planks of one width only. 'Herringbone Oak' is a medium oak parquet pattern. *M:* 'Village Plank', 'Old English', 'Cathedral Plank', w(random) 3, 5, 7in (7.5, 12.5, 18cm); l(random) 12–102in (30.5–260cm); 'Strip Oak' l9–96 × w2¼in (23–244 × 5.5cm); 'Herringbone Oak', strips l12 × w2in (30.5 × 5cm). *P:* 'Village Plank', 'Old English', 'Cathedral Plank' from £34.50 sq m; 'Strip Oak' from £50 sq m; 'Herringbone Oak' £59 sq m.

Wicanders' WOOD-O-CORK

PRICES AND INFORMATION WERE CORRECT AT THE TIME OF GOING TO PRESS

JAYMART RUBBER & PLASTICS LTD

Jaymart SG System studded and textured heavy duty, anti-slip rubber flooring is the 'safe and sound' recommendation for a whole range of public areas from department stores and leisure centres to schools, airports, swimming pool surrounds and many others. Meeting highest specifications, including BS 4790 (1972) burn resistance, and truly proven design standards, the tiles are supported by an array of accessories: nosings, trims, stringers, plus the new M104 nosing/round stud tread/smooth riser section for stairways.

Four variations of round stud design are available: Safe-t-step, Solo, Prolo and Safe-t-lay; plus square studded Safe-t-tread; floral pimpled Floraflor; textured slate Safe-t-tex; and Superfloor extra heavy gauge for ice-rink surrounds etc. Gauges range from 3 to 7.5mm according to type. SG System floortiles are in 36 easy-clean colours. Outdoor, oil-resistant and electrically conductive ranges are also available.

WOODLANDS TRADING ESTATE,
EDEN VALE ROAD,
WESTBURY,
WILTS. BA13 3QS.

Telephone: 0373 864926.

The Art of Kitchen Living

INTRODUCTION

Kitchens today are light years removed from their Victorian counterparts. The traditional larder or pantry has been overtaken by refrigerators and freezers. Floors are often cork, tiled or vinyl instead of stone or wood. The cooking range that could take up an entire wall has been fragmented into split ovens and hobs, eye-level grills and a host of gadgets. Nevertheless, it's still possible to opt for either a traditional or modern approach, depending primarily on the material and finish used for cabinet fronts.

Basically, there are four surfaces: solid wood, usually protected with a coat of clear sealer; wood veneer — thin sheets glued on to a cheaper base board — similarly protected and sometimes combined with solid wood frames; mock wood in plastic laminate; and coloured laminates in a matt finish or with the ultimate lacquer-like shine of gloss laminate. Solid wood kitchens are generally the most expensive, matt laminate the cheapest.

Although there is no such thing as a cheap kitchen, there are ways to cut the costs. If you're starting from scratch it's worth remembering that today's kitchen unit is essentially a simple box mounted on a plinth and fitted with shelves, wire storage baskets, racks, etc. One way to economize is to make your own housing and then fit the cabinets with the accessories you need. If you already have the units, and simply want to change the doors, invest in new drawer and door fronts in solid pine or oak, or go in search of discarded doors and/or panels from an architectural salvage supplier (see the listings at the end of the book).

If none of these options appeal, be prepared to part with a fair amount of cash. This can be substantially reduced if you invest in a self assembly kitchen — dealing direct with the manufacturer ensures good value for money and, although it may not be the cheapest kitchen on the market, it will almost certainly cost less that its 'fitted' counterpart. Whether you go for self-assembly or prefer to have your kitchen installed by an expert, first make an accurate floor plan, complete with measurements of all furniture and appliances that will be part of the new room. Alternatively, the manufacturer will arrange for a kitchen planner (his agent) to do the groundwork and installation.

Of course, the essential appliances should be planned in at an early stage. Hob-housing and appliance units are now standard elements in most kitchen ranges, and storage units for food processors, etc, are fairly common accessories. A number of manufacturers make appliances as well as units, or at least have co-ordinated their lines with appliances made by others, so can supply an entire kitchen from refrigerator to sink to spice rack. Lighting is another important design element in this most functional room of the house. Most manufacturers make matching panels to conceal strip lights mounted on top of cupboards, but other lighting is also necessary, both overall and specific over work areas.

Once the details have been finalized, discuss your requirements with a supplier. Usually, after taking accurate measurements, he will provide a plan and written quotation. It pays to shop around — or even ask more than one installer to quote on the same kitchen.

This section concentrates on *Units*, both fitted and self-assembly, and their custom-built alternatives (often nostalgic but incorporating some very contemporary features). Text about each firm describes the company's general approach, and focuses on outstanding ranges or details. The charts that follow the text give details of the finishes, handles and worktops in each range, with a sketch illustrating a typical top drawer/bottom cupboard combination. Study these charts once you have decided on the style, and then look through the company's brochure.

A brief sub-section on *Worktops* describes the major laminate ranges, which can be fitted to kitchens from many different manufacturers, plus a few of the more unusual alternatives on the market. Laminate worktops come in one of three ways: square-edged, 'postformed' or round-edged, or edged with solid wood.

Although most units are supplied in similar modules, proportions and sizes, measurements do differ slightly from company to company; once you have decided on the kitchen you want, it's really up to you or the planner to work out how you can fit the units into a given space.

There are also small sub-sections on *Sinks* and *Taps*. These, too, have come a long way. Though it's still possible to buy the traditional, heavy white ceramic trough, alternatives come in virtually any shape or combination — single, double, one and a half, two and a half — and in every imaginable colour — bright blue, dazzling yellow, beaten copper. Drainers as part of the sink, draining baskets that drop into the sink, fitted chopping boards and other accessories are also available. And the taps to go with them can be plain and functional, gaudily coloured, Edwardian or high tech.

● Prices are based on a combination of the following items: 45cm (17¾in) base unit with drawer; 90cm (35½in) sink base with two doors; half carousel with two baskets; 90cm (35½in) hob base with two doors; oven housing unit (oven h87.6cm/34½in); single 45cm (17¾in) wall unit; double 90cm (35½in) wall unit; single 60cm (23½in) wall unit. (If a specific width was not available, the nearest, larger, width was used.)

PRICES AND INFORMATION WERE CORRECT AT THE TIME OF GOING TO PRESS

UNITS

ABS CONTRACTS LTD
Exceptionally beautiful kitchen unit replacement doors and drawers in English oak, cherry, ash, or maple, for those who would like to transform their kitchen the easy way. Skilled cabinet-makers and joiners will make doors to the exact size specified, providing a very personalized service. For thorough kitchen modernization or alteration, ABS can provide extra carcases, solid wood infill pieces and any kind of hardwood or laminated worktop. They also make matching solid wood cornices, edging for tiled worktops, shelves, wine racks, display units, balustrades, and can provide a whole host of the most up-to-date kitchen accessories such as wire baskets, pull-out ironing boards and extending tables.

Doors and drawers from ABS

ACORN KITCHENS
All-British, all-timber kitchens installed by the company that makes them (they insist on that) and each bearing the bold acorn motif. More than 60 door designs can be ordered in oak, ash, pine, walnut, mahogany or — surely an exclusive — yew. Alternatively Acorn will design a one-off door for an individual customer. *P:* on application.

ALLMILMÖ
Dazzling kitchens whose outstanding good looks are firmly rooted in first-class practical design. CONTURA, with its ribbed surface and soft matt finish, remains a stylish classic. Besides their high quality solid wood and wood-laminate combinations Allmilmö have some innovative and beautiful panel ideas. FÜNEN has real parquet fronts and the OXFORD offers

KITCHENS

natural-looking soft grey wickerwork panels. The latest idea from this West German manufacturer is '3-D Design', intended as a tribute to British art deco. The system achieves its undulating appeal by using fronts that are 30 and 60cm (11¾ and 23½in) wide, with interconnecting pieces that form recesses for working in and at the same time create more space. This amazing '3-D Design' concept is not an alternative but a pleasing addition to existing Allmilmö kitchens and these undulating fronts are available in the OPTIMA (beige or light grey), MILANO (beige or white/grey), GOTLAND (Japan beige, pearl decor or light oak), BERLIN (beige-beech), KOPENHAGEN (natural ash, light oak or wenge-coloured oak), OXFORD (pewter grey, wood and wickerwork) ranges. Undulations in the wall cupboards provide more headroom in all work areas.

The unique Allmilmö door design also conserves space: all cupboard doors open right-back to lie flat against the adjoining ones.

Also exclusive to Allmilmö are some exceptionally beautiful 'roundline' wall cupboards, perfectly arched at the top to alleviate any harsh corners; these are available only for FÜNEN, BORNHOLM, OXFORD and MANILA. Ultra-modern ZEILOSET and CARAT kitchen furniture — bar stools with curved back rests, dining chairs and tables — create perfect kitchens and dining areas and co-ordinate with the units, being made in similar finishes, sometimes with the addition of gleaming metal frames and backs. Stylish to the last detail, Allmilmö also supply a ceramic collection: worktop and wall tiles with matching hobs and sinks and even matching crockery and tableware.

From Allmilmö. Top: OXFORD '3-D Design'; below: BORNHOLM; both with ZEILOSET furniture

Allmilmö's FINELINE

ALNO KITCHENS

Volume-produced German kitchens in 17 basic styles, plus infinite variations that are designed to be supremely functional. A particularly special and unique kitchen is ALNOLIFE, a complete kitchen that comes as a compact unit

Top: ALNOROY; below: 80 HOB. From Alno

that is perfect for small flats, attics, studio flats and office kitchens where space is at a premium. Of the exceptionally wide range of storage ideas, most striking is the immensely spacious corner larder with its own ventilation and interior lighting. Equally impressive is the versatile Alno shelving system that can be adjusted to personal needs and can incorporate lots of attractive solid wood spice boxes and rows of pull-out drawers. All kitchens come with five-year guarantee.

All kitchens can be fitted with Alno built-in appliances — built-under ovens, eye-level ovens, inset hobs, arranged as functional cooking centres, and refrigerators, freezers, dishwashers and sink units.

Worktops come in two thicknesses, 3 or 4cm (1¼ or 1½in) with a wide choice of styles: laminated with square-edged front and with contrasting coloured edging strip, rounded front edge, or rounded 'rustic-style' (moulded) solid wood edge. For wood-lovers a solid beechwood top with protective oiled surface is available.

ARC LINEA (UK) LTD
Bold, modern Italian kitchens made from unique materials in striking combinations. SURF is notable for its white, horizontally corrugated metal doors flanked by birchwood. Alternatively, in ALISSO an all-laminate look is relieved by the presence of birch units. KNOCK DOWN is a Meccano-like freestanding unit, providing an interesting change from the traditional kitchen idea. Accessories and shelves are attached to backing panels and can be used in lots of ways to create a completely new kind of kitchen combining cool glass and metal with the warmth of solid birchwood.

ARTISAN DESIGN
Individually-styled kitchens, an increasingly popular alternative to impersonal rows of kitchen units. Rick Baker of Artisan Design makes beautiful kitchens using traditional cabinet-making techniques. He works closely with the client, enthusiastically providing innovative design ideas for any kind of kitchen ranging from high tech to rustic cottage style. He will use any material — hardwoods including maple, oak, mahogany, cherry and walnut, plus pine and laminates. Worktops too come in any laminate or wood, in any thickness and can be round or square-edged or lipped in

wood to match the kitchen, depending on the customer's specification and budget. High quality special finishes such as stippling, rag-rolling and dragging, and also lacquering, hand-tinting and stencilling — for a totally individual look — can all be applied.

Tables, chairs, dressers and even upholstered sofas can be custom-built to set off a newly designed kitchen or made to order as individual pieces of furniture. Consultations, quotes and initial plans are drawn up free of charge and without any obligation. Since this is a small company with few overheads, superb kitchens can be created at a remarkably low price.

Kitchen furniture by Artisan Design

BAUKNECHT
Eighteen handsome, purposeful kitchens from a German manufacturer, including three intended for self-assembly. Even the more traditional designs like NIZZA and FLANDRIA exude robust practicality. In the modern idiom the all-white BIANCA — even the plinths are white — is strikingly attractive. SCANDINAVIA successfully forsakes pine in favour of oak, injecting warmth into what might otherwise have been a severe geometric design. Shallow drawers have a choice of inserts (for cutlery etc), while deeper ones can be fitted with clever adjustable divisions.

BOFFI
Sleek-looking, comfortable Italian kitchens. HOME PLANNING range comes in beech veneer and COLORE in white laminate with bright yellow, red, blue or grey plastic trimmings and handles. As an addition to the usual wall units, both feature very useful wall panels that support shelves at any height and are equipped with hanging racks or utensils, plate racks and bottle racks to give a more homely feel. Worktops come in white laminate, round or wood-edged, or in solid granite.

ARTHUR BONNET
From France, practical laminated kitchens, contemporary-look laminate and wood combination kitchens, and rustic-look solid oak

KITCHENS

kitchens, offering variety to meet the needs of varying lifestyles. Gallic design ingenuity is present in, for example, the electric towel drier (concealed behind a cupboard door) as well as little touches like the mid-level bread slicer unit and revolving hooks for hanging cups. The nine solid oak kitchens have a traditional appeal, typified by CHAMBORD with its antique style detailing, balustraded shelves and filigree escutcheons.

ROBERT BOSCH LTD
Twenty-three well designed kitchens, stylishly and cleverly integrated with Bosch's massive range of domestic appliances. The custom-built kitchens are designed with an eye to efficiency and include features such as pull-out tables and island units, as well as bottle and jar racks and inset trays for drawers. For those with less space or few pennies, there are some uncluttered, compact designs. FORMULA F range offers a simplified selection of units and, where space is a real problem, a mini-version, the COMPACT kitchen, can literally be built in a cupboard — it can accommodate a refrigerator or cupboard, two hot plates, sink and drainer, shelving, storage racks and drawers. The innovative SIXTY PROGRAMME, so called because it is based on 10 basic units 60cm (23½in) wide, is a smaller, inexpensive and flexible system; it can even be taken with you when you move house, says the brochure — new buyers permitting! Precise measurements are not critical to this system since variations in individual kitchens can be accommodated by using 'shelf elements' which come in 10cm (4in) increments. Other useful features include removable front panels and a drawer in the wider than usual plinth.

Left: COMPACT kitchen; top: CASA; below: DORINA M. All by Bosch

CESA
Over 20 delightful and original French kitchens, backed by a wealth of ideas, like the curved corner unit (more elegant than a square one and safer for children), the pull-out bottle rack and knife rack. The range of traditional wood designs — in pine, oak, ash, cherry, walnut and elm — in French rustic styles and stains is particularly impressive. Each kitchen may be complemented by a choice of tables and chairs, stained to match the panels.

CLARE KITCHENS
Practical, self-assembly laminated kitchen units with a good choice of oak or laminate fronts. Clare's luxury kitchen, CRESTALUX, has traditionally styled Canadian red oak doors with elaborate filigree metal handles and hinges to match — an unusual touch. All carcase interiors are magnolia with brown front edge and plinth and each base unit comes with a choice of four shelf heights.
There are nine laminate worktop designs, all chosen from the Formica and Wareite ranges; they have rounded front edge and are 3cm (1¼in) thick.

CROSBY KITCHENS LTD
Six excellent British self-assembly kitchens. The handsome CANADIAN, for example, is made from imported alder and stained by hand, while the recently-introduced PASTELLE range achieves a pleasing subtlety of tone. Crosby's comprehensive choice of accessories includes pull-out wire storage baskets and a telescopic towel rail. See following page for illustration.

DAVID KITCHENS
Exclusive handmade solid wood kitchens, each individually designed and custom-built to fit into any home. David Kitchens use a good variety of timbers — English oak, mahogany, walnut, pine, cherry and ash — each with several shade options plus various finishes — painted, dragged, sponged, marbled or tex-

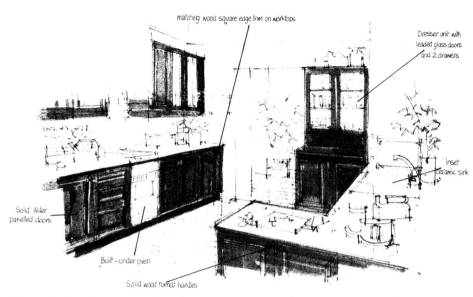

matching wood square edge trim on worktops

Dresser unit with leaded glass doors and 2 drawers

Inset ceramic sink

Solid Alder panelled doors

Built-under oven

Solid wood turned handles

Above: Crosby's CANADIAN; below: units from David Kitchens

tured — that may complement any existing decor or any new project. They can also create kitchens in a combination of solid wood and laminate. *P:* from £3000.

DEDECKER

A selection of interesting-looking, well designed and functional French kitchens. There is a wide choice of styles that range from the laminated softline look to the sleekness of the all-white 7000 or the 2200, in ocean green, glossy laminate framed by solid oak. Alternatively, BRETONNE and PROVENCE ranges are more traditional oak kitchens and PERIGORD is particularly splendid in solid cherry with a soft,

satin lacquered finish. Even the laminated kitchens have solid beech drawer interiors. The choice of worktops to match each kitchen is virtually limitless: granite, marble, Corian (a marble replica) or any laminate from the Resopal, Duropal, Wareite or Formica ranges. Dedecker kitchen specialists in this country are extremely helpful, providing a personalized advice, planning and installation service.

DIFFORD KITCHENS LTD

Self-assembly kitchens marketed through a network of 'factory shops' — a system that eliminates middlemen and expensive packaging so keeps prices down. There are fourteen attractive finishes to choose from and as wide a range of fittings and accessories as you would expect from a larger manufacturer. Standard handles are supplied with solid wood doors, but the holes are not pre-drilled at the factory so that the customer has the additional option of choosing and fitting any handle or knob on the market, according to personal preference.

EASTHAM

Sixteen sturdily-built British kitchens which can (but need not) be used in conjunction with gas and electrical appliances made by the same company. Choice of styles is impressively wide-ranging and backed up by a host of ideas: tall storage units with deep pull-out drawers, built-in laundry basket, matching stowaway chef's trolley, mixer lift (it swings the mixer into position or out of sight as required) and some excellent mid-wall units for smaller items. The quality of all Eastham kitchens is reflected in the five-year guarantee on all units plus a two-year guarantee on all worktops. See following page for illustration.

J T ELLIS & CO LTD

Seven solidly-crafted kitchens. YORK is a particularly versatile design with options of all-oak fronts or oak with contrasting laminate infill panels. All the usual storage accessories are available, plus a most unusual and useful white ceramic chopping board that can be inset into any worktop.

ENGLISH HARDWOOD DESIGN

Solid wood doors and drawer fronts with an attractive traditional design of deeply moulded frame surrounding a fielded panel. They can be supplied in standard sizes or special sizes to order in kiln-dried light, medium or dark oak, light or dark mahogany, ash or pine which is hand-sanded and finished with three coats of lacquer. Door furniture is supplied separately. The firm will make complete

PRICES AND INFORMATION WERE CORRECT AT THE TIME OF GOING TO PRESS

KITCHENS

Two Eastham kitchens. Top: CHELSEA; below: ABBEY

units if required. *M:* standard doors w29.5–59.5 × h45–89cm (11½–23½ × 17¾–35in). *P:* £23.44–£42.76 (ex VAT).

ENGLISH ROSE KITCHENS
Exceptional kitchens made by traditional craftsmen using modern manufacturing techniques plus good quality timber and materials. The solid oak ranges, WARWICK, WINCHESTER and CHELTENHAM, feature lovely country-style wall units, midway units, dresser units and shelves that create perfect displays

PRICES AND INFORMATION WERE CORRECT AT THE TIME OF GOING TO PRESS

plus storage space. All kitchen cabinets are faced in beige or white melamine, and there's the useful option of a child-proof safety-catch. Worktops are available with a choice of square, rolled or solid oak edges and kitchens come complete with all the most up-to-date

Units by English Hardwood Design

space-saving devices — pull-out tables, foldaway ironing boards, pop-out waste bins and double-hinged doors in corner units. All kitchens are beautifully tailor-made and the firm makes a point of designing according to individual needs and accommodating most makes of electric and gas hobs. The extremely careful quality control and high standards of craftsmanship are reflected in the five-year guarantee that comes with each kitchen.

FRAMFORD KITCHENS LTD
Four quite sophisticated, fully fitted modern kitchens in the medium price range. GEMINI, CONCORDE and APOLLO METRIC are laminated and TEAKFORM comes with an unusual wood laminate trim — teak veneer is combined with melamine to give extra durability plus the warm appeal of natural wood. An enormous advantage for versatility and design is that base units, wall units and tall wall units are available in any width from 21cm (8¼in) to 59cm (23¼in) in 1cm (½in) increments. Up-to-date accessories, pull-out larders, storage units, tables and ironing boards come with all ranges except APOLLO.
All worktops are custom-built. There is a choice of square-edged, which come in two thicknesses, 2cm (1in) or 4cm (1½in), teak-edged, both in a wide variety of laminates, and round-edged in selected finishes.

GIEFFE
Thirteen beautifully designed and hard-wearing kitchens, including the award-winning SILVER MOON: a stunning kitchen that looks best arranged in a full moon or half

moon shape. It comes with veneered oak fronts, lacquered and tinged in grey, retaining the grain of the wood and set off by a grey/white granite worktop and co-ordinating white bamboo trimmings.

Their other kitchens are equally striking. There's ARIANNA with fronts made of vertical strips of solid maple interspersed with fine mahogany lines, GABRIELLA in solid stained and lacquered walnut, plus pine, oak, birch and laminate kitchens with brightly lacquered wooden trimmings. All ranges come with a choice of round-edged or wood-edged laminates or granite in several colour variations. Interesting matching dining areas, benches, dressers and breakfast bars are available.

GOLDREIF KITCHENS UK LTD

Twenty well-made, elegant and extremely functional mass-produced German kitchens. They are available in laminate, plain or with wood edgings or veneer, in solid wood — ash, mahogany, pine and oak — in contemporary, traditional or rustic styles. Goldreif divides its kitchens into 10 price brackets rising from simple laminated styles to intricately moulded, higher grade solid wood units that suit all kinds of tastes and budgets; quality of design and manufacture are consistent throughout.

GOWER FURNITURE LTD

Five self-assembly kitchens: four simple laminate designs and more sophisticated REMBRANDT, in solid oak. All units have backs. REMBRANDT has an attractive period feel pro-

duced by the combination of leaded glass doors, balustrades on shelves and shelf units, oak-edged breakfast worktops and matching cornice. Varying combinations of base cabinets with either full doors or drawers are available in all ranges but maximum versatility in depth, width and height only comes in the higher price brackets. Similarly, the more expensive GOURMET, CASCADE and REMBRANDT worktops come in two depths, 50cm (19¾in) and 60cm (23½in), and some REMBRANDT worktops can be tailor-made.

JOHNNY GREY DESIGN

A totally different approach to kitchens for those who want an alternative to long counters and units — and are prepared to pay for it. Beautifully designed cabinets and freestanding pieces of furniture can be put together in a variety of ways to make a unique and practical kitchen that definitely has a personal touch. The furniture is made from solid ash with handle options of knobs set in a distinctive moulded circular 'dish' or of brightly coloured metalwork handles and trims. The designs loosely interpret traditional ones, and look good in both old and new houses.

Base and sink cabinets (with old-fashioned rectangular china sink) come in modules that have various door and drawer combinations. Rather than wall units there is a wall storage dresser and even the oven can be housed in an interesting curved corner unit. Additional pieces and accessories make the kitchen really stunning: a pastry dresser with ash or granite worktop, chopping block that has shelves for storage and for food mixers, and a wide range

Pastry dresser from Johnny Grey Design

PRICES AND INFORMATION WERE CORRECT AT THE TIME OF GOING TO PRESS

Gower's REMBRANDT

KITCHENS

Kitchen by Johnny Grey Design

alternative that is also economical. There are counterparts to these in the self-assembly range, plus low-budget contract kitchens for builders and hotels. Worktops may be laminated, sealed wood or tiled and come with a choice of rounded, square or matching wood edges. The kitchens come complete with co-ordinating doors for concealing appliances and space-saving storage solutions.

HABITAT DESIGNS LTD
Four simple, attractive, predominantly laminate and really practical kitchens. ARDENNES has a fresh appeal with pine drawer fronts and doors with mitred corners that surround white melamine panels; or, for a more traditional

Habitat's PRIMARY

Grovewood's ROMSEY

of smaller items such as saucepan racks, rolling-pin holders, waste bins, shelves and spice racks. To complement the kitchen furniture, matching tables, chairs and banquettes are available. Johnny Grey offer a design service, either a simple layout scheme or a full design proposal. The distinctive style and high quality craftsmanship is reflected in the price! *M:* module cupboard w60 × h103 × d60cm (23½ × 38¼ × 23½in); sink cabinet w200 × h103 × d62cm (78¾ × 40½ × 24½in); pastry dresser w120 × h87 × d70cm (47¼ × 34¾ × 27½); cupboard above dresser w108 × h88 × d29cm (42½ × 34¾ × 11½in). *P:* module cupboard £238, with four drawers £496; sink cabinet £1624 (sink from £130); pastry dresser £789, ash worktop £96, granite worktop £465; cupboard above dresser £657; rolling pin holder and shelf £120.

GROVEWOOD PRODUCTS LTD
Well-designed, good quality laminated or solid wood kitchens. The six in the tailor-made range include elegant DAINTYMAID, classical CAMEO and the more traditional solid wood designs, ROMSEY in mahogany and SALISBURY in oak; ELGIN provides a fashionable

country atmosphere, PROVENCE comes with solid knotted pine door and drawer fronts. PRIMARY and GRIS are versatile, basic and very economical kitchens with a choice of interchangeable finger grips.

All Habitat kitchens come in 11 units with white melamine interiors and white melamine worktops, and are designed for home assembly. Habitat do a huge range of accessories — from washing-up bowls to aprons that cheer up any kitchen. The latest colour scheme is a subtle grey to match the GRIS range.

HAMLET FURNITURE LTD

Standard, simple pine kitchen units in fielded panel or cottage door style, with either brass or wooden door knobs. Worktops are either solid wood — iroko teak or Brazilian mahogany — or laminated in olive green, chocolate brown or marble effect.

For those who would like merely to transform existing units, Hamlet have come up with the answer: they make solid timber door and drawer fronts that are pre-drilled with holes for hinges, ready to fit to the existing carcase. All the ironmongery — self closing hinges, brass or wooden door knobs or fancy brass handles — is supplied. Doors are 2cm (¾in) thick and come in oak or pine with natural or medium red stain and can be made up to any size specified.

Hamlet also make traditional Welsh dressers, oval and rectangular dining tables and chairs, in solid pine to complement their kitchen.

M & I J HARRISON LTD

Made-to-order kitchens in pine, mahogany or oak with a choice of 12 different finishes — natural, medium or antiqued pine; red, brown or golden mahogany; medium, dark or white oak; and white American oak, magnolia oak or magnolia American oak. They are based on a single attractive panel design, have brass handles and are competitively priced. An impressive array of wire-framed storage accessories is available.

Similarly well made are ALBERT dresser and table, in natural, medium or antiqued pine. Available in standard sizes or made to specifications. *M*: table d30 × w84, 60 or 72 × h30in (76 × 122, 152.5 or 183 × 76cm); dresser w55½ × d19 × h71in (139.5 × 48.5 × 180.5cm). *P*: table from £144; dresser £410.

IDEAL TIMBER PRODUCTS

PASSPORT range of practical kitchens either in solid wood, laminated with solid wood trims or simply laminated with metal strip handles. All worktops are laminated with rounded front edges in a choice of seven designs. EUROLINE 500 and EUROLINE 600 come in 50cm (19¾in) and 60cm (23½in) modules with a choice of

Pine kitchen from M & I J Harrison

two square-edged or six round-edged worktops and three door finishes; they are moderately priced basic kitchen units.

KINGSWOOD KITCHEN SYSTEMS

A choice of seven kitchens in solid wood (oak or mahogany), a combination of solid wood frame and veneered panels, or predominantly laminated. The units come in flat packs, with fittings, the doors being pre-drilled and drawers pre-grooved. The carcase is lined in beige melamine and exposed edges are finished in complementary brown; all units are a standard 60cm (23½in) in depth but this can be converted to 50cm (19¾in) if necessary and they are backed with a useful lift-out panel for easy access to pipes and cables once they have been installed. Leaded lights, balustrade units and display shelves from the solid wood ranges can be added to the laminated ranges to create a more luxurious effect.

There is an enormous choice of worktops with over one hundred designs and colours, tiles, and a complete choice of profiles — rolled-edged, square-edged, bull-nosed or hardwood tipped.

The company specializes in providing a 'complete kitchen package' for customers and so also offers gas and electric hobs in five colours or stainless steel with co-ordinating sinks, taps and tiles to complement their kitchens.

LADYLOVE

Seven competitively priced and well-made fitted kitchens in wood or laminate with solid wood or simulated wood handles and trims. Beautiful solid chestnut doors give COTSWOLD a warm and cosy look. Solid wooden doors and drawers with dovetail joints are also a feature of VINTAGE, and WESTMINSTER, though laminated, also has dovetailed wooden drawers. An advantage for kitchen design is that worktops and units come in two depths, 50 and 60cm (19¾ and 23½), except in COTSWOLD and DIANA. All ranges have pull-out ironing boards and COTSWOLD also has pull-out larder and storage rack. DIANA offers an economical alternative to the traditional kitchen, with a standard white finish and a choice of accessory colours.

LEICHT FURNITURE LTD

A huge choice of stunning, high-quality German kitchens — 29 ranges with 81 different fronts and handles. Work surfaces are designed for comfort at various levels, for example a lowered cooking area surrounded by heat resistant tiles or a raised, hardwood preparation centre. A new idea is their 'worktop' kitchen with knife depots and lots of open shelves and removable racks that, without looking cluttered, create a modern alternative to rows of closed fitted cupboards.

ARAGON/ACHAT exemplifies their innovative

KITCHENS

Leicht's BRISTOL

Manhattan's SEVEN-SIX

designs; ARAGON comes in white melamine and ACHAT in dark stained solid wood and the two contrasting tones can be combined in one kitchen for a really avant-garde effect. All ranges come with a choice of 18 designs of laminated, tiled or granite worktops; most include option of cabinets with frameless, framed, or framed and leaded glass door. Imaginative storage solutions include drawers concealed in cabinet bases, spice drawers, open wine cubicles, small shelf divisions and tall, thin pull-out cupboards.

MFI 'HYGENA' KITCHENS
Well-designed and colour co-ordinated kitchen ranges. Worktops are round-edged at the front and some match door panels. Units are a standard depth of 60cm (23½in) and wall units come in both 60cm (23½in) and 30cm (11¾in) depths with adjustable shelves; all carcase interiors have simulated light ash finish. Plinths are removable for easy access to plumbing and wiring. All the kitchens are self-assembled and come at a remarkably low price.

MANHATTAN FURNITURE
Well-made and practical kitchens with units that retain the appeal of furniture. The different surfaces used are matt-finish laminates, veneered oak panels or solid oak. The innovative SEVEN-SIX, with mitred, solid oak frame and contrasting oak beading, has reversible laminate panels: there's a different, but complementary pattern or colour on each side.

Worktops come with square or rounded edges, edged in solid oak, ash, afrormosia (Japanese oak), beech or teak, or with solid timber edge to accommodate a tiled surface. Kitchens come in flat self-assembly packs or can be delivered fully assembled. An extremely useful free planning service is available.

Manhattan's THREE-FIVE

JOHN MEAD COUNTRY KITCHENS

Individual solid wood kitchens specially designed for period and country houses with awkward beams and angles; plus three beautiful tailor-made kitchens: SHROPSHIRE, in oak; WILTSHIRE, in ash or pine, and VICTORIAN, in 'antiqued' pine, ash or oak.

The key to this unusual small company's success in custom kitchens has been to provide good value plus beauty by employing a network of creative designers scattered across the country, each of whom have a John Mead kitchen on display in their own home — eliminating the expense of showrooms and giving a genuinely personalized service. Kitchens are individually made in English hardwoods or Scots pine using high-class joinery techniques: wood colour and grain are carefully matched, frames have mortise and tenon joints, drawers are dovetailed, and doors are inset rather than laid on to a separate carcase, and hung on solid brass hinges. Shelves, cabinet floors and any other divisions are faced in melamine. Cabinet size can vary according to individual needs and height; cooker hoods and appliance door panels are individually made and fitted. Beautiful 'work islands' (with a preparation sink, marble inset chopping block, knife block, drawers, cupboards and seating area), lovely oak dressers, matching tables and benches plus unusual items like charcoal grills and decorative screens create the perfect practical kitchen.

MEISTER KITCHEN SUITES

A collection of seven good-looking made-to-measure kitchens. The laminated styles are distinctive and streamlined with either elegant oak handles and trims, or, to create totally different individual effects, a choice of five colours of handles and trims can be combined with varying door colours. DRAW FORM has a special additional choice of carcase case colours plus an enhanced drawer line created by slim oak trims. An alternative to the traditional styles in solid oak, mahogany or pine is CAMEO, a super white kitchen with beige, blue or brown trimmings that combines modern materials with classical design.

MIELE CO LTD

Huge range of attractive kitchens, each in a wide choice of colours and features. The kitchens range from the traditional look of PROGRAMME 26 in mahogany, oak or ash, to the cool elegance of PROGRAMME 56, where the white lacquered units with Provençal-style panels on the doors are finished to superb effect with a fine line in red or blue, picking out the edges of the doors and panels. Superbly integrated with kitchens are all the re-

PRICES AND INFORMATION WERE CORRECT AT THE TIME OF GOING TO PRESS

John Mead's WILTSHIRE

quisite appliances including the latest cookers and hobs, refrigerators, dishwashers, washing machines and dryers and even a rotary ironer. All appliances are made by Miele and incorporate the very latest technology.

MOBEN KITCHENS

Nine modern and attractive kitchens in a wide selection of colours and styles. Of the four wood kitchens, LOMBARDY is perhaps the most striking in solid white oak, giving the warmth of a traditional solid wood kitchen with an elegance to suit today's modern home. Among the laminate kitchens, the superb DRESDEN has panels painted in ivory enamel and details picked out in blue, green or brown. Sleek and stylish VIENNA has solid beech trim and comes in a choice of 22 colourways. Built-in appliances by Philips, New World, Cannon, NEFF, AEG and White-Westinghouse include refrigerators, freezers, cookers, electric and gas hobs, electric double ovens, dish washers and washing machines, as well as sinks and tap fittings that co-ordinate beautifully.

Moben's CARNIVAL

MOORES INTERNATIONAL

Cleanly-designed self-assembly kitchens of discreet appearance, with imaginative provision for storage and equipment. SAVANNA and CAMEO effectively match beige laminate doors with gently fluted trim; NATURAL OAK has a warm, traditional look with antiqued metal handles complementing the raised oak veneer door panels while the solid oak RENAISSANCE is backed up by a range of options which includes leaded glass doors, a matching cornice and a light pelmet. For each kitchen there is a choice of 11 characteristically tasteful worktops. See following page for illustration.

OPTIFIT

Six attractive self-assembly options with a standard of finish and detail more often associated with professional installation. Particularly fresh and bright is 100, in white with red trim

KITCHENS

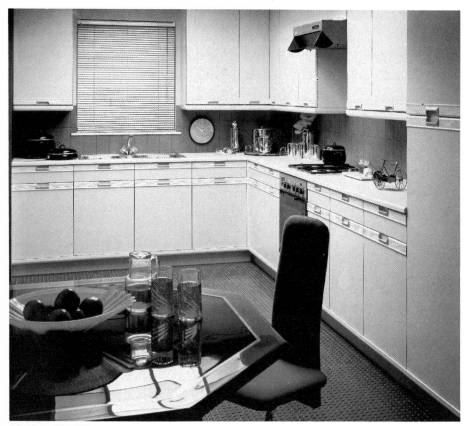

Moore's CAMEO

fitted but Pine Unlimited more usually supply Neff ovens and accessories. An additional plus is that a detailed and well designed floor plan is drawn up before the kitchen is made up, according to customer's specifications. *P:* on application.

PINEWOOD
Exclusive kitchens individually created by a small group of designers and carpenters; they work closely with customers and, being a small group, can be receptive to new ideas. They make traditional-style units in solid wood with finishes that range from a natural pine stain to coloured stains or dragged paint. They undertake any tiling, plumbing, or electrical work and supply and fit any kind of appliance. They offer a range of freestanding pieces of furniture like Welsh dressers, desks and wall units that can be built according to customer's specifications. Also, they give a free drawing and quotation. *P:* on application. See following page for illustration.

POGGENPOHL UK LTD
All kinds of seemingly perfect kitchens. In laminate, wood and laminate-wood mix, in rustic, ultra-modern, traditional and elegant styles, the kitchens have two things in common: all are functional and beautiful.
Wall units come with two shelves; plinths are

(plinths unusually matching the trim), although other colours may be chosen to complement the white panels. Wire baskets which swivel or slide out of sight are a decided asset.

PINE UNLIMITED COUNTRY KITCHENS
Beautiful solid pine kitchens with a real nineteenth-century farmhouse feel. The company prides itself on only using natural materials — those available prior to the advent of chipboard, melamine and plastic — and traditional manufacturing methods; all carcases are handmade using dovetailed joints. Rather than using plastic-coated wire racks and carousels, storage space is provided by functionally designed traditional larders, generous nests of drawers, a mobile work centre that pulls out from below the worktop and pull-out chopping blocks. Reproduction nineteenth-century pie cupboards with a slatted wood grill complete the authenticity of the kitchen.
Worktops are made from solid pine, green Westmorland slate or Welsh heather quarry tiles, hand-cut, with a moulded pine edge. Accessories include Sicilian marble insets for pastry making, solid brass sinks and taps and matching kitchen tables. Aga cookers can be

Kitchen by Pine Unlimited

Dresser by Pinewood

wall units — 'midway elements', housing essential items like cleaning materials, spices, perishable food and bread, can be fitted into most ranges. A similar, more decorative space-saving option housing essential items at eye level is the panel system — a series of appealing small shelves, neat spice boxes, kitchen roll holders, knife racks and towel racks made from solid ash that blends well with most Poggenpohl fronts.

Other good storage solutions are base units with tray partitions, pull-out shelves for blenders and slicers, extending tables and tall cupboard units, ideal for housing food supplies,

From Poggenpohl. Below: CR; bottom: MS

recessed for extra footspace and are detachable or can be fitted with drawers for extra storage space. A marvellous feature is that any work surface can easily be adjusted to any height between 74 and 90cm (29 and 35½in). The DIMENSION 75 programme is a novel way of using the space between work surface and

laundry and utensils. Matching chairs are available in all ranges and wardrobe units in all finishes; MA and MC also have matching oak table, corner bench and wall panelling.

Worktops are wood-edged, rounded or squared and come with or without splashbacks; they can be tiled or laminated in 13 designs including a mini-parquet in light or dark stained oak, mock marble, mock granite and stainless steel. Poggenpohl do a comprehensive range of sinks and appliances with co-ordinated front finishes.

PRIOR UNIT DESIGN

Individually designed kitchens made by a small group of skilled cabinet makers in a Devonshire workshop. They specialize in making made-to-measure furniture and fittings in pine, oak, ash, beech or any wood chosen by the customer. Typical Prior kitchens feature raised and fielded door panels (although plain doors can be made to order) and doors are made of solid kiln-dried timber sealed with a clear satin finish. All interiors are white melamine and units are fitted with brass knob door and drawer handles, unless otherwise specified. Worktops are solid wood, laminated (any design from the Formica, Wareite or Arborite ranges) or supplied ready for tiling. As each kitchen is made to order, any kind of kitchen appliance can be accommodated. Handmade, individually fitted copper cooker hoods can be supplied. Wire baskets, carousels and other accessories come with the units. Prior offer a kitchen planning and design service, the small charge being refunded if an order is subsequently placed; there is no charge for quotes based on a drawing of a specific item or complete kitchen. *P:* on application.

PRIOR also stock standard size units in Baltic pine and can make them up in other woods to order. *P:* (45cm/17¾in base unit, two-door sink base, half carousel, hob base, oven housing unit, single, double and tall wall units) pine £930, ash 20% extra, other timber prices on application.

Q A KITCHENS (IRONBRIDGE) LTD

Simple, modern self-assembly laminated units. All screw holes are pre-drilled and screws are concealed by a plastic cap. All units have back panels and all door backs match door fronts in colour and texture. Drawers are included as part of base units and handles are either moulded plastic or aluminium. Worktops have rounded edges and come in 12 standard lengths, although a non-standard length of up to 300cm (106in) can be cut. QA offer an extremely useful and unique three-year guarantee on all kitchens.

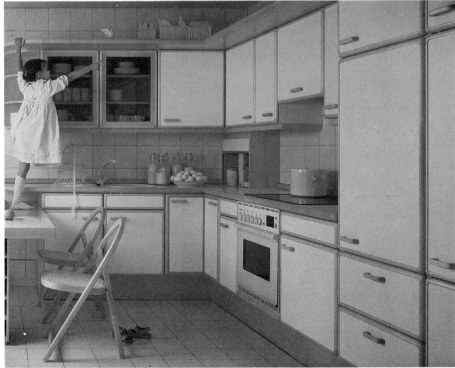

PRICES AND INFORMATION WERE CORRECT AT THE TIME OF GOING TO PRESS

KITCHENS

RAPINI

Ten elegant and practical Italian kitchens. ESPERIA in solid oak can be combined with units of ARETUSIA, a laminate kitchen with oak handles and trims, to give a greater mix of oak and laminate and a more individual effect. SILA is a beautiful kitchen at a reasonable price. It comes in a rich, warm chestnut with a natural stain and the handles are carved out of its solid wood frame.

All base units are 60cm (23½in) deep and wall units come in four heights, up to 106cm (41¾in). Rapini offer attractive accessories — open gallery units for straight runs or corners, chequered smoked glass doors (a special feature of the FEMINA range) and practical midway storage units with spice drawers.

SCHIFFINI MOBILI CUCINE

Classical Italian kitchens designed with typical Italian flare and emphasis on aesthetic appeal. Schiffini have certainly succeeded in giving all their ranges a sleek, cool and timeless feel. They also use a variety of stunning materials. DAMA in silk-screened glass framed in wood, ARNIA in 'Pantotex', a laminate with a polyester mirror-like gloss finish, combined with the warmth of birchwood shelves and carcase sides, and TIMO in white ash are just three options. All ranges have masses of storage space. There are good combinations of large and small drawers, tall units and wall cupboards fit together for wall-to-wall fitted storage and, for a more homely kitchen, laminate doors and drawers can be combined with birch, ash or oak shelving units. As wine is an important item in most Italian kitchens, a birchwood wine rack is an attractive feature of the COMBI-TEX kitchen.

TIMO and COMBI-MAX kitchens come with vibrant laminated worktops — bright green, yellow or red, with matching door and drawer handles. The more traditional kitchens are set off by mosaic tiled worktops, splendid pink or white African granite or white Carrara marble.

SCHREIBER FURNITURE

Robust kitchens from an established volume producer, with the emphasis on solid construction (all units have backs) and detail. The luxurious CHESTER, for example, boasts doors and drawer fronts made of real oak set off by handsome glass-fronted cupboard units. By contrast, the WHITE KITCHEN presents a more urban and contemporary look but still retains sculptured oak handles on doors and drawer fronts. All built-in appliances are by Hotpoint and come with a five-year guarantee on all parts, plus an efficient after-sales service. There is an impressive choice of twelve worktops and seven sink arrangements, including taps of differing design, as well as imaginative pull-outs for storage and food preparation.

Siematic's 1001 BE

SIEMATIC

High quality and very stylish kitchens in pine, oak and laminate and wood combinations plus the 9009 PR, an unusual laminated kitchen finished in an amazingly glossy polyester. The mirror-like coating creates an illusion of greater space while rounded pilasters and concave and convex curved corner units create flowing lines, the unit edges and sometimes the pilasters in a contrasting, slightly darker shade. The whole can be grandly set off by sparkling polished granite worktop and splashbacks.

Siematic's 4004 KL

The pine and oak ranges are more traditional with lovely Welsh-dresser-like storage units, shelves, rows of small wooden spice boxes, glass display units and moulded cornices. 1001 OP in pine is beautifully finished, taking advantage of the strength of the grain, and protected with a synthetic resin. The result is both natural and resilient.

The laminate and wood kitchens combine the warmth and beauty of solid wood trimmings, handles, shelves, carcase edges and pilasters, spice boxes and wine racks, with the practical advantages of laminated door and drawer fronts. The carcase doors of these kitchens — 4004 KS, 4004 KR, 4004 KL — are particularly solid, ¾in (2cm) thick.

SMALLBONE OF DEVIZES

Individually fitted kitchens in OLD PINE, ENGLISH OAK and HAND PAINTED ranges. All kitchen furniture is made by skilled carpenters from solid wood; drawers are dovetailed, doors are panelled and hinged on to solid wood frames with brass butt hinges. These handmade exteriors are combined with ultra-modern fittings and accessories. Wooden knobs are standard handles in the OLD PINE and ENGLISH OAK ranges and the HAND PAINTED range comes with porcelain handles. OLD PINE is a Victorian-style kitchen made from renovated second-hand timbers that have been cleaned, sanded and re-sealed;

solid, seasoned, stripped pine. Pine dressers, open shelves, glass-fronted display units and brass cup hooks between the work surface and wall units give the kitchen a Victorian feel although it is modern, convenient and compatible with sophisticated appliances.

The other five kitchens in the collection are self-assembled and reasonably priced. OLD ENGLISH has panelled pine exterior, parchment-coloured interior and brown-lipped front edges. Traditional dresser-style open shelf wall units and glass-fronted displays blend with the period-style wall panelling that can be fitted with a midway shelf between worktop and wall units. All the up-to-date storage accessories are available and, for design flexibility, all the units come in 30, 40, 50, 60 and 100cm (11¾, 15¾, 19¾, 23½, 39¼in) widths.

Worktops are laminated and can be edged in solid oak, pine or mahogany with or without a splashback. There are traditional stainless steel sinks with double drainers and round inset sinks in enamelled steel, both types with matching crockery basket and hardwood chopping board. As a final touch, under-cupboard lighting, concealed by moulded pelmets, cornices and intricately moulded panels, creates a warm and homely atmosphere in kitchens that are suitable for both modern and period houses.

Left: HAND PAINTED RANGE; below: ENGLISH OAK. Both by Smallbone

they are made into standard wall and base units plus Smallbone 'specials' like dog-kennel dressers, decorative plate racks, hand-carved wall friezes, rounded end shelves, cornices and spice drawers.

Their HAND PAINTED range is an eye-catcher. It is delivered with only an undercoat on to be hand-painted on site using Victorian techniques like dragging, rag-rolling and spongeing for different stunning effects. The kichens are painted in light airy colours — blues, ivory, apricot — and then varnished. For total individuality, stencils or *trompe l'oeil* decoration can be added.

The ENGLISH OAK range can be stained to blend with a customer's existing oak furniture or occasional pieces can be made up to blend with the new kitchen. The kitchens come with traditional carved panelling and all the latest ideas in accessories and interior fittings — from beautiful ceiling planters to hob controls that are concealed behind a drawer front. Smallbone offer a comprehensive design and installation service. *P: on application.*

SOLENT FURNITURE SYSTEMS ⚠

Solid pine kitchens with lots of character. COUNTRY DIARY kitchen is custom-built in

KITCHENS

STATELY HOME KITCHENS LTD
Solid oak frame kitchen with plenty of individual charm and character, made by craftsmen within a small company that provides a personalized service and installs each kitchen direct from the manufacturer.

All doors and drawer fronts are American red oak with natural, medium or dark stain and satin finish. Carcases are lined with mushroom-coloured melamine and plinths are recessed and laminated with a dark brown finish. Base units come in five different widths, wall units in three, tall units in two. Attractive solid oak cornice can be fitted above wall units, oak trims to conceal lighting on the underside of wall units, handmade leaded light windows are available and any other specialized items can be made to order. Worktops can be laminated or tiled, and are edged with a solid oak trim and come in two depths, 60 and 90cm (23½ and 35½in). *P:* (45cm/17¾in base unit, two-door sink base, half carousel, hob base, oven housing unit, single, double and tall wall unit) £1194.

STONEHAM DESIGNED KITCHENS
Solid oak, laminate and mixed oak-laminate kitchens, custom-built by a well established family firm that provides both good quality and good service.

The traditional solid oak dresser-like shelf units, end shelving with scalloped edges and cornices of the luxury, all oak PROVENCE range can be incorporated into the oak-laminate ranges (CAMARGUE, NATURA, STRATA and FLAIR) to give additional warmth and character, complementing the laminated units' oak handles and trims. The more economical kitchens such as FLAIR, the highly functional KINEA, and OPTICOLOR, still retain all the technical refinements and planning possibilities of the more expensive ranges.

Internal surfaces of all kitchen units are lined with beige melamine and edges are colour-matched with the door panel design. Units come in three widths: 30, 50 and 60cm (11¾, 19¾, 23½in). Worktops are 4cm (1½in) thick, and come with round, square edge or solid oak edge in designs chosen to co-ordinate perfectly with the door fronts of the 10 ranges. All the up-to-date accessories are available with each range — pull-out tables, ironing boards and larders plus fitted bottle racks and sliding shelves that glide forward out of base units so that items can be reached more easily.

TIBA
Most unusual incredibly hard-wearing stove-enamelled kitchen units, made in Germany specifically to complement Tiba's electric stoves, wood-burning stoves, central heating stoves and sink units. Doors are stove-enamelled in a choice of five colours — shaded beige, shaded orange, red, white or havana

(dark brown) and the interiors are also stove-enamelled in beige. Handles are equally hard-wearing plastic finger pulls, in light grey to match the white enamel or dark brown to match the coloured enamel doors. The units can incorporate various combinations of drawers and deeper shelves designed to store pots and pans, and are available in four widths: 55, 45, 27.5 and 15cm (21¾, 17¾, 10½ and 6in). Accessories include wood storage drawer — removable crate container on internal trolley base — plus bottle and towel units. *P:* base unit, white £134–£278, colours £146–£314.

TIELSA KITCHENS LTD
A whole host of German kitchens with more than 100 variations in front panel designs. Styles range from simple and basic to highly sophisticated, and the kitchens fall into 10 appropriate price brackets. Most are laminated with either solid wood — oak or ash — handles and trimmings or solid wood door and drawer fronts. Interesting wood stains (even turquoise, pale blue and a subtle ivory) are used to highlight the natural graining, and striking designs include TESSIN in lacquered, black-stained wood with panelling picked out

Tielsa's BIANCA

in brass.

Dining areas are cleverly integrated with each kitchen and other features are decorative, made-to-measure recess shelves above worktops, rounded corner and end shelf units, and very useful pegged wall boards. Worktops themselves come extra thick — 4cm (1½in) — in solid wood, laminated with round front edge or solid wood edge, or tiled with solid wood edge. The kitchens incorporate stainless steel and enamelled sinks by Franke (see *Kitchens, sinks*) and appliances by Philips.

UBM BUILDING SUPPLIES LTD
Good-looking, simple self-assembly kitchens: LORRAINE in solid oak or mahogany and VISCOUNT 80, VISCOUNT HARMONY and PARIS in laminate with either simulated wood or aluminium strip handles. UBM offer a choice of seven laminated worktops with either round front edge or wood front edge and either 3cm (1¼in) or 4cm (1½in) thick. They are practical kitchens and excellent value for money.

⚠ *INDICATES ONE OR MORE OF THE PRODUCTS MENTIONED ARE SELECTED BY THE DESIGN CENTRE*

Kitchens you can afford to cook in

Tielsa's AERA

WINCHMORE FURNITURE LTD

Nine styles of self-assembly kitchen, also equipment, accessories, chairs and tables. Several ranges are in natural wood, others include white and coloured elements. LAVENHAM has wooden framed doors with interchangeable central panels of red, white, blue or a small geometric pattern. DALHAM is a continuation of Winchmore's style for bedroom and bathroom storage units. Accessories include a retractable cook-book rest and plinth drawers for extra storage.

TOBY WINTERINGHAM

One-off fitted kitchens designed by Toby Winteringham or built to customer's own design. They are distinguished by their clean lines and the beauty of the wood. *P:* on application. See also *Furniture, made-to-order*.

WINTHER BROWNE & CO LTD

Useful kitchen accessories in solid wood — oak, pine or mahogany — designed to upgrade or finish an existing kitchen. Winther Browne do door trim moulding and matching full-length base unit handles, worktop edges with attractive profiles, light pelmets for concealed fluorescent light fittings, cornice mouldings that fit between the top of wall cabinets and the ceiling to fill a gap and create a visually pleasing finish plus gallery rails for a balustrade effect in wood or brass, fitted to the front of shelves. *P:* oak per foot: cornice £1.12, light pelmet £1.40, handle £1.10, door edge trim 42p, worktop edging 76p, gallery rail £2.

PRICES AND INFORMATION WERE CORRECT AT THE TIME OF GOING TO PRESS

WOODSTOCK WORKSHOPS

Superb, individually designed kitchens handmade in solid maple, cherry or walnut. The company enjoys all kinds of design challenges, with the aim of reflecting the period features of a home. There are no standard unit sizes or designs as each one is tailor-made to fit the available space and according to the customer's taste. Any appliance — including a well-loved old cooker or refrigerator — can be incorporated into the finished kitchen. The results are all unusually appealing, with designs that enhance the warm, honey tones of the beautiful maple worktops that are a Woodstock speciality (see separate entry). Free design and consultancy service offered without obligation. *P:* on application.

Woodstock do make a few standard pieces of furniture to complement the kitchens — a freestanding trolley, a moveable work centre plus kitchen tables, chairs, dressers and stools, all in solid hardwoods. The trolley features beautiful and immensely hard chopping surface, removable vegetable basket, spacious drawer and rack below, all in solid maple. *M:* trolley w27 × d22½ × h33in (w69 × 57 × 83cm). *P:* trolley, end grain top £255, face grain top £225.

WRIGHTON 🔥

Beautifully designed kitchens from a company that could reasonably claim to be the UK's foremost kitchen manufacturer — Wrighton are regular Design Council Award winners. They offer a choice of 14 kitchen designs with over 100 permutations of colour and finishes — from solid wood, painted wood and wood veneers to melamine laminates and high-gloss

Wrighton's PUGIN

polyesters. The brilliant mirror-like polyester finishes to the PAGEANT, HERALD, ENSIGN and VOYSEY DF ranges is softened and enhanced by natural wood trimmings. Each texture complements the other. The solid wood kitchens also offer great scope: there are fielded panels (VOYSEY), diagonally structured (PUGIN), profiled mouldings (ROSSETTI) and gothic panelling with sculptured mouldings (WALPOLE).

All ranges except ENSIGN can have base units fitted with either through doors or a drawer line. (ENSIGN units come with separate banks of drawers.) Carcase edges are colour co-ordinated and come with melamine interiors in white or stone. All units come in several sizes so they can fit any space within 5cm (2in). Worktops come in two thicknesses, standard 4cm (1½in) plus 6½cm (2¼in), with a choice of round or square-edged laminate or laminate with solid wood edge.

XEY

A wide selection of predominantly laminate and laminate-wood mix kitchens, all made in San Sebastian in northern Spain. They are well designed, some specially sleek and some more functional and traditional. For an ultra-modern streamlined effect, BENNY, DERBY, COLUMBIA 5 and JAVA come with bow-fronted doors on end units and corner wall and corner base units: besides being aesthetically pleasing, bow fronts give good storage space in corners and easy access. All 16 of Xey's kitchens come with all the latest labour-saving and functional accessories such as carousels and midway decor shelves. Worktops are laminated with solid wood front edges in a choice of 15 designs that complement the

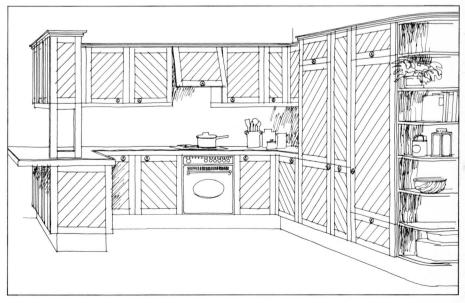

KITCHENS

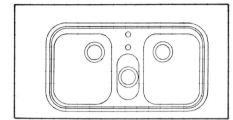

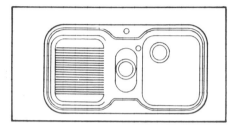

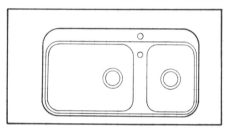

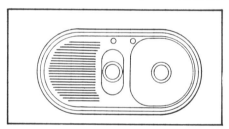

style of each kitchen. The quality of workmanship and materials is reflected in the five-year guarantee.

Xey's COLUMBIA 5

SINKS

ALLIA (UK) LTD
Durable ceramic sinks and drainers. Oval units are 'Loire' with single oval bowl and drainer, and similarly sized 'Moselle' with two oval bowls; rectangular units are 'Brittany' with single bowl and drainer, 'Picardy' with two bowls and the largest, 'Normandy', with two bowls and single drainer. In the round there are 'Alsace' bowls and drainers, sold individually. All come in white as well as two-tones: Carolina cream, Dakota brown and Missouri beige. Fitted wooden chopping boards with plastic-coated draining rack are available with 'Alsace', 'Loire' and 'Moselle'. *P:* £182–£283.

ATAG (UK) LTD
Colourful circular sinks in enamelled stainless steel to match Atag's large hob and oven range or just look good by themselves. Sinks and shallow, circular drainers are available in stainless steel or with tough enamelling in mocca brown, majolica brown, almond beige, white and grey-white (these two set off with attractive steel edging). The bowls are encased in an insulating cover which helps keep the water hot and cuts down noise of crashing cutlery, pots and pans. Accessories include fitted maple chopping board, plastic-coated draining rack and fine mesh, stainless steel sieve. *P:* Sink, stainless steel £67.85, coloured £79.35; drainer, stainless steel £56.35, coloured £67.85.

THE BATH STUDIO
Five ranges from Scandinavian Steel Sinks to cover almost every possibility — single, double and half bowls, central rinsing and waste disposal dips, and drainers, all in rounded and rectangular designs. Of the rectangular units, RESTEBECKEN comes in stainless steel or enamelled, RESTOLINE and SOFTINE COLOR enamelled only, the former also with option of white with coloured rim stripe. RESTOLUX oval units with 'D'-shape bowls and drainers come in stainless steel, coloured enamels or white with coloured rim stripe. Individual circular sinks come in stainless steel or a good range of enamels. Colours include red, green, cream, and various browns, with some two-tones, matching Scandinavian Steel's electric hob tops. Also available with each sink are fitted accessories such as parquet-style wooden chopping board and plastic-coated draining tray and basket. *P:* single bowl and drainer £63–£153; double bowl, single plus half bowl and drainer £73.80–£171; double plus half bowl £135–£187.20; circular sink with circular drainer £57.75–£70 (ex VAT).

BERGLEN PRODUCTS LTD
Circular, semi-circular, square, rectangular, single or double TAPMATE SILKFLEX enamelled steel sinks in a variety of sizes to give infinite scope for kitchen design. Half bowls are available with single and double sinks, and stylish drainers with waste outlet are standard on most models. Huge range of colours — many matching TAPMATE appliances — includes black, white, flannel (grey), emerald, mocca, peewit grey, red, Bermuda blue,

TAPMATE SILKFLEX from Berglen

bamboo, Bahama beige, and two-tone burnt sienna, bitter chocolate and green haze, while 'Contur' units have elegant blue, red or mocca stripe around the entire rim, offsetting the overall white. Plain stainless steel round bowl and drainer are also available. Match them all with Berglen's TAPMATE taps (see separate entry). *P:* round single bowl £53.20–£74, with drainer £87.70–£113.50; rectangular single bowl £47.80–£65, with drainer £113; single plus half bowl with drainer and inset £123.60–£157.70; double bowl £119.60–£145.20; double plus half bowl with inset £135–£162; two-tone and 'Contur' colourings 10% extra.

ROBERT BOSCH LTD
Two attractive enamel sinks and a built-in stainless steel sink unit specially for cooking areas from this well-known kitchen and domestic appliance manufacturer. The enamel sinks, rectangular with single drainer, come in

white or merian brown to complement other Bosch appliances and also in stainless steel. The small DIAMANT stainless steel built-in sink is intended for use alongside the cooker for preparing and draining vegetables, rinsing pulses etc. DIAMANT built-in parking plate, in stainless steel with ridged or linen-textured grip, matches the sink and provides a firm, heat resistant surface for pots and pans. Two elements can be joined with a special jointing strip. *P:* enamel sinks £112.70; DIAMANT sink unit £89.70.

COLSTON

Small collection of enamel sinks to match or co-ordinate with Colston's well-known range of built-in domestic appliances. SYMPHONY rectangular units come in three colours: mink brown — very dark and attractive — snow white and two-tone shaded sand. Units have one deep bowl plus left or right hand drainer/food preparation area with built-in waste outlet. *P:* £94.62.

FRANKE

Extensive collection of brightly coloured and stainless steel Swiss sinks. CLASSIC COLOR is a beautifully designed oval sink and drainer unit in plain stainless steel or enamelled in two-tone safari beige, emerald green or mahogany brown; and circular ROTONDO bowls and drainers come in stainless steel, white, Bahama beige, tabac and marron. Optional extras include fitted iroko wood chopping board, and strainer bowl, draining basket and inserts in coloured plastic. In stainless steel there are rectangular sinks of all sizes: the innovative, practical COMPACT, with option of small central rinsing sink suitable for waste disposal between main sink and drainer; the CONTINENTAL with a wide variety of bowl sizes and arrangements; and the UK with an unusually deep bowl. Single and double units with drainers, monobloc mixers (with sprayhead option), teak chopping boards and draining baskets are available with all these designs, plus Franke Kugler taps (see separate entry). *P:* CLASSIC COLOR (sink and drainer) £162–£183; ROTONDO (sink only) £69–£71; COMPACT (sink, drainer, coloured accessories) £132; CONTINENTAL, UK (sink and drainer) £122.

GAGGENAU

Very impressive range of enamelled steel sinks in good colours and with useful, large, deep bowls, from a German manufacturer of high-quality domestic appliances. There are round, square and rectangular bowls and round and rectangular drainers in a choice of eight colours — white, brown, Algarve, Brazil and terre d'Alsace (shades of brown), cappuccino, Bahama beige and majolica — or with large

3½in (9cm) waste outlets in brown, beige, white and majolica only. Rectangular models available with right or left-hand drainers. *P:* round bowl from £68.19; square bowl from £60.54; rectangular bowl from £64.34; drainer (all shapes) £53.

Gaggenau's units, all rectangular, consist of either a large square bowl and drainer with waste gutter and connection or a large square and smaller half bowl and drainer. Both have a pop-up waste assembly — so at long last one can open the drain without reaching into the sink! Units come in white, brown, terre d'Alsace, cappuccino, Algarve and Brazil. All sinks are available with fitted chopping board and draining basket. *P:* large bowl and drainer £227.70; large bowl, half bowl and drainer £313.95.

LEISURE

Stainless steel, coloured and patterned sinks, a really large range from a British manufacturer. In stainless steel, the practical and adaptable THINKING SINK range includes 13 different combinations of single, double and half bowls, drainers and central rinsing bowls to meet every need and fit any standard base unit. There's even a compact one and a half bowl model for small but busy kitchens. One model comes in an unusual, textured 'Diamond Leather' finish. Accessories are fitted chopping boards in melamine or teak, strainer bowl, scrap tray and plate rack in beige or brown plastic. *P:* single bowl unit £110.70–£139.50; double bowl unit £207.95–£287.10. In richly coloured enamels there are 'Prisma' and 'Prismaluxe' rectangular units with single

Leisure's 'Prisma'

Leisure's 'Prismaflex'

bowl and right- or left-hand drainer: 'Prisma' comes in white, mocca and two-tone sable, terre de France and shadow brown, 'Prismaluxe' in ivory, Sahara (beige) and unusual Wedgwood blue. 'Prismaplus' is similar but with central rinsing bowl; it comes in the same colours as 'Prisma'. 'Prismaflex' offers separate rectangular bowls and drainers that can be laid out in any combination. They come in cherry red, white and mocca, two-tone sable, sand and Brazil, and also in stylish 'Ritz' pattern — white with a border made up of blue or red diagonal stripes. Accessories include teak chopping board and wire draining basket, and ceramic tiles by Maw & Co (see *Ceramic tiles, walls*) to match the 'Ritz' design. *P:* 'Prisma', 'Prismaluxe' £103.15; 'Prismaplus' £142.75; 'Prismaflex' bowl, most colours £81.95, red £85.85, 'Ritz' £125.35; drainer, most colours £59.25, red £62, 'Ritz' £87.

Leisure also do an economical CONTRACT range with a basic, lay-on unit consisting of a single bowl sink and one or two drainers in plain stainless steel. *P:* on application.

PRICES AND INFORMATION WERE CORRECT AT THE TIME OF GOING TO PRESS

KITCHENS

MANHATTAN FURNITURE
Nine stainless steel sinks, including three of the cheaper lay-on units as well as the more popular inset versions. They come in all the usual combinations — single sink and double drainer; double sink and drainer; double sink and half sink etc. There is also a curved (but not quite circular) inset sink in stainless steel or a choice of three enamel colours — emerald, orange and mahogany. *P:* on application.

OPTIFIT
An exciting selection of tough, round enamelled-steel bowls in a range of eye-catching colours — white, burnt sienna or red for example — that complement an Optifit kitchen. Useful accessories include matching mixer taps, wooden chopping board, round plate rack, deep draining basket, detergent dispenser and waste kit. *P:* on application.

PROWODA KITCHEN APPLIANCES
Brightly coloured and even patterned sinks, part of a decorative range of kitchen appliances that covers everything from refrigerators to cooker hoods. Rectangular monobloc sinks, single or double with drainer, and sometimes half-bowl, come in white, six two-tone colours — terre de France (green/brown),

Prowoda's 'Manosque' sink with matching tiles and burner covers

terre de Rio (deep brown), val du Loire (sand), Provençal (terracotta), blue Pompadour, fern green — in white with red or blue coachline along the rim, and in white with two floral patterns — 'Vieux Chine' blue and white china motif, and 'Manosque' with blue and yellow flowers set against green leaves. Circular sinks and drainers, sold individually, are available in all the above plain and two-tone shades plus bright red; modular rectangular sinks and drainers in all these colours except white and val du Loire. Accessories with all sinks are co-ordinating COLORMIXER monobloc mixer tap, wooden chopping board and plastic-coated draining basket. *P:* single monobloc sink £135–£185; double monobloc £198–£281; circular £53.50–£60; modular £66–£72 (ex VAT).

SCHREIBER
A selection of stainless steel, round enamel and inset sinks in various configurations with a range of taps to match. Stainless steel sinks are available with either single or double drainer, with single bowl or double bowl and central half bowl. Enamel inset sinks come in brown and caramel, round with either single or double bowl in an oval unit. All options come with matching wooden chopping board and plastic-coated draining basket. *P:* on application.

TAPS

BARKING-GROHE LTD
A basic but useful range of taps in chrome or with bronze, satin gold or satin chrome metallic finish. The deck (two-hole) range offers a choice of nozzles and handles, including lever-action handles — useful when hands are full or covered with flour, and a must for anyone suffering from a disability such as arthritis. One-hole monobloc mixers also have a variety of co-ordinating nozzles and handles and a hot spray attachment is available for the second hole, to provide hot rinsing water whenever required. *P:* deck £64–£90; one-hole monobloc £63–£70.

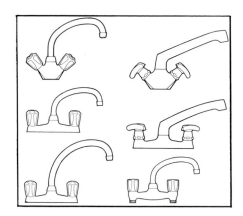

Barking-Grohe's deck and monobloc taps

THE BATH STUDIO
Modern, clean and colourful tap fittings designed by Danish architect Arne Jacobsen, as well as some more traditional fittings from Germany and Australia. Jacobsen's VOLA range offers three-hole and monobloc sink mixers with turning peg and right-angled spout in grey, red, orange, yellow, black, white, green, brown and blue as well as chrome or polished brass. And KLUDI offers a tremendous variety of modern forms and colours: single and dual control monoblocs with levers or handwheels, all chrome, chrome with bobbly coloured acrylic handles, or all-over coloured finish in white, avocado or mocca. *P:* (mixers) VOLA £123–£206; KLUDI £86.
In contrast, Dorf's MANOR HOUSE is a totally traditional three-hole mixer with cross-head handles raised on spindles and swan-neck spout, available in polished brass or chrome, and EL TORO has similar handles mixed with a modern spout, available in white and ivory with contrasting black spindle, royal blue, mission brown, chrome and gold with matching spindle, and beige, clay and grey with chrome spindle. Both ranges also include pillar taps, bib (wall-mounted) taps and a wall-mounted washing machine stop. BOOSTER three-hole sink set comes with chrome or gold-plate

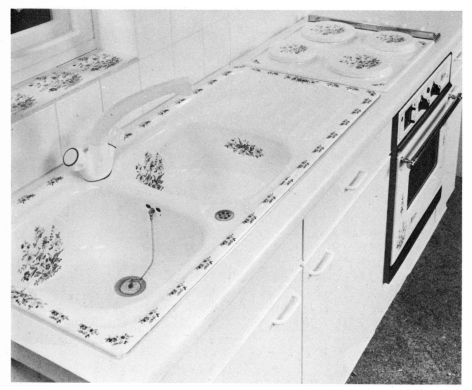

spout and similar handles or with ceramic handles in white, ivory, mission brown, royal blue, river gum green or white with 'Springtime' floral motif. *P:* (mixers) MANOR HOUSE £160; EL TORO £125; BOOSTER £125–£252.

BERGLEN PRODUCTS LTD
Stylish modern taps to match sinks and appliances in Berglen's TAPMATE programme (see *Kitchens, sinks*). 'Neotap' is a sleek, no-nonsense mixer with single lever control. Available chrome-plated or enamelled, in six colours, white, red, green haze, mocca, Bahama beige and burnt sienna, it gives an aerated stream of water and both temperature and flow of water can be pre-set. 'Futura', made by Damixa, has high-flown, angled neck with dual wheel controls in a bar across the base, operated by easy-to-turn grips that give full flow at a single 90° flip. Hand-cream dispenser and hot rinse attachment are available with 'Futura'. *P:* 'Neotap', chrome £95.50, coloured £106.80; 'Futura', chrome £49.98, coloured £57.48.

'Futura' from Berglen

CZECH & SPEAKE LTD
Two nostalgic sink mixers from the EDWARDIAN range in polished brass, chrome, or nickel with more unusual finishes like bronze, copper, gold and black chrome available to order. One is a pillar-mounted deck (two-hole) mixer with dual-flow swivel spout and quarter-turn white porcelain levers and the other a monobloc (one-hole) mixer with traditional brass and porcelain taps, also with swivel spout. *P:* deck £180; monobloc £105.

FRANKE KUGLER
Sleek chrome and coloured taps from Switzerland to complement Franke's own sinks (see separate entry) or give a finishing touch to any modern kitchen. 'Kuglodisc' is a stunning one-hole monobloc mixer with swan neck spout

and innovative right- or left-hand single lever control; available in white, beige, tabac, mocca, chrome and satin chrome. 'Kuglomix' one-hole mixer and 'Kuglotwin' deck (two-hole) mixer have dual control with swan-neck spout and semi-transparent acrylic handles in shades of brown; both are available in all the above colours plus safari beige, emerald green and mahogany brown, and 'Kuglomix' in bright red as well. 'Kuglette 2000' one-hole mixer has unusually angular lines; it is available in chrome, mocca, white, beige and red, all with contrasting black handles. Extendible shower spray-head is an optional extra with all types of spouts. *P:* 'Kuglodisc' coloured £112, chrome £92; 'Kuglomix' coloured £85, chrome £65; 'Kuglotwin' coloured £76, chrome £61; 'Kuglette 2000' coloured £61, chrome £51.

LEISURE
Exclusive, Scandinavian-designed tap from Britain's leading sink manufacturer. The 'Aquadisc' is a modern, angular, one-hole mixer available in chrome, white, mocca or beige to match Leisure's sinks. Like others of the new breed of taps, the control knobs, distinguished by a red or blue stripe at the base, use ceramic discs instead of washers, giving fingertip control and long life. *P:* £65.

'Aquadisc' from Leisure

MAMOLI
Very stylish chrome taps from this Italian manufacturer. Single mixer dual-flow, deck (two-hole) or one-hole, and simple hot and cold pillar taps are available for sinks. Some mixers can be supplied with swivel spouts, and one-hole models with separate hot rinse spray fitting that goes into the second sink hole. *P:* from £49.

SHAVRIN LEVATAP CO LTD
Variety of sleek modern pillar taps and mixer combinations operated by colourful levers (black, white, red, blue and soft green or

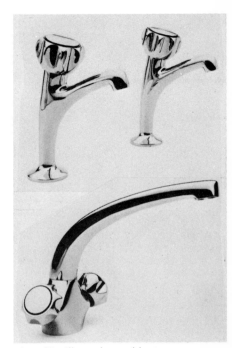

Mamoli's pillar and monobloc taps

duotone) which needs only a quarter turn and are guaranteed for 20 years. The chrome-plated dual-flow swivel spouts are available in cast or tubular, right-angled or swan-neck shapes, and extend to 9in (23cm) for twin-bowl sinks. *P.* sink mixer £60.

SPECTRUM
Modern sink mixers in bright red, yellow, green, blue, white and black. I BALOCCHI is a monobloc mixer with chunky cross-heads and

I BALOCCHI mixer from Spectrum

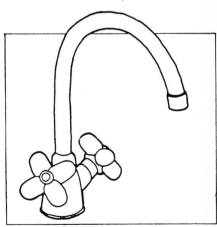

PRICES AND INFORMATION WERE CORRECT AT THE TIME OF GOING TO PRESS

swivelling spout. CALIBRO high-tech mono-control sink mixer, also with swivelling spout, is available for mounting on wall or sink. The control lever is a loop extending from the matt black head. *P:* I BALOCCHI £93.25; CALIBRO, sink-mounted £140, wall-mounted £153 (ex VAT).

WORKTOPS

ABET LAMINATI

Exciting and trend-setting designs for decorative high-pressure laminates, made in Italy with the typical Italian emphasis on design and visual appeal. PRINT range is reminiscent of the latest fabric designs in fashionable colour schemes and patterns. 'Serie R' has wide or narrow stripes in cool, fresh colourways: soft pink/white, grey/white, blue/white, blue/grey, green/white, light/darker blue. 'Quadretti' is similar but checked. There's also a grid pattern, 'Serie Misura', in grey, black or the four primaries on white; a polka dot pattern, 'Punti Misura', in red, green or black on white; a diagonal geometric, 'Serie Tecnica', in pink/white or grey/blue; and three stylish patterns of random squiggles, dots and splotches, 'Spugna', 'Bacteri' and 'Coriandolo', in similar colourways. The tones and styles would certainly enhance a clean-lined modern kitchen. Abet Laminati also make some beautiful, more delicate laminates that can be used for panels and infills, and sometimes for light-wear horizontal surfaces. TRAMA is a natural textile laminate with a surface of real yarns laid on to a cellulose base. LAMIKORK looks and feels like real cork. GRID is a silkscreened design available in a number of colourways. For a wilder look there's LAMINALL, surfaced in aluminium foil, and RELI-TECH also with metallic look but with embossed pattern, available in nine colourways. *P:* on application.

'Bacteri' and 'Coriandolo' from Abet Laminati's PRINT range

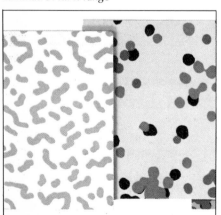

CERAMIC TILE DESIGN

Italian marble worktops cut to order. Some unusual colours such as black and green veining are available as well as the commoner grey and white. *P:* on application.

CORIAN DISTRIBUTORS C D (UK)

CORIAN, a unique marble-like material that has advantages over both laminates and marble itself. It comes in three subtle colours — opalescent cameo white, delicately veined dawn beige and almond. Like marble, it is solid and homogenous all the way through; it does not absorb moisture and is easy to fit. It can be cleaned using mild sandpaper and abrasives so any accidental damage such as knife cuts and cigarette burns can be removed, and it's generally weather-resistant. In kitchens CORIAN's a particularly durable worksurface, makes a superb pastry and chopping board and is totally stain resistant. What's more, it has no joins — seamless worktops even come with smoothly moulded integral sinks — making it the ultimate in terms of hygiene.
Kitchen worktops can be fitted in any width or length and in a variety of front edge turndowns and back upstands: square front, round, double round, Spanish, double Spanish, 'Imperial', recessed, bevelled, double bevelled, wood edge or a raised front edge to catch crumbs and spills. *P:* on application.

DUROPAL LTD

High quality and attractive high-pressure laminate that is easy to clean and trouble-free to maintain. Fifteen different surface textures are available, coming in 220 different styles — plain colours, patterns and wood or stone reproductions. Textures vary from high gloss

which creates interesting mirror-like effects, matt, 'Rhombic' (a linear structure), 'Ligna' and 'Foresta' (discreet 'wood grain') and 'Elm' (pronounced 'wood grain').
DUROPAL worktops are available in various profiles: double rounded, or with an additional slightly raised edge for splashback. Both kinds can be supplied with a useful wall upstand with a rounded top edge.
A practical idea is a new split-level worktop. It consists of a worktop with a double rounded profile plus a 'mezzanine shelf unit' which, besides increasing the overall depth of the working area, provides additional storage area on a separate level, useful during cooking.
Besides being perfect for kitchen worktops, DUROPAL high pressure laminates are popular for use in bathrooms, as window sills, bedroom furnishings, and in all kinds of domestic and office furniture.
P: on application.

FORMICA LTD

Vast choice of decorative laminates. COLOUR SYSTEM range consists of 72 plain colours in six chromatic colour families — green, blue, violet, red, orange and yellow — plus six neutral colour families. These colours are guaranteed to remain available for many years. There's also a COLOUR COMPLEMENT range of 16 particularly fashionable plain colours — fiesta bisque (grey-brown), rose ash, cameo pink, lilac mist, rose beige, new magnolia, sable, sherbet, calico, bamboo, aquamarine, ocean grey, Arctic blue, cloud blue, Folkestone, fog. This range is planned to be more flexible and reflect current trends.
Formica also market a standard collection of patterned, wood-design and marble-effect laminates designed for shopfitters and traders,

Formica's TOP PLAN 40

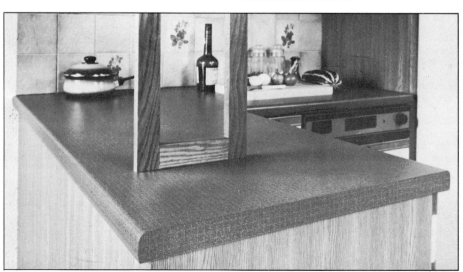

Marble drainer and sink surround from C P Hart

XCEL options are: medium oak, Adriatic marble, Buckingham tile, Chatsworth oak, pastiche grey, London tile, Padua tile, Moroccan leather, New Forest oak and hopsack. Besides these, XCEL hardwood-edged worktops are available in pastiche grey, hopsack, Padua tile, London tile, Buckingham tile and beige onyx marble with either dark mahogany or light oak solid wood edging. For complete colour co-ordination a choice of 57 plain colours are available in the ARCHITECT range and for something really exciting and different Wareite do all copper and aluminium embossed laminates in a choice of mirror gold, mirror bronze, autumn leaves, mirror copper, mirror aluminium, plus some interesting patterned copper effects. *P:* on application.

PETIT ROQUE LTD

Beautiful solid polished marble and granite kitchen worktops mostly imported from Italy, Spain, Portugal and Sicily, in many different colours with a choice of high gloss, semi-matt or matt finish. Petit Roque also supply finely rubbed sea green or black slate, 'Goldstone', an Italian sandstone in a buff colour with orange straight or swirled markings, and agglomerate marbles that have the advantage of being half the price of the natural material. Skilled craftsmen will cut sink, hob and tap holes, and polish the stone according to individual requirements at a minimal extra charge. *P:* (including cutting) marble and granite £8.90–£16.21 sq ft; slate £9.94–£11.94 sq ft; 'Goldstone' £12.39 sq ft; agglomerate marble £5.79–£11.94.

plus a more innovative SUPER range which also offers some very attractive craft designs and patterns. Specifically designed for the small builder and decorator is the economy STARTOPS range in 10 colours: dark mansion oak, light mansion oak, white, oyster Milano marble, almond quartz, pearl causeway, honey causeway, pink lattice, gold lattice, blue lattice. All these have a round front edge and velours finish, except for oyster Milano.

Good quality for the home is TOP PLAN 2, which comes in 12 colourways: classic onyx, Pacific stone, Polar white, peach scattercomb, minster pave, vellum, green vellum, brown vellum, warm haze and medium bridge oak, classic teak, planked teak. And the luxury range, TOP PLAN 40, is designed to cater for the studio kitchen market. The worktops are thicker than average, and rounded on either one or two edges. Colour options are classic onyx, harvest onyx, Alpine onyx, snowy haze, French check, green countercheck, honey ringlet, golden bridge oak, light morning oak, crystal beech, drift beige, drift blue, nimbus beige, vellum.
P: on application.

C P HART & SONS LTD

Marble worktops cut to order. A choice of marbles can be cut to fit over sinks and grooved to make efficient drainers. *P:* on application.

PERSTORP WAREITE LTD

Stylish decorative laminates in a huge selection of colours, patterns and marble and wood effects. GROSVENOR range offers some interesting natural-looking textures imitating jute and cork, leather, and Buckingham tiles, and fashionable patterns like the 'Checkmate Magnolia' and 'Checkmate Avocado', also some subtle abstract designs like 'Finaweave Buff' plus a good selection of warm wood prints and natural-looking marbles. Wareite XCEL range worktops come in two thicknesses, 3cm or 4cm (1¼ or 1½in). For islands or peninsular units, the larger two depth sizes are postformed along both front and back edges.

RESOPAL

Modern high-pressure laminates in more than 100 patterns and colours plus nine different textures. All are 3cm (1¼in) thick with either square edge or softline rounded edge. Spectrum of colours for the different designs includes white, grey linen, light and silver grey, beige, light, golden and dark brown, pale, bright and olive green, yellow, saffron, blues and reds. *P:* on application.

WOODSTOCK WORKSHOPS

Canadian maple worktops, as good-looking as they are practical. The advantage of maple is that it actually improves with use, building up a lovely patina with time. Also, unlike a lacquer or polyurethane finish, it can be renewed — simple rub a damaged area with wire wool and re-oil it — making maple perfect for a heavily used kitchen surface.

Woodstock worktops are 4½cm (1¾in) thick and custom made to any specification, shape or size; they come with optional maple upstand and cut-outs for sinks and hobs. *M:* widths, 65, 60, 45cm (25½, 23½, 17¾in). *P:* £91, £85, £75 per m; oil (1l) £5.

KITCHENS

Door and drawer-front designs for each range are illustrated, identified by the letters in bold type beneath each drawing and in the right-hand column.

KEY TO ABBREVIATIONS:

L =	Leaded-glass doors optional	C =	Clear-glass doors optional
S =	Smoked-glass doors optional	SA =	Self-assembly kitchen

KEY TO HANDLE DESCRIPTIONS:

Butterfly grip · 'D'-shape grip · Drop handle · Finger grip · Inset or recessed grip · Knob · Ring · Shell grip · Teardrop

ALLMILMÖ	PANELS	FINISHES	HANDLES	WORKTOPS	
BALI (£1106)	Laminate	Beige, savanne, gravel, oak reproduction, white	Shell-shape finger grip or 'D'-shape grip in light or dark oak	Laminates; round or square-edged or solid wood edge in profile or rounded style: pure white, white/grey, smoke blue, light beige (check), rush green (check), brown (check), pewter grey (check), Travertine decor, granite decor, wenge, medium brown; parquet-style wood in light oak, wenge, natural light reproduction ash, cherry-coloured reproduction beech; Allmilmö's 'Modula Ceramic System'; plus any laminates from Duropal and Resopal range	**A**
BAVARIA (£1736)	Pine	Natural sandblasted	Pine knob	As above	**B**
BERLIN (£1531)	Laminate; beech edging	Beige	Knob or extra length 'D'-shape grip in cherrywood stained beech	As above	**C**
BORNHOLM (£1662)	Wood veneer	Light stain	'D'-shape grip; wood knob	As above	**D**
BRABANT (£1661)	Oak frame	Medium light, medium brown stain	Wood knob; metal knob; escutcheon and key grip	As above	**E**
BRETAGNE (£1661)	Oak	Old brown stain	Burnished brass drop	As above	**E**
CAMARGUE (£2532, with smoked blue panelling or £2199 with natural lacquer)	Oak	Lacquered: white/grey with smoked blue panelling; light, medium brown or old brown lacquer	Porcelain or oak knob	As above	**B**
CONTURA (£1920)	Laminate	Fluted edelweiss (white) or pewter grey	Integrated chrome grip	As above	**F**
DUOFORM (£1342)	Laminate	Light grey, white, cherrywood, beech, ash, beige; all with contrasting edging	Vertical 'D'-shape grip or white porcelain knob	As above	**G**
EDELWEISS (£1342)	Laminate	White	Integrated chrome grip or 'D'-shape grip in white plastic or chrome	As above	**F**
FINELINE (£1531)	Laminate	Pewter grey, edelweiss	'D'-shape grip in chrome or white plastic; white porcelain knob	As above	**C**
FLORENZ (£2532)	Oak	Antique brown; natural sandblasted	Burnished antique drop	As above	**H**
FÜNEN (£1662)	Laminate; wood frame	Light oak, carrée, flecked, parquet (light oak or wenge)	Wood knob	As above	**I**

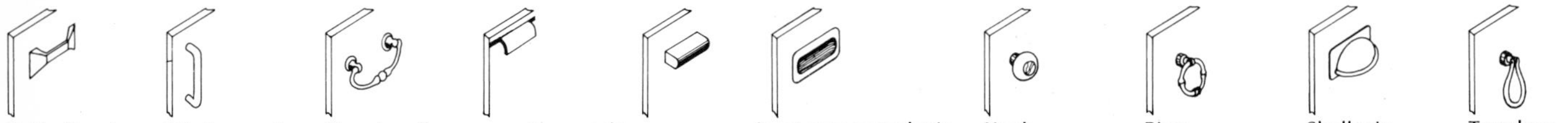

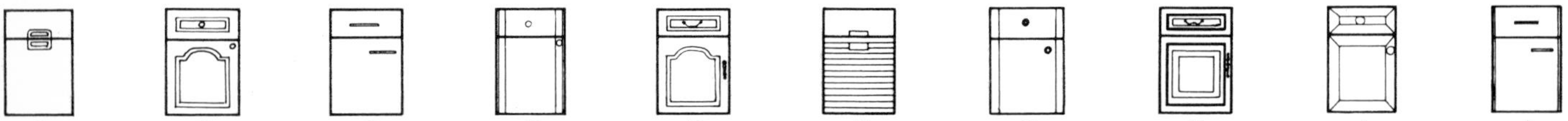

A **B** **C** **D** **E** **F** **G** **H** **I** **J**

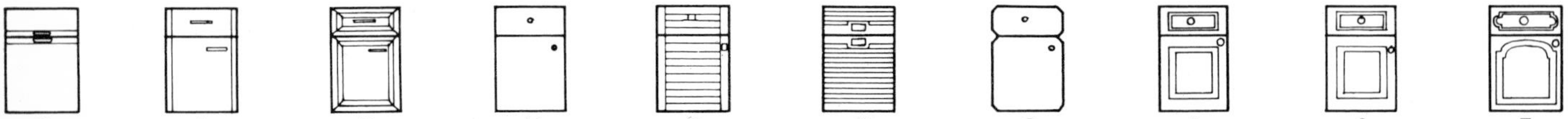

K **L** **M** **N** **O** **P** **Q** **R** **S** **T**

ALLMILMÖ CONT.	PANELS	FINISHES	HANDLES	WORKTOPS	
GOTLAND (£1481)	Laminate; wood edging	Beige, light oak, pearl decor	'D'-shape wood grip; wood knob	As above	J
JAPAN (£1231)	Laminate	Gold, beige	Shell-shape finger grip or 'D'-shape grip in light or dark oak	As above	K
JUTLAND (£1342)	Laminate	Beige, light wood veneer	'D'-shape grip; wood knob	As above	L
KOPENHAGEN (£1736)	Wood frame; oak or ash veneer	Light oak, wenge-coloured oak or natural ash	'D'-shape grip in chrome, oak or natural ash	As above	C
MANILA (£2532 for white/grey, £2372 for light or wenge stain)	Wood frame; matting front	White wood frame/grey bamboo wickerwork; light or wenge stain frame/bamboo wickerwork	Semi-circular white, light or wenge-stained grip	As above	M
MILANO (£1481)	Laminate	Lacquered: pewter grey, white/grey, beige	Knob with pewter grey, white/grey or beige inset in grey, natural ash or cherrywood stained beech; extra length 'D'-shape grip in white or pewter grey plastic, chrome, beige or cherrywood stained beech	As above	N
MOSELLE (£1736)	Oak	Light, medium brown stain	Wood knob	As above	B
NEVADA (£1920)	Oak, slatted	Light oak or wenge stain	Wood knob, chrome 'D'-shape grip or integrated grip	As above	O
NORDLAND (£2373)	Wood, slatted	Lacquered: white/grey	White porcelain knob; 'D' shape grip	As above	P
OCTAGON	Laminate	Finely textured: smoked blue/white edging, white/blue edging, pearl decor/white edging, white/brown edging, white/red edging, white/yellow edging, white/green edging	Porcelain knob with white, blue, beige, brown, red, yellow or green inset	As above	Q
OPTIMA (£1105)	Laminate	Finely textured: light grey, white, beige	'D'-shape grip in chrome, white plastic or light oak	As above	C
OXFORD (£2532 for white/grey with inlay and pewter grey, £2199 for mahogany)	Wood frame; mahogany veneer front	Lacquered: white/grey with gold or smoked blue inlay or English red/natural mahogany look or pewter grey, wood and wickerwork	Porcelain knob	As above	R
PIEMONT (£2373)	Oak	Old brown, medium brown stain	Burnished metal ring	As above	S
SOFT COLOUR DESIGN	Laminate	Pearl decor/white edge, smoked blue/white edge, white/blue, red, brown, yellow, green edge	White, blue, red, brown, yellow, green 'D'-shape grip	As above	J
TOSCANA (£2199)	Oak frame; oak veneer fronts	Medium patinated	Brass knob; antique drop	As above	T

ALNO	PANELS	FINISHES	HANDLES	WORKTOPS	
ALNO 80 HOB	Laminate	Simulated light oak, simulated brown oak, bast-beige	Wooden inset grip or 'D'-shape grip in brown or light oak	Round-edged or square-edged laminates: white, beige, blue, nova-white (flowered) nova-olive, nova-brown, apart-white (patterned), apart-sand, apart-green, simulated ash, simulated pine, simulated planked maple, simulated planked light oak, simulated planked brown oak, simulated light oak parquet, simulated brown oak parquet, simulated red-brown oak parquet, mosaic effect, marble effect, limestone effect, slate effect; solid beechwood	A

PRICES AND INFORMATION WERE CORRECT AT THE TIME OF GOING TO PRESS

KITCHENS

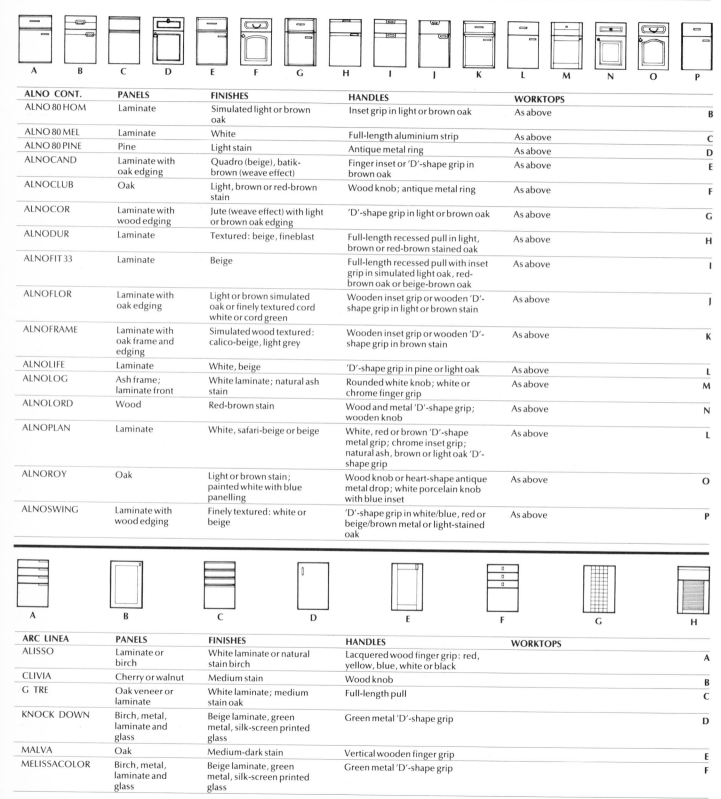

ALNO CONT.	PANELS	FINISHES	HANDLES	WORKTOPS	
ALNO 80 HOM	Laminate	Simulated light or brown oak	Inset grip in light or brown oak	As above	**B**
ALNO 80 MEL	Laminate	White	Full-length aluminium strip	As above	**C**
ALNO 80 PINE	Pine	Light stain	Antique metal ring	As above	**D**
ALNOCAND	Laminate with oak edging	Quadro (beige), batik-brown (weave effect)	Finger inset or 'D'-shape grip in brown oak	As above	**E**
ALNOCLUB	Oak	Light, brown or red-brown stain	Wood knob; antique metal ring	As above	**F**
ALNOCOR	Laminate with wood edging	Jute (weave effect) with light or brown oak edging	'D'-shape grip in light or brown oak	As above	**G**
ALNODUR	Laminate	Textured: beige, fineblast	Full-length recessed pull in light, brown or red-brown stained oak	As above	**H**
ALNOFIT 33	Laminate	Beige	Full-length recessed pull with inset grip in simulated light oak, red-brown oak or beige-brown oak	As above	**I**
ALNOFLOR	Laminate with oak edging	Light or brown simulated oak or finely textured cord white or cord green	Wooden inset grip or wooden 'D'-shape grip in light or brown stain	As above	**J**
ALNOFRAME	Laminate with oak frame and edging	Simulated wood textured: calico-beige, light grey	Wooden inset grip or wooden 'D'-shape grip in brown stain	As above	**K**
ALNOLIFE	Laminate	White, beige	'D'-shape grip in pine or light oak	As above	**L**
ALNOLOG	Ash frame; laminate front	White laminate; natural ash stain	Rounded white knob; white or chrome finger grip	As above	**M**
ALNOLORD	Wood	Red-brown stain	Wood and metal 'D'-shape grip; wooden knob	As above	**N**
ALNOPLAN	Laminate	White, safari-beige or beige	White, red or brown 'D'-shape metal grip; chrome inset grip; natural ash, brown or light oak 'D'-shape grip	As above	**L**
ALNOROY	Oak	Light or brown stain; painted white with blue panelling	Wood knob or heart-shape antique metal drop; white porcelain knob with blue inset	As above	**O**
ALNOSWING	Laminate with wood edging	Finely textured: white or beige	'D'-shape grip in white/blue, red or beige/brown metal or light-stained oak	As above	**P**

ARC LINEA	PANELS	FINISHES	HANDLES	WORKTOPS	
ALISSO	Laminate or birch	White laminate or natural stain birch	Lacquered wood finger grip: red, yellow, blue, white or black		**A**
CLIVIA	Cherry or walnut	Medium stain	Wood knob		**B**
G TRE	Oak veneer or laminate	White laminate; medium stain oak	Full-length pull		**C**
KNOCK DOWN	Birch, metal, laminate and glass	Beige laminate, green metal, silk-screen printed glass	Green metal 'D'-shape grip		**D**
MALVA	Oak	Medium-dark stain	Vertical wooden finger grip		**E**
MELISSACOLOR	Birch, metal, laminate and glass	Beige laminate, green metal, silk-screen printed glass	Green metal 'D'-shape grip		**F**

PRICES AND INFORMATION WERE CORRECT AT THE TIME OF GOING TO PRESS

ARC LINEA CONT.	PANELS	FINISHES	HANDLES	WORKTOPS	
SCACCO	Laminate	Grey or white with optional imprinted check pattern, yellow or red accessories	Finger grip: white, grey, yellow, red		G
SURF	Metal and birch	White corrugated aluminium; natural stain birch	Metal full-length recessed pull		H

A B C D E F G H I J K

BAUKNECHT	PANELS	FINISHES	HANDLES	WORKTOPS	
BELLA (£1210)	Laminate	White with blue or green edging	'D'-shape grip: blue or green	Laminates; square-edged: brown structured, beige, oak decor; round-edged: Travertine, beige Edo (olive square pattern), Rondo-terra, bamboo structure oak, natural oak decor, green trend, blue trend, Malaga, white, Lima (pale green)	A
BIANCA (£1210)	Laminate	White	Knob or inset grip: choice of colours	As above	B
COUNTRY (£1593)	Oak	Golden brown stain	Oak knob	As above	C
DIAGONAL (£1362)	Laminate	Textured: beige with grooved diagonal stripe	Round knob: oak or mahogany	As above	D
ELBA (£1362)	Laminate with oak edging	Textured: linen effect	Oak inset grip	As above	B
FLANDRIA (£1930)	Oak	Patina brown or antique brown stain	Oak, brass knob	As above	E
FORM SA	Laminate	Beige, white, Sahara beige, wood grain, greige (grey-beige)	Oak full-length pull: natural stain	As above	F
JAVA (£1414)	Oak frame; laminate front	Beige textured	Oak 'D'-shape grip: light, patina brown or antique stain	As above	G
LANDHAUS SA	Oak	Honey stain	Oak knob	As above	C
MODA (£1593)	Oak	Golden brown stain	Oak or brass knob	As above	H
NIZZA (£1930)	Oak	Patina brown, antique brown or natural oak stain	Oak or brass knob	As above	H
PRIMADONNA (£1414)	Laminate	White with blue inlay	White porcelain knob with blue insert	As above	I
RONDIS (£1414)	Laminate	Textured: cream	Oak full-length pull: patina brown	As above	F
SCANDINAVIA (£2392)	Oak	Natural, patina brown, cork brown, medium brown stain	Recessed circle in corner of door or drawer panel	As above	J
STANDARD SA	Laminate	White, Sahara, woodgrain	Plastic 'D'-shape grip	As above	K
STILFORM (£1210)	Laminate	Finely textured: beige	Oak full-length pull: antique brown or patina brown varnish	As above	F
WERKFORM (£943)	Laminate	Textured: white, beige, Sahara beige, woodgrain	Plastic knob or 'D'-shape grip to match finish	As above	K
WERKFORM WOOD (£1123)	Laminate with oak edging	Beige textured	Oak 'D'-shape grip: light, patina brown or antique stain	As above	A

ARTHUR BONNET	PANELS	FINISHES	HANDLES	WORKTOPS	
AVIGNON	Oak frame; veneered front	Medium stain	Antique metal drop on drawer; escutcheon and key on door		A
CALYPSO	Laminate	Grey-blue (woven effect)	Silver or blue aluminium strip		B

KITCHENS

| | A | B | C | D | E | F | G | H | I | J | K | L | M | N | O | P |

ARTHUR BONNET CONT.	**PANELS**	**FINISHES**	**HANDLES**	**WORKTOPS**	
CHAMBORD	Oak	Dark stain	Antique metal drop on drawer; escutcheon and key on door		A
CHINON	Oak	Light, dark or medium stain	As above		C
COGNAC	Laminate	White on dark blue	Plastic 'D'-shape grip: red, yellow, brown, white, grey		D
DERBY	Laminate	Dark green	Solid wood full-length recessed pull		E
FESTIVAL	Laminate with mahogany edging	White	Full-length recessed mahogany pull		E
FONTAINEBLEAU	Oak	Hand-distressed	Antique metal drop on drawer; escutcheon and key on door		F
ISBA	Oak (slatted)	Natural stain	Natural stain oak finger pull		G
LIMOUSIN	Oak	Antiqued, medium stain	Antique metal drop on drawer; escutcheon and key on door		H
NIAGARA	Oak	Light stain	Broad oak 'D'-shape grip		I
OHIO	Laminate and wood	White	Broad wooden 'D'-shape grip: light or dark stain		J
POMPADOUR	Oak	Light, dark or medium stain	Antique metal drop on drawer; escutcheon and key on door		A
RAMBOUILLET	Oak	Antiqued light or dark stain or grey stain	Antique metal drop on drawer; escutcheon and key on door		F
RICHELIEU	Oak	Medium or dark stain	Antique metal drop on drawer; escutcheon and key on door		K
ROUSSILLON	Laminate (grooved)	White with grey or green wide stripe	Knob: brass or grey-blue, brown, white or red		L
SAUMUR	Laminate	White or imitation pine	Plastic 'D'-shape grip: yellow, white, red, green, beige or chrome		M
SENLIS	Laminate with wood edging	White or blue-grey	Wooden knob: light, dark, red, white or grey-blue stain		N
VILLANDRY	Oak	Antiqued	Antique metal drop on drawer; escutcheon and key on door		O
VENDOME	Laminate	White, cream, grey-blue, burgundy	Wooden full-length pull: light, dark, white, grey-blue or red stain		P

| | A | B | C | D | E | F | G | H | I | J | K | L | M | N | O |

BOSCH	**PANELS**	**FINISHES**	**HANDLES**	**WORKTOPS**	
ALSACE (£2202)	Oak veneer, solid oak edging	Light, medium or antique stained oak	Solid wood knob; antique style metal ring	Laminate: oak strip effect, medium, light or cognac oak planking effect, Travertine, cirrus, montan, apricot, agave, Carrara white, Macao green, terracotta, sella grey, sabino beige.	A
ALSACE–L (£2559)	Lacquered oak veneer; solid oak edging	White, details in crystal (pale blue)	Metal pull; ceramic knob	As above	A
AVIGNON (£2559)	Solid oak	Light, medium or antique stained oak	Solid wood knob; antique-style metal ring	As above	B
CADRO (£1549)	Laminate	Pearl grey or sand	White metal round knob; 'D'-shape grip in nickelled metal	As above	C
CARAT (£1375)	Laminate	White, pearl grey	Coloured metal knob: blue, red, brown, white or green	As above	E
CASA (£1784)	Laminate; beech edging	Solid white, pearl grey, sand	Solid wood or metal pull; solid wood knob	As above	E

BOSCH CONT.	PANELS	FINISHES	HANDLES	WORKTOPS	
CLASSIC (£2202)	Oak veneer; solid oak edging	Light, medium cognac or antique stained oak	Solid wood or metal knob	As above	F
DORINA (£1419)	Laminate	Linen beige, Tonga beige, linen green	Oak recessed grip	As above	G
DORINA-M (£1549)	Laminate; solid oak edging	Tonga beige, linen beige linen green, Niagara beige	Solid oak 'D'-shape grip or rounded knob	As above	G
FAVORIT (£1671)	Laminate	Linen beige, Tonga beige, linen green	Full-length recessed pulls in oak effect or cognac (with Tonga beige)	As above	I
FLAIR (£2197)	Laminate	Crystal (off-white), sand, strato (pale blue), graphite, pearl grey	Knob or metal 'D'-shape grip	As above	D
FLAIR-M (£2255)	Ribbed laminate; solid beech edging	Pearl grey, graphite, sand	Nickel-plated vertical 'D' shape grip; rounded solid wood knobs	As above	J
OXFORD (£2937)	Solid oak	Antique stain	Antique-style metal rings	As above	K
RAVENNA (£1937)	Oak veneer	Light, medium, cognac or antique stained oak	Solid oak knob or 'D'-shape grip	As above	E
RUSTICA (£2158)	Oak veneer	Light, medium or antique stained oak or lacquered in crystal (off-white), sand, strato, graphite, pearl-grey	Oak recessed grip or 'D'-shape grip	As above	L
SIDENA (£1445)	Laminate	Beech effect	Solid beech or metal finger grip; beech knob	As above	E
SILIA (£1419)	Laminate	White, pearl, grey, sand	Solid beech or metal 'D'-shape grip or knob	As above	H
SOLIDA (£1288)	Laminate	Kyoto beige, quarto beige, quarto green, light oak, medium oak	Solid oak knob; recessed grip: light or medium oak effect	As above	M
SOLIDA-M (£1375)	Laminate	Kyoto or quarto beige, quarto green	Solid wood 'D'-shape grip or knob	As above	N
TARIO (£2021)	Rib-effect laminate; solid beech edging	White	Solid wood rounded knob	As above	N
TREND (£1446)	Laminate	White with red, blue, brown or white finishing	Plastic 'D'-shape grip: blue, red, brown or white	As above	O

A   B   C   D   E   F   G   H   I   J   K

CESA	PANELS	FINISHES	HANDLES	WORKTOPS	
ANGELIQUE (£1528)	Elm	Natural	Elm knob	Round-edged or square-edged laminates: white, cream, beige, fern green, red, olive green, midnight blue, brown, lined grey and various wood and grain effects; wood edged laminates; tiled with wood edge	A
AUDREY (£1391)	Laminate with oak trim	Olive green, cream, marbled brown	Full-length oak pull	As above	B
BERGERAC (£1059)	Laminate with wood trim	Textured: cream	Recessed full-length oak pull	As above	C
BIGORRE (£1324)	Chestnut	Champagne or cognac stain	Bronze drop	As above	D
BRESSANE (£2031)	Ash	Dark stain; semi-distressed	Pewter or bronze drop	As above	E
D'ARTAGNAN (£1455)	Oak	Light, medium or champagne stain	Bronze drop	As above	F
GASCOGNE (£1324)	Oak	Light, medium or cognac stain	Bronze drop	As above	G
GUYENNE (£1324)	Oak	Light, medium, champagne or cognac stain	Bronze drop	As above	D

KITCHENS

CESA CONT.	PANELS	FINISHES	HANDLES	WORKTOPS	
MOLIERE	Oak	Antiqued stain	Bronze drop	As above	F
MONTESQUIEU (£1926)	Oak	Champagne stain or lacquered: ivory	Bronze drop	As above	G
PAMELA (£1019)	Laminate	White	'D'-shape grip: natural ash, red, cloud grey; shell grip: natural oak	As above	H
POMPADOUR (£1455)	Cherrywood	Natural stain	Bronze drop	As above	F
RECAMIER (£1455)	Oak	Natural stain	Bronze drop	As above	I
RICHELIEU (£1981)	Walnut	Natural stain	Bronze drop	As above	F
ROUERGUE (£1574)	Oak	Cognac stain	Bronze drop	As above	G
TOURMALET (£1391)	Pine (slatted)	Natural	Recessed finger grip	As above	J
TURSAN (£1059)	Laminate	White	'D'-shape grip: natural ash; blue or red looped pull	As above	H
VANESSA (£1019)	Laminate with light oak edgings	Textured: creamy white	'D'-shape grip: light oak	As above	K

CLARE	PANELS	FINISHES	HANDLES	WORKTOPS	
CRESTALUX (£1066) SA	Laminate; solid Canadian red oak front	Natural stain	Antique bronze filigree knob	Solar white, silver Aztec, Adriatic marble, hopsack, Rio brown, smoky marble, warm haze, medium bridge oak, beech block	A
CUSINA (£665) SA	Laminate	High gloss polyester: burgundy, honey, sable stone, apple green; textured: folkweave	Natural oak full-length pull	As above	B
EUROPLAN (£560) SA	Laminate	Beige, patina green, teak	Aluminium strip	As above	B
ORION (£560) SA	Laminate	Rose, greystone, blue	Knob: white with coloured inset, chrome, wood, jet black	As above	C
PROVENCE (£1517) SA	Oak	Dark oak stain	Antique bronze knob	As above	D

A   B   C   D   A   B   C   D   E   F

CROSBY	PANELS	FINISHES	HANDLES	WORKTOPS	
CANADIAN (£896)	Alder	Natural stain	Knob	Laminates, square-edged: pastiche, rustic tile; round edged: peach, Waterford, planked oak; solid wood front edge in medium oak, antique oak, alder, mahogany	A
CAPRICE (£971)	Oak	Light stain	Oak and metal 'D'-shape grip	As above	B
CATHEDRAL (£813)	Oak	Natural stain	Oak knob	As above	C
CELESTE SA	Laminate; mahogany edging	Off-white	Mahogany inset grip	As above	D
COSMO- POLITAN (£685)	Laminate	Textured: sandweave, sageweave	Oak 'D'-shape grip	As above	E
PASTELLE SA	Laminate	Blue, beige, pink	Inset grip	Ravenna pink, Ravenna blue, classic onyx	F

PRICES AND INFORMATION WERE CORRECT AT THE TIME OF GOING TO PRESS

A B C D E F G H I J K L

DEDECKER	PANELS	FINISHES	HANDLES	WORKTOPS	
1500 DES (£1106)	Laminate	White	Plastic 'D'-shape grip: several colours		A
1500 E (£1106)	Laminate; oak edging	Matt or textured: white	Oak 'D'-shape grip		B
1600 (£1197)	Laminate; oak edging	Textured: several shades	Full-length oak pull		C
1800 (£1106)	Laminate; oak edging	White	White 'D'-shape grip; wooden finger pull: natural, medium stain		D
2000 (£1366)	Laminate; oak edging	White	Inset grip		E
2200 (£1366)	Laminate; oak edging	Anthracite imitation; bordeaux red	Oak ball-form knob		F
7000 (£1106)	Laminate	White	Full-length recessed pull		G
BRETONNE (£1921)	Oak; L	Dark stain	Pewterized knob		H
CHAMBORD (£2489)	Oak; L	Light, medium, dark stain	Antique drop		I
GASCOGNE (£2489)	Oak	Antiqued: light or dark oak	Coppered antique drop		I
PALLET (£1700)	Oak	Natural stain	Oak knob		J
PERIGORD (£1921)	Cherry; L	Satin lacquer	Bronze drop on drawer and escutcheon and key on door		K
PROVENCE (£1921)	Oak; L	Satin lacquer	Pewterized antique drop on drawers; escutcheon and key on doors		H
SAVOIE (£2263)	Oak; L	Light or dark patinated	Antique coppered drop		L
VENDEE (£1921)	Oak; L	Medium dark stain	Copper or tin antique drop on drawer; key and escutcheon on door		L
VENDEE K (£1921)	Oak and cherry; L	Medium dark stain	Copper or bronze antique drop on drawer and key and escutcheon on door		L

A B C D E

DIFFORD	PANELS	FINISHES	HANDLES	WORKTOPS	
ANTIQUE PINE (£527) SA	Pine	Polyurethane lacquer	Brass ring	Laminates, round front edge: beige leather, hopsack, cabana, onyx, Himalayan teak, New Forest oak, white, London tile	A
CABANA (£405) SA	Laminate	Textured: rustic beige	Oak full-length pull	As above	B
CHERRY (£572) SA	Cherry	Light stain	Brass ring	As above	A
CHESTNUT (£673) SA	Chestnut	Rich stain	Brass ring	As above	C

PRICES AND INFORMATION WERE CORRECT AT THE TIME OF GOING TO PRESS

KITCHENS

DIFFORD CONT.	PANELS	FINISHES	HANDLES	WORKTOPS	
CLASSIC OAK (£719) SA	Oak	Natural	Brass ring	As above	D
DE-LUXE WHITE (£473) SA	Laminate with mahogany trim	Textured: white	Mahogany 'D'-shape grip	As above	B
FAWN (£303) SA	Laminate	Fawn leather effect	Full-length oak pull	As above	B
HOPSACK (£406) SA	Laminate	Textured: corn colour	Oak full-length pull	As above	B
MEDIUM OAK (£569) SA	Oak	Natural stain	Brass ring	As above	A
PINE (£486) SA	Pine	Polyurethane lacquer: natural look	Brass ring	As above	E
ROYAL OAK (£550) SA	Oak	Light stain	Brass ring	As above	A
RUSTIC OAK (£655) SA	Oak	Medium stain	Brass ring	As above	A
WHITE (£292) SA	Laminate	White melamine	Oak full-length pull	As above	B

A B C D E F G H I J K L M

EASTHAM	PANELS	FINISHES	HANDLES	WORKTOPS	
ABBEY (£1158)	Wood	Light oak stain	Triangular antique-style metal pull	Laminates, round-edged: light oak, fawn tile, block cork, chocolate check, mosaic, classic onyx, autumn tile, green tile (wood-effect edge), medium oak; 'Modern' or 'Traditional' wood frame with Buckingham tiles	A
BERKELEY (£1352)	Oak	Light, dark stain	Nearly full-length pull in light or dark stain oak	As above	B
CANTERBURY (£1658)	Oak; L	Natural, stained	Metal ring on drawer and drop on door	As above	C
CARLTON (£1006)	Laminate; light oak trim	White check	Light oak finger grip	As above	D
CHELSEA (£1352)	Laminate	Cream with honey brown highlights	Porcelain knob	As above	E
COTTAGE (£1022)	Oak frame; laminate front	Green leather, barley	Brass effect antique-style ring	As above	F
E-LINE (£926)	Laminate	Satin: harvest check, cream pampas	Contoured finger grip: French beige, Congo brown	As above	G
EUROPEAN (£1145)	Laminate; oak trim	Lightly textured: bamboo, brown pampas	Recessed finger grip in oak trim	As above	F
HALLMARK (£1352;	Oak frame; oak veneer front	Reversible panel; quartered oak or plain oak in natural stain	Oak knob with metal inset	As above	H
KENDAL (£1006)	Laminate; oak trim	Yellow pampas, oatmeal parchment	Finger grip on oak trim	As above	I
MANOR (£731)	Laminate	Arctic white; wood-effect trim	Wood-effect inset grip	As above	J
MAYFAIR (£1225)	Laminate; oak trim	Beige check	Nearly full-length pull in light or medium stained oak	As above	K

Siematic's 1001 OP pine kitchen

The Beauty of Hardwood.
Oak, Mahogany, Cherry, Ash & Maple.

ABS offer a full range of standard size solid hardwood cupboard doors and matching drawer fronts plus a unique Made-to-Measure service.

If you're a DIY expert, builder, fitter or architect looking for good design, we can help you fit out your interiors quickly and easily and save pounds into the bargain.

Simply supply measurements of doors required (whether for the home or office), choose one of our fine hardwoods and leave the rest to us.

Or pop into our Hackney Road showroom and see for yourself the excellent quality,

alternative styles, different finishes and our extensive range of cabinets, fittings, worktops and hardware as well as a full range of shelving, mouldings, brackets, knobs and decor panels.

Or talk to us about our range of interior and exterior doors which we make to special order.

So for more information about our range of beautiful hardwood products please phone us on 01-739 8621 or call in anytime between 9 - 5.30 Monday to Friday or 9 - 4.00 on Saturday.

A·B·S

ABS CONTRACTS LIMITED, 257 HACKNEY ROAD, SHOREDITCH, LONDON E2. TELEPHONE 01-739 8621

EASTHAM CONT.	PANELS	FINISHES	HANDLES	WORKTOPS	
OAKLEAF (£1145)	Oak veneer	Light stain	Inset grip	As above	L
PAVILION (£769)	Laminate	Japanese grass	Oak full-length pull, light stain	As above	M
VILLA (£731)	Laminate	Brown pampas; wood effect trim	Wood-effect inset grip	As above	J
YORK (£1658)	Oak; L	Light, medium stain	Pewter knob	As above	E

ELLIS	PANELS	FINISHES	HANDLES	WORKTOPS	
CAMEO (£948)	Laminate	Biscuit, blue tweed, reed green	Oak full-length pull	Laminates; round-edged, square-edged or round-edged in solid oak: medium oak, Adriatic marble, buffalo, hopsack, pastiche, blue starlight, featherdown, rhinestone	D
ELGIN (£691)	Laminate	White	Red plastic 'D'-shape grip	As above	B
MENDIP (£1010)	Laminate; oak trim	Blue starlight, hopsack, white	Oak inset grip; ceramic knob	As above	C
METRO (£634)	Laminate	Raffia, coffee, safari, russet, white, pink mosaic, blue mosaic, grey mosaic	Aluminium strip	As above	A
WARWICK (£691)	Laminate	As above	Full-length oak pull	As above	D
WEDGWOOD (£1128)	Laminate; wood frame	Blue frame/blue inset, white frame/pink inset, white frame/grey inset	White porcelain knob	As above	E
YORK (£1171)	Oak; oak with laminate infill panel; L	Rustic oak stain	Antique metal ring	As above	F

A   B   C   D   E   F   A   B   C   D   E   F

ENGLISH ROSE	PANELS	FINISHES	HANDLES	WORKTOPS	
AVIEMORE (£1175)	Laminate; L	Beige with brown trim	Two-tone ceramic knob	Adriatic marble, blue mosaic, oasis, brown mosaic, linea (white), hessian, omega (beige)	A
CHELSEA (£1032)	Laminate; L	Grey, sand, brilliant white	Two-tone ceramic knob; solid wood recessed pull	As above	B
CHELTENHAM (£1338)	Solid oak; L	Medium stain	Oak knob with pewter inset	As above	C
KENSINGTON (£1175)	Laminate; L	White with blue trim	Two-tone (blue and white) ceramic knob	As above	D
WARWICK (£1338)	Solid oak; L	Golden stain	Antique-style bronze drop	As above	E
WINCHESTER (£1262)	Solid oak; L	Natural stain	Oak knob	As above	D
YORK (£1061)	Laminate, oak edging; L	Primrose, barley, meadow	Oak finger grip	As above	F

FRAMFORD KITCHENS	PANELS	FINISHES	HANDLES	WORKTOPS	
APOLLO METRIC (£815)	Laminate	Textured: nutmeg, mint, biscuit, Atlantic blue; gloss: glossy white, bamboo, cantaloupe; matt: ice, sunbeech, Bombay (light beige weave), planked teak, natural straw, green straw, elm	Aluminium strip	Round-edged: beige onyx marble, sunbeech, ice; teak-edged, square-edged: beige onyx marble, sunbeech, ice, matt white, natural slate, Victorian marble (pale green), syringa brown, nutmeg, mint, biscuit, Atlantic blue, Bombay (light beige weave), planked teak, natural straw, green straw, brown hide, olive cascade, athenaeum, elm	A

185

KITCHENS

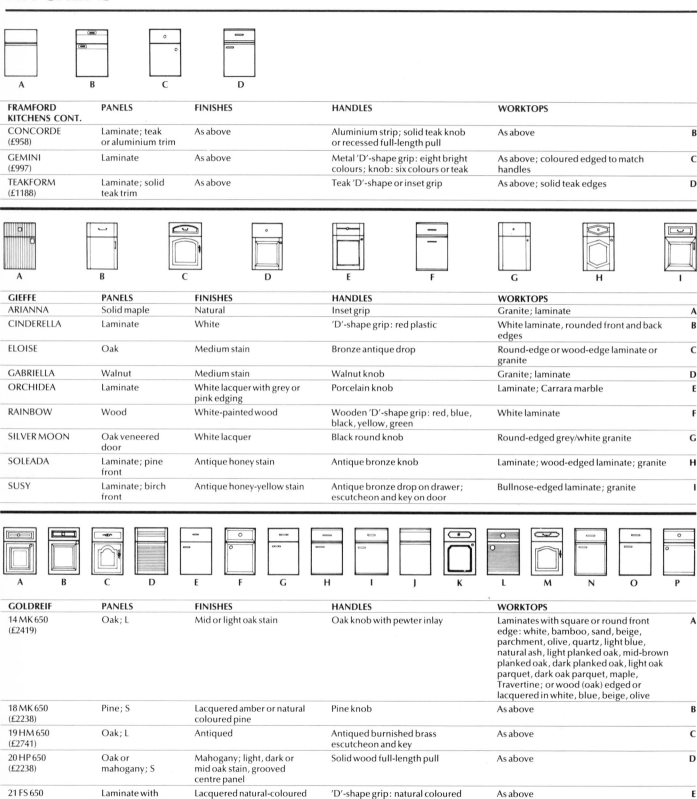

FRAMFORD KITCHENS CONT.	PANELS	FINISHES	HANDLES	WORKTOPS	
CONCORDE (£958)	Laminate; teak or aluminium trim	As above	Aluminium strip; solid teak knob or recessed full-length pull	As above	B
GEMINI (£997)	Laminate	As above	Metal 'D'-shape grip: eight bright colours; knob: six colours or teak	As above; coloured edged to match handles	C
TEAKFORM (£1188)	Laminate; solid teak trim	As above	Teak 'D'-shape or inset grip	As above; solid teak edges	D

GIEFFE	PANELS	FINISHES	HANDLES	WORKTOPS	
ARIANNA	Solid maple	Natural	Inset grip	Granite; laminate	A
CINDERELLA	Laminate	White	'D'-shape grip: red plastic	White laminate, rounded front and back edges	B
ELOISE	Oak	Medium stain	Bronze antique drop	Round-edge or wood-edge laminate or granite	C
GABRIELLA	Walnut	Medium stain	Walnut knob	Granite; laminate	D
ORCHIDEA	Laminate	White lacquer with grey or pink edging	Porcelain knob	Laminate; Carrara marble	E
RAINBOW	Wood	White-painted wood	Wooden 'D'-shape grip: red, blue, black, yellow, green	White laminate	F
SILVER MOON	Oak veneered door	White lacquer	Black round knob	Round-edged grey/white granite	G
SOLEADA	Laminate; pine front	Antique honey stain	Antique bronze knob	Laminate; wood-edged laminate; granite	H
SUSY	Laminate; birch front	Antique honey-yellow stain	Antique bronze drop on drawer; escutcheon and key on door	Bullnose-edged laminate; granite	I

GOLDREIF	PANELS	FINISHES	HANDLES	WORKTOPS	
14 MK 650 (£2419)	Oak; L	Mid or light oak stain	Oak knob with pewter inlay	Laminates with square or round front edge: white, bamboo, sand, beige, parchment, olive, quartz, light blue, natural ash, light planked oak, mid-brown planked oak, dark planked oak, light oak parquet, dark oak parquet, maple, Travertine; or wood (oak) edged or lacquered in white, blue, beige, olive	A
18 MK 650 (£2238)	Pine; S	Lacquered amber or natural coloured pine	Pine knob	As above	B
19 HM 650 (£2741)	Oak; L	Antiqued	Antiqued burnished brass escutcheon and key	As above	C
20 HP 650 (£2238)	Oak or mahogany; S	Mahogany; light, dark or mid oak stain, grooved centre panel	Solid wood full-length pull	As above	D
21 FS 650 (£2018)	Laminate with veneered front; S	Lacquered natural-coloured ash	'D'-shape grip: natural coloured ash	As above	E

GOLDREIF CONT.	PANELS	FINISHES	HANDLES	WORKTOPS	
31 HF 650 (£1748)	Oak frame; veneered front; S	Light oak, mid-brown, cream, or graphite oak lacquer	Wooden knob	As above	F
45 KB 650 (£1251)	Laminate; S	Finely textured: ocean green, parchment, white	Oak 'D'-shape grip: mid-brown stain	As above	G
48 FK 650 (£1379)	Laminate; S	Finely textured: light grey, light beige (both with small pattern)	White plastic 'D'-shape grip	As above	E
52 SV 650 (£1594)	Laminate; S	Finely textured: beige, white	'D'-shape grip: light oak, mid-brown oak, cream oak, graphite oak, mahogany, natural coloured ash	As above	H
60 CM 650 (£1379)	Laminate; S	Wood grain textured: white, beige, grey	Coloured metal 'D'-shape grip	As above	G
63 FB 650 (£1379)	Laminate; S	Finely textured: textile, ocean green, grafica, white	'D'-shape grip: oak (light stain), white plastic or natural stained ash	As above	G
66 FH 650 (£1509)	Laminate; S	Light beige, pastel blue	Oak 'D'-shape grip: light stain	As above	I
72 SG 650 (£1748)	Laminate; S	Finely textured: sand, antelope	Full-length pull: mid-brown oak, mahogany, natural ash	As above	J
81 CS 650 (£2419)	Laminate; L	White with blue inlay	White porcelain knob with blue inlay	As above	K
86 SH 650 (£1748)	Laminate; wood veneered front; S	Finely ribbed veneer in light or dark oak	Wooden knob	As above	L
87 HS 650 (£2238)	Oak; L	Antique mid or light oak stain	Antique metal pull	As above	M
90 HK 650 (£1748)	Laminate; oak edging; S	Textile-effect light beige	Wooden 'D'-shape grip: light or dark oak	As above	F
91 HK 650 (£1594)	Laminate; oak edging; S	Finely textured: white, light beige	Wooden knob	As above	N
92 SM 650 (£1509)	Laminate; S	Finely textured: white	Coloured metal 'D'-shape grip	As above	O
97 SK 650 (£1594)	Laminate; S	Finely ribbed; white, beige	'D'-shape grip or knob: white or beige	As above	P

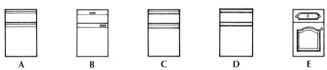

A　B　C　D　E

GOWER	PANELS	FINISHES	HANDLES	WORKTOPS	
CASCADE (£554) SA	Laminate	Textured: basket weave (beige); gloss: golden beige, summer green; English oak.	Gold-coloured metal strips	Laminate; roll-edged, textured: autumn baskette (light brown), manilla baskette (beige), Regency oak, classic onyx, Buckingham tile	A
GOURMET (£614) SA	Laminate	Textured: rustic weave (beige), antique oak; gloss: oyster, fresh olive, paprika. All with high gloss oyster drawer fronts	Solid wood strip with finger grip	As above	B
HOMESTYLE (£364) SA	Laminate	Textured: Sahara (pale brown), country weave (beige); gloss: polar white, velvet beige, golden oak	Metal strip in gold or silver finish	Laminate, roll-edged: chocolate, natural oak, classic onyx	C
MODULE 21 (£418) SA	Laminate	Apple, honeydew, mellow teak, polar white, sun beech	Aluminium strip	Laminate: chocolate, cremo marble, mellow teak, orange damask, sun beech	D
REMBRANDT (£1284) SA	Solid oak; L	Natural	Recessed brass ring	Laminate, roll-edged, textured: autumn baskette (light brown), manilla baskette (beige), Regency oak; classic onyx, Buckingham tile; manilla baskette, Buckingham tile with wood edging	E

KITCHENS

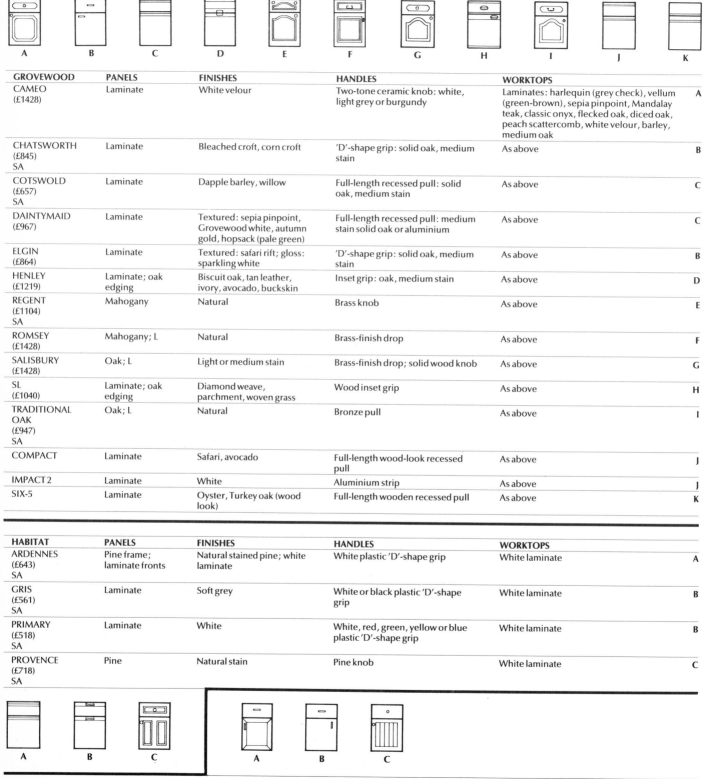

GROVEWOOD	PANELS	FINISHES	HANDLES	WORKTOPS	
CAMEO (£1428)	Laminate	White velour	Two-tone ceramic knob: white, light grey or burgundy	Laminates: harlequin (grey check), vellum (green-brown), sepia pinpoint, Mandalay teak, classic onyx, flecked oak, diced oak, peach scattercomb, white velour, barley, medium oak	A
CHATSWORTH (£845) SA	Laminate	Bleached croft, corn croft	'D'-shape grip: solid oak, medium stain	As above	B
COTSWOLD (£657) SA	Laminate	Dapple barley, willow	Full-length recessed pull: solid oak, medium stain	As above	C
DAINTYMAID (£967)	Laminate	Textured: sepia pinpoint, Grovewood white, autumn gold, hopsack (pale green)	Full-length recessed pull: medium stain solid oak or aluminium	As above	C
ELGIN (£864)	Laminate	Textured: safari rift; gloss: sparkling white	'D'-shape grip: solid oak, medium stain	As above	B
HENLEY (£1219)	Laminate; oak edging	Biscuit oak, tan leather, ivory, avocado, buckskin	Inset grip: oak, medium stain	As above	D
REGENT (£1104) SA	Mahogany	Natural	Brass knob	As above	E
ROMSEY (£1428)	Mahogany; L	Natural	Brass-finish drop	As above	F
SALISBURY (£1428)	Oak; L	Light or medium stain	Brass-finish drop; solid wood knob	As above	G
SL (£1040)	Laminate; oak edging	Diamond weave, parchment, woven grass	Wood inset grip	As above	H
TRADITIONAL OAK (£947) SA	Oak; L	Natural	Bronze pull	As above	I
COMPACT	Laminate	Safari, avocado	Full-length wood-look recessed pull	As above	J
IMPACT 2	Laminate	White	Aluminium strip	As above	J
SIX-5	Laminate	Oyster, Turkey oak (wood look)	Full-length wooden recessed pull	As above	K

HABITAT	PANELS	FINISHES	HANDLES	WORKTOPS	
ARDENNES (£643) SA	Pine frame; laminate fronts	Natural stained pine; white laminate	White plastic 'D'-shape grip	White laminate	A
GRIS (£561) SA	Laminate	Soft grey	White or black plastic 'D'-shape grip	White laminate	B
PRIMARY (£518) SA	Laminate	White	White, red, green, yellow or blue plastic 'D'-shape grip	White laminate	B
PROVENCE (£718) SA	Pine	Natural stain	Pine knob	White laminate	C

IDEAL TIMBER PRODUCTS SEE FOLLOWING PAGE

IDEAL TIMBER PRODUCTS CONT.	PANELS	FINISHES	HANDLES	WORKTOPS	
EUROLINE 500 (£304) SA	Laminate	Textured: white, beige, linen weave	Full-length metal recessed pull: brown or silver	Laminate, square-edged: Torino marble, sable teak; round-edged: Adriatic marble, teak, light oak, vellum, medium oak, bitter chocolate	A
EUROLINE 600 (£304) SA	Laminate	As above	As above	As above	A
PASSPORT DE LUXE (£642) SA	Laminate	Textured: oatmeal, tweed, vellum, raffia, white leather, pampas	Solid wood full-length recessed pull	Laminate: vellum, teak, medium oak, Adriatic marble, bitter chocolate, light oak, hopsack	B
PASSPORT LUXURY (£1069) SA	Solid wood	Cramond dark wood, Cramond light oak, cathedral dark oak, country oak, cathedral red oak	Solid wood knob or antique bronze ring	As above	C
PASSPORT QUALITY (£553) SA	Laminate	Textured: beige, white gloss, planked teak	Metal full-length recessed pull	As above	A

KINGSWOOD	PANELS	FINISHES	HANDLES	WORKTOPS	
CONISTON (£1330) SA	Solid oak; L	Dark, light or medium oak stain	Antique-style bronze ring	Beaumel, Resopal, Polyrey and Formica ranges	A
GRASMERE (£997) SA	Solid oak frame with matching veneered panels; L	Medium or light oak stain	Antique-style bronze ring	As above	B
LAKELAND (£725) SA	Laminate; L	Fawn leather, elegant square (off-white)	Solid light oak full-length recessed pull	As above	C
MILBURN (£997) SA	Laminate; L	Textured natural hessian	Solid, medium stain oak full-length recessed pull	As above	D
KENDAL (£1417) SA	Mahogany; L	Natural stain	Brass knob	As above	E
PENNINE (£1417) SA	Solid oak; L	Antique stain	Oak with brass inset knob	As above	F
WINDERMERE (£997) SA	Laminate; L	Antique leather, sparkling white	Mahogany full-length pull	As above	G

A B C D E F G   A B C D E F G

LADYLOVE	PANELS	FINISHES	HANDLES	WORKTOPS	
COTSWOLD (£1245)	Chestnut; L	Natural chestnut stain	Solid chestnut 'D'-shape grip	Laminate: onyx marble, vellum, medium oak, Baltic pine, block beech, Milano marble, minster pave, Buckingham tile, natural teak, white; textured: seaweed, browntone	A
DIANA (£485)	Laminate	White	Red, brown or blue 'D'-shape grip	As above	B
FORMULA I (£983)	Laminate	Hopsack (light beige)	Full-length recessed pull in solid polished oak	As above	C
SUPERB (£601)	Laminate	Tweed, sage green, sand	Full-length recessed pull in solid wood	As above	D
SYSTEM A DE LUXE (£485)	Laminate	Teak, olive, pine, orange, oak	Simulated wood strip	As above	E

KITCHENS

LADYLOVE CONT.	PANELS	FINISHES	HANDLES	WORKTOPS	
VINTAGE (£983)	Solid teak; L	Antique oak or honey stain	Brass knob	As above	F
WESTMINSTER (£601)	Laminate	Sage green, sand	Oak 'D'-shape grip	As above	G

A B C D E F G H I J
K L M N O P Q R S T

LEICHT	PANELS	FINISHES	HANDLES	WORKTOPS	
EXCELLENT COLLECTION					
CARAT-H (£1014)	Solid wood frame; laminated front; G	Simulated wood: dark or light	'D'-shape or inset grip: solid wood dark or light stain	Laminate: white, pearl grey, light grey, quartz. pearl beige, olive, terra brown, marble decor, Travertine marble, maple, light oak, block wood, oak parquet, dark oak	A
CARAT (£1014)	Solid wood frame, laminated front; G	Sisal, beige, light brown	'D'-shape or inset grip: solid wood, dark, light or cognac stain	As above	B
CHIC-G (£793)	Laminate; G	Hessian or natural or dark simulated wood	Knob, 'D'-shape or inset grip: solid wood, dark, natural or cognac stain	As above	C
COLORA (£957)	Laminate; G	Pure white, azure blue, ruby red, reseda green, stratos blue, jasmine	Knob or 'D'-shape grip: white, red, blue, green, jasmine, stratos blue	As above	D
CHALET (£1689)	Solid wood; L	Natural, dark or cognac stain	Natural, dark or cognac stained wooden knob	As above	E
DE LUXE-L (£897)	Laminate; G	Simulated natural oak, sisal, beige, cream	Full-length oak pull: natural, dark or cognac stain	As above	F
DE LUXE-S (£930)	Laminate; G	Hessian, Japanese beige, palma	'D'-shape grip: solid natural, dark or cognac stain; inset grip	As above	G
INTERFORM-S (£1244)	Laminate; G	Pearl white, Nevada, Gobi	As above	As above	H
INTERFORM-SH (£1333)	Oak; G	Natural, dark or cognac stain	As above	As above	G
MULTIFORM-F (£957)	Laminate; G	Simulated natural oak, hessian, pale olive	As above	As above	I
RUSTICA-2 (£1689)	Oak; L	Natural, dark or cognac stain	Oak knob: natural, dark or cognac stain	As above	J
SYLT (£1460)	Solid wood; L	White with pastel blue grooving	White and blue knob	As above	J
LUX COLLECTION					
AMARA (£1733)	Oak or ash; G	Natural or cognac stained oak; smoke blue or magnolia stained ash	'D'-shape grip: metal or wood; knob: oak (natural or cognac stain) or ash (smoke blue or magnolia stain)	As above	D
ARAGON/ ACHAT (£1440)	Laminate (ARAGON) and solid wood (ACHAT); G	White (ARAGON); dark brown stain (ACHAT)	'D'-shape grip: metal, white melamine, dark brown stained wood	As above	K
ASCONA-K (£1561)	Laminate; G	Safari, tweed	Solid wood 'D'-shape grip or knob, light or dark stain	As above	L
BOSCA-G (£1660)	Solid wood frame, veneered doors and drawers; G	Natural or dark stained oak	Oak 'D'-shape or inset grip; natural or dark stain	As above	M

CHART

LEICHT CONT.	PANELS	FINISHES	HANDLES	WORKTOPS	
BOSCA-K (£1332)	Solid wood frame, laminated doors and drawers; G	Sisal, orange, cream	Oak 'D'-shape or inset grip; natural or dark stain	As above	N
BRISTOL (£2344)	Oak; L	Natural, red or dark stain	Antique bronze ring or teardrop	As above	O
CAPRICE (£1995)	Solid wood frame, laminated doors and drawers; G	White with azure blue, mocca brown or white grooving	Two-tone ceramic knob	As above	P
CARONA (£1131)	Laminate; simulated ash or beech edging; G	Off-white	Solid wood knob with white centre	As above	Q
FORESTA-L/ TOSCANA (£1995)	Oak; G	Natural or dark stained wood (FORESTA-L); imprinted slats (TOSCANA)	Solid wood knob	As above	A
LINOVA (£1484)	Laminate; G	Textured: pearl, lava, sea blue	'D'-shape grip: pearl, beige or blue; knob: black or natural wood	As above	R
OPAL (£1131)	Laminate; G	Textured: light silver, lagoon, champagne, pale green	Knob: white, beige, grey or blue; 'D'-shape grip: white, metal	As above	D
OXFORD (£2250)	Oak; L	Dark or cognac stain	Solid wood knob with metal inlay	As above	S
SCALA (£1440)	Laminate with solid beech frame; G	Satin beige, platinum grey, basalt blue, agave green, anemone (white)	Beech 'D'-shape grip or knob	As above	A
TRADITION-2 (£1939)	Oak frame; veneered front; L	Natural, cognac or dark stain	Natural, cognac or dark stained oak knob	As above	P
WINDSOR (£2250)	Oak; L	Cognac stain	Antique bronze ring	As above	T

MFI HYGENA	PANELS	FINISHES	HANDLES	WORKTOPS	
CONTOUR (£280) SA	Laminate	Textured: chestnut weave; matt: cream ash (cream diagonal pattern); misty oak (grey)	Solid wood full-length recessed pull	Laminates: medium oak, light oak, ash, brown marble, grey marble, Tressca, granite	A
SILHOUETTE (£280) SA	Laminate	White	Butterfly grip; teak or ash	As above	B
WOODLAND (£280) SA	Solid pine frame; pine veneer doors	Natural lacquer	Pine knob	As above	C

A B C | A B C D E F G H

MANHATTAN	PANELS	FINISHES	HANDLES	WORKTOPS	
TWO-ONE	Laminate	White	Solid beech full-length pulls	Laminates, round-edged: textured white, white Milano, parchment, ochre, gaiety (grey pattern); square-edged: textured white, chamois, white, Milano, parchment, ochre, planked oak, island weave, reflections (grey pattern), gaiety, vulcan (beige pattern), woolsack, terrazzo	A
TWO-FIVE	Laminate	Scorched weave, bleached leather, chamois, planked oak, pampas (grey check)	Solid light or dark oak or afrormosia full-length pull	As above	A
THREE	Laminate	Chamois, mink, paprika, catkin, planked oak, ermine, camellia, flax, safari	Satin aluminium strip	As above	B

PRICES AND INFORMATION WERE CORRECT AT THE TIME OF GOING TO PRESS

191

KITCHENS

MANHATTAN CONT.	PANELS	FINISHES	HANDLES	WORKTOPS	
THREE-FIVE	Laminate	White with red or blue edging	Metal 'D'-shape grip: white stove-enamelled with red or blue collar	As above	C
FIVE	Laminate; ash edging	Chamois, mink, paprika, catkin, planked oak, ermine, camellia, flax, safari	Solid ash finger grip	As above	D
SIX	Laminate; teak edging	As above	Solid teak finger grip	As above	E
SEVEN-SIX	Laminate; pale oak mouldings; L; reversible	Safari/camellia (beige/red grids) panels with amontillado (dark red) beading, natural oak frame; flax/weave (narrow/broad blue grid) panels with haze blue beading, haze blue stained oak frame	Solid oak finger grip with pewter-coloured spacers	As above	F
EIGHT	Oak veneer with solid oak frame and mouldings; L	Natural oak	As above	As above	G
NINE	Solid oak; L	Oak knob with bronze inset	As above		H

JOHN MEAD	PANELS	FINISHES	HANDLES	WORKTOPS	
SHROPSHIRE	English oak	Clear or coloured lacquer, stained, antiqued	Brass or turned wood knob	Solid wood (1½in/4cm thick), tiles, Formica	A
VICTORIAN	Pine, oak or ash	As above	As above	As above	B
WILTSHIRE	Ash, cherry or pine	As above	As above	As above	C

A   B   C   A   B   C   D

MEISTER	PANELS	FINISHES	HANDLES	WORKTOPS	
CAMEO (£1457)	Laminate; L	White	Knob: sky blue, beige or coffee-coloured	Duracel range	A
COLOR (£1305)	Laminate	Magnolia	Oak full-length pull	As above	B
DRAW FORM (£1401)	Laminate	Jasmine, leaf green, white, magnolia	Oak 'D'-shape grip	As above	C
MELLA FORM (£1161)	Laminate	White, beige	'D'-shape grip: white, yellow, blue, red or brown	As above	D
MAHOGANY (£1409)	Solid mahogany; L	Rich dark stain	Brass knob	As above	A
OAK (£1490)	Solid oak; L	Light natural stain	Wooden knob	As above	A
PINE (£1387)	Solid pine; L	Natural stain	Brass knob	As above	A

A   B   C   D   E   F   G   H   I   J   K   L   M   N   O   P

MIELE	PANELS	FINISHES	HANDLES	WORKTOPS	
PROGRAMME 21	Laminate	Lotus white, Toscana sand, sylt brown, sylt green, sylt beige, pearl white, Sahara beige, lino white, lino blue, lino yellow	Aluminium strip	Laminates: Bali blue, Bali white, Bali brown, Bali green, golf white, golf sand, rustic oak, Kanton brown, Kanton sand, Sardo granite, Shetland granite, stained ash, Inka brown, Alpine white, Merano blue, dark oak	A

MIELE CONT.	PANELS	FINISHES	HANDLES	WORKTOPS	
PROGRAMME 24 (£2504.95)	Solid oak	Light, dark, rustic, black stained oak	Solid wood or metal finger grip	As above	B
PROGRAMME 26 (£2341.40)	Wood veneer, solid wood edges	Rustic and light stained oak, red mahogany, natural stained ash	Metal or wood knob	As above	C
PROGRAMME 27 (£2054.85)	Wood veneer	Red mahogany, wenge, light stained oak	Gold metal knob or solid wood 'D'-shape grip	As above	D
PROGRAMME 28	Laminate; solid oak or stained ash edging	Lotus white, Toscana sand, sylt brown, sylt green, sylt beige, pearl white, Sahara beige, lino white, lino blue, lino yellow	Metal ring pull	As above	E
PROGRAMME 29	Laminate; solid oak edging	As above	Solid oak full-length pull	As above	F
PROGRAMME 30	Laminate	Boston green, Boston blue, linen beige, pearl white, Sahara beige, Bahama white	Metal inset grip	As above	G
PROGRAMME 31	Laminate	As above	Solid wood finger grip	As above	H
PROGRAMME 32 (£1222.55)	Laminate	As above	Solid wood inset grip	As above	I
PROGRAMME 33 (£1222.55)	Laminate	As above	Solid wood 'D'-shape grip	As above	J
PROGRAMME 34 (£1781.40)	Wood veneer	Rustic oak, wenge, stained ash	Solid wood 'D'-shape grip	As above	K
PROGRAMME 35 (£1222.55)	Laminate	Boston green, Boston blue, pearl white, Sahara beige	Metal 'D'-shape grip: red, white, blue or Sahara beige	As above	L
PROGRAMME 36 (£1828.05)	Laminate; solid oak edging	Lotus white	Knob: marbled, plastic or solid wood	As above	M
PROGRAMME 37 (£1828.05)	Laminate; solid red mahogany, wengé or ash edging	Lino white, lino yellow	Solid wood 'D'-shape grip	As above	N
PROGRAMME 38 (£1596.90)	Laminate; solid oak, mahogany or ash edging	Lotus white, Toscana sand, sylt brown, sylt green, sylt beige, pearl white, Sahara beige, lino white, lino blue, lino yellow	Solid wood full-length pull	As above	K
PROGRAMME 39 (£1596.90)	Laminate; solid oak, mahogany or ash edging	As above	Solid wood inset grip	As above	O
PROGRAMME 45 (£1596.90)	Laminate, solid oak edging	Lotus white, simulated light oak	Knob: solid wood or marbled plastic	As above	M
PROGRAMME 46	Wood veneer	Rustic stained natural oak, stained ash, dark oak, mahogany	Knob: wood or metal	As above	P
PROGRAMME 56 (£2705.55)	Lacquered wood	Classic white	Wooden knob	As above	P
PROGRAMME 80 (£1222.55)	Laminate; solid oak edging	Pearl white, lotus white, Boston blue, Boston green, Bahama white, linen beige	Metal 'D'-shape grip: metal self-colour, white, blue, Sahara beige, copper red, cobalt blue, brown, platinum grey, green, lotus white, yellow	As above	L

MOBEN	PANELS	FINISHES	HANDLES	WORKTOPS	
ALBANY	Textured laminate; solid American oak trim	'Albany gold': autumn (gold), Manila (beige); American oak (natural) trim; 'Albany black': straw, harvest; American oak (black) trim	'Albany Gold': wood and metal 'D'- or 'L'-shape grip; 'Albany black': black ceramic knob with white inset	Laminates: Sienna topaz, white saddlecheck, Pacific stone, cool haze, graphic white, beige tweed, warm haze, cloud blue, red granite, fern green, blue saddlecheck, graphic green, polar white, Venetian onyx, cream raindrop, ocean green, ivory, green tweed	A
BRITTANY	Solid oak	Medium brown, ivory limed, natural limed, antique green	Antique-style metal knob	As above	B

KITCHENS

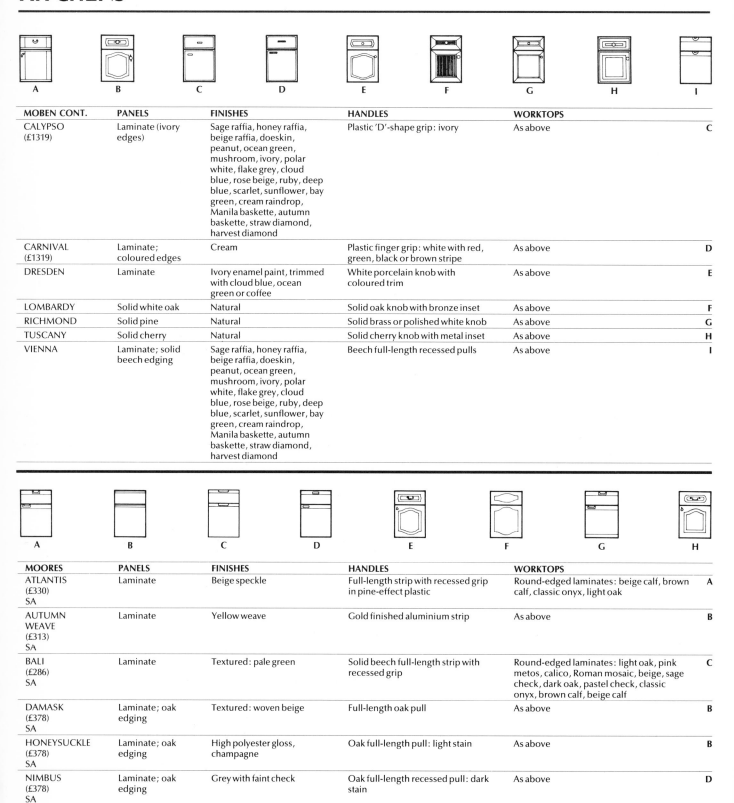

A B C D E F G H I

MOBEN CONT.	PANELS	FINISHES	HANDLES	WORKTOPS	
CALYPSO (£1319)	Laminate (ivory edges)	Sage raffia, honey raffia, beige raffia, doeskin, peanut, ocean green, mushroom, ivory, polar white, flake grey, cloud blue, rose beige, ruby, deep blue, scarlet, sunflower, bay green, cream raindrop, Manila baskette, autumn baskette, straw diamond, harvest diamond	Plastic 'D'-shape grip: ivory	As above	C
CARNIVAL (£1319)	Laminate; coloured edges	Cream	Plastic finger grip: white with red, green, black or brown stripe	As above	D
DRESDEN	Laminate	Ivory enamel paint, trimmed with cloud blue, ocean green or coffee	White porcelain knob with coloured trim	As above	E
LOMBARDY	Solid white oak	Natural	Solid oak knob with bronze inset	As above	F
RICHMOND	Solid pine	Natural	Solid brass or polished white knob	As above	G
TUSCANY	Solid cherry	Natural	Solid cherry knob with metal inset	As above	H
VIENNA	Laminate; solid beech edging	Sage raffia, honey raffia, beige raffia, doeskin, peanut, ocean green, mushroom, ivory, polar white, flake grey, cloud blue, rose beige, ruby, deep blue, scarlet, sunflower, bay green, cream raindrop, Manila baskette, autumn baskette, straw diamond, harvest diamond	Beech full-length recessed pulls	As above	I

A B C D E F G H

MOORES	PANELS	FINISHES	HANDLES	WORKTOPS	
ATLANTIS (£330) SA	Laminate	Beige speckle	Full-length strip with recessed grip in pine-effect plastic	Round-edged laminates: beige calf, brown calf, classic onyx, light oak	A
AUTUMN WEAVE (£313) SA	Laminate	Yellow weave	Gold finished aluminium strip	As above	B
BALI (£286) SA	Laminate	Textured: pale green	Solid beech full-length strip with recessed grip	Round-edged laminates: light oak, pink metos, calico, Roman mosaic, beige, sage check, dark oak, pastel check, classic onyx, brown calf, beige calf	C
DAMASK (£378) SA	Laminate; oak edging	Textured: woven beige	Full-length oak pull	As above	B
HONEYSUCKLE (£378) SA	Laminate; oak edging	High polyester gloss, champagne	Oak full-length pull: light stain	As above	B
NIMBUS (£378) SA	Laminate; oak edging	Grey with faint check	Oak full-length recessed pull: dark stain	As above	D

PRICES AND INFORMATION WERE CORRECT AT THE TIME OF GOING TO PRESS

MOORES CONT.	PANELS	FINISHES	HANDLES	WORKTOPS	
NATURAL OAK (£535) SA	Oak veneer; oak frame	Light oak stain, champagne	Antiqued metal drop or ring	As above	E
SUMMER TEAK (£313) SA	Laminate	Teak effect	Gold-finished aluminium strip	As above	B
TABASCO (£330) SA	Laminate	Tabasco	Full-length recessed pull: pine effect	As above	A
MEDIUM OAK (£519) SA	Oak veneer	Natural oak	Metal ring	As above	F
CAMEO (£286) SA	Laminate	Beige with small dots	Fluted beige strip with recessed grip	As above	G
CHAMPAGNE (£330) SA	Laminate	Champagne	Full-length recessed pull: pine effect	Laminate, round-edged: beige, calf, brown calf, classic onyx, light oak	A
CIRRUS (£378) SA	Laminate; oak edging	Pale pink (small check)	Full-length recessed pull: light oak stain	Laminate, round-edged: light oak, pink metos, calico, Roman mosaic, beige, sage check, dark oak, pastel check, classic onyx, brown calf, beige calf	D
RENAISSANCE (£712) SA	Oak; L	Natural	Brass antique drop	As above	H
PAPYRUS (£286) SA	Laminate	Textured: pale green	Beech full-length recessed pull	As above	C
SAVANNA (£286) SA	Laminate	Pale green, grass effect	Beige plastic full-length recessed pull	As above	G
WILD REED (£313) SA	Laminate	Pale yellow	Gold-finished aluminium strip	Laminate, round-edged: beige calf, brown calf, classic onyx, light oak	B

A B C D E F

OPTIFIT	PANELS	FINISHES	HANDLES	WORKTOPS	
OPTIFIT 100 POLAR WHITE (£459) SA	Laminate; coloured trim in red, blue, brown	Textured: white	Plastic 'D'-shape grip: red, blue, white, brown	Laminate; round edged: polar white, Saxon oak	A
OPTIFIT 200 SAHARA BEIGE (£459) SA	Laminated	Textured: beige	'D'-shape or inset grip: simulated oak	As above	B
OPTIFIT 500 TWEED (£580) SA	Laminate	Textured: beige weave	Oak full-length recessed pull	As above	C
OPTIFIT 600 SIERRA (£868) SA	Laminate; simulated oak trim	Finely textured: beige	'D'-shape grip: simulated oak	As above	D
OPTIFIT 700 NORDIC (£868) SA	Pine	Slatted; natural stain	Pine knob	As above	E
OPTIFIT 800 PROVENCAL (£1025) SA	Oak	Medium oak stain	Metal ring	As above	F

195

KITCHENS

A B C D E F G H I

J K L M N O P Q R

POGGENPOHL	PANELS	FINISHES	HANDLES	WORKTOPS	
CC (£897)	Laminate; S	Blossom white, beige	'D'-shape grip or knob, plastic; white, chrome, gold-yellow, cobalt-blue, burgundy-red, blue-grey, brown, beige; wood: light or dark stained oak, natural ash	Laminates: mini-parquet light-oak, mini-parquet dark oak, dark planked oak, light planked oak, planked ash, blossom white, olive, tobacco brown, blue-grey, sand, Corian beige, white or ivory marble quartz, Baltic brown or grey granite, grey-white, beige; tiled: white, beige, yellow-brown, honeycomb	A
CG (£897)	Laminate	Pearl-white, quartz	Inset aluminium strip	As above	B
CH (£1091)	Laminate; S	Blossom white, quartz, fineline sand	Inset grip in contrasting shade	As above	C
CF (£1091)	Laminate; S	Blossom white, quartz, fineline sand	Shell inset grip: light or dark brown oak; 'D'-shape grip: ash	As above	C
CI (£1144)	Laminate; S	Fineline ivory, fineline platinum grey, fineline sand	Knob or 'D'-shape grip: ash, grey stained oak, cherrywood	As above	D
CM (£1038)	Laminate; S	Blossom white, ivory, platinum grey	Finger grip, knob or 'D'-shape grip: red beech, grey stained oak, ash	As above	E
CR (£1194)	Laminate; oak edging; S	Blossom white, fineline sand	Knob or 'D'-shape grip: natural ash, light oak, dark brown oak	As above	F
FR (£1355)	Oak veneer; solid oak frame; S	Mid-brown, light oak stain	Oak knob	As above	G
FS (£1291)	Veneered or laminate; solid wood edges; S	Jasmine-white, ash veneer, oak veneer	Wooden knob or 'D'-shape grip	As above	H
MF (£1355)	Pine; S	Brushed and lightened pine	Pine knob	As above	I
ML (£1355)	Oak slats; S	Light oak	Oak knob	As above	J
MI (£1355)	Cherrywood; S	Cognac stain	Cherrywood knob	As above	K
MS (£1466)	Solid wood slats; metal side trim; S	Bleached oak, oak, burnt chestnut, mahogany, black oak	Metal 'D'-shape or rectangular finger grip; silver or brown	As above	L
FP (£1466)	Mahogany frame; matching veneer centre panel; S	Natural mahogany	Mahogany or burnished brass knob	As above	N
HR (£1466)	Laminate; oak edging; S	Light oak (textured wood-weave)	Oak knob or 'D'-shape grip	As above	F
KS (£1466)	Cherrywood veneer; S	Natural cherrywood	Cherrywood knob or 'D'-shape grip	As above	H
LP (£1762)	Laminate; S	White silk-matt with blue-grey or gold inlay	Knob: white with blue inlay or gold-plated with white inlay	As above	M
LT (£1575)	Oak; L	White oak with blue-grey inlay	Wooden knob with blue metal inlay	As above	O
MC (£1575)	Oak; L	Natural, light brown, dark brown oak	Wooden or pewter-finished knob	As above	P
MA (£1647)	Oak; L	Mid-brown oak	Antique metal drop with pewter finish	As above	Q
MT (£1466)	Oak; L	Rustic, mid-brown, natural stain	Oak knob with metal inlay	As above	O

POGGENPOHL	PANELS	FINISHES	HANDLES	WORKTOPS	
RP (£1724)	Cherrywood frame; cherrywood veneer front; S	Natural cherrywood	Cherrywood or brass knob	As above	R

QA KITCHENS	PANELS	FINISHES	HANDLES	WORKTOPS	
HYGENA NEW QA (£256) SA	Laminate	Polar white, seasoned teak, Tuscan leather, country mint	Plastic recessed grip	Laminate: Atlanta marble (grey-white), hessian (off-white), stripped oak, lemon damask, teak block, onyx, rustic planked oak	A

Diagrams labelled: A | A | B | C | D | E | F | G | H

RAPINI	PANELS	FINISHES	HANDLES	WORKTOPS	
ARETUSA (£956)	Oak frame; laminated front	Natural oak stain; cream laminate	Oak full-length recessed pull		A
ASTRA (£956)	Laminate	Cream	Oak, natural stain, full-length pull		B
ESPERIA (£1151)	Oak	Natural stain	As above		A
FEMINA (£1095)	Solid wood frame; glass front	White frame; chequered glass front	Grey wooden knob		C
GALA (£748)	Laminate; wood beading	Stripe-textured grey, white, silver; beading: red, yellow, pale blue, black, or white	Lacquered wooden finger grip in same colours as beading		D
IGEA (£1250)	Oak	Natural	Oak knob		E
NUVOLA (£956)	Laminate	White, pale green speckled, grey speckled	Plastic 'D'-shape grip		F
PERLA (£748)	Laminate	White	'D'-shape grip; red, blue-grey, yellow, light oak		G
SILA (£1095)	Chestnut frame and drawer front; veneered chestnut door front	Natural stain	Semi-circular recessed grip		H
SOLANGE (£1151)	Laminate	Vertical grey stripe	Wooden knob: grey with white inset		C

Diagrams labelled: A | B | C | D | E | F | G | H | I | J | K

SCHIFFINI	PANELS	FINISHES	HANDLES	WORKTOPS	
ARNIA (£2511)	Laminate and birch wood	Black, pink, white, blue	Full-length recessed pull	White Carrara marble, square or round edge; black or pink African granite, square edge; real copper or aluminium embossed laminate or any other laminate to order; aluminium trim to take any tiles; any solid wood to order	A
COMBI-LUX (£2171)	Solid wood	Lacquered white, green, blue, yellow	White, mocha knob	As above	B
COMBI-MAX (£1385)	Laminate	White	Black, green, half-moon knob	As above	C
COMBI-WOOD	Oak	Natural	Full-length recessed pull	As above	D

PRICES AND INFORMATION WERE CORRECT AT THE TIME OF GOING TO PRESS

KITCHENS

SCHIFFINI CONT.	PANELS	FINISHES	HANDLES	WORKTOPS	
COMBI-TEX (£1927)	Laminate and birch wood	'Pantotex' blue, white	Birch finger grip	As above	E
DAMA (£2989)	Wood and chequered smoked glass	Wood frame in varnished white or natural stain	Double inset finger grip	As above	F
GIARA (£1634)	Laminate or birch wood	White laminate; natural varnished birch; coloured edges to match handles	Birch finger grip: blue, black, red, yellow or varnished	As above	G
KROMOS (£2062)	Laminate and birch wood	'Pantotex' brown, black, white, grey	Natural stain birch knob	As above	H
PERSIANA (£2251)	Oak, louvered; G	White, natural or medium stain	Full-length recessed pull	As above	I
PRIMA (£3068)	Oak, smooth or louvered	Medium stain	Oak knob	As above	J
TIMO (£2253)	White ash	White; coloured edging: yellow, green, red, black	Yellow, green, red, black birch recessed pull	Round-edged laminate: yellow, green, red, navy blue	K

A   B   C   D   E

SCHREIBER	PANELS	FINISHES	HANDLES	WORKTOPS	
CHESTER	Oak	Natural or medium stain	Oak knob	Oak-edged laminate: Venetian marble; round-edged laminate: white, terrazzo, block teak look, medium oak look, light oak look, Verona Travertine, Venetian marble look; textured: Travertine, cherrystone, sandstone	A
EUROPA	Veneered teak or laminate	'Rich teak look' or textured vellum	Aluminium strip	As above	B
FESTIVAL	Laminate	Spring almond	Wood knob	As above	C
LONDONER	Laminate	Spring almond	Metal strip	As above	B
NEW YORKER	Laminate; oak edging	Beige	Oak-look 'D'-shape grip	As above	D
RUSTIQUE	Laminate; medium-stain oak surround	Spring almond	Oak knob, medium stain	As above	E
SCANDINAVIA	Oak veneer	Light stain	Wood knob	As above	E
TOWN & COUNTRY	Wood	Teak look stain	Wood knob	As above	E
THE WHITE KITCHEN	Laminate	White	Oak 'D'-shape grip	As above	D

A   B   C   D   E   F   G   H   I   J   K   L   M

SIEMATIC	PANELS	FINISHES	HANDLES	WORKTOPS	
1001 AL (£2938)	Wood; L	Hand-dragged; off-white with Delft blue or sepia brown frieze	Porcelain knob	Laminates: white, light oak, Travertine (brown speckled), granite, light beech, light pine, dark oak, medium oak; textured: white, beige, brown grey; white Corian marble; granite in black and white, white and brown, black and brown; solid wood: oak, wenge	A
1001 BE (£2703)	Oak	Dark oak	Antique bronze drop	As above	A
1001 NE (£2703)	Oak; L	Light, medium brown oak varnish	Wood or burnished metal knob	As above	A

SIEMATIC CONT.	PANELS	FINISHES	HANDLES	WORKTOPS	
1001 OP (£2703)	Pine	Weathered effect	Brass knob	As above	B
2002 V (£1107)	Laminate	Textured: grey, white, sand	White semicircular knob	As above	C
3003 GL (£2155)	Oak frame; oak veneer fronts	White, light oak stain, medium brown oak stain	Wood or metal knob	As above	D
3003 SK (£1910)	Pine	Mellow pine stain	Wooden knob	As above	A
3003 SE (£1910)	Oak	Light, medium brown oak stain	Wood or metal knob	As above	A
4004 EH (£1107)	Laminate	Textured: white, reed, sand, beige, sepia	Oak 'D'-shape grip or inset grip in light, dark or medium brown stain	As above	E
4004 EL (£1107)	Laminate; vertical oak edging	As above	As above	As above	F
4004 GR (£1107)	Laminate	Textured: white, reed, sand, beige, sepia, simulated light oak	Wooden 'D'-shape grip: light or dark oak stain, white	As above	G
4004 K (£1322)	Laminate	Textured: white, reed, sand, beige, sepia, light oak laminate	Oak full-length recessed pull, medium stain	As above	H
4004 KL (£1614)	Laminate; vertical oak edging	Grey, sand; grey, light, brown or dark oak	Oak 'D'-shape grip or knob	As above	G
4004 KR (£1522)	Laminate; oak trim	Sand	Oak full-length recessed pull, medium or light stain	As above	H
6006 (£1424)	Laminate	High gloss; grey, yellow	Aluminium strip	As above	I
7007 L (£1752)	Laminate with oak veneer	Light stain	Oak 'D'-shape or inset grip	As above	F
7007 MK (£1752)	Pine frame; veneered front	Knotty natural stain	Pine knob	As above	J
7007 RK (£1752)	Oak frame; laminate front	Grey, sand, white	Wooden 'D'-shape grip: light or dark oak stain, grey	As above	K
8008 RA (£3293)	Oak frame; rattan panels	Rattan in white or brown	Wooden knob with inlaid ceramic centre	As above	L
9009 PR (£2923)	Laminate	High gloss polyester: white, grey, sand	Metal knob	As above	M

SOLENT	PANELS	FINISHES	HANDLES	WORKTOPS	
BRETON (£605) SA	Solid oak frame; laminate front; L	Sage	Solid oak 'D'-shape grip	Laminate, round-edged: rustic planked oak, classic onyx; mahogany edge: nutmeg; oak edge: terrazzo, mosaic	A
CHATEAU (£901) SA	Oak; L	Mediun stain	Oak knob	As above	B
PANACHE (£492) SA	Laminate	Tarragon	Solid oak full-length recessed pull	As above	C
VERSAILLES (£546) SA	Mahogany frame; laminate front	Nutmeg	Mahogany knob	As above	D
OLD ENGLISH (£915) SA	Panelled pine; S	Natural stain	Pine knob	Laminate, moulded pine edge: mosaic (predominantly blue), terrazzo, stella gold-brown	E
COUNTRY DIARY (£1162)	Solid pine; S	Stripped pine	Brass knob on door; brass shell grip on drawer	Laminate, moulded pine edge: forest green, onyx	F

A B C D E F   A B C D E F G H

STONEHAM SEE FOLLOWING PAGE

KITCHENS

STONEHAM	PANELS	FINISHES	HANDLES	WORKTOPS	
CAMARGUE (£1534)	Solid oak frame; oak veneer front; L	Light or rustic oak stain	Solid oak knob	Laminate, square-edged, round-edged or oak-edged: fawn tweed, village oak, rawhide, palomino, light oak, diced oak, olive, white onyx, blue mosaic, ice ligna	A
CONTURA (£1067)	Laminate; L	Sable pampas, olive pampas	Solid oak full-length recessed pull: light or rustic stain	As above	B
FLAIR (£1067)	Laminate; L	As above	Solid oak full-length trim with oak 'D'-shape grip: light or rustic stain	As above	C
FINO (£1050)	Laminate; L	Textured: coffee crystal, cream crystal, Havana crystal, polar crystal	Solid oak full-length recessed pull: light or rustic stain	As above	D
LINEA (£1016)	Laminate; L	Textured: coffee crystal, cream crystal, Havana crystal, polar crystal	Aluminium strip	As above	E
NATURA (£1534)	Solid oak frame, laminated front; L	Textured: pencil cane, woven grass	Solid oak knob: light or rustic stain	As above	A
OPTICOLOR (£935)	Laminate; L	Textured: Arctic crystal	'D'-shape grip, plastic: white, red, green, Delft; oak: light or rustic stain	As above	F
PROVENCE (£1723)	Solid oak; L	Rustic stain	Antique brass finish drop	As above	G
STRATA (£1309)	Laminate; L	Textured: Sierra weave	Solid oak full-length recessed pull: light or rustic stain	As above	E
STUDIO (£1380)	Laminate; L	Textured: beige Samos, ice ligna	Solid oak inset grip: light or rustic stain	As above	H

A B C D E F G H I J K L M N

TIELSA	PANELS	FINISHES	HANDLES	WORKTOPS	
AERA	Laminate; oak veneered front	Natural oak, wenge, white, sand, grey, aquamarine, turquoise	Knob: natural oak, white, wenge, nickel	Round-edged laminate: white, blue, white/grey, beige, grey/white, beige/white, brown, green, travertia, granite, wenge, beech, natural oak, country oak; tiled; solid wood	A
ALPINA	Laminate; oak veneered fronts	Natural, limed, green, grey, black, blue, turquoise	Knob: green, white, light, medium, dark oak stain	As above	B
ALTERNA	Laminate	Textured: white, beige, ash	Wood inset grip: natural, wenge, anthracite, bordeaux	As above	C
ARIANE	Laminate	Textured: sapphire	Wood inset grip: natural, wenge	As above	D
AROSA	Laminate: oak front	Natural, medium, dark stain	Wooden knob: natural, medium, dark stain	As above	E
ASCONA	Laminate: wood front	White, ivory, grey, turquoise lacquer	Knob: white, beige lacquered wood	As above	F
BIANCA	Laminate: solid wood front	Diagonally lacquered: white, sand, grey, aquamarine, bordeaux, anthracite	Knob: white, nickel	As above	A
CARRARA	Oak frame; laminate front	Textured: hessian; white, natural oak, sand, wenge, grey	Knob: natural oak, wenge, nickel; 'D'-shape grip: natural oak, wenge, nickel	As above	G
COMO	Laminate; oak front	Natural, medium, dark oak stain	Knob: natural, medium, dark oak stain	As above	F
DAVOS	Laminate; oak front	As above	As above	As above	F
FIESTA	Laminate	Textured: beige	Inset grip: medium oak stain	As above	H

PRICES AND INFORMATION WERE CORRECT AT THE TIME OF GOING TO PRESS

TIELSA CONT.	PANELS	FINISHES	HANDLES	WORKTOPS	
FORMA	Laminate	White/blue, Bermuda beige	Knob: white, medium, light stain wood; inset grip: light, medium stain wood; finger grip: white, grey, bordeaux, brown, blue plastic; 'D'-shape grip: light, medium stain wood, silver-finish metal, white plastic	As above	I
FUTURA	Laminate	Textured: beige	Solid oak full-length recessed pull	As above	J
GOURMET	Laminate	White with blue, red, grey, brass inset	White porcelain knob	As above	K
LUGANO	Laminate: oak veneer front	Lacquered: white, ivory, grey, turquoise	Knob: white, beige	As above	E
MERAN	Laminate: oak veneer front	Lacquered: white, ivory, turquoise, grey	White, beige knob	As above	F
NOVA	Laminate	White, beige, ash	Knob: white, medium, light stain wood; inset grip: light, medium stain wood; finger grip: white, grey, brown, bordeaux, blue plastic; 'D'-shape grip: light, medium stain wood, silver-finish metal, white plastic	As above	I
POLO	Laminate	White, blue sand with white vertical profile	White porcelain knob	As above	L
RAVENNA	Laminate; oak veneer front	Hand finished: natural oak, wenge, grey, white, ivory, aquamarine, turquoise; textured: hessian	Round wooden knob: white, beige, wenge, natural	As above	M
SILVANA	Laminate: oak veneer front	Natural oak, wenge, white, sand, grey, aquamarine, turquoise	Knob: white, light, medium stain oak; nickel; inset grip: natural, wenge, bordeaux, anthracite; 'D'-shape grip: nickel, light or medium stain oak	As above	N
TESSIN	Laminate; wood veneer front	Lacquered: natural, limed, green, black, grey, blue, turquoise; white, brown, blue, red brass insets.	Knob: green, white, light, medium oak stain	As above	B

UBM	PANELS	FINISHES	HANDLES	WORKTOPS	
LORRAINE (£846) SA	Laminate frame; oak or mahogany front; L	Rustic oak, natural mahogany	Knob, with matching finish	Laminate, textured: planked oak, natural oak, dark English tile with real oak edge; smooth: classic onyx, Sienna vellum, classic onyx with real oak edge	A
VISCOUNT HARMONY (£457) SA	Laminate	Fawn, tawny reed, holly green	'D'-shape grip: simulated wood	As above	B
VISCOUNT 80 (£457) SA	Laminate	White, oak	Aluminium strip	As above	C
PARIS (£655) SA	Laminate	Textured: red leather, blue weave, green weave	Oak inset grip	As above	D

A   B   C   D   A   B   C   D   E   F   G   H

WINCHMORE	PANELS	FINISHES	HANDLES	WORKTOPS	
BARTON (£1328) SA	Oak; L	Nut brown stain, natural stain	Concealed groove	Laminate, round front and back edge (curveform): oak butcher block, russet leather, brown leather, planked maple, designers teak, planked west hickory, Winchester walnut, latigo leather, praline, natural rosewood, tangerine, doeskin, regimental red, solid frosty white, blue Atlantis, Java; wood-edged with laminate or Winchmore ceramic tile surface	A

WINCHMORE CONT.	PANELS	FINISHES	HANDLES	WORKTOPS	
CAVENDISH (£1540) SA	Laminate	White with blue or green inset panelling strips	White porcelain knob	As above	B
CLARE (£1540) SA	Laminate	White with sea grey, green or blue inset panelling strips	White porcelain knob	As above	A
DALHAM (£1260) SA	Maple	Natural or mahogany stain	Concealed groove	As above	C
LAVENHAM (£1052) L	Maple frame; laminated front;	Natural stain frame; red, white, blue or patterned (red, blue, green, yellow squares on white background) interchangeable panels	Concealed groove	As above	D
OAKLEY (£876) SA	Oak frame; laminated front	Natural stain oak; textured beige fronts	Oak, natural stain, inset grip	As above	E
RISBY (£1328) SA	Oak	Natural or nut brown stain	Concealed groove	As above	F
SAXHAM (£1328) SA	Oak	Natural or nut brown stain	Concealed groove	As above	G
SHELLEY (£812) SA	Maple frame; laminated front	White fronts; natural stain maple frame	Maple, natural stain, inset grips	As above	H

A   B   C   D   E   F   G   H   I   J   K

WRIGHTON	PANELS	FINISHES	HANDLES	WORKTOPS	
ACCENT (£1096)	Laminate	Pearl: white, stone	Diagonal or horizontal 'D'-shape grip: red, white, brown plastic; light, medium or dark oak	Laminates, round, square or wood edge: white, stone, white fleck, stone fleck, brown plaid, granite, white marble, Victorian marble, light oak woodgrain, medium oak woodgrain, dark oak woodgrain; tiled, wood edge	A
CHROMA	Laminate	High gloss polyester: Tuscan pink, dove grey, Paris blue, white, jet black	Rounded white acrylic	As above	B
DELFT (£1873)	Wood frame; laminated front	White painted wood; white, blue fronts	White porcelain knob	As above	C
ENSIGN (£1342)	Laminate	High gloss polyester: white, stone, Pompeian red, bitter chocolate, jet black	Wooden 'D'-shape grip or knob: light or dark oak	As above	D
ENSIGN DF (£1096)	Laminate	Textured: dark rattan, light rattan, denim beige	As above	As above	D
HERALD (£1244)	Laminate	High gloss polyester: white, stone, Pompeian red, bitter chocolate, jet black, Westminster grey, dove grey	Light, medium or dark oak full-length recessed pull	As above	E
HERALD DF (£1096)	Laminate	Textured: light rattan, dark rattan, denim beige	As above	As above	E
PAGEANT (£1244)	Laminate	High gloss polyester: white, stone, Pompeian red, bitter chocolate, Paris blue, jet black	Aluminium strip	As above	E

PRICES AND INFORMATION WERE CORRECT AT THE TIME OF GOING TO PRESS

CHART

WRIGHTON CONT.	PANELS	FINISHES	HANDLES	WORKTOPS	
PUGIN (£2154)	Oak	Light or dark oak stain	Brass inset ring or wooden knob	As above	F
ROSSETTI (£2154)	Oak	Dark oak stain	Wooden knob with brass inset	As above	G
TANA (£1244)	Laminate	Textured: blue/grey, beige	Light, medium or dark oak inset grip	As above	H
VOYSEY (£1659)	Laminate	High gloss polyester: white, stone, bitter chocolate, Pompeian red, jet black	Light, medium or dark oak knob	As above	I
VOYSEY DF (£1538)	Laminate	Textured: white, stone	Light or dark oak or mahogany knob	As above	I
VOYSEY FP (£1873)	Solid wood	Light or dark oak; mahogany	As above	As above	J
WALPOLE (£2154)	Oak	Medium oak	Bronze ring	As above	K

 A B C D E F G H I J K L M N

XEY	PANELS	FINISHES	HANDLES	WORKTOPS	
ARMAGNAC	Solid wood	Medium oak stain	Bronze antique drops on drawer; escutcheon and key on door	Laminates: white golfball, cream, leather matt marble, pearl grey golfball, green golfball, green (textured), light oak, medium oak, medium lath, light parquet, medium parquet, dark parquet, red granite, brown granite	A
BENNY	Laminate	White, horizontally reeded	Two-tone porcelain knob	As above	B
COLUMBIA 3	Oak frame; L	Textured: white, beige jute, beige korfu	Wooden 'D'-shape grip: medium or light oak stain	As above	C
COLUMBIA 4	Oak frame; veneered front; L	Light oak stain	Wooden 'D'-shape grip: light oak stain	As above	C
COLUMBIA 5	Oak frame; L	Textured: white, beige korfu, beige jute	Wooden knob: medium, light, dark oak stain	As above	D
DELTA	Laminate	Textured: cream, light oak, white, bamboo beige, rattan beige	Wooden inset grip: medium, light oak stain	As above	E
DERBY	Laminate	Textured: light linen, white, hay, moss green, brown linen	Wooden inset or 'D'-shape grip: medium or light oak stain	As above	F
FORMA	Laminate	Textured: brown linen, hay, moss green, light linen, white	Wooden inset or 'D'-shape grip: light or medium oak stain	As above	F
FINLAND	Oak frame	Oak veneer, reeded medium, light oak stain	Wooden 'D'-shape grip in medium oak or light oak stain	As above	G
JAVA	Oak frame; oak veneer	Reded veneer with light or medium oak stain	Wooden two-tone knob or finger grip	As above	H
LANGUEDOC	Oak frame; oak veneer	Medium or light stain	Wooden knob; brass handle	As above	I
LOUIS XIII	Oak; L	Medium stain	Cast iron drops on drawer; cast iron escutcheon and key on door	As above	J
ORLEANS	Oak; L	Medium oak stain	As above	As above	K
SAMBA	Laminate	White	'D'-shape grip: white, pearl grey, green	As above	L
VERSAILLES	Oak frame; veneer; L	Medium, light oak stain	Wooden knob or brass drops and key and escutcheon	As above	M
VIENA	Laminate	Textured: rattan beige, white, cream, bamboo beige	Oak full-length recessed pull: light or medium stain	As above	N

LIGHTING

INTRODUCTION

Whatever the furnishings, it is lighting that finally brings a room to life, so make lighting a prime consideration when decorating.

Start by making a sketch of the room, showing windows and doors, fireplace and other structural features, and the existing electrical points. Add the main pieces of furniture and mark the positions of specific objects, pictures or displays, that deserve highlighting. List special activities such as sewing or model-making. This plan should help you decide how much light you need (depending of course on the quality of the natural light and on your colour scheme) and where the fittings should go. Sketch additional electrical points where necessary. Finally, consult a qualified electrician who will advise you and also install new points (not a do-it-yourself job).

Obviously, special rooms have special needs. Kitchens need two levels of lighting: overall ceiling illumination and specific lights for work surfaces. Spotlights can be used for sink and stove illumination; wall mounted, or fixed on track systems, they're useful in any working room.

In the dining room, an attractive rise-and-fall pendant over the table, for example, can create a soft atmospheric light; and well placed wall lights are important over a serving table or sideboard. Bedrooms need overall lighting (with dimmer control as a luxury) and bedside lights, at eye level or higher, for reading in bed. Plastic or glass units that won't be affected by steam are best for the bathroom; enclosed fittings flush with the ceiling would be a good choice. Pull-cord switches are essential for safety, unless wall switches are outside; a low voltage razor point is the only exception.

Living room lighting depends on your lifestyle — and the impression you want to create. Downlighters, round or square metal canisters recessed or semi-recessed into the ceiling or ceiling-mounted, cast pools of light. Uplighters, their reverse, are equally dramatic, either freestanding or wall-mounted. Standard and table lamps are more conventional but no less effective. (But remember, trailing wires can be very dangerous — another reason for planning power points with an electrician).

Other possibilities, particularly useful for passages and halls, are surface fittings mounted directly on to walls and ceilings.

Recent technological developments have opened up new dimensions in lighting but have also created a bemusing world of jargon for the amateur. There is the trendy terminology of the sales assistant by which a light bulb becomes a 'lamp', a lamp becomes a 'light source' or 'luminaire'. And beyond that lies a plethora of different bulbs, each designed for a specific type of application.

The main distinguishing features of bulbs are whether they are mains or low voltage, tungsten or tungsten halogen, and whether they have a built-in reflector or require an independent one. (The standard 'GLS' bulbs are tungsten, mains voltage and need independent reflectors.)

Low voltage bulbs are energy-saving and have smaller filaments than standard bulbs so that the size of fittings can be reduced, although they can produce the same light. A transformer is necessary to reduce the voltage from the mains (240V) to that required by the fitting (usually 12V). This may either be built into the fitting or supplied separately, in which case it will probably be costed separately (so make sure you inquire in the shop). A dichroic bulb is one type of low voltage bulb.

Tungsten halogen (often simply halogen) bulbs are often, though not always, low voltage. Their advantage is that they give off a high brightness, white light that gives a truer colour rendering than the standard bulb.

Built-in reflectors can make it possible to accurately control the width of the beam emitted from the bulb, so are used to create narrow-spot, wide-spot, narrow-flood or wide-flood beams. Most are used for accent and task lighting rather than for general, diffused lighting. PAR-lamps are typical of these. The choice of fittings and bulbs grows increasingly complex but one thing remains constant: all lights are not all things to all rooms. If you know what you want your lighting to do, whether to flood a work area, highlight an object, create an atmosphere or simply fill a room with light, you immediately limit your choice considerably and are well on the way to solving your lighting problems. Measurements include shades, unless otherwise stated, and refer to the maximum dimension (the base of a shade, for example).

● Depth (d) is the projection from the wall.
● Recommended wattage (W) is given.

ANGLEPOISE LIGHTING LTD

Classic task lighting with a new dimension. '82' desk lighting will remain a favourite in offices and homes. Available in black or white with screw-down or freestanding table base, clamp, bracket for wall or drawing board, or freestanding, adjustable, trolley base. *M:* reach 106cm (41¼in); 100W. *P:* £40–£90. But the relatively new compact fluorescent bulbs from Philips and Thorn have given rise to sleek new-look Anglepoises.

'4.33PL' desk light with slim oblong head and reflector in aluminium is designed to complement the slimness of Philips PL single-ended fluorescent bulb. Available with clamp or table base in matt black satin aluminium or matt silver finish. The new bulb, the PL18, has the same light output as a 75W tungsten bulb but with an energy saving of up to 75 per cent and 5,000 (as compared with 1,000) hours life. A fluorescent bulb requires a 'choke' or 'control' box. In this case the choke is built into a special plug, designed by Anglepoise, which fits the

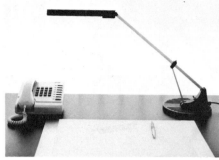

Anglepoise's '4.33PL' desk light with fluorescent bulb

standard three-pin socket. *M:* reach 77cm (30¼in); 11W. *P:* £65.12.

The T–range — '82T03', '82T', '433T', '82T10' — and the '3.33' — take the equally energy-efficient 2D bulb by Thorn. (2D is a flatter, square-shaped bulb consisting of a continuous fluorescent tube bent into a compact format with built-in choke.) '3.33' was the first to have the new-styled, finely lined polycarbonate shade in red, cadmium, yellow, bright green, matt black or white, with a special reflector that sits neatly over the bulb. Also available in clamp, wall-bracket, screw-down, floorstanding and drawing-board versions. *M:* reach 49cm (19¼in); 60W. *P:* £21.89.

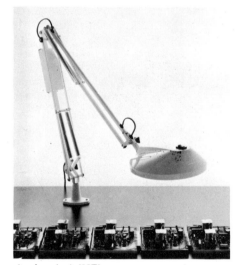

Anglepoise's '82T'

ARCHITECTURAL TRADING COMPANY

Oluce lights from Milan, demonstrating that Italian flair for distinctive but classic forms. Curves predominate; some fittings consist simply of a curve of chrome-plated metal along and around which the bulb and reflector can be moved. 'Coupé' lamps — desk, wall and floor-standing — make an almost complete arch from which the drum or hemisphere shades are suspended. Shades are aluminium, lacquered black or white. *M:* '3320' (floor-standing) h220 × reach 110cm (86½ × 43¼in); 150W. *P:* £338. 'Dogale' has round cast iron base and arching stem bearing opal or green Murano glass diffuser; the arch is tall in the floor-standing version, flattened in the desk lamp. *M:* '512' (desk) h45 × reach 65cm (17¾ × 25½in); '631' (floor-standing) h130 × reach 90cm (51¼ × 35½in); 50W. *P:* '512' £199–£205; '631' £229–£234. In the 'Slalom' lamp the stem is straight but moves within a 180-degree arc. Available in floor-standing or wall-hung, halogen or night-reading models, it has stem and three-sided right-angled base in black, with barrel-shaped bulb housing in black, white, yellow or red lacquered aluminium. *M:* stem l50cm (19¾in); 25W or 20W halogen. *P:* £34; halogen £60.

But not all Oluce lights use curves. 'Pascal 340' floor-standing uplighter consists of two cones, one set just above the other. Two bulbs throw light in the lower cone on to the white enamelled surface of the upper cone where one more powerful bulb throws light up to the ceiling. *M:* h200cm (78⅛in), base dia 40cm (15¾in); 2 × 100W and 1 × 150W. *P:* £199. 'Pascal 430' pendant has the cones inverted so that

Below: Architectural Trading Company. Left to right, from top: 'Atollo 233', 'Dogale 512', 'Coupé 3320', 'Pascal 340', 'Slalom 299', 'Pascal 430'

light shines downwards. *M:* max dia 42cm (16½in); 2 × 40W and 1 × 100W. *P:* £99. 'Atollo 233' is a superbly simple table lamp: the cylinder base tapers into a cone and is topped by a hemisphere shade, all in lacquered aluminium. Colours are white, brilliant black, sand and rust. *M:* h70 × dia 50cm (27½ × 19¾in); 2 × 100W. *P:* £175, £199 with dimmer.

ARGON

Neon brought down to earth, from the commercial hoardings to the home. Dazzling shapes or pictures can be individually mounted on a perspex board, mounted on a

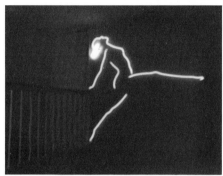

Above: Argon's neon 'Pink Lady'

wall or set in a perspex control box. Standard designs include POP IN range — freestanding 'Cocktail Glass', 'Ruby Lips', 'Palm Tree', 'Light Bulb', 'Blue Cat' and 'Blue Bird' — and TOUCAN — one or two giant toucans encased in perspex. *P:* POP IN from £95; TOUCAN from £398. The team of neon artists at Argon will work to commission, adapting into neon form designs ranging from logos to cartoon characters.

LAURA ASHLEY LTD

Glazed ceramic lamp bases, large and small. Simple, rounded 'Large' base comes in white or cream; similar 'Bedside' and 'Small' bases in white, cream, rose, terracotta, apricot, burgundy and sapphire. More elaborate but classic 'Octagonal' base comes in white only. *M:* 'Large' h28cm (11in); 'Small' h20cm (8in); 'Bedside' h18cm (7in); 'Octagonal' h32cm (10½in). *P:* 'Large' £11.95; 'Small' £8.95; 'Bedside' £5.95; 'Octagonal' £19.95.

Sold separately are conical, pleated and drum shades, available with either pendant or base carriers. Drum shades, which complement the 'Octagonal' base, are laminated cotton, some with contrasting binding, in five colourways: rose and candy, sapphire, burgundy, apricot and apricot wash, or with wickerwork design in white and sand. Conical shades, in three sizes, come in all these colours and also plain white, terracotta, rose-and-white candy stripe, and patterned with eleven of Laura Ashley's COUNTRY FURNISHINGS fabrics (see *Fabrics, Co-ordinates*). Pleated lampshades, available in all the same colourways, are supplied with a threaded ribbon for width adjustment. *M:* drum h35cm (13¾in); conical h23, 18 or 16cm (9, 7 or 6¼in); pleated h24cm (9½in). *P:* drum £9.95; conical £5.95–£6.95; pleated £9.95.

Laura Ashley's 'Large' base and pleated shade

LIGHTING

RALPH BALL

Minimal AERO LIGHT. Kite-like reflectors — anodized aluminium blades reflecting light from concealed halogen bulbs — seem to float on fine wires strung between floor and ceiling. Reflector blades are available in blue and silver, and two or more can be positioned anywhere on the support wire and angled in any direction. The wires carry safe low-voltage current from a transformer at the base of the unit. Ralph Ball will make up the lights to the required ceiling height. *M:* transformer base w.8.5 × d8.5 × h12.5cm (3¼ × 3¼ × 5in); reflector blades 15 × 15cm (6 × 6in); transformer capacity 100W (one 100W or two 50W halogen bulbs). *P:* standard unit (transformer, two reflector blades and two 50W bulbs) £164.90; additional reflector blades £16 each.

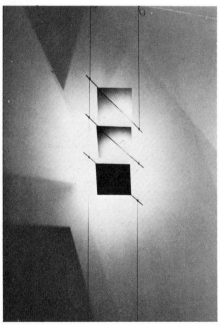

Ralph Ball's AERO LIGHT

BEST & LLOYD LTD

Brass light fittings, both traditional and modern, from contract lighting specialists. This long-established company still produces traditional candlestick wall sconces after Adam and Hepplewhite, and Victorian pendants, but is continually expanding the modern side of the collection, which includes floor-standing and table lamps, downlighters, flexible-arm wall bracket fittings, efficient task lighting, picture lights and some dramatically different new uplighters and swivel-head wall fittings. (Only picture lights are widely available retail.)
Practical if not ornamental, their new, sturdy, adjustable height 'Uplighter' incorporates the energy-saving SonDL bulb, one of the most efficient bulbs available — economical for

Best & Lloyd's 'Floor Lamp 43456'

offices and other areas where lights are invariably left on! *M:* h173–210cm (66–83¼in), base dia 45.5cm (18in). *P:* on application. '44012' series of semi-hemisphere wall bracket lights has been cunningly designed to take three different bulbs: Philips' PL9 low-energy bulb; tungsten halogen K13 bulb, which produces a very strong light excellent for bouncing off pale surfaces; and standard GLS bulb. *M:* '44012-4' dia 22 × d11cm (8¾ × 4¼in); '44015-6' dia 36 × d18cm (14¼ × 7in). *P:* on application. '43455' wall bracket fitting in solid brass can be used as reading or picture light. The squared-off reflector is pivot-jointed on to the arm of the lamp so that it can be swivelled through 80 degrees to direct light accurately. The same reflector on pivot joint is available as floor-standing light '43456', with brass stem and weighted base. *M:* '43455' total d49cm (19¼in), reflector w17.5 × l17.5cm (7 × 7in); '43456' h114cm (45in). *P:* on application.

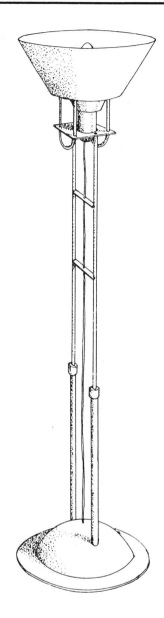

Best & Lloyd's 'Uplighter'

BIEFFEPLAST

Space age lighting, Bieffeplast's collection of hanging, floor, wall and table lights is characterized by pure geometrical shapes supported on slim, elegant structures, almost all in black or white. But the lights are also efficient and substantially built, suitable for domestic and office use.
'Semisfera' is a perfectly simple hanging light, a white hemisphere suspended on black, curly flex from a white, cylindrical ceiling attachment. *M:* dia 40 or 60cm (15¾ or 23½in). *P:* on application. 'Bipolo' reminds one of a flying

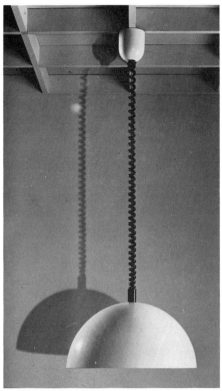

Bieffeplast's 'Semisfera'

saucer: two bulbs are housed in two small hemispherical extrusions, one on the top, one on the bottom of a flat central disc, and the whole structure hangs from an adjustable aluminium rod. Ingeniously, light is thrown both upwards and downwards. *M:* h70–170cm (27–67in); 'saucer' dia 35cm (13¾in); 100W. *P:* on application.

Equally futuristic is the design of 'Cuffia' table and floor-standing lamps. The small hemisphere housing the bulb faces into, and is partially covered by, a much larger hemisphere which acts as a reflector, reversing the direction of the light. The two hemispheres, both anodized aluminium, are mounted on a thick anodized stem with round base. *M:* table lamp h70cm (27½in); floor lamp h140cm (55in); both base dia 40cm (15¾in). *P:* on application. Aptly named 'Ciclope' has the bulb housed behind a transparent panel in a disc of anodized aluminium. This 'eye' is suspended midair: one thread attaches it to the ceiling but two more threads stretch up from the floor to prevent it swinging round. A curly black cable running up from the rounded base and transformer unit on the floor, carries the current. *M:* h400cm (157in), dia of suspended 'eye' 25cm (9¾in). *P:* on application.

PRICES AND INFORMATION WERE CORRECT AT THE TIME OF GOING TO PRESS

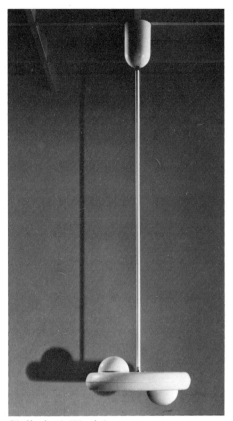

Bieffeplast's 'Bipolo'

BRILLANTLEUCHTEN

Brilliantly simple lighting distinguished by its colour, performance and price. Clip-on, ceiling-mounted, clamp, track, grouped or table-based spotlights dominate the collection. CLICK universal-jointed wall or clamp-on spotlight is the ultimate in cheeky simplicity, made of moulded plastic and metal in red, yellow, blue, white, brown or black. *M:* dia 9.4cm (37in); 40W. *P:* £12.25–£15.15. WASA combines, unusually, metal with wood: red or brown metal cowls are set into plain pine stems and attached by metal brackets to pine bases. *M:* dia 11cm (4¼in); 60W. *P:* from £13.95 (single spot) to £45.30 (three-spot pendant). Other spotlight ranges include halogen HIGHLIGHT; simple ROBUST; CLIP-SPOT and FESTIVAL, both colourful in red, yellow, blue, white or brown; and IDEAL lights with crimson, white, brown or beige cowls, some edged with contrasting triple stripe. ROBUST, HIGHLIGHT and WASA include floor-standing versions, IDEAL and FESTIVAL both floor-standing and table task lights. *M:* HIGHLIGHT w24cm (9½in), 300W; ROBUST dia 12cm (4¾in), 100W; CLIP-SPOT dia 8cm (3¼in), 40W; FESTIVAL dia 9cm (3½in) 60W; IDEAL dia 10cm (4in), 60W. *P:* HIGHLIGHT £73.05; others £5.74–£35.95.

Brillantleuchten also offer compact eyeball recessed downlighters and outdoor bulkhead lights that also fit well into bathrooms and halls. Their pendants include PENDELLEUCHTEN simple rise-and-fall models with conical metal shades in red, yellow, blue, black and white. *M:* dia 16.5 or 37cm (6½ or 14½in); 60W. *P:* from £22.75. LINIE pendant is a cone of opal plastic and red, blue, white or brown metal; the cone is also upturned to make wall-bracket and floor-standing uplighters with metal bracket and base. *M:* dia 33cm (13in); wall bracket d32.5cm (12½in); floor-standing h186cm (73¼in). *P:* £20.95–£47.05.

There are conventional PETIT bedside and table lamps with round metal base and matching shade in red, blue, white, beige, pink, brown and light blue. *M:* h25.5 × dia 22cm (10 × 8¾in); 60W. *P:* £18.05. And there are new-look desk lights: mantis-like STRING, an adjustable clamp-on drawing board light, and mechanical-looking MACH, available with digital clock and even desk tidy as part of base, also adjustable. STRING comes with blue, yellow, black, white or red metal fittings, MACH in black, brown, crimson, beige and white. *M:* STRING max h90cm (35½in), 60W or 9W PL; MACH max h45 × 14cm (17¾ × 5½in), 60W. *P:* MACH £21.05–32.15; STRING £17.20–£26.95.

Unique story-book collection of three-dimensional wall sculptures will please all children, real or make-believe. A cloud, stars, a balloon and an ice-cream cone of moulded, coloured plastic are lit from within. *P:* £20.60–£25.20. See illustration on following page.

Brillantleuchten's CLICK

C & R LIGHTING SYSTEMS

High tech structure for lighting and other electrical services from the Italian company Altalite, suitable for offices or contract display. STRUCTURA is a metal framework, triangular in section, with 'T', 'V', 'L' and curved corner joints and couplings. Framework can be suspended horizontally from the ceiling or free-standing sections can be used vertically, clamped to triangular metal plinth. Comes with white, black, gold, chrome or red epoxy finish. STRUCTURA can carry track, fluores-

LIGHTING

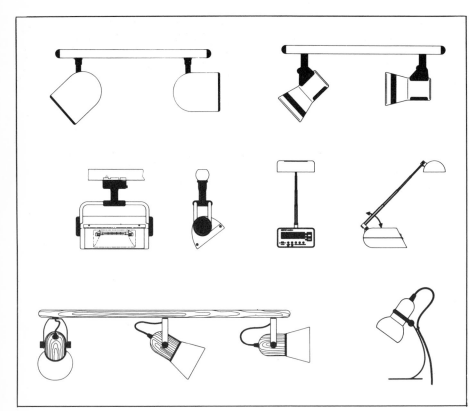

From Brillantleuchten. Left to right, from top: ROBUST spots, IDEAL DEKO spots (with decorated cowl), halogen HIGHLIGHT, MACH task light, WASA spots, FESTIVAL spot

cent and incandescent components along any of its length and can also carry power cables. Range of fittings includes four spots (in black or white) and two fluorescents (with and without louvres). *P:* '56033' 200cm (78¾in), frame section £40.50 (ex VAT).

Uplighter '56095' uses framework section set vertically, capped by triangular reflector plate supporting halogen bulb (with control gear housed in box in the base). *M:* h200cm (79in), base w52cm (20½in); 250W. *P:* on application.

C & R Lighting Systems' STRUCTURA ceiling light

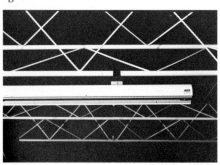

CANDLELIGHT PRODUCTS LTD

Elaborate flower shapes in metal and opal glass, and some simpler ceramics. In metal are 'Orchid' table lamp with perforated metal petals as shades set into leafy base, and 'Wistaria' table lamp with opal ball on plant-like stem. *M:* 'Orchid' h68cm (26¾in); 'Wistaria' h63cm (24¾in). *P:* £64 each. 'Pineapple' standard lamp has opal globe supported by metal leaves. *M:* h158cm (62¼in). *P:* £119. Metal colours are pink, peppermint, grey and white. In ceramic are two lamp bases with complementary pleated fabric shades: pyramidal 'Inca' and six-sided 'Classic'. *M:* h42cm (16½in); 'Classic' h44.5cm (17½in). *P:* 'Inca' £23; 'Classic' £21.85. Ceramic 'Conch Shell' lamp envelops an opal bulb. *M:* l24cm (9½in). *P:* £20. Ceramic colours are pink, peppermint, white, smoke and beige.

Below left: 'Pineapple' standard lamp; below 'Wistaria' table lamp. Both from Candlelight Products

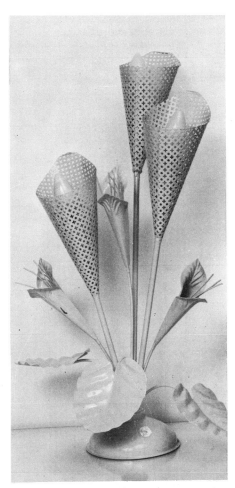

CASA FINA

Classic lamp bases and shades. Casa Fina's large ceramics collection includes Italian lamp bases with marbled glaze in pastel apricot, green, blue or grey; and straight-sided base with bamboo design in relief, in white on pink. All can be matched with cotton coolie shades in various colours and sizes. *M:* Italian bases h25, 30 or 40cm (9¾, 11¾ or 15¾in); 'Bamboo' base h42 × w20 × d20cm (16½ × 7¾ × 7¾in). *P:* Italian bases £28.45, £37.45, £45.75; 'Bamboo' base £37.45; shades £8.75–£23.95.

Casa Fina's classic Italian lamp bases with marbled glaze

R J CHELSOM & CO LTD

Solid brass chandeliers, wall lights and other fittings, based on traditional styles from sixteenth-century Flemish to Edwardian. More than 12 standard ranges are supplemented by Chelsom's specialist lighting service: they offer really imposing chandeliers of 26 lights or more, and will make to order for the contract market.

Stately FLEMISH range has chandeliers in 20 sizes, with from three to 32 lights. Each is solid brass and can be supplied with candle-bulbs or various tulip glasses. *M:* three-light '210/3' h16 × dia 18in (40 × 45cm); eight-light '240/8' h22 × dia 32in (56 × 80cm); 32-light '243/16+8+8' h48 × dia 74in (122 × 188cm). *P:* '210/3' £90; '240/8' £360; '243/16+8+8' £1,800. There are six matching wall lights. *M:* single 'A210/1' h12 × w3in (30 × 8cm); five light 'A240/5' h22 × w21in (54 × 53cm). *P:* 'A210/1' £32; 'A240/5' £140.

MARIA THERESA range has 11 chandeliers rich in the crystal drops and chains made popular

R J Chelsom's three-light, Victorian-style '1128/3' chandelier

by the empress who gave her name to the style. *M:* three-light '500/3' h15 × dia 16in (38 × 41cm); eight-light '6051/8' h22 × dia 25in (56 × 63cm); 18-light '490/12+6' h33 × dia 31in (84 × 79cm). *P:* '500/3' £56; '6051/8' £130; '490/12+6' £360. Again, there are six matching wall lights. *M:* single '500/A1' h5 × w4in (13 × 10cm); five-light '490/A5' h19 × w16in (48 × 40cm). *P:* '500/A1' £32; '490/A5' £80.

There are many Victorian-style fittings with decorative glass shades in imitation of gas lamps, 17 chandeliers and 15 wall lights in all. Five-light chandelier '1206/5' in the VICTORIAN range has rose, amber or plain tulip glass, and matching single wall light, '1206/A1'. *M:* '1206/5' h11 × dia 21in (28 × 53cm); '1206/A1' h7 × w6in (18 × 15cm). *P:* '1206/5' £54; '1206/A1' £9.75. In the DOMESTIC VICTORIAN range, '1222/3' chandelier has three spherical frosted glasses; '1224/5' has five suspended tulip shades in white, amber or clear glass; and ornate '3009/3+3' has two tiers, with six lights in all, of clear or white suspended tulip glasses. *M:* '1222/3' h11 × dia 18in (28 × 45cm); '1224/5' h16 × dia 23in (40 × 56cm); '3009/3+3' h20 × dia 22in (50 × 56cm). *P:* '1222/3' £55; '1224/5' £94; '3009/3+3' £146. The six wall lights in the range are similar; some, such as double '1224/1' with double white, amber or clear fluted tulip glasses, can be used either way-up, both as uplighters and downlighters. *M:* h11 × w11in (28 × 28cm). *P:* £20. DOMESTIC PERIOD range, which adapts various English styles to modern requirements (and budgets) includes simplified Victorian-style fittings with amber or white bulbous onion glasses, such as three-light '1128/3'. *M:* h13 × dia 16in (33 × 40cm). *P:* £60.

Chelsom's four designs of Georgian and Regency hanging lanterns would grace any entrance hall. Solid cast brass, highly polished and lacquered, they have thickly bevelled glass panels that slide out at the top for easy cleaning and maintenance. Like all Chelsom's pendants, they are suspended on brass chains. *M:* three-light '700' h16in × dia 10in (40 × 25cm); six-light '760' h38 × dia 20in (100 × 50cm). *P:* '700' £110; '760' £600.

Chelsom's six standard lamps and 12 table

Above: Candlelight Products' 'Orchid' table lamp; below: Casa Fina's 'Bamboo' ceramic lamp base

lamps, in solid brass, are sufficiently classic to blend with any conventional decor. *M: '526'* standard lamp h62 × dia 13in (157 × 33cm); '8495' standard lamp h60 × dia 11in (153 × 28cm); '523' table lamp h16 × dia 5½in (40 × 14cm); '8492' table lamp h18 × dia 7in (46 × 18cm). *P: '526'* £220; '8495' £170; '523' £68 '8492' £64.

CHINOISERIE LTD

High quality hand-painted table lamps with matching accessories such as cachepots, photograph frames, dishes and ginger jars. More than 40 designs, many using chinoiserie motifs such as 'Almond Blossom', 'Blue Peony', 'Canton' and 'Cherry Blossom', decorate a variety of base shapes including vase, ginger jar, basket, pumpkin, cylindrical and square. Most strikingly oriental is IMPERIAL DRAGON, available in four base shapes including red 'Heron' base matched with gleaming black 'Cut Corner' shade. *M:* total h38in (96.5cm). *P:* £134.

ZIGZAG design breaks from the Chinese style: 'Flame' has rough-edged zigzags in colours from burnt red to sand and cream, 'Icicle' has same design in cooler blue, green and beige. Each available with basket or ginger jar base and empire or coolie shade respectively. *M:* total h24–34in (61–86.5cm). *P:* £62.50–£104.

Chinoiserie's ZIGZAG range

SPECTRUM ginger-jar bases have graduated colour glaze: rich tones at the bottom pale towards the co-ordinated or contrasting empire shade. Easily matched to many colour schemes, the lamps come in caramel, sand, leaf green, rose and bluebell colourways. *M:* total h25in (65.5cm). *P:* £44.90.

In wood are lovely NEAPOLITAN candlestick and ginger-jar lamp bases, hand-marbled in strawberry, apricot, greengage, cassata and water ice colourways with matching marbled coolies. *M:* four sizes total h18–25in (45.5–

NEAPOLITAN hand-marbled collection from Chinoiserie

63.5cm) *P:* £32.70–£58.10.

With marvellous attention to detail, Chinoiserie have introduced unique HARLEQUIN flex from France which looks and feels like velvet and comes in 14 colours to co-ordinate with almost any lamp — a welcome alternative to the usual ugly wiring. All SPECTRUM lamps have this flex fitted, and it can be added to other lamps at slight extra cost. It is also available wholesale. *P:* 50m (54½yd) reel £13 on minimum order four reels.

Chinoiserie also sell individual lampshades. Hard shades come in empire, coolie, drum, hexagon, oval, rectangular pagoda, square pagoda, square wave, bowed band, cut corner and moon pagoda shapes. *M:* dia 10, 12, 14, 16, 18 and 20in (25.5, 30.5, 35.5, 40.5, 45.5 and 51cm); cut corner shade also dia 22in (56cm). *P:* £7.80–£42. Silk shades are also available. *M & P:* on application.

CIEL AT CHRISTOPHER LAWRENCE

Elegant pleated silk lamp shades on ceramic or wooden bases, giving a finishing touch to Christopher Lawrence's collection of fabrics and hand-painted furniture. Shades are 100 per cent silk, lined with silk in different weights and weaves: slub, wild silk or crepe de chine. They can be supplied in any shape or

Box-pleated silk lampshade on ceramic base, both by Ciel at Christopher Lawrence

PRICES AND INFORMATION WERE CORRECT AT THE TIME OF GOING TO PRESS

size with knife or box pleating in 130 different colours. *P:* £15–£75.

Lamp bases come in a variety of shapes and sizes. Ceramic 'Ostrich Egg Urn' may be ordered in any colour. *M:* base h14in (35.5cm). *P:* £86.25 (with shade). Classical 'Column', made of wood, is available in a variety of finishes — marbled, ragged, stained or simply varnished — as well as any colour. *M:* base h25in (63.5cm). *P:* £102.35 (with shade).

Marbled 'Column' base with knife-pleated silk shade, from Ciel at Christopher Lawrence

MARGERY CLINTON CERAMICS

Exquisitely detailed ceramic pendant, table and wall lights. Margery Clinton's range of ten table lamp bases (without shades) includes surprisingly lifelike 'Cabbage' and 'Cool Cat' in bone china, and simple but well-finished 'Single Gourd' and 'Double Gourd'. The other six, round, square, oblong or bottle-shaped, are delicately hand-painted with Chinese flowers or other motifs on mellow blue and green glazes. *M:* 'Cabbage' h18 × w20cm (7 × 7¾in);

Margery Clinton's 'Cabbage' lamp

'Fuchsia' and 'Harebell' pendants from Margery Clinton Ceramics

'Single Gourd' h16cm (6¼in); 'Double Gourd' h31cm (12¼in); 'Chinese Bottle' h50cm (19¾in); 'Small Square' h15cm (6in). *P:* 'Cabbage' £85; 'Gourds' £25 and £35; 'Chinese Bottle' £80; 'Small Square' £31.

Her unique pendant lamps are made in translucent bone china, each shade a perfect replica of the flower it is named after. *M:* 'Fuchsia' (from top to lowest stamens) h46cm (18in); 'Harebell' h20cm (7¾in); 'Lily' h21cm (8in). *P:* 'Fuchsia' £102; 'Harebell' £44; 'Lily' £52. 'Harebell' is also available as table lamp or wall fitting.

COLOURFLAIR FURNITURE LTD

Exclusive importers of the stylish American 'Tole 23' table lamps. Lamps and shades are made of metal painted in colours of the customer's choice and decorated with one of five traditional-style stencilled designs. Range includes a single light, a three-light candelabra and an unusual two-light desk lamp on a rectangular base with a shade echoing this shape. *M:* h23in (58.5cm). *P:* from £100.

Colourflair also stock a wide range of the American Paul Hanson table lamps. Slightly taller than average, they are ideal for lighting corners. The varied styles of the porcelain bases and the silk shades which can be made in colours of the customer's choice, ensure that almost any colour scheme can be matched. *M:* h32in (81cm). *P:* from £200.

△ *INDICATES AN ILLUSTRATED PRODUCT SELECTED BY THE DESIGN CENTRE*

Colourflair's 'Tole 23' two-light desk lamp with stencilled metal shade

CONCORD LIGHTING LTD △

Comprehensive but carefully researched collection of fittings. Initially specialists in track systems and accessories, Concord now manufacture seven different track systems; a fluorescent tube-track unit and a large range of accessories; and around 50 LYTESPOTS — recessed, suspended, freestanding or surface-mounted with rigid, curved or flexible couplings — most of which can be fitted with the appropriate adaptor for use with single or multicircuit track units. Impressive TUBETRACK 1 has slim tubes (said to be the slimmest on the market) that can be used both as track system and as freestanding three-dimensional display

Concord's TUBETRACK 1 system△

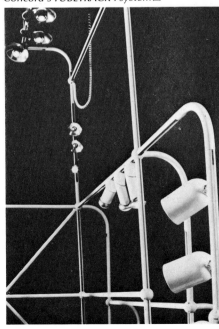

LIGHTING

structure. It can be hung, wall-mounted or stood on its own feet and LYTESPOTS can be attached at any point, aimed in any direction. *M:* tube dia 3cm (1¼in). *P:* on application. 'Beacon', a compact, low-voltage spotlight with integral transformer, accommodates a full range of bulbs from the very narrowest pin-spot to the widest flood beam. The black or white spun aluminium bulb housing is mounted on a rotating arm that is attached to the matching dual transformer housing, also in aluminium. Available track- or surface-mounted or in portable version with 2m (78¾in) coiled cable. *M:* l23.5 × d16 × w16cm (9½ × 6¼ × 6¼in). *P:* track and surface mounted £40; portable £42.

But tracks and spots now represent only a small proportion of Concord's collection. They make more than 70 different downlighters with varying light intensities, direction or non-directional beam distribution, recessed or surface-mounted, and eyeball or cone housing. Depending on the reflector and bulb, they can give anything from pin-spot to wall-wash illumination. 'Scoop Wallwasher' with broad reflector in white, polished silver or polished brass finish and adaptor with 100-degree swivel uses economical GLS bulbs and can be used in multiples to give a generous sweep of light. *M:* dia 18.5cm (7¼in). *P:* approx. £20–£25. Downlighter range also includes four different discharge lamps with integral or remote control units, all designed primarily for industrial application.

Concord's 'Scoop Wallwasher' △

Equally extensive is the range of fluorescent fittings for domestic, retail, office or industrial use. In each category Concord offer various reflectors, a choice of insets and diffusers or louvres to control glare. Twenty-two variable-length units are available. Range includes 'Top Eleven' fluorescent desk lamp made of tough, impact-resistant plastic in eggshell white finish with anodized asymmetrical reflector, using energy-saving PL11 bulb. The lamp is adjustable, will clamp on to desks or table tops up to 7cm (2¾in) thick and has built-in switch for easy light control. *M:* max h55cm (21¾in); IIW. *P:* approx. £180.

Innovative TOLTEC range of wall-mounted uplighters are specifically designed for the new

TOLTEC uplighter from Concord

linear metal halide bulbs, discharge lamps with refined colour rendering. The basic unit comprises cast aluminium V-shaped trough housing, asymmetric reflector finned for cooler operation and efficiency, wall-brackets with leads to remote control box, all finished in white stove enamel or other colours to order. *M:* d28.4 × h14.7 × w24cm (11 × 6 ×9½in); 150W or 200W. *P:* from £209.30 (without bulb).

THE CONRAN SHOP

Stockists of three simple styles of ceramic lamp base: spherical, cylindrical and melon jar. The spherical base comes in plain, ridged or crackle finishes and the cylinder and melon jar in the plain finish. Plain and ridged finishes come in burgundy, cream, grey, white, matt black and shiny black; crackle finish in grey, pink, cream and blue/grey. The crackle spherical base is also available in chrome colour. *M:* spherical and cylindrical h12in (30.5cm), melon jar h20in (51cm). *P:* spherical, plain and ridged, £16.95, crackle, £19.75, chrome, £28.00; cylindrical, £20.50; melon jar £21.50. Lampshades to team with the bases come in a number of styles. They can be covered with fabrics from the Conran range (see *Fabrics*), or, an extremely useful service, they can be covered in the customer's own fabric. *M:* small coolie dia 15in (38cm); large coolie dia 23in (58.5cm). *P:* small coolie in fabric £12; large coolie in paper laminate £23.

COURTNEY POPE LIGHTING LTD

Manufacturers of industrial and commercial light fittings. Courtney Pope continue to offer probably the largest selection of fluorescent fittings, with a fantastic choice of diffusers, surface or recessed mountings, slimline, compact multi-lamp units, grid and louvre ceiling systems and emergency lighting units. Keeping abreast of the times is their ALLOM STRADA linear lighting system with fluorescent and track inserts and built-in reflector. Distinctive, elliptical aluminium tracks, finished in red, green, brown or ivory, can be suspended or surface-mounted with a choice of rubber or rigid joints allowing complete flexibility in installation and layout. *M:* fluorescent module

'STDR 1' l126, 156, 186 or 216cm (49½, 61½, 73¼ or 85in); 'STDR/TR' spotlight module with standard track l126 or 216cm (49½ or 85in); integrated low voltage spot packs, single or double, 'STDR/12' l30 or 40 (11¾ or 15¾in). *P:* on application.

ALLOM TRACK 12 is the same low-voltage track used as an independent unit. It operates on 12V giving a low cost, precision spotlighting system to enhance any retail display. *M:* l120cm (48in). *P:* on application.

CRESSWELL SHADES LTD

Eclectic collection of 39 table lamps. There are classic spheres and ginger jars in different moods from luxurious burgundy with gold band decoration to elegant crackle ivory and fresh pastels. 'Estelle' has a simple ceramic base and tasselled satin shade giving a hint of Victoriana. *M:* h18in (45.5cm), shade dia 14½in (37cm). *P:* £37. 'Waldorf' and 'Astoria' lamps have white or stone-coloured round and square sided ceramic bases with clean-lined sculptured decoration that looks back to art deco. They have coolie and square shades

Below: 'Waldorf'; bottom: 'Astoria'. Both from Cresswell Shades

Cresswell's 'Adelphi'

respectively. *M:* 'Waldorf' h13½in (34.5cm), shade dia 13in (33cm); 'Astoria' h14½in (37cm), shade w13½in (34.5cm). *P:* £21–£25. 'Adelphi' draws on more modern influences with its geometric shape and horizontally banded square shade in monochrome grey or coffee. *M:* h17¾in (45cm), shade w13½in (34.5cm). *P:* £23.

MIX & MATCH range offers an opportunity to pair bases (shiny glazed spheres, bricks and cylinders) with shades (glossy one-colour, polka-dotted or lattice). Colours are bright - blue, green, red, yellow, black and white - or muted - beige, pale blue, pale pink and soft yellow. *M:* h12 or 16in (30.5 or 42cm), shade dia 9½ or 14½ (24 or 37cm). *P:* bases £9.50, £20.50.

'Estelle' and 'Adelphi' shades are also available as pendants and there are six other pendant shades. *P:* £3.15–£9.45. Cresswell also do six ranges of separate shades for table lamps: 'Dansk', oatmeal fabric in drum and coolie shapes; 'Chintz', glazed fabric in white, peach, cerise, green, blue, pink and cream in coolie shape; 'Canton', slubbed weave in neutral parchment, tobacco, pink and green

Bases and shades from Cresswell's MIX & MATCH range

with white balloon lining and trim, in bowed drum shape; 'Thai', a similar weave in beige, gold, pink, green or peach, with white balloon lining, trim and fringe, in bowed empire shape; 'Lisette', pleated, stiffened fabric in white, pink, cream or blue in empire shape; and 'New Silk', in white, gold, willow, sand and rose, with white balloon lining and trim, in bowed drum shape with additional skirt. *M:* most dia approx 10–20in (25.5–51cm); 'New Silk', 'Thai' and 'Canton' also dia approx 5, 8in (12.5, 20.5cm). *P:* 'Dansk', 'Chintz' £4–£15.60; 'New Silk', 'Thai' and 'Canton' £6.80–£34.40; 'Lisette' £5.50–£9.80.

CROMPTON PARKINSON LTD

Industrial, commercial and domestic lighting from a company known for their comprehensive range of light bulbs. SPOTRACK and SPOTLUX are carefully chosen ranges of spotlights and downlighters designed for interior display lighting. Matt black or satin silver spotlights, attached to sleeves, cowls or reflectors, are mounted on extruded aluminium track system. Tungsten halogen spotlight also available. *M:* SPOTLUX 'Series 40' surface-mounted unit dia 14cm (5½in); 40–100W ISL ES reflector bulb. *P:* £18.05. Crompton are also well known for fluorescent luminaires in a wide variety of sizes, styles and bulb configurations to cover all general lighting applications in offices: from workplace lighting — 'Modulux' recessed fluorescent with opal diffuser — to emergency systems — 'Dupurlite' non-maintained emergency lighting with one-hour life. *M:* 'Modulux' l180 or 60cm (70 or 23½in); two 65W or 58W fluorescent tubes. *P:* 'Modulux' £116.67; 'Dupurlite' £131.59.

Two spotlights from Crompton Parkinson's SPOTLUX series

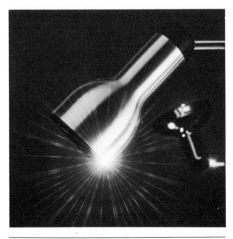

PRICES AND INFORMATION WERE CORRECT AT THE TIME OF GOING TO PRESS

JOHN CULLEN LIGHTING DESIGN LTD

Imaginative lighting consultants. John Cullen and his team of designers, draughtsmen and technicians will plan a lighting scheme to achieve a chosen effect, selecting and if necessary producing their own light fittings. Three original designs are available from their remarkable showroom, which has been set up to demonstrate the various effects and applications of uplighters, pin-spots, table and floor-standing lamps.

'Starlite' is an extremely discreet, low-voltage recessed light with integral transformer. *M:* dia ceiling plate 9.2cm (3½in), recess depth 4cm (1¾in), depth of light below ceiling plate 9cm (3¼in); tungsten halogen with choice of beam widths. *P:* from £35.55. 'Highlite' a versatile miniature uplighter, also capitalizes on the small dimensions of low voltage bulbs. Available with tungsten halogen bulb in three different beam widths, with straight or curly, white or colour-co-ordinated flex, in two-tone grey or beige-and-white finish. *M:* dia 9cm (3¼in), h20cm (7½in). *P:* from £50. 'Alabaster Urn' light, designed for John Cullen by Sally Settrington, is both a decorative object and lamp: light glows through the translucent bowl and reflects upwards to illuminate ceiling and walls. *M:* dia 25cm (9½in) h40cm (15½in). *P:* from £250.

'Highlite' uplighters from John Cullen Lighting Design

DERNIER & HAMLYN LTD

Decorative lighting in brass, gilt and silver finishes, recreating the magnificence of a bygone age both in style and craftsmanship. Dernier & Hamlyn were established in 1888 — before electricity — and continue to produce high quality fittings: crystal chandeliers, ceiling rose fittings, desk lamps, floor lamps, lanterns, pendants, picture lights, table lamps and wall brackets, are standard. In addition, Dernier & Hamlyn will create individual variations on any one of their numerous themes.

LIGHTING

Classic DUTCH range encompasses four separate chandelier designs, each with a choice in the number of lights. 'Rembrandt' chandeliers may have one, two or three tiers with up to 18 lights. To complement each pendant design are single and double wall brackets and an elegant table lamp — 17 fittings in all. *M:* '2906/12P' twelve-light pendant dia 86.3 × h94cm (33½ × 37in). *P:* £1,492. MAZARIN range comprises just five fittings, three pendants and two wall sconces, and is modelled on a seventeenth-century French design, the original of which hangs in the Bibliotheque Nationale in Paris. *M:* '7146/6P' six-light pendant dia 61 × h71cm (24 × 28in). *P:* £601. KNOLE comprises seven fittings including pendant, wall and table lamps. The decorative pineapple finial and finely detailed cherubs lighten this typically seventeenth-century English design. *M:* '2043/3W' three-light wall bracket w52 × h42 ×d22.8cm (20½ × 16½ × 9in). *P:* £350. CANTERBURY and YORK both consist of one six-light and one three-light pendant with matching wall sconce and table lamp. Simpler than the KNOLE design, both look more Georgian in style. *M:* YORK '7379/2T' two-light table lamp model h41.8cm (16½in) *P:* £135.

Chandeliers from the KNOLE range by Dernier & Hamlyn

Nine other ranges follow a similar pattern offering pendants with six, four or three lights and multiple or single light wall sconces and table lamps. The DUBARRY range introduces a single crystal glass tear-drop affixed to the underside of each light, and the VENEZIA range develops the idea, until the DIADEM range sparkling crystal becomes the most striking element in the structure. *M:* DIADEM three-light pendant '5153/3P' dia 38 × h34.2cm

(15 × 13½in) *P:* £188. The remaining chandeliers in the collection are HAMPTON, KEW and CHATSWORTH, based on the styles found in these great houses, and a classic ADAM range. Dernier & Hamlyn will also produce large crystal chandeliers to special order. The arrangement of the metal structure and the crystal formation are infinitely variable, so each chandelier can be constructed precisely to an individual's requirements. *P:* on application.

In addition to the table lamps in the chandelier ranges, there are 11 individual models with brass bases in a variety of traditional, particularly Georgian, styles with pagoda, square pagoda or drum fabric shades available in a wide range of fabrics, colours and trims. '7371/3T' has a candelabra base with three lights and a drum shade topped by a pineapple finial. *M:* '7371/3T' h43.2cm (17in). *P:* £83 (with shade). There are also four desk lamps, more Victorian in style, with a choice of brass or green glass trough or dome shade on simple upright or curved brass stem. *M:* '14898/D' with glass trough shade and upright stem h48.3cm (19in). *P:* £93.

The five floor lamps reflect details of the pendant designs with the same choice of shades as for the table lamps. '7675/F' has a fluted column on an elaborate rounded base with claw feet. *M:* h (to lamp-holder) 156.2cm (61½in). *P:* £334 (without shade).

There are six lantern designs, each a variation on the classic lantern style: a hexagonal or circular brass frame with clear glass panels and decorative brass, pagoda-shaped top. *M:* '14713/3L' (hexagonal with three lights) w45.7 × h53.3cm (18 × 21in). *P:* £626.
Dernier & Hamlyn also produce three models

Dernier & Hamlyn's '7371/3T' three-light table lamp

Dernier & Hamlyn's '7515/5C' downlighter

of picture light: one cylindrical and two trough (either plain or with curling ribbon decoration). *M:* '14880/A' cylindrical model l130.5cm (12in) *P:* £35.

To complete the collection, there are a number of reversed-arm downlight pendants and ceiling fittings, most of which reflect seventeenth-century shapes and detailing. '7515/5C' five-light ceiling fitting shows the distinctive pineapple and cherub decoration of the KNOLE range. *M:* dia 50.8 (20in), over all drop 35cm (14in) *P:* £234 (without shades).

DESIGNERS GUILD

Nice range of ceramic bases in 20 sizes from these inspiring showrooms — the perfect complement to their fabrics, wallpapers, furniture and soft furnishing. Bases come in several colours ranging from the pastels with which Designer's Guild made their name to the deeper tones they do now. Three styles of coolie shades are designed to go with them: fabric-covered, pleated fabric-covered and painted with a slight mottling. Bases and shades can also be made to order. *M:* bases h25–43cm (9¾–17in); shades dia 45–66cm (17¾–26in). *P:* bases £28–£164; fabric shades £17–£27; pleated fabric shades £29–£41; painted shades £16–£25.

Bases and shades from Designers Guild

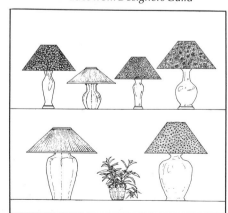

DOVERLIGHT LTD
Unique 'Light One' from specialists in custom lighting design and installation. 'Light One' uses tungsten halogen and high intensity lamps to provide a mix of general uplighting and task downlighting, by way of three inter-changeable controllers: a diffuser, a down-lighter cowl with small aperture (as illustrated) and an uplighter reflector contoured to reduce the concentration of brightness on the ceiling directly above the light source. Available in floor-standing, ceiling and wall-mounted ver-sions, with housing, reflector and cowl in alu-minium, and floor lamp base in cast iron. Housing and base have pearl grey crackle fin-ish. *M:* floor lamp h185cm (72¾in); ceiling drop to specification minimum 60cm (23.5in). *P:* upon application.

Doverlight's 'Light One'

EDISON HALO LTD
Specialists in commercial discharge lighting plus a selection of track fittings, downlighters, low voltage, outdoor and fluorescent units, and decorative fittings for restaurants, hotels and shops. 'SPX' indirect lighting meets the needs of today's office: it gives good general lighting, offsetting the hazards of VDU screens, and saves energy too. 'SPX' is a high intensity discharge uplighter made up of several components so the actual light unit is more compact than most, and easy to accommodate in a small workspace. The light unit can be positioned on a shelf, on top of filing cabinet, on a freestanding support stand or on a partition bracket. *M:* optical module

Edison Halo's 'SPX' freestanding unit

w34 × d34 × h15cm (13½ × 13½ × 6in), 250W SON DL or halogen; gear module w34 × d18.5 × h15cm (13½ × 7¼ × 6in). *P:* optical module £170; gear module £220; link cables from £6.30.
Edison also make an energy-saving track or surface-mounted low voltage fitting that is ideally suited for application in retail displays. Bulb and low-voltage transformer sit side by side in compact die-cast housing. *M:* track fit-ting w15.5 × d7cm (6 × 2¾in). *P:* £50.

ELIT LIGHTING LTD
Taking Britishness to an extreme, the BROLLY-LITE, an open brolly shade as pendant, floor or table lamp. Made of cotton, the shades come in two sizes and 24 plain colours, plus pat-terns: graph-paper grid of brown on cream; beige spots on brown; gingham checks in black, blue or red on white; white floral print on red or green; white polka dots on pastel blue, green, pink or yellow; and for the nursery, with pastel puppies or kittens! Table and floor lamps have natural wood stems, and an inexpensive converter kit consisting of shade carrier and brass finial allows shades to be hung from the ceiling or fitted to any other base. Shades can be covered in customer's own material at extra cost. *M:* shades h28.5 × dia 58.5cm (11¾ × 23in); or h39 × dia 66cm (15¼ × 26in); table lamp base h35cm (13¾in); floor lamp base h141cm (55½in). *P:* £6.95, £9.50; table lamp £9.95; floor lamp shades £19.95; converter kit 0.74p; special orders £4.75 extra.
Range of aluminium pendants includes ALFA,

a flat disc with cylindrical shade holder; func-tional conical shades in various sizes; and chunky PLUTO. All are available enamelled in red, white, green, yellow, brown, black, bright blue, pale blue, beige, pink and grey. *M:* ALFA dia 23in (58.5cm); conical shades dia 10, 12, 15 or 19in (25.5, 30.5, 38 or 49.5cm); PLUTO dia 13¾in (35cm). *P:* ALFA £40; conical shades £5–£10.50; PLUTO £12.

Elit's BROLLYLITE as table lamp and as pendant fitting

EMESS LIGHTING LTD
Manufacturers and importers of an enormous-ly varied range of lighting equipment and ex-clusive distributors of more than 1,000 Glass-hütte Limburg glass fittings. Of the five Emess ranges of track and spotlights, the nicest is MINI-SPOT in brown or black. Seven models comprise two sizes of track or 'lightbar', a clip spot, a three-light rise-and-fall pendant with ceiling plate, a table lamp and single spot. *M:* lightbars w38 or 60cm (16 or 23½in); 40W. *P:* £11.50, £17.50.
There are four ranges of Bohemian crystal chandelier fittings, all supplied with chain sets: 'Icicles' in three sizes with elongated drops. 'Baguettes' in four sizes with combina-tion drops, 'Almond and Rosette' in two sizes with the chunkiest drops, and ornate 'Classic' in three sizes. *M:* 'Icicles' dia 8, 10, 12in (21.5, 25.5, 30.5cm). *P:* £23, £30, £60. Art deco SBAD 2000 fittings are in solid brass with frosted glass panels decorated with etched motif. Varia-tions include five-light floor or table lamp, single and double wall fittings, plus pendants with up to eight lights. *M:* '2011' single-light pendant dia 17cm (6¾in). *P:* £58.
More utilitarian is the 'Shaverlight' in white plastic with prismatic diffuser, supplied with strip-lamp, pull-switch, transformer and shav-er socket. *M:* w44.5cm (17½in). *P:* £33.
From Glasshütte Limburg come 56 pendants. '4308/4310' is very contemporary with an angu-

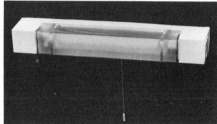

Top: Emess' versatile MINI-SPOT; below: the Emess 'Shaverlight' with concealed shaver socket

lar or rounded coolie shade in white or matt black metal over a lozenge-shaped diffuser in white opal glass. *M:* dia 34–60cm (13½ – 23½in); 60–100W. *P:* £125–£150. '1398' looks like a Victorian oil lamp, with opal white glass diffuser and base, crystal glass chimney, and matt black metal chain and scrolled globe support. *M:* dia 35cm (13¾in); 75W. *P:* £225. Slightly larger are '1259' with a fancier matt black globe support and authentic '1667', the same design with a real oil burner. *M:* dia 37cm (14½in). *P:* £270.

For stylishly simple wall lighting, there are several geometric shapes in white glass: a hemisphere, a U-shape, a square, a long, thin rectangle, a circle, and a snazzy triangle with gleaming brass base. Eighty more wall fittings include many splashproof ones in opal glass or crystal, such as '2605' and '2607' with white opal circle or hexagon enclosed within a square steel surround. *M:* 15 × 15cm (6 × 6in) or 20 × 20cm (7¾ × 7¾in); 40–60W. *P:* £43–£46. And there are scallop-shell sconces in frosted raindrop crystal or satin matt opal glass, in five sizes. *M:* '3087' w21.5 × d11.5cm (8½ × 4½in), 60W; '2991' w26 × d12cm (10¼ ×

4¾in), 75W. *P:* £50–£72. Ceiling lights are similarly simple and extensive, 104 in all, again featuring clean shapes in opal or crystal glass. Table and floor lamps show the same flair for form. There are seven floor-standing uplighters and standards with opal glass shades on stems of brass or metal with chrome or white finish. The 48 table lamps are distinctive shapes, some using opal glass and brass or metal, some with both base and shade of glass, some with glass base and white linen or black leather shade. '6328' and '6325' have a lovely mushroom shape, the former made with base and shade of satin matt opal glass, the latter satin matt opal glass with touches of colour. *M:* both h30 × dia 26cm (11¾ × 10¼in); 75W. *P:* on application.

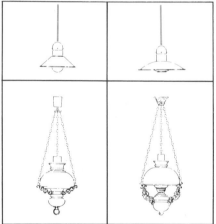

Top, left to right: Bohemian crystal chandeliers, 'Baguettes MS/10/B' and 'Icicles MS/12/B'; below, left to right: Glasshütte Limburg's pendants '4308', '4310', '1398', '1667'. All from Emess

NICHOLAS ENGERT INTERIOR DESIGN

Agents for low voltage light fittings designed and manufactured by Mole–Richardson of France for specialist and contract use, for art gallery, shop, discotheque or just the light-conscious home. Each fitting is designed for a particular bulb or range of bulbs and for a specific function, and is available with ceiling plate or track-mounting yoke suitable for a

wide range of track systems.

In the spotlight category there is a total of 31 different units, accommodating a full range from very narrow spot to wide flood bulbs; and in each case the bulb dictates the size of the fitting. Simplest are compact cubes such as 'Minimole 20/D' with remote transformer or 'Minicube 20/R' with transformer in separate housing attached to its side. Both are aluminium with brushed, black or gold finish. *M:* 'Minimole 20/D' d9 × h5 × w5cm (3½ × 2 × 2in), projection 7.5cm (3in); 'Minicube 20/R' d7.5 × h5 × w13.3cm) (3 × 2 × 5¼in), projection 9.3cm (3¾in). *P:* 'Minimole 20/D' £31.05; 'Minicube 20/R' £80.50.

More sophisticated are FINE ARTS spotlights, which accommodate a full range of attachments: filters, heat-absorbing glass, anti IR and UV glass, adjustable shields to prevent glare or direct the beam, and adjustable reflectors. 'Minos 75' has built-in transformer and anti-glare device; available in white, black, black and chrome, or black and gold finishes. *M:* h9 × w9 × d23.5cm (3½ × 3½ × 9¼in), projection 13.5cm (5¼in). *P:* £100.05.

Ideal for exhibition lighting are VARIMOLE framing projectors, available in three sizes with standard or long distance lenses (each fitting has recommended distance performance). 'Varimole 50T1', the middle one of the three, performs best over 3–5m (3¼ – 5½yd) or 4–7m (4¼ – 7¾yd), depending on the lens. *M:* h6.6 × w6.6 × d30cm (2½ × 2½ × 11¾in), projection 11.5cm (4½in). *P:* £151.11.

There are 28 recess downlighter units, and like the spotlights they have varying degrees of flexibility, with a choice of reflectors, filters, and low brightness, accent or general lighting. The smallest fits snugly into modular and louvred ceilings; it can be modified to meet various ceiling requirements and will accommodate four low voltage bulb types. It connects to a remote transformer. 'MD20/SP' takes the mini-dichroic bulb. *M:* recess 7cm (2¾in), bulb aperture dia 3.5cm (1½in) to fit 7.5 sq cm (3 sq in) ceiling cell. *P:* £25.

The most unusual downlighters are the DECOR range, where the standard circular housing accommodates narrow spot, or medium or wide flood bulbs but a cylindrical length of perspex protrudes from the aperture creating a gently diffused general or accent light depending on its length. All have remote transformers. *M:* 'MD 20/CX' recess d8.4cm (3¼in), bulb aperture dia 4cm (1½in) to fit opening dia 11.8cm (4½in). *P:* £44.39.

Mole–Richardson also produce a small collection of halogen units: four spots and two recess fittings, available with symmetrical or asymmetrical reflectors (the former for horizontal, the latter for vertical projection), all giving powerful ambient light. 'OCO 150/S' with integral transformer produces excellent low brightness. *M:* h10 × w18.8 × d15cm (3¼ × 7½ × 6in), projection 11.5cm (4½in). *P:* £109.25.

Left to right: Nicholas Engert's 'Minos 75', 'OCO-150/S' and 'Minimole 20/D'

EQUINOX INTERIORS LTD

Stockists of good range of original and unusual light fittings. Among the lights exclusive to Equinox are: 'Corner Light', pressed steel in black, white, red, yellow or chrome with an opal glass front; and 'Jerry Light', an unbreakable light suitable for hanging or standing, with a plastic waterproof body in black, red or yellow. *M:* 'Corner Light' h23cm (9in), 60W; 'Jerry Light' h36cm (14¼in), 100W. *P:* 'Corner Light' £21; 'Jerry Light' £32. There are also three BELUX lights: 'P50' floor light in black, red or white lacquered steel and aluminium, with linear halogen bulb; 'P70', also a floor light but with a fully adjustable angle, available in black, red or white lacquered steel and aluminium; and 'F21' clamped desk light in black, red or white lacquered steel and aluminium. *M:* P50' h180cm (70¾in), 300W; 'P70' max reach 60cm (23½in), 100W; 'F21' reach 50cm (19¾in), 100W. *P:* 'P50' £79 (with bulb); 'P70' £59; 'F21' £29.95.

Equinox's BELUX 'P50', 'F21' and 'P70'

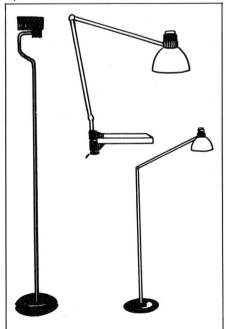

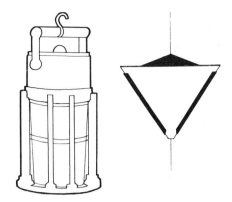

Equinox's 'Jerry Light' and 'Corner Light'

ERCO LIGHTING LTD

Sophisticated range of commercial and domestic light fittings from the genuinely simple to the most technically advanced: ceiling, floor and wall lights, spotlights, downlighters and uplighters, track and air-combination systems, accommodating fluorescent, low voltage, halogen and standard bulbs. Over the last five years Erco have worked with architects and designers to develop highly specialized fixtures while maintaining a comprehensive collection of purely domestic usage. This includes 15 different downlighters, 10 ranges of single and multiple spots and Hollywood-style mirror and bathroom fittings, emergency and outdoor lights, and low voltage track systems with a full range of fittings to include picture spots and framing projectors as well as the more universally known 360-degree eye-ball spot. Low voltage spotlights can be fitted on to Erco's low voltage flanged tracks and MONO-

Two of Erco's OSERIS spotlights with accessories including filters, sculpture and flood lenses, anti-dazzle screen and baffle

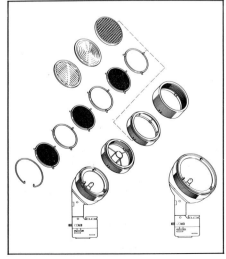

POLL tracks; both in white, bronze or polished aluminium. MONOPOLL track system offers a wide range of fittings for spotlights, spherical bulbs and fluorescent modules, and is also the basis of a freestanding version that can be fitted with any of Erco's spots. *M:* OSERIS spotlights h150 × dia 90cm to h200 × dia 120cm (59 × 35½ to 78¾ × 47¼in), 20W or 50W; standard MONOPOLL track l110, 170 or 230 × dia 5cm (43¼, 67 or 90½ × 2in). *P:* spots £45–£55, tracks £40–£90.

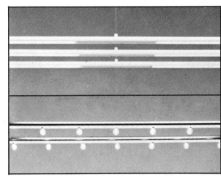

Fittings from Erco's MONOPOLL track system: fluorescent modules and modules for spherical bulbs

FORMA LTD

Exclusive range of lighting designed and made in Italy by iGuzzini showing an equal awareness of style, function and technology. Forma's collection is comprehensive and starts with a multi-phase thermoplastic track system, one of the smallest available, with three independent circuits and a good choice of couplers, accessories and fittings. *M:* w3 × d3cm (1¼ × 1¼in), available in 100, 200, 300 and 400cm (39, 78, 117 and 156in) lengths. *P:* '8391' 100cm section £12.60. The iGuzzini adaptor, which is the connecting element between track and light fittings, is suitable for use on four other track systems (Erco. Staff, Nova and Hoffmeister 3).

Track fittings include units for functional as well as decorative lighting — spots, projectors, and low voltage fittings with integral transformers. Although there are only nine different base units, all can be used with a wide range of bulbs, reflectors and anti-glare baffles, so that a unit can be made up to meet any requirement or application. Most are aluminium, variously with black, white, silver or gold finishes, and all are available with alternative base plate for ceiling–mounting. LEM '8420' base unit is phenolic resin and aluminium, adjustable to allow precise focusing of reflector attachments. Six different reflector shapes and sizes can be used, including parabolic reflector with colour options of red, green, blue, amber and magenta in addition to the usual silver; and there's a large variety of bulbs and diffusers. *M:* '8420' base unit d9 × dia 7cm (3½ ×

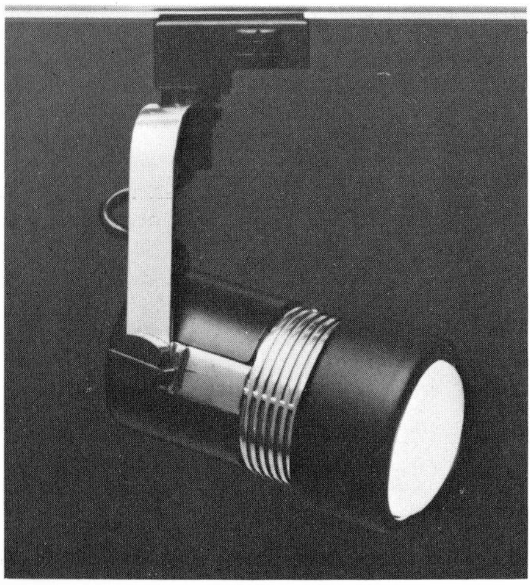

Forma's iGuzzini spotlight LEM '8420' with screen attachment '8604'

2¾in); '8607' parabolic reflector (silver) dia 20cm (7¾in). *P:* '8420' £42; '8607' £12.
Similarly, though there are 13 fully recessed downlighter units, with different sizes and recess depths, most will accommodate a choice of bulbs and integral reflectors to produce a much greater variety of lighting. The range also includes a ceiling-recessed wall-washer, in which a plate angled halfway across the aperture directs light towards the wall, and six semi-recessed, adjustable eyeball units. *M:* '8031' eyeball unit aperture dia 22.5cm (9in), recess d9.2cm (3½in). *P:* £43; '8630' aluminium reflector £20. In addition, iGuzzini produce a cylindrical surface-mounted downlighter in six sizes. '8051' is around the middle of the series. *M:* d8–25 × dia 7–20cm (3¼–9¾ × 2¾–7¾in). *P:* £87.
For a more general, diffused rather than directional, effect, iGuzzini make nine ceiling lights. All are white acrylic moulded in domed shapes reminiscent of science fiction architecture. 'Elpis', for example, is a softly rounded cone. *M:* d23 × dia 48cm (9 × 19in). *P:* £78.50. The same futuristic theme runs through a series of five wall lights, curved shapes made of clear and opaque, amber or black acrylic glass. *M:* 'Emi' d13.5 × h19 × w27cm (5 × 9½ × 10½in). *P:* £54.40. 12 other wall lights include cheeky 'Ping Pong', like a ping-pong bat in white acrylic; sculptural 'Bugia' fixed downlighter in white-painted metal; and multiple 'Linea' with six bulbs set in a strip of stainless steel. *M:* 'Ping Pong' h41 × w26cm (16¼ × 10¼in); 'Bugia' d19cm × h18 × w12.5 (7½ × 7 × 5in); 'Linea' h60 × w13cm (23½ × 5in). *P:* 'Bugia' £58; others on application.
Fifteen pendant fittings provide more clean, modern shapes, most in white, black, or ivory acrylic glass, some with rise-and-fall mechanisms. 'Gala' square acrylic glass coolie in black or white with clear rim is suspended on four thin wires. *M:* w53 × d53 × h18.5cm (20¾ × 20¾ × 7¼in). *P:* £205.
The 15 table and desk lamps and five floor-standing lamps can be divided between sculptural designs in acrylic and functional high tech designs in metal. 'Baobab' table lamp, with an acrylic hemisphere set on a tall conical metal base, is an example of the sculptural style. It comes in two versions, '4044' in black or white with deal rim and '4048' in white only. *M:* '4044' total h62cm (24½in), shade dia 45cm (17¾in); '4048' total h53cm (20¾in), shade dia 36cm (14¼in). *P:* on application. 'Praxis' adjustable task light in black, red or white polycarbonate and metal is totally functional by contrast, available freestanding, with clamp or with bracket base for fixing to the wall above a desk. *M:* h36–81 × reach 58–100cm (14¼–32 × 22¾–39in). *P:* £110.

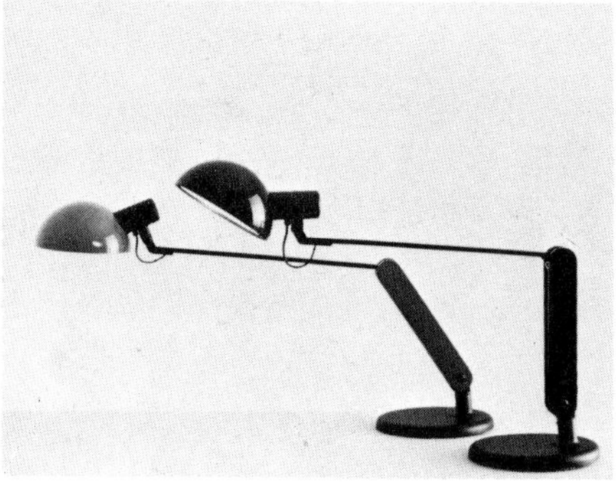

Forma's 'Praxis', from iGuzzini

GRAHAM & GREEN LTD

Delightful shop crammed with furnishing goodies, including an unusual selection of lamp bases and shades. There are hand-painted bases from France, some with dots in single colours such as blue and pink, others with multicoloured abstract motifs in several shades, another with swashes of colour in yellow or aqua with black small accents. All these are available with matching vases. *M:* 23 or 28cm (9 or 11in). *P:* £59 or £85. Also French is a crackle-glazed base in pastel shades, available in two sizes. *M:* 25 or 32cm (9¾ × 12½in). *P:* £21, £34. For fans of terracotta, there is an unusual urn-shaped base that is unglazed, distressed and hand-painted to look like an Italian antiquity. *M:* h42cm (16½in). *P:* £60. In terms of shades, there's always a selection of plain paper shades in coolie and drum shapes, and in various sizes, plus Italian marbled paper shades. *M:* h11.5 – 31cm (4½ – 12¼in). *P:* £2.95 – £22.50. Other pleated shades, from France, come in plain colours or in simple patterns. *M:* h17, 21, 25, 31cm (6¾, 8¼, 9¾, 12¼in). *P:* £12.85, £15.65, £22.50, £28.50.

PRICES AND INFORMATION WERE CORRECT AT THE TIME OF GOING TO PRESS

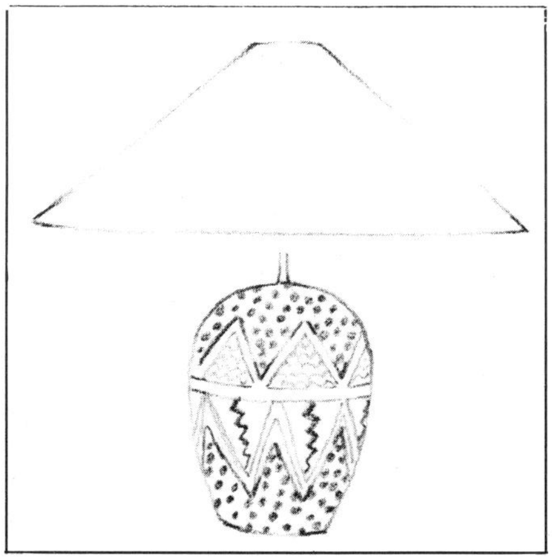

French hand-painted 'Tessalit' lamp base with coolie shade from Graham & Green

HABITAT DESIGNS LTD

From the famed and stylish chain store, a very good collection covering the entire lighting spectrum. There are six ranges of conventional table lamps. Spherical lamps include ceramic 'Cassata' in nine pastel colours and enamelled steel 'Bright Ball' in five bright colours; both with matching shades. *M:* h30cm (14¼in); 100W. *P:* 'Cassata' £7.95; 'Bright Ball' £8.95. There's also a simple white ceramic base to go with yellow, grey, white, blue or red cotton shade. *M:* base dia 21cm (8¼in), shade dia 45cm (17¾in); 100W. *P:* base £9.95, shade £4.95. 'Stirling' has ceramic base with pale green, Indian red or crackled cream glaze and complementary cotton shade. *M:* h41cm (16¾in); 100W. *P:* £12.95. 'Spice' has hand-thrown jar-shaped base, either natural or with white, peach or mushroom glaze, for use with one of their cotton coolie shades. *M:* h47cm, (18½in); 60W. *P:* natural £14.95; glazed £12.50. Cylindrical 'Drummer' has white ceramic base and cotton shade, both edged with a band of colour in pink, pale blue, grey or yellow. *M:* h36cm (14½in); 100W. *P:* £9.95. For a slick contrast, there's 'Cube', with square base and squared-off shade, both in black, red or white. *M:* h33cm (13in); 100W. *P:* £12.95.
Pendants include cotton 'Square Shades' in five colours (blue, yellow, natural, green and red). *M:* 45 × 45cm (17¾ × 17¾in); 100W. *P:* £7.50. In steel are 'Cone', in red, white or blue with matching lamp-holder and optional matching curly flex, and 'Darlington', in red, white or green. *M:* 'Cone' dia 38 or 45cm (15 or 17¾in), 60W; 'Darlington' dia 28cm (11in); 100W. *P:* 'Cone' £3.95, £6.95; 'Darlington' £6. In addition to Japanese-style round paper lanterns there are square 'Box Lanterns', made from white pleated paper and strips of red, black, blue or natural bamboo. *M:* h34 or 68cm (13½ or 26¾in). *P:* £3.95, £5.50. 'Ruffle' pendant is a splayed ruff of white china; 'Ripple'

Habitat's 'Flexi Desk light'

pendant a cone of white opal glass. *M:* 'Ruffle' dia 39cm (15¾in); 'Ripple' dia 25cm (9¾in); both 60W. *P:* 'Ruffle' £24.95; 'Ripple' £11.95. 'College' pendant is an opal glass globe with red, white or green ceiling cup and flex. *M:* dia 20cm (7¾in); 60W. *P:* £8.95. Two of Habitat's ceiling lights also make use of opal glass spheres, attached by means of stained wood or red or white collars that fit on to ceiling rose. *M:* dia 15 or 20cm (6 or 9½in); 60W or 100W. *P:* £3.95; £11.50.

Downlighters include 'Eyeball' and 'Mini Eyeball', which can be swivelled to any angle. *M:* dia 14 or 9.5cm (5½ or 3¾in); 100W or 60W. *P:* £7.95 or £9.95. 'Minispot' has chromed steel rim. *M:* dia 8cm (3¾in); 40W. *P:* £5.95. 'Recessed Downlight' with black, multi-groove surround gives a glare-free light. *M:* dia 15cm (6in); 60W. *P:* £8.50.

Four wall lights are vaguely art deco in style, simple shapes in white giving a soft, glare-free uplight: half-hemisphere 'Ceramic'; opal glass half-cone 'Cone'; shallow metal 'Light Bowl'; and fan-shaped metal and frosted glass 'Quad'. All would be best used with a dimmer switch. *M:* 'Ceramic' dia 31 × h15 × d15cm (12¼ × 6 × 6in), 60W; 'Cone' h21 × w35 × d8cm (8¼ × 13¾ × 3¼in), 100W; 'Light Bowl' h39 × w20 × 8cm (15¼ × 7¾ × 3¼in), 100W; 'Quad' h28 × w25cm (11 × 9¾in), 40W. *P:* £12.95–£21.95. 'Quad' is also available as a table lamp, standing on its side.

For really powerful uplighting, there is

'Halogen Wall Light', a functional upturned cone of black metal with circular bracket. *M:* w31cm (12½in); 200W. *P:* £19.95. There is also freestanding 'Halogen Uplighter', smoothly shaped in black or white metal. *M:* h175cm (69in); 200W. *P:* £34.95. Other freestanding lights include 'Glass Cone', with white metal stem and opal glass shade. *M:* h150cm (59in); 100W. *P:* £44.50. 'Synthesis Cowled Floorlight', also white metal, has adjustable-height steam and narrow shade. *M:* 40W. *P:* £17.95.

Well-designed, functional task lighting includes a version of the perennial anglepoise-type light, 'Worklamp', with clamp or base, or with sturdy rod extension to turn it into a floor-standing spot. As a desk lamp, it comes in bright red, yellow, green, blue, white or black; floor-standing it comes in white or red only. *M:* reach 92cm (36¼in) extension 83cm (32¾in); 60W. *P:* lamp with clamp £7.50; base £4.50; extension £3.95. 'Flexi Desk Light' has round swivel head in red or black, flexible black stem and round red or black base. *M:* h35cm (13¾in); 60W. *P:* £9.95. High tech 'Network Angle Light', spot with black mesh shade and chrome stem, clamps to desk top or shelf. *M:* reach 60cm (23½in); 40W. *P:* £9.95.

Selection of spotlights ranges from budget MONO single, twin or triple ceiling spots, to SUPERTRACK system with three different types of spot, including 'Mini Parabolic Track Spot' with concentrated beam for highlighting. *P:* MONO £5.95–£16.95; SUPERTRACK spots £7.95–£8.95.

To match their clear, bright colour scheme,

Habitat also have wall switches, single and double plugs and curly flex in red, blue, yellow or green.

HAMMOND WHOLESALE

Available only through decorators is the lovely collection of Anel Diffusion lamp-bases and shades from France. Bases are classical urn or jar shapes, moulded in ceramic or resin, and beautifully hand-painted in a wide range of stone and metallic finishes as well as mock wood and marble. CHAMOTTEX has five shapes finished in lustrous, luxury finishes such as tortoiseshell, malachite and lapis lazu-

By Anel Diffusion at Hammond. Below: 'Fontanges No 2'; bottom: 'Aragon'

LIGHTING

Hammond's 'Coeur No 4', by Anel Diffusion

li, some with white and black accent bandings. Some of the same shapes also come in semi-precious effects such as marble, ivory and gold-leaf. Urn-shaped 'Fontanges' can be supplied with mock ivory panelling and jet black banding. *M:* h40cm (15¾in). *P:* £435. 'Aragon' is panelled ceramic lamp with terracotta, corn, cream and 'agate' sections in Louis XIV style. *M:* h34cm (13½in). *P:* £571. 'Coeur No 4' with heart-shaped vase is ceramic with coral stipple finish and chocolate bandings. *M:* h30cm (11¾in). *P:* £140. (All prices ex VAT.)

HITECH (UK) LTD

High technology, low voltage fittings. Their small size, high control and efficiency, and low heat emission make them ideal for shop and exhibition displays as well as for domestic use. All are low voltage and all bar two require remote transformers, preferably housed close by. (Most of Hitech's transformers can be used to control more than one fitting; the largest in their range, for example, can power 15 50W units. *P:* £40–£99.) Each fitting can be supplied with yoke for track-mounting or with ceiling plate for independent use. All are available finished in black, white, chrome or gold (chrome and gold cost a little extra).
'Microspots' are the smallest range. They are designed to be concealed, with bulb and reflector sitting outside the main housing. Four designs are available, with square or smooth, reeded or corrugated round housing. *M:* 'S110C' round ceiling fitting d(without bulb) 9.6 × dia 6cm (3¾ × 2¼in). *P:* (white) £19.60. 'Minispots' are similar in principle but the bulb sits flush within the larger housing so the fitting need not be concealed. Four different housing designs are: smooth or reeded cylinder, smooth or corrugated cube. *M:* 'S240Y'

Some of Hitech's spotlights. From top: 'Minispot S240C', 'Ballspot S370C', round 'Modular Spot'

reeded cylinder track fitting d11.2 × dia 6cm (4 × 2¼in). *P:* (white) £18.50. Hitech's versatile 'Modular Spots' accept a variety of accessories

such as anti-glare baffles of various sizes, concentrating tubes to direct the beam more precisely, coloured filters, glass filters and diffusion materials (for effect and to minimize heat output). Again, the casing is available in round and square designs. Two versions are available with built-in transformers and correspondingly longer housings. *M:* 'S322C' square ceiling fitting, housing d10.8 × dia 6cm (4 × 2¼in); 'S410C' round ceiling fitting with built-in transformer, housing d18.5 × dia 6cm (7¼ × 2¼in); baffles ½, 1 and 1½in (1, 2.5 and 4cm). *P:* 'S322C' (white, with 1in baffle) £30; 'S410C' (white, no accessories) £72.60. 'Ballspot' is the popular eyeball housing scaled down for a low voltage bulb. *M:* 'S370C' ceiling fitting, housing dia 6.7cm (2½in). *P:* (white) £26.40.
'Multispot' and 'Multidownlighter' demonstrate a new concept — spotlight and downlighter that are identical in profile, with two straight sides and one curved. The semi-recessed downlighter has a directional versatility previously associated only with spotlights. It is mounted on a recessed ceiling plate than can rotate through 360 degrees, and the curved housing can be angled through 90 degrees. As a result it can also be used as a recessed, wall-mounted uplighter. *M:* 'D500' recess d9 × dia 12.5cm (3½ × 4¾in), max projection 6cm (2¼in). *P:* (white) £24.80.
As with the spotlights, there are 'Micro', 'Mini' and 'Modular' downlights. 'Mini' and 'Modular' both have an additional, outer bezel (rim) supporting the actual bulb housing, which facilitates bulb and accessory interchange. All take accessories such as anti-glare and concentrating tubes, baffles, and coloured, glass and diffusion filters; 'Mini' and 'Modular' take perspex rods too, and again 'Modular' is the most adaptable of the three. *M:* 'Modular D340' with concentrating tube, recess d5.4 × dia 12.5cm (2 × 4¾in); concentrating tube projection 7.6cm (2¾in). *P:* (white) £23.80. Hitech's directional downlighters have the same size as the 'Modular' outer bezel. 'Wall-washer', while flush to the ceiling, can rotate through 40 degrees; and semi-recessed 'Eyeball' allows maximum flexibility of movement with minimum depth of recess. *M:* 'Eyeball D380' recess d3.2 × dia 12.5cm (1¼ × 4¾in), projection 2.1cm (¾in). *P:* (white) £23.80. In the 'Flood Dome' downlighter the bulb is set back at the top of a fully recessed shallow dome so that the beam is thrown out over a wider area. *M:* 'D390' recess d7.7 × dia 12.5cm (3 × 4¾in). *P:* (white) £31.

OSWALD HOLLMAN LTD

From Germany, a sculptural and highly contemporary light-tube programme using fluorescent, track and incandescent modules for interiors and exteriors as well. KINKELDEY LIGHT TUBE offers all the options of other fluorescent and track light tubes — multidirectional couplings and corner joints,

Hitech's 'Eyeball' downlighter

emergency lights, interconnecting track, fluorescent and incandescent modules, a good selection of track fittings, variable-length, fluorescent tubes and end lights — plus some interesting additions. Double-length DUBLIX fluorescent modules have louvres or diffusers both top and bottom so that light shines up as well as down. Socket end pieces can also be inserted at module junctions so that regular three-pin plugs can be plugged in along the length of the lighting layout, bringing further flexibility to planning. A special rotary joint allows modules to be rotated to shed light in almost any direction. Cut-to-length modules, loudspeaker attachments, information lights and acrylic diffuser signs combine to make this a highly sophisticated system. But single light tubes, or small fluorescent tubes jointed at right angles into plain tubular stand, form satisfyingly simple lighting solutions for desks and worktops. All tubes are epoxy coated aluminium and come in standard yellow, orange or brown, and in special colours on request. *M:* standard light tube dia 9.5 × l110–209cm (3¾ × 43¼ – 82¼in); 18W–58W. *P:* from £35 per metre run. And not only is the KINKELDEY catalogue carefully thought out to assist plan-

Below: Oswald Hollman's DUBLIX light tube; bottom: DUBLIX with built-in three-phase track

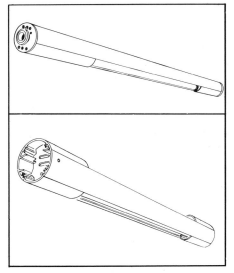

ning, but Hollman's consultancy service uses a computer to check light distribution in each lighting scheme!

HOMEWORKS LTD
Gorgeous glass lamp bases, imported from California by these stylish decorators. Two styles are available, both in clear or Venetian green glass. The bean jar comes in two sizes, the square-based column in three. *M:* bean jar h20, 24in (51, 61cm), square base h20, 28, 36in (51, 71, 91.5cm). *P:* from £130.

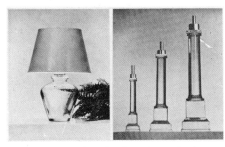

From Homeworks, glass bean jar and column lamp bases

ILLUMIN
Tiffany-style glass lighting: table, pendant and wall fittings made to order using handmade coloured glass and traditional materials and techniques. Although most of Illumin's lamps are one-off commissions there are a few standard designs. Of these, wall lights 'WL22', '23' and '24' are perhaps the most obviously 1920s and 1930s in style, while many of the pendants depict the luxurious shapes of fruit and flowers. *M:* 'WL22' w11 × h9in (28 × 25.5cm); 'Large Petal' pendant w4½ × h6in (11.5 × 15cm); 'Poppy' pendant w16 × h7in (40.5 × 18cm). *P:* 'WL22' £35.65; 'Petal' £12.50; Poppy' £114.

Illumin's 'Poppy' Tiffany-style pendant

JOHN LARKING
Versatile, multi-directional 'Javelin' light. The arm, a slim steel rod ingeniously suspended on a double loop of thread, can cantilever out from ceiling or wall at any angle, in any plane. The lamp itself is fixed into the free end of the rod and has anti-glare shade that can be ro-

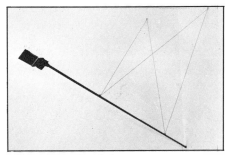

John Larking's 'Javelin'

tated to provide directional or reflected light. Available in black, white and stainless steel finishes. *M:* l166cm (65¼in); 60W. *P:* £39-£45.

THE LAST DETAIL
Lighting with a sense of humour. The Last Detail offer a range of unusual accessories for furnishing and decoration which includes some bizarre but functional light fittings. Of particular note is the life-size 'Goose' whose body glows with light. *M:* h24in (61cm). *P:* £35. The 'Goose' is just one, and the most expensive, of a collection of glowing animals and shapes; others are in the form of a duck, penguin, cockerel, rabbit, sheep, crescent moon and 'Shell Sign', like that of the petrol company.

The Last Detail. Top: miniature 'Hollywood' and 'Movie' lights; below: 'Goose' lights

LIGHTING

In miniature are the 'Hollywood Light', a scene light complete with adjustable tripod stand and adjustable baffles, and 'Movie Light', replica of a movie-camera, also on adjustable tripod stand, housing a bulb instead of a roll of film and lens. Both produce a finely controlled beam from low-energy halogen bulbs. *M:* 'Hollywood Light' max h14in (35.5cm); 'Movie Light' max h16in (40.5cm); both 40W. *P:* £35–£45. The Last Detail offer a mail order service.

LEAD & LIGHT
Opalescent and coloured glass 'Tiffany lights'. Lead & Light stained glass specialists offer 11 standard designs with tulip, floral and sunrise motifs in marvellously rich colours and some Tiffany-style table lamp bases. For a small additional charge shades can be made up in customer's own colour scheme. All pendant shades are sold wired and with brass chain and ceiling hook. *M:* eight-panel 'Tulip' w15¼in × h9¼in (38 × 24cm); six-panel 'Floral with Crown' w9½ × h12in (24 × 30.5cm); 'Double Tulip' table lamp shade w14½ × h9½in (37 × 24cm); table lamp base h15in (38cm). *P:* eight-panel 'Tulip' £69; six-panel 'Floral with Crown' £59.50; 'Double Tulip' £76; base £34.

Tiffany-style 'Double Tulip' shade and base from Lead & Light

THE LIGHTING WORKSHOP
Impressive retail range encompassing table and floor lights, downlighters, uplighters, clip and clamp spotlights, desk and task lights in a full range of colours, styles and sophistication. Imported from France is chic, compact 'Generation' light which uses the precision beam,

high output, multi-mirrored dichroic bulb (available with three different beam widths). The fitting can be mounted on wall or ceiling, with or without integral transformer, and given paint, chrome or gold finishes. *M:* d2¼ × l3¾ × w3¼in (5.5 × 9.5 × 8cm) with integral transformer l5 × d2¼ × w3¼in (12.5 × 5.5 × 8cm); 20W. *P:* from £48.85.

Designed primarily for architects and designers is the LUCIFER LINEAR SYSTEM: miniaturized display lighting developed to light the most delicate piece of jewellery or porcelain without the unsightly clutter of track and spot. The halogen bulbs clip onto an injection-moulded plastic strip with self-adhesive back and brass reflector. The self-adhesive strip allows the tiny tube to be concealed under a shallow shelf or perhaps inside the arch of a small recess. Available in maximum lengths of 79in (200cm), to be cut out as required. *M:* track 1.55 sq cm (¾ sq in). *P:* £40 per length (without bulbs).

The Lighting Workshop's 'Generation' Spot

LITA DISPLAY LTD
Primarily functional lighting in a choice of coloured finishes and sizes, developed to meet the requirements of architects and designers. SPACIOLITA is Lita's own tubular lighting system which can be suspended, surface-mounted or freestanding in any configuration. There are fluorescent and track units with a good range of couplers and other accessories, in standard anodized aluminium with matt black accessories or in more than 13 bright colours. *M:* fluorescent module 1m (39in); track module 1.5m (59in) *P:* fluorescent £85; track £90. In addition, Lita produce standard and flanged track lengths, twin and triple circuit. *M:* standard twin circuit 1.5m (59in); flanged triple circuit 2.5cm (99in). *P:* standard twin £18; flanged triple £43.

There are four different types of mains voltage track fitting: 'Ambient', 'Spot', 'Pinpoint' and 'Frame'. In total there is a choice of 47 different fittings in various colours and metallic finishes. As it is generally the bulb that dictates the application of each fitting, the range includes at least one fitting for each of the following bulbs: tungsten halogen, crown silvered, PAR, standard GLS and E-series. *P:* £10–£119.

Recessed downlighters with a visible source total seven with '602' in white designed for a miniature halogen reflector lamp, with optional anti-dazzle cowl. *M:* dia 97mm (3¾in); 50W, *P:* £13.90. Larger '642' has unusual feature of a silver reflector for the standard crown-silvered bulb. *M:* dia 23cm (9in) *P:* £10.25. Other recessed downlighters include: three concealed source fittings with round or square surrounds, all with white, brown, brass or nickel finishes; four with cone reflectors; one thin rectangular fluorescent fitting in steel; one round, low energy fluorescent; five halogen fittings; one linear discharge lamp; and two sodium and four mercury vapour fittings, all with polished gold reflectors. Semi-recessed fittings come in two basic styles: either a protruding shallow box '673' in white or brown or with a square base and tube projection. The latter come in eight variations, all in white, brown, brass or nickel finishes. *M:* '615' (the smallest) dia 11.5cm (4½in); 40W. *P:* (white) £8.50. There are seven recessed-eyeball fittings, two of the most unusual being '676' with a protruding rectangle rather than the usual hemisphere, adjustable in angle with anti-dazzle device; and '653' for miniature halogen lamp with framed beam and adjustable lens and mirror. '676' comes in white and brown, '653' in white only. *M:* '676' dia 12cm (4¾in) '653' dia 20cm (7¾in), 100W. *P:* '676' £21.80; '653' £34.35. Accessories for recessed fittings are: a wallwasher giving an asymmetrical shape, a louvre frill for cutting dazzle, a deflector to mask direct glare and a glass globe with ribbed or smooth surface.

Lita's 15 wall and ceiling fittings are functionally designed. There are slim cubes and tubes, and flatter round or square boxes, all in white finishes and many with anti-dazzle devices. From the range of 22 pendants, one of the most interesting is '6093' in black polycarbonate with opal white hemispherical bowl, with co-ordinated wall fitting, table lamp and standard lamp, all in this black-and-white scheme. *M:* '6093' dia 32cm (12½in). *P:* £18.25. Similarly stylish are '6044' with curly cable and steel coolie shade in white, amber or green with rise-and-fall mechanism, and '52167', a very elongated coolie shade in white, amber or yellow with black joints or in black with red joints. *M:* '6044' dia 50cm (19¾in); '52167' dia 52cm (20½in). *P:* '52167' £34.80; '6044' £32.60.

For fluorescent lighting tubes, there are two

Lita Display's '6093', '6044' and '52167' pendant fittings

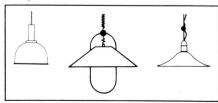

slim-line alternatives; '6206' in steel, aluminium and plastic with white lacquer finish, designed to be suspended from a wire at each end; and '3341' in matt aluminium which stands on a black end cap. *M:* '6206' w102cm (40¼in); may be reduced by 50cm (19¾in). *P:* '6206' £31; '3341' £61.95.

More than merely functional is Lita's ACCENT LIGHTING, developed for sophisticated display use. Fifteen low voltage fittings — track, fully recessed and semi-recessed downlighters — vary in size, complexity and beam width depending on their application. The different fittings come in black, white, gold, brown and chrome finishes; each has separate transformer unit. *P:* £25–£200.

MARLIN LIGHTING LTD ♠

Well-integrated fittings for both decorative and functional lighting schemes.

Sparkling CASCADE chandeliers consist of a myriad of interlocking crystalline glasses available in eight honeycomb-like configurations, either suspended or surface-mounted. *M:* d22–120cm (8¾–47¼in); 60–140W. *P:* £140–£300. Smaller units also available recessed or wall-mounted. Marlin make two other designs of chandelier, both in brass and both in three- and five-arm versions. T range in traditional Flemish style and V range in modern style with polished or silver-finished brass stems supporting distinctive cone, onion or semi-hemisphere glasses. Glasses come in clear, white crystalite, opal, amber, amber twist or honey options. *M:* T three- and five-light models dia 58cm (22in), each light 100W; V three-light model dia 52cm (20½in), five-light model dia 62cm (24½in), each light 100W. *P:* T£110–£160; V £70–£126. Matching single and twin wall fittings are also available and V range glasses also appear as individual pendants.

On a more functional note, LIGHTLINE SYSTEM 98–40, one of Marlin's five track systems, includes both fluorescent and track modules

Five of the configurations in Marlin's CASCADE range

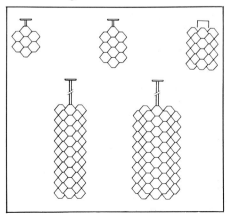

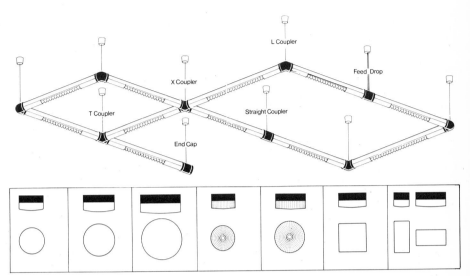

From Marlin. Top: LIGHTLINE SYSTEM 98-40; below: opal and prismatic units in the TRIMLINE range △

finished in chrome, brown or white. Track module can take any Marlin J-type spotlight at any point along its length. All modules can be rotated through 335 degrees and linked together using straight, 'T', 'X' or 'L' couplers, offering an infinite variety of light-grid options, from the simple rectangle suspended in the centre of the room to a more complex configuration to take light into the furthest corner. *M:* modules, l162 × dia 6.7cm (64 × 2½in); 18W, 36W or 58W. *P:* £64–£174. Individual pendant units also available.

In addition to tracks and spots — and there are many variations on Marlin's 15 cowl, drum, reflector and globe spot styles — there is an impressive range of directional lights and downlighters. These include cubes and cylinders that protrude from ceiling or wall, others that can be recessed at variable depths and completely recessed circles and squares. Type '2573' makes an unusual wall unit: twin cubes in oyster white or pale bronze with optional shining clear glass trim open at both ends to throw light up and down. *M:* w25 × h11.5 × d15.5cm (9¾ × 4½ × 6in); 2 × 60–100W. *P:* £44.

Left to right: Marlin Lighting's '2573' twin wall units, OPALIGHT surface fittings △, OPALIGHT pendant

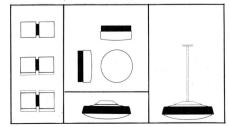

Other ranges include OPALIGHT ceiling and wall lights; round, square and rectangular crystalite ceiling and wall fittings for bathrooms; and well-known TRIMLINE square, rectangular or circular surface-mounted ceiling and wall fittings with opal or prismatic diffusers locked into slate black base; totally functional and almost unbreakable, they are said to be dust-free, weather, shock and vibration proof, and non-corrosive! TRIMLINE is available with either fluorescent or incandescent bulbs. *M:* circular dia 20, 25 or 32.5cm (7¾, 9¾ or 12½in); square 23 × 23cm (9 × 9in); rectangular w25 × d12.5cm (9¾ × 5in). *P:* £10–£50. Marlin also make emergency and sign lights.

ARNOLD MONTROSE LTD

Huge collection of decorative lighting with emphasis on the formal look of shining brass and glass. Many of Montrose's 80 or more chandelier designs would be ideal for function rooms or reception halls. On traditional lines there are 40 designs in cut lead crystal or Strass crystal and polished or gilt-finished brass, and 12 surface-mounted Strass crystal bowls; but there are also 23 striking modern designs — geometric, with sparkling pelmets in different coloured glass, and with vertical glass rods or crystal beads strung on straight or spiralling gilt chains producing a waterfall effect. *M:* '185/14/CR' Georgian-style 12-light crystal chandelier dia 38 × h52in (96.5 × 132cm); '349' Strass crystal bowls dia 22, 28 or 34in (56, 71 or 96.5cm); '249' modern pendant with Triedri glass spiral in four sizes dia 12-24 × h30–65in (30.5–61 × 76–165cm). *P:* '185/14/CR' £3,125; '349' £649–£1,820; '249' £348–£1,232.

Planners on a really grand scale might choose the STRASS CRYSTAL MODULAR SYSTEM, in which 20 sq cm (7¾ sq in) modules — gilded

LIGHTING

brass plates with Strass crystal chains of varying lengths suspended from them — can be combined in innumerable permutations on any scale. *P: on application.*

Less ostentatious than the crystal chandeliers are three elegant polished brass candlestick chandeliers in the Georgian and Adam styles; nine with arching polished brass stems and tulip glasses (available clear, frosted, cut or acid-etched, and in amber and amethyst shades); four angular modern designs; four in the elegant Empire style (in gilt and black, gilt and white, polished brass and bronzed metalwork or polished brass and dark green, with either candlestick lights or tulip glasses); three with opal glass spheres on brass frames; and even a mock Elizabethan flambeau pendant with gilt-finish 'torches' and frosted glass 'flames'. *M:* '115/8' Adam-style 18-light brass chandelier dia 38 × h37in (96.5 × 94cm); '110/6' Empire-style six-light chandelier dia 22 × h25in (56 × 63.5cm); '212/FLM/3' three-light flambeau pendant dia 17 × h24in (43 × 61cm). *P:* '115/18' £1,575; '110/6' £285; '212/FLM/3' £419.

From Arnold Montrose. Left to right, from top: '115' and '110' chandeliers, '212' flambeau pendant, '164', '183' and '155' pendants, '677', '633' and '665' table lamps

Also in crystal are six single pendants on gilt-finish or brass chains, and eight surface-mounted bowls. *M:* single pendant '177/1' dia 5 × h10½in (12.5 × 26.5cm); '331/2' surface-mounted bowl dia 10 × h6½in (25.5 × 16.5cm). *P:* '177/L' £94; '331/2' £172. Range of ceiling fittings also includes four square and hexagonal box fittings with brass frame and clear glass panes, and fourteen round and hexagonal designs in brass and frosted glass or opal perspex. *M:* '367/4' square box fitting with clear glass w13 × d13in (33 × 33cm). *P:* £216. There are ten brass pendant fittings with oval or round white, yellow or green fabric shades, most with gold metallic trim, on brass chains; plus single spheres and lanterns in opal, amber or smoked glass and functional cafe-style lights with opal spheres topped by rounded metal shades — '155/1' with small shade, '154/1' with larger shade, in green, polished chrome or yellow *M:* '164/2' brass pendant with shade dia 25 × h18in (63.5 × 45.5cm); '183/1' opal sphere pendant dia 10 × h20in (25.5 × 51cm); '1551/1' dia 12 × h18in (30.5 × 45.5cm). *P:* '164/2' £105; '183/1' £69; '155/1' £141–£191.

Many of the chandeliers and ceiling lights have matching wall fittings, giving co-ordinated lighting on different levels. Designs range from Georgian-style brass candlestick lights, tulip glasses, flambeaux, traditional and modern versions of Strass crystal curtains, brass wall brackets with oval or round fabric shades, and metal-shaded wall bracket to match '155/1' and '154/1'. There are also Louis XVI gilt candlestick lights with two, three or five curling foliate arms and, in contrast, art deco '534/3' in chrome and frosted glass. *M:* '405/02' Louis XVI wall sconce h14 × w11½ × d4½in (35.5 × 29 × 11.5cm); '534/3' h22 × w18 × d9in (56 × 45.5 × 23cm). *P:* '405/02' £99; '524/3' £280.

To light bathroom mirrors, there are more than 20 vertical and horizontal strips: in brass and crystal (even with crystal drops) gilt and crystal, chrome and crystal, brass and textured acrylic, and theatrically styled with brass plate and textured glass cubes. *M:* '558/3' brass strip with prismatic diffuser h4 × w23 × d4in (10 × 58.5 × 10cm). *P:* £91–£104.

Montrose offer 15 table and standard lamp sets, most making conventional decorative use of brass and gilt finishes but some more innovative. 1930s-inspired '715/2' standard and '673/2' table lamps, for example, have white opal hemisphere shades on slim polished chrome stems and circular base. *M:* '715/2' h65 × dia 10in (165 × 25.5cm); '673/2' h26 × dia 7in (66 × 18cm). *P:* '715/2' £105; '673/2' £59. More than 70 others repeat styles seen elsewhere in the Montrose collection, from elaborate cut crystal lamp bases (even in standard-lamp sizes) to gilded urns, clear and opal glass vases and Empire-style shaded candlestick lamps. There are also sleek, square chrome bases with square white shades, ceramic ginger jars and vases in white, ivory, deep blue and maroon, and gleaming metallic-finished ceramic columns, jars and vases, all with Montrose's characteristic gold-trimmed fabric shades. *M:* '677' chrome base with square shade h34 × dia 15in (86.5 × 38cm); '633' ginger jar h30 × dia 13in (76 × 33cm); '655' mirror-platinum-finished ceramic vase h29 × dia 12in (73.5 × 30.5cm). *P:* '677' £91; '633' £58–£119; '665' £93. (All prices ex VAT.)

MR LIGHT

Modern and traditional lighting with an emphasis on functional elegance. Large lighting retailers with three London shops, Mr Light are also sole agents for a number of ranges, many of which have been developed in conjunction with them as a result of demands made at the shops by interior designers and architects.

Exclusive ranges include traditional ceramic CRACKLE WARE table lamps in 10 to 15 different shapes, variations on classic forms, ancient Chinese fish-tail and ginger jars, all with contrasting coolie shades. Predominantly matt glazes come in four subtle, weathered tones — ivory crackle, peach crackle, raw terracotta, gold lustre — and the 'Moucheté' lamps have a finely stippled finish in pale yellow, peach, blue or pink or a matt, stone-like

Mr Light's CRACKLE WARE

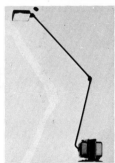

Top: plaster wall uplighters; below, left to right: 'Lili', 'Lumina'. From Mr Light

colour. *M:* h8–30in (20.5–76cm). *P:* £20–£150 (without shades).

Equally elegant is their series of solid brass lighting. Swing-arm lamps come in table, wall and floor-standing versions, one of the floor lamps with a telescopic stem. Brass base and stem are available with brass or chrome finish; fabric shades in black, white or red. *M:* table lamp '4010' h54 × reach 53cm (21¼ × 20¾in); shade dia 28cm (11in); wall fitting '1706' reach 62cm (24½in), shade dia 28cm (11in); telescopic floor lamp '3111' h133–167cm × reach 65cm (52¼–65 × 25½in), shade dia 38cm (15in). *P:* '4010' £125, shade £8.95; '1706' £89.95, shade £8.95; '3111' £215, shade £9.95. Rather more contemporary-looking are the brass wall and floor uplighters with shallow dish reflectors. The lights have halogen bulbs and dimmer control and are available in brass, black, white

or chrome finishes. *M:* '1138' wall fitting dish dia 25cm (9¾in), d35 × w21cm (13¾ × 8¼in); '3088' floor lamp h185cm (72¾in). *P:* '1138' £89.95; '3088' £225. In the 'Lili' table light, adapted from an original Bauhaus design, the shade is again a shallow dish, but upturned and with a circular hole cut in the top so that light and heat diffuse upwards as well as downwards. Shade is set on an adjustable stirrup-bracket and round stem and base, all in brass or chrome finish. *M:* h40 × dia 29cm (15¾ × 11½in). *P:* £125.

Mr Light are also exclusive agents for a number of high-tech task lights. Tiny 'Ego' reading light, with two light intensity settings, is deceptively simple with half-bullet base and similar shade connected by a slim metal stem that pivots at each end. Base and shade can be painted black, white, pink or blue, and wall-mounted version is also available. *M:* h42cm

(16½in). *P:* £49.95. DAPHINE halogen task light is just as simply designed, with slim, jointed extendable arm and neat, trough-shaped shade, all in metal painted red, white or black. It is available as a floor or table lamp (with weighted base) or as wall and desk lamp (with clamp or clip attachments); clamp desk lamp '01' has two light intensities. *M:* floor lamp '02', arm l150cm (58in), 50W; '01' arm l88cm (34¾in); both 50W. *P:* '02' £159.95; '01' £119.95. IGLOO is particularly stunning with a reflector closely fitted over the bulb, covered by a grill-work cowl. Shade and spindly stem are black, white, red, yellow or grey metal. It comes in floor, wall, ceiling, and clip, clamp

PRICES AND INFORMATION WERE CORRECT AT THE TIME OF GOING TO PRESS

LIGHTING

*Desk lamps from Mr Light. Above: 'Ego';
below: IGLOO*

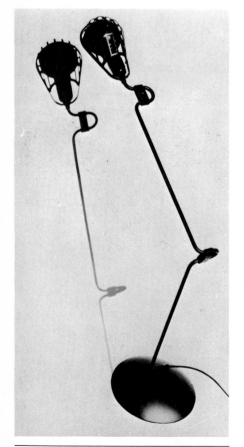

and freestanding table versions with stand in different lengths, down to tiny '38' with clip base attached almost directly to shade. *M:* '36' floor lamp h100 × reach 69.5cm (39¼ × 27¼in); '38' h26.5cm (10¼in), clip to fit 5cm (2in) desk top; both 75W. *P:* '36' £105, '38' £35. Mr Light's unique moulded plaster uplighters are unfinished so that they can be painted to match the rest of the decor. There are three distinctive designs, which owe their smooth lines to art deco. All are similar in size and one, '1340', can be corner as well as wall unit. *M:* '1340' w26 × d18cm (10 × 7in); 60W. *P:* £59.95.

MAXINE NAYLOR

PVC used to produce intriguing lighting effects. Maxine Naylor studied furniture design with special reference to the application of new materials, and her SHEET LIGHTING demonstrates this material's potential as a light diffuser. White sheet PVC, folded in geometric shapes, is held in place by polished or anodized aluminium rods, which also carry the

Maxine Naylor's 'Bow Light' and two pendants

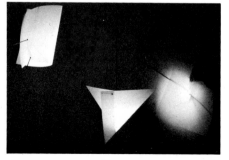

power cable. Five variations are: freestanding (with rod set into Portland stone base); 'Leaning' (to go against the wall); two different ceiling lights; and 'Bow Light' (to be mounted on the wall). *M:* freestanding, base w25 × d25 × h5.5cm (9¾ × 9¾ × 2in), rod h185cm (72¾in); leaning, rod 185cm (72¾in), shade 40 × 40cm (15¾ × 15¾in); ceiling, rods 50cm (19¾in), shade 30 × 30cm (11¾ × 11¾in), 40 × 40cm (15¾ × 15¾in) or 40 × 80cm (15¾ × 31½in); 'Bow Light', rod 150cm (59in), shade 50 × 60cm (19¾ × 23½in). *P:* freestanding £81; ceiling £31.20; 'Bow' and leaning lights £39.50.

NICE IRMA'S LTD (FABRICATION)

Importers since 1972 of the unusual from India, stocking two designs of brass lamp bases. Brass spheres engraved with concentric circles come in three sizes. *M:* dia 10, 12 and 14in (25.5, 30.5 and 35.5cm). *P:* £38, £46, £54. Tall brass cylinder comes in one size only. *M:* h10in × dia 5in (25.5 × 13cm). *P:* £45. To complement, a big selection of shades covered in Nice Irma's ikat-printed cotton, in various sizes and shapes. *P:* from £16.

Brass lamp base with ikat shade, both from Nice Irma's

OMK DESIGN LTD ♨

Sleek beauties from a purveyor of the pure modern line. Coolie–shaded SAN-PAN rise-and-fall pendant is in pressed steel with black, white, grey, red, yellow, duck egg blue or dark blue finish. *M:* shade h17 × w52 × d52cm (6¾ × 20½ × 20½in); rise-and-fall height adjustment 1m (1yd); 60W. *P:* £62. SAN-PAN table and standard lamps are also available. RITZ table and standard models are reminiscent of

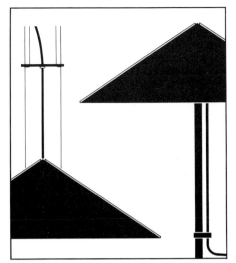

From OMK Design's SAN-PAN range△; rise-and-fall pendant and table lamp

the 1930s with hand-blown glass shades and bases. Table lamps come with white opal glass base and shade, satin matt glass base and shade, satin striped glass base and shade, chrome-and-black base and satin striped shade, or with metal base in the same colours as SAN-PAN and white opal glass shade. *M:* h36 × dia 33cm (14¼ × 13in), h41 × dia 33cm (16¼ × 13in) or h42 × dia 45cm (16½ × 17¾in); 100W. *P:* £50–£58. Standard lamps have chrome column and white opal or satin striped glass shade, or coloured column (choice as above) and plain white opal shade. *M:* h173 × dia 45cm (68 × 17¾in); 100W. *P:* £92–£104.

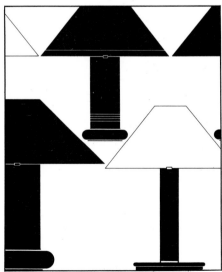

OMK's RITZ table lamps

⚫ *INDICATES ONE OR MORE OF THE PRODUCTS MENTIONED ARE SELECTED BY THE DESIGN CENTRE*

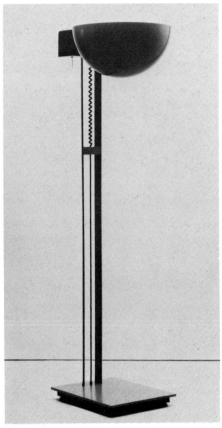

Orgatech's 'Bole' uplighter△

ORGATECH LTD ⚫

High intensity discharge uplighter for high tech offices — a real alternative to a blanket of fluorescents. Distinctively styled, energy-saving and glare-free, the 'Bole' uplighter consists of a compact discharge bulb mounted horizontally inside a large hemispherical reflector bowl, with control gear box attached. The basic design is freestanding, but variations include desk-mounting cantilever, and brackets for mounting on to a wall or substantially-built office partition; special designs such as ceiling versions can be produced to order. Bowl and stand are matt enamelled in combinations of vivid colours such as deep red, magenta, mid-blue, blue-green, black, dark brown and soft yellow. *M:* bowl dia 47cm (18½in), floor lamp h190cm (78in); 150–400W. *P:* £385 + bulb £32.

PERRINGS

Ceramic table lamps in six classic shapes, including ginger jar, sphere and hexagonal, with matching pagoda, empire or coolie shades, in ten colours: white, ivory, cafe au lait, celadon green, powder blue, pastel green, pastel pink, peach, burgundy and black. *M:* h18½–31in (45.5–78.5cm). *P:* £23.95–£49.95.

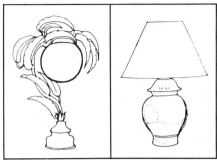

Left to right: Perrings' 'Metal Petal' and ceramic ginger jar with empire shade

There are also two unusual lamps, both art deco in inspiration. 'Metal Petal' has ornate metal stem and opal sphere, available in table, wall bracket and pendant versions in white, pastel pink or blue. *M:* h17in (43cm). 'Lady Lamp' is a white ceramic nude supporting an opal sphere. *M:* h26in (66cm). *P:* £49.95.

PIPE DREAMS LTD

Surreal bathroom lights. Pipe Dreams not only make bathroom fittings such as taps and shower-mixers (see *Bathrooms*) but a wall light to match, made of black or white china and shaped like a tap, with illuminated opal globe like a giant drip! *M:* h32 × d23cm (12½ × 9in); 40W. *P:* £22.50.

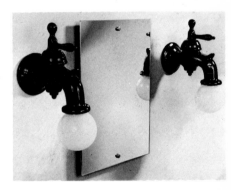

Pipe Dreams' bathroom lights

POOLE LIGHTING

Brass light fittings, many with a period feel. Among the latest introductions into the range are swivel-arm lights in solid brass, available as table, wall and standard lamps. Complementary shades come in three sizes and four colourways: black with gold liner, beige with gold liner, burgundy with gold liner and pink with white liner. *M:* '7401' h55cm (21¼in), max reach 50cm (19¾in); '7400' h29cm (11½in), max reach 53cm (20¾in); '7402' h154cm (60½in), max reach 55cm (21¼in). *P:* £32.10, £24.40, £52.50 (with shades). There are 26 styles of 'period' brass lights, each

LIGHTING

range consisting of two pendant lights, one with three, the other with five lights, and one single and one double wall sconce. Some styles also have matching table lamps. Apart from the three styles of chandelier which come with their own glass pendants, the glass shades are separate, with a choice of 16 shapes in a number of different colours and finishes. The different styles vary only slightly in size. *M:* '129' five- and three-light pendants h55 × dia 44cm (21¾ × 17¾in); single wall sconce h21 × d20 × w13cm (8¼ × 7¾ × 5in); double wall sconce h21 × d16 × w30cm (8¼ × 6¼ × 11¾in); table lamp h22 × dia 12cm (8¾ × 4¾in). *P:* £48.20, £31.90, £10.70, £18.30.

Poole also make brass-finish lights in the style of traditional oil lamps. There are five hanging and five table styles, with a choice of three shades in four colours: white, amber, coffee and green. *M:* hanging '7081' h60 × dia 40cm (23½ × 15¾in); table '7541' h39 × dia 30cm (15¼ × 11¾in). *P:* '7081' £22.90; '7541' £22.30. Twenty-one styles of lantern, from round to octagonal, complete the range of hanging lights; available with clear, smoked, clear etched or smoked etched glass. Solid brass standard and table lamps each come in seven styles. And the three brass individual picture lights come in two finishes — smooth and ridged — and three lengths. *M:* hanging lantern — '7215/3' h78 × dia 31cm (30¾ × 12¼in); brass standard lamp 'FS100' h140 × 35cm (55 × 13¾in); table lamp 'TL303' h42 × dia 13cm (16½ × 5in); picture light '7244' h11 × d19 × w29cm (4¼ × 7½ × 11½in). *P:* '7215/3' £36.70 (glass extra); 'FS100' £27.80; 'TL303' £18; '7244' £13.10.

Poole's '129' range

PRIMA LIGHTING LTD.

Colourful, innovative lighting from Italy. Reggiani manufacture one of the largest selections of recessed fittings available in Britain. Range includes recessed, captive eyeball and semi-recessed fittings, most with adjustable bulb-holders, anti-dazzle multi-grooves or finishing rings, and cone reflectors. Their de luxe BIJOU range in solid brass includes recessed eyeballs in three sizes, discreet but sturdy surface spotlights and track fittings, all designed for low-

Prima's BIJOU spotlights, by Reggiani

voltage dichroic light sources. All can be fitted with integral or remote transformers. Recess eyeball units can be set in linear strip ceilings without the need for adaptor plates. *M:* eyeball dia 9 × d14cm (3½ × 5½in). *P:* £69.68 (with integral transformer).

Reggiani's comprehensive range of halogen fittings are available fixed or adjustable, recessed or semi-recessed, and are small and light enough to be installed in any ceiling, linear or louvred. Series also includes surface spotlights, projectors, track and freestanding fittings, with or without integral transformers. All come in seven standard colour finishes: black, bronze, satin brass, polished brass, chrome, matt chrome and white. *M:* freestanding one-light unit h190cm (74¾in). *P:* £189.98.

ORIONE fittings, from Still 5, have been purpose-designed for the Philips' low energy bulbs and are particularly suitable for public buildings and amenity use (both interior and exterior). Modular pendant, wall- and post-mounted fittings have body of die-cast aluminium in red, white or brown finish, and clear or smoked globes. *M:* post fittings w35 × h33.5cm (13¾ × 13in). *P:* £64 (with bulb).

Bacchelli's modular fluorescent system incorporates track units suitable for either low or mains voltage. An unusual feature is the choice of silver, gold or white colours for reflectors and louvres, which help to modify the colour of the fluorescent tubes, so important in display lighting. Components can be assembled in any rigid configuration, and because each unit has an integral power unit there is no problem in forming long, continuous runs. *M:* basic fluorescent unit l180 × dia 9cm (70¾ × 3½in). *P:* £88.48.

Colourful ANACONDA fluorescent tube system by Programma Luce also includes matching table lamps, wall and ceiling lights and suspended fixture. The modular aluminium extrusion can be assembled in any number of configurations using rigid and flexible couplings plus two-, three- and four-way joints. It comes in seven standard colours: red, black, light blue, dark blue, green, yellow and white. *M:*

'Baby' table fitting w85 × h70cm (33½ × 27½in). *P:* £20 (without fluorescent tube). ANACONDA and many of Prima's other fittings can be supplied in other colours for an additional charge.

From Prima, freestanding halogen fitting by Reggiani

SANDERSON

Ceramic table lamps from Sanderson, long known for their textiles and wallpapers and now selling furniture, carpets and lighting as well in their lovely, re-designed showroom. Choose from nine base shapes: ginger jar, spiral vase, octagonal column, candlestick, large octagonal jar, large hexagonal spice jar and large jar. All can be glazed in five colourings — rose/beige, blue/grey, lilac/grey, neutral cream or pale green — and choice of

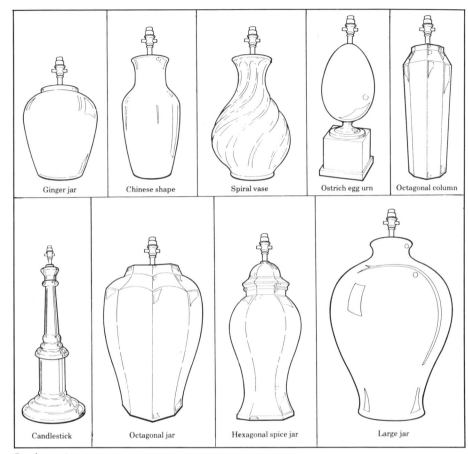

Ginger jar | Chinese shape | Spiral vase | Ostrich egg urn | Octagonal column

Candlestick | Octagonal jar | Hexagonal spice jar | Large jar

Sanderson's ceramic lamp bases

finishes includes crackle, spatter and mottle effects. In addition, unique glazed finishes can be created to commission. *M:* ginger jar h25cm (9¾in); octagonal jar h41cm (16¼in). *P:* ginger jar £28.50; octagonal jar £103.

These bases co-ordinate with natural Honan silk or glazed chintz lampshades in three classic shapes — 'Coolie', 'Empire' and 'Sanderson Coolie' — in small, medium or large sizes. Silk 'Coolie' comes in small and medium sizes with narrow or wide knife pleats. Silk 'Empire' comes in all three sizes with box pleats and in small and medium with narrow or wide knife pleats. 'Sanderson Coolie' comes in all sizes both in plain, glazed chintz (in 16 stock colours), with full gathered pleat or tight cover (giving a slight ribbed effect), and in silk with full gathered pleat, tight cover, narrow or wide knife pleats. All are handmade and lined with beige silk. Shades in any style or size can be made to special order in any of 60 colours of plain glazed chintz or 65 colours of Honan silk. *M:* 'Coolie' dia 46, 53 or 61cm (18, 20¾ or 24in); 'Empire'

41, 48 or 51cm (15¾, 19 or 20in); 'Sanderson Coolie' 43, 51 or 56cm (17, 20 or 22in). *P:* small 'Sanderson Coolie' glazed chintz, tight covered, £38; large 'Sanderson Coolie', glazed chintz, full gathered £63.

SC Products' 'WS1'

SC PRODUCTS

Elegant wall sconces based on a French design of the 1930s. 'WS1' is a bowl of polished chrome supported on an L-shaped wall bracket, with 3in (7.5cm) glass drops suspended through the base and backed by a reflecting chrome strip. 'WS2' is similar without the glass drops. *M:* w40.5 × h20 × d15cm (16 × 7¾ × 6in). *P:* 'WS1' £80; 'WS2' £60 (ex VAT).

Genuine 1930s lights are sometimes available; most have been renovated and adapted to meet current British standards and to take the standard GLS bayonet bulb.

SMITHBROOK LTD

Wrought iron lamps and lanterns made with traditional craftsmanship and attention to detail. Smithbrook produce a substantial range of lanterns for corner bracket, bracket or newel post mountings. There are more than 30 different shapes, all with standard matt black finish and clear glass, some with options of white finish and amber glass. Illustrated is 'S53', available with bracket or corner bracket mounting. *M:* d35.5cm (14in), lantern h58.5cm (23in). *P:* £66.50. In addition there are more than 35 wall light designs with single or double candle bulb-holders or with glasses, some

Smithbrook's 'S53'

LIGHTING

Smithbrook's 'S467'

available with white, pewter and antique finishes as well as matt black. *P:* £8.95–£49. Smithbrook's 21 pendant fittings are all forged metalwork, assembled by hand. Each model comes in a variety of sizes and finishes. Most have candle bulb-holders but a few are available with glasses and black canopies. One of the most ornate is 'S467' with five arms as illustrated. *M:* dia 48cm (19in). *P:* £66.

There are 18 styles of standard lamp with either upright candle bulb-holder or adjustable bridge and standard bulb-holder; and five styles of table lamp, all with candle bulb-holder. *P:* standards £37–£55; table lamps £14–£31.

SPECTRUM

Functional fluorescent lighting from the Swedish company AB Bruno Herbst. Suspended task lights come with a variety of louvres and plain or perforated steel reflectors specially designed for use with one or two slimline

Selection from Spectrum's range of luminaire and fluorescent fittings, all by AB Bruno Herbst

energy-saving tubes. Unusual 'H169' fluorescent task light has wing-like extended reflectors and anti-glare shades in perforated steel. Surface-mounted fittings — which can also be suspended on chains from the ceiling — are high standard sheet steel with metallicized plastic, metal or aluminium louvres. Standard colour for all fittings is white, and 'H169' comes in white only, but others are available in bright red, yellow, blue, brown and orange on request. *M:* task lights, l78–169cm (30¾–66½in), w9.5–26cm (3¾–10¼in), 18, 36 or 58W; 'H169' l97 or 58 × w44cm (38¼ or 62½ × 17¼in), 18 or 36W; surface-mounted fittings l62–153cm (24½–60¼in), w10–63cm (4–24¾in), 18, 36, 58W. *P:* task lights £41–£115.80; 'H169' £110.30–£141.40; surface-mounted fittings £21.70–£82.90. Herbst also design and manufacture fittings to suit specific requirements, and Spectrum can provide a lighting management system for maximum energy savings.

TAG DESIGN PARTNERSHIP ◮

Free-mounted wall lights in brightly painted steel with PVC 'screens' creating intriguing light patterns on ceilings and walls. Available in eight vibrant colours: red, pink, black, blue, yellow, grey, white and light blue. 'Hattie', the smallest, has a PVC strip curved into two parallel slots in the painted steel back-plate, forming an opaque screen over the golfball bulb. *M:* back-plate 17.2 sq cm (6½ sq in); 'screen' w36 × d17.2cm (14¼ × 6½ in); 40 or 60W. *P:* £13. 'Manta' produces more dramatic shafts of light across ceiling and wall, reminiscent of the deadly Manta-ray! The painted-steel back-plate is square and the square PVC screen fits

into slots at each corner. *M:* 45 sq cm (17¾ sq in). *P:* £21. 'Cobra' table lamp, the newest member of the collection, continues the sculptural theme. A golfball bulb on a thick steel stem stands apart from the sweeping polyester shade, like a stylized cobra-head, both linked by a circular steel base. *M:* dia 30 × h27cm (11¾ × 10½in). *P:* £30.

Tag Design's 'Hattie' △

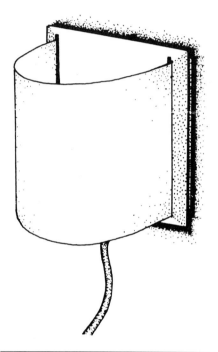

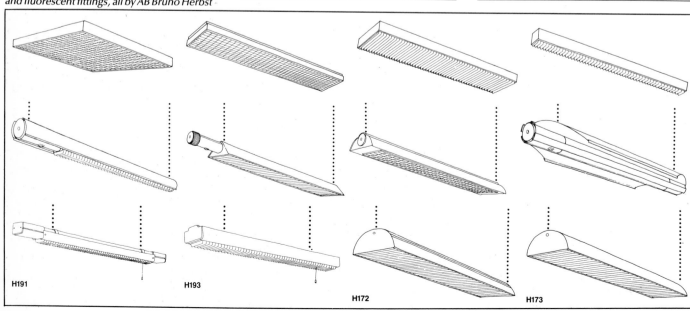

H191   H193   H172   H173

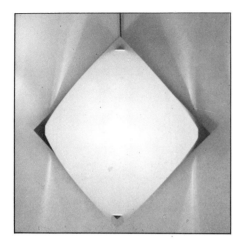

Top: 'Manta'△; below: 'Cobra'. Both from Tag

TEMPUS STET LTD

Extremely wide range of lights, mainly wall fittings, based on historical motifs and so particularly suitable for the room with a period feel. The 27 styles of wall sconce vary from the elaboration of 'L19', a candelabra with swag of fruit and flowers in the style of William Kent, and 'L27', a handsome light in the manner of Chinese Chippendale, to the simpler lines of 'L30' a bow and tassel with two candle-lights and 'L13', a Louis XVI oval supporting two small candle brackets decorated with an acanthus design. For extra style the range includes some combined mirrors and lights. There is 'L26', a handsome Adam sconce with tapered antique mirrors and, for a simpler setting, 'M16', a small Louis XV sconce. M: 'L19' h42 in (106.5cm); 'L27' h36in (91.5cm); 'L30' h23in (58.5cm); 'L13' h8in (20.5cm); 'L26' h37in (94cm); 'M16' h11¼in (28.5cm). P: 'L19' £200; 'L27' £160; 'L30' £80; 'L13' £70; 'L26' £200; 'M16' £75.

The five table lamp designs are based either on classical figures or candlesticks from historic churches. 'L22', a cherub and a swan, support a standard drum shade, as does 'L32', a winged sphinx. 'L23', a winged lion, supports a glass storm light. All three figures are gilt and rest on marble bases. 'L28' is a reproduction of an altar candlestick from St Martin's within Ludgate, London. M: 'L22' h18in (46cm); 'L32' h20in (51cm); 'L23' h24in (61cm); 'L28' h23in (58.5cm). P: 'L22' £150; 'L32' £220; 'L23' £150, storm glass £12, 'L28' £170.

These are three floor-standing lamps. 'L24' is a larger altar candlestick from Holkham Hall, Norfolk; 'L25' is a vestal virgin supporting a lamp and 'L55' is a fluted Edwardian standard lamp. M: 'L24' h45in (114cm); 'L25' h75in (190cm); 'L55' h56in (142cm). P: 'L24' £200; 'L25' £680; 'L55' £150 (gilt finish), £140 (wood).

Tempus Stet's 'L26'

△ *INDICATES AN ILLUSTRATED PRODUCT SELECTED BY THE DESIGN CENTRE*

SALLY TOWNSHEND (WRAPPA)

Square coolies, round coolies and geometrical shapes, on the wall, on the floor, from the ceiling or on the table. Sally Townshend creates furnishing fabric but has selected a few of her designs to make up into lights. Fabric panels are laced onto a painted metal frame to form lampshades on cylindrical or oblong handpainted bases; freestanding light fittings in the shape of a cube or pyramid; and pendant shades. Panels, plain or printed in soft pastel shades, have special finish that prevents burn from the bulb. Lights and lampshades available in various shapes, sizes and colourways.

Sally Townshend's lights. From top: handpainted square-sided lamp and coolie, round lamp and coolie, 'Tri-kite'

LIGHTING

M: cubes 43, 23 and 14 sq cm (17, 9 or 6 sq in); 'Tri-kite' wall light h42 × w26cm (16½ × 10¼in); round coolie shade dia 38 × h16cm (15 × 6¼in). P: cubes £36.80, £27.30 and £11.88; 'Tri-kite' £20.39; coolie £29.03.

CHRISTOPHER WRAY'S LIGHTING EMPORIUM LTD

Staggering selection of reproduction Victorian, Edwardian, Tiffany and art deco lighting, plus almost every imaginable accessory. Known for their turn-of-the-century brass fittings, Christopher Wray now produce some practical and modern lighting as well.

Most prosaic is the range of brass picture lights, clip-on CLIP LAMPS and three brass spotlights — moulded 'Edwardian', round 'Ball' and wide 'Reflector'. M: 'Edwardian' w8in (20.5cm). P: £24. For more decorative wall-mounting there are 32 brass brackets in varying neck styles and lengths. M: swan neck 6, 9 or 12in (15, 23 or 31cm). P: £9, £10, £11.50. Team these with any of 40 different glass shades. Twenty-five or more other wall fittings, mainly in brass, include ranges of SHIP'S GIMBALS, CLASSICAL CAST BRACKETS, and OIL STYLE BRACKETS which can be used with either paraffin or electricity. All these lamps can also be fitted with glass shades, except for the 'Waterford Oil Lamp' which has a fixed metal shade. M: 'Waterford' h23in (58.5cm). P: £82.50. For fans of deco, there's also a 'Deco' wall bracket.

Equally extensive range of desk and table lamps includes 20 or more typical oil-style lamps that can be fitted for paraffin or electricity; four classical brass COLUMN LAMPS with

Christopher Wray's 'Waterford Oil Lamp'

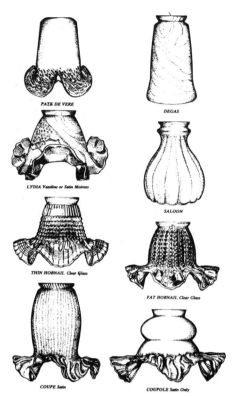

Selection of glass shades from Christopher Wray

PATE DE VERE

DEGAS

LYDIA *Vaseline or Satin Moirees*

SALOON

THIN HOBNAIL *Clear Glass*

FAT HOBNAIL *Clear Glass*

COUPE *Satin*

COUPOLE *Satin Only*

glass or fabric shades; two art deco lamps, 'Deco Column' and 'Palmist Hand'; useful, adjustable SPRING LAMPS with moulded shell-shaped brass shades on flexible arms; and a dozen others, including 'Queensbury Decorator', a double lamp that's fully adjustable in height. M: 'Deco Column' h15in (38cm); 'Hurlingham' SPRING LAMP max h17in (43cm); 'Queensbury Decorator' h32in (81.5cm). P: 'Deco Column' £37 (with shade); 'Hurlingham' £39.50 (with shade); 'Queensbury' £176 (without shades).

Six solid brass floor lamps echo the other ranges with brass, glass or fabric coolie shades. A seventh, 'Standfast', is more modern, an uplighter with upturned coolie shade in opal white glass. M: 'Standfast' h66in (167.5cm). P: £108.

Collection of pendants includes 20 or more traditional brass designs — ornate ones in the style of nineteenth-century oil and gas lamps, some matching wall bracket lamps; one billiard-table light; and HARP lamps with coloured glass globes suspended in a brass 'harp' shape (available in electric or paraffin-burning versions). M: HARP globes dia 5½–14in (14–35.5cm). P: £40–£115. For a total contrast, there

---

PRICES AND INFORMATION WERE CORRECT AT THE TIME OF GOING TO PRESS

Christopher Wray's 'Queensbury Decorator'

are three 1930s-style pendants that evoke a taste of Hollywood: 'Astaire' with perspex rings suspended on four chrome rods, 'Boulevard' and 'Adelphi' with fluted glass diffusers and chrome ends. M &P: on application.

Ever popular are Christopher Wray's TIFFANY shades, sold in 14 sizes and styles and 11 different colours — beige, honey, avocado, lilac, apple green, white, sky blue, hot orange, hot pink, dark blue and dark green. All can be combined with a range of 11 Tiffany-style bases featuring swirling nymphs and ivy. Other glass pendant shades are available with glass bead fringes in six designs.

Christopher Wray also stock an incredible variety of accessories for oil lamps, and one of Britain's largest ranges of light bulbs.

Left: 'Hurlingham' SPRING LAMP; right: 'Deco Column'. Both from Christopher Wray.

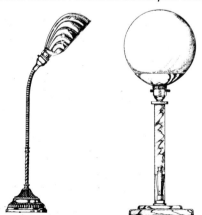

INTRODUCTION

Glass in its various forms can be used dramatically in decorative features or more subtly to create effects of space and light. A mirror hung opposite a window will bring light into an otherwise dark interior; a large one covering most of a wall can almost double the apparent size of a room. Stained, etched or sand-blasted glass can give interest to a window without a view or bring soft light and colour into a room; it can also be used as an unusual and translucent room divider.

This section gives a sample of the tremendous variety of products and services available in glass, from traditional mirrors to highly individual creations.

Craftspeople working in decorative glass today will create individual panels and windows both on traditional architectural lines and in unexpectedly contemporary designs. The price may be high depending on the techniques and the quality of the work involved, so it may be wise to ensure that a piece is removable and can be taken with you when you move house — most panels can be individually framed. The priority, however, is that the piece is securely installed.

When buying a mirror, check for distortion by looking into it from different distances and angles. Check the back too: it should be sealed to prevent scratching and exposed edges should be smooth.

• For period stained glass, see *Architectural salvage* at the end of the book.

MARK ANGUS

Distinctive contemporary architectural stained glass. Mark Angus has completed over 80 commissions for new and old buildings and examples of his work are held in the stained glass collections of the Victoria & Albert Museum and Ely Cathedral. *P:* approx £35 sq ft for design, execution and fixings.

Stained glass panels from Mark Angus

Door panels by Elaine C Bell

Chelsom's KRYSTAL mirror and console

ELAINE C BELL

Stained glass designed and made to order. Previous work includes free-hanging panels and room dividers as well as windows. All pieces are designed with attention to existing or planned decor, customer's personal taste, architecture and general environment. *P:* from £50 sq ft (minimum design fee £75).

ARTHUR BRETT & SONS LTD

Two elegant, eighteenth-century style mirrors from makers of fine reproduction English furniture — one landscape, one portrait. Both are mahogany with gilt enrichments, including gilt heraldic eagle on the top of the frame. *M:* landscape h86 × w109cm (33¾ × 43in); portrait h106 × w62cm (41¾ × 25½in). *P:* landscape £528; portrait £436 (ex VAT).

Arthur Brett's portrait mirror

CJ GLASS

Wide range of designs for stained glass windows. The designer, Charles Janson, specializes in work for private houses and conservatories. *P:* on application, estimates free. See colour illustration.

R J CHELSOM & CO LTD

From the KRYSTAL collection, a sophisticated mirror with frame of Plexiglass columns with shining brass corners; a perfect complement to the striking KRYSTAL console table, also in Plexiglass and brass. *M:* w20 × h35in (50 × 87cm). *P:* £170.

MIRRORS AND GLASS

Mirrors by The Conran Shop

THE CONRAN SHOP
Selection of simple beech-framed mirrors. *M:* square 120 × 120cm (47 × 47in); round dia 140cm (55in); rectangular w120 × h200cm (47 × 79in). *P:* £160, £350, £225.

ENVIRONMENT COMMUNICATION
Seven mirrors designed by Eugenio Carmi for the Italian firm Acerbis and conceived very much as works of art — the overall shape, drawn lines and planes of colour interact ever-changingly with whatever is reflected. Parallelogram-shaped 'No. 3' has diagonal bands of black, grey and white at the top and of brighter colours below. *M:* w70 × h90cm (27½ × 35½in). *P:* from £233. See colour illustration.

CELIA FRANK
Traditional and contemporary stained glass for domestic and architectural settings. This well-established artist specializes in large-scale modern work. *P:* on application.

PRICES AND INFORMATION WERE CORRECT AT THE TIME OF GOING TO PRESS

Traditional window by Goddard & Gibbs

GODDARD & GIBBS STUDIOS
Designers and restorers of decorated and leaded stained glass since 1868. Their work ranges from windows and roof-lights to interior panels using techniques of appliqué, *dalle-de-verre*, acid etching and sandblasting in addition to staining and painting. They provide a design service and will, if required, modify customers' own designs for interpretation in stained glass. *P:* on application.

HABITAT DESIGNS LTD
Wall, cheval and hand mirrors for bedrooms simply framed in wood, metal and plastic. Grid-patterned or plain mirror tiles can be used to cover a wall or bought singly with narrow frames in red, white or black. *M:* framed tile w40 × h40cm (15¾ × 15¾in). *P:* £7.25.

CHARLES HAMMOND
Large and varied Italian-made range reflecting English fashions from the Queen Anne period to the modern. Includes designs with bevelled glass, *oro-primo* (gilt), lacquer, bronzed and ornately carved frames. Lovely 'Florentine Necklace' frame is carved from cherrywood and can have plain wood, gold leaf or special painted finish. *M:* w33 × h40in (84 × 101.5cm). *P:* on application.

Charles Hammond's 'Florentine Necklace'

ED KING
Individually designed stained glass ranging from traditional leaded lights for front doors to more elaborate architectural stained glass. Previous pictorial designs have been based on such diverse subjects as a Yorkshire landscape, a fish and a skull. *P:* approx £35 sq ft. Ed King also does restoration work — estimates free. See following page for illustration.

Mirror by Sekon

Titchmarsh & Goodwin's 'RL22596'

Stained glass panel by Ed King

SEKON GLASSWORKS LTD
Really extensive range of decorative mirrors and glass from 'antique', marbleized and plain mirrors, acid embossing, brilliant cutting and bevelling to intricate stained glass panels in conjunction with their associate company Chicago Art Glass. Sekon take on a large amount of contract work for hotels, shops, restaurants etc. *P:* on application.

TEMPUS STET
Reproduction mirrors in a dazzling array of styles — early English, William and Mary, Chinese Chippendale, Regency, art nouveau etc — mainly produced in gilt or wood finish. Among the more restrained designs for large mirrors is 'M31' with acanthus leaves at the corners. *M:* w42 × h60in (106.5 × 152.5cm). *P:* £340 (ex VAT). Other sizes made to order.

TITCHMARSH & GOODWIN
Ogee-arched oak-framed mirror 'RL22596', part of an excellent range of handmade furniture in English oak. *M:* w23½ × h45½in (60 × 115.5cm). *P:* from £183.

PRICES AND INFORMATION WERE CORRECT AT THE TIME OF GOING TO PRESS

LAURENCE WHISTLER
Exquisite engraved panels of clear glass by the poet-artist responsible for the development of glass-engraving as an art form. His work tends towards symbolic interpretations of landscape with remarkable effects of light and shade. The panels can be set into windows or displayed in other ways. *P:* on application.

Engraved panel by Laurence Whistler

OFFICES

INTRODUCTION

The importance of a well-planned working environment is now widely recognized. Office-workers' morale and thus productivity is affected by the quality of their surroundings. Office furniture today reflects this attitude and is specifically designed to suit the tasks for which it is intended.

Offices can be arranged either on an open-plan system which makes for ease of communication, or in a 'cellular' style with separate working areas for small numbers or for individuals.

As with other areas of interior furnishing there is a huge choice — from traditional-style leather-topped partners' desks to the most sophisticated computer tables. The great computer boom of recent years has spurred the development of all types of furniture suitable for the 'electronic' office — VDU tables with split-level surfaces for screen and keyboard, printer tables, etc. Recent developments in style have been equally striking: on the one hand, high tech has made an aesthetic merit out of boldly functional design; on the other, laminates in bright or pastel colours — formerly considered too frivolous for a working environment — have been used to give a fresh look to standard desks and panels.

The section is divided into seven sub-sections: *Chairs, Co-ordinated furniture, Desks, Reception seating, Screens, Systems, Tables.* With a system a co-ordinated look can be created throughout thousands of square feet of office space. Systems include all the furniture from which individual work stations (comprising desks, extensions, storage and panels) can be made up. 'Wire management' facilities are often included so that all the necessary wiring for lighting, electrical and electronic equipment can be fitted and concealed. Panels are an efficient way of creating separate work areas with privacy and some degree of sound-proofing.

Reception desks are included in *Systems* while *Reception seating* is a separate sub-section.

Co-ordinated furniture covers smaller ranges which usually include desks, storage cabinets and tables.

Tables covers boardroom, conference and meeting tables.

Furniture with a more luxurious finish or in bigger sizes or both is often described by manufacturers as being suitable for 'executive' offices. However, there is no reason for such pieces to be used exclusively by management — so long as the company can afford it.

● All the furniture covered in the section is available on a contract basis. Most contract prices are negotiable depending on individual specifications and the size of the order. Many items are also available retail and retail prices are given where possible as a guide.

CHAIRS

● Measurements for desk chairs include both back and seat height, wherever both are available. The back height is always given first (e.g. if back height is 62cm and seat height 44cm, they are given as h62/44cm).

ANTOCKS LAIRN LTD △

Large choice of well designed chairs suitable for most office requirements.   Elegant ARTIC-ULA range combines aesthetics with advanced design. 'Articula III' has high articulating back, articulating seat with tilt, five-star swivel base, gas-operated height adjustment. It is scientifically designed to provide excellent back support and adjusts to user's weight and sitting position. Upholstered in a wide range of textures and colours including bright red. The aluminium sub-frame and base are available in polished chrome or black finish. *M*: w61 × d71 × h100cm (24 × 28 × 39¼in). *P*: £251.15–£280.80. Similar but with low back is 'Articula 211'. Twenty or so other models in the range offer fixed bases of various types, beam seating, and different adjustment mechanisms.

Antocks Lairn's 'Articula III' △

THE ARCHITECTURAL TRADING COMPANY LTD

DAVIS swivelling desk chair, a bold, chunky design from Italy. Full arms are in black-coated steel while seat and back, anatomically angled, are luxuriously cushioned with soft leather or

Architectural Trading's DAVIS

fabric covering. The chair swivels, is fully adjustable and rolls on castors. Colours include black, red, blue and cream. High- and low-backed versions are available. *M*: low back w65 × h85–93/44–52 × d67cm (25½ × 33½–36½/17¼–20½ × 26in); high back w65 × h104–112/44–52 × d73cm (25½ × 41–44/17¼–20½ × 28¾in). *P*: £335–£595.

H N BARNES (OFFICE SYSTEMS) LTD

HNB SEATING complementing an extensive office system (see *Systems*). Nine different designs range from visitor's chair to fully adjustable and flexible executive armchair. Ergonomically designed contoured back-rests and seats are featured in three distinct versions: secretarial chairs, desk/conference chairs with medium-height backs, and executive chairs with high backs and headrests. All chairs have steel frame and moulded polyurethane seat, back and armrests. All non-upholstered surfaces are finished in textured matt black epoxy and the upholstery is in a wool mix available in a wide selection of colours and weaves. *M*: executive chair w64 × d65 × h124–134/45–55cm (25½ × 25½ × 48¾–52¾/17¾–21¾in). *P*: £228. See following page for illustration.

BUSINESS INTERIORS LTD

Several excellent chair ranges by the Finnish firm Avarte.

SIRKUS comes in swivel and fixed-base versions with or without arms. All are beautifully simple with seat elements made from pressed birch plywood with laminate coating, gently curved. Slim seat and back cushioning is upholstered in Avarte's choice of 100% wool in eight shades or leather in five shades. The metal arms and bases, and the seat edges can be picked out in red, yellow, blue, or white, or

From left: HNB desk/conference, executive and secretarial models from H N Barnes

Business Interiors' SIRKUS '484MN'

left plain black. '484MN' chair has arms and fixed base. *M*: w53 × d60 × h96cm (20¾ × 23½ × 37¾in). *P*: £218.50–£249.50.

The secretarial chair, operating stool, desk chair, executive armchair and fixed–base armchair in the VARIUS range by the Spanish firm Casas have an original design. '254' swivel armchair has a spidery five-star pedestal base; for comfort it has a choice of mechanical or pneumatic seat–height adjustment, plus automatically adjusting back and seat. The metal base comes in black epoxy coating or chrome finish, while the central column and frame are available in eight varied colours including ter-

racotta and mint green. The colour interest is carried through to the upholstery which is available in a choice of four fabrics in several striking colours including bottle green and cognac. Contrasting colours can be used for interior and exterior and the leather armrests are in grey, black or terracotta. *M*: w64 × d60 × h87–95/45–53cm (25¼ × 23½ × 34¼–37½/17¾–20¾in). *P*: £321.50–£333. Can also be upholstered in customer's own material.

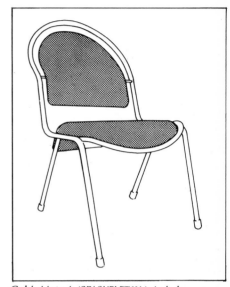

'254' and armless desk chair from Business Interiors' VARIUS

CUBIC METRE FURNITURE ⚠

Simple, well designed SKELETON chair range. The chairs include the simple stacking type with solid or metal-mesh back and seat, a five-star base swivel chair with gas–lift, and a beam-seat version linking two or three units. There's a full range of accessories for conferences including chair links, writing tablet, briefcase rest. Metal frames and fabric or leather seating

PRICES AND INFORMATION WERE CORRECT AT THE TIME OF GOING TO PRESS

come in attractive matching or contrasting colours including blue, red, yellow, black, grey and cream. 'SB' is the simple stacking chair without arms with solid back and seat. *M*: w51 × d62 × h84/44cm (20 × 24½ × 33/17¼in). *P*: £49.99.

Cubic Metre's 'SB' SKELETON chair △

HILLE INTERNATIONAL LTD ⚠

Large range of chairs including the award–winning SUPPORTO. This lives up to its appearance in providing comfort for the office–worker. It has a secure five-star base,

Hille's SUPPORTO 'LWB ASC' △

three options for the back-rest (high/wide, low/wide, narrow — all with or without arms) and instant gas-operated lever adjustment for both seat height and back-rest angle. The chair also adjusts automatically to the user's changes in sitting position, thus always providing maximum support. Frames are made from die-cast aluminium with burnished finish or nylon-coated in a choice of beige, light grey, red, white, black, green, yellow or blue. Upholstery is in herringbone or tweed weaves in neutral, bright and pastel colours, leather or PVC. 'LWB ASC' is a low wide-back version with arms and adjustable swivel base on castors. *M*: w58 × d58 × h79–85/41–50cm (23 × 23 × 31¼–33½/16¼–19¾in). *P*: from £198. The chair is also available with a fixed column height and can be fitted with glides as an alternative to castors. There is also an 'Executive' version — a high wide-back chair upholstered in soft leather with arm pads.

ISOPLAN

EUROPEAN chairs, guaranteed for five years. Five models range from the 'Senior Management Chair' to the 'Secretarial Chair'. 'Executive Chair 2001' has polypropylene shell with steel-reinforced arms and gas lift and tilt action. The five-star base has standard castors — glides are optional. The chair is upholstered in colour-fast Scottish wool tweed in 14 colours including corn husk and bottle blue. *M*: w66 × d65 × h80–87/46–53cm (26 × 25½ × 31½–34¼/ 18–20¾in). *P*: on application.

Isoplan's EUROPEAN '2001'

JUST DESKS

Collection of around 20 desk and visitors' chairs in traditional styles, all available in a choice of finish and a variety of leather colours. 'Court' swivel chair has adjustable height and tilt mechanism; leather comes in six colours — maroon, dark brown, dark green, olive, gold or chestnut. *M*: w23 × d20 × h18–21in (58.5 × 51 × 45.5–53.5cm). *P*: £180(ex VAT). Just Desks also make two- and three-seater leather-covered chesterfield sofas with matching armchair which would be suitable for reception seating.

Just Desks' 'Court'

LUCAS FURNITURE SYSTEMS

BODY CHAIR, designed to be compatible with PROGRAMME office systems (see separate entry). It has five-star pedestal base finished with stainless steel and fitted with castors or glides. Seat and back have double shell of moulded glassfibre finished in black or brown. Depending on the model, the chairs swivel or swivel and tilt, and all have a simple, reliable mechanical height adjustment. There is a good choice of fabrics for the upholstery which can be fitted in a variety of styles including a buttoned version; colours include yellow, red, green and blue. The chairs come in a variety of sizes and arm treatments. *M*: high-back swivel-tilt chair with open arms w66.5 × d48.5 × h92/45–51cm (26 × 19 × 36¼/17¾–20in). *P*: on application. See *Systems* for illustration.

MARTELA CONTRACT INTERIORS LTD

Large selection of chairs suitable for all office requirements. MASTER range consists of three basic models with different adjustment fea-

Martela's 'Master 3' with and without optional headrest

tures. 'Master 3' has seat and back that adjust automatically to the user's changes in sitting position. The five-star swivel base can be fitted with glides or castors. Wool-mix upholstery comes in 25 colours including black, browns, yellow, greens, reds and blues. There are four versions of the chair — the '272SB' has arms and headrest. *M*: w65 × d55 × h114–131cm (25½ × 21¾ × 45–51½in). *P*: on application.

A MURRAY (LONDON) LTD

FASTOFLEX wood-frame chairs made by Danish firm Farstrup. '2312' is a stackable chair without arms and '2313' a non-stackable armchair. Both models are available in natural or rosewood-stained beech with detachable upholstered back and seat. '2312' chairs can also be linked together to form multiple seating units. Upholstery is in a choice of 100% wool, wool mix, leather or customer's own fabric. *M*: w55 × d48 × h80/46cm (21¾ × 19 × 31½/18in). *P*: (wool mix) £91.35. A Murray also

A Murray's FASTOFLEX '2312'

have three other styles of FASTOFLEX chair and a complementary range of very simple tables in five sizes which can be put together in a variety of configurations.

NORFOLK MANOR FURNITURE LTD

Handmade, traditionally-styled executive and boardroom chairs in walnut and mahogany. 'C4' executive chair is available in swivel or fixed-base versions. Fixed-base model comes with or without arms, upholstered in leather in a choice of six colours including deep red and green, or in customer's own material. M: side chair w58 × d56 × h94cm (23 × 22 × 37in); armchair w62 × d56 × h94cm (24½ × 22 × 37in). P: side chair £443–£495; armchair £518–£583.

'C3' is an attractive plain boardroom chair in mahogany only, upholstered in the same leather colours with an antique finish brass stud trim. M: w54 × d67 × h97cm (21½ × 26¾ × 38½in). See *Tables* for illustration.

Norfolk Manor's 'C4'

OMK DESIGN LTD

STACK, a simple metal stacking chair of arresting design. Seat and back are in perforated pressed steel finished in polished chrome or baked epoxy in green, yellow, red, black or white; tubular frame comes in the same choice of finishes. Chairs can be joined at the bottom to form multiple seating units. M: w53.5 × d51 × h74/44.5cm (21 × 20 × 29/17.5in). P: £55–£108.

ORGATECH LTD

Ergonomically designed SYNCHRO-SIT range by Sitag in various versions from typist's to

OMK's STACK △

luxurious executive model. Seat backs are designed to give the user maximum support and there are different options for seat and back adjustment. '55' is equipped with the Sitag synchronized mechanism so that seat and back adjust automatically to the user's changes in

Orgatech's SYNCHRO-SIT '55'

position. A unique feature is the patented 'Schukra' design which allows the curve of the back-rest to be adjusted so that each individual can set it to the preferred position. The chair has gas-powered height adjustment. Upholstery is in fabric or leather and over 50 colours are available. M: w55 × d53 × h125–137/43–55cm (21¾ × 20¾ × 49¼–54/17–21¾in). P: £570–£627.

PLANULA (UK) LTD

Distinctive squared design for Italian KAPPA chairs, six models from typist's to executive's. '6' director's chair has five-star, polished aluminium swivel base, is height-adjustable and has rocking mechanism which adjusts to changes in the sitter's position. It has tall narrow back with round cushion headrest, and is upholstered in fabric in reds, greens, cream, beiges, brown and black, or leather in tan, medium and dark brown and black. Can be supplied with castors or glides. M: w71 × d70 × h120–128/48–56cm (28 × 27½ × 47¼–50½/19–22in)   P: £388.50–£709. See *Co-ordinated furniture* for illustration.

PROJECT FURNITURE LTD

Comfortable EUROMAT swivel chairs with adjustable seat and back-rests to accommodate all sitting positions. Available with or without arms in different sizes. Five-star pedestal base is in polished aluminium, upholstery in wool or wool-mix fabrics, PVC or cus-

Project Furniture's EUROMAT 'EBR 729'

tomer's own material. *M*: swivel chair with arms 'EBR 729' w63 × d53–68 × h88–100/42–54cm (24¾ × 20¾–26¾ × 34¾–39¼/16½–21¼in). *P*: (tweed) £192.58. Chairs are also available with a fixed cantilever skid frame in chrome or enamel.
Project make several other chair ranges and a range of reception seating.

RACE FURNITURE LTD

STORK chairs suitable for boardroom, conference or office use. Frames are all-steel covered in highly resilient, fire-resistant moulded polyurethane foam. Upholstery is in a wide choice of fabrics including PVC, hide, 100% wool and wool mix in an enormous range of colours. 'HBA/TG' chair with arms has five-star swivel base finished in black or brightly polished aluminium fitted with castors or glides. Like all the chairs in the range it has gas-operated height adjustment and optional tilt action. *M*: w62.5 × d65 × h105–117/44–56cm (24½ × 25½ × 41¼–46/17¼–22in). *P*: on application. Can also be upholstered in customer's own material.

Race's STORK 'HBA/TG' △

A REASON & SONS LTD

Executive, visitors' and conference chairs. DORADO '1' is a high-back executive desk chair with headrest, combining maximum support with superb comfort. It has five-star aluminium base with twin-wheel castors or glides, gas-operated adjustable seat height and tilting action which can be set to a fixed position. Upholstered in 100% wool weave or tweed in parchment, oatmeat, barley, sand,

A Reason's DORADO '1'

nutmeg, orange and red; or soft supple hide in six standard shades — light caramel, golden tan, desert sand, russet brown, dark coffee and black. Alternative shades of hide are available on request. *M*: w84 × h117–127/44–54cm (33 × 46–50/17¼–21¼in). *P*: £698–£895. DORADO '2' is a lower back version and DORADO '3' is a conference and visitors' armchair.

GORDON RUSSELL LTD

CONFERENCE chairs for management suites and executive offices. There is a choice of three armchairs and one armless chair. 'R252' armchair is available in American black walnut or stained beech with hide or fabric covers. *M*: w59 × d59 × h84/43cm (23¼ × 23¼ × 33/17⅛in). *P*: (American black walnut) £390.

SCOTT HOWARD ASSOCIATES LTD

Large range of beautifully designed chairs from the long-established Danish firm Fritz Hansen. MINSKER chair has a very distinctive but simple design with back and seat made of moulded laminated wood and base of solid steel. Available in natural oak or beech, in oak in five stained colours including orange, and also lacquered in ten stunning colours including magenta and ultramarine, which would brighten up any office. Frame is finished in chrome, lacquered models with frames in matching or slightly paler colours. The chair stacks and the bases can be linked together to form multiple seating. *M*: w51 × d49 × h73cm (20 × 19¼ × 28¾in). *P*: £64.

Gordon Russell's CONFERENCE 'R252' △

Scott Howard's MINSKER

There are six basic styles in Comforto's SYSTEM 15 range, from secretary's chair to executive armchair, plush-upholstered in fabric or leather. All have five-star base and options for seat and back-rest adjustment. Frames are made of polypropylene with PVC protective edge banding, bases are steel in a chrome finish or in all-black or dark-brown matt enamel finish and can be fitted with castors or glides. 'Executive Operational Chair' comes with or without arms and with a choice of mechanical or gas-operated height adjustment and back-rest angle control or automatic seat and back-rest adjustment. *M*: w69 × d72 × h104–116/42-50cm (27¼ × 28¼ × 41-45¾/16½–19¾in). *P*: £500. See following page for illustration.

CO-ORDINATED FURNITURE

SYSTEM 15 'Executive' model from Scott Howard

STEELCASE STRAFOR UK LTD

Ergonomically designed CONCENTR'X 454. The chairs have polypropylene shell and steel structure on five-star welded steel base fitted with castors. There are three basic models: operator's chair with and without arms, and managerial chair with arms. All are height-adjustable and designed to adjust with the user's body thus providing maximum support whatever the sitting position. Frame and base are available in beige, brown or black, base also in chrome finish. Upholstery is in 100% wool tweed in eight pastel colours, a wool and cotton mix in 14 colours ranging from grey to bright red, or polyester in 24 colours. The cantilevered arms for the operator's chair are constructed of cast aluminium and finished in textured vinyl with optional armrest pads. *M*: operator's chair w60 × d59 × h86.4–96.5cm (23½ × 23¼ × 33¾–37¾in). See *Systems* for illustration. Steelcase Strafor make several other chair ranges.

CO-ORDINATED FURNITURE

ASTROHOME LTD

Cheerful Meccano-like SPEED-RACK system designed and made in Belgium. Extremely flexible SPEED-RACK can provide desks, tables, shelves and shelving systems, counters, work surfaces and benches in a great variety of sizes and heights. There are three primary components: metal uprights and crossbars, and melamine tops; all very easily assem-

bled by means of fitting lugs into slots on the uprights. No nuts and bolts are required — a rubber mallet is the ideal tool for assembly. The metal components are available in four standard colours — yellow, red, blue and white — and any other colour can be ordered. The white melamine work surfaces come in a wide range of sizes. *M*: work surfaces w75–200 × d38–90cm (29½–78¾ × 15–35½in). *P*: on application. A variety of accessories augments the basic components.

Astrohome's SPEED-RACK

BFE BUSINESS FURNITURE & EQUIPMENT LTD

BIEFFE OFFICE RANGE, a stylish solution to office furnishing designed by Conran Associates. Standard range, which includes shelves, desks, chairs, filing cabinets, tables and partition screens, creates a harmonious impression with its clean lines and subtle colours. Executive range of desks, chairs, tables, shelving and storage units is more luxurious and manufactured from high quality materials. 'SN/1' executive desk comes in teak or laminated teak with chrome tubular steel base. *M*: w178 × d75 × h73.5cm (70 × 29½ × 29in). *P*: £182. BFE also supply a wide selection of drawing boards and draughtsman's chairs.

'SN/1' from BFE's BIEFFE OFFICE RANGE

H N BARNES (OFFICE SYSTEMS) LTD

Smart, wooden EXECUTIVE COLLECTION which includes elegant 'Mensa' desk, drawer and filing pedestals, credenza, round tables and wall storage unit. The well-proportioned desk has a slim slab top which carries two hanging pedestals for drawers and filing; alternatively it can be supplied with two mobile pedestals. Design details include fluted supporting panels, satin-aluminium drawer handles, bevelled edging on the top and Lebanon cedar lining for the three sizes of drawers. Available in a choice of 12 different finishes ranging from natural oak and coloured lacquers on oak to beautifully figured ash, satinwood, wenge, walnut and burr maple. *M*: w200 × d100 × h73cm (78¾ × 39¼ × 28¾in). *P*: on application.

BUSINESS INTERIORS LTD

Exclusive modern office system. Randers, one of the best known furniture firms in Denmark, produces a wide-ranging collection of architect-designed furniture finished in attractive colours. The good-looking system includes seating, conference tables, typewriter tables, drawer units, writing/drawing tables with adjustable tops. Storage is catered for by stationery boxes, filing trolleys and storage

'Mensa' from H N Barnes' EXECUTIVE COLLECTION

241

OFFICES

'Working Tables' and chairs by Randers from Business Interiors

cabinets with easily adaptable fitments. The 'Working Table' has work surface in beech veneer or black or grey lacquered mahogany, mounted on steel frame in plum red, bright red, mint green, dark green, navy blue, white or black. Table tops are also available in plastic laminate in white, beige, grey or olive green. Other colours are available on application. *M*: 'Working Table', five sizes, w140–200 × d80–100 × h70–74cm (55–78¾ × 31½–39¼ × 27½–29¼in). *P*: £192–£316. Randers also manufacture reception seating upholstered in a good range of fabrics.

FLEXIFORM▲

FLEXIBURO system — an attractive, good value range of desks, storage and linking units — from well known storage suppliers. FLEX-IBURO computer work station accommodates the computer terminal on a split-level machine

Flexiform's FLEXIBURO △

table linked to the main work surface. There is an over-desk storage shelf and complementary FLEXIFORM storage units can be installed to house related software, print-outs etc. Desks and triangular linking units are steel and wood with PVC work surfaces. Desk frames, linking modules and drawer fronts are in dark brown; work surfaces in light beige. *M*: machine table w105 × d75 × h68cm (41¼ × 29½ × 26in) or w120 × d75 × h72cm (47¼ × 29½ × 28⅓in). *P*: £187, £190.

JOHNNY GREY DESIGN

For an office that doesn't look like an office, the HOME OFFICE collection — individual pieces distinctively styled in natural ash contrasted with black lacquer and red metalwork handles. See *Furniture, made-to-order*.

HABITAT & HEAL'S CONTRACTS

Very attractive ASH range from this firm well known for excellent design. The range comprises desks, desk extension, mobile and fixed pedestals, credenza and conference and meeting tables. Crown-cut ash veneer is used

'AD 1' and other pieces from ASH range by Habitat & Heal's Contracts

for all surfaces which are lipped in solid ash; solid ash is also used for the legs. 'AD 1 Chairman's Desk' has lockable drawers lined with ebonized wood which is also used for drawer handles and removable paper trays. *M*: w210 × d95 × h73cm (82¾ × 37½ × 28¾in). *P*: £1256–£1381. The whole range is also available in black-ash finish with contrasting natural ash and can be modified to suit individual requirements. Habitat & Heal's also supply the luxurious HC 2000 range, handmade with Rio rosewood or natural oak veneers.

HILLE INTERNATIONAL LTD

Unusually styled FOCUS range including pieces suitable for all offices from secretarial to executive. The furniture is available in two contrasting veneers — light oak and dark brown wenge — with solid wood lipping; there is a further choice of finishes to order. Optional 'Perlato' cream-coloured marble for table and credenza tops adds an elegant and luxurious touch. Range includes desks, secretarial furniture, mobile pedestals, credenzas, boardroom and conference tables in several sizes seating from four to eighteen people. The original 'Enigma Desk' has one circular end suited to round-table discussions, and one pointed end enabling mobile storage extensions and work surfaces to be placed on either side. *M*: 'Enigma Desk' w225 × d100 × h73cm (88½ × 39½ × 28½in); 'Mobile Storage Extension' w70 × d70 ×h71cm (27½ × 27½ × 27¾in). *P*: (oak) desk £1240, extension £729. Hille's custom-made furniture unit can also manufacture individual pieces such as reception desks and boardroom tables to match the FOCUS range. See following page for illustration.

Hille also make the SENATOR GROUP — high quality desk, credenza and boardroom/conference table with rosewood veneers and stainless steel bases; also LEEWAK VARIATIONS, an executive range with a wide choice of surfaces for furniture tops including natural or colour-stained wood veneers, leather and marble.

customers' specifications). All pieces can be finished in a choice of veneers — mahogany, burr walnut, burr oak, bird's eye maple, rosewood and madrona, or specially polished to tone with existing furniture. Pedestal desks in the LONDON COLLECTION come in five sizes plus an 'L'-shaped secretary's desk. They are finished by hand with leather tops in a choice of colours including brown, green and red with gilding in different patterns; drawers are lockable with solid brass handles. *M*: from w42 × d24 × h30in (106.5 × 61 × 76cm). *P*: (rosewood) from £680 (ex VAT).

LONDON COLLECTION filing cabinets are available with two to four drawers and can be built in banks to stand up to four abreast. *M*: three-drawer w21 × d25 × h43in (53.5 × 63.5 × 109cm). *P*: (burr oak) £455 (ex VAT).

Just Desks also stock a selection of antique desks and run a re-leathering service.

Hille's FOCUS featuring 'Enigma Desk'

ISOPLAN △

ISOPLAN SYSTEM, a co-ordinated range of desks, storage units, acoustic screens, screen-hung furniture, chairs and planters. The furniture is made with pale European quartered oak veneers. Storage units can be fitted up for all office filing and shelving needs and are open-fronted or closed by hinged door or tambour shutter. Screens can be glazed with bronze perspex or upholstered with wool-mix tweed available in 12 colours including blue, yellow, green and red. Tambour shutters are covered in the same fabric to match or co-ordinate with screens and chairs. All screens have a cable duct and cable access can be provided for desk and table tops. 'Q6000' desk can be used with mobile pedestals or fixed single or double pedestals with two or three drawers in any configuration. *M*: w157 × d79 × h74cm (62 ×

Isoplan's ISOPLAN SYSTEM △

31 × 29¼in). *P*: £332.

Isoplan also make FORUM senior management furniture in Rio rosewood, American walnut and Burma teak; VISCOUNT high-quality desks and tables in American walnut, teak and other woods to order; and also a range of boardroom and conference tables.

JUST DESKS

High-quality desks, tables, cabinets and book-cases in two ranges — STANDARD REPRODUCTION (finished to customers' specifications); and LONDON COLLECTION (Just Desk's own design and manufacture, built to

Rosewood pedestal desk from Just Desks' LONDON COLLECTION

Burr oak filing cabinet from Just Desks' LONDON COLLECTION

KEWLOX

Attractive, robust DRIAD range. Different elements allow varying configurations. Tops and work surfaces are finished in textured post-formed laminate; side panels are finished with tough melamine coat. Variety of storage elements include over-desk storage and units fitted with tambour shutters. There are compatible screening systems. Desks come in three sizes and are delivered packed flat for easy assembly. Side panels are in chocolate or white, teamed with worktops in cream, black,

OFFICES

Kewlox's DRIAD

white or brown leather look. 'Executive' desks have similar design with oak sides and oak or any of the above worktop colours for the top. *M*: 'D1' desk w179 × d74 × h72cm (70 × 30 × 29in). *P*: standard £236.40; 'Executive' £297.65.

MAGPIE FURNITURE LTD ⚠

Comprehensive range of studio, office and drawing office furniture, constructed of welded-steel frames with lacquered-pine drawers and pine or plastic-laminate tops. All

From Magpie's S RANGE △

frames are finished in a tough epoxy coating in a choice of seven bright colours — red, yellow, green, blue, grey, black or white. S RANGE tables come in 13 standard sizes. Desks are available in the same sizes as the tables and have single or double pedestals — each pedestal consists of three shallow drawers or one shallow drawer with a deep filing drawer under, fitted with rails to hold foolscap suspended files. *M*: w60–100 × d100–180 × h71cm (23½–39¼ × 39¼–70¾ × 28in). *P*: tables from £111.69; desks from £200.48.
Studio furniture includes plastic-faced drawing boards, three draughting stands, draughtsman's chairs and plan chests in four sizes. *M*: plan chest w55–150 × d70–100 × h71cm (21¾–59 × 27½–39¼ × 28in). *P*: from £210.99. (All prices ex VAT.)

MARTELA CONTRACT INTERIORS LTD

CONTI range — a wide choice of desks, storage cabinets, chairs and executive furniture. The range is designed to integrate fully with Martela's INTEAM OFFICE system (see separate entry) and includes computer furniture. Ideal for small spaces, 'Micro-terminal' table is freestanding with split-level top for VDU and keyboard; the keyboard surface slides in and out. Worktops are in beige laminate and the cantilever metal frame is finished in dark brown. The table is height-adjustable. *M*: w60 × d60 × h65–80cm (23½ × 23½ × 25½–31½in). *P*: on application.

A MURRAY (LONDON) LTD

Good quality office furniture from the Dutch firm Teska, suitable for all types of office from secretarial and clerical to executive. Teska furniture is robustly constructed, a high proportion of solid wood being used in its manufacture. The range includes desks, storage cabinets and mobile bookcases and is available in brown or black stained or white lacquered ash or in African walnut veneers and solids. *M*: '7000 Series' double pedestal executive desk w200 × d100cm (78¾ × 39¼in); circular table dia 143cm (56¼in). *P*: (African walnut) desk £1069; table £748.
Teska also make a wide range of boardroom tables with square, circular, rectangular or oval tops and matching wooden-framed boardroom chairs in the same wood finishes.
From Uffix comes the attractive and functional TEAM LINE range. Desks, storage cabinets and shelving are made of melamine with plastic laminate stain-, scratch- and heat-resistant working surfaces, tops and doors. All the furniture has rounded edges and is available in

Martela's CONTI 'Micro-terminal' table and work station

A Murray's TEAM LINE

white or coffee, both with brown edging. Desks are available in three sizes and can be joined with linking segments to form oval or square conference tables. *M*: 'S160' desk w160 × d75 × h75cm (63 × 29½ × 29½in). *P*: £142. There is also a range of five-star base swivel chairs to match.

OMK DESIGN LTD

Small, well-designed range of co-ordinated office furniture, easily assembled from tough epoxy-coated steel components linked by polished aluminium knuckle joints. Informal screening is achieved by the use of perforated steel panels which allow light and ventilation. The desk has oven-baked epoxy frame with polished chrome, epoxy or aluminium knuckle joints and perforated steel 'modesty' panel, with top in a choice of reversible laminate, tinted or clear glass. Colours (which apply to the other components as well) are yellow,

Work station with screen from OMK

white, red, brown, black, green, dove grey and duck-egg blue. *M*: w161 × d84.5 × h74cm (63 × 33 × 29in). *P*: £292–£320. An office planning service is available from OMK.

PLANULA (UK) LTD

Well designed Italian furniture.
Sophisticated LETTURA executive range comprises tables, desks and storage units. The furniture is made from stained ash with metal legs and trim in grey with black trim or all black. *M*: table 'TR/240' w240 × d80 × h72cm (94½ × 31½ × 28¼in). LETTURA M range has exactly the same components but is in all wood. The main surfaces are lacquered very dark brown and the trim is Italian walnut.

Planula's LETTURA 'TR/240' and KAPPA 'E' chair

Attractive STUDIO range in natural walnut has clean lines accentuated by flush-fitting handles. It comprises desks, tables and a good selection of storage units available open-

fronted, or with doors or drawers. The largest desk, the 'S/200', would be suitable for a managerial office. Desks can be used in conjuction with two- and three-drawer mobile storage units. Tall storage cupboards are available in two depths. *M*: 'S/200' w200 × d100 × h73cm (78¾ × 39¼ × 28¾in); tall cupboard w90 × d37 or 50 × h146cm (35½ × d14½ or 19¾ × 57½in). *P*: 'S/200' £273; cupboard £284, £304.

Planula's STUDIO featuring 'S/200' desk

GORDON RUSSELL LTD ⚠

High-quality co-ordinated office furniture.
SERIES 1 boardroom and senior executive office furniture uses veneers of specially selected Rio rosewood or teak, hand-polished. Leg frames are steel with bright chrome finish. Double pedestal desk has a choice of two pedestals which can be fitted on either side: two drawers, the top one with sliding pen tray, or one deep drawer fitted for foolscap and A4 filing. All drawers fitted with standard locks. This desk is also available with wider kneehole or with a smaller top. *M*: 'R984 Mark 1' w213.5 × d91.4 × h72.5cm (84 × 36 × 28in). *P*: £1050–£1539.

SERIES 80 △ desk from Gordon Russell

SERIES 80 modern-style furniture, intended for senior management, includes desks, tables, sideboards, credenzas and drawer pedestals in Rio rosewood or American black walnut veneers. Steel legs and drawer handles are finished in bright chrome. The double pedestal desk has the same choice of drawer pedes-

tals as in SERIES 1. Each pedestal is fitted with locks inside the kneehole which lock all drawers. *M*: w213.5 × d91.5 × h72.5cm (84 × 36 × 28½in). *P*: (rosewood) £2046.
These and other ranges from Gordon Russell can be complemented by custom-made designs including desks, storage units and conference tables.

SCANDIA
Large contract range of stylishly simple co-ordinated desks and chairs, size to order, including 'LH 7624' desk and 'LH 7512' chair. Suitable anywhere from a director's office to a reception area, the desk and chair come in oak or mahogany, with the desk top veneered on wood block. The chair has cane back and seat and is available with a leather cushion. Other desk/chair combinations include lino-top and curved-top desks with matching chairs. *M*: 'LH 7624' w185 × d92.5 × h73.5cm (72¾ × 36½ × 29in). *P*: £897.

Scandia's 'LH 7624' and 'LH 7512'

TURBERVILLE SMITH & SON LTD
Several small ranges of high quality furniture in rosewood or teak from the Danish firm Dyrlund. SUPER SKY LINE range comprises two sizes of desk, side extension and conference tables in six sizes. The desks have three drawers and a lock. The extension has a tambour door and lock with five drawers and file drawer inside. *M*: desks w83 × d39 × h28½in (210 × 100 × 72cm), w94½ × d43 × h28½in (240 × 110 × 72cm); extension w55 × d20½ × h24in (140 × 55 × 61cm). *P*: on application.
SUPREME range in rosewood only consists of

Turberville Smith's SUPREME desk

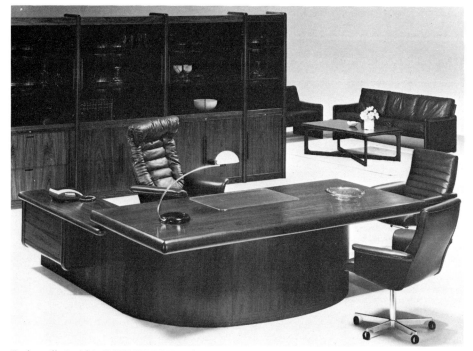

Turberville Smith's SUPER SKY LINE with UNIQUE wall units

desk with or without extension, credenza and conference tables in two sizes. The desk has two drawers with lock and the top is in a choice of rosewood, smoked glass, leather or marble. *M*: w94½ × d47½ × h29in (240 × 110 × 73.5cm). *P*: on application.
UNIQUE wall units in rosewood or teak complement the desks. Base cabinets can be used alone or with glass-fronted cabinets placed on top. Base cabinets come with file drawers or tambour doors concealing shelves or trays, or a combination of both. Top cabinets have glass sliding doors and interior light fittings. *M*: base cabinet w42½ × d16½ × h32in (106 × 40 × 80cm); top cabinet w42½ × d16½ × h46in (106 × 40 × 115cm). *P*: on application.

R TYZACK LTD
Contract furniture both in a standard range of period styles and to order.
Writing table '2037' has three locking drawers and yew or mahogany veneer. *M*: w48 × d26 x h30in (122 × 66 × 76cm). *P*: on application.
'Gainsborough' chairs are made with legs ('1056') or pedestal base ('1056R') and can be covered in plain or buttoned, hand-antiqued hide or customer's own fabric. *M*: w26 × d25 × h39in (66 × 65.5 × 99cm). *P*: on application. Smaller versions suitable for dining and conference rooms are available, and Tyzack make some hide-covered sofas and armchairs and occasional tables that would be suitable for reception areas.

Tyzack's '2037' with 'Gainsborough' chairs

WESTRA OFFICE EQUIPMENT LTD ⚠
Furniture specially designed for the 'electronic' office. The range includes work stations, storage modules, VDU table and turntables,

Westra's 'Adjustable Video Station-2' △

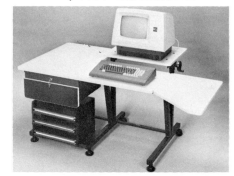

printer tables and accessories such as acoustic printer hoods, data trays, print-out trolleys and cabinets. Supporting frames are made of dark brown metal and all work surfaces are in cream melamine. 'Adjustable Video Station-2' has a large work surface into which is built a screen platform enabling the VDU to be adjusted for both height and tilt. Storage such as a lockable personal storage drawer with three translucent brown file trays can be fitted under the working surface on the operator's left. *M*: w120 × d80 × h69–84cm (47¼ × 31½ × 27–33in). *P*: £217.50

WILTSHIER CONTRACT FURNISHING LTD
Complete contract furnishing service for companies. Wiltshier have several ranges of exclusive products to meet all needs. They are the sole distributors of GALO BEN office furniture from Spain. There are eight complete ranges — from general office layout to executive suite. Available in cream laminate with beech drawer fronts, oak laminate or in all-wood (walnut). Storage units are basically simple but can be arranged in many different ways, with drawers on metal runners. *M*: desk w160 × d80 × h72cm (63 × 31½ × 28¼in). *P*: on application.

DESKS

THE DESK SHOP
Desks and a valuable range of services from specialist shop. The Desk Shop restore and sell antique desks and also offer an antique-desk finding service for customers with particular requirements. Bespoke desks are also made. OXFORD REPRODUCTION RANGE is a range of good value reproduction desks, soundly

OXFORD pedestal desk from The Desk Shop

constructed and excellently finished with solid brass handles and matched veneers. The mahogany pedestal desk has eight drawers including a deep filing drawer and is also available in pine, yew, burr walnut, myrtle burr and oak. *M*: w152 × d91 × h77cm (60 × 36 × 30½in). *P*: £495.
The company makes chairs to complement the desks and provides a free interior design service for contracts over a certain size.

FLEXIFORM ▲
Unique 'Lock-up Work Station', a lockable unit to house microcomputer, telex machine etc. Special features are: integral cable channels, ventilated back panel for heat dispersion, plastic-coated steel tambour shutter and roll-out worktop. The unit and components come in sandstone or brown with the tambour in sandstone only. *M*: w100 × d60 × h188cm (40 × 24 × 74in). *P*: £452.50.

NORFOLK MANOR FURNITURE LTD
Handmade range of traditionally-styled furniture in mahogany and walnut. Range of desks includes a secretary's desk and 'work stations'

Flexiform's 'Lock-up Work Station' △

with typing extensions as well as more imposing models. The 'President's Desk' has lockable drawers and can include a deep file drawer in the right-hand pedestal; has an optional gilt-tooled leather top in a choice of five colours including light tan and black. *M*: w182 × d106 × h77.5cm (72 × 42 × 30½in). *P*: £2569–£2776.
Norfolk Manor will also supply custom-made furniture to fit in with individual schemes. Alternative finishes (such as oak, yew, ash, pine, cherry or rosewood) are also available to special order.

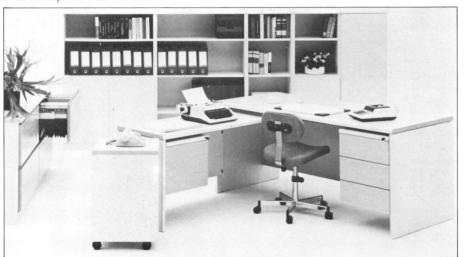
GALO BEN system from Wiltshier

Norfolk Manor's 'President's Desk'

G T RACKSTRAW
Solid oak pedestal desks in various sizes and with a choice of hide tops from the largest volume supplier of reproduction cabinet furniture in the UK. Each desk is gently distressed

Rackstraw's 'D780'

and hand waxed. *M*: 'D780' w168 × d91.5 × h76cm (66 × 36 × 30in). *P*: £2178. Other designs are available in solid mahogany (see *Furniture, desks*).

RECEPTION SEATING

ANTOCKS LAIRN LTD
Extensive range of reception seating, both modular and individual pieces, including the versatile CASCADE. 'C 185' armchair and 'C 285' and 'C 385' two- and three-seater sofas have integrally moulded seat and back in high-resilience foam upholstered in a wide choice of fabrics. Upholstered rectangular end panels form the arms. *M*: 'C285' two-seater w152 × d80 × h64cm (59¾ × 31½ × 25¾in). *P*: (pure wool upholstery) £489.60. For a more solid appearance, similarly upholstered infill panels can be added beneath the seat at the front and at the back. Or for a simpler look, the seat element is available mounted on a polished chrome frame as the 'CO 85' chair, which can be linked with others to form multiple units. Matching low-level square, rectangular or quarter-circle tables are available, with chrome legs and white melamine tops.

Antocks Lairn's CASCADE

BUSINESS INTERIORS LTD
Comfortable and stylish seating by the Finnish firm Avarte. REMMI upholstered chair, sofas and ottoman have tubular-steel frames with polished chrome finish; optional armrests are finished in black plastic or laminated birch in natural, dark brown or black. Detachable upholstery with zipped cushions comes in a

choice of four plain fabrics in an excellent range of colours, an attractive patterned cotton mix in three colourways including a soft grey green with a bright green and pink motif, soft leather in five shades including black, or customer's own material. All elements are fitted with black polyamide base glides. *M*: three-seater sofa with arms w192 × d92 × h84cm (75½ × 36¼ × 33in). *P*: £1099-£1472. Avarte also make the original-looking ATELJEE range which includes sofas, chair and ottoman all with tubular-steel sub-frames with arms, back and optional headrest panels veneered in birch. The exposed leg tubes are covered in birch or metal. Birch colours and upholstery options are the same as for REMMI. *M*: three-seater sofa w223 × d83 × h70cm (87¾ × 32¾ × 27½in). *P*: £1114-£1487.50. Both these ranges would look equally at home in a domestic setting.
There are six other AVARTE ranges suitable for reception areas, and Business Interiors also stock ranges from the Danish firm Randers.

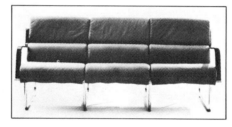

Three-seater sofas from Business Interiors. Top: REMMI; below: ATELJEE

FRAYLING FURNITURE LTD △
Versatile GEMINI contoured foam seating specifically designed for the contract field. Range comprises armchairs, units with or without an arm on either side, and corner units, upholstered in a wide choice of durable, fire-retardant fabrics. Frames are made of beech and fibreboard. *M*: unit w68 × d85 × h67cm (26¾ × 33½ × 26½in). *P*: on application.

HILLE INTERNATIONAL LTD
Several ranges of reception seating. THETA can be arranged in many different ways; the units are supplied in one, two, three or four modules without arms or with narrow or wide arms. There is also an armchair and three-

Frayling's GEMINI △

seater sofa with the same choice of arms. The seating has a timber frame with webbed seats and foam upholstery, and is covered in a large range of fabrics, including 100% wool and a wool mix, in an enormous choice of colours from subtle shades to more vibrant hues. Sofas are available with two or three cushions. *M*: sofa with narrow arms w203 × d91 × h64cm (80 × 36 × 25in). *P*: from £730. Corner units are also available.

Hille's THETA

HITCH/MYLIUS
Modern unit seating with sofas and armchairs in a number of styles and coverings, for domestic or contract use. HM181 is a range of contract seating based on fibreglass shell frames upholstered in fire-retardant polyester foam and Courtelle fibre. Single units can be connected in curves of almost any radius by plastic segmental shelves of 30°, 45° or 60°, or in straight runs by rectangular shelves of three

Hitch/Mylius's HM181

Office Kit's office system in Formica

45 SERIES by Fantoni from Scott Howard

widths. Single-armed end units and armchairs are available, plus tables and a planter in the same gloss-finished cream or brown plastic as the shelves. *M*: single unit '181/A' w68 × d71 × h67cm (26¾ × 28 ×26½in). *P*: on application. See also *Furniture, upholstered*.

KINGCOME CONTRACTS
An almost infinite variety of high-quality up-holstered seating made to specification. The contract division of L M Kingcome Ltd offers their made-to-order service in a special trade price structure, plus some standard-sized sofas and armchairs. There's also an interior design and decorating department and an on-site cleaning and Scotchgard fabric and carpet protection service. See *Furniture, upholstered* for design details.

ORGATECH LTD
SWISSFORM reception seating by Sitag. 'In-tern' sofa and chairs have solid oak or ano-dized aluminium base and flexible webbing. Seats and backs are made from extra-thick, high quality foam covered with cotton wad-ding. Upholstery is in leather in a choice of nine colours including pale cream, rust and black, or in fabric. There are matching stools, tables, infill tops and planters.*M*: chair with arms w66 × d54 × h76cm (26 × 21¼ × 30in). *P*: (leather) £602.

Orgatech's 'In-tern'

PLANULA (UK) LTD
Luxurious SERIE P reception seating from this Italian firm. Range comprises easy chair with or without arms, two- and three-seater sofas upholstered in leather or fabric over polyurethane foam. Easy chair without arms, 'P/86', has an unusual pyramidal base in black resin glass. Leather upholstery comes in tan, medium and dark brown and black; fabric in red, greens, cream, beiges, brown and black. *M*: 'P/86' w77 × d78 × h70cm (30¼ × 30¾ × 27½in). *P*: £423–£709. Matching black lac-quered occasional table and planter are avail-able. Planula also make reception desks, see *Systems*.

Planula's SERIE P seating with EP & F reception desk

RACE FURNITURE LTD
Extremely flexible MOLECULA seating system. Comprises seven upholstered elements (in-cluding a round stool) plus a circular table which fit together in innumerable permuta-tions. Supported by a rigid frame, the seats and backs are made from highly resilient polyurethane foam. Upholstery is in 100%

Race's MOLECULA △

wool, wool mix, hide or vinyl in a wide choice of colours. *M*: corner unit w68 × d84 × h̄70cm (26¾ × 33 × 27½in); centre unit w76 × d84 × h70cm (30 × 33 × 27½in); stool dia 62.5 × h34cm (24½ × 13½in). *P*: on application.

A REASON & SONS LTD
Several ranges of reception seating. By varying the different components of OSCAR seating it is possible to create an infinite number of per-mutations. OSCAR is strongly constructed with elasticated, rubber-webbed seats and backs and upholstered in a high resilience foam and Dacron combination. The units are covered in soft, supple hide available in six standard shades including desert sand, russet brown and black; they can also be covered in 100% wool weave or flame-retardant tweed in parchment, oatmeal, barley, sand, nutmeg, orange and red. Single, double or treble sea-ting units come in four variations: with or with-out arms or with left or right arm only. There are matching table and angle units. *M*: double seat with left and right arm w162 × d94 × d76cm (63½ × 37 × 30in). *P*: £762–£1176.

A Reason's OSCAR

OFFICES

GORDON RUSSELL LTD ⚖

Two versatile ranges of seating covered in Gordon Russell's selected fabrics or in customer's own material.

SERIES 50 has upholstered seat and back resting on base of Rio rosewood, American black walnut or teak veneer. Single units can be supplied with two narrow or wide arms or one-armed components can be bolted together to form multiple seating. Integral end and corner tables or separate occasional tables mounted on castors are available. *M*: three-seater sofa (wide arms) w248 × d86 × h73cm (97¾ × 33¾ × 28¾in). *P*: rosewood (fabric upholstery) £304.

SERIES 55 offers fully upholstered seating as individual armchair or sofa units or multiple configurations. There is a matching table unit veneered in Rio rosewood or American black walnut, also a lower occasional table mounted on castors. *M*: single unit seat w60 × d84 × h68.5cm (23½ × 33 × 27in). *P*: £460.

Gordon Russell's SERIES 55 △

STEELCASE STRAFOR UK LTD

Luxurious D800 range. Armchair and two- and three-seater sofas have tubular steel structure with metallic spring suspension. Cushion seats and backs are made of polyurethane foam and goose down, and the lower back, which provides exceptional support, of polyurethane foam only. Available covered in leather in a choice of seven colours including off-white, black, burgundy and brown with

Steelcase Strafor's D800 two-seater

self-piping. *M*: D800 two-seater sofa w150 × d85 × h78cm (82¾ × 33½ × 30¾in). *P*: on application. Steelcase Strafor make several other ranges of reception seating.

SCREENS

CUBIC METRE FURNITURE

Attractive FIRST screen system, either free-standing or fixed to the floor, in sturdy but light-weight metal mesh. Any number of screens can be fitted together to create different spaces. Screens come in standard black (other Cubic Metre colours available on request) and in two sizes. Accessories include metal-mesh shelf, coat-hooks, magnetic 'pins', ashtray and pencil holder. *M*: w75 × h150cm (29½ × 59in); w75 × h180cm (29½ × 70¾in). *P*: £87.99, £107.99.

IDEAS FOR LIVING

From Seccose in Italy, informal QUINTA screens to be used independently or joined together. Screens have metal frame in bright red, white or black and can be equipped with wire netting, metal or glass panels or off-white canvas. Hinges are available for joining screens together and allow a maximum angle of 90°. *M*: w73 × h163cm (28¾ × 64¼in). *P*: basic screen £49.40. Wire netting in black,

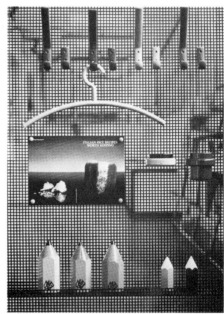

FIRST screen from Cubic Metre

white, red or yellow is also available for attachment to walls, and there's an extensive range of accessories to clip on to the netting — spotlights, pen trays and hooks of all types.

Seccose also make a variety of beautifully functional metal shelving, tables, chairs, storage units, hat stands and trolleys, all with the same bright, rather high tech look. (See *Furniture, chairs, shelving, storage, tables.*)

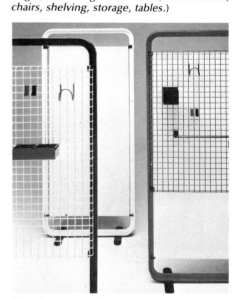

Ideas for Living's QUINTA screens

PRICES AND INFORMATION WERE CORRECT AT THE TIME OF GOING TO PRESS

Gordon Russell's SERIES 50 △

STORAGE

ESTIA DESIGNS LTD

For high-tech offices and studios, F12 plan chests and document-drawer units. With tubular steel frames in a choice of seven colours and colour-matched handles to the white plastic drawers, they come in 7-, 10- or 19-drawer units for sizes A1, A2, A3 and A4. The 7-drawer A1 plan chest can be fitted with a white melamine adjustable drawing board which slides out to give leg room. *M*: A1 plan chest (with drawing board flat) w38 × d26 × h28in (96.5 × 66 × 71cm). *P*: £135.

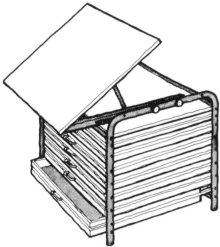

F12 plan chest from Estia

FLEXIFORM ⚠

Well-known storage system composed of units in four standard heights. All are based on the 100 × 50cm (39½ × 19¾in) module which makes for ease of planning. Units can be open-fronted or closed by six different methods and have a large range of fittings to provide all

Flexiform's storage system △

types of filing including shelf systems and more specialized storage for items such as stationery and artwork. Standard colours are brown and sandstone but 'Architectural' texture finish in red, blue, green, grey and white is also available. In addition to the normal steel the units can be supplied in wood veneer or laminate finishes. *M*: bulk storage unit 'A5' with metal tambour w100 × d50 × h221cm (39½ × 19¾ × 87in); screen-height storage unit 'B5' with metal tambour w100 × d50 × h162cm (39½ × 19¾ × 64in). *P*: standard £253–£295, special colours £285–£332. Flexiform also provide a survey and planning service for customers — they will produce floor plans with recommended cabinet layouts and a detailed quotation.

ISOPLAN ⚠

STORAGE FURNITURE, extensive range of storage cabinets suitable for general or management offices. Comes in teak, oak, American walnut or Rio rosewood in two heights (desk- and full-height) and can be packed flat for removal. With the exception of a telephone console and glass-fronted bookcase, all cabinets are fitted with height adjusters and locks. Doors are hinged; alternatively rigid PVC tambour shutters in matching colours are used. Cabinets can be fitted with drawers for a variety of filing needs. 'C78DV' full-height storage unit will take a full range of accessories: roll-out suspension filing frames, compu-

Isoplan's 'C78DV' △

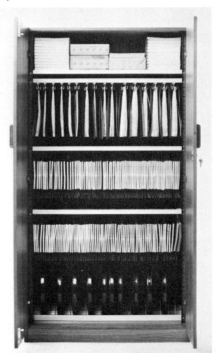

ter binders and reels, shelf division storage etc. *M*: w95 × d52 × h175cm (37½ × 20½ × 69in). *P*: (teak) £511.

MORESECURE LTD

Really functional steel shelving suitable for a myriad uses — storage of papers, lateral filing, print-outs, boxes etc. CLEAR STORE shelving is available in standard pre-packed units. It is quick and simple to assemble (no nuts and bolts); the basic unit can be built in five minutes or less! Shelves are fully adjustable and come in four widths and five depths, and units can be fitted with lockable doors if required. Available in two-tone finish in dark chocolate/beige. *M*: six sizes, w39¼ × d12 × h75in (100 × 30.5 × 190cm) to w39¼ × d18 × h87in (100 × 46 × 221cm). *P*: basic unit £54.32–£75.61. The shelving can also be supplied to customer's own specifications. It can also be converted to a mobile system by means of wheels fitted on to a track, so that units can be moved aside to reveal more shelving and so maximise the use of space.

Moresecure also make two further ranges of shelving suitable for offices and a range of cupboards.

Moresecure's CLEAR STORE

NORFOLK MANOR FURNITURE LTD

Attractive plain mahogany filing cabinets from Norfolk Manor's range of handmade furniture. Available in two- and three-drawer versions. Optional extra is a gilt-tooled leather top. *M*: three drawers w55 × d66 × h114cm (21¾ × 26¼ × 45in). *P*: £735, gilt-tooled top

Mahogany filing cabinet from Norfolk Manor

£44 extra. The filing cabinets can also be made in multi-width versions. Norfolk Manor also make bookcases and storage units suitable for boardrooms.

OMK DESIGN LTD ▲

GRAFFITI, a really original shelving, hanging and storage system. It is made in metal and consists of uprights which are rested against the wall in a sloping position, supported by rubber feet at top and bottom. Shelves in six sizes are hung to the uprights by means of met-

OMK's GRAFFITI △

al hooks. The components are finished in oven-baked epoxy in blue, two shades of grey, white, green, red, duck-egg blue, dove grey, black, brown or yellow. The hooks can also be finished in chrome. *M*: uprights h200, 220, 240cm (78¾, 86½, 94½in). *P*: £58, £63, £67.

SYSTEMS

ALL-STEEL SYSTEMS FURNITURE

Comprehensive standard office system which includes panels, desks, tables, storage units etc suitable for open-plan or cellular offices, plus a more sophisticated system for electronic equipment, all in laminate and fabric finishes over strong steel structures.

All the components in the standard system are compatible, allowing areas of any size to be furnished. There is an excellent screen system, into which doors can be fitted if required. The panels, which come pre-packed, are straight or curved with efficient hingeing and are particularly easy to install and re-arrange. They are available fabric-covered in dozens of colours including beige, soft green, grey-blue and mauve; also in painted metal or laminate, or tinted or clear glass. *M*: straight panels w18–60 × h33–78in (46–153 × 84–198cm).

All-Steel's standard office system

All-Steel's SYNTRAX system is specially designed for the 'electronic office' and is fully compatible with their standard office system. Components include worktops, linking tops, storage pedestals and a full range of functional accessories. The whole system is designed for maximum flexibility and is suited to both individual and group requirements. There is a VDU carriage which can be fitted to the worktops and can be moved laterally along their total width; the carriage also rotates through 355° and moves in and out. The computer work station can be fitted with an articulating keyboard arm which swivels through 180° to allow the keyboard to be stored under the work surface;

it also has a height adjustment. An easily accessible trough in the worktops holds and conceals two- or three-circuit electrical wiring. All the system components have vinyl-coated bevelled edges and are available in four paint colours with co-ordinating laminate work surfaces and drawer fronts: taupe/taupestone, frost/greystone, slate/greystone, warm beige/beigestone with matching paint or polished chrome bases. *M*: work-surfaces w36, 42, 48, 60, 66, 72 × d30 × h29in (91.5, 106.5, 122, 152.5, 167.5, 183 × 76 × 73.5cm). *P*: on application.

H N BARNES (OFFICE SYSTEMS) LTD

Comprehensive range of freestanding and panel-based furniture with a flexible modular design. The furniture is manufactured in oak, left natural or stained to almost any colour and finished in polyurethane lacquer; colours can be co-ordinated with the fabrics covering the screen panels. There is an integral wall tracking system between each wall panel designed

From H N Barnes. Top: panels and system furniture; below: small VDU table

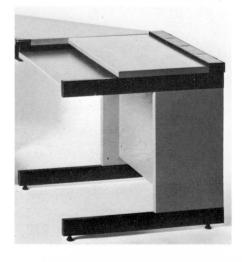

to carry shelving, work surfaces, storage units and lighting at any height and position while a capacious two-way wire-management facility allows for all necessary socket outlets and cabling. Computer furniture includes printer stand with paper-feed grille and rear collection tray, VDU tables with sliding panels, operator's/typist's desk and tambour-fronted stationery pedestal. *M*: small VDU table with cantilever frame w80 × d80 × h68-73cm (31½ × 31½ × 26¾-28¾). *P*: on application. TASK-AM complete lighting system is designed to fit the furniture layout exactly. It provides two levels of energy-saving workspace lighting — task lights for well-lit work surfaces and ambient light for a more softly lit background.

IDEAS FOR LIVING

Stylishly designed OP/7 system from the Italian firm Coopsette. Includes tables, desks, mobile pedestals, storage cabinets and screens, all constructed on a modular system allowing great flexibility. Frames for desks and tables are metal finished in reddish-brown or black. Worktops are in cream-coloured laminate or beech veneer. Tables and desks, provided with or without wire-management facilities, include various VDU and printer tables. 'T14N09' table has special lower height for keyboard or typewriter; available with cream laminate top only. *M*: w140 × d80 × h65cm (55 × 31½ × 25½in). *P*: £196. Screens are available in four widths, all sound-proofed and covered in flame-resistant fabric in blue, beige, black, red, green, brown or rust. They too can be fitted with concealed wiring.

For meetings, a variety of tables are available: square, oval, 'D'-ended and rectangular, with black metal base (each support consisting of a pair of right-angled panels) and cream lamin-

'T14N09' table from Ideas for Living's OP/7

ate tops with black edging. Large oval and open-centred conference tables can be created using rectangular tables plus curved linking sections with angles of 90° or 120°.

The system also includes a multi-functional reception desk with counter, fitted with a distinctive metal-mesh front panel. It can be constructed in various sizes by combining different components.

LUCAS FURNITURE SYSTEMS △

Well-designed, really complete office systems flexible enough to adapt to changing circumstances in today's office. PROGRAMME 1 comprises desks, work stations, linking units, computer terminal furniture and screens; also storage units catering for all types of filing system including storage for computer print-outs and software. Innumerable combinations suitable both for cellular and open-plan offices can be achieved. Furniture is solidly con-

Lucas's PROGRAMME 1 △ featuring '8ST/VDU' table

structed from timber panels and steel components, available in light oak solids or veneers with cantilevered steel frames for desks and tables in black finish. Cableways and cable outlets can be incorporated into the system so that electronic equipment can be easily installed. The computer terminal furniture comprises a small number of basic components which can be adjusted to accommodate different equipment. The range includes '8ST/VDU' freestanding table with split-level top, work station with compact sliding worktop, and turntable units. The system can be set up for a single operator or for sharing. *M*: '8ST/VDU' w80 × d80 × h72/66cm (31½ × 31½ × 28¼/26in). *P*: on application.

PROGRAMME 2 was the winner of a Design Council Award in 1984, the first complete office system to do so. It is designed to combine good-looking furniture with all the needs of the electronic office such as safely concealed, but accessible wiring. Desks, storage units, partitioning and lighting all work together to create an integrated environment. The system is easily installed or re-arranged. Oak-veneered furniture comes in natural, cool or warm oak finishes, complementing the black steel supports and black melamine-faced outer panels. The extensive range of screens (common to both PROGRAMMES 1 and 2) can be used to create an infinite variety of working areas. There is a wide choice of desks, work tables and machine tables, allied to six types of drawer pedestal, mobile pedestals, backfile units, over-desk shelves and typing extensions to create an almost inexhaustible supply of different work stations. These work stations can be linked with six sizes of linking triangles to form different configurations. *M*: desks/tables w80-160 × d80 × h72cm (31½-63 × 31½ × 28¼in); storage units w100 × d50 × h72–230cm (39¼ × 19 × 28¼–40½in). *P*: on application.

OP/7 reception desk from Ideas for Living

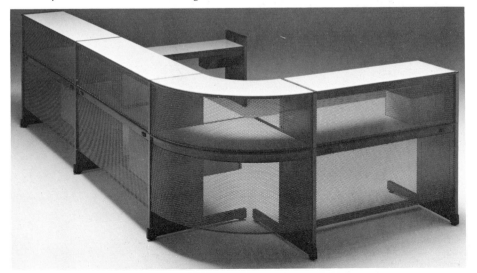

OFFICES

PROGRAMME 2 also includes full-height partitioning, which allows even more choice in planning office space. There are four ranges, all demountable and all accepting a wide range of screen-supported storage and shelving components. Partition panels and doors can be glazed or solid with paint, wallpaper, fabric, laminate or veneer finish. Full wire-management facilities are available. The most luxurious partitioning, 'P290', has hung panels over a supporting metal framework; the frame is erected on a floor channel with two skirting-level cable ducts behind clip-on covers. This partitioning can be specified in any combination of solid, door, partial or full height glazed panels. *M & P:* on application.

Lucas also make wall panels and wall liners in a huge choice of materials which can be used with wall track straight on to existing walls and are compatible with the other partitioning.

A complete office furnishing service from initial survey, design and space planning to final maintenance contract is also available.

Martela's INTEAM

Lucas's PROGRAMME 2 furniture and partitioning plus BODY CHAIR

MARTELA CONTRACT INTERIORS LTD

Good-looking INTEAM complete office system from this Finnish company. It includes easily-assembled screens in three heights and three widths, available in a wide choice of textures, tones and fabrics or glazed with tinted glass (which is also used for a sliding door). *M:* w20, 60, 80 × h110, 158, 209cm (7¾, 23½, 31½ × 43¼, 62¼, 82¼in). *P:* on application. Work surfaces are freestanding or screen-mounted and are all height-adjustable. Standard tops are in beige laminate and can also be supplied in oak. The frames have brown uprights and polished aluminium feet. Modular-sized storage cabinets can take all kinds of storage — computer, lateral, suspension, box files, card

indexes etc. The cabinets can be open-fronted or closed by doors or tambour shutters. There are also mobile and fixed units, all with different drawer options, and over-desk storage. Full wire-management facilities are incorporated in the system — electrical, telephone and computer cable trunking can be fitted to any level on the screens. Efficient ambient and task lighting is also available.

Martela also provide a complete design and planning service.

OFFICE KIT

Comprehensive and sophisticated range of components, with Formica laminate surfaces in nine original colourways, to meet many different requirements for cellular offices. The system comes in kit form and can be assembled and rearranged quickly. Comprises desking and storage in a variety of heights and widths, screens in four heights, adjustable lighting for ambient and task illumination, wire and cable ducts, and a multiplicity of accessories. Colourways include pretty pastel blue/grey, cream/scarlet and two tones of pink. *M:* standard desk w80–160 × d80 × h72cm (31½–63 × 31½ × 28¼in). *P:* on application. See colour illustration.

ORGATECH LTD

Highly flexible ERGODATA office system by Fortschritt designed to adapt easily to changing circumstances. The basic work-station components are two identical cantilever-form side-pieces with a cross-section available in varying lengths. Work stations can be easily adapted for computer use by fitting 'drop-on' height-compensating tops which raise the work surface to the correct height for a VDU unit. The special feature of the system is that all

work stations and desks can be adjusted for both height and inclination so that every individual has a working surface fixed at the correct height for them. Extension elements can be fitted to the back of work stations so that the viewing distance between the user and the VDU is increased. Computer furniture includes printer tables with a feed for the paper and basket to catch the print-out. There is an excellent range of storage cabinets, the MODULAR ROOM SYSTEM, which allows for all types of filing in all configurations. The whole system, including the storage cabinets, has concealed cable ducting. All furniture is finished with smooth rounded edges. There are two standard frame colours — terra and mocca; surfaces are available in eleven colours and three oak veneers. For orders of 150 or more work stations the surfaces can be in the unusual — for offices — colours of rose

ERGODATA work station from Orgatech

pink and lavender blue. *M*: standard desk w160 × d80 × h72cm (63 × 31½ × 28¼in). *P*: from £401.

The less sophisticated AZ-DATA system is designed to co-ordinate with ERGODATA, but is 25% cheaper; it can of course also be used independently. It incorporates many of ERGO-DATA'S versatile features, such as rear extensions to desking, cable channels and easy assembly. It is reinforced by the huge range of AZ-MODUL storage cabinets fitted with drawers, or shelves and racks closed by tambour doors, catering for all storage requirements. Orgatech also provide a complete planning and design service which takes into consideration all the elements required such as carpeting, screening, curtains and organisational fittings of all kinds.

Orgatech's AZ-DATA

PLANULA (UK) LTD

Small well-designed office system SERIE EP & F (Equipped Panels and Furniture) for the 'electronic office'. Sound-absorbent panels are available in four sizes, glazed or covered in the same fabrics as Planula's chairs (see separate entry). Supply cables are housed in PVC conduits with snap-on covers which run along the upper edge and both sides of the bottom of the panels and are connected vertically by specially equipped uprights. *M*: w90, 135 × d10.5 × h108, 181cm (35½, 53¼ × 4 × 42½, 71¼in). *P*: on application. The furniture, which includes desks and linking units, is equipped to carry power, data and telephone cables; even the surfaces have been developed to reduce reflections on computer screens. 'EF/VDT/120' computer table has split-level, height-adjustable surfaces for keyboard and terminal which can be placed to the right or left of the operator. Available in cream or darker beige laminate with contrasting black inset sections. *M*: w120 × d75 × h73cm (47¼ × 29½ × 28¾in). *P*: £370.88.

The system also includes receptionist's desk with work surface and counter with rounded

Planula's SERIE EP & F

edges and corners, also equipped with conduits for cables and in the same striking two-tone laminate finish. See *Reception furniture* for illustration.

PROJECT OFFICE FURNITURE LTD ⚠

PROJECT 4000, very well designed complete office system mainly in natural light oak with dark brown trim, some pieces also available in other woods. The components can be set up for clerical, secretarial, microcomputer and VDU work stations, also for executive, conference and reception areas. All incorporate an excellent wire-management system. Range of computer tables includes '4KOEE'. Its work surface provides enough room for both machine and clerical work, while the keyboard well can be set left or right to suit the operator and is very rigid to minimize vibration. It can be linked to a printer table such as '479EES', which has a slotted top to allow paper feed from beneath and can be fitted with detachable baskets mounted on mobile trolley to catch the print-out. *M*: '4KOEE' w120 × d80 × h72cm (47¼ × 28¼ × 31½in); '479EES' w80 × d72 × h80 (31½ × 31½ × 28¼in). *P*: £174.50; £184.81. The system includes a good range of storage cabinets in four heights which can be fitted for all types of filing. All cabinets can be open-fronted or closed by hinged, space-saving retractable doors or roll-up tambour. Desk-top storage, bookcase units and filing trolleys are also available. *M*: cabinet with retractable door '64452' w100 × d52.4 × h156cm (39¼ × 20½ × 61½in); all cabinets w100cm (39¼in). *P*: £255.34–£271.88. See following page for illustration.

MATRIX systems are panel-based. Basic panel

units come in five heights and four widths. They can be fabric-covered or glazed and can have an acoustic infill for greater sound absorption. Additional panels can extend the partitioning to the ceiling for complete privacy. Special features can be created using shaped, coloured or textured infills for panels; fully lockable glazed doors can also be fitted. There is a vast array of work surfaces which can be mounted on the panels at different heights to suit the job being done; plus freestanding desks and tables including a fully-adjustable VDU table. MATRIX PLUS is a refinement of the basic system — screen uprights are reduced to a fine line and hinge segments are in a choice of three colours: grey, terracotta and ivory. Work surfaces are in a slightly textured grey in a faint checked pattern with darker grey shades for the structural elements and edge trim. Exactly the same components are included as in the basic system. A useful 'D'-

Project's MATRIX PLUS

OFFICES

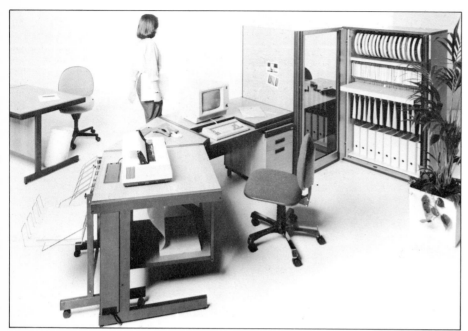

Project's PROJECT 4000 △ featuring '479EES' and '4KOEE'

ended work surface comes in three sizes. *M*: w120, 140, 160 × d80cm (47¼, 55, 63 × 31½in). *P*: on application. MATRIX AURA has an even softer appearance: screen hinges are fabric-covered and work tops are finished in oak.

GORDON RUSSELL LTD
Attractively designed complete office system, SYSTEM 100. Elements include desks, storage units, linking units and screens, plus task and ambient lighting. The system is made in solid oak and veneer with a natural finish or stained to choice. Low-reflection grey linoleum is standard for all work surfaces though oak veneer tops and other linoleum colours are available. Screens are covered in all-wool fab-

'SY 139' from Gordon Russell's SYSTEM 100

ric in choice of colours including dusky pink. All types of filing are catered for by wide range of fittings for the storage units. All the cables and wires needed for electronic and electrical equipment can be fitted into furniture and screens. A turn-table unit is available for VDU equipment. Machine table 'SY 139' has a split top with both working surfaces independently adjustable for height and angle. *M*: 'SY 139' w108 × d80 × h72cm (42½ × 31½ × 28¼in). *P*: £531. Gordon Russell also provide a complete office planning service.

SCOTT HOWARD ASSOCIATES LTD
Elegant CONCEPT office system by German firm Planmöbel. The system includes desks, storage units, computer tables, screens and room dividers, with wire-management facilities. The highly flexible partitioning screens allow office planners to arrange their space in virtually any way they please. The screens come in three heights and can be continued up to the ceiling if a complete room partition is required. Doors can be fitted into partitions and angled sections are available. Standard screen colour combinations for metal frames and panels respectively are light grey with red or grey fabric, grey-brown with beige fabric, black-brown with blue fabric; or light grey with white, light grey, grey-brown or black-brown perforated metal panels. Glass panels are also available. *M*: h110, 165, 205cm × w45, 80, 120cm (43¼, 65, 80¾ × 17¾, 31½, 47¼in). *P*: on application. Furniture comes in the following colour combinations for laminate surfaces and metal frame respectively: light grey/

'System-work' desk and additions, from Scott Howard's CONCEPT

pebble beige, grey-brown/pebble beige or oak veneer, black-brown/pebble beige or oak veneer. 'System-work' adjustable desk comes in five widths and can be set to three heights. *M*: w80, 120, 160, 180, 200 × d80 × h68, 72, 75cm (31½, 47¼, 63, 70¾, 78¾ × 31½ × 26¾, 28¼, 29½in). *P*: work station including desk, storage and screen £1000–£1500.

45 SERIES from Fantoni has the excellent design so typical of many Italian products. This stylish but relatively inexpensive range includes desks, work stations, storage cabinets and conference tables all made with rounded edges. The system is totally flexible and constructed from panels covered by a special plastic material in white or pale grey. Work surfaces are in non-glare laminate resistant to heat, wear, ink, alcohol etc and are also available in natural oak. Desks and tables pack flat for storage or transportation and are easily assembled. The system incorporates built-in wire-management channels and includes computer and printer tables. Storage cabinets are available in four heights and can be fitted for all types of filing; they are supplied open-fronted or with glass or solid doors. Acoustic

HALLER SYSTEM from Scott Howard

Scott Howard's 45 SERIES

wall panels can be used independently or with the other components to divide office space, and can be equipped with shelves on both sides. There are three sizes of work station, consisting of high-level desk and lower-level extension on one or both sides, which may also be used in conjunction with mobile storage pedestals. *M*: with left-hand extension w150 or 165 × d75 (desk) d165 (extension) × h75/65cm (59 or 65 × 29½/65 × 29½/25½in), with extensions both sides w165 × total d165 × h75/65cm (65 × 65 × 29½/25½in). *P*: work station including desk, storage and screen £700-£1200.

Swiss-designed HALLER SYSTEM offers an enormous range of integrated elements including frames, panels, organization components with accessories, tables, screens, wire-management facilities and ambient lighting. Chromed steel is used for frames and table legs; panels are stove-enamelled and drawers are enamelled steel. The system is very flexible and the different elements are easily assembled using simple tools, and as easily rearranged if required. The standard colours used in the system are pure white, light grey, gold yellow, pure orange, Haller green, gentian blue, Haller brown, graphite black, ruby red (other colours available to order); work surfaces are laminated or veneered. Work tables are rectangular or square, with triangular linking tops. *M*: rectangular w150 × d75 × h74cm (60 × 30 × 29in), w175 × d75 × h74cm (69 × 30 × 29in), w200 × d100 × h74cm (78 × 40 × 29in). *P*: on application. Similar lower tables are available at slightly lower height to store underneath, and also low-level occasional tables. The system also incorporates ambient lighting using energy-saving high intensity discharge lamps integrated into the furniture at any position.

STEELCASE STRAFOR UK LTD

SERIES 9000 system suitable for all office situations from secretarial to managerial. The modular system is highly flexible, all the elements being interchangeable and mutally compatible. An exceptional feature is the enormous choice of colours for panel-covering, furniture

elements and trims, so that the customer really can create the exact type of office environment that is required. Panels can be straight or curved in five heights and several widths and are covered in a choice of several materials: 100% wool tweed in eight pastel colours or a highly fire-resistant polyester in 24 colours which range right across the spectrum. Other options are lacquered steel in nine neutral shades, or laminates in the same neutrals plus brick red, pine green, navy, oak or walnut. The panels can also be glazed with tinted glass, and fitted with doors if necessary. The colour choice carries through to the furniture components which are all constructed of steel and finished in the same nine neutral shades with trim options of chrome, neutrals, bright yellow, blue and green. The furniture is freestanding and panel-hung and finished with rounded edges. Work surfaces can have real oak or wenge veneers or be laminated in grey, sand, beige, airforce blue, navy, grass and pine green, yellow, burgundy or rust. Seating can be upholstered to match or co-ordinate with panels and trims. Filing and storage units are freestanding or panel-hung, high- or low-level, and can be fitted to accept all kinds of

filing including computer print-outs. Full account is taken of the needs of the 'electronic office'. Wire-management channels run both horizontally and vertically and ambient and task lights can be incorporated into the office layout. Computer furniture includes VDU table with split-level surfaces for screen and keyboard. The screen surface is height-adjustable with the angle of inclination variable by 10°; the keyboard slides backwards and forwards so that it can be placed at the optimum distance from the screen for the individual operator. *M*: screen top w80 × d50 × h74–90cm (31½ × 19¾ × 29¼–35½in), keyboard top w80 × d30 × h66.8cm (31½ × 19¾ × 26in). *P*: on application. The table can be fitted with side units. There is also a printer unit with paper feed.

Steelcase Strafor make several desking ranges which can be used independently or in conjunction with the SERIES 9000 system.

Steelcase Strafor's SERIES 9000 VDU work station and CONCENTR'X 454 chair

TURBERVILLE SMITH & SON LTD

Good-looking GLOBAL office system from Norwegian firm Hov Møbelindustri A/S. The

Turberville Smith's GLOBAL with 'Flexiterm' VDU table

finely-graded modular system is in laminated light beech and comprises desking, VDU work stations, storage furniture, counters and partitions. All the furniture is built with softly rounded corners and edges. Desks come in 10 different standard sizes all with adjustable height. Typing tables and pedestals can be supplied for each desk size as required. Cable conduits can also be fitted where necessary. 'Flexiterm' VDU table has five standard settings for individual arrangement of keyboard and screen, plus the capacity of coding individual work positions for up to eight people — when each person inputs his or her own code the table will automatically adjust to the correct position. *M*: w82 × d60 × h72cm (32¼ × 23½ × 28¼in). *P*: on application. Alternatively, the system includes a swinging 'arm' that will support a VDU and can be clamped on to any work surface.

A full range of storage cabinets, roll-front cabinets and bookcases is available. Screen partitioning is available in three standard heights in straight or curved sections (45° and 90°), made either from sound-absorbent materials covered with flame-retardant fabric or from smoke-tinted Plexiglass. The solid panels will take suspended shelving, cabinets etc. *M*: straight w41, 62, 82, curved w70, Plexiglass w82 × h120, 150, 180cm (straight 16¼, 24½ 32¼, curved 27½, Plexiglass 32¼ × 47¼, 59, 70¾in). *P*: on application. Counters provide an extra element for fitting out an office. They can be curved round by 90° or 45° to enclose the working area. The work surfaces on the inner side harmonize with other components. The system also includes conference tables.

UNITY DESIGNS (UK) LTD

Distinctive-looking system comprising tables, mobile storage pedestals, high and low storage units, screens and chairs. All items may be used independently or in conjunction and the system is equally suitable for open-plan and cellular office schemes. Storage is well catered for by two- and three-drawer mobile pedestals in two depths, also two-, three- and four-drawer side units. There are also desk-height cupboards with sliding doors and high cupboards, tambour-fronted or with hinged doors. All storage units are available in a choice of nine colours including dove blue and pink. Screens can be fabric-covered, half glazed or fully glazed and come in two heights and five widths; there is also a smaller version which is fabric-covered only. The aluminium screen frames can be finished to match the storage units and the upholstery of the chairs. Tables come in six sizes and have off-white, low-glare laminate work surfaces protected by black moulded polyurethane safety edges. Wire management is via an optional patented slide-in separator pack. *M*: tables w80–113 × d56.5, 80 × h72cm (31½–44½ × 22, 31½ × 28¼in). *P*: on application.

System layout from Unity

TABLES

BUSINESS INTERIORS LTD

Functional chrome and wood tables by the Finnish firm Avarte. Versatile SP-SYSTEM tables have a wide choice of tops — rectangular, round, semicircular and 'D'-ended in various sizes — with tubular steel supports in varying lengths. They can be put together in many different configurations. Bases are finished in polished chrome; birch plywood tops are available in natural birch or stained black or brown. *M*: 'D'-ended table '730-858' w250 × d140 × h71cm (98½ × 55 × 28in). *P*: £397–£429.50. Avarte make five other ranges of tables, all equally well designed.

Business Interiors' SP-SYSTEM '730-858'

MARTIN J DODGE

Exceptionally good range of solid mahogany reproduction English furniture, much of which is suitable for boardrooms and directors'

offices. 'T15' three-pedestal table with optional cross-banded border comfortably seats 16, but all lengths of boardroom tables can be made to suit customers' requirements. *M*: (extended) w168 × d48 × h29½in (426.5 × 122 × 75cm) *P*: £2486–£2910. Various chairs are available to go with it (see *Furniture, chairs*).

FRAY DESIGN ▲

REFLEX TABLE SYSTEM with highly practical folding and linking frames and tops to allow many different layouts and easy removal. The tables are basically square or rectangular in shape; triangular and segmental linking junctions and interchangeable round tops give them greater adaptability. Tubular steel frames are coated in black, white or brown epoxy, with other colours or chrome available on request. Tops come in melamine, laminate or various wood veneers. *M*: standard tables and tops w60–75 × d60–180 × h72cm (23½–29½ × 23½–70¾ × 28¼in) *P*: tables £40–£123; link tops and frames £36–£103 (ex VAT). Larger tables are also built to special requirements.

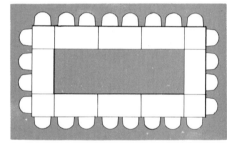

An arrangement of Fray Design's REFLEX TABLE SYSTEM △

PETER HAXWORTH ▲

Custom-built tables with high-quality wood veneer tops and high-tech UTS supports. Finished in polished chrome (or special finishes such as bronze), these supports are adjustable in height and fold flat for removal and storage. Any shape and size of table can be made, the larger ones being built in several sections so that they can be reduced in size or

Martin J Dodge's 'T15'

TABLES

rearranged in different formations. *M*: to order. *P*: on application. Occasional tables and desks can be made in matching veneers with the same adjustable supports. See *Furniture, made-to-order* for illustration.

HILLE INTERNATIONAL LTD
Fine quality boardroom table in the DELPHI GROUP. Standard veneers are Santos rosewood or oak with solid wood lipping; base is in polished chrome. There are five standard sizes. *M*: w244–550 × d114–148 × h71cm (96–216 × 45–58 × 28in). *P*: (oak) from £112. The table can be custom-made in other veneers and sizes. There is a matching credenza and luxuriously upholstered chair to provide all the furniture needed for the boardroom.

Hille's DELPHI GROUP

R E H KENNEDY LTD
Solid mahogany extending boardroom table with three pedestals '1569'. Part of a large range of top-quality handmade and hand-polished reproduction furniture. *M*: w135–180 × d48 × h29in (343–457 × 122 × 73.5cm) *P*: on application.

LUCAS FURNITURE SYSTEMS
Simple, well constructed PROGRAMME meeting tables designed as part of the PROGRAMME system (see separate entry). Tables are supplied fully assembled and ready for use. 'Meeting' and 'Conference' designs offer round and rectangular tables in a variety of different sizes to seat up to eight people. Tops are oak-veneered chipboard in clear-lacquered natural

R E H Kennedy's '1569'

PROGRAMME meeting tables from Lucas

finish and tubular steel frames are finished in satin chrome or epoxy powder coating in amber or buffalo. *M*: rectangular w120–200 × d80–100 × h72cm (47¼–78¾ × 31½–39¼ × 28¼in) *P*: on application. Lucas also make square and round low occasional tables in a similar style.

NORFOLK MANOR FURNITURE LTD
High quality boardroom and conference tables. 'T86' boardroom table has a four-piece mahogany top and stands on four pedestals. Additional options are cross-banding and brass claw feet. *M*: w564 × d206 ×h72cm (222 × 81 × 28¼in). *P*: on application.

Norfolk Manor's 'T86' with 'C3' chairs

GORDON RUSSELL LTD △
An excellent choice of conference tables and boardroom furniture. SERIES 40 tables have folding frames which allow storage in the minimum of space. Standard tables are made with Rio rosewood or teak veneers, but other suitable veneers or plastic laminate can be supplied to order. Standard legs are steel with bright chrome finish but other metals and finishes can be supplied. Table clips can be fitted to link up multiple assemblies. *M*: 'R989

Mark 1' w213.5 × d91.5 × h72.5cm (84 × 36 × 28¼in). *P*: (rosewood) £962.
Gordon Russell also make SERIES 45, a flexible conference table system in wood or wood and chromed steel which has tables and leaves that can be fitted together in many different configurations. There are five further ranges of boardroom and conference tables, all equally high quality.

SERIES 40 △ table from Gordon Russell

SCOTT HOWARD ASSOCIATES LTD
SERIES 2R range from Danish firm Fritz Hansen. Tables come in a variety of sizes and can be extended literally into infinity by fitting flaps and leaves. Leaves in 45° and 90° segments enable the tables to be curved; if these segments are used independently, a circular table can be created. The tables are available in natural beech, natural teak, black or dark-brown stained teak, or white laminate with solid-beech edging. All the tops are lipped in solid wood. Supporting brackets and all fittings are in chromed steel. *M*: tables w80 × d80 × h70cm (31½ × 31½ × 27½in) to w200 × d100 × h70cm (78¾ × 39¼ × 27½in); leaves w80 × d80 × h70cm (31½ × 31½ × 27½in) to w160 × d80 × h70cm (63 × 31½ × 27½in); h75cm (29½in) optional. *P*: from £200. Scott Howard have other Fritz Hansen tables in circular, oval, square and rectangular shapes.

SERIES 2R conference table arrangement from Scott Howard

PAINT

INTRODUCTION

Painting is undoubtedly the cheapest and quickest way to change the atmosphere, or even the apparent shape, of a room.

Before changing an existing scheme, decide which of the predominant colours in furniture, carpets and curtains are most suitable for walls and ceilings. The size and shape of the room will narrow your choice still further: strong, intense colours will create a sense of cosiness in a large room, apparently bringing the walls forward and lowering the ceiling; cool, pale shades give a feeling of space. Light is also important. A sunlit room will accommodate dark shades but warm, light tones are usually best for shaded northern exposure.

If in doubt, stick to one main colour. Apply this rule throughout the house if space is confined: a sunny sitting room emphasized in soft gold could lead to a hallway in a brighter, yellower shade, and a beige kitchen.

Aesthetic considerations apart, there are practical benefits in selecting one type of paint in preference to another.

Plastics, or vinyls, have largely superseded traditional cellulose-based paints, and are generally much easier to apply. (Non-drip paints that give a smooth, glossy finish without runs and snags are an offshoot.) They come in matt, silk and gloss finishes. Most other household paints for interior use are water-borne like emulsions, or oil-based like traditional gloss paints. Emulsions are easy to apply, quick drying, and have virtually no smell. Gloss paint, generally tougher, is recommended for windows, skirtings, doors etc, and comes in full shine, eggshell or silk (mid-sheen) finishes. It tends to highlight imperfections so requires a well-prepared surface — generally an oil-based undercoat — and it takes hours to dry. Modern eggshell or silk finishes can also be water based, and are more resistant to condensation and wear than water-based matt paints.

Most manufacturers produce the 88 British Standard colours but combine them to achieve their own shades. Paints mixed to order are obviously more expensive than standard ranges. To avoid this extra expense, try creating your own colour by adding a commercial tinter, available in tubes from hardware shops and builders' merchants, to a manufacturer's shade. These strong pigments can be used with water-, oil- and vinyl-based paints, and are perfect for creating a host of pastels from one large tin of white.

A variety of textured paints or wall coatings are available, giving high or low relief spattered or patterned finishes. They are applied to all kinds of concrete and brickwork, to plaster (particularly ceilings), and old paintwork, concealing cracks and flaws. Functional if not always beautiful, most are washable and dirt-repellent.

Also included here are specialist paints such as aluminium paints, luminous and fluorescent paints, black paints (including stove black) and enamels.

● For wood stains, varnishes and other finishes, see *Useful products*.

ARDENBRITE PRODUCTS LTD

Fourteen beautiful shades of metallic paint for indoor or outdoor use. Applied by brush or spray, the paint dries in 30 minutes but remains slightly flexible to resist cracking. For a glossier finish, cover with one or two coats of protective glaze. May be used on wood, stone and expanded polystyrene as well as metal. Ideal to add a classy look to iron railings, these paints are used on the Houses of Parliament, Liberty in Regent Street and on the 10,000 rosettes and ornamental mouldings on Hammersmith Bridge, but they would also be suitable for picture frames, lamps, radiators and pipes. Colours include five golds, two bronzes, silver, pewter grey, two coppers and gunmetal (a lovely silvery brown). *M:* 50ml–5l (1¾ fl oz–8¾pt). *P:* £1.35–£62.45 (ex VAT).

ARTEX LTD

Paints and texture coatings for professional and DIY use. AX is a new asbestos-free texture coating for indoor use. Mix with warm water, apply to walls or ceilings and give the desired textured finish using special roller, sponge or brush. In white only, but may be painted over in any colour. READYMIX is similar but has the

Artex's READYMIX with stipple pattern

Artex's AX with scroll pattern

advantage of being washable, making it particularly suitable for kitchens and bathrooms; in ivory, magnolia or cream. *P:* AX (5kg) (11lb) approx £6; READYMIX 5l (8¾pt) approx £12. Other products are available to the trade only, mostly for contract use. SPRAYTEX is a ready-mixed texture coating for spraygun application; EMULSION is a competitively priced paint range and HYCLAD is a long-lasting texture coating for inside or outside use. Artex also make a range of sealers, primers, stabilizers and a wide selection of laying-on and texturing tools. *P:* on application.

LAURA ASHLEY

Good range of satin gloss and vinyl matt emulsion paints in some unusual shades, to co-ordinate with Laura Ashley wallpapers, fabrics and furnishings. Satin gloss is available in terracotta, kingfisher, apricot, sand, tropical green, cream, moss, china blue, poppy, plum, navy, smoke, sapphire, burgundy, rose, white and stone, while the vinyl matt emulsion comes in terracotta, apricot, cream, moss, sand, sapphire, smoke, aquamarine, plum, rose, burgundy, stone, kingfisher, tropical green and white. *P:* (1l) satin gloss, white £2.95, colours £3.75; vinyl matt emulsion, white £1.95, colours £2.75.

BERGER DECORATIVE PAINTS

MAGICOTE paints for home decorators and BROLAC paints for professionals. MAGICOTE vinyl matt and vinyl silk come in 16 colours including six shades of 'Natural Whites', plus brilliant white and black in vinyl matt only. *M:*

1, 2.5l (1¾, 4⅜pt); brilliant white and black also in 5l (8¾pt). *P:* (2.5l) white approx £3.99; colours approx £5.25; 'Natural Whites' approx £4.50.
MAGICOTE non-drip gloss and liquid gloss come in 22 colours including brilliant white. *M:* 500ml, 1l (17½ fl oz, 1¾pt); brilliant white also in 2.5l (4⅜pt). *P:* (1l) white approx £2.49; colours approx £3.
Also for the home decorator but used a lot by interior decorators and architects is BERGER COLORIZER range — more than 400 colours

Top: Berger's TARTARUGA with 'Spearhead' design roller; below: TARTARUGA'S peelable backing

that are mixed to order in the desired shade, quantity and finish. Prices vary, but expect to pay rather more than for standard MAGICOTE colours.
BROLAC trade range is enormous, covering full gloss in 84 colours plus white, brilliant white, jet black and aluminium; low-odour eggshell in brilliant white, jet black and all British Standard colours; PEP vinyl silk and vinyl matt emulsions in 78 colours including 'Country Whites' plus brilliant white and jet black, the vinyl matt also in white; exterior paint and an extensive range of primers, undercoats and enamels. *M:* 500ml–10l (17½ fl oz – 17½pt). *P:* on application.
Finally, there's TARTARUGA, a texture paint originally developed in Portugal for use inside or outside. In 10 subtle colours, the paint is applied by brush and then stippled or patterned with one of four special TARTARUGA DESIGN ROLLERS. It can be used over a special strippable backing paper: when the textured surface is no longer required, simply cut a corner or edge of the paper and peel away the entire top face, paint and all; the underside of the paper remains as a base for future decoration. *P:* on application.

BLUNDELL-PERMOGLAZE LTD
Very comprehensive PERMOGLAZE range aimed mainly at the trade market, but also available retail. Washable, hard-wearing vinyl silk comes in a good choice of about 70 colours. *M:* 1, 2.5, 5l (1¾, 4⅜, 8¾pt). Glossy vinyl, in a choice of 13 colours, gives a slightly subdued gloss finish for interior use. It has no residual odour, so is particularly suitable for food processing and storage areas where paint smells must be avoided. *M:* 2.5, 5l (4⅜, 8¾pt). 'High Opacity' matt is an economical smooth coating for interior contract use in 17 colours. *M:* 5, 10, 15l (8¾, 17½, 26⅜pt). Gloss comes in about 80 colours. *M:* 500ml, 2.5, 5l (17½ fl oz, 4⅜, 8¾pt). The eggshell is particularly easy to apply and comes in about 90 colours. *M:* 1, 2.5, 5l (1¾, 4⅜, 8¾pt). PAMMASTIC vinyl matt is durable enough for kitchens and bathrooms and comes in around 70 colours. *M:* 1, 2.5, 5, 10l (1¾, 4⅜, 8¾, 17½pt). *P:* all on application.
Blundell-Permoglaze also make paint rollers

and ancillary equipment. Roller heads can be made from long, short and medium pile or woven pile for applying oil paints on smooth surfaces, and there is also a texture roller head in two sizes for heavy texture water-based paint. *M:* roller frames 7, 9, 12in (18, 23, 30.5cm). A variety of paint trays and a ladder/staging bucket are also made and there is a useful PERMOGLAZE ROLLER WASHER, designed to save time when cleaning roller heads that have been used for water-based paints. *P:* on application.

J W BOLLOM & CO LTD
Terrific BROMEL paints and wall coatings from this old-established company. Mainly suppliers to the trade, J W Bollom also sell to the public at their five trade counters.
Vinyl silk and vinyl matt emulsion come in an extensive range of colours. *M:* 1, 2.5, 5l (1¾, 4⅜, 8¾pt). Oil-based paints include the usual gloss and eggshell plus 'Triple-milled Gloss Enamel' and 'Eggshell Enamel', particularly recommended for industrial and coastal regions. These come in the full British Standard range of colours plus the 104 shades in the *Architects' Dictionary of Colour. M:* 1, 2.5, 5l (1¾, 4⅜, 8¾pt). A good selection of colours is also available in cellulose paint. *M:* 5l (8¾pt). *P:* all on application.
Flame retardant paints of varying British Standard strengths include gloss, eggshell, and emulsion as well as varnish systems which should not be over-painted, for a natural effect. BROGUARD NL flame-proofing solution for use on textiles should be used to complement the paints and varnishes.
BRO-SPRAY acrylic wall coating is lightly textured to disguise imperfections and irregularities, and is odourless, non-toxic and flame retardant. For interior use only, it is recommended for use in the food and catering industries, schools, hospitals, garages and public buildings. Satin and gloss are available in 86 colours, and different decorative effects can be achieved by spraying contrasting flecks or spots on top. BROMATEX textured wall coating is another flame retardant finish also available in 86 colours, may be used inside or out, and the final finish can be stippled or combed. Both coatings can be applied either by brush or spray.
Finally, there's DRYWALL exterior and interior wall coating, originally formulated in Scandinavia to withstand extreme weather conditions and now manufactured in Great Britain under licence. There are four grades — non-textured, fine textured, medium textured and pebble dash — to suit all applications. Non-textured and fine textured versions can be applied by brush, roller or airless spray; other textures by hopper feed spray gun. All come in white and 59 lovely colours, offering a really good choice for commercial or domestic users. *M:* all wall coatings 5l (8¾ pt). *P:* on application.

PAINT

CEMENTONE-BEAVER LTD
BEAVER paints for the amateur and professional decorator. Trade range includes contract emulsion suitable for all interior walls and ceilings in 17 colours; liquid gloss in 54 colours; trade vinyl matt emulsion for exterior and interior use in 41 colours; SHEENCOTE emulsion in 20 colours, offered as an alternative to conventional eggshell and semi-gloss paints for subtle sheen on interior and exterior surfaces; and the usual undercoats and primers. *M:* contract emulsion 5l (8¾pt), brilliant white and magnolia also 10l (17½pt); liquid gloss, 1, 2.5l (1¾, 4⅜pt), brilliant white, magnolia and black also 5l (8¾pt); trade vinyl matt emulsion 2.5, 5l (4⅜, 8¾pt), brilliant white also 10l (17½pt); SHEENCOTE emulsion 2.5, 5l (4⅜, 8¾pt).

For a textured wall finish, choose from two products: TEXIT, a dry powder that is mixed with water and applied to interior walls or ceilings only; and FLEXITEX, a ready-mixed product for interior or exterior use. Both cover small cracks and imperfections and can be textured after application with brush or roller. *M:* TEXIT 5, 10, 25kg (11, 22, 55lb), FLEXITEX 5, 10l (8¾, 17½pt).

For the amateur decorator there's a choice of BEAVER vinyl silk emulsion, vinyl matt emulsion, liquid gloss and non-drip gloss. Silk emulsion comes in 25 colours including brilliant white; matt emulsion in 26 colours including brilliant white and jet black; and gloss paints in 20 colours including brilliant white and jet black. *M:* vinyl silk and vinyl matt 1, 2.5, 5l (1¾, 4⅜, 8⅜pt); non-drip gloss 500ml, 1, 2l (17½ fl oz, 3½pt); liquid gloss 500ml, 1, 2.5, 5l (17½ fl oz, 1¾, 4⅜pt).
P: all on application.

CROWN DECORATIVE PRODUCTS LTD
CROWN PLUS TWO emulsion and gloss paints as well as a huge choice of colours in the COLOUR CUE range. CROWN PLUS TWO emulsions are divided into four tonal groups — 'Misty Shades', 'Pretty Pastels', 'Summer Tints' and 'Country Colours' — each with six colours

in vinyl matt or vinyl silk, plus three Whisper Whites'. All are available in small 'Matchpots' size to test at home. CROWN PLUS TWO non-drip gloss comes in a good range of 24 colours including some fashionable soft shades. *P:* emulsion (2½l) £4.99; gloss (1l) £3.49; 'Matchpot' 25p refundable on purchase of 2½l can). If you can't find something to your taste in PLUS TWO, then the 980 colours of vinyl silk and matt emulsion, gloss and eggshell in the COLOUR CUE system should provide the answer. *P:* emulsion (2½l) £7.95; gloss and eggshell (1l) £3.95.

FINNIGANS SPECIALITY PAINTS LTD
Two answers to rust. HAMMERITE enamel finish obliterates rust in a single coat applied directly to metal — no primer or undercoat is needed. The resulting siliconized surface is dirt repellent, waterproof and capable of withstanding temperatures of up to 300°F, as well as being lead-free and non-toxic. HAMMERITE is available with glossy hammered enamel finish in 11 colours — black, silver grey, light blue, red, dark blue, bronze, gold, light green, mid green, dark green and violet — or with smooth

HAMMERITE enamel finish by Finnigans

PRICES AND INFORMATION WERE CORRECT AT THE TIME OF GOING TO PRESS

finish in white only. Ideal for everything from wrought iron gates to radiators and kitchen scales, the smooth white in particular for touching up cookers and freezers and washing machines. Can also be applied to magnesium alloy, aluminium, galvanized iron, bitumen and woodwork, even cardboard, and a heavy coat applied to damp concrete, walls and stone floors will stop dusting and damp. Hammered finish is touch dry within 15 minutes, rainproof in 30; smooth finish is touch dry in 30 minutes. *M:* 250ml, 1l (8¾ fl oz, 1¾pt). *P:* £2.12, £6.99 (ex VAT).

NO 1 is a really advanced metal primer. It kills rust, primes and undercoats all in one, making surfaces ready for almost all top-coat paints. And the formula goes on working to prevent rust re-activating. NO 1 contains no lead, zinc or acid and can also be used on wood and even concrete, where it makes a very hard-wearing, non-slip floor paint. Available in beige or brown, the primer is touch dry in 20 minutes and ready for most over-coats in 2-4 hours. Available in cans or aerosols. *M:* cans 250ml, 1l (8¾ fl oz, 1¾pt). *P:* £2.63, £8.60; aerosol £2.15 (ex VAT).

HABITAT DESIGNS LTD
Paint colours specially mixed to co-ordinate with Habitat's fabrics and wallpapers. Emulsion comes in white plus 18 colours: pollen, sunflower yellow, cantaloup, apricot, powder blue, forget-me-not, cornflower blue, marine blue, moonshine, almond pink, poppyfield red, Indian red, pistachio, peppermint green, sage green, forest green, vanilla and fleet grey. Gloss colours are: sunflower yellow, cantaloup, forget-me-not, marine blue, poppyfield red, pistachio, and chalk white. Undercoat comes in red, yellow, grey and white. *M:* undercoat 1l (1¾pt); gloss 1l (1¾pt), white also 2.5l (4⅜pt); white emulsion 5l (8¾pt); vinyl matt emulsion 2.5l (4⅜pt). *P:* undercoat £3.15; gloss £3.15, £5.95; white emulsion matt £6.95, silk £7.25; vinyl matt emulsion £5.95.

HUMBROL LTD
Staggering selection of enamel paints, intended for model-making. There are about 20 gloss colours, 40 satin, 10 metallics and more than 200 matt and semi-matt colours. Available in tiny tins and in aerosol spray cans. All are completely non-toxic so safe for use on toys, children's furniture etc. *M:* tins 14–250ml (½–8¾ fl oz); aerosols 113, 397g (4, 14 oz). *P:* 40p–£1.95; aerosols £1.55, £2.80.

U-SPRAY GLOSS PAINT, a non-toxic paint in aerosol form, dries in seven minutes and is perfect for furniture and household appliances. Ten colours include black, white and four metallics. *M:* 13, 397g (4, 10 oz). *P:* £1.55, £2.80.

Humbrol's ALUMINIUM PAINT gives a bright, silvery finish to metal and other surfaces,

RADIATOR PAINT is specially formulated to stay dazzling white for years, and LUMINOUS paint in red, green or white is useful for door bells, light switches, or even fishing floats. *M:* ALUMINIUM PAINT 250ml (8¾ fl oz); RADIATOR PAINT 250ml (8¾ fl oz); LUMINOUS PAINT 50ml (1¾ fl oz). *P:* ALUMINIUM PAINT £1.80; RADIATOR PAINT £2.45; LUMINOUS PAINT £1.90.

Finally, not so much a paint, more a wall and ceiling coating, come Humbrol's TEXTURED FINISH and SILK TEXTURE FINISH, both for indoor or outdoor use. TEXTURED FINISH's crunchy, textured effect will normally last 10 years. Covering small cracks in walls or ceilings, it has a flexibility which allows it to move with the surface so that any new cracks developing underneath are also disguised. SILK TEXTURE FINISH also covers cracks and produces an elegant, easy-to-clean sheen. *M:* 2.5, 5l (4⅜, 8¾pt). *P:* TEXTURED FINISH £5.25, £8.95; SILK TEXTURE FINISH £7.25, £11.95.

IMPERIAL CHEMICAL INDUSTRIES PLC

Paints for the trade and retail market sold under the well known brand name DULUX. Range includes vinyl silk and vinyl matt, each in 26 colours plus brilliant white and six 'Natural Whites' — slightly tinted with beige, blue, pink, apricot or cream; gloss and non-drip gloss in 22 colours plus brilliant white and 'Natural Whites'; and Silthane silk in 20 colours plus brilliant white. MATCHMAKER range offers an even greater choice of colour: 575 shades in all, mixed to order in gloss, matt or silk. *M:* vinyl silk, vinyl matt 2.5, 5l (4⅜, 8¾pt); gloss paints, colours 500ml, 1, 2.5l (17½ fl oz, 1¾, 4⅜pt), brilliant white also 5l (8¾pt); Silthane silk 1, 2.5l (1¾, 4⅜pt); MATCHMAKER undercoat, gloss, Silthane silk 480ml, 960ml, 2.4l (16¾ fl oz, 1¾, 4¼pt); MATCHMAKER vinyl matt, vinyl silk 960ml, 2.4, 4.8l (1¾, 4¼, 8½pt). *P:* on application.

There are some useful leaflets for amateur decorators, and even a video entitled *Colouring Your Home* to help with colour planning; failing that, a colour consultant can create individual colour schemes for customers. *P:* video £9.95 (inc p & p); colour scheming service £5 (allow four weeks for delivery).

Products for the trade cover an enormous selection: primers, undercoats, eggshell (44 colours), high gloss (93 colours), vinyl matt (79 colours), vinyl silk (47 colours), SUPERMATT (13 colours), economical ICI CONTRACT EMULSION (white and magnolia only), semi-gloss floor paint (six colours), quick-drying enamel (six colours) and MATCHMAKER range. Comprehensive technical literature and advice available. *M:* most in standard sizes 2.5, 5l (4⅜, 8¾pt), vinyl matt white and magnolia, SUPERMATT selected colours and CONTRACT EMULSION also 10l (17½pt). *P:* on application.

Other useful DULUX painting products are a universal primer for wood, metal and plaster surfaces, an aluminium sealer for treated wood, a rust-inhibiting metal primer, a primer sealer, an aluminium finish paint and a paint-brush cleaner.

JOY PRODUCTS

Paints for special purposes. JOY ENAMEL is a lead-free paint in 18 intermixable colours. Ideal for use on toys, tins, etc. For hot water pipes and radiators choose HEAT RESISTING ENAMEL PAINT in cream, blue, beige, black and white or HEAT RESISTING METALLIC paint in golds, bronzes and silvers. *M:* 250ml (8¾ fl oz). *P:* JOY ENAMEL £2.03; HEAT RESISTING ENAMEL PAINT £1.84; HEAT RESISTING METALLIC PAINT £3.66.

Black paints come in a huge choice which includes HEATPROOF STOVE BLACK for a glossy finish or BERLIN BLACK for an eggshell finish on cookers and stoves, FLAT BLACK for decorative ironwork and BLACKBOARD BLACK — for use as its name implies. *M:* 250ml (8¾ fl oz). *P:* all £1.39.

Finally there is the wonderful FLUORESCENT PAINT in orange, red, yellow and green which can be used on most indoor and outdoor surfaces including paper, and LUMINOUS PAINT in green which comes as a kit consisting of base reflecting coat and luminous top coat. *M:* FLUORESCENT PAINT 50ml (1¾ fl oz); LUMINOUS PAINT 2oz (57g). *P:* FLUORESCENT PAINT £1.27; LUMINOUS PAINT £1.63. (All prices ex VAT.)

LANGSTON JONES & SAMUEL SMITH LTD

SIGNPOST paints and wall coatings for domestic and industrial use. Matt emulsion gives the perfect finish for walls and ceilings, inside or out, and comes in 25 colours including six subtle shades of white. Silk emulsion gives a beautiful silk finish that is easy to clean; available in the same 25 colours. Gloss with polyurethane and silicones gives a tough high-gloss finish for wood and metal surfaces indoors and out. Gloss and non-drip comes in 24 colours plus brilliant white. *M:* vinyl matt,

vinyl silk 1–5l (1¾–8¾ pt); gloss 250ml–5l (8¾ fl oz–8¾pt).

TEXIFLEX is a self-texturing finish for walls and ceilings, and its companion SMOOTHEX gives a smooth textured finish that doesn't hold or attract dust and dirt. TEXIFLEX can be applied by brush for smooth finish or roller for coarser finish. It covers small cracks, is steam-resistant and can be combed, stippled or sponged for more decorative effects. For interior use only, its white finish may be left plain or over-painted to tone with other decorations. SMOOTHEX is for indoor or outdoor use and is best applied with a good quality coarse foam roller. It covers small cracks and holes and can be wiped clean with warm soapy water. In white only. *M:* 2.5, 6l (4⅜–10½pt). *P:* all on application.

LEYLAND PAINT AND WALLPAPER PLC

Enormous range of paints for home decorators and for the trade. Home decorators can choose from the popular vinyl silk or vinyl matt emulsions, mainly in gentle pastel shades plus a new range of 'Softer Shades' — very pale blue, green, pink, peach and cream. Gloss finish and non-drip gloss come in 24 colours, plus black and brilliant white. Eggshell is a low-odour oil-based paint in 36 colours including brilliant white, black and the complete BS4800 basic colour range. *M:* vinyl silk and vinyl matt emulsions, 1, 2.5 5l (1¾, 4⅜, 8¾pt), 'Softer Shades' 2.5l (4⅜pt); gloss 500ml (17½ fl oz) 1, 2.5, 5l (1¾, 4⅜, 8¾pt); non-drip gloss 500ml (17½fl oz), 1, 2.5l (1¾, 4⅜pt); eggshell 1, 2.5, 5l (1¾, 4⅜, 8⅜pt).

The size of the trade paint range is staggering. As well as including the usual vinyl paints, gloss, eggshell and emulsion finishes in more than 100 colours, primers and exterior wall paints, there is also MULTICOLOUR SPRAYING FINISH, a satin sheen finish that looks and feels like jointless vinyl wall cover-

PRICES AND INFORMATION WERE CORRECT AT THE TIME OF GOING TO PRESS

PAINT

ing, CELLAR PAINT, FLOOR PAINT in red or grey and SPRELUX SPRAYING PLASTIC for a textured, multi-flecked effect inside or out in 21 colours. *M:* MULTICOLOUR SPRAYING FINISH, CELLAR PAINT and SPRELUX SPRAYING PLASTIC 5l (8¾pt).
P: all on application.

DONALD MACPHERSON & CO LTD

Comprehensive range from the people who make the much-praised COVER PLUS paints for Woolworth (see separate entry). Macpherson's paints for the trade cover vinyl matt and vinyl silk emulsions in 64 colours plus black and brilliant white, and gloss and eggshell paints in 75 colours plus black and brilliant white. *M:* vinyl matt and vinyl silk emulsions 2.5, 5l (4⅜, 8¾pt); gloss 1, 2.5, 5l (1¾, 4⅜, 8¾pt); eggshell 2.5, 5l (4⅜, 8¾pt). *P:* on application.

MANDERS PAINTS LTD

Very comprehensive range from a company with over 200 years of paint-making experience. For professionals there is gloss in 11 colours including brilliant white; vinyl matt in 107 colours; vinyl silk in 67 colours; eggshell in 105 colours and undercoat in 23 colours. Fungicidal quality is available in all except undercoat. POPULAR COLOUR RANGE for home decorators covers the same paint finishes, but in a smaller choice of colours and with the addition of a non-drip gloss and 'Easitex' flexible textured vinyl coating to cover hairline cracks and uneven surfaces on walls or ceilings. In white only, 'Easitex' may be textured with brush, roller or comb and may be over-coated with most types of paint. *M:* gloss 500ml–5l (17½ fl oz–8¾pt); vinyl matt, vinyl silk, eggshell 1–5l (1¾–8¾pt); 'Easitex' 2.5, 5l (4⅜, 8¾pt). For good coverage at an economical price, Manders make trade matt and silk emulsions in ten basic, pale colours. *M:* 5, 10l (8⅜, 17½pt). A technical services department offers a free survey facility and advice to trade users and specifiers. *P:* all on application.

JOHN OLIVER LTD

Enormous range of exclusive JOHN OLIVER COLOURS, 1300 Spectrum paint colours and the full British Standard range, plus an exact paint matching service — all from one supplier. The 35 JOHN OLIVER COLOURS all come in emulsion and vinyl silk finish and many are also available in gloss and eggshell. Colours include daring scarlets, bright blues, greens and yellows, shocking pink or black, plus easier-to-live-with pinks, beiges, greys and whites. Spectrum paint colours and British Standard range can be supplied in any finish

PRICES AND INFORMATION WERE CORRECT AT THE TIME OF GOING TO PRESS

and it takes John Oliver only seven days to mix a special colour to match existing furnishings. *M:* 1, 2.5, 5l (1¾, 4⅜, 8¾pt). *P:* (2½l) emulsion and vinyl silk £10.90, eggshell and gloss £13; special mix surcharge £10.50. (All prices ex VAT.)

E PARSONS & SONS

Good range of specialist paints. BLACKFRIAR black paints include 'Semi Gloss Black' for interior and exterior use on wood or metal, 'Stove Bright' gloss paint for interior use on metal and 'Dull Black' for interior wood and metal. *P:* (2.5l/4⅜pt) 'Semi Gloss Black', 'Dull Black', £11.93; 'Stove Bright' £14.16.
Other BLACKFRIAR paints include heat-resistant 'Aluminium Paint' for exterior or interior use, 'Metallic Paint' for interior use only in pale gold, deep gold, copper, bronze and silver, and quick-drying 'Enamel Paint' in eight colours. *P:* (2.5l/4⅜pt). *M:* 'Aluminium Paint' and 'Metallic Paint' 125ml—2.5l (4½ fl oz–4⅜pt); 'Enamel Paint' 125–500ml (4½–17½ fl oz). *P:* (2.5l) 'Aluminium Paint' £14.17; 'Metallic Paint' £29.14; (500ml) 'Enamel Paint' £3.69.

ARTHUR SANDERSON & SONS LTD

Amazing choice of 1350 colours in SANDERSON SPECTRUM PAINTS, each in four finishes — gloss, eggshell, vinyl matt emulsion and vinyl silk emulsion. Impossible to describe the range and even more impossible to make a choice, so Sanderson have cleverly produced a leaflet to help the home decorator select the right colour scheme. Seven colour themes have been chosen — cool hues, natural shades, warm hues, pastel shades, contemporary colours, shades of white and accent colours — and 261 colours have been grouped according to these themes. Paints are all mixed to order in a range of can sizes. *P:* (1l) gloss, eggshell £5.75; vinyl matt, vinyl silk emulsion £5.25.

SILEXINE PAINTS LTD

Wide range of specialist paints. SANDCOTE is a finely textured paint for internal or external use on dry, smooth or textured cement, plaster or bricks. It covers fine cracks, is water-resistant and the manufacturers claim that, being made with crushed marble, it will retain its appearance for up to seven years. Apply by brush or spray, choosing from white or 24 colours — among them are some good beiges, greens and browns and pale coral. SMOOTH-COTE is a smooth acrylic weather-resistant paint with fungicide available in all the same colours. *M:* SANDCOTE 5, 10l (8¾, 17½pt); SMOOTHCOTE 5l (8¾pt). *P:* (5l) SANDCOTE white £13.20, colours £13.95; SMOOTHCOTE white £17.40, colours £18.67.
TEXIDEC, for interior use, provides a tough, durable, monotone, two-tone or multi-

coloured high or low relief texture finish to building blocks, brickwork, concrete or even old paintwork. It comes in 12 basic colours in matt, silk, and TEXIGLAZE for shiny finish; combinations can be used for different effects, smooth or spattered. Odourless, dirt-repellent and washable, the surface is recommended for commercial and public buildings, for entrance halls and staircases in blocks of flats, and for prefabricated concrete and all types of ceilings. *M:* 5l (8¾pt). *P:* £19.62.
Other Silexine paints that would be useful around the home include ANTICON, an anti-condensation coating, and antifungal FUNGI-CHEK, available as primer, undercoat, tile grout, and gloss or emulsion paint. *M:* 1–5l (1¾–8¾pt). *P:* £5.50–£25.
(All prices ex VAT.)

UBM BUILDING SUPPLIES LTD

Basic colours at competitive prices available through UBM's own retail outlets. Vinyl silk emulsion comes in a choice of magnolia, blush stone, fawn, honeysuckle, ice green, milk white, new blue, peach and brilliant white; matt emulsion in the same colours plus jet black. *M:* 2.5, 5l (4⅜, 8¾pt). *P:* (2.5l) vinyl silk, brilliant white £4.22, colours £4.78; matt, brilliant white £4.09, colours £4.66.
UBM gloss is available in brilliant white, magnolia and black. *M:* white 1, 2.5, 5l (1¾, 4⅜, 8¾pt); magnolia and black 2.5l (4⅜pt). *P:* (2.5l) £5.13.
For real economy when painting large areas in just white or magnolia, go for HIGH COVER Matt Emulsion. *M:* 10l (17½pt). *P:* £14.22.
UBM make an oil-based primer and an acrylic primer/undercoat, both in white only. *M:* 2.5l (4⅜pt). *P:* oil-based primer £6.08; acrylic primer/undercoat £4.53.
UBM undercoat comes in white or grey. *M:* white 1, 2.5, 5l (1¾, 4⅜, 8¾pt); grey 2.5l (4⅜pt). *P:* (2.5l) white £5.13; grey £5.96.
(All prices ex VAT.)

WOOLWORTH

COVER PLUS paint made exclusively for Woolworth by Donald Macpherson & Co Ltd. This much-praised paint range consists of full gloss, non-drip gloss, matt vinyl and silk vinyl finishes, undercoat and an exterior wall finish in five colours. Gloss and vinyl paints come in 24 colours including brilliant white. Six 'Tinted Whites' come in full gloss and matt and silk vinyl. *M:* full and non-drip gloss 500ml–1l (17½ fl oz, 1¾pt), brilliant white 2.5l (4⅜pt), matt and silk vinyl 1, 2.5l (1¾, 4⅜pt), brilliant white 5l (8¾pt). *P:* full gloss (1l) brilliant white £2.49, colours £3.09; non-drip gloss (1l) brilliant white £2.59, colours £3.09; matt vinyl (2.5l) brilliant white £4.15, colours £6.19; silk vinyl (2.5l) brilliant white £4.39, colours £6.39; 'Tinted Whites' full gloss (1l) £3.09, matt and silk vinyl (2.5l) £4.99.

INTRODUCTION

A staircase may not be a decoration but it can be a striking decorative element. This section includes traditional designs as well as some unusual spirals, in wood, steel and cast iron, to carry you in style from one level to another. Many have been designed with split-level and loft conversions in mind, and most are supplied in kit form.

Of course, if you're looking for something really unique, the answer is to commission a good joiner to create it for you.

● Entire salvaged staircases or parts can be obtained from many of the dealers listed in *Architectural salvage* at the end of the book.

ALBION DESIGN OF LONDON

Variety of spiral, open spiral and straight cast iron stairs reproduced to a Victorian pattern. Attractive basic design features treads pierced with a floral motif, slender cast spindles with leaf mouldings and a plain mild steel handrail. The pattern can be supplied as a conventional tight spiral around a central column, as straight flights, and as an open well spiral with inner edge supported on cast iron columns every 12

Treads with floral motif by Albion Design

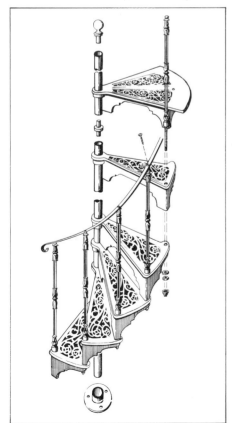

Range of cast iron spindles by Albion Design

treads, outer edge on a suitably curved wall. Albion also supply an unusual softwood spiral staircase in kit form. Treads, balusters and handrail are timber but the central drum has a veneer of timber over a concrete core and an interlocking system of tubular steel post tensioning rods. *M:* cast iron spiral stairs dia 91–244cm (36–96in); timber spiral stairs dia 154–207cm (60½–81½in). *P:* cast iron spiral stairs £69–£116 per rise of 20.5cm (8in); other prices on application.

ARCHITECTURAL COMPONENTS LTD

Three timber spiral stairs. 'Stybrez' is a simple modern design with two square section balusters per tread and a deep handrail, all in pine. More economical, 'Styvel' is made of laminated wood to similar design. Although 'Stylarmor' has balusters and newel posts of traditional turned design, it has a hidden structure of galvanized steel tubing. Available in movingui, sapele or oak. *M:* 'Stybrez' dia 119, 139, 160cm (47, 55, 63in); Styvel 109–249cm (43–98in) in 10cm (4in) increments; 'Stylarmor' 109–249cm (43–98in) in 10cm (4in) increments. *P:* on application.

Spiral staircase by Architectural Components

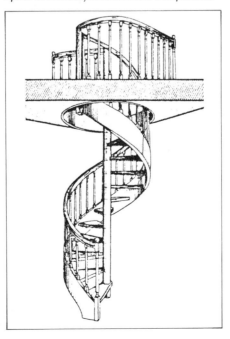

THE BIRMINGHAM GUILD LTD

Spiral and straight staircases with steel frames and hardwood or steel plate treads. 'Guild' spiral stairs are supplied to client's specifications. The bolt-together structure is mild steel, with a choice of mild steel, aluminium, bronze, brass or stainless steel for the balustrade. For internal spirals, iroko hardwood treads are carried on steel tread brackets and all metal is painted with red zinc oxide primer. For fire escapes or other external use, mild steel chequer-plate treads are employed and the metalwork can be shotblasted and zinc sprayed. Square landings are supplied which allow maximum head clearance. The company will also manufacture straight staircases to order from the same materials. *M:* spiral staircase dia 48–72in (122–183cm) in 6in (15cm) increments. *P:* on application.

Spiral staircase by Birmingham Guild

BRITANNIA ARCHITECTURAL METALWORK

Specialist casters of eighteenth- and nineteenth-century metalwork. Britannia claim to have the largest collection in the country of Georgian and Victorian patterns for railings, balusters, brackets, gratings, verandas, roof ridge cresting, balconies, and window box retainers. Their cast iron staircase is to a Victorian pattern with treads and balustrade incorporating leaf motifs. The firm will also clean up old castings and even reproduce them in either cast aluminium or iron. *M:* cast iron staircase dia 118–213cm (48–84in). *P:* on application.

STAIRCASES

CONSCULPT

Concrete spiral stairs for internal or external use. Consculpt spirals have well-moulded concrete treads on threaded steel core. Balustrade, of three posts per tread, and handrail are made from anodized aluminium. Treads are supplied as grey or white concrete with non-slip nosings. Alternatively, polished granite surface or carpet recesses may be chosen. The stairs, designed for domestic, hotel or school use, can easily cope with a rise of several floors and are supplied as kits or fixed by Consculpt. *M:* dia 76, 92, 100, 115, 165, 230cm (30, 36¼, 39¼, 45, 65, 90in). *P:* on application.

External concrete staircase by Consculpt

E A HIGGINSON & CO LTD

Seven solid wood spiral staircases made by Effebi in Italy. 'B3', 'B4', 'B5' and 'PS' are simply styled with straight balusters and plain handrails ('B5' with plank handrail), while 'B1/L', 'B2/L' and 'B6' have traditionally turned balusters and newels with moulded handrails. All except 'PS' are available in standard treated Slav or Rumanian beech, and also in Sipo mahogany, Slavonian oak, Swedish pine, elm, ash and Tanganyika walnut. 'PS' comes in Swedish pine only, with PVC handrail. *M:* 'B1/L' dia 110–300cm (43¼–118in); 'B2/L', 'B4', 'B5,', 'B6,' dia 110–220cm (43¼–86½in); 'B3' dia 110-160cm (43¼–63in), 'PS' dia 110–140cm (43¼–55in). *P:* on application.

E A Higginson will also supply custom-made architectural joinery including hardwood and softwood staircases within reasonable travelling distance of their north-west London works.

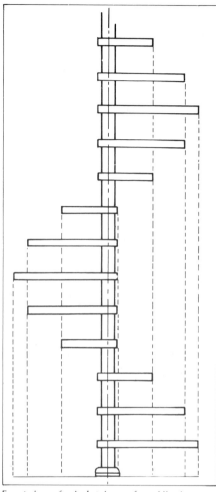

Front view of spiral staircase from Higginson

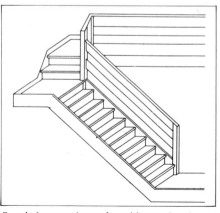

Ranch-fence staircase from Magnet Southerns

MAGNET SOUTHERNS

Straight wooden stairs, spiral stairs in kit form and component pieces from a company with more than 250 branches. 'Standard' stairs have either open treads or continuous risers and traditional balustrade with turned spindles and newel posts. Range of components includes spindles and newels in hemlock (softwood) or mahogany turned to Georgian, Victorian or American colonial patterns, and all the handrail parts needed for fancy turns and terminations. 'Special' staircases are also made to order with 'ranch fence' balustrade with longitudinal members instead of vertical spindles. *M:* 'Standard' stairs w36in (91.5cm). *P:* 'Standard' stairs 12 treads in softwood £350 (open treads) £300 (continuous risers); other prices on application.

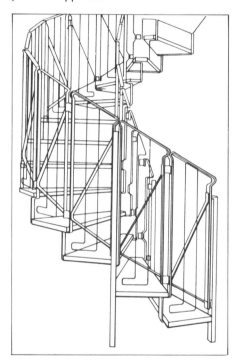

Spiral stairs in kit form by Magnet Southerns

W H NEWSON & SONS LTD

BURBIDGE machine-made staircase parts, to make up standard staircases. There is a variety of newel posts, handrails, base rails, turned spindles and corner fittings for all types of

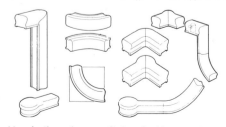

Handrails and corner fittings by Newson & Sons

turns and configurations. All are traditionally styled and available in kiln-dried hemlock, ready to be polished, painted or stained, and in mahogany. *M:* spindle h80, 90, 110cm·(31½, 35½, 43¼in). *P:* spindles £4.25–7.38; rails £11–£26.88 per 180cm (70¾in) run.

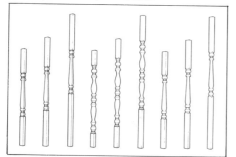

Turned spindle designs by Newson & Sons

PEDLEY WOODWORK LTD

SPIROTRED range of wood and steel spiral stairs, supplied in kit form. For main stairs there are 'E2' and slightly smaller 'E1', both with black-coated steel central column and balustrading, 'E2' with pine, sapele or teak finish to handrail and treads, 'E1' with pine or teak only. 'LC1' and 'LC2' are designed specifically for economical loft conversions. 'LC1' has fibreboard treads, black-coated steel central column and balusters, and pine handrail; 'LC2' has solid sapele treads and handrail. *M:* 'E2' dia 212cm (84in), 'E1' dia 183cm (72in); 'LC1', 'LC2' dia 120cm (47½in). *P:* 'E2', 'E1' £550–£1050; 'LC1' £229; 'LC2' £399.

SPIROTRED wood and steel stairs by Pedley

THE SPIRAL STAIRCASE COMPANY

Antique and reproduction cast iron spiral stairs from this small family business. The genuine antique is cheaper than the reproduction but finding one to fit can be difficult. This firm supply a most attractive cast iron reproduction with traditional pierced treads, delicate balustrade spindles and a plain wrought iron handrail. Also available is salvaged ironwork for balconies, terrace balustrading etc. Callers by appointment only. *M:* reproduction staircase dia 42–54in (107–137cm) in 6in (15cm) increments. *P:* antique staircases £300–£500; reproduction staircase £48 per tread, with 8in. (20.5cm) rise (typical 8ft/2.4m rise £528).

Spiral Staircase Company's reproduction stairs

STUART INTERIORS

Imposing reproduction Jacobean balustrading in solid English oak, made by West Country master craftsmen. For use on balconies or staircases, the range incorporates a variety of features: flat and turned balusters, carved newel posts, finials and bosses, and moulded handrails. Staircases are made in the workshop and assembled on site. Restoration of existing staircases is also undertaken. *P:* £115–£190 per 12in (30.5cm) run. Stuart also make panelling and all kinds of Jacobean woodwork (see *Architectural ornaments*).

WINTHER BROWNE & CO LTD

WINBRON staircase kits for traditional stairs in pine or mahogany. Each kit consists of two newel posts, 40 spindles, and 420cm (165in) lengths of handrail and of base rail. Newels come in three standard patterns though others can be twisted or turned to customer's design. Spindles come in two patterns, plain turned or barley twist; the latter reflecting the cost of the extra machining required. Both newels and

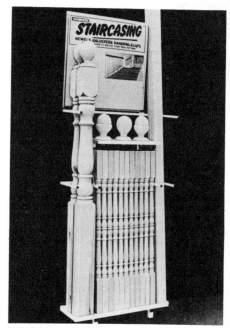

Oak balustrade designs by Stuart Interiors

WINBRON staircase kits by Winther Browne

spindles can be trimmed to fit. *M:* spindles h90cm (35½in); newels h150cm (59in). *P:* WINBRON staircasing kit £240–£338; spindles (plain) £2.95–£9; newels £31–£50; handrail £2.40–£4.30 per 12in (30.5cm) run.

INTI

Hearth
point
mode
Nothir
it will
heatin
chimn
mode
heate
these,
adapte
dome:
fashio
this ar
Stove:
iron f
more
Two v
firepla
workr
result
Secor
ideally
firepla
Firepl
some
log- a
sets
comp
dogs
the h
Mant
firepl
deco
a fire
stone
Stove
and c
fuels.
• Per
from
salva

FIR

ACQ

Antic
sorie
Shell
Acqu
mod
GAZ
dard
avail
ginal
fire i
sets.

AM/
Vast
stylis
bras

268

with Burmese lustre door; inset model in this colourway or all-over Burmese lustre. *M:* h61.8 × w62 × d43.3cm (24½ × 24½ × 17in). *P:* inset £530; freestanding £580.

PARKRAY 29 open fire boiler has specially designed inset open fire with bronze lustre or matt black front. Will burn both smokeless fuels and house coal and will heat hot water and up to five radiators. *M:* h56 × w46 × d35cm (22 × 18 × 13¾in). *P:* £167.
(All prices ex VAT.)

QUEBB STOVES

Well designed, solidly constructed cast iron freestanding stoves which can burn solid fuel, wood or peat. Boilers can be provided to supply ample domestic hot water.

MASTER range is the most powerful. Models vary from woodburning without boiler to multifuel with large boiler, with total heat output available from 12–25KW. Stoves can be used with doors open or closed. Finishes are matt black or stove-enamelled in either pewter-grey or copper. *M:* h33 × w35 × d19in (84 × 89 × 48.5cm). *P:* £475–£615.

Similar but smaller are MISTRALE (output 12–15KW) and MISTRESS (output 7.5–10KW), both multifuel only. *M:* MISTRALE h45 × w60 × d40cm (17¾ × 23½ × 15¾in); MISTRESS h58.2 × w52.2 × d35.9cm (22¾ × 20½ × 14¼in). *P:* MISTRALE £395; MISTRESS £295; boilers £35–£70.

Standard range comprises smaller double and single door stoves for wood or solid fuel. All can be fitted with boilers for hot water and radiators and have hotplates for cooking. Side shelves topped with ceramic tiles are an optional extra. 'Minor' single door woodburning stove is the smallest with output of 3–5KW, 'Magnum', available in single and double door, woodburning and solid fuel versions, is the largest; wood and solid fuel ver-

Left to right, from top: MASTER, MISTRALE, 'Magnum', 'Minor'. All from Quebb

sions give outputs of 10–15KW and 17–25KW respectively. *M:* 'Minor' h25 × w13½ × d14½in (63.5 × 34.5 × 37cm); 'Magnum' h27 × w16½ × d27½in (68.5 × 42 × 37cm). *P:* £235–£490; boilers £40–£140 according to model.
(All prices ex VAT.)

RAYBURN △

Highly efficient fires suitable for both smokeless and bituminous coal. SOFONO FULL VIEW is a well designed drop-front inset fire finished in pewter-coloured vitreous enamel. TUDOR, also inset, has traditional lines and matt black finish. It is inexpensive and simple to install. REMBRANDT is a classically designed open fire with canopy, made of solid cast iron with corrugated look, also in matt black but with polished brass finials. Rayburn's 'Plus 31' back boiler is available as an option with both SOFONO and TUDOR fires, and the luxury 'Rembrandt C' model comes with the boiler built in. 'Plus 31' can provide enough energy to heat all domestic hot water and up to seven radiators. All come in two sizes to fit standard 16in (40.5cm) and 18in (45.5cm) fire openings. *M:* (approx) SOFONO, TUDOR w38–44.5 × d17–18.5cm (15–17 × 6¾–7¼in); REMBRANDT h(to top of hood) 91.5–99 × w57–62 × d36cm (36–39 × 22½–24½ × 14¼in); 'Rembrandt C' h91.5–99 × w38 × d44.5cm (36–39 × 15 × 17½in). *P:* SOFONO £57–£69, with boiler £193; TUDOR £29.95–£35.96, with boiler £179; REMBRANDT £306; 'Rembrandt C' £419.

There are also five room heaters. RAYBURN 70 is designed for smokeless fuel and comes freestanding or inset, vitreous-enamelled in pewter or grey. There are two models, '70B' and '70C', the latter capable of providing central heating as well as domestic hot water and space heating. *M:* w51 × h58 × d36.5cm (20 × 22¾ × 14¼in). *P:* £195–£245, freestanding kit £40 extra.

REMBRANDT open fire from Rayburn

The RAYBURN 70

RAYBURN 80, similar, comes in four vitreous enamel colours: copper, pewter, two-tone sable and silver mist. There are three models, to power up to 10 radiators as well as heating water. *M:* w69.2 × h60 × d33.5–39cm (27¼ × 23½ × 13¼–15in). *P:* £305–£345, freestanding kit £45 extra.

Uniquely, PRINCE 76 can be both room heater and open fire. Raise the closure plate to make it an open fire while still providing central heating; close the plate for really economical heating. 'Smoke-burning' feature enables bituminous coal to be burnt even in a smokeless zone. Available in pewter surround with copper or pewter decor panels. *M:* w59.7 × h63.5 × d39.5 (23½ × 25 × 15½in). *P:* £509.

COALGLO can heat up to eight radiators (as well as water), is thermostatically controlled, and again can burn bituminous coal in a smokeless zone. Available in four vitreous enamel colours: sable, pewter, copper and silver mist. *M:* w69.2 × h60 × d38cm (27¼ × 23½ × 15in). *P:* £509, freestanding kit £45 extra.

GEORGIAN is traditionally styled, made from strong, heat-resistant cast iron in matt black finish. But it's as efficient as any modern heater — the biggest model can provide all domestic hot water and heat up to 10 radiators. Thermostatically controlled, it is very simple to look after (correctly set, it will burn for up to 10 hours without any attention whatsoever). *M:* w55 × h58.5 × d40–43.5cm (21¾ × 23 × 15¾–17in). *P:* £325–£365.

Rayburn's GEORGIAN

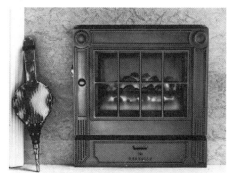

turns and configurations. All are traditionally styled and available in kiln-dried hemlock, ready to be polished, painted or stained, and in mahogany. *M:* spindle h80, 90, 110cm (31½, 35½, 43¼in). *P:* spindles £4.25–7.38; rails £11–£26.88 per 180cm (70¾in) run.

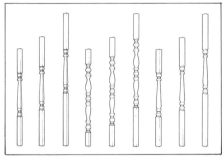

Turned spindle designs by Newson & Sons

PEDLEY WOODWORK LTD

SPIROTRED range of wood and steel spiral stairs, supplied in kit form. For main stairs there are 'E2' and slightly smaller 'E1', both with black-coated steel central column and balustrading, 'E2' with pine, sapele or teak finish to handrail and treads, 'E1' with pine or teak only. 'LC1' and 'LC2' are designed specifically for economical loft conversions. 'LC1' has fibreboard treads, black-coated steel central column and balusters, and pine handrail; 'LC2' has solid sapele treads and handrail. *M:* 'E2' dia 212cm (84in), 'E1' dia 183cm (72in); 'LC1', 'LC2' dia 120cm (47½in). *P:* 'E2', 'E1' £550–£1050; 'LC1' £229; 'LC2' £399.

SPIROTRED wood and steel stairs by Pedley

THE SPIRAL STAIRCASE COMPANY

Antique and reproduction cast iron spiral stairs from this small family business. The genuine antique is cheaper than the reproduction but finding one to fit can be difficult. This firm supply a most attractive cast iron reproduction with traditional pierced treads, delicate balustrade spindles and a plain wrought iron handrail. Also available is salvaged ironwork for balconies, terrace balustrading etc. Callers by appointment only. *M:* reproduction staircase dia 42–54in (107–137cm) in 6in (15cm) increments. *P:* antique staircases £300–£500; reproduction staircase £48 per tread, with 8in rise (20.5cm) rise (typical 8ft/2.4m rise £528).

Spiral Staircase Company's reproduction stairs

STUART INTERIORS

Imposing reproduction Jacobean balustrading in solid English oak, made by West Country master craftsmen. For use on balconies or staircases, the range incorporates a variety of features: flat and turned balusters, carved newel posts, finials and bosses, and moulded handrails. Staircases are made in the workshop and assembled on site. Restoration of existing staircases is also undertaken. *P:* £115–£190 per 12in (30.5cm) run. Stuart also make panelling and all kinds of Jacobean woodwork (see *Architectural ornaments*).

WINTHER BROWNE & CO LTD

WINBRON staircase kits for traditional stairs in pine or mahogany. Each kit consists of two newel posts, 40 spindles, and 420cm (165in) lengths of handrail and of base rail. Newels come in three standard patterns though others can be twisted or turned to customer's design. Spindles come in two patterns, plain turned or barley twist; the latter reflecting the cost of the extra machining required. Both newels and

Oak balustrade designs by Stuart Interiors

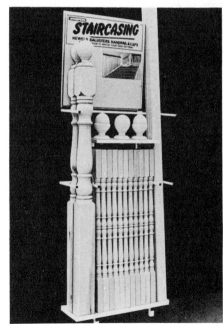

WINBRON staircase kits by Winther Browne

spindles can be trimmed to fit. *M:* spindles h90cm (35½in); newels h150cm (59in). *P:* WINBRON staircasing kit £240–£338; spindles (plain) £2.95–£9; newels £31–£50; handrail £2.40–£4.30 per 12in (30.5cm) run.

STOVES AND FIREPLACES

INTRODUCTION

Hearth and home. A fireplace can be the focal point of a house, whether it is traditional or modern, functional or purely decorative.

Nothing quite compares with an open fire. But it will never be the world's most efficient heating method — too much heat goes up the chimney. For really economical heating, modern answers are convector fires and room heaters, usually inset fires with glass doors; these, and other modern designs, can be adapted to take a back boiler which can heat domestic water and radiators. The old-fashioned answer is a stove, which can do all this and even provide a hotplate for cooking. Stoves are decorative in their traditional cast iron form and also in the sleek new lines of more up-to-date designs.

Two words of warning. First, installing a new fireplace is a job for a reliable expert. Shoddy workmanship or inappropriate materials can result in chimneys or floors catching fire. Second, always get the chimney swept and, ideally, relined before using a re-opened fireplace — caked soot is a major hazard.

Fireplace accessories includes grates, sometimes called fire baskets or dog grates; log- and coal-effect gas fires and conversion sets for standard grates; fire irons or companion sets (tongs, poker and shovel); fire dogs or andirons to support burning wood on the hearth; and wood baskets.

Mantels and surrounds deals with complete fireplaces and their constituent parts: the decorative mantel; the protective surround in a fireproof material like cast iron, marble, stone or tiles; and the hearth or base.

Stoves and fires covers stoves, room heaters and other heat-efficient fires for all types of fuels.

• Period fireplaces and stoves can be obtained from some of the dealers listed in *Architectural salvage* at the end of the book.

FIREPLACE ACCESSORIES

ACQUISITIONS (FIREPLACES) LTD

Antique and reproduction grates and accessories. Stock varies, but the cast iron 'Cameo Shell Grate' is always available. Like most of Acquisitions' other grates, both antique and modern, it can be fitted with their KOHLAN-GAZ coal-effect gas fire. (The fires, in 12 standard sizes or special sizes to order, are also available separately.) Other items include original brass or cast iron fenders, coal buckets, fire irons, trivets, fire guards and companion sets. *P:* 'Cameo Shell Grate' £555.

AMAZING GRATES

Vast range of original accessories plus nine stylish reproduction cast iron grates with solid brass ornamentation. All are suitable for solid

fuels or for coal-effect gas fires. Choice ranges from classical 'Adam' to flamboyant 'Mayfair'. Standard grates can be converted for coal-effect gas fires, and coal-effect fires can be made to order.

Amazing Grates specialize in high quality reproduction brass fenders and fireplace accessories. Particularly unusual — and practical — is their large but elegant nursery mesh fireguard.

P: on application.

ARISTOCAST LTD

Small but useful range of coal- and log-effect electric and gas fires. Electric fires, manufactured using solid brass and aluminium castings, come in five freestanding models: 'Victorian', 'Elizabethan', 'Windsor', 'Regency', and 'Adam' (also available as insert). Gas fires available with inset grate or fire basket. *P:* electric

Left: selection of grates from Acquisitions; below: Amazing Grates' reproduction grates

Left to right, from top: 'Hambledon', 'Philippe', 'Fawley', 'Hurley', 'Sandford' and 'Frilford'. All from Carved Pine Mantelpieces

fires £166–£333; coal-effect fire with inset grate £138, with fire basket £188; log-effect fire with inset grate £148, with fire basket £202.

A BELL & CO LTD

Good range of brass and wrought iron accessories including grates, fire irons, companion sets, fire guards and brass coal scuttles. Canopies (both functional and ornamental) are another speciality; available in copper, brass, stainless steel and black iron. Conversion sets for log- or coal-effect fires available for 18in (45.5cm) Bell fires and for other fires to order. *P:* '3526' dog grate £372; companion sets £33–£42; spark guards £10.80–£54.60; fire dogs £28.80; canopies £156.60–£214.80; standard conversion set £117.60.

CARVED PINE MANTELPIECES LTD

More than 25 brass grates, all in traditional English and French styles. Suitable for open fires, grates can be converted for electricity or gas, with mock coal or logs, at extra cost. Other accessories include a wide range of antique fenders, fire irons, fire dogs and fire screens. *P:* on application.

NICHOLAS ENGERT

Totally transparent fire guards. Made from specially tempered glass, 6mm (3/8in) thick, these fire guards are freestanding, tough and durable, and naturally very unobtrusive. *M:* w73 × h49cm (28¾ × 19¼in) or w92.5 × h51cm (36¼ × 20in). *P:* £50.85; £65.95 (ex VAT).

FEATURE FIRES LTD

Small but varied selection of accessories. Two sizes each of 'Chestnut' and 'Castle' baskets are stocked, as well as log baskets with dogs, a Spanish-style basket, fire screens, fire irons, fire guards and a coal scuttle. HEATRAE gas logs are available in three standard sizes. Special gas logs and coals can be made to order. *P:* on application.

GALLEON CLAYGATE LTD

Wide range of hearth furniture in wrought iron, brass, copper etc. Suitable for modern fireplaces is bi-parting, sliding fire screen with fine mesh curtains in black, stainless steel or bronze, and pelmet in anodized aluminium, stainless steel or brass. *P:* from £58.

PRICES AND INFORMATION WERE CORRECT AT THE TIME OF GOING TO PRESS

Four types of basket from Feature Fires

INTEROVEN LTD

Grates and other accessories from specialists in cast and wrought iron. More than ten grates, in either black or polished finish, include 'French', 'Adam', 'Regency', 'Chestnut', and 'Castle' designs, some with decorative brass knobs and fascias. Most come in two standard sizes. There are three sizes of fire baskets,

STOVES AND FIREPLACES

Left to right, from top: 'French', 'Castle', 'Adam', 'Apollo', 'Regency' and 'Chestnut' from Interoven

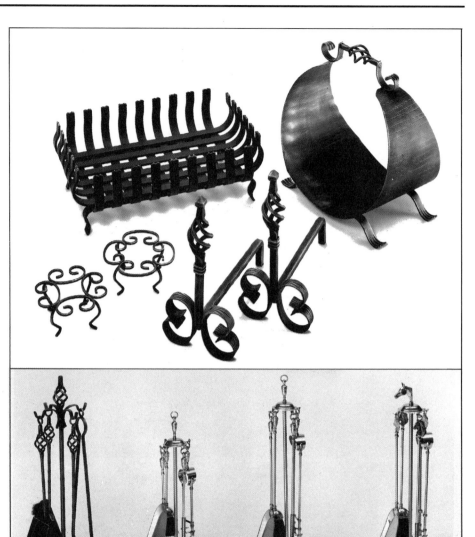

Above, left to right: 'Tindell' grate, log holder, trivets and 'Latimer' dogs; below: a selection of companion sets. All from Petit Roque

three styles of fire dogs ('Regency', 'Gothic' and 'Button') and seven designs of fire backs, including 'Lion and Shield' and 'Medallion'. A speciality is the 'Log-o-Loop', a wrought iron construction with matt black finish for carrying or storing logs. *P:* grates £18.50–£166.50; fire baskets £32.50–£70.50; fire dogs £32.25–£50.75; fire backs £32.75–£83.50; 'Log-o-Loop' £17.50.

ROGER PEARSON & CO LTD
Select range of brass accessories and cast iron grates to complement Pearson's mantels. Brass fenders, fire dogs (one set depicting lions) and a brass electric fire with solid brass back-plate are available, and there are four designs of cast iron grates. *P:* brass electric fire £198; cast iron products from £79.

PETIT ROQUE LTD
Very extensive selection of grates for burning either logs or coal. Designs cover both classical and modern, in metals including wrought iron and bright polished steel with brass finish; they range from ostentatious 'Aristocrat' in brass, to simple 'Regency' cast iron insert and 'Tindell' wrought iron fire basket. Fire dogs, fire screens, fire backs, companion sets, coal buckets, log holders, trivets and miscellaneous brass accessories (lamps, kettles, bellows etc) are all available. *P:* on application.

PURITAN FORGE LTD
INSTAMOUNT fire curtain screen, a flexible curtain of specially woven wire mesh which can be gathered or drawn like conventional curtains. The openness of the weave has been calculated to provide optimum protection from flying sparks without any heat loss. The mesh is finished in a matt black epoxy coating. The glide rod is held in position under spring tension so no drilling is required, and it is disguised by a decorative top bar, available in either satin black (to match the curtain) or polished brass. INSTAMOUNT is custom-made to fit both square and arched top fire-

places. *P:* (for standard fireplace opening, up to 24in/61cm wide) £49.50; decorative kerb bar £8.50.
See following page for illustration.

JAMES SMELLIE LTD
Canopies in hand-hammered copper or brass, plain or hand-hammered stainless steel, and steel finished black. Only the highest quality heavy-gauge metal is used. There are four basic shapes: 'Westbury', 'Stratton', 'Cromwell', and 'Monmouth', the first three being ornamental whilst the 'Monmouth', lined with asbestos and sheet steel, is designed to fit above a dog grate in an open fireplace. Three made-to-order cooker hoods are available. *P:*

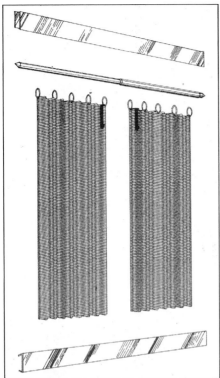

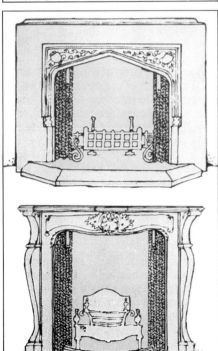

Puritan Forge's INSTAMOUNT fire curtain screen; below: the screen in position on arched top and square fireplaces

from £75.

There are also 15 different designs of basket dog grates as well as a number of reproduction seventeenth-century fire backs, and two superb canopy dog grates — 'Kenilworth' and 'Windsor'. *P:* dog grates from £80; canopy dog grates from £229.

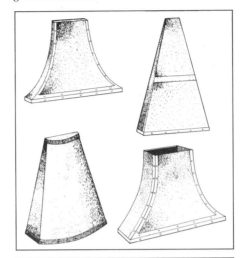

Top: James Smellie's range of canopies; below: 'Monmouth' in position

MANTELS AND SURROUNDS

ACQUISITIONS (FIREPLACES) LTD

Specialists in original and reproduction Victorian and Edwardian fireplaces. Reproduction cast iron mantels are made from moulds taken from original castings, such as the Victorian 'Serpentine' and 'Peace and Plenty'. They can be supplied with burnished cast iron finish or painted to order. Reproduction mantels are available in pine or solid mahogany. They range from a simple large roundel pine mantel to the ornate 'Sherwood Kennedy' in solid mahogany with hand-carved Adam-style detailing. Particularly unusual is the 'Parkfield Grosvenor', made of solid pine japanned black and lacquered with two marquetry inlays. Ori-

Top: 'Peace and Plenty' cast iron mantel; below: Victorian tiled inset. Both from Acquisitions

ginal restored Victorian tiled inserts can be fitted into these reproduction mantels or there is now a reproduction Victorian tiled insert made using original techniques and materials. *P:* 'Serpentine' and 'Peace and Plenty' cast iron surround £555; large roundel pine mantel £198.50; 'Sherwood Kennedy' £395; 'Parkfield Grosvenor' £198.50; inserts approx £245–£395. There is a wide choice of highly decorative original cast iron and pine fireplaces, all beautifully restored and many with original hand-decorated tiled inserts. Among the stock are usually some very fine art nouveau pieces. *P:* art nouveau fireplaces £195–£850.

AMAZING GRATES

Vast range of period fireplaces in cast iron, wood and marble, plus some elegant reproduction mantels and fireplace tiling. Solid pine mantels come in four traditional designs — large and small, 'Georgian', 'Regency' and 'Victorian' — available painted, in natural pine or with dark 'mahogany' finish. Amazing Grates stock a unique selection of reproduction hand-painted Victorian majolica glazed tiling, perfect for fireplace panels and hearths. They also undertake restoration work and

Left to right, from top: Amazing Grates' large 'Georgian', small 'Georgian', 'Regency' and 'Victorian'

'Picobell' fire from A Bell

have a fitting service in London. *M:* mantels in three sizes only, internal w36 × h36in (91 × 91cm), w33 × h35in (84 × 89cm) or w35 × h37in (89 × 94cm). *P:* mantels on application; tile sets £25–£69.

ARISTOCAST LTD
Eleven cast plaster mantels with black, green or beige marble hearths and back panels cut to

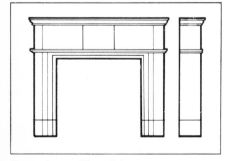

'Regent' mantel from Aristocast

order. Styles range from the slim 'Regent', for small rooms and narrow chimney-breasts, to the decorative, French-style 'Louis' and important 'Large Georgian'. Made from strong Herculite plaster, mantels are suitable for use with gas, electric and open fires. *P:* mantels £108–£253; marble back panels and hearth approx £250.

A BELL & CO LTD
Extensive range of modern fireplaces combining polished marble, slate and other stones; also marble, whitewood and natural pine reproduction mantels and surrounds. Simple hole-in-the-wall fireplaces are faced in stainless steel, copper or bronze. Polished marbles for hearths and facings can be supplied in white, rose, grey, grey-green, dark green, dark beige, dark red and black. All made to measure. *P:* standard fireplaces £392.40–£1,668; hole-in-the-wall fireplaces £314.40–£918; reproduction mantels £449.40–£1,065.60.
There are also attractive metal canopy fireplaces. Particularly good value is the angular 'Picobell' fire in sheet-metal, for use freestand-

ing, fitted into a recess or attached to the wall with just two fixing bolts. 'Centrobell' is designed for installation in the centre of a room, has two open sides and comes complete with curtain. 'Fire-in-the-middle', also for the centre of a room, has a gleaming metal cone suspended above a separate marble hearth. *P:* (standard without curtains) 'Picobell' £376; 'Centrobell' £2,069.80; 'Fire-in-the-middle' £2,296.

CARVED PINE MANTELPIECES LTD
More than 40 mantels in Russian pine, coloured and waxed. There's a varied selection of beautiful designs depicting urns, flowers, festoons etc, ranging from the charmingly simple 'Edenhall' to elaborately carved models such as 'Debden', 'Heyford' and 'Pyrton'. All designs can be made to measure. Marble slips, surrounds and hearths come in a good choice of colorations. *P:* on application.
See following page for illustration.

CATHEDRAL WORKS ORGANIZATION
Beautiful stone fireplaces from Rocamat in France, who produce an amazing range of stones, granites and marbles for all uses. Fireplace elements are delivered in a kit form and are simple to install. *P:* on application.

'Debden' from Carved Pine Mantelpieces

CERAMIC TILE DESIGN

Marble cut for fireplace slips and hearths. Colours include red, black, green veining and the commoner grey-and-white. Stone is cut in Italy and normally delivered in two to three weeks. *P:* on application.

DELABOLE SLATE LTD

Custom-built fireplaces in lovely, natural slate. The stone is supplied from Delabole's own quarry and cut to order. *P:* on application.

FEATURE FIRES LTD

Varied selection of individually designed fireplaces and flue systems. Traditional timber or fibreglass mantels with marble or stone surrounds, plain or carved, are made to order; also complete carved stone fireplaces. In stock are modern hole-in-the-wall frames and brick-built fireplaces, plus SPINCRAFT freestanding

Left to right, from top: handmade stone fireplace, stone fireplace with oak beam, mantel in fibreglass or timber, SPINCRAFT freestanding fire. All from Feature Fires

fireplaces, in five models, with metal chimney and conical canopy with semicircular opening. Standard-sized hoods and COLT cowls are readily available, and special hoods and cowls can be ordered. *P:* on application.

GALLEON CLAYGATE LTD

Huge range of reproduction and modern surrounds. Materials include polished or riven marble (choose between genuine, reconstituted and simulated, the latter suitable for electric fires), stone, sand-faced or smooth briquettes, ceramic tiles, slate and quartzite. Briquette and stone kits are available separately. Mantels come in hardwood, waxed pine or fibreglass, and are based on Georgian or Regency designs scaled down for the modern home. More than 100 fireplaces are available, including rustic brick, continental and contemporary designs; others can be made to order. *P:* period-style £389–£734; stone and riven marble £249–£1,092; rustic brick £462–£848; continental £355–£480; contemporary £154–£208.

'Kingsbridge' period-style fireplace from Galleon Claygate

G J GREEN & VERONESE

Classic Adam-style mantel from craftsmen in decorative plaster. Others can be made to order. *P:* on application.

HAMPTON GARDEN ACCESSORIES (HGA) LTD

Cast Cotswold stone fireplaces. In traditional styles are three ready assembled ranges: the CLASSIC (in 'Tewkesbury' and 'Tintern' models); the larger COUNTRY CLASSIC with broad oak mantel (and options including pine, iroko and sapele shelves and even a canopy); and the MODULAR, built of ashlar-faced blocks (in three variations). Five modern designs come in kit form, all in blocks of cast stone: 'Malmes-

Green and Veronese's Adam-style mantel

Top to bottom: COUNTRY CLASSIC, CLASSIC 'Tintern' and CLASSIC 'Tewkesbury'. All from Hampton Garden Accessories

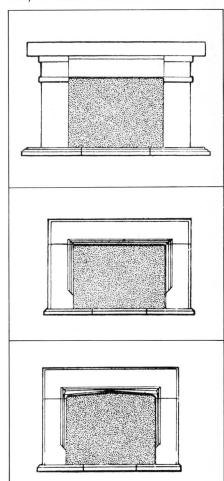

bury', 'Tetbury', 'Raglan', 'Sterling' and 'Berkeley'. Options such as hearths, shelves and stone side extensions allow adaptations in style and size. Extensions, and complete fireplaces, can also be designed to order. *P:* CLASSIC £268-£296; COUNTRY CLASSIC £293; MODULAR £186-£270; kits £109-£225.

HART OF KNIGHTSBRIDGE
Twenty-two classic carved pine mantels, some very imposing with elaborate detailing. All come in natural, waxed or white finish, and marble slips and hearths can be supplied. 'Clovelly', 'Melton', 'Bradwell' and 'Canterbury' are some of the more ornate designs. Made-to-measure fireplaces can be supplied. Electric and coal grates are also available. *P:* (including marble) £225-£1150.

Hart of Knightsbridge mantels. Top: 'Clovelly'; below: 'Canterbury'

GEORGE JACKSON & SONS LTD
Adam-style fireplace from the firm who worked for Robert Adam in the eighteenth century. Designed in Jackson's studios, the composition enrichments are handmade from Jackson's original moulds. Dimensions can be slightly varied to suit individual requirements. *M:* inner h39 × w42in (99 × 106.5cm), outer h51 × w67in (129.5 × 170cm). *P:* on application. Jackson's will also design to order.

KEDDDY HOME IMPROVEMENTS LTD
Scandinavian warm air open fires. Some can be fitted with back boilers to heat radiators and domestic water. See *Stoves*.

OCEES COMPONENTS & STRUCTURES LTD
ACORN solid fuel convector fires. See *Stoves*.

PATRICKS OF FARNHAM
Very large range of both traditional and modern fireplaces. Regency- and Georgian-style mantels can be supplied in fibreglass, white painted wood, carved waxed wood and polished white statuary marble. Illustrated are 'Wetherby' in carved waxed wood and 'Venice' in white statuary marble. Patricks have a stock of more than 30 different col-

Below: 'Wetherby'; bottom: 'Venice'. Both from Patricks of Farnham

oured marbles and slates from which to choose hearth and slips. Also available are four attractive Tudor-style fireplaces hand-carved from Ancaster stone quarried in Lincolnshire. Any dimension or motif can be altered to suit individual requirements on all Patricks' fireplaces. *P:* 'Wetherby' £599; 'Venice' (with slips only) £995.
Modern random-stone fireplaces, and also several traditional designs in natural stone (including Ancaster, Cotswold, York and Portland) are available. There are also several designs using natural Lakeland green slate. All fire frames come in brass, copper or stainless steel. *P:* £249-£995.

ROGER PEARSON & CO LTD
Unusual range of fibrous plaster mantels, many reproduced from period designs. More than 30 styles include a variety of Victorian and Edwardian designs such as 'Seymour', neat 'Cameo', ideal for a small room, early Victorian 'Rosenbury' with slender niches for displaying objects, and scroll-sided 'Lambourn'. All come in white only, except 'Lambourn' which is also available with an antique steel grey finish. Available on special order is the 'Brampton', a flamboyant chimney-piece in solid white Carrara marble, designed by Roger Pearson. Marble back panels and hearths can be supplied for all fireplaces. In addition the range includes three unusual ornate overmantels suitable for mirrors, plaques or pictures. *P:* mantels £59-£295; 'Brampton' £1,995; overmantels £55-£150.

Roger Pearson's 'Seymour'

PETIT ROQUE LTD
Wide-ranging collection including 11 period-style mantels in pine, plain or primed white ready for painting. Good range of styles includes hand-carved designs such as 'Leverstock' and 'Sunningdale'. Marble for slips and hearths, available also in sheet form, comes in a variety of colorations and in three qualities, only one of which is suitable for open fires (the others may suffer cracking and smoking and allow excess heat loss). *P:* 'Leverstock' (mantel

Hand-carved 'Leverstock' from Petit Roque

only) £418.60, (with marble etc for open fire) £648; 'Sunningdale' (mantel only) £605.82, (with marble etc for open fire) £842.83.
More than a dozen modern fireplace designs range from the 'Weekender', where the whole chimney breast is clad in quartzite, to the 'Spacesaver' and other hole-in-the-wall fires where the fire hole is simply framed in polished brass, copper or stainless steel with a slender marble hearth. There are also some unusual and imposing special designs such as the 'Waddesdon' with white fibrous plaster canopy and corbels. These fireplaces can also be supplied in do-it-yourself kits, with instructions. Components sold separately include copper, brass and stainless steel canopies, oak beams, copper and stainless steel smoke hoods, shelves, corbels, bricks, slate and quartzite cladding, quarry tiles, fire frames, and marble and sandstone slabs (to be fixed with Petit Roque's own adhesive). *P:* 'Weekender' (including fitting within 50 mile radius) £1,115, (DIY) £470; 'Spacesaver' (fitted) £303, (DIY) £149; special designs (fitted) from £875, (DIY) from £440; canopies £116.70–£182.58; smoke hoods £7.85–£18.20.

RAYBURN
Efficient open fires with optional burners. See *Stoves.*

JAMES SMELLIE LTD
Made-to-order hole-in-the-wall fireplaces in six different designs — 'Original', 'Dovedale', 'Welwyn', 'Tudor', 'Regency' and 'Lansdowne' in copper, brass, bronze or stainless steel. 'Firex' under-draught fire with optional boiler is included; it will burn any solid fuel. Matching canopies are another option. Fires can be surrounded by stone, tile, brick or marble. *P:* from £140.

PRICES AND INFORMATION WERE CORRECT AT THE TIME OF GOING TO PRESS

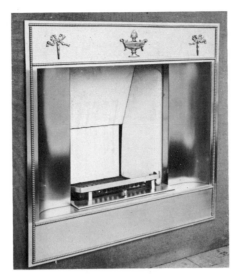

STUART INTERIORS
Beautiful reproduction overmantels from Jacobean specialists. Ornately carved, in oak with yew or holly insets, each piece is designed individually to suit its surroundings, incorporating insignias and coats of arms as required. Simple chamfered stone fireplaces installed beneath. *P:* on application. See also *Architectural ornaments.*

Jacobean-style overmantel from Stuart Interiors

VERINE PRODUCTS & CO
Faithful reproductions of eighteenth-century mantels. Made in fibreglass, they won't crack, warp or distort with heat and are suitable for solid fuel, gas or electric fires. Twelve traditional designs are available including 'Regency', 'Wheatsheaf Adam', 'Louis XV', 'Athenian' and 'Fluted Adam'. Most ostentatious is 'Artemis', a pure white mantel with quiver, bow and arrow motif, supported on white or hand-marbled Doric columns. All other mantels come in white, except for 'Athenian' which has dark wood finish. Verine can supply all man-

Left: James Smellie's 'Regency'; above: Verine's 'Wheatsheaf Adam'

tels with polyester resin slips — VERINE MARBLE or VERIMAR, hand-marbled in seven convincing shades, or GREEK KEY, with golden Greek key border on ivory, brown or green — but these are suitable for gas or electric fires only. Stockists can cut and polish real marble slips on request. *P:* mantels only £138–£362; including VERINE MARBLE hearth and slips £295–£540.

WYVERN FIREPLACES
Large selection of mainly modern fireplaces. Designs combine such materials as tiles, brick, natural slate or stone, and polished or riven marble. Solid polished hardwood shelves are a regular feature. Canopies supplied with some designs. Wyvern's contract range comprises ten small, typically 1950s tiled fireplaces. *P:* £127–£550.

Tiled fireplace from Wyvern

STOVES AND FIREPLACES

STOVES

A BELL & CO
One of the first patented woodburning stoves, designed by Benjamin Franklin in 1741. Made from heavy cast iron, FRANKLIN has a flat top, two doors with double hinges, and a removable swing-in barbecue grill. Flue pipe can be connected to back or top of stove. The stove is designed for slow burning: use of coal should be limited because the stove can become red hot. Three models are available, 'Baby Ben', 'Large Ben' and 'Giant Ben'. *M:* h75 × w85 × d31cm (29½ × 33½ × 12¼in); h79 × w95 × d36cm (31 × 37½ × 14¼in); h79 × w106 × d36cm (31 × 41¾ × 14¼in) (d excludes front tray). *P:* £246, £276, £294.

COALBROOKDALE
Four traditional woodburning and multifuel stoves; all cast iron in matt black with glass panels and lined with firebricks, all front-loading and with secondary air control making them suitable for bituminous coals. Smallest is 'Little Wenlock', with single door. Different models burn multifuel or wood or peat only, and provide space heating or boiler for hot water as well. Larger 'Much Wenlock', also with single door, can provide part central heating in addition to this, burning coal, smokeless fuel or wood. A space heater only, two-door 'Severn' has distinctive decorative panels in matt black or optionally enamelled burgundy, ivory or blue. Powerful, multifuel 'Darby', also with double doors, can heat six large radiators as well as providing hot water and space heating. All have top and rear flue outlets except 'Darby', with rear outlet only. *M:* (without boilers) 'Little Wenlock' h21 × w15¾ × d17in (53.5 × 40 × 43cm); 'Much Wenlock' h26½ × w20¼ × d19in (67 × 51.5 × 48.5cm); 'Severn' h28¼ × w26½ × d17in (72 × 67.5 × 43cm);

Coalbrookdale's 'Little Wenlock'

Coalbrookdale's 'Much Wenlock'

'Darby' h30 × w32½ × d18in (76 × 82.5 × 45.5cm). *P:* 'Little Wenlock' £198–£289; 'Much Wenlock' £379–£451; 'Severn' £493, enamelled panels £23; 'Darby' £663–£810.

HEAT APPLIANCES LTD
LOGFIRES woodburning stove available in three sizes, which can also burn peat or be adapted for solid fuel. The squat, double-door, front-loading stoves are in matt black cast iron. The largest, 'Warwick', gives a maximum heat output of 15KW, 'Avon' gives 11KW and the smallest, 'Gloucester', gives 8KW. Back boiler can be added to provide hot water, sufficient in the case of the two larger stoves to supply complete home central heating. *M:* 'Warwick' h78.5 × w87 × d44.5cm (31 × 34 ×17½in); 'Avon' h69.5 × w81 × d36cm (27½ × 32 × 14¼in); 'Gloucester' h71.5 × w70.5 × d33cm (28 × 27.5 × 13in). *P:* 'Warwick' £535.90, boiler £181.80; 'Avon' £476.10, boiler £151.80; 'Gloucester' £363.40, boiler £69.
HEATSTREAM convector fires include four inset open fires — either standard inset or 'Picture Frame' models suitable for hole-in-the-wall fireplaces or wherever the fire is raised off the hearth — four freestanding open fires suitable for inglenooks, and inset, 'Picture Frame' and freestanding models with glass doors making them closed stoves. All are suitable for coal, smokeless fuels or even log- and coal-effect gas fires, and are estimated to produce double the heat output of a similarly sized conventional fire. All have functional modern styling with matt black finish and (except one freestanding model) polished brass frame. Non-standard sizes are available. Fires can be installed by a competent DIY handyman, and can be supplied with factory-fitted back boilers as optional extra. *M:* (frame size) inset and 'Picture Frame' h56–64 × w40–72.5 × d35cm (22–25¼ × 15¾–28½ × 13¾in); freestanding h58–67 × w47–74 × d36.2cm (22¾–26½ × 16½–29¼ × 14½in). *P:* inset £265.65–£380.65; freestanding £378.35–£483; closed £346.15–£458.85. See following page for illustration.

HUNTER STOVES
British-made multifuel and woodburning stoves in traditional and modern styles. MIDI multifuel stoves burn solid and smokeless fuel, dry wood or peat, and provide both radiant and convected heat. Air supply is thermostatically controlled and safety features include exterior-operated dust-free riddling and protective insulated canopy. Boilers can be fitted. There are three models, '8', '14' and '20', giving outputs of 8KW, 15KW and 20KW respectively; all come in either textured black or bronze. *M:* '8' h25 × w26 × d13in (63.5 × 66 × 33cm); '14' h29 × w29 × d14¾in (74 × 74 × 37.5cm); '20' h33 × w32½ × d16½in (84 × 82.5

HEATSTREAM inset and freestanding open and closed fires from Heat Appliances

Top: SELECT; below: RELIANT; from Hunter

× 55cm). *P:* '8' £393, with boiler £497; '14' £469, with boiler £575; '20' £519, with boiler £635.
The original Hunter woodburning stove, available in three sizes, provides heat plus hot water and central heating if required. It features primary and secondary air supplies and damper controls. Front-loading design allows it to take large logs so that it can burn through the night. Finished in textured black or bronze, this sturdy, simple design fits well in all settings. Available in three sizes with outputs of 6.75KW, 12KW and 18KW. *M:* h29 × w23½ × d13½in (74 × 60 × 34.5cm); h37 × w29½ × d18in (94.5 × 75 × 46cm); h40 × w33 × h19½in (101.5 × 84.5 × 49.5cm). *P:* £343, £416, £468; optional boiler approx £100.
POPPY and SELECT stoves are attractively old-

Hunter's MIDI multifuel stove

fashioned in appearance, though POPPY is in fact a modern design, produced with the assistance of the National Coal Board for maximum efficiency. SELECT is a reproduction of an elegant Franch design of the 1880s. In cast iron, POPPY has a bowed door and enamelled tile decoration. It can burn both smokeless and bituminous coals, and comes with optional high output boiler. SELECT, in black cast iron with brass fittings, comes in solid fuel and

Hunter's POPPY solid fuel stove

woodburning versions with optional boiler. *M:* POPPY h31¾ × w18 × d19in (80.5 × 45 × 48cm); SELECT h22 × w22 × d14½in (56 × 56 × 37cm). *P:* POPPY £667, with boiler £756; SELECT £364, with boiler £457.
RELIANT is a basic radiant room heater combining efficiency and economy at a very reasonable price. It can burn solid fuel, smokeless fuel or wood with an output of 8KW, four times more efficient than a similarly sized open fire. *M:* h24½ × w24 ×d13½in (62 × 61 × 24.5cm). *P:* £276, with boiler £367. (All prices ex VAT.)

INTEROVEN LTD
A variety of well designed stoves. Woodburning 'Goodwood', made from ¼in (6mm) thick steel plate, is designed for small fireplaces. It has hotplate facility and is available with built-in boiler. Two large steel or glass panel doors can accommodate 18in (46cm) logs. Multifuel conversion kit available. *M:* w21 × h24 × d18in (53.5 × 61 × 46cm). *P:* £299; conversion kit £32. 'Sovereign' is similar but with curved doors to fit narrower fireplaces.

STOVES AND FIREPLACES

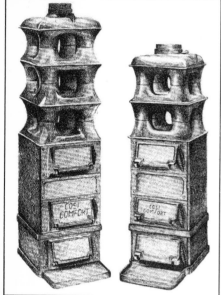

Top: 'Goodwood'; below, from left: COSI COMFORT 'Major' and 'Minor'; by Interoven

Unusual-looking cast iron COSI COMFORT comes in kit form. Quick and easy to assemble, it's economical and will burn coal, coke or peat as well as wood. Two models are available. *M:* 'Minor' w13⅞ × h45 × d13¼in (35.5 × 114.5 × 33.5cm); 'Major' w17½ × h68 × d25in (44.5 × 173 × 63.5cm). *P:* £290; £355.
Most exceptional is the RAIS 6 multifuel stove, designed in Denmark with clean, Scandinavian good looks. Its rounded body is divided into three levels; a fuel storage section at the base, a central burning section and a slow cooking plate at the top. *M:* w50 × h100 × d45cm (19¾ × 39¼ × 17¾in). *P:* £274.

KEDDDY HOME IMPROVEMENTS LTD
Scandinavian warm air open fires. Fresh outside air is brought in through a separate channel, heated, and expelled into the room to boost the warmth provided by the open fire. Some of the fires can be fitted with back boilers to heat radiators and domestic water.
SUPERFIRE burns all solid fuels including peat

and turf. Made from lightweight concrete blocks, it comes in six different sizes and shapes — for straight walls or corners, for chimney connection straight up or at the back — and can be used as it is or with any surround or mantel. It is supplied as a complete kit and is easy to assemble and install. Options include sturdy back boiler. *M:* w45–75 × h55–64 × d35cm (17¾–29½ × 21¾–25¼ × 13¾in). *P:* £360–£785, with back boiler £438–£453.
WINDFIRE burns wood or coal and can be sited almost anywhere in a room provided there's a chimney. Made of high grade steel, fire box, convector and flue are finished in matt black, with yellow firebricks on the inside and with double sidewalls for economy. Optional glass door increases efficiency even further. Fire comes in a kit form but installation requires some skill. *M:* h(to top of hood) 109 × d53.4 × w64cm (43 × 21 ×25¼in). *P:* £415; back boiler £69; glass door £68.
SUNFIRE can be either a highly efficient open fire providing radiated and convected heat or, when fitted with airtight glass doors, an inset stove for maximum efficiency and overnight burning. It comes in three sizes, each with optional back boiler. *M:* w45–75 × h55–64 × d35cm (17¾–29½ × 21¾–25¼ × 12¾in). *P:* £118; back boiler £59; glass door and frame kit £109.
Freestanding CONTURA fireplace combines efficiency with elegance. It is available in black or white satin finish with optional glass sliding

Kedddy's WINDFIRE

Kedddy's CONTURA fireplace

doors, and is suitable for either top or back connection. *M:* h(to top of hood) 123 × d65 × w75cm (48½ × 25½ × 29½in). *P:* black £560; white £635; glass doors £115–£145.
FEATUREFIRE is a pre-cast firechest in lightweight leca concrete and can be assembled in only 30 minutes. Suitable for any location, including corners, it offers controlled under-hearth air supply, cast iron grate and fire back, flue damper, built-in lintel and flue gather, all as standard items. May be faced with bricks, stone, plasterboard or any other suitable material. *M:* h(to top of hood) 113 × d45 × w90cm (44½ × 17¾ × 35½in). *P:* £290.
Kedddy also supply the ISO-KAERN chimney system, suitable for any fuel (including wood and straw), designed to minimize condensation, tar and soot deposits, and to be safe against chimney fires. (It is insulated to withstand continuous flue gas temperatures of 650°C.) Has an estimated minimum 60 years' life. Linings and casing can be cut to any angle and the chimney is simple to install. *M & P:* on application.
(All prices ex VAT.)

MORLEY MARKETING
OAKFIRE woodburning or multifuel stove. Made from heavy gauge cast iron and available in matt black, vitreous enamelled in brown, green, pewter or unusual bright blue, or with pewter or bronze lustre finish, and with polished solid brass fittings, the stove combines up-to-date design and sturdy British construction with an attractively traditional appearance. Side and top loading for wood

From left: PETIT GODIN, 'Belle Epoque'. Both from Morley

allows logs up to 18in (45cm) to be burned, or smokeless fuel can be used. Top surface forms a hotplate for boiling a kettle or emergency cooking and a back boiler can be fitted to provide up to 30 gallons of domestic hot water. A gas-fired coal/log effect version also exists. *M:* w21 × d13 × h20in (53.5 × 33 × 51cm). *P:* woodburning, matt black £203, enamelled £260, lustre £278, with boiler £270, £327, £345; multifuel £276, £332, £350, with boiler £343, £399, £418; gas coal £344, £432, £450; downward opening front door £50–£60 extra.

Imported from France are typically French GODIN stoves. Most beautiful is the nostalgic 'Belle Epoque'. This freestanding stove has black vitreous enamelled finish with swirling period embellishments and front and sides decorated with ceramic tiles. The steel panels holding the tiles are removable: lift them out and slide in any standard 15 × 15cm (6 × 6in) tiles up to 6mm (¼in) thick. Burns wood or coal. *M:* h90 × w42 × d48cm (35½ × 16½ × 19in). *P:* £385.

Four models of freestanding PETIT GODIN stoves also burn wood or coal. Small or large, round or oval, all have smooth black steel body with ornately cast top, door, feet, base and ash-catcher vitreous enamelled in cedar green, brown or caviar grey. One small round PETIT GODIN stove is made for gas, available in matt black only. *M:* small round '3720A' h32¼ × w16 × d21 (82 × 40.5 × 53.5cm); large round '3721' h39 × w21 × d27in (99 × 53.5 × 68.5cm); small oval '3726' h30¼ × w24½ × d22¼in (76 × 62 × 56.6cm); large oval '3727' h37 × w22¼ × d24½in (94 × 56.5 × 62cm); gas stove '3420' h32¼ × dia 23½in (82 × 60cm). *P:* '3720A' £230; '3721' £295; '3726' £275; '3727' £295; '3420' £335.

COLONIAL large cast iron stove can be used with its glass-paned double doors open or closed. Burns wood, peat or lignite. Available in three sizes with choice of flue outlets including decorative triangular and square flue adaptors. Cast iron, swivelling barbecue grill and braising pan are optional extras, the grill with all models, braising pan with two larger models only. *M:* '3215' h76 × w85 × d60cm (30

× 33½ × 23½in); '3126' h79 × w95 × d66cm (31 × 37½ × 26in); '3127' h79 × w105 × d66cm (31 × 41¼ × 26in). *P:* £292, 332, £358.

There are also some functional modern stoves. Largest is wood stove '3112' in black enamelled steel with brass fittings and glass panel in door. Has thermostatic control and produces output to heat 13000 cu ft (368 cu m). Model '4112' has high output boiler for central heating and domestic hot water. *M:* h33 × w34 × d23in (84 × 86.5 × 58.5cm). *P:* '3112' £620; '4112' £765. Simplest of all is '3716' coal stove, a small cast iron box with glass panel door, in caviar grey or terracotta. Output heats 3100 cu ft (88 cu m). *M:* h24 × w15 × d15in (61 × 38 × 38cm). *P:* £230.

(All prices ex VAT.)

OCEES COMPONENTS AND STRUCTURES LTD ♠

ACORN solid fuel convector fires, designed to be wall-hung on brackets or freestanding on legs. Large area of metal body increases radiated output of the fire and makes it suitable for use in rooms of up to 2250 cu ft (63.6 cu m). Fires are finished in vitreous enamel in five standard colours — black, white, grey, red and matt black — or other colours to order. Convection casings available in lacquered copper or plain or hammered aluminium. Hoods, spark guards and gas ignition sets are optional accessories. *M:* w 24 × h25 × d16in (61 × 63 × 40cm). *P:* £260.

ACORN fire from Ocees

PARKRAY ♠

Large range of solid fuel room heaters and open fires with boilers, all suitable for smokeless zones.

CONSORT range includes inset and freestanding models, from simple room heaters and room heaters supplying domestic hot water and a heated towel rail to the powerful 'Consort III' (output 13.6 KW), which can heat 10 radiators and domestic water. Vitreous enamel fascia available in three shades: autumn dusk, Kashmir mist and sepia. A special feature of the design is that there's no need to bend down to empty the ash. *M:* h62.6 × w57 × d36cm (24½ × 22½ × 14¼in). *P:* £186–£390.

CAPRICE is similar but with the addition of real

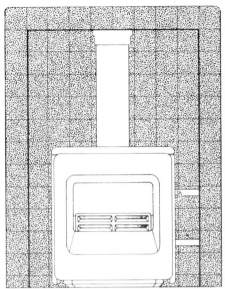

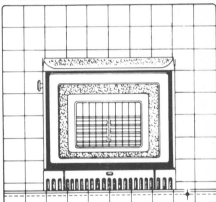

Top: CONSORT△; below: COALMASTER II. Both by Parkray

wood surround, in teak to complement sepia and tawny enamelled doors, or mahogany for Kashmir mist and clove silk doors. (All enamels are shades of brown.) Decorative fronts are separately packaged and interchangeable, so can be changed later to match the decor. *M:* h71.7 × w70.4 × d35cm (28¼ × 27½ × 13¾in). *P:* £273–£390.

G RANGE is one of Britain's biggest-selling room heaters, offering reliability and efficiency at an economical price. In addition to space heating and domestic hot water, '88G' supplies heat for five to six radiators, '99G' eight to nine radiators, '111G' ten radiators. *M:* h61 × w56 × d36cm (24 × 22 × 14¼in). *P:* '88G' £280; '99G' £302; '111G' £331.

COALMASTER II inset or freestanding room heater differs from the other models in burning ordinary house coal rather than smokeless fuels, but as it is designed to consume its own smoke it is approved for use in smoke control zones. Freestanding model comes in ebony

STOVES AND FIREPLACES

with Burmese lustre door; inset model in this colourway or all-over Burmese lustre. *M:* h61.8 × w62 × d43.3cm (24½ × 24½ × 17in). *P:* inset £530; freestanding £580.
PARKRAY 29 open fire boiler has specially designed inset open fire with bronze lustre or matt black front. Will burn both smokeless fuels and house coal and will heat hot water and up to five radiators. *M:* h56 × w46 × d35cm (22 × 18 × 13¾in). *P:* £167.
(All prices ex VAT.)

QUEBB STOVES
Well designed, solidly constructed cast iron freestanding stoves which can burn solid fuel, wood or peat. Boilers can be provided to supply ample domestic hot water.
MASTER range is the most powerful. Models vary from woodburning without boiler to multifuel with large boiler, with total heat output available from 12–25KW. Stoves can be used with doors open or closed. Finishes are matt black or stove-enamelled in either pewter-grey or copper. *M:* h33 × w35 × d19in (84 × 89 × 48.5cm). *P:* £475–£615.
Similar but smaller are MISTRALE (output 12–15KW) and MISTRESS (output 7.5–10KW), both multifuel only. *M:* MISTRALE h45 × w60 × d40cm (17¾ × 23½ × 15¾in); MISTRESS h58.2 × w52.2 × d35.9cm (22¾ × 20½ × 14¼in). *P:* MISTRALE £395; MISTRESS £295; boilers £35–£70.
Standard range comprises smaller double and single door stoves for wood or solid fuel. All can be fitted with boilers for hot water and radiators and have hotplates for cooking. Side shelves topped with ceramic tiles are an optional extra. 'Minor' single door wood-burning stove is the smallest with output of 3–5KW, 'Magnum', available in single and double door, woodburning and solid fuel versions, is the largest; wood and solid fuel ver-

sions give outputs of 10–15KW and 17–25KW respectively. *M:* 'Minor' h25 × w13½ × d14½in (63.5 × 34.5 × 37cm); 'Magnum' h27 × w16½ × d27½in (68.5 × 42 × 37cm). *P:* £235–£490; boilers £40–£140 according to model.
(All prices ex VAT.)

RAYBURN ⚠
Highly efficient fires suitable for both smokeless and bituminous coal. SOFONO FULL VIEW is a well designed drop-front inset fire finished in pewter-coloured vitreous enamel. TUDOR, also inset, has traditional lines and matt black finish. It is inexpensive and simple to install. REMBRANDT is a classically designed open fire with canopy, made of solid cast iron with corrugated look, also in matt black but with polished brass finials. Rayburn's 'Plus 31' back boiler is available as an option with both SOFONO and TUDOR fires, and the luxury 'Rembrandt C' model comes with the boiler built in. 'Plus 31' can provide enough energy to heat all domestic hot water and up to seven radiators. All come in two sizes to fit standard 16in (40.5cm) and 18in (45.5cm) fire openings. *M:* (approx) SOFONO, TUDOR w38–44.5 × d17–18.5cm (15–17 × 6¾–7¼in); REMBRANDT h(to top of hood) 91.5–99 × w57–62 × d36cm (36–39 × 22½–24½ × 14¼in); 'Rembrandt C' h91.5–99 × w38 × d44.5cm (36–39 × 15 × 17½in). *P:* SOFONO £57–£69, with boiler £193; TUDOR £29.95–£35.96, with boiler £179; REMBRANDT £306; 'Rembrandt C' £419.
There are also five room heaters. RAYBURN 70 is designed for smokeless fuel and comes freestanding or inset, vitreous-enamelled in pewter or grey. There are two models, '70B' and '70C', the latter capable of providing central heating as well as domestic hot water and space heating. *M:* w51 × h58 × d36.5cm (20 × 22¾ × 14¼in). *P:* £195–£245, freestanding kit £40 extra.

REMBRANDT open fire from Rayburn

The RAYBURN 70

RAYBURN 80, similar, comes in four vitreous enamel colours: copper, pewter, two-tone sable and silver mist. There are three models, to power up to 10 radiators as well as heating water. *M:* w69.2 × h60 × d33.5–39cm (27¼ × 23½ × 13¼–15in). *P:* £305–£345, freestanding kit £45 extra.
Uniquely, PRINCE 76 can be both room heater and open fire. Raise the closure plate to make it an open fire while still providing central heating; close the plate for really economical heating. 'Smoke-burning' feature enables bituminous coal to be burnt even in a smokeless zone. Available in pewter surround with copper or pewter decor panels. *M:* w59.7 × h63.5 × d39.5 (23½ × 25 × 15½in). *P:* £509.
COALGLO can heat up to eight radiators (as well as water), is thermostatically controlled, and again can burn bituminous coal in a smokeless zone. Available in four vitreous enamel colours: sable, pewter, copper and silver mist. *M:* w69.2 × h60 × d38cm (27¼ × 23½ × 15in). *P:* £509, freestanding kit £45 extra.
GEORGIAN is traditionally styled, made from strong, heat-resistant cast iron in matt black finish. But it's as efficient as any modern heater — the biggest model can provide all domestic hot water and heat up to 10 radiators. Thermostatically controlled, it is very simple to look after (correctly set, it will burn for up to 10 hours without any attention whatsoever). *M:* w55 × h58.5 × d40–43.5cm (21¾ × 23 × 15¾–17in). *P:* £325–£365.

Rayburn's GEORGIAN

Left to right, from top: MASTER, MISTRALE, 'Magnum', 'Minor'. All from Quebb

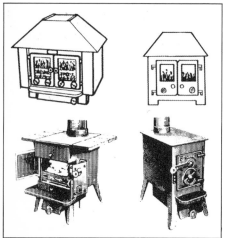

PERRINGS. WHERE YOU CAN ALWAYS AFFORD TO FEEL AT HOME.

At Perrings, we've everything you need to furnish a house and make it feel like a home. Carpets to complement wallpapers. Made to measure curtains to match sofas and lamps to highlight furniture in bedrooms, living rooms and dining rooms.

We've more than 30 stores where each and every one of our experienced staff will make you feel at home the minute you walk in the door.

If you would like to see more of our furnishing selection, visit any Perrings store or send for our furnishing leaflets.

Shown here are Santana wall units, dining table and chair. Nicci white leather chrome chair. Three seater Martine sofa. Co-ordinating with Stardust Pearl carpet, Constantine curtain fabric and wallpaper from the Sanderson Collection.

For leaflets and details of your nearest store write to: Design Studio, Perrings, Avenue House, Malden Road, Worcester Park, Surrey KT4 7ND or telephone 01-337 0951.

Perrings
Home Furnishing

FURNITURE

INTRODUCTION

Whatever the setting created by wall coverings, curtains, flooring, it is the furniture that finally defines a room's purpose and character. Choosing first the kind of things you want and then the individual designs can be both one of the most difficult and one of the most enjoyable aspects of decorating. There's a bewildering variety of furniture to look at, but it gives you the opportunity to indulge any taste – traditional, avant-garde or eclectic.

Requirements will be determined by way of life as much as by aesthetic leanings. For example, entertaining might be a prime consideration; you may want to seat a lot of people easily, want scattered occasional chairs you can move around in the sitting room, and find an extending table most practical for dining. Or a lively family may mean you have to forgo some of the finer touches, children not being compatible with delicate pieces.

Once requirements are settled, consider the comfort and practicality of each comparable piece. The furniture you buy usually stays with you and moves with you from house to house. This may also be a good reason for choosing fairly classic designs for the major pieces. Before buying a large item, be sure to check that it is the right size for the room. A fail-safe method when choosing a dining table for instance is to make an exact copy of the table top in paper and lay it on the floor to see how much space it will take up and what will fit around it.

The furniture here is divided into 12 categories: *Beds, Bedroom furniture, Chairs, Desks, Dining suites, Made-to-order, Screens and partitions, Shelving, Storage, Tables (dining), Tables (occasional)* and *Upholstered furniture.* Inevitably there is a degree of overlap but cross-references direct you to other sections.

Beds covers items ranging from four-posters to bunks, and also includes individual headboards, decorative extras that can be used with any divan. Don't skimp here — after all your bed is where you spend about a third of your life. The base (and mattress) will affect the quality of your sleep, so decide whether you want a simple divan (available in varying degrees of softness), a traditional sprung base or simple wooden slats. If space is limited or you want a convertible spare bed, consider a Japanese-style futon — a cotton-padded mattress that the Japanese lay out on a straw-matted floor at night and roll up to store away during the day — available in Westernized versions that roll up into sofas and rest on special wooden bases. The other alternative is an upholstered sofa bed that folds out into a conventional divan (for these see *Upholstered furniture).*

Bedroom furniture includes dressing tables, specifically bedroomy chairs, chests of drawers and wardrobes (others can be found in *Chairs, Storage* and *Upholstered furniture),*

fitted cupboards, suites including beds as well as matching bedside tables and other furniture, and systems with built-in beds — the last often the answer for one-room living.

Chairs covers dining and other upright or hard chairs, and also stools — in materials as diverse as plastic, fibreglass, wood, bamboo and tubular steel, cane-backed and seated, slung with leather or canvas, or partially upholstered. With dining and desk chairs in particular it is vital to make sure that the chair is the right size. Seat height should be comfortable in relation to table or desk top, and if possible the arms should fit underneath.

Desks contains a variety of models both decorative and workmanlike. There are elegant period-style writing tables and bureaux, sturdier partners' desks, and some very practical, sleekly designed modern desks and work tables, down to a children's work and play-table in superbly functional plastic. When buying a desk, look for smooth-running drawers, a comfortable height and sufficient storage for supplies and papers. The working surface should be a practical size and covered in an appropriate material — high-quality laminates are probably best for heavy use.

Dining suites covers matching dining tables and chairs (often in ranges that extend to sideboards and wall units). With the tables, surface is all-important. Again, high quality laminates form a good surface; cheaper ones may scratch more easily. Traditional painted lacquers and their modern polyester counterparts are wonderfully glossy but difficult to maintain. Glass is beautifully cool-looking, fairly tough and reasonably priced. As for wood, waxed or polyurethane-sealed solid wood is far more practical than either French-polished wood, which marks very easily, or veneer.

The next section, *Made-to-order furniture,* is devoted to people and firms who supply more unusual, or unique, furniture. A number of the items covered elsewhere can be made up to customer's specification of size and finish, but the designs here are models that can be adapted in a variety of ways to suit individual requirements, one-offs, or special designer pieces not normally available 'off the shelf'. Some of the designers and craftspeople in this section work only to their own designs but will accept a commission for a piece to suit a specific purpose or fit a particular space; others are specialists in their own medium — be it wood, cane or acrylic — but will follow specifications on size, colour and finish or even make to customer's own design. Although these pieces generally cost more than their mass-produced equivalents, they are not always as expensive as you might think, and certainly compare favourably with items at the top end of the manufactured market.

Screens and partitions shows a variety of the room dividers available, both traditional decorative screens and simple modern partitioning. (See also *Mirrors and glass* for

some unusual room-dividing panels.)

Shelving includes straightforward shelving as well as traditional bookcases and modular systems with components (sometimes including storage facilities) that can be combined to suit your space and purpose. Before making a final choice make sure that the shelves will bear the weight you intend them to support. As a general rule, metal and solid wood make the strongest shelving, followed by metal mesh, plywood and glass. And before fitting wall-mounted shelves, check that the wall will bear the weight.

Storage covers some similar modular units — this time those designed primarily for storage in closed compartments — and also more conventional items such as dressers, chests of drawers, rug and campaign chests.

Tables, dining covers all kinds of standard-height dining tables; there are also some small-topped café-style tables that would seat no more than two or three. A standard place setting for dining is considered to be 24in (61cm) wide, a useful point to bear in mind when considering size.

Tables, occasional ranges from tall consoles and sofa tables to small lamp and side tables, and low coffee tables; there are also such things as a games table and, for the indecisive, a split-level table you could use for almost anything.

Finally there's *Upholstered furniture,* dealing with traditional deeply stuffed sofas, armchairs, ottomans and chaise-longues, lighter modern versions and alternatives such as sag bags. Here more than anywhere else, aesthetics must be weighed against comfort and practicality. Sadly, the prettiest design may not always be the most appealing to stretch out in. Structure and covering must also be taken into account. There are traditional pieces handmade with elaborately lashed springs and layers of wadding, or less expensive modern designs with pre-made spring units, separate rubber webbing and stuffing in latex or plastic foam, or with rigid shells in light, strong, expanded polystyrene. Cushion fillings too range from down, long-lasting and luxurious, to cheaper foams which will tend to sag with wear. For the covers, wool is most hard-wearing, rivalled by man-made acrylic; cotton and linen cost less than wool but do not wear as well. Leather is virtually maintenance-free but colours are not always fast. Go for dark, patterned covers, or for loose covers that are easily cleaned if you favour a lighter-coloured fabric.

● All pieces detailed have been selected as representative of a company's range. As far as possible, measurements and prices are given for each illustrated item.

● See also *Offices, desks, reception seating* and *tables.* Though intended primarily for the contract market many of the items covered here are available retail and could happily be used in the home.

FURNITURE

BEDS

ASTROHOME
Multipurpose SPEED-RACK SYSTEM, Meccano-like metal elements that are linked by lugs on the horizontal surfaces and slots on the uprights. Primarily for desks and shelving, the elements can also be used to construct standard, platform and bunk beds. They can be put together in all kinds of ways, from a simple single bed to a complete 'bedroom system' with bunks, platforms, desks, shelving and ladders. Astrohome can design structures to order, but don't provide the mattresses. *M:* single bed l200 × w90 × h45cm (78¾ × 35½ × 17¾in); bunk h200cm (78¾in). *P:* simple bed base £100; system with two linked beds, shelving and cupboards approx £1000. See also *Offices, co-ordinated furniture.*

BEAUDESERT
Four-poster beds copied from original antique beds and made to order. They can be produced in almost any wood to almost any size. The 'Hepplewhite' is sturdily built in solid mahogany or hand-painted pine with bed-hangings from Beaudesert's own range of chintzes. *M:* standard w66 × l78 × h84in (167.5 × 198 × 213.5cm). *P:* approx £3500 with fabric. Beaudesert also provide a full interior design service.

Beaudesert's 'Hepplewhite'

ARTHUR BRETT & SONS LTD
Beautiful eighteenth-century style mahogany headboards, made by fine craftsmen. A variety of styles and sizes are available. *M:* '1634' and '1793' w100, 152, 198cm (39¼, 59¾, 78in). *P:* '1634' £485, £612, £732; '1793' £448, £588, £707.

PRICES AND INFORMATION WERE CORRECT AT THE TIME OF GOING TO PRESS

From top: '1793', '1634' headboards by Arthur Brett

MICHAEL J COX
Four-posters in period styles, or freestanding four-poster surrounds made to transform customer's own beds. Nine different styles include 'Elizabethan', 'Hepplewhite', 'Seventeenth Century', 'Chippendale', 'Late Georgian' and 'Eighteenth Century'. Four-posters, all made to order, usually come with turned mahogany front posts and mahogany fascia with matching stained pine frame, and, if required, a covered strung base. Surrounds are available in mahogany, natural pine, or medium or dark stain pine, and can be made to fit around any standard 3–5ft (91.5–152.5cm) bed. Cox can make up ruched or pyramid-style canopies in white net or customer's own fabric. *P:* bed (including base and mattress) pine £510, mahogany £597; surround, pine from £325, mahogany £425; net drapes, valance and canopy £95; make-up charge for customer's fabric £75.

Michael J Cox's four-posters

DRAGONS
Children's delightfully-decorated bedheads in solid wood with or without cut-out hearts. Almost any painted design can be carried out by one of the 21 artists working for the shop. *M:* any size. *P:* from £150 ex VAT. Complete beds, bunks, four-posters and dropside cots are available too from this inspired supplier of children's furniture (see *Bedrooms, furniture* for illustration).

DUNLOP LTD
Carefully designed beds by one of the foremost manufacturers. Traditionally styled DUNLOPILLO VARIATIONS range offers six different mattresses and four different bases which can be put together in different permutations to provide the comfort and support each individual needs. Bases are available with storage drawers (in teak, mahogany or white finish) underneath. To help even the most ill-matched couple sleep well, a 'Zip and Link' facility enables two different 190 × 90cm (74¾

DUNLOPILLO VARIATIONS set from Dunlop

× 35½in) or 200 × 100cm (78¾ × 39¼in) mattresses to be zipped together. *M:* l190 × w90cm (74¾ × 35½in) to l215 × w215cm (84¾ × 84¾in). *P:* standard double (w135cm/53¾in) approx £360.

The modern STYLISTIC bed offers a total package of bed, padded headboard and bedding. The divan is a spring-edge unit topped by a 15cm (6in) deep 'Strataflex Support' mattress. Accessories include patterned covers for divan and headboard, matching king-size, polyester-fibre-filled duvet and two pillows, and sheets and pillow-slips in two complementary plain colours. *M:* l200 × w150cm (78¾ × 59in). *P:* £499.

Dunlop's STYLISTIC

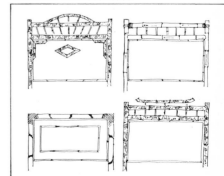

Dux's 'Ulla'

DUX INTERIORS LTD

Unusual steel and cane beds by Scandinavian designers. 'Ulla', Bruno Mathsson's innovative bed in chrome tubing, is strikingly contemporary. *M:* four sizes w105–165 × l200cm (41¼–65 × 78¾in). *P:* £638–£1000.

'Soraya' is an attractive modern four-poster in cane with cane lattice canopy. It is available in natural finish or lacquered white, blue, green, yellow and red, and can be hung with a variety of Dux's own choice of fabrics with matching bedlinen. *M:* four sizes w120–183 × l200cm (47¼–72 × 78¾in). *P:* £1356–£1619.

Dux also make a semicircular headboard in woven rattan, 'Daisy', available in white, black, bright red, pink, green, blue and yellow. *M:* w120, 140, 165, 183cm (47¼, 55, 65, 72in). *P:* £164–£270.

Dux's 'Soraya'

Pine beds from Warren Evans

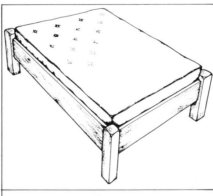

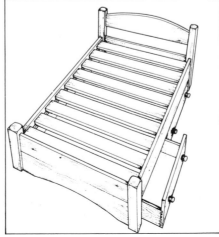

WARREN EVANS

Simple, low, solid pine bed with slatted base. Headboard in a choice of designs, low pillow board, footboard and standard or scooped design storage drawers under the bed are all optional extras. Can be supplied with interior sprung, natural fibre mattress or with foam mattress. *M:* to order. *P:* from £38–£65.

FAULKNERS

Cane bedheads in four styles: 'Victorian Sunray', 'Parallel', 'Plains' and 'Chinese'. Can be made single or double to customer's specifications. *M:* to order. *P:* from £39. Faulkners make a wide range of cane furniture to specification, including wardrobes, bedside tables, dressing tables and stools. See *Special furniture* for details.

Faulkners' cane bedheads

FURNITURE

FUTON COMPANY

Bed bases designed for the 'futon' — a Japanese mattress made from three thin layers of pure cotton or cotton with 30% wool. The futon needs no springs, giving firm, comfortable support in itself, and it is meant to be aired and rolled up each day. It comes in six sizes and in a calico or canvas case. Cotton covers are available in seven colours — brown, beige, grey, yellow, pale green, royal blue and bright red. *M:* futons w76–198 × l198 × d8cm (30–78 × 78 × 3¼in). *P:* £44.75–£169, covers £34–£55.

The ordinary futon bed base comes in four sizes and consists of two stackable units and headboard in natural or black finish. *M:* w103–157 × l201 × h (without headboard) 15cm (40½–61¾ × 79¼ × 6in). *P:* £119–£199. It can also be supplied as a sofa bed (see *Upholstered furniture*).

The new 'Gaijin' double bed base is built from brightly coloured medium density fibreboard (MDF) struts and slats which interlock in Japanese cross-halving joints. A combination of any two colours from a choice of red, blue, apricot, grey and black is possible. *M:* w137 × l198 × h (without headboard) 30cm (54 × 78 × 11¾in). *P:* £269. There is a matching bedside table and also a chair and table (see *Chairs*).

Futon Company's standard bed

GOLDEN PLAN LTD

Fold-away beds, raised beds and other space-saving ideas from this specialist bed company. Most original is the bunk-height HIGH SLEEPER, with a functional frame and ladder in blue or red tubular steel. The space beneath is utilized with a built-in wardrobe with shelves and rail and an adjustable writing desk, both in grey laminate. A stereo unit and bookshelf in similar colours and style are also available. *M:* l84 × w38½ × h71in (213.5 × 98 × 180cm). *P:* £395.

The WENTELBED (the word is Dutch for a bed

Golden Plan's HIGH SLEEPER

Golden Plan's WENTELBED

that pivots away flat against the wall, can be folded up, either on end (vertically), or sideways (horizontally). The frame is made in strong tubular steel with non-sag steel mesh bases and will take any standard divan mattress (though sprung interior or foam mattresses can be provided). All models except the horizontal 'Ambassador' require base units to be screwed into the floor. Melamine-faced cupboard and shelf surrounds can be provided to accommodate any of the vertical models. *M:* w30–54 × h75–78in (76–137 × 190.5–198cm). *P:* (w36in/91.6cm) horizontal £121, vertical £125; cupboard surround, single from £115.50, double from £140.

GOOD IDEAS

Good quality and reasonably priced futons (Japanese-style mattresses) now being made in this country by Devon-based mail-order company. The hand-made 100% cotton bed-rolls can be bundled into a roll only 12in (30.5cm) thick, so are the ultimate in space-saving beds, great for guests, but still excellent for those suffering from back conditions or allergies. The futons are covered in black, white, brown or red cotton, come in four standard widths but can be made to measure if required. Matching pillows, zabutons (cushions) and

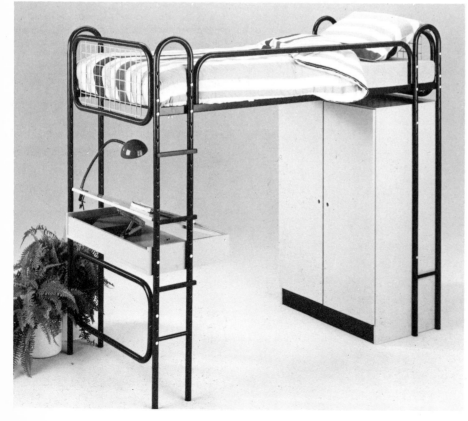

Good Ideas' futons

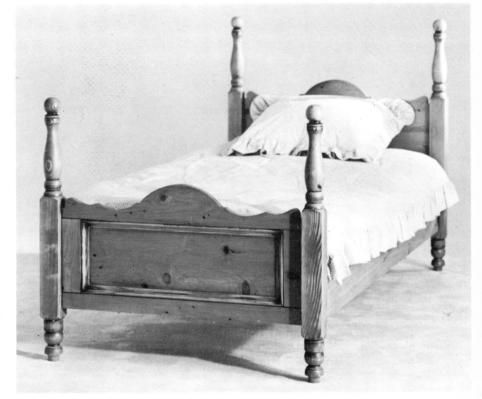

Grange's IRLANDE 'B42'

bolsters are also available. *M:* w30–56 × l78in (76–142 × 198cm). *P:* £45–£75; pillows etc from £4.50 each; p&p extra.

GRANGE

Stunning beds from this French firm, with designs inspired by nineteenth-century French and Irish styles.

The simple, elegant lines fashionable in post-Napoleonic France can be seen in the CALECHE galley-shaped double bed 'LG32', with its cherrywood veneer in stain or decorator (darker) finish. *M:* w151 × l214 × h100cm (59½ × 84¼ × 39¼in). *P:* on application. Available in four other sizes.

IRLANDE is a more informal range based on Irish country furniture and veneered in waxed cypress pine. The bed, which comes in seven sizes, has extended, knobbed corner posts. *M:* single 'B42' w100 × l204 × h117cm (39¼ × 80¼ × 46in). *P:* on application.

'LG32' in Grange's CALECHE range

Grange make various other styles of bed as parts of different ranges, each of which also includes a collection of bedroom furniture (see *Bedrooms, furniture*).

HABITAT DESIGNS LTD

Well-designed, reasonably priced beds, bunks and futons.

Modern and economical is a tubular steel bedstead in red with interior-sprung mattress. Single, double and bunk versions are available. *M:* single h50 × w98 × l190cm (19¾ × 38½ × 74¾in). *P:* bedstead £49.95, mattress £44.50.

Solid-pine four-poster bed is made with stark simplicity from square-edged timbers. Curtains are tied on with tapes. *M:* w198 × l147 × h189cm (78 × 57¾ × 74½in). *P:* frame £185, interior-sprung mattress £89.50.

Pine bunk beds stack in double tier or can be

Habitat's tubular steel bed

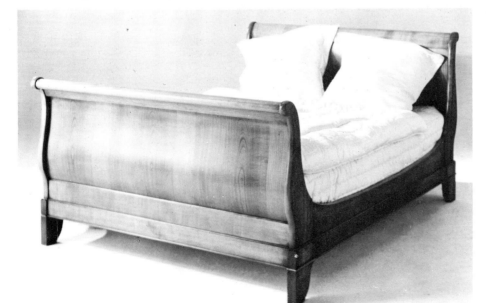

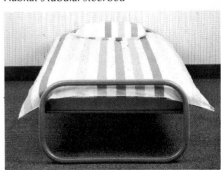

FURNITURE

Habitat's pine four-poster

used separately. *M:* h132 × w99 × l195 (52 × 39 ×76¾in). *P:* £139.

Cotton futons covered in cream calico with red arrowhead pattern and base in solid ash with red legs turn into a low sofa with two side tables during the day. *M:* as bed w155 × l204 × h39cm (61 × 80¼ × 15¼in). *P:* complete £339. See *Screens and partitions* for illustration.

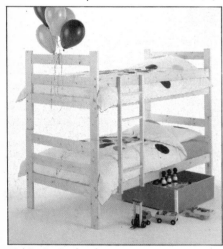

Habitat's pine bunk

HAMLET

Sturdy solid-pine beds in two styles, each with a timber slat base and a choice of foam or sprung mattress if required, plus bunk beds. 'Fjord' bed has a headboard and footboard with shallow scallop top and comes in three sizes. *M:* double 'BDF2' w147 × l200.5 × h75cm (57¾ × 79 × 29½in). *P:* £157.50 (without mattress). Hamlet sell their furniture by mail order and prices include delivery in the UK.

HYPNOS

An old-established firm producing high-quality handmade beds (for use in British

Top: 'Heidi'; above: 'Wheatley'. Both from Hypnos

Embassies among other places). 'Wheatley' high-specification pocketed-spring mattress can be supported by a spring-edge, a spring-edge with drawers, or a firm-edge divan, all on castors. A number of different headboards can be supplied, covered in customer's own fabric if desired. *M:* small double w135 × l190cm (53¼ × 74¾in). *P:* £262–£445.30. Standard double also available.

Range of wooden bedsteads and bunks includes the attractive 'Heidi' in antiqued solid pine, with thick, square bedposts and shaped head- and footboards. The open-sprung mattress, covered in traditionally striped fabric, rests on a slatted wooden base. *M:* standard double w166 × l218 × h104cm (65¼ × 85¾ × 41in). *P:* £325; mattress £158.

IDEAS FOR LIVING

Steel-frame beds and bunks from Seccose in Italy. Headboards and footboards are coloured metal bent into a rectangular shape; the rest of the frame is black metal, and the base is wooden slats. Available in white, red, black, blue and grey. Extras include clip-on bedside tables for the beds and wire protective panels for the upper bunk. *M:* 'Solo' singles l200, 210 × w89, 109 × h55cm (78¾, 82¾ × 35, 43 × 21¾in); 'Duo' doubles l200, 210 × w164, 159 × h55cm (78¾, 82¾ × 64½, 62½ × 21¾in); 'Tandem' bunks l200, 210 × w89, 109 × h153cm (78¾, 82¾ × 35, 43 × 60¼in). *P:* 'Solo' £109.20; 'Duo' £186.60; 'Tandem' £252.20; bedside table £24.70.

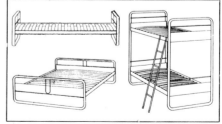

Ideas for Living's Seccose beds

INTEK ⚠

NATURE bed, simply and functionally designed and ideal for sleepers with back problems. It has a well-made wooden frame and the

NATURE bed from Intek △

mattress is supported by wooden slats suspended in a 'ladder' of rubber strips, providing a firm, resilient base. Though single beds only are produced, linking bolts and zipped mattresses can be used to couple them into doubles. The bed's unusual 'ski' legs — designed to glide laterally over carpets for bed-making but not to move longitudinally — can be cut to required height, and spare legs in different heights as well as solid beech headboards can be provided. The beds stack neatly and can be quickly dismantled when necessary. Intek recommend, and can supply, DUNLOPILLO mattresses in 'firm' and 'very firm' qualities for use with the bed. *M:* w90 × l190 or 200cm (35½ × 74¾ or 82¾in). *P:* £211.

INTERLÜBKE

Bright new INTERLÜBKE DUO bedroom collection with colourful beds in two styles. 'Upholstered' bed has a low, padded, spring-interior base zipped to a spring-interior top mattress with either fixed or adjustable padded headboard, all covered in matching cotton or satin. Bedding fabrics, plain, spotted or striped, come variously in dark blue, bright red, grey, sun yellow, light blue and beige. Duvets, pillows and co-ordinated covers are also available. *M:* (without headboard) w110–

Interlübke's DUO 'Upholstered' beds

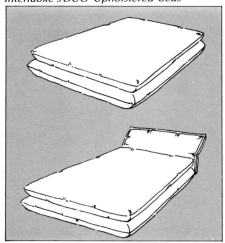

VICTORIAN king-size bed and furniture from Jaycee

200 × l210 × h40cm (43¼–78¾ × 82¾ × 15¾in). *P:* £564.50–£1072.50.
Alternatively there is the more conventional plinth base in natural ash or finished in white, grey or black lacquer; and there are many more beds (including folding-away ones) in other ranges from this design-conscious German firm (see *Bedrooms, furniture*)

JAYCEE FURNITURE

Old-fashioned wooden beds from the VICTORIAN COLLECTION, in solid Scandinavian redwood in gold, mellow or antique finishes. Each piece is polished and finished by hand and incorporates hand-carving. There is a single, double and king-size bedframe. *M:* king-size bedframe w200 × d150cm (78¾ × 59in). *P:* £348 (mellow and gold); £368 (antique). See also *Bedrooms, furniture.*

LONDON BEDDING CENTRE

Luxurious beds designed and made exclusively for the store by leading manufacturers. There are back-care beds, sofa beds, four-posters, fashion and storage beds, electrically operated beds and a range of headboards and bedlinen to fit every size. More than six brass bedsteads include the unusual 'Iris' bedstead from Italy with head and foot made from solid brass polished to resist fingermarks. Side rails support the bed base with pocketed spring interior mattress by Relyon. *M:* w66 × l78 × h50in (167.5 × 198 × 127cm). *P:* £3486.

WILLIAM L MACLEAN

Well-made reproduction furniture designed primarily for the top end of the contract mar-

'Iris' bedstead from London Bedding Centre

ket, but so nice that it would fit equally well in private homes. For those fond of headboards, there are seven styles: a fully upholstered one, two caned styles and two *faux* bamboo which are also available with an upholstered central panel, plus fancy fretwork '12–4014/5' and Empire-style '12–4007–13' with a solid panel topped by a Grecian vase at the apex. In addition, there are three four-posters: one with a cross-bar headboard, '12–4021', as well as those with posts in 'French' or 'English' style. All designs are made in solid beech, available in around 100 decorator finishes, and come in single, double, queen- or king-sized widths. All headboards can also be fitted with side support rails. *M:* '12–4021' w150 × d200 × h210cm (59 × 78¾ × 82¾in). *P:* on application. See following page for illustrations.

FURNITURE

Oakleaf's four-poster

Above: '12–4021' four-poster; left, from left: 'English' and 'French' posts. All from Macleans

black, silver or grey epoxy, and rigid wire mesh bases in red, black, or zinc finish. Platform beds can be single, double or king size, with optional desk units.

'Platform C' is a standard double bed supplied with full-length hanging rail, shelves and chrome Venetian fine blinds. *M:* w54 × l75 × h72in (137 × 190.5 × 183cm). *P:* coloured £544, unpainted approx £484.

Closer to the floor there's the 'Round Rail Bed' with sprung metal base and tubular steel semicircular head and foot rail, available single, double or king-size. *M:* double 54 × 75in (137 × 190.5cm). *P:* £220. See colour illustration.

OAKLEAF REPRODUCTIONS LTD

Reproduction seventeenth-century four-poster. Moulded in rigid polyurethane foam, it's an exact copy of an original bed — down to the carving marks and riven panels. Oakleaf also make very ornate headboards in a range of finishes (antique gold, antique silver, magnolia and gold tips, dark wood and light wood) and with different coloured Dralon buttoned pads. *M:* four-poster w54 or 60in (137 or 152.5cm); headboards w36, 54 or 60in (91.5, 137 or 152.5cm). *P:* beds £645.15, £688.60; headboards £49.46–£55.08.

One-Off's 'Platform C'

ONE OFF LTD

Functional chic in space-saving platform and bunk beds. Supplied in kit form, standard tubular frames and clamps come unpainted or finished in red, yellow, blue, green, white,

RELYON LTD ♨

Well-established manufacturers of versatile range of good quality interior-sprung beds. Over 30 styles of bed with mattress are available, including the magnificent oval 'La Ronde' and several special 'back-care' beds. Eight provide under-bed storage, including 'Hollywood' which combines extra-deep storage drawer with fully sprung edge divan base. Headboards come in 16 styles, upholstered in Dralon (usually deep-buttoned), with polished oak, mahogany, walnut or teak veneer, or with rattan panel in a pine frame. *M:* 'Hollywood' w120, 135 × l190cm (47¼, 53¼ × 74¾in). *P:* £487.

Relyon's 'Hollywood'

Simpler, stylish 'Cane' bedstead has similar rattan-panelled head- and footboards attached to pine frame and base; neatly fitted pine drawers slide out from underneath on castors. The idea is repeated in the lovely cane bunk beds which can be used in a double tier with ladder or separately as full-size single beds. Range of simple wooden beds also includes a plain wooden bunk bed. *M:* 'Cane' w135 × l190cm (53¼ × 74¾in). *P:* from £399.
For the child who's too old for a cot but not yet ready for a full-size bed there's the 'Junior Bed', available with protective side rails and easy-to-clean PVC headboard. *M:* w68 × l150 or 165cm (26¾ × 59 or 65in). *P:* £137–£162.50.

Relyon's 'Cane' bed △

SC PRODUCTS
Classic 1930s furniture in gleaming chrome. 'B4' bed, a reproduction of a design first manufactured in 1933, has double head and foot rails formed from tubular steel curved in a horseshoe shape. *M:* w152 ×l200 × h99cm (59¾ × 78¾ × 39in). *P:* £714.

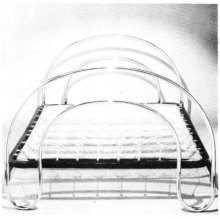

SC Products' 'B4'

SLEEPEEZEE LTD
SLEEPEEZEE SPACESAVERS, for children's bedrooms or guest rooms where space is at a premium. There are comfortably-sized single beds that can be converted to two singles or a double quickly and easily, plus a compact 'Chestabed' with capacious storage space underneath. The 'Twosome' comes in two widths with one bed tucking neatly under the other during the day. The beds have a sturdy hardwood frame with beech slatted base. They are available in black, red, green or natural finish. *M:* w30 or 36 × 75in (76 or 91.5 × 190.5cm). *P:* from £214.
Sleepeezee are best known for their large range of high quality divans with BEAUTYREST pocketed springs or open springs in various degrees of firmness.

STAPLES & CO LTD
Large range from well-known bed-makers, encompassing luxury divans in a variety of tensions, space-saving foldaway and two-in-one

Staples's '523'

beds, and some lovely traditional brass bedsteads and four-posters. The four-posters can be supplied with pure white Nottingham lace bedspreads and curtains, giving them a romantic, Victorian look. And any Staples bed base and mattress can be chosen to fit.
'523' is a brass four-poster, available in polished brass or white enamelled steel with brass top rails and ornamentation. *M:* w36–72 × l78 × h83in (91.5–183 × 200 × 211cm). *P:* on application.
There's also a very good selection of separate headboards in solid wood — oak, walnut, mahogany, curl mahogany or teak — polished brass in Georgian and Victorian styles, and white-enamelled metal in simpler modern designs. *M:* most w36–72in (91.5–183cm). *P:* (standard 36in single) wood £42–£131; brass £132–£265; metal £42–£99.

STEELUX ZEDBEDS LTD △
Cheerful and stylish tubular steel beds, bunk beds and fold-away guest beds in a variety of designs, all finished with a non-chip epoxy powder coating. Available in red, dark blue, pale blue, pale pink, and white, and with matching sidetables. The range includes the streamlined 'Italia', single or double with curved head- and footboards. *M:* w36 or 54 × l77½ × h46in (92 or 137 × 197 × 117cm). *P:* on application.

Steelux's 'Italia', single △ and double

STUART INTERIORS
Craftsman-made reproduction Elizabethan and Jacobean oak four-poster beds, made to customers' requirements and designed to fit modern mattresses and bedlinen. The 'Six-

FURNITURE

Stuart's 'Sixteenth Century' four-poster

teenth Century' bedstead is inlaid with walnut, holly or yew and hand-carved. It features a detailed tester typical of the era. *M:* w60 × h84 × l78in (153 × 214 × 198cm). *P:* £3300 (ex VAT).

CHRIS TRIPPEAR
Glass-fibre versions of seventeenth-century beds, faithfully reproducing the intricate carving. They are backed with wood and stained or painted and even gilded as required. *M:* small four-poster w54 × l74 × h78in (137 × 188 × 198cm). *P:* approx £1750. Chests, wardrobes etc can be made to match the beds.

TUDOR OAK
Traditional English furniture made from kiln-dried solid English oak, hand-finished and distressed. '210' eighteenth-century four-poster

Tudor Oak's '210' four-poster

has turned posts and panelled headboard. *M:* w68 × l88 × h82½in (172.5 × 223.5 × 209.5cm). *P:* on application. Tudor Oak's other four-posters include '200', in a heavier, earlier style with panelled sides, ceiling and full tester, the tester hand-carved with Tudor rose motif.

VERARDO
Vast, regularly changing choice of glamorous Italian lacquered furniture. Ranges include double and single beds, bed-surround units, separate headboards, and matching furniture such as chests of drawers, dressing tables, bedside tables, fitted (self-assembly) wardrobes and storage cupboards, and mirrors.
PAOLA bed has sleek, curving lines and comes in white, black or grey lacquer or in birdseye maple veneer with walnut or mink stain. *M:* w137–198 × l200cm (54–78 × 78¾in). *P:* £950 (without mattress).
MANOLA bed is lacquered in black, creamy beige, burgundy or white, with fine gold trim on headboard and footboard. There is a single

From Verardo. Below: MANOLA; bottom: PAOLA

bed and six sizes of double bed, each available with either standard metal or slatted wooden base. *M:* double w137–198 × 1200cm (54-78 × 78¾in); chest of drawers with four long drawers w120 × d50 × h73cm (74¼ × 19¾ × 28¾in); bedside table w50, 70 × d44 × h46cm (19¾, 27½ × 17¼ × 18in). *P:* 150cm double bed £480, metal base £68, mattress £122; chest of drawers £374; bedside table £184.

WESLEY-BARRELL LTD
Craftsman-built beds. 'Monarch' has a mattress with densely-packed 'micro-pocketed' springs, a deep sprung base, and a choice of three covering fabrics. It can be fitted with deep-buttoned upholstered headboards or

Wesley-Barrell's 'Monarch' with 'Abdale' headboard and bedside table

with 'Abdale', pine and cane or mahogany and cane headboard. Matching 'Abdale' bedside table is available. *M:* bed w36, 54 × l75in (91.5, 137 × 190.5cm) or w60 × l78in (152.5 × 198cm). *P:* bed £465–£760, headboard £47–£66. Wesley-Barrell make three other qualities of sprung bed (with optional drawers in the bases) as well as wooden and brass bedsteads, convertible bunk beds, 'Hide-away' twin beds (one stored beneath another) and sofa beds.

WOOD BROS FURNITURE LTD
Contrasting beds from the extensive OLD CHARM range of reproduction furniture — a baby's cradle and a 'Great Bed of Ware'. Both are made from mainly solid oak with a light oak, Tudor oak or antiqued finish.
The cradle has rockers and solid sides topped by a hand-turned rail doubled at one end to support a curved hood. For a delightful finishing touch the baby's name can be carved on a heart motif at the base. *M:* l36 × w18 ×

Below: OLD CHARM cradle; bottom: 'Great Bed of Ware'. Both from Wood Bros

h29in (91.5 × 45.5 × 73.5cm); *P:* £372–£410.
The 'Great Bed of Ware', scaled down from the famous bed in the Victoria and Albert Museum, is a grand four-poster with canopy, decorative finials and a linenfold panelled headboard. *M:* w79 × l83 × h90in (200 × 190 × 228cm). *P:* £2559–£2724.

BEDROOM FURNITURE
ARC LINEA (UK) LTD
PUNTO & LINEA wall or freestanding storage and partitioning system, including wardrobes, shelves and even tip-up divan beds. See *Storage* for details.

ARCHITECTURAL COMPONENTS LTD
Traditional Tyrolean bedroom furniture in pine, finished in antique green or antique rose, and hand-painted with swags and urns of flowers, birds and curlicues. Beds come in several dimensions from single to king-size; and can be combined with matching bedside cupboards, chests of drawers, pedimented wardrobes, and a shoe-chest with a swing-out rack to hold shoes inside. *M:* single bed w90 × l200cm (35½ × 78¾in); double bed w145-206 × l200cm (57-81 × 78¾in); two-door wardrobe w91 × h 204 × d49cm (35¾ × 80¼ × 19¼in). *P:* single bed £286; standard (180cm) double bed £556; wardrobe £762 (ex VAT). See *Storage* for illustration.

PUNTO & LINEA partitioning and storage with tip-up bed, from Arc Linea

BEAUDESERT
Dressing tables and stools in 15 styles redolent of Edwardian country houses. The kidney-shaped table and matching stool have full-skirted frills in glazed chintz from Beaudesert's own collection (see *Fabrics*) or in any other suitable fabric. Among the less expensive models, it has three drawers on one side and a cupboard on the other with a shelf between. *M:* w46 × d33 × h28in (117 × 84 × 71cm). *P:* table and stool approx £700 depending on fabric chosen.

Beaudesert's multi-tiered, kidney-shaped dressing table

△ *INDICATES AN ILLUSTRATED PRODUCT SELECTED BY THE DESIGN CENTRE*

FURNITURE

PAPILLON suite from Candlelight

BEHR INTERNATIONAL
Complete bedroom systems from an innovative and stylish German manufacturer, giving versatile and space-saving storage plus double and single beds with built-in surround and bedside table. HEADLINE beds, supported on thin metal columns, come in a wide range of colours from soft to bright. SWINGFORM beds come in light, havana or black oak, cherrywood, mahogany or lacquered white or brown. *M:* both w90, 100, 160, 180 × l200cm (35½, 39¼, 63, 70¾ × 78¾in). *P:* on application. See also *Storage*.

CANDLELIGHT PRODUCTS LTD
PAPILLON bedroom suite in bentwood and rattan. Comprises decorative headboard, oval-mirrored dressing table, glass-topped bedside table, chest of drawers and old-fashioned wash-stand with oval mirror, towel rails and traditional jug and bowl. There's also a simply styled dressing table stool from the FORM range, with bentwood base and upholstered seat. All available in natural finish or sprayed in pastel shades: white, smoke, pink, peach, peppermint or beige. *M:* headboard w92, 132 or 152cm (36¼, 52 or 59¾in); dressing table d46 × w54 × h56cm (18 × 21¼ × 22in); bedside table d41 × w54 × h56cm (16¼ × 21¼ × 22in); stool w40 × h40 × d40cm (15¾ × 15¾ × 15¾in). *P:* 92cm headboard £80; dressing table £210; bedside table £100; stool £54. Candlelight's extensive range of co-ordinated rattan furniture and accessories also includes laundry baskets and bedlinen.

PRICES AND INFORMATION WERE CORRECT AT THE TIME OF GOING TO PRESS

CHARTA FURNITURE
Compact, laminated bedroom furniture units. Each range includes the conventional storage, dressing tables and stools, shelving and corner units. And both fun and eminently practical for children's bedrooms, there are raised, bunk-style beds with ingenious cupboard combinations — even a pull-out desk — underneath. CAPRICE MAGNOLIA units are magnolia with

Charta's CAPRICE MAGNOLIA units and bed

wooden trim and wooden full-length recessed pulls rather than handles. Chests range from a single two-drawer unit to a double four-drawer unit; wardrobes have single or double doors, some with two drawers in the base or with optional top cupboard unit. *M:* chests w45 × h53cm (17¾ × 20¾in), w90 × h89cm (35½ × 35in); wardrobes w90 × h124cm (35½ × 48¾in), w45 × h182cm (17¾ × 71¾in); bunk-style bed w198 × h156 or 102cm (78 × 61½ or 40¼in). *P:* chests £46, £99; wardrobes £101, £151; beds £420, £317. All come in flat, self-assembly packs.

Two other ranges are similar, and similarly priced. CHAMELEON is white with a choice of coloured handles — white, pink, blue or red — to match decor; RED II is white with red edging and handles. Instead of a ladder, access to the raised bed is provided by semicircular footholds cut into the side of the pull-out desk. Both are available in kits, CHAMELEON also ready-assembled.

CHILTERN HILLS UPHOLSTERY
Very Sanderson UPSTAIRS range of deep-frilled chairs, ottomans, tables and headboards covered in any print from Sanderson's 'Options' collection (see *Co-ordinates*) or customer's own fabric. *M:* 'Ascot' chair w26 × d30 × h33in (66 × 76 × 84cm); 'Chartwell' ottoman w37 × d19 × h16in (94 × 49.5 × 40.5cm). *P:* 'Ascot' £179.50–£199.50; 'Chartwell' £109.50–£129.50.

Chiltern Hills' 'Ascot' and 'Chartwell'

RICHARD CULLINAN JOINERY LTD
One design of fitted wardrobes in three standard sizes — 'Aintree', 'Goodwood' and 'Sandown' — made up in any wood of customer's choice. The wardrobes can be installed by fitters in innumerable combinations. Each has top storage space and hanging rail in the lower cupboard; and two larger ones also have a six drawer unit inside. Additional fittings are available. Doorknobs and rails are made of brass. *M:* all h95½ × d24in, 'Aintree' single w18in (46cm), 'Goodwood' single w20in (51cm), 'Sandown' single w22in (56cm). *P:* double £298; double plus single £480; three doubles £980. Richard Cullinan will also make wardrobes and other furniture to customer's own design.

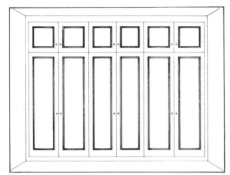

Fitted wardrobe from Richard Cullinan

Garlanded chest of drawers by Dragons

Wardrobe doors by English Hardwood

DRAGONS

Everything imaginable in painted solid wood furniture for a child's room, plus soft furnishings to order. Tables, chairs, wardrobes, chests of drawers, toy boxes, shelves, wastepaper bins etc can be painted with characters from Beatrix Potter, A A Milne or almost any non-copyright nursery fiction, or with flowers, circuses, soldiers or what you will by one of the 21 artists working for the shop. The virtually kick- and slam-proof toy box has a heavy moulded base, a full-length piano hinge to the top and solid brass grab handles at each end. A little more grown-up is a medium-size chest of drawers painted with garlands. *M:* chest of drawers h27 × w33 × d18in (68.5 × 84 × 45.5cm); toy box w31 × d15½ × h16½in (79 × 40 × 42cm). *P:* chest of drawers from £335;

toy box from £130 (ex VAT). Dragons can also supply furniture unpainted for would-be hand-painters to decorate themselves.

ENGLISH HARDWOOD DESIGN

Attractive fielded-panel wardrobe doors in kiln-dried solid pine, light/dark mahogany or ash. Wooden knobs or brass drop handles are supplied separately, and there's an option of rattan cane panels. Whole units can also be supplied if required. *M:* standard w30.5–61 × h46–198cm (12–24 × 18–78in). *P:* £24.18–£71.49 (ex VAT).

GRANGE

Several delightful ranges of bedroom furniture produced by this French firm. They include designs inspired by nineteenth-century French and Irish styles but intended to fit as well into eclectic modern rooms as into period ones.
The IRLANDE range is derived from Irish rural models and all pieces are veneered in waxed cypress pine. The four-door wardrobe with two drawers 'IR700' successfully evokes the functional elegance of the originals. *M:* w181 × d60 × h202cm (71¼ × 23½ × 79½in). *P:* on application. Also available in three- and six-door form.

IRLANDE 'IR700' wardrobe from Grange

In the same range is attractive '3D710' dressing table shaped like an old-fashioned wash-stand with two drawers and cut-away lower shelf. It is available with a swivel mirror but, without this, would be equally suitable as a writing table. *M:* w105 × d54 × h102cm (41¼ × 21¼ × 40¼in). *P:* on application.

Bedroom by Dragons

FURNITURE

IRLANDE '3D710' dressing table from Grange

In contrast, CALECHE (ROMANTIQUE) domed-cornice wardrobe 'FR200' is as French in its appearance as the name given to its shape (*chapeau de gendarme*). Like all the CALECHE range it has cherrywood veneer in satin or decorator (darker) finish. *M:* w153 × d63 × h207cm (60¼ × 24¾ × 81½). *P:* on application. The various Grange bedroom ranges also include bedside cabinets and chests of drawers (see *Storage*).

CALECHE 'FR200' wardrobe from Grange

HAMLET

Pleasant solid-pine chests of drawers, wardrobes, bedside cabinets, a dressing table and a marble-topped vanitory unit, in two ranges. The first has fielded panel doors and brass or wooden knobs, while the second, slightly cheaper, range has 'cottage-style' doors and brass drop handles. Bedside cabinet 'BC OD/F' has one fielded panel drawer with a wooden knob and one shelf. *M:* w50 × d46 × h72.5cm (19¾ × 18 × 28½in). *P:* £96.50. Hamlet sell their furniture by mail order and prices include delivery in the UK.

Hamlet's 'BC OD/F' bedside cabinet

CHARLES HAMMOND

KINGSTON HALL range of bedroom furniture with a touch of chinoiserie from these leading interior designers and wholesale suppliers. Range includes matching bedside and lamp tables, dressing tables and stools, all of which can be finished and decorated to customer's requirements. *M:* single-drawer bedside table with shelf w54 × d49 × h61cm (21¼ × 19¼ × 24in). *P:* on application.

HAMMONDS FURNITURE

A comprehensive collection of built-in or freestanding bedroom furniture in seven styles. Furniture includes wardrobes, square or kidney dressing tables, padded headboards, bridging units, chests of drawers, bedside tables, mirrors, mirror doors and niches. CHARLOTTE in pale ivory has raised and fielded panels on doors and drawer fronts which can be picked out with a fine line of co-ordinating colour if required. *M:* 'CH1' two-door master wardrobe w35½ × d22½ × h89in (90 × 57 × 44cm); 'CH60DT' dressing table with triple mirror w60 × d18 × h28½in (152.5 × 45 × 72.5cm). *P:* 'CH1' £288.80, with mirrored doors £361; 'CH60DT' £399.

Bedside table from Charles Hammond

CHARLOTTE 'CH60DT' from Hammonds Furniture

INTERLÜBKE

Elegant modular bedroom systems from these pioneers in modern furnishing.
STUDIMO PLUS has a multiplicity of components for the whole house but is especially suitable for studio living where cupboards can double up as room dividers. There are many depths, widths and heights to choose from for cupboards, open shelves and drawers, and

PRICES AND INFORMATION WERE CORRECT AT THE TIME OF GOING TO PRESS

Interlübke's STUDIMO PLUS

numerous accessories, as well as seven different finishes — white-grey or Jersey cream lacquer, natural or black stained ash, brown stained oak, cherrywood and mahogany. Slide-away cupboard doors can have matching finishes or they can be glass, mirrored or fabric-covered. *M:* module d24, 36, 49, 60, 63cm (9½, 14¼, 19¼, 23½, 24¾in). *P:* on application. See also *Storage*.

Other ranges include MEDIUM PLUS with wood veneer or lacquer shells, and tops either in matching finishes or travertine or polished granite; MUTARO freestanding units, curved back panels and matching beds, most sensational in high-shine black lacquer partnered with rattan or fabric; and the original STORAGE WALL units combining starkly simple exteriors with infinitely variable interiors.

JAYCEE FURNITURE

Old-fashioned bedroom furniture to match the beds in the VICTORIAN COLLECTION (see separate entry). Range includes dressing table and stool, triple mirror, bedside cabinets, chests of drawers (see *Storage*), all in Scandinavian redwood in gold, mellow and antique finishes. *M:* one-drawer bedside cabinet w46 × d38 × h59cm (18 × 15 × 23in); dressing table w121 × d46 × h75cm (47¾ × 18 × 29½in); triple mirror w60 × d17 × h106cm (23¾ × 6¾ × 42in). *P:* £138, £200, £138 (mellow and gold); £146, £212, £146 (antique).

WILLIAM L MACLEAN

Well-made, period-inspired furniture designed primarily for the top end of the contract market, but so nice that it would look equally happy in private homes. To go with their beds (see separate entry) there are occasional and

bedside tables (see separate entry), bed-end stools, seven styles of chest of drawers and seven styles of dressing tables, in styles as varied as stripped pine, Georgian, French provincial, *faux* bamboo, and more than 100 other wood and painted finishes.

However, what distinguishes the collections are the possibilities for wardrobes: in addition to two wardrobes with floral carvings, in French provincial style, and '2-4005' with lattice-work slatted doors, there are four types of individual wardrobe doors: '13-4010' with fine canework fronts, '13-4011' with slatted lattice, '13-4012' with diagonals, and '13-4013' with ornate panels and carving. *M:* single doors h173–200 × w48–51cm (68–78¾ × 19–20in). *P:* on application.

MANHATTAN FURNITURE

Fully-fitted, practical and good-looking bedroom storage systems. Wardrobes come in varying lengths with lots of different cupboard and drawer combinations. SAVANNAH, with internal and external melamine surfaces in textured snow or chamois, has sleek full-length cherrywood trims and handles; TUXEDO is similar but has simpler looped cherrywood handles. All ranges have matching dressing tables, headboards, bedside units, chests of drawers and accessories — down to tie and shoe racks and rails. Furniture is usually delivered fully assembled but can be self-assembled and the company offers an extremely useful free planning and design service. *M:* double wardrobe w100 × h245 × d62cm (39¼ × 96½ × 24½in); double three-drawer chest of drawers w100 × h70½ × d47½ (39¼ × 27½ ×18½in). *P:* on application.

Manhattan's TUXEDO

FURNITURE

Manhattan's SAVANNAH

MEREDEW △

Several smart bedroom ranges in traditional and more modern styles. Colourful FAME is designed especially but not exclusively for teenage bedrooms. Honey-coloured wood veneers combine with chocolate-brown, pink or blue melamine frames and moulded handles. The range includes a bunk bed which can incorporate large and small drawer units and a slide-out desk/bookcase unit; a sofa bed; hi-fi storage; and a lock-up cupboard. *M:* '648' bunk bed with desk/storage unit and clip-on light w192 × d95 (extended 180) × h122cm (75½ × 37½ (70¾) × 48in). *P:* £249.
Crown sapele veneers characterize RENAISS-ANCE range. All wood is kiln-dried to guard against central heating, and these veneers are stained by hand to dark or light finish. *M:* 'RM/RL428' three-drawer chest w89.5 × d42 × h75cm (35¼ × 16½ × 29½in). *P:* £154.

PANAVISTA

Made-to-measure wardrobes with either mirror or wood-finished sliding doors. Mirror doors come in silver or bronze finish with the wood alternative in rosewood, teak, sapele woodgrain, sapele veneer, ash veneer or white. Mirrors and wood-finished doors can be combined as required and all are available with a choice of three frames — gold, ivory/white or polished brass. System can be installed in any size of room, even an alcove or area under the stairs, regardless of irregular ceiling heights or 'out-of-true' walls. Wardrobe interiors of rails, adjustable shelving and drawers can be made almost totally to customer's specifications. *P:* on application.

PERRINGS

FANTASY range of modern style bedroom furniture ideal for a teenage bedroom. It includes wardrobes, chests of drawers, TV/hi-fi unit and a single bed. Available in grey or white

From top: FAME △, RENAISSANCE from Meredew

finish. Perrings also make co-ordinating quilt covers, pillow-cases and fitted sheets. *M:* single bed (without mattress) w100 × d196 × h67cm (39½ × 26½ × 77¼in). *P:* £139.50.
Traditional style VICTORIA range of antique pine finish furniture. The range includes wardrobes (all hanging or with fitted shelves), a

'linen chest' (cupboard above six drawers), dressing-table with mirror and single or double beds. Each piece is made with solid moulded panels and beautifully proportioned smooth wooden knobs and curved feet. Co-ordinating bedlinen, curtains and carpets are also available. *M:* double bed (without mat-

△ *INDICATES AN ILLUSTRATED PRODUCT SELECTED BY THE DESIGN CENTRE*

One Off's 'Round Rail Bed'

Margaret Martin's beach hut wardrobe

From top: Personal Touch's BALMORAL, WINDSOR

From top: FANTASY, VICTORIA from Perrings

tress) w147 × d200cm (58 × 79in). *P:* £269. Perrings also make several other ranges of bedroom furniture varying in style from pieces suitable for children to a semi-fitted look.

PERSONAL TOUCH

Made-to-measure wooden bedroom furniture, including headboards, wardrobes, dressing tables, bedside units and chests of drawers. The whole bedroom can be fitted out in such styles as LOUIS, with ornate scrolling and elaborate detail, or the much simpler ranges WINDSOR and BALMORAL. The interior of the standard two-door wardrobe is fitted with hat-shelf, storage shelf and hanging rail; other options are two-tier hanging space, vertical division and shelves, shoe racks, and internal drawers. All units are spray-paint finished in white, magnolia, dawn mist (greenish) or mushroom. *M:* up to w120cm (47¼in), any h, any d. *P:* on application.

RELYON LTD

PINEWOOD, for complete country look. This well-designed range includes chests with eight, five (the bottom drawer being double, it appears to be six), four and three drawers, bedside chest, two- or three-door wardrobes,

dressing table, ottoman and four headboards. The range even includes cheval mirror, triple mirror, dressing-table mirror and hanging mirror. The pine comes in two finishes: 'Town' style in natural or the 'Village' style in a light 'antique' stain. Handles can be either a round knob or a thick 'D'-shape. *M:* four-drawer chest w77 × d42 × h71cm (30¼ × 16½ × 28in); two-door wardrobe w89 × d57 × h185cm (35 × 22½ × 72¾in). *P:* chest £163; wardrobe £295.

Relyon's PINEWOOD furniture

⚠ *INDICATES ONE OR MORE OF THE PRODUCTS MENTIONED ARE SELECTED BY THE DESIGN CENTRE*

FURNITURE

Mirrored wardrobes from Sharps

Bedroom by Trüggelmann

SHARPS BEDROOM DESIGN
Inexpensive tailor-made modern bedroom furniture, designed to customer's specification to fit any size room, includes sliding mirrored wardrobes. The mirrors visually enlarge and lighten the room, whilst providing considerable storage space; they can be set in a gold matt frame. Internal fittings are flexible, allowing hanging rails, shelving, sliding drawers and shoe racks in melamine veneer. Other wardrobes can also be designed in a wide variety of wood/melamine veneers, with a total complementary range of bedroom furniture. *M:* doors w24–28 × h to 96in (61–71 × 244cm). *P:* on application.

STAG
Complete ranges for the bedroom, from basic melamine flat-packed units to more luxurious wood-veneered pieces. The new, melamine SAVANNA range includes 14 freestanding pieces with plain white carcases and grey basketweave-textured doors, plus a padded headboard and matching stool covered in grey cotton. Dressing table '730' consists of a large shallow drawer fitted on to deep-drawered pedestals. *M:* w45½ × d17 × h31½in (115.5 × 43 × 80cm). *P:* from £120.

TRÜGGELMAN
An astonishing range of furnishings from 'total concept' custom-made bedrooms in period styles: from Louis XV and Louis XVI to art

Stag's SAVANNA

nouveau. Inspired perhaps by the grandeur of their native schlosses, this German company can make beds, cabinets, dressing tables and stools, wardrobes, mirrors, even panelling, columns and cornices, in truly palatial styles and proportions. *P:* on application. See also *Made-to-order.*

WINCHMORE FURNITURE LTD
DALHAM storage units in maple, with natural polished finish or darker mahogany staining. Drawers, wardrobe and cupboard doors have a simple rectangular carved panelling design. The range includes four wardrobes/cupboards with various shelves and interior drawers,

three chests of drawers, a dressing table and mirror with or without cupboards above, and open shelf units. These can be assembled together in any arrangement or used singly, freestanding. Units can be topped by either a flat pelmet or an architrave. *M:* base units mostly multiples of w40, 50cm (15¾, 19¾in) × d55cm (21¼in); full units h226cm (89in). *P:* single wardrobe doors from £83; chests of drawers from £148 (ex VAT).

DALHAM units by Winchmore

CHAIRS

• When considering a chair's measurements it is often just as important to know the seat height as the back height (particularly with dining chairs). Wherever available, both measurements are given together, back height first (e.g, if seat height is 44cm and back height 62cm, they are stated as h62/44cm).

ANTIQUES OF TOMORROW

A choice of nine reproduction dining chairs in Victorian, Queen Anne and Louis XVI designs. Like the other furniture from this manufacturer, chairs can be polished to customers' specifications and upholstered in a range of fabrics, or provided plain as required. '37/S' Victorian-style dining chairs have upholstered seats and back, and partly cushioned arms on the armchair. *M:* w19¼ × d18¾ × h42in (49 × 48 × 106.5cm). *P:* side chair, plain £37.61, polished and upholstered £78.37.

'37/S' armchair from Antiques of Tomorrow

THE ARCHITECTURAL TRADING COMPANY LTD

Zanotta furniture, designed by Italy's best. For those who like to be in the driving seat, 'Mezzadro' is simply a tractor seat set on an angled stem of lacquered or chromium-plated steel with a beech footrest. It was designed by the Castiglioni brothers and has been exhibited in the Museum of Modern Art in New York. *M:* w49 × d51 × h51cm (19¼ × 20 × 20in). *P:* lacquered £99; chromium £108.
'Giotto' is a classic adjustable stool with a re-

From top, left to right: Architectural Trading's 'Mezzadro', 'Safari', 'Giotto' and 'Tripolina'

volving seat that can be moved up and down by means of a steel screw. It's made from kiln-dried beech. *M:* dia 45 × h45–66cm (17¾ × 17¾–21¾in). *P:* £87.
Other ranges include a natural canvas and bay oak version of a 'director's chair', 'Safari'. It has a tilting back with removable bolster headrest, and is completely demountable. *M:* w66 × d61 × h92/39cm (26 × 24 × 36½/15¼in). *P:* £285.

Also demountable is 'Tripolina' with strong canvas or fabric cover slung over hinged stainless steel frame. *M:* w70 × h106 × d70cm (27½ × 41¾ × 27½in). £402.

BAKER, KNAPP & TUBBS LTD

From the STATELY HOMES OF ENGLAND AND SCOTLAND collection — a range of the highest quality reproduction furniture, replicas of pieces housed in stately homes — exquisitely made '5043–D' Chinese Chippendale open armchair. It is hand-carved in imitation of bamboo with interlaced ovals on back and sides, and hand-painted with sprays of gilt flowers on a dark lacquered ground. The original was made circa 1760. *M:* w26 × d23 × h39in (66 × 58.5 × 99cm). *P:* £3618.

H J BERRY & SONS LTD

Traditional English chairs from a family firm founded in 1840. There are Lancashire spindle-backs and Yorkshire ladderbacks with either rush or upholstered (often tapestry) seats; Windsors; rockers with rush or loose cushion seats; and a useful child's rocker with ladder or spindle back — all with medium or dark 're-pro' finish. Shades for contract orders also in-

PRICES AND INFORMATION WERE CORRECT AT THE TIME OF GOING TO PRESS

Baker, Knapp & Tubbs '5043-D'

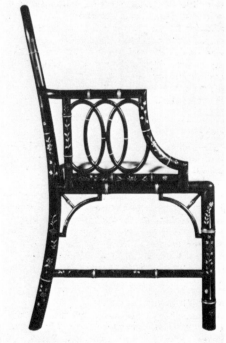

FURNITURE

clude natural beech, sapele and medium mahogany. There are also more sophisticated Regency-style dining chairs in beech with mahogany finish. *M:* '1' Lancashire chair w22½ × d18 × h36in (57 × 47 × 108cm); '246' Windsor w16¾ × d18 × h35½in (42.5 × 45.5 × 90cm); '14' rocker w22½ × d30 × h39in (57 × 76 × 99cm); '17' child's rocker w16½ × d17 × h30/12½in (41 × 43 × 76/32cm). *P:* '1' £137; '246' £39.90; '14' £137; '17' £93.

There are also some inexpensive modern designs and a large contract range, aimed at pubs and hotels that includes dining chairs and 18 different high and low stools, plus matching bar tables.

From top, left to right: Berry's '1', '246', '14', '17'

BOSS DESIGN

Sophisticated leather-covered seating in out-of-the-ordinary colours, the product of an imaginative collaboration between three British manufacturers: Tarian Design (see *Fabrics*), Connolly's (suppliers of leather upholstery for Rolls Royce and Jaguar cars) and Boss. The leather comes in unusual shades including bilberry, grape, almond and forest green, to match Tarian's fabric range.

Graceful IBIS stools are constructed in sweeps of chrome with leather seat and back support.

Three sizes are available, one at bar-stool height (with additional chrome footrest) and two smaller, occasional versions. *M:* w50 × d55 × h88/68cm (19¾ × 21¾ × 34¾/26¾in), w50 × d55 × h73/50cm (19¾ × 21¾ × 28¾/19¾), w50 × d50 × h62/44cm (19¾ × 19¾ × 24½/17¼in). *P:* £90–£137.

DELPHI dining, conference and desk chairs have chrome frame and slim, soft leather cushioning on back and seat offset by contrasting piping. Variations include low and high back, with and without arms, and swivelling desk chair on castors. *M:* low back with arms, w61 × h80 × d61cm (24 × 31½ × 24in); high back without arms w51 × h102 × d68cm (20 × 40¼ × 26¾in). *P:* from £198.

Boss's DELPHI

Boss's IBIS stools

ARTHUR BRETT & SONS LTD

Fine reproduction English furniture in classic eighteenth-century styles. Extensive range of dining chairs includes examples of the styles of Chippendale, Sheraton, Hepplewhite and others. In Chippendale style is '1539' in Brazilian mahogany, with fine acanthus leaf carving. Can be upholstered in customer's own fabric. Side chair and armchair are available. *M:* w57 × h98cm (22½ × 38½in). *P:* side chair £632; carver £796 (ex VAT).

Brett's also make open armchairs and corner chairs with upholstered seats, stools, and desk and reading chairs covered in antiqued hide.

Brett's '1539'

CANDLELIGHT PRODUCTS LTD

Quality rattan and bentwood furniture in natural finish or sprayed in pastel shades — white, smoke, pink, peach, peppermint and beige. Designs range from cosily rounded, basketwork 'Nuage' to throne-like 'Petal', and also include an elaborate bentwood bar stool. All have cushion seats upholstered in Candlelight's own delicately patterned fabrics. *M:* 'Nuage' w86 × d64 × h107cm (33¾ × 25¼ ×

From left: Candlelight's 'Nuage', 'Petal', bentwood bar stool

From left: Cotswold's 'A1C', 'C10'

42¼in); 'Petal' w120 × d83 × h98cm (47¼ × 32¾ × 38½in); stool h100cm (39¼in). *P:* 'Nuage' £180; 'Petal' £300; stool £86 (ex VAT).

CIANCIMINO INTERNATIONAL LTD

'Ming' dining chair in simplified Chinese style, made from beech with walnut or ebonized finish or natural sycamore. Ideal for long dinners, the chair has a cushion upholstered to customer's choice. There is a matching armchair. *M:* seat h17¼in (44cm). *P:* walnut finish £312.80.

Ciancimino's 'Ming'

COTSWOLD FURNITURE COMPANY

Wide-ranging collection of reproduction chairs made in well-seasoned beechwood and available in Cotswold's amazing variety of wood and painted finishes. There are 18 styles of side chair, most with matching armchairs. 'M20' is an unusually elegant side chair with upholstered seat and back, the frame forming a smoothly curved, elongated 'swan's neck' on the sides. Armchair, smaller than standard dining chairs and a bergère chair with loose cushion are available in the same design. *M:* 'M20' w20 × d16 × h34/18in (51 × 40.5 × 86.5/45.5cm). *P:* £144.90.

Cotswold's 'M20' and armchair

'A1C' is elegant but imposing: a Louis XVI spoonback armchair with upholstered or woven cane back. There's a side chair to match. *M:* w21 × h37½/18½in (53.5 × 95/48cm). *P:* £154.20.
On the traditionally English side, there's a familiar Hepplewhite wheatear side chair, 'C10', with armchair to match. *M:* w20 × d19 × h38½/17in (51 × 48.5 × 98/43cm). *P:* £129.50. Other styles of dining chair include Chippendale, Regency, Georgian, Victorian and Louis XV. There are six chairs specifically designed for bedrooms, including Louis XV and XVI gilded boudoir chairs, and a selection of nine stools. See also *Upholstered furniture.*

DEVALAKE LTD

Small but attractive range of dining chairs in Regency, Victorian and Jacobean styles. Mahogany or yew-finish 'Regency' side chair and armchair have upholstered seats in Dralon or 'Regency Stripe', and either upholstered or brass inlaid back. *M:* side chair w50 × d49 × h83cm (19¾ × 19¼ × 32¾in). *P:* £98.

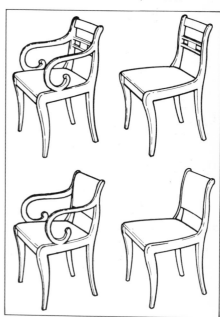

Devalake's 'Regency' chairs

MARTIN J DODGE

Exceptionally good reproduction English furniture, including Chippendale, Sheraton and Adam, using solid mahogany. All the chairs are available with or without arms; seats are upholstered in calico or customer's material. 'Chippendale' chair 'C11' has a pierced back splat and finely carved 'C' scrolls and foliage. *M:* carver w28 × d22 × h40in (71 × 56 × 101.5cm). *P:* £602.
'Hepplewhite' shield-back chair 'C9' has a carved wheatear top rail and serpentine front

FURNITURE

From top: Martin J Dodge's 'C11', C9'

rail. *M:* carver w23 × d18 × h39in (58.5 × 45.5 × 99cm). *P:* £335.

A more fanciful design is 'C24' 'Regency' painted chair with cane seat, sabre legs and

Martin J Dodge's 'C24'

curling arm and back rails. The chair can be painted any colour with mouldings and the lion paws on the end of the arms highlighted in gold leaf. It can also be made in mahogany and gold-leaf. A matching side chair is available. *M:* w22 × h34 (56 × 86.5cm). *P:* £455.

NICHOLAS ENGERT

Minimalist dining chairs in acrylic. Two designs are available: 'Z' in 25mm (1in) thick acrylic, and 'Classic' in 20mm (¾in) thick acrylic. *M:* w17 × d17 × h35in (43 × 43 × 89cm). *P:* 'Z' £554.40; 'Classic' £319.20 (ex VAT).

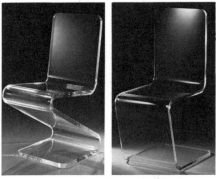

From left: 'Z' and 'Classic' from Nicholas Engert

ENVIRONMENT COMMUNICATION

Charles Rennie Mackintosh designs reproduced by Cassina in Italy. 'Argyle' chair, originally designed in 1897, has ebonized ash frame and seat upholstered in blue fabric. *M:* w48 × d47 × h136cm (19 × 18½ × 53½in). *P:* £607.

'Willow 1' from Environment

'Willow 1', designed in 1904, is almost semi-circular, with a tall, grid-patterned lattice back. It too comes in ebonized ash, with seat cushion upholstered in green or beige fabric. *M:* w94 × d41 × h119cm (37 × 16¼ × 46¾in). *P:* £1619.

Other classic Mackintosh pieces available from Cassina include dining tables (see *Dining suites*), sideboards, and an armchair and sofa.

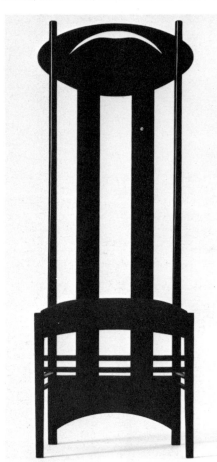

'Argyle' from Environment

EQUINOX INTERIORS LTD

Elegantly simple 'Arc' chair, designed by the Frenchman Pascal Mourgue. The adjustable back and removable leg-rest combine with the gentle resilience of woven cane seating to create comfort and support. The chair is available in either natural ash or beech or black beech. *M:* w57 × d82 × max h84cm (22½ × 32 × 33in), leg-rest d73cm (28½in). *P:* £195. See illustration on following page.

FUTON COMPANY ⬥

Low-level 'Gaijin' chair inspired by Japanese models. Made from medium density fibre-

Above: Equinox's 'Arc'; below: Futon Company's 'Gaijin' △ with table and sofa bed

Glenister's '5138A'

Grange's 'A29'

board in red, blue, apricot, grey or black, or from natural ash, it is angled so that the body automatically shifts into the correct sitting position and weight is evenly distributed. For storage the back slides out and slots underneath the seat and the whole thing can be hung up. *M:* w37 × d43 × h59cm (14½ × 17 × 23¼in). *P:* £29.50, ash £55. A matching table is available, and also a bed and bedside table (see *Beds*).

THE THOMAS GLENISTER COMPANY
Traditional chairs made by an old-established firm freely employing modern machinery and techniques. Most models are finished in medium mahogany colour but they can also be polished to customer's required colour and distressed. Among eight different wheelback designs is '5138A' double-bow armchair with curved 'crinoline' stretcher. *M:* w23½ × d26 × h39in (60 × 66 × 99cm). *P:* from £150.

GRANGE
Chair designs in several delightful ranges from this French firm, all intended to fit as well into modern eclectic rooms as into period ones. Sabre-legged scroll armchair 'A29' is part of the CALECHE range in the simple elegant style of post-Napoleonic France. It is veneered in cherrywood with a satin or decorator (darker) finish, and can have a leather or fabric seat. *M:* w50 × d43 × h87cm (19¾ × 17 × 34¼in). *P:* on application.

IRLANDE designs are derived from nineteenth-century Irish rural models. Smoker's bow or captain's chair 'A49' is finished in waxed cypress pine. *M:* w67 × d55 × h78cm (26½ ×

FURNITURE

Grange's 'A49'

21¾ × 30¾in). *P:* on application.
Dining tables are available in both these ranges.

HABITAT DESIGNS LTD

Excellent range of traditional and modern chairs distinguished by good, simple design. 'Toad' with curved woven rattan back and chestnut frame makes a delightful chair outdoors or in. *M:* w58 × d60 × h75cm (22¾ × 23½ × 29½in). *P:* £39.95. There's a table to match (see *Tables, occasional*).
'Ludwig Tall Stool' in cheerful red-stained

Habitat's 'Toad' chair and table

beech can be adjusted in height by screwing the seat up or down. *M:* dia 32 × h66–78cm (12½ × 26–30¾in). *P:* £19.95. There is also a lower version in natural beech.
Folding 'Director's Chair' in black beech with black canvas back and seat can be stored away when not in use. *M:* w54 × d48 × h88cm (21¼ × 19 × 34¾in). *P:* £24.95. See *Desks* for illustration. Similar but in natural-coloured rubber tree wood is the 'Director's Orient Chair'.

Habitat's 'Ludwig'

CHARLES HAMMOND

Among many and varied styles of furniture from these leading interior designers and wholesale suppliers, a large range of French reproduction dining chairs. One of the earliest designs in the range is that of the Louis XIII

period: side chair and armchair are available with carved frame polished to a dark oak colour, seat and back covered in Hammond's own fabrics (see *Fabrics*). *M:* w57 × d68 × h112cm (22½ × 26¾ × 44in). *P:* on application.

Louis XIII armchair from Charles Hammond

HOMEWORKS LTD

WOODWORKS dining chairs. Six styles include 'L-15' and oval-backed '7413', both reminiscent of classic French furniture; and

From top, left to right: Homeworks' 'L15', '7413', '7411', 'C500'

more rustic pieces like rush-seated 'C500', and '7411' with a square caned back, rush seat. Some chairs have upholstered sides and backs. Hand-carved solid oak or cherry frames look as though they've faded with age. *M:* 'L-15' w26 × d26 × h39in (66 × 66 × 99cm); '7413' w24 × d24 × h39in (61 × 61 × 99cm); 'C500' w19 × d18 × h34in (48.5 × 46 × 86.5cm); '7411' w24 × d24 × h36in (61 × 61 × 91.5cm). *P:* on application.

IDEAS FOR LIVING

Stunning contemporary designs imported from Italy.

Sculptural 'Lizie' chair was designed for the Paris Museum of Modern Art — to be sat in at the café rather than admired in the gallery. The designer was Régis Protière and it's made by Pallucco. The frame is two arched steel tubes connected by a network of steel threads, creating a play of curve and tension; the seat is natural beech or aluminium. Framework and seat can be finished in black, light, dark or hammered grey. *M:* w50 × d51 × h71.5/41.5cm (19¾ × 20 × 28/16¼in). *P:* on application.

Pallucco's 'Lizie' from Ideas for Living

From Seccose comes 'Quadra', a functionally styled armchair with metal frame — coloured metal bent into a rectangle to form the sides, linked by thin black metal traverse rods — and slim, cotton cushions on seat and back resting on semi-elastic plasticized netting. The chair comes in contrasting colourways: black frame with écru fabric or black fabric with red, yellow, white or grey frame. *M:* w52 × d53 × h80cm (20½ × 20¾ × 31½in). *P:* £65–£85.80.

From Kartell, masters of modern materials, comes a versatile range of stools in injection-moulded plastic, '4822'–'4826'. The stools have curved backrests or handles (which can also be used to hang them away on the wall), and

From top: Seccose's 'Quadra', Kartell's stools. Both from Ideas for Living

come in various heights for bars, worktops and dining tables. The frame is metal and plastic; seats are glass-reinforced, semi-expanded polypropylene with central hole (a thin cushion can also be placed over the hole). Stools with plain polypropylene seats come in various combinations of black, white and red; there's a large choice of colours for the cushions. *M:* dia 39.5 × h45, 55, 75cm (15½ × 17¾, 21¾, 29½in). *P:* £75, £89.50, £92.50, £95. Related to the stools are stacking, easy and dining chairs in injection-moulded plastic in bright colours and special colours to order (see *Dining suites*).

Kartell also make a neatly folding armchair, '4820', with a frame of moulded polypropylene and stainless steel, and red, yellow or brown linen or cotton back, seat and sides. *M:* w54 × d50 × h72cm (19¾ × 21¼ × 28¼in). *P:* £125.

JAYCEE

Large contract and domestic ranges of traditional reproduction furniture, predominantly in oak, with an emphasis on Tudor styles and hand-carving. BROADLEAF TRUST collection

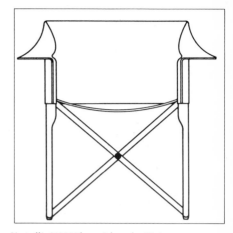

Kartell's '4820' from Ideas for Living

includes a solid oak double bow armchair and matching side chair, available in a choice of three coloured finishes, warm Tudor, autumn gold and antique. *M:* 'L745' armchair w52 × d52.5 × h102cm (20½ × 20½ × 40¼in); 'L744' side chair w45 × d52.5 × h90cm (17¾ × 20½ × 35½in). *P:* 'L745' from £189; 'L744' from £104.

Jaycee's 'L745' and 'L744'

R E H KENNEDY LTD

Large collection of good quality reproduction dining chairs, both Georgian designs in mahogany and earlier designs in English oak. Oak range includes 'Elizabethan', Stuart', 'Cromwellian', 'Yorkshire' and 'Derbyshire' designs in solid oak with studded hide seats and backs. 'Stuart 2143' has high back and is elaborately turned and carved. *M:* '2143' w19 × d16 × h46in (49.5 × 40.5 × 117cm). *P:* on application. See following page for illustration.

JAMES LUPTON & SONS LTD

Oak dining chairs and other furniture in familiar English styles, available with traditional medium oak stain or white stain for a lighter, more modern effect. Range of side chairs and armchairs includes 'Georgian' with uphol-

FURNITURE

Kennedy's 'Stuart 2143'

Maclean's '47-4003'

From top: Maclean's '48-4107' and '48-4072' with side chairs

stered back and seat, and scrolled arms on the armchair; 'Quaker Back' with carved back panel and buttoned cushions; high 'Five Ladder Back'; plus Stuart and Cromwellian designs. *M:* (side chairs) 'Georgian' w51 × d59 × h101cm (20 × 23¼ × 39¾in); 'Quaker Back' w37 × d46 × h100cm (14½ × 18 × 39¼in); 'Five Ladder Back' w51 × d42 × h103cm (20 × 16½ × 40½in). *P:* 'Georgian' £195; 'Quaker Back' £71; 'Five Ladder Back' £99.

From left: Lupton's 'Georgian', 'Quaker Back' and 'Five Ladder Back'

WILLIAM L MACLEAN
Well-made, period inspired furniture designed primarily for the top end of the contract market but so nice that it would look equally happy in private homes. From the huge range of 39 styles of side and armchairs come many distinctive and individual styles as well as the perennial favourites — Louis XV and XVI, chinoiserie and Georgian. All pieces are made from kiln-dried beech and available in more

than 100 finishes. Many of the chairs have caned backs (either broad-weave 'Jumbo' or standard) and all come with an optional feather cushion. Customer's own fabric can be used for upholstery.

Among the most unusual is '47-4003' side chair with slender curving sides and claw feet, particularly striking in a dark lacquered finish. *M:* w51 × d56 × h94cm (20 × 22 × 37in). *P:* from £320.

In art nouveau style is side chair '47-4050', with characteristically serpentine curves and upholstered seat and back. *M:* w50 × d61 × h107cm (19¾ × 24 × 24¼in). *P:* from £380.

Simpler is Quaker-back armchair '48-4107' with rush seat and carved flower motif across the front. *M:* w61 × d63 × h105cm (24 × 24¾ × 41¼in). *P:* from £235.

There's also a rare 1930s design, '48-4072' armchair with upholstered seat and back and typically angular frame. *M:* w59 × d60 × h99cm (23¼ × 23½ × 39in). *P:* from £230.

Maclean's '47-4050' and armchair

Both side chairs and armchairs are available in all the above designs.
(All prices ex VAT.)

HERMAN MILLER
EAMES FIBREGLASS CHAIRS, the original early 1950s design for such seating. Several different models available in six colours with or without upholstery. 'La Fonda' side and armchairs have full seat and back pad and chrome-plated or white epoxy-coated four-star base. *M:* w47 × d54 × h81cm (18½ × 21¼ × 32in). *P:* £102.50–£122.50.

Herman Miller's EAMES FIBREGLASS CHAIRS

Unusual, and expensive, oiled walnut stool '413' turned from a solid wood block to produce an individual random wood grain pattern. Three variations on a cotton reel shape are available. *M:* dia 33 × h38cm (13 × 15in). *P:* £349. See following page for illustration.

PRICES AND INFORMATION WERE CORRECT AT THE TIME OF GOING TO PRESS

Herman Miller's '413'

NEVILLE NEAL

Strong and graceful rush-seated chairs made from natural ash or oak, lightly waxed or stained. Neville Neal learnt the craft from a pupil of Ernest Gimson, who was responsible for its revival during the Arts and Crafts movement. Nine different designs are available with

Neville Neal's 'Gimson 3'

or without arms, plus rocking chairs, children's chairs and stools.

The 'Gimson' ladderback design in wax-polished ash has an unassuming yet finely detailed simplicity. There are three full-size versions: with arms ('3'), without arms ('3A') and fireside ('3B'). *M:* '3' w20 × d16 × h46in (51 × 40.5 × 117cm); '3A' w17 × d15 × h42in (43 × 38 × 106.5cm); '3B' w22 × d19 × h47in (56 × 49.5 × 119.5cm). *P:* £79.50, £60.50, £91.20.

PIRA

Modern, lightweight and elegant furniture from Italy.

Black-coated steel and brightly coloured plastic 'Cricket' in the MAGIS range strikingly combines form and function. When not in use its thin but strong legs fold completely flat into a series of rectangles behind the seat and back, and the carrying hold can be used to hang it Shaker-style on the wall as an intriguing piece of graphic art. *M:* w40 × d47 × h82cm (15¾ × 18½ × 32¼in). *P:* £37.

A slender frame of polished steel supports seat and back of perforated sheet metal to form the stacking 'X-line' chair in the same range. It comes in a variety of bright colours with optional armrests and fittings for linking several together. *M:* w41 × d44 × h75cm (16¼ × 17¼ × 29½in). *P:* £30.

Pira's 'Cricket'

Pira's 'X-line'

PRICES AND INFORMATION WERE CORRECT AT THE TIME OF GOING TO PRESS

FURNITURE

G T RACKSTRAW

Well-made solid mahogany dining chairs from the largest volume supplier of reproduction cabinet furniture in the UK. 'M14850' armchair with sabre leg and scroll arm is one of eight designs in the range based on Georgian and Regency styles, all of which are also available in yew veneer. *M:* w21¼ × d21½ × h34in (54 × 54.5 × 85.6cm) *P:* £254–£344.
Rackstraw also make solid oak chairs in six designs including ladderback, Windsor and Cromwellian.

South Bank's '900' with armchairs

Rackstraw's 'M14850'

SOUTH BANK DESIGNS

Many different period styles from Italy in pickled pine finish (from stock) or a variety of special finishes including lacquer (to order). Seats can be covered in fabric from three price ranges, in leather or suede, or in customer's own fabric. Most designs are available both with and without arms.
Georgian-style wheelback armchair '1429' looks sensational in black lacquer with the central motif picked out in gold. *M:* w56 × d49 × h99cm (22 × 19¼ × 39in). *P:* £238–£310.
'900' side chair is in Louis XV style with carved flowers. *M:* w50 × d44 × h97cm (19¾ × 17¼ × 38¼in). *P:* £184–£258.
The carved back of the '1600' side chair has a charming balloon design. *M:* w50 × d48 × h97cm (19¾ × 19 × 38¼in). *P:* £208–£248.

South Bank's '1429'

Upholstered armchair from Stuart

South Bank's '1600' with armchair

STUART INTERIORS

Painstaking reproductions of Jacobean and early American chairs in oak and yew, realistically antiqued with a wax finish.
Typical of the Stuart period is an upholstered side chair and armchair copied from a mid-seventeenth century design. Can be upholstered in customer's own fabric or a period-correct fabric from Stuart's own collection. *M:* armchair w22 × h38in (56 × 96.5cm) *P:* £180 (ex VAT).

Stuart's Yorkshire wainscot chair

A handsome Yorkshire wainscot chair in oak features fine carving and inlay. *M:* w24 × h54in (61 × 137cm). *P:* £665 (ex VAT).

WILLIAM TILLMAN

Fine reproduction Hepplewhite, Chippendale and Regency chairs in solid mahogany. Hepplewhite-style 'HC' chair is available as side chair or armchair, and can be upholstered in customer's choice of fabric. *M:* side chair w21 × d20 × h37in (53.3 × 51 × 94cm). *P:* on application.

William Tillman's 'HC'

TITCHMARSH & GOODWIN

Reproduction furniture from an exemplary firm of cabinet-makers. The entire range of

oak furniture is handmade from their own air-dried and kiln-finished timber, individually polished and distressed to an antique finish. 'RL8256' chairs have carved rails on the back and their seats can be covered in hide or customer's own fabric. *M:* side chair w18 × d16 × h36½in (45.5 × 40.5 × 92.5cm), armchair w22 × d17 × h38in (56 × 43 × 96.5cm). *P:* from £232, £285.

Titchmarsh & Goodwin's 'RL8256'

'RL53' chairs have back as well as seat upholstered in hide or fabric, and upholstered arms on the armchair, with studding. Front rails are turned in the Cromwellian manner. *M:* side chair w18½ × d16½ × h36in (47 × 42 × 91.5cm), armchair w23 × d17 × h38in (58.4 × 43 × 96.5cm), *P:* (hide) £255, £345.
There is also a large range of mahogany and yew furniture in late eighteenth-century styles made to the same high standard.

Titchmarsh & Goodwin's 'RL53'

R TYZACK LTD

Reproduction furniture both in a standard range and to order, from a small independent manufacturer. Dining chairs in eighteenth- and nineteenth-century styles include the '5020' with elegant rope-stay back. Matching armchair with scrolled arms is available. Seat can be covered in hand-antiqued hide or customer's own fabric. *M:* side chair w18 × d21 × h33in (45.5 × 53.5 × 84cm). *P:* on application.

Tyzack's '5020'

WESTNOFA

BALANS 'alternative sitting' range, designed on the principle that kneeling is a more relaxed and natural posture than sitting, keeping the spine upright and discouraging slumping. The idea came from observation of small children — who kneel before they sit — and was developed by Norwegian designers. The basic design of tilted seat and knee-rests (distributing the weight between the knees and the base of the spine) has been adapted in a dozen or more ways for use in offices, on factory assembly lines, in therapeutic clinics and for the home. 'Scandi' is the teak frame 'luxury' version for the dining or sitting room; it's upholstered in 100% wool in a wide choice of colours. It may look unusual but sitting is believing! *M:* w52 × d73 × h50cm (20½ × 28¾ × 19¾in). *P:* from £171.35. See also *Upholstered furniture.*

Westnofa's BALANS

FURNITURE

DESKS

BAKER, KNAPP & TUBBS LTD
Large but elegant '88' three-drawer desk in hand-polished mahogany with cross-banding and solid brass drop handles. *M:* w72 × d36 × h30in (183 × 91.5 × 76cm). *P:* £2678. Baker, Knapp & Tubbs make a large collection of very fine reproduction desks for both contract and domestic use.

Baker, Knapp & Tubbs's '88'

Brett's '2113'

ARTHUR BRETT & SONS LTD
Wide range of desks from makers of high quality reproduction English furniture, from important partners' desks to simpler kneehole bureaux.
'2113' is an elegant mahogany writing table in Chippendale style. The three-sectioned top is lined with individual panels of finest selected gilt-tooled hide, subtly antiqued; the brass fittings are cast in Brett's own workshops. *M:* w183 × d107 × h74cm (72 × 42¼ × 29¼in). *P:* £2952 (ex VAT).
'2063', an eighteenth-century-style partners' desk in walnut, also has antiqued and gilt-tooled hide top, plus additional leather writing tablets fitted to the top drawers, and hand-made brassware. The bottom right-hand drawer is deep enough to hold files. *M:* w183 × h76 × d102cm (72 × 30 × 40¼in). *P:* £4952 (ex VAT).

Brett's '2063'

PRICES AND INFORMATION WERE CORRECT AT THE TIME OF GOING TO PRESS

CANDLELIGHT PRODUCTS LTD
'Balmoral' desk with bentwood frame and woven rattan panels on side and back. Comes in natural finish or sprayed in pastel shades — white, smoke, pink, peach, peppermint or beige — to match Candlelight's other bentwood and rattan furniture. *M:* w123 × d62 × h76cm (48½ × 24½ × 30in). *P:* from £180.

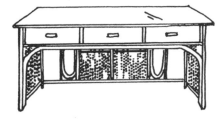

Candlelight's 'Balmoral'

DESIGN WORKSHOP
'TD2' desk in gleaming aluminium, wood and leather, dubbed the 'executive' desk in the TOMMASO system on account of its size and glamour. The base is satin or polished aluminium, the top ash, sycamore, Indian rosewood or wenge with leather inlay, and the desk has two shallow, leather-lined drawers. *M:* w220 × d100 × h73cm (86½ × 39¼ × 28¾in). *P:* £1250–£1311 (ex VAT). The TOMMASO system also includes dining suites, occasional tables, storage cabinets and upholstered seating (see separate entries).

THE DESK SHOP
See *Offices, desks.*

Design Workshop's 'TD2'

DEVALAKE
Reproduction desks, bureaux and writing tables. Most unusual is French-style 'Bonheur du Jour' fall-front writing table with two small drawers and vertical storage for papers. It has a leather inlaid writing surface and is finished in mahogany or yew with tulipwood inlay. *M:* w64 × d40 × h117cm (25¼ × 15¾ × 46in). *P:* mahogany £220, yew £239. See following page for illustration.

MARTIN J DODGE
Among an exceptionally good range of reproduction English furniture, a classic solid mahogany bureau 'H28' raised from bracket feet with four long drawers. The front opens to reveal a centre door with a column each side, pigeon-holes and small, shaped drawers. *M:* w34 × d20 × h40in (86.5 × 51 × 101.5cm). *P:* £1259.
More exotic desks include 'H29' a lacquered bureau bookcase with gilt chinoiserie decora-

Devalake's 'Bonheur du Jour' writing table

Martin J Dodge's 'H28'

tions. The desk has seven drawers and a central kneehole cupboard; behind the fall front there is a centre door with pigeon-holes and drawers arranged on each side. The upper double-domed section has shelving behind panelled doors. *M:* w48 × d23 × h86in (122 × 58.5 × 218.5cm). *P:* £4761.

MARY FOX LINTON LTD
Classically simple desk from a company that makes superb quality furniture to order. In blue and black lacquered wood with a silver gilt trim, the standard version has three drawers in each pedestal and a central pen tray. *M:* w180 × d80 × h75cm (70¾ × 31½ × 29½in). *P:* £2800 (ex VAT).

Martin J Dodge's 'H29'

GOSTIN OF LIVERPOOL
Mahogany pedestal desk '42A' from a small firm specializing in period oak, walnut, mahogany and marquetry using traditional techniques. Hand-distressed, coloured and waxed,

Mary Fox Linton's lacquered desk

the desk has a shaped, tooled leather top in green, brown or red, solid brass handles, quarter columns either side of each plinth, and ogee feet. *M:* w155 × d95 × h76cm (62 × 38 × 30in). *P:* from £1200.

Gostin's '42A'

GRANGE
Elegant and individual desks and bureaux from an exceptional range of period-style furniture made in France.

For those with literary leanings, Grange make a replica of Balzac's desk from his chateau at Saché. Surprisingly light and simple for such a literary giant, the desk is beautifully made with a solid oak frame and cherrywood top. The wood is tinted and waxed by hand to create the patina of age. Grange are producing only a limited edition of this desk. *M:* on application. *P:* £700.

A similar limited edition is the replica of George Sand's desk, a very unusual piece with scalloped kneehole and tiered shelves at the back. It's made from solid cherrywood, again

tinted and waxed by hand. *M:* on application. *P:* £1200. See colour illustration.

Grange's standard designs include attractive 'F2000' in the REJANNE range, a fall-front writing table with tooled leather top, made in cherrywood with dark decorator or light satin stain. *M:* w106 × d49 × h105cm (41¾ × 19¼ × 41¼in). *P:* £830.

IRLANDE range of charmingly rustic Irish furniture in waxed cypress pine includes a simple writing desk 'IB100' with two drawers and a cupboard on one side. *M:* w131 × d70 × h76cm (51½ × 27½ × 30in). *P:* £528.

Grange's replica of Balzac's desk

Grange's 'F2000'

Grange's 'IB100'

HABITAT DESIGNS LTD

Desks mainly for the home — for housekeeping, dressmaking, study or the home computer, in pine, beech or ash veneers, white lacquer or black metal.

'Computech' desk has three deep shelves on a black, tubular steel frame. The top shelf can hold a VDU; the second shelf, at table-top height, pulls out to hold printer and keyboard; and the bottom shelf stores software. Trailing wires can be kept in place by snap-on metal clips. This eminently practical and space-saving unit runs on castors. *M:* w73 × d69 × h108cm (28¾ × 27¼ × 42½in). *P:* £69.

'Altona', veneered in black ash with chromed metal handles, is a larger, conventional desk, suitable for home or office. Top and side units with drawers or cupboards come separately, to be assembled as required. *M:* complete w182 × d76 × h74cm (71¾ × 30 × 29¼in). *P:* desk top £39, cupboard unit £59, three-drawer unit £71.

Habitat's 'Altona'

PRICES AND INFORMATION WERE CORRECT AT THE TIME OF GOING TO PRESS

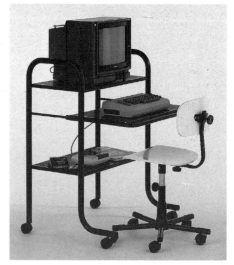

Habitat's 'Computech'

M & I J HARRISON

Reproduction Victorian country furniture in pine. Sturdy kneehole desk has nine drawers and is offered in natural, medium or antiqued finish. *M:* w50 × d22 × h32in (127 × 56 × 81.5cm). *P:* £360.50 (ex VAT).

IDEAS FOR LIVING

From Kartell in Italy, a practical desk made up from stacking drawer elements and a separate top. Made in semi-expanded shockproof polystyrene, the elements and top are available in white, black, brown and bright red, green and yellow. *M:* top w136 × d42cm (53½ × 16½in). *P:* four-drawer stacking element £25.05, top £35. See *Storage* for illustration.

For children, there's '5312' work or play table in easy-to-clean, knockabout plastic, with basket attachment for crayons and paints. It's part of a marvellous complete nursery school sys-

Ideas for Living's '5312' child's work table, by Kartell

Grange's replica of George Sand's desk

FOR INSPIRATION WE NEED LOOK NO FURTHER THAN OUR LOCAL PALACE

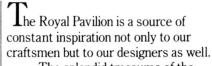

The Royal Pavilion is a source of constant inspiration not only to our craftsmen but to our designers as well.

The splendid treasures of the Pavilion, the elegant Regency architecture of the crescents, the seafront and the fields and farms of the rolling Downs are all reflected in our new collection.

Furniture, hand-carved in the best traditions of British craftsmanship, which recreates the best of the past in the idiom of today.

Our factory shop in Brighton has a wide range of furniture on display and new designs are always being added.

William L Maclean

William L Maclean Ltd.
3 New England Street
Brighton, Sussex, BN1 4GQ
Tel: (0273) 695411
Telex: 877167 DESDEC G
A Wenstrom House Company

Our clients include:
Design Unit Dubai
Champneys at Tring Health Resort
Gleneagles Hotel
Helsinki Intercontinental
Tivoli Gardens, Copenhagen

David Hicks International
The Royal Opera House,
Covent Garden
Richmond Design Group
Forgacs, Reardon Ray
Design Consultants

DINING SUITES

BATH CABINET MAKERS

Dining suites designed specifically to co-ordinate with a well-known range of wall cabinets (see *Storage*). ROYAL BATH extending dining table in dark mahogany repeats the classic theme of a rectangular top with rounded corners set on twin pedestals with claw feet. Armchair and side chair come in dark or light mahogany, either with upholstered seat and back or with upholstered seat and open back with two wooden cross members. *M:* table w63–78 × d35½ × h28⅜in (160–198 × 90 × 71cm). *P:* table £360; side chair £116.

ROYAL BATH from Bath Cabinet Makers

H J BERRY & SONS LTD

Inexpensive modern and traditional kitchen or dining room tables and chairs, plus a large contract range for bars and hotels. MATES suite comprises a plain round table with turned legs and four curved-back chairs with turned rails, legs and stretchers. Available with natural finish or polished to medium and dark reproduction shades; table top is wood-grain melamine in matching shade. *M:* table dia 42 × h48in (106.5 × 122cm). *P:* table £108.70, chair £66.80.

H J Berry's MATES

R J CHELSOM & CO LTD

Formal brass or lacquered steel and glass dining tables and matching chairs.
BAMBOO collection includes a rectangular

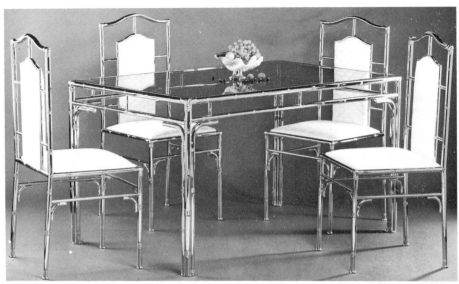

Chelsom's BAMBOO

table with smoked plate-glass top and high-backed, upholstered side chairs. Their Chinese-style design uses polished brass or ivory lacquered steel in imitation of bamboo. Chairs can be upholstered in a wide range of fabrics, including an attractive grey and white fan design. *M:* table '1100' w56 × d34 × h30in (142 × 86.5 × 76cm); chair '1099' w18 × d17 × h39in (45.5 × 43 × 99cm). *P:* table £388–£430; chair £170. The collection includes a number of matching pieces such as a mirror, occasional tables, telephone table and chair, trolleys and shelving.

COLOURFLAIR

WHEATSHEAF dining table with oval glass top on hand-carved pedestal, and matching chairs with upholstered seat and back, and slender frames and arms carved to match the table. A matching console table is available. *M:* w200 × d110 × h78cm (78¾ × 43¼ × 30¾in). *P:* dining table £2148; chair £482.
Colourflair's varied collection of dining tables

Colourflair's WHEATSHEAF

PRICES AND INFORMATION WERE CORRECT AT THE TIME OF GOING TO PRESS

also includes circular tables in a variety of different marbles (see *Tables, occasional*). *M:* dia 90–122 × h78cm (35½–48 × 30¾in) *P:* £722.50–£1262.30.

CONFETTI

BOSTON dining suites, part of a colour-co-ordinated furniture system that also includes coffee tables and shelf units (see separate entries). Circular tables have pedestal composed of a cluster of three lacquered tubular metal supports; square and rectangular tables have four tubular metal legs, both with tops of 1in (2.4cm) thick birch ply. Chairs, with or without arms, have lacquered tubular metal frame, lacquered wooden seat, back surround and armrest, with upholstered seat and back pads (see illustration on cover). Table tops are laminated in white, black, dove grey, pale blue, red or yellow with profile edges in grey, pink, pale blue or natural wood; table legs and chair frame and arms can be lacquered in the same colours as the tops, or chrome. Select matching frames, profile edges and tops. Or mix and match: try contrasting profile edges

Confetti's BOSTON

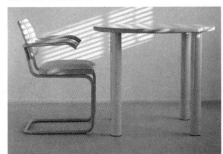

FURNITURE

and surfaces, chair and table — the combinations are stunning and designed to cater for all colour schemes. *M:* square and rectangular tables, five sizes, w48 × d16 × h29in (122 × 40.5 × 73.5cm) to w60 × d36 × h29in (152.5 × 91.5 × 73.5cm); round table dia 36 or 48 × h29in (91.5 or 122 × 73.5cm); chair w18 × h32/19in (45.5 × 81.5/48.5cm). *P:* rectangular and square tables £98–£190; round tables £150, £190; armchair £50, side chair £46.

High-tech MANHATTAN dining suites similarly match or contrast coffee tables and cabinets in the same range (see also *Tables, occasional; Storage*). Each element in the range is decorated with a grid pattern. Dining tables have broad metal base perforated with square holes, lacquered in black, white, dove grey, red, powder blue or yellow, with a toughened clear glass top with black or white printed grid. 'X-line' chair has welded steel frame and metal seat and back also perforated with square holes; frame, seat and back are available in chrome or colours as above. This light, simply designed chair is stackable and would be as useful in a conference hall as in the home. *M:* table, three sizes w48 × d33 × h29in (122 × 84 × 73.5cm) to w72 × d36 × h29in (183 × 91.5 × 73.5cm); chair w17 × h29/17in (43 × 73.5/43cm). *P:* table £240–£320; chair £36–£39.

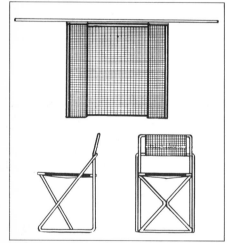

Confetti's MANHATTAN

THE CONRAN SHOP
Simple but very unusual HAVANA table, in burr ash veneer with solid ash rails and lippings. Comfortable curved-back HAVANA chair can be upholstered in customers' own material. *M:* table w200 × d100 × h72cm (79 × 39 × 28¼in). *P:* table £675; chair from £250.

DENMOR FURNITURE CO LTD
Octagonal table and contemporary-look side chairs which nevertheless have near-gothic arches in their backs. The table extends for

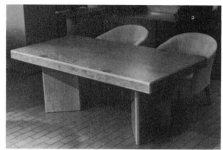

Conran's HAVANA

dinner parties and the seats are covered in fabric to harmonize with the three finishes — grey lacquer, grey polyester and mahogany colour. The suite forms part of Denmor's modular CONCEPT system (see *Storage*). *M:* table (extended) w159.5 × d119.5 × h73cm (63 × 47 × 28¾in). *P:* table £80–£120; chair £22.75–£35.50.

Denmor's CONCEPT

DESIGN FURNITURE △
Stylish, well-made modern furniture, classic enough for any interior.

'Blandford' dining table has extending rectangular top and crossed trestle legs in white, black or natural ash or Rio or Santos rosewood veneers. Matching 'Sandford' side chairs are solid beech colour-matched to rosewood or ash finishes, with upholstered seat and back. *M:* 'Blandford' (extended) w200 or 235 × d98 × h70cm (78¾ or 92½ × 38 × 27½in); 'Sandford' w47 × d57 × h100cm (18½ × 22½ × 39½in). *P:* 'Blandford' £640–£860; 'Sandford' £132.

'Cordova' is an extending table that's oval when closed, circular when open; available in Rio or Santos rosewood veneers, with match-

From Design Furniture. Top: 'Sandford', 'Blandford' △; below: 'Studland', 'Cordova'

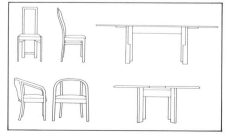

ing 'Studland' armchairs. *M:* 'Cordova' (closed) w138 or 164 × d114 or 134 × h68cm (54¼ or 64½ × 45 or 52¾ × 26¾in), (open) dia 138 or 164cm (54¼ or 64½in); 'Studland' w62 × d62 × h76cm (24½ × 24½ × 30in). *P:* 'Cordova' £660–£950; 'Studland' £135.

DESIGN WORKSHOP
Square-form TOMMASO suite in rich materials. 'TBIW' table has square top and broad, square base veneered in sycamore, Indian rosewood or wenge; a contrasting aluminium plate can be inset into the top. *M:* w130 × d130 × h73cm (51¼ × 51¼ ×28¾in). *P:* £651–£714 (ex VAT). Variations come with satin or polished aluminium base, or with rectangular top and two pedestals in the same materials. Clear or tinted glass tops are available.

Design Workshop's 'TBIW'

Plush 'TDGW' chair on castors has plywood shell veneered in the same woods as the table. Seat, back and sides are upholstered in fine, soft leather in a variety of shades. *M:* w66 × d55 × h69cm (26 × 21¾ × 27¼in). *P:* £276–£312 (ex VAT). Again, there are variations: 'TDG' with shell clad in aluminium and 'TDGL' with shell covered in leather.

Similar materials and sections are used

Design Workshop's 'TDGW'

throughout the TOMMASO system (see also *Desks; Storage; Tables, occasional; Upholstered furniture*).

MARTIN J DODGE

Exceptionally good range of solid mahogany reproduction English furniture, particularly notable for fine carving and marquetry. Many sizes and shapes of pedestal tables are available, as well as many chair designs (see *Chairs*). Individual designs can be made up. 'T8' circular dining table on pedestal with brass plain or claw feet can be finished in rosewood, satinwood, yew or mahogany with an optional crossbanded border. 'Sheraton' cross-splat chairs 'C14' have a rosewood or satinwood inlay top rail and drop-in seats. Side chairs and armchairs are available. Both table and chairs are hand-polished and then waxed. *M:* table dia 48 × h29½in (122 × 75cm); side chair w19 × d17 × h35in (49.5 × 43 × 89cm). *P:* table £530–£645; side chair £187.

Martin J Dodge's 'T8' and 'C14'

ENVIRONMENT COMMUNICATION
Modern classics made in Italy.
Massive rectangular table 'La Basilica' is made from three or four staves of natural ash or walnut with six or eight legs. Designed by Mario Bellini and produced by Cassina in Italy, its primitive severity is accentuated by the box-like 'Break' chairs made from steel-framed panels and polyurethane foam covered in fabric with leather piping. They are available with or without arms. *M:* table w280 × d78.5 or 105 × h74cm (110¼ × 31 or 41¼ × 29¼in); arm

Environment's 'La Basilica' and 'Break'

Environment's 'DS1' and 'DS4'

chair w56 × d51 × h85cm (22 × 20 × 33½in). *P:* table from £1240; chair from £462.
From Cassina come beautifully made reproductions of furniture by earlier twentieth-century masters. Charles Rennie Mackintosh designs include 'DS1' grid-pattern gateleg table with folding oval top, and 'DS4' armchairs and 'DS3' side chairs with the grid pattern repeated on the extended back. All come in ebonized or walnut-stained ash; chairs have mother-of-pearl inlay on the back and rush seat. *M:* table (extended) w177 × d125 × h75cm (69¾ × 49¼ × 29½in); chairs w49 or 52 × h75 × d45cm (19¼ or 20½ × 29½ × 17¾in). *P:* 'DS1' £1231; 'DS3' £425; 'DS4' £459. Mackintosh's square 'DS2' table in two sizes continues the grid theme in the same wood. *M:* w75 × d75 or w100 × d100 × h75cm (29½ × 29½ or 39¼ × 39¼ × 29½in). *P:* £769, £850.

Environment's 'DS2' and 'DS3'

ESTIA
Unique LINX integrated table and seating system. Each seat incorporates a table support so that triangular, square, rectangular or polygonal shapes are possible. Tubular frames come in red, black or blue, tops in melamine or glass, and seats can be upholstered in Estia fabrics (cotton, corduroy, velour or wool/viscose in many colours) at no extra cost. *M:* four-seater w122 × d122 × h71cm (48 × 48 × 28in). *P:* (with glass top 'L4GT') £135.

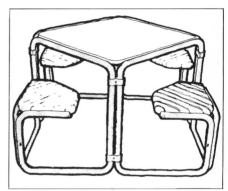

Estia's LINX

GRANGE
Delightful period furniture from France.
The elegant CALECHE range includes circular pedestal table '3Q660'. The table extends with the addition of two central leaves, the resulting 'D'-ends each supported by two additional slim legs. It's available in cherrywood with light satin or dark decorator finish, or in walnut. *M:* (closed) dia 115 × h75cm (45¼ × 29½in), (extended) w160, 204 × d115 × h75cm

Grange's '3Q660' and 'A83'

FURNITURE

(63, 80¼ × 45¼ × 29½in). *P:* £670.
The table can be matched with 'A83' buckle back chair, one of five dining chairs in the range. An attractive side chair with curved back and legs it comes in solid beech tinted satin cherry, decorator cherry or walnut to match the table. *M:* w36 × d39 × h46cm (14¼ × 15¼ × 18in). *P:* £105.

HABITAT DESIGNS LTD
Excellent range of dining tables in ash, beech, elm, oak and pine with solid, veneered or melamine tops. Dining chairs present the whole gamut of good, simple design from Windsor through Bauhaus to high tech.
At the traditional end the QUAKER dining table is made from natural ash with an oak veneer top and can seat up to eight people. The matching side chairs and armchairs in ash can have rush or grey wool upholstery seats. *M:* table w202 × d93 × h72cm (79½ × 36½ × 28¼in); side chair w52 × d45 × h89cm (20½ × 17¾ × 35in). *P:* table £149; chair £39.

Habitat's QUAKER

'Vigo' extending table in black ash veneer seats up to 10 people at full size; the thick rectangular top stands on a simple underframe. To match there are 'Manzano' side chairs, in black ash with tall curved backs; backs and seats are in natural-coloured woven rattan. *M:*

Habitat's 'Vigo' and 'Manzano'

'Vigo' w180–232 × d90 × h72cm (70¾–91¼ × 35½ × 28¼in); 'Manzano' w45 × d51 × h99cm, (17¾ × 20 × 39in). *P:* 'Vigo' £195; 'Manzano' £59.95.

HAMLET
Simple solid-pine tables in five styles, with chairs or benches to match. The rectangular, straight-legged 'Space Saver' table comes in three sizes to allow four, six or eight 'Standard' chairs to tuck under it. The chairs have low backs with flat top-rails and seats upholstered in a choice of six tweedy fabrics or customer's own. 'Standard' carvers are also available, though they won't tuck away. *M:* medium table 'TASL60' w152.5 × d76 × h75cm (60 × 30 × 29½in); side chair 'CHS1' w44.5 × d43 × h45cm (17½ × 17 × 17¾in). *P:* table £138.50; side chair £39.50. Hamlet sell their furniture by mail order and prices include delivery in the UK.

HOMEWORKS LTD
'DC-166B' chairs and 'ST-325' table, part of the WICKERWORK suite handmade in Italy. Well constructed and good-looking, they come in a natural or dark brown finish. Loose, reversible chair cushions are plain or tufted. *M:* table w18 × l50 × h28in (46 × 127 × 71cm), chair w22 × h38 × d22in (56 × 96.5 × 56cm). *P:* from £414 (fabric extra).

Homeworks' 'DC-166B' and 'ST-325'

'4400' and '4875' from Ideas for Living

IDEAS FOR LIVING
From Kartell of Italy, bright, functional and inexpensive tables in sturdy plastic and polyurethane. Range of square and rectangular expanded polyurethane tables with laminated plastic tops comes in three heights — as dining, children's and coffee table — in white, black or grey. The children's version is available with black top and red or yellow legs. *M:* rectangular '4400' w120 × d80 × h30, 46, 72cm (47¼ × 31½ × 11¾, 18, 28¼in); square '4500' w80 × d80 × h30, 46, 72cm (31½ × 31½ × 11¾, 18, 28¼in). *P:* '4400' £175, £185, £195; '4500' £155, £159, £165.
Tables can be matched with '4875' chairs in moulded polypropylene, available in black, white, brown and bright green, red and yellow. The legs are detachable. *M:* w48 × d50 × h71cm (19 × 19¾ × 28in). *P:* £22.

JAYCEE
Large contract and domestic ranges of traditional reproduction furniture. VICTORIAN collection of dining and occasional furniture in solid Scandinavian pine includes an attractive rectangular centre-leaf dining table with turned legs. The sides are decorated with a hand-carved acanthus motif, a feature of all the pieces in the range. There are ladderback armchairs and side chairs to match. *M:* table w136 × d90 × h75cm (53½ × 35½ × 29½in); side and armchairs w52 × d52.5 × h102cm (20½ × 20½ × 40¼in). *P:* table £340; side chair £92; armchair £110. See following page for illustration.
In solid oak, Jaycee make refectory and draw-leaf tables with Tudor-style hand-carved bulbous legs, and a large contract range including smaller tables and chairs popular for pubs and restaurants.
See following page for illustration.

PRICES AND INFORMATION WERE CORRECT AT THE TIME OF GOING TO PRESS

DINING SUITES

Jaycee's VICTORIAN

R E H KENNEDY LTD
Solid mahogany circular pedestal table with mostly solid mahogany side chairs and armchairs in the Hepplewhite style. Part of a large range of top-quality handmade and hand-polished reproduction furniture. *M:* table '1510' dia 54 × h28½in (137 × 72.5cm); side chair '1585' w21 × d17 × h37in (53.5 × 43 × 94cm). *P:* on application.

Kennedy's '1510' and '1585'

MEREDEW
Five ranges of dining-room furniture that also include wall units (see *Storage*).
Top of these ranges is CHARTWELL in crown sapele veneer. Extending table 'CM769' is rectangular with slightly curved ends and turned legs. Chair seats are covered in a choice of striped or plain fabrics. *M:* table w151–202 × d94 × h73cm (59½–79½ × 37 × 28¾in);

Meredew's CHARTWELL

armchair 'CM556' w55 × d56 × h86cm (21¾ × 22 × 33¾in). *P:* table £249; armchair £106. Two-pedestal table is also available.
REMBRANDT sapele-veneered extending table and chairs provide a simpler alternative. Chairs have Dralon seat covers in a choice of colours. *M:* table 'BM768' w151–202 × d94 × h73cm (59½–79½ × 37 × 28¾in); armchair 'BM546' w57 × d51 × h86.5cm (22½ × 20 × 34in). *P:* £237, £99. There are high-backed chairs in the same range, which is also available in teak veneer as VICEROY. See *Storage* for illustration.

⚠ INDICATES ONE OR MORE OF THE PRODUCTS MENTIONED ARE SELECTED BY THE DESIGN CENTRE

PETER MILES ⚠
Outstanding handmade dining tables and chairs designed by Ronald Carter RDI. Traditional timber techniques are used, with a choice of solid English or imported hardwoods, all of which are sealed and then waxed. Customer's own fabric can be used for seat covers.
WITNEY range includes a graceful circular table with a planked one-piece top, traditional English underframe with button fixing from the top, and shaped and scalloped legs. Standard version seats eight people. The basic side chair has a deep, shaped back-rail, slim legs and a wool seat cover over a foam webbing frame. A high-back armchair is available in a slightly different design. *M:* table dia 145 × h72cm (57 × 28¼in); chair w52 × d46 × h80cm (20½ × 18 × 31½in). *P:* table £778–£978; chair £115–£135 (excluding fabric).

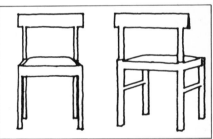

WITNEY table and chairs △ from Peter Miles

HAARLEM trestle table has a solid-timber and veneered top with two trestles positioned at the time of making to planned seating arrangements. Dining chair has a narrow, sloped back echoing the shape of the trestles, and a sturdy, square seat with a wool cover over foam and webbing base. *M:* table w244 × d122 × h72cm (96 × 48 × 28¼in); chair w48 × d55 × h92cm (19 × 21¾ × 36¼in). *P:* table £438–£538; chair £95–£125 (excluding fabric).

Peter Miles's HAARLEM

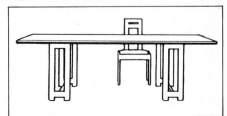

FURNITURE

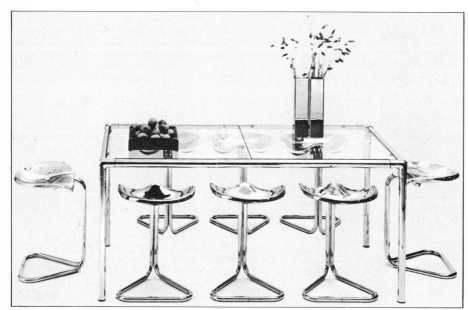

OMK's 'T10' △ and 'Tractor Seats' △

OMK DESIGN LTD △
High-tech modular table system with tractor-seat stools, for domestic or contract use. You can choose your own kit of parts from chrome or epoxy frames (colours on request), chrome or aluminium knuckle joints, and clear, bronze or mirrored glass or laminate tops. 'T9' has a single square of glass, 'T10' has two squares to form a rectangle. The contoured 'Tractor Seats' are available in polished chrome or red/black epoxy, and store away within the table frame. This elegant system also includes low tables in four sizes and a conference table. *M:* 'T9' w85 × d85 × h74cm (33½ × 33½ × 29¼in), 'T10' w161 × d85 × h74cm (63½ × 33½ × 29¼in). *P:* £130–£152, £186–£234.

PIRA
Modern, lightweight and elegant furniture from Italy
Flat-folding PLIAVIVA rectangular table comes in three versions: 'TP1' with natural ash frame and black or white melamine top, 'TP2' with natural or ebonized ash frame and top, and 'TP3' in natural beech with white melamine top. *M:* w165 × d76 × h72cm (65 × 30 ×28¼in).

Pira's PLIAVIVA 'TP1'

P: 'TP1' £170.
PLIAVIVA folding side chairs come in three versions to match the table: 'CH1' in natural or ebonized ash with solid, scooped seat, 'CH2' in natural or ebonized ash with grid cut into the seat, and 'CH3' in beech, natural or coloured black, green, yellow, red or blue. Armchairs are also available. *M:* side chair w47 × seat h45 × d36cm (18½ × 17¾ × 14¼in). *P:* 'CH2' £45.
This pleasingly functional range also includes a folding desk, console table, shelves and a trolley (see separate entries).

PRETTYGATE TRADERS LTD
Medium-priced modern furniture in lacquered finishes, imported from Holland and Italy. AZS circular dining table, with either single-piece top or with flip-over centre leaf,

Top and below: AZS table and chairs from Prettygate

Pira's PLIAVIVA 'CH2'

has a pure and simple design set off by the curved-back chairs. All come in grey, black, white or red lacquer; chairs, available with or without arms, come with scooped ply, woven cane or fabric pad seat. *M:* table dia 105 × h72cm (41¼ × 28¼in), centre leaf w35cm (13¼in). *P:* table £160, with centre leaf £180; side chair £70; armchair £85.

G T RACKSTRAW

Well-made tables of traditional types in solid mahogany or oak from the largest volume supplier of reproduction cabinet furniture in the UK. All wood used is dried to 10% moisture content.

The top of the 'M16905' two-pedestal extending table is crossbanded with boxwood line inlay and the hand-turned pedestals are fitted with brass claw castors. *M:* w72–90 × d36 × h30in (183–228 × 91 × 76cm). *P:* £766–£1018. A wide range of pedestal tables are available in solid mahogany or mahogany with a yew veneer.

Rackstraw's 'M16905'

SCOTT HOWARD ASSOCIATES LTD

From a wide range of modern furniture imported from Denmark, CAFE series of streamlined, steel-frame chairs and tables. Designed originally for use in cafés, they are suitable both inside and out at home. All have steel

Scott Howard's 'P465'

Scott Howard's '9600'

tube frames in galvanized finish or painted red, white or blue. 'P465' rectangular table has either anthracite-grey lacquered metal or clear-lacquered brass top; '9600' chair has seat and curved back-rail in metal covered with grey rubber. Useful for small but sociable homes, two or more tables could be pushed together for a larger dining table, and the chairs stack easily. *M:* table w60 × d70 × h70cm (23½ × 27½ × 27½in); chair w49 × d49 × h70cm (19¼ × 19¼ × 27½in). *P:* table from £148; chair £71. There's also a small, round café table (see *Tables, occasional*).

SOUTH BANK DESIGNS

Many different period styles of dining chairs and some tables from Italy in pickled pine finish (from stock) or a variety of special finishes including lacquer. '1376' circular dining table with a look of turn-of-the-century Vienna has a Calacatta (white) or Travertine (beige) marble

South Bank's '1376' and '1354'

top. '1354' matching chair, also available with arms, can be covered in fabric from three price ranges, in leather or suede, or in customer's own fabric. *M:* table dia 124 × h76cm (48¾ × 30in); chair w57 × d51 × h108cm (22½ × 20 × 42½in). *P:* table £628–£822; chair (customer's own fabric) £210.

STAG

Dining suites in three stylish living/dining ranges, veneered in mahogany, oak or teak. Rectangular extending dining table '880' in the oak-veneered OVERTURE range has a marquetry chequered top. Dining chairs '871/2' have high backs upholstered, like the seats, in beige herringbone fabric. *M:* table w62½–86 × d38½ × h29in (158.5–218.5 × 98 × 73.5cm); side chair w19 × d21½ × h38½in (49.5 × 54.5 × 98cm). *P:* table from £240; chair from £100. Matching wall cabinets and a coffee table are available (see *Storage*).

Stag's OVERTURE '880' and '871/2'

WILLIAM TILLMAN

Fine reproduction Sheraton, Chippendale, Regency and gothic tables and chairs in solid mahogany with waxed finish. Sheraton-style

Tillman's 'SJ1' and 'SJSC'

FURNITURE

two-pedestal table 'SJ1' will seat 12 people, The shield-back Hepplewhite-style side chairs and armchairs 'SJSC' can be upholstered in customer's choice of fabric. *M:* table w72–120 × d45 × h28½in (183–305 × 114.5 × 72.5cm); side chair w20½ × d20 × h36½in (52 × 51 × 92.5cm). *P:* on application.

TOWN & COUNTRY PINE
Traditional-looking tables and chairs in solid pine coloured to resemble old stripped pine. '3202' oval table has centre leaf for extension, and turned legs. '3322' armchair has upholstered seat and back, and there's a matching side chair, '3312'. *M:* table w150–196 × d105 × h72.5cm (59–77¼ × 41¼ × 28½in); armchair w54 × d53.5 × h81cm (21¼ × 21 × 32in). *P:* table £279.50; armchair £129.50. Other designs include round and rectangular tables and ladderback and stick-back chairs with upholstered seats.

Town & Country's '3202' and '3322'

TOWNHOUSE INTERIORS
Invisible assets from Italy exclusive to Townhouse Interiors. FABIAN range includes a dining table in solid acrylic perspex with a brass

FABIAN from Townhouse

chair upholstered in white silk, chintz, leather or suede. *M:* table dia 40 × h75cm (55 × 29½in); chair w43 × d45 × h110cm (17 × 17¾ × 43¼in). *P:* on application.

TULLEYS OF CHELSEA
A small range of hand-finished reproduction tables and chairs in yew or mahogany veneers. Pedestal table '810' seats up to 10 people. Matching cross-stick arm and side chairs come in a wide choice of seat coverings. *M:* table w64–84 × d39 × h30in (162.5–213.5 × 99 × 76cm); side chair w19 × d19 × h34in (49.5 × 49.5 × 86.5cm). *P:* table from £229; chair from £89.

Tulleys' '810'

VERARDO
Glamorous lacquered furniture from Italy. EMPIRE range in black, beige, rose or white lacquer includes octagonal dining table on broad fluted pedestal base with veneered marquetry top; it has an extension leaf. The matching side chairs have lacquered frame and upholstered seat and back panel. *M:* table dia

Verardo's EMPIRE

130–174 × h73cm (51¼–68½ × 28¾in). *P:* table £550; chair £130. EMPIRE range also includes a versatile system for storage and much more — even a corner bar with wall units, a separate counter and stools.

WEBBER FURNITURE
Oak reproduction furniture. CROYDON range includes 17 different chairs and 15 tables. Typical are '60' solid oak truss table, '360' side chair and '361' armchair, which could well be combined with '257/377' lead-light dresser (see *Storage*). Available with medium to dark oak finishes or with distressed finish. *M:* '60' w63 × d30 × h28in (160 × 76 × 71cm). *P:* '60' £338.25; '360' (customer's cover) £68.50; '361' (customer's cover) £87; distressed finish extra.

Webber's '60', '360' and '361'

MADE-TO-ORDER FURNITURE

ROBERT & COLLEEN BERY

Beautifully decorated furniture and mirrors, which the Berys design, make and finish themselves. Two distinct finishes are available: richly stained wood with hardwood edging and highly lacquered surface; or gesso ground, with sponged, dragged or stippled paintwork in pastel shades and matt lacquered surface. Stencilled decoration of birds, flowers, flower-filled baskets or jardinières, Japanese fans and other motifs is then added. One-off orders to client's own specifications are welcome. Furniture designs include desk, wardrobe, Welsh dresser, cabinet, chest, bookshelves and various occasional tables. Certain pieces, such as the desk, are made only to order. Delivery takes 4–8 weeks. *M:* dresser w39 × h84 × d16in (99 × 213.5 × 40.5cm); cabinet w39 × h37 × d18in (99 × 94 × 45.5cm); octagonal table dia 48 × h15½in (122 × 39.5cm); chest w36 × h20 × d20in (91.5 × 51 × 51cm). *P:* dresser £480; cabinet £320; octagonal table £420; chest from £150. Matching doors and panels are stocked and can be trimmed to size. See also *Decorative painters.*

Stencilled cabinet, dresser, table and chest by Robert & Colleen Bery

BROWNS OF WEST WYCOMBE

Traditional chairs handmade to customers' specifications. Patterns, all reproduction, include beautiful Regency lyre-back dining chairs, Chippendale ladderbacks and traditional Gainsborough chairs. Upholstered models are hand-stitched, webbed and filled with horse hair. Examples include George III and Queen Anne fully upholstered comfortable lounge chairs, ladies' fireside chairs and traditional wing chairs. Wood for the frames and fabric can be specified by the customer. Browns also do high quality repairs and restoration of period furniture. *P:* on application.

Two chair patterns from Browns

CABOCHON FURNITURE LTD

High quality laminate-finished furniture designed and manufactured by a small British company. Cabochon's classically simple design concept with its clean, squared lines could be applied throughout a room or in individual pieces, in either domestic or commercial interiors — and the hard-wearing finish makes it as functional as it looks. Dining tables, coffee, side and console tables, storage and display units with glass shelves, mirrors, two- and three-seater sofas and a desk are all made either in standard sizes or to customer's own specification. The standard finish is matt white laminate but innumerable other colours and finishes are possible. Particularly attractive and versatile is the 'CN101' small nest of tables. *M:* w27 × d15 × h24in (68.5 × 38 × 61cm). *P:* £420.

Cabochon's 'CN101'

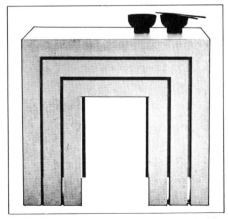

ASHLEY CARTWRIGHT

Beautifully made original furniture, usually in English hardwoods. Both interior and garden furniture is designed to commission, from individual pieces to university and boardroom scale. A most unusual chest of drawers in sycamore has a coloured inset handle running up its entire length. *M:* h36in (91.5cm). *P:* £1500.

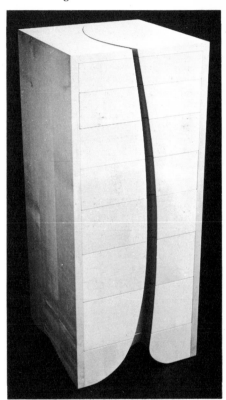

Chest of drawers by Ashley Cartwright

CARVED PINE MANTELPIECES LTD

Pine corner cupboards, bookcases, bureaux and wardrobes. In selected Russian pine, items can be built to individual drawing or reproduced in eighteenth-century style, to complement Carved Pine's panelling and mantels. *P:* on application. See also *Fireplaces.*

CASA FINA

Really extensive range of cane furniture which can be bought off-the-peg or ordered in one of 50 Dulux gloss colours as well as natural, black or white! Delivery is six to eight weeks for the colours but the range is so big that if you love the look of cane, it would be worth waiting for. Casa Fina will also design one-off pieces in cane. Available items include sofas, tables and shelves for the sitting room, dining suites and

PRICES AND INFORMATION WERE CORRECT AT THE TIME OF GOING TO PRESS

FURNITURE

Above: cane pieces from Casa Fina; below: Ciancimino's 'TLC'

chairs, plinths, obelisks and lamp-bases (see *Lighting*). All are made from marine beech and the possible finishes include plain paint, stippling, lacquering and all kinds of *faux* finishes — marble, tortoiseshell, lapis (dark blue with gold flecks), malachite and ivory. A two-door cabinet in a faintly Chinese style demonstrates combinations of marbled, stippled and plain finishes. *P: £517.50*

JOHN COLEMAN
Contemporary furniture designed by John Coleman and handmade in veneer or solid timber, both to commission and from previous designs.

Below: 'Gentleman's Dresser'; bottom: 'Stripe'. By John Coleman

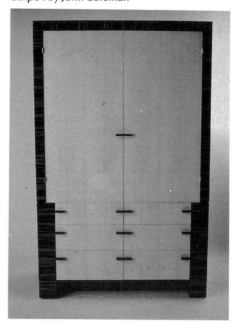

sideboards, headboards and storage for the bedroom plus lots of smaller accessories such as mirrors and shelves for the bathroom — there's even a toilet-roll holder! *M:* tall chest of drawers w16 × d16 × h40in (40.5 × 40.5 × 101.5cm). *P: £200. M:* round coffee table with glass top dia 42 × h16½in (106.5 × 42cm). *P: £108.*

CIANCIMINO INTERNATIONAL LTD
'TLC' dining table, a sleek bare minimum, with smoked glass top and anodized aluminium base. It is available in black, bronze and light bronze and is made to customer's own specification. *P: on application.*

CIEL AT CHRISTOPHER LAWRENCE
Painted wooden furniture made to order. Any item can be made; pieces to date include tallboys, occasional tables, stereo cabinets,

Ciel's painted cabinet plus chair and cubes

PRICES AND INFORMATION WERE CORRECT AT THE TIME OF GOING TO PRESS

'Gentleman's Dresser' has doors and drawers of fiddle-back sycamore strikingly framed in Macassar ebony. *M:* w120 × d60 × h190cm (47¼ × 23½ × 74¾in). *P:* approx £2250.
'Stripe' coffee table in sycamore and coloured veneer is part of a range including occasional and hall tables and mirrors, all offered in various sizes and colours — pink, olive, blue, red, green etc. *M:* w60 × d60 × h36cm (23½ × 23½ × 14¼in). *P:* approx £185.

RICHARD EPSOM

Furniture designed and constructed for contemporary and traditional interiors. Richard Epsom specializes in large-scale wood carving — from exotic figures to copies of carved furniture — but he will also design to order. Another speciality is water-gilded mirrors in any period style. *P:* on application. See *Architectural ornaments* for illustration.

FAULKNERS

Specialists in modern cane and reproduction Victorian bamboo furniture made to clients' specifications. There are a number of storage pieces including bookcases, open shelving units, stereo units, dressers, three-drawer chests, dressing tables and single wardrobes. An unusual combination wardrobe with drawers on one side exploits an asymmetrical

Faulkners' dressing table and stool

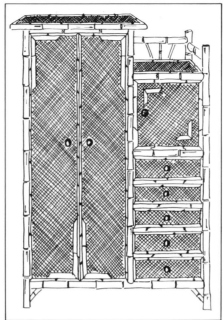

Combination wardrobe by Faulkners

Japanese look which can be emphasized with black or red lacquer. Otherwise the handles themselves or decorative diamonds of bamboo increase the charm of the natural material. *P:* bookcases from £60; chests from £167; wardrobes from £201.
Also available are dining tables, occasional tables (with glass, laminate or raffia tops), easy

chairs, sofas and bedheads, as well as Victorian novelties such as hallstands. *P:* chairs from £145; sofas £201 (framework only).

FORMICA ⚠

Dramatic 'Broken Length' table with grey surface and pink core revealed along its jagged edge. It was specially commissioned from Massimo and Lella Vignelli to demonstrate Formica's new surfacing material COLOUR-CORE. This has colour all the way through, thus eliminating the usual dark seams and giving an illusion of solidity. Of course, it can be put to more everyday uses. Further information from Formica. *P:* on application. See colour illustration.

JOHNNY GREY DESIGN

The HOME OFFICE collection, individual and appealing pieces of furniture for use both in the office and at home. Items, all made to order, include bookcase, drinks cabinet, trestle table, round dining table, coffee table, 'Cricket' occasional table, display cabinet, adjustable shelves and sideboard, upright chair with wooden stretchers, desks and even lamps. There's also a small filing cabinet and a table with special lower shelf for VDU and keyboard. Solid wooden surfaces and moulded wooden legs contrast sharply with black polyester lacquer and bright red metalwork handles and trims. *M:* trestle table with reversible top w80–120 × h130 × d160–230cm (31½–47 × 51¼ × 63–90½in). *P:* trestle table £579; chair £273; shelves £861. Johnny Grey will design and make complementary pieces of

From Johnny Grey's HOME OFFICE range

FURNITURE

furniture and even entire offices to customer's requirements, all in his distinctive but functional style.

PETER HALL WOODCRAFT
A small family business making high-quality individual furniture, both traditional and contemporary, in local Cumbrian oak and imported mahogany, mainly to commission. Members of the Guild of Lakeland Craftsmen, they also restore antiques and re-upholster chairs and sofas using horsehair and a wide range of authentic fabrics. Another branch of their work is the production of unusual, delicate turnery. *P:* on application.

CHARLES HAMMOND
Amazing furniture made to individual customers' requirements by these leading interior designers. Gilt eagle console table in the William

Console table from Hammond

Dresser by Peter Hall

Kent style demonstrates the more fantastic end of their range, which also extends to cool modern designs. *M:* w36 × d15 × h31in (91.5 × 38 × 78.5cm). *P:* on application.

PETER HAXWORTH ▲
Custom-built tables with high-quality wood veneer tops and high-tech UTS supports. Finished in polished chrome (or special finishes such as bronze), these supports are adjustable in height and fold flat for removal and storage. Any shape and size of table can be made, the larger ones being built in sections for extra adaptability. *M:* to order. *P:* on application. Tables can also be made with laminate tops of any colour.

Table by Peter Haxworth △

MARGARET MARTIN
Exclusive pieces that combine function with startling dramatic effect. A wardrobe disguised as a beach hut evokes Georgian esplanades and far-off summers, in softly stained and bleached ash. A pinnacled and turreted Strawberry Hill extravaganza incongruously houses a television and video. In a less flamboyant spirit, an austere cabinet of whitened oak and

Oak and ebony cabinet by Margaret Martin

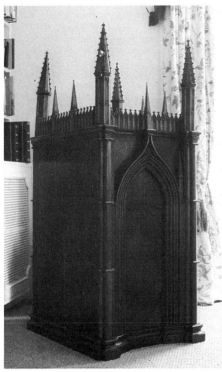

Margaret Martin's gothic television cabinet

Elm table by Charles Matts

ebony plays boldly on the contrast between the two woods, a contrast heightened by intricate cross-hatching and paint-finishing.

Each design, quite original, is developed after much discussion with the client, and then made up in carefully chosen woods by cabinet-maker Brian Moxom. The painstaking and highly skilled nature of the work involved in each commission means, however, that none of these pieces come cheap. *P:* on application. See also colour illustration.

CHARLES MATTS
Individual and traditional dressers, tables, chairs, desks, bookcases, display units etc, made from local hardwoods air-dried and kiln-conditioned on the premises.

Solid elm circular table has an unusual design which can be varied according to customers' requirements. *M:* dia 67 × h29in (170 × 73.5cm). *P:* £800. Chairs and a dresser can be made to match, in elm or other hardwoods.

MAXINE NAYLOR
Strangely ethereal furniture inspired by industrial techniques and employing such materials as mild steel, slate, aluminium and glass. 'Trestle' table consists of a sheet of glass supported at each end by a sheet of mild steel formed into an 'A' shape with a tie bar. *M:* w137 × d45.5 × h34cm (54 × 18 × 13½in). *P:* on application.

'Tilting' occasional tables or whatnots involve pairs of triangular aluminium plates threaded on to chromed aluminium rods with steel ball bearings between each pair of plates. These allow the tables to lean in any direction while the plates remain horizontal, parallel to the triangular slate base. *M:* plates and base 30 × 30 × 30 × h70cm (11¾ × 11¾ × 11¾ × 27½in). *P:* on application.

Maxine Naylor's 'Tilting' tables

Maxine Naylor's 'Trestle' table

Maxine Naylor will make variations on these pieces to order, as well as other intriguing designs, for example storage cubes made from steel sheets wrapped round mirror-glass panels.

CHRISTIAN NIMMO
Striking chests of drawers and other furniture produced in limited runs by a designer craftsman. Several sizes of drawer are sprayed a very dark brown satin finish and then fit into a red oxide framework to create a satisfying geometrical pattern. Accompanying the chest is a matching sideboard, sofa-end unit, various sizes of coffee table, and bedside unit, so it can be used in bedrooms as well as living rooms. There is another possible version in stained sycamore and paduak veneers with drawers lined with cedar of Lebanon. *M:* chest of drawers w110 × d50 × h85cm (43½ × 19½ × 37½in). *P:* £475 (ex VAT). See following page for illustration.

⚠ *INDICATES ONE OR MORE OF THE PRODUCTS MENTIONED ARE SELECTED BY THE DESIGN CENTRE*

FURNITURE

Chest of drawers by Christian Nimmo

ONE OFF LTD
Brilliantly original punk-influenced high-tech designs for glass tabletops on trestles. Glass is cut, enamelled and sand-blasted to any shape, size and thickness. Tubular or wire trestles finished in chrome or epoxy can be made to any height. *P:* on application.

PATRICKS OF FARNHAM
Tables made up in more than 50 types of marble and onyx. Any size of shape of top can be cut for a variety of frames and legs. *P:* on application.

ALAN PETERS
Solid wood furniture by a master craftsman. Unashamedly of the late twentieth century yet not ignoring the best traditions of the past, Alan Peters' furniture reflects two main influences: his early training with Edward Barnsley and his recent visits to the Far East.
Oriental-looking hall table is in solid Indian rosewood with a fluted fan-shaped top on radiating gate legs. *M:* w42 × d21 × h30in (106.5 × 53.5 × 76cm). *P:* on application.
Architectural chest of drawers is solid English

Alan Peters's hall table

walnut with brass handles on ebony inlay. *M:* w42 × d18 × h36in (106.5 × 45.5 × 91.5cm). *P:* on application.
While producing some set pieces, Alan Peters designs most of his furniture individually, and is as happy making a single piece for a sixteenth-century farmhouse as planning a director's office in a tower block.

Alan Peters's chest of drawers

QUADRANT 4 ⚠
Classically sleek acrylic pieces. A clever table base composed of two curved pieces of acrylic joined back to back can be used in different positions as a coffee or dining table base; the top in both cases is an oblong piece of acrylic with curved ends. Other pieces include a whatnot shelf. The medium, and the difficulties of working with it, however, make this furniture fairly expensive. *P:* on application.

J SHARD LTD
Fine furniture made to specification. Standard period-style designs include a Cupid's-bow sofa table in Brazilian mahogany with Rio rose-

Sofa table by J Shard

wood veneer, and with crossbanding and marquetry inlays using burr walnut, boxwood and Coromandel ebony. *M:* w60 × d24 × h30in (152.5 × 61 × 76cm). *P:* on application.
Most of Shard's work is undertaken for interior designers and architects, commissions including homes, offices, boardrooms, and hotels.

STUART INTERIORS
Entire rooms, and all the furniture in them, designed or restored in Elizabethan or Jacobean style by master craftsmen in association with a consultant historian. Stuart can reproduce any furniture or fittings from the period, including stone fireplaces, window and door surrounds, tapestries, wallpapers, handmade iron hinges, handles and nails, pewter and stoneware, or will trace original pieces on the client's behalf. They can work in a grand manner or produce plainer pieces such as the early turned chair, in yew, turned table, and cupboard with geometrically moulded doors. *P:* on application. See following page for illustration.

JANE THOMAS
Furniture with an oriental simplicity, in natural and stained sycamore and other hardwoods. Jane Thomas usually works to one-off commission, although she will copy existing pieces.
An ebonized coffee table with four drawers has blue-stained sycamore inlay edging the top and the round cut-out drawer pulls, and contrasting ebonized and blue-stained stretchers. *M:* w39¼ × d31½ × h15¾in (100 × 80 × 40cm). *P:* on application. See back cover for illustration.

KENNETH TOPP
Sculptural furniture with an ethnic influence. CLIFFTOP range, at a knock-down price, includes a console table in limed ash with strik-

Kenneth Topp's stylized figure console table

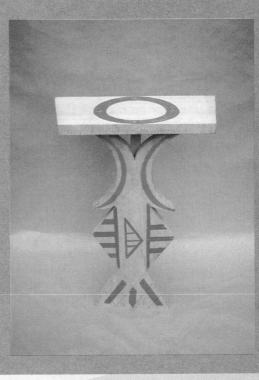

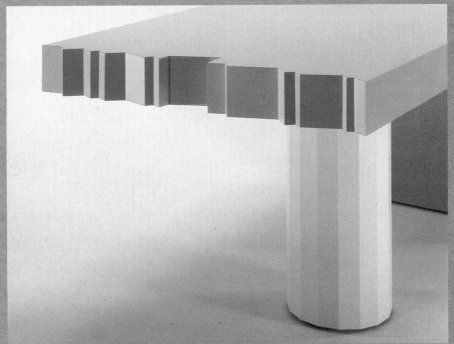

Top: Kenneth Topp's CLIFFTOP console; below: Formica's 'Broken Length' table in COLOURCORE

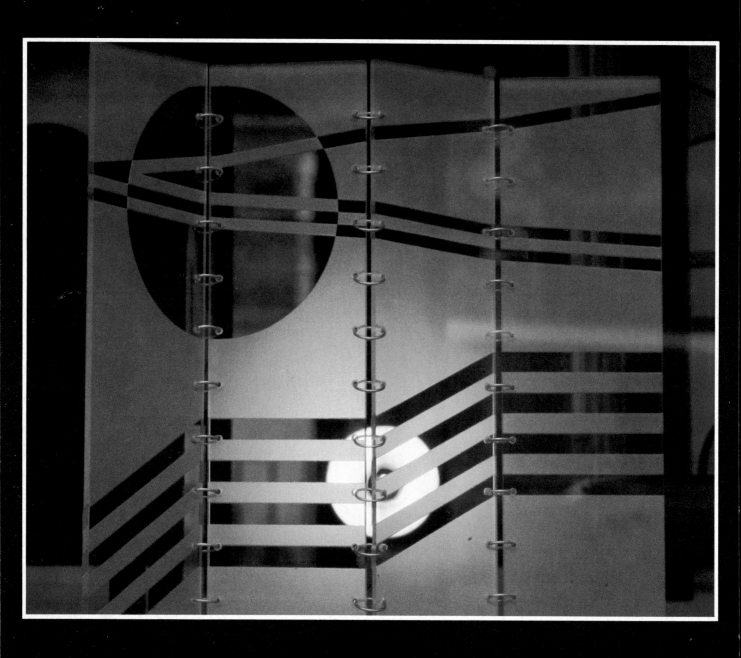

Screen in sandblasted glass by Catherine Lalau-Keraly (see Screens and partitions*)*

Trüggelmann fittings and furniture

Jacobean furniture by Stuart Interiors

ing outline and painted decoration. *M:* w26 × d13 × h33in (66 × 33 × 84cm). *P:* from £95. Also available uncoloured. See colour illustration. Stylized figure console table carved from water-stained hardwood has a semi-matt black melamine finish. *M:* w33¼ × d16¾ × h35¼in (84.5 × 42.5 × 89.5cm). *P:* from £800. Kenneth Topp's other work has ranged from a grand bed to a sculptural balustrade.

CHRIS TRIPPEAR
Glass-fibre versions of seventeenth-century furniture faithfully reproducing the intricate carving. There are four-poster beds, chests, wardrobes, bars, fireplaces and other composite pieces which are assembled to order, backed with wood, and stained or painted as required. Existing panelling etc can be matched. A cast of a seventeenth-century Italian carving is used for a striking desk which is painted green with detail picked out in gold. *M:* w72 × d24 × h30in (183 × 61 ×76cm). *P:* approx £1200.

TRÜGGELMANN
An astonishing range of furniture, panelling, columns, decorations etc for 'total concept' custom-made interiors in period styles: Louis XV, Louis XVI, Transitional and art nouveau. Bedrooms, living and dining rooms can all be transformed with the help of Trüggelmann's interior design service. *P:* on application. See also following page.

TUKAN HARDWOOD FURNITURE
High quality pieces made to specification by a group of Suffolk craftsmen. Whether a client wants a copy of an existing piece, has an exact design, or a vaguer idea of what he wants, Tukan provide an attentive service, discussing each commission with the client and developing a design if necessary. Their work includes carving, lacquering and marbling as well as cabinet-making, and furniture is usually made up from their own stocks of hardwoods. An example of their work is a copy of a Sheraton chair made for a client who had seven originals

'Sheraton' chair by Tukan

but wanted a set of 18; work included chair-making, caning, distress gilding, and painting — there's a different cherub in the back panel of each chair. *P:* on application. Tukan provide a door-to-door service — and not just confined to Suffolk!

PRICES AND INFORMATION WERE CORRECT AT THE TIME OF GOING TO PRESS

FURNITURE

Cabinet by Toby Winteringham

array of drawers and pigeon holes inside, is made from sycamore and kingwood. *M:* w62 × d30 × h135cm (24½ × 11¾ × 53¼in). *P:* on application.
Austere coffee table owes its beauty to the grain of the cherrywood from which it is made. *M:* w140 × d70 × h40cm (55 × 27½ × 15¾in). *P:* on application.

ARNOLD ZELTER
Music stands and cabinets plus any high-quality handmade furniture to order. Arnold Zelter works mainly in oak, mahogany, rosewood and walnut, and will incorporate carving and turning. *M:* music cabinet w35 × d14½ × h27in (89 × 37 × 68.5cm) *P:* from £609; music stands £140–£700 (ex VAT).

Music cabinet by Arnold Zelter

Top: Trüggelmann interior; below: Toby Winteringham's coffee table

WHITNEY LACQUER LTD
Specialists in polyester lacquer and Europe's leading designers and producers of custom-built lacquered furniture ranging from coffee tables to bathrooms and to banking halls. *P:* on application.

TOBY WINTERINGHAM
Clean-lined designs, usually in English hardwoods, ranging from street furniture to kitchens and bedrooms to small mirrors. Toby Winteringham can also make up items to customer's own design.
Fascinating cabinet on a stand, with four doors opening in different directions and a useful

SCREENS AND PARTITIONS

ROBERT & COLLEEN BERY

Beautifully decorated screens with stencilled flowers, birds, fans and flower-filled jardinières applied on to a lacquered or gesso ground. Three types of screen are usually available: solid wood panels in *faux* cane framing; solid birch panels stained in deep blue or black; pastel-coloured solid wood panels with gilt-inlaid hardwood framing and brass hinges. Three-panel screens are standard but extra panels can be added. The Berys can also make a Georgian-style screen with calico wrapped over a wooden frame. *M:* solid wood screens (three panels) h72 × w54in (183 × 137cm). *P:* 'Swaying Irises', 'Garden Trellis' £210, extra panels £60 each. See also *Special furniture, Decorative painters.*

Robert & Colleen Bery's 'Garden Trellis' and 'Swaying Irises'

CANDLELIGHT PRODUCTS LTD

Graceful four-section screen with cane frame, fabric panels and cane bars top and bottom. Panels can be covered in Candlelight's own fabrics. Cane available in natural finish or sprayed in pastel shades (white, pink, smoke, peach, peppermint or beige). *M:* l180 × max h196cm (70¾ × 77¼in). *P:* from £200.

CUBIC METRE FURNITURE

Metal mesh screens for a high-tech interior. See *Offices, screens.*

SUSANNE GARRY LTD

Unique sliding panels made to any width in Susanne Garry's own fabrics (see *Fabrics & wall coverings, co-ordinates*) — a Japanese idea that this company has even sold to a restaurant in Japan. Processed, rigid fabric is fitted to an adaptation of Silent Gliss's sliding screen system to make unusual room dividers,

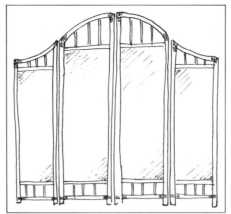

Cane screen from Candlelight

decorative panels or screens for windows. Panels can be stacked to left, right or centre, hand-, cord- or electronically-operated. *P:* on application.

DAVID GILLESPIE ASSOCIATES LTD

Carved timber panels for use as screens, partitions, grilles, or as suspended ceilings or even bedheads. Lattice patterns include small square, star-shaped and rectangular apertures, and Moorish-style designs. The panels can be carved on one or both sides. Most panels are in Californian redwood, though the MANDARIN range includes some in araucaria. *M:* MANDARIN range, module size 180 × 55cm (70¾ × 21¾in). *P:* on application. Gilles-

Gillespie's MANDARIN carved screen

Laser-cut screen from Gillespie

pies also make laser-cut screens, which can be produced in almost any pattern, however intricate, to order.

HABITAT DESIGNS LTD

'Quadrille' lattice-work three-panel screen in solid pine. In a natural finish, it has a particularly elegant simplicity. *M:* w138 × d2 × h171cm (54¼ × ¾ × 67¼in). *P:* £59.

Habitat's 'Quadrille' screen with futon bed

IDEAS FOR LIVING

Functional screens with coloured metal frame from Seccose. See *Offices, screens.*

CATHERINE LALAU-KERALY

Highly individual modernist partitions, made to commission by a stained-glass artist. A typical piece is a decorative small glass screen with a

PRICES AND INFORMATION WERE CORRECT AT THE TIME OF GOING TO PRESS

FURNITURE

Canvas screen from Catherine Lalau-Keraly

sandblasted design. The four sections are joined by brass rings fed through holes drilled in the glass. Other glass screens come in wood frames and can be etched, painted, enamelled or stained to create many designs. *M:* w80 × h70cm (31½ × 27½in). *P:* from £450. See colour illustration in *Made-to-order*.
Less expensive but quite as effective screens can be commissioned in canvas. The abstract painted canvas in three sections on a wooden frame is joined by double-sided hinges and creates a large area of screening. *M:* w400 × h180cm (157 × 70¾in). *P:* from £500.

MAXINE NAYLOR
Severely simple screen made from four paper panels tensioned with glass-fibre rods. Tubular aluminium uprights are bedded in a Portland stone base. *M:* each panel w22 × h150cm (8¾ × 59in), base w75 × d25 × h5cm (29½ × 9¾ × 2in). *P:* on application. Maxine Naylor will make variations on this design as well as other screens to commission. See also *Made-to-order*.

W H NEWSON & SONS LTD
PELLA folding doors. Made of high-density particle board, they are faced with mahogany,

Maxine Naylor's paper screen

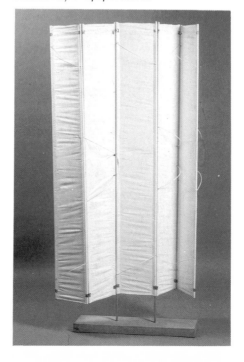

limba, pine, makoré, oak, teak and brown oak veneers, and bonded with water-resistant synthetic adhesives. Exclusive inner-spring connectors ensure that they open and close uniformly without bunching, jamming or noise. All doors are available single, as a pair, or as sliding panel doors for recessed installation. Made to order, they come either with plain faces, with smoked, translucent, sculptured or clear acrylic panels — ACRILOOK range — or with raised and fielded solid wood panels — DESIGNER doors. *P:* on application.

RICHMOND INTERIORS
Stockists of beautifully hand-painted screens from CHINESE COLLECTION. Solidly made from wooden panels, the screens are decorated by carving a layer of clay baked on the wood and then hand-painting them using 24ct gold leaf. There are about 100 designs to choose from, and the screens can be made up of as many panels as required, the panels also coming in a variety of sizes. *M:* four-panel 'Crane' screen, each panel h72 × w16in (183 × 40.5cm). *P:* £624.

CHINESE COLLECTION screen from Richmond

SILENT GLISS
Fabric-covered sliding panels that move on a system derived from curtain tracks. This Japanese-inspired product can be used as a room divider or a screen for windows. Panels can be stacked left or right, drawn from both sides like conventional curtains, or even centre stacked; and can be hand-, cord- or electronically operated. Fabrics come in a wide range, including hand-painted and hand-printed designs; alternatively, screens can be made up in customer's own fabric. *M:* w66–96cm (26–37¾in). *P:* on application.

SHELVING

ALTERNATIVE PRODUCTIONS LTD △

Simple, inexpensive cord shelving. Shelves are suspended on two lengths of cord attached to two wall screws; they can be fixed in place at any height by looping the cord around a chrome tube that also serves as a bookend. Cord is pre-stretched and strong — manufacturers state breaking strain at 1300lb (590kg). Shelves and cord come in six colours — blue, grey, pink, black, red and green — that can be combined as desired. Easy to assemble, the set comprises six shelves and all necessary fittings. *M:* shelves w65 × d21.5cm (25½ × 8½in). *P:* £24.50 plus p&p.

Alternative Productions' cord shelving △

△ *INDICATES AN ILLUSTRATED PRODUCT SELECTED BY THE DESIGN CENTRE*

ARTHUR BRETT & SONS LTD

Beautiful reproduction furniture from specialists in eighteenth-century styles. '1999L' is an attractive mahogany freestanding open bookshelf fitted with two slim lower drawers. *M:* h122 × w92 × d23cm (48 × 36¼ × 9in). *P:* £472 (ex VAT). Also available are a smaller version with single drawer, and four designs of mahogany hanging shelves.

Brett's '1999L'

CANDLELIGHT PRODUCTS LTD

Arched shelving units in sets of three with varying heights, either with woven rattan sides and wooden shelves or with open bentwood and glass shelves. Available in natural finish or sprayed in pastel shades (white, smoke, peppermint, pink, peach or beige). *M:* woven w52, 57, 65 × h185, 198, 208 × d31cm (20½,

Candlelight's bentwood shelving units

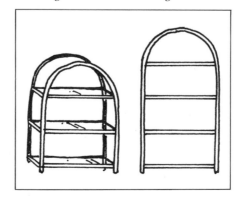

22½, 25½ × 72¾, 78, 82 × 12¼in); bentwood w60, 71, 91 × h111, 150, 188 × d46cm (23½, 28, 35¾ × 43¾, 59, 74 × 18in). *P:* set of three woven units from £150; individual bentwood unit from £120.

CHAINPORT LTD △

CLIFFHANGER, an exceptionally neat shelf support. It is screwed horizontally to the wall and then a standard 15-16mm (⅝in) board is slotted into it. Once the shelf is in place, the support becomes 'invisible' — no brackets, no uprights. CLIFFHANGER is surprisingly strong, and can cope easily with all normal domestic uses. Made of extruded aluminium, it is available in silver, white or brown finish. It's also ideal for displays and hanging signs. *M:* w24, 36 or 48in (61, 91.5 or 122cm). *P:* from £5.49 with screws, wall plugs and plastic end caps.

R J CHELSOM & CO LTD

BAMBOO étagère or bookcase with frame in polished brass or ivory lacquered steel

Chelsom's BAMBOO étagère

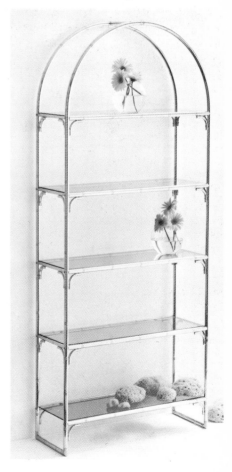

FURNITURE

moulded and shaped in a curve to imitate bamboo. The piece has five smoked glass display shelves. *M:* w33 × d13 × h78in (84 × 33 × 198cm). *P:* £219. Chelsom do a similar étagère in the EMPEROR collection with frame lacquered in cream or rich vintage burgundy with polished brass corner pieces and feet. Both ranges also include trolleys, occasional tables and dining suites.

CONFETTI

BOSTON shelf unit, part of a colour-co-ordinated furniture system that also includes dining suites and occasional tables (see separate entries). Shelves of 1in (2.4cm) thick birch ply, coated in heavy duty laminate, rest on lacquered tubular metal supports. Shelves come in white, black, dove grey, pale blue, red or yellow with profile edges in grey, pink, pale blue or natural; tubular supports can be chrome or lacquered in the same colours as the shelves. Select matching shelves, profile edges and supports, and match them with the rest of the system; or mix — try contrasting profile edges with top surfaces or with frame, or contrasting pieces of furniture. *M:* h60 × w36 × d12in (152.5 × 91.5 × 30.5cm), 14in (35.5cm) between shelves; additional shelves are available. *P:* standard unit £254.

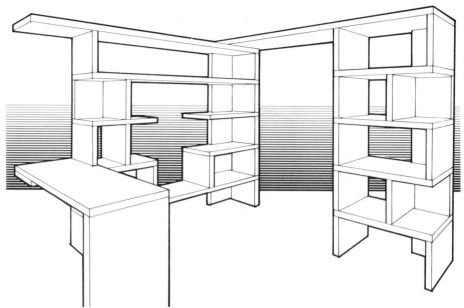

Above: Conran shelving system; right: Cubestore's CUBESHELF △

accommodate music systems, television, and books, and the 'box girder' construction of the shelves permits long unsupported spans of over 200cm (79in). Horizontal shelves are finished in grey laminate with ash lippings, while upright panels are available in grey, red, blue or yellow, so that interesting colour accents may be added. *P:* on application.

CUBESTORE ⚠

CUBESHELF, an adjustable, wall-mounted shelving system. Wall uprights, standard and heavy-duty brackets, shelves and special fittings come in a wide range of lengths, or can be cut to size for awkward places such as alcoves. The uprights project only 10mm (³⁄₈in) from the walls, and have smooth surfaces. Shelves are chipboard, faced in satin white melamine with optional brown edgings. Uprights, brackets and fittings are satin anodized aluminium. Screws, wallplugs, etc are supplied with each order. *M:* uprights 24–72in (61.5–183cm); brackets 6–18in (15–46cm); shelves w36–72in × d7in (91.5–183 × 17.5cm). *P:* uprights from £2.40; shelves from £2.75. STACK is a simple basic shelf system whereby units can be used alone, wall-mounted, stacked or included in a CUBEBOX scheme (see *Storage*). The units are made of white melamine-faced chipboard; the shelves can be adjusted in 32mm (1¼in) increments. Shelves are sold separately, so you need only buy the quantity you require. Doors are an optional extra. Another option is an aluminium strip which can be fitted to the front edge of the shelves so that they can be installed at a slope for displaying leaflets or books. Because

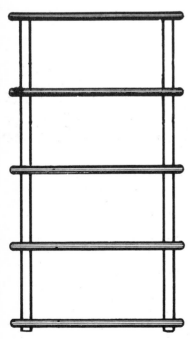

Confetti's BOSTON shelf unit

THE CONRAN SHOP

Flexible stylish shelving at low cost. The dimensions have been carefully calculated to

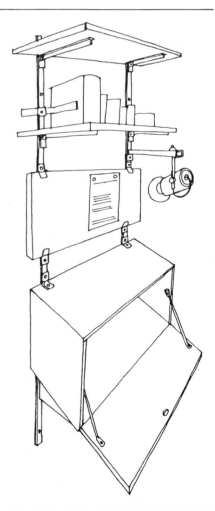

CubeStore's STACK

STACK units have solid back panels that are finished on both sides the system is also suitable for use as a room divider or other double-sided installation. *M:* w22 or 32 × h20 × d6, 10 or 14in (56 or 81.5 × 51 × 15, 25.5 or 35.5cm). *P:* basic unit (w22 × d6in) £6.50; shelves from £1.30 each; doors from £7.50 pair.

CUBIC METRE FURNITURE ⚠
Modern self-assembly metal shelving in lively colours.

Cubic Metre's 'Unit' bookcases △

'Unit' bookcase has simple tubular metal frame in red, green, yellow, white or black with natural coloured plywood or wire shelves. It can be leant against the wall or two units can be joined back to back to form a freestanding shelf or display unit. *M:* w85 × d41 × h195cm (33½ × 16¼ × 76¾in). *P:* £110. 'Brooklyn' is a freestanding wire shelf system, offered in two different shelf sizes in Cubic Metre's primary colour finishes. *M:* shelves w75 × d26cm (29½ × 10¼in), w120 × d31cm (47¼ × 12½in). *P:* shelves £15, £27; brackets £7 each; feet £3.60 each; uprights £4.50 each; bookends £4.20 each.
'Shelf System' is in very strong metal mesh and comprises two upright brackets and shelf. It is offered in two sizes in blue, red, green, yellow, white and black. Units can be joined vertically. *M:* w76 × d31 × h71cm (30 × 12¼ × 28in), w121 × d31 × h71cm (47¾ × 12¼ × 28in). *P:* £52.60, £68.59.

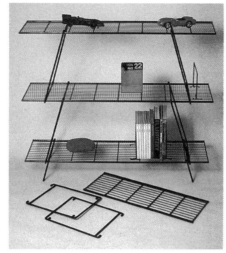

From top: 'Brooklyn' △*, 'Shelf System'* △ *from Cubic Metre*

NICHOLAS ENGERT
Four-shelf acrylic étagère. *M:* w18 × h51 × d18in (46 × 130 × 46cm). *P:* £630 (ex VAT).

⚠ INDICATES ONE OR MORE OF THE PRODUCTS MENTIONED ARE SELECTED BY THE DESIGN CENTRE

Étagère from Engert

ENVIRONMENT COMMUNICATION
From Acerbis International in Italy, MADISON PROGRAM shelving system, square or rectangular modules making shelves, drawers and cupboards. Shelf fronts come in natural wood or shiny lacquered finishes, standing out against the contrastingly painted sides and horizontal surfaces; for a softer look, sides can be fabric-covered. Plate glass inner shelves hook into slots spaced at 3cm (1¼in) intervals in a vertical aluminium rail on the wooden frame. Cupboard doors are available in wood (in same finishes as shelves) or plate glass; and come with special hinges as flap tops for bars or desks. Freestanding double-sided unit is available for centre room displays and can also be fixed from ceiling to floor. There is a facility for concealed lighting within the units, using fluorescent or low-voltage bulbs. *M:* uprights

FURNITURE

h215.3, 250.5, 285.7 × d42.2cm (84¾, 98½, 112½ × 16½in); horizontal tops w34.8, 66.8, 137.2cm (13½, 26¼, 54in); double-sided d46.9cm (18¼in); uprights and tops can also be cut to length as desired. *P:* MADISON 1 unit as illustrated below £4500. See also colour illustration.

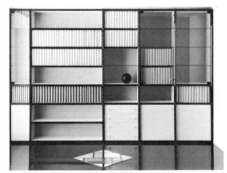

MADISON 1 unit from Environment

ESTIA
Cunningly devised 'F1' tubular-metal-framed shelving system in black, blue, grey, white, red, green or yellow with white melamine shelves. The 'U'-shaped frames in two-shelf 'A' or three-shelf 'B' units can be fitted with castors to make trolleys or joined end-to-end to make a long range of shelving. Shelves, or optional drawers and baskets, can be connected either side of the frames and at varying intervals, so many arrangements are possible. *M:* 'A', 'B' w30¼ × d17 × h24, 36in (77 × 43 × 61, 91.5cm). *P:* £24, £34; trolleys £27.50, £37.50. Estia also make leaning shelves with tubular uprights, and hanging shelves in metal or pine.

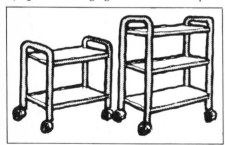

Estia's 'A' and 'B' unit trolleys

HABITAT DESIGNS LTD
Excellent range of basic open shelving. 'Prop' is a clever tech style of shelving cum room divider using two blue metal struts which can be cut to height and screwed into the ceiling for added security. The four shelves are veneered in ash. *M:* w107 × d28 × h248cm (42¼ × 11 × 97¾in). *P:* £109.
TECH system, ideal for storage of technological paraphernalia, comes in black or white tubular metal providing shelf units with or without

Habitat's 'Prop'

castors, trolleys, closed units (with black-ash veneered sides) for stereos, even a computer desk unit (see *Desks*). 'Tech Tower' has tall tube frame and four strong metal shelves; the middle two shelves are adjustable. It comes in red too. *M:* w66 × d38 × h154cm (26 × 15 × 60½in). *P:* £62.50. See *Upholstered furniture* for illustration.
'Faro' strikingly contrasts metal shelves in gloss white or matt black (or both) with natural-ash veneered uprights. Elements are supplied separately and can be assembled at home in many arrangements. *M:* uprights h83 or 188 × d33cm (32¾ or 74 × 12½in); shelves w68 × d33cm (26¾ × 12½in); wooden plinth h8 (12½in). *P:* uprights £14.50, £27.50; shelves £14 pair; plinth £8.95.
Other simple and economical Habitat shelving comes in solid pine, plain white melamine, beech (with a ladder-like folding frame), white melamine with beech edging, or more sombre black ash veneer.

M & I J HARRISON
Radiator shelves to match the whole range of furniture and fittings offered by this firm. To prevent warping they are made from 18mm ply

veneered in natural, medium or antiqued pine, red, brown or golden mahogany, or medium, dark, white or magnolia oak. The edges are lipped in solid timber. *M:* max w96 × d4–12in (244 × 10–30.5cm). *P:* £2.89–£5.20 per 12in (ex VAT).

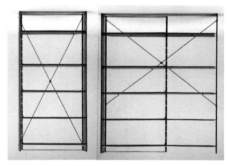

Radiator shelves from M & I J Harrison

IDEAS FOR LIVING
Simple shelving from Italy.
From Pallucco comes 'Fra' Dolcino' extensible library. It consists of two vertical frames with a

Below: 'Fra' Dolcino'; bottom: 'Vertica'. Both from Ideas for Living

cross-shaped brace that is hinged to the base of the frames but attached to rails higher up — as the frames are extended the brace lowers and widens progressively. The four shelves consist of two telescopic tops, one sliding upon the other when not extended. *M:* w100–180 × d33.6 × h200cm (39¼–70¾ × 13¼ × 78¾in). *P:* on application.

Seccose make a number of strong, modern shelving units in boldly coloured metal. Among them is the VERTICA metal bookcase, in white, black, red, grey or yellow. The bookcases are available in a number of heights and widths, with options of bookends in the form of a curved black metal strip, inclined wire racks for display, hanging cabinets with sliding glass doors, and screens to convert it into a cupboard; stop-book rods can also be supplied. *M:* 'Vertica H 73' w60, 80 × d35 × h73cm (23½, 31½ × 13¾ × 28¾in); 'Vertica H 93' w60, 80 × d35 × h93cm (23½, 31½ × 13¾ × 36½in); elements also available separately in other sizes, max h223cm (87¾in). *P:* 'Vertica H 73' £78.75, £85; 'Vertica H 93' £82.50, £87.50.

LEIDA SYSTEMS LTD

Strong, wall-mounted '6/700' hardwood shelf support system, in Leida's 500 SERIES. Can be used to support any normal type of shelving. A steel clip locks together upright bars and brackets, enabling brackets to be adjusted at 7cm (2¾in) intervals. Uprights and wedge-shaped brackets come in ramin, Brazilian mahogany and African walnut with high-quality sanded finish ideal for paint, stain, varnish or wax. *M:* upright h35–105cm (13¾–41¾in); bracket d14.5–28cm (5¾–11in). *P:* upright from £1.17; brackets from £2.47 pair.

Leida's '6/700' shelf supports

NICHOLL & WOOD LTD

Functional, Meccano-like ZAMBA steel shelving for homes, workshops or garages. Pre-packed units come in two sizes: 'Continental 4' with four steel shelves and 'Standard 6' with six shelves. Both are available in brown and beige or black and orange. *M:* 'Continental 4' w12, 31½ × h65in (30, 80 × 165cm); 'Standard

6' w12, 31½ × h73in (30, 80 × 185.5cm). *P:* 'Continental 4' £13.99; 'Standard 6' £17.99. Even simpler are 'Easily Assembled' units consisting of two steel 'ladders' with shelves resting on the 'rungs'.

ONE OFF LTD

Versatile rigid wire mesh shelving system using tubular-steel uprights and cast-iron clamps finished in zinc or any colour of epoxy. Shelves are available in four different lengths. Uprights are cut to the required height. *M:* shelves w25–57 × d12in (63.5–145 × 30.5cm); uprights max h108in (274.5cm). *P:* shelves £18.65–£32.99 each; uprights £10.50–£19.50 each.

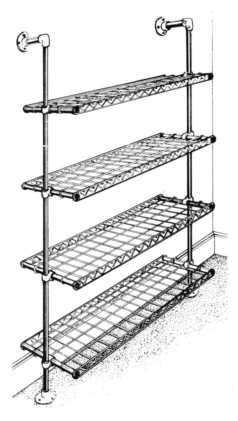
One Off's wire mesh shelving

PIRA

Simple bookcase that can be folded away for moving or storage, part of the functional PLIAVIVA range (see also *Desks, Dining suites*). 'BL4' is multicoloured with black frame and cross-pieces and two blue, two yellow shelves, all in ash. Other versions come in plain natural or ebonized ash or in natural ash with black or white melamine surfaces. *M:* w172 × h172 × d37cm (67¾ × 67¾ × 14½in). *P:* £260.

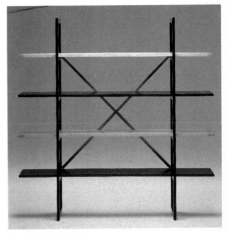
Pira's PLIAVIVA bookcase

TITCHMARSH & GOODWIN

Individually handmade reproduction furniture from an exemplary firm of cabinet-makers. Mahogany display cabinet 'RL21773' has 'Chinese Chippendale' glazing bars and carved cornice. The doors are fastened with twin locks. *M:* w38 × h17½ × h72in (96.5 × 44.5 × 183cm). *P:* from £3075.

Titchmarsh & Goodwin's 'RL21773'

FURNITURE

VERARDO

Glamorous lacquered furniture from Italy. Heberard's ZEUS range in black, white or grey lacquer includes a versatile collection of storage and shelving elements. The bookcase featured combines three shelving units with a plinth storage unit containing four shallow and two deep drawers. *M:* w190 × d63 × h208cm (74¾ × 24¾ × 82in). *P:* £1250. See *Storage.*

Verardo's ZEUS bookcase by Heberard

STORAGE

ARC LINEA (UK) LTD
Very adaptable PUNTO & LINEA wall or free-standing partition and storage system, smoothly styled in birch, white lacquer, or an eye-catching combination of white lacquer

Arc Linea's PUNTO & LINEA

with bright red and yellow drawer and door fronts. The system includes shelves, cupboards (with glass or wooden fronts), wardrobe units, partition shelf and storage units, tip-up writing desks, tables, even tip-up divan beds. Equally suitable for living room, bedroom or kitchen, the system is designed to give a co-ordinated look throughout a whole flat or house. *M:* standard door 48, 64, 80, 128, 144, 208 and 256cm (19, 25¼, 31½, 50½, 56¾, 82, and 100¾in). *P:* on application.

ARCHITECTURAL COMPONENTS LTD
Hand-painted Tyrolean furniture made from pine finished in antique green or antique rose. Voglauer's ANNO 1800 range includes a num-

'EKAS' and other pieces from Architectural Components' ANNO 1800

ber of storage items — wardrobe with drinks cabinet inside, chest of drawers, dresser, sideboard, corner cupboard and corner unit — plus other pieces such as chairs and stools, a table and and even an umbrella stand. Most pieces have scalloped pediments and plinths, panels painted with roses in urns or similar floral motifs, and other strips of decoration and medallions. 'EKAS' corner unit has closed compartments top and bottom, with drawers and shelves in between. *M:* h185 × w84 (72¾ × 33in). *P:* £710.

BAKER, KNAPP & TUBBS LTD
Beautiful reproduction furniture in English and continental styles.

A particularly fine example from the CONTINENTAL collection is '4102' chest of drawers in maple solids and white ash burr veneer with a generous black and gold marble top. The three drawers are fitted with solid brass lion pulls. *M:* w50½ × d20¼ × h35¼ (128.5 × 51.5 × 89.5cm). *P:* £2094.

Baker, Knapp & Tubbs's '4102'

In the same range there's '4231', a capacious Louis XVI buffet in maple with French walnut veneer and solid brass handles and decoration. *M:* w64 × d19 × h32in (162.5 × 48.5 × 81.5cm). *P:* £1815.

Baker, Knapp & Tubbs's '4231'

BATH CABINET MAKERS

Large storage cabinets for dining or living rooms, made in good quality woods and combining cupboards, shelving and drop-flap drinks cabinets. GEORGETOWN, in light or dark mahogany, offers eight cabinets with different combinations of drawers, shelving, cupboards and glazed display areas. Concealed lighting can be fitted. An octagonal dropleaf table and centre-leaf dining table, plus side and armchairs, are made to match. *M:* cabinet 'GEO 9656' w75 × d18 × h74in (190.5 × 45.5 × 188cm). *P:* £990. Bath make three other collections, all including matching dining suites. Notable among them is MING, which follows the fashion for lighter woods with a painted yellow finish that allows the wood grain to show through.

Behr's HEADLINE

GEORGETOWN from Bath Cabinet Makers

BEHR FURNITURE

Stunning system furniture for storage and much more, designed for a modern lifestyle. In the brilliantly simple HEADLINE system, thin metal columns replace conventional solid uprights and act as axes for pivoting shelves, clothes rails, even table tops. Elements can be manoeuvred out for use then pushed back to the wall or concealed behind folding doors. Units have been designed with television and audio equipment in mind, with deep shelves, space behind for wiring, cut-out panels for speakers. System includes wardrobes, drawers, shelving, cabinets and sideboards, plus tables and other furniture for complete continuity; and Behr can provide anything else to individual requirements. Made from ash, the system comes in 14 different finishes: natural, pigmented, brown and black ash, and lacquered grey, Sahara, natural (off-) white,

white, black, dark blue, pigeon blue, pink, yellow and rusty red. *M:* standard module h213, 110.5, 72.1, 33.8cm (83¾, 43½, 28¼, 13½in) w50, 100cm (19¾, 39¼in). *P:* on application. Equally functional and all-inclusive is SWINGFORM. Cupboards and shelving can be hidden behind elegant wooden swing doors with smooth or corrugated panels and round inset handles; the doors open right back to give access to every corner. Cabinets provide ideal storage for bars and music centres — small pull-out drawers hold audio and video cassettes, and units can be planned to house speakers for optimum performance. All are made to measure in natural light, havana or black oak, cherrywood or mahogany, or lacquered white or brown. Other options include clear or

Behr's SWINGFORM

SWINGFORM hi-fi storage from Behr

smoked glass, full mirror or fabric-covered doors. *M:* standard wall unit h258.8, 235.5 (101¾, 92¾in). *P:* on application.

ARTHUR BRETT & SONS LTD

Fine reproduction English furniture from well established firm of cabinet-makers. Impressive range includes magnificent secretaires and bureau bookcases, tallboys, corner cabinets and cupboards, plus classic chests of drawers, campaign chests, cabinets and commodes and, for the dining room, serving cabinets and sideboards fitted with cutlery trays.

PRICES AND INFORMATION WERE CORRECT AT THE TIME OF GOING TO PRESS

FURNITURE

'2104' mahogany inlaid bookcase has been adapted from an eighteenth-century design to the smaller dimensions practical for most modern homes. It is constructed from finest selected mahogany and mahogany veneers, and inlaid with satinwood. *M:* w112 × d47 × h221cm (44 × 18½ × 87in). *P:* £2712 (ex VAT).

Brett's '2104'

COLOURFLAIR

From the DECORATIVE COLLECTION, an attractive sideboard in a Chinese-influenced style. Part of an extensive collection (see also *Tables, occasional*) it comes in polished wood or 22 different colours, with contrast line, feather finish or special colours to order. Two-three- and four-door models are available. *M:* four-door w183 × d50 × h76cm (72 × 30 × 19¾in). *P:* £1285; contrast line £26.70; feather finish 7½% extra; special colours 10% extra.

CONFETTI

Smart, modern MANHATTAN cabinet to match dining suite and coffee table in this grid-patterned furniture. Tall and low rectangular cabinets are available with metal sides perforated with square holes, lacquered wooden

Sideboard from Colourflair's DECORATIVE COLLECTION

top and base, grid-printed wooden back, and doors and shelves in thick clear glass with black or white grid. Available in black, white, dove grey, red, powder blue or yellow. *M:* w48 × d15 × h29 or 60in (122 × 38 × 73.5 or 152.5cm). *P:* £480, £580.

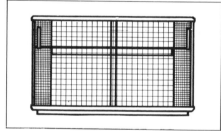

Confetti's MANHATTAN

CUBESTORE ⚠

Inexpensive storage systems based on cube modules. The simplest, CUBEKIT, has a special joint that allows you to add one cube to the next with shared sides; to the basic open cube can be added doors, shelves, drawers, wine rack/pigeon-hole compartments etc. Cubes can face in any direction so large display units, bed bases, room dividers, coffee tables etc can be assembled. The cubes come in plain chipboard (for painting, varnishing or colour staining) or with white or dark brown melamine-faced door and drawer fronts, panels and edges. Because all parts are interchangeable, brown doors can be combined with white cubes or white drawers with self-painted colours. *M:* module w15 × d15 × h15in (38 × 38 × 38cm). *P:* white basic cube £7.80; shelf £1.15; brown cube £8.20; brown shelf £1.25.
A similar but more extensive system is CUBEBOX. Some of the units are already double-sized, and there is even a wardrobe unit. Units can be used alone or stacked together, using special plugs, in any combination to make lar-

Cubestore's CUBEKIT △

ger arrangements. Freestanding or wall-mounted, the range includes vertical and horizontal partitions, two- and three- drawer units, cupboards and wardrobes. Units are made from all-white melamine-faced panels; door and drawer fronts are available in white or dark brown melamine. The standard units can be modified using the range of fittings which includes stays, plinths, castors, locks, doors, shelves, desk-tops, and wine-rack compartments. *M:* module w16 × d16 × h16in (40.5 × 40.5 × 40.5cm). *P:* open 16in cube £13.95; three-drawer unit (double module) £32.75.
CUBEBOX 'Super' has standard finger-holes replaced by a choice of coloured handles (red, blue, yellow, green, black, white, grey, brown and beige.) The units come edged in the same choice of colours, and handles can either match or contrast. *P:* handles 50p each.

Cubestore's CUBEBOX

CUBIC METRE FURNITURE ▲
'The Batman', a portable wardrobe alternative. It has a dark blue metal frame, yellow coat-hanger accessories and blue canvas storage compartments. *M:* w120 × d55 × h165cm (47½ × 21¾ × 65in). *P:* £250.

Cubic Metre's 'Batman' △

DESIGN FURNITURE
SIERRA storage cabinets and bench units, simply styled in Rio or Santos rosewood or black, white or natural ash.
Storage cabinets come in seven different combinations of shelves, drawers and cupboards. 'SRT 036' drinks cabinet has two-door upper cupboard with mirrored back and two glass shelves, two central drawers, and two-door lower cupboard with two wooden shelves; it has an interior light. *M:* w91 × d37 × h160cm (35¾ × 14½ × 63in). *P:* (ash) £540.
Each of the four bench units comprises a large two-drawer unit plus up to four smaller additional units; these can be fitted with one deep drawer (with optional internal fittings for

Design Furniture's 'SRT 036' and bench units

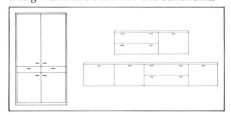

home filing or record storage) or two drawers (with optional video recorder storage fittings). *M:* all d50 × h41cm (19¾ × 16¼in), two-drawer unit w80cm (31½in), additional unit w55cm (21¾in). *P:* (Rio rosewood) 'SRB 060' (two units) £515; 'SRB 062' (four units) £895.

DESIGN WORKSHOP
'THF' hi-fi cabinet with gleaming frame in satin or polished aluminium, and top and compartments in ash, sycamore, Indian rosewood or wenge. It provides storage for records and cassettes, with additional space for magazines at the rear, and runs on castors for easy access. *M:* w90 × d42 × h57cm (35½ × 16½ × 22½in). *P:* £716 (ex VAT). Similar conventional two-door cabinets are available with leather-covered doors and with outer shell either aluminium or wood veneer. The cabinets are part of the TOMMASO system (see also *Desks, Dining suites, Tables, occasional, Upholstered furniture*).

DEVALAKE LTD
Huge range of reproduction furniture that includes both conventional pieces and pieces that have been modified to meet modern requirements. A tallboy unit in mahogany or yew finish looks quite traditional when closed but the top lifts and doors open to reveal an area for a hi-fi system and drawers for cassette tapes, and below is a compartment for record storage. *M:* w63 × d44 × h134cm (24¾ × 17¼ × 52¾in). *P:* mahogany £256, yew £279. Other chests and cabinets discreetly house videos, televisions and records.
There's a large range of glass-fronted and open display cabinets, including a carved corner cupboard in solid oak with two open upper display shelves framed by carvings, and below a panelled cupboard door with inset carving. *M:* w71 × d41 × h188cm (28 × 16¼ × 74in). *P:* on application.

From left: Devalake's tallboy hi-fi unit and carved corner cupboard

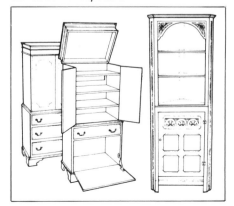

Other storage items include solid oak Welsh dresser, sideboard and rug chest, plus chests of drawers and sideboards in flat and serpentine styles with mahogany or yew finish.

MARTIN J DODGE
Exceptionally good range of solid mahogany reproduction English furniture particularly notable for fine carving and marquetry. 'Chippendale' double breakfront bookcase 'H82' is of magnificent quality. Made from Cuban mahogany, it has carved plinth, waist and cornice mouldings and a wonderful broken-arch fretted swan's neck pediment. There are cupboards and drawers in the base and adjustable glass or wood shelving in the glazed upper section. *M:* w100 × d18 × h108in

From top: Martin J Dodge's 'H80', 'H82'

PRICES AND INFORMATION WERE CORRECT AT THE TIME OF GOING TO PRESS

FURNITURE

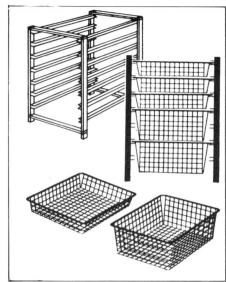

Elfa's storage baskets and racks

(254 × 45.5 × 274.5cm). *P:* £10262.
Classic 'H80' breakfront bookcase has a drawer above each of the four shelved cupboards in the base and a glazed upper section. *M:* w80 × d16 × h90in (203 × 40.5 × 228.5cm). *P:* £4020. Martin Dodge also make a wide variety of sideboards, chests of drawers, commodes and cabinets.

DUX INTERIORS LTD

AVANTI storage system with a multitude of elements to combine smoothly and strongly together. It comes in beech, mahogany or light oak veneer and lacquered grey, white, black, red, blue, amber and green, as well as an aluminium finish; handles are satinized aluminium. Shelves and cupboards can be glass-fronted, with or without frames, and there are excellent interior fittings for desks and hi-fi equipment. Tall cupboards and deep as well as shallow drawers make this range suitable for luxury bedrooms as well as living rooms and studies. *M:* small base unit w56 × d42 × h64cm (22 × 16½ × 25in). *P:* £220–£325.

PRICES AND INFORMATION WERE CORRECT AT THE TIME OF GOING TO PRESS

AVANTI storage units with desk fittings, from Dux

ELFA

Self-assembly modular storage system. Metal frames (in three widths) have four, seven or ten runners from which wire baskets or racks are suspended. Baskets and racks come in six different sizes, and the frames can be cut to size, so the units can be fitted anywhere, by themselves or built into existing cupboards. Runners can also be bought separately and fixed beneath a shelf to hold a single basket. Accessories include castors, label holders and hanging-rail brackets. Standard colour is white but other colours are available. *M:* seven-runner unit w35, 45, 55 × d54 × h74cm (13¾, 17¾, 21¾ × 21¼ × 29¼in). *P:* £29–£35 complete with baskets.

MARY FOX LINTON LTD

Stunningly simple and finely made chest on a stand. The clear perspex up-and-over base is as self-effacing as possible beneath the stark elegance of the chest itself, which is silver gilt with a navy lacquer interior. The set is available to order. *M:* w76 × d51 × h186cm (30 × 20 × 73¼in). *P:* £2500 (ex VAT).

Mary Fox Linton's silver-gilt chest

THE THOMAS GLENISTER COMPANY

Reproductions of classic English styles by an old-established firm freely employing modern machinery and techniques. Most models are finished in medium mahogany colour but they can also be polished to customer's required colour and distressed. Among a small range of sideboards, cupboards etc is the '5286' glazed hanging corner cabinet with swan's-neck pediment. *M:* w22 × d12 × h36in (56 × 30.5 × 91.5cm). *P:* £225.

Glenister's '5286'

GOSTIN OF LIVERPOOL

Early eighteenth-century-style oak dresser base 'GA3', suitable as a small buffet or serving piece, from traditional cabinet-makers and marquetry specialists. All pieces, period designs in oak, walnut and mahogany, are hand-coloured and waxed, and have solid brass fittings. *M:* w142 × d41 × h79cm (54 × 16 × 31in). *P:* £660.

Gostin's 'GA3'

GRANGE

Several stunning ranges of furniture produced by this French firm. They include designs inspired by nineteenth-century French and Irish styles but intended to fit as well into modern eclectic rooms as into period ones.

The simple elegant lines fashionable in post-Napoleonic France can be seen in the CALECHE range. The chest of drawers '3M600' conceals a slim fourth drawer in its doucine ('S'-section) moulding. The tall dresser 'IN605' has the same unostentatious good looks while providing generous storage with its five cupboards, four drawers and three open shelves. Like all the range, both pieces are veneered in cherrywood with a satin or decorator (darker) finish. *M:* chest w119 × d52 × h48cm (46¾ × 20½ × 19in), dresser w189 × d50 × h213cm (74½ × 19¾ × 83¾in). *P:* on application.

From top: Grange's 'IN605', '3M600'

The design of the IRLANDE range is derived from Irish rural models and all pieces are veneered in waxed cypress pine. The four-drawer chest '3M770' characteristically combines robust function with refined detail. *M:*

Grange's '3M770'

w91 × d47 × h86cm (35¾ × 18½ × 33¾in). *P:* on application.

The Grange collections also include bookcases, sideboards, tallboys and display cabinets.

HABITAT DESIGNS LTD

Some of the best design ideas for practical and reasonably priced storage.

For the home or office there is 'Alfa' in pale grey lacquer trimmed with natural birch. Lacquered doors or drawers with white handles can be fitted to the shelves and uprights as needed. *M:* large shelf unit with eight sections w75 × d42 × h149cm (29½ × 16½ × 58¾in); set of three drawers w37 × d33 × h35cm (14½ × 13 × 13¾in). *P:* £99; £39.

In the QUAKER range of more traditional furniture made from solid and veneer oak and ash is a five-drawer chest suitable for living room or bedroom. *M:* w114 × d45 × h84cm (45 × 17¾ × 33in). *P:* £169. Range includes two other base units, three top units, a six-drawer chest, blanket box, bedside cabinet and wardrobe.

Habitat's QUAKER chest of drawers

FURNITURE

There's also a cube storage system in black, white and red plastic, ideal for children's rooms, another cube storage system in pine veneer, and — if function's the object — a system of wire baskets on a metal trolley frame.

HAMLET
Pleasant solid-pine dressers, cupboards, chests and book and video units in two ranges, with fielded panel or 'cottage-style' doors. Corner dresser 'CDB/F+CDT/F' has a cupboard base with fielded panel door and an open top with scallop surround and two shelves. *M:* w76 × d51 × h194.5cm (30 × 20 × 76½in). *P:* £237. Hamlet sell their furniture by mail order and prices include delivery in the UK.

M & I J HARRISON
Reproduction Victorian country furniture in pine. 'Albert' dresser has three drawers and cupboards in the base and two small cupboards with shelves between in the upper part. *M:* w55½ × d19 × h71in (141 × 49.5 × 180cm). *P:* £410 (ex VAT). See *Tables, dining* for illustration.

HYPERION WALL FURNITURE
Versatile unit system of cabinets, shelving and wall panels assembled to order or made to measure, with incorporation of hi-fi systems a

Habitat's 'Alfa'

Hyperion's wall units with swivelling television shelf

speciality. Five different wood finishes are available: teak, walnut, oak, mahogany and rosewood. A typical arrangement could include a corner unit (made to order) and an extending swivel shelf for a television. Lighting can be fitted under shelves or in cabinets. *M:* single cabinet w16¾ × d9, 14, 18 × h14–73in (42.5 × 23, 35.5, 45.5 × 35.5–185.5cm). *P:* on application.

IDEAS FOR LIVING
From Kartell of Italy, functional brightly coloured stacking drawers in tough plastic. The square drawers are simply stacked — there's no need for screws or tools — and the unit can be fitted with castors. Each unit has a separate top. Drawers can be stacked to open in any direction; and units can be used singly as desk pedestals (see *Desks*) or in groups to support, perhaps, a kitchen worktop. Available in brown, green, white, red, black and yellow. *M:* drawers w42 × d42 × h14cm (16½ × 16½ × 5½in), lid h2.5cm (1in). *P:* single drawer £13.90; three-drawer unit £52.85; five-drawer unit £80.65. Kartell also make an ingenious 'Revolving Tower' of stacking open elements, with castor base, ideal for books.

Drawers units from Ideas for Living

INTERLÜBKE
Elegant modular storage systems from these pioneers in modern furnishing.
STUDIMO PLUS has a multiplicity of components for the whole house, with many depths, widths and heights to choose from, and comes in seven finishes — white-grey or Jersey cream lacquer, natural or black stained ash, brown-stained oak, cherrywood and mahogany. Slide-away cupboard doors can have matching finishes or they can be glass, mirrored or

Environment Communication's MADISON PROGRAM shelving by Acerbis

Legs and Tops to Mix or Match.

estia

ESTIA DESIGNS LTD   5-7 TOTTENHAM STREET   LONDON W1   01 636 5957

Interlübke's STUDIMO PLUS

Kennedy's '2034'

OAK ranges.
ENGLISH OAK sideboard '2034' has four doors with carved fielded panels and four drawers with ornate brass handles. *M:* w80 × d19 × h32in (203 × 49.5 × 81.5cm). *P:* on application.

MILITARY Wellington chest '1415' in mahogany veneer has inset brass handles like the other pieces in this particularly attractive range, which is also available in yew veneer. *M:* w28 × d18 × h53in (71 × 45.5 × 134.5cm). *P:* on application.

Kennedy's '1415'

fabric-covered. Components include television and hi-fi storage, a fold-away table, and numerous accessories. *M:* module d24, 36, 49, 60, 63cm (9½, 14¼, 19¼, 23½, 24¾in). *P:* on application. See also *Bedrooms, furniture*.
Offshoots from STUDIMO PLUS are STUDIMO PROFIL units with projecting side panels and STUDIMO SOLITAR freestanding units, both available in the same finishes as the main range; and there are several other equally stylish ranges including the original STORAGE WALL living-room units concealing sophisticated design elements within classically simple white-grey lacquer shelving, cupboards and drawers.

JAYCEE

Attractive chest of drawers 'B541' in the VICTORIAN collection. Like the other pieces in this extensive range, the chest is made from Scandinavian pine with gold, mellow or antique finish, polished and finished by hand, and is decorated with a hand-carved acanthus motif. *M:* w104 × d46 × h83.5cm (41 × 18 × 32¾in). *P:* £394.
Jaycee also make a variety of large storage units, bars and dressers in oak, hand-carved in a Tudor-influenced style.

Jaycee's 'B541'

R E H KENNEDY LTD

A large collection of top-quality reproduction sideboards, dressers, cabinets, chests of drawers etc in ENGLISH GEORGIAN mahogany, MILITARY mahogany or yew, and ENGLISH

PRICES AND INFORMATION WERE CORRECT AT THE TIME OF GOING TO PRESS

FURNITURE

LEMA

Superbly flexible wooden storage systems. Open shelves, closed units with solid, louvered or glass doors, partition columns — deep, double-sided shelving designed to divide, say, living from dining areas — and wall partitions, can be designed and made up in various woods including birch, walnut, oak and black-tinted oak, with natural varnish finishes, glossy or opaque white lacquer or black lacquer, and 'D'-shaped handles in matching woods, aluminium or tortoiseshell. Lema make furniture to match, with an emphasis on compact items such as bunks, slide-out and folding beds and folding tables, all suited to studio living. *M:* to order. *P:* on application.

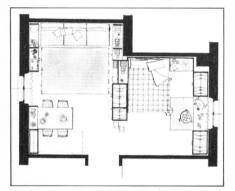

Studio room plan with Lema storage system

JAMES LUPTON & SONS LTD

Oak dressers, sideboards, cabinets and chests in British provincial styles.
The most capacious dresser is '508' in the medium-oak CARDINAL range. It has two central shelves set between cupboards with leaded glass doors, and the base, sold separately as sideboard '507', has four doors and four drawers. *M:* '508' w190 × d46 × h188cm (74¾ × 18 × 74in); '507' w190 × d46 × h87cm

Lupton's '508'

(74¾ × 18 × 34¼in). *P:* '508' £1115; '507' £730. Similar designs are available in the more sophisticated CHATSWORTH range, in oak with a fashionable whitened finish, and in an economy veneered range.

WILLIAM L MACLEAN

Impressive range of storage options from suppliers of well-made period-inspired furniture for the top end of the contract market. The extensive collection of sideboards, cabinets and dressers for the dining room and bookcases for the sitting room offers a choice spanning *faux* bamboo, Chinese, French provincial and Empire styles, all pieces made from kiln-dried beech and available in more than 100 different finishes.
One of the most unusual sideboards is '1–95' in Empire-inspired style with a single, wide upper drawer and two doors below; sides and legs are elegantly reeded. *M:* w98 × d50 × h89cm (38½ × 19¾ × 35in). *P:* from £880.

Maclean's '1-95'

A variety of cabinets includes '2-4009', a French provincial design with two lattice-work upper doors, two plain lower doors, carved detail and long, ornamental hinges and escutcheons. *M:* w110 × d56 × h150cm (43¼ × 22 × 59in). *P:* from £995.
Maclean's also make a number of chests of drawers and a varied range of wardrobes (see *Bedrooms, furniture*).
(All prices ex VAT.)

MEREDEW

Wall units in smart veneers, five ranges that also include dining suites (see separate entry). Top of these ranges is CHARTWELL, finished in crown sapele veneer. Seven full-height cabinets, a sideboard and a hi-fi storage cabinet are available. Breakfront display cabinet 'CM886' has three glass doors and concealed lighting. *M:* w202 × d40 × h174cm (79½

Maclean's '2-4009'

× 15¾ × 68½in). *P:* £649. See *Dining suites* for illustration.
Simpler REMBRANDT sapele-veneered cabinets can be fitted into runs with varying heights. There are three high wall storage and 'home entertainment' units, a high display cabinet with full-length glass doors in arched wood frame, high corner units, a low bookcase, low bureau, low display and television/video cabinets, plus small television/video display and storage units. Bureau 'BK/BM960' has a drop

Meredew's REMBRANDT with 'BK/BM960' bureau

flap revealing pigeon holes and two small drawers, plus two large drawers, a cupboard and an adjustable glass shelf with concealed lighting. *M:* w112.5 × d40 × h126cm (44¼ × 15¾ × 49½in). *P:* £325. The same designs are available in teak veneer in the VICEROY range.

PETER MILES

Excellently made WITNEY tallboy in stained oak, ash or mahogany, designed by Ronald Carter RDI. It has scalloped, solid-timber uprights at each corner, a flyover top, and cupboard doors and drawers with detailed solid-timber surrounds and veneered or solid inset panels. Its six drawers are surmounted by a cupboard with two adjustable shelves, a pull-out, glass-covered half-shelf at serving height, and two 'secret' compartments. *M:* w95 × d53.5 × h179cm (36 × 21 × 70½in). *P:* £1098–£1198. Can be made in other timbers or to other specifications, along with sideboard, cupboard, chest of drawers and bookcase in the same range.

Pira's 'Teseo'

offices. Starting from freestanding white, yellow, red or grey metal frames consisting simply of four uprights with crossbars at top and bottom, it adds three main types of shelving — glass, metal or wire-mesh baskets — strung on steel wires at any height. Extras include lights, sliding partitions and book-holders, tiltable desks and clothes-hanging rails. Stability on uneven surfaces is ensured by adjustable feet. *M:* basic unit w103 × d30 or 45 × h202cm (40½ × 11¾ or 17¾ × 79½in). *P:* on application.

PRETTYGATE TRADERS LTD

MADOCA simple lacquered furniture from Holland. A wide selection of shelving, storage units and occasional pieces come in eight lacquer finishes — grey, white, Alpine white, red, black, blue, beige and yellow. A specialized hi-fi unit has a sliding top shelf for the deck, a

Peter Miles's WITNEY tallboy

PIRA

Modern, lightweight and elegant furniture from Italy.

'Teseo' in the MAGIS range provides a technological solution to the problem of storage in the home as well as in shops, schools and

deep shelf for amplifier, tuner and tape deck, two drawers for cassettes and vertical record storage at the bottom. It can be combined with a two-shelf bookcase. *M:* (both) w136 × d40 × h136cm (53½ × 15¾ × 53½in). *P:* £395.

G T RACKSTRAW

A wide variety of well-made cabinets, bookcases, sideboards and chests of drawers from the largest volume supplier of reproduction cabinet furniture in the UK. Most are made in solid mahogany except for a few designs in solid oak, and all timber is dried to 10% moisture content.

Classic 'M16780' four-door breakfront bookcase in mahogany has a fine curl veneer to the lower doors and adjustable shelves throughout. *M:* w81 × d18 × h82cm (206 × 46 ×

Rackstraw's 'M16780'

Prettygate's MADOCA bookcase and hi-fi unit

FURNITURE

208cm). *P:* £3538–£4306. Other versions of this cabinet are available with yew veneer, different glazing pattern or a decorative pediment.

ROSET (UK) LTD

Sleek modern storage units by a team of European designers.

FIRST range comprises 37 standard units — tall and short, including a tremendous variety of shelving, drawers and cupboards. All have sycamore veneer with polyurethane lacquer surfaces in subtle contrasts: grey sycamore with grey lacquer or light sycamore with beige lacquer. Contrasting dividers are finished in bordeaux, blue or red lacquer. Standard units include '5', a six-drawer chest, '13', a large wall cabinet with deep and shallow shelves, pigeonholes and drawers of varying depths, and distinctive '15' cabinet with two-door cupboard (the doors with glass panels) and shelving above, topped by a semicircular lacquered pediment. *M:* '5' w139.5 × h116cm (55 × 45¾in); '13' w184.5 × h207cm (72½ × 81½in); '15' w95 × h188.5cm (37½ × 74in). *P:* '5' £530–£558; '13' £809–£860; '15' £563–£611. Other elements can be bought individually to make up further storage settings.

Roset's other wall storage ranges include the attractively plain TANA, airy in light ash or austere in ebonized ash.

Left to right, from top: '15', '5' and '13' from Roset's FIRST range

---

STAG

Wall cabinets for the living/dining room in three ranges, veneered in mahogany, oak and teak. OVERTURE range is finished in medium oak with solid oak edgings and solid brass inset handles. It includes three wall units, a sideboard and dresser top, a video cabinet, two bridging units, and tables and chairs (see *Dining suites*). Bookcase unit '840' has a cupboard base and top section with glass doors, sides and shelves and a top light. *M:* w23½ × d16 × h77½in (60 × 40.5 × 197cm). *P:* from £280.

Stag's OVERTURE with '840' bookcase

STUART INTERIORS

Faithful replicas of joined Jacobean cupboards, seventeenth- and eighteenth-century sideboards and dressers, all in oak.

Jacobean 'Livery Cupboard' copied from a sideboard in the possession of the Shakespeare Birth Trust at Stratford-on-Avon, comprises two doors and a potboard beneath. It is hand-carved with a 'lunette' frieze just under the top, and wax-finished to achieve an antique appearance. *M:* w50 × h54in (127 × 137cm). *P:* £1595 (ex VAT).

Stuart's 'Livery Cupboard'

Dresser from Stuart

Replica of late eighteenth-century open high dresser has four drawers in the base and a potboard. The three-shelf rack has a narrow cupboard at each end. *M:* w96 × h84 (244 × 214cm). *P:* £3800 (ex VAT).

WILLIAM TILLMAN

Fine reproduction Sheraton chiffoniers and sideboards in solid mahogany with waxed finish. Breakfront chiffonier 'Z1' has satinwood cross-banded top. *M:* w62 × d18 × h36in (157.5 × 45.5 × 91.5cm). *P:* on application. Any size chiffonier or sideboard can be made to order.

Tillman's 'Zl'

TITCHMARSH & GOODWIN

Individually handmade reproduction furniture from an exemplary firm of cabinet-makers. 'RL22408' dresser is made from their own solid oak with mahogany cross-banding around the doors and drawers in the style of North Country oak furniture during the Regency. Locks and brass escutcheons on all doors and swan-neck drawer handles are also in keeping with

Titchmarsh's 'RL22408'

R TYZACK LTD

Reproduction furniture both in a standard range of eighteenth- and nineteenth-century styles and to order, from a small independent manufacturer. Classically simple low bookcase with mahogany veneer is suitable for home or office. *M:* w48 × d12 × h38in (122 × 30.5 × 96.5cm). *P:* on application.

Tyzack's '2056'

Webber's '416'

gothic carved doors on elaborate brass hinges, and a single drawer above. *M:* w30 × d16½ × h32in (76 × 42 × 81.5cm). *P:* £305; distressed finish extra.

this style. *M:* w54 × d18 × h75in (137 × 45.5 × 190.5cm). *P:* from £1375. Can be supplied with a boarded back.

TOWN & COUNTRY PINE

Three-door sideboard or dresser base '3111' in solid pine coloured to look like old stripped pine, with brass handles. One of a wide range of cupboards, chests and dressers for the living room and bedroom. *M:* w146 × d46.5 × h78cm (57½ × 18¼ × 30¾in). *P:* £395. See back cover for illustration.

TULLEYS OF CHELSEA

A small range of hand-finished reproduction chests, cupboards, bookcases etc in yew or mahogany veneers. Television and video cabinet '871' will accommodate any television up to 26in (66cm) screen and has a false-drawered front which slides away out of sight. *M:* w34 × d20 × h40in (86.5 × 51 × 101.5cm). *P:* from £299. Smaller size available.

Tulleys' '871' television cabinet

VERARDO

Glamorous lacquered furniture from Italy. Heberard's clean-lined ZEUS range includes storage elements that can be put together with glass or wooden doors and shelves as cupboards, wall units and sideboards. The sideboard unit featured has two cupboards, four drawers and a flying top; like the rest of the range, it is available in white, black or grey lacquer. *M:* (excluding top) w190 × d51 × h81cm (74¾ × 20 × 32in). *P:* £630. See also *Shelving*.

Sideboard unit from Verardo's ZEUS range

WEBBER FURNITURE

Oak furniture in traditional rustic styles. CROYDON range includes a number of storage items such as corner cupboards, canopied bar, dressers, bookcases, sideboards and television/video cabinet. All are available in three medium-to-dark oak shades, with optional distressed finish in the 'traditional' shade. Small credence cupboard '416' has two

WOOD BROS FURNITURE LTD

Extensive OLD CHARM range of solid oak furniture. Storage items include sideboards, dressers, cabinets, chests and a court cupboard, plus three richly-carved wall units in Tudor, Elizabethan and turn-of-the-century styles incorporating bookcases, display shelves and cupboards, and drawers. One attractive piece is the '1234' rug chest carved with romanesque arches. Like the other pieces in the range, the rug chest is available with light, medium 'Tudor' or antiqued finish. *M:* w45 × d17½ × h20½in (114.5 × 44.5 × 52cm). *P:* £253–£296.

'1234' from Wood Bros

PRICES AND INFORMATION WERE CORRECT AT THE TIME OF GOING TO PRESS

Devalake's 'Pembroke Table'

mounted on a single pedestal with claw feet. Available in mahogany or yew finish. *M:* w153 × d93 × h77cm (60¼ × 36½ × 30¼in). *P:* mahogany £225, yew £250. Other tables in the range are Regency-style two-pedestal table, also in mahogany or yew finish, and gateleg table and refectory tables in solid oak.

NICHOLAS ENGERT
Acrylic dining-table bases, simply a sheet of thick acrylic in 'V'-shape or extended semicircle. Would complement almost any material on top. *M:* h29in (73.5cm). *P:* on application.

EQUINOX INTERIORS LTD
From a sophisticated range of European furniture, the English designed and extremely versatile 'Compass' folding table. It will seat four or fold in half to create a writing/drawing desk or music rest. Though inexpensive, it is constructed in high quality black or natural ash and finished superbly. *M:* dia 91 × h72cm (35¾

Equinox's 'Compass'

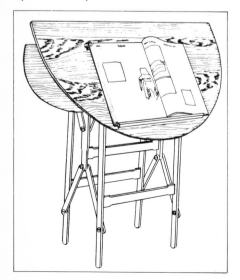

× 28in). *P:* £150.
From Italy comes the 'Flapjack' dining table. Expertly manufactured, the top swivels and opens to twice the folded size. It is available in natural or black stained ash, but other models also come with a black or white melamine top. *M:* (open) w165 × d76 × h71cm (65 × 29¾ × 28in). *P:* £158.

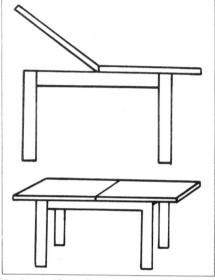

Equinox's 'Flapjack'

ESTIA
Tubular trestles and table legs for your own table top, whatever that may be, in black, blue, grey, white, red, green or yellow. The 'F7' tripod trestle gives more leg room than the usual trestle and comes apart for storage. White or black laminate tops can be supplied. *M:* w16 × d27 × h28in (40.5 × 68.5 × 71cm). *P:* £16 set of two. See *Tables, occasional* for Estia's adjustable-height coffee or dining table.

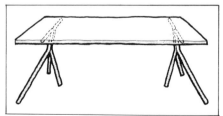

Estia's 'F7' trestles

MARY FOX LINTON LTD
A shimmering, futuristic circular table in silver gilt on two semi-circular clear perspex bases, cleverly designed to seat four people. Like other pieces made to order by this company, it is breathtaking in its simplicity. *M:* dia 137 × h76cm (54 × 30in). *P:* £3000 (ex VAT).

Circular table from Mary Fox Linton

THE THOMAS GLENISTER COMPANY
Reproductions of classic English styles by an old-established firm freely employing modern machinery and techniques. Most models are finished in medium mahogany colour but they can also be polished to customer's required colour and distressed. One of the more uncommon items in the range is the oval-topped 'Sutherland' gateleg table '5370T', with slim turned legs and claw feet. *M:* (extended) w54 × d33 × h29in (137 × 84 × 73.5cm). *P:* from £450. Range also includes oval and rectangular pedestal tables.

Glenister's '5370T'

M & I J HARRISON
Reproduction Victorian country furniture in pine. Tables are available in three standard sizes with natural, medium or antiqued finish. *M:* w48, 60, 72 × d30 × h30in (122, 152.5, 183 × 76 × 76cm). *P:* from £144 (ex VAT).

IDEAS FOR LIVING
Chic Italian furniture that combines simple forms, modern materials and bold colours. 'Achab' extending table by Pallucco has

Ideas for Living's '4300' tables by Kartell

Jaycee's '0261'

Lupton's '527'

wooden structure with supports in turned steel and brass, available in striking colour combinations: natural birchwood with red metal, top with black laminated centre panel and white laminated end panels; natural birchwood with grey metal and grey and white laminated top; black lacquered wood with black metal and birch veneer top; natural birchwood with black metal and white laminated top. *M:* w120–210 × d90 × h75–72cm (47¼–82¾ × 35½ × 29½–28¼in). *P:* £534.30. See colour illustration.

'4300' by Kartell is functional and inexpensive in tough, injection-moulded plastic with anti-scratch paint finish in gleaming yellow, red, green, white, brown and black. The square top is fitted to the round legs by means of conical housings; and top, connecting cones and legs come in different shades of the same colour. *M:* w80 × d80 × h72cm (31½ × 31½ × 28¼in). *P:* £125. Kartell make chairs to match and a number of other tables in the same materials, high, low, rectangular and on pedestals (see *Dining suites*). All the furniture can be used indoors or out, for dining room, canteen, patio or café.

Other tables in this exceptional range include simple rectangular tables by Seccose with met-

al frame (often in bright colours) and a variety of maple, laminate and granite tops, plus unusually constructed tables from Ciatti, both wooden folding tables with parts in different colours and ROLLING tables with high-tech chrome frame, glass or laminate top, and option of castor feet.

JAYCEE

From a wide range of traditional reproduction furniture, '0261' circular extending 'Jacobean' table. Like most other pieces in the TUDOR collection, the table is made from solid oak, partially hand-carved and hand-finished. *M:* (closed) dia 120 × h73cm (47¼ × 28¾in), (extended) w170 × d120 × h73cm (67 × 47¼ × 28¾in). *P:* from £556.

JAMES LUPTON & SONS LTD

Seven solid oak dining tables in two distinct finishes — medium-dark CARDINAL and silver-white CHATSWORTH. '527' twin pedestal table has a rectangular flip top with slightly scalloped corners and bevelled edges. *M:* (extended) w98 × d92 × h74cm (78 × 36¼ × 29¼in). *P:* £720. Lupton's other dining tables

are a circular extending table, round-ended flip-top table, oval dropleaf table, and three refectory and drawleaf designs.

WILLIAM L MACLEAN LTD

From a large range of high quality contract furniture, 12 dining tables, all made from kiln-dried beech and available in more than 100 different finishes.

'26-150' is Regency in inspiration, an elegant oval table with slim, reeded legs. *M:* w175 × d128 × h75cm (69 × 50½ × 29½in). *P:* from £840 (ex VAT).

'26-159' is a modern design with a touch of

Maclean's '26-150'

FURNITURE

Chippendale, its simple lines enlivened by fretwork corner brackets; it is supplied with wood or bronzed glass top. It matches '27-87' console table (see *Tables, occasional*). *M:* w200 × d90 × h75cm (78¾ × 35½ × 29½in). *P:* from £590 (ex VAT).

OMK DESIGN LTD ▲

Sophisticated high-tech look for the familiar design of 'Trestle', suitable as a dining or work table, for domestic or contract use. The tubular-steel frame and legs are finished in matt black or white epoxy, and the top is of clear, tinted or 'Georgian' wire glass. *M:* w168 × d76 × h76cm (66¼ × 30 × 30in). *P:* clear or tinted glass £196, wire glass £308.

OMK's 'Trestle' △

BOB PULLEY ▲

Round-topped 'Shiguchi' table with fascinatingly jointed legs (*shiguchi* being Japanese for 'connecting joint)'. The legs, which can be made from ash, beech or oak, disassemble like a mathematical puzzle. The top can have a matching veneered surface or a grey plastic laminate one. *M:* dia 120 × h72cm (47¼ × 28¼in). *P:* £180.
Bob Pulley designs and manufactures a small range of furniture. His studio also designs prototypes for larger manufacturing companies.

SC PRODUCTS

Stunning dining table from a firm that specialises in 1930s reproductions. 'HT21', first manufactured in 1933, has chromium-plated tubular steel frame with triple tubes forming curved legs and straight stretcher. Top is available in glass, black lacquer or other finishes to order. Comes in three sizes. *M:* w183 or 214 × d92 × h75.5cm (72 or 84¼ × 36¼ × 29¾in) or w244 × d107 × h75.5 (96 × 42¼ × 29¾in). *P:* (lacquer) £2106–£2444.

Refectory table from Stuart Interiors

Bob Pulley's 'Shiguchi' △

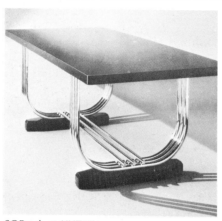

SC Products' 'HT21'

STUART INTERIORS

Majestic replicas of seventeenth-century dining tables in oak and yew, from a company that specializes in Jacobean and Elizabethan woodwork of all kinds. Stuart will make tables to customer's specification and seating requirements and will faithfully reproduce any design from the period. Their standard designs of refectory tables include one with a fluted frieze and carved 'inverted baluster' legs. *M:* w84 × d32 × h29in (213.5 × 81.5 × 73.5cm). *P:* £1310 (ex VAT).

TAG DESIGN PARTNERSHIP

Well-designed modern tables for contract or domestic use. Circular and rectangular dining tables, and also a tea table and desk, all share the same modular construction: tops are finished in grey or black textured plastic laminate with stained beechwood edges in red, yellow or blue, while the tubular steel legs are

Tag's dining and tea tables

finished in grey or black epoxy with coloured feet also in red, yellow or blue. *M:* circular dining table dia 122 × h76.5cm (48 × 30in); rectangular dining table w183 × d91 × h76.5cm (72 × 35¾ × 30in); tea table dia 61 × h33 or 76.5cm (24 × 13 or 30in). *P:* circular dining table £247.04; rectangular dining table £180.39; tea tables £93.69.

TITCHMARSH & GOODWIN

Reproduction furniture from an exemplary firm of cabinet-makers. The entire range of oak furniture is handmade from their own air-dried (kiln-finished) timber and individually polished and distressed to an antique finish. 'RL42' gateleg table has turned legs and a central drawer. *M:* w66 × d48 × h29½in (167.5 × 122 × 75cm). *P:* from £845. Various other versions available. There is also a large range of mahogany and yew furniture in late eighteenth-century styles made to the same high standard.

Titchmarsh & Goodwin's 'RL42'

R TYZACK LTD

Reproduction furniture both in a standard range of eighteenth- and nineteenth-century styles and to order, from a small independent manufacturer. '2043' two-pedestal table has a solid mahogany top with one leaf. *M:* w72–90 × d39 × h30in (183–228.5 × 99 × 76cm). *P:* on application. Also available in standard two-leaf version.

Tyzack's '2043'

PRICES AND INFORMATION WERE CORRECT AT THE TIME OF GOING TO PRESS

WINDMILL FURNITURE ⚓

Simple square-legged wooden dining tables in almost any size, regular shape, and colour. Frames are beech or oak; beech frames have tops veneered in ash, beech, linoleum or laminate, oak frames have oak veneered tops. Windmill will make their design in any other hardwood upon request and will stain tables to any colour (at least 5% surcharge). All tables except those with linoleum or laminate tops are finished with a matt lacquer which Windmill claims will withstand staining and marking even under very heavy usage. There are four standard sizes but others are available to specification. *M:* w75 × d75 × h72cm (29½ × 29½ × 28¼in) to w180 × d90 × h72cm (w70¾ × d35½ × h28½in). *P:* £120–£224.

Dining table from Windmill △

OCCASIONAL TABLES

THE ARCHITECTURAL TRADING COMPANY LTD

Highly original CANTONE corner and console tables, from the Italian company Zanotta. CANTONE's separate elements — semicircular for console table, half that for corner table — can be used individually or piled on top of one another in decreasing sizes to form three tiers.

CANTONE console from Architectural Trading

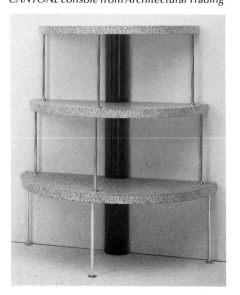

Or they could be used back to back to make a round table. Tops are plywood coated in speckled black and white plastic laminate. Front legs are slim, silvered steel tubes with rubber feet; broad central hind legs are black lacquered wood. *M:* corner element, three sizes, w66–80 × d66–80 × h60cm (26–31½ × 26–31½ × 23½in), three tiers h180cm (70¾in); console element, three sizes w132–160 × d66–80 × h60cm (52–63 × 26–31½ × 23½in), three tiers h180cm (70¾in). *P:* corner elements £289, £319, £348; console elements £467, £530, £580.

BAKER, KNAPP & TUBBS LTD

Extensive range of reproduction furniture of the highest quality, in classic English and continental styles.

One fine example from the CONTINENTAL collection is '4162' round lamp table in maple solids and American walnut veneers with black and gold marble top; the three legs have cast brass collars. *M:* dia 24¾ × h25½in (63 × 65cm). *P:* £714.

From the same collection comes '4234' Louis XVI console in maple with French walnut veneer and cast brass inlay, collar and ferrule. *M:* w42 × d14 × h33in (106.5 × 35.5 × 84cm). *P:* £908. See following page for illustration.

Baker, Knapp & Tubbs's '4162'

ARTHUR BRETT & SONS LTD

Fine reproduction English furniture from a well-established firm of cabinet-makers.

Exquisite '2083' oval inlaid tray on stand in the Sheraton manner features a central oval panel of thuya wood surrounded by a 'fan' of shaded fruitwood; there are additional inlays of satinwood, rosewood and other exotic woods. The tray has a shaped gallery and brass lifting handles, and rests on a matching inlaid satinwood

Baker, Knapp & Tubbs's '4234'

Brett's '1912'

Brett's '2083'

table. The model is also available as an oval coffee table without tray or lifting handles but with the same elaborate inlay and gallery edge. *M:* w97 × d66 × h48cm (38¼ × 26 × 19in). *P:* £2419.

In simpler taste is '1912' mahogany inlaid end table with one drawer and undershelf, attractively cross-banded in thuya wood veneer. *M:* w61 × d44 × h69cm (23½ × 17¼ × 27¼in). *P:* from £566 (ex VAT).
Brett's impressive collection includes many more end, lamp and bedside tables, plus consoles, tripod tables, library, serving and card tables — even, for games fanatics, a beautiful satinwood-inlaid gaming table fitted with backgammon and chess boards. They also make a range of coffee tables so cleverly adapted from traditional designs — butler's trays, coaching, sofa and side tables — that they look almost authentic.

CANDLELIGHT PRODUCTS LTD
Rattan and bentwood tables in natural finish or sprayed in pastel shades — colours include white, smoke, peach, peppermint and beige. FORM coffee table and set of two nesting tables have simple bentwood frame and glass top. The coffee table has a useful slatted undershelf. *M:* coffee table w130 × d61cm (51¼ × 24in); nesting tables w53 × d50 × h50cm (20¾ × 19¾ × 19¾in), w45 × d42 × h46cm (17¾ × 16½ × 18in). *P:* coffee table from £50; two nesting tables from £136.
Candlelight also make an occasional table with a woven rattan top, and a wide range of co-ordinated furniture and accessories, including planters that, with glass tops, make simple and serviceable occasional tables.

R J CHELSOM & CO LTD
Extensive collection of formal lacquered metal or brass and glass furniture.
The LORD collection, designed by the Italian

company Orsenigo, includes rectangular coffee and side tables with solid brass legs, gold-plated galleries and smoked plate glass tops. *M:* coffee table '1111' w36 × d21 × h18in (91.5 × 53.5 × 45.5cm); side table '1111/S' w16 × d16 × h14in (40.5 × 40.5 × 35.5cm). *P:* coffee table £304; side table £84. The rest of the range comprises a console table, round and rectangular trolleys with smoked glass top and undershelf, round and oblong dining tables with smoked glass top, upholstered dining chairs and an elegant mirror.

Chelsom's LORD coffee and side tables

COLOURFLAIR
From the DECORATIVE COLLECTION, Chinese-influenced coffee tables. Matching pieces include console, side and lamp tables (one lamp table with two built-in drawers), stools, dining tables, chairs and sideboards. All are available in polished wood or 22 different coloured finishes, with options of contrast line, feather finish or special colours to order. *M:* '42–42' w107 × d107 × h40cm (42¼ × 42¼ × 15¾in); '48–48' w122 × d122 × h40cm (48 × 48 × 15¾in); '48–22' w120 × d56 × h40cm (47¼ × 22 × 15¾in). *P:* £470.60; £498.80; £437.30; contrast line £17; feather finish 7½% extra; special colours 10% extra.
From the MARBLE COLLECTION comes a

PRICES AND INFORMATION WERE CORRECT AT THE TIME OF GOING TO PRESS

Candlelight's FORM tables

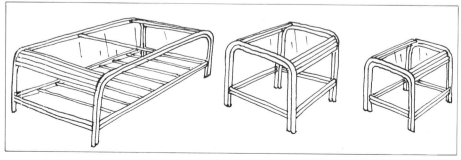

Coffee and side tables from Colourflair's DECORATIVE COLLECTION

clean-lined coffee table with round top on hexagonal base. The collection includes four other coffee table designs, side table designs, console table, circular dining table and two desks. All are available in Travertine, rose aurore, Sicilian, Perlato, Bottocino or creme Valencia marble, or five other stones (including onyx) at a surcharge. Tops for coffee and side tables are available separately. *M:* hexagonal and circular tables, five sizes, dia 90–122cm (35½–48in). *P:* £520.75–£872.90.

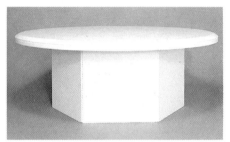

Circular coffee table from Colourflair's MARBLE COLLECTION

CONFETTI

BOSTON coffee tables, square with tubular metal legs or round with pedestal composed of a cluster of three tubular metal supports. Similar nesting tables are available. Tops are birch ply covered in white, black, dove grey, pale blue, red or yellow laminate, with profile edges in grey, pink, pale blue or natural; legs are chrome or lacquered in the same colours as the tops. Try mixing and matching different elements with each other or with other items in the BOSTON furniture system (see *Shelving, Dining suites.*) *M:* square w16 × d16 × h15in (40.5 × 40.5 × 38cm) to w36 × d36 × h15in (91.5 × 91.5 × 38cm); round dia 24, 36 × h15in (61, 91.5 × 38cm). *P:* £65–£128.
Matching other pieces in the MANHATTAN range are coffee tables with broad base of metal perforated with square holes and toughened clear glass top with black or white

⚠ INDICATES ONE OR MORE OF THE PRODUCTS MENTIONED ARE SELECTED BY THE DESIGN CENTRE

printed grid. Colours are black, white, dove grey, red, powder blue and yellow. (See also *Storage, Dining suites.*) *M:* w48 × d33 × h14in (122 × 84 × 35.5cm) or w60 × d36 × h14in (152.5 × 91.5 × 35.5cm). *P:* £120, £160.

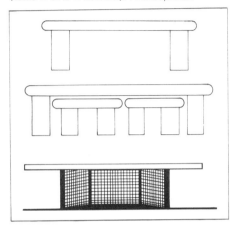

From top: BOSTON coffee table; BOSTON nest; MANHATTAN coffee table. All from Confetti

COTSWOLD FURNITURE COMPANY

All types of occasional tables in reproduction styles, made from solid seasoned timber with a varied selection of wood and painted finishes. Many are designed to match Cotswold's occasional, upholstered and dining chairs (see separate entries).
Among a number of bamboo tables is 'D12' rectangular coffee table with woven cane top. *M:* w37 × d19½ × h18in (94 × 49.5 × 45.5cm). *P:* £112.25.

Cotswold's 'D12'

In contrast is 'A525' Louis XVI circular lamp table. It is particularly attractive in an antique-style white finish, one of the painted finishes at which Cotswold excel. *M:* dia 23½in (60cm). *P:* £109.70.

CUBIC METRE FURNITURE ⚠

Three all-purpose tables with simple, modern designs by Minale, Tattersfield and Partners. 'Split Level' table has a low, semi-circular cof-

Cotswold's 'A525'

Cubic Metre's 'Split Level' table

fee table at one end and a higher, semi-circular, two-person dining table at the other. It could also be a perfect television, hi-fi or telephone table. Structure is in blue, red, green, yellow, white or black metal, with midway open metal tray in same colours or drawer in natural coloured wood; tabletops are glass. *M:* dia 50 × h40/75cm (19¾ × 15¾/29½in). *P:* £250.
'TR' table has black or grey metal frame and top in wired glass or stratified laminate with a different colour on each face. Colour combinations are black/white, red/white, blue/white, green/white. It comes in three sizes as a console, cof-

FURNITURE

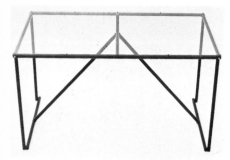

Cubic Metre's 'TR' △

fee or dining table. *M:* console w120 × d40 × h82cm (47¼ × 15¾ × 32¼in); coffee w80 × d80 × h40cm (31½ × 31½ × 15¾in); dining w140 × d70 × h72cm (55 × 27½ × 28¼in). *P:* (excluding glass) console £79.99; coffee £69.99; dining £79.99.
'Cubic Metre Table' has round chrome or coloured legs (various combinations of yellow, blue, green, red, black and white) with rectangular grey or white melamine or tiled top in Cubic Metre's own tiles (see separate entry). It looks striking with a black and white chequerboard top and alternate black and white legs. *M:* dining w130 or 84 × d84 × h75cm (51¼, 33 × 33 × 29½in); coffee w84 × d84 × h42cm (33 × 33 × 16½in). *P:* dining £300, £400; coffee £220–£250.

The 'Cubic Metre Table'

DESIGN WORKSHOP
TOMMASO square-form tables in contrasting materials. 'TT' low table has satin or polished aluminium frame with square top in aluminium, tinted glass, travertine marble or various woods (ash, wenge, sycamore, rosewood). Corners are gently rounded. *M:* w87 × d87 × h35cm (34¼ × 34¼ × 13¾in). *P:* £276–£312 (ex VAT). The same materials and sections are used for desks, storage cabinets, dining suites and upholstered seating throughout the TOMMASO system (see separate entries).

Design Workshop's 'TT'

DEVALAKE LTD
Reproduction occasional tables in familiar English styles.
'Hunt Table' in mahogany or yew finish is oval with two drop leaves and a sturdy rectangular frame. *M:* (extended) w150 × d99 × h50cm (59 × 39 × 19¾in). *P:* mahogany £149, yew £157.

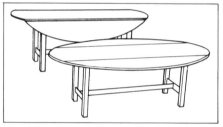

Devalake's 'Hunt Table'

There are two versions of the 'Butler's Tray', one with crossed folding legs, the other with a rectangular base. The oval, detachable top converts to a tray by raising four flaps which then act as handles. It, too, comes in mahogany or yew finish. *M:* cross-leg style w87 × d64 × h50cm (34¼ × 25¼ × 19¾in). *P:* mahogany £117, yew £124.

Devalake's 'Butler's Tray', folding model

MARTIN J DODGE
Exceptionally good range of solid mahogany reproduction English furniture, particularly notable for fine carving and marquetry.

'Adam' serving/hall table 'T42' is raised from six square-sided tapering legs to a fluted frieze, with a rosette carved at the top of each leg. *M:* w66 × d18 × h35in (167.5 × 45.5 × 89cm). *P:* £910.

Martin J Dodge's 'T42'

'T30' is a classic mahogany-inlaid sofa table with rosewood cross-bandings. It has two real and two dummy drawers. *M:* w40 × d20 × h60in (101.5 × 51 × 152.5cm). *P:* £1877. See following page for illustration.
Another classic is 'T22' nest of three tables with tops veneered in curl mahogany with optional double cross-banded border in satinwood and rosewood, and edge beading. *M:* (largest) w19 × d13 × h25in (48.5 × 33 × 63.5cm). *P:* plain £450, cross-banded £550.

Martin J Dodge's 'T22'

△ INDICATES AN ILLUSTRATED PRODUCT SELECTED BY THE DESIGN CENTRE

Martin J Dodge's 'T30'

Environment's 'Sindbad'

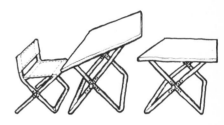

Estia's 'E32'

NICHOLAS ENGERT

Elegant and stylish acrylic furniture.
Typical designs are the superbly simple UP AND OVER tables. There is a coffee table with turned-under feet, a console table and side table, available clear or smoked. *M:* coffee w52 × d30 × h16in (132 × 76 × 40cm); console w42 × d15 × h29in (107 × 38 × 74cm); side w42 × d15 × h15in (107 × 38 × 38cm). *P:* £1008, £588, £453.60.
Low-level, 'Two-tier Pillar Leg Table' in 3cm (1¼in) thick acrylic is another example from the range. *M:* w38 × d26 × h18in (96 × 66 × 45cm). *P:* £984.20.
Range also includes sofa tables, writing desks, stools, hi-fi storage units and many small objects. In some cases acrylic is used in conjunction with other materials, including wood, slate, marble and lacquerwork.

Engert's 'Two-tier Pillar Leg Table'

ENVIRONMENT COMMUNICATION

Oriental-inspired semi-oval 'Sindbad' table from the Italian firm Cassina, designed by Vico Magistretti to be used singly or in a pair. It is made in ash with oak finish, in ebonized ash or in natural walnut. *M:* w185 × d47 × h38cm (72¾ × 18½ × 15in). *P:* from £391.

ESTIA

For studio dwellers, multi-purpose 'E32' table adjustable to coffee or dining table height and tiltable at several angles for use as a drawing

Engert's UP AND OVER tables

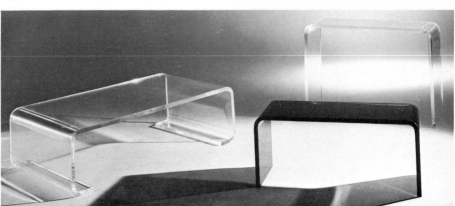

board. The white melamine top rests on a tubular frame in black, blue, grey, white, red, green or yellow. *M:* w48 × d30 × h18–35in (122 × 76 × 45.5–89cm). *P:* £35.

MARY FOX LINTON

Hand-carved marble table-top on square clear perspex base. Except for those with extraordinary sang-froid, this must be more of an art object than a functional coffee table. It is just one of the finely made pieces available to order from this company. *M:* w122 × d44 × h40cm (48 × 17¼ × 15¾in). *P:* £16000 (ex VAT). See following page for illustration.

GIPSY TABLES

Inexpensive, highly popular round tables with cloths. Made entirely from chipboard or with chipboard tops and pine legs, the tables come in several sizes. Cloths can be made from cus-

FURNITURE

Mary Fox Linton's marble coffee table

tomer's own fabric, and can be lined, braided, fringed or ruffled, with padded or glass tops. *M:* standard chipboard dia 18–30 × h24, 30in (45.5–76 × 61, 76cm); chipboard with pine legs dia 18–60 × h24, 30in (45.5–152.5 × 61, 76cm).

Round table from Gipsy

P: (excluding cloths etc) £18, £24–£60. Tables with simple felt cloths can be ordered by mail. Gipsy make various other fabric-covered items such as bed-bases, headboards and stools.

THE THOMAS GLENISTER COMPANY

Reproductions of classic English styles by an old-established firm freely employing modern machinery and techniques. Most models are finished in medium mahogany colour but they can also be polished to customer's required colour and distressed. Among a small range of occasional tables is the 'Chippendale' cluster-leg '5315T'. *M:* w27 × d18 × h18in (68.5 × 45.5 × 45.5cm). *P:* from £140.

Glenister's '5315T'

GRANGE

Several delightful period furniture ranges produced by this French firm. The collection includes oval and scalloped sofa tables, nests, coffee tables, a lovely two-drawer, drop-leaf sewing table and other occasional pieces, variously in walnut, cypress pine and cherry. The CALECHE range of elegant French furniture of the Empire period includes '3P650' cherrywood games or tea table with folding top. It's available in a light satin or dark decorator finish. *M:* (closed) w83 × d56 × h75cm (32¾ × 22 × 29½in), (open) w112 × d83 × h73cm (44 × 32¾ × 28¾in). *P:* £260.

Grange's '3P650'

In the same range is 'B28' tilt-top breakfast table, perfect as a generous side table or in a bow window. It comes in the same finishes. *M:* w103 × d66 × h78cm (40½ × 26 × 30¾in). *P:* £340.

Grange's 'B28'

HABITAT DESIGNS LTD

Lots of good, functional designs in wood, laminate, metal and rattan.
Semi-circular 'Tony' wall table folds down when not in use. It has a white melamine top and beech frame. *M:* w90 × d15 × h46cm (35½ × 6 × 18in). *P:* £19.95.
'Toad' rattan-topped low square table is de-

PRICES AND INFORMATION WERE CORRECT AT THE TIME OF GOING TO PRESS

Top: hall table by Kartell; below: 'Achab' dining table by Pallucco. Both from Ideas for Living

Adeptus for the
Continental look
in furniture

lightful for the garden or can be painted in Habitat's vinyl matt paint to fit in with any interior colour scheme. *M:* w67 × d67 × h37cm (26½ × 26½ × 14½in). *P:* £39.95. See *Chairs* for illustration.

Habitat's 'Tony'

CHARLES HAMMOND

SHAW range of brass furniture designed exclusively for these leading interior designers and wholesale suppliers. Sleekly modern in outline, the solid brass frames can have a highly polished or satin finish with lacquer coating to prevent tarnishing. The range includes glass-topped coffee and end tables, an étagère with glass shelves, and a Travertine-topped console table. *M:* end table w56 × d56 × h40cm (22 × 22 × 15¾in). *P:* on application.

SHAW end table from Charles Hammond

NEIL HENDERSON ⚠

Self-descriptive LINEAR range in sycamore or mahogany with a black line, or in a semi-matt grey lacquered finish with a pink, yellow, red or blue line. Other colours are available to order. The contrasting line gives an elegant art-deco effect to the '3 in 1' nest of tables. There are several different sizes of table in the range, including a console table. *M:* nest w60 × d60 × h41.5cm (23½ × 23½ × 16½in); con-

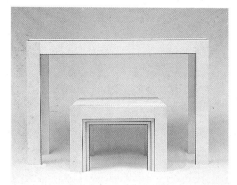

Neil Henderson's LINEAR △ console and nest

sole w120 × d40 × h80cm (47¼ × 15¾ × 31½in). *P:* nest £360–£575; console £266–£480 (ex VAT). Neil Henderson makes other furniture to order.

HOMEWORKS LTD

Exciting collection of imports. Lovely Italian wickerwork coffee-table bases include cotton-reel 'RT206' and cross-shaped 'XT281', both in natural or dark brown finish with glass top. *M:* dia 36 × h16in (91.5 × 40.5cm). *P:* 'RT 206' £303; 'XT 281' £263, glass top extra.

From left: Homeworks' 'RT206' and 'XT281'

IDEAS FOR LIVING

From a superb range of highly contemporary Italian furniture, plastic tables by Kartell.

An elegant hall table comes in black or white plastic; it has a square top and circular low undershelf and is available in three heights. *M:* w42 × d42 × h40, 70, 100cm (16½ × 16½ × 15¾, 27½, 39¼in). *P:* from £94. See colour illustration.

Also in black or white is a nest of three tables, '4905–7', a design selected for the New York Museum of Modern Art. *M:* dia 48 × h32, 37 and 42cm (19 × 12½, 14½ and 16½in). *P:* £59 (ex VAT).

Kartell also make square and rectangular tables in expanded polyurethane with laminated plastic tops, in white, black and grey, available in three heights as dining, side and coffee tables (see *Dining suites*).

⚠ *INDICATES ONE OR MORE OF THE PRODUCTS MENTIONED ARE SELECTED BY THE DESIGN CENTRE*

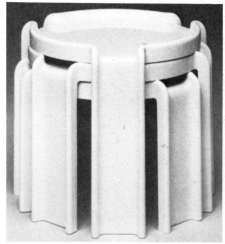

'4905-7' by Kartell from Ideas for Living

JAYCEE

A large range of reproduction and traditionally styled furniture. In the solid oak BROADLEAF TRUST range is 'L754' coffee table with tapering shape and turned legs. It's available in warm Tudor, autumn gold or antique finish. *M:* w122 × d61 × h48cm (48 × 24 × 19in). *P:* £259.

Jaycee's 'L754'

R E H KENNEDY LTD

A large collection of top-quality reproduction tables in ENGLISH GEORGIAN mahogany, MILITARY mahogany and ENGLISH OAK ranges. Octagonal MILITARY library table '1196/H' has tooled hide top and inset brass handles. *M:* w44 × d44 × h29in (112 × 112 × 73.5cm). *P:* on application. See following page for illustration.

JAMES LUPTON & SONS LTD

Traditional-style solid oak occasional tables in 13 different designs including hall, Pembroke and lamp tables, and various nests of tables. Five coffee tables include '580' oval table with glass top and cross-stretchers. There's a matching end table, '581', with glass top and dark-stained woven rattan undershelf. Available with medium-dark CARDINAL finish or

FURNITURE

Kennedy's MILITARY library table

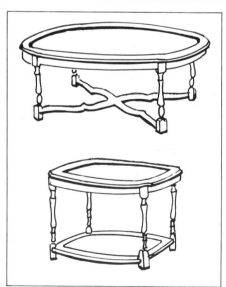

Lupton's '580' and '581'

with lighter silver-white CHATSWORTH finish. *M:* '580' w108 × d69 × h42cm (42½ × 27¼ × 16½in); '581' w69 × d48 × h51cm (27¼ × 19 × 20in). *P:* '580' £239; '581' £195.

WILLIAM L MACLEAN

Well-made, period-inspired furniture designed primarily for the top end of the contract market though it would fit equally well in private homes. Massive range of occasional tables offers a choice of 10 console tables, in-

Maclean's '27-4002'

cluding two in *faux* bamboo and one with a marble top, dozens of coffee and side tables, and seven bedside tables, two of which are designed to be fitted to the wall and are without back legs. Most pieces are available in about 100 different finishes, all timber is kiln-dried and hand-polished, and marble tops are an option with many designs.

Console tables include Georgian '27–4002' with a single drawer and cabriole legs. *M:* w82 × d55 × h77cm (32¼ × 21¾ × 30¼in). *P:* from £420.

Modern by contrast is '27–87' console table, plain in line but with fretwork detailing at the corners. It comes with wood or bronzed glass top. *M:* w115 × d45 × h75cm (45¼ × 17¾ × 29½in). *P:* from £335.

Maclean's '27-87'

Among the side tables there's an attractive French provincial design, '28–4031' with solid beech top, flower motif and cabriole legs. *M:* w58 × d58 × h49cm (22¾ × 22¾ × 19¼in). *P:* from £195.
(All prices ex VAT.)

Maclean's '28-4031'

△ *INDICATES AN ILLUSTRATED PRODUCT SELECTED BY THE DESIGN CENTRE*

PETER MILES △

Handmade tables designed with admirable restraint by Ronald Carter RDI. Traditional timber techniques are used, and a choice of solid English or imported hardwoods, all of which are sealed and then waxed.

WITNEY range includes a severely simple display table with square glass top over a fabric-covered base (customer's own fabric can be used). *M:* w71 × d71 × h47.5cm (28 × 28 × 18¾in). *P:* £158–£198. Can be made in other sizes to order.

SCARTHIN NICK nest of tables consists of one rectangular table with two square ones beneath, timber or glass topped. The beauty of the wood and the attention to detail make a virtue of austerity. *M:* w91 or 41 × d41 × h48.5 or 40.5cm (35¾ or 16¼ × 16¼ × 19 or 16in). *P:* £258–£298. Equally practical in this range is a serving trolley.

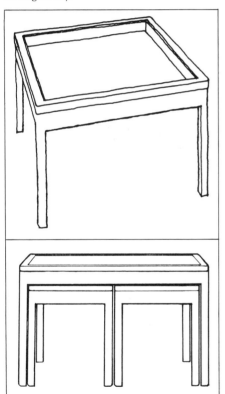

From top: Peter Miles's WITNEY display table △, SCARTHIN NICK nest

HERMAN MILLER

Functional modern design shown in low pedestal table '5452' with white laminate top, maple veneer edge, sculpted white epoxy-coated aluminium base and white nylon glides. One of a range of tables of various heights and sizes with wood veneer, laminate or marble tops, for domestic or contract use. *M:* dia 72 × h42cm (28¼ × 16½in). *P:* £157.50.

Herman Miller's '5452'

OMK DESIGN LTD △

High-tech modular table system for domestic or contract use. You can choose your own kit of parts from chrome or epoxy frames (colours on request), chrome or aluminium knuckle joints, and clear, bronze or mirrored glass or laminate tops. 'T11' and 'T13' each have a single square of glass, 'T12' and 'T14' have two squares to form a rectangle. *M:* 'T11' w85 × d85 × h31cm (33½ × 33½ × 12¼in), T12' w161 × d85 × h31cm (63½ × 33½ × 12¼in), 'T13' w60 × d60 × h31cm (23½ × 23½ × 12¼in),

'T14' w115 × d60 × h31cm (45¼ × 23½ × 12¼in). *P:* £122–£142, £176–£224, £66–£88, £84–£110. The system also comes in a dining-table height (see *Dining suites* for illustration).

PIRA

Modern, lightweight and elegant furniture from Italy.

Multi-purpose 'Trio P10' with brightly coloured plastic-coated base on wheels and round black laminated top is particularly useful as a bedside table. Its base slides under the bed and the height can be adjusted for breakfasting off or, with the top inclined, for reading (the book is supported by two buttons which pop out). It stows away compactly with the top in vertical position. *M:* dia 49 × h63–80cm (19¼ × 24¾–31½in). *P:* approx £70. A cheaper non-adjustable model is also available.

PLIAVIVA console table folds away when not in use, like other pieces in this pleasingly functional range. It comes in three versions: 'CS1' with natural ash frame and white or black melamine top, 'CS2' with natural or ebonized ash frame and top, and 'CS3' in natural beech with white melamine top. *M:* w130 × d42 × h80cm (51¼ × 16½ × 31½in). *P:* approx £115. See following page for illustration.

Pira's 'Trio P10'

FURNITURE

Pira's PLIAVIVA console

G T RACKSTRAW LTD
Well-made coffee, sofa, lamp, tray tables etc from the largest volume supplier of reproduction cabinet furniture in the UK.
The COUNTRY CHIPPENDALE range is especially attractive, using provincial eighteenth-century designs for models. All pieces are made in solid mahogany dried to 10% moisture content with a waxed antique mahogany or yew finish. The three-drawered 'M17173' coffee table comes in other sizes too. *M:* w51¼ × d23½ × h19in (130 × 60 × 48cm). *P:* approx £426. Rackstraw have extensive experience in dealing with interior decorators and contract furnishers.

Rackstraw's 'M17173'

RAINFORD HOUSE OF ELEGANCE
Console and corner tables in fibrous plaster with Georgian motifs, from specialists in period mouldings. The curved tops are fixed to the wall with brackets and tile adhesive. *M:* console w29½ × d11½in (75 × 29cm); corner d12½in (31.5cm). *P:* console £28; corner £16 (ex VAT).

RICHMOND INTERIORS
Classic-style square side table, marbled and lacquered, available in any colour or paint finish required. There is also a coffee table in the same style. *M:* side table w80 × d80 × h50cm (31½ × 31½ × 19¾in); coffee table w120 × d120 × h43cm (47¼ × 47¼ × 17in). *P:* £630, £1104.

PRICES AND INFORMATION WERE CORRECT AT THE TIME OF GOING TO PRESS

Square side table from Richmond

ROSET (UK) LTD
Simple and stylish occasional tables from a firm of European designers. BOWLING tables have square or rectangular glass or travertine marble tops with rounded corners, and tubular, lacquered metal legs that project into a small dome on the table top. Legs come in four colours: sand, grey, black and bordeaux. *M:* three sizes, w110 × d70cm (43¼ × 27½in), w90 × d90cm (35½ × 35½in), w70 × d70cm (27½ × 27½in), all h30 or 36cm (11¾ or 14¼in). *P:* from £174.

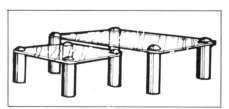

Roset's BOWLING tables

SC PRODUCTS
Sleek reproduction 1930s side tables in chrome, black lacquer and black glass 'ST2 Savoy Table' has a circular top of solid black glass supported on three tubular steel legs which meet in a ring at the base. Similar tables are available with black glass shelf mid-way and with black lacquered wood bases. *M:* dia 56 × h57 or 73cm (22 × 22½ or 28¾in). *P:* £156.
In the same vein, rectangular 'SU2' has black lacquered wood top and black glass lower shelf fitted into a tubular steel frame. *M:* w76 × d39.5 × h60cm (30 × 15½ × 23½in). *P:* £208. A taller version with another shelf is available as 'SU1' shelf unit.

SC Products' 'SU2' and 'ST2'

SCOTT HOWARD ASSOCIATES LTD
Simple, steel-frame 'P60' café table. Three-legged frame comes galvanized or painted

364

red, white or blue; round top is anthracite-grey lacquered metal or clear-lacquered brass. Suitable for cafés or anywhere around the home. *M:* dia 55 × h70cm (21¾ × 27½in). *P:* from £100. There's a chair to match (see *Dining suites*).

Scott Howard's 'P60'

Tempus Stet's 'B19'

Titchmarsh & Goodwin's 'RL22510'

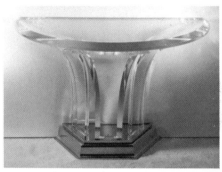

'Lotus CT' from Townhouse

TAG DESIGN PARTNERSHIP
Circular tea or coffee table with laminate top and tubular steel legs in very contemporary grey or black with bright red, yellow or blue edging. See *Tables, dining*.

TEMPUS STET
Amazing reproduction brackets, pedestals and table legs in seventeenth, eighteenth- and nineteenth-century styles, many of which can be produced in gilt, antiqued silver, bronze or wood finishes. There are also complete tables with scagliola or composite 'Temstone' tops; the OSTERLEY range, for example, based on Robert Adam's side and console tables at Osterley Park in Middlesex.
'B19' matching boy and girl console table legs or brackets are available gilded or in wood effects. *M:* h28in (71cm). *P:* wood effect £75 each; gilded £80 each.
Special commissions form a major part of Tempus Stet's work.

WILLIAM TILLMAN
Fine reproduction Sheraton and Chippendale tables for many purposes, including a satinwood sofa gaming table with leathered backgammon board and reversible top with inlaid chessboard. *M:* w37–60 × d23 × h29½in (94–152.5 × 58.5 × 75cm). *P:* on application.

Gaming table from Tillman

TITCHMARSH & GOODWIN
Individually hand-made reproduction furniture from an exemplary firm of cabinet-makers.
'RL22510' English yew butler's tray table has hinged sides. *M:* w50 × d27½ × h17½in (127 × 70 × 75cm). *P:* from £765. Also available in mahogany.

TOWNHOUSE INTERIORS
Almost invisible STAMM 'Lotus CT' console table in acrylic perspex with brass base. An exclusive from Italy. *M:* w120 × d60 × h75cm (47¼ × 23½ × 29½in). *P:* on application.

WINDMILL FURNITURE ⬕
Simple square-legged wooden coffee tables in almost any size, regular shape, and colour. Frames are beech or oak; beech frames have tops veneered in ash, beech, linoleum or laminate, oak frames have oak veneered tops. Windmill will make their design in any other hardwood on request and will stain tables to any colour (at least 5% surcharge). All tables except those with linoleum or laminate tops are finished with a matt lacquer which Windmill claims will withstand staining and marking even under very heavy usage. There are five standard sizes but other sizes are available to specification. *M:* square w60 × d60 × h40cm (23½ × 23½ × 15¾in) to w90 × d90 × h40cm (35½ × 35½ × 15¾in); rectangular w120 × d60 × h40cm (47¼ × 23½ × 15¾in); round dia 90 × h40cm (35½ × 15¾in). *P:* £83–£122.60.

Windmill's coffee tables △

FURNITURE

UPHOLSTERED FURNITURE

ADEPTUS DESIGNS LTD
Well-designed multi-density foam furniture from a firm that arguably pioneered the use of this material. Adeptus are continually developing new ranges to add to their collection of double and single sofa beds, sofas, chairs and modular units. All are available covered in 20 or so different fabrics — cotton, tweed or cord, plain or printed with geometric or abstract patterns — or in customer's own fabric. One simply styled range is TREVI, with armchair and two sizes of sofa bed. *M:* sofa beds w60 × d32 × h25½in (152.5 × 81.5 × 65cm), w74 × d29 × h25½in (188 × 73.5 × 65cm); armchair w38 × d32 × h25½in (96.5 × 81.5 × 65cm). *P:* sofas from £166, £181; armchair from £122.

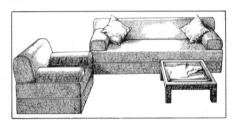

Adeptus's TREVI

ANTIQUES OF TOMORROW
Reproduction suites plus occasional chairs, window seats and footstools. Any item can be purchased with or without French polishing, covered or uncovered, so that customers can finish the furniture to their own requirements. VICTORIAN suite includes balloon-back chaise-longue, 'Ladies Chair' with quarter-length arms and 'Gents Chair' with full arms. All have moulded wooden frame and deep-buttoned backs. *M:* chaise-longue w66 ×

Antiques of Tomorrow's VICTORIAN

d27½ × h33½in (167.5 × 70 × 85cm); 'Ladies Chair' w23 × 28¼ × h34¾in (58.5 × 72 × 88cm); 'Gents Chair' w27¼ × d31 × h35½in (70 × 78.5 × 90cm). *P:* (polished and upholstered in Dralon) chaise-longue £277.31; 'Ladies Chair' £122; 'Gents Chair' £135.73.

THE ARCHITECTURAL TRADING COMPANY LTD
Zanotta furniture from Milan, Italian to the core.
There are two stunning easy chairs in steel and leather. Low-line 'Maggiolina' has stainless steel frame and black or white leather cushions in a matching cowhide sling. *M:* w71 × d102 × h83cm (28 × 40 × 32¾in). *P:* £989.
The second is 'Genni', a classic 1930s design now made in the most up-to-date materials, with a motor-age bolster headrest attached on leather straps. Adjustable frame can be chrome-plated or lacquered, and fabric upholstery is also offered. There's a footstool to match. *M:* w57 × d109 × h76cm (22½ × 43 ×

Architectural Trading's 'Genni'

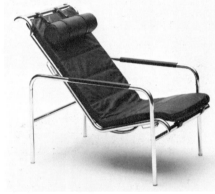

Architectural Trading's LOIRA

30in). *P:* (fabric) £507, (leather) £623–£685.
More conventional is plain, square LOIRA range of two- and three-seater sofas, armchair and unit seating. With leather or fabric cover over upholstered steel frame, the range also includes sofa beds in three widths. *M:* three-seater sofa w224 × d85 × h77cm (88¼ × 33½ × 30¼in). *P:* (fabric) £1510–£1804.
DINAMO range has light, clean lines with angled cushions as armrests. Two-seater sofas, armchair and day bed are upholstered in leather or lovely classic grey/white or candy pink/white striped fabric, with black or light grey steel legs and frame. *M:* sofas w195, 230 × d83 × h80cm (76¾, 90½ × 32¾ × 31½). *P:* (fabric) £1441–£1723.
Elite among sag bags is 'Sacco' anatomical chair, held in the collections of the Victoria and Albert Museum in London and the Museum of Modern Art in New York. The pear-shaped envelope of leather or fabric is filled with expanded polystyrene pellets. Some fabric covers are removable for washing. *M:* w80 × d80 × h68cm (31½ × 31½ × 26¾in). *P:* (fabric) £77, (leather) £389–£547.

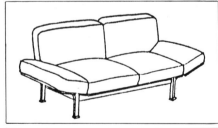

From Architectural Trading. Top: DINAMO; left: 'Maggiolina'; right 'Sacco'

ARKANA
Comfortable-looking modern suites in seven ranges, each including armchair, two- and three-seater sofas covered in a choice of 20 different fabrics. A rectangular ottoman can be

Arkana's MISTRALE △

combined with most ranges. Simply styled MISTRALE has hardwood base frame with deep foam-core cushions and detachable arm bolsters. Available in hide as well as fabric. *M:* sofas w150, 208 × d94 × h81cm (59, 82 × 37 × 32in); armchair w94 × d94 × h81cm (37 × 37 × 32in). *P:* two-seater £420–£490; three-seater £556–£650; armchair £282–£338.

LAURA ASHLEY LTD
Square and roomy loose-covered sofa and armchair with solid beech frame and feather-filled cushions made for Laura Ashley by a well-known manufacturer. They are available by mail order in a choice of four 100% cotton fabrics of varying weight and quality from the COUNTRY FURNISHING, UPHOLSTERY and DRAWING ROOM ranges (see *Fabrics*). *M:* sofa w168 × d89 × h74cm (66¼ × 35 × 29¼in); armchair w92 × d89 × h74cm (36¼ × 35 × 29¼in). *P:* sofa £445–£495; armchair £245–£295. Additional and replacement loose covers can also be ordered.

Laura Ashley's sofa and armchair

PRICES AND INFORMATION WERE CORRECT AT THE TIME OF GOING TO PRESS

BEAUDESERT
Handmade armchairs and sofas in classic European styles. The best upholstery materials are used, and each piece is available to order in chintz from Beaudesert's own collection or in any suitable fabric. The 'Library Chair' demonstrates the comfortable old-fashioned elegance of their style. *M:* w29 × d25 × h36in (73.5 × 63.5 × 91.5cm). *P:* approx £720.

Beaudesert's 'Library Chair'

BOSS DESIGN
Sophisticated leather seating, the product of an imaginative collaboration between three British manufacturers: Tarian Design (see *Fabrics*), Connolly's (suppliers of leather upholstery for Rolls Royce and Jaguar cars) and Boss. Ten colourways for leather include unusual shades such as bilberry, grape, aqua, almond and forest green, all complementing fabrics in the Tarian collection. CAROUSEL is a typically luxurious suite in leather and chrome.

Armchair and two- and three-seater sofas have leather cushions and leather-padded arms with contrasting piping. Back-rests on each section are easily adjustable to five positions. *M:* armchair w89 × d82–98 × h77–89cm (35 × 32¼–38½ × 30¼–35in); sofas w152, 193 × d82–98 × h77–89cm (59¾, 76 × 32¼–38½ × 30¼–35in). *P:* armchair from £410; three-seater sofa from £880.

Boss's CAROUSEL

ARTHUR BRETT & SONS LTD
Fine reproduction furniture from cabinet-makers who specialize in eighteenth-century styles. Extensive range includes open armchairs in Queen Anne, Georgian and Regency designs, beautifully turned and carved, with upholstered backs and seats; a tall Queen-Anne style wing armchair, two chair-back settees, a formal Hepplewhite-style 'loveseat'; and tub and desk chairs upholstered in antiqued hide.

'1919' is a superb carved walnut open armchair, from a George I original. It can be upholstered in customer's own fabric. *M:* w70 × d53 × h99cm (27½ × 20¾ × 39in). *P:* £1069 (ex VAT).

'1660' is a very elegant formal settee in the

Brett's '1919'

FURNITURE

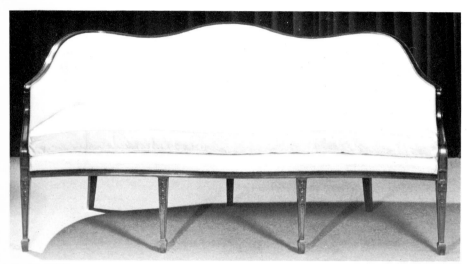

Brett's '1660'

son's OPTIONS collection (see *Fabrics*) or customer's own fabric. *M:* sofas w55, 75 × d36 × h37in (139.5, 190.5 × 91.5 × 94cm); armchair w35 × d36 × h36in (89 × 91.5 × 91.5cm). *P:* (with Sanderson fabric) sofas £415, £550.50; armchair £299.50.

Newly launched 'Sesame' sofa bed is streamlined in appearance. It adjusts to an intermediate reclining angle, offers storage space for bedding and has removable seat, back and bolster covers. *M:* w79 × d39 × h35in (200.5 × 99 × 89cm). *P:* from £200.

Chiltern Hills' SESAME

Hepplewhite manner. It is available in fruitwood or mahogany, with loose feather-and-down cushion. *M:* w183 × d74 × h89cm (72 × 29¼ × 35in). *P:* (customer's own fabric, with loose cushion) £2682 (ex VAT).

CANDLELIGHT PRODUCTS LTD
Rattan and bentwood suites in natural finish or sprayed in pastel shades — white, smoke, pink, peach, peppermint and beige. SIX has smooth, classic lines; MOOD is simple styled with woven rattan side panels; while FRENCH

From top: Candlelight's SIX, MOOD, FRENCH THRONE

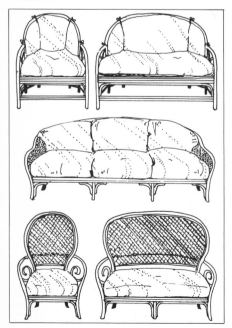

THRONE has elaborately curling arms and high lattice backs. Each suite includes armchair and two-seater sofa; MOOD also includes a three-seater. All can be upholstered in Candlelight's own delicately patterned fabrics. *M:* SIX armchair w57 × d50 × h88cm (22½ × 19¾ × 34¾in), sofa w107 × d50 × h88cm (42¼ × 19¾ × 34¾in); MOOD chair w69 × d68 × h71cm (27¼ × 26¾ × 28in), sofas w132, 190 × d68 × h71cm (52, 74¾ × 26¾ × 28in); FRENCH THRONE chair w72 × d53 × h104cm (28¼ × 20¾ × 41in), sofa w148 × d53 × h104cm (58¼ × 20¾ × 41in). *P:* sofas from £250; chairs from £140.

CHILTERN HILLS UPHOLSTERY
Very Sanderson HARMONY range of armchair, two- and three-seater sofa, table and ottoman covered in any print from Sander-

CIANCIMINO INTERNATIONAL LTD
Stylishly simple WING sofas and armchair designed by George Ciancimino. Made in timber to customer's specification of size, they are firmly but comfortably upholstered in a good range of materials including wool and leather. Other styles can be designed from customers' own ideas. *M:* to order (sofa max w96in/244cm). *P:* on application. See following page for illustration.

PRICES AND INFORMATION WERE CORRECT AT THE TIME OF GOING TO PRESS

Chiltern Hills' HARMONY

Ciancimino's WING

COLLINS & HAYES LTD

Collections in very different styles from major manufacturer.

Very traditional ROMANTIC collection comprises six different sofa designs and nine armchairs to go with them. All can be covered in a wide range of fabrics — cotton prints, jacquards, damasks, acrylic velvets and moirés — chosen with co-ordination in mind. The fabric is also sold by the metre for curtaining etc, and for a complete look, there are co-ordinating round tables with floor-length tablecloths, scatter cushions, lamps, lampshades and even ceramic ornaments. One of the most distinctive of the sofas is 'Longfellow' with angled arms and slightly pointed back. Two- and three-seater sofas have hardwood frame, seat cushions of foam wrapped in polyester fibre and back cushions filled with polyester fibre or feathers on customer's request. *M:* w179, 235 × d102 × h90cm (70½, 92½ × 40¼ × 35½in). *P:* two-seater from £779. See front cover for illustration.

TRIO from Collins & Hayes

THEME collection provides sleek modern designs. TRIO armchair and two- and three-seater sofas have contoured arms and floppy back cushions, their slim line accentuated by diagonal stitching. All have timber frame with elasticated webbing supporting cushions made from foam wrapped in polyester fibre. They can be covered in a wide range of fabrics and a colourful range of leathers (including soft blue, green, cream and apricot as well as bright red and shades of brown) or in custom-

er's own material. *M:* sofas w159, 219 × d103 × h76cm (62½, 86¼ × 40½ × 30in). *P:* two-seater from £523; three-seater from £615.

Other collections from Collins & Hayes include VARIATIONS, three classic but informal designs with practical loose covers.

COLOURFLAIR

Large range of sofas, armchairs and occasional chairs in a massive choice of fabrics or in customer's own fabric.

Occasional chair from Colourflair's DECORATIVE COLLECTION

For the most traditional settings there's a classic occasional chair from the DECORATIVE COLLECTION, available in polished wood or 22 different painted finishes. *M:* w63 × d63 ×

Colourflair's FELICITY

h97cm (24¾ × 24¾ × 38¼in). *P:* (without fabric) £562.90 (ex VAT).

Modern and plain by contrast are FELICITY single-seat, two-seat, three-seat and corner units. *M:* two-seat unit w142 × d89 × h76cm (56 × 35 × 30in); three-seat unit w213 × d89 × h76cm (83¾ × 35 × 30in). *P:* two-seat unit £490; three-seat unit £639.

CONFETTI

ALABAMA, a modern and practical upholstered suite. Armchair, mini, standard and 'executive' sofas have fully reversible cushions and removable, washable covers in customer's own or Confetti's range of fabrics. Sturdy metal frame and exposed legs are lacquered white. *M:* sofas w48, 60 or 84 × d34 × h27in (122, 152.5 or 213.5 × 86.5 × 68.5cm); armchair w36 × d34 × h27in (91.5 × 86.5 × 68.5cm). *P:* (without fabric) sofas £260–398; armchair £198.

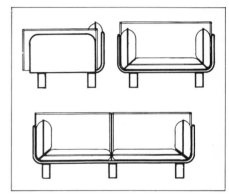

Confetti's ALABAMA

CONNAUGHT FURNITURE LTD

Soft-look suites in simple styles. All can be covered in almost any of Connaught's selection of washable acrylics, pure wool and leather. Chunky LUCY chair has snug quilted cover, featured here in acrylic velvet with diagonal stripe and bound edges over tough polyester

Connaught's LUCY

FURNITURE

filling. Matching two- and three-seater sofas are available. *M:* w102 × d104 × h78cm (40¼ × 41 × 30¾in). *P:* from £235.

Connaught's duvet-style, polyester-filled, loose-lay covers over scaled-down bases create an expansive look in a small space. PENELOPE chair, teamed with two- and three-seater sofas, looks fresh and modern with a checked cover reversible to plain, in acrylic fabric in yellow/blue/grey, red/grey, pink/grey and two beige tones. *M:* w112 × d117 × h78cm (44 × 41 × 30¾in). *P:* from £229.

Connaught's PENELOPE

COTSWOLD FURNITURE COMPANY

Wide-ranging collection of reproduction armchairs, occasional chairs and settees, made in well-seasoned beechwood and available in Cotswold's amazing variety of wood and painted finishes. Upholstery is made from

Top: 'A42'; below 'A132'. Both from Cotswold Furniture Company

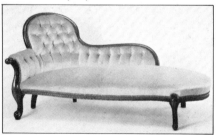

traditional materials — hair, coir fibre and coil springs — covered in Cotswold's own high quality fabrics or those supplied by the customer. Collection includes 18 settees and 36 armchairs.

Plush Victorian button-backs are well represented, including balloon-back chaise-longue 'A42' and matching armchair. *M:* 'A42' w63 × d32 × h36in (160 × 81.5 × 91.5cm). *P:* 379.75. Extensive range of Louis XV and Louis XVI seating includes formal 'A132', a Louis XVI spoonback two-seater settee with gilded frame. *M:* w43 × d17 × h38in (109 × 43 × 96.5cm). *P:* £262.40.

'D3' wing chair has faux bamboo carved frame; it comes with loose cushion seat and plain upholstered back and with option of woven cane sides. *M:* w27 × d23 × h43in (68.5 × 58.5 × 109cm). *P:* £295–£306.95.

Cotswold's 'D3'

LIBERTY 'L112' settee and matching armchair show the fluid lines of art nouveau. *M:* settee w53 × d19 × h40in (134.5 × 48.5 × 101.5cm). *P:* £416.80.

DELCOR FURNITURE LTD

Traditional suites hand-built in Northumberland and delivered direct to customers throughout the UK mainland.

SUNDANCE suite offers a choice of standard or high back two-, three- and four-seater sofas and armchair. Frames are hardwood with plywood facings; seating supports are Pirelli's resilient webbing covered with foam and reinforced at the front edge; standard cushions are filled with Terylene wrapped around a foam core. Optional extras include skirt, side

Cotswold's LIBERTY 'L112'

cushions, feather and/or down fillings, loose armcaps, self-piping and Scotchgard fabric protection. Can be upholstered in selected fabrics — prints, cottons, unions and Dralon velvet — from major manufacturers including Sanderson, G P & J Baker and Warner (see separate entries) or in customer's own choice of material. *M:* standard three-seater w79 × d35 × h29in (200.5 × 89 × 73.5cm). *P:* (uncovered) £252 plus delivery. See following page for illustration.

Delcor's DESIGNER collection goes even further and leaves the designing to you, offering an armchair and two, two-and-a-half-, three- and four-seater sofas with a choice of back height, back style and arm length as well as trimming and covering.

DESIGN FURNITURE

Four stylish and well-made modern suites. JASMINE two- and three-seater sofas, armchair and footstool have solid beech frames, steel seat springing and castor feet. Available in Design Furniture's wide range of fabrics. *M:* sofas w157, 211 × d100 × h80cm (61¾, 83 × 39½ × 31½in); armchair w100 × d100 × h80cm (39½ × 39½ × 31½in). *P:* sofas £490, £592; armchair £352.

Design Furniture's JASMINE

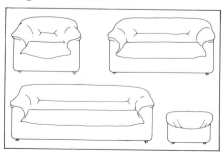

PRICES AND INFORMATION WERE CORRECT AT THE TIME OF GOING TO PRESS

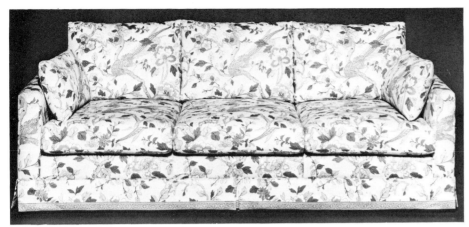

Delcor's SUNDANCE

DESIGN WORKSHOP

Square-form seat units in leather and aluminium. The units have aluminium plinths with polished or satin finish in silver, champagne, bronze or black (to order); seats are upholstered in fine, soft leather in a variety of shades. Large chrome castors allow the units to move freely even on deep pile carpets. Armless and one-armed units can be joined in a variety of formations, including right-angled arrangements, and the units are firmly joined by special connectors at the sides of the plinths. Ottomans are also available, and three of these can be combined to make a comfortable day bed. *M:* two-seater (combining 'T1L' and 'T1R' one-armed units) w226 × d87 × h68cm (89 × 34¼ × 26¾in). *P:* £1626 (ex VAT). The section of the aluminium seat unit plinth is the basis for all the components in the TOMMASO furniture system (see also *Desks, Dining suites, Storage, Tables, occasional*).

Design Workshop's TOMMASO two-seater

DESIGNERS GUILD

Attractive suites to be covered in Designers Guild's fashionable fabrics (see separate entries) or alternatively in customer's own material. All have well-made, seasoned beechwood frames and are sprung with either serpentine springs or Duflex spring units. Cushion fillings can be specified to comfort and design requirements, with flame-retardant materials used wherever possible. All cushions have zipped, removable covers. Fabrics can be quilted to order, Designers Guild recommending that

glazed chintzes be quilted for longer life. Designs range from the old-world HUMPHREY with deep-buttoned backs to modern CHRISTOPHER, armless with simple separate cushions for back and seat, and similar COLUMBUS unit seating. Some ranges include ottomans, but Designers Guild make a classic cushioned ottoman that could be added to any of their suites.

In the middle of the range is CLUB, two- and three-seater sofas and armchair with curved backs and scrolled arms. (Featured here in 'Anemone' fabric.) *M:* three-seater w234 × d97 × h89cm (92½ × 38¼ × 35in); armchair w109 × d97 × h89cm (43 × 38¼ × 35in). *P:* (without fabric) three-seater £1030; armchair £600.

PETER DUDGEON

Top-notch handmade furniture upholstered in customer's own fabric. Among a wide range of mainly traditional styles of sofas and chairs is

Peter Dudgeon's RAEBURN

Designers Guild's CLUB

FURNITURE

the 'Raeburn' chair, available with or without arms. It can be covered in leather or velvet with close brass nailing, or in a soft cover. *M: w24 × d28 × h40in (61 × 71 × 101.5cm) P: (without fabric) £399–£428 (ex VAT).*

DUNLOP LTD

From a design by Dunlopillo France, the LE WEEKEND range of all-foam sofa beds for occasional rather than nightly use. The three models each have a tight-upholstered fold-out base topped with fashionable 'floppy look' upholstery that doubles as a duvet. By day the cover is fastened into place by concealed zips. 'Domenica' is covered in acrylic velvet in three colourways — mushroom/ivory, turquoise/grey green and rust/peach, with the base in plain mushroom, turquoise or rust. Bolsters can be fitted into the sides of the unit to form armrests. *M: w142 × d98 × h73cm (56 × 38½ × 28¾in). P: £375.50.* The other two models in the range, both slightly less expensive, are 'Venerdi', covered in floral cotton, and 'Sabato', covered in plain needlecord.

Dunlop's LE WEEKEND

DUX INTERIORS LTD

Tubular-steel upholstered chairs manufactured in Scandinavia.
'Jetson' chair is a distinctive design by Bruno Mathsson. Its leather or fabric cradle seat is stretched over a tubular steel frame with chromed steel swivel base. The slim uphol-

Dux's SPIDER recliner

Dux's 'Jetson'

stery is buttoned and there's a bolster headrest. *M: w65 × d83 × h97cm (25½ × 32¾ × 38¼in). P: £654–£861.*
For a modern day bed there's the SPIDER recliner, more like a caterpillar with ten individually-sprung cushions on six spindly metal legs in chrome or black finish. The range also includes a sofa and chair. All can be covered in a choice of 15 shades of leather, in suede-look Alcantara, 15 different fabrics, or customer's own material. *M: recliner w177 × d72 × h67cm (69¾ × 28¼ × 26½in). P: £678–£1348.*

ENVIRONMENT COMMUNICATION

Wonderful furniture by outstanding designers, from the Italian firm Cassina.
'Sunset in New York' is an extravagant design by Gaetano Pesce. The three-seater sofa with multi-plywood frame and seat constructed of blocks of polyurethane and polyester padding is covered in skyscraper-like fabric surmounted by a back-rest representing a lurid red setting sun. *M: w225 × d105 × h120cm (88½ × 41¼ × 47¼in). P: from £3204.* See colour illustration.
Le Corbusier's 'LC2' uncompromisingly right-angular armchair and two- and three-seater sofas have steel frames coated in polished chrome or matt black, glossy basalt, grey, light blue, green, bordeaux or ochre enamel. The loose cushions are padded with polyurethane and polyester and covered in fabric or leather. *M: armchair w76 × d70 × h67cm (30 × 27½ × 26½in). P: from £871.*

Environment's 'LC2'

More sybaritic VERANDAH armchair and two-seater sofa designed by Vico Magistretti can be adjusted to three alternative back positions with a footrest extension that can be folded under the seat. The frame is made of steel units with polyurethane and polyester padding covered in fabric or leather. The base is made of glossy dark green or matt black enamelled steel. *M: armchair w96 × d85–155 × h75–110cm (37¾ × 33½–61 × 29½–43¼in). P: £764.*

Environment's VERANDAH

PRICES AND INFORMATION WERE CORRECT AT THE TIME OF GOING TO PRESS

ESTIA

Wide range of no-nonsense comfortable suites, seating units and sofa beds of multi-density foam construction covered in fabric which can be chosen from five price brackets: plain cotton, striped cotton, cotton corduroy, velours or wool/viscose mix, and Dartington Hall wool tweed (see *Fabrics*). 'E5' deep seating with high backs comes in modular units with or without arms or with left or right arms only to make sofas. *M:* armchair w36 × d33 × h29in (91.5 × 84 × 73.5cm). *P:* £130–£167.50.

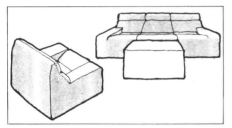

Estia's 'E5'

MARY FOX LINTON LTD

Excellent furniture made to order and covered in a variety of special design fabrics by this company.

Handsome 'Geneva' sofa has a conventional design with comfortable deep seats and ample space for two people. *M:* w160 × d90 × h85cm (63 × 35½ × 33½in). *P:* (without fabric) £625 (ex VAT).

Armless two-seater 'Cushion Sofa' looks more informal but equally inviting. Each seat con-

Top: 'Geneva'; below: 'Cushion Sofa'. Both from Mary Fox Linton

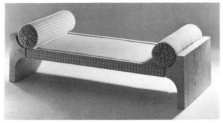

Day bed from Mary Fox Linton

sists of three piled-up cushions, and the back is divided to look like two vertical cushions. *M:* w152 × d66 × h91cm (89¾ × 26 × 35¾in). *P:* (without fabric) £650 (ex VAT).

Successfully combining classical and modern forms, an elegant day bed designed by Mary Fox Linton and Colin Golding is supported by sycamore-veneered blocks curved to hold bolsters at each end. *M:* w210 × d90 × h51cm (82¾ × 35½ × 20in). *P:* (without fabric) £1200 (ex VAT).

FRAYLING△

Versatile DOMINGO unit seating for any size of room. The required number of armless units can be fastened together, with arms at each end (reversible for longer life) and optional corner units, stool and table. Frames are made of beech with particle-board panels and moulded foam seat, back and arms. All items are upholstered in wool or Dralon in a choice of colours. *M:* unit w72 × d96.5 × h77cm (28¼ × 38 × 30¼in). *P:* on application. Frayling also make contract seating (see *Offices, reception seating*).

Frayling's DOMINGO △

FUTON COMPANY

Japanese-influenced sofa bed formed from two rolled futons and bed base (see *Bedrooms, beds* for details). It comes in four sizes ranging from an armchair to a three-seater sofa, with bolsters and cushions supplied separately. Cotton covers come in a choice of seven colours. *M:* w103–157 × d103 × h46cm (40½–61¾ × 40½ × 18in). *P:* £297–£449. Futon Company also make Japanese-style screens, tables and mats. See *Chairs* for illustration.

△ *INDICATES AN ILLUSTRATED PRODUCT SELECTED BY THE DESIGN CENTRE*

FUTON FACTORY

Cheap and cheerful sofa beds and unit seating using pure cotton and multi-density (part coconut fibre) futons. 'Double Decker' comprises two slatted softwood units which stack to make a sofa with the addition of a back-rest and straps and a folded six-layer futon. Futons are covered in cotton drill or calico in a variety of plain colours and hand-printed designs which can also be used for reversible bedcovers and curtains. *M:* w30–60 × d36 × h26in (76–152.5 × 91.5 × 66cm). *P:* £68–£129.

Futon Factory's 'Double Decker' as sofa and as futon base

GRAHAM & GREEN

From this delightful shop, the 'Cranbrook' chesterfield sofa. Comes in two sizes, covered in nubby, woolly fabric with diagonal weave in various soft, neutral shades. *M:* w157, 183 × d94 × h75cm (w61¾, 72 × 29½ × 37in). *P:* £335, £375. See following page for illustration.

GRANGE

Out-of-the-ordinary designs from this French firm, all intended to fit as well into modern eclectic rooms as into period ones. Grange or customer's own fabric can be used for the upholstery.

The design of the IRLANDE range is derived from nineteenth-century Irish rural models,

Grange's IRLANDE 'AL42'

FURNITURE

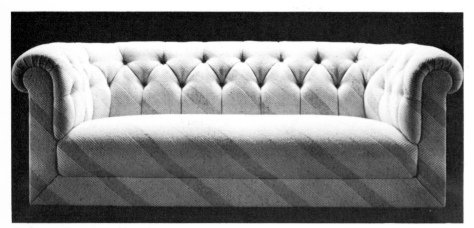

Graham & Green's Cranbrook

and the two-seater sofa bed 'AL42' has a cosy cottagey look. It is finished in waxed cypress pine. *M:* w168 × d71–190 × h99cm (66¼ × 28–74¾ × 39in). *P:* on application.
The luxurious round-backed 'FS2' two-seater sofa in the EMA range has solid beech frame, webbed seat, sprung back and goose-feather cushions. *M:* w142 × d92 × h83cm (56 × 36¼ × 32¾in). *P:* on application.

Grange's EMA 'FS2'

HABITAT DESIGNS LTD
Around 20 styles of sofas, sofa beds, armchairs and unit seating, with 48 fabrics to choose from for some models. Customer's own fabric can also be used if suitable.

Habitat's ALBA

Clean-lined 'Alba' sofa with an interior-sprung hardwood frame can be covered in red, yellow, pastel blue or oatmeal textured-weave fabric. *M:* w158 × d84 × h74cm (62¼ × 33 × 29¼in). *P:* £245.

Habitat's 'Zöe'

'Zöe' sofa or sofa bed has curved back and piped scroll arms with interior-sprung hardwood frame. It's available in the full range of fabrics. *M:* w176 × d91 × h83cm (69¼ × 35¾ × 32¾in). *P:* sofa £380–£465, sofa bed £520–£605.

Habitat's 'Butterfly Chair'

Metal-framed 'Butterfly Chair' has a black canvas sling seat and either red or blue cushions to match the frame. *M:* w90 × d65 × h87cm (35½ × 25½ × 34¼in). *P:* £65.

CHARLES HAMMOND
A collection of luxurious, hand-built, hand-finished chairs and sofas in around 20 basic styles from the early eighteenth-century to the present, from these leading interior designers and wholesale suppliers. 'Knaresborough' two-seater sofa has a fully stuffed back with feather-and-down seat cushions. Like the rest of the range it can be upholstered in fabrics from Hammond's wholesale collection (see *Fabrics*); it is featured here in 'Hollyhock Major' hand-block printed chintz. *M:* w150 × d89 × h82cm (59 × 33¾ × 35in). *P:* on application. There are many possibilities for variations on piping, fringes, skirts and borders.

'Knaresborough' from Charles Hammond

HITCH/MYLIUS
Modern and classically simple unit seating and suites suitable for domestic or contract use. 'HM151' units (armless or with right or left arms only), armchair and two- and three-seater sofas have solid beech frames with seats suspended on elastic webbing. Upholstery is in Dacron and Courtelle fibre. Loose covers, piping, arm-caps and Scotchgard soil-proofing treatment are available on request. *M:* two-seater 'HM151/S' w211 × d94 × h74cm (83 × 37 × 29¼in). *P:* on application. See also *Offices, reception seating*

'HM151/S' from Hitch/Mylius

PRICES AND INFORMATION WERE CORRECT AT THE TIME OF GOING TO PRESS

HOMEWORKS LTD

'SB107' day bed and 'SO178' ottoman by Wickerworks, handmade in Italy. Both come in a natural or dark brown finish, with loose, reversible buttoned upholstery; also with pleated or tufted and buttoned seats and backs. Five similar sofas, four armchairs, a chaise-longue and seven side tables are available. *M:* day bed w85 × h29 × d40in (216 × 73.5 × 101.5cm). *P:* (without fabric) £1755.

BUMPER NO 10 modular seating is available in single, double, triple and corner units with three-tier foam-padded 'bumpers' or with low skirts. Covered in client's own fabric, units can be supplied with hand-webbed, coil-sprung seats. *M:* single unit w31 × d31 × h35in (78.5 × 78.5 × 89in). *P:* from £240.

Homeworks' 'SB107' and 'SO178'

IDEAS FOR LIVING

Sofas and armchairs that combine high tech with comfort, from an extensive collection of modern Italian furniture.

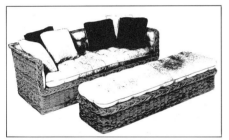

TAMISO from Ideas for Living

Seccose make TAMISO armchair and two- and three-seater sofas from simple elements: a metal frame bent into rectangles at the sides to form arms, and plastic-coated semi-elastic wire netting supporting the generously stuffed cushions for seat and back. Sides come in red, black or blue, netting in black, covers in off white or black. *M:* two-seater w128 × d75 × h66cm (50½ × 29½ × 26in); armchair w70 × d75 × h66cm (27½ × 29½ × 26in). *P:* sofa £202.50; armchair £125.50. The range from Seccose also includes shelving and storage units, tables, chairs and beds with brightly coloured metal frames (see separate entries).

G & A KELLY LTD

High-quality handmade sofas, armchairs and chaise-longues. G & A KELLY have a small standard range of designs but usually make furniture to client's specification. All the frames are made from beech, cushions are fibre-filled and wrapped in Dacron. The client generally supplies the fabric. *P:* sofas, chaise-longues from £400.

Chaise-longue from Kelly

L M KINGCOME LTD

Almost any style you could want made to your own specification. Kingcome's brochure illustrates the basic styles: 24 sofas, 4 armchairs with square ottomans, a round footstool, 14 armchairs, 2 chaise-longues, 4 corner units, plus reproduction pieces such as Regency and Louis XVI bergères, a Georgian wing chair, two Regency open armchairs and two upholstered dining chairs. These or any permutation of them can be handmade to any size, though Kingcome do quote average sizes for reference. Number of sofa seat and back cushions, back heights and seat depths, loose or tight covers, fillings ranging from synthetics to feather and down, ball feet (polished, fabric-

Kingcome's 'Wilton'

Kingcome's 'Armless Bedroom Chair'

covered or lacquered), plinths, fringes and braid are all supplied to order; and most sofas can be supplied as sofa beds. Covers can be any fabric specified from any source in the UK or most pieces can be covered in hide, either leather or suede, all supplied by Kingcome at normal retail prices. Or you can supply your own material for 20% on the basic price.

'Wilton' basic design offers an impeccably elegant formal sofa. It can be scaled up or down in length, within reason, yet maintain its graceful proportions. *M:* (average) w200 × d93 × h86cm (78¾ × 36½ × 33¾in). *P:* from £999.

'Armless Bedroom Chair' is prettily traditional. *M:* (average) w94 × d97 × h80cm (37 × 38¼ × 31½in). *P:* from £175.

Any style can be made up into corner units, with square, rounded or rectangular corner pieces or alternatively with a fabric-covered

FURNITURE

Kingcome's 'Oxford Corner Unit'

corner table with polished glass top. 'Oxford Corner Unit' has a long, clean look. *M:* to order. *P:* on application.

THE LONDON SOFA-BED CENTRE
Varied collection of well-designed sofa beds and matching sofas, armchairs and units from sofa bed specialists.
Traditionally-styled OXFORD three-seater sofa (with two cushions) and sofa bed, and larger 'Queensize' sofa (with three cushions) and sofa bed all have hardwood frames with Dacron-wrapped polyester seat cushions and feather-filled back cushioning. Bun feet are covered in the same fabric. All sofa beds have interior-sprung mattresses and are upholstered to order either from the hundreds of showroom fabrics or in customer's own materials. *M:* three-seater w76 × d36 × h31in (193 × 91.5 × 78.5cm). *P:* (without fabric) £495.
Versatile ISOLDE unit seating provides co-ordinated upholstered seating and sofa beds plus tables. One system, available as a package, consists of armless three-seater sofa bed, corner unit and seat unit. Matching upholstered table has plate glass top. All units have 'glide' feet to facilitate movement. *M:* sofa bed

From The London Sofa-bed Centre. Top: OXFORD; below: 'ISOLDE'

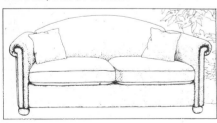

w52 × d37 × h26in (132 × 94 × 66cm); corner unit w37 × d37 × h26in (94 × 94 × 66cm); seat unit w36 × d37 × h26in (91.5 × 94 × 66cm). *P:* entire system £860.

WILLIAM M MACLEAN LTD
Well-made period-inspired furniture for the top end of the contract market or for private houses. The range of upholstered furniture is vast with styles ranging from French provincial to Queen Anne, Georgian or Chinese — even a faux bamboo upholstered deck chair! All are available in more than 100 decorator finishes which are oven-baked, heat and spirit resistant. Customer's own fabric can be used for upholstery, and most sofas come with matching armchairs.
Charmingly curvaceous '48.4059' has cabriole legs and frame carved to resemble bamboo. *M:* w63 × d60 × h84cm (24¾ × 23½ × 33in). *P:* from £350.
A Regency-style imitation bamboo frame is

Maclean's '48.4059'

also used for the elegant spindle-backed '48.4136'. *M:* w55 × d57 × h85cm (21¾ × 22½ × 33½in). *P:* from £225.
The '48.4135 Glen' chair with its sabre legs provides an updated version of a neo-classical model. *M:* w62 × d57 × h72cm (24½ × 22½ × 28¼in). *P:* from £190.

From top: Maclean's '48.4136', '48.4135 Glen'

PETER MILES
SCARTHIN NICK range of conference and occasional chairs designed by Ronald Carter RDI and excellently made with solid-timber frames upholstered in wool, hide or customer's own fabric. 'III' occasional chair has curved back with timber top-rail, and fabric-covered side panels and armrests with a wavy profile. *M:* w62 × d69 × h80cm (24½ × 27¼ × 31½in). *P:* £278–£298 excluding fabric. See following page for illustration.

Environment Communication's 'Sunset in New York' sofa by Gaetano Pesce

Suite from Michael Tyler. SCENE 5

Peter Miles's '111'

Hermann Miller's 'EA116'

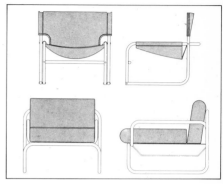

OMK's T RANGE △

HERMANN MILLER LTD

Modern classics from a company well-known for its contract and domestic ranges.
'Eames Lounge Chair ES670' by Charles Eames was first produced in 1956, a revolutionary and influential piece in twentieth-century design. It has a framework of moulded wood-veneered shells (rosewood or black ash) supporting luxurious soft leather cushions. There's a matching ottoman, 'ES671'. *M:* chair w85 × d84 × h84cm (33½ × 33 × 33in); ottoman w66 × d53.5 × h41cm (26 × 21 × 16¼in). *P:* on application.
EAMES ALUMINIUM GROUP functional designs would be ideal in home or office. Swivel lounge armchair 'EA116' has polished or dark-tone epoxy-coated aluminium arms and four-star base; seat and tall, curving back are covered in quilted leather or tough fabric in off-white, dark blue or brown, orange, light green or black. *M:* w62 × d69 × h 90cm (24½ × 27¼ × 35½in). *P:* on application.

'Eames Lounge Chair ES670' from Hermann Miller △

MORGAN GILDER FURNITURE

Hand-built two- and three-seater sofas, armchairs and ottomans in four pleasant styles from a small personal company. Removable or fixed covers, and curtains if wanted, are made from the customer's own fabric; cushions can be filled with fire-retardant foam or feathers at a few pounds extra cost per cushion. Right-angled frame, cushions and valance produce the stylish, rather 1930s look of ADAM, especially when covered in plain fabric with contrasting piping. *M:* two-seater w56 × d35 × h36in (142 × 89 × 91.5cm). *P:* (without fabric) £345.

Morgan Gilder's ADAM

OMK DESIGN LTD △

High-tech elegance in seating for domestic or contract use.
Macho T RANGE goes in for clean lines with strong tubular-steel frames finished in polished chrome or epoxy (colours on request). 'T1' armless chair has a self-assembly frame with slung seat in cow hide or heavy-duty canvas. 'T2' armchair and matching 'T6' and 'T3' two- and three-seater sofas have more curving frames, rubber webbing and cushions

covered in soft hide, corduroy, velours, simulated hide or customer's own fabric. *M:* 'T1' w75 × d75 × h70cm (29½ × 29½ × 27½); 'T2' w82 × d82 × h72cm (32¼ × 32¼ × 28¼in). *P:* 'T1' £106–£233, 'T2' £196–£304.

CASSIS creates a surprisingly pretty effect from curved panels of perforated sheet steel with rigid tubular trim and ample cushions contoured to the frame. 'PS1' armchair, 'PS2' two-seater sofa and 'PS3' three-seater sofa come in black, white, green, brown or terra-cotta epoxy finish with a wide choice of zipped covers. The light-weight frame comes boxed for self-assembly; individual panels are interchangeable. Prices include scatter cushions. *M:* 'PS1' w100 × d110 × h74cm (39¼ × 43¼ × 29¼in); 'PS2' w160 × d110 × h74cm (63 × 43¼ × 29¼in); 'PS3' w222 × d110 × h74cm (87½ × 43¼ × 29¼in). *P:* 'PS1' £390–£520; 'PS2' £610–864; 'PS3' £910–£1302.

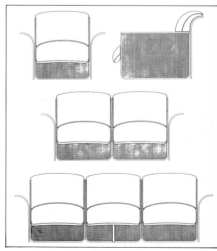

OMK's CASSIS △

ONE OFF LTD

Witty transformation of luxurious car seating into high tech 'Rover' chairs. Reclining leather Rover V8 2000 front seats are mounted on

FURNITURE

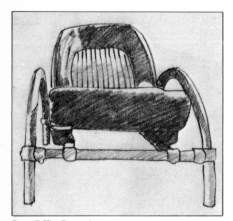

One Off's 'Rover'

semicircular tubular-steel frames coated in epoxy. *M:* w27 × max d36in (68.5 × 91.5cm) *P:* £260. Two-seater version also available.

PARKER & FARR FURNITURE LTD
Luxury suites of armchairs, two- and three-seater sofas and corner units in a wide choice of designs and sizes, upholstered in customer's own fabric or in one of the 100 designs in Parker & Farr's collection.
VALENTINO is attractively curvilinear with scalloped cut-away base, lightly scrolled arms and rounded backs. Range includes a cushioned stool. *M:* sofas w187, 217 × d85 × h88, 90cm (73½, 85½ × 33½ × 34¾, 35½in); armchair w100 × d85 × h85cm (39¼ × 33½ × 33½in). *P:* on application.

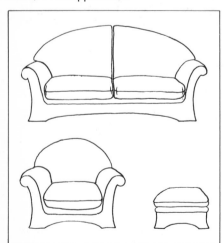

Parker & Farr's VALENTINO

PALAMEDES has contrastingly sharp, square lines and offers models in either standard or high-backed styles. There are four two-seater sofas (one a sofa bed), one three-seater, two armchairs and a stool. A wing chair, 'Chipps', and a button-backed occasional chair, 'Rock-

Parker & Farr's PALAMEDES. Top: standard back; below: high back

ford', are available to complement the range. *M:* sofas w180, 210, 271 × d93 × h76, 96cm (70¾, 82¾, 106¾ × 36½ × 30, 37¾in); armchair w92 × d88 × h76, 92cm (36¼ × 34¾ × 30, 36¼in). *P:* on application.

PARKER KNOLL FURNITURE LTD
Contemporary and traditional styles with the emphasis on quality and comfort. Nine suites, all with armchairs and one sofa, are available in a wide range of Parker Knoll's own fabrics.

Parker Knoll's BEVERLEY 'PK1103'

BEVERLEY includes an ingenious two-seater sofa with drop-ends, 'PK1103', which converts, progressively, into a lounger, five-seater or single bed. *M:* w151–206 × d83 × h75cm (59½–81 × 32¾ × 29½in). *P:* from £454.
More formal are FROXFIELD two-seater sofa

Parker Knoll's FROXFIELD and 'Frith'

and armchair with high backs and wooden legs, which are complemented by the 'Frith' wing chair. *M:* FROXFIELD sofa w121 × d79 × h81cm (47¾ × 31 × 32in), armchair w56 × d79 × h81cm (22 × 31 × 32in); 'Frith' w56 × d86 × h96cm (22 × 33¾ × 37¾in). *P:* FROXFIELD sofa £375, armchair £218; 'Frith' £283.

PERRINGS
Four suites selected to span styles both old and new, part of an updated and fully co-ordinated collection from established furnishers.
HANNAH is quietly traditional. Two- and three-seater sofas, armchair and ottoman have removable loose covers with pleated skirts available in a variety of Perrings' patterned fabrics with plain or contrast piping (featured here in 'Ribbons and Bows'). *M:* three-seater w198 × d94 × h89cm (78 × 37 × 35in). *P:* three-seater £399.

Perrings' HANNAH

MARTINE offers plainer modern lines with high backs and fashionable folded-cushion arms. Two- and three-seater sofas, armchair and ottoman come in a selection of contempory fabrics including the diagonal weave 'Bonita' (featured here). *M:* three-seater w190 × d101 × h89cm (74¾ × 39¾ × 35in). *P:* £345.

Perrings' MARTINE

RELYON LTD
Sofa beds and matching armchairs in varied styles from well known bed manufacturers. There are 19 designs; some unfold into a low, all-foam bed, others into a standard-height

bed with sprung-interior mattress.
'Manhattan' is an elegant, conventional three-seater sofa with splayed back and arms, fully skirted to floor, with two matching scatter cushions; a spring-balanced folding mechanism allows it to convert into a double bed with Relyon spring-interior mattress. Available with a variety of plain or patterned covers. *M:* w195 × d98 × h78cm (76¾ × 38½ × 30¾in). *P:* from £812.

Relyon's 'Manhattan'

'Monaco' is a modern three-seater which transforms in one easy movement into an all-foam bed. The cover, in two-tone 100% cotton, doubles as a duvet and is removable for cleaning. The box base provides generous linen storage. *M:* w197 × d97 × h85cm (74 × 38 × 33in). *P:* £409.

Relyon's 'Monaco'

REST ASSURED
Comfortable but reasonably priced sofa beds and suites in a variety of fabrics from manufacturers best known for their beds. One of nine straightforward sofa bed designs is the box-shaped ESTELLE. An armchair in the same range converts into a single bed. *M:* sofa bed w164 × d87.5 × h88cm (64½ × 34½ × 34¾in). *P:* £227.95.

Rest Assured's ESTELLE

ROSET (UK) LTD
Informal modern suites and sofa beds from European design team. Most ranges comprise chair, two sizes of sofa and ottoman.
Stylish AMAK range was inspired by the principle of a hammock: the cushioned seat, covered in black or grey leather, is suspended between base supports made from strong black polystyrene. *M:* sofa w200 × d105 × h68cm (78¾ × 41¼ × 26¾in); chair w112 × d105 × h68cm (44 × 41¼ × 26¾in). *P:* sofa £700; chair £505.
Deep-cushioned GAO range includes a three-seater sofa with a base that converts into a double bed while the cover becomes a duvet. *M:* sofa w200 × d110 × h88cm (78¾ × 43¼ × 34¾in); chair w85 × d94 × h71cm (33½ × 37 × 28in). *P:* sofa £603; chair £256.
Simpler in line, MODULY armchair and two sizes of sofa have pull-out single and double beds concealed in a drawer in the base. *M:* sofas w152, 175 × d95 × h79cm (59¾, 69 × 37½ × 31in); armchair w93 × d95 × h79cm (36½ × 37½ × 31in). *P:* sofas from £501; armchair £407.

From Roset. Top: AMAK with ottoman; centre: GAO with sofa bed extended; bottom: MODULY with ottoman

SAG BAGS
Durable seating bags filled with expanded polystyrene beads, available in a variety of sizes, shapes and materials. All the coverings — canvas, hide, and polyurethane-coated nylon and cotton — and fillings are flame-retardant and non-toxic. The range comprises 'Flan', the largest and recommended as a substitute sofa; 'Pear' for lengthways lounging; smaller 'Junior Pear'; round 'Onion'; and 'Penta', round with a hollower centre. The polystyrene beads compact through long use so Sag Bags can supply packs of beads for topping up old bags — the beads are inserted through a zip opening. *M:* 'Pear' w54in (137cm). *P:* £55.

SLEEPEEZEE
Attractive selection of two- and three-seater sofas that convert easily into single and double beds. HYDABEDS all have Sleepeezee's standard interior-sprung mattresses but a more luxurious and bulkier 'Beautirest' pocketed

Sleepeezee's 'Cuddler'

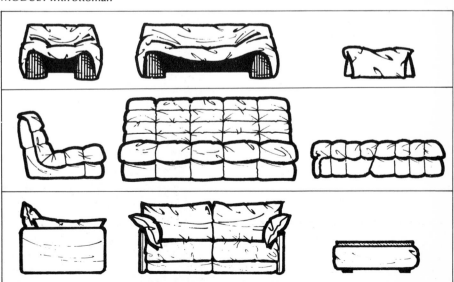

FURNITURE

mattress can be supplied if required. Sofas can be covered in a wide choice of fabrics — prints, tweeds, velvets and weaves from major European manufacturers. Two-seater 'Cuddler' is simply styled and unobtrusive; the fabrics available include a pretty small-scale Italian print (featured here). *M:* w136 × d90 × h82cm (53½ × 35½ × 32¼in). *P:* from £626.

SOUTH BANK DESIGNS
Many different period designs from Italy in pickled pine finish (from stock) or a variety of special finishes including lacquer. Covers can be made up in a wide selection of fabrics in three price brackets, leather or suede, or customer's own fabric.
'1303' cane wing chair in Louis XV style with carved flowers has a fitted seat cushion. *M:* w71 × d61 × h107cm (28 × 24 × 42¾in). *P:* £484–£838.
South Bank's only sofa is the charmingly compact '1338' with straight sides and back and carved frame. *M:* w123 × d56 × h96cm (48½ × 22 × 37¾in). *P:* £698–1140. A matching armchair is available.

From South Bank. Top: '1303'; below: '1338'

TITCHMARSH & GOODWIN
Individually made reproduction furniture from exemplary cabinet-makers. 'RL22374' mahogany tub chair with carved frame can be covered in hide or customer's own fabric. *M:* w25 × d18 × h34in (63.5 × 45.5 × 86.5cm). *P:* from £725. See *Desks* for illustration.

TULLEYS OF CHELSEA
Calico-upholstered seating with hardwood frames and spring units, supplied uncovered or tight- or loose-covered in a choice of 8000 fabrics. Among more than 20 models is ENMORE design with a padded, gently rounded back and feather-filled cushions. It is available as an armchair and as a two- or three-seater sofa, with a kick pleat or bun feet. *M:* three-seater w206 × d89 × h79cm (81 × 35 × 31in). *P:* (uncovered) £525.

Tulleys' ENMORE

MICHAEL TYLER FURNITURE LTD
SCENES collection of bold, simply designed sofa beds and chairs, covered in bright modern fabrics selected by Michael Tyler. SCENE 4 chair and sofa extend into single and double beds. The frame of beech and black metal is padded with polyether foam overlaid with a quilt covering filled with 100% polyester siliconized fibre. The quilt is used for bedding and the large back cushions, covered in contrast fabric, double as pillows. *M:* double sofa bed w64 × d46 × h27in (163 × 117 × 69cm); *P:* £572. SCENE 5 chair and sofa have frame of beech with plywood panels supported on cylindrical lacquered legs. Seat suspension is Pirelli webbing and fillings are good quality polyether foam. Again, the covering is in the form of a quilt. *M:* sofa w58 × d37 × h26.5in (146 × 94 × 67cm). *P:* £311. See colour illustration.

R TYZACK LTD
Reproduction furniture with leather upholstery a speciality, from a small independent manufacturer. '1053' tub chair in mahogany with carved details on arms and legs can be covered in hand-antiqued hide or customer's own fabric. *M:* w24 × d25 × h32in (61 × 63.5 × 81.5cm). *P:* on application.

Tyzack's '1053'

ULFERTS OF SWEDEN LTD
Varied collection of suites and plush easy chairs designed and made in Sweden.
There are 10 suites, each comprising armchair, two- and three-seater sofas, and three are available as corner groupings. NOVA sofas and armchairs have floppy, fibre-filled cushions loosely buttoned and draped over a resilient foam base. The result is attractively casual and looks very comfortable. Like all suites in the collection, NOVA is available in Ulfert's wide selection of fabrics; it is also one of four in the range available in leather. *M:* three-seater w210 × d92 × h81cm (82¾ × 36¼ × 32in). *P:* three-seater from £656.
For additional lounge seating there are static and swivelling easy chairs deeply upholstered in hide or fabric, some with matching footstools. 'Stressless Royal' has floppy upholstery in a choice of three different leathers and a wooden frame with unusual circular base available in a variety of wood and coloured stains (including red, grey and black). *M:* w87 × d85 × h97cm (34¼ × 33½ × 38¼in). *P:* from £510. See following page for illustration.

NOVA from Ulferts

'Stressless Royal' from Ulferts

WADE SPRING & UPHOLSTERY COMPANY LTD

Twenty or more conventionally-styled suites upholstered in fabric or hide, plus some occasional seating.

In fabric, LISA suite includes two- and three-seater sofas, upright armchair, reclining armchair (with adjustable back and extendible footrest) and a square stool with lifting top. Each sofa comes with two scatter cushions. Suites are available upholstered in Dralon (in 20 or so colours), wool (in four colours) or a wide variety of typically English cotton prints. If desired, Dralon and wool can be supplied with contrast piping and scatter cushions can be supplied also in reverse colourway. *M:* sofas w137, 188 × d89 × h90cm (54, 74 × 35 ×35½in) *P:* on application.

In hide there are suites such as KENDAL with chesterfields, club chair and wing chair, and also a dozen or so swivel, easy and desk chairs in familiar styles.

Wade's LISA

△ *INDICATES AN ILLUSTRATED PRODUCT SELECTED BY THE DESIGN CENTRE*

WESLEY BARRELL LTD

Beautifully made, classic suites. Among 18 designs is BIBURY, available in 'High Back' style with wing sides or in 'Low Back' style with roll arms. Armchairs and two- and three-seater sofas and sofa beds come in both styles and there's a 'High Back' reclining armchair, and a 'Low Back' chaise-longue with adjustable arm and three scatter cushions. Range also includes a large square ottoman that converts into a single bed. Like all Wesley Barrell's suites, BIBURY comes in a wide variety of fine fabrics — cotton chintzes, tapestries and plains — from well-known companies including G P & J Baker, Tissunique, Warners, Sanderson and Moygashel (see separate entries). *M:* 'Low Back' three-seater and sofa bed w71 × d37 × h34in (180 × 94 × 86.5cm). *P:* sofa £630–£874, sofa bed £827–£1070.

Wesley Barrell's BIBURY 'Low Back'

WESTNOFA

'Tripos', a versatile variation on the revolutionary BALANS kneeling chair (see *Chairs*). The design offers three chairs in one; positioned on the front section of the base it is suitable as a work chair (the knees are bent and supported, the spine upright and relaxed); eased back into the central position it becomes a recliner; eased back further it becomes a full

Westnofa's BALANS 'Tripos'

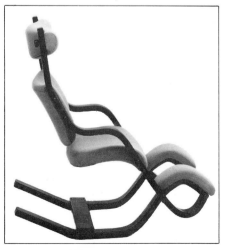

lounger. The centres of gravity are calculated so that you can change the position while seated simply by applying pressure, but without danger of the chair toppling over. The adjustable headrest adapts to each position. The frame, of laminated beech, comes in natural finish or rosewood, teak or black stain; upholstery is in 100% wool in a good choice of colours. *M:* w52 × d116 × h120/46cm (20½ × 45¾ × 47¼/18in). *P:* from £384.

Westnofa also distribute an award-winning 1960s classic, 'Tiara' chair and footstool in laminated beech, now available with upholstery in fabric as well as leather. Fabrics (either 100% wool or wool mixes) and leather are available in a range of pastel shades. *M:* (chair only) w60 × d85 × h100/42cm (23½ × 33½ × 39¼/16½in). *P:* from £332.25.

Westnofa's 'Tiara'

WINDMILL FURNITURE △

Elegant 'Isokon Long Chair' and similar but shorter 'Isokon Short Chair' recreated from the 1930s design by Marcel Breuer. Frame in both models is laminated Finnish birch with a lacquer finish. Seat is laminated beech and high quality fire retardant foam. For the chairs' upholstery there is a choice of six mothproofed pure wool tweeds: charcoal (chosen by Breuer himself), moor (mid-brown), chestnut, oatmeal, elephant (mid-grey) and putty mix (slightly dappled light grey). Alternatively, a suitable fabric selected by the customer could be used. *M:* 'Isokon Long Chair' w24 × d56 × h34in (61 × 142 × 86.5cm) *P:* £483.

'Isokon Long Chair' from Windmill △

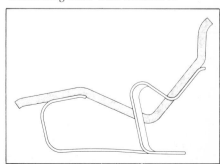

ARCHITECTURAL SALVAGE

ROBERT AAGAARD LTD
Frogmire House
Stockwell Road
Knaresborough
North Yorkshire HG5 0JP
Tel: (0423) 864805
Specialists in period chimneypieces and marble interiors for same, plus appropriate fireside accessories.

ABENBURY BRICKWORKS
Wrexham
Clwyd
Tel: (074 571) 4112 sales office or (0978) 361179 yard
Large quantities of carefully reclaimed period bricks which have been sorted, graded, cleaned and packed.

ACQUISITIONS (FIREPLACES) LTD
269 Camden High Street
London NW1 7BX
Tel: (01) 485 4955
Original specialists in Victorian and Edwardian cast iron and wooden fireplace surrounds, plus fireplace tiles and accessories. Fitting service.

AMAZING GRATES
Antique Fireplace Specialists
61–63 High Road, London N2 8AB
Tel: (01) 883 9590
Specialists in fireplace surrounds in marble, cast iron and wood, accessories in brass and iron, grates in cast iron, and tiles. Restoration and installation service available.

THE ARCHITECTURAL ANTIQUE MARKET
133 Upper Street
London N1
Tel: (01) 226 5565
Architectural salvage items including fireplaces, stained glass, doors, tiles and ironwork, 17th–20th century.

ARCHITECTURAL HERITAGE OF CHELTENHAM
Dept I/FS
Boddington Manor
Boddington, Nr Cheltenham, Glos
Tel: (024268) 741
Suppliers of period and Victorian items suitable for refurbishment and restoration of houses, bars, restaurants and gardens. Panelled rooms, doors, stained glass, bathroom fittings and beams always stocked.

ARCHITECTURAL SALVAGE
Netley House
Gomshall
Surrey GU5 9QA
Tel: (048641) 3221
Maintains index of all kinds of architectural items and for a £10 registration fee will put buyer in touch with appropriate seller. No items directly for sale or on display.

BAILEYS ARCHITECTURAL ANTIQUES
The Engine Shed
Ashburton Industrial Estate
Ross-on-Wye
Herefordshire
Tel: (0989) 63015
Purchase, renovate and install: fireplaces, bathrooms, stained glass, panelling, pews, staircase balustrading and newel posts, columns, lighting, doors and door furniture.

DON BATEMAN
Home Farm
Pulham St Mary
Norfolk
Tel: (037 976) 784
Period building services in Norfolk and suppliers of old beams and studs, pamment, bricks, tiles, flooring, even oak barns for re-erection.

BEACON ARCHITECTURAL SALVAGE
Nr Stratford-upon-Avon
Telephone for directions
Tel: (078987) 616
Original Edwardian through Art Deco bathroom sanitaryware and fittings, plus architectural items such as doors, stained glass, fireplaces, gas radiators and building materials.

BRIDGWATER RECLAMATION LTD
Monmouth Street
Bridgwater
Somerset
Tel: (0278) 424636
Windows, doors, panelling, sinks, wash-basins, architraves, moulding, fire surrounds.

BRIGHTON ARCHITECTURAL SALVAGE
33 Gloucester Road
Brighton
Sussex
Tel: (0273) 681656
Warehouse of architectural antiques including period fireplaces and surrounds in marble, pine, mahogany and cast iron, stained glass, panelling, decorative ironwork, light fittings and garden ornaments.

BRITAINS HERITAGE
13 Meadway
Weston Park
Leicestershire
Tel: (0533) 857747
Original Victorian and Edwardian fireplaces in marble, wood and cast iron; all expertly restored.

BROADLAND TIMBER MART
Norwich Road
Lowestoft
Norfolk
Tel: (0502) 4599
Good choice of timber plus doors, window frames, slates and occasionally fire surrounds.

BROMLEY DEMOLITION
75 Siward Road
Bromley
Kent
Tel: (01) 464 3610
Limited stock of basic demolition items – bricks, doors, floorboards and joists.

BUCKINGHAM ANTIQUES
274–276 Queenstown Road
London SW8
Tel: (01) 627 1410
Specialists in cast iron fireplaces and pine mantelpieces with full restoration and installation service.

T F BUCKLE LTD
427 Kings Road
London SW10
Tel: (01) 352 0952
Antique pine, marble and stone fireplaces and reproduction spiral staircases. Occasionally other architectural features.

ROBIN BURGE
333 Kennington Road
London SE11
Tel: (01) 587 1478
Period style panelling in old pine including features such as bookcases.

ANDRE BUSEK ARCHITECTURAL ANTIQUES
Savoy Showrooms
New Road
South Moulton
Devon
Tel: (076 95) 3342
Based in a disused cinema, featuring a showhouse built entirely with reclaimed materials. Specialists in quality items rather than basic supplies, and have a complete restoration service.

CANTABRIAN ANTIQUES
16 Park Street
Lynton
N Devon
Tel: (05985) 3282
Internal and external decorative architectural items – bathroom fittings, doors, oak beams, panelling, stained glass, bar and shop fittings. Good selection of quality salvage particularly of fireplaces and surrounds.

THE CAST IRON FIREPLACE COMPANY LTD
99–103 East Hill
Wandsworth London SW18 2QB
Tel: (01) 870 1630
Fully restored cast iron fireplaces from 1830 on, some with decorative tile panels.

ALFRED G CAWLEY & SONS LTD
Havering Farm
Worplesdon
Surrey
Tel: (0483) 232398

Building materials – doors, bricks, timber, floorboards.

CHAPEL HOUSE FIREPLACES
Telephone for appointment
Tel: (0484) 682275
Supply and delivery of antique and Victorian fireplaces and mantelpieces in cast iron, marble, pine, oak and mahogany.

CHESHIRE RECLAIMED BUILDING MATERIALS LTD
Leak Street
Old Trafford
Manchester
Tel: (061) 872 2352
Good choice of bricks and flagstones.

CIVIL ENGINEERING DEVELOPMENTS LTD
728 London Road
West Thurlock
Grays
Essex RM16 1LU
Tel: (04026) 7237
Suppliers of reclaimed stones and aggregates including cobbles, pebbles, knapped flints, setts and York flagstones.

THE COMPLETE BATHROOM
16 Roundtree Close
Roundtree Way
Norwich
Norfolk
Tel: (0603) 486298
Specialists in period bathrooms, including installation and design service.

CONSERVATION BUILDING PRODUCTS
Forge Works
Forge Lane
Cradley Heath
Warley
W Midlands B64 5AL
Tel: (0384) 64219 or (052 784) 497 evenings/ weekends
Stockists of period roofing tiles, fittings, finials, hand or machine-made bricks, oak beams, joists, complete trusses, quarry floortiles, paving, coping, stripped pine doors, panelling, sandstone and architectural ironwork.

COUNTERPARTS DEMOLITION LTD
Station Yard
Station Road
Topsham
Exeter Devon
Tel: (039 287) 5995
Stock of basic items – timber, slates, doors, galvanised sheeting; sometimes fire surrounds.

COVENTRY CONSERVATION STORE
78 Whitefriars Street
Coventry
Tel: (0203) 25555 ext 2816

Small selection of items across the range – bricks, tiles, quarry tiles, parquet flooring, roofing materials, cast-iron fire surrounds, tiled fireplaces, bric-a-brac.

CROWTHER OF SYON LODGE
Syon Lodge
Busch Corner
London Road
Isleworth
Middx TW7 5BH
Tel: (01) 560 7978
Specialists in 18th and 19th century English and French fireplaces in marble, pine and stone.

T CROWTHER & SON LTD
282 North End Road
London SW6 1NH
Tel: (01) 385 1375/7
Dealers in antique architectural items such as oak and pine panelling, wood and marble mantelpieces and garden ornaments.

DALLING ANTIQUES
63 Dalling Road
London W6
Tel: (01) 748 5102
Specialists in restoration and renovation of Continental solid fuel stoves and cooking ranges in a wide variety of styles including ornate cast iron and vitreous enamel models.

STAN DAWSON (WYLAM) LTD
Bythorne Farm
Wylam
Northumberland
Tel: (066 14) 3195
Good stock of slates, timber, trusses.

EDINBURGH NEW TOWN CONSERVATION COMMITTEE
13A Dundas Street
Edinburgh
Tel: (061) 556 7054
Stock available only to residents within the district council's boundaries. Wide range of salvage includes chimney pots, doors, balconies, balustrades, French lime for pointing, fire surrounds, tiles.

AN ENGLISHMAN'S HOME
56 Stokescroft
Bristol 7
Avon
Tel: (0272) 424257
or
113 East Street
South Moulton
North Devon
Tel: (07695) 3342
Comprehensive range of pub and shop fittings plus restored marble fire surrounds, Victorian and Georgian grates, stained glass light fittings, and ironwork.

FAIRWATER YARD
Staplegrove Road
Taunton Somerset
Tel: (0823) 87035
Slates, roof tiles, timber, basins, toilets.

FLOYDS
349 Ilderton Road
London SW15
Tel: (01) 639 6991
Reclaimed building materials such as London stock bricks, Welsh slates, timber and tiles.

FROM DOOR TO DOOR
The Old Smithy
Cerrigydrudion
N Wales
Tel: (0490 82) 491
Architectural fittings including doors, spindles, newel posts, pews and fire surrounds.

GLENFIRST LTD
Chettles Industrial Estate
Ilkeston Road
Nottingham
Tel: (0602) 703140
Enormous range of building materials – literally everything from roof tiles to asbestos sheeting plus kitchen unit tops and garden seating.

GLOVER & STACEY
Malt House Premises
Main Road
Kingsley
Bordon
Hants
Tel: (042 03) 5754
Specialists in fireplaces, surrounds, stained glass, timber moulding and doors, as well as several restoration services.

HALLIDAYS CARVED PINE MANTELPIECES LTD
28 Beauchamp Place
London SW3 1NJ
Tel: (01) 589 5534
Carved pine and marble mantelpieces, grates, corner cupboards, and panelling.

HAVENPLAN'S ARCHITECTURAL EMPORIUM
The Old Station
Station Road
Killamarsh Nr Sheffield
Specialists in staircase pieces plus old doors in oak, pine or mahogany, fire inserts and surrounds, water pumps, cast iron gates, railings, church fittings, old panelling and planking, even postboxes.

HERITAGE WOODCRAFT
Victor Works
Station Street
Atherstone
Warwicks CV9 1BY
Tel: (08277) 5792

ARCHITECTURAL SALVAGE

Reclaimed and reconditioned hardwood flooring of all types.

EDWARD KING STAINED GLASS
37 Northfield Road
London E6 2AJ
Tel: (01) 472 2507
Small firm offering range of services from on-site repairs to removing complete windows for restoration.

KNIGHT'S OF LONDON
2A Belsize Park Mews
London NW3 5BL
Tel: (01) 431 2490
Independent service covering every aspect of antique and period fireplace design including planning, discovery and purchase for both private and commercial clients.

LAMONT ANTIQUES
Newhams Row
175 Bermondsey Street
London SE1
Tel: (01) 403 0126
Architectural items including leaded light windows, bar and restaurant fittings.

A LANDAU
45 Mill Lane
London NW6
Tel: (01) 794 3028
    (01) 452 3993 (Home)
Late Victorian and Edwardian fire surrounds, stained glass panels and tiles.

LANGHAM ARCHITECTURAL MATERIALS
Langham Farm
East Nynehead
Wellington
Somerset TA21 0DD
Tel: (082346) 297
A wide range of period fixtures and fittings including hardwood and softwood beams, hobs, grates, fire surrounds in stone, marble, cast iron and pine, brassware etc.

LASCO TIMBER LTD
Mark Street (off Paul Street)
London EC2
Tel: (01) 729 3620
18th and 19th century pitch pine and yellow pine floor boarding in widths up to 16in (40cm). Also Georgian and Victorian skirting, architraving, cornicing and other mouldings machined from original patterns.

LIVERPOOL ARCHITECTURAL WORKSHOP
7 Head Street
St James's Place
Liverpool L8 1YU
Tel: (051) 708 7518
Collection of stained glass, Victorian bathrooms and fireplaces.

LONDON ARCHITECTURAL SALVAGE & SUPPLY CO LTD
Mark Street (off Paul Street)
London EC2A 4ER
Tel: (01) 739 0448/9
Architectural salvage specialists for domestic and contract clients. Items include red and black quarry tiles, church pews, panelled doors, marble fireplace surrounds, cast iron grates, panelling, bathroom sanitaryware, ironwork and joinery, leaded glass and shop fittings.

MARBLE HILL GALLERY
72 Richmond Road
Twickenham
Middx
Tel: (01) 892 1488
Pine and French marble mantels.

OLD WORLD TRADING COMPANY
565 Kings Road
London SW6
Tel: (01) 731 4708
18th and 19th century marble fireplaces supplied and fitted, complete with hearths and grates.

B OLDS
Site 1
Mercury Way
off Cold Blow Lane
London SE14
Tel: (01) 732 6640
Stock of basic building materials – bricks, tiles, concrete slabs, timbers and doors.

PAGEANT ANTIQUES
122 Dawes Road
London SW6
Tel: (01) 385 7739
Architectural fittings, fireplaces, panelling, period architraves, doors, plus wrought and cast iron staircases.

PERIOD RECLAMATION & RESTORATION SERVICES
205 Salisbury Road
Burton
Christchurch
Dorset BH23 7JT
Tel: (0202) 473300
Architectural and period dismantling specialists. Suppliers of reclaimed property and restoration materials such as tiles, slates, bricks, oak beams plus marble and pine fireplace surrounds.

E S PHILLIPS AND SON
99 Portobello Road
London W11
Tel: (01) 229 2213
Stained glass windows, architectural fittings, panelling, flooring, and fireplaces.

THE PINE MINE
100 Wandsworth Bridge Road
London SW6
Tel: (01) 736 1092
Chimneypieces, mantels, doors and fittings in pine.

PITCH PINE LTD
Wellington Road
Ashton-under-Lyme
Manchester OL6 7EG
Tel: (061) 339 0047
Second hand pitch pine timber, seasoned, selected and graded, free of rot, infestation, nails and bolts, sawn all round and cut to order.

POSTERITY ARCHITECTURAL EFFECTS
Baldwins Farm
Newent
Glos
Tel: (053185) 597
Stockists of cast iron columns, panelling, bar fittings, fireplace surrounds, doors and windows, bathroom fittings, garden ornaments and conservatory fittings.

D S & A G PRIGMORE
Mill Cottage
Mill Lane
Colmworth,
Bedford
Tel: (023 062) 264
Good selection of bricks, slates, ridge tiles, timber, cupboards, panelling, fireplaces, wood blocks.

A L RATTRAY
The Garden House
Craighall
Blairgowrie
Perthshire
Scotland
Tel: (0250) 4749
Architectural recyclers of Victorian bathroom fittings, doors, mantelpieces, panelling, iron and wood staircases, balconies, balustrades plus stained, etched and cut glass doors.

RECLAIMED MATERIALS
Northgate
White Lund Industrial Estate,
Morecambe
Tel: (0524) 69094
Good selection of slates plus flagstones, timber flooring, steel and fire surrounds.

REDUNDANT CHURCH FURNISHINGS
The Warren
Church Road
Woldingham
Surrey
Tel: Woldingham 905 2366
Victorian ecclesiastical fixtures and fittings.

RELIC ANTIQUES
Brillscott Farm
Lea
Nr Malmesbury
Wilts
Tel: (06662) 2332
Architectural antiques including fairground art and animals plus shop and pub fittings.

THE RICHMOND ANTIQUARY
28 Hill Rise
Richmond
Surrey
Tel: (01) 948 0583 and Egham 7229 (Home)
Architectural antiques including doors, mantelpieces and panelling.

ROBERTSON & PARTNERS LTD
Jodrell Street
Nuneaton
Warks
Tel: (0203) 384110
Timber, some flooring and steel sheeting

ROGERS DEMOLITION AND DISMANTLING SERVICE
Belgrave Road
Portswood
Southampton
Tel: (0703) 449173
Will dismantle whole houses from top to bottom. Salvage material includes bricks, chimney pots, panelling, pumps, flagstones, steel girders, slates, skirting boards and even complete period rooms.

SCALLYWAG
Wren Road
Camberwell Green
London SE5
Tel: (01) 701 5353
Architectural items including doors, panelling, mouldings, church furnishing, staircases and fire surrounds.

SOLID PRODUCTS
Unit 4
158–206 Western Avenue
Acton
London W3 6RW
Tel: (01) 993 6093
Vast stock of tongue-and-groove secondhand flooring in excellent condition. Both large and small orders welcomed.

SOLOPARK LTD
The Old Railway Station
Station Road
Pampisford
Cambs CB2 4HB
Tel: (0223) 834663
Specialist suppliers of reclaimed building materials including bricks (soft reds, handmades, Tudors, stocks), internal and external doors, staircases, window frames, panelling, mouldings, oak and hardwood

rafters, fireplaces, chimneypots, York stone pavings, floor panels plus roofing tiles and slates.

SOUTHBRIDGE BUILDING SUPPLIES LTD
Kingscote Railway Station Yard
East Grinstead
W Sussex
Tel: (0342) 313244
Suppliers of scaffolding, asbestos, corrugated panels, doors.

STOVE SHOP
181 Kings Cross Road
London WC1
Tel: (01) 833 3534
Original antique stoves from the Continent, and some English models. Renovated and restored to working order in various styles made from cast iron or coloured vitreous enamel.

SUSSEX DEMOLITIONS SERVICES
Oxted Station Car Park
Oxted
Surrey
Tel: (08833) 5413
Salvage specialists with building materials, fire surrounds, doors and brass fittings.

SWADLINGS
13 Dragon Street
Petersfield
Hants
Tel: (0730) 64634
Extensive selection of period bathroom fittings, accessories and sanitaryware.

SYMONDS BROTHERS
Colt Yard
Pluckley Road
Bethersden
Kent
Tel: (023 382) 724
Good supply of bricks, doors, tiles; some timber and cast-iron surrounds.

ANDY THORNTON ARCHITECTURAL ANTIQUES LTD
Ainleys Industrial Estate
Ellan,
W Yorkshire HX5 9JP
Tel: (0422) 78125/6
Large-scale architectural fittings including pulpits, shop fronts, staircases, stained glass and doors.

TIMBER RECLAMATION (DEMOLITION) LTD
25 Redcliffe Street
Bristol
Tel: (0272) 297479
Specialists in timber – stock includes floorboards and joists.

WALCOT RECLAMATION
108 Walcot Street
Bath
Avon BA1 5BG
Tel: (0225) 66291
Architectural antiques with good selection of fireplaces and accessories from all periods, plus grates, stoves and ranges. Stained glass, panelled doors, flooring, roofing, beams, architectural joinery and bathrooms also stocked.

WHITEWAY AND WALDRON LTD
305 Munster Road
London SW6
Tel: (01) 381 3195
Stained glass and architectural fittings, such as church pews, doors, fire surrounds.

WINKLEIGH TIMBER
Old Sawmills
Winkleigh
Devon
Tel: (083 783) 573
Timber, joists. Window and door frame seconds (new).

DAVID WOODS ANTIQUES
The Chimneys
Dauntsey Lock
Chippenham
Wilts
Tel: (0249) 891234 evenings (06662) 2976
Specialists in original Victorian and Edwardian bathroom fittings.

WOODSTOCK (TOTNES) LTD
Station Road
Totnes
Devon
Tel: (0803) 864610
Doors, windows, toilets, timber, sheet materials and fire surrounds.

WOOLAWAY & SONS
Junction Yard
Seven Brothers Bank
Barnstaple
Devon
Tel: (0271) 74191
Small selection of architectural salvage – doors, slates and fire surrounds.

USEFUL ADDRESSES

ARCHITECTURE AND DESIGN ASSOCIATIONS

Architectural Association
34–36 Bedford Square
London WC1
Tel: (01) 636 0974

British Institute of Interior Design
1c Devonshire Avenue
Beeston
Nottingham
Tel: (0602) 221255

Design Council
The Design Centre
28 Haymarket
London SW1
Tel: (01) 839 8000

Interior Decorators and Designers Association
4–5 Sheen Lane
London SW14
Tel: (01) 876 4415

International Wool Secretariat
Wool House
Carlton Gardens
London SW1
Tel: (01) 930 7300

CONSUMER INFORMATION SOURCES

British Standards Institution
2 Park Street
London W1
Tel: (01) 629 9000

Building Centre
26 Store Street
London WC1
Tel: (01) 637 1022 (administration) (0344) 884999 (information)

Building Centre
Colston Avenue
The Centre
Bristol
Tel: (0272) 22953

Building Centre
115 Portland Street
Manchester
Tel: (061) 236 9802

Building Centre
47 High Street
Paisley
Renfrewshire
Tel: (041) 840 1199

Building Information Centre
Cauldon College of Further Education
The Concourse
Stoke Road
Shelton
Stoke-on-Trent
Staffs
Tel: (0782) 29561

Building Materials Information Service
22 The Broadway
Peterborough
Cambridgeshire
Tel: (0733) 314239

Building Research Advisory Service
Building Research Station
Bucknalls Lane
Garston
Watford WD2 7JR
Tel: (0923) 676612

Building Research Establishment
Scottish Laboratory
Kelvin Road
East Kilbride
Glasgow
Tel: (035 52) 33941

Consumers' Association
14 Buckingham Street
London WC2
Tel: (01) 839 1222

Solid Fuel Advisory Service
The Building Centre
26 Store Street
London W1
Tel: (01) 637 1189

CONSERVATION GROUPS

The Building Conservation Trust
Apartment 39
Hampton Court Palace
East Molesey
Surrey KT8 9BS
Tel: (01) 943 2277

Conservation Bureau
Conservation Officer
Scottish Development Agency
102 Telford Road
Edinburgh
Tel: (031) 343 1911/6

Conservation Sourcebook
Crafts Council
8 Waterloo Place
London SW1
Tel: (01) 930 4811

The Georgian Group
37 Spital Square
London E1 6DY
Tel: (01) 377 1722

SPAB
(The Society for the Protection of Ancient Buildings),
37 Spital Square
London E1 6DY
Tel: (01) 377 1644

The Thirties Society,
3 Park Square West,
London NW1
No telephone

Victorian Society
1 Priory Gardens
Bedford Park
London W4 1TT
Tel: (01) 994 1019

TRADE ASSOCIATIONS AND GUILDS

Art Metalware Manufacturers' Association
27 Frederick Street
Birmingham
Tel: (021) 236 2657/9

Association of Master Upholsterers
348 Neasden Lane
London NW10
Tel: (01) 205 0465

British Antique Dealers' Association
20 Rutland Gate
London SW7
Tel: (01) 589 4128

British Bath Manufacturers' Association
Fleming House
Renfrew Street
Glasgow
Tel: (041) 322 0826

British Blind and Shutter Association
5 Greenfield Crescent
Edgbaston
Birmingham B1
Tel: (021) 454 2177

British Carpet Manufacturers' Association
72 Dean Street
London W1
Tel: (01) 734 9853

British Floorcovering Manufacturers'
Association
125 Queens Road
Brighton
Sussex
Tel: (0273) 29271

British Foundry Association
14 Pall Mall
London SW1
Tel: (01) 930 7171

British Wood Preserving Association
Premier House
150 Southampton Row
London WC1
Tel: (01) 837 8217

Builders' Merchants' Federation
15 Soho Square
London W1
Tel: (01) 439 1753

Ceramic Tile Council
Federation House
Stoke-on-Trent
Staffs
Tel: (0782) 45147

Electrical Contractors' Association
32 Palace Court
London W2
Tel: (01) 229 1266

Federation of Master Builders
33 John Street
London WC1
Tel: (01) 242 7583/7

Glazing and Glass Federation
6 Mount Row
London W1
Tel: (01) 629 8334

Guild of Architectural Ironmongers
8 Stepney Green
London E1
Tel: (01) 790 3431

The Guild of Master Craftsmen
170 High Street
Lewes
East Sussex
Tel: (0273) 477374

Institution of Electrical Engineers
Savoy Place
Victoria Embankment
London WC2
Tel: (01) 240 1871

Kitchen Furniture Manufacturers' Association
82 New Cavendish Street
London W1
Tel: (01) 580 5588

The National Fireplace Council
P O Box 35
Stoke-on-Trent ST4 7NU
Tel: (0782) 44311

USEFUL PRODUCTS

INTRODUCTION

Successful decorating depends largely on using the right product for a specific job. This section is devoted to a few valuable products for the decorator or handyman, from general-purpose adhesives to specialized cleaners and polishes for marble or chrome, from basic grouts to coloured ones, from wood varnishes to coatings for restoring enamel, plus a few gadgets you may not know even exist. It is broken down into the following parts: *Adhesives, Miscellaneous, Sealants, Tiling* and *Wood care.*

ADHESIVES

CIBA-GEIGY

ARALDITE epoxy resin adhesive. It forms extremely strong, durable bonds on metal, glass, wood, rubber, china, leather and most hard, rigid plastics. It resists heat and corrosion, is waterproof and electrically insulating. Two tubes are supplied, adhesive and hardener, which have to be mixed before use. Ordinary ARALDITE sets in 12 hours and is ideal for glueing complicated structures or large areas because it allows plenty of time for positioning the pieces and clamping or taping them together. ARALDITE RAPID, which sets in 10 minutes, is better for smaller jobs, especially those that are hard to clamp. *M:* 30g (1oz). *P:* ARALDITE £1.56, ARALDITE RAPID £1.91.

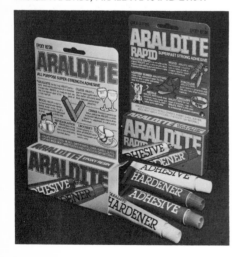

DUNLOP LTD

Useful selection of contact adhesives for general purposes and special products for woodwork, floors and ceilings. Non-drip THIX-OFIX immediately forms strong bonds with many materials. UNIVERSAL ADHESIVE AND PRIMER is a strong, versatile adhesive which bonds most materials in the home. POWERFIX is a versatile, water-based contact adhesive suitable for wood, cork, rubber, leather,

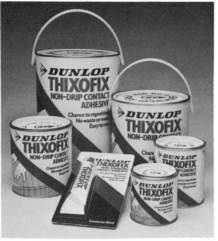

laminates, paper and other materials. It brushes on like paint so can be used to bond large areas, and it dries faster than other water-based adhesives. WOODWORKER is a ready-to-use PVA glue suitable with most woods, while waterproof EXTRA STRONG WOOD GLUE can be used indoors or out, and is ideal for areas where conditions are damp, such as kitchens and bathrooms. For walls, non-drip WALLCOVERING ADHESIVE is suitable for vinyl, textile, hessian and polystyrene wallcoverings. Water- and heat-resistant FLOOR-ING ADHESIVE can be used to fix vinyl, linoleum and carpet flooring. *M:* THIXOFIX 40ml (1½oz), 250ml–5l (8¾ fl oz–8¾pt); UNIVERSAL ADHESIVE AND PRIMER 500ml (17½ fl oz), 1l (1¾pt); POWERFIX 30, 120, 250, 500ml (1½, 4¼, 8¾, 17½ fl oz); WOODWORKER 100ml (3½ fl oz), 500ml (17½ fl oz), 1l (1¾pt); EXTRA STRONG WOOD GLUE 125ml (4½ fl oz), 250ml (8¾ fl oz), 500ml (17½ fl oz), 5l (8¾pt); WALLCOVERING ADHESIVE 1, 2½, 5k (2.2, 5.5, 11lb); FLOORING ADHESIVE 500ml–5l (17½ fl oz–8¾pt). *P:* on application.

HUMBROL

Broad range of home repair adhesives. WON-DERBOND cyanoacrylate gives a super-strong, quick bond to metal, glass, plastic, china and other materials. It comes in three forms: 'Universal', 'Glass and Ceramic' and 'Wood and Modelling'. FLEXIBOND latex adhesive gives a flexible but strong bond to textiles; it is useful for laying carpets, carpet tiles or felt. Humbrol also make a rapid-setting SUPERFAST EPOXY two-part epoxy resin adhesive for almost all rigid materials; EPOXY PUTTY for heavier repairs to wood, metal, rigid plastics (including UPVC), even stonework or glass; and SUPER-STIK contact adhesive for laying laminates and also for metal, plaster, wood, hardboard, leather, PVC and other plastics — it is usually adjustable so that surfaces can be repositioned before bonding. Their MULTIPURPOSE FLOORING ADHESIVE can be used for all

kinds of floor coverings — its acrylic formulation will bond vinyl tiles and sheet, carpet and cork tiles, rubber, linoleum and other materials bonded to hardboard, wood, cement or concrete. *P:* WONDERBOND 3g (¹⁄₁₀oz) £1.50; FLEXIBOND 24ml (¾ fl oz) 99p; SUPERFAST EPOXY 130g (4½oz) £1.55; EPOXY PUTTY pack £1.65; SUPERSTIK 24ml (¾ fl oz) 77p; MULTIPURPOSE FLOORING ADHESIVE 500ml (17½ fl oz) £2.15, 1l (1¾pt) £3.40, 2.5l (4⅜pt) £7.50.

MISCELLANEOUS

ATTRACTA PRODUCTS LTD

ROLLERMATE painting machine designed to take time and trouble out of painting. The twin-roller system is fed from a valve-controlled paint reservoir which ensures an even flow of paint, without drips or splashes. The paint flow can be adjusted to eliminate matting, clogging and streaking, and a simulated lamb's-wool outer roller gives a smooth, professional finish. The angle of the rollers can be altered to suit different conditions and a lightweight aluminium extension pole is available for reaching high walls and ceilings. The reservoir will cover about 35 sq yd (30 sq m) before refilling. The machine is suitable for use with most gloss paints and emulsions. *P:* £8.95 plus £1.05 p&p (mail order only).

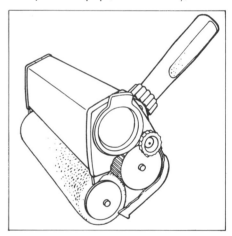

ROLLERMATE painting machine by Attracta

A BELL & CO

Useful range of cleaners and polishers. BELL 1967 CLEANER is a multipurpose cleaner and degreaser for all materials and general household use. BELL MARBLE POLISH is a good all round wax polish where a tough surface is required, while SPECIAL MARBLE CLEANER is for a more rigorous cleaning job. To clean stainless steel, bronze or copper use STAINLESS STEEL CARE; for iron and steel surfaces BELL ARMOUR BRIGHT POLISH and for black metal BLACKLEAD TYPE POLISH. *P:* BELL 1967 CLEANER ½pt (280ml) £2.90; BELL MARBLE

POLISH ½lb (226g) £3.60; SPECIAL MARBLE CLEANER 10oz (283g) £2.65; STAINLESS STEEL CARE 170g (6oz) £3.60; BELL ARMOUR BRIGHT POLISH ¾lb (340g) £2.20; BLACKLEAD TYPE POLISH 28.4g (1oz) £1.40.

DYLON INTERNATIONAL LTD
DYLON POLYESTER DYE to revitalize polyester fabrics. The dye is suitable for use on all common polyesters and it can even be used on mixtures of polyester and cotton. Six bright colours are available — apricot, bluebell, apple, rose, lemon and lilac — and the dyeing can be done quickly and cleanly in an automatic washing machine. *P:* 75ml (1½fl oz) bottle £1.99.
Other useful products from Dylon include fabric paint which will bring fresh, permanent colour to all kinds of dull or faded fabrics; fabric colour and stain remover plus a rain and stain repellent; fabric whiteners; shoe dyes and cleaners; and a wide range of clothes dyes.

HUMBROL
Two unusual home repair products. PLASTIC WOOD allows easy repairs to damaged wood; it can be stained with wood dye and sanded when dry. VINYL MENDER is a kit containing adhesive and a collection of flexible PVC patches to mend PVC sheetings, mouldings and coated fabrics such as leather cloth. *P:* PLASTIC WOOD 24ml 99p; VINYL MENDER 24ml £1.45.

NORTH WESTERN LEAD CO LTD
DECRA-LED pliable strip lead for applying to glass to create leaded windows. By applying self-adhesive DECRA-LED to windows you can give your home a period feel and, by using TRANSPARENT GLASS STAIN, create your own designs in imitation of stained glass. DECRA-LED can also be used in the home itself on, for example, display cabinets, mirrors and coffee tables. *P:* on application.

PORCELAIN NEWGLAZE LTD
NEWGLAZE EPOXY COATING for reglazing vitreous enamel surfaces. It can be used to restore worn baths, basins, sinks and tiles for a fraction of the cost of replacement. It can also be used to transform the look of battered refrigerators and washing machines, and can even be applied to steel furniture and other equipment. The epoxy-resin compound overcomes the difficulty of getting a durable paint coating to adhere to hard, enamelled surfaces. Two coats painted on to a well-prepared surface will produce a gleaming, abrasion-resistant finish that will last for years. Each

PRICES AND INFORMATION WERE CORRECT AT THE TIME OF GOING TO PRESS

mail-order kit comes with step-by-step instructions and contains enough NEWGLAZE to cover a bath. Colours include white, turquoise, rose pink, sky blue, avocado, primrose, jade green and pampas. *P:* kit £14.95 inc p&p.

S-KITCHEN CONTRACTS LTD
Ingenious room-planning system and telescopic measuring rods from specialists in aids for kitchen design. SKC PLANNING SYSTEM takes the hard labour out of designing kitchens, bathrooms, living rooms and offices. Each layout consists of a scaled grid-planning board with magnetic rubber strips and pieces for indicating walls, furniture and fixtures. These pieces can be moved about and fixed on top of each other in order to build up a detailed, representative design. Then the board with pieces attached can be photocopied to provide a permanent record. Alterations can be made easily and immediately, without tedious redrafting, and the finished plan is bound to be professionally clean and precise. *P:* from £130.

Living Room Planner · Office Planner · Bath Planner · Kitchen Planner

Telescopic measuring rods avoid the inaccuracies of sagging, shifting tape measures and the awkwardness of folding rules. They ensure absolutely precise measurement in even the trickiest of corners because they can be extended at any angle, and they are easy for one person to use. MESSFIX measuring rod has rectangular telescopic sections and built-in tape measure which gives a clear reading through a viewing window. TELEMESS measuring rule, which works on the same telescopic principle, is less sophisticated but more robust. ANGLEFIX is an aid for measuring angles quickly and precisely, even in awkward positions. It comes complete with a built-in digital indicator for accuracy and easy read-off. Two versions are available: 'Mini' and 'Maxi'. *P:* MESSFIX 3m (3¼yd) £49.50, 4m (4¼yd) £54; TELEMESS 3m (3¼yd) £30; 5m (5½yd) £48; ANGLEFIX 'Mini' £45, 'Maxi' £49. All prices ex VAT.

SOLVOLENE LUBRICANTS LTD
AUTOSOL chrome cleaner and chrome, aluminium and metal polish, to enhance all kinds of metalwork. It removes rust and tarnish and produces a brilliant shiny finish. In the home it is ideal for polishing brass knockers, letterboxes, door handles and taps; and it can also be used to restore the look of plastic and ceramic surfaces. SOLVOL MULTI-PURPOSE

Solvolene's AUTOSOL

Left: room-planning system; below: MESSFIX measuring rod. Both from S-KITCHEN CONTRACTS

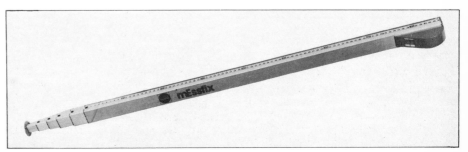

USEFUL PRODUCTS

LIGHT OIL is intended for particularly trouble-some hinges and sliding joints. *M:* AUTOSOL polish (tube) 75g (2½oz); SOLVO MULTI-PURPOSE LIGHT OIL 125ml (4½ fl oz). *P:* AUTOSOL polish £1.26; SOLVOL 55p.

STAPRO & WELLDEN
SPRAYCLEAN acoustic tile cleaner to remove stains from absorbent ceiling tiles. The strong chemical solution emulsifies and disperses ingrained dirt and grease, including nicotine, without reducing the acoustic or fire-retardant properties of the tiles. An extra-strong formula is available to attack the thick grime that collects around air vents, grills and heating systems. It is particularly effective against cooking grease and will even dissolve water marks. Spray shields and extension rods are supplied with the basic spray apparatus so that the most inaccessible corners can be cleaned easily and without mess. *P:* £6.95 (ex VAT).

SEALANTS

A BELL & CO
BELSEALER, suitable for all slightly porous surfaces, is excellent for stone, unpolished marble and slate. *P:* ½pt (280ml) to cover 3 sq yd (2.5 sq m) £4.95.

DUNLOP LTD
Three sealants in handy mini-cartridge form. Silicone BATH AND KITCHEN SEALANT is fully waterproof and has 10-year guarantee. Colours include white, avocado, sun king (orange), ivory, Kashmir beige, Alpine/Bermuda blue. MASTIC SILICONE provides excellent adhesion to ceramic, metal, plastic, glass etc, and is available in white, clear, grey, black and brown. *M:* BATH AND KITCHEN SEALANT 78g (2¾ oz) MASTIC SILICONE 310ml (11 fl oz). *P:* on application.

HANSIL LTD
Dow Corning BATH AND KITCHEN SEAL. A pressurized cartridge, long nozzle and T-bar control make this silicone rubber sealant particularly economical and convenient to use. A clean, effective and professional-looking finish is easy to achieve. A range of seven colours is available — white, avocado, champagne, ivory, sun king (orange), pampas, clear, wild sage. *P:* 78g (2¾oz) £2.45 (ex VAT).

PLASTICS AND RESINS LTD
POLAGARD range of weatherproof polymeric coatings for walls and ceilings, inside and out. These are for areas where extra protection is needed and all contain a fungicide to prevent spoilage by mildew, fungus and lichen. Satin-finish 'Polagard' protective wall covering also

comes in an extra-fungicidal version, 'Polagard S'. These coatings act as breathing membranes, allowing escape of moisture from within while preventing penetration of water from outside. *P:* 'Polagard', 'Polagard S' 5l (8¾pt) £6.74, 25l (43¾pt) £33.74.

TILING

BLUNDELL-PERMOGLAZE LTD
Range of adhesives for DIY tiling: PERMOGLAZE DRY MIX TILE ADHESIVE, PERMOGLAZE CERAMIC WALL TILE ADHESIVE, PERMOGLAZE WATER RESISTANT CERAMIC WALL TILE ADHESIVE (use this round baths and in shower cubicles), and PERMOGLAZE GROUT to finish the job off. *P:* on application.

BUILDING ADHESIVES LTD
Selection of water-resistant grouts for use with all kinds of ceramic tiles. BAL-GROUT is a white compressible cement-based grout for general interior and exterior applications. Grey BAL-GROUT FLOORING will fix glazed and unglazed ceramic tiles in most domestic situations. BAL-SUPERGROUT is ideal for waterproofing showers and splashbacks. Water-impervious BAL-EPOXY GROUT will seal tiled work surfaces and table-tops where hygiene is particularly important. Sachets of BAL-GROUT COLOUR MIX can be added to these grouts to complement the colour of the tiles. BAL-BROWN GROUT is suitable for general use with wall or floor tiles. *M:* BAL-GROUT 0.5, 1.5, 3.5, 12.5kg (1, 3⅓, 7½, 27½lb); BAL-GROUT FLOORING 2.5, 3.5, 12.5kg (5½, 7½, 55lb); BAL-SUPERGROUT 1l (1¾pt); BAL-EPOXY GROUT 0.5, 1, 6kg (1, 2¼, 12lb); BAL-BROWN GROUT 1, 3.5, 12.5kg (2¼, 7½, 27½lb); BAL-GROUT COLOUR MIX 35g (1¼oz) sachet to mix with 3.5kg (7½lb) of grout. *P:* BAL-GROUT 3.5kg £2.09; BAL-GROUT FLOORING 3.5kg £1.46; BAL-SUPERGROUT £2.45; BAL-EPOXY GROUT 1kg £7.79; BAL-BROWN GROUT 3.5kg £2.50; BAL-GROUT COLOUR MIX sachet £1.08.

DUNLOP LTD
Selection of adhesives and grouts for wall, ceiling and floor tiles. Ready-mixed CERAMIC WALL TILE ADHESIVE for fixing tiles to dry interior surfaces also comes in a waterproof version suitable for bathrooms, showers and kitchens. On porous surfaces use TILE PRIMER before the adhesive. There is a dual-purpose tile adhesive and grout, FIX & GROUT, which dries to a resistant, white finish. For a high-quality waterproof finish for ceramic wall tiles use their GROUTING. For fixing foam polystyrene tiles, sheet and coving there is CEILING TILE ADHESIVE and for cork tiles and sheeting, CORK ADHESIVE. WATERPROOF MORTAR is a power adhesive for wall and floor tiles,

mosaics, stone and brick slips. To prepare surface before fixing self-adhesive tiles use FLOOR PRIMER. *M:* CERAMIC WALL TILE ADHESIVE 500ml–10l (17½ fl oz–17½pt); WATERPROOF CERAMIC WALL TILE ADHESIVE 1–10l (1¾–17½pt); TILE PRIMER 5l (8¾pt); FIX & GROUT 500ml–5l (¾–8¾pt); GROUTING 500g–12kg (1–26lb); CEILING TILE ADHESIVE 250ml–2.5l (8¾ fl oz–4⅜pt); CORK ADHESIVE 500ml–2.5l (17½ fl oz–4⅜pt); WATERPROOF MORTAR 20kg (44lb); FLOOR PRIMER 500ml (17½ fl oz). *P:* on application.

NICOBOND LTD
Comprehensive range of adhesives and grouts for fixing ceramic tiles. THIKBED ADHESIVE combines rendering and fixing in one operation and can cope with rough as well as smooth surfaces. White WORKTOP ADHESIVE is designed to give a hygienic, water-resistant bond to tiles and mosaic on kitchen worktops. Joints can be sealed and coloured with READY MIXED COLOURED GROUT. This is available in 12 strong permanent colours, is highly water-resistant and sets slowly, which makes it particularly easy to use. The range of colours can be increased by mixing sachets of COLOUR BLEND with grey or white grout. *M:* THIKBED ADHESIVE 2.5, 5, 10l (4⅜, 8¾, 17½pt); WORKTOP ADHESIVE 1, 2.5, 5l (1¾, 4⅜, 8¾pt); READY MIXED COLOURED GROUT 500ml, 1l (17½ fl oz, 1¾pt); COLOUR BLEND small sachet 30g (1oz). *P:* THIKBED ADHESIVE 2.5l £3.74; WORKTOP ADHESIVE 2½l £5.55; READY MIXED COLOURED GROUT 500ml £1.56; COLOUR BLEND £1.05.

RAMUS TILE CO LTD
SCHONOFOAM and SCHONOX TS lightweight, flexible, compound sheet matting for laying between wood or metal sub-floors and ceramic or quarry tiles flooring. SCHONOFOAM is a mixture of foam and polystyrene in sheet form and SCHONOX TS is a cork and

rubber compound available on a roll. Both act as a buffer between sub-floor and tiles to absorb movement, which can ultimately crack the grout and sometimes the tiles too. SCHO-NOX TS is also an effective sound barrier and when used together with a layer of SCHONO-FOAM can reduce noise levels by as much as 50%. For either product to be totally successful SCHONOFLEX K adhesive and SCHONOFLEX F grout should be used in securing the matting compounds to the sub-floor and the tile to the matting. SCHONOFLEX K and F allow a degree of movement as both have a degree of elasticity. *M:* SCHONOX TS (roll) w1 × l20m (39in × 65ft), d4mm (¼in); SCHONOFOAM (sheet) w50cm × l1m (19½ × 39in), d4mm (¼in). *P:* SCHONOX TS £5.35 sq m; SCHONOFOAM £1.23 sheet, £2.46 sq m; SCHONOFLEX K £22.75 for 25kg bag to cover 27.7 sq m; SCHONOFLEX F £7.90 for 25kg bag to cover 15–35 sq m.

VITREX TOOLS
Handy TILE SAW for cutting the most awkward shapes out of wall and floor tiles. Durable tungsten carbide blade will saw through all kinds of tiles, whatever their size or thickness, and it can be used to cut any slot, curve or angle. Also available from the comprehensive range of tiling tools is a simple TILE FILE to smooth and shape the rough-cut edges. *P:* TILE SAW £4.95, TILE FILE 75p.

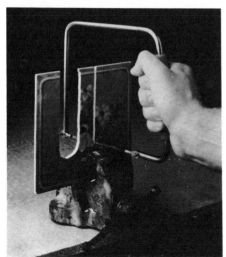

Vitrex's tile saw

WOOD CARE

BLUNDELL-PERMOGLAZE LTD
PERMOGLAZE varnishes. Choose from 'Clear Varnish' (an exceptionally pale, general-purpose varnish), 'Polyurethane Varnish' (in gloss for inside or outside and eggshell or matt for inside), 'CLEAR GLAZE' (a water-based,

tough, clear finish to apply over suitable wall-paper or bare interior wood) and TIMBER-COTE (a very durable clear finish for exterior woodwork that absorbs ultraviolet light). *M:* 500ml–5l (17½ fl oz–8¾pt). *P:* on application.

J W BOLLOM & CO LTD
All sorts of wood finishing products sold under the Bromel and Henry Flack Ltd trade names. For furniture restorers there are 19 different French polishes, ranging from transparent to ebonite. ANGLO-YANKEE SHINE polishes give a very high gloss and come in extra pale, pale and dark. For a heat-resistant finish MEL-POL comes in transparent, white and button finishes. The range of wax polishes is staggering. BRIWAX gives stripped pine furniture a lovely sheen. Colours are natural, medium brown, Jacobean, mahogany, elm, antique brown and antique mahogany. SHERADALE ANTIQUE WAX POLISH in light or dark is a fine quality beeswax polish for antique furniture. HARRACKS WAX POLISH in light or dark is for maximum penetration on old timber, and for floors there is 'P' and 'P32'.
MR FLACK'S OLDE ENGLISH COLLECTION provides small sizes of basic products to help you achieve a professional finish. The range consists of MR FLACK'S WAX, SANDING SEA-LER, WOOD ADHESIVE, FRENCH POLISH KIT, WAX POLISHING KIT, BUTTON POLISH, FRENCH POLISH, WHITE POLISH, SHELLAC SANDING SEALER, LIQUID GLASS, PINE POLISHING KIT and also POLISHING MITTS. For staining and waxing in one go there is STAYNWAX for use on bare timber, especially stripped pine. Other stains available are NUS-TAIN, COLOUR FAST WOOD STAIN NO 143 and SPRAY SHADE NO 12 — all in a wide range of colours.
Other wood finishes include seven different cellulose lacquers to enhance timber grain and colour, gloss or satin finish polyurethane varnish and spirit varnishes in a selection of colours and finishes.
P: all on application.

CEMENTONE-BEAVER LTD
A wide range of preservatives, varnishes and wood stains. WOOD PRESERVER is available in a choice of clear, green and light and dark oak finishes. EXTERIOR WOOD PRESERVATIVE in rustic brown is both decorative and protecting at the same time. POLYURETHANE VARNISH is in a choice of gloss or satin finish, and if you want to stain and varnish at the same time, choose the POLYURETHANE COLOURED VARNISH for interior use only in teak, mid oak, dark oak, walnut or mahogany. For staining wood, there is BEAVER WOOD STAIN in six colours. *M:* WOOD PRESERVER 1, 2.5, 5, 25l (1¾, 4⅜, 8¾, 43¾pt); EXTERIOR WOOD PRE-SERVATIVE 2.5, 5, 25l (1¾, 8¾, 43¾pt); YACHT VARNISH, POLYURETHANE VARNISH 250ml–

5l (8¾ fl oz–8¾pt); POLYURETHANE COL-OURED VARNISH 250, 500ml (8¾–17½ fl oz); BEAVER WOOD STAIN 500ml, 1, 2.5l (17½ fl oz, 1¾, 4⅜pt). *P:* on application.

D FARMILOE
TOUCH AND GO French polish kit. Each kit contains six bottles of French polish stains — dark and light mahogany, medium and dark oak, and medium walnut and teak — plus wax stopping, in four shades, to fill deep scratches and dents before repolishing. Easy-to-follow instructions are also supplied. *P:* kit £8.37 inc p & p, bottle of stain 4 fl oz (140ml) £1.94.

IMPERIAL CHEMICAL INDUSTRIES PLC
INTERIOR VARNISH in clear, pine or teak is a polyurethane varnish in a choice of three finishes — gloss, satin or matt. If you want to add more colour to your wood, Dulux do a wonderful range of specially mixed INTERIOR VARNISH in a choice of 40 colours. Choose from blues, greens, yellows, reds or pinks and produce your own shades by applying more or fewer coats for a paler or a more intense look. *M:* INTERIOR VARNISH 250ml (8¾ fl oz), 750ml (26¼ fl oz). *P:* on application.

INTERNATIONAL PAINT PLC
Really comprehensive range of wood pre-servatives, stains and varnishes. WOODPLAN products cover the three steps of preserving, colouring and varnishing. 'Double Action Tim-ber Preservative' gives clear, deeply penetrat-ing finish that prolongs the life of the timber, and of the finish applied over it. 'Stains' come in green plus several natural colours — pine, mahogany, teak, dark oak, mid oak, light oak and rosewood. They are for indoor or outdoor use and the colours resist fading well. The last step is to apply 'Woodplan Gloss Varnish' or 'Clear Diamond Varnish'. *M:* 'Double Action Timber Preservative' 500ml (17½ fl oz), 2.5l (4⅜pt); 'Stains' 250ml (8¾ fl oz), 500ml (17½ fl oz); 'Gloss Varnish' 250ml (8¾ fl oz), 500ml (17½ fl oz), 1l (1¾pt), 2.5l (4⅜pt); 'Satin Var-nish' 250ml (8¾ fl oz), 500ml (17½ fl oz), 1l (1¾pt); 'Clear Diamond Varnish' 750ml (26 fl oz) two-part pack. *P:* (for 500ml cans) 'Stains' £4; 'Gloss Varnish' £3.45; 'Satin Varnish' £3.45; 'Clear Diamond Varnish' 750ml can £6.59.
With so many people choosing exterior doors in natural wood finishes, International Paint have come up with two special door finishing kits, one to give a clear finish and the other to stain the door in either mid-oak, teak or maho-gany. STAIN DOOR FINISHING KIT consists of wood preservative, stain and gloss varnish; CLEAR DOOR FINISHING KIT of wood pre-servative, gloss varnish and satin varnish — use both varnishes in different combinations to acquire the desired finish. *M:* STAIN KIT 500ml (17½ fl oz) preservative, 250ml (8¾ fl oz)

USEFUL PRODUCTS

stain, 500ml (17½ fl oz) varnish; CLEAR KIT 500ml (17½ fl oz) preservative, 500ml (17½ fl oz) gloss, 250ml (8¾ fl oz) satin. *P:* STAIN KIT £8.31; CLEAR KIT £8.52.

JOY PRODUCTS
An enormous and interesting range of varnishes and stains for special purposes. Varnishes include GENERAL PURPOSE VARNISH for indoor or outdoor use, SHELLAC VARNISH for finishing furniture, UNIVERSAL POLYURETHANE VARNISH and POLYURETHANE GLAZE for a shining protective coat. *P:* (for 250ml/8¾ fl oz unless otherwise stated) GENERAL PURPOSE VARNISH £1.66, SHELLAC VARNISH 4 fl oz (110ml) £1, UNIVERSAL POLYURETHANE VARNISH £1.71, POLYURETHANE GLAZE £1.88.
For staining new wood choose HIGH SPEED PENETRATING WOOD DYE in light, mid or dark Jacobean, golden oak, walnut, teak, mahogany or ebony. FLOOR STAIN in dark, light and mid oak gives a high-gloss, non-scratch finish and colours at the same time. *M:* 280ml (8¾ fl oz). *P:* HIGH SPEED PENETRATING WOOD DYE £1.55, FLOOR STAIN £1.32. (All prices ex VAT.)

LANGSTON JONES & SAMUEL SMITH LTD
Good range of varnishes. Choose from HIGH GLOSS VARNISH for almost all interior and exterior timber, POLYURETHANE MATT, SATIN and GLOSS VARNISH, again for indoor or outdoor use, but easier to apply and quicker drying than conventional varnish, or YACHT VARNISH, specially formulated for coastal areas and recommended for front doors and any indoor or outdoor applications where an extra tough high gloss finish is required. The varnishes form part of the 'Craftsman Range' which also includes wood preservatives, French polish and knottings and other products. *M:* HIGH GLOSS VARNISH, YACHT VARNISH 250ml–2.5l (8¾ fl oz–4⅜pt); POLYURETHANE MATT, SATIN and GLOSS VARNISH 125ml – 2.5l (4½ fl oz – 4⅜pt). *P:* on application.

LEYLAND PAINT & WALLPAPER PLC
Stains and varnishes in the LEYLAND WOODCARE range. For varnish, choose from extra pale EXTERIOR GLOSS VARNISH and POLYURETHANE VARNISH in gloss, eggshell or flat finishes. For staining and preserving timber, Leyland produce PRESERVATIVE WOOD STAIN in eight colours — red, cedar, medium oak, dark oak, opaque black, beech, yellow, pine, opaque white and forest green. *M:* EXTERIOR GLOSS VARNISH 500ml, 1, 2.5l (17½ fl oz, 1¾, 4⅜pt); POLYURETHANE VARNISH 500ml, 1, 2.5l (17½ fl oz, 1¾, 4⅜pt). *P:* on application.

MANDERS PAINTS LTD
TIMBERCARE products for the professional or home decorator. INTERIOR VARNISH in gloss or eggshell finish is a fast-drying polyurethane varnish that comes in clear, teak or pine, or 16 colours — pinks, blues, greens and browns. For exterior work there is durable, microporous EXTERIOR SATIN FINISH in six natural wood colours. For a preservative effect on external wood, choose EXTERIOR PRESERVATIVE which protects for years against the effects of sunlight, rot and mould growth. In green and four natural wood colours. *M:* INTERIOR VARNISH 500ml, 1, 2.5l (17½ fl oz, 1¾, 4⅜pt); EXTERIOR SATIN FINISH 1, 2.5, 5l (1¾, 4⅜, 8¾pt); EXTERIOR PRESERVATIVE 2.5, 5l (4⅜, 8¾pt).
If you want to try your hand with scumble glaze over a painted ground for some really lovely decorative effects, then use Manders' MATSINE — a series of translucent, flat-drying colours that are used mainly as a stain on bare wood. In six natural wood colours. *M:* 250, 500ml (8¾, 17½ fl oz).

E PARSONS & SONS
BLACKFRIAR wood treatment products. For interior woodwork the BLACKFRIAR POLYURETHANE VARNISH range includes clear varnish in high gloss, semi-gloss or matt finishes and stained varnish in a choice of 10 wood colours — light oak, medium oak, dark oak, sapele, dark Jacobean, dark mahogany, deep red mahogany, Jacobean oak, walnut and teak. These varnishes produce a finish that is ideally suited for use on kitchen surfaces, worktops, furniture, floors, doors and bar counters. *M:* clear varnish 125ml–5l (4½ fl oz–8¾pt); stained varnish 125ml–2.5l (4½ fl oz–4⅜pt). *P:* clear varnish 2.5l (4⅜pt) £12.82; stained varnish 2.5l (4⅜pt) £14.26.
For something more colourful, use one of the polyurethane COLOURED MATT STAINS underneath the varnish. In yellow, red, green, bright orange, blue or magenta. *M:* 250ml, 1l (8¾ fl oz–1¾pt). *P:* 250ml (8¾ fl oz) £2.06, 1l (1¾pt) £7.87.

STERLING RONCRAFT
Extensive COLRON refinishing range for restoring and protecting wooden furniture and timber. 'Restorer and Cleaner' removes layers of wax, shellac, lacquer, oil and varnish without spoiling the natural patina of the wood. 'Hard Finish Remover' dissolves the tougher finishes — such as paint, plastic coatings, polyurethane varnishes — down to the bare wood. 'Wood Reviver' penetrates deep into the grain of the wood to replace lost natural oils and to prevent warping and splitting. 'Liquid Wax', a blend of beeswax and hard-polishing waxes, enriches the colour and tone of dulled wood and gives lasting sheen finish. To achieve the same effect without altering the

Sterling Roncraft's RONSTRIP

colour of the wood there is 'Finishing Wax', a natural dressing that combines pure waxes, yellow beeswax and Brazilian carnauba wax. A durable alternative to wax is 'Antique Oil', a mixture of resins and pure tung-oil, which produces an easily-cleaned glossy finish. Three new products are available to treat badly damaged wood. 'Scratch Remover', a rub-on wax stick, covers up small scratches, dents and water marks. 'Woodfiller' fills in larger cracks, nail holes, joints and chips with an adhesive finish that is hard enough to be planed, sanded or nailed. Spray-on 'Wormwood Killer' cures wood attacked by all species of wood-borers, can be applied to all wood surfaces, and guards against reinfestation. *P:* Restorer and Cleaner' 500ml (17½ fl oz) £3.14; 'Hard Finish Remover' 500ml (17½ fl oz) £3.59; 'Wood Reviver' 250ml (8¾ fl oz); 'Liquid Wax' 250ml (8¾ fl oz) £2.04; 'Finishing Wax' 70g (2½oz) £1.58; 'Antique Oil' 250ml (8¾ fl oz); 'Scratch Remover' blister pack £1.37; 'Woodfiller' 125ml (4½ fl oz) £1.99; 'Wormwood Killer' 200ml (7 fl oz) aerosol £2.29.
In the RONSTRIP range is thick, non-drip 'Varnish Remover'. The solution is painted on to old varnish, left for 15 minutes and then scraped off, bringing the old varnish with it. Particularly good for large flat surfaces such as doors, kitchen furniture, skirtings and floors, it can also be used on polyurethanes, lacquers and other transparent finishes. *M:* 850ml (30 fl oz). *P:* £4.99.
RONSEAL range includes 'Wood Repair System' consisting of hardener to reinforce decayed wood, high performance filler and wood preservative tablets to protect timber against wet rot — they are placed into pre-drilled holes in areas where moisture is likely to enter the joinery. RONSEAL polyurethane clear varnishes come in hard glaze, satin and matt finishes, in tough 'Outdoor' quality, and in 'Woodshades' natural coloured varnishes in teak, oak, chestnut, antique oak, pine, walnut, dark oak, red mahogany and olive shades. *M:* wood hardener 250, 500ml, (8¾, 17½ fl oz); filler 250, 500g (8¾, 17½oz); clear varnishes 250, 500ml, 1l, 2.5l (8¾, 17½ fl oz, 1¾, 4⅜pt), hard glaze only also 20l (35pt); 'Outdoor' 500ml, 1, 2.5l (17½ fl oz, 1¾, 4⅜pt); 'Woodshades' 250, 500ml, 1l (8¾, 17½ fl oz, 1¾pt).

NOTE TO READER

Listed on the following pages are the names, addresses and telephone numbers of all companies included in this book. Enquiries concerning specific ranges or products, requests for catalogues etc, should normally be directed to the sales or customer services departments.

Listed in italic type after each name and address are the different sections of the book in which that company's products are described, followed by the relevant sub-section, e.g. Carpeting (Rugs).

It has been unavoidable that during the production of this book a few of the companies included have changed their trading name, been subject to take-over or gone out of business. We have included here all such information which was available to us immediately before going to press. We apologise to the reader and to the companies concerned for any inconvenience caused.

Should you discover other changes, or simply that a company has moved to a new address, we would appreciate hearing from you. Please write to:
The Decorator's Directory,
Michael Joseph Ltd,
44 Bedford Square,
London WC1B 3DU

ABS CONTRACTS LTD, 257 Hackney Road, Shoreditch, London E2; tel: (01) 739 8621; *Kitchens (Units)*

AG TILES LTD, Dividy Road, Bucknall, Stoke-on-Trent ST2 0JB; tel: (0782) 313981; *Ceramic tiles (Floor)*

ABET LAMINATI, 238 Grand Buildings, Trafalgar Square, London WC2 5EZ; tel: (01) 367 3545; *Kitchens (Worktops)*

ACORN KITCHENS, Pages Industrial Park, Billington Road, Leighton Buzzard, Bedfordshire LU7 8TP; tel: (0525) 370080; *Kitchens (Units)*

ACQUISITIONS (FIREPLACES) LTD, 269 Camden High Street, London NW1 7BX; tel: (01) 485 4955; *Stoves and fireplaces (Accessories, Mantels and surrounds)*

ADAM CARPETS LTD, Greenhill Works, Birmingham Road, Kidderminster, Worcestershire DY10 2SH; tel: Kidderminster 2247; *Carpeting (Flecked, Made-to-order, Plain)*

W ADAMS & SONS LTD, Westfield Works, Spon Lane, West Bromwich, West Midlands B70 6BH; tel: (021) 553 2161; *Bathrooms (Fittings)*

ADEPTUS DESIGNS LTD, 110 Tottenham Court Road, London W1; tel: (01) 388 5965; *Furniture (Upholstered)*

AFIA CARPETS, 60 Baker Street, London W1M 1DJ; tel: (01) 935 0414/2982; *Carpeting (Coir, Flecked, Made-to-order, Patterned, Plain)*

ALBION DESIGN OF LONDON LTD, 12 Flitcroft Street, London WC2H 8DJ; tel: (01) 836 0151; *Staircases*

ALBION HARDWARE LTD, Merridale House, Merridale Street, Wolverhampton WV3 0RB; tel: (0902) 27532; *Bathrooms (Fittings), Ceramic tiles (Wall), Fittings (Door), Lighting*

ALLIA (UK) LTD, Whieldon Road, Stoke-on-Trent ST4 4HN; tel: (0782) 49191; *Bathrooms (Fittings, Sanitaryware, Showers); Kitchens (Sinks)*

ALLIANCE FLOORING CO LTD, 36 Maxwell Road, Fulham, London SW6; tel: (01) 736 3811; *Flooring (Cork, Wood)*

ALLMILMÖ LTD, Station Road, Thatcham, Nr Newbury, Berkshire RG13 4RD; tel: (0635) 68181; *Kitchens (Units)*

ALL-STEEL SYSTEMS FURNITURE, 18 Verney Road, London SE16 3DH; tel: (01) 639 8931; *Offices (Systems)*

ALNO KITCHENS, Byron House, Wallingford Road, Uxbridge, Middlesex UB8 2RU; tel: (0895) 52131; *Kitchens (Units)*

ALTERNATIVE PRODUCTIONS LTD, 220 Farmers Road, London SE5 0TW; tel: (01) 582 2767/3979; *Furniture (Shelving)*

AMAZING GRATES, Phoenix House, 61-63 High Road, London N2 8AB; tel: (01) 883 9590; *Stoves and fireplaces (Accessories, Mantels and surrounds)*

AMTICO, National Plastics Ltd, Foleshill Road, Coventry CV6 5AG; tel: (0203) 8 88771; showroom: 17 Great George St, London W1R 9DE; tel: (01) 629 6258; *Flooring (Vinyl tiles)*

SALLY ANDERSON TILES, Parndon Mill, Harlow, Essex CM20 2HP; tel: Harlow 20982; *Ceramic tiles (Floor, Wall)*

ANGLEPOISE LIGHTING LTD, Enfield Industrial Estate, Redditch B97 6DR; tel: (0527) 63771; *Lighting*

MARK ANGUS, The Manor, Woolavington, Near Bridgwater, Somerset; tel: Bridgwater 684233; *Mirrors and glass*

ANTIFERENCE LTD, Bicester Road, Aylesbury, Buckinghamshire HP19 3BJ; tel: (0296) 82511; *Fittings (Curtain)*

ANTIQUES OF TOMORROW, 17 Tower Street, Rye, East Sussex TN31 7AU; tel: (0797) 224252; *Furniture (Chairs, Upholstered)*

ANTOCKS LAIRN LTD, Lancaster Road, Cressex, High Wycombe, Buckinghamshire HP12 3HZ; tel: (0494) 24912; London showroom: 15 Rathbone Street, London W1; tel: (01) 636 3248; *Offices (Chairs, Reception seating)*

ARC LINEA (UK) LTD, 13 Cheval Place, London SW7; tel: (01) 584 0646; *Kitchens (Units), Furniture (Bedrooms, Storage)*

ARCHITECTURAL COMPONENTS LTD, 4–10 Exhibition Road, London SW7 2HF; tel: (01) 584 6800; *Bathrooms (Fittings, Sanitaryware), Staircases, Furniture (Bedrooms, Storage)*

ARCHITECTURAL HERITAGE OF CHELTENHAM, Boddington Manor, Boddington, Nr Cheltenham, Gloucestershire GL51 0TJ; tel: (02468) 741; *Bathrooms (Fittings, Sanitaryware)*

ARCHITECTURAL TEXTILES, 25 Old Street, London EC1V 9HL; tel: (01) 253 3993/4183; *Fabrics and wall coverings (Wall coverings)*

ARCHITECTURAL TRADING COMPANY, 1/2 Cosser Street, London SE1; tel: (01) 633 0819; *Lighting, Offices (Chairs), Furniture (Chairs, Dining tables, Occasional tables, Upholstered)*

ARDENBRITE PRODUCTS LTD, 57 Farringdon Road, London EC1M 3JH; tel: (01) 405 2487; *Paint*

ARGON, 17 Neal Street, London WC2; tel: (01) 240 5051; *Lighting*

ARISTOCAST LTD, Bold Street, Sheffield S9 2LR; tel: (0742) 448581 (10 lines); *Architectural ornaments (Wood), Stoves and fireplaces (Accessories, Mantels and surrounds)*

ARKANA, Lower Bristol Road, Bath, Avon BA2 1ET; tel: (0225) 316564; *Furniture (Upholstered)*

MARTHE ARMITAGE, 1 Strand-on-the-Green, Chiswick, London W4 3PQ; tel: (01) 994 0160; *Fabrics and wall coverings (Wall coverings)*

ARMITAGE SHANKS LTD, Armitage, Rugeley, Staffordshire WS15 4BT; tel: (0543) 490253; *Bathrooms (Fittings, Sanitaryware)*

ARMSTRONG WORLD INDUSTRIES LTD, Armstrong House, 3 Chequers Square, Uxbridge, Middlesex UB8 1NG; tel: (0895) 51122; *Architectural ornaments (Suspended ceilings), Flooring (Vinyl sheet, Vinyl tiles)*

BERNARD J ARNULL LTD, 17–21 Sunbeam Road, Park Royal, London NW10 6JP; tel: (01) 965 6094; showroom: 13/14 Queen Street, London W1; tel: (01) 499 3231; *Bathrooms (Fittings, Sanitaryware, Showers), Ceramic tiles (Floor, Wall)*

ARTEX LTD, Artex Avenue, Newhaven, East Sussex BN9 9DD; tel: Newhaven 513100; *Paint*

ARTISAN DESIGN, 13 Palace Road, London N8 8QL; tel: (01) 348 9159; *Bathrooms (Fittings), Decorative painters, Kitchens (Units)*

LAURA ASHLEY LTD, Carno, Powys, Mid Wales SY17 5LQ; tel: (05514) 301/2; *Blinds (Roller, Roman), Ceramic tiles (Wall), Fabrics and wall coverings (Fabrics, Co-ordinates, Bed linen), Lighting, Paint, Furniture (Upholstered)*

ASTROHOME LTD, 47/49 Neal Street, London WC2; tel: (01) 240 0420; *Offices (Co-ordinated furniture), Furniture (Beds, Dining tables)*

ATAG (UK) LTD, 19-20 Hither Green, Clevedon, Avon BS21 6XU; tel: (0272) 877301; *Kitchens (Sinks)*

ATTRACTA PRODUCTS LTD, 120-132 Cricklewood Lane, London NW2 2DP; tel: (01) 200 7751; *Useful products (Miscellaneous)*

AVENA CARPETS LTD, Bankfield Mill, Haley Hill, Halifax HX3 6ED, West Yorkshire; tel: (0422) 44096; *Carpeting (Made-to-order)*

AXMINSTER CARPETS LTD, Axminster, Devon EX13 5PQ; tel: Axminster 33533; *Carpeting (Flecked, Patterned, Rugs)*

B C SANITAN LTD, 30/31 Lyme Street, London NW1; tel: (01) 485 8545; *Bathrooms (Sanitaryware)*

B & E MARKETING LTD, 5 The Crescent, Worlebury, Weston-super-Mare, Avon; tel: (0934) 25437/ 25095; *Bathrooms (Fittings)*

BFE BUSINESS FURNITURE & EQUIPMENT LTD, Unit 9, Great Western Industrial Park, off Windmill Lane, Armstrong Way, Southall, Middlesex UB2 4SD; tel: (01) 843 9993; *Offices (Co-ordinated furniture)*

BMK LTD, PO Box 9, Kilmarnock KA1 1SX; tel: (0563) 21100; London showroom: 87–91 New Bond Street, London W1Y 9LA; tel: (01) 408 2220; Manchester showroom: 24 Lever Street, Manchester M1 1DX; tel: (061) 236 9936; *Carpeting (Flecked, Made-to-order, Patterned, Plain)*

H & F BADCOCK LTD, Highshore Road, Peckham, London SE15 5AB; tel: (01) 639 0304; *Architectural ornaments (Plaster)*

BAKER, KNAPP & TUBBS LTD;
no longer trading

G P & J BAKER LTD, 18 Berners Street, London W1P 4JA; West End Road, High Wycombe, Buckinghamshire HP11 2QD; tel: (01) 636 8412; tel: (0494) 33422; *Fabrics and wall coverings (Fabrics, Co-ordinates)*

LEONARD BALL, H L & J S Ball, 44 Market Street, Lutterworth, Leicestershire; tel: (04555) 4942; *Fittings (Door and cabinet)*

RALPH BALL, 177 Waller Road, London SE14; tel: (01) 635 8792; *Lighting*

BALTERLEY BATHROOMS LTD, Silverdale Road, Newcastle-under-Lyme ST5 6EL; tel: (0782) 633118/9/20; *Bathrooms (Fittings, Sanitaryware)*

BARBEE CERAMICS LTD, Merton Works, Church Road, Welling, Kent DA16 3DZ; tel: (01) 855 9644; *Ceramic tiles (Floor, Wall)*

BARKING–GROHE LTD, 1 River Road, Barking, Essex IG11 0HD; tel: (01) 594 7292; *Bathrooms (Fittings, Showers), Kitchens (Taps)*

H N BARNES (OFFICE SYSTEMS) LTD, London showroom: 365 Euston Road, London NW1 3AR; tel: (01) 580 2080; production: Oaks Lodge, Fordham Road, Newmarket, Suffolk; tel: (0638) 669911; *Offices (Chairs, Co-ordinated Furniture, Systems)*

SUPPLIERS' ADDRESSES

JACQUELINE BATEMAN, 7 Rylett Crescent, London W12 9RP; tel: (01) 749 3596; *Decorative painters*

BATH CABINET MAKERS, Lower Bristol Road, Bath BA2 1ET; tel: (0225) 318523; *Furniture (Dining suites, Storage)*

THE BATH STUDIO, 332 Uxbridge Road, Hatch End, Pinner, Middlesex HA5 4HR; tel: (01) 421 0522; *Bathrooms (Fittings, Sanitaryware), Kitchens (Units, Taps)*

BAUKNECHT, Beekay Kitchen Furniture Ltd, 455 Walton Summit, Bamber Bridge, Preston, Lancashire PR5 8AU; tel: (0772) 324242; *Kitchens (Units)*

BAUMANN FABRICS LTD, 41/42 Berners Street, London W1P 3AA; tel: (01) 637 0253; *Blinds (Vertical)*

J D BEARDMORE & CO LTD, Field End Road, Ruislip, Middlesex HA4 0QG; tel: (01) 864 6811; 3 Percy Street, London W1; tel: (01) 637 7041; *Fittings (Door and cabinet)*

BEAUDESERT, 8 Symons Street, London SW3; tel: (01) 730 5102; *Fabrics and wall coverings (Fabrics), Furniture (Beds, Bedrooms, Upholstered)*

BEHR FURNITURE, 148 Regent's Park Road, London NW1; tel: (01) 722 6081; *Furniture (Bedrooms, Storage)*

A BELL & CO, Kingsthorpe, Northampton NN2 6LT; tel: (0604) 712505; *Stoves and fireplaces (Accessories, Mantles and surrounds, Stoves), Useful products (Miscellaneous, Sealants)*

ELAINE C BELL, 27 Cornwell House, 21 Clerkenwell Green, London EC1R 0DP; tel: (01) 608 1205; *Mirrors and glass*

Wm H BENNETT & SONS LTD, 79 Piccadilly, Manchester M1 2BX; tel: (061) 236 3551; *Fabrics and wall coverings (Fabrics)*

BENTLEY & SPENS, Studio 25, 90 Lots Road, London SW10 0QD; tel: (01) 352 7454 ext 5; *Fabrics and wall coverings (Fabrics)*

BERGER DECORATIVE PAINTS, Petherton Road, Hengrove, Bristol BS99 7JA; tel: Bristol 836110; *Paint*

BERGLEN PRODUCTS LTD, Masons House, Kingsbury Road, Kingsbury, London NW9 9HQ; tel: (01) 206 1366; *Bathrooms (Fittings, Sanitaryware), Kitchens (Taps); See also DAMIXA LTD*

H J BERRY & SONS LTD, Kirk Mills Chipping, Preston PR3 2RA, Lancashire; tel: (99956) 226; *Furniture (Chairs, Dining Suites)*

ROBERT & COLLEEN BERY, 8 Rosehill Road, London SW18 2NX; tel: (01) 874 5542; *Decorative painters, Furniture (Made-to-order, Screens and partitions)*

BEST & LLOYD LTD, William Street West, Smethwick, Warley, West Midlands B66 2NX; tel: (021) 558 1191; *Lighting*

BIEFFEPLAST, OMK Design Ltd, The Stephen Building, 30 Stephen Street, London W1; tel: (01) 631 1335; *Lighting*

THE BIRMINGHAM GUILD LTD, Grosvenor Works, Sherborne Street, Birmingham B16 8HL; tel: (021) 632 6311; *Staircases*

BISQUE LTD, 244 Belsize Road, London NW6; tel: (01) 328 2225; *Bathrooms (Fittings)*

BLIND ALLEY LTD, 27 Chalk Farm Road, London NW1 8AG; tel: (01) 485 8030; *Blinds (Roller, Roman, Venetian, Vertical)*

BLOSSOM (FABRICS) LTD, 24 Duncan Terrace, London N1 8BS; tel: (01) 837 5856/7; *Fabrics and wall coverings (Co-ordinates)*

BLUNDELL-PERMOGLAZE LTD, Sculcoates Lane, Hull, HU5 1RU; tel: Hull 492241; *Paint, Useful products (Tiling, Wood)*

BOFFI, 17/18 Devonshire Close, London W1N 1LF; tel: (01) 631 0655; *Kitchens (Units)*

J W BOLLOM & CO LTD, PO Box 78, Beckenham, Kent BR3 4BL; tel: (01) 658 2299; *Fabrics and wall coverings (Wall coverings), Paints, Useful products (Wood)*

ARTHUR BONNET, Taylor Alden Ltd, 226/228 Haydons Road, London SW19 5TT; tel: (01) 543 3866/9; *Kitchens (Units)*

BONSACK BATHS LTD, 14 Mount Street, London W1Y 5RA; tel: (01) 629 9981/493 3240; *Bathrooms (Sanitaryware)*

ROBERT BOSCH LTD, PO Box 98, Broadwater Park, North Orbital Road, Denham, Uxbridge, Middlesex UB9 5HJ; tel: (0895) 833633; *Kitchens (Units, Sinks)*

BOSS DESIGN, 60 Wellington Road, Dudley, West Midlands DY1 1RE; tel: (0384) 236230; *Furniture (Chairs, Dining tables, Occasional tables, Upholstered)*

CHRISTOPHER BOULTER, 43 Goodrich Road, London SE22; tel: (01) 299 2219; *Decorative painters*

BOYDEN & CO LTD, Cumberlow Avenue, London SE25 6AF; tel: (01) 771 0141; *Ceramic tiles (Floor, Wall)*

ANDREW BRADLEY, 24 Kensington Gardens, Camden, Bath BA1 6LH; tel: (0225) 317025; *Decorative painters*

ARTHUR BRETT & SONS LTD, Haslips Close, Midland Street, Norwich NR2 4PX; tel: (0603) 620522; wholesale showroom for the trade: Hammond Wholesale, 7b Harriet Walk, London SW1 9JP; tel: (01) 235 0634/5; *Mirrors and glass, Furniture (Beds, Chairs, Desks, Shelving, Storage, Dining tables, Occasional tables, Upholstered)*

BRILLIANTLEUCHTEN, 35/36 Floral Street, London WC2 9DJ: tel: (01) 240 0461; *Lighting*

BRINTONS LTD, PO Box 16, Kidderminster, Worcestershire DY10 1AG; tel: Kidderminster 3444; *Carpeting (Flecked, Patterned, Plain)*

BRISTOL INTERNATIONAL, Euroway Industrial Park, Swindon, Wiltshire SN5 8YW; tel: Swindon 615961; *Carpeting (Coir, Flecked, Made-to-order, Patterned, Plain)*

BRITANNIA ARCHITECTURAL METALWORK, 5 Normandy Street, Alton, Hampshire; tel: (0420) 84427; *Staircases*

BROCKWAY CARPETS LTD, Hoobrook, Kidderminster DY10 1XW; tel: Kidderminster 4737/8/9; *Carpeting (Patterned, Plain)*

BROWNS OF WEST WYCOMBE, Church Lane, West Wycombe, High Wycombe, Buckinghamshire HP1 3AH; tel: (0494) 24537; *Furniture (Made-to-order)*

BUILDING ADHESIVES LTD, Longton Road, Trentham, Stoke-on-Trent ST4 8JB; tel: (0782) 659921; *Useful products (Tiling)*

BUSBY & BUSBY, 57 Salisbury Street, Blandford Forum, Dorset DT11 7PY; tel: (0258) 55221; *Fabrics and wall coverings (Fabrics)*

BUSINESS INTERIORS LTD, Broad Quay House, Broad Quay, Bristol BS1 4DJ; tel: (0272) 279137; *Offices (Chairs, Co-ordinated furniture, Reception Seating, Tables)*

CJ GLASS, Stansbatch Barn, Staunton-on-Arrow, Leominster HR6 9LG; tel: Kington 260073; *Mirrors and glass*

C P CARPETS (KIDDERMINSTER), PO Box 21, Stour Buildings, Green Street, Kidderminster, Worcestershire DY10 1HF; tel: Kidderminster 755311; London showroom: 14 Goodwins Court, 55–56 St Martin's Lane, London WC2 4LL; tel: (01) 240 1096; *Carpeting (Made-to-order)*

C & R LIGHTING SYSTEMS, Southfields Road, Dunstable, Bedfordshire LU6 3EJ; tel: (0582) 62423; *Lighting*

CABOCHON FURNITURE LTD, 7 Tyers Gate, London SE1 3HX; tel: (01) 403 5404; *Furniture (Made-to-order)*

CAMBORNE FABRICS LTD, Crown Works, Paddock, Huddersfield HD3 4EY; tel: (0484) 643111; *Fabrics and wall coverings (Fabrics)*

ROSEMARY CAMDEN, 42 Limerston Street, London SW10 0HH; tel: (01) 352 7838; *Decorative painters*

CANDLELIGHT PRODUCTS LTD, 3/4 Parkhouse Lane, Tinsley, Sheffield S9 1XA; tel: (0742) 447515; *Bathrooms (Fittings), Lighting, Furniture (Bedrooms, Chairs, Desks, Screens and partitions, Shelving, Occasional tables, Upholstered)*

CAPITAL CERAMICS, Priors House, Beaumont Road, London E13 6RJ; tel: (01) 471 8121; *Ceramic tiles (Floor, Wall), Flooring (Stone)*

CARPETS INTERNATIONAL CONTRACTS, PO Box 24, Mill Street, Kidderminster, Worcestershire DY10 6XE; tel: Kidderminster 740802; *Carpeting (Made-to-order)*

CARPETS OF WORTH LTD, Severn Valley Mills, Stourport-on-Severn, Worcestershire; tel: Stourport 4122; *Carpeting (Patterned, Tiles)*

CARRON CABINET & JOINERY MANUFACTURING CO LTD, PO Box 45, Carron, Falkirk, Scotland; tel: (0324) 29894; *Bathrooms (Fittings)*

CARRON PLASTICS LTD, PO Box 32, Carron, Falkirk, Scotland FK2 8DW; tel: (0324) 38407; *Bathrooms (Sanitaryware, Showers)*

CARRON STEELYNE LTD, PO Box 37, Carron, Falkirk, Scotland FK2 8DW; tel: (0324) 38313; *Bathrooms (Sanitaryware, Showers)*

CARTERS (J & A) LTD, Alfred Street, Westbury, Wiltshire BA13 3DZ; tel: (0373) 822203; *Bathrooms (Fittings)*

ASHLEY CARTWRIGHT, 1 Banbury Road, Brackley, Northamptonshire; tel: (0280) 704104; *Furniture (Made-to-order)*

CARVED PINE MANTELPIECES LTD, High Street, Dorchester on Thames, Oxford OX9 8HL; tel: (0865) 340028; 28 Beauchamp Place, London SW3 1NJ; tel: (01) 589 5534; *Stoves and fireplaces (Accessories, Mantels and surrounds), Furniture (Made-to-order)*

CASA FINA, 132 Notting Hill Gate, London W11; tel: (01) 221 9112; *Carpeting (Rugs), Lighting, Furniture (Made-to-order)*

CATHEDRAL WORKS ORGANISATION, Terminus Road, Chichester, Sussex PO19 2TX; tel: (0243) 784225; *Bathrooms (Fittings), Flooring (Stone), Stoves and fireplaces (Mantels and surrounds)*

CAVALCADE WALLCOVERINGS LTD, PO Box 78, Beckenham, Kent BR3 4BL; tel: (01) 658 2299; *Fabrics and wall coverings (Wall coverings, Co-ordinates)*

CELMAC DISTRIBUTORS LTD, Unit 3, Ferry Lane, Brentford, Middlesex TW8 0BG; tel: (01) 586 7963; *Bathrooms (Fittings)*

CEMENTONE BEAVER LTD, Cementone Division, Tingewick Road, Buckingham MK18 1AN; tel: (0280) 814000; *Paint, Useful products (Wood care)*

CERAMIC TILE DESIGN, 56 Dawes Road, London SW6; tel: (01) 381 1455; *Bathrooms (Fittings), Ceramic tiles (Floor, Wall), Kitchens (Worktops), Stoves and fireplaces (Mantels and surrounds)*

CESA, Unit C1 Brookway, Leatherhead, Surrey; tel: (0372) 376144; *Kitchens (Units)*

CHAINPORT LTD, 12 Aviation Way, Southend on Sea SS2 6UN; tel: (0702) 549626; *Furniture (Shelving)*

CHARTA FURNITURE LTD, Westhampnett Mill, Chichester, West Sussex PO18 0NP; tel: (0243) 78081; *Furniture (Bedrooms)*

CHECKMATE INDUSTRIES LTD, Bridge House, Bridge Street, Halstead, Essex CO9 1HT; tel: Halstead 477272; *Carpeting (Flecked, Tiles)*

R J CHELSOM & CO LTD, Squires Gate Industrial Estate, Blackpool, Lancashire FY4 3RN; tel: (0253) 46324; *Lighting, Mirrors and glass, Furniture (Dining suites, Shelving, Occasional tables)*

CHILTERN HILLS UPHOLSTERY, William S Toms Ltd, Station Road, Princes Risborough, Buckinghamshire HP17 9DN; tel: (08444) 2233; *Furniture (Bedrooms, Upholstered)*

CHINOISERIE LTD, 11-15 Headfort Place, Belgrave Square, London SW1X 7DE; tel: (01) 235 6104; *Lighting*

CHLORIDE SHIRES LTD, Park Road, Guiseley, Leeds LS20 8AP; tel: (0943) 73232/77821; *Bathrooms (Fittings, Sanitaryware, Showers)*

CIANCIMINO INTERNATIONAL LTD, 307-311 Kings Road, London SW3 5EP; tel: (01) 352 2016; *Furniture (Chairs, Made-to-order, Upholstered)*

CIBA-GEIGY, Plastics Division, Ciba-Geigy Plastics and Additives Company, Duxford, Cambridge CB2 4QA; tel: (0223) 832121; *Useful products (Adhesives)*

CIEL AT CHRISTOPHER LAWRENCE, 281 Lillie Road, London SW6; tel: (01) 385 5167; *Lighting, Furniture (Made-to-order)*

E A CLARE & SON LTD, 46-48 St Anne Street, Liverpool L3 3DW; tel: (051) 207 1336; *Furniture (Dining tables)*

CLARE KITCHENS, Bowater Ripper, Castle Hedingham, Halstead, Essex CO9 3EP; tel: (0787) 60676; *Kitchens (Units)*

KENNETH CLARK CERAMICS, The North Wing, Southover Grange, Lewes, East Sussex BN7 1TP; tel: (0273) 476761; *Ceramic tiles (Wall)*

MARGERY CLINTON CERAMICS, The Pottery, Newton Port, Haddington, East Lothian; tel: (062) 082 3584; *Ceramic tiles (Floor, Wall), Lighting*

COALBROOKDALE, Glynwed Consumer & Building Products Ltd, PO Box 30, Ketley, Telford TF1 1BR; tel: (0952) 51177; *Stoves and fireplaces (Stoves)*

COLE & SON (WALLPAPERS) LTD, PO Box 4BU, 18 Mortimer Street, London W1A 4BU; tel: (01) 580 1066; *Fabrics and wall coverings (Wall coverings)*

JOHN COLEMAN, 11 Colville Mews, London W11 2DA; tel: (01) 221 2533; *Furniture (Made-to-order)*

COLLINS & HAYES LTD, Ponswood, Hastings, East Sussex TN34 1FX; tel: (0424) 430186; *Furniture (Upholstered)*

COLOURFLAIR FURNITURE LTD, 29 Bruton Street, London W1; tel: (01) 493 2178; *Furniture (Dining suites, Storage, Occasional tables, Upholstered)*

COLSTON, Ariston House, London Road, High Wycombe, Buckinghamshire HP11 1BQ; tel: (0494) 33499; *Kitchens (Sinks)*

NAOMI COLVIN, 16 Malford Road, Camberwell, London SE5 8DQ; tel: (01) 274 2843; *Decorative painters*

CONCORD LIGHTING LTD, Concord House, 241 City Road, London EC1V 1JD; tel: (01) 253 1200; *Lighting*

CONFETTI, Banks Heeley Plastics Ltd, Unit 1, Orchard Road, Royston, Hertfordshire SG8 5HD; tel: (0763) 42346; *Furniture (Dining suites, Shelving, Storage, Occasional tables, Upholstered)*

CONNAUGHT FURNITURE LTD, First Avenue, Weston Road, Crewe, Cheshire CW1 1BG; tel: (0270) 584911; *Furniture (Upholstered)*

THE CONRAN SHOP, 77/79 Fulham Road, London SW3 6RE; tel: (01) 589 7401; *Fabrics and wall coverings (Fabrics), Lighting, Mirrors and glass, Furniture (Dining suites, Shelving)*

CONSCULPT, Froghill, Ponsanooth, Truro, Cornwall; tel: (0872) 863578; *Staircases*

CONTINENTAL TILES (SPECIALISTS) LTD, 8 Haycroft Road, Stevenage, Hertfordshire; tel: (0438) 724808; *Fabrics and wall coverings (Wall coverings)*

COPLEY MOULDINGS, Thorney Grange, Spennithorne, Leyburn, North Yorkshire DL8 5PW; tel: (0969) 23410; *Architectural ornaments (Plaster)*

CORIAN DISTRIBUTORS CD (UK), Richmond House, 16 Blenheim Terrace, Leeds LS2 9HN; tel: (0532) 439651; *Kitchens (Worktops)*

COTSWOLD FURNITURE CO, Carterton, Oxfordshire; tel: (0933) 845464; *Furniture (Chairs, Occasional tables, Upholstered)*

COURTNEY POPE LIGHTING LTD, Amhurst Park Works, Tottenham, London N15 6RB; tel: (01) 800 1270; *Architectural ornaments (Suspended ceilings), Lighting*

MICHAEL J COX, Lower Washbourne Barton, Ashprington, Totnes, Devon; tel: Harbentonford 488; *Furniture (Beds)*

CRAYONNE LTD, Windmill Road, Sunbury-on-Thames, Middlesex TW16 7EE; tel: (76) 85644; *Bathrooms (Fittings)*

CRESSWELL SHADES LTD, 7 Green Drift, Royston, Hertfordshire SG8 5DD; tel: (0763) 41166; *Lighting*

CROMPTON PARKINSON LTD, Woodlands House, The Avenue, Cliftonville, Northampton NN1 5BS; tel: (0604) 30201; *Lighting*

CROSBY KITCHENS LTD, Orgreave Drive, Handsworth, Sheffield S13 9NS; tel: (0742) 697371; *Kitchens (Units)*

JOHN CROSSLEY & SONS LTD, PO Box 15, Mill Street, Kidderminster DY11 6XE; tel: Kidderminster 3434; *Carpeting (Flecked, Patterned)*

CROWN DECORATIVE PRODUCTS LTD, Crown House, Hollins Road, Darwen, Lancashire BB3 0BG; tel: Darwen 74951; *Fabrics and wall coverings (Wall coverings, Co-ordinates)*

CUBESTORE, 38 Grosvenor Road, London W4; tel: (01) 994 6016; *Furniture (Shelving, Storage, Dining tables)*

CUBIC METRE FURNITURE, 17-18 Great Sutton Street, London EC1; tel: (01) 251 2437/8; *Ceramic tiles (Wall), Offices (Chairs, Screens), Furniture (Shelving, Storage, Dining tables, Occasional tables)*

RICHARD CULLINAN (JOINERY) LTD, 1b Yukon Road, London SW12 9PZ; tel: (01) 675 3437/8; *Furniture (Bedrooms)*

RICHARD CULLINAN (JOINERY) LTD, 1b Yukon Road, London SW12 9PZ; tel: (01) 675 3437/8; *Furniture (Bedrooms)*

CZECH & SPEAKE LTD, 39c Jermyn Street, London SW1; tel: (01) 980 4567/8; *Bathrooms (Fittings, Sanitaryware), Kitchens (Taps)*

DLW (BRITAIN) LTD, Block 38C, Milton Trading Estate, Milton, Nr Abingdon, Oxfordshire OX14 4RT; tel: Abingdon 831296; *Carpeting (Flecked, Patterned, Plain, Tiles), Flooring (Vinyl sheet)*

DAMIXA LTD, The Woodcock Estate, Warminster, Wiltshire; tel: (0905) 214683/214783; *Bathrooms (Fittings, Showers).* Accessories distributed by Damixa; fittings now distributed by Berglen Products Ltd (see above)

DANGLES & CO, 30 Home Close, Kibworth, Leicestershire LE8 0JT; tel: (053 753) 2066; *Fittings (Curtains)*

DARTINGTON HALL TWEEDS LTD, Shinners Bridge, Dartington, Totnes, South Devon TQ9 6JE; tel: (0803) 864388; *Fabrics and wall coverings (Fabrics)*

DAVID KITCHENS, David House, Jubilee Close, Townsend Lane, London NW9 8TR; tel: (01) 200 1444; *Kitchens (Units)*

DAVIES KEELING TROWBRIDGE, 18 Glenshaw Mansions, South Island Place, Brixton Road, London SW9 0DS; tel: (01) 582 0427; *Decorative painters*

DECARTE, 268 Gloucester Terrace, London W2 6HU; tel: (01) 727 8294; 74 Calvert Road, Greenwich, London SE10; *Decorative painters*

DEDECKER, Holloway Furniture Group, Jenna House, 101 Blackhorse Lane, Walthamstow, London E17 6DJ; tel: (01) 523 1321; *Kitchens (Units)*

DELABOLE SLATE LTD, Pengley House, Delabole, Cornwall PL33 9AZ; tel: (0840) 212242; *Flooring (Stone), Stoves and fireplaces (Mantels and surrounds)*

DELCOR, Delcor House, Double Row, Seaton Delaval, Northumberland NE25 0PR; tel: (0632) 371303/372395; *Furniture (Upholstered)*

EDITH DE LISLE, see QUENBY PRINTS LTD

SUPPLIERS' ADDRESSES

DENMOR FURNITURE CO LTD, Riverside House, Leaside Road, London E5 9LU; tel: (01) 806 3155/6/7; *Furniture (Dining suites)*

DERNIER & HAMLYN LTD, 62 Kimber Road, Southfields, London SW18; tel: (01) 870 0011; *Lighting*

DESCAMPS, 197 Sloane Street, London SW1; tel: (01) 235 7165; *Fabrics and wall coverings (Bed linen)*

DESIGN FURNITURE, Cowley, Oxford OX4 2SJ; tel: (0865) 777261; *Furniture (Dining suites, Storage, Upholstered)*

DESIGN WORKSHOP, 150 Penistone Road, Shelley, Huddersfield, Yorkshire HD8 8JQ; tel: (0484) 602996; *Furniture (Desks, Dining suites, Storage, Occasional tables, Upholstered)*

DESIGNERS CHOICE, PO Box 114, Weybridge, Surrey KT13 0LW; tel: (0932) 55821; *Carpeting (Made-to-order, Rugs)*

DESIGNERS GUILD, 271–277 Kings Road, London SW3 5EN; tel: (01) 743 8744; *Carpeting (Patterned, Plain, Rugs), Fabrics and wall coverings (Fabrics, Co-ordinates), Lighting, Furniture (Upholstered)*

THE DESK SHOP, 41 St Clements, Oxford OX4 4AG; tel: (0865) 45524; *Offices (Desks), Furniture (Desks)*

DEVALAKE LTD, Lincoln Road, Cressex Industrial Estate, High Wycombe, Buckinghamshire; tel: (0494) 28002/3; *Furniture (Chairs, Desks, Storage, Dining tables, Occasional tables)*

DIFFORD KITCHENS LTD, Southam Road, Banbury, Oxfordshire; tel: (0295) 59565; *Kitchens (Units)*

ALAN DODD, 295 Caledonian Road, London N1 1EG; tel: (01) 607 8737; *Decorative painters*

MARTIN J DODGE, Southgate, Wincanton, Somerset BA9 9EB; tel: (0963) 32388; *Offices (Tables), Furniture (Chairs, Desks, Dining suites, Storage, Occasional tables)*

DOMUS LTD, 260-266 Brompton Road, London SW3 2AS; tel: (01) 589 9457/8; *Ceramic tiles (Wall)*

DONALD BROTHERS LTD, Wallace Craigie Works, Dundee, Scotland DD4 6BB; tel: (0382) 40309; *Fabrics and wall coverings (Fabrics)*

DORMA, CV Home Furnishing Ltd, PO Box 7, Lees Street, Swinton, Manchester M27 2DD; tel: (061) 794 4781; *Fabrics and wall coverings (Bed linen)*

DOVERLIGHT LTD, 47 Rudall Crescent, London NW3 1RR; tel: (01) 794 1057; *Lighting*

DRAGONS, 23 Walton Street, London SW3; tel: (01) 589 3795/0548; *Furniture (Beds, Bedrooms)*

PETER DUDGEON, 1a Brompton Place, London SW3 1QE; tel: (01) 589 0322; *Furniture (Upholstered)*

DUNLOP LTD, Dunlop House, Ryder Street, St James's, London SW1 6PX; tel: (01) 930 6700; *Carpeting (Tiles), Flooring (Vinyl sheet, Vinyl tiles), Furniture (Beds, Upholstered)*

DUNLOP LTD, Chemical Products Division, Consumer Products, Chester Road, Birmingham B35 7AL; tel: (021) 373 8101; *Useful products (Adhesives, Sealants, Tiling)*

DUROPAL LTD, 131 St Peter's Court, Chalfont St Peter, Gerrards Cross, Buckinghamshire SL9 9QJ; tel: (0753) 886557; *Kitchens (Worktops)*

DUX INTERIORS LTD, 19–30 Alfred Place, London WC1E 7EA; tel: (01) 637 2778/9; *Furniture (Beds, Storage, Upholstered)*

DYLON INTERNATIONAL LTD, UK Division, London SE26 5HD; tel: (01) 650 4801; *Useful products (Miscellaneous)*

EASTHAM, Holmes Road, Thornton, Blackpool FY5 2SQ; tel: (0253) 856771; *Kitchens (Units)*

ELIZABETH EATON, 25a Basil Street, London SW3 1BB; tel: (01) 589 0118/9; *Ceramic tiles (Floor)*

EATON BAG CO LTD, 16 Manette Street, London W1V 5LB; tel: (01) 437 9391; *Blinds (Paper)*

EDISON HALO LTD, Eskdale Road, Uxbridge Industrial Estate, Uxbridge, Middlesex UB8 2RT; tel: (0895) 56561; *Lighting*

EGETAEPPER (UK) LTD, PO Box 115, Oak Street, Preston, Lancashire PR1 3YR; tel: (0772) 23451/5; *Carpeting (Flecked, Made-to-order, Patterned, Plain)*

ELFA, Penallta Industrial Estate, Ystrad Mynach, Mid Glamorgan CF8 7QZ; tel: Hengoed 814831; *Furniture (Storage)*

ELIT LIGHTING LTD, 279 Wimbledon Park Road, London SW19 6NW; tel: (01) 788 9191; *Lighting*

J T ELLIS & CO LTD, Crown Works, Wakefield Road, Huddersfield HD5 9BA; tel: (0484) 514212; *Kitchens (Units)*

ELON TILES (UK) LTD, 8 Clarendon Cross, Holland Park, London W11 4AP; tel: (01) 727 0884; *Bathrooms (Sanitaryware), Ceramic tiles (Floor, Wall), Fittings (Door and cabinet)*

EMESS LIGHTING LTD, 6 Anderson Road, Roding Lane South, Woodford Green, Essex, IG8 8ET; tel: (01) 551 4156; *Lighting*

NICHOLAS ENGERT INTERIOR DESIGN, 2 Inch's Yard, Market Street, Newbury, Berkshire; tel: (0635) 32414; *Lighting, Stoves and fireplaces (Accessories), Furniture (Chairs, Shelving, Dining tables, Occasional tables)*

ENGLISH HARDWOOD DESIGN, Kellet Road, Carnforth, Lancashire LA5 9XP; tel: Carnforth 735076/7; *Kitchens (Units), Furniture (Bedrooms)*

ENGLISH ROSE KITCHENS, Ideal Timber Products Ltd, Broadmeadow Industrial Estate, Dumbarton, Scotland; tel: (0389) 61777; *Kitchens (Units)*

ENVIRONMENT COMMUNICATION, Heath Hall, Heath, Wakefield WF1 5SL; tel: (0924) 366446; London showroom: 17 Rosemont Road, London NW3; tel: (01) 435 3827; *Mirrors and glass, Furniture (Chairs, Dining suites, Shelving, Occasional tables, Upholstered)*

RICHARD EPSOM, 16 The Mint, Harbledown, Canterbury; tel: (0227) 61363; *Architectural ornaments (Wood), Furniture (Made-to-order)*

EQUINOX INTERIORS LTD, 64–72 New Oxford Street, London WC1; tel: (01) 636 2345; *Carpeting (Rugs), Lighting, Furniture (Chairs, Dining tables)*

ERCO LIGHTING LTD, 38 Dover Street, London W1X 3RB; tel: (01) 408 0320; *Lighting*

ERICSON BLINDS LTD, Canal Wharf, Langley, Slough SL3 6EW; tel: Slough 46080/46868; *Blinds (Venetian)*

ESTIA DESIGNS LTD, 5–7 Tottenham Street, London W1; tel: (01) 636 5957; *Offices (Storage), Furniture (Dining Suites, Shelving, Dining tables, Occasional tables, Upholstered)*

WARREN EVANS, 4A Sans Walk, London EC1; tel: (01) 251 4687; *Furniture (Beds)*

EXCLUSIVE ART, 4 Nettlestead Cottages, Maidstone Road, Paddock Wood, Kent TN12 6DB; tel: (089283) 6231; *Decorative painters*

FABER (VENETIAN BLIND SERVICE LTD), Oakdale Trading Estate, Ham Lane, Kingswinford, West Midlands DY6 7AY; tel: (0384) 293714; *Blinds (Roller, Special, Venetian, Vertical), Fittings (Curtain)*

FABRICATION see NICE IRMA'S

D FARMILOE, 15 Kent Close, Bexhill-on-Sea, Sussex TN40 2LD; tel: (0424) 214943; *Useful products (Wood care)*

FAULKNERS, Lombard House, Lombard Street, Quayside, Newcastle upon Tyne; tel: (0632) 323780; *Furniture (Beds, Made-to-order)*

FEATURE FIRES LTD, 32 High Street, Northwood, Middlesex; tel: (65) 26699; *Stoves and fireplaces (Accessories, Mantels and surrounds)*

FILTRASOL LTD, A10 Beaver Industrial Estate, Ashford, Kent; tel: (0233) 31055; *Blinds (Roller, Venetian, Vertical)*

FINNIGANS SPECIALITY PAINTS LTD, Eltringham Works, Prudhoe, Northumberland NE24 6LP; tel: (0661) 32411; *Paints*

CHRISTIAN FISHBACHER (LONDON) LTD, Threeways House, 40/44 Clipstone Street, London W1P 8AL; tel: (01) 580 8937; *Fabrics and wall coverings (Fabrics)*

JOHN FISHER, 15 Effingham Road, Lee, London SE12 8NT; tel: (01) 852 7003; *Decorative painters*

FLEXIFORM, head office: 67 Wellington Street, Leeds LS1 1JL; tel: (0532) 441026; London sales centre: 16 Duncan Terrace, London N1 8BZ; tel: (01) 278 0671; *Offices (Co-ordinated Furniture, Desks, Storage)*

FORBO KROMMENIE (UK) LTD, Leet Court, 14 Kings Street, Watford, Hertfordshire; tel: (0923) 52323; *Flooring (Linoleum, Vinyl sheet, Vinyl tiles)*

FORBO TAPIJT BV, UK Sales Manager, Gordon Wareham, Orchard Farm House, Filands, Malmesbury, Wiltshire; tel: Malmesbury 3028; *Carpeting (Flecked, Plain)*

FORMA, Victor Mann & Co Ltd, Unit 3, Mitcham Industrial Estate, 85 Streatham Road, Mitcham, Surrey; tel: (01) 640 6811; *Lighting*

FORMICA LTD, Shearwater House, 21 The Green, Richmond, Surrey TW9 1PJ; tel: (01) 940 6055; *Kitchens (Worktops), Furniture (Made-to-order)*

FOURSQUARE DESIGNS, 1 Dale Close, London SE3 9BB; tel: (01) 852 7820; *Fabrics and wall coverings (Fabrics)*

MARY FOX LINTON LTD, 249 Fulham Road, London SW3 6HY; tel: (01) 351 0273; *Carpeting (Patterned, Rugs), Fabrics and wall coverings (Fabrics), Furniture (Desks, Storage, Dining tables, Occasional tables, Upholstered)*

FRAMFORD KITCHENS LTD, Sandy, Bedfordshire; tel: (0767) 80831; *Kitchens (Units)*

CELIA FRANK, The Stained Glass Studio, 31 Clerkenwell Close, London EC1; tel: (01) 253 4143; *Mirrors and glass*

FRANKE, Petrate Ltd, Unit 21, Eldon Way, Crick, Northamptonshire NN6 7SL; tel: (0788) 823771/2; *Bathrooms (Fittings), Kitchens (Sinks)*

SUPPLIERS' ADDRESSES

FRANKE KUGLER, Petrate Ltd, Kitchen Division, Unit 21, Eldon Way, Crick, Northamptonshire NN6 7SL; tel: (0788) 823771/2; *Kitchens (Taps)*

FRAY DESIGN, Church Street, Addingham, Ilkley, West Yorkshire LS29 0QT; tel: (0493) 831333; *Offices (Tables)*

FRAYLING, Davenport Street, Burslem, Stoke-on-Trent ST6 4LN; tel: Stoke-on-Trent 811041; *Offices (Reception seating), Furniture (Upholstered)*

FUTON COMPANY, 82–83 Tottenham Court Road, London W1; tel: (01) 729 0670; *Furniture (Beds, Chairs, Upholstered)*

FUTON FACTORY, 192 Balls Pond Road, Islington, London N1; tel: (01) 226 4477; *Furniture (Upholstered)*

GAGGENAU, Gaggenau Electric (UK) Ltd, Colville Road, London W3 BB1; tel: (01) 993 2332/7; *Kitchens (Sinks)*

GALLEON CLAYGATE LTD, 216-230 Red Lion Road, Tolworth, Surbiton, Surrey KT6 7RB; tel: (01) 397 3456/9; *Stoves and fireplaces (Accessories, Mantels and surrounds)*

GARDEX LTD, Cromwell Road, Bredbury, Stockport SK6 2RX; tel: (061) 430 5269; *Bathrooms (Fittings, Showers)*

SUSANNE GARRY LTD, 152a Walton Street, London SW3; tel: (01) 584 1091/0459; *Blinds (Roller, Roman), Fabrics and wall coverings (Co-ordinates), Furniture (Screens and partitions)*

GASKELL BROADLOOM CARPETS LTD, Wheatfield Mill, Rishton, Blackburn, Lancashire BB1 4NU; tel: (0254) 885566; *Carpeting (Flecked, Made-to-order, Patterned, Plain, Rugs, Tiles), Fabrics and wall coverings (Wall coverings)*

GEORGIAN CARPETS LTD, Glensmore Mills, Kidderminster, Worcestershire DY10 2LH; tel: Kidderminster 69921; London showroom: Bowater House, Knightsbridge, London SW1X 7LR; tel: (01) 584 7070; *Carpeting (Plain, Rugs)*

GERLAND LTD, 90 Crawford Street, London W1H 2AP; tel: (01) 723 6601; *Flooring (Rubber, Vinyl sheet, Vinyl tiles)*

GIEFFE, 15 Kennard Road, Stratford, London E15; tel: (01) 555 7393/4; *Kitchens (Units)*

DAVID GILLESPIE ASSOCIATES LTD, Dippenhales Crossroads, Farnham, Surrey GU1 5DW; tel: (0252) 723531; *Architectural ornaments (Suspended ceilings), Decorative painters, Furniture (Screens and partitions)*

GILT EDGE CARPETS, PO Box 5, Mill Street, Kidderminster, Worcestershire DY11 6XQ; tel: Kidderminster 748600; *Carpeting (Flecked, Patterned, Plain)*

GIPSY TABLES, 12A Napier Avenue, London SW6 3PT; tel: (01) 731 0703; *Furniture (Occasional tables)*

THE THOMAS GLENISTER COMPANY, Hughenden Road, High Wycombe, Buckinghamshire HP13 5DP; tel: High Wycombe 21988; *Furniture (Chairs, Storage, Dining tables, Occasional tables)*

GODDARD & GIBBS STUDIOS, 41-49 Kingsland Road, London E2 8AD; tel: (01) 739 6563; *Mirrors and glass*

GOLDEN PLAN LTD, 14 Golden Square, London W1R 3AG; tel: (01) 343 2066; *Furniture (Beds)*

GOLDREIF KITCHENS UK LTD, Thames House, 63 Kingston Road, New Malden, Surrey; tel: (019) 429347/8; *Kitchens (Units)*

GOODACRE CARPETS LTD, Castle Mills, Kendal, Cumbria; tel: (0539) 23601; Kidderminster showroom: Bowater Carpets Ltd, Glensmore Mills, Glenmore Street, Kidderminster, Worcestershire; tel: (0562) 2287/3659; London showroom: Bowater House, Knightsbridge, London SW1X 7LR; tel: (01) 584 7070; *Carpeting (Patterned)*

GOOD IDEAS, Moles Cottages, Exminster, Exeter, Devon; tel: (0392) 833019; *Furniture (Beds)*

GORDON, WATTS & CO LTD, Kern House, 36–39 Kingsway, London WC2B 6HA; tel: (01) 405 8372; *Fabrics and wall coverings (Wall coverings)*

GOSTIN OF LIVERPOOL, Portway, off 2A Higher Road, Halewood, Liverpool L25 0QQ; tel: (051) 486 1703/6175; *Furniture (Desks, Storage)*

GOWER FURNITURE LTD, Holmfield Industrial Estate, Halifax, West Yorkshire HX2 9TN; tel: (0422) 246201; *Kitchens (Units)*

SUSIE GRADWELL STENCILS, 1 The Old Bakery, Long Street, Croscombe, Nr Wells, Somerset; tel: Shepton Mallet (0749) 2429; *Decorative painters*

GRAHAM & GREEN LTD, 4 & 7 Elgin Crescent, London W11; tel: (01) 727 4594; *Carpeting (Rugs), Lighting, Furniture (Upholstered)*

GRANGE, David Marshall, 7–9 Bridge Street, St Ives, Huntingdon, Cambridgeshire PE17 4EH; tel: Huntingdon 61796; *Furniture (Beds, Bedrooms, Chairs, Desks, Dining suites, Storage, Occasional tables, Upholstered)*

G J GREEN AND VERONESE, 24 Edison Road, London N8 8AE; tel: (01) 348 4461/2; *Architectural ornaments (Plaster), Stoves and fireplaces (Mantels and surrounds)*

GREENWOOD & COOPE LTD, Brookhouse Mill, Greenmount, Nr Bury, Lancashire BL0 9AU; tel: Tottington 2241; *Carpeting (Flecked, Patterned, Plain)*

ELEANOR GREEVES, 12 Newton Grove, Bedford Park, London W4 1LB; tel: (01) 994 6523; *Ceramic tiles (Wall)*

JOHNNY GREY DESIGN, Hampshire Farm, South Harting, Petersfield, Hampshire GU31 5LP; tel: (073085) 394; *Kitchens (Units), Offices (Co-ordinated furniture), Furniture (Made-to-order)*

GROVEWOOD PRODUCTS LTD, Tipton, West Midlands DY4 7UZ; tel: (021) 557 3955; *Kitchens (Units)*

GUILD OF LAKELAND CRAFTSMEN, c/o Rosemary Russell, Secretary, 33 Entry Lane, Kendal, Cumbria; tel: (0539) 27917; *Carpeting (Rugs)*

HABITAT DESIGNS LTD, The Heal's Building, 196 Tottenham Court Road, London W1P 9LD; tel: (01) 631 3880; mail order: PO Box 2, Wallingford, Oxfordshire OX10 9DQ; tel: (0491) 35511; *Bathrooms (Fittings), Blinds (Paper, Roller, Roman, Venetian), Carpeting (Coir, Flecked, Plain, Rugs), Ceramic tiles (Floor, Wall), Fabrics and wall coverings (Fabrics, Wall coverings, Co-ordinates, Bed linen), Flooring (Linoleum, Vinyl sheet, Vinyl tiles), Kitchens (Units), Lighting, Mirrors and glass, Paint, Furniture (Beds, Chairs, Desks, Dining suites, Screens and partitions, Shelving, Storage, Occasional tables, Upholstered)*

HABITAT & HEAL'S CONTRACTS, 22/24 Torrington Place, London WC1E 7LH; tel: (01) 631 3464; *Offices (Co-ordinated furniture)*

PETER HALL WOODCRAFT, Danes Road, Staveley, Kendal, Cumbria LA8 9LP; tel: Kendal 821633; *Furniture (Made-to-order)*

JAMES HALSTEAD LTD, PO Box 3, Radcliffe New Road, Whitefield, Manchester M25 7NR; tel: (061) 766 3781; *Carpeting (Tiles)*

HAMILTON WESTON WALLPAPERS, 11 Townshend Road, Richmond, Surrey TW9 1XH; tel: (01) 940 4850; *Fabrics and wall coverings (Wall coverings)*

HAMLET FURNITURE LTD, Unit 2, Waverley Road, Yale, Bristol BS17 5QT; tel: (0454) 319090; *Kitchens (Units), Furniture (Beds, Bedrooms, Dining suites, Storage)*

CHARLES HAMMOND, 7b Harriet Walk, London SW1X 9JQ; tel: (01) 235 0634/5; *Mirrors and glass, Furniture (Bedrooms, Chairs, Made-to-order, Occasional tables, Upholstered)*

HAMMOND WHOLESALE LTD, 7b Harriet Walk, London SW1X 9JQ; tel: (01) 235 0634; *Fabrics and wall coverings (Fabrics), Lighting*

HAMMONDS FURNITURE, 1 Fleming Road, Harrowbrook Industrial Estate, Hinckley, Leicestershire LE10 3DT; tel: (0455) 39487; *Furniture (Bedrooms)*

HAMPTON GARDEN ACCESSORIES (HGA) LTD, Cirencester Road, Chalford, Gloucestershire; tel: (0453) 883828; *Stoves and fireplaces (Mantels and surrounds)*

HAMPSTEAD DECORATIVE ARTS, 82 Belsize Park Gardens, London NW3; tel: (01) 586 1810; *Decorative painters*

HAND PAINTED STENCILS, 6 Polstead Road, Oxford OX2 6TW; tel: (0865) 56072 or (01) 701 5647; *Decorative painters*

HANDY DIRECT SUPPLIES, Stephenson Street, London E16; tel: (01) 474 0106; *Architectural ornaments (Suspended ceilings)*

HANSIL LTD, 19 Wintersells Road, Byfleet, Surrey KT14 7LH; tel: (09323) 51911; *Useful products (Sealants)*

M & I J HARRISON LTD; no longer trading

HARRISON BEACON, Harrison of Birmingham Ltd, PO Box 233, Bradford Street Works, Birmingham B12 0PE; tel: (021) 773 1111; *Fittings (Door and cabinet)*

HARRISON DRAPE, Harrison of Birmingham Ltd, Bradford Street, Birmingham B12 0PE; tel: (021) 773 1111; *Fittings (Curtain)*

HART OF KNIGHTSBRIDGE, 3 Beauchamp Place, London SW3 1NG; tel: (01) 584 5770; *Architectural ornaments (Wood), Stoves and fireplaces (Mantels and surrounds)*

C P HART & SONS LTD, Newnham Terrace, Hercules Road, London SE1; tel: (01) 928 5866; *Bathrooms (Fittings, Sanitaryware), Ceramic tiles (Wall), Kitchens (Worktops)*

HATEMA (UK) LTD, 70/72 Old Street, London EC1V 9AN; tel: (01) 253 5433/4; *Carpeting (Flecked, Plain), Fabrics and wall coverings (Wall coverings)*

SUPPLIERS' ADDRESSES

PETER HAXWORTH, 17 Islip Road, Oxford OX2 7SN; tel: Oxford 511831; *Offices (Tables), Furniture (Made-to-order)*

HEAT APPLIANCES LTD, Heat House, 4 Brighton Road, Horsham, West Sussex RH13 5BA; tel: (0403) 56227; *Stoves and fireplaces (Stoves)*

HEATHERLEY FINE CHINA LTD, Unit 3, Ferry Lane, Brentford, Middlesex TW8 0BG; tel: (01) 568 7963; *Bathrooms (Fittings), Fittings (Door and cabinet)*

NEIL HENDERSON, The Workshop, Eastgate, Hornton, Banbury, Oxfordshire OX15 6BT; tel: (0295) 87 531; *Furniture (Occasional tables)*

HEUGA UK LTD, Heuga House, 1 Oxford Road, Aylesbury, Buckinghamshire HP19 3EP; tel: Aylesbury 33244; *Carpeting (Tiles)*

E A HIGGINSON & CO LTD, Binns Lane Works, Mill Hill, London NW7 2AJ; tel: (01) 959 2808; *Staircases*

HILL & KNOWLES LTD, 133 Kew Road, Richmond, Surrey TW9 2PN; tel: (01) 948 4010; *Fabrics and wall coverings (Co-ordinates)*

HILLE INTERNATIONAL LTD, Whittington House, 19/30 Alfred Place, London WC1 7EA; tel: (01) 580 2080; *Offices (Chairs, Co-ordinated Furniture, Reception seating, Tables)*

HIPPO HALL, 65 Pimlico Road, London SW1; tel: (01) 730 5532; *Fabrics and wall coverings (Bed linen)*

HITCH/MYLIUS, Spencer House, Brettenham Road, London N18 2EU; tel: (01) 807 9324; *Offices (Reception seating), Furniture (Upholstered)*

HITECH (UK) LTD, Tower House, Lea Valley Trading Estate, Edmonton, London N18 3HR; tel: (01) 884 3333; *Lighting*

OSWALD HOLLMAN LTD, 208 Kent House Road, Beckenham, Kent BR3 1JN; tel: (01) 778 5888/7994; *Lighting*

HOMETEX TRADING LTD, Sedbergh Chambers, Chantry Drive, Ilkley, West Yorkshire LS29 9HU; tel: Ilkley 608197; *Carpeting (Flecked, Made-to-order)*

HOMEWORKS LTD, 107a Pimlico Road, London SW1; tel: (01) 730 9116; *Architectural ornaments (Wood), Carpeting (Patterned), Lighting, Furniture (Chairs, Dining suites, Occasional tables, Upholstered)*

HOPE WORKS LTD, Pleck Road, Walsall WS2 9HH; tel: (0922) 27175; *Fittings (Door and cabinet)*

IDEAL STANDARD LTD, PO Box 60, National Avenue, Kingston-upon-Hull HU5 4JE; tel: (0482) 46461; *Bathrooms (Fittings, Sanitaryware, Showers)*

IDEAL TIMBER PRODUCTS LTD, Broadmeadow Industrial Estate, Dumbarton G82 2RG, Scotland; tel: (0389) 61777; *Bathrooms (Fittings), Kitchens (Units)*

IDEAS FOR LIVING, 5 Kensington High Street, London W8; tel: (01) 937 3738; *Offices (Screens, Systems), Furniture (Beds, Chairs, Desks, Dining suites, Shelving, Storage, Dining tables, Occasional tables, Upholstered)*

ILLUMIN, 82 Bond Street, Macclesfield, Cheshire SK11 6QS; tel: (0625) 613600; *Lighting*

IMPERIAL CHEMICAL INDUSTRIES PLC, Wexham Road, Slough SL2 5DS; tel: (75) 31151; *Paint, Useful products (Wood care)*

INSIDE STORY LTD, Crest, Ducks Hill Road, Northwood, Middlesex HA6 2SQ; tel: (65) 22858; *Decorative painters*

INTEK, 52 Kings Road, Alton, Hampshire GU34 1PY; tel: (0420) 83146; *Furniture (Desks)*

INTERFACE FLOORING SYSTEMS LTD, Shelf Mills, Halifax, West Yorkshire HX3 7PA; tel: Halifax 676261; *Carpeting (Flecked, Plain, Tiles)*

INTERIOR SELECTION, 240 Blythe Road, London W14 0HJ; tel: (01) 602 6616; *Fabrics and wall coverings (Co-ordinates)*

INTERLÜBKE, 239 Greenwich High Road, London SE10 8NB; tel: (01) 858 3325; *Furniture (Beds, Bedrooms, Storage)*

INTERNATIONAL PAINT PLC, 24-30 Canute Road, Southampton, Hampshire SO9 3AS; tel: Southampton 37838; *Useful products (Wood)*

INTEROVEN LTD, 70-72 Fearnley Street, Watford, Hertfordshire WD1 7DE; tel: (92) 46761; *Stoves and fireplaces (Accessories, Stoves)*

ISOPLAN LTD, Icknield Way, Tring, Hertfordshire HP23 4JX; tel: (044 282) 4111; *Offices (Chairs, Co-ordinated furniture, Storage)*

GEORGE JACKSON & SONS LTD, Rathbone Works, Rainville Road, Hammersmith, London W6 9HD; tel: (01) 385 6616/381 5297; *Architectural ornaments (Plaster, Wood) Stoves and fireplaces (Mantels and surrounds)*

JONATHAN JAMES, New Road, Rainham, Essex; tel: (76) 56921–5; *Architectural ornaments (Plaster)*

KATHARINE JAMES LTD, The Mail House, Eldon St, Tuxford, Newark, Nottinghamshire NG22 1DO; tel: (0777) 871550; *Fabrics and wall coverings (Co-ordinates)*

SARAH JANSON, 49 Drayton Gardens, London SW10 9RX; tel: (01) 373 2867; *Decorative painters*

JAYCEE FURNITURE (BRIGHTON) LTD, Bexhill Road, Brighton, Sussex BN2 6QQ; tel: (0273) 34081/5; *Furniture (Beds, Bedrooms, Chairs, Desks, Dining suites, Storage, Dining tables, Occasional tables)*

JAYMART RUBBER & PLASTICS LTD, Woodlands Trading Estate, Eden Vale Road, Westbury, Wiltshire BA13 3QS; tel: (0373) 864926; *Carpeting (Coir, Patterned, Rugs), Flooring (Rubber, Vinyl sheet)*

LAURA JEFFREYS, 29 Brunswick Gardens, London W8 4AW; tel: (01) 727 9517; *Decorative painters*

H & R JOHNSON LTD, Highgate Tile Works, Tunstall, Stoke-on-Trent ST6 4JX; tel: Stoke-on-Trent 85611; *Ceramic tiles (Floor, Wall)*

JOY PRODUCTS, Turnbridges Ltd, 72 Longley Road, London SW17; tel: (01) 672 6581; *Paint, Useful products (Wood care)*

JUST DESKS, 20 Church Street, London NW8; tel: (01) 723 7976; *Offices (Chairs, Co-ordinated Furniture), Furniture (Desks)*

KEDDDY HOME IMPROVEMENTS LTD, 198 High Street, Egham, Surrey; tel: (0784) 37 357; *Stoves and fireplaces (Mantels and surrounds, Stoves)*

G & A KELLY LTD, 1b Yukon Road, London SW12 9PZ; tel: (01) 675 3437/3438; *Furniture (Upholstered)*

R E H KENNEDY LTD, Halifax Works, 427 Wherstead Road, Ipswich, Suffolk IP2 8LH; tel: Ipswich 53802/51797; *Offices (Tables), Furniture (Chairs, Dining suites, Storage, Occasional tables)*

KEWLOX FURNITURE LTD, Driad House, Bideford Avenue, Perivale, Middlesex UB6 7QB; tel: (01) 997 5444; *Offices (Co-ordinated furniture)*

KIBBLEWHITE & BLACKMUR LTD, Long Reach Road, Barking, Essex; tel: (01) 594 5591; *Flooring (Vinyl tiles, Wood)*

ED KING, 37 Northfield Road, London E6 2AJ; tel: (01) 472 2507; *Mirrors and glass*

L M KINGCOME LTD, 304 Fulham Road, London SW10 9EP; tel: (01) 351 3998; *Furniture (Upholstered)*

KINGSWOOD KITCHEN SYSTEMS, Allied Manufacturing Co (London) Ltd, Sarena House, Grove Park, Colindale, London NW9; tel: (01) 205 8844; *Kitchens (Units)*

KNOBS & KNOCKERS, 30-40 York Way, London N1 9AB; and branches throughout England and Wales; tel: (01) 278 8925; *Fittings (Door and cabinet, Windows)*

LADYLOVE, Preston & Rowland Ltd, Century House, Widnes, Cheshire; tel: (051) 423 2551; *Kitchens (Units)*

CATHERINE LALAU KERALY, 104 Hereford Road, London W2; tel: (01) 727 4998; *Mirrors and glass, Furniture (Screens and partitions)*

LANGLEY LONDON LTD, 161-167 Borough High Street, London SE1 1HU; tel: (01) 407 4444; *Bathrooms (Showers), Ceramic tiles (Floor, Wall)*

LANGSTON JONES & SAMUEL SMITH LTD, Haverhill, Suffolk CB9 8PQ; tel: Haverhill 703611; *Paint, Useful products (Wood care)*

JOHN LARKING, No 3, 290 Muswell Hill Broadway, London N10; tel: (01) 883 3302; *Lighting*

THE LAST DETAIL, 341 Kings Road, London SW3 5ES; tel: (01) 351 6294; *Lighting*

CHRISTOPHER LAWRENCE, Christopher Lawrence Textiles & Lighting Ltd, 283 Lillie Road, London SW6 7LN; tel: (01) 385 5167; *Fabrics and wall coverings (Fabrics)*

LYN LE GRICE STENCIL DESIGN, Alsia Mill, St Buryan, Cornwall TR19 6HG; tel: (0736) 72765; *Decorative painters*

LEAD & LIGHT, 15 Camden Lock, Commercial Place, London NW1 8AF; tel: (01) 485 4568; *Lighting*

LEICHT FURNITURE LTD, Leicht House, Lagoon Road, Orpington, Kent BR5 3QG; tel: Orpington 36413/4; *Kitchens*

LEIDA SYSTEMS LTD, Beddington House, 203 Biscot Road, Bedfordshire LU3 1BJ; tel: (0582) 429111; *Furniture (Shelving)*

LEISURE, Glynwed Consumer & Building Products Ltd, Meadow Lane, Long Eaton, Nottingham NG10 2AT; tel: (0602) 73414; *Bathrooms (Showers), Kitchens (Sinks, Taps)*

LEMA, c/o I & I, 47 Rudall Crescent, London NW3 1RR; tel: (01) 435 2922; *Furniture (Storage)*

JOHN LEWIS PARTNERSHIP, 4 Old Cavendish Street, London W1A 1EX; tel: (01) 637 3434; *Ceramic tiles (Wall)*

LEYLAND PAINT & WALLPAPER PLC, Northgate, Leyland, Preston PR5 2LT; tel: Leyland 421481; *Fabrics and wall coverings (Wall coverings, Co-ordinates), Paints, Useful products (Wood)*

B LILLY & SONS, Baltimore Road, Birmingham B42 1DJ; tel: (021) 357 1761; *Fittings (Door and cabinet, Windows)*

THE LIGHTING WORKSHOP, 35-36 Floral Street, Covent Garden, London WC2E 9DJ; tel: (01) 240 0461; *Lighting*

LITA DISPLAY LTD, 190 City Road, London EC1V 2QR; tel: (01) 251 8844; *Lighting*

NICHOLAS LLEWELYN DECORATIONS, 27 Klea Avenue, London SW4; tel: (01) 673 2072; *Decorative painters*

LOCKS & HANDLES, Architectural Components Ltd, 8 Exhibition Road, London SW7 2HF; tel: (01) 584 6800; *Fittings (Doors and cabinet)*

LONDON BEDDING CENTRE, 26-27 Sloane Street, London SW1X 9NE; tel: (01) 235 7541; *Furniture (Beds)*

THE LONDON SOFA-BED CENTRE, 236 Fulham Road, London SW10 9NB; tel: (01) 352 1358; *Furniture (Upholstered)*

CATHERINE LOVEGROVE MURALS, 21 Cumberland Street, Pimlico, London SW1V 4LS; tel: (01) 834 8987; *Decorative painters*

LUCAS FURNITURE SYSTEMS, 616 Wick Lane, London E3 2JJ; tel: (01) 980 3232; *Offices (Chairs, Systems, Tables*

JAMES LUPTON & SONS LTD, Wellington Street, Long Eaton, Nottingham NG10 4HT; tel: (0602) 730730; *Furniture (Chairs, Storage, Dining tables, Occasional tables)*

LUXAFLEX LTD, Hunter Douglas Ltd, Industrial Estate, Larkhall, Lanarkshire ML9 2PD; tel: (0698) 881281; *Blinds (Roller, Special, Venetian, Vertical); and* 15–16 Bellsize Close, Walsall Road, Norton Canes, Cannock WS11 3TQ, Staffordshire; tel: (0543) 75757; *Fittings (Curtain)*

LUXURIOUS TEXTILES LTD, Roban House, 255 Low Lane, Horsforth, Leeds LS18 5NY; tel: (0532) 584666; *Fabrics and wall coverings (Wall coverings)*

MFI 'HYGENA' KITCHENS, Ludgate House, 107 Fleet Street, London EC4 2AB; tel: (01) 583 2723; *Kitchens (Units)*

J G MCDONOUGH LTD, 347 New King's Road, London SW6 4RJ; tel: (01) 736 5146; *Architectural ornaments (Plaster)*

HUGH MACKAY PLC, PO Box No 1, Durham City, DH1 2RX; tel: Durham 64444; London showroom: Roman House, Wood Street, London EC2Y 5BU; tel: (01) 606 8491; *Carpeting (Made-to-order, Patterned)*

WILLIAM L MACLEAN LTD, 3 New England Street, Brighton BN1 4GQ; tel: (0273) 695411; *Furniture (Beds, Bedrooms, Chairs, Storage, Dining tables, Occasional tables, Upholstered)*

DONALD MACPHERSON & CO LTD, Warth Mills, Radcliffe Road, Bury, Lancashire BL9 9NB; tel: (061) 764 6030; *Paint*

MAGNET SOUTHERNS, Magnet Southern Joinery Ltd, Keighley, West Yorkshire; tel: (0535) 661133; *Architectural ornaments (Wood), Fittings (Door and cabinet), Staircases*

MAGPIE FURNITURE LTD, Four Marks, Alton, Hampshire GU34 5HN; tel: (0420) 63535; *Offices (Co-ordinated furniture)*

MALLINSON DENNY (BUSHBOARD) LTD, Pine End Works, Lydney, Gloucestershire GL15 4EW; tel: (0594) 42213; *Flooring (Wood)*

MAMOLI, Petrate Ltd, Kitchen Division, Unit 21, Eldon Way, Crick, Northamptonshire NN6 7SL; tel: (0788) 823771/2; *Bathrooms (Fittings), Kitchens (Taps)*

MANDERS PAINTS LTD, PO Box 9, Mander House, Wolverhampton WV1 3NH; tel: (0902) 871028; *Paint, Useful products (Wood)*

MANHATTAN FURNITURE, Dennis & Robinson Ltd, Churchill Industrial Estate, Lancing, West Sussex BN15 8UH; tel: (0903) 755321; *Kitchens (Units, Sinks), Furniture (Bedrooms)*

MARBLE STYLE LTD, Trafalgar Works, Station Road, Chertsey, Surrey KT16 8BE; tel: (09328) 63718; *Bathrooms (Fittings, Sanitaryware Showers)*

MARLBOROUGH CERAMIC TILES, Packard & Ord Ltd, Marlborough, Wiltshire; tel: (0672) 52422; *Ceramic tiles (Floor, Walls)*

MARLIN LIGHTING LTD, Hanworth Trading Estate, Hampton Road West, Feltham, Middlesex TW13 6DR; tel: (01) 894 5522; *Lighting*

MARGARET MARTIN, The Cottage, Manningford Abbots, Nr Pewsey, Wiltshire; tel: (0672) 63191; *Furniture (Made-to-order)*

MARTELA CONTRACT INTERIORS LTD, Rooksley, Milton Keynes MK13 8PD; tel: (0908) 667418; London showroom: 210 High Holborn, London WC1V 7PB; tel: (01) 831 8771; *Offices (Chairs, Co-ordinated furniture, Systems)*

MARVIC TEXTILES LTD, 12–14 Mortimer Street, London W1N 7RD; tel: (01) 580 7951; *Fabrics and wall coverings (Fabrics)*

MATKI LTD, Molly Millar Bridge, Wokingham, Berkshire RG11 2RF; tel: (0734) 790909; *Bathrooms (Showers)*

CHARLES MATTS, Manor Farm Workshops, School Road, Aldborough, Norwich, Norfolk NR11 7AA; tel: Cromer 768060/761422; *Furniture (Made-to-order)*

MAW & CO, 342 High Street, Tunstall, Stoke-on-Trent ST6 5EL; tel: (0782) 817341; *Ceramic tiles (Wall)*

MAYBRIK (UK) LTD, PO Box 114, Weybridge, Surrey KT13 0LW; tel: Weybridge 55821; *Flooring (Stone)*

JOHN MEAD COUNTRY KITCHENS, Roadside Farm, Little Salisbury, Pewsey, Wiltshire; tel: (0672) 6235; *Kitchens (Units)*

MEISTER KITCHEN SUITES, John Knowles (London) Ltd, Brickfield's Wallage Lane, Rowfant, Crawley, Sussex RH10 4NQ; tel: (0342) 712135; *Kitchens (Units)*

MERCIA WEAVERS LTD, 57 Brindley Road, Astmoor, Runcorn, Cheshire WA7 1PS; tel: Runcorn 64054/72575; London showroom: 17–18 Berners Street, London W1P 4AY; tel: (01) 636 8412; *Carpeting (Patterned, Plain);* also SIGNATURE RUGS

MEREDEW, Dunhams Lane, Letchworth Garden City, Hertfordshire SG6 1LG; tel: (04626) 2381; *Furniture (Bedrooms, Dining suites, Storage)*

METLEX INDUSTRIES LTD, Metlex House, 29 Vicarage Road, Croydon, Surrey CR9 3BQ; tel: (01) 688 1133; *Bathrooms (Fittings)*

MIELE CO LTD, Fairacres, Marcham Road, Abingdon, Oxfordshire OX14 1TW; tel: Abingdon (0235) 28585; *Kitchens (Units)*

PETER MILES, Millers Green, Wirksworth, Derbyshire DE4 4BG; tel: (062) 982 3853/8; *Furniture (Desks, Dining suites, Storage, Occasional tables, Upholstered)*

SALLY MILES, 37 Englewood Road, London SW12; tel: (01) 675 4264; *Decorative painters*

HERMANN MILLER, 149 Tottenham Court Road, London W1P 0JA; tel: (01) 388 7331; *Furniture (Chairs, Occasional tables, Upholstered)*

MOBEN KITCHENS LTD, Maclaren House, Talbot Road, Stretford, Manchester M32 0FP; tel: (061) 872 5966; *Kitchens (Units)*

MONKWELL FABRICS, Semple & Company Ltd, 10–12 Wharfdale Road, Bournemouth, Dorset BH4 9BT; tel: (0202) 762456; *Fabrics and wall coverings (Fabrics)*

ARNOLD MONTROSE LTD, 47/48 Berners Street, London W1P 3AD; tel: (01) 580 5316/8; *Lighting*

MOORES INTERNATIONAL, Moores Furniture Group Ltd, Queen Mary House, Thorp Arch Trading Estate, Wetherby, West Yorkshire LS23 7BR; tel: (0937) 844300; *Kitchens (Units)*

MOORHOUSE ASSOCIATES, 240 Camden High Street, London NW1; tel: (01) 267 9714; *Fabrics and wall coverings (Fabrics)*

MORESECURE LTD, Holyhead Road Factory Centre, Western Way, Wednesbury, West Midlands WS10 7BN; tel: (021) 556 3311; *Offices (Storage)*

MORGAN & OATES, Church Lane, Ledbury, Herefordshire HR8 1DW; tel: Ledbury 2718; *Carpeting (Rugs)*

MORGAN GILDER FURNITURE, The Mill, Mill Lane, Stony Stratford, Milton Keynes, Buckinghamshire; tel: Milton Keynes 568674; *Furniture (Upholstered)*

MORLEY MARKETING, C J Kershaw Ltd, Victoria Maltings, Broadmeads, Ware, Herts SG12 9HS; tel: (0920) 68001; *Stoves and fireplaces (Stoves)*

GEORGE MORRIS, 221 Fir Tree Road, Epsom Downs, Surrey; tel: (07373) 59558, eves (27) 76440; *Decorative painters*

MR LIGHT, 275 Fulham Road, London SW10 9PZ; tel: (01) 352 7525; *Lighting*

MUNDET CORK & PLASTICS LTD, Vicarage Road, Croydon CR9 4AR; tel: (01) 688 4142; *Flooring (Cork)*

A MURRAY (LONDON) LTD, head office: Murray House, 10 Lawrence Way, Yorktown Industrial Estate, Camberley, Surrey GU15 3DL; tel: (0276) 27261/7; London sales office: 92–93 St Martin's Lane, London WC2N 4AP; tel: (01) 836 6161; *Offices (Chairs, Co-ordinated Furniture)*

NAIRN COATED PRODUCTS LTD, Lune Mills, Lancaster LA1 5QN; tel: (0524) 65222; *Fabrics and wall coverings (Wall coverings, Co-ordinates)*

NAIRN FLOORS LTD, Old Loom House, Back Church Lane, London E1 1LS; tel: (01) 480 0144; *Flooring (Linoleum, Vinyl sheet);* see also NAIRN-FLAIR LTD

NAIRNFLAIR LTD, PO Box 1, Kirkcaldy KY1 2SB, Scotland; tel: (0592) 261111; *Carpeting (Tiles)*

SUPPLIERS' ADDRESSES

MAXINE NAYLOR, 177 Waller Road, London SE14; tel: (01) 635 8792; *Lighting, Furniture (Made-to-order, Screens and partitions)*

NEVILLE NEAL, School House, Stockton, Nr Rugby CV23 8JE; tel: Southam (092 681) 3702; *Furniture (Chairs)*

NEWMAN-TONKS HARDWARE LTD, Newman-Tonks Consumer Division, Merridale House, Merridale Street, Wolverhampton, West Midlands WV3 0RB; tel: (0902) 27532; *Fittings (Door and cabinet)*

W H NEWSON & SONS LTD, 61 Pimlico Road, London SW1W 8NF; tel: (01) 730 6262/8; also Reigate and Sunbury on Thames; *Architectural ornaments (Plaster, Wood), Staircases, Furniture (Screens and partitions)*

NICE IRMA'S (FABRICATION) LTD, 46 Goodge Street, London W1P 1FJ; tel: (01) 580 6921; *Carpeting (Rugs), Fabrics and wall coverings (Fabrics), Lighting*

NICHOLL & WOOD LTD, Netherton Works, Holmfield, Halifax, West Yorkshire HX3 6ST; *Furniture (Shelving)*

NICOBOND LTD, 310 Shoreditch High Street, London E1 6PE; tel: (01) 247 8838/9; *Ceramic tiles (Floor, Wall), Useful products (Tiling)*

CHRISTIAN NIMMO, Lindalls, Church Street, Amberley, Nr Arundel, West Sussex; tel: (079) 881644; *Furniture (Made-to-order)*

NORFOLK MANOR FURNITURE LTD, Main Cross Road, Great Yarmouth, Norfolk NR30 3NZ; tel: (0493) 856418/856865; *Offices (Chairs, Desks, Storage, Tables)*

NORTH WESTERN LEAD COMPANY LTD, Newton Moor Industrial Estate, Mill Street, Hyde, Cheshire SK14 4LF; tel: (061) 368 4491; *Useful products (Miscellaneous)*

OMK DESIGNS LTD, Stephen Building, 30 Stephen Street, London W1P 1PN; tel: (01) 631 1335; *Lighting, Offices (Chairs, Co-ordinated furniture, Storage) Furniture (Dining suites, Dining tables, Occasional tables, Upholstered)*

OAKLEAF REPRODUCTIONS LTD, Ling Bob, Main Street, Wilsden, Bradford BD15 0JP; tel: (0535) 272878; *Architectural ornaments (Wood), Furniture (Beds)*

GILBERT O'BRIEN, Flat G, 22 Montague Street, London WC1; tel: (01) 580 8305; *Decorative painters*

OCEES COMPONENTS AND STRUCTURES LTD, 49 Knightsbridge Court, Sloane Street, London SW1X 9LL; tel: (01) 225 0777; *Stoves and fireplaces (Mantels and surrounds, Stoves)*

OFFICE KIT LTD, 15 Macklin Street, London WC2B 5NH; tel: (01) 242 5722; *Offices (Systems)*

JOHN S OLIVER LTD, 33 Pembridge Road, London W11 3HG; tel: (01) 221 6466; *Fabrics and wall coverings (Wall coverings, Co-ordinates), Paint*

OLIVER & PINK, 359 New Kings Road, London SW6; tel: (01) 736 6299; *Decorative painters*

THE OLLERTON HALL DECORATING SERVICE, Ollerton, Knutsford, Cheshire; tel: Knutsford 2740; *Carpeting (Flecked, Patterned, Plain)*

ONE OFF LTD, 56 Neal Street, London WC2; tel: (01) 379 7796; *Furniture (Beds, Made-to-order, Shelving, Upholstered)*

OPTIFIT, Berglen Distributors Ltd, Masons House, Kingsbury Road, London NW9 9NQ; tel: (01) 204 3434; *Kitchens (Units, Sinks)*

ORGATECH LTD, 42 Gorst Road, London NW10 6LD; tel: (01) 965 5611; *Lighting, Offices (Chairs, Reception seating, Systems)*

OSBORNE & LITTLE, 304 Kings Road, London SW3 5UH; tel: (01) 352 1456; *Fabrics and wall coverings (Fabrics, Co-ordinates)*

P & O CARPETS LTD, 63 South Audley Street, London W1; tel: (01) 629 9678; *Carpeting (Rugs)*

PAINTED PATTERNS, 16 Trevecca, Liskeard, Cornwall; tel: Liskeard 46750; *Decorative painters*

PALLU & LAKE LTD, 18 Newman Street, London W1; tel: (01) 636 3743; *Fabrics and wall coverings (Fabrics, Co-ordinates)*

PANAVISTA, Fircroft Way, Edenbridge, Kent TN8 6EL; tel: Edenbridge (0732) 865371/3; *Furniture (Bedrooms)*

PANORAMA (PEEL & CAMPDEN LTD), 4 Ashbourne Parade, Finchley Road, London NW11 0AD; tel: (01) 458 5585; *Blinds (Roller, Venetian)*

PAPER MOON, 12–13 Kingswell, 58–62 Heath Street, London NW3; tel: (01) 431 3035; *Fabrics and wall coverings (Co-ordinates)*

PARALLEL LINES, Unit 9, Llambed Industrial Estate, Lampeter, Dyfed SA48 8LT; tel: (0570) 423152; *Fabrics and wall coverings (Fabrics)*

PARKER & FARR, Wollaton Road, Beeston, Nottingham N99 2NW; tel: (0602) 252131; *Furniture (Upholstered)*

PARKER KNOLL FURNITURE LTD, PO Box 22, Frogmoor, High Wycombe, Buckinghamshire HP13 5DJ; tel: (0494) 21144; *Furniture (Upholstered)*

PARKERTEX LTD, 18 Berners Street, London W1P 4JA; tel: (01) 636 8412; West End Road, High Wycombe, Buckinghamshire HP11 2QD; tel: (0494) 33422; *Fabrics and wall coverings (Fabrics)*

PARKRAY, TI Parkray Ltd, Park Foundry, Belper, Derbyshire DE5 1WE; tel: (0773) 82 3741; *Stoves and fireplaces (Stoves)*

E PARSONS & SONS LTD, Blackfriars Road, Nailsea, Bristol BS19 2BU; tel: (0272) 854911; *Paint, Useful products (Wood care)*

PATRICKS OF FARNHAM LTD, Guildford Road, Farnham, Surrey GU9 9QA; tel: (0252) 722345; *Bathrooms (Fittings), Stoves and fireplaces (Mantels and surrounds), Furniture (Made-to-order)*

ROGER PEARSON & CO LTD, see RAINFORD HOUSE OF ELEGANCE; *Stoves and fireplaces (Accessories, Mantels and surrounds)*

PEDLEY WOODWORK LTD, Shirehill Works, Saffron Walden, Essex; tel: (0799) 22461; *Staircases*

PEMBROKE SQUARES, 28 Westmoreland Place, London SW1; tel: (01) 834 9739; *Fabrics and wall coverings (Bed linen)*

PENBRICE INTERIORS, 239 Maida Vale, London W9 1QJ; tel: (01) 328 3546; *Blinds (Roman)*

PERKINS & POWELL LTD, Leopold Street, Birmingham B12 0UJ; tel: (021) 772 2306; *Fittings (Door and cabinet, Window)*

PERMA BLINDS LTD, Prospect Row, Dudley, West Midlands DY2 8SE; tel: (0384) 214231; *Blinds (Special, Venetian, Vertical)*

PERRINGS, Avenue House, Malden Road, Worcester Park, Surrey KT1 7ND; tel: (01) 337 0951; *Lighting, Furniture (Bedrooms, Upholstered)*

PERSONAL TOUCH, 55 Beckenham Lane, Shortlands, Bromley, Kent BR2 0DA; tel: (01) 464 2196; *Furniture (Bedrooms)*

PERSTORP WAREITE LTD, Wareite Sales Department, Aycliffe Industrial Estate, Newton Aycliffe, County Durham DL5 6EF; tel: (0325) 31541; *Kitchens (Worktops)*

ALAN PETERS, Aller Studios, Kentisbeare, Collompton, Devon TX15 2BU; tel: Kentisbeare (088 46) 251; *Furniture (Made-to-order)*

PETIT ROQUE LTD, 5a New Road, Croxley Green, Rickmansworth, Hertfordshire WD3 3EJ; tel: (0923) 779291/720968; *Bathrooms (Fittings), Kitchens (Worktops), Stoves and fireplaces (Accessories, Mantels and surrounds)*

PILKINGTON'S TILES LTD, PO Box 4, Clifton Junction, Manchester M27 2LP; tel: (061) 794 2024; *Ceramic tiles (Floor, Wall)*

PINE UNLIMITED COUNTRY KITCHENS, 13A Greenwich South Street, London SE10; tel: (01) 858 0506; *Kitchens (Units)*

PINEWOOD, 4 Harcourt Road, Redland, Bristol BS6 7RG; tel: (0272) 49654; *Kitchens (Units)*

PIPE DREAMS, 103 Regent's Park Road, London NW1 8UR; tel: (01) 586 4337/8663; *Bathrooms (Fittings), Lighting*

PIRA, 10 Hoxton Square, London N1 6NU; tel: (01) 739 7865; *Furniture (Chairs, Desks, Dining suites, Shelving, Storage, Occasional tables)*

TIMOTHY PLANT, 7 Bramham Gardens, London SW5; tel: (01) 370 2945; *Decorative painters*

PLANTATION SHUTTERS, 93 Antrobus Road, London W4 5NQ; tel: (01) 994 2886; *Blinds (Paper)*

PLANULA (UK) LTD, 37 Great Portland Street, London W1; tel: (01) 631 0464; *Offices (Chairs, Co-ordinated furniture, Reception seating, Systems)*

PLASTIC FINISHES LTD, Bridge Road, Camberley, Surrey; tel: (0276) 27141; *Bathrooms (Fittings, Showers)*

PLASTICS & RESINS LTD, Cleveland Road, Wolverhampton WV2 1BU; tel: (0902) 53215; *Useful products (Sealants)*

DANIEL PLATT & SONS LTD, Brownhills Tileries, Tunstall, Stoke-on-Trent ST6 4NY; tel: (0782) 86187; *Ceramic tiles (Floors)*

PLUSH FLUSH, 27 Sackville Street, London W1X 1DA; tel: (01) 437 7677; *Bathrooms (Fittings, Sanitaryware)*

POGGENPOHL UK LTD, Thames House, 63 Kingston Road, New Malden, Surrey KT3 3PB; tel: (01) 949 5716; *Kitchens (Units)*

S POLLIACK LTD, Norton Industrial Estate, Norton, Malton, North Yorkshire YO17 9HQ; tel: (0653) 5331; *Bathrooms (Fittings, Sanitaryware), Ceramic tiles (Wall)*

POOLE LIGHTING, Cabot Lane, Creekmoor, Poole, Dorset BH17 7BY; tel: (0202) 697344; *Lighting*

POPPY LTD, 44 High Street, Yarm, Cleveland TS15 9AE; tel: (0642) 783892/782017; *Fabrics and wall coverings (Co-ordinates)*

PORCELAIN NEWGLAZE LTD, 91 Godolphin Road, London W12 8JN; tel: (01) 749 0720; *Useful products (Miscellaneous)*

PRETTYGATE TRADERS LTD, 111 Prettygate Road, Colchester CO3 4DZ; tel: (0206) 570851; *Furniture (Desks, Dining suites, Storage)*

PRIMA LIGHTING LTD, 151 Deans Lane, Edgware, Middlesex HA8 9NY; tel: (01) 959 0277; *Lighting*

PRIOR UNIT DESIGN, A P & P M Hammick, Woodbury, Exeter, Devon; tel: (0395) 32237; *Kitchens (Units)*

PROJECT OFFICE FURNITURE LTD, Hamlet Green, Haverhill, Suffolk CB9 8QJ; tel: (0440) 705411; *Offices (Chairs, Systems)*

PROWODA KITCHEN APPLIANCES LTD, Headbrook, Kington, Herefordshire HR5 3DZ; tel: (0544) 230789; *Kitchens (Sinks)*

BOB PULLEY, 4 Ranelagh Mansions, New Kings Road, London SW6 4RH; tel: (01) 736 2831; *Furniture (Dining tables)*

PURITAN FORGE LTD, PO Box 287, London SE23 3TN; tel: (01) 669 8281; *Stoves and fireplaces (Accessories)*

Q A KITCHENS (IRONBRIDGE) LTD, Lightmore, Telford, Shropshire; tel: (0952 45) 2071; *Kitchens (Units)*

QUADRANT 4, Shakenhurst, Cleobury Mortimer, Nr Kidderminster, Worcestershire; tel: Clows Top 300/406; *Furniture (Made-to-order)*

QUEBB STOVES, ABT Products Ltd, Alton Road, Ross-on-Wye, Herefordshire HR9 5NF; tel: (0989) 63656; *Stoves and fireplaces (Stoves)*

QUENBY PRINTS LTD, 90 Baggrave Street, Leicester LE5 3QT; tel: (0533) 23056/7; *Fabrics and wall coverings (Fabrics)*

RACE FURNITURE LTD, New Road, Sheerness, Kent ME12 1AX; tel: (0795) 662311; London showroom: 15 Rathbone Street, London W1P 1AF; tel: (01) 636 3248; *Offices (Chairs, Reception seating)*

G T RACKSTRAW LTD, St Martin's Works, Castle Street, Worcester WR1 3EX; tel: (0905) 27388; *Offices (Desks), Furniture (Chairs, Desks, Dining suites, Storage, Occasional tables)*

RAINBOW PRODUCTS LTD, Albion Wharf, Hester Road, London SW11; tel: (01) 228 9321; *Bathrooms (Sanitaryware, Showers)*

RAINFORD HOUSE OF ELEGANCE, Wentworth House, Birdwell, Nr Barnsley S70 5UN; tel: (0226) 75129/747871/748565; *Architectural ornaments (Plaster), Furniture (Occasional tables); see also* ROGER PEARSON LTD

RAMUS TILE COMPANY LTD, Palace Road, Bounds Green, London N11 2PX; tel: (01) 881 2345/889 4631; *Ceramic tiles (Floor, Wall), Useful products (Tiling)*

RAPINI, Purley Kitchens Ltd, 952 Brighton Road, Purley, Surrey CR22 LP; tel: (01) 660 6939; *Kitchens (Units)*

RAYBURN, Glynwed Consumer & Building Products Ltd, PO Box 30, Ketley, Telford TF1 1BR; tel: (0952) 51177; *Stoves and fireplaces (Mantels and surrounds, Stoves)*

A REASON & SONS LTD, Weardale Road, Lewisham, London SE13 5QD; tel: (01) 852 3344/5; *Offices (Chairs, Reception seating)*

PETER REED, Springfield Mill, Blacko, Nelson, Lancashire; tel: Nelson 66992/692416; *Fabrics and wall coverings (Bed linen)*

REGENCY BATHROOM ACCESSORIES LTD, Credenda Road, Bromford Road Industrial Estate, West Bromwich B70 7JE; tel: (021) 544 6633; *Bathrooms (Fittings)*

RELYON LTD, Wellington, Somerset TA21 8NN; 1 St James Street, London SW1A 13J; tel: (01) 839 4584; *Furniture (Beds, Bedrooms, Upholstered)*

RESOPAL, 42 Jordangate, Macclesfield, Cheshire SK10 1EW; tel: (0625) 612966; *Kitchens (Worktops)*

REST ASSURED, Bembridge Drive, Northampton NN2 6NB; tel: (0604) 716000; *Furniture (Upholstered)*

RICH & SMITH, Bower House, Bower Hinton, Nr Martock, Somerset; tel: (0935) 824696; London showroom: 12 Ellerby Street, London SW6; tel: (01) 736 5324; *Fabrics and wall coverings (Co-ordinates)*

RICHMOND INTERIORS, 5 Langley Street, London WC2H 9JA; tel: (01) 240 8469; *Furniture (Screens and partitions, Occasional tables)*

JAMES ROBERTSHAW & SONS LTD, Albion Works, Lark Hill, Farnworth, Lancashire; tel: Farnworth 74764; *Blinds (Paper)*

SYLVIA ROBINSON, 29 Middlebridge Street, Romsey, Hampshire; tel: Romsey 514930; *Ceramic tiles (Wall)*

ROOKSMOOR MILLS, Bath Road, Nr Stroud, Gloucestershire GL5 5ND; tel: Amberley 2577; *Carpeting (Coir)*

ROSET (UK) LTD, 95a High Street, Great Missenden, Buckinghamshire HP16 0BA; tel: (02406) 5001; *Furniture (Storage, Occasional tables, Upholstered)*

ROTHLEY BRASS LTD, Newman-Tonks Consumer Division, Merridale House, Merridale Street, Wolverhampton WV3 0RB; tel: (0902) 27532; *Fittings (Door and cabinet, Window)*

ROUNTON DESIGN LTD, 31–32 Camden Lock, London NW1 8AF; tel: (01) 267 9741; *Fabrics and wall coverings (Wall coverings)*

DENNIS RUABON LTD, Hafod Tileries, Ruabon, Wrexham, Clwyd LL14 6ET; tel: (0978) 843484; *Ceramic tiles (Floor)*

GORDON RUSSELL LTD, Broadway, Worcestershire WR12 7AD; tel: (0386) 853345/858211; *Offices (Chairs, Co-ordinated furniture, Reception seating, Systems, Tables)*

RUSSELL & CHAPPLE LTD, 23 Monmouth Street, London WC2H 9DE; tel: (01) 836 7521; *Fabrics and wall coverings (Fabrics)*

E RUSSUM & SONS LTD, Edward House, Tenter Street, Rotherham S60 1LB; tel: Rotherham 65005; *Carpeting (Coir, Patterned, Rugs)*

RUSTICHIANA LTD, 42 Pimlico Road, London SW1W 8LP; tel: (01) 730 6607; *Ceramic tiles (Wall), Fabrics and wall coverings (Co-ordinates, Bed linen)*

RYE TILES, Ceramic Consultants Ltd, The Old Brewery, Wishward, Rye, Sussex TN31 7DH; tel: (0797) 223038; *Ceramic tiles (Floor, Wall)*

SC PRODUCTS, 79 Westbourne Park Road, London W2 5QH; tel: (01) 727 8606; *Lighting, Furniture (Beds, Dining tables, Occasional tables)*

ST MARCO'S LTD, 45 Sloane Street, London SW1X 9LU; tel: (01) 235 4832/3; *Bathrooms (Fittings, Sanitaryware)*

SAG BAGS, 4 Elephant Lane, London SE16; tel: (01) 237 8818/231 2001; *Furniture (Upholstered)*

SAHCO-HESSLEIN UK LTD, 58-59 Margaret Street, London W1N 7FG; tel: (01) 636 3552; *Fabrics and wall coverings (Fabrics)*

SAINT LEGER FABRICS, World's End Studios, 134 Lots Road, London SW10 0RJ; tel: (01) 351 4333; *Fabrics and wall coverings (Fabrics)*

T F SAMPSON LTD, Tomo House, Creeting Road, Stowmarket, Suffolk IP14 5BA; tel: Stowmarket (0449) 613535; *Blinds (Paper, Venetian)*

ARTHUR SANDERSON & SONS LTD, 52/53 Berners Street, London W1P 3AD; tel: (01) 636 7800; *Carpeting (Made-to-order, Patterned, Plain, Rugs), Fabrics and wall coverings (Fabrics, Co-ordinates, Bed linen), Lighting, Paint*

SCANDIA, Per Jorgensen Ltd, Dorton Park, Dorton, Aylesbury, Bucks HP18 9NR; tel: (0844) 237561; *Offices (Co-ordinated Furniture)*

SCHIFFINI MOBILI CUCINE, Robert McCreanor Ltd, 147 Sloane Street, London SW1X 9BZ; tel: (01) 730 0926/7/8; *Kitchens (Units)*

SCHREIBER FURNITURE LTD, Caparo House, 101-103 Baker Street, London W1; tel: (01) 935 0280; *Kitchens (Units, Sinks)*

SCOTT HOWARD ASSOCIATES LTD, 32 Broadwick Street, London W1V 1FG; tel: (01) 437 5792; *Offices (Chairs, Systems, Tables), Furniture (Dining suites, Occasional tables)*

SEKERS FABRICS LTD, 15–19 Cavendish Place, London W1M 9DL; tel: (01) 636 2612; *Carpeting (Plain), Fabrics and wall coverings (Fabrics)*

SEKON GLASSWORKS LTD, Essian Street, London E1 4QE; tel: (01) 790 5001; *Mirrors and glass*

J SHARD LTD, 1b Yukon Road, London SW12 9PZ; tel: (01) 675 3437/3438; *Furniture (Made-to-order)*

SHARPS BEDROOM DESIGN, Albany Park, Frimley, Camberley, Surrey GU15 2PL; tel: (0276) 685366; *Furniture (Bedrooms)*

SHAVRIN LEVATAP CO LTD, 25 Hatton Garden, London EC1N 8BA; tel: (01) 952 2558; *Bathrooms (Fittings), Kitchens (Taps)*

SHEARDOWN ENGINEERING LTD, South Road, Templefields, Harlow, Essex CM20 2AP; tel: (0279) 21788; *Bathrooms (Fittings)*

SHELLEY TEXTILES LTD, Barncliffe Mills, Shelley, Nr Huddersfield, Yorkshire HD8 8LU; tel: Huddersfield 604336; *Carpeting (Rugs)*

SHEPPARD DAY DESIGNS LTD, 12 Nimrod Way, Elgar Road, Reading, Berkshire RG2 0EB; tel: (0734) 869900; *Flooring (Cork, Linoleum, Wood)*

ROBERT SHIMIELD, 24 Whitehall Park, London N19; tel: (01) 992 4477, 263 9862; *Decorative painters*

SHIRES see CHLORIDE SHIRES

SIEMATIC, 11/17 Fowler Road, Hainault, Ilford, Essex LG6 3UU; tel: (01) 500 1944; *Kitchens (Units)*

SIGNATURE RUGS see MERCIA WEAVERS LTD

SILENT GLISS LTD, 5 Brewery Road, London N7 9QJ; tel: (01) 609 2646; *Bathrooms (Showers), Blinds (Roman, Vertical), Fittings (Curtain), Furniture (Screens and partitions)*

SILEXINE PAINTS LTD, Bio-Kil Chemicals, Brickyard Industrial Estate, New Road, Gillingham, Dorset SP8 4BR; tel: Gillingham 3121/2; *Paint*

SUPPLIERS' ADDRESSES

JAYNE SIMCOCK, 49 St Margarets Grove, Twickenham, Middlesex TW1 1JF; tel: (01) 892 9238; *Ceramic tiles (Wall), Decorative painters*

SITTING PRETTY LTD, 131 Dawes Road, London SW6; tel: (01) 381 0049; *Bathrooms (Fittings, Sanitaryware)*

S-KITCHEN CONTRACTS LTD, 5 Fox Lane, Palmers Green, London N13 4AB; tel: (01) 886 5599; *Useful products (Miscellaneous)*

SKOPOS FABRICS, Skopos Design Ltd, Providence Mills, Earlsheaton, Dewsbury, West Yorkshire WF12 6HT; tel: (0924) 465191; London showroom: 87 York Street, London W1; tel: (01) 402 5532; *Fabrics and wall coverings (Fabrics)*

SKYE CERAMICS, 240 Brompton Road, London SW3 2BB; tel: (01) 584 9818; West Country Tiles, 76 Huish, Yeovil; tel: (0935) 74827; *Ceramic tiles (Wall)*

SLEEPEEZEE, Morden Road, Merton, London SW19 3XP; tel: (01) 540 9171; *Furniture (Beds, Upholstered)*

SMALLBONE OF DEVIZES, Unit 10-11 Nimrod Way, Elgar Road, Reading, Berkshire; tel: (0734) 868044; *Kitchens (units)*

JAMES SMELLIE LTD, Stafford Street, Dudley, West Midlands DY1 2AD; tel: (0384) 52320; *Stoves and fireplaces (Accessories, Mantels and surrounds)*

H & E SMITH LTD, Britannic Works, Broom Street, Hanley, Stoke-on-Trent ST1 2ER; tel: (0782) 21617/8; *Ceramic tiles (Wall)*

PETER SMITH ASSOCIATES (WILTSHIRE) LTD, Vorda Works, Highworth, Swindon, Wiltshire SN6 7AJ; tel: Swindon 764301; *Carpeting (Coir, Rugs)*

SMITHBROOK LTD, Smithbrook, Cranleigh, Surrey; tel: (0483) 272744; *Lighting*

SOLENT FURNITURE SYSTEMS, Solent Furniture Ltd, Pymore Mills, Bridport, Dorset DT6 5PJ; tel: (0308) 22305; *Kitchens (Units)*

SOLVOLENE LUBRICANTS LTD, Solvol Works, Reginald Square, London SE8 4RX; tel: (01) 692 2241; *Useful products (Miscellaneous)*

SOMMER ALLIBERT (UK) LTD, Berry Hill Industrial Estate, Droitwich, Worcestershire WR9 9AB; tel: (0905) 774221; *Bathrooms (Fittings), Carpeting (Patterned, Plain), Flooring (Vinyl sheet)*

SOULEIADO, 171 Fulham Road, London SW3; tel: (01) 589 6180; *Fabrics and wallcoverings (Co-ordinates)*

SOUTH BANK DESIGNS, 23–24 The South Bank Business Centre, 1 Ponton Road, London SW8; tel: (01) 622 1727; *Furniture (Chairs, Dining suites, Upholstered)*

SPECTRUM, 122 Drury Lane, London WC2B 5SU; tel: (01) 836 1104; *Bathrooms (Fittings), Kitchens (Taps), Lighting*

SPHINX TILES LTD, Bath Road, Thatcham, Newbury, Berkshire RG13 4HQ; tel: (0635) 65475; *Ceramic tiles (Floor, Wall)*

THE SPIRAL STAIRCASE COMPANY, 42 Spencer Road, Twickenham, Middlesex TW2 5TO; tel: (01) 894 4568; *Staircases*

STAG, Haydn Road, Nottingham NG5 1DU; tel: Nottingham 605007; *Furniture (Bedrooms, Dining suites, Storage)*

STAPLES & CO LTD, Windover Road, Huntingdon, Cambridgeshire PE18 7EF; tel: (0480) 5211; *Furniture (Beds)*

STAPRO & WELLDEN, Stapro Ltd, 15 Ditchling Rise, Brighton, Sussex BN1 4GL; tel: (0273) 680132/3; *Useful products (Miscellaneous)*

BRUCE STARKE & CO LTD, PO Box 92, Brentwood, Essex CM14 4AF; tel: Brentwood 218833; *Carpeting (Coir)*

STATELY HOME KITCHENS LTD, Coronation Parade, 54 Cannon Lane, Pinner, Middlesex HA5 1HW; tel: (01) 866 0973/4; *Kitchens (Units)*

STEELCASE STRAFOR UK LTD, 100 Avenue Road, London NW3; tel: (01) 586 5933; *Offices (Chairs, Reception seating, Systems)*

STEELES CARPETS LTD, Bloxham, Nr Banbury, Oxfordshire OX15 4HA; tel: Banbury 720556; 45 Great Russell Street, London WC1B 3PA; tel: (01) 631 4842; *Carpeting (Made-to-order, Tiles)*

STEELUX ZEDBEDS LTD, Rood End Road, Oldbury, Warley, West Midlands B69 4HN; tel: (021) 552 3377; *Furniture (Beds)*

STERLING RONCRAFT, Chapeltown, Sheffield S30 4YP; tel: (0742) 467171; *Useful products (Wood care)*

STODDARD CARPETS LTD, Glenpatrick Carpet Works, Elderslie, Johnstone, Renfrewshire PA5 9UJ; tel: (0505) 27100; *Carpeting (Flecked, Made-to-order, Patterned, Plain, Tiles)*

STONEHAM DESIGNED KITCHENS, Stoneham & Son (Deptford) Ltd, Powerscroft Road, Sidcup, Kent DA14 5DZ; tel: (01) 300 8181; *Kitchens (Units)*

STOREYS DECORATIVE PRODUCTS LTD, Southgate, White Lund, Morecambe LA3 3DA; tel: (0524) 65981; *Fabrics and wall coverings (Wall coverings, Co-ordinates)*

STUART INTERIORS, South Pemberton, Somerset TA13 5LR; tel: (0460) 40349; *Architectural ornaments (Wood), Staircases, Stoves and fireplaces (Mantels and surrounds), Furniture (Beds, Chairs, Made-to-order, Storage, Dining tables)*

SUNDOUR FABRICS, Robin Hood Mill, Lever Street, Bolton BL3 6NY; tel: (0204) 387802; *Fabrics and wall coverings (Fabrics)*

SUNSTOR LTD, G Hall & Co Ltd, St George's Square, Portsmouth, Hampshire PO1 3AT; tel: (0705) 750212; *Blinds (Roller, Venetian, Vertical)*

SUNVENE LTD, 7 Greenheys Lane, Manchester M15 6NQ; tel: (061) 226 4636; *Blinds (Roller, Venetian, Vertical)*

SUNWAY BLINDS LTD, Mersey Industrial Estate, Heaton, Mersey, Stockport, Cheshire SK4 3EG; *Blinds (Roller, Roman, Special, Venetian, Vertical)*

LUDVIG SVENSSON (UK) LTD, Riverside Way, Nottingham NG2 1LJ; tel: (0602) 866641; *Fabrics and wall coverings (Bed linen)*

SWISH PRODUCTS LTD, Tamworth, Staffordshire B79 7TW; tel: (0827) 3811; *Fittings (Curtain)*

TAG DESIGN PARTNERSHIP, 39–41 North Road, Islington, London N7 9DP; tel: (01) 607 9374; *Lighting, Furniture (Dining tables, Occasional tables)*

TAMESA FABRICS LTD, 343 Kings Road, London SW3 5ES; tel: (01) 351 1126–9; *Carpeting (Patterned), Fabrics and wall coverings (Fabrics)*

TARIAN DESIGN LTD, No 2 Senlan Rhymney, Rhymney Bridge Road, Cardiff CF3 7AS; tel: Cardiff 460 625; *Fabrics and wall coverings (Fabrics)*

TASSO DECOR INTERNATIONAL LTD, 146 New Cavendish Street, London W1M 7FG; tel: (01) 631 4742; sales office; Hollis Road, Grantham, Lincolnshire NG31 7QH; tel: (0476) 74401; *Fabrics and wall coverings (Wall coverings)*

TEMPUS STET LTD, Trinity Business Centre, 305–309 Rotherhithe Street, London SE16 1EY; tel: (01) 231 0955; *Fittings (Curtain), Lighting, Mirrors and glass, Furniture (Occasional tables)*

TEROYDECOR LTD, 10 Vincent Street, Bradford BD1 2NT; tel: (0274) 735431; *Fabrics and wall coverings (Wall coverings)*

JANE THOMAS, Garden Flat, 65 Mount Ararat Road, Richmond, Surrey TW10 6PL; tel: (01) 948 4805; *Furniture (Made-to-order)*

THOMSON SHEPHERD see ARTHUR SANDERSON & SONS LTD

TIBA, C J Kershaw Ltd, Morley Marketing, Victoria Maltings, Broadmeads, Ware, Hertfordshire SG12 9HS; tel: (0920) 68001; *Kitchens (Units)*

TIDMARSH & SONS LTD, 1 Laycock Street, London N1 1SW; tel: (01) 226 2261; *Blinds (Paper)*

TIELSA KITCHENS LTD, Wakefield Road, Gildersome, Leeds LS27 0QW; tel: (0532) 524131; *Kitchens (Units)*

WILLIAM TILLMAN, Crouch Lane, Borough Green, Kent TN15 8LT; tel: Borough Green 883278; *Furniture (Chairs, Desks, Dining suites, Storage, Occasional tables)*

TIMNEY FOWLER PRINTS, 8 Portobello Green, 281 Portobello Road, London W10; tel: (01) 968 5626; *Fabrics and wall coverings (Fabrics)*

TINTAWN LTD, Richfield Avenue, Reading, Berkshire RG1 8NZ; tel: Reading 56321; *Carpeting (Patterned, Plain, Rugs)*

TISSUNIQUE LTD, 10 Princes Street, Hanover Square, London W1R 7RD; tel: (01) 491 3386; *Fabrics and wall coverings (Fabrics, Co-ordinates)*

TITCHMARSH & GOODWIN, Trinity Works, Back Hamlet, Ipswich IP3 8AL; tel: Ipswich 52158; *Mirrors and glass, Furniture (Chairs, Desks, Shelving, Storage, Dining tables, Occasional tables, Upholstered)*

TODAY INTERIORS LTD, Hollis Road, Grantham, Lincolnshire NG31 7GH; tel: (0476) 74401; *Fabrics and wall coverings (Wall coverings, Co-ordinates)*

TOMKINSONS CARPETS LTD, PO Box 11, Duke Place, Kidderminster, Worcestershire DY10 2JR; tel: Kidderminster 745771; *Carpeting (Made-to-order, Patterned, Plain, Rugs)*

KENNETH TOPP, 14 Star and Garter Mansions, Lower Richmond Road, London SW15; tel: (01) 785 9208; *Furniture (Made-to-order)*

TOULEMONDE-BOCHART AT DIVERTIMENTI, 139/141 Fulham Road, London SW3; tel: (01) 581 8064; *Carpeting (Rugs)*

TOWN AND COUNTRY PINE, William S Toms Ltd, Station Road, Princes Risborough, Buckinghamshire HP17 9DN; tel: (08444) 2233; *Furniture (Dining suites, Storage)*

TOWNHOUSE INTERIORS, 25G Lowndes Street, London SW1; tel: (01) 235 3189/3180; *Furniture (Dining suites, Occasional tables)*

SALLY TOWNSHEND (WRAPPA), 14 Upland Road, London SE22 9EE; tel: (01) 299 2050; *Lighting*

CHRIS TRIPPEAR, Old Shap Wells Cottage, Shap, Nr Penrith, Cumbria; tel: Shap 264; *Furniture (Beds, Made-to-order)*

TROMPLOY DESIGN, 8 Smithbrook Kilns, Cranleigh, Guildford, Surrey; tel: Cranleigh 273232; *Decorative painters*

TRÜGGELMANN, 13 Eccleston Street, London SW1; tel: (01) 352 3998; *Furniture (Bedrooms, Made-to-order)*

STEVEN TUBB, Craigmore Farm, Stockiemuir Road, Blanefield, Stirling G63 9AU; tel: (0360) 70010; *Bathrooms (Fittings)*

TUDOR OAK, Bakers Cross, Cranbrook, Kent TN17 3AL; tel: Cranbrook 712465; *Furniture (Beds)*

TUKAN HARDWOOD FURNITURE, 2 High Street, Saxmundham, Suffolk IP17 1DD; tel: (0728) 3377; *Furniture (Made-to-order)*

TULLEYS OF CHELSEA, 289–297 Fulham Road, London SW10 9PZ; tel: (01) 352 1078; *Furniture (Desks, Dining suites, Storage, Upholstered)*

TURBERVILLE SMITH & SON LTD, 72–94 Park Road, Crouch End, London N8 8JP; tel: (01) 340 8201; showroom: 16–17 Hay Hill, Berkeley Square, London W1; tel: (01) 499 1638; *Carpeting (Made-to-order), Offices (Co-ordinated furniture, Systems)*

TURNELL & GIGON LTD, Room G/04, 250 Kings Road, London SW3 5UE; tel: (01) 351 5142/3; *Fabrics and wall coverings (Fabrics, Co-ordinates)*

TWYFORDS LTD, PO Box 23, Stoke-on-Trent ST4 7AL; tel: Stoke-on-Trent 289777; *Bathrooms (Fittings, Sanitaryware, Showers)*

MICHAEL TYLER FURNITURE LTD, Woodlands Way, The Ridge, Hastings, East Sussex TN34 2RY; tel: (0424) 53331; *Furniture (Upholstered)*

R TYZACK LTD, Kitchener Road, High Wycombe, Buckinghamshire HP11 2SH; tel: (0494) 23265/20993; *Offices (Co-ordinated Furniture), Furniture (Chairs, Storage, Dining tables, Upholstered)*

UBM BUILDING SUPPLIES LTD, Avon Works, Winterstoke Road, Bristol BS99 7PL; tel: (0272) 664611; *Bathrooms (Fittings, Sanitaryware), Kitchens (Units), Paint*

ULFERTS OF SWEDEN LTD, St George's House, 128 St George Street, London W1R 9DE; tel: (01) 499 8537; *Furniture (Upholstered)*

ULSTER CARPET MILLS LTD, Castleisland Factory, Portadown, Craigavon, Northern Ireland; tel: Portadown 34433; *Carpeting (Patterned)*

UNITY DESIGNS (UK) LTD, Downley, High Wycombe, Buckinghamshire HP13 5TX; tel: (0494) 34411; *Offices (Systems)*

VALLI & COLOMBO LTD, St Mary's Chambers, Station Road, Stone, Staffordshire ST15 8AS; tel: (0785) 817 331; *Fittings (Door and cabinet)*

VERARDO, 36 The Precinct, Letchworth Drive, Bromley BR2 9BE, Kent; tel: (01) 460 5790, 464 8605; *Furniture (Beds, Dining suites, Shelving, Storage)*

VERINE PRODUCTS & CO, Folly Faunts House, Goldhanger, Maldon, Essex CM9 8AP; tel: (0621) 88611; *Architectural ornaments (Plaster), Stoves and fireplaces (Mantels and surrounds)*

VERTIKA INTERNATIONAL LTD, Sutton Mill, Byrons Lane, Cross Street, Macclesfield, Cheshire SK11 6TF; tel: Macclesfield 611622; *Blinds (Vertical)*

VITREX TOOLS, 457–463 Caledonian Road, London N7 9BB; tel: (01) 609 0011; *Useful products (Tiling)*

VIXEN-SMITH LTD, Unit 7/10 Exbridge Industrial Estate, Exbridge, Dulverton, Somerset; tel: Dulverton (0398) 23060; *Blinds (Paper, Roller, Roman, Venetian, Vertical);* now trading as VIXEN BLINDS

VOGUE BATHROOMS, Bilston Works, Batmans Hill Road, Bilston, West Midlands WV14 8UA; tel: (0902) 43121; *Bathrooms (Sanitaryware)*

V'SOSKE JOYCE (UK) LTD, 54 Linhope Street, London NW1 6HL; tel: (01) 724 0182; *Carpeting (Made-to-order, Rugs)*

WADE SPRING & UPHOLSTERY CO LTD, Wellington Street, Long Eaton, Nottingham NG10 4HT; tel: (06076) 2135; *Furniture (Upholstered)*

WALLPAPER ORIGINALS, 37 Old Hall Road, Salford, Manchester M7 0JJ; tel: (061) 740 1140; *Fabrics and wall coverings (Wall coverings)*

WARNER & SONS LTD, 7–11 Noel Street, London W1V 4AL; tel: (01) 439 2411; *Fabrics and wall coverings (Fabrics, Co-ordinates)*

WEAVERCRAFT CARPETS LTD, Toftshaw Lane, Bradford BD4 6QW; tel: Bradford 681881; *Carpeting (Patterned)*

WEBBER FURNITURE, 115 Sydenham Road, Croydon CR9 2TD, tel: (01) 688 6178; *Furniture (Dining suites, Storage)*

WESLEY-BARRELL (WITNEY) LTD, Park Street Factory, Charlbury, Oxfordshire; tel: (0608) 810481; *Furniture (Beds, Upholstered)*

WESTNOFA, Wiltshier Contract Furnishing Ltd, Allard House, 18 Verney Road, London SE16 3DH; tel: (01) 639 8931/8; *Furniture (Chairs, Upholstered)*

WESTRA OFFICE EQUIPMENT LTD, The Green, Southall, Middlesex UB2 4DE; tel: (01) 843 1122; *Offices (Co-ordinated furniture)*

LAURENCE WHISTLER, The Old Manor, Alton Barnes, Marlborough, Wiltshire SN8 4LB; tel: Woodborough 515; *Mirrors and glass*

WHITNEY LACQUER LTD, 174–192 Estcourt Road, London SW6 7HD; tel: (01) 385 8324/8677; *Furniture (Made-to-order)*

WICANDERS LTD, Maxwell Way, Crawley, Sussex RH10 2SE; tel: (0293) 27700; *Fabrics and wall coverings (Wall coverings), Flooring (Cork, Wood)*

WILTON ROYAL CARPET FACTORY LTD, Wilton, Salisbury SP2 0AY; tel: Salisbury 742441/743711; London showroom: The British Carpet Trade Centre, Third Floor, 99–105 Kensington High Street, London W8 5SB; tel: (01) 937 3914; *Carpeting (Flecked, Made-to-order, Patterned, Plain)*

WILTSHIER CONTRACT FURNISHING LTD, 18 Verney Road, London SE16 3DH; tel: (01) 639 8931; *Offices (Co-ordinated furniture)*

WINCHMORE FURNITURE LTD, Mildenhall, Suffolk IP28 7BE; tel: (0638) 712082; *Bathrooms (Fittings), Kitchens (Units), Furniture (Bedrooms)*

WINDMILL FURNITURE, Turnham Green Terrace Mews, Chiswick, London W4 1QU; tel: (01) 994 7032; *Furniture (Dining tables, Occasional tables, Upholstered)*

TOBY WINTERINGHAM, 1 King Staithe Lane, King's Lynn, Norfolk PE30 1LZ; tel: King's Lynn 66529; *Kitchens (Units), Furniture (Made-to-order)*

WINTHER BROWNE & CO LTD, Nobel Road, Eley's Estate, Edmonton, London N18 3DX; tel: (01) 803 3434; *Architectural ornaments (Wood), Kitchens (Units), Staircases*

WOOD BROS FURNITURE LTD, London Road, Ware, Hertfordshire; tel: (0920) 3147/8; *Furniture (Beds, Desks, Storage)*

R WOODLAND & SON, 2 The Avenue, Loughton, Essex; tel: (01) 508 6882; *Decorative painters*

WOODSTOCK WORKSHOPS, Pakenham Street, Mount Pleasant, London WC1; tel: (01) 837 1818; *Kitchen (Units, Worktops)*

WOODWARD GROSVENOR & CO LTD, Stourvale Mills, Green Street, Kidderminster, Worcestershire DY10 1AT; tel: Kidderminster 745271; London showroom: 8/9 Giltspur Street, London EC1A 9DE; tel: (01) 236 7156; *Carpeting (Rugs)*

WOOLWORTH, F W Woolworth & Co Ltd, 242 Marylebone Road, London NW1; tel: (01) 262 1222; *Paint*

WORLD'S END TILES, 9 Langton Street, World's End, Chelsea, London SW10 0JL; tel: (01) 351 0279; British Rail Yard, Silverthorne Road, Battersea, London SW8 3HE; tel: (01) 720 4489; *Ceramic tiles (Floor, Wall)*

WRAPPA see SALLY TOWNSHEND

CHRISTOPHER WRAY'S LIGHTING EMPORIUM LTD, 600–604 Kings Road, London SW6 2DX; tel: (01) 736 8434; *Lighting*

WRIGHTON, F Wrighton & Sons Ltd, Nazeing Road, Nazeing, Essex EN9 2JD; tel: (0992) 445544; *Kitchens (Units)*

B & P WYNN & CO, 18 Boston Parade, Boston Road, London W7 2DG; tel: (01) 567 8758; *Bathrooms (Fittings, Sanitaryware)*

WYVERN FIREPLACES, Grove Trading Estate, Dorchester, Dorset DT1 1SU; tel: (0305) 64716/7; *Stoves and fireplaces (Mantels and surrounds)*

XEY, Rex Stewart Gordon Scott Ltd, 31 St Leonards Road, Eastbourne, East Sussex BN21 4SWE; tel: (0323) 22933; *Kitchens (Units)*

BRIAN YATES (INTERIORS) LTD, 3 Riverside Park, Lancaster LA1 3PE; tel: (0524) 35035; *Fabrics and wall coverings (Fabrics, Co-ordinates)*

ARNOLD ZELTER, Valley Workshops, Valley Farmhouse, East Runton, Cromer, Norfolk; tel: Cromer 512049; *Furniture (Made-to-order)*

INDEX

INDEX

INDEX